Management Information Systems

Managing The Digital Firm

First Canadian Edition

Management Information Systems

Managing The Digital Firm

First Canadian Edition

Kenneth C. Laudon

New York University

Jane P. Laudon

Azimuth Information Systems

Canadian Adaptation by

Mary Elizabeth Brabston

Asper School of Business, University of Manitoba

Prentice Hall

Toronto

National Library of Canada Cataloguing in Publication Data

Laudon, Kenneth C., 1944–
   Management information systems: managing the digital firm

1st Canadian ed.
Includes index.
ISBN 0-13-033809-5

1. Management information systems. I. Laudon, Jane Price
II. Brabston, Mary Elizabeth, 1948–   III. Title

T58.6.L38 2002   658.4'038   C2001-902025-2

ISBN 0-13-033809-5

Vice President, Editorial Director: Michael Young
Acquisitions Editor: Kelly Torrance
Marketing Manager: Cas Shields
Developmental Editor: Maurice Esses
Production Editor: Marisa D'Andrea
Copy Editor: Catherine Haggert
Production Coordinator: Janette Lush
Page Layout: Hermia Chung
Photo Research: Susan Wallace-Cox, Beth McAuley
Art Director: Mary Opper
Interior and Cover Design: Anthony Leung
Cover Image: PhotoDisc

1 2 3 4 5   05 04 03 02 01

Printed and bound in U.S.A.

Statistics Canada information is used with the permission of the Minister of Industry, as
Minister responsible for Statistics Canada. Information on the availability of the wide range
of data from Statistics Canada can be obtained from Statistics Canada's Regional Offices, its
World Wide Web site at http://www.statcan.ca, and its toll-free access number 1-800-263-1136.

For

Erica and Elisabeth

– K.C.L. AND J.P.L. –

To my parents,

Donald Campbell Brabston and Mary Jane Coolman Brabston,

whose love, support, and example

have encouraged me in all my endeavours.

– M.E.B. –

ABOUT THE AUTHORS

Kenneth C. Laudon is a Professor of Information Systems at New York University's Stern School of Business. He holds a B.A. in Economics from Stanford and a Ph.D. from Columbia University. He has authored eleven books dealing with information systems, organizations, and society. Professor Laudon has also written over forty articles concerned with the social, organizational, and management impacts of information systems, privacy, ethics, and multimedia technology.

Professor Laudon's current research is on the planning and management of large-scale information systems and multimedia information technology. He has received grants from the National Science Foundation to study the evolution of national information systems at the Social Security Administration, the IRS, and the FBI. A part of this research is concerned with computer-related organizational and occupational changes in large organizations, changes in management ideology, changes in public policy, and understanding productivity change in the knowledge sector.

Ken Laudon has testified as an expert before the United States Congress. He has been a researcher and consultant to the Office of Technology Assessment (United States Congress) and to the Office of the President, several executive branch agencies, and Congressional Committees. Professor Laudon also acts as an in-house educator for several consulting firms and as a consultant on systems planning and strategy to several Fortune 500 firms. Ken works with the Concours Group to provide advice to firms developing enterprise systems.

Ken Laudon's hobby is sailing.

Jane Price Laudon is a management consultant in the information systems area and the author of seven books. Her special interests include systems analysis, data management, MIS auditing, software evaluation, and teaching business professionals how to design and use information systems.

Jane received her Ph.D. from Columbia University, her M.A. from Harvard University, and her B.A. from Barnard College. She has taught at Columbia University and the New York University Graduate School of Business. She maintains a lifelong interest in Oriental languages and civilizations.

The Laudons have two daughters, Erica and Elisabeth.

ABOUT THE CANADIAN ADAPTER

Mary Elizabeth Brabston, B.A., M.B.A., Ph.D. is tenured Assistant Professor of Management Information Systems at the University of Manitoba's Asper School of Business. Prior to the Asper School, Dr. Brabston taught at the University of Tennessee at Chattanooga. Dr. Brabston received her doctorate at Florida State University. Having spent her working life as a banker, political staffer, development officer, and academic, Dr. Brabston brings a comprehensive view to her analysis of how information systems can help organizations to achieve their potential. Her teaching and research interests involve strategic planning and applications of information systems and information resource management. Her work has appeared in such publications as the *Journal of Computing and Information Technology, Journal of Computer Information Systems, Journal of Information Systems Education,* and *Human Relations.*

Management Information Systems: Managing the Digital Firm reflects a deep understanding of MIS research and teaching as well as practical experience designing and building real-world systems.

BRIEF CONTENTS

CONTENTS

CHAPTER 4   ELECTRONIC COMMERCE AND ELECTRONIC BUSINESS   110

CHAPTER 5   SOCIAL, POLITICAL, AND ETHICAL ISSUES IN THE
INFORMATION AGE   150

PREFACE

WELCOME TO THE DIGITAL FIRM

Management Information Systems: Managing the Digital Firm (First Canadian Edition) is based on the premise that knowledge about information systems is essential for creating competitive firms, managing global corporations, and providing useful products and services to customers. This book provides an introduction to management information systems that undergraduate and MBA students will find essential to their professional success.

THE INFORMATION REVOLUTION IN BUSINESS AND MANAGEMENT: THE EMERGING DIGITAL FIRM

The growth of the Internet, the globalization of trade, and the rise of information economies have recast the role of information systems in business and management. The Internet has become the foundation for new business models, new business processes, and new ways of distributing knowledge. Companies can use the Internet and networking technology to conduct more of their work electronically, seamlessly linking factories, offices, and sales forces around the globe. Leading-edge firms such as Nortel, Celestica, and Cisco Systems are extending these networks to suppliers, customers, and other groups outside their organizations so they can react instantly to customer demands and market shifts. Cisco Systems corporate managers can use information systems to "virtually close" their books at any time, generating consolidated financial statements based on up-to-the-minute figures on orders, discounts, revenue, product margins, and staffing expenses. Executives can constantly analyze performance at all levels of the organization. Digital integration, both within the firm and without, from the warehouse to the executive suite, from suppliers to customers, is changing how we organize and manage a business firm. Ultimately, these changes are leading to fully digital firms in which all internal business processes and relationships with customers and suppliers are digitally enabled. In digital firms, information to support business decisions is available any time and anywhere in the organization. Accordingly, we have subtitled this text *Managing the Digital Firm*.

NEW TO THE FIRST CANADIAN EDITION

In comparison with the first six U.S. editions, this first Canadian edition more fully explores the digital integration of the firm and the use of the Internet to digitally enable business processes for electronic commerce and electronic business. The text provides a complete set of tools for integrating the Internet and multimedia technology into the MIS course and for promoting active problem solving. The Canadian edition focuses on Canadian companies, people, events, trends, markets, cases, and costs. Where appropriate, differences between Canada and other countries are discussed. In particular, because the United States is Canada's largest and closest trading partner, the differences between Canada and the United States are highlighted. The following features and content reflect this new direction.

NEW COVERAGE OF THE DIGITAL FIRM

Chapter 1 introduces and defines the emerging digital firm, using examples of leading-edge companies such as Cisco Systems and Nygård International. Chapter 3 explains how information systems and business strategy have changed as a result of digital firm technology, and Chapter 14 describes digital firm applications of decision support systems and executive support systems. The entire text details the management, organization, and technology issues surrounding the digital integration of the firm and the formation of industry-wide networks and global supply chains.

DETAILED COVERAGE OF CUSTOMER RELATIONSHIP MANAGEMENT, SUPPLY CHAIN MANAGEMENT, AND ENTERPRISE SYSTEMS

Chapter 2 provides detailed treatment of customer relationship management, supply chain management, enterprise systems, and the digital integration of business processes. Subsequent chapters include additional descriptions, discussions, and case studies of these topics, emphasizing the importance of integrating information across business processes and electronically linking the firm to suppliers, customers, and other business partners. "Before and after" snapshots throughout the text illustrate how firms have changed their business processes using digital technology.

INCREASED COVERAGE OF ELECTRONIC COMMERCE, ELECTRONIC BUSINESS, AND THE INTERNET

The Internet, electronic commerce, and electronic business are introduced in Chapter 1 and integrated throughout the text and the entire learning package. The text now features two full chapters on these topics. Chapter 4, "Electronic Commerce and Electronic Business," discusses electronic commerce, Internet business models, e-business, and the management and organizational transformations driving the move toward digital firms. Chapter 10, "The Internet and the New Information Technology Infrastructure," describes the underlying technology, capabilities, and benefits of the Internet, with new coverage of the wireless Web, m-commerce, and digital firm infrastructure. Every chapter contains a Window On box or a case study devoted to electronic commerce, electronic business, or digital firm issues, as well as in-text descriptions of how Internet technology is changing a particular aspect of information systems.

MORE ACTIVE HANDS-ON LEARNING PROJECTS AND PROBLEM SOLVING

This edition is problem-solving and project oriented, with active hands-on learning projects to help make text concepts more meaningful to students.

New Canadian Case Studies

We have added four new, comprehensive Canadian Case Studies, each with an accompanying video, to conclude each of the four parts of the text. These cases provide students with a more in-depth, integrated, real-world view of the material covered in the preceding part. Classroom discussion of the part-ending cases should help the students to integrate the material learned in that part with preceding material.

New Hands-on Application Exercises

Each chapter now features a hands-on Application Software Exercise in which students can develop a solution using spreadsheet, database, expert system, CASE, or electronic presentation software. Some of these exercises require students to use these application software tools in conjunction with Web activities. The Application Exercises give students the opportunity to apply their software skills and text concepts to management problem solving. Complete application exercises are included in each chapter and also on the Laudon, Laudon, and Brabston Web site, along with required data files. The Application Exercises include business problems such as

- Developing a Web page for a business (Chapter 6 and Chapter 15)
- Developing a hotel reservation database and management reporting system (Chapter 2)
- Developing a spreadsheet application for information technology risk assessment (Chapter 14)

New Management Decision Problems

We have added a Management Decision Problem to each chapter to encourage students to apply what they have learned to a real-world management decision-making scenario. These problems can be used for practical group or individual learning both in and outside of the classroom. The problems require students to make decisions based on real-world MIS issues such as

▌ Analyzing enterprise process integration (Chapter 2)

▌ Measuring the effectiveness of Web advertising (Chapter 4)

▌ Monitoring how much time employees spend on the Web (Chapter 15)

NEW LEADING-EDGE TOPICS

In addition to the new digital firm coverage we have already described, this edition includes up-to-date treatment of topics such as

▌ M-commerce and the wireless Web (Chapter 10)

▌ Optical networks and broadband access (Chapter 9)

▌ Application service providers and online storage service providers (Chapters 6 and 7)

▌ Peer-to-peer computing (Chapter 6)

▌ B2B exchanges (Chapter 4)

▌ Scalability and high-availability computing (Chapters 6, 10, and 12)

▌ Middleware and enterprise application integration software (Chapter 7)

▌ Application development for e-commerce (Chapter 11)

▌ XML (Chapter 7)

▌ Web-enabled databases and elements of SQL (Chapter 8)

BOOK OVERVIEW

Part One is concerned with the organizational foundations of systems, their strategic role, and the organizational and management changes driving electronic commerce, electronic business, and the emerging digital firm. It provides an extensive introduction to real-world systems, focusing on their relationship to organizations, management, and business processes, including social, ethical, and legal impacts of information systems.

Part Two provides the technical foundation for understanding information systems, describing the hardware, software, data storage, and telecommunications technologies that compose the organization's information technology infrastructure. Part Two concludes by describing how all of these information technologies work together with the Internet to create a new infrastructure for the digital integration of the enterprise.

Part Three focuses on the process of redesigning organizations using information systems, including reengineering of critical business processes and development of Web applications. This part focuses on the management of information as a critical resource with particular attention to developing systems, maintaining systems quality and security, and managing information systems professionals and processes. Attention is given to systems analysis and design as an exercise in organizational design, requiring sensitivity to the right tools and techniques to use, quality assurance, and change management.

Part Four describes the role of information systems in capturing and distributing organizational knowledge and in enhancing management decision making across the enterprise. It shows how knowledge management, workgroup collaboration, and individual and group decision making can be supported by the use of knowledge work, group collaboration, artificial intelligence, decision support, and executive support systems.

In addition, international issues and issues relating to the most recent developments in information systems are incorporated throughout the text. International issues are covered primarily in Chapters 3, 10, and 13. Issues related to knowledge management are found in Chapter 15, while issues related to electronic commerce, supply chain management, and customer relationship management are incorporated throughout the text.

CHAPTER OUTLINE

Each chapter contains the following:

- A detailed outline at the beginning to provide an overview
- An opening vignette describing a real-world organization to establish the theme and importance of the chapter
- A diagram analyzing the opening vignette in terms of the management, organization, and technology model used throughout the text
- A list of learning objectives
- Management Challenges related to the chapter theme
- Marginal definitions of key terms in the text
- A Management Decision Problem presenting a real-world management decision scenario
- An Application Software Exercise requiring students to use application software tools to develop solutions to real-world business problems based on chapter concepts
- A Management Wrap-Up tying together the key management, organization, and technology issues for the chapter, with questions for discussion
- A chapter summary keyed to the learning objectives
- A list of key terms that the student can use to review concepts
- Review questions for students to test their comprehension of chapter material
- A group project to develop teamwork and presentation skills
- An Internet Connection section that refers to the Companion Website for this Canadian edition and that lists additional sites of interest
- A chapter-ending case study that illustrates important themes

COMPANION WEBSITE (WWW.PEARSONED.CA/LAUDON)

The first Canadian edition of the text is accompanied by a robust Companion Website created for students and instructors. One section of the site consists of an online Study Guide to facilitate and enhance learning. It includes Self-Test Questions, E-Commerce Exercises, Part-Ending Projects, and files for the Application Exercises in the textbook. Another section of the site provides alternative approaches and supplementary discussions for some of the topics in the textbook. This section of the site will also contain regular updates of material in the book to ensure that the real examples and discussions of technology are current. Another section of the site is reserved for Instructor's Resources. Finally, the site also includes links to other relevant Web destinations and the posting of the CBC video segments that supplement the Canadian Case Studies in the book.

UNIQUE FEATURES OF THIS TEXT FOR THE STUDENT

Management Information Systems: Managing the Digital Firm (First Canadian Edition) has many unique features designed to create an active, dynamic learning environment.

A special diagram accompanying each chapter-opening vignette illustrates how management, technology, and organization elements work together to create an information system solution to the business challenges discussed in the vignette.

INTEGRATED FRAMEWORK FOR DESCRIBING AND ANALYZING INFORMATION SYSTEMS

An integrated framework portrays information systems as comprising of management, organization, and technology elements. This framework is used throughout the text to describe and analyze information systems and information system problems.

REAL-WORLD EXAMPLES

Real-world examples drawn from business and public organizations are used throughout to illustrate text concepts. Numerous companies in Canada and around the world are discussed.

Each chapter opens with a vignette illustrating the themes of the chapter by showing how a real-world organization meets a business challenge using information systems. Each chapter also contains two or three Window On boxes (Window on Management, Window on Organizations, Window on Technology) that present real-world examples illustrating the management, organization, and technology issues in the chapter. Each Window On box concludes with a section called To Think About, containing questions for students to apply chapter concepts to management problem solving. The themes for each box are as follows:

Window on Management

Management problems raised by systems and their solutions; management strategies and plans; careers and experiences of managers using systems

Window on Organizations

Activities of private and public organizations using information systems; experiences of people working with systems

Window on Technology

Hardware, software, telecommunications, data storage, standards, and systems development methodologies

MANAGEMENT WRAP-UP OVERVIEWS OF KEY ISSUES

Management Wrap-Up sections at the end of each chapter summarize key issues using the authors' management, organization, and technology framework for analyzing information systems.

MANAGEMENT WRAP-UP

Selection of a systems development approach can have a large impact on the time, cost, and end product of systems development. Managers should be aware of the strengths and weaknesses of each systems development approach and the types of problems for which each is best suited.

Organizational needs should drive the selection of a systems development approach. The impact of application software packages and outsourcing should be carefully evaluated before either is selected because these approaches give organizations less control over the systems development process.

Various software tools are available to support the systems development process. Key technology decisions should be based on the organization's familiarity with the technology and its compatibility with the organization's information requirements and information architecture.

For Discussion
1. Why is selecting a systems development approach an important business decision? Who should participate in the selection process?
2. Some have said that the best way to reduce system development costs is to use application software packages or fourth-generation tools. Do you agree? Why or why not?

Management Wrap-Up provides a quick overview of the key issues in each chapter, reinforcing the authors' management, organization, and technology framework.

A TRULY INTERNATIONAL PERSPECTIVE

All chapters are illustrated with real-world examples from nearly one hundred corporations in the United States, Europe, Asia, Latin America, Africa, Australia, and the Middle East. Each chapter contains at least one Window On box, case study, or opening vignette drawn from a non-Canadian firm, and often more. International issues are interwoven throughout the text and are emphasized in Chapters 3, 10, and 13.

ATTENTION TO SMALL BUSINESSES AND ENTREPRENEURS

A cube-shaped symbol identifies in-text discussions and specially designated chapter-opening vignettes, Window On boxes, and chapter-ending case studies that highlight the experiences and challenges of small businesses and entrepreneurs using information systems.

PEDAGOGY TO PROMOTE ACTIVE LEARNING AND MANAGEMENT PROBLEM SOLVING

Management Information Systems: Managing the Digital Firm (First Canadian Edition) contains many other features that encourage students to learn actively and to engage in management problem solving.

Group Projects

At the end of each chapter is a group project that encourages students to develop teamwork and oral and written presentation skills. The group projects make even better use of the Internet. For instance, students might be asked to work in small groups to evaluate the Web sites of two competing businesses or to develop a corporate ethics code on privacy that considers e-mail privacy and the monitoring of employees using networks.

Management Challenges Section

Each chapter begins with several challenges relating to the chapter topic that managers are likely to encounter. These challenges are multifaceted and sometimes pose dilemmas. They make excellent springboards for class discussion. Some of these Management Challenges are finding the right Internet business model, overcoming the organizational obstacles to building a database environment, and agreeing on quality standards for information systems.

Case Studies

Each chapter concludes with a case study based on a real-world organization. These cases help students synthesize chapter concepts and apply this new knowledge to concrete problems and scenarios.

INSTRUCTIONAL SUPPORT MATERIALS

The following support materials have been carefully prepared to assist adopters of the textbook in their teaching of the course.

INSTRUCTOR'S MANUAL

The Instructor's Manual includes teaching objectives and suggestions, detailed lecture outlines, and answers to all the Review Questions, Group Projects, Case Studies, and Canadian Case Studies in the textbook.

TEST ITEM FILE

The Test Item File provides a set of true/false questions, multiple-choice questions, fill-in-the-blank questions, and essay questions for each chapter of the textbook. Each question is accompanied by the correct answer, a level-of-difficulty rating (i.e., easy, medium, or hard), and a cross-reference to the relevant section of the textbook.

PEARSON TEST MANAGER (FOR WINDOWS)

The Pearson Test Manager is a special computerized version of the Test Item File that enables instructors to edit existing questions, add questions, and generate tests. The Pearson Test Manager also combines a powerful database with special tests so that instructors can process and analyze test results. In addition, the Pearson Test Manager offers the Online Testing System, which instructors can use to administer, correct, record, and return computerized exams over a variety of networks.

ELECTRONIC TRANSPARENCIES (IN POWERPOINT)

Electronic colour slides illuminate and build upon key concepts in the text.

CBC/PEARSON EDUCATION CANADA VIDEO LIBRARY FOR MIS

The CBC and Pearson Education Canada have combined their experience in global reporting and academic publishing to create a special video ancillary to the textbook. The video consists of four segments from the CBC programs *Venture* and *UNDERcurrents*. Each segment has been chosen to supplement a Canadian Case Study presented at the end of the parts of the textbook.

COMPANION WEBSITE (WWW.PEARSONED.CA/LAUDON)

As described earlier in this Preface, a robust Companion Website has been created to accompany this first Canadian edition of the textbook. One of the most notable features of the site is that it will be updated regularly to ensure that material presented in the book remains current. The site also includes a password-protected faculty area from which instructors can download some of the text's supplements.

ACKNOWLEDGMENTS

The production of any book is a team effort and involves many valued contributions from a number of persons. I am particularly grateful to the staff of Pearson Education Canada for their vision, encouragement, and collegiality in producing this first Canadian introductory MIS text. I would like to thank Michael Young, who came late into the project but offered a steady hand, and Kelly Torrance. Particular thanks are owed to Maurice Esses, whose patience, encouragement, support, and knowledgeable advice were always in abundant supply. Special thanks are also due to Marisa D'Andrea and Cat Haggert, who are responsible for the "look and feel" of this text as well as for producing the text under a most ambitious schedule. This text is the result of their collective hard work.

Students and former students helped with this project as well. Special thanks are due to Joe Kwan and Zach Zahradnik, who worked on research and editing. Thanks also to Alana Yaren, who assisted with preliminary research.

I am also grateful to the following instructors who provided formal reviews of parts of the manuscript:

Susan Birtwell, Kwantlen University College

David Chan, York University

Len Fertuck, University of Toronto

Dale Foster, Memorial University of Newfoundland

Milena Head, McMaster University

Dennis Kira, Concordia University

Ron Murch, University of Calgary

Daniel Scott, Langara College

Leiser Silva, University of Alberta

Anthony Wensley, University of Toronto

One of our goals was to write a book that was authoritative, that synthesized diverse views in the MIS literature, and that helped to define the field of MIS for Canadian business students. Canadian business leaders, in particular the chief information officers at a variety of Canadian businesses, were generous in confirming and enriching the details of specific cases and examples mentioned in the text.

It is our hope that this team endeavour contributes to a shared vision and understanding of the MIS field in Canada and throughout the world.

A Great Way to Learn and Instruct Online

The Pearson Education Canada Companion Website is easy to navigate and is organized to correspond to the chapters in this textbook. Whether you are a student in the classroom or a distance learner you will discover helpful resources for in-depth study and research that empower you in your quest for greater knowledge and maximize your potential for success in the course.

[www.pearsoned.ca/laudon]

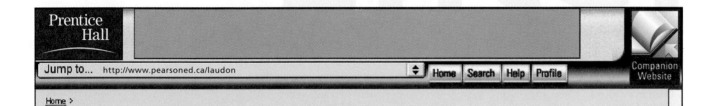

Jump to...   http://www.pearsoned.ca/laudon   ⬍   Home   Search   Help   Profile

Home >

PH Companion Website

Management Information Systems: Managing the Digital Firm, First Canadian Edition, by Laudon, Laudon, and Brabston

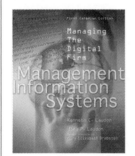

Study Resources

The modules in this section provide students with tools for learning course material. These modules include:
- Self-Test Questions
- Application Exercises
- Internet and E-Commerce Projects
- Comprehensive Projects

In the quiz modules students can send answers to the grader and receive instant feedback on their progress through the Results Reporter. Coaching comments and references to the textbook may be available to ensure that students take advantage of all available resources to enhance their learning experience.

Updates and Other Resources

The modules in this section are designed for students and instructors alike. These modules include:
- Updates
- Alternative Models
- Technical Topics
- Web Destinations
- Cumulative Glossary

Instructor Resources

The modules in this section provide instructors with additional teaching tools. Downloadable PowerPoint Presentations, Electronic Transparencies, and an Instructor's Manual are available in this section. Where appropriate, this section will be password protected. To get a password, simply contact your Pearson Education Canada Representative or call Faculty Sales and Services at 1-800-850-5813.

PART I

THE ROLE OF INFORMATION SYSTEMS IN BUSINESS TODAY

MANAGING THE DIGITAL FIRM: CANADA AND BEYOND

OBJECTIVES

After completing this chapter, you will be able to:

1. *Analyze the role of information systems in today's competitive business environment.*

2. *Define an information system from both a technical and business perspective and distinguish between computer literacy and information systems literacy.*

3. *Explain how information systems are transforming organizations and management.*

4. *Assess the relationship between the digital firm, electronic commerce, electronic business, and Internet technology.*

5. *Identify the major management challenges of building and using information systems in organizations.*

Technology and Fashion Working Hand in Glove

In the late 1960s, he borrowed $8000 and financed the purchase of a Winnipeg-based ladies' apparel manufacturing firm, renaming it "Tan Jay." Today, Finnish-born Peter J. Nygård heads Nygård International, Canada's largest manufacturer and distributor of women's apparel.

It's a $300 million, privately held fashion empire with factories and distribution centres in Canada, the United States, Mexico, and Asia that produces about 15 million garments annually. The enterprise includes research and design facilities in New York, Montreal, Europe, and Hong Kong. Nygård has their own retail outlets, but their apparel is also at Eatons, The Bay, and at leading American retail stores, including Dillard's, Sears, and Saks Fifth Avenue.

Peter Nygård's need to keep performance facts and figures within easy reach has led him to invest over $50 million in building a streamlined computerized operation, with the goal of eliminating traditional, paper-based manufacturing methods. This commitment to technology has fuelled impressive results, with Nygård International achieving annual exports to the United States totalling $120 million.

Nygård's work with information technology dates back to the early 1980s. When the company was founded, the apparel industry was a nightmare of paperwork. In this paper-based industry, key information was hard to locate, transmit, share, and analyze.

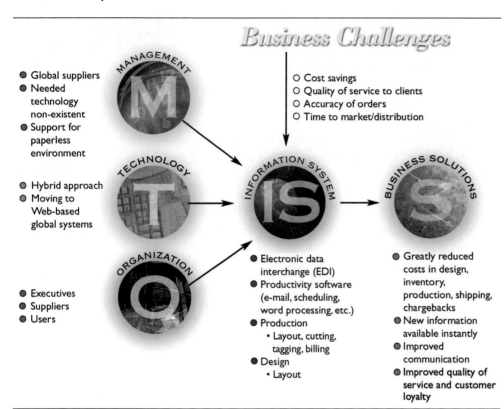

Nygård turned to information technology for help, but he foresaw dangers in uncharted waters. "Many pioneered the use of technology and failed because the technology wasn't developed enough or because they exhausted themselves being first," Nygård said. "Too often in pioneering, you can go from being the 'cutting-edge' to 'bleeding-edge.' Timing is everything... Don't just use technology to repeat the traditional process. You have to rethink how you can use technology to do things in a completely different way."

This insight led Nygård to develop a new kind of manufacturing system called NS2000. A collection of best-of-breed and Nygård proprietary software, this hybrid system orchestrates all of the firm's resources, drawing upon methodologies embedded in supply chain management (SCM) and enterprise resource planning (ERP) systems.

A major component of NS2000 is Automatic Reorder To Sale (ARTS 2), which is both a physical factory and a network that links all Nygård stores and major retail accounts. Whenever Nygård clothes are sold, the cash register transaction at the retail outlets triggers reorder forms filed instantly on computer. Reorders from all over the world are flashed electronically to the ARTS 2 plant in Winnipeg. From this information, supply and production schedules are coordinated for speed and efficiency.

Here's how a typical day of production works. Before dawn, Nygård's Resources Planning system compiles all the instructions needed to pull the fabrics and schedule manufacturing processes. The Continuous Replenishment (CR) module then

(continued)

scans all orders and, using inventory sizes and shapes, lays out the outline markers that make optimum use of material for production that morning.

Giant bolts of fabric are positioned by machine in sequence as computerized spreaders roll the cloth back and forth like layered pastry over long tables. Then a Gerber cutter "cookie-cuts" the layers of fabric into stacks of pant legs, collars, sleeves, and dress panels. The new shapes are bundled over to modular sewing stations for assembly. Each finished garment is inspected, bar-coded, tagged, and finally prepared for packing and shipment.

Orders that used to take three weeks now go out within a few hours of first notification. With ARTS 2, garments are made only when needed, reducing the high cost of warehousing.

Nygård's system also links to their major suppliers, which are notified as orders are placed, coordinating the flow of all component parts, including zippers, trims, buttons, and hangers. At present, the firm is linked via electronic data interchange (EDI) to about 85 percent of its customers and suppliers.

Computer-aided design and computer-aided manufacturing (CAD/CAM) technology is also employed. Designers create designs on screen, including cloth patterns. From there, it's easy to calculate how much material is needed to make a full run of sizes, to compare this amount with available inventory stock, and to cost manufacturing to the penny.

"Almost any garment can be produced quickly," Nygård observed. He estimates that 85 percent of the lead-time to production came from administrative delays. IT has reduced this dramatically. The saving of time and labour has, according to Nygård, prevented clothing prices from rising for the past decade. "The cost of goods falls as electronics drive the economy."

Historically, lack of organization and the high incidence of theft or loss in the garment industry led retailers to routinely demand millions of dollars annually in refunds or chargebacks from manufacturers for items they claimed as missing from incoming shipments. In response, Nygård created a surveillance system to monitor every aspect of production.

The system bar-codes and tracks each item, videotaping the clothes as they are packed, and weighs each shipment so that any change in weight along the way signals alarms and stops the whole process. The system is so secure that Dillard's American chain exempted Nygård from chargebacks altogether.

IT has also changed the way that stores and retail outlets physically handle shipments of Nygård's designs. In the past, Nygård International would make a single, bulk shipment to a giant retailer such as The Bay. All garments were sorted, reticketed, relabelled, and then repacked for shipment to the chain's individual stores. Now, with electronic surveillance, bar-coding, and tracking, shipments are prepacked for a given store. Once they leave a Nygård plant, they travel to a chain's warehouse. There, the unopened boxes are simply transferred to a waiting truck and delivered locally.

Nygård invests heavily in technology training. All non-manufacturing employees must spend approximately one-third of their time on computer training. At Nygård, eliminating paper-based communications has become the goal. For example, photocopiers require user codes, e-mail messages are mandated to fit single screens, and hardcopy facilities are centralized. Laptops are the medium for minutes in meetings. To stop reams of paper faxes, e-mail addresses replace fax numbers on all Nygård business cards.

As always, Peter Nygård is looking ahead. According to Nygård, the potential of the Internet is not fully realized. "When people talk about e-commerce, they often mean little more than Web-based retail, selling sweaters and pants. But the biggest gains to be made in e-commerce are in the back-office. Probably 70 percent of administrative work can be done via the Web. This is where one can make fantastic savings, slashing the cost of communications, production, and delivery." Nygård so believes in his vision that he has partnered with the city of Winnipeg's Development Authority, the Canada/Manitoba Economic Development Partnership, the Manitoba Industrial Opportunities Program, and the fashion industry to create distance and multimedia training facilities, a manufacturing pilot plant, research laboratories, and other information technology resources for the fashion industry, so that even his own competition can receive training in state-of-the-art fashion technology.

Sources: Ian Mount and Brian Caulfield, "The Missing Link: What You Need to Know about Supply-Chain Technology," *eCompany Now*, May 2001; Burke Campbell and Murray Conron, "Going Paperless Is In Fashion," *ComputerWorld Canada*, August 13, 1999; Sarah Yates, "Commitment to Technological Change Pays Dividends at Nygård," *Trade & Commerce*, Spring 2001; "Three Levels of Government Fund International Fashion Technology Centre," *Winnipeg Development Authority Press Release*, June 4, 1999, www.wda.mb.ca/new/news41.html, accessed July 29, 2001.

The changes taking place at Nygård International exemplify the transformation of business firms throughout the world as they re-build themselves as fully digital firms. These digital firms use the Internet and networking technology to make data flow seamlessly among different parts of the organization, streamline the flow of work, and create electronic links with customers, suppliers, and other organizations.

All types of businesses, both large and small, are using information systems, networks, and Internet technology to conduct more of their business electronically, achieving new levels of efficiency and competitiveness. Information systems, the Internet, and other global networks are creating new opportunities for organizational coordination and innovation. Information systems can help companies extend their reach to faraway locations, offer new products and services, reshape jobs and work flows, and perhaps profoundly change the way they conduct business. This chapter starts our investigation of information systems and organizations by describing information systems from both technical and behavioural perspectives and by surveying the changes they are bringing to organizations and management.

1.1 WHY INFORMATION SYSTEMS?

Until recently, information itself was not considered an important asset for a firm. The management process was considered a face-to-face, personal art and not a far-flung, global coordination process. Today, it is widely recognized that understanding information systems is essential for managers because most organizations need information systems to survive and prosper.

THE COMPETITIVE BUSINESS ENVIRONMENT AND THE EMERGING DIGITAL FIRM

Four powerful worldwide changes have altered the business environment. The first change is the emergence and strengthening of the global economy. The second change is the transformation of industrial economies and societies into knowledge- and information-based service economies. The third is the transformation of the business enterprise. The fourth is the emergence of the digital firm. These changes in the business environment and climate, summarized in Table 1.1, pose a number of new challenges to business firms and their management.

Emergence of the Global Economy

A growing percentage of the North American economy—and other advanced industrial economies in Europe and Asia—depends on imports and exports. Foreign trade, both

TABLE 1-1	THE CHANGING CONTEMPORARY BUSINESS ENVIRONMENT

Globalization	Transformation of the Enterprise
Management and control in a global marketplace	Flattening
Competition in world markets	Decentralization
Global work groups	Flexibility
Global delivery systems	Location independence
	Low transaction and coordination costs
Transformation of Industrial Economies	Empowerment
Knowledge- and information-based economies	Collaborative work and teamwork
Productivity	**Emergence of the Digital Firm**
New products and services	Digitally enabled relationships with customers, suppliers, and employees
Knowledge as a strategic asset	Core business processes accomplished via digital networks
Time-based competition	
Shorter product life	Digital management of key corporate assets
Turbulent environment	Rapid sensing of and responding to environmental changes
Limited employee knowledge base	

exports and imports, accounts for a little over 25 percent of the goods and services produced in North America, and even more in countries like Japan and Germany. The success of firms today and in the future depends on their ability to operate globally.

Today, information systems provide the communication and analytic power that firms need for conducting trade and managing businesses on a global scale. Controlling the far-flung global corporation—communicating with distributors and suppliers, operating 24 hours a day in different national environments, servicing local and international reporting needs—is a major business challenge that requires powerful information system responses.

Globalization and information technology also bring new threats to domestic business firms. Because of global communication and management systems, customers now can shop in a worldwide marketplace, obtaining price and quality information reliably, 24 hours a day. This phenomenon heightens competition and forces firms to play in open, unprotected worldwide markets. To become effective and profitable participants in international markets, firms need powerful information and communication systems.

Transformation of Industrial Economies

Canada, the United States, Japan, Germany, and other major industrial powers are being transformed from industrial economies to knowledge- and information-based service economies, while manufacturing has been moving to low-wage countries. In a knowledge- and information-based economy, knowledge and information are the key ingredients in creating wealth.

The knowledge and information revolution began at the turn of the twentieth century and has gradually accelerated. Today, most people no longer work on farms or in factories but instead are found in sales, education, healthcare, banks, insurance firms, and law firms; they also provide business services like copying, computer programming, or making deliveries. In 2000, almost three times as many Canadians worked in the services-producing sector as the goods-producing sector of the economy (Statistics Canada, 2001). These services-producing jobs primarily involve working with, distributing, or creating new knowledge and information.

Knowledge and information are the foundations for many new services and products. **Knowledge- and information-intense products** such as computer games require a great deal of knowledge to produce. Entire new information-based services have sprung up, such as Lexis, Dow Jones News Service, and America Online. These fields employ millions of people.

knowledge- and information-intense products
Products that require a great deal of learning and knowledge to produce.

Knowledge is used more intensively in the production of traditional products as well. In the automobile industry, for instance, both design and production now rely heavily on knowledge and information technology. During the past 15 years, automobile producers have hired more computer specialists, engineers, and designers while reducing the number of blue-collar production workers.

In a knowledge- and information-based economy, information technology and systems take on great importance. Knowledge-based products and services of great economic value, such as credit cards, overnight package delivery, and worldwide reservation systems, are based on new information technologies. Information technology constitutes more than 70 percent of the invested capital in service industries like finance, insurance, and real estate.

Across all industries, information and the technology that delivers it have become critical, strategic assets for business firms and their managers (Leonard-Barton, 1995). Information systems are needed to optimize the flow of information and knowledge within the organization and to help management maximize the firm's knowledge resources. Because employees' productivity will depend on the quality of the systems serving them, management decisions about information technology are critically important to the firm's prosperity and survival.

Transformation of the Business Enterprise

There has been a transformation in the possibilities for organizing and managing the business enterprise. Some firms have begun to take advantage of these new possibilities.

The traditional business firm was—and still is—a hierarchical, centralized, structured arrangement of specialists that typically relies on a fixed set of standard operating procedures to deliver a mass-produced product (or service). The new style of business firm is a flattened (less hierarchical), decentralized, flexible arrangement of generalists who rely on nearly instant information to deliver mass-customized products and services uniquely suited to specific markets or customers.

The traditional management group relied—and still does—on formal plans, a rigid division of labour, and formal rules. It appeals to loyalty to ensure the proper operation of a firm. The new manager relies on informal commitments and networks to establish goals (rather than formal planning), a flexible arrangement of teams and individuals working in task forces, and a customer orientation to achieve coordination among employees. The new manager appeals to the knowledge, learning, and decision-making of individual employees to ensure proper operation of the firm. Once again, information technology makes this style of management possible.

The Emerging Digital Firm

The intensive use of information technology in business firms since the mid-1990s, coupled with equally significant organizational redesign, has created the conditions for a new phenomenon in industrial society—the fully digital firm. The **digital firm** can be defined along several dimensions. A digital firm is one where nearly all of the organization's *significant business relationships* with customers, suppliers, and employees are digitally enabled and mediated. *Core business processes* are accomplished through digital networks spanning the entire organization or linking multiple organizations. **Business processes** are the unique ways in which work is organized, coordinated, and focused to produce a valuable product or service. Developing a new product, generating and fulfilling an order, or hiring an employee are examples of business processes, and the way organizations accomplish their business processes can be a source of competitive strength. (A detailed discussion of business processes can be found in Chapter 2.) *Key corporate assets*—intellectual property, core competencies, financial and human assets—are managed through digital means. In a digital firm, any piece of information required to support key business decisions is available at anytime and anywhere in the firm. Digital firms *sense and respond* to their environments far more rapidly than traditional firms, giving them more flexibility to survive in turbulent times. Digital firms offer extraordinary opportunities for more global organization and management. By digitally enabling and streamlining their work, digital firms have the potential to achieve unprecedented levels of profitability and competitiveness.

digital firm

An organization where nearly all significant business processes and relationships with customers, suppliers, and employees are digitally enabled, and key corporate assets are managed through digital means.

business processes

The unique ways in which organizations coordinate and organize work activities, information, and knowledge to produce a product or service.

Digital firms are distinguished from traditional firms by their near total reliance on a set of information technologies to organize and manage. For managers of digital firms, information technology is not simply a useful handmaiden, an enabler, but rather it is the core of the business and the primary management tool.

There are very few fully digital firms today. Yet inexorably, it is the direction that nearly all firms—especially larger traditional firms—are being driven by a number of business forces and opportunities. When your customers, suppliers, and competitors become digital firms, your firm either becomes equally digital or perishes. The Window on Organizations illustrates one digital firm in the making.

Simply investing in information technology does not make a digital firm or automatically produce high levels of profitability and efficiency. Moving from a traditional firm

WINDOW ON ORGANIZATIONS

CISCO SYSTEMS: A DIGITAL FIRM IN THE MAKING

Cisco Systems loves to advertise that it is the company on which the Internet runs. Headquartered in San Jose, California, it dominates the sale of network routers and switching equipment used for Internet infrastructure. Under the leadership of CEO John Chambers, it has become one of the most valuable companies on earth. One key to its success is that Cisco is an organization that uses the Internet in every way it can. To turn its advertising slogan around, it would be equally accurate to say that Cisco runs on the Internet.

Cisco is very close to becoming a digital firm, using Internet technology to drive every aspect of its business. Customers, suppliers, distributors, and other business partners have access to portions of Cisco's private internal Web site as well as its public Web site. Over 90 percent of Cisco's sales come via the Internet. Three quarters of Cisco products are manufactured by contract suppliers, and Cisco does not order from them from sales projections. Instead, production is based on actual customer orders. Customers use the Cisco Web site to configure and price their systems and then to place the order. The order is then routed directly to one of Cisco's manufacturers, such as Flextronics International in Singapore, which produce the product and ship it directly to the customer. The same Web site is linked directly to Federal Express and UPS so customers can track their shipments. Using this method to build products on order, Cisco has cut delivery time by 70 percent while reducing its own inventory. As Karen Brunett of Cisco's Internet business solutions group put it, "We don't touch the product at all." For those customers who feel they do need handholding when ordering, Cisco sales personnel gladly provide it.

Customer service also occurs on the Net. Cisco receives about 800 000 customer queries monthly, and 85 percent of those are handled satisfactorily on the Net, eliminating thousands of customer service representative positions and saving the company $600 million in the year 2000 alone. Cisco does make available personal service when the customer wants it, however. Charles Schwab Corp., for example, cannot afford network downtime under any circumstances, and so it pays Cisco to keep engineers available by telephone 24 hours per day. Meanwhile, customer satisfaction has risen by 25 percent since 1995.

Management is on top of all the financial numbers because their computers update sales and related figures three times daily, and those numbers are instantly available over the Web on a need-to-know basis. Executives can even see net income, margins, orders, and expenses. Due to their using the Internet to obtain and store all these numbers, the company can even close their books within 24 hours after the end of a quarter. This rate of speed is almost unheard of for a function that is usually so slow that the Securities and Exchange Commission gives companies 90 days after a quarter to report.

Similarly, human resource functions are managed through Internet technology. For example, Cisco receives about 25 000 employment applications monthly, and almost all come in through Cisco's public Web site (see Figure 1-1). If the applications were submitted by paper, Cisco probably could not handle them all. Cisco employees can fill out all human resource forms (such as expense reports or changes to healthcare benefits) on the Web and update them whenever necessary. The company has also moved almost 80 percent of its training to the Web and is very pleased with the results. Cisco even is using the Internet to operate what may be the largest daycare centre in Northern California, where 450 youngsters can be cared for while their parents work. Parents can monitor their children on the Web while at work via two cameras installed in the daycare centre.

Interestingly, according to *Fortune*'s 2001 Most Admired Companies ranking, Canada's Nortel Networks ranks a close second behind Cisco, besting Cisco in the categories of product quality and innovativeness. Though Nortel is under pressure from new economy giants like Cisco and Lucent, the company isn't overly worried, for its optical backbones carry an estimated 75 percent of North America's Internet traffic and 50 percent of Europe's.

To Think About: How is the Internet driving organizational and management changes at Cisco? To what extent is Cisco a digital firm? To what extent does market competition from other companies like Nortel or Lucent drive these changes at Cisco?

Sources: Scott Thurm, "Eating Their Own Dog Food," *The Wall Street Journal*, April 19, 2000; John Markoff, "Ignore the Label, It's Flextronics Inside," *The New York Times*, February 15, 2001; Andy Serwer, "There's Something About Cisco," *Fortune*, May 15, 2000; Lee Sherman, "A Matter of Connections" *Knowledge Management*, July 2000; Ahmad Diba and Lisa Munoz, "America's Most Admired Companies," *Fortune*, February 19, 2001; and Harikrishnan Menon and Aruna Vaidayanathan, "On Wings of Light," *The Economic Times Online*, November 10, 2000.

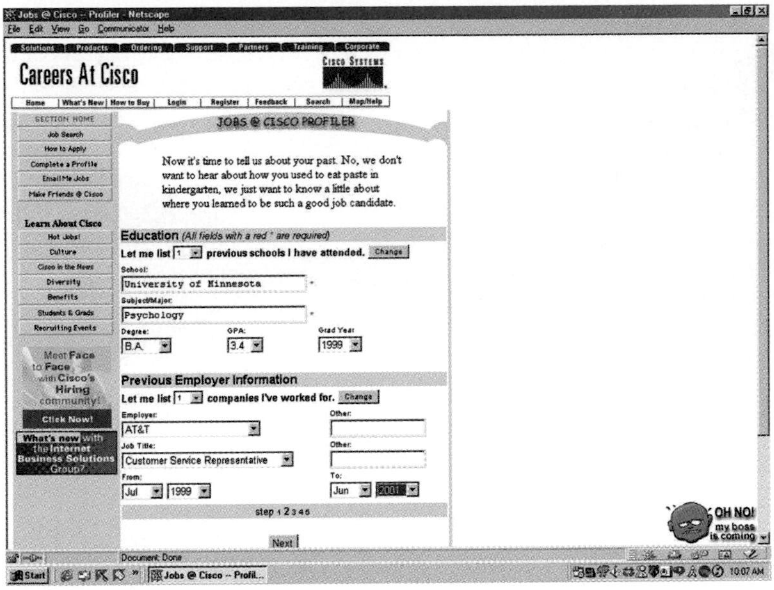

FIGURE 1-1 Cisco Systems uses the Web to recruit almost all of its employees. With many of its business processes enabled by the Internet, Cisco is becoming a digital firm.

toward a digital firm requires insight, skill, and patience. Managers need to identify the challenges facing their firms, discover the technologies that will help them meet these challenges, organize their firms and business processes to take advantage of the technology, and create management procedures and policies to implement the required changes. This book is dedicated to helping managers prepare for these tasks.

WHAT IS AN INFORMATION SYSTEM?

An **information system** can be defined technically as a set of interrelated components that collect (or retrieve), process, store, and distribute information to support decision making and control in an organization. In addition to supporting decision making, coordination, and control, information systems may also help managers and workers analyze problems, visualize complex subjects, and create new products.

Information systems contain information about significant people, places, and things within the organization or in the environment surrounding it. By **information** we mean data that have been shaped into a form that is meaningful and useful to human beings. **Data**, in contrast, are raw facts representing events occurring in organizations or the physical environment before they have been organized and arranged into a form that people can understand and use.

A brief example contrasting information to data may prove useful. Supermarket checkout counters ring up millions of pieces of data such as product identification numbers or the cost of each item sold. These pieces of data can be totalled and analyzed to provide meaningful information such as the total number of bottles of dish detergent sold at a particular store, which brands of dish detergent were selling the most rapidly at that store or sales territory, or the total amount spent on that brand of dish detergent at that store or sales region (see Figure 1-2).

Four activities in an information system produce the information that organizations need to make decisions, control operations, analyze problems, and create new products or services. These activities are input, processing, output, and feedback (see Figure 1-3). **Input** captures or collects raw data from within the organization or from its external environment. **Processing** converts this raw input into a more meaningful form. **Output** transfers the processed information to the people who will use it or to the activities for which it will be used. Information systems also require **feedback**, which is output that is returned to appropriate members of the organization to help them evaluate or correct the input or processing activities.

In Nygård's information system for apparel buying, the raw input for an order from retailers consists of the item number, item description, and amount of each item ordered

information system
Interrelated components working together to collect, process, store, and disseminate information to support decision making, co-ordination, control, analysis, and visualization in an organization.

information
Data that have been shaped into a form that is meaningful and useful to human beings.

data
Raw facts representing events occurring in organizations or the physical environment before they have been organized and arranged into a form that people can understand and use.

input
The capture or collection of raw data from within the organization or from its external environment for processing in an information system.

processing
The conversion, manipulation, and analysis of raw input into a form that is more meaningful to humans.

output
The distribution of processed information to the people who will use it or to the activities for which it will be used.

feedback
Output that is returned to the appropriate members of the organization to help them evaluate or correct input or processing.

FIGURE 1-2 Data and information. Raw data from a supermarket checkout counter can be processed and organized in order to produce meaningful information such as the total unit sales of dish detergent or the total sales revenue from dish detergent for a specific store or sales territory.

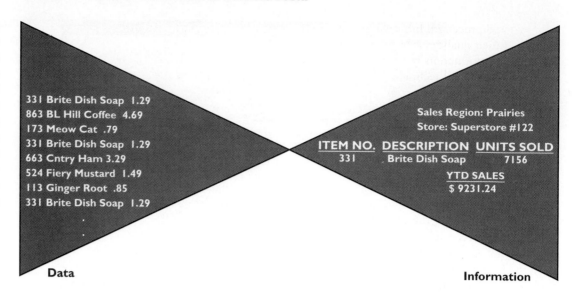

331 Brite Dish Soap 1.29
863 BL Hill Coffee 4.69
173 Meow Cat .79
331 Brite Dish Soap 1.29
663 Cntry Ham 3.29
524 Fiery Mustard 1.49
113 Ginger Root .85
331 Brite Dish Soap 1.29

Sales Region: Prairies
Store: Superstore #122

ITEM NO.	DESCRIPTION	UNITS SOLD
331	Brite Dish Soap	7156

YTD SALES
$ 9231.24

Data   **Information**

along with the retailer's name and identification number. The computer processes these data by comparing the item number on the order to item numbers in Nygård's master catalogue and supplying the correct item number when discrepancies are found. The system schedules the production and shipment of orders to the retailer. Shipping documents, invoices, and online reports to the retailer showing delivery date and location of the order in transit become outputs. The system thus provides meaningful information such as lists of which retailer ordered what items, the total number of each item ordered daily, and the total number of each item ordered by each retailer.

Our interest in this book is in formal, organizational, **computer-based information systems (CBIS)** like those designed and used by Nygård and its customers, suppliers, and employees. **Formal systems** rest on accepted and fixed definitions of data and procedures for collecting, storing, processing, disseminating, and using these data. The formal systems we describe in this text are structured; that is, they operate in conformity with predefined rules that are relatively fixed and not easily changed. For instance, Nygård's system requires that all orders include the retailer's name and identification number and a unique number for identifying each item.

Informal information systems (such as office gossip networks) rely, by contrast, on unstated rules of behaviour. There is no agreement on what is information or on how it will

computer-based information systems (CBIS)
Information systems that rely on computer hardware and software for processing and disseminating information.

formal system
A system resting on accepted and fixed definitions of data and procedures, operating with predefined rules.

FIGURE 1-3 Functions of an information system. An information system contains information about an organization and its surrounding environment. Four basic activities—input, processing, output, and feedback—produce the information organizations need. Environmental actors such as customers, suppliers, competitors, stockholders, and regulatory agencies interact with the organization and its information systems.

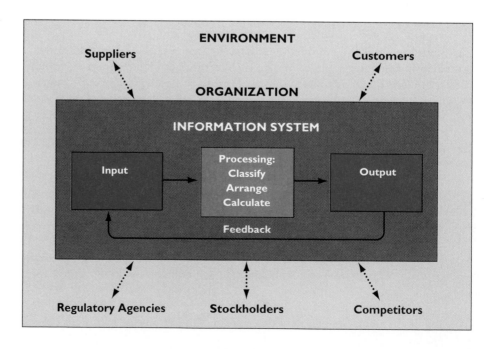

ENVIRONMENT
Suppliers   Customers
ORGANIZATION
INFORMATION SYSTEM

Input → Processing: Classify Arrange Calculate → Output

Feedback

Regulatory Agencies   Stockholders   Competitors

be stored and processed. Informal systems are essential for the life of an organization, but an analysis of their qualities is beyond the scope of this text.

Formal information systems can be either computer-based or manual. Manual systems use paper-and-pencil technology. Manual systems serve important needs, but they too are not the subject of this text. Computer-based information systems, in contrast, rely on computer hardware and software technology to process and disseminate information. From this point on, when we use the term information systems, we will be referring to computer-based information systems—formal organizational systems that rely on computer technology. The Window on Technology describes some of the typical technologies used in computer-based information systems today.

Although computer-based information systems use computer technology to process raw data into meaningful information, there is a sharp distinction between a computer and a computer program on the one hand, and an information system on the other. Electronic computers and related software programs are the technical foundation of modern information systems. Computers provide the equipment for storing and processing information. Computer programs are sets of operating instructions that direct and control computer processing. Knowing how computers and computer programs work is important in designing

UPS COMPETES GLOBALLY WITH INFORMATION TECHNOLOGY

United Parcel Service, the world's largest air and ground package distribution company, started out in 1907 in a closet-sized basement office. Jim Casey and Claude Ryan—two teenagers from Seattle with two bicycles and one phone—promised the "best service and lowest rates." UPS has used this formula successfully for over 90 years.

Today UPS delivers more than 13 million parcels and documents daily to Canada and the United States and more than 200 other countries and territories. The firm has been able to maintain its leadership in small package delivery services in the face of stiff competition from Federal Express and Airborne Express by investing heavily in advanced information technology. Over the past decade, UPS has spent over $1 billion a year to boost customer service while keeping costs low and streamlining overall operations.

Using a handheld computer called a Delivery Information Acquisition Device (DIAD), UPS drivers automatically capture customers' signatures along with pickup, delivery, and time-card information. The drivers then place the DIAD into their truck's vehicle adapter, an information-transmitting device that is connected to the cellular telephone network. (Drivers may also transmit and receive information using an internal radio in the DIAD.) Package tracking information is then transmitted to UPS's computer network for storage and processing in UPS's main computers in Mahwah, New Jersey, and Alpharetta, Georgia. From there, the information can be accessed worldwide to provide proof of delivery to the customer or to respond to customer queries.

Through its automated package tracking system, UPS can monitor packages throughout the delivery process. At various points along the route from sender to receiver, a bar code device scans shipping information on the package label; the information is then fed into the central computer. Customer service representatives can check the status of any package from desktop computers linked to the central computers and are able to respond immediately to inquiries from customers. UPS customers can also access this information from the company's Web site using their own computers or wireless devices such as pagers and cell phones.

Anyone with a package to ship can access the UPS Web site to track packages, check delivery routes, calculate shipping rates, determine time in transit, or schedule a pickup. Businesses anywhere can use the Web site to arrange UPS shipments and bill the shipments to the company's UPS account number or to a credit card. The data collected at the UPS Web site are transmitted to the UPS central computer and then back to the customer after processing. UPS also provides tools that enable its customers such as Cisco Systems, described in the Window on Organizations, to embed UPS functions, such as tracking and cost calculation, into their own Web sites so that they can track shipments without visiting the UPS site. UPS started a new service called UPS Document Exchange to deliver business documents electronically using the Internet. The service provides a high level of security for important documents as well as document tracking.

To Think About: What are the inputs, processing, and outputs of UPS's package tracking system? What sort of feedback does UPS receive from the system? What technologies are used? How are these technologies related to UPS's business strategy? What would happen if these technologies were not available?

Sources: Rick Brooks, "Outside the Box," *The Wall Street Journal E-Commerce Section*, February 12, 2001; Bob Brewin, "FedEx, UPS Vie to Offer Wireless Tracking Services," *Computerworld*, July 3, 2000; Kelly Barron, "Logistics in Brown," *Forbes*, January 10, 2000; Art Jahnke, "Deliverance," *CIO Web Business Magazine*, July 1, 1999; and David Baum, "UPS: Keeping Track, *Oracle Magazine*, May/June 1999.

Using a handheld computer called a Delivery Information Acquisition Device (DIAD), UPS drivers automatically capture customers' signatures along with pickup, delivery, and time-card information.

solutions to organizational problems, but computers are only part of an information system. A house is an appropriate analogy. Houses are built with hammers, nails, and wood, but these do not make a house. The architecture, design, setting, landscaping, and all of the decisions that lead to the creation of these features are part of the house and are crucial for solving the problem of putting a roof over one's head. Computers and programs are the hammer, nails, and lumber of CBIS, but alone they cannot produce the information a particular organization needs. To understand information systems, one must understand the problems they are designed to solve, their architectural and design elements, and the organizational processes that lead to these solutions.

A BUSINESS PERSPECTIVE ON INFORMATION SYSTEMS

From a business perspective, an information system is an organizational and management solution, based on information technology, to a challenge posed by the environment. Examine this definition closely because it emphasizes the organizational and managerial nature of information systems: To fully understand information systems, a manager must understand the broader organization, management, and information technology dimensions of systems (see Figure 1-4) and their power to provide solutions to challenges and problems in the business environment. We refer to this broader understanding of information systems,

FIGURE 1-4 Information systems are more than computers. Using information systems effectively requires an understanding of the organization, management, and information technology shaping the systems. All information systems can be described as organizational and management solutions to challenges posed by the environment.

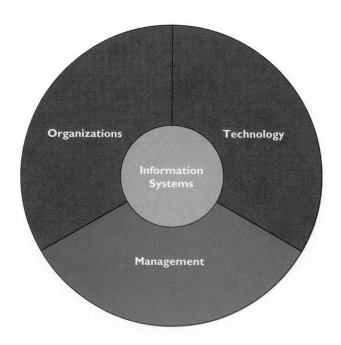

which encompasses an understanding of the management and organizational dimensions of systems as well as the technical dimensions of systems, as **information systems literacy**. Information systems literacy includes a behavioural as well as a technical approach to studying information systems. **Computer literacy**, in contrast, focuses primarily on knowledge of information technology.

Review the diagram at the beginning of the chapter, which reflects this expanded definition of an information system. The diagram shows how Nygård's apparel buying information system solves the business challenges of rapid growth, intensifying competition, and opportunities presented by new technology—in this case, the Internet. The diagram also illustrates how management, technology, and organization elements work together to create the system. Each chapter of this text begins with a diagram like this one to help you analyze the opening case. You can use this diagram as a starting point for analyzing any information system or information system problem you encounter.

Organizations

Information systems are an integral part of organizations. Indeed, for some companies, such as credit reporting firms, without the information system there would be no business. The key elements of an organization are its people, structure, operating procedures, politics, and culture. We introduce these components of organizations here and describe them in greater detail in Chapter 3. Organizations comprise different levels and specialties. Their structures reveal a clear-cut division of labour. Experts are employed and trained for different functions. The major **business functions**, or specialized tasks performed by business organizations, consist of sales and marketing, manufacturing, finance, accounting, and human resources (see Table 1-2). Chapter 2 provides more detail on these business functions and the ways in which they are supported by information systems.

An organization coordinates work through a structured hierarchy and formal, standard operating procedures. The hierarchy arranges people in a pyramid structure of rising authority and responsibility. The upper levels of the hierarchy consist of managerial, professional, and technical employees, while the lower levels consist of operational personnel.

Standard operating procedures (SOPs) are formal rules that have been developed over a long time for accomplishing tasks. These rules guide employees in a variety of procedures, from writing an invoice to responding to customer complaints. Most procedures are formalized and written down, but others are informal work practices, such as a requirement to return telephone calls from co-workers or customers, that are not formally documented. The firm's business processes, which we defined earlier, are based on its standard operating procedures; many business processes and SOPs are incorporated into information systems, such as how to pay a supplier or how to correct an erroneous bill.

Organizations require many different kinds of skills and people. In addition to managers, **knowledge workers** (such as engineers, architects, or scientists) design products or services and create new knowledge, and **data workers** (such as secretaries, bookkeepers, or clerks) process the organization's paperwork. **Production or service workers** (such as machinists, assemblers, or packers) actually produce the organization's products or services.

information systems literacy
Broad understanding of computer-based information systems, encompassing the management and organizational dimensions of systems as well as their technical dimensions.

computer literacy
Knowledge of the technical dimensions of computer-based information systems.

business functions
Specialized tasks performed in a business organization, including manufacturing and production, sales and marketing, finance, accounting, and human resources.

standard operating procedures (SOPs)
Formal rules for accomplishing tasks, which have been developed to cope with expected situations.

knowledge workers
People such as engineers or architects who design products or services and create knowledge for the organization.

data workers
People such as secretaries or bookkeepers who process the organization's paperwork.

production or service workers
People such as machinists or packers who actually produce the products or services of the organization.

TABLE 1-2	MAJOR BUSINESS FUNCTIONS
Function	**Purpose**
Sales and marketing	Selling the organization's products and services
Manufacturing and production	Producing products and services
Finance	Managing the organization's financial assets (cash, stocks, bonds, etc.)
Accounting	Maintaining the organization's financial records (receipts, disbursements, paycheques, etc.); accounting for the flow of funds
Human resources	Attracting, developing, and maintaining the organization's labour force; maintaining employee records

senior managers
People occupying the topmost hierarchy in an organization who are responsible for making long-range strategic decisions.

middle managers
People in the middle of the organizational hierarchy who are responsible for carrying out the plans and goals of senior management.

operational managers
People who monitor the day-to-day activities of the organization.

computer hardware
Physical equipment used for input, processing, output, and feedback activities in an information system.

computer software
Detailed, preprogrammed instructions that control and coordinate the work of computer hardware components in an information system.

storage technology
Physical media and software governing the storage and organization of data for use in an information system.

communications technology
Physical devices and software that link various computer hardware components and transfer data from one physical location to another.

network
Two or more computers linked to share data or resources such as a printer.

information technology (IT) infrastructure
The portfolio of shared information technology resources for the organization that comprises computer hardware, software, data and storage technology, and networks.

Each organization has a unique culture, or fundamental set of assumptions, values, and ways of doing things, that has been accepted by most of its members. Parts of an organization's culture can always be found embedded in its information systems. For instance, UPS's concern with customer service is an aspect of its organizational culture that can be found in the company's package tracking systems.

Different levels and specialties in an organization create different interests and points of view. These views often conflict. Conflict is the basis for organizational politics. Information systems come out of this cauldron of differing perspectives, conflicts, compromises, and agreements that are a natural part of all organizations. In Chapter 3, we will examine these features of organizations in greater detail.

Management

Managers perceive business challenges in the environment, they set the organizational strategy for responding to these challenges by allocating the human and financial resources to achieve the strategy and coordinate the work. Throughout, they must exercise responsible leadership. Management's job is to "make sense" out of the many situations faced by organizations and to formulate action plans to solve organizational problems. The business information systems described in this book reflect the hopes, dreams, and realities of real-world managers.

But managers must do more than manage what already exists. They must also create new products and services and even re-create the organization from time to time. A substantial part of management responsibility is creative work driven by new knowledge and information. Information technology can play a powerful role in redirecting and redesigning the organization. Chapter 3 describes managers' activities and management decision making in detail.

It is important to note that managerial roles and decisions vary at different levels of the organization. **Senior managers** make long-range strategic decisions about which products and services to produce. **Middle managers** carry out the programs and plans of senior management. **Operational managers** are responsible for monitoring the firm's daily activities. All levels of management are expected to be creative, to develop novel solutions to a broad range of problems. Each level of management has different information needs and information system requirements.

Technology

Information technology is one of many tools managers use to cope with change. **Computer hardware** is the physical equipment used for input, processing, output, and feedback activities in an information system. It consists of the following: the computer processing unit; various input, output, and storage devices; and connections and physical media to link these devices together. Chapter 6 describes computer hardware in greater detail.

Computer software consists of the detailed, preprogrammed instructions that control and coordinate the computer hardware components in an information system. Chapter 7 explains the importance of computer software in information systems.

Storage technology includes both the physical media for storing data, such as magnetic or optical disk or tape, and the software governing the organization of data on these physical media. More detail on physical storage media can be found in Chapter 6, while Chapter 8 covers data organization and access methods.

Communications technology, consisting of both physical devices and software, links the various pieces of hardware and transfers data from one physical location to another. Computers and communications equipment can be connected in networks for sharing voice, data, images, sound, or even video. A **network** links two or more computers to share data or resources such as a printer. Chapters 9 and 10 provide more details on communications and networking technology and issues.

All of these technologies represent resources that can be shared throughout the organization and constitute the firm's **information technology (IT) infrastructure**. The IT infrastructure provides the foundation or platform on which the firm can build its specific information systems. Each organization must carefully design and manage its information technology infrastructure so that it has the set of technology services it needs for the work it wants to accomplish with information systems. Chapters 6 through 10 of this text examine each major technology component of information technology infrastructure and show how they all work together to create the technology platform for the organization.

Let us return to UPS's package tracking system in the Window on Technology and identify the organization, management, and technology elements. The organization element anchors the package tracking system in UPS's sales and production functions (the main product of UPS is a service—package delivery). It specifies the required procedures for identifying packages with both sender and recipient information, taking inventory, tracking the packages en route, and providing package status reports for UPS customers and customer service representatives. The system must also provide information to satisfy the needs of managers and workers. UPS drivers need to be trained in both package pickup and delivery procedures and in how to use the package tracking system so that they can work efficiently and effectively. UPS customers may need some training to use UPS in-house package tracking software or the UPS Web site. UPS's management is responsible for monitoring service levels and costs and for promoting the company's strategy of combining low cost and superior service. Management decided to use automation to increase the ease of sending a package via UPS and of checking its delivery status, thereby reducing delivery costs and increasing sales revenues. The technology supporting this system consists of handheld computers, bar code scanners, wired and wireless communications networks, desktop computers, UPS's central computer, storage technology for the package delivery data, UPS in-house package tracking software, and software to access the World Wide Web. The result is an information system solution to the business challenge of providing a high level of service with low prices in the face of mounting competition.

1.2 CONTEMPORARY APPROACHES TO INFORMATION SYSTEMS

Multiple perspectives on information systems show that the study of information systems is a multidisciplinary field. No single theory or perspective dominates. Figure 1-5 illustrates the major disciplines that contribute problems, issues, and solutions to the study of information systems. In general, the field can be divided into technical and behavioural approaches. Information systems are sociotechnical systems. Though they comprise machines, devices, and "hard" physical technology, they still require substantial social, organizational, and intellectual investments to make them work properly.

TECHNICAL APPROACH

The technical approach to information systems emphasizes mathematically based models to study information systems as well as the physical technology and formal capabilities of these systems. The disciplines that contribute to the technical approach are computer science, management science, and operations research. Computer science is concerned with establishing theories of computability, methods of computation, and methods of efficient data

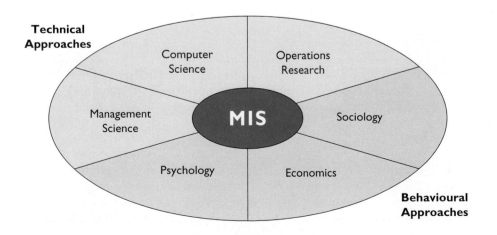

FIGURE 1-5 Contemporary approaches to information systems. The study of information systems deals with issues and insights contributed from technical and behavioural disciplines.

storage and access. Management science emphasizes the development of models for decision-making and management practices. Operations research focuses on mathematical techniques for optimizing selected parameters of organizations, such as transportation, inventory control, and transaction costs.

BEHAVIOURAL APPROACH

An important part of the information systems field is concerned with behavioural issues that arise in the development and long-term maintenance of information systems. Issues such as strategic business integration, design, implementation, utilization, and management cannot be explored usefully with the models used in the technical approach. Other behavioural disciplines contribute important concepts and methods. For instance, sociologists study information systems with an eye toward how groups and organizations shape the development of systems and also how systems affect individuals, groups, and organizations. Psychologists study information systems with an interest in how human decision makers perceive and use formal information; they also study how people deal with the changes brought about by new technology. Economists study information systems with an interest in the impact systems have on control and cost structures within the firm and within markets.

The behavioural approach does not ignore technology. Indeed, information systems technology is often the stimulus for a behavioural problem or issue. But the focus of this approach is generally not on technical solutions. Instead it concentrates on changes in attitudes, management and organizational policy, and behaviour (Kling and Dutton, 1982).

APPROACH OF THIS TEXT: SOCIOTECHNICAL SYSTEMS

management information systems (MIS)
The study of information systems, focusing on their use in business and management.

The study of **management information systems (MIS)** arose in the 1970s to focus on computer-based information systems aimed at managers (Davis and Olson, 1985). MIS combines the theoretical work of computer science, management science, and operations research with a practical orientation toward building systems and applications. It also focuses on behavioural issues raised by sociology, economics, and psychology.

Our experience as academics and practitioners leads us to believe that no single perspective effectively captures the reality of information systems. Problems with systems—and their solutions—are rarely all technical or all behavioural. Our best advice to students is to understand the perspectives of all disciplines. Indeed, the challenge and excitement of the information systems field is that it requires an appreciation and tolerance of many different approaches.

Adopting a sociotechnical systems perspective helps to avoid a purely technological approach to information systems. For instance, the fact that information technology is rapidly declining in cost and growing in power does not necessarily or easily translate into productivity enhancement or bottom-line profits.

In this book, we stress the need to optimize system performance as a whole. Both the technical and behavioural components need attention. This means that technology must be

FIGURE 1-6 A sociotechnical perspective on information systems. In a sociotechnical perspective, the performance of a system is optimized when both the technology and the organization mutually adjust to one another until a satisfactory fit is obtained.

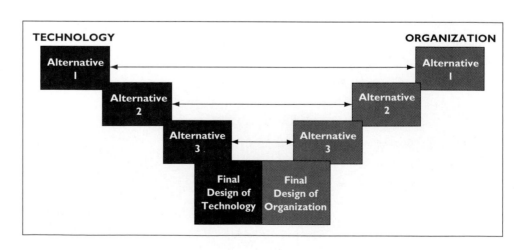

changed and designed in such a way as to fit organizational and individual needs. At times, the technology may have to be "de-optimized" to accomplish this fit. Organizations and individuals must also be changed through training, learning, and planned organizational change to allow the technology to operate and prosper (see, for example, Liker et al., 1987). People and organizations change to take advantage of new information technology. Figure 1-6 illustrates this process of mutual adjustment in a sociotechnical system.

1.3 TOWARD THE DIGITAL FIRM: THE NEW ROLE OF INFORMATION SYSTEMS IN ORGANIZATIONS

Because they play such a critical role in contemporary organizations, managers cannot ignore information systems. Information technology is transforming the possibilities for managing and organizing, and managers of business firms need to understand these new opportunities. Today's systems directly affect how managers decide, plan, and manage their employees and increasingly shape what products are produced, where, when, and how. Therefore, responsibility for systems cannot be delegated to technical decision-makers.

THE WIDENING SCOPE OF INFORMATION SYSTEMS

Figure 1-7 illustrates the new relationship between organizations and information systems. There is a growing interdependence between business strategy, rules, and procedures on the one hand, and information systems software, hardware, databases, and telecommunications on the other. A change in any of these components often requires changes in other components. This relationship becomes critical when management plans for the future. What a business would like to do in five years often depends on what its systems will be able to do. Increasing market share, becoming the high-quality or low-cost producer, developing new products, and increasing employee productivity depend more and more on the kinds and quality of information systems in the organization.

A second change in the relationship between information systems and organizations results from the growing reach and scope of systems projects and applications. Developing and managing systems today involves a much larger part of the organization than it did in the past. As firms become more like digital firms, the system enterprise extends to customers, vendors, and even industry competitors (see Figure 1-8). Where early systems produced largely technical changes that affected just a few people in the firm, contemporary systems bring about managerial changes (who has what information about whom, when, and how often) and institutional "core" changes (what products and services are produced, under what conditions, and by whom). As companies move toward digital firm organizations, nearly all

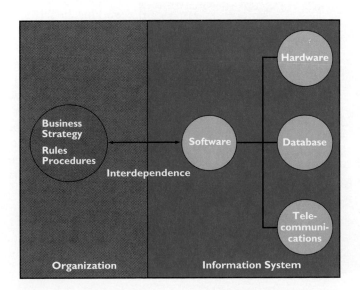

FIGURE 1-7 The interdependence between organizations and information systems. In contemporary systems, there is a growing interdependence between organizational business strategy, rules, and procedures and the organization's information systems. Changes in strategy, rules, and procedures increasingly require changes in hardware, software, databases, and telecommunications. Existing systems can act as a constraint on organizations. Often, what the organization would like to do depends on what its systems will permit it to do.

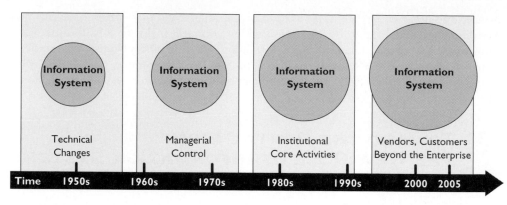

FIGURE 1-8 The widening scope of information systems. Over time, information systems have come to play a larger role in the life of organizations. Early systems brought about largely technical changes that were relatively easy to accomplish. Later systems affected managerial control and behaviour and subsequently "core" institutional activities. In the digital-firm era, information systems extend far beyond the boundaries of the firm to encompass vendors, customers, and even competitors.

the firm's managers and employees—as well as customers and vendors—participate in a variety of firm systems, tied together by a digital information web. For instance, what a customer does on a firm's Web site can trigger an employee to make an on-the-spot pricing decision or alert a firm's suppliers of potential "stock out" situations.

THE NETWORK REVOLUTION AND THE INTERNET

Internet

An international network of networks that is a collection of hundreds of thousands of private and public networks.

One reason information systems play such a large role in organizations and affect so many people is the soaring power and declining cost of computer technology. Computing power, which has been doubling every 18 months, has improved the performance of microprocessors 25 000 times since their invention 30 years ago. With powerful, easy-to-use software, the computer can crunch numbers, analyze vast pools of data, or simulate complex physical and logical processes with animated drawings, sounds, and even tactile feedback.

The soaring power of computer technology has spawned powerful communication networks that organizations can use to access vast storehouses of information from around the world and to coordinate activities across space and time. These networks are transforming the shape and form of business enterprises, creating the foundation for the digital firm.

The world's largest and most widely used network is the **Internet**. The Internet is an international network of networks that are both commercially and publicly owned. The Internet connects hundreds of thousands of different networks from over 200 countries around the world. More than 500 million people working in science, education, government, and business use the Internet to exchange information or to perform business transactions with other organizations around the globe.

The Internet. This global network of networks provides a highly flexible platform for information sharing. Digital information can be distributed at almost no cost to millions of people throughout the world.

The Internet is extremely elastic. If networks are added or removed, or if failures occur in parts of the system, the rest of the Internet continues to operate. Through special communication and technology standards, any computer can communicate with virtually any other computer linked to the Internet using ordinary telephone lines. Companies and private individuals can use the Internet to exchange business transactions, text messages, graphic images, and even video and sound, whether they are located next door or on the other side of the globe. Table 1-3 describes some of the Internet's capabilities.

TABLE 1-3   WHAT YOU CAN DO ON THE INTERNET

	Function	Description
	Communicate and collaborate	Send electronic mail messages; transmit documents and data; participate in electronic conferences
	Access information	Search for documents, databases, and library card catalogues; read electronic brochures, manuals, books, and advertisements
	Participate in discussions	Join interactive discussion groups; conduct voice transmission
	Supply information	Transfer computer files of text, computer programs, graphics, animations, sound, or video
	Find entertainment	Play interactive video games; view short video clips; listen to sound and music clips; read illustrated and even animated magazines and books
	Exchange business transactions	Advertise, sell, and purchase goods and services

The Internet has created a new "universal" technology platform on which to develop all sorts of new products, services, strategies, and organizations. It has reshaped the way information systems are being used in business and daily life. By eliminating many technical, geographic, and cost barriers obstructing the global flow of information, the Internet is accelerating the information revolution, inspiring new uses of information systems and new business models (see the Window on Management). The Internet provides the primary technology platform for the digital firm.

Because it offers so many new possibilities for doing business, the Internet capability (or function, area, or service) known as the **World Wide Web** is of special interest to organizations and managers. The World Wide Web is a system with universally accepted standards for storing, retrieving, formatting, and displaying information in a networked environment. Information is stored and displayed as electronic "pages" that can contain text, graphics, animations, sound, and video. These Web pages can be linked electronically to other Web pages, regardless of where they are located, and viewed by any type of computer. By clicking on highlighted words or buttons on a Web page, a user can link to related pages to find additional information, software programs, or even more links to other pages on the Web. The Web can serve as the foundation for new kinds of information systems such as Midnight Sun Plant Food's system for placing orders over its Web site (see Figure 1-9).

All of the Web pages maintained by an organization or individual are called a **Web site**. Businesses are creating Web sites with stylish design, colourful graphics, push-button interactivity, and often sound and video to disseminate product information widely, to "broadcast" advertising and messages to customers, to collect electronic orders and customer data, and increasingly to coordinate far-flung sales forces and organizations on a global scale.

In Chapters 4 and 10, we describe the Web and other Internet capabilities in greater detail. We also discuss relevant features of the Internet throughout the text because the Internet affects so many aspects of information systems in organizations.

World Wide Web
A system with universally accepted standards for storing, retrieving, formatting, and displaying information in a networked environment.

Web site
All of the World Wide Web pages maintained by an organization or an individual.

WINDOW ON MANAGEMENT

YUKON NETREPRENEURS

How do you make a business grow when you live within the Arctic Circle? That was the problem faced by Herbie Croteau, the founder and CEO of Midnight Sun Plant food. He lives in Faro, which has a population of 500. Faro is in Yukon Territory, which has a population of 31 000, two-thirds of whom live in the capital, Whitehorse. And, of course, being north of the Arctic Circle, it has very long winters with an average winter temperature of −26° Celsius and average snowfall around 1.5 m. A truck driver for the local zinc mine, Croteau found himself out of a job when the mine closed in 1992. To pass the time he began developing a fertilizer from local ingredients for his wife to use to feed both her indoor and her outdoor plants. When neighbours saw the size of her plants and vegetables, they began asking Croteau to sell them some of his fertilizer, and he found himself in business.

Because Croteau lived in such a small town, his natural market was almost non-existent. In 1993 he started to bring his fertilizer to Whitehorse, a town of 22 000, five hours away from Faro. In business terms, Whitehorse also presented only a tiny market, and so by 1998, Croteau's annual sales had only grown to $15 000. However, the Internet had reached the Yukon, and when it arrived in Faro, Croteau began to see it as a way to expand his business.

Yukon residents are relatively educated, with nearly 20 percent of adults holding college degrees, making it a fertile territory for the Internet. Recognizing this, a small group of computer enthusiasts founded YKkNnet in 1994, bringing the Internet to the region. With the help of the government and a Canadian telephone giant (Northwestel), the company eventually brought Internet service to 38 percent of Yukon households. In 1998 Croteau put his company on the Web (www.midnightsunplantfood.com) in an attempt to broaden his market.

At first, Croteau's site got only two visitors per day, and so Croteau spent much of his time searching out sites that offered free links to other Web sites. Quickly, his visitors rose to hundreds each week. Then his site began accepting credit cards enabling online sales, and his site even included a currency converter and video testimonials from happy customers. He has already redesigned his site several times to make it easier to reach. Croteau claims that 90 percent of the people visiting his site purchase his plant food and he expected his revenue to perhaps reach as high as $100 000 in 2000.

In Haines Junction, another Yukon Territory business turned to the Internet for aid. Roland and Susan Shaver had founded Bear North Adventures, which offered guided snowmobile tours of the breathtaking mountains and pristine snow-covered lakes. Their problem was finding ways to publicize their magnificent territory and their tours. After investing $2000 to establish a Web site (www.yukonsnowmobile.com), they can provide visitors with pictures of the touring area along with information on the prices of their tours. Web users find the Bear North site through links on other travel and snowmobile sites.

To Think About: What are the business problems that an entrepreneur can address through the use of the Internet? What problems can use of the Internet create for a business? Do you think using the Internet mandated changes in these entrepreneurs' business processes?

Source: David H. Freedman, "Cold Comfort," *Forbes.com*, May 29, 2000; "Success Stories," December 13, 2000, http://www.economicdevelopment.yk.ca/exports/Exports%20Home/Success%20Stories.htm, accessed August 19, 2001.

FIGURE 1-9 Midnight Sun Plant Food uses their Web site to promote sales of their product globally.

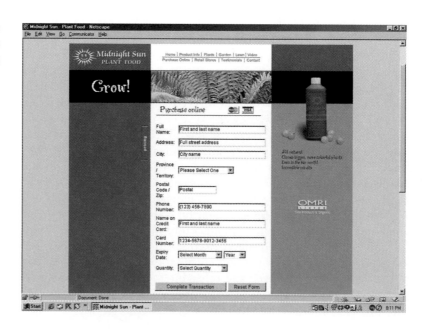

NEW OPTIONS FOR ORGANIZATIONAL DESIGN: THE DIGITAL FIRM AND THE NETWORKED ENTERPRISE

The explosive growth in computing power and networks, including the Internet, is turning organizations into networked enterprises, allowing information to be instantly distributed within and beyond the organization. This capability can be used to redesign and reshape organizations, transforming their structure, scope of operations, reporting and control mechanisms, work practices, workflows, products, and services. The ultimate end product of these new ways to conduct business electronically is the digital firm.

Flattening Organizations

Large, bureaucratic organizations, which primarily developed before the computer age, are often inefficient, slow to change, and less competitive than newly created organizations. Some of these large organizations have "downsized," reducing the number of employees and the number of levels in their organizational hierarchies. In digital firms, hierarchy and organizational levels do not disappear. There are legitimate reasons for maintaining hierarchies. But digital firms develop "optimal hierarchies" that balance the decision-making load across an organization, resulting in flatter organizations. Flatter organizations have fewer levels of management, with lower-level employees being given greater decision-making authority (see Figure 1-10). Those employees are empowered to make more decisions than in the past, they no longer work standard 9-to-5 hours, and they no longer necessarily work in an office. Moreover, such employees may be scattered geographically, sometimes working half a world away from the manager.

Contemporary information technology can make more information available to line workers so they can make decisions that previously had been made by managers. Networked computers have made it possible for employees to work together as a team, another feature of flatter organizations. With the emergence of global networks such as the Internet, team members can collaborate closely even from distant locations. These changes mean that management's "span of control" has also been broadened, allowing high-level managers to manage and control more workers spread over greater distances. Many companies have eliminated thousands of middle managers as a result of these changes. AT&T, IBM, and General Motors are just a few of the organizations that eliminated more than 30 000 middle managers in one fell swoop from their global operations.

Separating Work from Location

It is now possible to organize globally while working locally. Information technologies such as e-mail, the Internet, and videoconferencing on the desktop permit tight coordination of

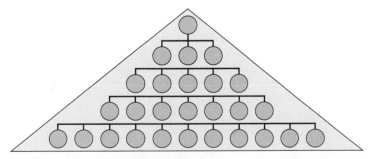

A traditional hierarchical organization with many levels of management

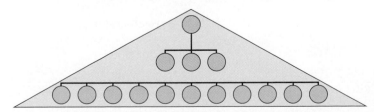

An organization that has been "flattened" by removing layers of management

FIGURE 1-10 Flattening organizations. Information systems can reduce the number of levels in an organization by providing managers with information to supervise larger numbers of workers and by giving lower-level employees more decision-making authority.

geographically dispersed workers across time zones and cultures. Entire parts of organizations can disappear: inventory, and the warehouses to store it, can be eliminated as suppliers tie into the firm's computer systems and deliver just what is needed just in time.

Communications technology has eliminated distance as a factor for many types of work in many situations. Salespersons can spend more time in the field with customers and have more up-to-date information with them while carrying much less paper. Many employees can work remotely from their homes or cars, and companies can reserve space at smaller central offices for meeting clients or other employees.

Collaborative teamwork across thousands of miles has become a reality as users work together even if they are located in different provinces or states or on different continents. Affinity IT Contracting and Search is a geographically distributed Australian online recruitment company with head offices in Glebe and locations throughout Australia. Affinity IT uses Lotus Sametime, an IBM software application, to bring employers and job candidates together for virtual interviews over the Internet (www.affinityit.com.au). The virtual interview takes place while the candidate's resume is being displayed using Sametime's document sharing feature. Affinity IT also uses Sametime's instant messaging and application sharing functions to speak with colleagues and to share information quickly.

Reorganizing Workflows

Information systems have been progressively replacing manual work procedures with automated work procedures, workflows, and work processes. Electronic workflows have reduced the cost of operations in many companies by displacing paper and the manual routines that accompany it. Improved workflow management has enabled many corporations not only to cut costs significantly, but also to improve customer service at the same time. For instance, insurance companies can reduce processing of applications for new insurance from weeks to days (see Figure 1-11).

Redesigned workflows can have a profound impact on organizational efficiency and can even lead to new organizational structures, products, and services. We discuss the impact of restructured workflows on organizational design in greater detail in Chapters 3 and 11.

Increasing Flexibility of Organizations

Companies can use communications technology to organize in more flexible ways, increasing their ability to sense and respond to changes in the marketplace and to take advantage of new opportunities. Information systems can give both large and small organizations additional flexibility to overcome some of the limitations posed by their size. Table 1-4 describes some of the ways in which information technology can help small companies act "big" and help big companies act "small." Small organizations can use information systems to acquire some of the muscle and reach of larger organizations. They can perform coordinating activities, such as processing bids or keeping track of inventory, and many manufacturing tasks with very few managers, clerks, or production workers. For example, Beamscope Canada, a Toronto distributor of electronic and computer parts, competes effectively against global giants such as Ingram Micro Inc. and Merisel Inc. because its Beamscope Online system offers customers online service and 24-hour ordering capabilities (Engler, 1999).

FIGURE 1-11 Redesigned workflow for insurance underwriting. An application requiring 33 days in a paper system would only take 5 days using computers, networks, and a streamlined workflow.

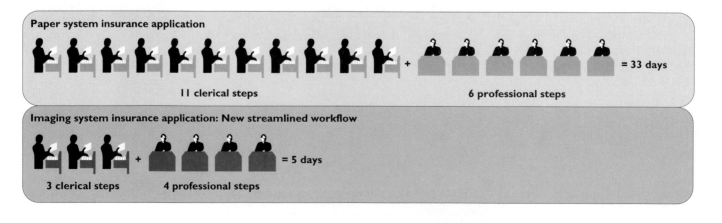

Paper system insurance application

11 clerical steps   6 professional steps   = 33 days

Imaging system insurance application: New streamlined workflow

3 clerical steps   4 professional steps   = 5 days

TABLE 1-4	HOW INFORMATION TECHNOLOGY INCREASES ORGANIZATIONAL FLEXIBILITY

Small Companies

Desktop machines, inexpensive computer-aided design (CAD) software, and computer-controlled machine tools provide the precision, speed, and quality of giant manufacturers.

Information immediately accessed by telephone and communications links eliminates the need for research staff and business libraries.

Managers can easily obtain the information they need to manage large numbers of employees in widely scattered locations.

Large Companies

Custom manufacturing systems allow large factories to offer customized products in small quantities.

Massive databases of customer purchasing records can be analyzed so that large companies can know their customers' needs and preferences as easily as local merchants do.

Information can be easily distributed down the ranks of the organization to empower lower-level employees and workgroups to solve problems.

Large organizations can use information technology to achieve some of the agility and responsiveness of small organizations. One aspect of this phenomenon is **mass customization**, to which software and computer networks are used to link the plant floor tightly with orders, design, and purchasing and to finely control production machines. The result is a dynamically responsive environment in which products can be turned out in greater variety and can be easily customized with no added cost for small production runs. For example, Levi Strauss has equipped its stores with an option called Personal Pair, which allows customers to design jeans to their own specifications, rather than picking them off the rack. Customers enter their measurements into a personal computer, which then transmits the customer's specifications over a network to Levi's plants. The company is able to produce the custom jeans on the same lines that manufacture its standard items. There are almost no extra production costs because the process does not require additional warehousing, production overruns, or inventories.

A related trend is **micromarketing**, in which information systems can help companies pinpoint tiny target markets for these finely customized products and services—as small as individualized "markets of one."

The Changing Management Process

Information technology is recasting the management process, providing powerful new capabilities to help managers plan, organize, lead, and control. For instance, it is now possible for managers to obtain information on organizational performance down to the level of specific transactions from just about anywhere in the organization at any time. Recall the variety of information that Nygård International is able to use by connecting electronically throughout their supply chain, from their suppliers to their customers and even their own stores and online store. The greater availability and detail of information make possible far more precise planning, forecasting, and monitoring than ever before.

Information technology has also opened new possibilities for managers to lead. By distributing information through electronic networks, a manager can effectively and frequently communicate with thousands of employees and even manage far-flung task forces and teams—tasks that would be impossible in face-to-face organizations.

Redefining Organizational Boundaries

A key feature of the emerging digital firm is the ability to conduct business across firm boundaries almost as efficiently and effectively as it can conduct business within the firm. Networked organizations allow companies to coordinate with other organizations across great distances. Transactions such as payments and purchase orders can be exchanged electronically among different companies, thereby reducing the cost of obtaining products and

mass customization
Use of software and computer networks to finely control production so that products can be easily customized with no added cost for small production runs.

micromarketing
Defining tiny target markets for finely customized products and services.

services from outside the firm. Organizations can also share business data, catalogues, or mail messages through networks. These networked information systems can create new efficiencies and new relationships between an organization, its customers, and suppliers, redefining their organizational boundaries. For example, Nygård has reduced not only its own costs, but also the costs of its suppliers. In addition, their corporate customers can check on their orders. Nygård's customers have also learned to trust Nygård, knowing they will receive their shipments on time and that the shipments will be accurate. Nygård and its suppliers have thus become linked business partners with mutually shared responsibilities.

interorganizational systems
Information systems that automate the flow of information across organizational boundaries and link a company to its customers, distributors, or suppliers.

The information system linking Nygård and its suppliers is called an interorganizational information system. Systems linking a company to its customers, distributors, or suppliers are termed **interorganizational systems** because they automate the flow of information across organizational boundaries. Digital firms use interorganizational systems to link people, assets, and ideas, partnering with suppliers and customers (and sometimes even competitors) to create and distribute new products and services without being limited by traditional organizational boundaries or physical locations. For example, Cisco Systems does not manufacture the products it sells, using other companies such as Flextronics for this purpose. Cisco uses the Internet to transmit orders to Flextronics and to monitor the status of orders as they are being shipped.

ELECTRONIC COMMERCE AND ELECTRONIC BUSINESS

The changes we have just described represent new, electronic ways of conducting business both inside and outside the firm that can ultimately result in the creation of digital firms. Increasingly, the Internet provides the underlying technology for these changes. The Internet can link thousands of organizations into a single network, creating the foundation for a vast electronic marketplace. An **electronic market** is an online marketplace linked by an information system whereby many buyers and sellers can exchange information, products, services, and payments. Through computers and networks, these e-markets function like electronic intermediaries, with lowered costs for typical marketplace transactions such as

electronic market
A marketplace that is created by computer and communication technologies that link many buyers and sellers.

TABLE 1-5	EXAMPLES OF ELECTRONIC COMMERCE AND ELECTRONIC BUSINESS

Electronic Commerce

Drugstore.com operates a virtual pharmacy on the Internet, selling prescription medicine and over-the-counter health, beauty, and wellness products. Customers can input their orders via Drugstore.com's Web site and have their purchases shipped to them.

Travelocity.ca provides a Web site that can be used by consumers for travel and vacation planning. Visitors can find out information on airlines, hotels, vacation packages, and other travel and leisure topics, and they can make airline and hotel reservations online through the Web site.

Enlogix, a subsidiary of Vancouver-based Westcoast Energy Inc., the country's largest diversified energy company, develops systems for all of the Westcoast family of companies, and for other utilities outside the Westcoast group facing the same competitive pressures. Enlogix evolved into an application service provider (ASP), which provides applications online to businesses so that the businesses do not have to purchase and maintain the applications themselves. Today Enlogix supports more than three million end customers. Enlogix lets its customers offer their customers Web-based billing and payment among many other services

Electronic Business

Roche Bioscience scientists around the world use an intranet to share research results and discuss findings. The intranet also provides a company telephone directory and newsletter.

Famili-Prix, a Québec City-based pharmaceutical products distributor, took advantage of a recently implemented intranet that is accessible from all their affiliated drugstores to make all the material normally found in sales binders available from a Web interface, so buyers can start their ordering work even before the "Carrefour des achats" or buying day. Sales representatives are equipped with notebook computers that wirelessly access the corporate network, pull out the order forms of each drugstore, and complete their sales. At the end of the day, everyone knows exactly what the sales figures are—rather than having to wait a couple of weeks for the data to be entered in the system.

EDS Systemhouse Corporation uses an intranet to provide 70 000 employees with access to personalized health benefits information based on location, age, salary, and family status. Employees can compare benefits of different medical plans before enrolling.

Dream Works SKG uses an intranet to check the daily status of projects, including animation objects, and to coordinate movie scenes.

matching buyers and sellers, establishing prices, ordering goods, and paying bills (Bakos, 1998). Buyers and sellers can complete purchase and sale transactions digitally, regardless of their location.

A vast array of goods and services are being advertised, bought, and exchanged worldwide using the Internet as a global marketplace. Companies create eye-catching electronic brochures, advertisements, product manuals, and order forms on the World Wide Web. All kinds of products and services are available on the Web, including fresh flowers, books, real estate, musical recordings, electronics, and steaks, along with sheet metal, business consulting services, and potential employees.

Many retailers maintain their own site on the Web, such as HBC.com, the online store of the Hudson's Bay Company. Others offer their products through electronic shopping malls, such as Alberta's canam-mall.com. Customers can locate products in online malls either by retailer, if they know what they want, or by product type, and then order the products directly. Even electronic financial trading (see for example www.baystreet.ca) has arrived on the Web so that investors can purchase stocks, bonds, mutual funds, and other financial instruments.

Increasingly, the Web is being used for business-to-business transactions as well. For example, airlines can use Boeing Corporation's Web site to order parts electronically and check the status of their orders.

The global availability of the Internet for the exchange of transactions between buyers and sellers is fuelling the growth of electronic commerce. **Electronic commerce** is the process of buying and selling goods and services electronically with computer-based business transactions using the Internet, networks, and other digital technologies. It also encompasses activities supporting those market transactions, such as advertising, marketing, customer support, delivery, and payment. By replacing manual and paper-based procedures with electronic alternatives, and by using information flows in new and dynamic ways, electronic commerce can accelerate ordering, delivery, and payment for goods and services while reducing operating and inventory costs.

The Internet is emerging as the primary technology platform for electronic commerce. Equally important, Internet technology is starting to facilitate the management of the rest of the business—publishing employee personnel policies, reviewing account balances and production plans, scheduling plant repairs and maintenance, and revising design documents. Companies are taking advantage of the connectivity and ease of use of Internet technology to create internal corporate networks called **intranets** that are based on Internet technology. Earlier in this chapter, the Window on Organizations described how Cisco Systems is using a private intranet to provide reports to management and human resources services to

electronic commerce
The process of buying and selling goods and services electronically via computer-based business transactions using the Internet, networks, and other digital technologies.

intranet
An internal network based on Internet and World Wide Web technology and standards.

FIGURE 1-12 Famili-Prix provides customers with a wide variety of health and beauty information on its Web site. Its intranet is also available to its employees.

electronic business

The use of the Internet and other digital technology for organizational communication and coordination and the management of the firm.

extranet

A private intranet that is accessible to authorized outsiders.

employees. The number of these private intranets for organizational communication, collaboration, and coordination is rapidly escalating. In this text, we use the term **electronic business** to distinguish these uses of Internet and digital technology for management and coordination of business processes from electronic commerce.

The Window on Organizations also showed how Cisco Systems allows its suppliers and distributors access to portions of its private intranet. Private intranets extended to authorized users outside the organization are called **extranets,** and firms use these networks to coordinate their activities with other firms for electronic commerce and electronic business. Table 1-5 lists some examples of electronic commerce and electronic business.

Famili-Prix's Web site is user friendly and links to a wide variety of information for customers and potential employees (see Figure 1-12). Figure 1-13 illustrates a digital firm making intensive use of Internet and digital technology for electronic commerce and electronic business. Information can flow seamlessly among different parts of the company and between the company and external entities—its customers, suppliers, and business partners. Organizations will move toward this vision of a digital firm as they use the Internet, intranets, and extranets to manage their internal processes and their relationships with customers, suppliers, and other external entities.

Both electronic commerce and electronic business can fundamentally change the way business is conducted. To use the Internet and other digital technologies successfully for electronic commerce, electronic business, and the creation of digital firms, organizations may have to redefine their business models, reinvent business processes, change corporate cultures, and create much closer relationships with customers and suppliers. We discuss these issues in greater detail throughout the text.

FIGURE 1-13 Electronic commerce and electronic business in the emerging digital firm. Electronic commerce uses Internet and digital technology to conduct transactions with customers and suppliers while electronic business uses these technologies for the management of the rest of the business.

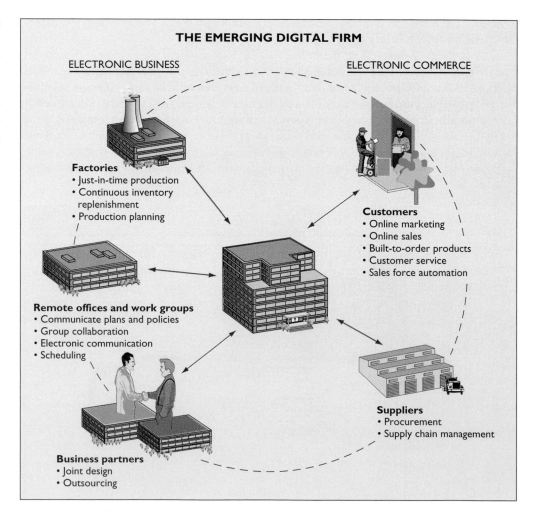

THE EMERGING DIGITAL FIRM

ELECTRONIC BUSINESS

ELECTRONIC COMMERCE

Factories
• Just-in-time production
• Continuous inventory replenishment
• Production planning

Customers
• Online marketing
• Online sales
• Built-to-order products
• Customer service
• Sales force automation

Remote offices and work groups
• Communicate plans and policies
• Group collaboration
• Electronic communication
• Scheduling

Suppliers
• Procurement
• Supply chain management

Business partners
• Joint design
• Outsourcing

MANAGEMENT DECISION PROBLEM

PLANNING A NEW INTERNET BUSINESS

You would like to create a new business on the Web that provides cat and dog owners with advice on animal health, behaviour, and nutrition and that sells products such as pet beds, carriers, dishes, toys, flea treatments, and grooming aids. Your Web site would also have capabilities for pet owners to exchange electronic messages about their pets and pet care with other pet owners. In researching the Canadian market for your business, you have determined that the only applicable data is found for the U.S. market in the U.S. Commerce Department's *Statistical Abstract of the United States*. You decide to use the U.S. data and attempt to collect your own Canadian data on those who visit your Web site.

Household Pet Ownership by Income Level:

Annual Income	Dog Owners	Cat Owners
Less than $12 500	14%	15%
$12 500 to $24 999	20%	20%
$25 000 to $39 999	24%	23%
$40 000 to $59 999	22%	22%
Over $60 000	20%	20%
Total	**100%**	**100%**

Internet Usage by Income Level

Annual Income	Percent Using the Internet
Less than $20 000	5%
$20 000 to $49 999	26%
$50 000 to $74 999	28%
$75 000 and over	41%
Total	**100%**

1. What are the implications of this information for starting your business on the Internet?

2. What additional information might be useful to help you decide whether your business could be profitable and what type and price range of products to sell?

1.4 LEARNING TO USE INFORMATION SYSTEMS: NEW OPPORTUNITIES WITH TECHNOLOGY

Although information systems create many exciting opportunities for both businesses and individuals, they are also a source of new problems, issues, and challenges for managers. In this text, you will learn about both the challenges and opportunities information systems pose, and you will be able to use information technology to enrich your learning experience.

THE CHALLENGE OF INFORMATION SYSTEMS: KEY MANAGEMENT ISSUES

Although information technology is advancing at a blinding pace, there is nothing easy or mechanical about developing and using information systems. There are five key challenges confronting managers:

1. **The Strategic Business Challenge: Realizing the Digital Firm. How can businesses use information technology to become competitive, effective, and digitally enabled?** Creating a digital firm and obtaining its benefits is a long and difficult journey for most organizations. Investment in information technology amounts to more than half of the annual capital expenditures of most large service-sector firms. Yet despite these heavy investments, many organizations do not obtain significant business benefits, nor do they become digitally enabled. The power of computer hardware and software has grown much more rapidly than the ability of organizations to apply and use this technology. To stay competitive, realize genuine productivity, and take advantage of digital firm capabilities, many organizations actually need to be redesigned. They will have to make fundamental changes in organizational behaviour, develop new business models, and eliminate the inefficiencies of outmoded organizational structures. If organizations merely automate what they are doing today, they are largely missing the potential of information technology. To fully benefit from information technology, including the Internet, organizations need to rethink and redesign the way they design, produce, deliver, and maintain goods and services.

2. **The Globalization Challenge: How can firms understand the business and systems requirements of a global economic environment?** The rapid growth in international trade and the emergence of a global economy call for information systems that can support the production, marketing, and distribution of goods in many different countries. In the past, each regional office of a multinational corporation focused on solving its own unique information problems. Given language, cultural, and political differences among countries, this focus frequently resulted in chaos and the failure of central management controls. To develop integrated, multinational information systems, businesses must develop global hardware, software, and communications standards and create cross-cultural accounting and reporting structures (Roche, 1992).

3. **The Information Architecture and Infrastructure Challenge: How can organizations develop an information architecture and information technology infrastructure that can support their goals when business conditions and technologies change so rapidly?** Meeting the business and technology challenges of today's digital economy requires redesigning the organization and building a new information architecture and information technology (IT) infrastructure.

information architecture
The particular design that information technology takes in a specific organization to achieve selected goals or functions.

Information architecture is the particular form that information technology takes in an organization to achieve selected goals or functions. It is a design for the business application systems that serve each functional specialty and level of the organization and the specific way that they are used by each organization. As firms move toward digital firm organizations and technologies, information architectures are increasingly being designed around business processes and clusters of system applications spanning multiple functions and organizational levels. Because managers and employees directly interact with these systems, it is critical for organizational success that the information architecture meet business requirements now and in the future.

Figure 1-14 illustrates the major elements of information architecture that managers will need to develop now and in the future. The architecture shows the firm's business application systems for each of the major functional areas of the organization, including sales and marketing, manufacturing, finance, accounting, and human resources. It also shows application systems supporting business processes spanning multiple organizational levels and functions within the enterprise and extending outside the enterprise to systems of suppliers, distributors, business partners, and customers. The

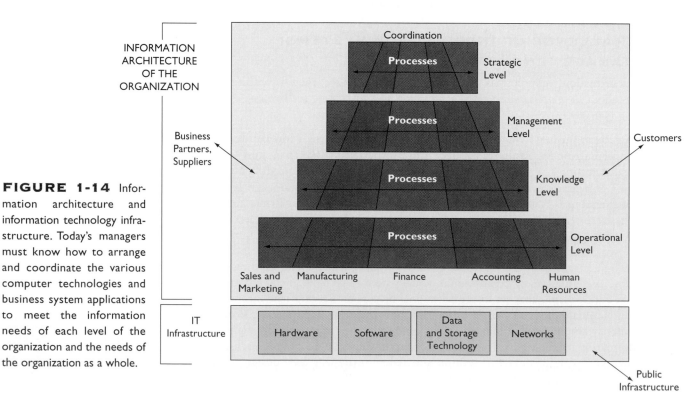

FIGURE 1-14 Information architecture and information technology infrastructure. Today's managers must know how to arrange and coordinate the various computer technologies and business system applications to meet the information needs of each level of the organization and the needs of the organization as a whole.

firm's information technology infrastructure provides the technology platform for this architecture. Computer hardware, software, data and storage technology, networks, and human resources required to operate the equipment constitute the shared IT resources of the firm that are available to all of its applications. Although the technology platform is typically operated by technical personnel, general management must decide how to allocate the resources it has assigned to hardware, software, data storage, and telecommunications networks to make sound information technology investments (Weill and Broadbent, 1997 and 1998).

Typical questions regarding information architecture and IT infrastructure facing today's managers include: Should the corporate sales data and function be distributed to each corporate remote site, or should they be centralized at headquarters? Should the organization develop systems to connect the entire enterprise or separate islands of applications? Should the organization extend its infrastructure outside its boundaries to link to customers or suppliers? There is no one right answer to these questions (see Allen and Boynton, 1991). Moreover, business needs are constantly changing, which requires the IT architecture to be reassessed continually (Feeny and Willcocks, 1998).

Creating the information architecture and information technology infrastructure for a digital firm is an especially formidable task. Most companies are crippled by fragmented and incompatible computer hardware, software, telecommunications networks, and information systems that prevent information from flowing freely between different parts of the organization. Although Internet standards solve some of these connectivity problems, creating enterprise-wide data and computing platforms is rarely as seamless as promised. Many organizations still struggle to integrate their islands of information and technology into a coherent architecture. Chapters 6, 7, 8, 9, and 10 provide more detail on information architecture and IT infrastructure issues.

4. **The Information Systems Investment Challenge: How can organizations determine the business value of information systems?** A major problem raised by the development of powerful, inexpensive computers involves not technology but management and organizations. It's one thing to use information technology to design, produce, deliver, and maintain new products. It's another thing to make money doing it. How can organizations obtain a sizable payoff from their investments in information systems?

Engineering massive organizational and system changes in the hope of positioning a firm strategically is complicated and expensive. Is this an investment that pays off? How can you tell? Senior management can be expected to ask these questions: Are we receiving the kind of return on investment from our systems that we should be? Do our competitors get more? Understanding the costs and benefits of building a single system is difficult enough; it is daunting to consider whether the entire systems effort is "worth it." Imagine, then, how a senior executive must think when presented with a major transformation in information architecture—a bold venture in organizational change costing tens of millions of dollars and taking many years.

5. **The Responsibility and Control Challenge: How can organizations ensure that their information systems are used in an ethically and socially responsible manner?** How can we design information systems that people can control and understand? Although information systems have provided enormous benefits and efficiencies, they have also created new problems and challenges that managers should be aware of. Table 1-6 describes some of these problems and challenges.

Many chapters of this text describe scenarios that raise these ethical issues and Chapter 5 is devoted to this topic. A major management challenge is to make informed decisions that are sensitive to the negative consequences of information systems as well to the positive ones.

Managers will also be faced with ongoing problems of security and control. Information systems are so essential to business, government, and daily life that organizations must take special steps to ensure that they are accurate, reliable, and secure. A firm invites disaster if it uses systems that don't work as intended, that don't deliver information in a form that people can interpret correctly and use, or that have control rooms where controls don't work or where instruments give false signals. Information

TABLE 1-6 BENEFITS AND NEGATIVE IMPACTS OF INFORMATION SYSTEMS

Benefit	Negative Impact
Information systems can perform calculations or process paperwork much faster than people	By automating activities that were previously performed by people, information systems may eliminate jobs
Information systems can help companies learn more about the purchase patterns and preferences of their customers	Information systems may allow organizations to collect personal details about people that violate their privacy
Information systems provide new efficiencies through services such as automated teller machines (ATMs), telephone systems, or computer-controlled airplanes and air terminals	Information systems are used in so many aspects of everyday life that system outages can cause shutdowns of businesses or transportation services, paralyzing communities
Information systems have made possible new medical advances in surgery, radiology, and patient monitoring	Heavy users of information systems may suffer repetitive stress injury, technostress, and other health problems
The Internet distributes information instantly to millions of people across the world	The Internet can be used to distribute illegal copies of software, books, articles, and other intellectual property

systems must be designed so that they function as intended and so that humans can control the process.

Managers will need to ask: Can we apply high quality assurance standards to our information systems as well as to our products and services? Can we develop information systems that respect people's rights to privacy while still pursuing our organization's goals? Should information systems monitor employees? What do we do when an information system designed to increase efficiency and productivity eliminates people's jobs? Chapters 5 and 12 address these issues.

This text is designed to provide future managers with the knowledge and understanding required to deal with these challenges. To further this objective, each succeeding chapter begins with a Management Challenges box that outlines the key issues of which managers should be aware.

INTEGRATING TEXT WITH TECHNOLOGY: NEW OPPORTUNITIES FOR LEARNING

In addition to the changes in business and management that we have just described, we believe that information technology creates new opportunities for learning that can make the MIS course more meaningful and exciting. We have provided a Web site for integrating the text with leading-edge technology. Observant readers may notice that this section of each chapter is titled "Companion Website," with *Website* written as one word. Although *Web site* is usually written as two words, the software used to compile our interactive Web site is called *Companion Website*, so we have used this as our section title.

As you read each chapter of the text, you can visit the Pearson Education Canada, Laudon, Laudon, and Brabston Web site and use the Internet for interactive learning and management problem solving. For each chapter, you will find an Electronic Commerce project where you can use Web research and interactive software at various company Web sites to solve specific problems. We have also provided an online interactive Study Guide that contains questions to help you review what you have learned and test your mastery of chapter concepts. Our Web site also includes regular updates to examples discussed in the book and to discussions of the use of technology. You will find links to additional sites of interest listed near the end of each chapter. You will find it useful to visit these sites to see how what has been described in the chapter looks in a real-world setting.

Application exercises concluding each chapter require students to use spreadsheet, database, and other application software in hands-on projects related to chapter concepts. Students can apply the application software skills they have learned in other courses to real-world business problems. You can find these exercises before the Management Wrap-Up of each chapter and both the exercises and their data files on the Laudon, Laudon, and Brabston Web site.

On our Web site, we have posted the CBC videos that relate to the four Canadian Case Studies at the ends of the parts of the textbook. We have also added a comprehensive project for each of the four major parts of the textbook. These projects require you to apply what you have learned to more extensive problems, such as developing an Internet business model, calculating the Total Cost of Ownership (TCO) of a Web site, redesigning business processes, and designing a corporate knowledge intranet. Some of these projects require use of the Web.

This is Canada's own text. While it is an adaptation of the Laudon and Laudon U.S. edition, it contains significant Canadian content, including examples, statistics, cases, organizations, and legal and societal implications. Without omitting significant U.S. material (for example, Wal-Mart or UPS as examples), the focus of this edition is on Canadian material, Canadian technology, Canadian organizations, and Canadians themselves. In addition, there is a significant amount of non-North American content, focusing on the international flavour of information systems in today's global marketplace.

APPLICATION SOFTWARE EXERCISE

WEB BROWSER AND SPREADSHEET EXERCISE: INVESTING IN ELECTRONIC RETAILING

You recently watched a news broadcast extolling the virtues of electronic commerce and the fortunes that have been made in this new form of commerce. The report mentioned such retailing companies as Indigo.com and HBC.com. You are interested in learning more about these companies and would also like to learn more about other popular retailing stores.

Besides the companies mentioned above, identify and investigate five additional e-tailers. For each of the seven e-tailers, locate the company's stock symbol and current selling price. This information is easily located on the Web.

Assume you want to purchase 10 shares of each company's stock. Create a spreadsheet that lists the following information: stock name, stock symbol, number of shares for each stock purchased, purchase price per share, total investment for each stock, and overall total investment. You should also create a pie chart that compares the total investment for each stock. After one week, check each stock's current value. Have any stocks gained value? Have any stocks lost value? Modify your spreadsheet to include these findings. Prepare a report for your instructor. In this report, discuss your findings regarding each company and your stock investment. Your report should include copies of your modified spreadsheet and pie chart.

MANAGEMENT WRAP-UP

Managers are problem-solvers who are responsible for analyzing the many challenges confronting organizations and for developing strategies and action plans. Information systems are one of their tools, delivering the information required for solutions. Information systems both reflect management decisions and serve as instruments for changing the management process.

Information systems are rooted in organizations, an outcome of organizational structure, culture, politics, workflows, and standard operating procedures. They are instruments for organizational change, making it possible to recast these organizational elements into new business models and redraw organizational boundaries. Advances in information systems are accelerating the trend toward global, knowledge-driven economies and flattened, flexible, decentralized organizations.

A network revolution is under way. Information systems technology is no longer limited to computers but consists of an array of technologies that enable computers to be networked together to exchange information across great distances and organizational boundaries. The

Internet provides global connectivity and a flexible platform for information sharing, creating new uses for information systems, and revolutionizing the role of information systems in organizations.

For Discussion

1. Information systems are too important to be left to computer specialists. Do you agree? Why or why not?

2. As computers become faster and cheaper and the Internet becomes more widely used, most of the problems we have with information systems will disappear. Do you agree? Why or why not?

SUMMARY

1. *Analyze the role of information systems in today's competitive business environment.* Information systems have become essential for helping organizations deal with changes in global economies and the business enterprise. Information systems provide firms with communication and analytic tools for conducting trade and managing businesses on a global scale. Information systems are the foundation of new knowledge-based products and services in knowledge economies and help firms manage their knowledge assets. Information systems make it possible for businesses to adopt flatter, more decentralized structures and more flexible arrangements of employees and management. Organizations are trying to become more competitive and efficient by transforming themselves into digital firms where nearly all core business processes and relationships with customers, suppliers, and employees are digitally enabled.

2. *Define an information system from both a technical and business perspective and distinguish between computer literacy and information systems literacy.* The purpose of a CBIS is to collect, store, and disseminate information from an organization's environment and internal operations to support organizational functions and decision-making, communication, coordination, control, analysis, and visualization. Information systems transform raw data into useful information through three basic activities: input, processing, and output. From a business perspective, an information system represents an organizational and management solution based on information technology to a challenge posed by the environment.

Information systems literacy requires an understanding of the organizational and management dimensions of information systems as well as the technical dimensions addressed by computer literacy. Information systems literacy draws on both technical and behavioural approaches in studying information systems. Both perspectives can be combined into a sociotechnical approach to systems.

3. *Explain how information systems are transforming organizations and management.* The kinds of systems developed today are very important for the organization's overall performance, especially in today's highly globalized and information-based economy. Information systems drive both daily operations and organizational strategy. Powerful computers, software, and networks, including the Internet, help organizations become more flexible, eliminate layers of management, separate work from location, and restructure workflows, giving new powers to both line workers and management. Information technology provides managers with tools for more precise planning, forecasting, and monitoring of the business. To maximize the advantages of information technology, there is a much greater need to plan the organization's information architecture and information technology infrastructure.

4. *Assess the relationship between the digital firm, electronic commerce, electronic business, and Internet technology.* The Internet provides the primary technology infrastructure for electronic commerce, electronic business, and the emerging digital firm. The Internet and other networks have made it possible for businesses to replace manual and paper-based processes with the electronic flow of information. In electronic commerce, businesses can exchange electronic purchase and sale transactions with each other and with individual customers. Electronic business uses the Internet and digital technology to expedite the exchange of information that can facilitate communication and coordination both inside the organization and between the organization and its business partners. Digital firms use Internet technology intensively for electronic commerce and electronic business to manage their internal processes and relationships with customers, suppliers, and other external entities.

5. *Identify the major management challenges to building and using information systems in organizations.* There are five key management challenges in building and using information systems: (1) designing systems that are competitive and efficient; (2) understanding the system requirements of a global business environment; (3) creating an information architecture that supports the organization's goals; (4) determining the business value of information systems; and (5) designing systems that people can control, understand, and use in a socially and ethically responsible manner.

KEY TERMS

Business functions, 13

Business processes, 7

Communications technology, 14

Computer-based information systems (CBIS), 10

Computer hardware, 14

Computer literacy, 13

Computer software, 14

Data, 9

Data workers, 13

Digital firm, 7

Electronic business, 26

Electronic commerce, 25

Electronic market, 24

Extranet, 26

Feedback, 9

Formal system, 10

Information, 9

Information architecture, 28

Information system, 9

Information systems literacy, 13

Information technology (IT) infrastructure, 14

Input, 9

Internet, 18

Interorganizational systems, 24

Intranet, 25

Knowledge- and information-intense products, 6

Knowledge workers, 13

Management information systems (MIS), 16

Mass customization, 23

Micromarketing, 23

Middle managers, 14

Network, 14

Operational managers, 14

Output, 9

Processing, 9

Production or service workers, 13

Senior managers, 14

Standard operating procedures (SOPs), 13

Storage technology, 14

Web site, 19

World Wide Web, 19

REVIEW QUESTIONS

1. Why are information systems essential in business today? Describe four trends in the global business environment that have made information systems so important.

2. What is an information system? Distinguish between a computer, a computer program, and an information system. What is the difference between data and information?

3. Name and describe the four activities that constitute an information system.

4. What is information systems literacy? How does it differ from computer literacy?

5. What are the organization, management, and technology dimensions of information systems?

6. Distinguish between a behavioural and a technical approach to information systems in terms of the questions asked and the answers provided.

7. What major disciplines contribute to an understanding of information systems?

8. What is the relationship between an organization and its information systems? How does this relationship change over time?

9. What are the Internet and the World Wide Web? How have they changed the role played by information systems in organizations?

10. Describe some of the major changes that information systems bring to organizations.

11. How do information systems change the management process?

12. What is the relationship between the network revolution, the digital firm, electronic commerce, and electronic business?

13. What do we mean by information architecture and information technology infrastructure? Why are they important concerns for managers?

14. What are the key management challenges involved in building, operating, and maintaining information systems today?

GROUP PROJECT

In a group with three or four classmates, find a description in a computer or business magazine of an information system used by an organization. Look for information about the company on the Web to gain further insight into the company and prepare a brief description of the business. Describe the system you have selected in terms of its inputs, processes, outputs, and feedback, and in terms of its organization, management, and technology features and the importance of the system to the company. Present your analysis to the class.

INTERNET CONNECTION

■ COMPANION WEBSITE

At www.pearsoned.ca/laudon, you'll find an online study guide with two quizzes to test your knowledge of the role of information systems in business today. You'll also find updates to the chapter and online exercises and cases that enable you to apply your knowledge to realistic situations.

CASE STUDY   *Saskatchewan Wheat Pool Lab Reaps Healthy Harvest with E-Business Tools*

While the transformation of seeds into fruitful bounties generally relies on human nurturing and help from Mother Nature, Canadian farmers have an additional resource to strengthen their odds of having a bountiful harvest—the Saskatchewan Wheat Pool Lab. Established in 1924, the Saskatchewan Wheat Pool (www.swp.com) is Canada's top agricultural co-operative, with more than 70 000 members. Saskatchewan Wheat Pool is a publicly traded agribusiness co-operative headquartered in Regina, Saskatchewan.

Anchored by a prairie-wide grain handling and agri-products marketing network, the Pool channels prairie production to end-use markets in North America and around the world. These core business operations are complemented by food processing and value added businesses that allow the Pool to leverage its pivotal position between prairie farmers and destination customers. By developing strategic partnerships and supply agreements, the Pool is expanding market opportunities for agri-food products.

At its seed quality testing lab in Saskatoon, technicians and testers examine growers' samples for disease, germination potential, and purity, certifying those that meet government standards. Business at the Saskatoon Lab has climbed steadily after two of the Pool's testing facilities merged in September 1997. The two facilities had been handling up to 30 000 samples a year. However, it became apparent that the eight-year-old system the Lab was using for simple test tracking could no longer keep pace with their growth, creating backlogs and hampering customer service.

To improve productivity and enhance service, the Pool's information technology staff sought an automated, Year 2000-compliant solution for seed test tracking. Working with LGS Group Inc., a Canadian information systems consulting firm, the IT staff created a workflow automation system using Lotus Notes and Lotus Domino that enables lab technicians to enter and track seed sample and testing information in Lotus Notes databases, which are accessible through the company intranet.

The organization's new system, which handles a far larger volume of test samples per year—up to 70 000 compared with the previous system's 30 000—is already demonstrating its value in eliminating production backlog and improving customer service. In fact, the turnaround for testing certificates is so quick that many customers no longer need to request status reports. As a result, the Lab has achieved a 15 to 20 percent reduction in call volume. And, when customers do call, they can get their answers right away.

To date, 90 percent of the lab's manual reporting has been automated by the system. As a result, managers can use Lotus Notes to retrieve a wealth of information—from statistics on sample testing to data sorted by grower or seed type for strategic planning and decision making. According to Harrison Webster, Program Manager for Workflow, Saskatchewan Wheat Pool, "This [Lotus Notes and Domino] solution is demonstrating not only a staggering return on investment, but also adding value to the business process by helping us find new ways of getting and using mission-critical information…The results we've achieved using Lotus Notes and Domino, including an annual operating cost saving of $300 000 to $400 000, have far exceeded our expectations." Says Arlen Olson, senior consultant with LGS Group: "We have provided Notes and Domino expertise to the Pool for the past two years. The seed test tracking system is another excellent example of a Notes application that provides a high return on investment."

Faster, less cumbersome processes mean that the Saskatoon lab is equipped to handle the increasing volume of test samples far more efficiently. The old system, designed for simple record keeping of test samples, worked in concert with a paper filing system. As samples arrived, lab technicians entered information on file cards and into a database. And each time samples went through different tests, technicians had to fill out new file cards. When customers called for status reports on their samples, technicians had to search through files for the appropriate cards—which meant that customers generally weren't able to get an answer until hours or even days later when all of their information was in place.

As the volume of business grew, the technicians found themselves putting in many extra hours just for routine housekeeping tasks while a backlog of tests piled up. With the automated system, not only have they cleared the backlog, they have also eliminated the possibility of falling behind in the future. New samples can be categorized, appropriate tests conducted, and the results tracked at each stage, without the need to re-enter information time and again. "Now people know exactly what to do—where to go for the sample and obtain information on the results," explains Bob Whiting, the Pool's Manager of Quality Assurance. "Everything comes up on the screen for them. Before Notes and

Domino, too much time was spent on door-to-door searches for data because test samples can be located in a number of areas within the lab."

The Pool and LGS Group selected Lotus products for their solution because the Pool wanted to leverage its investment in Lotus Notes, which was already being used by several divisions for e-mail and groupware. Alongside the test tracking system, the Pool has also launched several new applications at the Saskatoon lab to further enhance efficiency and staff productivity. Among these is an electronic institutional memory whereby reference materials as well as information that previously existed only on paper or within employees' minds are now stored in the Lotus Notes database. "Now, we won't lose business-critical information if someone leaves the organization," says Webster. "This information is built into our system." According to Whiting, "Our Notes- and Domino-based workflow automation system has provided us the ability to strengthen our leadership position, promote our services and really deliver on what we promise— prompt service and seed testing results."

In another application, lab technicians are using their Lotus Notes-based system to calculate invoice fees for their customers. After testing data is entered for a sample, the system calculates the fee and stores this data in Lotus Notes. Previously, these invoices were calculated manually, with technicians searching through records of each test conducted for every sample. Under this system, the organization estimates it lost up to $15 000 each year due to lost or misplaced information. "One of the strengths of the Lotus Notes and Lotus Domino solution is its ability to handle complex processes, pulling together specific information scattered in different areas of the system," says Webster. "Not only does this make a basic function like invoice preparation much more efficient, it also enables more effective reporting."

New risk management capabilities, made possible by the test tracking system, portend even greater savings. Because it deals with living organisms, the seed business can be very risky, so it's important to assess growth potential early on. Lotus Notes gives the Pool's seed marketing professionals quick, convenient access to information about the Pool's own seed products, which are tested at Saskatoon for certification and sold on the retail market.

Equipped with this information, the marketing staff can evaluate, in a timely manner, whether the seeds are marketable. In the past, the sales force relied on a binder stacked with paper spreadsheets containing the data. Often, by the time they found the right spreadsheets and determined whether or not the seed made the grade, it was too late to stop the sales process. "This poses a risk that can cost us customers. So, being able to eliminate such an improper sale can help us maintain our customer base and could save us millions of dollars a year," notes Whiting.

Saskatchewan Wheat Pool projected 100 percent return on investment for this project within a year. But the returns came much sooner considering the risk management benefits. As Webster notes, "If we can reduce our risk by even 25 percent, then we've paid for this application five or six times in the first year." What's more, the organization is confident that word about the improvements in customer service resulting from the new seed test tracking system will spread. Whiting says, "People are already talking about the seed lab and how happy they are with the results. This word-of-mouth advertising will help us grow."

The Lab's successes are evidence of what can be done with computer-based information systems to improve quality, productivity, creativity, communication, and even marketing. However, use of information technology is not a panacea for all that may be wrong in an organization. At the time of this writing, the Saskatchewan Wheat Pool itself (not the Lab) has been undergoing financial hard times for over a year. Over-expansion and over-investment hurt the Pool, but through divesting some of the investments and improving efficiency and marketing throughout the organization, the Pool is expected to survive and prosper.

It is easy for any information systems professional or author to promote information technology as the greatest thing since Cartier discovered Canada. But, as you read this text and perhaps continue your MIS studies, always remember that it is people who make decisions—even with the help of computer-based information systems, and sometimes, people are only human. Computer-based information systems will not cure cancer or make a firm profitable, but they can help to do so—just as they helped the Saskatchewan Wheat Pool Lab.

Sources: Dave Bedard, "Sask Pool Will Survive," *Grainews*, March 23, 2001; *"Saskatchewan Wheat Pool Lab Reaps Healthy Harvest With E-Business Tools,"* IBM Case study, www2.software.ibm.com/casestudies/, accessed July 28, 2001; Hoover's Online Company Capsules, www.hoovers.com/co/capsule/, accessed July 28, 2001; Saskatchewan Wheat Pool Web site, www.swp.com, accessed July 28, 2001.

CASE STUDY QUESTIONS

1. What were the reasons that the Saskatchewan Lab had to change its business processes?

2. Why did the Lab choose the Lotus solution? What do each of these products do?

3. What management, organization, and technology issues did the Lab have to address?

4. By what measure(s) would you evaluate the success of this initiative? Was this initiative successful?

5. Do you think the changes the Lab made have made the Lab a digital organization? Why or why not?

2

INFORMATION SYSTEMS IN THE ENTERPRISE

OBJECTIVES

After completing this chapter, you will be able to:

1. *Analyze the role played by the six major types of information systems in organizations and their relationship to each other.*

2. *Describe the types of information systems supporting the major functional areas of the business.*

3. *Analyze the relationship between business processes, including those for supply chain management, organizations, and information systems.*

4. *Explain how enterprise systems and industrial networks create new efficiencies for businesses.*

5. *Evaluate the benefits and limitations of enterprise systems and industrial networks.*

Cara Airport Services Dishes It Out—Better and Cheaper!

Cara Operations Limited (www.cara.com) is the largest integrated food service company in Canada. Cara's Cara Airport Services division has over 60 percent of the airline business in Canada, supplying over 100 000 meals every day to over 50 airlines. Cara's daily production schedule was prepared by an in-house mainframe system and amounted to educated guesses. After the schedule was prepared, changes could not be entered on the system. However, meal orders change up until takeoff, and many meal orders were being sent to Cara's 11 airport kitchen facilities on slips of paper.

Passengers got their food, but not very efficiently. Orders were processed by extra labour or by making extra meals, even when the meals were not needed.

Today Cara is attempting to save money for both the airlines and its own company by implementing a combination of enterprise resource planning (ERP) and supply chain management (SCM) software to produce more precise production schedules. The UNIX-based software (J.D. Edwards & Company's One World ERP applications linked to a planning package by SynQuest

Inc. of Atlanta) was implemented early in 2000. With more than 500 000 changes to orders every day, Cara will use SynQuest's software's real-time execution capability to track changing meal counts and configurations for all flights, up to five minutes before the aircraft is ready to depart.

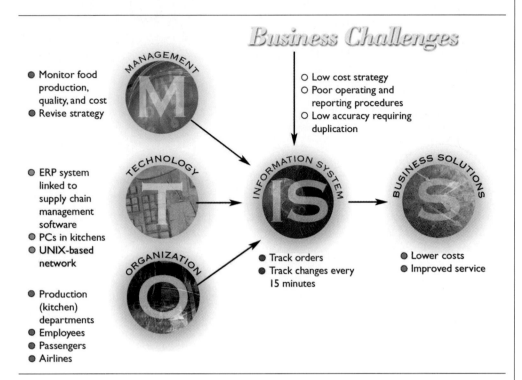

Business Challenges

- Monitor food production, quality, and cost
- Revise strategy

MANAGEMENT

- ERP system linked to supply chain management software
- PCs in kitchens
- UNIX-based network

TECHNOLOGY

- Production (kitchen) departments
- Employees
- Passengers
- Airlines

ORGANIZATION

INFORMATION SYSTEM

- Track orders
- Track changes every 15 minutes

○ Low cost strategy
○ Poor operating and reporting procedures
○ Low accuracy requiring duplication

BUSINESS SOLUTIONS

- Lower costs
- Improved service

Fred Cress, senior vice president of Cara Airport Services, explains, "SynQuest software will help us financially optimize production by giving us the information we need to determine the financial impact of various supply chain planning scenarios. For example, if lemon pepper chicken is on one line, SynQuest will provide a plan that recommends the right number of lemon pepper chicken meals on that line, taking into account all the appropriate financial and customer service variables."

New meal orders are processed on the fly and sent electronically to PCs in the kitchens, rather than on slips of paper that can get lost. The new real-time capability enables Cara to assign employees to monitor menu changes for only the last 15 minutes before a flight, rather than the hour they spent before.

Cara believes large savings will occur from the ERP/SCM implementation: a potential 7 percent reduction in the $130 million spent on meal production each year. They expect payback on the $13 million project within four or five years. Cara expects their new system will not only save them money but will also save them the business of their airline clients—in essence, saving their business.

Sources: Craig Stedman, "Airline Food Vendor Seeks 7% Savings on Production," *ComputerWorld*, June 14, 1999; Jamie Muir, "Cara Selects SynQuest Supply Chain Management Software for 11 Site Contract," SynQuest, Inc., March 1, 1999, www.synquest.com/press_template.cfm?ID=308, accessed January 2001; Jerry W. Bird, "Flying Gourmet: Cara's Airline Food Caters to Every Taste," *Food in Canada*, January 2001; Jack Kohane, "Cara Airport Services Invests in Supply Chain Management System to Improve Production Efficiencies and Customer Service," *Food in Canada*, April 1999.

Cara Airport Services Dishes It Out—Better and Cheaper!

MANAGEMENT CHALLENGES

2.1 **Key Information Systems Applications in the Organization**
- Different Kinds of Systems
- Six Major Types of Systems
- Relationship of Systems to One Another

2.2 **Information Systems from a Functional Perspective**
- Sales and Marketing Systems
- Manufacturing and Production Systems

Window on Management:
Mining for Profitable Products, Customers, and Performance
- Finance and Accounting Systems
- Human Resources Systems

2.3 **Integrating Functions and Business Processes: Enterprise Systems and Industrial Networks**
- Business Processes and Information Systems
- Customer Relationship Management
- Supply Chain Management
- Enterprise Systems
- Benefits and Challenges of Enterprise Systems

MANAGEMENT DECISION PROBLEM:
Analyzing Enterprise Process Integration

Window on Organizations:
Nestlé Turns to Enterprise Systems for Global Coordination
- Extended Enterprises and Industrial Networks

APPLICATION SOFTWARE EXERCISE:
Database Exercise: Tracking Reservations at Macdonald's Midnight Inn

MANAGEMENT WRAP-UP

• *Summary* • *Key Terms* • *Review Questions* • *Group Project* • *Internet Connection* • *Case Study: Tooling up for SCM*

MANAGEMENT CHALLENGES

Businesses need different types of information systems to support decision making and work activities for various organizational levels and functions. Many may also need enterprise-wide systems that integrate information and business processes from different functional areas. Cara, for instance, needed information systems that would allow it to produce more precise production schedules and to do so at the last minute. This involved the entire supply chain. It found a solution in building systems that could link important business processes for production and logistics. The opening vignette presents the potential rewards to firms with well-conceived systems linking the entire enterprise. These enterprise-wide systems typically require a significant amount of organizational and management change and raise the following management challenges:

1. **Integration:** Although it is necessary to design different systems serving different levels and functions in the firm, more and more firms derive benefits from integrating their systems. However, integrating systems so that different organizational levels and functions can freely exchange information can be difficult and costly. Managers need to determine what level of system integration is required and how much it is worth in dollars.

2. **Enlarging the scope of management thinking:** Most managers are trained to manage a product line, a division, or an office. They are rarely trained to optimize the performance of the organization as a whole and often are not given the means to do so. But enterprise systems and industrial networks require managers to take a much larger view of their own behaviour—to include other products, divisions, departments, and even outside business firms in their planning. Investments in enterprise systems are huge, they must be developed over long periods of time, and they must be guided by a shared vision of the firm's objectives.

I n this chapter, we examine the role of the various types of information systems in organizations. First we look at ways of classifying information systems based on the organizational level they support. Next we look at systems in terms of the organizational function they serve. We show how systems can support major business functions and processes that span more than one function, such as supply chain management. Finally we examine enterprise systems and industrial networks, which enable organizations to integrate information and business processes across entire firms and even entire industries.

2.1   KEY INFORMATION SYSTEMS APPLICATIONS IN THE ORGANIZATION

Because there are different interests, specialties, and levels in an organization, there are different kinds of information systems. No single system can provide all the information an organization needs. Figure 2-1 illustrates one way to depict the kinds of systems found in an organization. In the illustration, the organization is divided into strategic, management, knowledge, and operational levels and then is further divided into functional areas such as sales and marketing, manufacturing, finance, accounting, and human resources. Systems are built to serve these different organizational interests (Anthony, 1965).

DIFFERENT KINDS OF SYSTEMS

operational-level systems
Information systems that monitor the elementary activities and transactions of the organization.

Four main types of information systems serve different organizational levels: operational-level, knowledge-level, management-level, and strategic-level systems. **Operational-level systems** support operational managers by keeping track of the elementary activities and transactions of the organization, such as sales, receipts, cash deposits, payroll, credit decisions, and the flow of materials in a factory. The principal purpose of systems at this level is to answer routine questions and to track the flow of transactions through the organization.

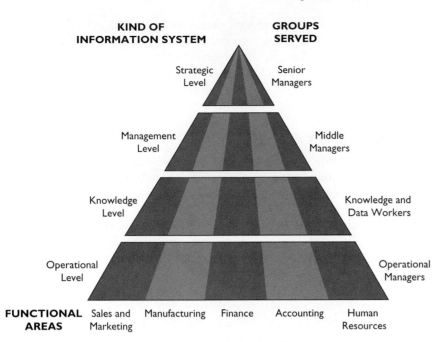

KIND OF
INFORMATION SYSTEM

GROUPS
SERVED

Strategic
Level

Senior
Managers

Management
Level

Middle
Managers

Knowledge
Level

Knowledge and
Data Workers

Operational
Level

Operational
Managers

**FUNCTIONAL
AREAS**   Sales and   Manufacturing   Finance   Accounting   Human
Marketing   Resources

How many parts are in inventory? What happened to Mr. Williams's payment? To answer these kinds of questions, information must be easily available, current, and accurate. Examples of operational-level systems include a system to record bank deposits from automatic teller machines or one that tracks the number of hours worked each day by employees on a factory floor.

Knowledge-level systems support the organization's knowledge and data workers. The purpose of knowledge-level systems is to help the business integrate new knowledge and to help the organization control the flow of paperwork. Knowledge-level systems, especially in the form of workstations and office systems, are the fastest-growing applications in business today. These systems support knowledge workers at all levels of the organization. Some knowledge workers are also managers located at a variety of levels in the organization's hierarchy.

Management-level systems serve the monitoring, controlling, decision making, and administrative activities of middle managers. The principal question addressed by such systems is, Are things working well? Management-level systems typically provide periodic reports rather than instant information on operations. An example is a relocation control system that reports on the total moving, house-hunting, and home financing costs for employees in all company divisions, noting wherever actual costs exceed budgets.

Some management-level systems support non-routine decision making (Keen and Morton, 1978). They tend to focus on less-structured decisions for which information requirements are not always clear. These systems often answer "what if" questions: What would be the impact on production schedules if we were to double sales in the month of December? What would happen to our return on investment if our factory schedule were delayed for six months? Answers to these questions frequently require new data from outside the organization as well as data from inside that cannot be easily drawn from existing operational-level systems.

Strategic-level systems help senior management address strategic issues and long-term trends, both in the firm and in the external environment. Their principal concern is matching changes in the external environment with existing organizational capabilities. What will employment levels be in five years? What are the long-term industry cost trends, and where does our firm fit in? What products should we be making in five years?

Information systems also serve the major business functions, such as sales and marketing, manufacturing, finance, accounting, and human resources. A typical organization has operational-, management-, knowledge-, and strategic-level systems for each functional area. For example, the sales function generally has a sales system on the operational level to record daily sales figures and to process orders. A knowledge-level system designs promotional displays

knowledge-level systems
Information systems that support knowledge and data workers in an organization.

management-level systems
Information systems that support the monitoring, controlling, decision-making, and administrative activities of middle managers.

strategic-level systems
Information systems that support the long-range planning activities of senior management.

for the firm's products. A management-level system tracks monthly sales figures by sales territory and reports on territories where sales exceed or fall below anticipated levels. A system to forecast sales trends over a five-year period serves the strategic level.

We will first describe the specific categories of systems serving each organizational level and their value to the organization. Then we will show how organizations use these systems for each major business function.

SIX MAJOR TYPES OF SYSTEMS

Figure 2-2 shows the specific types of information systems that correspond to each organizational level. The organization has executive support systems (ESS) at the strategic level, management information systems (MIS) and decision support systems (DSS) at the management level, knowledge work systems (KWS) and office automation systems (OAS) at the knowledge level, and transaction processing systems (TPS) at the operational level. Systems at each level in turn are specialized to serve each of the major functional areas. Thus, the typical systems found in organizations are designed to assist workers or managers at each level in the functions of sales and marketing, manufacturing, finance, accounting, and human resources.

Although we present here one model of categorizing information systems, there are other models, ranging from two types of systems to eight or more types. All of the models incorporate the same basic systems, simply assigning them to different categories. For example, we assign expert systems to decision support systems here while others may make expert systems a separate category. For another generally accepted model of categorizing information systems, see our Web site.

Note that each of these systems may have components that are used by organizational levels and groups other than their main constituencies. A secretary may find information on an MIS, or a middle manager may need to extract data from a TPS. It is important to remember as we proceed with this discussion and throughout the text that any type of system may actually be

FIGURE 2-2 The six major types of information systems, TPS, OAS, KWS, DSS, MIS, and ESS, showing the level of the organization and business function that each supports.

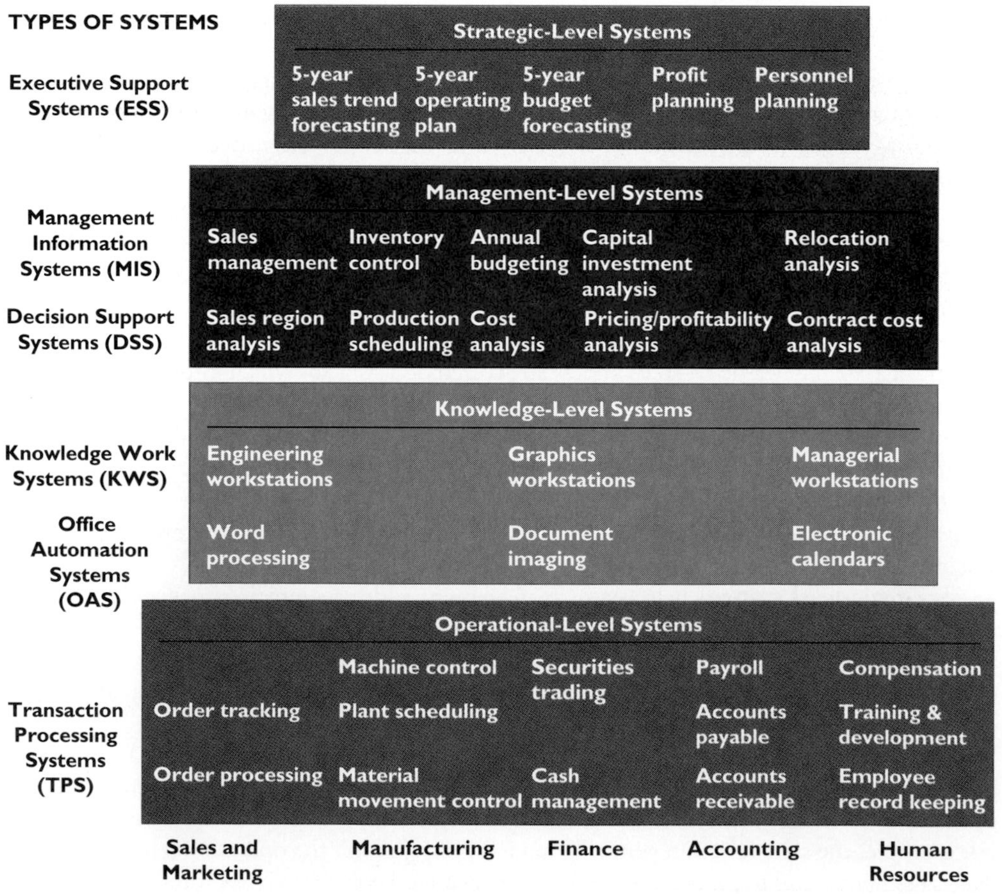

TYPES OF SYSTEMS

Strategic-Level Systems

Executive Support Systems (ESS)

| 5-year sales trend forecasting | 5-year operating plan | 5-year budget forecasting | Profit planning | Personnel planning |

Management-Level Systems

Management Information Systems (MIS)

| Sales management | Inventory control | Annual budgeting | Capital investment analysis | Relocation analysis |

Decision Support Systems (DSS)

| Sales region analysis | Production scheduling | Cost analysis | Pricing/profitability analysis | Contract cost analysis |

Knowledge-Level Systems

Knowledge Work Systems (KWS)

| Engineering workstations | Graphics workstations | Managerial workstations |

Office Automation Systems (OAS)

| Word processing | Document imaging | Electronic calendars |

Operational-Level Systems

| | Machine control | Securities trading | Payroll | Compensation |

Transaction Processing Systems (TPS)

| Order tracking | Plant scheduling | | Accounts payable | Training & development |
| Order processing | Material movement control | Cash management | Accounts receivable | Employee record keeping |

| Sales and Marketing | Manufacturing | Finance | Accounting | Human Resources |

used by a variety of workers and managers at almost all levels in the organization's hierarchy, depending on how the information system is implemented in a particular organization. Some information systems may be used as subsets of other systems, too. For example, a spreadsheet or database, normally considered an OAS system, may be part of a decision-support system or a transaction processing system. Table 2-1 summarizes the features of our model of six types of information systems.

Transaction Processing Systems

Transaction processing systems (TPS) are the basic business systems that serve the operational level of the organization. A transaction processing system is a computerized system that performs and records the daily routine transactions necessary to conduct business. Examples are sales order entry, hotel reservation, payroll, employee record keeping, and shipping systems.

At the operational level, tasks, resources, and goals are predefined and highly structured. The decision to grant credit to a customer, for instance, is made by a lower-level supervisor according to predefined criteria. All that must be determined is whether the customer meets the criteria.

Figure 2-3 depicts a payroll TPS, which is a typical accounting transaction processing system found in most firms. A payroll system keeps track of the money paid to employees. The master file comprises discrete pieces of information (such as a name, address, or employee number) called data elements. Data are keyed into the system, updating the data elements. The elements in the master file are combined in different ways to make up reports of interest to management and government agencies, and paycheques are sent to employees. These TPS can generate other report combinations of existing data elements.

Other typical TPS applications are identified in Figure 2-4. The figure shows that there are five functional categories of TPS: sales/marketing, manufacturing/production, finance/accounting, human resources, and other types of TPS that are unique to a particular industry. The UPS package-tracking system described in Chapter 1 is an example of a manufacturing TPS. UPS sells package delivery services; the system keeps track of all of its package shipment transactions.

Transaction processing systems are often so central to a business that a TPS failure for a few hours can spell a firm's demise and perhaps other firms linked to it. Imagine what would happen to UPS if its package tracking system were not working! What would airlines do without computerized reservation systems?

transaction processing systems (TPS)
Computerized systems that perform and record the daily routine transactions necessary to conduct business; they serve the organization's operational level.

TABLE 2-1	CHARACTERISTICS OF INFORMATION SYSTEMS

Type of System	Information Inputs	Processing	Information Outputs	Users
ESS	Aggregate data; external, internal	Graphics; simulations; interactive	Projections; responses to queries	Senior managers
DSS	Low-volume data or massive databases optimized for data analysis; analytic models and data analysis tools; rules	Interactive; simulations; analysis; graphics	Special reports; decision analyses; responses to queries; decisions enacted; recommendations	Professionals; staff managers
MIS	Summary transaction data; high-volume data; simple models	Routine reports; simple models; low-level analysis	Summary and exception reports	Middle managers
KWS	Design specifications; knowledge bases	Modelling; simulations	Models; graphics; responses to queries	Professionals; technical staff
OAS	Documents; schedules	Document management; scheduling; communication	Documents; schedules; e-mail	Clerical workers
TPS	Transactions; events	Sorting; listing; merging; updating	Detailed reports; lists; summaries	Operations personnel; supervisors

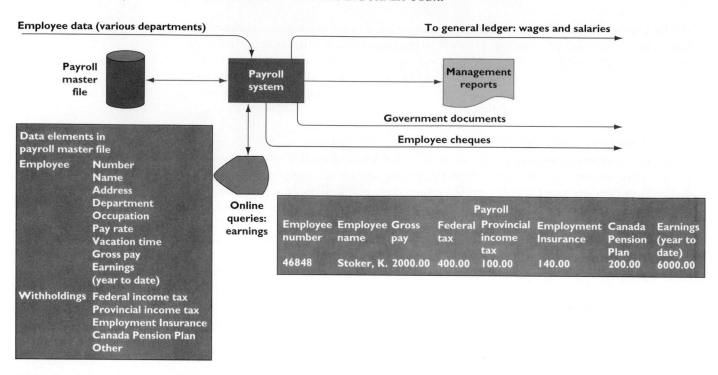

FIGURE 2-3 A symbolic representation of a payroll TPS.

Managers need TPS to monitor the status of internal operations and the firm's relations with the external environment. TPS are also major producers of information for the other types of systems. (For example, the payroll system illustrated here and other accounting TPS supply data to the company's general ledger system, which is responsible for maintaining records of the firm's income and expenses and for producing reports such as income statements and balance sheets.)

FIGURE 2-4 Typical applications of TPS. There are five functional categories of TPS: sales/marketing, manufacturing/production, finance/accounting, human resources, and other types of systems specific to a particular industry. Within each of these major functions are subfunctions. For each of these subfunctions (e.g., sales management), there is usually a TPS.

	TYPE OF TPS SYSTEM				
	Sales/ marketing systems	Manufacturing/ production systems	Finance/ accounting systems	Human resources systems	Other types (e.g., university)
Major functions of system	Sales management	Scheduling	Budgeting	Personnel records	Admissions
	Market research	Purchasing	General ledger	Benefits	Grade records
	Promotion	Shipping/receiving	Billing	Compensation	Course records
	Pricing	Engineering	Cost accounting	Labour relations	Alumni
	New products	Inventory operations		Training	
Major application systems	Sales order information system	Machine control systems	General ledgers systems	Payroll systems	Registration system
	Market research system	Purchase order systems	Accounts receivable/ payable systems	Employee records systems	Student transcript system
	Sales commission system	Quality control systems	Budgeting systems	Benefit systems	Curriculum class control systems
		Engineering systems	Funds management systems	Career path systems	Alumni benefactor system
		Supply chain management systems			

Knowledge Work and Office Automation Systems

Knowledge work systems (KWS) and **office automation systems (OAS)** serve information needs at the knowledge and other levels of the organization. Knowledge work systems aid knowledge workers, while office automation systems primarily aid data workers (although they are also used extensively by knowledge and other workers).

In general, *knowledge workers* are people who hold formal university degrees and who are often members of a recognized profession, like engineers, doctors, lawyers, and scientists. Their jobs consist primarily of creating new information and knowledge. Knowledge work systems, such as scientific or engineering design applications, promote the creation of new knowledge and ensure that new knowledge and technical expertise are properly integrated into the business. *Data workers* typically have less advanced educational degrees and tend to process rather than create information. They are primarily secretaries, accountants, filing clerks, or managers whose jobs are principally to use, manipulate, or disseminate information. Office automation systems are information technology applications designed to increase data workers' productivity by supporting the coordinating and communicating activities of the typical office. Office automation systems coordinate diverse information workers, geographic units, and functional areas. These systems communicate with customers, suppliers, and other organizations outside the firm and serve as a clearinghouse for information and knowledge flow.

Typical office automation systems handle and manage documents (through word processing, desktop publishing, document imaging, and digital filing), scheduling (through electronic calendars), and communication (through electronic mail, voice mail, or videoconferencing). **Word processing** refers to the software and hardware that create, edit, format, store, and print documents (see Chapter 7). Word processing systems represent the single most common application of information technology to office work because all offices produce documents. **Desktop publishing** produces professional publishing-quality documents by combining output from word processing software with design elements, graphics, and special layout features. Companies are now starting to publish documents in the form of Web pages for easier access and distribution. We describe Web publishing in more detail in Chapter 15.

Document imaging systems convert documents and images into digital form so that they can be stored and accessed by the computer.

Management Information Systems

In Chapter 1, we defined management information systems as the study of information systems in business and management. The term *management information systems (MIS)* also designates a specific category of information systems serving management-level functions. **Management information systems (MIS)** serve the management level of the organization, providing managers with reports and, in some cases, with on-line access to the organization's current performance and historical records. Typically, they are oriented almost exclusively to internal, not environmental or external, events. MIS primarily support the functions of planning, controlling, and decision making at the management level. Generally, they depend on underlying transaction processing systems for their data.

MIS summarize and report on the company's basic operations. The basic transaction data from TPS are summarized and filtered and are usually presented in long reports that are produced on a regular schedule. Figure 2-5 shows how a typical MIS transforms transaction level data from inventory, production, and accounting into MIS files that are used to provide managers with reports. Figure 2-6 shows a sample report from this system.

Graphics designers use desktop publishing software to design a page for "La Opinion." Desktop publishing software enables users to control all aspects of the design and layout process for professional-looking publications.

knowledge work systems (KWS)
Information systems that aid knowledge workers in the creation and integration of new knowledge in the organization.

office automation systems (OAS)
Computer systems, such as word processing, electronic mail systems, and scheduling systems, that are designed to increase the productivity of data workers in the office.

word processing
Office automation technology that facilitates the creation of documents through computerized text editing, formatting, storing, and printing.

desktop publishing
Technology that produces professional-quality documents combining output from word processors with design, graphics, and special layout features.

document imaging systems
Systems that convert documents and images into digital form so that they can be stored and accessed by the computer.

management information systems (MIS)
Information systems at the management level of an organization that support the functions of planning, controlling, and decision making by providing routine summary and exception reports.

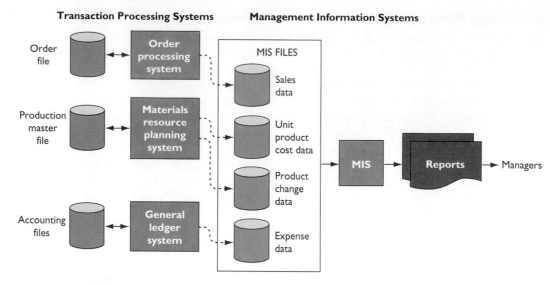

FIGURE 2-5 How management information systems obtain their data from the organization's TPS. In the system illustrated by this diagram, three TPS supply summarized transaction data at the end of the time period to the MIS reporting system. Managers gain access to the organizational data through the MIS, which provides them with the appropriate reports.

MIS usually serve managers interested in weekly, monthly, and yearly results—not day-to-day activities. MIS generally provide answers to routine questions that have been specified in advance and have a predefined procedure for answering them. For instance, MIS reports might list the total pounds of lettuce used this quarter by a fast food chain or, as illustrated in Figure 2-6, compare total annual sales figures for specific products to planned targets. These systems are generally not flexible and have little analytical capability. Most MIS use simple routines such as summaries and comparisons as opposed to sophisticated mathematical models or statistical techniques.

Decision Support Systems

decision support systems (DSS)

Information systems at the organization's management level that combine data and sophisticated analytical models or data analysis tools to support semi-structured and unstructured decision making.

Decision support systems (DSS) also serve the management level of the organization. DSS help managers make decisions that are unique, rapidly changing, and not easily specified in advance. They address problems when the procedure for arriving at a solution may not be fully predefined. While DSS use internal information from TPS and MIS, they often bring in information from external sources as well, such as current stock prices or product prices of competitors. While DSS primarily serve the managerial levels of the firm, they may be used at any level in the organization's hierarchy.

FIGURE 2-6 A sample report that might be produced by the MIS in Figure 2-5.

Canadian Consumer Products Corporation
Sales by Product and Region: 2001

Product Code	Product Description	Sales Region	Actual Sales	Planned Sales	Actual vs. Planned
4469	Carpet Cleaner	Atlantic	1 066 700	2 000 000	0.53
		East	4 867 001	4 750 000	1.02
		Prairies	3 150 000	3 000 000	1.05
		West	4 100 500	4 000 000	1.03
	TOTAL		13 184 201	13 750 000	0.96
5674	Room Freshener	Atlantic	2 066 700	2 000 000	1.03
		East	3 902 001	4 250 000	0.92
		Prairies	3 350 000	3 000 000	1.12
		West	4 002 500	4 000 000	1.00
	TOTAL		13 321 201	13 250 000	1.01

Clearly, DSS have more analytical power than other systems. They are built with a variety of models to analyze data, or they may condense large amounts of data into a form that can be analyzed by decision makers. DSS are designed so that users can work with them directly; these systems, therefore, include user-friendly software. DSS are interactive; the user can change assumptions, ask new questions, and include new data. **Group decision support systems (GDSS)** use computer-mediated communication tools, such as networks, anonymous input and voting, and whiteboards, to support groups as they make decisions. **Expert systems** provide what appears to be intelligence, with the ability to make decisions and reach conclusions. Expert systems are used in a wide variety of applications, from spell- and grammar-checking to tax programs and credit card authorization. We discuss these cutting-edge applications in Chapter 15.

A DSS for assessing patients under long-term care has been implemented in Ontario. Patients receiving healthcare at home or in nursing homes can be assessed using standardized categories developed at the University of Waterloo and the University of Alberta in conjunction with MED e-care Healthcare Solutions, Inc., a Toronto-based software development firm (www.mede-care.com). Patients can be assessed using the new DSS, and their records can be transmitted electronically from one agency to another as needed, such as when a patient moves from home healthcare to a nursing home. Patients can be assessed repeatedly to determine how they are responding over time. Among the data elements that are assessed are cognitive abilities, memory, depression, history of falls, pressure ulcers, and incontinence. Using the assessment tools, patient care can be planned before the patient even arrives at the nursing home. MED e-care is also partnering with other Canadian firms, such as Momentum Software of Winnipeg, Manitoba, to provide its MDS software to nursing homes throughout North America. Figure 2-7 illustrates the type of DSS now being built; interestingly, using the MDS and other standards being developed for patient assessment, many vendors can develop a variety of DSS tools for long-term care applications (Zeidenberg, 2000). We will describe other types of DSS in Chapter 14.

Executive Support Systems

Senior managers use **executive support systems (ESS)** to make decisions. ESS serve the strategic level of the organization. They address non-routine decisions requiring judgment, evaluation, and insight because there is no agreed-upon procedure for arriving at a solution. ESS create a generalized computing and communications environment rather than providing any fixed application or specific capability. ESS are designed to incorporate data about external events such as new tax laws or competitors, but they also draw summarized information from internal MIS and DSS. They filter, summarize, and track critical data, reducing the time and effort required to obtain information useful to executives. ESS employ advanced graphics software and can immediately deliver graphs and data from many sources to a senior executive's office or to a boardroom.

Unlike the other types of information systems, ESS are not designed primarily to solve specific problems. Instead, ESS provide a generalized computing and telecommunications capacity that can be applied to a changing array of problems. While DSS are designed to be highly analytical, ESS tend to make less use of analytical models.

group decision support systems (GDSS)
A form of decision support system that supports the decision-making processes of groups through computer-mediated communication tools.

expert systems
Information systems that provide what appears to be intelligence or expertise, with the ability to make decisions and reach conclusions.

executive support systems (ESS)
Information systems at the organization's strategic level designed to address unstructured decision making through advanced graphics and communications.

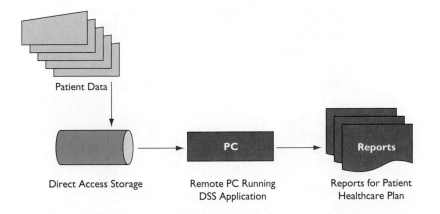

Patient Data

Direct Access Storage → PC (Remote PC Running DSS Application) → Reports (Reports for Patient Healthcare Plan)

FIGURE 2-7 DSS for assessing and monitoring patients. It is used daily by healthcare professionals responsible for providing healthcare to patients who require long-term care.

FIGURE 2-8 Model of a typical ESS. This system pools data from diverse internal and external sources and makes them available to executives in an easy-to-use form.

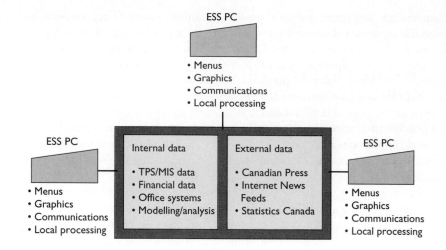

Questions ESS assist in answering include the following: What business should we be in? What are our competitors doing? What new acquisitions would protect us from cyclical business swings? Which units should we sell to raise cash for acquisitions (Rockart and Treacy, 1982)? Figure 2-8 illustrates a model of an ESS. It consists of PCs with menus, interactive graphics, and communications capabilities that can access historical and competitive data from internal corporate systems and external databases such as the Canadian Press or Statistics Canada (www.statcan.ca). Because ESS are designed to be used by senior managers who often have little, if any, direct contact or experience with computer-based information systems, they incorporate easy-to-use graphic interfaces. More details on leading-edge applications of DSS and ESS can be found in Chapter 14.

RELATIONSHIP OF SYSTEMS TO ONE ANOTHER

Figure 2-9 illustrates how the systems serving different levels in the organization are related to one another. TPS are typically a major source of data for other systems while ESS are primarily a recipient of data from lower-level systems. The other types of systems may exchange data with each other as well. Data may also be exchanged among systems serving different functional areas. For example, an order captured by a sales system may be transmitted to a manufacturing system as a transaction for producing or delivering the product specified in the order.

Although it is definitely advantageous to have some measure of integration among these systems so that information can flow easily between different parts of the organization, integration costs money. Integrating many different systems is extremely time-consuming and complex. Each organization must weigh its needs for integrating systems against the difficul-

FIGURE 2-9 Interrelationships among systems. The various types of systems in the organization have interdependencies. TPS are a major producer of information that is required by the other systems, which, in turn, produce information for other systems. These different types of systems are only loosely coupled in most organizations.

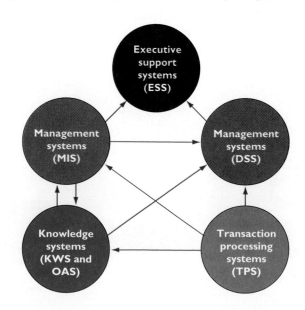

ties of mounting a large-scale systems integration effort. The discussion of enterprise systems in Section 2.3 explores this issue in greater detail.

2.2 INFORMATION SYSTEMS FROM A FUNCTIONAL PERSPECTIVE

Information systems can be classified by the specific organizational function they serve as well as by organizational level. We now describe typical information systems that support each of the major business functions and provide examples of functional applications for each organizational level.

SALES AND MARKETING SYSTEMS

The sales and marketing function is responsible for selling the organization's product or service. Marketing is concerned with identifying customers for the firm's products or services, determining what they need or want, planning and developing products and services to meet their needs, and advertising and promoting these products and services. Sales is concerned with contacting customers, selling the products and services, taking orders, and following up on sales. **Sales and marketing information systems** support these activities.

> **sales and marketing information systems**
> Systems that help the firm identify customers for the firm's products or services, develop products and services to meet their needs, promote and sell these products and services, and provide ongoing customer support.

Table 2-2 shows that information systems are used in sales and marketing in a number of ways. At the strategic level, sales and marketing systems monitor trends affecting new products and sales opportunities, support planning for new products and services, and monitor the performance of competitors. At the management level, sales and marketing systems support market research, advertising and promotional campaigns, and pricing decisions. They analyze sales performance and the performance of the sales staff. Knowledge-level sales and marketing systems support marketing analysis applications. At the operational level, sales and marketing systems assist in locating and contacting prospective customers, tracking sales, processing orders, and providing customer service support. A sales expert system might inform a customer service representative that, based on the customer's purchase history, the customer ordering merchandise should be cross-sold on a different product as well.

Review Figure 2-6. It shows the output of a typical sales information system at the management level. The system consolidates data about each item sold (such as the product code, product description, and price) for further management analysis. Company managers examine these sales data to monitor sales activity and buying trends. In addition, sales and marketing systems are used for customer relationship management (CRM). The Window on Management describes how a few Canadian businesses are using typical CRM sales and marketing systems that might be found in a larger business.

MANUFACTURING AND PRODUCTION SYSTEMS

The manufacturing and production function is responsible for actually producing the firm's goods and services. Manufacturing and production deal with the planning, development, and maintenance of production facilities; the establishment of production goals; the acquisition,

TABLE 2-2	EXAMPLES OF SALES AND MARKETING INFORMATION SYSTEMS

System	Description	Organizational Level
Order processing	Enter, process, and track orders	Operational
Market analysis	Identify customers and markets using data on demographics, markets, consumer behaviour, and trends	Knowledge
Pricing analysis	Determine prices for products and services	Management
Sales trend forecasting	Prepare five-year sales forecasts	Strategic
Cross-selling	Cross-sell customers based on purchase history	Expert

MINING FOR PROFITABLE PRODUCTS, CUSTOMERS, AND PERFORMANCE

Royal Bank's search for adequate performance measures, including customer profitability, began years ago. They partnered with Inea Corporation, a small, Toronto-based software firm, to develop an off-the-shelf business reporting and intelligence product. Large, multinational companies like Royal Bank (www.royalbank.com) operate businesses that carry a lot of risk, so they need a flexible system to enable them to measure and report business metrics adjusted for the risk they bear at any given time. They also have to work with multiple currencies, exchange rates, inflation rates, economic assumptions, and so on.

Alain Simard, the bank's current vice president of finance information technology, wanted to be able to break down profitability and performance by product, customer, channel, and line of business. The system developed by Inea and Royal Bank does just that. Today, Royal Bank is changing its use of the Inea software. They want to better understand customer service metrics as well as the financial picture of the bank. Royal Bank is counting on using Inea to help them develop discretionary pricing for customers, changing the way the bank sells its products and services.

One datamining tool is customer relationship management (CRM) software. Bill Comeau, senior director of database marketing services for Bell Canada International Inc. in Toronto, says, "Delivering products to customers becomes more complicated all the time. CRM software can help." Bell Canada (www.bell.ca) recently implemented NCR Corp.'s Worldmark Server and Teradata Relational Database Management System, a decision support parallel relational database capable of supporting databases of more than 500 gigabytes. Comeau says he hopes the system will help Bell Canada build better customer profiles, based on call-detail records and customer and billing histories stored in the database.

Bell Canada can also reduce "churn" by building accurate predictive models to determine which customers are most likely to switch to a competitor. Bell Canada also uses KnowledgeStudio, one of Angoss Software Corp.'s datamining tools, along with Seagate Software Inc.'s Holos, which includes tools for customer profiling, planning, budgeting, forecasting, and performance management, and SAS Institute Inc.'s Enterprise Miner, to identify patterns, group customers with similar characteristics, and create predictive target models that help determine which customers should receive a particular offer. Bell Canada also uses predictive models to guide them in determining where to place their network facilities.

Schwab Canada Inc. (www.schwabcanada.com) has attempted to capture every one of its customer transactions, tying them all back into Siebel Inc.'s CRM suite of applications. When a customer contacts Schwab in Toronto, a representative can look at all the information relating to that customer, including records of conversations and copies of letters and statements. "When you have that kind of information, you can do a much better job of serving the customer," says Schwab Canada CIO Steve Kruste.

To Think About: How can datamining change the way organizations conduct their business? What benefits does datamining provide? What problems might it create?

Sources: Saroja Girishankar, "Customer Service for Business Partners," *InformationWeek*, April 17, 2000; Candee Wilde, "Telcos Turn to Analytical Tools to Stay in Touch," *InformationWeek*, March 13, 2000; Martin Slofstra, "Analyze This," *InfoSystems Executive*, August 2000; Jeff Sweat, "The Well-Rounded Customer," *InformationWeek*, April 10, 2000.

---

manufacturing and production information systems
Systems that help with the planning, development, and production of products and services and with controlling the flow of production.

storage, and availability of production materials; and the scheduling of equipment, facilities, materials, and labour required to fashion finished products. **Manufacturing and production information systems** support these activities.

Table 2-3 shows some typical manufacturing and production information systems arranged by organizational level. Strategic-level manufacturing systems deal with the firm's long-term manufacturing goals, such as where to locate new plants or whether to invest in new manufacturing technology. At the management level, manufacturing and production systems analyze and monitor manufacturing and production costs and resources. Knowledge manufacturing and production systems create and distribute design knowledge or expertise to drive the production process, and operational manufacturing and production systems deal with the status of production tasks. A production expert system could determine when a machine needed recalibration, based on its past history.

Most manufacturing and production systems use some sort of inventory system, illustrated in Figure 2-10. Data about each item in inventory, such as the number of units depleted because of a shipment or purchase or the number of units replenished by reordering or returns, are either scanned or keyed into the system. The inventory master file contains basic data about each item, including the unique identification code for each item, the description of the item, the number of units on hand, the number of units on order, and the reorder point (the number of units in inventory that triggers a decision to reorder to prevent

TABLE 2-3 EXAMPLES OF MANUFACTURING AND PRODUCTION INFORMATION SYSTEMS

System	Description	Organizational Level
Machine control	Control the actions of machines and equipment	Operational
Computer-aided design (CAD)	Design new products using the computer	Knowledge
Production planning	Decide when and how many products should be produced	Management
Facilities location	Decide where to locate new production facilities	Strategic
Capacity scheduling	Decide how many shifts of how many workers must be scheduled to complete production on time	Expert

a stock-out). Companies can estimate the number of items to reorder, or they can use a formula for calculating the least expensive quantity to reorder called the *economic order quantity*. The system produces reports such as the number of each item available in inventory, the number of units of each item to reorder, or items in inventory that must be replenished.

FINANCE AND ACCOUNTING SYSTEMS

The finance function is responsible for managing the firm's financial assets—cash, stocks, bonds, and other investments—to maximize the return on these financial assets. The finance function is also in charge of managing the capitalization of the firm (finding new financial assets in stocks, bonds, or other forms of debt). To determine whether the firm is getting the best return on its investments, the finance function must obtain a considerable amount of information from sources external to the firm.

The accounting function is responsible for maintaining and managing the firm's financial records—receipts, disbursements, depreciation, and payroll—to account for the firm's flow of funds. Finance and accounting share related problems—how to keep track of a firm's financial assets and fund flows. They provide answers to questions such as these: What is the current inventory of financial assets? What records exist for disbursements, receipts, payroll, and other fund flows?

Table 2-4 shows some of the typical **finance and accounting information systems** found in large organizations. Strategic-level systems for the finance and accounting function establish long-term investment goals for the firm and provide long-range forecasts of the firm's financial performance. At the management level, information systems help managers

finance and accounting information systems
Systems that keep track of the firm's financial assets and fund flows.

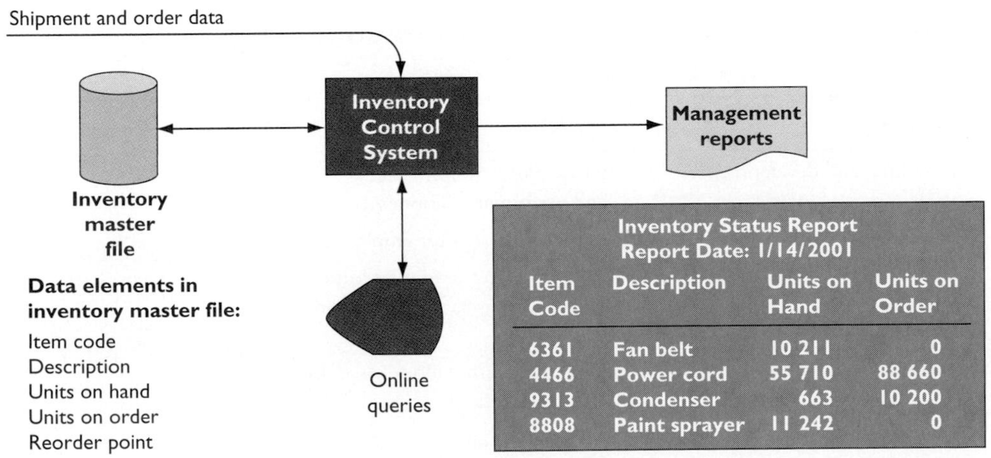

FIGURE 2-10 Overview of an inventory system. This system provides information about the number of items available in inventory to support manufacturing and production activities.

Shipment and order data

Inventory
Control
System

Management
reports

Inventory
master
file

Data elements in inventory master file:
Item code
Description
Units on hand
Units on order
Reorder point

Online
queries

Inventory Status Report Report Date: 1/14/2001			
Item Code	Description	Units on Hand	Units on Order
6361	Fan belt	10 211	0
4466	Power cord	55 710	88 660
9313	Condenser	663	10 200
8808	Paint sprayer	11 242	0

TABLE 2-4   Examples of Finance and Accounting Information Systems

System	Description	Organizational Level
Accounts receivable	Track money owed to the firm	Operational
Portfolio analysis	Design the firm's portfolio of investments	Knowledge
Budgeting	Prepare short-term budgets	Management
Profit planning	Plan long-term profits	Strategic
Temporary funds investment	Invest temporary funds based on parameters set by funds managers	Expert

oversee and control the firm's financial resources. Knowledge systems support finance and accounting by providing analytical tools for designing the right mix of investments to maximize returns for the firm. Operational systems in finance and accounting track the flow of funds in the firm through transactions such as paycheques, payments to vendors, securities reports, and receipts. A finance expert system could trigger investment purchases and sales based on market volatility or the prime rate. Review Figure 2-3, which illustrates a payroll system—a typical accounting TPS found in all businesses with employees.

HUMAN RESOURCES SYSTEMS

human resources information systems

Systems that maintain employee records, track employee skills, job performance, and training, and support planning for employee compensation and career development.

The human resources function is responsible for attracting, developing, and maintaining the firm's work force. **Human resources information systems** support activities such as identifying potential employees, maintaining complete records on existing employees, and creating programs to develop employees' talents and skills.

Strategic-level human resources systems identify the workforce requirements (skills, educational level, types of positions, number of positions, and cost) for meeting the firm's long-term business plans. At the management level, human resources systems help managers monitor and analyze the recruitment, allocation, and compensation of employees. Knowledge systems for human resources support analysis activities related to job design, training, modelling employee career paths, and reporting relationships. Human resources operational systems track the recruitment and placement of the firm's employees. A human resources expert system might determine cost-of-living salary increments based on a variety of external data (see Table 2-5).

Figure 2-11 illustrates a typical human resources TPS for employee record keeping. It maintains basic employee data, such as the employee's name, age, sex, marital status, address, educational background, salary, job title, date of hire, and date of termination. The system can produce a variety of reports, such as lists of newly hired employees, employees who are

TABLE 2-5   Examples of Human Resources Information Systems

System	Description	Organizational Level
Training and development	Track employee training, skills, and performance appraisals	Operational
Career pathing	Design career paths for employees	Knowledge
Compensation analysis	Monitor the range and distribution of employee wages, salaries, and benefits	Management
Human resources planning	Plan the long-term labour force needs of the organization	Strategic
Benefits analysis	Recommend changes in benefits to the company or to individual employees	Expert

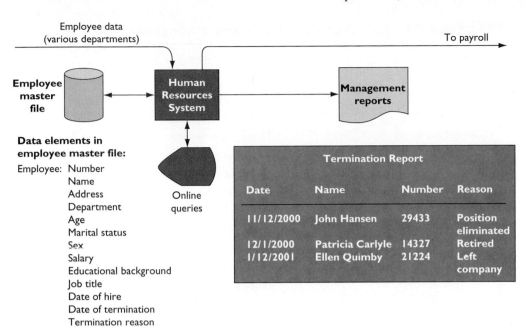

FIGURE 2-11 An employee record-keeping system. This system maintains data on the firm's employees to support the human resources function.

terminated or on leave of absence, employees classified by job type or educational level, or employee job performance evaluations. These systems are typically designed to provide data that can satisfy federal and provincial record-keeping requirements for employment equity and other purposes.

2.3 INTEGRATING FUNCTIONS AND BUSINESS PROCESSES: ENTERPRISE SYSTEMS AND INDUSTRIAL NETWORKS

With today's technology, information systems scattered across organizations can talk to each other, moving them toward computer integration. Today organizations are using information systems to coordinate activities and decisions across entire firms and even entire industries.

BUSINESS PROCESSES AND INFORMATION SYSTEMS

The functional systems we have just described support workflows and activities called business processes. **Business processes** refer to the manner in which work is organized, co-ordinated, and focused to produce a valuable product or service. On one hand, business processes are concrete workflows of material, information, and knowledge—sets of activities. However, business processes also refer to the unique ways in which organizations coordinate work, information, and knowledge. Table 2-6 describes typical business processes for each of the functional areas.

business processes
The unique ways in which organizations coordinate and organize work activities, information, and knowledge to produce a product or service.

Although each of the major business functions has its own set of business processes, many other business processes are cross-functional, transcending the boundaries between sales, marketing, manufacturing, and research and development. These cross-functional processes cut across the traditional organizational structure, grouping employees from different functional specialties to complete a piece of work. For example, the order fulfillment process at many companies requires cooperation between the sales function (receiving and entering the order), the accounting function (credit checking and billing for the order), and the manufacturing function (assembling and shipping the order). Figure 2-12 illustrates how this cross-functional process might work. Information systems support these cross-functional processes as well as processes for stand-alone business functions.

Information systems can help organizations achieve great efficiencies by automating parts of these processes or by helping organizations rethink and streamline these processes. However, redesigning business processes requires careful analysis and planning. When systems are used to strengthen the wrong business model or business processes, the business can

TABLE 2-6	EXAMPLES OF BUSINESS PROCESSES
Functional Area	**Business Process**
Manufacturing and Production	Assembling the product
	Checking for quality
	Producing bills of materials
Sales and Marketing	Identifying customers
	Making customers aware of the product
	Selling the product
Finance and Accounting	Paying creditors
	Creating financial statements
	Managing cash accounts
Human Resources	Hiring employees
	Evaluating employees' job performance
	Enrolling employees in benefits plans

become more efficient at doing what it should not do. As a result, the firm becomes vulnerable to competitors who may have discovered the right business model. Therefore, one of the most important strategic decisions that a firm can make is not deciding how to use computers to improve business processes, but instead understanding what business processes need improvement (Keen, 1997). Chapter 11 will treat this subject in greater detail, since it is fundamental to systems analysis and design.

CUSTOMER RELATIONSHIP MANAGEMENT

Instead of treating customers as exploitable sources of income, businesses are now viewing them as long-term assets to be nurtured through customer relationship management (CRM). **Customer relationship management** focuses on managing all of the ways that a firm deals with its existing and potential customers. CRM is both a business discipline and a technology discipline that uses information systems to coordinate all of the business processes surrounding the firm's interactions with its customers in sales, marketing, and service. The ideal CRM system provides end-to-end customer care from receipt of an order through product delivery.

In the past, a firm's processes for sales, service, and marketing were highly compartmentalized and did not share very much essential customer information. Some customer information might be stored and organized in terms of that person's account with the company. Other pieces of information about the same customer might be organized by products that were purchased. There was no way to consolidate all of this information to provide a unified view of a customer across the company. CRM tools try to solve this problem by integrating

customer relationship management (CRM)
Managing all of the ways that a firm deals with its existing and potential customers.

FIGURE 2-12 The order fulfillment process. Generating and fulfilling an order is a multi-step process involving activities performed by the sales, manufacturing and production, and accounting functions.

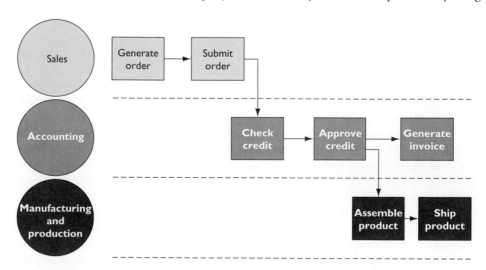

Keying data from tax returns into the Canada Customs and Revenue Agency's tax computer system is an important activity in the tax collection process. Business processes coordinate work, information, and knowledge.

the firm's customer-related processes and consolidating customer information from multiple communication channels—the telephone, e-mail, wireless devices, and the Web—so that the firm can put one coherent face on the customer (see Figure 2-13).

Good CRM systems consolidate customer data from multiple sources and provide analytical tools for answering questions such as, What is the value of a particular customer to the firm over his or her lifetime? Who are our most loyal customers? (It costs six times more to sell to a new customer than it does to an existing customer [Kalakota and Robinson, 2001]). Who are our most profitable customers? (Typically 80%–90% of a firm's profits are generated by 10%–20% of its customers.) What do these profitable customers buy? Firms can then use the answers to these questions to acquire new customers, to provide better service and support, to customize offerings more precisely to customer preferences, and to provide ongoing value to retain profitable customers. Chapters 3, 4, 10, and 14 provide additional detail on customer relationship management applications and technologies.

SUPPLY CHAIN MANAGEMENT

There are also important business processes that flow between two different organizations, such as those for supply chain management. **Supply chain management (SCM)** is the close linkage of activities involved in buying, making, and moving a product. It integrates supplier, distributor, and customer logistics requirements into one cohesive process to reduce time,

supply chain management (SCM)
The integration of supplier, distributor, and customer logistics requirements into one cohesive process.

FIGURE 2-13 Customer relationship management. CRM applies technology to view customers from a multifaceted perspective. CRM uses a set of integrated applications to address all aspects of the customer relationship, including customer sales, service, and marketing.

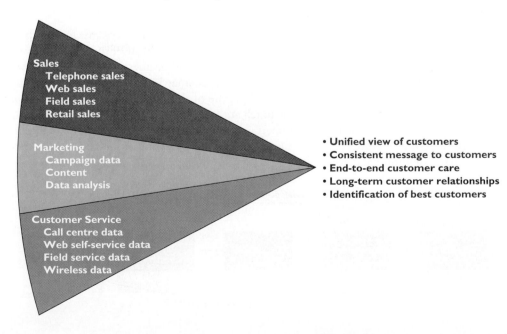

Sales
  Telephone sales
  Web sales
  Field sales
  Retail sales

Marketing
  Campaign data
  Content
  Data analysis

Customer Service
  Call centre data
  Web self-service data
  Field service data
  Wireless data

• Unified view of customers
• Consistent message to customers
• End-to-end customer care
• Long-term customer relationships
• Identification of best customers

supply chain
A collection of entities, such as manufacturing plants, distribution centres, retail outlets, people, and information, which are linked together into processes supplying goods or services from source through consumption.

redundant effort, and inventory costs (see Figure 2-14). The **supply chain** is a network of activities, processes, and parties that procure materials, transform raw materials into intermediate and finished products, and distribute the finished products to customers. It links manufacturing plants, distribution centres, delivery mechanisms and channels, retail outlets, people, and information through processes such as procurement or logistics to supply goods and services from source through consumption. Goods and services start out as raw materials and move through the company's logistics and production systems until they reach customers. To manage the supply chain, a company tries to eliminate redundant steps, delays, and the amount of resources tied up along the way.

Companies that skillfully manage their supply chains get the right amount of their products from their source to their point of consumption within the least amount of time and at the lowest cost. (Note that while these are desirable goals, they may not be able to be attained at the same time. For example, it may cost more to have materials available within the least amount of time.) Information systems make supply chain management more efficient by helping companies coordinate, schedule, and control procurement, production, inventory management, and delivery of products and services to customers. Information systems can integrate demand planning, production forecasting, materials requisition, order processing, inventory allocation, order fulfillment, transportation services, receiving, invoicing, and payment. Companies can benefit from using information systems for supply chain management by helping supply chain participants:

- Decide when and what to produce, store, and move
- Rapidly communicate orders
- Track the status of orders
- Check inventory availability and monitor inventory levels
- Track shipments
- Maintain a high degree of accuracy
- Reduce paperwork
- Plan production based on actual customer demand
- Rapidly communicate changes in product design
- Provide product specifications
- Share information about defect rates and returns

Many firms find that they can compete more effectively by using supply chain management to lower their inventory costs while delivering products or services more rapidly to customers.

ENTERPRISE SYSTEMS

A large organization typically has many different kinds of information systems that support different functions, organizational levels, and business processes. Most of these systems were originally built around different functions, business units, and business processes and do not "talk" to each other. Under these circumstances, managers may have a hard time assembling the data they need for a comprehensive, overall picture of the organization's operations. For instance, sales personnel might not be able to tell at the time they place an order whether the items they ordered are in inventory; customers could not track their orders; and manufacturing could not communicate easily with finance to plan for new production. This fragmentation of data in hundreds of separate systems could thus have a negative impact on

FIGURE 2-14 Supply chain management. The major entities in the supply chain use the flow of information to coordinate the activities involved in buying raw materials, and making and moving a product.

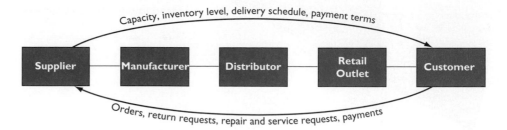

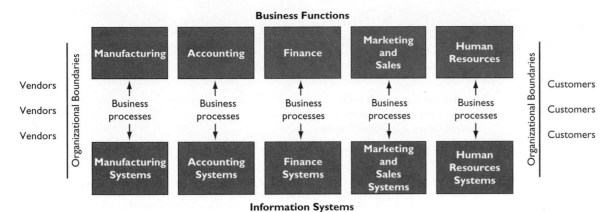

FIGURE 2-15 Traditional view of systems. In most organizations, separate systems were originally built over a long period of time to support discrete business processes and discrete segments of the business value chain. The organization's systems rarely include vendors and customers.

organizational efficiency and business performance. Figure 2-15 illustrates the traditional arrangement of information systems.

Systems for CRM and SCM are a step forward in solving this problem. Many organizations are also building **enterprise systems**, also known as enterprise resource planning (ERP) systems, to solve this problem. Enterprise software automates and models many business processes, such as filling an order or scheduling a shipment, with the goal of integrating information across the company and eliminating complex, expensive links between computer systems in different areas of the business. Information that was previously fragmented in different systems can flow seamlessly throughout the firm so that it can be shared by business processes in manufacturing, accounting, human resources, and other areas of the firm. Discrete business processes from sales, production, finance, and logistics can be integrated into company-wide business processes that flow across organizational levels and functions. An enterprise-wide technical platform serves all processes and levels. Figure 2-16 illustrates how enterprise systems work.

An enterprise system collects data from various key business processes (see Table 2-7) and stores the data in a single comprehensive data repository where they can be used by other parts of the business. Managers emerge with more precise and timely information for coordinating the daily operations of the business and with a firm-wide view of business processes and information flows.

For instance, when a sales representative in Brussels enters a customer order, the data flows automatically to others in the company who need to see it. The factory in Hong Kong receives the order and begins production. The warehouse checks its progress online and schedules the shipment date. The warehouse can also check its stock of parts and replenish whatever the factory has depleted. The enterprise system stores production information

enterprise systems
Firm-wide information systems that integrate key business processes so that information can flow freely between different parts of the firm. Also known as enterprise resource planning systems (ERP).

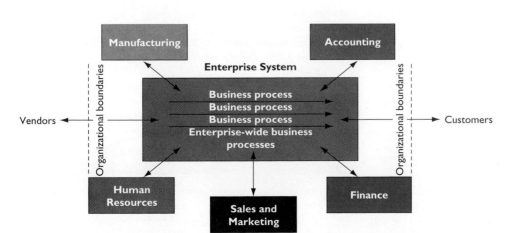

FIGURE 2-16 Enterprise systems. Enterprise systems can integrate the key business processes of an entire firm into a single software system that allows information to flow seamlessly throughout the organization. These systems may include transactions with customers and vendors.

TABLE 2-7	BUSINESS PROCESSES SUPPORTED BY ENTERPRISE SYSTEMS

Manufacturing processes including inventory management, purchasing, shipping, production planning, material requirements planning, and plant and equipment maintenance.

Financial and accounting processes including accounts payable, accounts receivable, cash management and forecasting, product-cost accounting, cost-centre accounting, asset accounting, general ledger, and financial reporting.

Sales and marketing processes including order processing, pricing, shipping, billing, sales management, and sales planning.

Human resource processes including personnel administration, time accounting, payroll, personnel planning and development, benefits accounting, applicant tracking, and travel expense reporting.

where it can be accessed by customer service representatives who track the progress of the order through every step of the manufacturing process. Updated sales and production data automatically flow to the accounting department. The system transmits information for calculating the salesperson's commission to the payroll department. The system also automatically recalculates the company's balance sheets, accounts receivable and payable ledgers, cost centre accounts, and available cash. Corporate headquarters in Ottawa can view up-to-the-minute data on sales, inventory, and production at every step of the process as well as updated sales and production forecasts and calculations of product cost and availability. The Window on Organizations shows how Nestlé benefited from a program that standardized and coordinated its information systems and business processes.

BENEFITS AND CHALLENGES OF ENTERPRISE SYSTEMS

Enterprise systems promise to integrate the diverse business processes of a firm into a single integrated information architecture. Because of the cost and complexity of integrating stems, there must be significant benefits to integration and significant planning to reduce the costs in terms of time, effort, and money.

Benefits of Enterprise Systems

Enterprise systems promise to greatly change four dimensions of business: firm structure, management processes, technology platform, and business capability.

Firm Structure and Organization: One Organization   Companies can use enterprise systems to support organizational structures that were not previously possible or to create a more disciplined organizational culture. For example, they might use enterprise systems to

MANAGEMENT DECISION PROBLEM

ANALYZING ENTERPRISE PROCESS INTEGRATION

Management at your agricultural chemicals corporation has been dissatisfied with production planning. Production plans are created using best guesses of demand for each product that are based on how much of each product has been ordered in the past. If a customer places an unexpected order or requests a change to an existing order after it has been placed, there is no way to adjust the production plans. The company may have to tell customers it can't fill their orders or may run up extra costs maintaining additional inventory to prevent stock-outs.

At the end of each month, orders are totalled and manually keyed into the company's production planning system. Data from the past month's production and inventory systems are manually entered into the firm's order management system. Analysts from the sales and production departments analyze the data from the respective systems to determine what the sales and production targets should be for the next

month. These estimates are usually different. The analysts then meet at a high-level planning meeting to revise the sales and production targets to take into account senior management's goals for market share, revenues, and profits. The outcome of the meeting is a finalized production master schedule.

The entire production planning process takes 17 business days to complete. Nine of these days are required to enter and validate the data. The remaining days are spent developing and reconciling the sales and production targets and finalizing the master production schedule.

1. Draw a diagram of the production planning process.

2. Analyze the problems this process creates for the company.

3. How could an enterprise system solve these problems? In what way could it lower costs? Diagram what this process might look like if the company implemented an enterprise system.

NESTLÉ TURNS TO ENTERPRISE SYSTEMS FOR GLOBAL COORDINATION

Nestlé SA, headquartered in Vevey, Switzerland, is a giant food and pharmaceuticals company that operates virtually all over the world, with over 230 000 employees at 500 facilities in 80 countries. Although best known for its chocolate, coffee, and milk products, Nestlé sells thousands of other items, which are adapted to fit local markets and culture.

The firm had been allowing each factory to conduct business as it saw fit, taking into account differing local conditions and business cultures. With 80 different information technology units, Nestlé's information technology infrastructure has been described as a veritable Tower of Babel. Its operations around the world run on nearly 900 IBM AS/400 midrange computers, 15 mainframes, and 200 UNIX systems. There is no corporate computer centre.

Nestlé's management found that allowing these local differences created inefficiencies and extra costs that could prevent the company from competing effectively in electronic commerce. The lack of standard business processes prevented Nestlé from, for example, leveraging its worldwide buying power to obtain lower prices for its raw materials because each factory negotiated its own deals and prices even though each factory used the same global suppliers.

Several years ago, Nestlé embarked on a program to standardize and coordinate its information systems and business processes. The company initially installed SAP's R/3 enterprise resource planning (ERP) software to integrate material, distribution, and accounting applications in the United States, Europe, and Canada. Now it is extending its enterprise systems to all of its facilities to make all 500 facilities act as a single-minded e-business.

In June 2000 Nestlé contracted with SAP to deploy mySAP.com, which extends SAP's enterprise software to the Web. The new system will allow each Nestlé employee to start work from a personalized Web page linked to his or her job function. The employee's job will be structured to conform to the "best practices" defined by SAP for each of 300 work roles. These roles mandate precise steps for executing a business process that must be followed in the prescribed sequence. For instance, an invoice for an order can't be referred to accounts payable until the system shows that the order was received. According to Jean Claud Dispaux, senior vice president for group information systems, "it's an exceptionally simple way to make sure that everyone does the same job the same way."

Nestlé is also creating up to five computer centres around the world to run mySAP.com enterprise financial, accounts payable, accounts receivable, planning, production management, supply chain management, and business intelligence software. Once this project is completed, Nestlé will be able to use sales information from retailers on a global basis to measure the effectiveness of its promotional activities and reduce overstocking and spoilage caused by having products sit too long on grocery shelves.

Implementing the enterprise software throughout the company will take about three years and cost nearly $300 million. Many employees will have to change the way they work to conform to the roles defined by the new system. Nestlé is providing individualized training to help employees make the transition. "It won't be a nice project," Dispaux says, "but it's necessary."

To Think About: What motivated Nestlé to implement an enterprise system? Why would Nestlé invest in mySAP within just a few years of implementing SAP R/3? What international aspects of their systems (currency and taxation differences, cultures, infrastructure differences) do you think influenced Nestlé's ability to introduce an enterprise system? What did Nestlé do to overcome the reluctance of the "locals" to implement an ERP? Do you think this was the same for the second round with mySAP? Do you think it was enough? What else could Nestlé have done to "soften the blow" of implementing an enterprise system?

Sources: Steve Konicki, "Nestlé Taps SAP for E-Business," *Information Week*, June 26, 2000.

---

integrate the corporation across geographic or business-unit boundaries or to create a more uniform organizational culture in which everyone uses similar processes and information. An enterprise-enabled organization does business the same way worldwide, with functional boundaries de-emphasized in favour of cross-functional coordination and information flow.

Management: Firm-Wide, Knowledge-Based Management Processes In addition to automating many essential business transactions, such as taking orders, paying suppliers, or changing employee benefits status, enterprise systems can also improve management reporting and decision making. Information supplied by an enterprise system is structured around cross-functional business processes and it can be obtained more rapidly. For example, an enterprise system might help management more easily determine which products are most or least profitable. No longer would general managers be stuck without any hard data on firm performance or with data that applies only to their own immediate department. An enterprise system could supply management with better data about business processes and overall organizational performance.

Technology: Unified Platform   Enterprise systems promise to provide firms with a single, unified, and all-encompassing information system technology platform and environment. Enterprise systems promise to create a single, integrated repository that gathers data on all the key business processes. The data have common, standardized definitions and formats that are accepted by the entire organization. We will discuss more about the importance of standardizing organizational data in Chapter 8.

Business: More Efficient Operations and Customer-Driven Business Processes   Enterprise systems can help create the foundation for a customer-driven or demand organization. By integrating discrete business processes such as sales, production, finance, and logistics, the entire organization can more efficiently respond to customer requests for products or information, forecast new products, and build and deliver them as demand appears. Manufacturing has better information to produce only what customers have ordered, to procure exactly the right amount of components or raw materials to fill actual orders, to stage production, and to minimize the time that components or finished products are in inventory. By using enterprise systems to capture unit cost and quality data, firms can improve the quality of their products and services.

The Challenge of Enterprise Systems

Although enterprise systems can improve organizational coordination, efficiency, and decision making, they have proven very difficult to build. Enterprise systems require complex pieces of software and large investments of time, money, and expertise. They require not only investments in technology but also fundamental changes in the way a business operates. Companies will need to rework their business processes to make information flow smoothly between them. Employees will have to take on new job functions and responsibilities. Enterprise systems raise serious challenges for firms: a daunting implementation process, surviving a cost/benefit analysis, inflexibility, and realizing strategic value.

Daunting Implementation   Enterprise systems bring dramatic changes to business. They require not only deep-seated technological changes but also fundamental changes in the way the business operates. Business processes change dramatically as do organizational structure and culture. Firms implementing enterprise systems have to come up with organization-wide definitions of data, retrain thousands of workers, and redesign their fundamental business processes, all at once, while carrying on business as usual. It might take a large company three to five years to fully implement all of the organizational and technology changes required by an enterprise system. Organizations that don't understand that such changes will be required or that are unable to make them will have problems implementing enterprise systems, or they may not be able to achieve a higher level of functional and business process integration.

High Upfront Costs and Future Benefits   The costs of enterprise systems are large, upfront, highly visible, and often politically charged. Although the costs to build the system are obvious, the benefits often cannot be precisely quantified at the beginning of an enterprise project. One reason is that the benefits often accrue from employees using the system after it is completed and gaining the knowledge of business operations previously impossible to learn.

Inflexibility   Enterprise system software tends to be complex and difficult to master, with a worldwide shortage in people with the expertise to install and maintain it. The software is deeply intertwined with corporate business processes. If companies need to make major changes, the system will have to be changed. Because enterprise systems are integrated, it is difficult to make a change in only one part of the business without affecting other parts as well. The new enterprise systems could eventually prove as brittle and hard to change as the old systems they replaced—a new kind of "digital concrete" that could bind firms to outdated business processes and systems.

Realizing Strategic Value   Companies may also fail to achieve strategic benefits from enterprise systems if the integration of business processes using the generic models provided by standard ERP software prevents the firm from using unique business processes that had been sources of advantage over competitors. If an enterprise system is not compatible with the way the company does business, the company may lose a way to perform a key business process that may be related to its competitive advantage. Enterprise systems promote centralized organizational coordination and decision making that may not be the best way for some firms to operate. There are companies that clearly do not need the level of integration provided by enterprise systems (Davenport, 2000 and 1998). Chapter 11 provides more detail on the organizational and technical challenges of enterprise system implementation.

EXTENDED ENTERPRISES AND INDUSTRIAL NETWORKS

In some industries, companies are extending their enterprise systems beyond the boundaries of the firm to share information and coordinate business processes with other firms in their industry. **Industrial networks**, sometimes called *extended enterprises*, link together the enterprise systems of firms in an entire industry (see Figure 2-17). J.D. Edwards' WorldSoftware Energy and Chemical Solutions ERP package is helping Shell Canada manage its entire supply chain, from the procurement of raw materials through delivery to the customer. In addition, the company can now utilize a complete, fully integrated, scalable ERP system with multi-language, multi-currency capabilities. Shell has already benefited from J.D. Edwards' ERP system, achieving a 50% reduction in IT costs in those areas where WorldSoftware is implemented.

There are two kinds of industrial networks. **Vertical industrial networks** integrate the operations of the firm with its suppliers and can be used for supply chain management. **Horizontal industrial networks** link firms across an entire industry. An example would be the OASIS network of utility industry firms, which uses the Web to help OASIS's North American members sell surplus electrical power. A few industry networks coordinate the activities of competitors. For example, in the airline industry, American, Continental, Delta, Northwest, and United came together to develop Orbitz, a travel Web site that would list all of the airfares and schedules of over 22 airlines, providing customers with easy access to their own information without using a travel agent. Since travel agents collect a commission for every flight or trip they book, member airlines can save the cost of the commissions by encouraging their customers to use Orbitz.com. Table 2-8 provides examples of both types of industrial networks. Most industrial networks today are vertical and do not link together competitors in the same industry.

Many of these industrial networks are currently dedicated to supply chain management. Enterprise systems have primarily focused on helping companies manage their internal manufacturing, financial, and human resource processes and were not originally designed to support supply chain management processes involving entities outside the firm. However, enterprise software vendors are starting to enhance their products so that firms can link their enterprise systems with vendors, suppliers, manufacturers, distributors, and retailers.

Enterprise systems can enable integration among internal supply chain processes such as sales, inventory, and production that makes it easier for the firm to coordinate its activities with manufacturing partners and customers. Manufacturing can be informed about exactly what to produce based on sales orders, reducing the need to keep excess stock in inventory. If participants in the supply chain use the same enterprise software systems, their systems can

industrial networks
Networks linking systems of multiple firms in an industry; also called extended enterprises.

vertical industrial networks
Industrial networks linking firms with their suppliers.

horizontal industrial networks
Industrial networks linking firms across an entire industry, including competing firms.

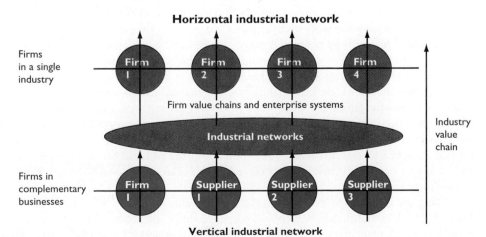

FIGURE 2-17 Industrial networks. Industrial networks link the enterprise systems of firms in an entire industry into an industry-wide system. Horizontal industrial networks link firms in the same industry, including competitors, while vertical industrial networks link a firm with suppliers in the same industry.

TABLE 2-8	EXAMPLES OF INDUSTRIAL NETWORKS	
Organization(s)	**Type of Industrial Network**	**Description**
Coca-Cola	Vertical	Installed an enterprise system using SAP software and extended the system to its bottling partners. Coke and its partners can pool resources, share sales information, and leverage their combined size to obtain lower raw material costs. The extended enterprise system enables Coca-Cola to react more rapidly to market changes and to deploy products more efficiently to places where they are most likely to sell.
OASIS	Horizontal	Web sites link North American electrical utility companies in regional power pool groups to sell their surplus power to wholesalers and to locate the transmission facilities for moving the power between its source and the customer.
Ford, General Motors, and DaimlerChrysler	Horizontal	Shared Internet purchasing system enables them to obtain parts online from suppliers, reducing costs and saving time.
Safeway UK	Vertical	Has electronic links to suppliers where it can share information about forecasts, shelf space, and inventory so they can track demand for their products, adjust production, and adjust the timing and size of deliveries. Suppliers can download Safeway's information into their enterprise systems or production planning systems. Suppliers send Safeway information about product availability, production capacity, and inventory levels.
Canadian Eco-Industrial Network	Horizontal	A membership association of public and private organizations designed to serve as an information clearinghouse for eco-industrial network developers and practitioners in Canada.

exchange data without manual intervention. Companies can also use Internet technology to create industrial networks because it provides a platform across which systems from different companies can seamlessly exchange information.

APPLICATION SOFTWARE EXERCISE

DATABASE EXERCISE: TRACKING RESERVATIONS AT MACDONALD'S MIDNIGHT INN

Macdonald's Midnight Inn is a family-owned and -operated bed and breakfast in Kenora, Ontario. After inheriting the Macdonald Mansion eight years ago, James and Peggy Macdonald decided to renovate the mansion and establish a bed and breakfast. The bed and breakfast has 14 rooms, five of which overlook a private lake, five of which overlook the woods, with the remaining four rooms overlooking the gardens. Room rates are based on room choice, length of stay, and number of guests per room. Guests staying for seven days or more are given a 15 percent discount on their daily room rates. Each additional guest is charged $20.00 per day, and a maximum of four guests are permitted in each room.

Business has grown steadily over the past eight years. In the early years, the establishment was frequented primarily by couples; however, the bed and breakfast now caters to a variety of clientele, including families, executives, and locals. The bed and breakfast's growing popularity is due in part to its location, the activities available to its visitors, and its affordability.

Currently, all records are kept manually. Their manual record-keeping system has caused many problems for James and Peggy. For instance, just last week, Peggy had two families booked into the Laurier room. Luckily, she was able to reassign one of the families to the Mackenzie room and avoid upsetting a valuable customer. Similarly, James does not have immediate access to management information about the bed and breakfast's operations. He would like to have information about current room occupancy, average length of stay, and weekly income by room.

Using the information provided in the scenario and in the accompanying tables on the Laudon, Laudon, and Brabston Web site, prepare a simple database to track reservations and generate management reports. In addition to the 10 transactions provided, add at least ten more transactions to the database. You may make any assumptions you feel are necessary; however, please document these assumptions in writing and provide them to your professor.

In addition to the data provided, what other data should be captured and stored in the database? As mentioned above, James requires managerial information about the bed and breakfast's operations. What reports would provide the necessary information? Identify at least two other reports that would be beneficial for James. Prepare these reports. Finally, write a brief paragraph describing how an enterprise system could enhance the B&B's business.

MANAGEMENT WRAP-UP

Enterprise systems and industrial networks require management to take a firm-wide view of business processes and information flows. Managers need to determine which business processes should be integrated, the short- and long-term benefits of this integration, and the appropriate level of financial and organizational resources to support this integration.

There are many types of information systems in an organization supporting different organizational levels, functions, and business processes. Some of these systems span more than one function or business process. Enterprise systems integrating information from different organizational functions and business processes often require extensive organizational change.

Information systems that create firm- or industry-wide information flows and business processes require major technology investments and planning. Firms must have an information technology (IT) infrastructure that can support organization-wide or industry-wide computing.

For Discussion:

1. Review the payroll TPS illustrated in Figure 2-3. How could it provide information for other types of systems in the firm?

2. Adopting an enterprise system is a key business decision as well as a technological decision. Do you agree with this statement? Why or why not? Who should make this decision?

SUMMARY

1. *Analyze the role played by the six major types of information systems in organizations and their relationship to each other.* There are six major types of information systems in contemporary organizations that are designed for different purposes and different audiences. Operational-level systems are transaction processing systems (TPS), such as payroll or order processing, that track the flow of daily routine transactions necessary to conduct business. Knowledge-level systems support clerical, managerial, and professional workers. They consist of office automation systems (OAS), for increasing data workers' productivity, and knowledge work systems (KWS), for enhancing knowledge workers' productivity. Management-level systems (MIS and DSS) provide the management control level with reports and access to the organization's current performance and historical records. Most MIS reports summarize information from TPS and are not highly analytical. Decision support systems (DSS) help management make decisions that are unique, rapidly changing, and not specified easily in advance. They have more advanced analytical models and data analysis capabilities than MIS and often draw on information from external as well as internal sources. Two

particular types of DSS are group decision support systems (GDSS) that are designed for use by groups to enhance group decision-making, and expert systems that are designed to mimic human intelligence to make decisions.

Executive support systems (ESS) support the strategic level by providing a generalized computing and communications environment to assist senior management's decision making. ESS have limited analytical capabilities but can draw on sophisticated graphics software and various sources of internal and external information.

The various types of systems in the organization exchange data with one another. TPS are a major source of data for other systems, especially MIS and DSS. ESS primarily receive data from lower-level systems. The different systems in an organization have traditionally been loosely integrated.

2. *Describe the types of information systems supporting the major functional areas of the business.* At each level of the organization, there are information systems supporting the major functional areas of the business. Sales and marketing systems help the firm identify customers for the firm's products or services, develop products and services to meet their needs, promote and sell these products and services, and provide ongoing customer support. Manufacturing and production systems deal with the planning, development, and production of products and services, and with controlling the flow of production. Finance and accounting systems keep track of the firm's financial assets and fund flows. Human resources systems maintain employee records, track employee skills, job performance and training, and support planning for employee compensation and career development.

3. *Analyze the relationship between organizations, information systems, and business processes, including those for customer relationship management and supply chain management.* Business processes refer to the manner in which work is organized, coordinated, and focused to produce a valuable product or service. Business processes are concrete workflows of material, information, and knowledge; they represent unique ways in which organizations coordinate work, information, and knowledge, and the ways in which management chooses to coordinate work. While each of the major business functions has its own set of business processes, many other business processes are cross-functional, such as fulfilling an order. Information systems can help organizations achieve great efficiencies by automating parts of these processes or by helping organizations rethink and streamline these processes, especially those for customer relationship management and supply chain management. CRM uses information systems to co-ordinate all of the business processes surrounding a firm's interactions with its customers. SCM is the close linkage of activities involved in buying, making, and moving a product. Information systems make supply chain management more efficient by helping companies coordinate, schedule, and control procurement, production, inventory management, and delivery of products and services to customers.

4. *Explain how enterprise systems and industrial networks create new efficiencies for businesses.* Enterprise systems integrate the key business processes of a firm into a single software system so that information can flow throughout the organization, improving coordination, efficiency, and decision making. Industrial networks link other organizations in the same industry in a single industry-wide system. Vertical industrial networks consist of an organization and its suppliers, while horizontal industrial networks link competitors in the same industry.

5. *Evaluate the benefits and limitations of enterprise systems and industrial networks.* Enterprise systems and industrial networks promise greater efficiency through better coordination of both internal and external business processes. Enterprise systems can help create a more uniform organization in which everyone uses similar processes and information and measures their work in terms of organization-wide performance standards. An enterprise system could supply management with better data about business processes and overall organizational performance. Enterprise systems feature a single information technology platform where data definitions are standardized across the organization. The coordination of sales, production, finance, and logistics processes provided by enterprise systems helps organizations respond more rapidly to customer demands.

The reality is that firm- and industry-wide systems are very difficult to implement successfully. They require extensive organizational change, complicated technologies, and large upfront costs for long-term benefits that are difficult to quantify. Once implemented, enterprise systems are very difficult to change. Management vision and foresight is required to take a firm- and industry-wide view of problems and to find solutions that realize strategic value from the investment.

KEY TERMS

Business processes, 51

Customer relationship management (CRM), 52

Decision support systems (DSS), 44

Desktop publishing, 43

Document imaging systems, 43

Enterprise systems, 55

Executive support systems (ESS), 45

Expert systems, 45

Finance and accounting information systems, 49

Group decision support systems (GDSS), 45

Horizontal industrial networks, 59

Human resources information systems, 50

Industrial networks, 59

Knowledge-level systems, 39

Knowledge work systems (KWS), 43

Management information systems (MIS), 43

Management-level systems, 39

Manufacturing and production information systems, 48

Office automation systems (OAS), 43

Operational-level systems, 38

Sales and marketing information systems, 47

Strategic-level systems, 39

Supply chain, 54

Supply chain management, 53

Transaction processing systems (TPS), 41

Vertical industrial networks, 59

Word processing, 43

REVIEW QUESTIONS

1. Identify and describe the four levels of the organizational hierarchy. What types of information systems serve each level?

2. List and briefly describe the six major types of systems in organizations.

3. What are the five types of TPS in business organizations? What functions do they perform? Give examples of each.

4. Describe the functions performed by knowledge work and office systems and some typical applications of each.

5. What are the characteristics of MIS? How do MIS differ from TPS? from DSS?

6. What are the characteristics of DSS? How do they differ from those of ESS?

7. Describe the relationship between TPS, OAS, KWS, MIS, DSS, and ESS.

8. List and describe the information systems serving each of the major functional areas of a business.

9. What is a business process? Give two examples of processes for stand-alone functional areas of a business and one example of a cross-functional process.

10. What is customer relationship management? Why is it so important to businesses? How do information systems facilitate customer relationship management?

11. What is supply chain management? What activities are involved in SCM? Why is it so important to businesses?

12. How do information systems facilitate supply chain management?

13. What are enterprise systems? How do they change the way an organization works?

14. What are the benefits and challenges of implementing enterprise systems?

15. What are industrial networks? Define and describe the two different types of industrial networks.

16. How can organizations benefit from participating in industrial networks?

GROUP PROJECT

With a group of three or four other students, select a business using an industrial network for supply chain management. Use the Web, newspapers, journals, and computer or business magazines to find out more about the industrial network and its use of information technology to provide links to other organizations. If possible, use presentation software to present your findings to the class.

 **INTERNET CONNECTION**

■ **COMPANION WEBSITE**

At www.pearsoned.ca/laudon, you'll find an online study guide with two quizzes to test your knowledge of information systems in the enterprise. You'll also find updates to the chapter and online exercises and cases that enable you to apply your knowledge to realistic situations.

■ **ADDITIONAL SITES OF INTEREST**

There are many interesting Web sites to enhance your learning about enterprise systems. You can search the Web yourself, or just try the following sites to add to what you have already learned.

Brint

www.brint.com

Search for interesting articles on a variety of business and technology topics

TechTutorials

www.techtutorials.com

Offers free tutorials on a variety of PC applications

ComputerWorld and *ComputerWorld Canada*

www.computerworld.com and **www.computerworld.ca**

The leading computer periodical for IS managers

Computing Canada

www.itbusiness.ca

Canada's leading computer periodical; the site also hosts other Canadian computer-related periodicals

CASE STUDY *Tooling up for SCM*

What do Cisco Systems, Dell, EMC Corporation, Hewlett-Packard, IBM, ICL, Sequent, and Sun Microsystems have in common? They're all industry giants that outsource all or part of their manufacturing processes. In fact, some of them have never even owned a factory.

In a marketplace where product life cycles span a mere six to nine months, some original equipment manufacturers (OEMs) prefer to focus on their core businesses—typically front-end design and marketing—and outsource their back-end factory operations to gain a competitive advantage.

Approximately 15 percent of the world's $750-billion electronics manufacturing services (EMS) market is already working this way; that figure is expected grow rapidly during the foreseeable future.

In the race for customers, organizations that can deliver their products to a global market ahead of the competition are positioned for success, which is why some firms are forming partnerships with EMS companies. Incredibly, more than 50 OEMs—including every one of the industry leaders mentioned above—are dealing with the same EMS partner, Celestica.

Established in 1917 as the manufacturing arm of IBM Canada Ltd., Celestica was incorporated as a wholly owned subsidiary in 1994. Then Gerry Schwartz's Onex Corp. bought the company for $750 million and launched it on an acquisition spree before taking it public in 1998. Today, its nearly 1.5 million square metres of manufacturing space is the launch pad for a broad range of products, including mainframes, terminals, personal computers, servers, routers, and set-top boxes. The company supplies customers with a broad range of integrated EMS, from printed circuit assembly and system build, to memory and power solutions. Add to that some very compelling value-added services such as quick-to-market supply chain management, global component-purchasing power, and industry-leading design and prototyping capabilities, and it is clear why Celestica is thriving. Celestica's annualized revenues for 1999 were $5.3 billion.

So, if major OEMs are principally dealing with the same supplier, how are innovation and product distinction derived? "Although we're involved in the design, the fundamental new product idea still rests with the OEM," explains Lisa Colnett, Senior Vice-President Worldwide Process Management and Chief Information Officer for Celestica. Colnett is responsible for key corporate functions including IT, manufacturing, and human resources. Colnett says that OEMs are increasingly bringing their designs and product specifications to Celestica to be translated into products. "The innovation that we bring to the table is how to make them more manufacturable and get them through our processes more quickly."

Mass Customization

Yet manufacturing can be just the tip of the iceberg. To gain the full strategic impact of working with the EMS giant, many customers avail themselves of Celestica's "mass customization" opportunities. Ironically, what sounds like an oxymoron is actually practicable and ingenious. Some of the staunchest competitors in the OEM marketplace leverage collective sourcing and purchasing power for components and related services through Celestica, all the while designing and building a customized product. Colnett describes what she considers to be her firm's critical differentiator in the EMS market:

> "We have to be the best-of-class manufacturer with the latest techniques, but increasingly it's the supply chain that customers are buying from us, of which manufacturing is one component, " she remarks. "Our objective is to reach earlier into that process and farther into our customer's customer chain so that we're managing the process end-to-end. We place a lot of emphasis on after-sales support to further streamline the whole supply chain process. The argument being if you've built the product, then you're likely to have some special capability and knowledge to help repair the product."

The Circle of Life

Supply chain management (SCM) is the manufacturing sector's "circle of life." In an ideal world, manufacturers provide seamless connectivity to their customers, suppliers, and partners, linking the entire trading group in increasingly tighter bonds of information flow, business cooperation, and ultimately, profitability. A well-oiled supply chain management system supports just-in-time manufacturing with flexible dynamic replenishment.

For the most part, SCM applications execute operations such as managing warehouses, inventory supplies, and distribution channels. There are two basic categories of SCM software: planning and execution. Execution applications track product storage and movement and help manage materials, information, and financial data among suppliers, manufacturers, distributors, and customers. Advance planning applications, or optimization software, applies sophisticated algorithms to identify the best way to fill an order based on set operation constraints.

Celestica's Toolkit

Celestica employs a spectrum of IT tools to address virtually every stage of its customers' supply chain processes. For example, collaborative design tools such as Valor help customer-designers develop products to Celestica's manufacturing tolerances and design capabilities. Another important tool, Aspect Component and Supplier Management (CSM) solution, provides the company with the decision support capability to determine preferred parts, designs, and suppliers and to make them accessible for enterprise reuse. This information enables Celestica representatives to define the fastest route for sourcing a customer's product and getting it into the market. The product also enables customers to configure their outsourced products directly over the Internet, leveraging Celestica's buying power through online access to Celestica-preferred components found in the Aspect CSM system.

Another important tool, Matrix, is the company's common bill of materials repository. It assists with product data management and rapid parts sourcing. i2 Technologies' RHYTHM software advance planning tool provides real-time product demand information and allows Celestica to simulate a range of order decisions to meet customers' needs cost effectively. Celestica also builds Web interfaces across these tools to make them more easily accessible to customers and suppliers. Operating within an AS/400 environment, transaction-based tools such as BPCS from SSA, and SAP, are used for Enterprise Resource Planning (ERP) applications, and SFDM software from Genrad is used for shop-floor applications.

"Our whole business is about time to market and velocity of information," comments Bernie Uhlich, Celestica's Manager of Global SCM Web Commerce. "Effectively managing the supply chain enables customers to get improvements in inventory turns, material flow, improved planning, and ultimately, reduces the time to market significantly.

"Traditional EDI [electronic data interchange, or transactions that occur electronically between a buyer and seller, not on the Web, but through other networks established between companies and their suppliers and customers based on industry-specific standards] is good for high-volume transactions but only 3 [percent] to 10 percent of the North American marketplace uses it," he remarks. "How do you get into the remaining huge untapped supplier and customer base?" Uhlich says that Internet-based EDI (or Web EDI) and XML information standards are the answer. With the caveat that users must maintain the same degree of discipline and legal standards as in traditional EDI, he stresses that both project and connectivity development can be expedited tremendously over the Web.

"I wouldn't be too concerned about the costs of implementing it," he advises. "It's a very strategic investment. We have some 2000-plus suppliers. By implementing Web EDI we opened up the opportunity to electronically trade with a huge portion of our supply base that we otherwise wouldn't be able to access." He adds that there are other significant benefits such as alleviating the need for human intervention with suppliers and the ability to process all supplier-related information electronically. "Once everyone is connected, you can hook these suppliers up with the same back-end systems that you're using internally. That speeds up the time, and it's a huge win. It also enables you to manage by exception."

Demand Planning

With short product life cycles, the speed of reaction and response has become more important than even a good long-term forecast. Forecasts tend to be derived from historical demand patterns. Colnett says that a better way to determine a customer's future requirements is to leverage the supply chain strategy by creating closer customer ties. She cites the example of a customer with a six-month supply chain that wished to significantly shorten its time to market.

"The first thing we did was diagnose their supply chain from end-to-end, searching for opportunities for earlier and better information. We applied our ability to influence the design so that we could build it better, faster, and more cost-effectively. "We explained to the customer that we could help them get to market faster if we and they used a certain set of tools. Once we were in production, we applied some advance planning tools to enable us to look at forecasts sooner and prepare earlier for the next version of the product. The outcome was absolutely amazing."

Acquisition Strategy

With more than 20 000 employees worldwide, the company operates 27 manufacturing and design facilities in Canada, the United States, Mexico, the United Kingdom, Ireland, Italy, Thailand, Hong Kong, and China. To put it mildly, Celestica is growing in leaps and bounds—approximately 40 percent year-over-year, in a market sector whose average growth rate is about 27 percent. Much of their growth is through acquisition of the facilities and staff of other companies. This is both a blessing and a challenge organizationally.

"Using common part numbering schemes and bill of material systems is not negotiable," Colnett stresses. "They can interface to many ERP systems. We use Matrix as our common bill of materials repository. Everyone in the corporation has to keep their master bills of material there. From there, we can make strategic business decisions."

Another major consideration is to determine what applications are "customer-touching." In other words, what applications will the customer reasonably expect to be the same in its interactions with a new acquisition?

"Our goal is to be a global player," explains Harv Sembhi, Director of Corporate Supply Chain Integration at Celestica. "That's why companies like Dell, Lucent, HP, and IBM are coming to us. To that effect, our design point is to provide our customers with a common look and feel across our organization. That's why it's important that all of our locations are using similar platforms."

Sembhi uses the example of a customer that needs to transfer a product from Toronto to Mexico. If both locations of Celestica were using the same application, processing the transfer electronically would be absolutely straightforward. "I think that's what our customers are expecting us to have," he stresses: "a very well-defined, clear, integrated application and ERP strategy with similar business systems and processes across the globe. That's really what we're bringing to the table. We're very actively involved in migrating these sites where it makes sense. In some cases we're integrating them through data warehousing systems."

Sembhi adds, "Internal to our company, we need to minimize the investment we make in different IT platforms. We need to standardize and minimize the costs. Externally, we need to be able to link these standard applications through business-to-business processes that are customized to specific customers. It's kind of like trying to operate a central kitchen with personalized dining."

What the Future Holds

Sembhi stresses that from an IT perspective, the design point for the future is to compress the information pipeline to days, if not hours, by using applications that have intelligence. To that end, Celestica began partnering in 2000 with SAP, an ERP vendor headquartered in Germany, for their ERP system. Celestica is integrating all of their manufacturing and supply chain management in accordance with SAP standards.

"Through business-to-business applications you can develop very tightly linked processes where customers, Celestica representatives, and suppliers can come together and in one swoop do a full pass on an entire supply chain plan. By doing so, you can eliminate the lumps out of the supply chain. On top of that, if you bring together your top eight to ten major suppliers based on product complexity or lead time and collectively plan everything before firing up your execution engines to place purchase orders, then you've taken an enormous amount of time and inventory out of the process. It's mass customization—when you want it, you've got it. The whole question of virtual corporations and virtual integration is becoming more important. Companies will have to be able to make decisions very quickly based on what is available through their SCM pipelines."

Sources: Pat Atkinson, "Tooling Up for SCM," *CIO Canada*, March 1, 2000; Sean Silcoff, "An Old Economy, Low-Return Company Lurks Beneath Celestica's Flashy Exterior," *Canadian Business*, May 1, 2000; "mySAP.com® Brings eBusiness Solutions to Celestica Inc," SAP Press Release, available http://wwwext03.sap.com/canada/press/releases/2000/pr081700.asp, accessed June 6, 2001.

CASE STUDY QUESTIONS

1. Describe how Celestica uses enterprise systems for supply chain management.

2. If SAP uses different standards and processes than Celestica, how difficult will it be for Celestica to change to the SAP model? Who should be responsible for the conversion?

3. What management, organization, and technology factors are associated with Celestica acquiring additional companies and facilities? with their mass customization capabilities for their customers?

3

INFORMATION SYSTEMS, ORGANIZATIONS, MANAGEMENT, AND STRATEGY

OBJECTIVES

After completing this chapter, you will be able to:

1. *Identify the salient characteristics of organizations.*
2. *Analyze the relationship between information systems and organizations.*
3. *Contrast the classical and contemporary models of managerial activities and roles.*
4. *Describe how managers make decisions in organizations.*
5. *Evaluate the role of information systems in supporting various levels of business strategy.*
6. *Explain why it is difficult for firms to sustain a competitive advantage.*
7. *Compare global strategies for developing business.*
8. *Demonstrate how information systems support different global strategies.*

Karmax Stamps "Quality" on Information Technology

For Karmax Heavy Stamping of Milton, Ontario, quality is a way of life. From its ISO 9001, QS 9000, and ISO 14001 certifications, to its company quality programs targeted to deliver 100 percent quality products to its customers—the "Big 3" North American automotive manufacturers—Karmax owes its success to its focus on quality processes and products.

Founded in 1988, Karmax Heavy Stamping, a division of the Cosma International Group of Magna International, manufactures and assembles sheet metal components for sale to major automotive companies such as DaimlerChrysler, General Motors, and Ford Motor. To be successful in the highly competitive world of automotive suppliers, its 74 400 m² stamping facility is heavily dependent on technology for automation.

Making parts for automotive manufacturers' production lines running multiple shifts (with just-in-time inventory) requires a tightly controlled logistical supply chain. In fact, a key measurement for suppliers to the automotive industry is delivery performance. And the numbers involved are not small.

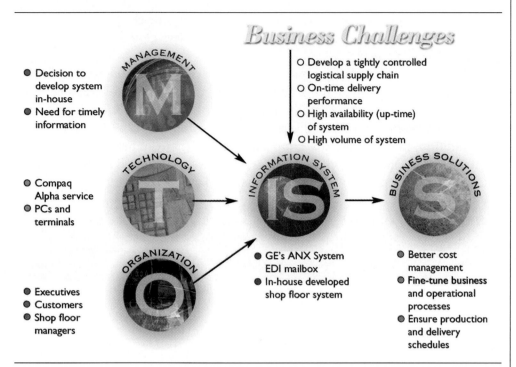

Business Challenges

MANAGEMENT
- Decision to develop system in-house
- Need for timely information

TECHNOLOGY
- Compaq Alpha service
- PCs and terminals

ORGANIZATION
- Executives
- Customers
- Shop floor managers

INFORMATION SYSTEM
- GE's ANX System EDI mailbox
- In-house developed shop floor system

○ Develop a tightly controlled logistical supply chain
○ On-time delivery performance
○ High availability (up-time) of system
○ High volume of system

BUSINESS SOLUTIONS
- Better cost management
- Fine-tune business and operational processes
- Ensure production and delivery schedules

Karmax makes more than 30 million individual parts each year for its customers. These include body side apertures, fenders, tailgates, doors, and roofs. "Approximately 200 shipments each day leave our loading docks for customers," says Steve Harwood, Manager of Information Systems at Karmax. "Each shipment must be preceded by an Advance Ship Notice (ASN). The ASN is an electronic notification of the departure and contents of the shipment. Without that ASN reaching the customer, they will turn the truck away."

Karmax developed its own in-house shop floor system to track production and inventory. "Through the Karmax Manufacturing System (KMS), we are able to monitor the flow of material from the time it arrives as raw material until it is shipped out as finished product on a real-time basis," says Graham Postma, Business Manager for Karmax. Karmax is able to collect, monitor, and analyze critical shop floor data and operations.

Shop floor data collection includes information on inventory transition gathered through an INTERMEC Radio Frequency Data Collection system. The company can also collect data from its stamping presses, yielding valuable information such as number of pieces, speed, if the machine is up or down, and run rates. In addition, they can monitor the flow of draw lube—the fluid's pressure and availability—which is a critical factor in the stamping process.

"The last area where we are doing shop floor data collection is through our automated material handling system," says Harwood. This is an eight-story highrise inventory system composed of 4500 bin locations that are accessed through cranes, conveyors, and automatic guided vehicles picking up or storing work in progress or shippable parts.

(continued)

67

When they chose a new information technology infrastructure to further streamline and automate its production, inventory, and delivery systems, Karmax implemented three Compaq AlphaServers, 250 Compaq Deskpros, and hundreds of other terminals connected via a local area network to improve collection of data and streamline communications among itself, its suppliers, and its customers. "Utilizing GE's ANX solution, we now receive information from our electronic data interchange (EDI) mailbox in seconds instead of minutes," says Don Robinson, a senior systems analyst at Karmax.

According to Michael Long, Operations Analyst, Karmax has enjoyed a competitive advantage through high availability, meaning their systems are available more than 99.99 percent of the time. Without this level of availability, Karmax could not guarantee its customers prompt delivery of the right product.

In addition, through data collection and analysis, they can better manage costs, fine-tune business and operational processes, and ensure their production and delivery schedules meet the needs of their customers.

Sources: "Karmax Stamps 'Quality' on Information Technology," Compaq Case Study, www6.compaq.ca/English/enterprise/success/corporate/karmax.htm, accessed June 10, 2001; "GE Logs a First on Automotive Network," *Link@GE News Brief,* March 2000, www.keystrokes.net/proofs/linkage/nb-anx-020100.htm, accessed June 10, 2001.

MANAGEMENT CHALLENGES

Karmax's experience illustrates the interdependence of business environments, organizational culture, management strategy, and the development of information systems. Karmax developed a series of supply chain management systems in response to changes in competitive pressures from its surrounding environment, but its systems effort could not succeed without a significant amount of commitment to quality and organizational and management change. The new information system is changing the way Karmax runs its business and makes management decisions.

1. **Sustainability of competitive advantage.** The competitive advantages strategic systems confer do not necessarily last long enough to ensure long-term profitability. Because competitors can retaliate and copy strategic systems, competitive advantage isn't always sustainable. Markets, customer expectations, and technology change. The Internet can make competitive advantage for companies disappear very quickly (Yoffie and Cusumano, 1999). Classic strategic systems such as American Airlines' SABRE computerized reservation system, Citibank's ATM system, and Federal Express' package tracking system benefited by being the first in their industries. Then rival systems emerged. Information systems alone cannot provide an enduring business advantage. Systems originally intended to be strategic frequently become competitive necessities, something required by every firm to stay in business, or they may even inhibit organizations from making the strategic changes essentials for future success (Eardley, Avison, and Powell, 1997).

2. **Fitting technology to the organization (or vice-versa).** On the one hand, it is important to align information technology to the business plan, to the firm's business processes, and to senior management's strategic business plans. Information technology is, after all, supposed to be the servant of the organization. On the other hand, these business plans, processes, and management strategy all may be very outdated or incompatible with the envisioned technology. In such instances, managers will need to change the organization to fit the technology or to adjust both the organization and the technology to achieve an optimal "fit."

This chapter explores the relationships between organizations, management, information systems, and business strategy. We introduce the features of organizations that you will need to understand when you design, build, and operate information systems, and the relationship of these organizational features to information systems. We also scrutinize the role of a manager and the management decision-making process, identifying areas where information systems can enhance managerial effectiveness. We conclude by examining the problems firms face from competition and the ways in which information systems can provide competitive advantage.

3.1 ORGANIZATIONS AND INFORMATION SYSTEMS

Information systems and organizations influence one another. On the one hand, information systems must be aligned with the organization to provide information that important groups within the organization need. At the same time, the organization must be aware of and open to the influences of information systems in order to benefit from new technologies.

The interaction between information technology and organizations is very complex and is influenced by a great many mediating factors, including the organization's structure, standard operating procedures, politics, culture, surrounding environment, and management decisions (see Figure 3-1). Managers must be aware that information systems can markedly alter life in the organization. They cannot successfully design new systems or understand existing systems without understanding organizations. Managers do decide what systems will be built, what they will do, how they will be implemented, and so forth. Sometimes, however, the outcomes are the result of pure chance and of both good and bad luck.

WHAT IS AN ORGANIZATION?

An **organization** is a stable, formal social structure that takes resources from the environment and processes them to produce outputs. This technical or *microeconomic* definition focuses on three elements of an organization. Capital and labour are primary production factors provided by the environment. The organization (the firm) transforms these inputs into products and services in a production function. The products and services are consumed by environments in return for supply inputs (see Figure 3-2). An organization is more stable than an informal group (such as a group of friends that meets every Friday for lunch) in terms of longevity and routine. Organizations are formal legal entities, with internal rules and procedures, that must abide by laws. Organizations are also social structures because they are a collection of social elements, much as a machine has a structure—a particular arrangement of valves, cams, shafts, and other physical elements.

The technical definition of organizations is powerful and simple, but it is not very descriptive or even predictive of real-world organizations. A more realistic behavioural definition of an **organization** is that it is a collection of rights, privileges, obligations, and responsibilities that are delicately balanced over a period of time through conflict and conflict

organization (technical definition)
A stable, formal, social structure that takes resources from the environment and processes them to produce outputs.

organization (behavioural definition)
A collection of rights, privileges, obligations, and responsibilities that are delicately balanced over a period of time through conflict and conflict resolution.

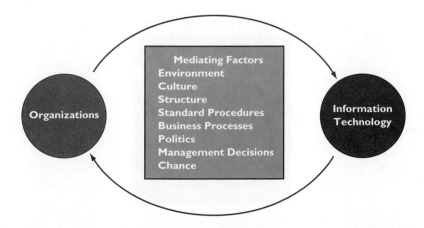

FIGURE 3-1 The two-way relationship between organizations and information technology. This complex two-way relationship is mediated by many factors, not the least of which are the decisions made—or not made—by managers. Other factors mediating the relationship are the organizational culture, bureaucracy, politics, business fashion, and pure chance.

FIGURE 3-2 The technical (microeconomic) definition of the organization. In the microeconomic definition of organizations, capital and labour (the primary production factors provided by the environment) are transformed by the firm through the production process into products and services (outputs to the environment). The products and services are consumed by the environment, which supplies additional capital and labour as inputs in the feedback loop.

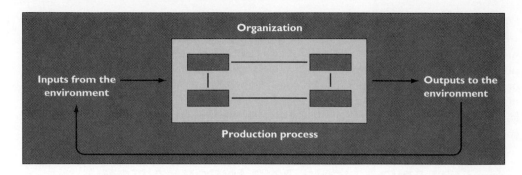

resolution (see Figure 3-3). In the behavioural view of the firm, people who work in organizations develop customary ways of working; they gain attachments to existing relationships; and they make arrangements with subordinates and superiors about how work will be done, how much work will be done, and under what conditions. Many of these arrangements are not described in any formal rule book or procedures.

How do these definitions of organizations relate to information system technology? A technical view of organizations encourages us to focus on the way inputs are combined into outputs when technology changes are introduced into the company. The firm is seen as infinitely malleable, with capital and labour substituting for each other quite easily. But the more realistic, behavioural definition of an organization suggests that building new information systems or rebuilding old ones involves much more than a technical rearrangement of machines or workers—that some information systems change the organizational balance of rights, privileges, obligations, responsibilities, and feelings that has been established over a long period of time.

Technological change requires changes in who owns and controls information, who has the right to access and update that information, who makes decisions about whom to assign to jobs, when the jobs should be done, and how the jobs are accomplished. This more complex view forces us to look at the way work is designed and the procedures used to achieve outputs.

The technical and behavioural definitions of organizations are not contradictory. Indeed, they complement each other: The technical definition tells us how thousands of firms in competitive markets combine capital, labour, and information technology, while the behavioural model takes us inside the individual firm to see how technology affects the organization's inner workings. Section 3.2 describes how each of these definitions of organizations can help explain the relationships between information systems and organizations.

Some features of organizations are common to all organizations; others distinguish one organization from another. Let us look first at the features common to all organizations.

COMMON FEATURES OF ORGANIZATIONS

Aside from all being Canadian, you might not think that the Hudson's Bay Company, Air Canada, and the Royal Canadian Mounted Police have much in common, but they do. In

FIGURE 3-3 The behavioural view of organizations. The behavioural view of organizations emphasizes group relationships, values, and structures.

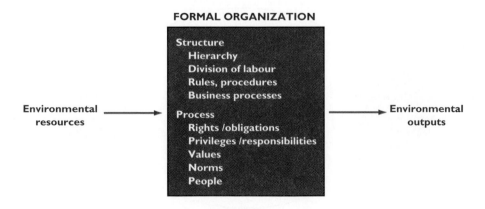

some respects, all modern organizations are alike because they share the characteristics that are listed in Table 3-1. A German sociologist, Max Weber, was the first to describe these "ideal-typical" characteristics of organizations in 1911. He called organizations **bureaucracies** that have certain "structural" features.

According to Weber, all modern bureaucracies have a clear-cut division of labour and specialization. Organizations arrange specialists in a hierarchy of authority in which everyone is accountable to someone and authority is limited to specific actions. Authority and action are further limited by abstract rules or procedures (standard operating procedures, or SOPs) that are interpreted and applied to specific cases. These rules create a system of impartial and universalistic decision making; everyone is treated equally. Organizations try to hire and promote employees on the basis of technical qualifications and professionalism (not personal connections). The organization is devoted to the principle of efficiency: maximizing output using limited inputs.

According to Weber, bureaucracies are prevalent because they are the most efficient form of organization. Other scholars have extended Weber's work, identifying additional features of organizations. All organizations develop standard operating procedures, politics, and cultures.

Standard Operating Procedures

Organizations that survive over time become very efficient, producing a limited number of products and services by following standard routines. These standard routines become codified into reasonably precise rules, procedures, and practices called **standard operating procedures (SOPs)** that are developed to cope with virtually all expected situations. Some of these rules and procedures are written, formal procedures. Most are "rules of thumb" to be followed in selected situations.

These standard operating procedures have a great deal to do with efficiency. For instance, in the assembly of a car, managers and workers develop complex standard procedures to handle the thousands of motions in a precise fashion, permitting the finished product to roll off the assembly line. Any change in SOPs requires an enormous organizational effort. Indeed, the organization may need to halt the entire production process before the old SOPs can be retired.

Difficulty in changing standard operating procedures is one reason North American automakers have been slow to adopt Japanese mass-production methods. For many years, North American automakers followed Henry Ford's mass-production principles. For example, Ford believed that the cheapest way to build a car was to churn out large numbers of autos by having sequences of workers repeatedly perform one simple task on each car as it moved along an assembly line. By contrast, Japanese automakers have emphasized "lean production" methods whereby a smaller number of workers, each performing several tasks, can produce cars with less inventory, less investment, and fewer mistakes. Workers have multiple job responsibilities and are encouraged to stop production in order to correct a problem.

Organizational Politics

People in organizations occupy different positions with different specialties, concerns, and perspectives. As a result, they naturally have divergent viewpoints about how resources, rewards, and punishments should be distributed. For most organizations, these resources are limited and must be allocated by management. The different viewpoints held by employees based on their position or access to resources matter to both managers and employees, and they result in political struggle, competition, and conflict within every organization. Political resistance is one of the great difficulties of bringing about organizational change—especially the development of new information systems. Virtually all information systems that bring about significant changes in goals, procedures, productivity, and personnel are politically charged and will elicit serious political opposition. The chapter-opening vignette could

bureaucracy
A formal organization with a clear-cut division of labour, abstract rules and procedures, and impartial decision making that uses technical qualifications and professionalism as a basis for promoting employees.

standard operating procedures (SOPs)
Precise rules, procedures, and practices developed by organizations to cope with virtually all expected situations.

TABLE 3-1	STRUCTURAL CHARACTERISTICS OF ALL ORGANIZATIONS
Clear division of labour	
Hierarchy	
Explicit rules and procedures	
Impartial judgment	
Technical qualifications for positions	
Maximum organizational efficiency	

imply that Karmax had to persuade its partners to participate in its new enterprise system to prevent political resistance from occurring; in Karmax' case, however, it was the Big 3 automotive companies who required the use of specific EDI standards by all of their suppliers.

Organizational Culture

organizational culture
The set of fundamental assumptions about what products the organization should produce, how and where it should produce them, and for whom they should be produced.

All organizations have rock-solid, unassailable, unquestioned (by the members) assumptions that define their goals and products. **Organizational culture** is this set of fundamental assumptions about what products the organization should produce, how it should produce them, where, and for whom. Generally, these cultural assumptions are taken totally for granted and are rarely publicly announced or spoken about. (Schein, 1985).

You can see organizational culture at work by looking around your university or college. Some assumptions of campus life are that professors know more than students, that the reason students attend school is to learn, and that classes follow a regular schedule. Organizational culture is a powerful unifying force that restrains political conflict and promotes common understanding, agreement on procedures, and common practices. If we all share the same basic cultural assumptions, then agreement on other matters is more likely.

At the same time, organizational culture is a powerful restraint on change, especially technological change. Most organizations will do almost anything to avoid making changes in basic assumptions. Any technological change that threatens commonly held cultural assumptions usually meets a great deal of resistance. On the other hand, there are times when the only sensible thing to do is to employ a new technology that directly opposes an existing organizational culture. When this occurs, the technology implementation is often delayed while the culture slowly adjusts.

UNIQUE FEATURES OF ORGANIZATIONS

Although all organizations do have common characteristics, no two organizations are identical. Organizations have different structures, goals, constituencies, leadership styles, tasks, and surrounding environments.

Different Organizational Types

One important way in which organizations differ is in their structure or shape. The differences among organizational structures are characterized in many ways. Mintzberg's classification, described in Table 3-2, identifies five basic kinds of organizations (Mintzberg, 1979).

TABLE 3-2   ORGANIZATIONAL STRUCTURES

Organizational Type	Description	Example
Entrepreneurial structure	Young, small firm in a fast-changing environment. It has a simple structure and is managed by an entrepreneur serving as its single chief executive officer.	Small start-up business
Machine bureaucracy	Large bureaucracy existing in a slowly changing environment, producing standard products. It is dominated by a centralized management team and centralized decision making.	Mid-sized manufacturing firm
Divisionalized bureaucracy	Combination of multiple machine bureaucracies, each producing a different product or service, all topped by one central headquarters.	Fortune 500 firms
Professional bureaucracy	Knowledge-based organization where goods and services depend on the expertise and knowledge of professionals. Dominated by department heads. Weak centralized authority.	Law firms, school systems, hospitals
Adhocracy	"Task force" organization that must respond to rapidly changing environments. Consists of large groups of specialists organized into short-lived multidisciplinary teams. Weak central management.	Consulting firms

Organizations and Environments

Organizations reside in environments from which they draw resources and to which they supply goods and services. Organizations and environments have a reciprocal relationship. On the one hand, organizations are open to, and dependent on, the social and physical environment that surrounds them. Without financial and human resources—people willing to work reliably and consistently for a set wage or revenue from customers—organizations could not exist. Organizations must respond to legislative and other requirements imposed by government as well as the actions of customers and competitors. On the other hand, organizations can influence their environments. Organizations form alliances with others to influence the political process; they advertise to influence customer acceptance of their products.

Figure 3-4 shows that information systems play an important role in helping organizations perceive changes in their environments and also in helping organizations act on their environments. Information systems are key instruments for *environmental scanning*, helping managers identify external changes that might require an organizational response.

Environments generally change much faster than organizations. The main reasons for organizational failure are an inability to adapt to a rapidly changing environment and a lack of resources—particularly among young firms—to sustain even short periods of troubled times (Freeman et al., 1983). New technologies, new products, and changing public tastes and values (many of which result in new government regulations) put strains on any organization's culture, politics, and people. Most organizations do not cope well with large environmental shifts. The inertia built into an organization's standard operating procedures, the political conflict raised by changes to the existing order, and the threat to closely held cultural values typically inhibit organizations from making significant changes. It is not surprising that only 10 percent of the Fortune 500 companies in business in 1919 still exist today.

Other Differences Among Organizations

Organizations have different shapes or structures for many other reasons also. They differ in their ultimate goals and the types of power used to achieve them. Some organizations have coercive goals (e.g., prisons); others have utilitarian goals (e.g., businesses). Still others have

FIGURE 3-4 Environments and organizations have a reciprocal relationship. Environments shape what organizations can do, but organizations can influence their environments and decide to change environments altogether. Information technology plays a critical role in helping organizations perceive environmental change and in helping organizations act on their environment. Information systems act as a filter between organizations and their environments. They do not necessarily reflect reality but instead refract environmental change through a number of built-in biases.

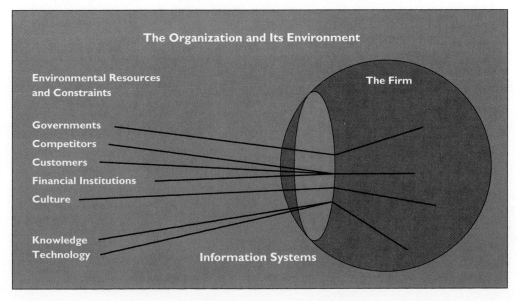

TABLE 3-3	A SUMMARY OF SALIENT FEATURES OF ORGANIZATIONS
Common Features	**Unique Features**
Formal structure	Organizational type
Standard operating procedures (SOPs)	Environments
Politics	Goals
Culture	Power
	Constituencies
	Function
	Leadership
	Tasks
	Technology
	Business processes

normative goals (e.g., universities, religious groups). Organizations also serve different groups or have different constituencies, some primarily benefiting their members, others benefiting clients, stockholders, or the public. The nature of leadership differs greatly from one organization to another—some organizations may be more democratic or authoritarian than others. Another way organizations differ is by the tasks they perform and the technology they use. Some organizations perform primarily routine tasks that could be reduced to formal rules that require little judgment (such as manufacturing auto parts) while others (such as consulting firms) work primarily with non-routine tasks.

As you can see in Table 3-3, the list of unique features of organizations is longer than the common features list. It stands to reason that information systems will have different impacts on different types of organizations. Different organizations in different circumstances will experience different effects from the same technology. The Window on Organizations shows, for example, how Japan's unique environment, culture, and organizational characteristics have affected Internet use and electronic commerce. A close analysis of a specific organization is necessary before a manager can effectively design and manage information systems for that organization.

3.2 THE CHANGING ROLE OF INFORMATION SYSTEMS IN ORGANIZATIONS

Information systems have become integral, online, interactive tools deeply involved in the minute-to-minute operations and decision making of large organizations. We now describe the changing role of information systems in organizations and how it has been shaped by the interaction of organizations and information technology.

INFORMATION TECHNOLOGY INFRASTRUCTURE AND INFORMATION TECHNOLOGY SERVICES

information systems department
The formal organizational unit that is responsible for the information systems function in the organization.

programmers
Highly trained technical specialists who write computer software instructions.

One way that organizations can influence how information technology will be used is through decisions about the technical and organizational configuration of systems. Previous chapters described the ever-widening role of information systems in organizations. Supporting this widening role have been changes in information technology (IT) infrastructure, which we defined in Chapter 1. During the 1950s, organizations were dependent on computers for a few critical functions. The 1960s witnessed the development of large centralized machines. By the late 1970s and into the 1980s, IT infrastructure became complex, and information systems included telecommunications links to distribute information. Today's new IT infrastructure is designed to make information flow across the enterprise and

E-COMMERCE, JAPANESE STYLE

In Japan, many people don't have credit cards or are reluctant to give out their credit card numbers over the Internet. Internet access charges are very high compared to North America and other areas. While many Japanese own PCs, most still don't surf the Web from their homes. So how can e-commerce flourish? The answer, at least for now, lies in the old neighbourhood convenience store.

Convenience stores—called "conbini"—have a special place in Japan. Most people have tiny homes or apartments with minimal space for storage or refrigerators. Frequent shopping is a necessity. Japanese convenience stores are very small, averaging about 100 square metres and outside the radar of Japanese regulators. They can thus be more responsive to changing customer tastes than larger competitors. What's more, most conbini are open round the clock. There are more than 33 000 convenience stores throughout Japan and the average 7-Eleven store attracts 900 visitors each day.

The ubiquity and popularity of these stores make them attractive partners for e-commerce companies that need marketing and promotion. The convenience stores don't have promotional expenses because so many customers come to them on their own. People can pay by cash for e-commerce goods when they pick them up at the convenience stores, and the product orders can be handled by the conbini's existing distribution systems. A newcomer would have trouble finding temporary warehousing to store goods for delivery to customers, but convenience stores already have warehouses and can act as the final pick-up point. The conbini also provide computer terminals with Internet access. According to Kenyu Adachi, director of the Ministry of Trade and Industry distribution industry division, "Without the convenience store, e-commerce in Japan would have more trouble taking off."

The convenience stores are counting on the Internet, too. With no more room to expand physically and relentless competition from new stores, the neighbourhood convenience store is betting on e-commerce to keep afloat. By offering access to e-commerce sites, the convenience stores can expand their range of product offerings without expanding their space. All of the major Japanese convenience store chains have adopted Internet strategies.

7-Eleven Japan, the country's largest convenience store chain, lets a customer select titles from the eShopping Books Web site. Several days later, the customer can pick up the selection and pay for it at the local 7-Eleven. eShopping Books uses 7-Eleven's warehouses and pays for the books only after they have been sold, so it does not bear the cost of warehousing merchandise. Its cost structure may be even lower than Amazon.com's.

To Think About: What factors explain why convenience stores are centres of Internet use and electronic commerce in Japan? Would this structure work in Canada? in any part of North America?

Sources: Stephanie Strom, "E-Commerce the Japanese Way," *The New York Times*, March 18, 2000; and "The Web@Work/Lawson Co.," *The Wall Street Journal*, March 13, 2000.

---

includes links to customers, vendors, and public infrastructures, including the Internet. Each organization determines how its infrastructure will be configured.

Another way that organizations affect information technology is through decisions about who will design, build, and maintain the organization's IT infrastructure. These decisions determine how information technology services will be delivered.

The formal organizational unit or function responsible for technology services is called the **information systems department**. The information systems department is responsible for maintaining the hardware, software, and networks that compose the firm's information technology (IT) infrastructure.

The information systems department consists of specialists such as programmers, systems analysts, project leaders, and information systems managers (see Figure 3-5). **Programmers** are highly trained technical specialists who write the software instructions for the computer. **Systems analysts** constitute the principal liaison between the information systems group and the rest of the organization. It is the systems analyst's job to translate business problems and requirements into information requirements and systems. **Information systems managers** are leaders of teams of programmers and analysts, project managers, physical facility managers, telecommunications managers, and heads of office automation groups. They are also managers of computer operations and data entry staff. **End users** are representatives of departments outside of the information systems group for whom applications are developed. These users play an increasingly large role in the design and development of information systems.

systems analysts
Specialists who translate business problems and requirements into information requirements and systems, acting as the liaison between the information systems department and the rest of the organization.

information systems managers
Leaders of the various specialists in the information systems department.

end users
Representatives of departments outside the information systems group for whom applications are developed.

FIGURE 3-5 Information technology services. Many types of specialists and groups are responsible for the design and management of the organization's information technology (IT) infrastructure.

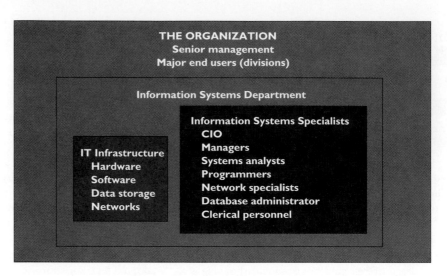

chief information officer (CIO)
The senior manager in charge of the information systems function in the firm.

In many companies, the information systems department is headed by a **chief information officer (CIO)**. The CIO is a senior manager who oversees the use of information technology in the firm. Finally, external specialists, such as hardware vendors and manufacturers, software firms, and consultants also frequently participate in the day-to-day operations and long-term planning of information systems.

When IT infrastructure was in its infancy, the information systems group was composed mostly of programmers and performed very highly specialized but limited technical functions. Today a growing proportion of staff members are systems analysts and network specialists, with the information systems department acting as a powerful change agent in the organization. The information systems department suggests new business strategies and new information-based products and services and coordinates both the development of the technology and the subsequent planned changes in the organization.

In the past, firms generally developed their own software and managed their own computing facilities. Today, many firms are turning to external vendors to provide these services (see Chapters 7 and 11) and use their information systems departments to manage these service providers.

HOW INFORMATION SYSTEMS AFFECT ORGANIZATIONS

How have changes in information technology affected organizations? To find answers, we will draw on research and theory based on both economic and behavioural approaches.

Economic Theories

From an economic standpoint, information technology can be viewed as a factor of production that can be freely substituted for capital and labour. As the cost of information system technology falls, it is substituted for labour, which historically has been a rising cost. Hence, in the **microeconomic model of the firm**, information technology should result in a decline in the number of middle managers and clerical workers as information technology substitutes for their labour.

microeconomic model of the firm
Economic view of organizations that posits that technology is another factor of production that can be substituted for capital and labour.

Information technology also helps firms contract in size because it can reduce transaction costs—the costs incurred when a firm buys on the marketplace what it cannot make itself. According to **transaction cost theory**, firms and individuals seek to economize on transaction costs, much as they do on production costs. Using markets is expensive (Williamson, 1985) because of costs such as locating and communicating with distant suppliers, monitoring contract compliance, buying insurance, obtaining information on products, and so forth. Traditionally, firms have tried to reduce transaction costs by getting bigger, hiring more employees or buying their own suppliers and distributors, as General Motors used to do.

transaction cost theory
Economic theory stating that firms grow larger because they can conduct marketplace transactions internally more cheaply than they can with external firms.

Information technology, especially the use of networks, can help firms lower the cost of market participation (transaction costs), making it worthwhile for firms to contract with

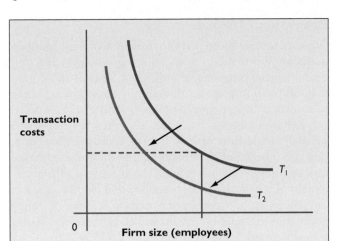

FIGURE 3-6 The transaction cost theory of the impact of information technology on the organization. Firms traditionally grew in size in order to reduce transaction costs. IT potentially reduces the costs for a given size, shifting the transaction cost curve inward, opening up the possibility of revenue growth without increasing size, or even revenue growth accompanied by shrinking size.

external suppliers instead of using internal sources. For example, by using computer links to external suppliers, a company can achieve economies by obtaining the majority of its parts from the outside. Figure 3-6 shows that as transaction costs decrease, firm size (the number of employees) should shrink because it becomes easier and cheaper for the firm to contract the purchase of goods and services in the marketplace rather than to make the product or service itself. Firm size can stay constant or contract even when the company increases its revenues. (For example, in the early 1980s, General Electric reduced its workforce from about 400 000 people to about 230 000 while increasing revenues 150 percent.)

Information technology also can reduce internal management costs. According to **agency theory**, the firm is viewed as a "nexus of contracts" among self-interested individuals rather than as a unified, profit-maximizing entity (Jensen and Meckling, 1976). A principal (owner) employs "agents" (employees) to perform work on his or her behalf. However, agents need constant supervision and management because they will otherwise tend to pursue their own interests rather than those of the owners. As firms grow in size and scope, agency costs or coordination costs rise because owners must expend more and more effort supervising and managing employees.

agency theory
Economic theory that views the firm as a nexus of contracts among self-interested individuals who must be supervised and managed.

Information technology, by reducing the costs of acquiring and analyzing information, permits organizations to reduce agency costs because it becomes easier for managers to oversee a greater number of employees. Figure 3-7 shows that by reducing overall management costs, information technology allows firms to increase revenues while shrinking the numbers of middle management and clerical workers. We have seen examples in earlier chapters where information technology expanded the power and scope of small organizations by allowing them to perform coordinating activities such as processing orders or keeping track of inventory with very few clerks and managers.

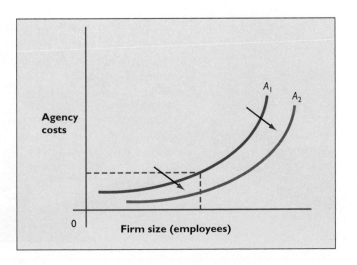

FIGURE 3-7 The agency cost theory of the impact of information technology on the organization. As firms grow in size and complexity, traditionally they experience rising agency costs. IT shifts the agency cost curve down and to the right, allowing firms to increase size while lowering agency costs.

Behavioural Theories

While economic theories try to explain how large numbers of firms act in the marketplace, behavioural theories from sociology, psychology, and political science are more useful for describing the behaviour of individual firms. Behavioural research has found little evidence that information systems automatically transform organizations although the systems may be instrumental in accomplishing this goal once senior management decides to pursue this end.

Behavioural researchers have theorized that information technology could change the hierarchy of decision making in organizations by lowering the costs of information acquisition and broadening the distribution of information (Malone, 1997). For example, information technology can bring information directly from operating units to senior managers, thereby eliminating middle managers and clerical support workers. Information technology can permit senior managers to contact lower-level operating units directly through the use of networked telecommunications and computers, eliminating middle management intermediaries. Alternatively, information technology can distribute information directly to lower-level workers, who could then make their own decisions based on their own knowledge and information without any management intervention. Some research even suggests that computerization increases the information given to middle managers, empowering them to make more important decisions than in the past, thus reducing the need for large numbers of lower-level workers (Shore, 1983).

In postindustrial societies, authority increasingly relies on knowledge and competence, and not on mere formal position. Hence, the shape of organizations should "flatten," since professional workers tend to be self-managing; and decision making should become more decentralized as knowledge and information become more widespread throughout the organization (Drucker, 1988). Information technology may encourage "task force" networked organizations in which groups of professionals come together—face to face or electronically—for short periods of time to accomplish a specific task (e.g., designing a new automobile); once the task is accomplished, the individuals join other task forces. More firms may operate as *virtual* organizations where work no longer is tied to geographic location.

Who makes sure that self-managed teams do not head off in the wrong direction? Who decides which person works on what team and for how long? How can managers judge the performance of someone who is constantly rotating from team to team? New approaches for evaluating, organizing, and informing workers are required; not all companies can make virtual work effective (Davenport and Pearlson, 1998).

No one knows the answers to these questions, and it is not clear that all modern organizations will undergo this transformation. Pearson Education Canada, for example, may have many self-managed knowledge workers in certain divisions, but it still will have a publishing division structured as a large, traditional bureaucracy. In general, the shape of organizations historically changes with the business cycle and with the latest management fashions. When

In virtual offices, employees do not work from a permanent location. Here, workspaces are temporary with employees moving from desk to desk as vacancies open.

times are good and profits are high, firms hire large numbers of supervisory personnel; when times are tough, they let go many of these same people (Mintzberg, 1979).

Another behavioural approach views information systems as the outcome of political competition between organizational subgroups for influence over the organization's policies, procedures, and resources (Laudon, 1974; Keen, 1981; Kling, 1980; Laudon, 1986). Information systems inevitably become bound up in organizational politics because they influence access to a key resource—namely, information. Information

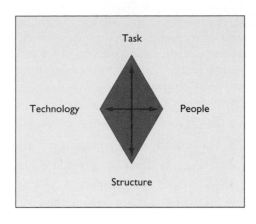

FIGURE 3-8 Organizational resistance and the mutually adjusting relationship between technology and the organization. Implementing information systems has consequences for task arrangements, structures, and people. According to this model, in order to implement change, all four components must be changed simultaneously. Source: Leavitt, 1965.

systems can affect who does what to whom, when, where, and how in an organization. For instance, the Canadian government was tracking the lives of its citizens with a sophisticated computer software program and storing the data collected in what it called a Longitudinal Labour Force file. The system held up to 2000 pieces of information on almost every Canadian citizen or landed immigrant. When the Canadian public became aware of the existence of the system, concerns were raised over the use of this information. As a result of the public outrage and the flood of access requests filed by Canadians, the Human Resources Development Minister ordered the dismantling of the database.

Because information systems potentially change an organization's structure, culture, politics, and work, there is often considerable resistance to them when they are introduced. There are several ways to visualize organizational resistance. Leavitt (1965) used a diamond shape to illustrate the interrelated and mutually adjusting character of technology and organization (see Figure 3-8). Here, changes in technology are absorbed, deflected, and defeated by organizational task arrangements, structures, and people. In this model, the only way to bring about change is to change the technology, tasks, structure, and people simultaneously. Lewin (1951) and Schein (1969) discussed the need to "unfreeze" organizations and people before introducing an innovation, quickly implementing it, and "refreezing" or institutionalizing the change (Kolb, 1970; Alter and Ginzberg, 1978; Schein, 1987).

THE INTERNET AND ORGANIZATIONS

The Internet, especially the World Wide Web, has an important impact on the relationships between firms and external entities and even on the organization of business processes inside a firm. The Internet increases the accessibility, storage, and distribution of information and knowledge for organizations. In essence, the Internet can dramatically lower the transaction and agency costs facing most organizations. For instance, brokerage firms and banks in Toronto can now "deliver" their internal operations procedures manuals to their employees at distant locations by posting them on their corporate Web site, saving millions of dollars in distribution costs. A global sales force can receive nearly instant price and product information updates via the Web or instructions from management via e-mail. Vendors of some large retailers can access their retailers' internal Web sites directly for up-to-the-minute sales information and initiate replenishment orders instantly.

Businesses are rapidly rebuilding some of their key business processes based on Internet technology, and are making this technology a key component of their information technology infrastructures. If prior networking is any guide, one result will be simpler business processes, fewer employees, and much flatter organizations than in the past.

IMPLICATIONS FOR THE DESIGN AND UNDERSTANDING OF INFORMATION SYSTEMS

In order to reap the benefits of technology, changes in organizational culture, values, norms, and interest-group alignments must be managed with much planning and effort as technology changes. It is entirely possible that a technological change would meet all of the technical specifications and run bug-free but still not accomplish its purpose. New information systems often mandate changes in business processes, individual tasks or task-sequencing, reporting relationships, richness of job tasks, and skill sets. It is frequently these changes that are the biggest obstacles to implementing a new or significantly upgraded information system. In our experience, the central organizational factors to consider when planning a new system are these:

- The environment in which the organization must function.
- The structure of the organization: hierarchy, specialization, standard operating procedures.
- The organization's culture and politics.
- The type of organization.
- The nature and style of leadership.
- The extent of top management's support and understanding of the impacts of technology.
- The principal interest groups affected by the system.
- The kinds of tasks, decisions, and business processes that the information system is designed to assist.
- The sentiments and attitudes of workers in the organization who will be using the information system.
- The history of the organization: past investments in information technology, existing skills, important programs, and human resources.

3.3   MANAGERS, DECISION MAKING, AND INFORMATION SYSTEMS

To determine how information systems can benefit managers, we must first examine what managers do and what information they need for decision making and their other functions. We must also understand how decisions are made and what kinds of decisions can be supported by formal information systems.

THE ROLE OF MANAGERS IN ORGANIZATIONS

Managers play a key role in organizations. Their responsibilities range from making decisions, to writing reports, to attending meetings, to arranging birthday parties. We can better understand managerial functions and roles by examining classical and contemporary models of managerial behaviour.

Classical Descriptions of Management

classical model of management
A traditional description of management that focused on its formal functions of planning, organizing, coordinating, deciding, and controlling.

The **classical model of management** was largely unquestioned for the more than 70 years. In the 1920s Henri Fayol and other early writers first described the five classical functions of managers as planning, organizing, coordinating, deciding, and controlling. This description of management activities dominated management thought for a long time, and it is still popular today.

But these terms actually describe managerial functions and are unsatisfactory as a description of what managers actually do. The terms do not address what managers do when they plan, decide things, and control the work of others. We need a more fine-grained understanding of how managers actually behave.

Behavioural Models

Contemporary behavioural scientists have observed that managers do not behave as the classical model of management led us to believe. Kotter (1982), for example, describes the morning activities of the president of an investment management firm as follows.

> 7:35 a.m. Richardson arrives at work, unpacks her briefcase, gets some coffee, and begins making a list of activities for the day.

7:45 a.m. Bradshaw (a subordinate) and Richardson converse about a number of topics and exchange pictures recently taken on summer vacations.

8:00 a.m. They talk about a schedule of priorities for the day.

8:20 a.m. Wilson (a subordinate) and Richardson talk about some personnel problems, cracking jokes in the process.

8:45 a.m. Richardson's secretary arrives, and they discuss her new apartment and arrangements for a meeting later in the morning.

8:55 a.m. Richardson goes to a morning meeting run by one of her subordinates. Thirty people are there, and Richardson reads during the meeting.

11:05 a.m. Richardson and her subordinates return to the office and discuss a difficult problem. They try to define the problem and outline possible alternatives. She lets the discussion roam away from and back to the topic again and again. Finally, they agree on a next step.

In this example, it is difficult to determine which activities constitute Richardson's planning, coordinating, and decision making. **Behavioural models** state that the actual behaviour of managers appears to be less systematic, more informal, less reflective, more reactive, less well-organized, and much more frivolous than students of information systems and decision making generally expect it to be.

Observers find that managerial behaviour actually has five attributes that differ greatly from the classical description: First, managers perform a great deal of work at an unrelenting pace—studies have found that managers engage in more than 600 different activities each day, with no break in their pace. Second, managerial activities are fragmented; most activities last for less than nine minutes, and only 10 percent of the activities exceed one hour in duration. Third, managers prefer speculation, hearsay, gossip—they want current, specific, ad hoc information (printed information will often be too old). Fourth, they prefer oral forms of communication to written forms because oral media provide greater flexibility, require less effort, and bring a faster response. Fifth, managers give high priority to maintaining a diverse and complex web of contacts that acts as an informal information system.

From his real-world observations, Kotter argues that effective managers are actually involved in only three critical activities:

▌ First, general managers spend significant time establishing personal agendas and both short- and long-term goals.

▌ Second—and perhaps most important—effective managers spend a great deal of time building an interpersonal network composed of people at virtually all organizational levels, from warehouse staff to clerical support personnel to other managers and senior management.

▌ Third, Kotter found that managers use their networks to execute personal agendas to accomplish their own goals.

behavioural models
Descriptions of management based on behavioural scientists' observations of what managers actually do in their jobs.

A corporate chief executive learns how to use a computer. Many senior managers still lack computer knowledge or experience and require systems that are extremely easy to use.

managerial roles
Expectations of the activities that managers should perform in an organization.

interpersonal roles
Mintzberg's classification of managerial roles where managers act as figureheads and leaders of the organization.

informational roles
Mintzberg's classification of managerial roles where managers act as the nerve centres of their organizations, receiving and disseminating critical information.

decisional roles
Mintzberg's classification of managerial roles where managers initiate activities, handle disturbances, allocate resources, and negotiate conflicts.

Analyzing managers' day-to-day behaviour, Mintzberg found that it could be classified into 10 managerial roles. **Managerial roles** are expectations of the activities that managers should perform in an organization. Mintzberg found that these managerial roles fell into three categories: interpersonal, informational, and decisional.

Interpersonal Roles   Managers act as figureheads for the organization when they represent their companies to the outside world and perform symbolic duties such as giving out employee awards. Managers act as leaders, attempting to motivate, counsel, and support subordinates. Managers also act as a liaison between various organizational levels; within each of these levels, they serve as a liaison among the members of the management team. Managers provide time and favours, which they expect to be returned.

Informational Roles   Managers act as the nerve centres of their organization, receiving the most concrete, up-to-date information and redistributing it to those who need to be aware of it. Managers are therefore information disseminators and spokespersons for their organization.

Decisional Roles   Managers make decisions. They act as entrepreneurs by initiating new kinds of activities, they handle disturbances arising in the organization, they allocate resources to staff members who need them, and they negotiate conflicts and mediate between conflicting groups in the organization.

Table 3-4, based on Mintzberg's role classifications, is one look at where systems can and cannot help managers. The table shows that information systems do not yet contribute a great deal to important areas of management life. These areas provide great opportunities for future systems efforts. (Note that it could be argued that e-mail and the Internet can assist managers in all of their roles.)

MANAGERS AND DECISION MAKING

Decision making is often a manager's most challenging role. Information systems have long helped managers communicate and distribute information; however, they have provided only limited assistance for management decision making. Because decision making is an area that system designers have sought most of all to affect (with mixed success), we now turn our attention to this issue.

TABLE 3-4   MANAGERIAL ROLES AND SUPPORTING INFORMATION SYSTEMS

Role	Behaviour	Support Systems
Interpersonal Roles		
Figurehead		None exists
Leader	Interpersonal	None exists
Liaison		Electronic communication systems
Informational Roles		
Nerve centre		Management information systems, ESS
Disseminator	Information	Mail, office systems
Spokesperson	processing	Office and professional systems, workstations
Decisional Roles		
Entrepreneur		None exists
Disturbance handler	Decision	None exists
Resource allocator	making	DSS systemss
Negotiator		None exists

Source: Kenneth C. Laudon and Jane P. Laudon; and Mintzberg, 1971.

The Process of Decision Making

Decision making can be classified by organizational level, corresponding to the strategic, management, knowledge, and operational levels of the organization introduced in Chapter 2. **Strategic decision making** determines the objectives, resources, and policies of the organization. **Management control decision making** (also known as middle or tactical level management) is principally concerned with how efficiently and effectively resources are used and how well operational units are performing. **Operational control decision making** determines how to carry out the specific tasks set forth by strategic and middle-management decision makers. **Knowledge-level decision making** deals with new ideas for products and services, ways to communicate new knowledge, and ways to distribute information throughout the organization.

Within each of these levels of decision making, researchers classify decisions as structured and unstructured. **Unstructured decisions** are those in which the decision maker must provide judgment, evaluation, and insights into the problem definition. All of these decisions are novel, important, and non-routine, and there is no well-understood or agreed-upon procedure for making them (Gorry and Scott-Morton, 1971). **Structured decisions**, by contrast, are repetitive and routine and involve a definite procedure for handling them so that they do not have to be treated each time as if they were new. Some decisions are **semi-structured**; in such cases, only part of the problem has a clear-cut answer provided by an accepted procedure.

Combining these two views of decision making produces the grid shown in Figure 3-9. In general, operational control personnel face fairly well-structured problems while strategic planners tackle highly unstructured problems. Many of the problems knowledge workers encounter are fairly unstructured as well. Nevertheless, each level of the organization contains both structured and unstructured problems. Note that there are information systems to support or execute each of these types of decisions.

Stages of Decision Making

Making decisions consists of several different activities. Simon (1960) described four different stages in decision making: intelligence, design, choice, and implementation.

FIGURE 3-9 Different kinds of information systems at the various organization levels support different types of decisions.

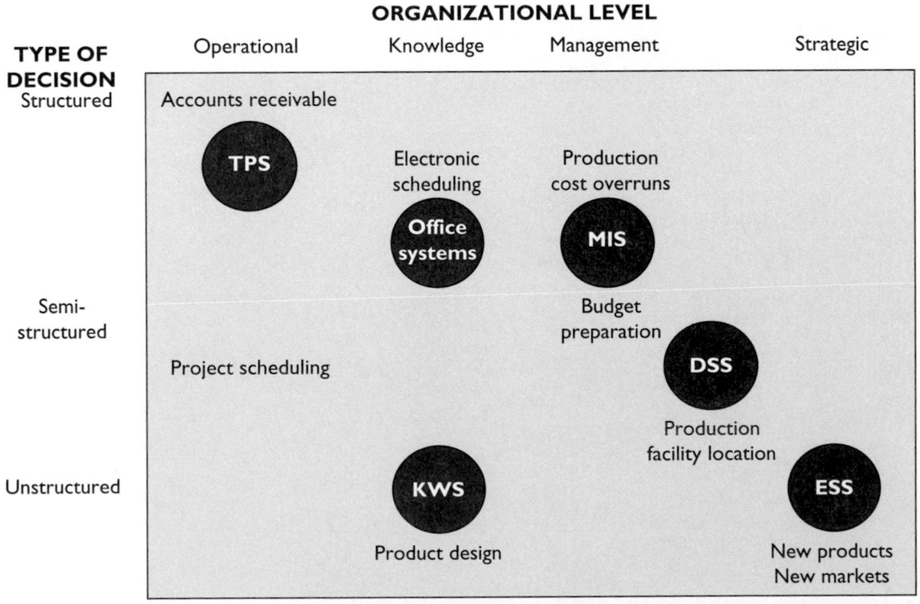

Key: TPS = Transaction processing system; KWS = Knowledge work system; MIS = Management information system; DSS = Decision support system; ESS = Executive support system

strategic decision making Determining the long-term objectives, resources, and policies of an organization.

management control decision making Monitoring and guiding how efficiently or effectively resources are utilized and how well operational units are performing (also known as middle- or tactical-level management).

operational control decision making Deciding how to carry out specific tasks set forth by upper and middle management and establishing criteria for completion and resource allocation.

knowledge-level decision making Evaluating new ideas for products and services, ways to communicate new knowledge, and ways to distribute information throughout the organization.

unstructured decisions Non-routine decisions in which the decision maker must provide judgment, evaluation, and insights into the problem definition; there is no agreed-upon procedure for making such decisions.

structured decisions Decisions that are repetitive, routine, and have a definite procedure for handling them.

semi-structured decisions Decisions where only part of the problem has a clear-cut answer provided by an accepted procedure.

intelligence
The first of Simon's four stages of decision making: when the information is collected to identify problems occurring in the organization.

design
Simon's second stage of decision making: when the possible alternative solutions to a problem are developed.

choice
Simon's third stage of decision making: when one among the various solution alternatives is selected.

implementation
Simon's final stage of decision making: when the decision is put into effect and reports on the progress of the solution are evaluated.

Intelligence consists of identifying and understanding the problems occurring in the organization—whether there is a problem, what is the real problem (not just its symptoms), why there is a problem, where the problem is, and what are the effects of the problem. Traditional MIS systems that deliver a wide variety of detailed information can help identify problems, especially if the systems report exceptions.

During solution **design**, the decision maker designs possible solutions to the problems. Smaller DSS systems are ideal in this stage of decision making because they operate on simple models, can be developed quickly, and can be operated with limited data.

Choice consists of choosing among solution alternatives. Here the decision maker might need a larger DSS or a GDSS to develop more extensive data on a variety of alternatives and complex models or data analysis tools to account for all of the choice's costs, consequences, and opportunities.

During the **implementation** of the solution, when the decision is put into effect, managers can use a reporting system that delivers routine reports on the progress of a specific solution. Support systems can range from full-blown MIS systems to much smaller systems as well as project-planning software operating on personal computers.

In general, the stages of decision making do not necessarily follow a linear path. Think again about the decision you made to attend a specific school. At any point in the decision-making process, you may have to loop back to a previous stage (see Figure 3-10). For instance, one can often come up with several designs but may not be certain about whether a specific design meets the requirements for the particular problem. This situation requires additional intelligence work. Alternatively, one can be in the process of implementing a decision, only to discover that it is not working. In that case, one is forced to repeat the design or choice stage. Again, there are information systems to assist the decision maker at each stage of decision making, from handling the data for a benchmarking study to ascertain what the problem is, to evaluating alternative solutions, to communicating the decision, to monitoring the results of implementing the decision.

Individual Models of Decision Making

A number of models attempt to describe how people make decisions. Some of these models focus on individual decision making while others focus on decision making in groups.

FIGURE 3-10 The decision-making process. Decisions are often arrived at after a series of iterations and evaluations at each stage in the process. The decision maker often must loop back through one or more of the stages before completing the process.

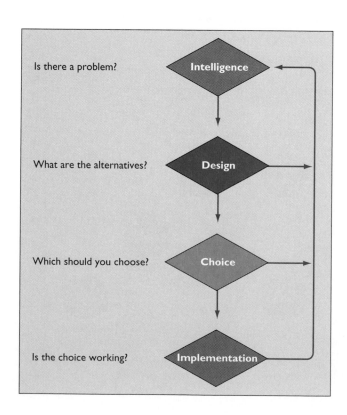

The basic assumption behind individual models of decision making is that human beings are in some sense rational. The **rational model of human behaviour** is built on the idea that people engage in basically consistent, rational, value-maximizing calculations. Under this model, an individual identifies goals, ranks all possible alternative actions by their contributions to those goals, and chooses the alternative that contributes most to those goals.

Criticisms of this model show that most individuals do not have singular goals and so are unable to rank all alternatives and consequences. In fact, people cannot specify all of the alternatives. Many decisions are so complex that calculating the choice (even if done by computer) is virtually impossible. One modification to the rational model states that instead of searching through all alternatives, people actually choose the first available alternative that moves them toward their ultimate goal. Another modification alters the rational model by suggesting that in making policy decisions, people choose policies most like the previous policy (Lindblom, 1959). Finally, some scholars point out that decision making is a continuous process in which final decisions are constantly being modified.

Modern psychology has further qualified the rational model by research that finds that humans differ in how they maximize their values and in the frames of reference they use to interpret information and make choices. **Cognitive style** describes underlying personality dispositions toward the treatment of information, the selection of alternatives, and the evaluation of consequences. McKenney and Keen (1974) described two decision-making cognitive styles: systematic versus intuitive. **Systematic decision makers** approach a problem by structuring it in terms of some formal method. They evaluate and gather information in terms of their structured method. **Intuitive decision makers** approach a problem with multiple methods, using trial and error to find a solution. They tend not to structure information gathering or evaluation. Neither style is considered superior to the other. They are different ways of being rational. More recent psychological research shows that humans have built-in biases that can distort decision making. People can be manipulated into choosing alternatives that they might otherwise reject simply by changing the frame of reference (Tversky and Kahneman, 1981). Information systems can be used to organize information and to help evaluate alternatives for the systematic decision makers while they can be used for what-if scenarios for intuitive decision makers.

Organizational Models of Decision Making

Decision making often is not performed by a single individual but by entire groups or organizations. **Organizational models of decision making** take into account the structural and political characteristics of an organization. Bureaucratic, political, and even "garbage can" models have been proposed to describe how decision making takes place in organizations. We shall now consider each of these models.

Bureaucratic Models According to **bureaucratic models of decision making**, an organization's most important goal is the preservation of the organization itself. The reduction of uncertainty is another major goal. Policy tends to be incremental, only marginally different from the past, because radical policy departures involve too much uncertainty. These models depict organizations generally as not "choosing" or "deciding" in a rational sense. Rather, according to bureaucratic models, whatever organizations do is the result of standard operating procedures (SOPs) honed over years of active use.

Organizations rarely change these SOPs because they may have to change personnel and incur risks (who knows if the new techniques work better than the old ones?). Although senior management and leaders are hired to coordinate and lead the organization, they are effectively trapped by the organization's standard solutions. Some organizations do, of course, change; they learn new ways of behaving; and they can be led. But all of these changes usually require a long time. Look around and you will find many organizations doing pretty much what they did 10, 20, or even 30 years ago.

Political Models of Organizational Choice Power in organizations is shared; even the lowest-level workers have some power. In **political models of decision making**, what an organization does is a result of political bargains struck among key leaders and interest groups. Organizations do not come up with "solutions" that are "chosen" to solve some

rational model of human behaviour
A model of human behaviour based on the belief that people, organizations, and nations engage in basically consistent, value-maximizing calculations or adaptations within certain constraints.

cognitive style
Underlying personality dispositions toward the treatment of information, selection of alternatives, and evaluation of consequences.

systematic decision makers
Individuals with a cognitive style that approaches a problem by structuring it in terms of some formal method.

intuitive decision makers
Individuals with a cognitive style that approaches a problem with multiple methods in an unstructured manner, using trial and error to find a solution.

organizational models of decision making
Models of decision making that take into account the structural and political characteristics of an organization.

bureaucratic models of decision making
Models of decision making where decisions are shaped by the organization's standard operating procedures (SOPs).

political models of decision making
Models of decision making where decisions result from competition and bargaining among the organization's interest groups and key leaders.

"problem." They come up with compromises that reflect the conflicts, the major stakeholders, the diverse interests, the unequal power, and the confusion that constitute politics.

"Garbage Can" Model   A more recent theory of decision making, called the **"garbage can" model of decision making**, states that organizations are not rational. Decision making is largely accidental and is the product of a stream of solutions, problems, and situations that are randomly associated. If this model is correct, it should not be surprising that the wrong solutions are applied to the wrong problems in an organization or that, over time, a large number of organizations make critical mistakes that lead to their demise.

IMPLICATIONS FOR SYSTEMS DESIGN

The research on decision making shows that it is not a simple process even in the rational individual model. Information systems do not make decisions for humans but rather support the decision-making process. How this is done will depend on the types of decisions, decision makers, and frames of reference.

Research on organizational decision making should alert students of information systems to the fact that decision making in a business is a group and organizational process. Systems must be built to support group and organizational decision making. As a general rule, information systems designers should design systems that have the following characteristics:

▌ They are flexible and provide many options for handling data and evaluating information.

▌ They are capable of supporting a variety of styles, skills, and knowledge.

▌ They are powerful in the sense of having multiple analytical and intuitive models for the evaluation of data and the ability to keep track of many alternatives and consequences.

▌ They reflect understanding of group and organizational processes of decision making.

▌ They are sensitive to the bureaucratic and political requirements of systems.

3.4 INFORMATION SYSTEMS AND BUSINESS STRATEGY

Certain types of information systems have become especially critical to firms' long-term prosperity and survival. These systems are powerful tools for staying ahead of the competition and are called *strategic information systems*. **Competitive advantage** means staying ahead of the competition. It means that a company is ahead of its competition in terms of cost/price, market share, or some other measure of competitive success.

WHAT IS A STRATEGIC INFORMATION SYSTEM?

Strategic information systems change the goals, operations, products, services, or environmental relationships of organizations to help them gain an edge over competitors. Systems that have these effects may even change the business of organizations. For instance, the Bank of Montreal transformed its core business from traditional banking services, such as customer chequing and savings accounts and loans, to electronic commerce, money management, and financial information services, providing online access to individuals and businesses to handle their financial record keeping, cash management, and investment information and transactions. The Bank of Montreal provides online services that include point-of-sale automobile financing; recruiting and hiring their own employees; consumer financing for small- to medium-sized businesses, permitting the companies' customers to finance purchase of their products and services immediately; and wireless services for cellular phone- and personal-digital-assistant-using bank customers. The Bank of Montreal also developed the first *virtual bank* in Canada. ("CIT, BMO Launching Auto Financial Portal," 2000; "What Banks Are Doing to Help Capitalize on the Web," 2000; Ray, 2000; Baroudi, 2000).

Strategic information systems should be distinguished from strategic-level systems for senior managers that focus on long-term decision-making problems. Strategic information systems can be used at all organizational levels and are more far-reaching and deep-rooted

---

"garbage can" model of decision making
Model of decision making that states that organizations are not rational and that decisions are solutions that become attached to problems for accidental reasons.

competitive advantage
Being ahead of the competition in terms of cost/price, market share, or some other measure of competitive success.

strategic information systems
Computer systems at any level of the organization that change goals, operations, products, services, or environmental relationships to help the organization gain a competitive advantage

than the other kinds of systems we have described. Strategic information systems profoundly alter the way a firm conducts its business, or even the very business of the firm itself. As we will see, organizations may need to change their internal operations and relationships with customers and suppliers to take advantage of new information systems technology.

Traditional models of strategy are being modified to accommodate the impact of digital firms and new information flows. Before the emergence of the digital firm, business strategy emphasized head-to-head competition against other firms in the same marketplace. Today, the emphasis is increasingly on exploring, identifying, and occupying new market niches before competitors can do so, understanding the customer value chain better, and learning more quickly and more deeply than competitors.

There is generally no single all-encompassing strategic system, but instead there are a number of systems operating at different levels of strategy—the business, the firm, and the industry level. For each level of business strategy, there are strategic uses of systems. And for each level of business strategy, there is an appropriate model used for analysis.

BUSINESS-LEVEL STRATEGY AND THE VALUE CHAIN MODEL

At the business level of strategy, the key question is "How can we compete effectively in this particular market?" The market might be light bulbs, utility vehicles, or cable television. The most common generic strategies at this level are (1) to become the low-cost producer, (2) to differentiate the product or service, and/or (3) to change the scope of competition by either enlarging the market to include global markets or narrowing the market by focusing on small niches not well served by competitors. Digital firms provide new capabilities for supporting business-level strategy by managing the supply chain, building efficient customer "sense and response" systems, and participating in "value webs" to deliver new products and services to market.

Leveraging Technology in the Value Chain

At the business level the most common analytic tool is value chain analysis. The **value chain model** highlights specific activities in the business where competitive strategies can best be applied (Porter, 1985) and where information systems are most likely to have a strategic impact. The value chain model identifies specific, critical leverage points where a firm can use information technology most effectively to enhance its competitive position. Exactly where can it obtain the greatest benefit from strategic information systems? What specific activities can be used to create new products and services, enhance market penetration, lock in customers and suppliers, and lower operational costs? This model views the firm as a series or "chain" of basic activities that add a margin of value to a firm's products or services. These activities can be categorized as either primary activities or support activities.

Primary activities are most directly related to the production and distribution of the firm's products and services that create value for the customer. Primary activities include inbound logistics, operations, outbound logistics, sales and marketing, and service. Inbound logistics includes receiving and storing materials for distribution to production. Operations transforms inputs into finished products. Outbound logistics entails storing and distributing products. Sales and marketing includes promoting and selling the firm's products. The service activity includes maintenance and repair of the firm's goods and services. **Support activities** make the delivery of the primary activities possible and consist of organization infrastructure (administration and management), human resources (employee recruiting, hiring, and training), technology (improving products and the production process), and procurement (purchasing input).

Organizations have competitive advantage when they provide more value to their customers or when they provide the same value to customers at a lower price. An information system could have a strategic impact if it helped the firm provide products or services at a significantly lower cost than competitors or if it provided products and services at the same cost as competitors but with greater value. The value activities that add the most value to products and services depend on the features of each particular firm.

value chain model
A model that highlights the primary or support activities where information systems can best be applied to achieve a competitive advantage.

primary activities
Activities most directly related to the production and distribution of a firm's products or services.

support activities
Activities that make the delivery of a firm's primary activities possible. Consists of the organization's infrastructure, human resources, technology, and procurement activities.

value web
The digitally enabled network of a firm and its suppliers and business partners.

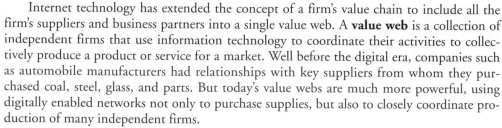

Internet technology has extended the concept of a firm's value chain to include all the firm's suppliers and business partners into a single value web. A **value web** is a collection of independent firms that use information technology to coordinate their activities to collectively produce a product or service for a market. Well before the digital era, companies such as automobile manufacturers had relationships with key suppliers from whom they purchased coal, steel, glass, and parts. But today's value webs are much more powerful, using digitally enabled networks not only to purchase supplies, but also to closely coordinate production of many independent firms.

For instance, in the Italian sweater industry, Bennetton is the design, marketing, and distribution side of a much larger number of independent firms that collectively produce sweaters and other apparel for the U.S. market. Dyers, weavers, assemblers—all operating as independent businesses—obtain production information from Bennetton systems and efficiently produce the ingredients needed for the Bennetton marketing business.

Figure 3-11 illustrates the activities of the value chain and the value web, showing examples of strategic information systems that could be developed to make each of the value chain activities more cost effective.

The industrial networks we introduced in Chapter 2 form the infrastructure for these value webs. A firm can achieve a strategic advantage by providing value, not only through its internal value chain processes but also through powerful, efficient ties to value web partners as well.

Businesses should try to develop strategic information systems for both the internal value chain activities and the external value web activities that add the most value. A strategic analysis might, for example, identify sales and marketing activities where information systems could provide the greatest boost. The analysis might recommend a system to reduce marketing costs by targeting marketing campaigns more efficiently or by providing information for developing products more finely attuned to a firm's target market. A series of systems, including some linked to systems of other value web partners, might be required to create a strategic advantage.

FIGURE 3-11 The value chain and the value web. Various examples of strategic information systems for the primary and support activities of a firm and its value web that would add value to a firm's products or services.

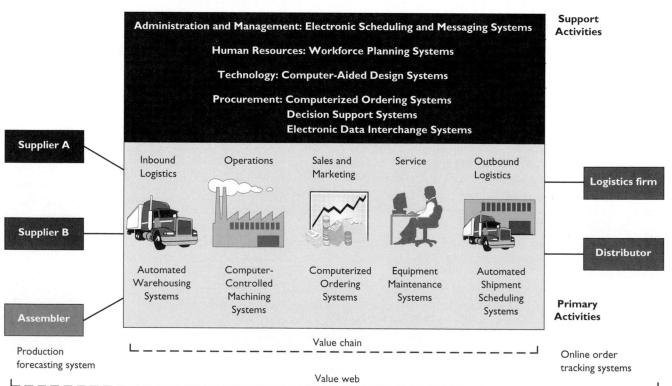

CANADA'S LEADING INVESTMENT HOUSE GETS CLOSER TO ITS CLIENTS

Established in 1964, Phillips, Hager & North (PH&N) has grown to become one of the largest independent investment-counselling firms in Canada. The company currently manages over Can$35 billion in assets. With 250 employees in three offices nationwide, PH&N prides itself on delivering consistent, conservative, long-term investment performance. The company's client advisors deliver detailed and objective investment support. PH&N has made it a policy not to advertise its services, preferring to rely instead on word-of-mouth referrals from its clients.

Unfortunately, PH&N's existing legacy system was unable to leverage information across multiple offices and lines of business. The company had no simple method in place for sharing notes and summaries among its employees, so if a client moved from Toronto to Vancouver, for example, the new client advisor spent countless hours creating a new customer file. What the firm needed was a complete view of the customer that would span geography and traverse business units.

With that in mind, PH&N set out to develop an effective customer relationship management (CRM) solution to keep both current and future clients truly satisfied. "We want each of our 50 000 customers to have an exceptional relationship with PH&N," says Ron Matthews, Vice President, Information Technology, at PH&N. "That means making sure all of our departments are on the same page, have access to the same complete customer information, and are functioning as a cohesive whole. You need the right tools to put that in place."

Today, PH&N has implemented a CRM system that is helping to improve client service, reduce response times, and cut operating costs.

PH&N contracted with Onyx software, which had a proven track record in developing and tailoring applications for the financial services industry as well as a willingness to collaborate closely with PH&N's internal team during the development and deployment of the solution. Onyx supplied PH&N with an enterprise-wide data solution based on the Microsoft Windows® operating system and SQL Server™ platform. "We were on the verge of seeing different business areas adopt different strategies," recalls Matthews. "The power of the Onyx/Microsoft combination allowed us to create an enterprise-wide solution that would benefit the entire company."

A complete view of every customer is now immediately accessible. Every decision made by the company is now based on the most complete information available. When a client calls PH&N today, the service representative views the client's entire profile on-screen, with all preferences, business interactions, and relationships clearly laid out and easy to understand. By integrating the CRM solution with a document management system, client advisors in any location can pull up a fax sent by the client the previous day. In the future, using this platform, the information can be distributed wherever it is needed—perhaps to a monthly client statement, a cell phone, or e-mail.

"Retention of a client means meeting or exceeding their expectations," says Matthews. "With our CRM tools, we have increased the probability that we will understand what the client needs from us and successfully meet those needs whenever and whoever they call within our firm. Being a business that seeks its clients through word-of-mouth referral, this is very important to us. It's part of the commitment we make to our clients."

Finally, the CRM system has also improved systems management within the company considerably. Matthews says his group used to spend between 12 and 20 hours per week—or 50 percent of their time—supporting PH&N's previous technology environment. Still, the system was only operational 80 percent of the time, and only a handful of people could use it before unsatisfactory performance was encountered. "Today, I'd be surprised if we've spent 20 hours in the last two years keeping the system up and running," says Matthews. "It has been available almost 100 percent of the time with good strong performance and response time."

To Think About: How does PH&N's new CRM system address their organizational strategy? Has the CRM system permitted PH&N advisors to focus on the customer? How? Should every company have a CRM system?

Sources: "Canada's Leading Investment House Gets Closer to Its Clients," Microsoft Canada Case Studies, www.microsoft.com/canada/casestudies, accessed July 5, 2001; Steve Campbell, "Yaletown Technology Group: Taking CRM Lessons to Heart," *BCTIA Monitor*, www.yaletech.com/news/articles/crm.htm, accessed July 5, 2001.

The role of information technology at the business level is to help the firm reduce costs, differentiate product, and serve new markets.

Information System Products and Services

Firms can use information systems to create unique new products and services that can be easily distinguished from those of competitors. Strategic information systems for **product differentiation** can prevent the competition from responding in kind so that firms with these differentiated products and services no longer have to compete on the basis of cost.

Many of these information technology-based products and services have been created by financial institutions. Citibank developed automatic teller machines (ATMs) and bank debit cards in 1977. Citibank became at one time the largest bank in the United States. Citibank

product differentiation
Competitive strategy for creating brand loyalty by developing new and unique products and services that are not easily duplicated by competitors.

competitive necessity
The result of something that formerly yielded a competitive advantage becoming a requirement for doing business.

ATMs were so successful that Citibank's competitors were forced to develop their own ATM systems just to keep up—ATMs had become a **competitive necessity**. Banks have continued to innovate by providing online electronic banking services so that customers can do most of their banking transactions with home computers linked to proprietary networks or the Internet. Some companies, such as ING Direct, Citizens Bank of Canada, and even the traditional Bank of Montreal, have used the Web to set up "virtual banks," offering a full array of banking services without any physical branches. (Customers mail in their deposits and receive cash at ATMs.)

Manufacturers and retailers are starting to use information systems to create products and services that are custom-tailored to fit the precise specifications of individual customers. Dell Computer Corporation's Canadian subsidiary, like its U.S. parent, sells directly to customers using build-to-order manufacturing. Individuals, businesses, and government entities can buy computers directly from Dell customized with exactly the features and components they need. They can place their orders directly using a toll-free telephone number or Dell's Canadian Web site (see Figure 3-12). Once the Dell factory receives an order, it assembles the computer based on the configuration specified by the customer. Chapter 1 describes other instances in which information technology is creating customized products and services while retaining the cost efficiencies of mass-production techniques.

Systems to Focus on Market Niche

Businesses can create new market niches by identifying a specific target for a product or service that it can serve in a superior manner. Through **focused differentiation**, the firm can provide a specialized product or service for this narrow target market better than competitors.

focused differentiation
Competitive strategy for developing new market niches for specialized products or services where a business can compete in the target area better than its competitors.

An information system can give a company a competitive advantage by producing data for finely tuned sales and marketing techniques. These systems treat existing information as a resource that the organization can "mine" to increase profitability and market penetration. Information systems enable companies to finely analyze customer buying patterns, tastes, and preferences so that they efficiently pitch advertising and marketing campaigns to smaller and smaller target markets.

Sophisticated software tools find patterns in large pools of data and infer rules from them that can be used to guide decision making. For example, mining data about purchases at supermarkets might reveal that when potato chips are purchased, soft drinks are also purchased 65 percent of the time. When there is a potato chips promotion, soft drinks are purchased 85 percent of the time people purchase potato chips. This information could help firms design better sales promotions or product displays. Table 3-5 describes how businesses are benefiting from customer data analysis. More detail on this topic can be found in Chapters 8 and 14.

FIGURE 3-12 Customers can place their orders directly using a toll-free telephone number or Dell Canada's Web site.

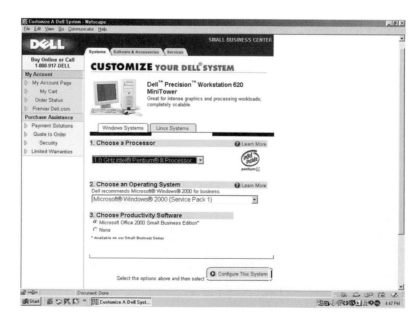

TABLE 3-5	HOW BUSINESSES ARE USING CUSTOMER DATA ANALYSIS
Organization	**Application**
Canadian Imperial Bank of Commerce (CIBC)	Customer profitability system helps the bank identify its most profitable customers so that it can offer them special sales and services.
Ceridian Canada Ltd.	Data generated by customers enables customer service representatives to interact with clients without the client having to repeat their entire history with Ceridian. CRM data will point out trends, including why Ceridian wins a contract and why it loses the contract.
Xerox Canada	Uses data gathered on customer dissatisfaction and ways to correct deficiencies. Helps to identify profitable customers and to motivate customer loyalty by meeting customer requirements even before the customer has contacted the company for additional services.

The data come from a range of sources—credit card transactions, demographic data, purchase data from checkout counter scanners at supermarkets and retail stores, and data collected when people access and interact with Web sites. Analysis of these data can drive one-to-one marketing where personal messages can be created based on individualized preferences. The level of fine-grained customization provided by these data analysis systems parallels that for mass customization described in Chapter 1.

The cost of acquiring a new customer has been estimated to be five times that of retaining an existing customer. By carefully examining transactions of customer purchases and activities, firms can identify profitable customers and win more of their business. Likewise, companies can use these data to identify unprofitable customers (Clemons and Weber, 1994).

Supply Chain Management and Efficient Customer Response Systems

Digital firms have the capabilities to go far beyond traditional strategic systems by taking advantage of digital links with other organizations. A powerful business-level strategy available to digital firms involves linking the value chains of vendors and suppliers to the firm's value chain. Linking the customer's value chain to the firm's value chain in an "efficient customer response system" can further enhance integration of value chains. Firms using systems to link with customers and suppliers can reduce their inventory costs while responding more rapidly to customer demands.

By keeping prices low and shelves well stocked using a now legendary inventory replenishment system, Wal-Mart has become the leading retail business in the United States. Wal-Mart's

MANAGEMENT DECISION PROBLEM

ANALYZING CUSTOMER ACQUISITION COSTS

Companies that sell products directly to consumers over the Web need to measure the effectiveness of their Web site as a sales channel. Web sites are often expensive to build and maintain, and firms want to know if they are getting a good return on their investment. One way to measure Web site effectiveness is to analyze new customer acquisition costs. In other words, how much must the company spend in advertising, marketing, or promotional discounts to turn an online browser into an online buyer? Are the firm's customer acquisition costs higher or lower than for other companies selling online? (The average new customer acquisition cost for companies that sell online is $42 per customer although these costs may be higher or lower for certain types of businesses.) If new customer acquisition costs continue to rise, this could be an indicator that the company is facing higher marketing costs because of increased competition or because they are not meeting their customers' needs. The following is the information on quarterly new customer acquisition costs for four different Web companies:

**New Customer Acquisition Costs:
July 1, 2001, to July 1, 2002**

Company	Q3 '01	Q4 '01	Q1 '02	Q2 '02
Internet Software City	81.82	84.70	92.98	142.65
Online Garage Sale	8.79	9.22	10.60	7.73
Books and More Books	24.77	26.88	31.20	36.17
Online Travel and Vacation	5.11	5.14	5.98	5.61

1. Are any of these companies experiencing customer acquisition problems? Explain your answer.

2. What can companies facing competitive pressure do to lower their customer acquisition costs and to compete more effectively in a virtual environment?

Wal-Mart's continuous inventory replenishment system uses sales data captured at the checkout counter to transmit orders to restock merchandise directly to its suppliers. The system enables Wal-Mart to keep costs low while fine-tuning its merchandise to meet customer demands.

"continuous replenishment system" sends orders for new merchandise directly to suppliers as soon as consumers pay for their purchases at the cash register. Point-of-sale terminals record the bar code of each item passing the checkout counter and send a purchase transaction directly to a central computer at Wal-Mart headquarters. The computer collects the orders from all Wal-Mart stores and transmits them to suppliers. Suppliers can also access Wal-Mart's sales and inventory data using Web technology. Because the system can replenish inventory with lightning speed, Wal-Mart does not need to spend much money on maintaining large inventories of goods in its own warehouses. The system also allows Wal-Mart to adjust purchases of store items to meet customer demands. Competitors such as Kmart spend 21 percent of sales on overhead. But by using systems to keep operating costs low, Wal-Mart pays only 15 percent of sales revenue for overhead.

Wal-Mart's continuous replenishment system is an example of efficient supply chain management, which we introduced in Chapter 2. To manage the supply chain, a company tries to eliminate delays and cut the amount of resources tied up along the way. This can be accomplished by streamlining the company's internal operations or by asking suppliers to put off delivery of goods—and their payments—until the moment they are needed.

Supply chain management systems not only lower inventory costs, but they also deliver the product or service more rapidly to the customer. Supply chain management can thus be used to create efficient customer response systems that respond to customer demands more efficiently. An **efficient customer response system** directly links consumer behaviour back to distribution, production, and supply chains. Wal-Mart's continuous replenishment system provides this type of efficient customer response.

The convenience and ease of using these information systems raise **switching costs** (the cost of switching from one product to a competing product). This discourages customers from going to competitors. For example, Allegiance Corporation's "stockless inventory" and ordering system uses supply chain management (SCM) to create an efficient customer response system. Originally developed by American Health Supply Company, the stockless inventory information system survived a series of spinoffs and mergers to be offered eventually by Source Medical, Canada's largest medical products distributor. Hospitals that participate in a program such as the stockless inventory information system become unwilling to switch to another supplier because of the system's convenience and low cost. Source Medical and its U.S. parent, Allegiance Corporation, supply nearly two-thirds of all products used by North American hospitals.

Terminals tied to Allegiance's own computers are installed in hospitals. When hospitals want to place an order, they do not need to call a salesperson or send a purchase order—they simply use an Allegiance computer terminal on-site to order from the full Allegiance supply catalogue. The system generates shipping, billing, invoicing, and inventory information, and the hospital terminals provide customers with an estimated delivery date. With more than 80 distribution centres in North America, Allegiance can make daily deliveries of its products, often within hours of receiving an order.

Allegiance delivery personnel no longer drop off their cartons at a loading dock to be placed in a hospital storeroom. Instead, they deliver orders directly to the hospital corridors, dropping them at nursing stations, operating rooms, and supply closets. This has created in effect a "stockless inventory," with Allegiance serving as the hospitals' warehouse.

Figure 3-13 compares stockless inventory with the just-in-time supply method and traditional inventory practices. While just-in-time inventory allows customers to reduce their inventories by ordering only enough material for a few days' inventory, stockless inventory allows them to eliminate their inventories entirely. All inventory responsibilities shift to the

efficient customer response system
System that directly links consumer behaviour back to distribution, production, and supply chains.

switching costs
The expense a customer or company incurs in lost time and expenditure of resources when changing from one supplier or system to a competing supplier or system.

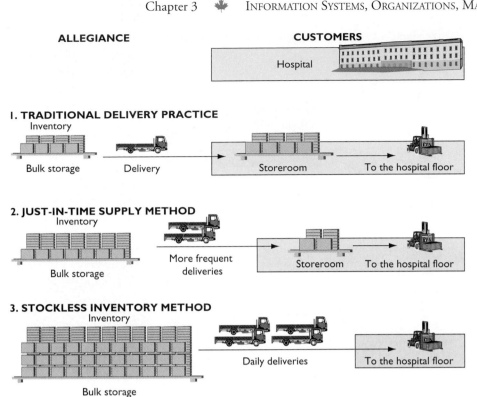

ALLEGIANCE

CUSTOMERS

Hospital

1. TRADITIONAL DELIVERY PRACTICE
Inventory

Bulk storage   Delivery   Storeroom   To the hospital floor

2. JUST-IN-TIME SUPPLY METHOD
Inventory

Bulk storage   More frequent deliveries   Storeroom   To the hospital floor

3. STOCKLESS INVENTORY METHOD
Inventory

Bulk storage   Daily deliveries   To the hospital floor

FIGURE 3-13 Stockless inventory compared to traditional and just-in-time supply methods. The just-in-time supply method reduces inventory requirements of the customer while stockless inventory allows the customer to eliminate inventories entirely. Deliveries are made daily, sometimes directly to the departments that need supplies.

distributor, who manages the supply flow. Stockless inventory is a powerful instrument for "locking in" customers, thus giving the supplier a decided competitive advantage.

Supply chain management and efficient customer response systems are two examples of how digital firms can engage in business strategies not available to "analog" or traditional firms. Both types of systems require network-based IT infrastructure investment and software competence to make customer and supply chain data flow seamlessly among different organizations. Both of these types of strategies have greatly enhanced the efficiency of individual digital firms by moving toward a *demand-pull production system*, away from the *traditional supply-push economic system* in which factories were managed on the basis of 12-month official plans, rather than on near-instantaneous customer purchase information. Figure 3-14 illustrates the relationships between supply chain management, efficient customer response, and the various business-level strategies.

FIRM-LEVEL STRATEGY AND INFORMATION TECHNOLOGY

A business firm is typically a collection of businesses. Often, the firm is organized financially as a collection of *strategic business units (SBUs)*, and the returns to the firm are directly tied to strategic business unit performance. The questions are, "How can the overall performance of these business units be maximized?" and "How can information technology contribute?"

There are two answers in the literature to these questions: synergy and core competency. The idea driving synergies is that when some units can be used as inputs to other units, or when two organizations can pool markets and expertise, these relationships can lower costs and generate profits. Recent mergers such as those of Air Canada and Canadian Airlines, Rogers and Cantel, and the Toronto Dominion Bank and Canada Trust occurred precisely for this purpose.

How can IT be used strategically here? One use of information technology in these synergy situations is to tie together the operations of disparate business units so that they can act as a whole. These systems lower costs, increase customer access to new products and services, and speed up the process of marketing new products and services. Simply being able to integrate or merge information systems and data means lower IT and computer operating costs as well as permitting customers of one company to conduct business with the merged company as they had previously done with the predecessor company.

FIGURE 3-14 Business-level strategy. Efficient customer response systems are often inter-related, helping firms "lock in" customers and suppliers while lowering operating costs. Other types of systems can be used to support product differentiation, focused differentiation, and low-cost producer strategies.

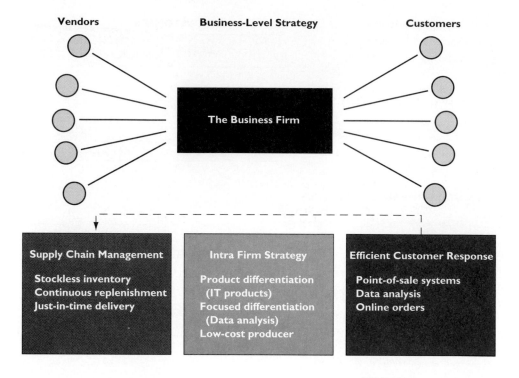

core competency
An activity at which a firm excels as a world-class leader.

Enhancing Core Competencies

A second concept for firm-level strategy involves the notion of **core competency**. The argument is that the performance of all business units can increase insofar as these business units develop a central core of competencies. A core competency is an activity at which a firm is a world-class leader. Core competencies may involve being the world's best fibre-optic manufacturer, the best miniature parts designer, the best package delivery service, or the best thin film manufacturer. In general, a core competency relies on knowledge that is gained over many years of experience (*embedded knowledge*) and a first-class research organization or simply key staff who stay abreast of new external knowledge (*tacit knowledge*).

How can IT be used to advance or create core competencies? Any system that encourages the sharing of knowledge across business units enhances competency. These systems might encourage or enhance existing competencies and help employees become aware of new external knowledge; they might also help a business leverage existing competencies in related markets.

INDUSTRY-LEVEL STRATEGY AND INFORMATION SYSTEMS: INFORMATION PARTNERSHIPS, COMPETITIVE FORCES, AND NETWORK ECONOMICS

Firms together compose an industry, such as the automotive, telecommunications, television broadcasting, and forest products industries, to name a few. The key strategic question at this level of analysis is: "How and when should we compete as opposed to cooperate with others in the industry?" While most strategic analyses emphasize competition, a great deal of money can be made by cooperating with other firms in the same industry or firms in related industries. For instance, firms can cooperate to develop industry standards in a number of areas; they can cooperate by working together to build customer awareness and by working collectively with suppliers to lower costs (Shapiro and Varian, 1999). The three principal concepts for analyzing strategy at the industry level are information partnerships, the competitive forces model, and network economics.

information partnership
Cooperative alliance formed between two or more corporations for the purpose of sharing information to gain strategic advantage.

Information Partnerships

Firms can form information partnerships, and even link their information systems to achieve unique synergies. In an **information partnership**, both companies can join forces, without actually merging, by sharing information (Konsynski and McFarlan, 1990). Air Canada has an arrangement with Canadian Imperial Bank of Commerce (CIBC) to award one mile in its frequent flyer program for every dollar spent using a CIBC Aerogold credit card. Air Canada benefits from increased customer loyalty, and CIBC gains new credit card subscriptions and a highly creditworthy customer base for cross-marketing. Air Canada has also allied with Primus Canada, awarding five frequent flyer miles for each dollar of long distance billing when a customer spends over $15 a month.

These partnerships help firms gain access to new customers, creating new opportunities for cross-selling and targeting products. Companies that have been traditional competitors may find such alliances to be mutually advantageous. Allegiance Healthcare Canada offers its customers medical supplies from competitors and office supplies through its electronic ordering channel.

The Competitive Forces Model

In the **competitive forces model**, illustrated in Figure 3-15, a firm faces a number of external threats and opportunities: the threat of new entrants into its market, the pressure from substitute products or services, the bargaining power of customers, the bargaining power of suppliers, and the positioning of traditional industry competitors.

Competitive advantage can be achieved by enhancing the firm's ability to deal with customers, suppliers, substitute products and services, and new entrants to its market, which in turn may change the balance of power between a firm and other competitors in the industry in the firm's favour.

How can information systems be used to achieve strategic advantage at the industry level? By working with other firms, industry participants can use information technology to develop industry-wide standards for exchanging information or business transactions electronically (see Chapter 10), which forces all market participants to subscribe to similar standards. Earlier we described how firms can benefit from value webs with complementary firms in the industry. These efforts increase efficiency at the industry level as well as the business level—making substitute products less possible and perhaps raising entry costs—thus discouraging new entrants. Also, industry members can build industry-wide, IT-supported consortiums, symposiums, and communications networks to coordinate activities vis-à-vis government agencies, foreign competition, and competing industries.

An example of this type of industry-level cooperation can be found in the Chapter 4 Window on Organizations describing Covisint, an electronic exchange shared by the major automobile manufacturers for procurement of auto parts. While the Big 3 North American auto manufacturers aggressively compete on such factors as design, service, quality, and price, they can raise the industry's productivity by working together to create an integrated supply chain. Covisint enables all manufacturers and suppliers to trade on a single Internet site, sparing manufacturers the cost of setting up their own Web-based marketplaces.

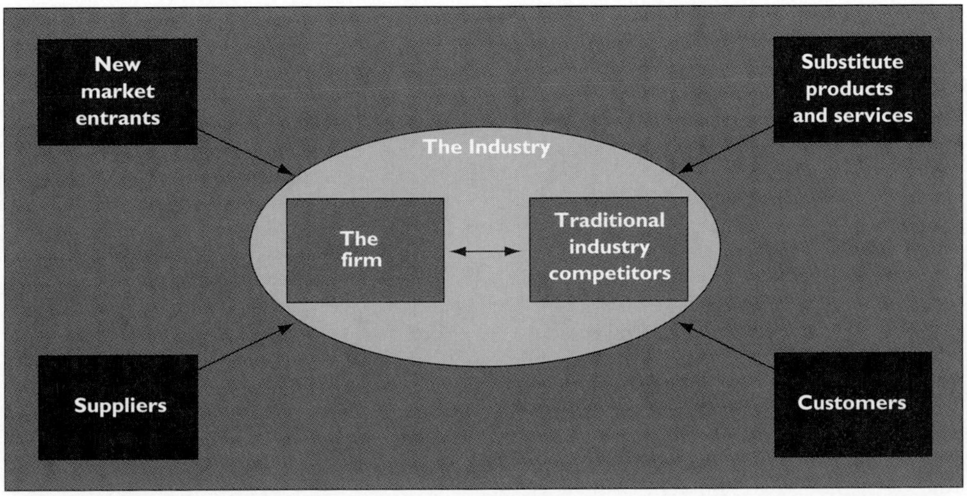

competitive forces model
Model used to describe the interaction of external influences, specifically threats and opportunities, that affect an organization's strategy and ability to compete.

FIGURE 3-15 The competitive forces model. There are various forces that affect an organization's ability to compete and therefore greatly influence a firm's business strategy. There are threats from new market entrants and from substitute products and services. Customers and suppliers wield bargaining power. Traditional competitors constantly adapt their strategies to maintain their market positioning.

In the digital firm era, the competitive forces model needs modification. The traditional Porter model assumes a relatively static industry environment, relatively clear-cut industry boundaries, and a relatively stable set of suppliers, substitutes, and customers. Instead of participating in a single industry, today's firms are much more aware that they participate in "industry sets"—multiple related industries that consumers can choose from to obtain a product or service (see Figure 3-16). For instance, automobile companies compete against other automobile companies in the "auto industry," but they also compete against many other industries in the transportation industry "set" such as train, plane, and bus transportation companies. Success or failure for a single auto company may depend on the success or failure of various other industries, such as the current Firestone tire recall debacle and its impact on Ford Motor Company (see Chapter 8). Universities may think they are in competition with other traditional schools, but in fact they are in competition with electronic distance-learning schools, publishing companies that have created online courses, and private training firms that offer technical certificates—all of whom are members of a much larger "education industry set." In the digital firm era, we can expect greater emphasis on building strategies to compete—and cooperate—with members of the firm's industry set.

Network Economics

network economics
New economics model where the marginal costs of adding another participant are negligible while the marginal gain is much greater.

A second strategic concept useful at the industry level is **network economics**. In traditional economics—the economics of factories and agriculture—production experiences diminishing returns. The more any given resource is applied to production, the lower the marginal gain in output until a point is reached where the additional inputs produce no additional outputs. This is the law of diminishing returns, and it is the foundation for most of modern economics.

In some situations, the law of diminishing returns does not work. For instance, in a network, the marginal costs of adding another participant are about zero while the marginal gain is much larger. The larger the number of subscribers in a telephone system or on the Internet, the greater the value to all participants. It's no more expensive to operate a television station with 1000 subscribers than with 10 million subscribers. The value of a community of people grows with size even though the cost of adding new members is inconsequential.

From the network economics perspective, information technology can be strategically useful. Internet sites can be used by firms to build "communities of users"—like-minded customers who want to share their experiences. This can build customer loyalty and enjoyment and build unique ties to customers. Microsoft Corporation—the world's dominant PC software manufacturer—uses information technology to build communities of software developers around the world. Using the Microsoft Developer's Network, these small software development firms work closely with Microsoft to debug Microsoft's operating system software, to provide new applications ideas and extensions, to supply customers with tips and new software applications, and in general to participate in a powerful and useful network.

FIGURE 3-16 The new competitive forces model. The digital firm era requires a more dynamic view of the boundaries between firms, customers, and suppliers, with competition occurring among industry sets.

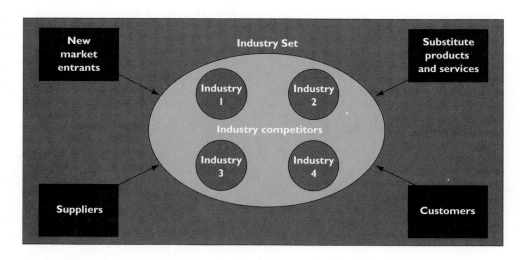

USING SYSTEMS FOR COMPETITIVE ADVANTAGE: MANAGEMENT ISSUES

Strategic information systems often change the organization as well as its products, services, and operating procedures, driving the organization into new behaviour patterns. Using technology effectively for strategic benefit requires careful planning and management.

Managing Strategic Transitions

Adopting the kinds of strategic systems described in this chapter generally requires changes in business goals, relationships with customers and suppliers, internal operations, and information architecture. These sociotechnical changes, affecting both social and technical elements of the organization, can be considered **strategic transitions**—a movement between levels of sociotechnical systems.

These changes often entail blurring of organizational boundaries, both external and internal. Suppliers and customers must become intimately linked and may share each other's responsibilities. For instance, in Allegiance Healthcare Canada's stockless inventory system, Allegiance has assumed responsibility for managing its customers' inventories (Johnston and Vitale, 1988). Managers need to devise new business processes for coordinating their firms' activities with those of customers, suppliers, and other organizations. The organizational change requirements surrounding new information systems are so important that they merit attention throughout this text.

strategic transitions
A movement from one level of sociotechnical system to another. Often required when adopting strategic systems that demand changes in the social and technical elements of an organization.

What Managers Can Do

Information systems are too important to be left entirely to a small technical group in the corporation. Managers must identify the systems that could provide a strategic advantage to the firm. Some of the important questions managers should ask themselves are as follows:

▌ What are some of the forces at work in the industry? What strategies are being used by industry leaders?

▌ How is the industry currently using information and communication technology? Which organizations are the industry leaders in the application of information systems technology?

▌ What is the direction and nature of change within the industry? From where is the momentum and change coming?

▌ Are significant strategic opportunities to be gained by introducing information systems technology into the industry? What kinds of systems are applicable to the industry?

Once the nature of information systems technology in the industry is understood, managers should turn to their organization and ask other important questions:

▌ Is the organization behind or ahead of the industry in its application of information systems?

▌ What is the current business strategic plan, and how does that plan mesh with the current strategy for information services?

▌ Does the firm have sufficient technology and capital to develop a strategic information systems initiative (Kettinger et al. 1994)?

▌ Where would new information systems provide the greatest value to the firm?

Once these issues have been considered, managers can gain a keen insight into whether their firms are ready for strategic information systems.

SUSTAINING COMPETITIVE ADVANTAGE

A firm achieving a competitive advantage typically has "first mover" advantages. While the risks and costs associated with achieving a competitive advantage can be formidable, the first mover advantages can enable the business to beat their competition. These first mover advantages include enhancing customer and brand loyalty, having one's name forever associated

strategic intent

The concept of constantly looking for additional ways to achieve a competitive advantage, even when one already has that advantage.

with a product (much like snowmobiles have been called "SkiDoos" for years), and simply becoming the "go to" company, as Wal-Mart did.

Once a competitive advantage is achieved, it is only rarely sustained over the long term. While the business that is leapfrogging ahead of its competition has considerable first mover advantages, other firms observe what the competitive advantage is and how it was achieved. They then determine how to copy that core competency, to do it even better, perhaps by adding bells and whistles to a product or service, and they can almost always do it cheaper since most of the research and development work has already been done by the first company.

Nevertheless, the first mover company must continually seek to maintain its competitive advantage. They must commit themselves to the concept of **strategic intent**, constantly looking for additional ways to achieve a competitive advantage even when they already have that advantage (Hamel & Pralahad, 1989). Frequently, this means looking for new strategic information system opportunities or ways to enhance existing strategic information systems.

3.5   THE GROWTH OF INTERNATIONAL INFORMATION SYSTEMS

We already have described two powerful worldwide changes driven by advances in information technology that have transformed the business environment and posed new challenges for management. One is the transformation of industrial economies and societies into knowledge- and information-based economies. The other is the emergence of a global economy and global world order.

Many firms will be replaced by fast-moving networked corporations that transcend national boundaries. The growth of international trade has radically altered domestic economies around the globe. About $1 trillion worth of goods, services, and financial instruments—the equivalent of the annual Canadian gross domestic product—changes hands each day in global trade.

Consider a laptop computer purchased in Canada as an example: The CPU is likely to have been designed and built in the United States; the DRAM (or dynamic random access memory, which makes up the majority of primary storage in a computer) was designed in the United States but built in Malaysia; the screen was designed and assembled in Japan, using American patents; the keyboard is from Taiwan; and it was all assembled in Japan, where the case also was made. Management of the project, located in Silicon Valley, California, along with marketing, sales, and finance, all supporting those same functions in Canada, coordinated all the activities from financing and production to shipping and sales efforts. None of this would be possible without powerful international information and telecommunication systems, an international information systems infrastructure.

To be effective, managers need a global perspective on business and an understanding of the support systems needed to conduct business on an international scale.

DEVELOPING THE INTERNATIONAL INFORMATION SYSTEMS INFRASTRUCTURE

international information systems portfolio

The basic information systems required by organizations to coordinate worldwide trade and other activities.

business driver

A force in the environment to which businesses must respond and that influences the direction of business.

An infrastructure is the constellation of facilities and services, such as highways or telecommunications networks, required for organizations to function and prosper. An **international information systems portfolio** consists of the basic information systems required by organizations to coordinate worldwide trade and other activities. Figure 3-17 depicts the major dimensions of an international information systems portfolio.

Building an effective international information systems portfolio is a process comprising six important steps, listed below, that should be carried out in sequence.

1. Understanding the overall market forces or business drivers that are pushing an industry toward global competition is critical. A **business driver** is a force in the environment to which businesses must respond and that influences the direction of the business.

2. Careful examination of the inhibitors or negative factors that create *management challenges*—factors that could scuttle the development of a global business is also critical.

3. A corporate strategy for competing in that environment must be developed.

4. How to structure the organization so it can pursue the strategy is the next step. How will it accomplish a division of labour across a global environment? Where will production, administration, accounting, marketing, and human resource functions be located? Who will handle the systems function?

5. The management issues in implementing the strategy and making the organization design come alive must be evaluated. The key here is the design of business procedures. How can the organization discover and manage user requirements? How can it induce change in local units to conform to international requirements? How can it reengineer on a global scale, and how can it coordinate systems development?

6. The technology platform must be determined. Although changing technology is a key driving factor leading toward global markets, a corporate strategy and structure is needed before choosing the right technology.

International Information Systems Portfolio

FIGURE 3-17 International information systems portfolio. The major dimensions for developing an international information systems portfolio are the global environment, the corporate global strategies, the structure of the organization, the management and business procedures, and the technology platform.

After this process of reasoning has been completed, the organization is moving toward an appropriate international information systems portfolio capable of achieving its corporate goals. Let us begin by looking briefly at the overall global environment.

THE GLOBAL ENVIRONMENT: BUSINESS DRIVERS AND CHALLENGES

Table 3-6 lists the global business drivers that are leading all industries toward global markets and competition.

Global business drivers can be divided into two groups: general cultural factors and specific business factors. A lengthy discussion of each of these factors is beyond the scope of this text. For our purposes, let us consider each of these drivers as factors that complicate the development and implementation of global information systems.

All of the major business functions can be coordinated on a global scale. Each business function should be located where it is best accomplished. Global markets, production, and administration create the conditions for powerful, sustained global economies of scale. Not all industries are similarly affected by these trends.

Business Challenges

Although the possibilities of successful globalization are significant, fundamental forces are operating to inhibit a global economy and to disrupt international business. Table 3-7 lists the most common and powerful challenges to the development of global systems.

TABLE 3-6	GLOBAL BUSINESS DRIVERS	
General Cultural Factors	**Specific Business Factors**	
Global communication and transportation technologies	Global markets	
Development of global culture	Global production and operations	
Emergence of global social and educational norms	Global coordination	
Political stability or instability	Global workforce	
Global knowledge base	Global economies of scale	

Again, a lengthy discussion of these challenges is beyond the scope of our text. Understanding that these challenges and obstacles vastly increase the development and implementation of information systems is our main point here. For a further discussion of the global business drivers, challenges, and obstacles, consult our text's Web site.

GEOGRAPHICALLY-BASED INTERNATIONAL STRATEGIES

Many countries, regions, provinces, or even cities and towns are developing and implementing strategic initiatives using advanced information technology to "grow" their area. We are aware of U.S. technology centres such as Silicon Valley in Northern California, the area in Massachusetts around the Massachusetts Institute of Technology, and the Research Triangle in North Carolina. But Canada has technology centres, too, fostered and supported by local governments. The following are just a few examples from Canada and abroad that illustrate this dynamic approach to community renewal.

The City of Winnipeg, Manitoba, is trying to build an "information corridor" in the older part of the city known as the Exchange District. Already several buildings in the District house multiple Internet or multimedia companies. CanWest Global, headquartered in Winnipeg, recently announced that they were bringing their call centre with 1200 employees and a wealth of technology to Winnipeg and locating in the Exchange District. Many call centres, such as Royal Bank and Faneuil Marketing, call Winnipeg home.

Despite the emergence in the Ottawa region of a Silicon Valley North and other e-business clusters in Toronto, Waterloo, Ont., Montreal, Calgary, and Vancouver, there are few other successful cluster activities in the rest of Canada because the linkages among universities, business, and the financial community are generally not as strong or as focused as their American counterparts. Factors that create tight linkages—directed research, the cross-pollination among university faculty, business management, and technology staff, and active early-stage venture capitalists—are infrequent and too small to drive new-business creation. Moreover, Canadian Internet start-ups in all locales face a set of common challenges in gaining access to financing and in attracting and retaining IT talent.

Nonetheless, Vancouver has created a niche for the computer graphics industry along with many other high-tech companies, according to George Hunter, Executive Director of the British Columbia Technology Industries Association. Hunter also feels that Kelowna and Victoria have thriving software industries. Ottawa's advanced technology industry created the area known as Silicon Valley North, with a broad range of emerging firms, including multi-million-dollar players like Nortel Networks (Northern Telecom), Newbridge Networks Corporation (bought in 2000 by Alcatel S.A.), and Corel Corporation. Today, Ottawa is home to a number of industry giants, such as JDS Uniphase, Mitel Corporation, Cognos Inc., GSI Lumonics Inc., EDS/SHL Systemhouse, Accelio Corporation, Simware Inc., and more.

Other countries are also taking major strategic IT initiatives to attract business to their shores—or deserts. Dubai Internet City is the first complete Information Technology and Telecommunications centre in the world to have been built inside a free trade zone. "I had a

TABLE 3-7	CHALLENGES AND OBSTACLES TO GLOBAL BUSINESS SYSTEMS	
General	**Specific**
Cultural particularism: regionalism, nationalism, language differences	Standards: different EDI, e-mail, telecommunications standards
Social expectations: brand-name expectations; work hours, and ethics	Reliability: telephone network not uniformly reliable
Political laws: transborder data and privacy laws, commercial regulations	Speed: different data transfer speeds, many slower than in Canada
Environmental: regulations, societal expectations	Personnel: shortages of skilled consultants
	Development of local IT infrastructure: political issues, financial investments

vision to transform the old economy by making Dubai a hub for the new economy," Dubai's Crown Prince Mohammad bin Rashid said. Dubai Internet City offers modern, ready-to-operate, fully serviced office space with cutting edge technology and both wired and wireless networks. Dubai Internet City allows 100% foreign ownership of companies, and laws relating to partnerships with local sponsors have been relaxed. Sales, company earnings, and private income are exempt from any form of taxation. Companies can also take land on a renewable lease of up to 50 years and build their own offices. Dubai Internet City's infrastructure uses Sun Microsystems' server platforms, iPlanet software, Lucent cabling, and Cisco components. Siemens was project integrator. Dubai Internet City is the biggest IT-build in the Middle East and has the largest generation Internet Protocol telephony system in the world.

In Malaysia, the government built a Multimedia SuperCorridor outside the capital city of Kuala Lumpur to serve as the springboard for the information technology industry. It appears that their vision lacked the infrastructure and partnerships with local and national business to achieve the success of their neighbour, Singapore. Spurred by its role as a transportation centre in Asia, Singapore has become one of the world's most competitive air, sea, and telecommunications hubs. Years ago, Singapore's government committed to educating their populace on advancing information technologies; their educational commitment spurred development in this area so that their infrastructure is as robust and fast as that found in North America. Promoting their Free Trade Zone also signalled the world that Singapore was open for IT business.

Back in Canada, a federal initiative known as CANARIE is Canada's advanced Internet development agency—it is roughly analogous to the Internet2 effort in the United States. Two of its main projects are CA*Net2 and CA*Net3. Headquartered in Ottawa, CANARIE has already succeeded in enhancing Canadian R&D Internet speeds by a factor of almost one million since its inception in 1993. More information on CA*Net2 and CA*Net3 initiatives will be found in Chapter 9.

STATE OF THE ART

One might think that most international companies should have rationally developed, logical, integrated international systems architectures. Nothing could be further from the truth. Most companies have inherited patchwork international systems from the distant past. Still other companies have recently built technology platforms for an international infrastructure but cannot use them effectively because they lack a global strategy.

As it turns out, there are significant difficulties in building appropriate international infrastructures. The difficulties involve planning a system appropriate to the firm's global strategy, structuring the organization of systems and business units, solving implementation issues, and choosing the right technical platform. Let us examine these problems in greater detail.

3.6 ORGANIZING INTERNATIONAL INFORMATION SYSTEMS

There are three organizational issues facing corporations seeking a global position: choosing a strategy, organizing the business, and organizing the systems management area. The first two are closely connected, so we will discuss them together.

GLOBAL STRATEGIES, ORGANIZATIONS, AND INFORMATION SYSTEMS

Four main global strategies form the basis for global firms' organizational structure. These strategies are domestic exporter, multinational, franchiser, and transnational. Each of these strategies is pursued with a specific business organizational structure (see Table 3-8). There are also other types of governance patterns observed in specific companies (e.g., authoritarian dominance by one unit, a confederacy of equals, a federal structure balancing power among

TABLE 3-8	GLOBAL BUSINESS STRATEGY AND STRUCTURE STRATEGY				
Business Function	**Domestic Exporter**	**Multinational**	**Franchiser**	**Transnational**
Production	Centralized	Decentralized	Networked	Networked
Finance/Accounting	Centralized	Centralized	Centralized	Networked
Sales/Marketing	Mixed	Decentralized	Networked	Networked
Human Resources	Centralized	Centralized	Networked	Networked
Strategic Management	Centralized	Decentralized	Centralized	Networked

strategic units, and so forth; see Keen, 1991). The configuration, management, and development of systems tend to follow the global strategy chosen by the organization (Roche, 1992; Ives and Jarvenpaa, 1991). Figure 3-18 depicts the typical arrangements.

By *systems*, we mean the full range of activities involved in building information systems: conception and alignment with the strategic business plan, systems development, and ongoing operation. For the sake of simplicity, we consider four types of systems configuration. *Centralized systems* are those in which systems development and operation occur totally at the domestic home base. *Duplicated systems* are those in which development occurs at the home base, but operations are handed over to autonomous units in foreign locations. *Decentralized systems* are those in which each foreign unit designs and operates its own unique solutions and systems. *Networked systems* are those in which systems development and operations occur in an integrated and coordinated fashion across all units.

domestic exporter
A strategy characterized by heavy centralization of corporate activities in the country of origin.

multinational
A global strategy that concentrates financial management and control out of a central home base while decentralizing production, sales, and marketing operations to units in other countries.

The **domestic exporter** strategy is characterized by heavy centralization of corporate activities in the home country of origin. Nearly all international companies begin this way, and some move on to other forms. Production, finance/accounting, sales/marketing, human resources, and strategic management are set up to optimize resources in the home country. International sales are sometimes dispersed using agency agreements or subsidiaries, but even here foreign marketing is totally reliant on the domestic home base for marketing themes and strategies. Winnipeg's MacDon Industries, Ltd. and other heavy capital-equipment manufacturers fall into this category of firm. As can be seen in Figure 3-18, domestic exporters tend to have highly centralized systems in which a single domestic systems development staff develops worldwide applications.

The **multinational** strategy concentrates financial management and control out of a central home base while decentralizing production, sales, and marketing operations to units in other countries. The products and services on sale in different countries are adapted to suit local market conditions. The organization becomes a far-flung confederation of production and marketing facilities in different countries. Many financial services firms, such as Assante Corporation, along with a host of manufacturers such as General Motors, DaimlerChrysler,

FIGURE 3-18 Global strategy and systems configurations. The large Xs show the dominant patterns, and the small Xs show the emerging patterns. For instance, domestic exporters rely predominantly on centralized systems, but there is continual pressure and some development of decentralized systems in local marketing regions.

SYSTEM CONFIGURATION	STRATEGY			
	Domestic Exporter	**Multinational**	**Franchiser**	**Transnational**
Centralized	X			
Duplicated			X	
Decentralized	x	X	x	
Networked		x		X

and Intel fit this pattern. Multinationals offer a direct and striking contrast to domestic exporters. Here foreign units devise their own systems solutions based on local needs with few if any applications in common with headquarters (the exceptions being financial reporting and some telecommunications applications).

Franchisers are an interesting mix of old and new. On the one hand, the product is created, designed, financed, and initially produced in the home country, but for product-specific reasons must rely heavily on foreign personnel for further production, marketing, and human resources. Food franchisers such as McDonald's, Mrs. Fields Cookies, and Kentucky Fried Chicken fit this pattern. Generally, foreign franchisees are clones of the mother country units, but fully coordinated worldwide production that could optimize factors of production is not possible. For instance, potatoes and beef can generally not be bought where they are cheapest on world markets but must be produced reasonably close to the area of consumption. Franchisers have the simplest systems structure. Like the products they sell, franchisers develop a single system, usually at the home base, and then replicate it around the world. Each unit, no matter where it is located, has identical applications.

Transnational firms are the stateless, truly globally managed firms that may represent a larger part of international business in the future. Transnational firms have no single national headquarters but instead have many regional headquarters and perhaps a world headquarters. In a **transnational** strategy, nearly all the value-adding activities are managed from a global perspective without reference to national borders, optimizing sources of supply and demand wherever they appear and taking advantage of any local competitive advantages. Transnational firms take the globe, not the home country, as their management frame of reference. The governance of these firms has been likened to a federal structure in which there is a strong central management core of decision making but considerable dispersal of power and financial muscle throughout the global divisions. Few companies have actually attained transnational status, but BASF, Citicorp, Sony, Ford, and others are attempting this transition. Finally, the most ambitious form of systems development is found in the transnational. Networked systems are those in which there is a solid, singular global environment for developing and operating systems. This usually presupposes a powerful telecommunications backbone, a culture of shared applications development, and a shared management culture that crosses cultural barriers. The networked systems structure is the most visible in financial services where the homogeneity of the product—money and money instruments—seems to overcome cultural barriers.

REORGANIZING THE BUSINESS

How should a firm organize itself for doing business on an international scale? To develop a global company and an information systems support structure, a firm needs to follow these principles:

1. Organize value-adding activities along lines of comparative advantage. For instance, marketing/sales functions should be located where they can best be performed, for least cost and maximum impact; the same is also true for the production, finance, human resources, and information systems functions.

2. Develop and operate systems units at each level of corporate activity—regional, national, and international. To serve local needs, there should be host country systems units of some magnitude. Regional systems units should handle telecommunications and systems development across national boundaries that take place within major geographic regions (e.g., Europe, Asia, North America). Transnational systems units should be established to create the linkages across major regional areas and to coordinate the development and operation of international telecommunications and systems development (Roche, 1992).

3. Establish at world headquarters a single office and individual responsible for the development of international systems (e.g., a global chief information officer, CIO, position).

franchiser
A firm where a product is created, designed, financed, and initially produced in the home country, but for product-specific reasons must rely heavily on foreign personnel for further production, marketing, and human resources.

transnational
Truly globally managed firms that have no national headquarters; value-added activities are managed from a global perspective without reference to national borders, optimizing sources of supply and demand and taking advantage of any local competitive advantage.

APPLICATION SOFTWARE EXERCISE

SPREADSHEET EXERCISE: DETERMINING MONTHLY LOAN PAYMENTS FOR ROBERTO'S PLACE

Roberto's Place is a chain of pizza delivery stores, owned and operated by Roberto Lunsford. Customers often remark on the quality, variety, and low price of Roberto's pizzas. For each store, Roberto has three delivery vehicles. During the past year, Roberto has noticed an increase in the repair and maintenance costs associated with several of his delivery vehicles. Under normal circumstances, Roberto will purchase two cars each year. However, because of the increased repair and maintenance problems, he must now purchase at least six new vehicles.

After visiting several dealerships, he determines that each vehicle will cost approximately $20 000. He knows that he can borrow up to $125 000 from a local bank; the interest rate is 9 percent; he will need to arrange financing for at least 4 years, and he has $25 000 available for a down payment. Organize this information in a spreadsheet. What is Roberto's approximate monthly payment?

If Roberto finances his new pizza delivery vehicles for 5 years instead of 4 years, what is the new monthly payment? If Roberto wishes to keep his payment below $2 000 a month, should he finance the loan for 5 years instead of 4 years? What is the difference in monthly payments? Also, what is the difference in total interest between the 4- and 5-year payoff options?

After speaking with a loan officer at the local bank, Roberto is told that the available interest rates vary between 8 and 9 percent. Using your spreadsheet product's help feature, investigate how to build input tables. Next, build one input table, outlining the interest rates and associated monthly payments. Your interest rates should increase in quarter percent increments. Prepare a written analysis of your findings. What recommendations would you give Roberto?

MANAGEMENT WRAP-UP

Information technology provides tools for managers to carry out both their traditional and newer roles, allowing them to monitor, plan, and forecast with more precision and speed than ever before and to respond more rapidly to the changing business environment. Finding ways to use information technology to achieve competitive advantage at the business, firm, and industry level is a key management responsibility. In addition to identifying the business processes, core competencies, and relationships with others in the industry that can be enhanced with information technology, managers need to oversee the sociotechnical changes required to implement strategic systems. Finally, managers need to consider the international business aspects of their organizations and ensure that the organization's information systems support the firm's international strategy and structure.

Each organization has a unique constellation of information systems that results from its interaction with information technology. Contemporary information technology can lead to major organizational changes—and efficiencies—by reducing transaction and agency costs. IT can also be a source of competitive advantage. Developing meaningful strategic systems generally requires extensive changes in organizational structure, culture, and business processes that often encounter resistance. Globalization requires that the organization consider how it will conduct business in the international marketplace; these decisions affect organizational strategy and structure.

Information technology offers new ways of organizing work and information that can promote organizational survival and prosperity. Technology can be used to differentiate existing products, create new products and services, nurture core competencies, and reduce operational costs. Selecting an appropriate technology for the firm's competitive strategy is a key decision. Global information systems require information technology that can be used in a variety of different countries with different cultures and laws and different infrastructures.

For Discussion:

1. A number of information system experts have claimed that there is no such thing as a sustainable strategic advantage. Do you agree? Why or why not?

2. How has the Internet changed the management process? Are all Internet-based systems strategic? Why or why not?

3. Does globalization change the way information technology decisions are made? Does globalization change what those decisions are?

SUMMARY

1. *Identify the salient characteristics of organizations.* All modern organizations are hierarchical, specialized, and impartial. They use explicit standard operating procedures to maximize efficiency. All organizations have their own culture and politics arising from differences in interest groups. Organizations differ in goals, groups served, social roles, leadership styles, incentives, surrounding environments, and types of tasks performed. These differences create varying types of organizational structures.

2. *Analyze the relationship between information systems and organizations.* The impact of information systems on organizations is not unidirectional. Information systems and the organizations in which they are used interact with and influence each other. The introduction of a new information system will affect organizational structure, goals, work design, values, competition between interest groups, decision making, and day-to-day behaviour. At the same time, information systems must be designed to serve the needs of important organizational groups and will be shaped by the organization's structure, tasks, goals, culture, politics, and management. The power of information systems to transform organizations radically by flattening organizational hierarchies has not yet been demonstrated for all types of organizations, but information technology can reduce transaction and agency costs. The Internet has a potentially large impact on organizational structure and business processes because it can dramatically reduce transaction and agency costs.

3. *Contrast the classical and contemporary models of managerial activities and roles.* Early classical models of management stressed the functions of planning, organizing, coordinating, deciding, and controlling. Contemporary research has examined the actual behaviour of managers to show how managers get things done. Mintzberg found that managers' real activities are highly fragmented, varied, and brief in duration, with managers moving rapidly and intensely from one issue to another. Other behavioural research has found that managers spend considerable time pursuing personal agendas and goals and shy away from making grand, sweeping policy decisions.

4. *Describe how managers make decisions in organizations.* Decisions can be structured, semistructured, or unstructured, with structured decisions clustering at the operational level of the organization and unstructured decisions at the strategic planning level. The nature and level of decision making are important factors in building information systems for managers.

Decision making itself is a complex activity at both the individual and the organizational level. Individual models of decision making assume that human beings can accurately choose alternatives and consequences based on the priority of their objectives and goals. The rigorous rational model of individual decision making has been modified by behavioural research that suggests that rationality is limited. People select alternatives biased by their cognitive style and frame of reference. Organizational models of decision making illustrate that real decision making in organizations takes place in arenas where many psychological, political, and bureaucratic forces are at work. Thus, organizational decision making may not necessarily be rational.

5. *Evaluate the role of information systems in supporting various levels of business strategy.* A strategic information system changes the goals, operations, products, services, or environmental relationships of organizations to help gain an edge over competitors. Information systems can be used to support strategy at the business, firm, and industry level. At the business level of strategy, information systems can be used to help firms become the low-cost producer, differentiate products, or serve new markets. Information systems can also be used to "lock in" customers and suppliers using efficient customer response and supply chain management applications. Value chain analysis is useful at the business level to highlight specific activities in the business where information systems are most likely to have a strategic impact.

At the firm level, information systems can be used to achieve new efficiencies or to enhance services by tying together the operations of disparate business units so that they can function as a whole or by promoting shared knowledge across business units. At the industry level, systems can promote competitive advantage by facilitating cooperation with other firms in the industry, creating consortiums or communities for sharing information, exchanging transactions, or coordinating activities. The competitive forces model and network economics are useful concepts for identifying strategic opportunities for systems at the industry level.

Not all strategic systems make a profit; they can be expensive and risky to build. Many strategic information systems are easily copied by other firms, so that strategic advantage is not always sustainable. Implementing strategic systems often requires extensive organizational change and a transition from one sociotechnical level to another. Such changes are called *strategic transitions* and are often difficult and painful to achieve.

6. *Explain why it is difficult for firms to sustain a competitive advantage.* While the risks and costs associated with achieving a competitive advantage can be formidable, the first mover advantages can enable a business to beat their competition. Once a competitive advantage is achieved, however, it is only rarely sustained. The competition determines how to copy the core competency that yields the competitive advantage, to do it even better and almost always more cheaply. The original firm must commit to strategic intent by constantly looking for additional ways to achieve a competitive advantage even when they already have that advantage.

7. *Compare global strategies for developing business.* There are four basic international strategies: domestic exporter, multinational, franchiser, and transnational. In a domestic exporter strategy, almost all operations and information systems are centralized in the headquarters' country. In a multinational strategy, foreign operations are managed locally and use their own local information systems with the exception of financial reporting applications and some telecommunications systems. In a franchiser strategy, the company duplicates its operations and information systems wherever it is located outside the headquarters' country. In a transnational strategy, all factors of production are coordinated on a global scale. However, the choice of strategy is a function of the type of business and product.

8. *Demonstrate how information systems support different global strategies.* There is a connection between firm strategy and information systems design. Domestic exporters typically are centralized in domestic headquarters with some decentralized operations permitted. Multinationals typically rely on decentralized independence among foreign units with some movement toward development of networks. Franchisers almost always duplicate systems across many countries and use centralized financial controls. Transnational firms must develop networked system configurations and permit considerable decentralization of development and operations.

KEY TERMS

Agency theory, 77

Behavioural models, 81

Bureaucracy, 71

Bureaucratic models of decision making, 85

Business driver, 98

Chief information officer (CIO), 76

Choice, 84

Classical model of management, 80

Cognitive style, 85

Competitive advantage, 86

Competitive forces model, 95

Competitive necessity, 90

Core competency, 94

Decisional roles, 82

Design, 84

Domestic exporter, 102

Efficient customer response system, 92

End users, 75

Focused differentiation, 90

Franchiser, 103

"Garbage can" model of decision making, 86

Implementation, 84

Information partnership, 94

Information systems department, 75

Information systems managers, 75

Informational roles, 82

Intelligence, 84

International information systems portfolio, 98

Interpersonal roles, 82

Intuitive decision makers, 85

Knowledge-level decision making, 83

Management control decision making, 83

Managerial roles, 82

Microeconomic model of the firm, 76

Multinational, 102

Network economics, 96

Operational control decision making, 83

Organization, 69

Organizational culture, 72

Organizational models of decision making, 85

Political models of decision making, 85

Primary activities, 87

Programmers, 75

Product differentiation, 89

Rational model of human behaviour, 85

Semi-structured decisions, 83

Standard operating procedures (SOPs), 71

Strategic decision making, 83

Strategic information systems, 86

Strategic intent, 98

Strategic transitions, 97

Structured decisions, 83

Support activities, 87

Switching costs, 92

Systematic decision makers, 85

Systems analysts, 75

Transaction cost theory, 76

Transnational, 103

Unstructured decisions, 83

Value chain model, 87

Value web, 88

REVIEW QUESTIONS

1. What is an organization? Compare the technical definition of an organization with the behavioural definition.

2. What features do all organizations have in common? In what ways can organizations differ?

3. How has information technology infrastructure in organizations evolved over time?

4. How are information technology services delivered in organizations? Describe the role played by programmers, systems analysts, information systems managers, and the chief information officer (CIO).

5. Describe the major economic theories that help explain how information systems affect organizations.

6. Describe the major behavioural theories that help explain how information systems affect organizations.

7. Why is there considerable organizational resistance to the introduction of information systems?

8. Compare the descriptions of managerial behaviour in the classical and behavioural models.

9. What specific managerial roles can information systems support? Where are information systems particularly strong when supporting managers, and where are they weak?

10. What are the four stages of decision making described by Simon?

11. Describe each of the organizational models of decision making. How would the design of systems be affected by the choice of model employed?

12. What is the impact of the Internet on organizations and the process of management?

13. What is a strategic information system? What is the difference between a strategic information system and a strategic-level system?

14. Describe appropriate models for analyzing strategy at the business level, and the types of strategies and infor-mation systems that can be used to compete at this level.

15. How can the competitive forces and network economics models be used to identify strategies at the industry level?

16. How can information systems support strategies at the firm and industry levels?

17. Why are strategic information systems difficult to implement?

18. How can managers find strategic applications for their firms?

19. Can competitive advantage be sustained over time? How?

20. How do the differences among various countries affect the development and implementation of information systems in multinational companies?

21. How does organizational structure in global organizations affect the type of information systems found in those organizations? Describe the relationship of each type of organizational structure to the information systems most commonly found in that type of organization.

GROUP PROJECT

With a group of three or four students, research a local business using annual reports, newspapers, or business publications, such as the *Financial Post*, *Canadian Business*, and the *Globe and Mail*. Visit the company's Web site to gain further insights into how they achieve a competitive advantage and how their information systems appear to their customers. Analyze the business and iden-tify what level or levels of strategy the firm is pursuing (business,

firm, or industry). Can you apply any of the models discussed in this chapter to what the company is doing? Analyze how the company is using information systems to pursue its strategy. Can you suggest additional strategic information systems for that business, including those that use the Internet? Is that business active in global markets? How does that change their strategy and/or structure? Present your findings to the class.

INTERNET CONNECTION

■ COMPANION WEBSITE

At www.pearsoned.ca/laudon, you'll find an online study guide with two quizzes to test your knowledge of information systems, organizations, management, and strategy. You'll also find updates to the chapter and online exercises and cases that enable you to apply your knowledge to realistic situations.

■ ADDITIONAL SITES OF INTEREST

There are many interesting Web sites to enhance your learning about these concepts. You can search the Web yourself, or just try the following sites to add to what you have already learned.

Harvard Business Review

www.hbr.com

A must-read for business majors. Includes articles on a variety of business issues, including strategic information systems.

Canadian Pacific Hotels

www.cphotels.ca

Canadian Pacific Hotels' Web site is a part of the Fairmont Hotels Web site and includes their Activity Planner. Using the Activity Planner, users can tell the Web site where they need a hotel room, what activities they would like to do while there, and what ameni-ties and facilities they would like to find there. The Web site will then post a screen giving detailed information on the hotel, nearby activities, and location.

Source Medical

www.sourcemedical.ca

The Canadian spinoff of Baxter Travenol's medical products dis-tribution operation is a well-organized Web site for the casual viewer. Source Medical's customers access part of their Web site that is not available to the general public to find out what they need to know about Canada's largest medical products distributor.

Assante Corporation

www.assante.com

How one Canadian financial firm presents itself to the world, with links to its customized local Web sites within the United States and other countries.

CASE STUDY   *The Air Canada/Canadian Airlines Merger: What Happens to the Frequent Flyer?*

Air Canada was already Canada's largest airline before it merged with Canadian Airlines. Air Canada wanted to be a truly world-class airline—in terms of market share, quality, and safety. Today the combined Air Canada carries 85% of Canadian passengers within Canada. When Air Canada took over Canadian Airlines in December 1999, Air Canada said that the two airlines would continue to operate separately for a short time while they planned how to integrate their operations, schedules, personnel, and information systems.

As Air Canada began to absorb Canadian Airlines, many observers felt that they forgot their customers—and most important, their frequent flyer customers. Air Canada's frequent flyer program is called Aeroplan; 3 800 000 individuals are members of Aeroplan. Aeroplan also has more than 50 partnerships in the hotel, car rental, financial services, and telecommunication sectors. Canadian Plus had slightly fewer members and partners, many of whom were different from those of Aeroplan. Integration of Aeroplan with Canadian Airlines' Canadian Plus frequent flyer program was originally scheduled for April 2000, at the same time they were to begin integrating the routes and schedules into one expanded network. At that same time, they were to introduce 32 new routes and 12 new destinations.

It turns out that integrating two different airlines is not as easy as it sounds! Simply turning a key and assuming that personnel from both former airlines can access information from both airlines and that the information systems and personnel will respond appropriately does not happen without a plan. The integration plan had been omitted from the merger plans! It took a while for the integration "problems" to begin cropping up.

Passengers who tried to check in for one airline at the other merged airline's counters were told they had to go to the counter for the other airline. Ticket agents at Canadian counters could not tag Air Canada passenger bags nor could they check them in for Air Canada flights. The Canadian ticket agents could not even access Air Canada schedules, including departure gate information, from their terminals. The same was true for Air Canada personnel. Passengers also found that customer service personnel for both airlines were not as friendly, helpful, or well informed as had previously been their reputation. For the first few months of the merger, the new Air Canada experienced a virtual torrent of consumer complaints about almost everything related to customer service.

There were thousands of consumer complaints about lost baggage, long check-in delays, cancelled flights, and cranky service at major airports. It turns out that if you displease a customer about one aspect of service, they will more readily identify and complain about other areas that are not perfect as well. Several months into the integration, airline customers were so dissatisfied with progress in integrating the systems that government agencies, Parliament, and the media talked about investigating Air Canada for failure to deliver what it had promised! Air Canada's problems made the newspapers, radio, and television and affected financial forecasts for the merged airline. Robert Milton, Air Canada's CEO, finally took out advertisements asking for 180 days to straighten everything out.

Milton took over as Air Canada's chief executive in 1999, but had been a senior executive with the airline since the mid-1990s. In August 2000, toward the beginning of the 180-day commitment, the Montreal-based airline announced record operating profits of U.S.$224 million, up U.S.$70 million from the previous year.

Milton said Air Canada would hire 2000 additional personnel and institute other measures to deal with bottlenecks and service disruptions caused by rapid growth and the takeover of Calgary-based Canadian Airlines. "We know what has to be done, and we're sparing no effort to achieve it," he told a news conference in Toronto. "It's also important we keep our customers informed every step of the way so we're going to be upfront about the improvements we're making and when."

While warning that "there is no quick fix or Band-Aid solution to this situation," Milton said most of the 2000 additional workers would be in customer service functions such as call centres, airports, and in-flight operations.

"Staffing is the key to improve customer service and end congestion," he said, striving to counter the massive complaints by travellers about service at Canada's dominant airline.

As part of Air Canada's "180-day commitment," changes to major terminals, such as Pearson Terminal in Toronto, were implemented, including kiosk check-in. Additional personnel were hired and trained to deal with the onslaught of customer activity and complaints. Integration was finally begun on merging the frequent flyer programs and information systems of the two airlines.

The most profitable customers for an airline are those passengers who fly the most miles and display customer loyalty by flying most of their miles with only one carrier. These are their frequent flyers. Among the most profitable customers are those who also purchase memberships to the VIP lounges airlines host at many airports. Air Canada and Canadian had separate VIP lounges. Both airlines also had priority check-in for certain of their most profitable customers, including tagging bags for priority status to come off the airplane first upon arrival. Both lounge memberships and priority baggage access could be earned with frequent flyer points/miles.

Many Canadians held both Canadian Plus and Aeroplan status and were interested in how the merger would affect their miles. Canadian Plus members were notified in January 2000 that Canadian Plus and Aeroplan members could earn points/miles on either airline, and three months later, could redeem their points/miles on either airline. In February, top-tier reciprocal lounge access and priority check-in was granted. Unfortunately, while the airlines' personnel agreed with passengers that the integration had "technically" taken place, gaining access to the lounges, using priority status, and redeeming points/miles was at best troublesome and frequently impossible.

In July, it was announced that by January 2001, Canadian Plus points would be fully converted to Aeroplan miles on a one-to-one basis, allowing passengers to combine their Aeroplan miles and Canadian Plus points.

Sources: "Air Canada To Hire 2000 Workers To Improve Customer Service," *CanoeMoney*, August 3, 2000, www.canoe.ca/AirMergers/aug3_aircanservice.html, accessed January 2001; "Status—Pearson Airport and Frequent Flyer Miles," *Rider Travel Corporation*, www.ridertbi.ca/News_And_Advisories/Pearson_Airport_Status.asp, accessed January 2001; Lisa S. Levstein, "Advantex To Form Internet Alliance For Online Shopping Portal With Air Canada," Advantex press release, February 10, 2000, www.advantex.com, accessed January 2001; "British Trade Body Clears Air Canada-Canadian Merger At Heathrow," *CanoeMoney*, August 31, 2000, www.canoe.ca/AirMergers/aug31_ukoksairmerger.html, accessed January 2001.

CASE STUDY QUESTIONS

1. Evaluate the Air Canada–Canadian merger using Porter's competitive forces model. How is competition at the business, firm, and industry levels affected by the merger?

2. How did the merger with Canadian Airlines fit in with Air Canada's strategy?

3. What steps might Air Canada have taken so that the "virtual torrent" of complaints did not materialize? Why did Air Canada not take these steps?

4. Air Canada targeted Pearson Airport for major operational changes. Why? What changes in information systems would these airport changes necessitate? Could information systems be used to help make these changes?

5. How could information systems be used to accomplish Milton's 180-day commitment to the Canadian flying public?

6. What do you think were the problems Air Canada experienced in attempting to integrate the information systems of two different, but similar airlines? How would you have overcome these problems?

7. What strategic information systems do you think most airlines already have? Can you think of others that would benefit one airline over another? Evaluate these systems in terms of the models and discussion in the chapter.

4

ELECTRONIC COMMERCE AND ELECTRONIC BUSINESS

OBJECTIVES

After completing this chapter, you will be able to:

1. *Explain how Internet technology has transformed organizations and business models.*

2. *Compare the categories of electronic commerce, and explain how electronic commerce is changing consumer retailing and business-to-business transactions.*

3. *Evaluate the principal electronic payment systems.*

4. *Demonstrate how Internet technology can support electronic business, supply chain management, and customer relationship management.*

5. *Assess the managerial and organizational challenges posed by electronic commerce and electronic business.*

6. *Explain Canadian trends in e-commerce.*

Electronic Commerce for Students: U-Swap.com

When Eduardo Mandri moved to Montreal from Mexico in the fall of '98 to earn his MBA at McGill University, he needed the usual gear a student requires—apartment, books, bed—and he had a hard time finding it. "All the ads were on different bulletin boards, and a lot of them were outdated. I thought: There must be a better way." At first, Mandri, who was a veteran of three business start-ups in Mexico, considered a store where students could resell their used goods, but then he realized "there's no reason for a shop if there's an Internet." So in May 1999, he recruited MBA classmate Allison Dent, who was experienced as an IT consultant, and together they created U-Swap, which is now the most popular interactive student classified ad Internet site in

Canada. At www.u-swap.com, students can buy or sell furniture, books, and bikes, find an apartment or a tutor, or hitch a ride home the holidays.

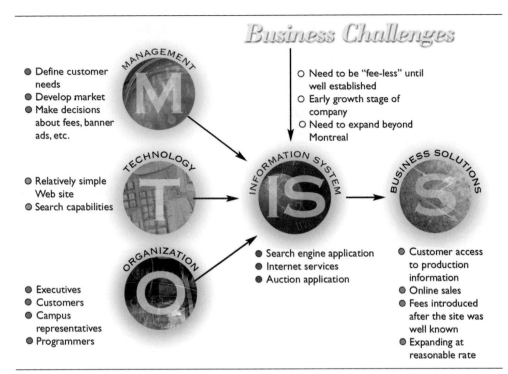

Business Challenges

MANAGEMENT
- Define customer needs
- Develop market
- Make decisions about fees, banner ads, etc.

TECHNOLOGY
- Relatively simple Web site
- Search capabilities

ORGANIZATION
- Executives
- Customers
- Campus representatives
- Programmers

- ○ Need to be "fee-less" until well established
- ○ Early growth stage of company
- ○ Need to expand beyond Montreal

INFORMATION SYSTEM
- Search engine application
- Internet services
- Auction application

BUSINESS SOLUTIONS
- Customer access to production information
- Online sales
- Fees introduced after the site was well known
- Expanding at reasonable rate

With the help of two McGill professors, Mandri and Dent did an online marketing study of 350 students to determine what form a classified-ad site for students should take. Although half the students said they would be willing to pay for ads, the U-Swap team decided to offer the service free to keep volume up. Revenue would come from banner ads, commissions on referrals to other sites, and strategic alliances. Student information, though, would be kept private. Not only would this policy protect students from unwanted advertising, it also would let them avoid giving out their e-mail address, phone number, or street address until they became comfortable with a buyer. This is especially popular with female students who don't want to post their phone number campus-wide just to sell a futon. The marketing study also told Mandri and Dent what classified categories to provide. Most popular are computer hardware, apartments, "catch a ride," textbooks, and tutors (at exam time). The wide variety of categories would make U-Swap useful year-round, unlike competitors that just sell textbooks.

With the programming expertise of Wojtek Banas of Montreal, Mandri and Dent added such features as a quick search of the entire site, for example, a search for a specific book title, automatic notification, which tells a shopper when an ad meeting their requirements is placed, and links to a range of shopping and information sites. After extensive testing by family and friends, U-Swap launched smoothly in September 1999. Student reaction was enthusiastic, Dent says. "People come up to us and say, 'I sold my computer in less than 24 hours.' Or 'I got 112 e-mails for my apartment.'"

By summer 2000, U-Swap had 7000 ad listings at 18 universities. Their listings have expanded to include furniture and appliances, sports equipment, motor vehicles, parties and events, and jobs. U-Swap has the largest user base in its market. There are many descriptive options when posting an item for sale, including posting a picture of the item when appropriate. In 2001, expansions were planned for a

(continued)

111

total of 75 institutions in Canada, the United States, Mexico, and France, all served from one site. U-Swap covers most of the major universities in Canada, including Concordia, McGill, Carleton, York, the University of Toronto, Queens, and the University of Ottawa. Interestingly, the site is not just for students. Anyone can post or purchase an item.

Advertisers can now pay $3–$5 for a bold heading or featured ad, or they can try an eBay-style auction for a small commission fee. U-Swap has added five undergraduates to its Montreal staff as well as part-time representatives at each of the 75 schools. Meanwhile, Mandri and Dent managed to graduate with honours in the spring of 2000 so they could dedicate themselves full-time to their burgeoning business. And if they need any used desk lamps for their growing office space, they'll know where to look.

Sources: "Students Shop Without a Store," *Information Strategy*, Winter 2000; "Students Put Online Commerce to Work in a Thriving Classified-Ad Site," Canadian Information Productivity Awards Web site, www.cipa.com/winners/small4_story.html, accessed April 30, 2001.

MANAGEMENT CHALLENGES

Like U-Swap.com, many companies are starting to use the Internet to communicate with both their customers and suppliers, creating new digital electronic commerce networks that bypass traditional distribution channels. Businesses like U-Swap.com take advantage of new business models that have emerged during the development of e-commerce. They are using Internet technology to streamline internal business processes as well. Digitally enabling business processes and relationships with other organizations and parties can help companies achieve new levels of competitiveness and efficiency, but it raises the following management challenges:

1. **Electronic commerce and electronic business require a complete change of mindset.** Digital firms require new organizational designs and management processes. To implement electronic commerce and electronic business successfully, companies must examine and perhaps redesign entire business processes rather than throwing new technology at existing business practices. Companies must consider a different organizational structure, changes in organizational culture, a different support structure for information systems, different procedures for managing employees and networked processing functions, and perhaps a different business strategy.

2. **Finding a successful Internet business model.** Companies have raced to put up Web sites in the hope of increasing earnings through electronic commerce. However, many if not most electronic commerce sites have yet to turn a profit or to make a tangible difference in sales and marketing efforts. Cost savings or access to new markets promised by the Web may not materialize. Companies need to think carefully about whether they can create a genuinely workable business model on the Internet and how the Internet relates to their overall business strategy.

Internet technology is creating a universal technology platform for buying and selling goods and for driving important business processes inside the firm. The Internet has inspired new ways of organizing and managing that are transforming businesses and the use of information systems in everyday life. Along with bringing many new benefits and opportunities, electronic commerce and electronic business have created a new set of management challenges. We describe these challenges so that organizations can understand the management, organization, and technology issues that must be addressed to benefit from electronic commerce, electronic business, and the emerging digital firm.

4.1 ELECTRONIC COMMERCE, ELECTRONIC BUSINESS, AND THE EMERGING DIGITAL FIRM

Throughout this edition we emphasize the benefits of integrating information across the enterprise, creating an information technology infrastructure where information can flow seamlessly from one part of the organization to another and from the organization to its customers, suppliers, and business partners. The emerging digital firm requires a high level of information integration, and companies increasingly depend on an integrated infrastructure to remain efficient and competitive. Internet technology has emerged as the key enabling technology for this digital integration.

INTERNET TECHNOLOGY AND THE DIGITAL FIRM

For a number of years, companies used proprietary or homegrown systems to integrate information from their internal systems and to link to their customers and trading partners. These systems were expensive and based on technology standards that only a few could follow. The Internet is rapidly becoming the infrastructure of choice for electronic commerce because it offers businesses a much easier way to link to other businesses and individuals at low cost. It provides a universal and easy-to-use set of technologies and technology standards that can be adopted by all organizations, no matter what computer system or information technology platform they are using and no matter what their size or capitalization.

Trading partners can communicate directly with each other, bypassing intermediaries and inefficient, multi-layered procedures. Web sites are available to consumers 24 hours a day. Some information-based products, such as software, music, and videos, can actually be electronically distributed via the Internet. Vendors of other types of products and services can use the Internet to distribute information about their products, such as pricing, availability, options, and delivery time. The Internet can replace existing distribution channels or extend them, creating outlets for attracting and serving customers who otherwise would not patronize the company. For example, Web-based discount brokerages have attracted new customers who do not want to pay the high commissions and fees charged by conventional brokerage and financial services firms.

Companies can use Internet technology to radically reduce their transaction costs. Chapter 3 introduced the concept of transaction costs, which include the costs of searching for buyers and sellers, collecting information on products, negotiating terms, writing and enforcing contracts, and transportation costs. Information on buyers, sellers, and prices for many products is immediately available on the Web. For example, manually processing a purchase order can cost $100 to $125, but purchasing goods over the Internet can reduce these costs by nearly 80 percent. Figure 4-1 provides other examples of transaction cost reductions from the Internet. Handling transactions electronically can reduce transaction costs and delivery time for some goods, especially those that are purely digital (such as software,

DISTRIBUTION SAVINGS ON E-GOODS IS DRAMATIC			
E-commerce Savings by Category			
	Traditional System	Internet	Percent Savings
Airline Tickets	$12	$1.50	87%
Banking	$1.62	$0.20	88%
Bill Payment	$3.33 – $4.80	$1 – $1.60	70% – 67%
Term Life-Insurance Policy	$600 – $1050	$300 – $525	50%
Software	$22	$0.30 – $0.70	97% – 99%

FIGURE 4-1 Internet technology can radically reduce transaction costs in many industries.

Source: "Distribution Savings on E-Goods is Dramatic," from "Spotlight: The Economic Impact of E-Commerce," *The Industry Standard,* May 15, 1999. Reprinted by permission.

text products, images, or videos) because these products can be distributed over the Internet as electronic versions.

Equally important, Internet technology provides the infrastructure for electronic business because its technology and technology standards can also be used to make information flow seamlessly from one part of the organization to another. Internet technology provides a much lower-cost and easier-to-use alternative for coordination activities than proprietary networks. Managers can use e-mail and other Internet communication capabilities to manage larger numbers of employees, to manage projects, and to coordinate the work of multiple teams working in different parts of the world. Internet standards can be used to link disparate systems, such as ordering and logistics tracking, that previously could not communicate with each other. The Internet also reduces other agency costs such as the cost to coordinate activities of the firm with suppliers and other external business partners. The low-cost connectivity and universal standards provided by Internet technology are the driving force behind the explosion of electronic business and the emergence of the digital firm.

NEW BUSINESS MODELS AND VALUE PROPOSITIONS

The Internet has introduced major changes in the way companies conduct business. It brings about a dramatic drop in the cost of creating, sending, and storing information while making that information more widely available. Millions of people can exchange massive amounts of information directly, instantly, and for free.

In the past, information about products and services was usually tightly bundled with the physical value chain for those products and services. If a consumer wanted to find out about the features, price, and availability of a refrigerator or an automobile, the consumer had to visit a "bricks and mortar" store that sold those products. The cost of comparison shopping was very high because people had to physically travel from store to store or telephone each store.

The Internet has changed that relationship. Once everyone is connected electronically, information about products and services can flow directly and instantly to consumers. The traditional link between the flow of the product and the flow of product-related information is broken. Information is not limited to traditional physical methods of delivery. Customers can find out about products on their own on the Web and buy directly from product suppliers instead of using intermediaries such as retail stores.

The unbundling of information from traditional value chain channels is having a disruptive effect on old business models and creating new business models as well. A **business model** describes how the enterprise delivers a product or service, showing how the enterprise creates wealth. Some of the traditional channels for exchanging product information have become unnecessary or less economical, and business models based on the coupling of information with products and services may no longer be necessary.

For example, before the Internet, people who wanted to purchase books had to go to a physical bookstore in order to learn what titles were available, the books' contents, and prices. The bookstore had a monopoly on this information. When Amazon.com opened as an online bookstore, it provided visitors to its Web site with a vast electronic catalogue containing close to three million titles, along with tables of contents, reviews, and other information about those titles. People could order books directly using their PCs. Amazon.com was able to sell books at lower cost because it did not have to pay rent, employee salaries, warehousing, and other overhead to maintain physical retail bookstores. Amazon had almost no inventory costs because it relied on book distributors to stock most of its books although today it does maintain an inventory. Traditional booksellers who maintained physical storefronts were threatened. Selling books and other goods directly to consumers online without using physical storefronts represents a new business model. Publishers such as FirstPrint and Armand Press are now challenging this business model by selling digital electronic books directly to consumers without any intermediaries at all.

Financial service business models underwent a similar revolution. In the past, people wishing to purchase stocks or bonds had to pay high commissions to full-service brokers such as Merrill Lynch. Individual investors relied on these firms both to execute their trading transactions and to provide them with investment information. It was difficult for individual

business model

An abstraction of how the enterprise delivers a product or service, showing how the enterprise creates wealth.

investors to obtain stock quotes, charts, investment news, historical data, investment advice, and other financial information on their own. This information can now be found in abundance on the Web, and investors can use financial Web sites to place their own trades directly for very small transaction fees. The unbundling of financial information from trading has sharply reduced the need for full-service retail brokers. Figure 4-2 shows the many services available at just one Canadian financial services provider.

The Changing Economics of Information

The Internet shrinks information asymmetry. An **information asymmetry** exists when one party in a transaction has more information that is important for the transaction than the other party. Possession of that information can determine their relative bargaining power. For example, until auto retailing sites appeared on the Web, there was a pronounced information asymmetry between auto dealers and customers. Only the auto dealers knew the manufacturers' prices, and it was difficult for consumers to shop around for the best price. Auto dealers' profit margins depended on this asymmetry of information. Now consumers have access to a legion of Web sites providing competitive pricing information, and many auto buyers use the Internet to shop around for the best deal. Thus the Web has reduced the information asymmetry surrounding an auto purchase. The Internet has also helped businesses seeking to purchase from other businesses reduce information asymmetries and locate better prices and terms.

Before the Internet, businesses had to make tradeoffs between the richness and reach of their information. **Richness** refers to the depth and detail of information—the amount of information the business can supply to the customer as well as information the business collects about the customer. **Reach** refers to how many people a business can connect with. Rich communication occurs, for example, when a sales representative meets with a customer, sharing information that is very specific to that interaction. Such an interaction is very expensive for a business because it can only take place with a small audience. Newspaper and television ads could reach millions of people quite inexpensively, but the information they provide is much more limited. It used to be prohibitively expensive for traditional businesses to have both richness and reach. Few if any companies could afford to provide highly detailed, cus-

information asymmetry
Situation where the relative bargaining power of two parties in a transaction is determined by one party in the transaction possessing more information essential to the transaction than the other party.

richness
A measurement of the depth and detail of information that a business can supply to the customer as well as information the business collects about the customer.

reach
A measurement of how many people a business can connect with and how many products it can offer those people.

FIGURE 4-3 The changing economics of information. In the past, companies have had to trade off between the richness and reach of their information. Internet connectivity and universal standards for information sharing radically reduce the cost of providing rich, detailed information to large numbers of people, reducing the trade-off.

Source: Philip B. Evans and Thomas Wurster, *Blown to Bits: How the New Economics of Information Transforms Strategy,* (Boston, MA: Harvard Business School Press, 2000), p. 31. Reprinted by permission.

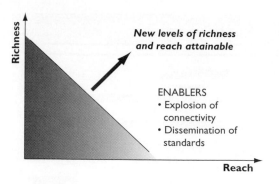

tomized information to a large mass audience. The Internet has transformed the richness and reach relationship (see Figure 4-3). Using the Internet and Web multimedia capabilities, companies can quickly and inexpensively provide detailed product information and detailed information specific to each customer to very large numbers of people simultaneously (Evans and Wurster, 2000).

Internet-enabled relationships between richness and rich are changing internal operations as well. Organizations can now exchange rich, detailed information among large numbers of people, making it easier for management to coordinate more jobs and tasks. In the past, management's span of control had to be much narrower because rich communication could only be channelled among a few people at a time using cumbersome, manual, paper-based processes. Digitally enabled business processes have become new sources of organizational efficiency, reducing operating costs while improving the accuracy and timeliness of customer service. For our purposes, we define electronic business as the digitizing of internal processes, primarily using intranets, e-mail, and other Web-based tools. Electronic commerce is defined as the digitizing of external processes, primarily using the Internet and its many capabilities.

Internet Business Models

The Internet can help companies create and capture profit in new ways by adding extra value to existing products and services or by providing the foundation for new products and services. Table 4-1 describes some of the most important Internet business models that have emerged. All in one way or another add value: They provide the customer with a new product or service; they provide additional information or service along with a traditional product or service; or they provide a product or service at much lower cost than traditional means.

Some of these new business models take advantage of the Internet's rich communication capabilities. eBay is an online auction forum, using e-mail and other interactive features of the Web. People can make online bids for items such as computer equipment, antiques and collectibles, wine, jewellery, rock-concert tickets, and electronics that are posted by sellers from around the world. The system accepts bids for items entered on the Internet, evaluates the bids, and notifies the highest bidder. eBay collects a small commission on each listing and sale. Keep in mind that not all items offered for auction are based in good ethics. People have tried to auction off human livers for transplantation on eBay as well fraudulent works of art.

Business-to-business auctions are proliferating as well. Bid.com in Toronto, which started out hosting consumer cyberauctions, now has Web-based auction services for business-to-business sales of items such as agricultural equipment. Many business-to-business sites have sprung up to help companies dispose of surplus inventory. Online bidding is expected to grow rapidly, representing as much as 40 percent of total online transactions by 2004, because buyers and sellers can interact so easily through the Internet to determine what an item is worth at any particular moment (Dalton, 1999).

The Internet has created online communities, where people with similar interests can exchange ideas from many different locations. Some of these virtual communities provide the foundation for new businesses. Tripod, Lupus Online (an Italian site for owners of German shepherd dogs), and FortuneCity (which started out in the United Kingdom and whose CEO, Peter Macnee, received his bachelor's degree from the University of Western Ontario) provide communities for people wishing to communicate with others about arts, careers, health and fitness, sports, business, travel, and many other interests (see Figure 4-4). Members can post their own personal Web pages, participate in online discussion groups, and join online "clubs" with other like-minded people. Revenue for these communities comes mostly from providing ways for corporate clients to target customers, including the placement of banner ads on their Web sites. A **banner ad** is a graphic display on a Web page

banner ad
A graphic display on a Web page used for advertising. The banner is linked to the advertiser's Web site so that a person clicking on it will be transported to the advertiser's Web site.

TABLE 4-1 INTERNET BUSINESS MODELS

Category	Description	Examples
Virtual Storefront	Sells physical goods or services online instead of through a physical storefront or retail outlet. Delivery of non-digital goods and services takes place through traditional means.	Amazon.com Norstarmall Ubiquityfinancial
Marketplace Concentrator	Concentrates information about products and services from multiple providers at one central point. Purchasers can search, comparison-shop, and sometimes complete the sales transaction.	DealerNet Canadashop
Online Exchange	A bid-ask system where multiple buyers can purchase from multiple sellers.	U-Swap.com Procuron Autotrader Covisint
Information Broker	Provides product, pricing, and availability information. Some facilitate transactions, but their main value is the information they provide.	XE.com, The Universal Currency Converter Travelocity BayStreet.ca
Transaction Broker	Buyers can view rates and terms, but the primary business activity is completing the transaction.	E*Trade AccessToyota TDWaterhouse
Auction	Provides an electronic clearinghouse for products where price and availability are constantly changing, sometimes in response to customer actions.	eBay Auction4IT WeShopCanada
Reverse Auction	Consumers submit a bid to multiple sellers to buy goods or services at a buyer-specified price.	Priceline ICGcommerce Yourprice
Aggregator	Groups of people who want to purchase a particular product sign up and then seek a volume discount from vendors.	Buyers Accompany WHNX
Digital Product Delivery	Sells and delivers software, multimedia, and other digital products over the Internet.	1st-spot.net National Air Photo Library of Canada CompuSmart.com
Content Provider	Creates revenue by providing content. The customer may pay to access the content, or revenue may be generated by selling advertising space or by having advertisers pay for placement in an organized listing in a searchable database.	Financial Post BayStreet.ca[1] Yahoo.ca Canada.com
Online Service Provider	Provides service and support for hardware and software users.	Global Dental Archive by Bytedental PCSupport @Backup
Virtual Community	Provides an online meeting place where people with similar interests can communicate and find useful information.	Kidshelp.simpatico Lupus Online & Virtual Community FROGnet for French speaking researchers in non-French speaking countries FortuneCity Tripod
Portal	Provides an initial point of entry to the Web along with specialized content and other services.	Yahoo.ca UNIServe
Syndicator	Aggregates content or applications from multiple sources and resells them to other companies.	Sportsline Screaming Media Yournews
Virtual desktop	Provides online calendars, calculators, address books, word processing, and other office productivity software.	Hotmail MyPalm

[1] Some Web sites fall into more than one category, such as BayStreet.ca.

used for advertising. The banner is linked to the advertiser's Web site so that a person clicking on the banner will be transferred to a Web page with more information about the advertiser.

Even traditional retailing businesses are enhancing their Web sites with chat rooms, message boards, and community building features as a means of encouraging customers to spend more time, return more frequently, and hopefully make more purchases online. For example, iGo (www.iGo.com), a Web site selling mobile computing technology, found that its average sale increased by more than 50 percent after it added the ability to communicate interactively online with customer service representatives (Bannan, 2000).

The Web's information resources are so vast and rich that special business models called **portals** have emerged to help individual and organizations locate information more efficiently. A portal is a Web site or other service that provides an initial point of entry to the Web or to internal company data. Yahoo! is an example. It provides a directory of information on the Internet along with news, sports, weather, telephone directories, maps, games, shopping, e-mail, and other services. Yahoo! also has a Canadian portal that offers exclusively Canadian content. There are also specialized portals to help users with specific interests. For example, Barrabes (www.barrabes.com) is a bilingual portal for mountaineering and snow sports featuring weather reports, ski trail reports, a magazine, expert reviews, advice, instruction, and online shopping for 14 000 items of skiing and mountaineering gear. (Companies are also building their own internal portals to provide employees with streamlined access to corporate information resources—see Chapter 15.)

Yahoo! and other portals and Web content sites often combine content and applications from many different sources and service providers. Other Internet business models use syndication as well to provide additional value. For example, E*Trade, the discount Web trading site, purchases most of its content from external sources such as Reuters (news), Bridge Information Systems (quotes), and BidCharts.com (charts). Companies can also purchase electronic commerce services such as shopping cart ordering and payment systems from syndicators to use on their Web sites. Online **syndicators** who aggregate content or applications from multiple sources, package them for distribution, and resell them to third-party Web sites, are emerging as another new Internet business model (Werbach, 2000). The Web makes it much easier for companies to provide these information-based services.

Chapter 7 describes Application Service Providers (ASPs) that provide software that runs over the Web. *Virtual desktop* services that provide online calendars, calculators, address books, word processing, and other office productivity software, as well as facilities to store users' data on remote computers are proliferating.

Most of the business models described in Table 4-1 are called **pure-play** business models because they are based purely on the Internet. These firms did not have an existing bricks-and-mortar business when they designed their Internet business. However, many existing

portal

A Web site or other service that provides an initial point of entry to the Web or to internal company data.

syndicator

A business that aggregates content or applications from multiple sources, packages them for distribution, and resells them to third-party Web sites.

pure-play

Businesses that are based solely on the Internet.

FIGURE 4-4 Fortune City is an Internet business based on online communities for people sharing similar interests, such as sports, health, or music. The company generates revenue from advertising banners on its Web pages.

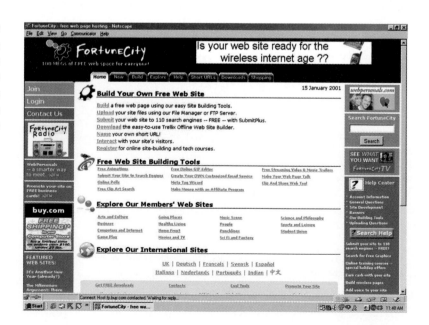

retail firms such as The Bay, Canadian Tire, and the *Wall Street Journal* have developed Web sites as extensions of their traditional bricks-and-mortar businesses. These businesses represent a hybrid **clicks-and-mortar** business model.

4.2 ELECTRONIC COMMERCE

Although most commercial transactions still take place through conventional channels, rising numbers of consumers and businesses are using the Internet for electronic commerce. Projections show that by 2004, over 640 million people, representing 14 percent of the world's population, will be active Internet users and total e-commerce spending could reach $4.5 to $6 trillion.

CATEGORIES OF ELECTRONIC COMMERCE

There are many ways in which electronic commerce transactions can be classified. One is by looking at the nature of the participants in the electronic commerce transaction. The three major electronic commerce categories are business-to-consumer (B2C), business-to-business (B2B), and consumer-to-consumer (C2C).

▌ **Business-to-consumer (B2C) electronic commerce** involves retailing products and services to individual shoppers. Indigo.ca, which sells books, gifts, flowers, and music to individual consumers, is an example of B2C e-commerce.

▌ **Business-to-business (B2B) electronic commerce** involves sales of goods and services among businesses. Merx, the flagship service of the Bank of Montreal's e-commerce subsidiary, Toronto-based Cebra Inc., has changed the shopping habits of the federal and provincial governments and hundreds of municipalities, academic institutions, schools and hospitals through B2B e-commerce.

▌ **Consumer-to-consumer (C2C) electronic commerce** involves consumers selling directly to consumers. For example, eBay, the giant Web auction site, allows people to sell their goods to other consumers by auctioning them off to the highest bidder.

Another way of classifying electronic commerce transactions is in terms of the participants' physical connection to the Web. Until recently, almost all e-commerce transactions took place over wired networks. Now cell phones and other wireless handheld digital appliances are Internet enabled so that they can be used to send e-mail or access Web sites. Companies are rushing to offer new sets of Web-based products and services that can be accessed by these wireless devices. For example, in Britain, customers of Virgin Mobile can use their cell phones to browse Virgin's Web site and purchase compact discs, wine, TV sets, and washing machines. Subscribers to Japan's NTT DoCoMo Internet cell phone service can send and receive e-mail and tap into online news, purchase airplane tickets, trade stocks, and browse through restaurant guides, linking to Web sites that have been redesigned to fit on tiny screens. The use of handheld wireless devices for purchasing goods and services has been termed **mobile commerce** or **m-commerce**. Chapter 10 discusses m-commerce and wireless Web technology in detail.

CUSTOMER-CENTRED RETAILING

The Internet provides companies with new channels of communication and interaction that can create closer yet more cost-effective relationships with customers in sales, marketing, and customer support. Companies can use the Web to provide ongoing information, service, and support, creating positive interactions with customers that can serve as the foundation for long-term relationships and repeat purchases.

Direct Sales over the Web

Manufacturers can sell their products and services directly to retail customers, bypassing intermediaries such as distributors or retail outlets. Eliminating intermediaries in the distribution channel can significantly lower purchase transaction costs. Operators of virtual storefronts

clicks-and-mortar
A business model where the Web site is an extension of a traditional bricks-and-mortar business.

business-to-consumer electronic commerce (B2C)
Electronic retailing of products and services directly to individual consumers.

business-to-business electronic commerce (B2B)
Electronic sales of goods and services among businesses.

consumer-to-consumer electronic commerce (C2C)
Consumers selling goods and services electronically to other consumers.

mobile commerce (m-commerce)
The use of wireless devices such as cell phones or handheld digital information appliances to conduct e-commerce transactions over the Internet.

such as Indigo.ca or Pickupngo.com do not have expenditures for rent, sales staff, and the other operations associated with a traditional retail store. Airlines can sell tickets directly to passengers through their own Web sites or through travel sites such as Travelocity.ca without paying commissions to travel agents.

To pay for all the steps in a traditional distribution channel, a product may have to be priced as high as 135 percent of its original cost to manufacture (Mougayar, 1998). Figure 4-5 illustrates the savings that can result from eliminating each of these layers in the distribution process. By selling directly to consumers or reducing the number of intermediaries, companies should be able to achieve higher profits while charging lower prices. The removal of organizations or business process layers responsible for intermediary steps in a value chain is called **disintermediation**.

The Internet accelerates disintermediation in some industries and creates opportunities for new types of intermediaries in others. In certain industries, distributors with warehouses of goods or intermediaries such as real estate agents may be replaced by new intermediaries or "infomediaries" specializing in helping Internet users efficiently obtain product and price information, locate online sources of goods and services, or manage/maximize the value of the information captured in electronic commerce transactions (Hagel III and Singer, 1999). The information brokers listed in Table 4-1 are examples. The process of shifting the intermediary function in a value chain to a new source is called **reintermediation**.

Interactive Marketing and Personalization

Marketers can use the interactive features of Web pages to hold consumers' attention or to capture detailed information about their tastes and interests for one-to-one marketing (see Chapter 3). Web sites have become a bountiful source of detailed information about customer behaviour, preferences, needs, and buying patterns that companies can use to tailor their promotions, products, services, and pricing. Some customer information may be obtained by asking visitors to "register" online and provide information about themselves, but many companies also collect customer information by using software that tracks the activities of Web site visitors. Companies can use special Web site auditing software capable of tracking the number of times visitors request Web pages, the Web pages of greatest interest to visitors after they have entered their sites, and the path visitors followed as they clicked from Web page to Web page. They can analyze this information about customer interests and behaviour to develop more precise profiles of existing and potential customers, and to maximize the effectiveness of their Web site design and content.

For instance, TravelWeb, a Web site offering electronic information and online reservations for more than 16 000 hotels in 138 countries, learns about customer preferences by tracking the origin of each user and the screens and hypertext links the user accesses. The Hyatt hotel chain found that Japanese users are most interested in the resort's golf facilities, which was valuable information in shaping market strategies and for developing hospitality-related products.

Communications and product offerings can be tailored precisely to individual customers (Bakos, 1998). Generic Web sites that force users to wade through options and content that

disintermediation

The removal of organizations or business process layers responsible for certain intermediary steps in a value chain.

reintermediation

The shifting of the intermediary role in a value chain to a new source.

FIGURE 4-5 The benefits of disintermediation to the consumer. The typical distribution channel has several intermediary layers, each of which adds to the final cost of a product, such as a sweater. Removing layers lowers the final cost to the consumer.

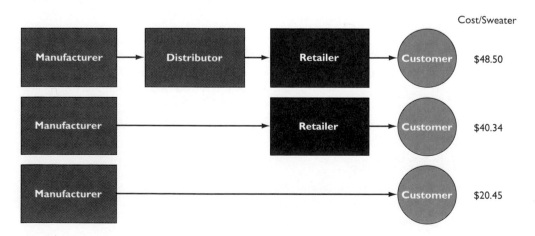

MANAGEMENT DECISION PROBLEM

MEASURING THE EFFECTIVENESS OF WEB ADVERTISING

You head an Internet company called Baby Boomers Online, which features articles of interest to people aged 40 to 60 on subjects such as travel, discount shopping, health, and financial planning, with links to Web sites selling related products and services. Your revenue comes from banner ads that other companies place on your Web site for a fee. You would like to generate more revenue by raising your advertising rates. You can do this by increasing the quantity and quality of visitors to your site to justify charging more for ads placed there. One way to measure the success of ads placed on a Web site is by measuring the *click-through rate*, which is the percentage of ads that Web visitors view on a Web page and then click on to explore. Software on the computer running your Web site provided the following weekly report.

1. Calculate the click-through rate (expressed as a percentage) for each ad by dividing the number of ad clicks by the number of ad views. *Ad clicks* are the number of times a visitor clicks on a banner ad to access the advertiser's Web site. *Ad views* are the number of times visitors call up a page with a banner during a specific time period, such as a day or a week. Rank order the ads with the highest click-through rates.

2. What categories of ads are the most successful at your Web site? least successful? Using this information, what kinds of companies should you solicit as advertisers on your site?

3. According to industry news sources, more than 27 percent of the visitors to the Travelocity international Web site were 50 or older as were over 31 percent of the visitors to Priceline.com, which offers discount airline tickets. How can you use this information to increase click-throughs and revenues at your own Web site?

Web Usage Report for the Week Ending February 16, 2001

Ad Title	Ad Views	Ad Clicks	Click-Through Rate (%)
Soy Foods and Vitamins	321	19	
Budget Trips Inc.	674	228	
Budget Books Online	79	5	
No-Frills Getaways	945	311	
Computers for Less	118	5	
Boomer Financial Planners Inc.	63	16	

---

are irrelevant to them are considered frustrating, but firms can create unique personalized Web sites that display content or ads for products or services of special interest to each user, improving the customer's experience and creating additional value (see Figure 4-6). By using **Web personalization** technology to modify the Web pages presented to each customer, marketers can achieve the benefits of using individual salespeople at dramatically lower costs.

Personalization can also help firms form lasting relationships with customers by providing individualized content, information, and services. Here are some examples:

- Amazon.com retains information on each customer's purchases. When a customer returns to the Amazon.com Web site, that person will be greeted with a Web page recommending books based on that person's purchase history or past purchases of other buyers with similar histories.

- Air Canada is using personalization to reduce its cost structure by encouraging customers to manage their frequent flyer accounts and purchase tickets through its Web site instead of from a travel agent. Air Canada e-mails a weekly Websaver bulletin with discounted fares for the week.

Web personalization
Tailoring Web content directly to a specific user.

FIGURE 4-6 Firms can create unique personalized Web sites that display content or ads for products or services of special interest to each user, improving the customer's experience and creating additional value.

FIGURE 4-7 Web site personalization. Web sites can tailor their content to the specific interests of their visitors or permit their visitors to customize the content themselves.

▋ Dell Computers' Canadian Web site allows users to create their own personal "Dell sites" where Dell can offer them special prices and deals based on the information they provide about their interests and computing requirements. Users can buy exactly what they want without having to call a representative, hunt down the products available, and try to work out deals.

Many other Web sites are using personalization technologies to deliver Web pages with content and banner ads geared to the specific interests of the visitor (see Figure 4-7). Chapters 10 and 14 describe additional technologies that gather information on Web site visitors to make such personalized advertising and customer interaction possible. They also describe how companies are trying to combine Web visitor data with customer data from other sources such as off-line purchases, customer service records, or product registrations to create detailed profiles of individuals. Critics worry that companies gathering so much personal information on Web site visitors pose a threat to individual privacy, especially when so much of this information is gathered without the customer's knowledge. Chapter 12 provides a detailed discussion of Web site privacy issues raised by these practices while Chapter 5 discusses the international differences in privacy issues and laws.

The cost of customer surveys and focus groups is very high. Learning how customers feel or what they think about one's products or services through electronic visits to Web sites is much cheaper. Web sites providing product information also lower costs by shortening the sales cycle and reducing the amount of time sales staff must spend on customer education. The Web shifts more marketing and selling activities to the customer as customers fill out their own online order forms. By using the Web to provide vendors with more precise information about their preferences and suggestions for improving products and services, customers are being transformed from passive buyers to active participants in creating value (Prahalad and Ramaswamy, 2000).

M-Commerce and Next Generation Marketing

Within the next few years, the Web will be accessible from almost anywhere as consumers turn to wireless telephones, handheld digital appliances, interactive television, and other information appliances to link to the Internet. Chapter 10 will discuss m-commerce and new wireless Internet devices in greater detail. Travellers will be able to access the Internet in automobiles, airports, hotels, and train stations. Mobile commerce will provide businesses with additional channels for reaching customers and with new opportunities for personalization. Location tracking software in some of these devices will enable businesses to track users' movements and supply information, advertisements, and other services while they are on the go, such as local weather reports or directions to the nearest restaurant. Instead of focusing on how to bring a customer to a Web site, marketing strategies will shift to finding ways of bringing the message directly to the customer at the point of need (Kenny and Marshall, 2000). Figure 4-8 illustrates how personalization can be extended via the ubiquitous Internet and m-commerce.

Customer Self-Service

The Web and other network technologies are inspiring new approaches to customer service and support. Many companies are using their Web sites and e-mail to answer customer questions or to provide customers with helpful information. The Web provides a medium through which customers can interact with the company, at their convenience, and find information on their own that previously required a human customer-support representative. Automated self-service or other Web-based responses to customer questions, such as *frequently asked question (FAQ)* pages, cost one-tenth the price of using a live customer service representative on the telephone.

Companies are realizing substantial cost savings from Web-based customer self-service applications. Air Canada, WestJet, and other major airlines have created Web sites where customers can review flight departure and arrival times, seating charts, and airport logistics, check frequent-flyer miles, and purchase tickets online. Microsoft has reduced customer calls concerning questions or problems by allowing customers to access technical solutions information from the service and support area of its Web site. If they can't find answers on their own, they can send e-mail to a live technician. Chapter 1 described how customers of UPS can use its Web site to track shipments, calculate shipping costs, determine time in transit, and arrange for a package pickup. FedEx and other package delivery firms provide similar Web-based services.

New products are even integrating the Web with customer call centres where customer service problems have been traditionally handled over the telephone. A **call centre** is an organizational department responsible for handling customer service issues by telephone and

call centre
An organizational department responsible for handling customer service issues by telephone and other channels.

Target	Platform	When	Content and Service
Traveller	Computer-equipped car 	Whenever car is moving	Provide maps, driving directions, weather reports, ads for nearby restaurants and hotels.
Parent	Cell phone 	During school days	Notify about school-related closings: Hello, Caroline. Your children's school is closing early. Press 1 for closure reason Press 2 for weather reports Press 3 for traffic reports
Stock Broker	Pager 	During trading days. Notify if unusually high trading volume.	Summary portfolio analysis showing changes in positions for each holding.

FIGURE 4-8 Customer personalization with the ubiquitous Internet. Companies can use mobile wireless devices to deliver new value-added services directly to customers at any time and place, extending personalization and deepening their relationship.

other channels. For example, visitors can click on a "push to talk" link on the e-Trade Canada Web site that uses voice-over IP to connect users with customer service representatives. NBTel is using LiveContact software from Toronto's Balisoft to link customers and call centres via text, voice chat, or multimedia. Vancouver-based Uniglobe.com uses an online chat function to enable potential customers to chat in real time with one of 75 cruise travel specialists; Uniglobe.com also promises to respond to e-mail questions within 20 minutes.

BUSINESS-TO-BUSINESS ELECTRONIC COMMERCE: NEW EFFICIENCIES AND RELATIONSHIPS

The fastest growing area of electronic commerce is not retailing to individuals but the automation of purchase and sale transactions between businesses. Some analysts estimate that B2B transactions represent 80 percent of all e-commerce transactions and could represent as much as 87 percent by 2004. That year worldwide B2B e-commerce revenues are expected to reach nearly $2.8 trillion. For a number of years, companies have used proprietary electronic data interchange (EDI) systems for this purpose; now they are turning to the Web and Internet technology. By eliminating inefficient paper-based processes for locating suppliers, ordering supplies, and delivering goods, and by providing more opportunities for finding the lowest-priced products and services, business-to-business Web sites like Bellzinc.ca can save participants anywhere from 5 percent to 45 percent. B2B commerce can also reduce errors in commerce-related documents from 20 percent to less than 1 percent (Keen, 2000).

Corporate purchasing traditionally has been based on long-term relationships with one or two suppliers. The Internet makes information about alternative suppliers more accessible so that companies can find the best deal from a wide range of sources, including those overseas. A purchasing manager might consult the Web when he or she needs to buy from an unfamiliar supplier or locate a new type of part. Identifying and researching potential trading partners is one of the most popular procurement activities on the Internet. Suppliers themselves can use the Web to research competitors' prices online. Organizations also can use the Web to solicit bids from suppliers online. Table 4-2 describes some examples of business-to-business electronic commerce.

TABLE 4-2	EXAMPLES OF BUSINESS-TO-BUSINESS ELECTRONIC COMMERCE
Business	**Electronic Commerce Application**
Cebra, Inc. (a division of the Bank of Montreal)	Operates MERX, Canada's official electronic tendering service. With 1500 open tender opportunities on any given day, MERX connects together a community of over 50 000 businesses and government purchasers.
Hydro One	Uses the Ariba Dynamic Trade system to hold secure, Web-based reverse auctions with selected suppliers of equipment and construction material, allowing suppliers to bid online, see the bids of other participants but not their names, and make multiple competing bids. Hydro One has enjoyed substantial savings resulting from lower purchase prices and reduced processing costs. Their suppliers benefit from the paperless bidding process and shorter transaction cycle.
Empori	Operates an electronic marketplace that sells goods from 21 consumer retailers and a dozen B2B vendors. Empori fulfills orders placed at its site through depots in downtown office buildings in Toronto and Western Canada. Empori also delivers directly to businesses.
Procuron	A national e-procurement site founded by Bell Canada, CIBC, Scotiabank, and Mouvement des caisses Desjardins. Procuron offers business products such as office supplies, equipment, and furniture, computer hardware, and accessories. The company will also soon offer business services such as travel, personnel, promotional items, and courier services.
General Electric Information Services	Operates a Trading Process Network (TPN) where GE and other subscribing companies can solicit and accept bids from selected suppliers over the Internet. TPN is a secure Web site developed for internal GE use that now is available to other companies for customized bidding and automated purchasing. GE earns revenue by charging subscribers for the service and by collecting a fee from the seller if a transaction is completed.

For business-to-business electronic commerce, companies can use their own Web sites, like Alliant Exchange (www.alliantexchange.com), a large U.S. food distribution company, or they can conduct sales through Web sites set up as online marketplaces. Online marketplaces, also termed *electronic hubs* or *e-hubs,* represent some of the new Internet business models we introduced earlier in this chapter. Using online marketplaces, companies can connect to many buyers without having to create point-to-point connections to each and can potentially find new customers. Many marketplaces have capabilities for integrating product information stored in disparate vendor systems. Companies purchasing products don't have to manage four or five different systems for buying from various suppliers and can save money by comparing prices and purchasing from a wider range of companies (Dalton, 1999).

One type of online marketplace or e-hub called an exchange has attracted special interest because so many businesses are turning to Internet exchanges to automate their purchases and sales. **Exchanges** are online marketplaces where multiple buyers can purchase from multiple sellers using a bid-ask system (see Figure 4-9). E-Steel (www.esteel.com) is an example. Buyers log in and create inquiries, specifying details, terms, and suppliers for the steel they wish to purchase. Suppliers respond with specifications for their wares. Buyers can also search for certain types of steel, offer bids, and negotiate online with suppliers.

There are several categories of exchanges (see Figure 4-10). *Vertical exchanges,* also known as *industry exchanges*, are set up to service specific industries such as automobiles, forest products, or energy. Vertical exchanges are available for many industries including chemicals and plastics, metals, machine tools, energy, telecommunication capacity, paper products, agriculture, and loans and mortgage products. PMmarketplace is a vertical exchange for the Canadian commercial real estate/property manager industry.

Horizontal exchanges focus on specific functions that can be found in many different industries, such as purchasing office equipment or maintenance, human resources, repair, and operating supplies. Actijob.com is an international job exchange headquartered in Laval, Quebec, to assist businesses in filling job vacancies. Companies can also create their own private exchanges called *branded exchanges*, in order to add value for customers by providing marketplace services. For example, Cable & Wireless Hong Kong Telecom (CWHKT), a full-service communications provider, created an exchange for the Greater China region. Now known as Pacific Century Cyberworks, the exchange provides services for increasing purchasing and supply chain efficiencies for a broad range of industries.

By enabling buyers and sellers to share information about supply, demand, and production, exchanges can sharply reduce inefficiencies among all the participants in the supply chain—suppliers, manufacturers, distributors, logistics companies, even billing companies. Exchanges are proliferating, but analysts believe that many cannot be sustained. Many exchanges were built to serve the same industry, and not all of them can survive. Exchanges facilitate competitive bidding among many suppliers to provide purchasers with the lowest price. Suppliers may be reluctant to participate in exchanges if their profit margins erode. Moreover, companies, especially those with lean production systems, must consider timing of deliveries, customization, and other factors besides price when making purchases. Most B2B exchanges support relatively simple transactions that cannot address these complexities (Wise and Morrison, 2000). The Window on Organizations explores some of the challenges facing exchanges as they struggle to become sustainable businesses.

exchange
A type of online marketplace where multiple buyers can purchase from multiple sellers using a bid-ask system.

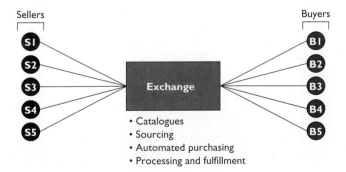

FIGURE 4-9 Exchanges are online marketplaces where multiple buyers can purchase from multiple sellers using a bid-ask system.

FIGURE 4-10 Bellzinc uses an *e-tendering* system where small- and medium-sized business buyers can use an online request-for-proposal service to obtain products and services.

ELECTRONIC COMMERCE PAYMENT SYSTEMS

electronic payment system
The use of digital technologies such as electronic funds transfer, credit cards, smart cards, debit cards, and Internet-based payment systems to pay for products and services electronically.

Special **electronic payment systems** have been developed to handle ways of paying for goods electronically on the Internet. Electronic payment systems on the Internet include systems for credit card payments, digital cash, electronic wallets, electronic cheques, and electronic billing systems.

The more sophisticated electronic commerce software (see Chapter 10) has capabilities for processing credit card purchases on the Web. Businesses can also contract with services such as PC Authorize, WebAuthorize, Qunara, and IC Verify to process their credit card transactions. These services accept merchant transactions containing customer credit card information, authenticate the credit card to make sure that it is valid and that funds are available, and arrange for the bank that issued the credit card to deposit money for the amount of the purchase in the merchant's bank account. Chapter 12 describes the technologies for secure credit card processing in more detail.

digital wallet
An application that stores credit card, electronic cash, and owner identification information and identifies that information at an electronic commerce site's checkout counter.

Digital wallets make paying for purchases over the Web more efficient by eliminating the need for shoppers to repeatedly enter their address and credit card information each time they buy something. A **digital wallet** stores credit card, electronic cash, and owner identification information and provides that information at an electronic commerce site's "checkout counter" (see Figure 4-11). The electronic wallet enters the shopper's name, credit card number, and shipping information automatically when invoked to complete the purchase. Amazon.com's 1-Click shopping, which enables a consumer to automatically fill in shipping and credit card information by clicking one button, uses electronic wallet technology. Digital wallet systems include Microsoft Passport, Securelynx, Gator, and America Online's Quick Checkout (which is accepted at many different electronic commerce sites).

micropayment
Payment for a very small sum of money, often $1.00 or less

electronic cash (e-cash)
Currency represented in electronic form that moves outside the normal network of money (paper currency, coins, cheques, and credit cards).

Micropayment systems have been developed for purchases of less than $10 that would be too small for conventional credit card payments. If one needed to pay an Internet service $1.50 to search for a specific piece of information or several dollars to reprint an article, electronic cash or smart cards would be useful for this purpose. **Electronic cash** or **e-cash** (also known as digital cash) is currency represented in electronic form that is moving outside the

CAN COVISINT SUCCEED AS AN AUTO INDUSTRY EXCHANGE?

On February 25, 2000, General Motors, Ford, and Daimler-Chrysler announced the formation of a new automotive industry business-to-business trading exchange called Covisint. The three rivals agreed to work cooperatively on this exchange to squeeze excess costs out of the process of purchasing of auto parts. (General Motors and Ford together spend about $375 billion a year on purchasing of raw materials and components.) Lower prices could be achieved by requiring suppliers to bid for orders over the Covisint Web site, which would reduce the cost of each purchase order transaction by reducing administrative costs. Covisint is expected to reduce the transaction cost of each purchase order from $150 to $15 or $20. Covisint includes an analysis tool to help the manufacturers weigh competing bids from suppliers using attributes such as quality, price, and delivery date. The automobile producers believe they will save billions every year, trimming costs by $1800 to $4500 per car. The rival automakers believe they could realize additional savings by sharing one common industry exchange rather than bearing the costs of setting up their own exchanges. Covisint could also provide savings to suppliers by providing a low-cost point of entry for trading with manufacturers. Covisint is controlled by the Big Three automobile manufacturers (later joined by Renault and Nissan Motors) and two companies supplying the software to power the Web site—Oracle, which is Ford's software teammate, and Commerce One, which has partnered with General Motors.

Covisint has been controversial from the beginning. Many observers and analysts doubt that it can ever succeed. The United States Federal Trade Commission (FTC) started investigating whether the giant automobile manufacturers were using Covisint to control parts prices. The two giant software vendors have been squabbling over specifications. The main reason for skepticism has probably been the lack of participation by most of the approximately 40 000 auto industry suppliers. Covisint's board is made up only of representatives of the automobile producers and so excludes parts suppliers. Eventually, Covisint did agree to the formation of a Customer Advisory Council of suppliers that will have some input into decisions.

Another issue is that many of the about 8000 first-tier suppliers (those who sell directly to the automobile companies) had already built their own private exchanges to be used with their lower-tier suppliers. Covisint has now assured these suppliers that Covisint is being designed to enable the suppliers to use their own exchanges in conjunction with Covisint. Another concern of the suppliers is that Covisint could impose high transaction fees. (As of this writing, that issue has not been resolved.) The suppliers also fear their products will become commodities, that they will lose the benefit of loyalty to their brands. The reaction of Covisint is that suppliers will be given the opportunity to build their own company-branded portals on the site. Yet another problem is the lack of communication; thousands of suppliers have been left with little or no information on Covisint. One advantage seen by the smaller suppliers is that Covisint will enable them to participate in e-commerce; previously, more than 60 percent of them could not afford their own electronic networks.

On September 12, 2000, the FTC announced the end of its Covisint investigation, enabling the exchange to proceed. The approval was tentative, however, because, according to the U.S. FTC, Covisint was not yet in operation and did not even have bylaws or operating rules. The FTC announced they would monitor its operation because "the founders represent such a large share of the automobile market, the Commission cannot say that implementation of the Covisint venture will not cause competitive concerns." Soon thereafter, the Bundeskartellamt, the German equivalent of the FTC, also granted its approval.

To Think About: Do you think Covisint can succeed, and if so, how and why, and if not, why not? What problems do you see in the way the Covisint project was managed?

Sources: Ruhan Memishi, "Covisint's Starts and Stops," *Internet World,* January 1, 2001; Clare Ansberry, "Let's Build an Online Supply Network," *The Wall Street Journal,* April 17, 2000; Dow Jones Newswires, "Honda Considers Joining Covisint Parts Exchange," *The Wall Street Journal,* November 21, 2000; "Covisint: Reinventing Procurement and Supply," *The New York Times,* November 6, 2000; Paul Elias, "Feds Can't Call Covisint Antitrust-worthy—Yet," *Red Herring Magazine,* September 12, 2000; Gail Kachadourian, "Covisint is Up and Running," *Automotive News,* October 9, 2000; Steve Konicki, "Covisint's Rough Road," *Information Week,* August 7, 2000; Sarah L. Roberts-Witt, "Proposed Auto Exchange Hits Bumps," *Knowledge Management,* July 2000.

---

normal network of money (paper currency, coins, cheques, and credit cards). Users are supplied with client software and can exchange money with another e-cash user over the Internet or a retailer accepting e-cash. CyberCash, e-Coin, and InternetCash offer digital cash services. In addition to facilitating micropayments, digital cash can be useful for people who don't have credit cards and wish to make Web purchases or for people who want to give gift certificates for online shopping.

Smart cards offer an alternative system for processing micropayments since the smart card's microchip can contain electronic cash as well as other information. A **smart card** is a plastic card the size of a credit card that stores digital information. The smart card can store health records, identification data, or telephone numbers, or it can serve as an "electronic purse" in place of cash. The Mondex smart card contains electronic cash and can be used to

smart card
A credit-card-sized plastic card that stores digital information and that can be used for electronic payments in place of cash.

FIGURE 4-11 Gator (www.gator.com) is a digital wallet system that stores personal information securely on the user's computer. When the user encounters a registration or order form on the Web, Gator Form Helper pops up and fills in the form with one or just a few clicks. Users should know that Gator has been accused of guerilla-marketing tactics by allowing companies to serve a pop-up ad to users, even though they may be on a rival's site, and of replacing banner ads with their own sponsor's ads.

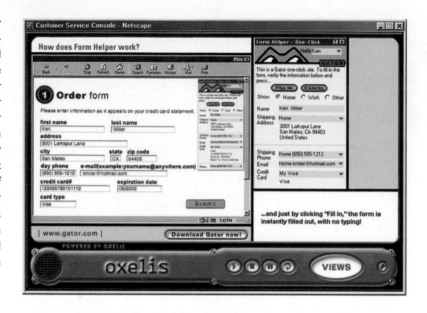

person-to-person payment system

An electronic payment system for people who want to send money to vendors or individuals who are not set up to accept credit card payments.

transfer funds to merchants in physical storefronts and to merchants on the Internet. Mondex cards can accept electronic cash transferred from users' bank accounts over the Web. The card requires use of a special card reading and writing device whenever the card needs to be "recharged" with cash or whenever the card needs to transfer cash to either an online or offline a merchant. Internet users must attach a Mondex reader to their PC to use the card. To pay for a Web purchase, the user would swipe the smart card through the card reader.

Micropayment systems have been developed to let consumers bill small purchases to their credit cards or telephone bills. Qpass collects all of a consumer's tiny purchases for monthly billing on a credit card. *The New York Times* uses Qpass to bill consumers wishing to access articles from its Web site (www.nytimes.com). ECharge and Trivnet let consumers charge small purchases to their monthly telephone bills.

New Web-based **person-to-person payment systems** have sprung up to serve people who want to send money to vendors or individuals who are not set up to accept credit card

---

TABLE 4-3   EXAMPLES OF ELECTRONIC PAYMENT SYSTEMS FOR E-COMMERCE

Payment System	Description	Commercial Example
Credit cards	Secure services for credit card payments on the Internet protect information transmitted between users, merchant sites, and processing banks	PC Authorize, Web Authorize, and IC Verify by Cybercash Qunara's Commerce Exchange
Electronic cash (e-cash)	Digital currency that can be used for micropayments	CyberCash e-Coin Beenz
Person-to-person payment systems	Software service that sends money over the Web to individuals who are not set up to accept credit card payments	PayPal BillPoint Yahoo! PayDirect
Digital [electronic] wallet	Software that stores credit card and other information to facilitate payment for goods on the Web	Passport Gator AOL Quick Checkout by AOL
Electronic cheque	Cheque with an encrypted digital signature	NetCheck PaybyCheck
Smart card	Microchip can store electronic cash to use for online and offline micropayments	Mondex
Electronic bill payment	Software that supports electronic payment for online and physical store purchases of goods or services after the purchase has taken place	EPost.ca CheckFree

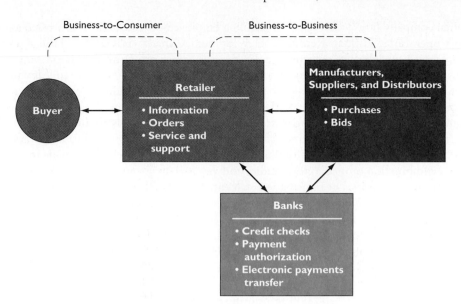

FIGURE 4-12 Electronic commerce information flows. Individuals can purchase goods and services electronically from online retailers, which in turn can use electronic commerce technologies to link directly to their suppliers or distributors. Electronic payment systems are used in both business-to-consumer and business-to-business electronic commerce.

payments. The party sending money uses his or her credit card to create an account with the designated payment at a Web site dedicated to person-to-person payments. The recipient "picks up" the payment by visiting the Web site and supplying information about where to send the payment (a bank account or a physical address). PayPal, Billpoint, and Yahoo!'s PayDirect (http://paydirect.yahoo.com) are popular person-to-person payment systems.

Online merchants and financial service companies offer bill presentment and payment services over the Web as well as over proprietary networks. These services support payment for online and physical store purchases of goods or services after the purchase has taken place. They notify purchasers about bills that are due, present the bills, and process the payments, and some of these services, such as CheckFree, consolidate subscribers' bills from various sources so that they can all be paid at one time.

Payment systems, such as NetCheck and PaybyCheck, that use electronic cheques are also available. These cheques are encrypted with a digital signature that can be verified and can be used for payments in electronic commerce. Electronic cheque systems are especially useful in business-to-business electronic commerce. Table 4-3 summarizes the features of these payment systems.

The process of paying for products and services purchased on the Internet is complex and merits additional discussion. We discuss electronic commerce security in detail in Chapter 12. Figure 4-12 provides an overview of the key information flows in electronic commerce.

4.3 ELECTRONIC BUSINESS AND THE DIGITAL FIRM

Businesses are finding some of the greatest benefits of Internet technology come from applications that lower agency and coordination costs. Although companies have used internal networks for many years to manage and coordinate internal business processes, intranets quickly are becoming the technology of choice for electronic business.

HOW INTRANETS SUPPORT ELECTRONIC BUSINESS

Intranets are inexpensive, scalable to expand or contract as needs change, and accessible from most computing platforms. While most companies, particularly the larger ones, must support a variety of computer platforms that cannot communicate with each other easily, intranets provide instant connectivity, uniting all computers in a single, virtually seamless network. Web software presents a uniform interface that can be used to integrate different processes and systems throughout the company. Companies can connect their intranets to internal company transaction systems, enabling employees to take actions central to a company's operations. Human Resources Development Canada (HRDC) in Hull, Quebec, negotiates a new collective agreement every two to three years. With that frequency, it was difficult to keep the agreement document up to date. Keeping copies of the collective agreement current, up-to-date, and available to all interested clients became a never-ending paper-issuing and notification exercise, so HRDC now posts the collective agreement on their intranet where any clients needing to access the agreement can easily find it.

Intranets can help organizations create a richer, more responsive information environment. Internal corporate applications based on the Web page model can be made interactive using a combination of media, text, audio, and video. A major use of intranets has been to create online repositories of information that can be updated as often as required. Product catalogues, employee handbooks, telephone directories, policy manuals, and benefits information can be revised immediately as changes occur. This "event-driven" publishing allows organizations to respond more rapidly to changing conditions than traditional paper-based publishing, which requires a rigid production schedule. Intranet documents can always be up-to-date, eliminating paper, printing, and distribution costs. For instance, Sun Healthcare, a chain of nursing and long-term care facilities headquartered in Albuquerque, New Mexico, saved U.S.$400 000 in printing and mailing costs when it put its corporate newsletter on an intranet. The newsletter is distributed to 69 000 employees in 49 states (Mullich, 1999).

Intranets have provided cost savings in other application areas as well. Glaxo Wellcome of Mississauga, Ontario, decided to move from a portfolio of two or three "blockbuster" drugs to a roster of 30 or more mid-range new drugs. In order to manage the change, its information technology specialists developed an intranet-based relationship management capability (RMC) for its marketing and sales departments, a system with information sharing as its underlying theme. Research and strategic planning have been streamlined and enhanced to reduce costs by $3 million and have cut the time for a drug to be added to the company's repertoire from 12 months to less than nine. Conservative studies of returns on investment (ROIs) from intranets show ROIs of 23 percent to 85 percent, and some companies have reported ROIs of more than 1000 percent. More detail on the business value of intranets can be found in Chapter 10.

The intranet provides a universal e-mail system, remote access, group collaboration tools, electronic library, application sharing, and company communications network. Some companies are using their intranets for virtual conferencing. Intranets are simple, cost-effective communication tools. Table 4-4 summarizes the organizational benefits of using intranets.

INTRANETS AND GROUP COLLABORATION

Intranets provide a rich set of tools for creating collaborative environments in which members of an organization can exchange ideas, share information, and work together on common projects and assignments regardless of their physical location. Others use intranets to create enterprise collaboration environments linking diverse groups, projects, and activities

TABLE 4-4	**ORGANIZATIONAL BENEFITS OF INTRANETS**

Accessible from most computing platforms

Can be tied to internal corporate systems and core transaction databases

Can create interactive applications with text, audio, and video

Scalable to larger or smaller computing platforms as requirements change

Easy to use, universal Web interface

Low start-up costs

Richer, more responsive information environment

Reduced information distribution costs

Up-to-date, accurate information

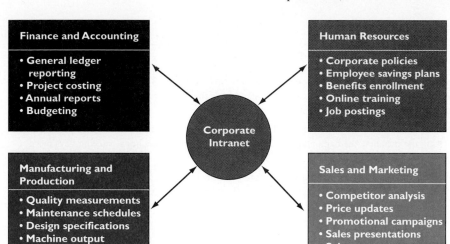

FIGURE 4-13 Functional applications of intranets. Intranet applications have been developed for each of the major functional areas of business.

throughout the organization. For example, Noranda Inc., a large Canadian mining company, uses an intranet to keep track of its mineral exploration research in a dozen offices in North and South America, Australia, and Europe.

INTRANET APPLICATIONS FOR ELECTRONIC BUSINESS

Intranets are springing up in all the major functional areas of business, allowing an organization to manage more of its business processes electronically. Figure 4-13 illustrates some of the intranet applications that have been developed for finance and accounting, human resources, sales and marketing, and manufacturing and production.

Finance and Accounting

Many organizations have extensive transaction processing systems that collect operational data on financial activities, but their traditional management reporting systems, such as general ledger systems and spreadsheets, often cannot bring this detailed information together for decision-making and performance measurement. Intranets can be valuable for finance and accounting because they can provide an integrated view of financial and accounting information online in an easy-to-use format. Table 4-5 provides some examples.

TABLE 4-5   INTRANETS IN FINANCE AND ACCOUNTING

Organization	Intranet Application
Gulf Canada Resources (www.gulf.ca)	Intranet-based corporate budgeting system helps Gulf improve its cash flow forecasting and its ability to integrate acquisitions quickly. Users are able to check field-level production figures against forecast numbers to help them react to under-performing or over-performing recovery sites and to add or subtract capital where needed.
Maple Leaf Sports & Entertainment Limited (MLSEL) (www.torontomapleleafs.com)	Intranet-based accounting system capable of streamlining all of its venues, services, and products while maintaining high performance. Using Great Plains eEnterprise software, MLSEL achieves a seamless integration of all their data and achieved enhanced performance, ease of reporting, and scalability while combining 170 000 general ledger accounts. The new system creates customized reports for a diverse group of users.
Bell Canada	By using software and Web-based training techniques, Bell Canada provides its managers with basic financial training before introducing them to more complex shareholder value concepts. Managers are able to gain far more knowledge and benefit from shareholder value learning because they now understand basic finance. With the online Finance Series, the company has been able to cover in half a day the same learning that would take two days in a traditional classroom environment.

TABLE 4-6	INTRANETS IN HUMAN RESOURCES
Organization	Intranet Application
Falconbridge Ltd.	Employees with access to the corporate intranet can update their addresses, beneficiary information, and sick days. They can also schedule vacation days and have that reflected in the production applications where information on labour availability is needed for work teams.
CIBC	Web-enabled StaffSmart coordinates staffing needs at more than 1200 branches via the corporate intranet. Using the intranet, the bank allocates employees to different branches at varying days or times to meet fluctuating demand.
TD Canada Trust	The bank's People Development site has three major segments: Know Yourself, Know TD, and Taking Action. Within these three modules, employees across Canada can assess their skills, interests, and values; write a development plan; access competency information; learn more about the bank's business units and goals; link to online course registration; and study a host of online tools and tips.
Microsoft	HR Web is a secure Intranet site that provides Microsoft employees with secured access to various benefit enrollment forms, support for investment programs, retirement savings planning, and healthcare. The easy-to-use application makes it convenient for employees to electronically submit timecards, report absences, view pay stubs, and access human resources (HR)-related news and information, campus maps, commuting options, and community volunteer opportunities.

Human Resources

One of the principal responsibilities of human resources departments is to keep employees informed of company policies and issues as well as to provide information about their personnel records and employee benefits (see Figure 4-14). Human resources can use intranets for online publishing of corporate policy manuals, job postings and internal job transfers, company telephone directories, and training classes. Employees can use an intranet to enrol in healthcare, employee savings, and other benefit plans if they are linked to the firm's human resources or benefits database, or to take online competency tests. (See the Window on Technology.) Human resource departments can rapidly deliver information about upcoming events or company developments to employees using newsgroups or e-mail broadcasts. Table 4-6 lists examples of how intranets are used in the area of human resources.

Sales and Marketing

Earlier we described how the Internet and the Web can be used for selling to individual customers and to other businesses. Internet technology also can be applied to the internal management of the sales and marketing function. One of the most popular applications for

FIGURE 4-14 Enwisen's Employee Information System enables employees to maintain their own human resources data over a corporate intranet. Self-service human resources intranets can give employees more control over their own information while reducing human resources administration costs.

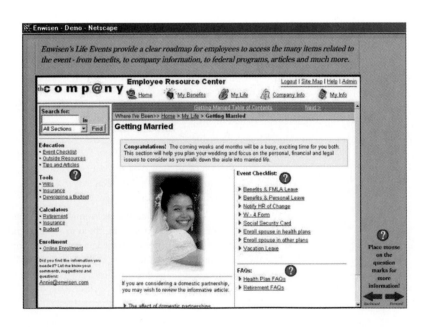

SELF-SERVICE INTRANETS FOR HUMAN RESOURCES

While most of a company's efforts are usually directed toward customers, the human-resources department is challenged with managing and developing strategies for the internal customer—employees and job candidates. To that end, HR sometimes ranks low on the list of priorities for e-business efforts. Today, however, many companies are installing self-service HR systems on their intranets, and the results benefit both the companies and their employees. A recent survey by Watson Wyatt Worldwide found that more than 79 percent of corporations are now using their intranets to deliver HR-related services to their employees. One reason for this popularity is that today employees of many corporations are spread throughout the country or the world. Even companies with employees scattered around nearby locations can benefit from the use of an intranet-based self-service HR system.

The University Health Network (UHN) is made up of the Toronto General Hospital, the Toronto Western Hospital, and the Princess Margaret Hospital, and is the primary teaching hospital for the University of Toronto. With over 9000 employees and with students coming and going along with regular employee turnover, the UHN telephone directory was already out of date when it was printed. The UHN decided it was time to eliminate the paper telephone directory and create an electronic version over a corporate intranet, accessible to all 9000+ employees.

"By linking up various databases throughout the hospitals we're able to have a staff directory that's up to date all the time," said UHN CIO Matthew Anderson in Toronto.

Now all members can access the intranet and the hospitals can control the information each employee can access through a roles-based security system. Along with the telephone directory, the hospital has also put its administrative manuals, infection control manual, and codes (e.g., Code Blue) on the intranet.

This means that staff members who need to look up a particular policy no longer have to hunt down a manual and wonder if it's the latest version or not. "Now they don't have to worry about someone reading the incorrect policy and not knowing which policy is correct. They know the one that's on the intranet is a live policy and can be used by everyone," said Steven Rodin, president of systems integrator Davinci Technologies, Inc. in Toronto.

Now that the directory, policies, and codes are online, Anderson is concentrating on placing financial reporting capabilities on the intranet as well as automating certain hospital functions. For example, hiring and outfitting an employee can be a long, drawn-out process, so instead of having to fill out several different forms, the hospital creates a single form on the intranet. A completed form triggers e-mail notifications requesting various actions.

The hospital would also like to spend time putting a nicer face on the intranet to facilitate employee buy in. "Selling the intranet to our users has been a bit more of struggle than most people anticipated. Originally, it was more of a 'build it, and they will come' approach, and we're finding that generally, users don't do that. Selling them on good graphics and good usability is important," Fobe said.

To Think About: What are the benefits of using intranets for human resources applications? What management, technology, and organization issues must be addressed in installing an intranet-based self-service human resources system in a national or international organization? How do you make users use the intranet?

Sources: Norbert Turek, "Automation Transforms Human Resources," *Information Week,* July 10, 2000; Poonam Khanna, "UHN's Intranet Lets Hospital Leave World of Paper Behind," www.itworld.ca, accessed May 14, 2001; "Davinci Technologies Inc. Implements Intranet at University Health Network (UHN)," www.sackepr.com/DavNov16-99.html; accessed May 14, 2001.

---

corporate intranets is the oversight and coordination of sales force activities. Sales staff can dial in for updates on pricing, promotions, rebates, or customers or obtain information about competitors. They can access presentations and sales documents and customize them for customers. Table 4-7 describes some of these uses.

Manufacturing and Production

In manufacturing, information-management issues are highly complex, involving massive inventories, capturing and integrating real-time production data flows, changing relationships with suppliers, and volatile costs. The manufacturing function typically uses multiple types of data including graphics and text that are scattered in many disparate systems. Manufacturing information is often very time-sensitive and difficult to retrieve because files must be continuously updated. Developing intranets that integrate manufacturing data under a uniform user interface is more complicated than in other functional areas.

Despite these difficulties, companies are launching intranet applications for manufacturing. Intranets coordinating the flow of information between lathes, controllers, inventory systems, and other components of a production system can make manufacturing information

TABLE 4-7 INTRANETS IN SALES AND MARKETING	
Organization	**Intranet Application**
Xerox Canada	Using NetXpert, a Web-based application, Xerox executives and senior managers can access all demographic data on national accounts via the Xerox intranet. This includes information such as total revenue, installed equipment, sales cycles, business year-to-date, as well as other customer contact information—names of senior management personnel, location of offices, etc.
Bell Canada (www.bell.ca)	Working with CGI Inc., North America's fifth-largest IT services company, Bell Canada (whose parent, BCE Inc., owns 45% of CGI) is migrating 650 customer-care representatives to a new system called ARCHI that provides the latest in marketing campaign data, customer and product information, and service availability. ARCHI reduces customer handling time by 30 seconds and training time to four hours from three days. Full rollout of ARCHI will affect more than 10 000 Bell representatives.
Rogers AT&T (www.rogers.com)	Using a BackWeb application, the intranet can "pop up" a box or flash on the employee's display screen, displaying information in text, audio, video, or multimedia format. The intranet can also send employees information at crucial times, such as pushing new deals for cell phones or special offers to call centre employees before they can even take the next customer call.
Microsoft	MS Sales consolidates data in data warehouses on worldwide sales, inventory, distributors, resellers, and customers within a single solution optimized for complicated online analytical processing (OLAP) queries. This solution provides Microsoft employees with an up-to-date, accurate, and consistent picture of the state of Microsoft's business, allowing them to make better strategic decisions.

more accessible to different parts of the organization, increasing precision and lowering costs. Table 4-8 describes some of these uses.

COORDINATION, SUPPLY CHAIN MANAGEMENT, AND CUSTOMER RELATIONSHIP MANAGEMENT

Intranets can also be used to simplify and integrate business processes spanning more than one functional area. These cross-functional processes can be coordinated electronically, increasing organizational efficiency and responsiveness. One area of great interest to companies is the use of Internet technology to facilitate supply chain management.

TABLE 4-8 INTRANETS IN MANUFACTURING AND PRODUCTION	
Organization	**Intranet Application**
Noranda Inc.	Intranet for its Magnola magnesium production facility in Quebec monitors plant operations remotely using a virtual control panel and video cameras.
Sony Corporation	Intranet delivers financial information to manufacturing personnel so that workers can monitor the production line's profit-and-loss performance and adapt performance accordingly. The intranet also provides data on quality measurements, such as defects and rejects, as well as maintenance and training schedules.
Mobility Canada	A custom-designed Lotus Notes/Domino application routes documents through a customizable workflow profile—which means the approval process never gets overlooked. The document, which could be authored anywhere in the country, must receive a digital signature from approvers listed in a profile before being automatically published on the Web. An archive date can be set to pull the document from the Web and any links pointing to it are removed, automatically. This simplifies the creation and management of WWW content. The Web pages are created by the owners of the information, rather than by a dedicated HTML editor. This gives the business area greater control and responsibility over information destined for the public and HTML bottlenecks are eliminated because Domino does the coding.
Rockwell International	Intranet improves process and quality of manufactured circuit boards and controllers by establishing home pages for its Milwaukee plant's computer-controlled machine tools that are updated every 60 seconds. Quality control managers can check the status of a machine by calling up its home page to learn how many pieces the machine output that day, what percentage of an order that output represents, and to what tolerances the machine is adhering.

Chapter 2 introduced the concept of supply chain management, which integrates procurement, production, and logistics processes to supply goods and services from their source to final delivery to the customer. The supply chain links material suppliers, distributors, retailers, customers, and manufacturing facilities.

In the pre-Internet environment, supply chain coordination was hampered by difficulties in making information flow smoothly between many different kinds of systems servicing different parts of the supply chain, such as purchasing, materials management, manufacturing, and distribution. Enterprise systems could supply some of this integration for internal business processes, but ERP systems are difficult and costly to build. Some of this integration can be supplied more inexpensively using Internet technology. Firms can use intranets to improve coordination among their internal supply chain processes, and they can use extranets to coordinate supply chain processes shared with their business partners (see Figure 4-15). An **extranet** is a private intranet that is extended to authorized users outside the company. Many of the industrial networks we introduced in Chapter 2, which link a company's systems with those of other companies in its industry, are based on extranets for streamlining supply chain management.

extranet
A private intranet that is accessible to authorized outsiders.

Through a Web interface, a manager can tap into suppliers' systems to see if inventory and production capabilities match demand for the manufacturer's products. Business partners can use Web-based supply chain management tools to collaborate online about forecasts. Sales representatives can tap into suppliers' production schedules and logistics information to monitor customers' order status (see figure 4-16). As extended supply chains start sharing production, scheduling, inventory, forecasting, and logistics information online instead of by phone or fax, companies can respond more accurately and in a more timely manner to changing customer demand. The low cost of providing this information with Web-based tools instead of costly proprietary systems encourages companies to share critical business information with a greater number of suppliers. Table 4-9 provides examples of Web-based SCM and CRM applications.

Extranets are also used in customer relationship management. As customers interact with the company online, data is gathered about customers that can enable the company to determine which customers are profitable. Profitability information can then be used to target these customers further to ensure that they are retained as customers and that their needs are met. Additional data gathered during online interactions can be used to fine-tune the Web site, to target new markets or to add additional niches to the firm's current base, and to cross-sell customers. Online interactions permit customers to receive improved service, providing timely, accurate, user-friendly information on questions about products and services and the status of current orders.

FIGURE 4-15 Intranet linking supply chain functions. Intranets can be used to integrate information from isolated business processes so that they can be coordinated for supply chain management. Access to private corporate intranets can be extended to distributors, suppliers, logistics services, and customers to improve coordination of external supply chain processes.

TABLE 4-9	EXAMPLES OF WEB-BASED SUPPLY CHAIN MANAGEMENT AND CUSTOMER RELATIONSHIP MANAGEMENT APPLICATIONS

Organization	Application
Hudson Bay Company	HBC.net (intranet) and HBC.biz (extranet) for B2B relationships were launched in 2000. This e-business transformation made HBC a complete e-business and effects everything from store operations to administration and supply chain management. The extranet allows suppliers to log on daily to existing sales systems and gather details on how much of their product has been sold, and reduces people, equipment, and management costs while improving service. HBC.com is the Bay's B2C e-commerce site that collects data on customers to be used in improving marketing and sales efforts.
Pratt and Whitney Canada (www.pwc.ca)	An extranet allows both suppliers and customers to access a variety of information and approvals, cutting lead time for purchasing, production, and distribution.
Bombardier Aerospace (www.bombardier.com)	Business Aircraft Customer Support's extranet for their clients includes a number of communication tools for them as well as a proprietary Part Ordering tool (with over 20 000 parts), that allows their clients to order plane parts online. Using their extranet, Bombardier technicians not only learn specifically how to repair or overhaul a certain item but also can order the necessary parts online.
Celestica	An extranet permits Celestica to link with suppliers and customers, enabling customers to stay in close touch with product development; Celestica's Repetitive Supplier Scheduling (RSS) program ensures that supplies are available when needed; RSS connects Celestica with over 30 major suppliers.
Nortel	Nortel's extranet includes Factory Planner, Collaboration Planner, Supply Chain Planner, and Demand Planner to conduct real-time planning with suppliers based on customer demand for Nortel products. Nortel also uses their extranet for customer relationship management, to anticipate customer buying needs.

The Web-based B2B marketplaces and exchanges we described earlier also provide supply chain management functions. When completed, Covisint, the giant automotive industry exchange described in the Window on Organizations, will help the participating automotive manufacturers view their supply chains as components move through the system. Purchase orders, supplier ship dates, and production schedules are all available on the Covisint Web site. The auto manufacturers and their suppliers can use this real-time information to reduce their inventories and respond more quickly to customers.

Internet-based supply chain management applications are clearly changing the way businesses work internally and with each other. In addition to reducing costs, these supply chain management systems provide more responsive customer service, allowing the workings of the business to be driven more by customer demand. Earlier supply chain management systems were driven by production master schedules based on forecasts or best guesses of demand for products. With the new flow of information made possible by Web-based tools, supply chain management can follow a demand-driven model.

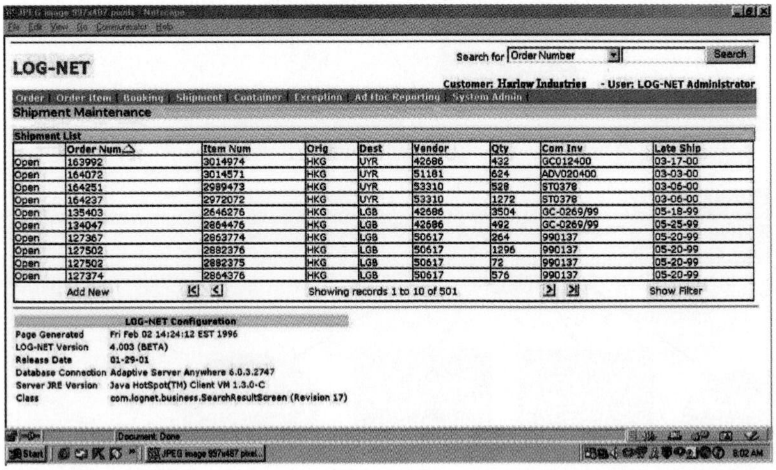

FIGURE 4-16 LOG-NET Inc. provides software for tracking purchase orders and shipments from any location over the Internet. Companies can use such Web-based tools to improve their supply chain management.

4.4 MANAGEMENT CHALLENGES AND OPPORTUNITIES

Although electronic commerce and electronic business offer organizations a wealth of new opportunities, they also present managers with a series of challenges. Many new Internet business models have yet to prove to be enduring sources of profit. Web-enabling business processes for electronic commerce and electronic business requires far-reaching organizational change. The legal environment for electronic commerce has not yet solidified, and companies pursuing electronic commerce must be vigilant about security and consumer privacy.

UNPROVEN BUSINESS MODELS

Not all companies make money on the Web. Hundreds of dot-com firms, including MyKidsBenefit.com, Pop.com (now located at www.countingdown.com), WinePlanet.com.au, Bid.com, Boo.com, Productopia.com, and Pets.com have laid off employees, changed their missions, or closed their doors. Fleetscape.com, M-Xchange.com, IndustrialVortex.com, Chemdex, and Promedix, and other exchanges have shut down. As of this writing, Internet bellwethers such as Amazon.com and Travelocity have yet to turn a profit. Dot-com stock prices have collapsed after these companies failed to generate enough revenue to sustain their costly marketing campaigns, infrastructure, and staff salaries, losing money on every sale they made. Business models built around the Internet are new and largely unproven. The chapter-ending case study on the failure of Boo.com is devoted to this topic.

Doing business over the Net is not necessarily more efficient or cost-effective than traditional business methods. Virtual retailers may not need to pay for costly storefronts and retail workers, but they require heavy outlays for advertising, warehousing, customer service call centres, and customer acquisition.

Challenges also confront businesses that are trying to use the Web to supplement or enhance a traditional business model. Many businesses are finding that it is not enough to "get on the Web." Businesses that are unclear about their online strategy can waste thousands and even millions of dollars building and maintaining a Web site that fails to deliver the desired results. Even successful Web sites can incur extremely high costs. For example, The Bay, the flagship chain of Hudson's Bay Company's department stores, has brick and mortar retail stores and a profitable Web site. It has hefty payroll expenditures to pay for the skilled technical staff supporting the Web site and additional shipping expenses to make sure Web orders are delivered to customers in a timely fashion. Hudson's Bay spends $40 million annually on upgrading and remodelling its Web site.

BUSINESS PROCESS CHANGE REQUIREMENTS

Electronic commerce and electronic business require careful orchestration of the firm's divisions, production sites, and sales offices, as well as close relationships with customers, suppliers, and other business partners. Essential business processes must be redesigned and more closely integrated, especially those for supply chain management. Traditional boundaries between departments and visions can be an impediment to collaboration and relationship-building between companies and suppliers. The digitally enabled enterprise must transform the way it conducts business on many levels to act rapidly and with precision.

Channel Conflicts

Using the Web for online sales and marketing may create **channel conflict** with the firm's traditional channels, especially for less information-intensive products that require physical intermediaries to reach buyers (Palmer and Griffith, 1998). Its sales force and distributors may fear that their revenues will drop as customers make purchases directly from the Web or that they will be displaced by this new channel. The Window on Management describes how several companies are dealing with this problem.

Channel conflict is an especially troublesome issue in B2B electronic commerce where customers buy directly from manufacturers via the Web instead of through distributors or sales representatives. Milacron Inc. operates one of the heavy equipment industry's most

channel conflict
Competition between two or more different distribution chains used to sell the products or services of the same company.

CONTROLLING CHANNEL CONFLICT

When Canada's largest book retailer, Chapters Inc., decided it had to establish a Web site, it created another way for its customers to purchase its products. Unfortunately it also created the threat of channel conflict. Chapters Inc. had several strong reasons for selling on the Web. For one, management feared it was losing sales to Web sites such as Amazon.com. Also, research has shown that most Web customers are new to the given company, having never purchased at the stores of the site owners. In addition, management believed the Web would enable it to expand into new areas such as used and out-of-print books. However, a Web site could steal customers from its own bricks-and-mortar stores, and Chapters management wanted a strategy to avoid channel conflict.

Chapters decided to integrate its Web site with its stores to give its customers good experiences regardless of which channel they chose. To prevent cross-channel rivalry, the company created a special new "retail ambassador" position to troubleshoot the relationship between the two channels and ensure that both organizations took a holistic view of the customer retail experience.

The new Chapters Web site gives its visitors information on books and enables them to shop online, much as other booksellers do. In addition, however, the company uses the Web to improve the experiences of in-store customers by placing computer kiosks in each store linked to the specific store's inventory. Each kiosk is so easy to use that even customers with no Web experience can find out if a book is in stock and if so determine its shelf location. Customers can also order books not in stock through the kiosks and have them delivered to their homes. Because the kiosks' back ends are integrated with Chapters' e-commerce systems, all customer service functions are integrated, enabling customers to return online purchases at any store. Soon the company will start selling other products through the kiosks and the Web, including e-books, videos, CDs, and DVDs.

Has Chapters' integrated approach been effective? According to David Hainline, the Chief Operating Officer of Chapters Online, consumers rated its bookstores the number one retail brand in Canada in 1999. Chapters Online has been able to stop the leakage of its business to other online booksellers. Management is obviously pleased. So, apparently, was management at Indigo Books and Music, which merged with Chapters in 2001.

Other companies have had more difficulty managing channel conflict. When Levi Straus & Co. began selling its Levi and Dockers brands online, it was potentially stealing business from the very retail stores where most people purchase Levi products. After a year Levi Straus abandoned online sales, converting its Web site to information only, thus eliminating the channel conflict. When Avon Products, the U.S.$6 billion cosmetics company, experienced powerful online competition from Estée Lauder Inc., Avon decided it must begin selling online. In the United States, Avon mainly sells its products through about 500 000 independent saleswomen who go door-to-door announcing, "Avon calling." These representatives felt threatened when their customers suddenly had another venue to purchase Avon cosmetics. In this case, Avon management concluded it could not abandon Web sales and so decided to give the reps a commission of its online sales to their customers. The reps did not find the solution to be totally satisfactory—they receive a much lower percentage than if their customers had purchased directly from them. Only time will tell if Avon's solution has been successful in addressing Avon's channel conflict.

To Think About: What management, organization, and technology issues should be addressed when considering whether to use the Web for direct sales to consumers?

Sources: Stephanie Wilkinson, "Melding Clicks and Bricks," *Datamation*, August 29, 2000; Alorie Gilbert and Beth Bacheldor, "The Big Squeeze," *Information Week*, March 27, 2000; Minda Zetlin, "Channel Conflicts," *Computerworld*, September 25, 2000.

extensive Web sites (www.milpro.com) for selling machine tools to contract manufacturers. To minimize negative repercussions from channel conflict, Milacron is paying full commissions to its representatives for online sales made in their territory even if they have not done any work on the sale or met the buyer. Other companies are devising other solutions, such as offering only a portion of their full product line on the Web. Using alternative channels created by the Internet requires very careful planning and management.

LEGAL ISSUES

Laws governing electronic commerce are still being written. Legislatures, courts, and international agreements are just starting to settle such questions as the legality and force of e-mail contracts, the role of electronic signatures, and the application of copyright laws to electronically copied documents. Moreover, the Internet is global and is used by individuals and organizations in hundreds of different countries. If a product were offered for sale in Thailand via a server in Singapore and the purchaser lived in Hungary, which country's law would apply?

TABLE 4-10	**DIGITALLY ENABLING THE ENTERPRISE: TOP QUESTIONS FOR MANAGERS**

1. How much digital integration does our business need to remain competitive? How can the digital integration provided by Internet technology change our business model? Should we change our business model?

2. How can we measure the success of digitally enabling the enterprise? Will the benefits outweigh the costs?

3. How will business processes have to be changed to use Internet technology seriously for electronic commerce or electronic business? How much process integration is required?

4. How will we have to recast our relationships with customers, suppliers, distributors, employees, and other business partners to take advantage of digitally enabled business processes?

5. Do we have the appropriate information technology infrastructure for digitally enabling our business? What technical skills and employee training will be required to use Internet technology? How can we integrate Internet applications with existing applications and data?

6. How can we make sure our intranet is secure from entry by outsiders? How secure is the electronic payment system we are using for electronic commerce?

7. Are we doing enough to protect the privacy of customers we reach electronically?

The legal issues surrounding intellectual property are discussed in Chapter 5. The legal issues of companies such as Napster (discussed in Chapters 5 and 6), and the Canadian company IcraveTV, are but an indicator of a few of the legal issues involved in e-commerce. The legal and regulatory environment for electronic commerce has not been fully established.

SECURITY AND PRIVACY

Internet-based systems are even more vulnerable to penetration by outsiders than private networks because the Internet was designed to be open to everyone. Any information, including e-mail, passes through many computer systems on the Net before it reaches its destination. It can be monitored, captured, and stored at any of these points along the route. Valuable data that might be intercepted include credit card numbers and names, passwords, private personnel data, marketing plans, sales contracts, product development and pricing data, negotiations between companies, and other data that might be of value to competition. Hackers, vandals, and computer criminals have exploited Internet weaknesses to break into computer systems, causing harm by stealing passwords, obtaining sensitive information, electronic eavesdropping, or "jamming" corporate Web servers to make them inaccessible. We explore Internet security, computer crime, and technology for secure electronic payments in greater detail in Chapters 5 and 12.

The Web provides an unprecedented ability to learn about and target customers. Throughout the text, we have emphasized customer relationship management and the use of the Web to implement CRM. But the same capability can also undermine individual privacy. Through the use of Web site monitoring software and other technology for tracking Web visitors, companies can gather detailed information about individuals without their knowledge. In other instances, Web site visitors knowingly supply personal information such as their name, address, e-mail address, and special interests in exchange for access to the site, without realizing how the organization owning the Web site may use the information. Companies collecting detailed customer information over the Web will need to balance their desire to profit from the information with the need to safeguard individual privacy. Chapter 5 discusses privacy from a legal and an ethical viewpoint.

Digitally enabling the enterprise with Internet technology requires careful management planning. Table 4-10 lists what we believe are the top questions managers should ask when exploring the use of the Internet for electronic commerce and electronic business.

4.5 STATUS OF CANADIAN ELECTRONIC COMMERCE

Commercial use of the Internet—electronic commerce—began in the United States and rapidly spread to other parts of the world. As a close trading partner, Canada began e-commerce shortly after the United States but was slower to embrace this new trading method. While a higher percentage of Canadians than Americans use the Internet, the percentage of e-commerce use per capita or per business is lower in Canada than the United States. What trends are there in Canada regarding e-commerce? What barriers are there to conducting e-commerce in Canada? How are taxation issues addressed? Is another country deliberately cannibalizing Canadian e-commerce sales?

CURRENT STATISTICS ON CANADIAN AND INTERNATIONAL E-COMMERCE

In an April 2001 report, Statistics Canada reported that the total value of private sector sales over the Internet soared in 2000, but the proportion of businesses selling online actually fell. Canadian businesses received $7.2 billion in customer orders over the Internet in 2000, up 71.4 percent from $4.2 billion in 1999. However, only 6 percent of businesses reported selling goods and services online in 2000, down from 10 percent in 1999. For every two Canadian companies that started selling online over the Net in 2000, five actually stopped selling online.

The survey covered 21 000 companies and found that e-commerce sales accounted for 0.4 percent of company total operating revenue in 2000, up from 0.2 percent in 1999. Large Canadian businesses are more likely to sell over the Internet and are responsible for a large proportion of online sales. In 2000, 31 percent of Canadian businesses with more than 500 employees sold goods or services over the Net but accounted for 43 percent of total online sales while only 6 percent of businesses with 1 to 19 employees sold online. In spite of the declining number of Canadian firms selling online, more and more Canadian firms are purchasing online, 18 percent in 2000 compared to 14 percent in 1999. According to a report by the Boston Consulting Group (Canada), Canada has the highest share of global e-commerce revenues after the United States with an Internet economy representing $28 billion in revenues and 95 000 jobs.

Measured by value, Canadian e-commerce sales were highest in manufacturing, followed by wholesale trade, transportation and warehousing, and retail trade. Overall, 20 percent of Canadian sales over the Internet were to consumers. Seventeen percent of Canadian e-commerce sales went to customers (businesses or households) outside Canada.

Interestingly, according to Forrester Research, Canada's e-commerce sales volume is only 4 percent of that of North America, with global growth of almost 200 percent between 2000 and 2001. Tables 4-11, 4-12, and 4-13 provide a clearer view of the global growth of e-commerce. Table 4-11 shows the differences in Internet access between English- and non-English speaking peoples. The statistics reveal that although English-speaking peoples only make up 8 percent of the world's population, they make up 45 percent of those with Internet access. Table 4-12 reveals that the United States will have 47 percent of the world's e-commerce, Japan 13 percent, Canada 2.3 percent, and Germany 5.7 percent. Finally, Table 4-13 reveals the proportion of Web content provided in various languages. Today, almost 69 percent of Web content is provided in English even though only 45 percent of the world's on-line

TABLE 4-11   GLOBAL INTERNET ACCESS

	Internet Access (M)	Percentage of World Online Population	Total Population (M)	GDP ($B)	Percentage of World Economy
English	220.4	43.0%	860	$13 812	33.4%
Non-English	292.7	57.0%	5340	$27 590	66.6%
European Languages (non-English)	163.0	31.8%	1162	$14 112	34.1%
Asian Languages	129.5	25.3%	N/A	N/A	N/A
TOTAL WORLD	505.0		6200	$41 400	

Source: Adapted from Global Reach, www.glreach.com/globstats, accessed November 22, 2001.

TABLE 4-12   WORLDWIDE E-COMMERCE GROWTH

	2000	2001	2002	2003	2004	% of Total Sales in 2004
Total ($ B)	$657.0	$1 233.6	$2 231.2	$3 979.7	$6 789.8	8.6%
North America	$509.3	$908.6	$1 498.2	$2 339.0	$3 456.4	12.8%
United States	$488.7	$864.1	$1 411.3	$2 187.2	$3 189.0	13.3%
Canada	$17.4	$38.0	$68.0	$109.6	$160.3	9.2%
Mexico	$3.2	$6.6	$15.9	$42.3	$107.0	8.4%
Asia Pacific	$53.7	$117.2	$286.6	$724.2	$1 649.8	8.0%
Japan	$31.9	$64.4	$146.8	$363.6	$880.3	8.4%
Australia	$5.6	$14.0	$36.9	$96.7	$207.6	16.4%
Korea	$5.6	$14.1	$39.3	$100.5	$205.7	16.4%
Western Europe	$87.4	$194.8	$422.1	$853.3	$1 533.2	6.0%
Germany	$20.6	$46.4	$102.0	$211.1	$386.5	6.5%
United Kingdom	$17.2	$38.5	$83.2	$165.6	$288.8	7.1%
France	$9.9	$22.1	$49.1	$104.8	$206.4	5.0%
Italy	$7.2	$15.6	$33.8	$71.4	$142.4	4.3%
The Netherlands	$6.5	$14.4	$30.7	$59.5	$98.3	9.2%
Latin America	$3.6	$6.8	$13.7	$31.8	$81.8	2.4%

Source: Adapted from Global Reach (www.glreach.com/globstats)

population is English speaking and only 8 percent of the world's total population is English speaking.

E-COMMERCE BUSINESS SALES TO CANADIANS BY U.S. FIRMS

Several studies have shown that Canadian consumers and businesses conduct a significant amount of their electronic purchases with U.S. firms. Many of these U.S. firms, such as Amazon.com, established early pre-eminence in the online marketplace and are difficult for any similar firm located anywhere in the world to compete with. Were it not for e-commerce, those sales would have taken place with Canadian companies. These lost sales are significant and could result in the restructuring of entire industries and the demise of some Canadian companies. Considering the North American Free Trade Act (NAFTA) and other trade agreements between Canada and other countries, there is little that can be done at present to prevent Canadian sales going to other countries, primarily those in the United States. There is little if any reason to believe that non-Canadian firms are deliberately cannibalizing Canadian sales, any more than there is reason to believe that Canadian firms engaged in foreign trade are deliberately cannibalizing the sales in those countries. But many U.S. companies have Canadian Web sites, open for e-commerce, such as Yahoo.ca and Travelocity.ca; other firms like IBM and Microsoft have purchased the domain names for Canadian versions of their Web sites and route those addresses to a Canadian area of the URL (e.g., www.ibm.ca routes the user immediately to www.ibm.com/ca). These companies are certainly attempting to serve the Canadian market.

Not all of the impacts of the Internet and electronic commerce are positive, and not all of these globally positive impacts are beneficial to individual countries. Canada,

TABLE 4-13   WEB CONTENT BY LANGUAGE

English	68.4%
Japanese	5.9%
German	5.8%
Chinese	3.9%
French	3.0%
Spanish	2.4%
Russian	1.9%
Italian	1.6%
Portuguese	1.4%
Korean	1.3%
Other	4.6%
Total Web pages:	313 B

Source: eMarketer, Inc.

Regional Global E-Commerce as Projected for 2001

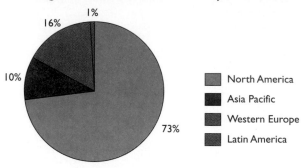

- North America
- Asia Pacific
- Western Europe
- Latin America

FIGURE 4-17 An interesting view of global e-commerce projected for 2001 ranked by regions.

unfortunately, is not an exception to the potential for negative impacts of lost sales. What other barriers are there to Canadian e-commerce?

BARRIERS TO E-COMMERCE IN CANADA

Among businesses that did not buy or sell over the Net, 56 percent said they believe their goods or services do not lend themselves to Internet transactions. Thirty-six percent preferred to maintain their current business model. Fourteen percent felt that security was a concern, and 12 percent said the cost of development and maintenance was too high. Finally, 10 percent of non-e-commerce businesses said there was a lack of skilled employees while 9.6 percent said that their customers are not ready to buy online. Canada is a country with a much larger percentage of small- and medium-sized businesses (SMEs) than the United States. The SMEs typically do not have the expertise or staff to transform the nature of their business into electronic commerce. With a widely dispersed population, Canada's broadband access is also a barrier to electronic commerce among that portion of Canadians who live in outlying areas. Although Canada's densely populated areas have long had access to low bandwidth, and are rapidly becoming wired for high bandwidth, its rural and sparely populated areas (primarily northern Canada, including northern Manitoba, Nunavut, the Northwest Territories, and Yukon) are just now gaining some access to low bandwidth. Many of the people living in these areas cannot afford high bandwidth Internet access, and unless someone can fund the implementation of satellite transmission to these areas, the situation will not soon change.

The Boston Consulting Group (Canada) report, titled *Fast Forward: Accelerating Canada's Leadership in the Internet Economy*, was the result of meetings of the Canadian E-Business Roundtable, whose membership includes Gaylen Duncan, the CEO of the Information Technology Association of Canada, and John Roth, the former CEO of Nortel Networks. The study maintains that—in spite of its warnings—Canada is poised to lead the Internet economy, given its sophisticated infrastructure, highly connected population, early Internet policy initiatives, and skilled workforce, but warns that Canada has not yet embraced the opportunities to lead.

The report warns of several significant barriers to becoming a major global player in e-commerce. These barriers include a lack of urgency among Canadian business leaders to make the Internet a strategic priority, a growing shortage of skilled IT talent to fill critical positions, and a false sense of security in Canadian retail circles that have been sheltered from U.S. competition to date by the high costs of cross-border shipping, currency conversion, and taxes. Another constraint is that investment decisions in Canada are largely based on traditional return on investment (ROI) models, which may not be appropriate for this type of investment decision.

Canadian businesses must leverage the broad reach of the Internet to move into larger markets or to establish themselves in promising new niche markets. This is problematic since many small- and medium-sized businesses lack managers with e-business expertise or the in-house IT staff to handle technical challenges. Even more troubling is the conservative investor culture in Canada. The Canadian investor environment is far less dynamic than the United States because the venture capital market is dominated by passive and semi-public investors. Labour-sponsored funds, government funds, and hybrid funds—none of which are permitted to take a large ownership stake in the companies in which they invest—make up over 60 percent of the Canadian venture capital pool. In contrast, only one percent of U.S. funds are managed by non-private investors.

Despite the emergence in the Ottawa region of Silicon Valley North and other e-business clusters in Toronto, Waterloo, Ontario, Montreal, Calgary, and Vancouver, there are few other successful cluster activities in the rest of Canada because the linkages among universities, businesses, and the financial community are generally not as strong or as focused as their American counterparts. Canadian Internet start-ups across Canada face a set of common challenges in gaining access to financing and in attracting and retaining IT talent.

The report also criticized the lack of emphasis Canadian universities place on entrepreneurship and new business creation. The Roundtable made a series of recommendations involving the development of a national e-business strategy. These recommendations include:

- Put all levels of government services completely online
- Offer financial incentives to businesses to get wired
- Lower business and legacy taxes
- Restructure current tax and securities regulations that create barriers to early-stage capital formulation on a large scale.

The Roundtable has identified six priority areas for accelerating Canada's e-business leadership:

1. Establish Canada's brand in e-business.
2. Accelerate the transformation of existing business.
3. Foster e-business creation and growth.
4. Expand the e-business talent pool.
5. Make government services online a priority.
6. Build Canada's e-business leadership profile internationally.

The risks of inertia in these initiatives, according to the report, are forfeiting first mover advantages, competing at a scale disadvantage, getting shut out of traditional supply relationships, and missing global market opportunities. Finally, the Roundtable identified five opportunities for Canada to lead in e-business.

1. Network infrastructure: Canada's historic investments in leading-edge research in network technologies are evident today in the quality and breadth of its Internet backbone. Canada also has a growing number of innovative new technology companies supplying the Internet. The continued growth of these companies and their progeny will establish Canada as an important source of technologies that will accelerate the performance of Internet networks around the world.

2. Multimedia North: As broadband capacity grows, the demand for animation and Web-based graphics will expand exponentially. Canada is well-positioned to be a leading multimedia supplier. Internationally, Canada's animation and design schools are renowned and feed a growing multimedia industry.

3. Global customer care centres: The Internet has created a new type of call centre that integrates online and telephone solutions for customer service. Given the rapid decline in telecommunications costs, global call centres are now feasible—if they can be staffed by sophisticated response teams with higher-order technical, language, and service skills. Other countries, such as Ireland, are Canada's competition in this arena.

4. Remote service provider: Canada's experience in remote delivery of healthcare and educational services is promising for extending existing services to global markets and for developing new programs and services that can be delivered over the Web. Canada already ranks second globally in the development of remote learning programs with over 1800 online courses in place.

5. Web tools developer. Many niche markets are still open to new dot-coms that Web-enhance the offerings of leading global Internet players. Canadian companies are already creating and commercializing a variety of Web tools, such as navigation tools, site performance enhancers and testers, new search technologies, and new payment solutions.

If the Canadian government, business, educational institutions, and the general public can focus on these issues, Canada can take its place at the head of the e-commerce movement and help to lead the world in the latest industrial revolution.

E-COMMERCE TAXATION ISSUES

If borders are meaningless in the Internet economy, buyers and sellers can be anywhere. For governments that have long defined their consumer taxation powers along geographical lines, this is a scary premise. With Canadians making an estimated $3 billion in online purchases in 2000, lost tax revenue is a problem that will only grow with time.

The problem goes like this. In the old economy, you paid tax on a purchase—a CD, say—at the store where you bought it because it was assumed you would use it in the same tax jurisdiction. The music store then remitted that tax to the appropriate governments. But things get tricky the moment you order that CD online from another jurisdiction or, worse still, download it as a digital file directly to your home computer. Who collects the tax? Who remits it? Should there be any tax at all?

In Canada, online orders coming from another country are supposed to be taxed just like traditional mail order items: Canadian Customs should hold them at the border until you pay the tax. But that seldom happens in reality. As for digital downloads? How does Canadian Customs monitor these sales?

APPLICATION SOFTWARE EXERCISE

ANALYZING WEB MARKETING CAMPAIGNS

Your firm is attempting to increase the number of online customers by placing advertising banners for your Web site at other Web sites. When users click on these banner ads, they are automatically transported to your Web site. Data from this advertising campaign are summarized in the weekly Marketing Trends Report produced by your Web site analysis software, which can be found on our Web site for Chapter 4.

- Total visitors are the number of people who visited your Web site by clicking on a banner ad for your site that was placed on an affiliated Web site.
- Total shoppers are the number of visitors referred by banner ads who reached a page in your Web site designated as a shopping page.
- Total attempted buyers are the number of potential buyers referred by banner ads who reached a Web page designated as a page for summarizing and paying for purchases.
- Total buyers are the number of buyers referred by banner ads who actually placed an order from your Web site

Management would like to use these data to identify which Web sites directed the most visitors to your Web site and which sites were the most effective in referring visitors who actually became buyers.

Use spreadsheet software to do the following:

1. For each referring Web site, calculate the conversion rate, which is the percentage of visitors who actually become buyers.
2. Calculate the total number of visitors, shoppers, attempted buyers, and buyers who came to your site that week.
3. Prepare a bar graph for management showing which Web sites provided the most visitors and which provided the highest conversion rates.
4. Create an electronic slide of your graph using electronic presentation software.

MANAGEMENT WRAP-UP

Managers need to carefully review their strategy and business models to determine how to maximize the benefits of Internet technology. Managers should anticipate making organizational changes to take advantage of this technology, including new business processes and relationships with the firm's value partners and customers, and even new business designs. Determining how and where to digitally enable the enterprise with Internet technology is a key management decision.

The Internet can dramatically reduce transaction and agency costs and is fuelling new business models. By using the Internet and other networks for electronic commerce, organizations can exchange purchase and sale transactions directly with customers and suppliers, eliminating inefficient intermediaries. Organizational processes can be streamlined by using the Internet and intranets to make communication and coordination more efficient. To take advantage of these opportunities, organizational processes must be redesigned.

Internet technology has created a universal computing platform that has become the primary infrastructure for electronic commerce, electronic business, and the emerging digital firm. Web-based applications integrating voice, data, video, and audio are providing new products, services, and tools for communicating with employees and customers. Intranets enable companies to make information flow between disparate systems, business processes, and parts of the organization.

For Discussion
1. How does the Internet change consumer and supplier relationships?
2. The Internet may not make corporations obsolete, but they will have to change their business models. Do you agree? Why or why not?

SUMMARY

1. *Explain how Internet technology has transformed organizations and business models.* The Internet is rapidly becoming the infrastructure of choice for electronic commerce and electronic business because it provides a universal, easy-to-use set of technologies and technology standards that can be adopted by all organizations, no matter what computing platform they use. Internet technology provides a much lower cost, easier to use alternative for coordination activities than proprietary networks. Companies can use Internet technology to radically reduce their transaction costs.

The Internet radically reduces the cost of creating, sending, and storing information while making that information more widely available. Information is not limited to traditional physical methods of delivery. Customers can find out about products on their own on the Web and buy directly from product suppliers instead of using intermediaries such as retail stores. Some of the traditional channels for exchanging product information have become unnecessary or uneconomical, and business models based on the coupling of information with products and services may no longer be necessary. The unbundling of information from traditional value chain channels has a disruptive effect on old business models and even on new business models as well.

The Internet shrinks information asymmetry and has transformed the richness and reach relationship. Using the Internet and Web multimedia capabilities, companies can quickly and inexpensively provide detailed product information and information specific to each customer to very large numbers of people simultaneously. The Internet can help companies create and capture profit in new ways by adding extra value to existing products and services or by providing the foundation for new products and services. Many different business models for electronic commerce on the Internet

have emerged, including virtual storefronts, marketplace concentrators, information brokers, portals, content providers, digital content delivery, online exchanges, auctions, syndicators, and online service providers.

2. *Compare the categories of electronic commerce, and explain how electronic commerce is changing consumer retailing and business-to-business transactions.* The three major types of electronic commerce are business-to-consumer (B2C), business-to-business (B2B), and consumer-to-consumer (C2C). Another way to classify electronic commerce transactions is in terms of the participants' physical connection to the Web. Conventional e-commerce transactions over wired networks can be distinguished from mobile commerce or m-commerce, the purchase of goods and services using hand-held wireless devices.

The Internet provides a universally available set of technologies for electronic commerce that can be used to create new channels for marketing, sales, and customer support and to eliminate intermediaries in buy and sell transactions. Interactive capabilities on the Web can be used to build closer relationships with customers in marketing and customer support. Firms can use various Web personalization technologies to deliver Web pages with content geared to the specific interests of each user, including technologies to deliver personalized information and ads through m-commerce channels. Companies can also reduce costs and improve customer service by using Web sites to provide helpful information as well as e-mail and even telephone access to customer service representatives.

B2B e-commerce generates efficiencies by enabling companies to locate suppliers electronically, solicit bids, place orders, and track shipments in transit. Businesses can use their own Web sites to conduct B2B e-commerce or use online marketplaces. Exchanges are online marketplaces where multiple buyers can purchase from multiple sellers using a bid-ask system. The two major types of exchanges are vertical exchanges for specific industries and horizontal exchanges providing common functions for many different industries such as maintenance, repair, and operating supplies.

3. *Evaluate the principal electronic payment systems.* The principal electronic payment systems for Internet commerce are credit cards, electronic cash (e-cash), electronic wallets, electronic cheques, person-to-person payment systems, smart cards, and electronic billing systems. Smart cards and e-cash are useful for small micropayments. Electronic chequing and billing systems are useful in business-to-business electronic commerce.

4. *Demonstrate how Internet technology can support electronic business, supply chain management, and customer relationship management.* Private, internal corporate networks called intranets can be created using Internet connectivity standards. Extranets are private intranets that are extended to selected organizations or individuals outside the firm. Intranets and extranets support electronic business by providing a low-cost technology that can run on almost any computing platform. Organizations can use intranets to create collaboration environments for coordinating work and information sharing, and they can use intranets to make information flow between different functional areas of the firm. Intranets also provide a low-cost alternative for improving coordination among organizations' internal supply chain processes. Extranets can be used to coordinate supply chain processes shared with external organizations and to permit customers to check on the status of their orders. The data gleaned from online customer interactions can be used to target customers, to determine which customers are profitable and which are not, to investigate new markets and new market niches, as well as a host of other CRM capabilities.

5. *Assess the managerial and organizational challenges posed by electronic commerce and electronic business.* Many new business models based on the Internet have not yet found proven ways to generate profits or reduce costs. Digitally enabling a firm for electronic commerce and electronic business requires far-reaching organizational change, including redesign of business processes, recasting relationships with customers, suppliers, distributors, and other business partners, and new roles for employees. Channel conflicts may erupt as the firm turns to the Internet as an alternative outlet for sales. Security, privacy, and legal issues, and integration of Internet-based applications with the firm's core transaction systems pose additional electronic commerce challenges.

6. *Explain Canadian trends in e-commerce.* More Canadian businesses are purchasing online, but fewer of them are selling online. Larger businesses are more likely to purchase online as are manufacturing firms. Barriers to e-commerce include the view that a particular set of goods and services are not suitable for e-commerce or that customers are not ready for e-commerce. Some businesses prefer to maintain their current business model, and security, taxation, maintenance and development issues all provide barriers. Due to their prominence in the electronic marketplace, U.S. companies find it easy to cannibalize Canadian companies' e-commerce sales.

KEY TERMS

Banner ad, 116

Business model, 114

Business-to-business electronic commerce (B2B), 119

Business-to-consumer electronic commerce (B2C), 119

Call centre, 123

Channel conflict, 137

Clicks-and-mortar, 119

Consumer-to-consumer electronic commerce (C2C), 119

Digital wallet, 126

Disintermediation, 120

Electronic cash (e-cash), 126

Electronic payment system, 126

Exchange, 125

Extranet, 135

Information asymmetry, 115

Micropayment, 126

Mobile commerce (m-commerce), 119

Person-to-person payment system, 128

Portal, 118

Pure-play, 118

Reach, 115

Reintermediation, 120

Richness, 115

Smart card, 127

Syndicator, 118

Web personalization, 121

REVIEW QUESTIONS

1. What are the advantages of using the Internet as the infrastructure for electronic commerce and electronic business?

2. How is the Internet changing the economics of information and business models?

3. Name and describe six Internet business models for electronic commerce. Distinguish between a pure-play Internet business model and a clicks-and-mortar business model.

4. Name and describe the various categories of electronic commerce.

5. How can the Internet facilitate sales and marketing to individual customers? Describe the role played by Web personalization.

6. How can the Internet help provide customer service?

7. How can Internet technology support business-to-business electronic commerce?

8. What are exchanges? Why do they represent an important business model for B2B e-commerce?

9. Name and describe the principal electronic payment systems used on the Internet.

10. Why are intranets so useful for electronic business?

11. How can intranets support organizational collaboration?

12. Describe the uses of intranets for electronic business in sales and marketing, human resources, finance and accounting, and manufacturing.

13. How can companies use Internet technology for supply-chain management? for customer relationship management?

14. Describe the management challenges posed by electronic commerce and electronic business on the Internet.

15. What is channel conflict? Why is it becoming a growing problem in electronic commerce?

16. What is important about differences in individual countries in terms of electronic commerce? Why should Canadians care about how much of Canadian e-commerce dollars are used to purchase goods from U.S. Web sites?

GROUP PROJECT

Form a group with three or four of your classmates. Select two businesses that are competitors in the same industry, and that have Web sites and use them for electronic commerce. Visit their Web sites. You might compare, for example, the Web sites for virtual banking created by Bank of Montreal and TD Canada Trust, or the Internet trading Web sites of E*Trade and BayStreet.ca. Prepare an evaluation of each business's Web site in terms of its functions, user-friendliness, and how well it supports the company's business strategy. Which Web site does a better job? Why? What are your recommendations to improve these Web sites, either by making them more consistent with the organization's strategy or by improving on their design? Check out our Web site for tips on good Web design. Use an electronic presentation to demonstrate your recommendations to the class.

INTERNET CONNECTION

■ **COMPANION WEBSITE**

At www.pearsoned.ca/laudon, you'll find an online study guide with two quizzes to test your knowledge of e-commerce business models. You'll also find updates to the chapter and online exercises and cases that enable you to apply your knowledge to realistic situations.

■ **ADDITIONAL SITES OF INTEREST**

There are many interesting Web sites to enhance your learning about electronic commerce. You can search the Web yourself, or just try the following sites to add to what you have already learned.

Ecommerce Times

www.ecommercetimes.com

The latest news on electronic commerce technologies, business models, and companies

Internet Week

www.interntwk.com/

A weekly publication of the latest happenings on the Internet

Search e-business

searchebusiness.techtarget.com

A wealth of news and hyperlinks about the Internet and e-commerce

CASE STUDY *Boo.com: Poster Child for Dot-Com Failure?*

Boo.com arrived on the Internet scene promising its investors and online shoppers the treat of a profitable Web site with high-quality, stylish, designer sportswear purchased easily from their office or home. Thanks to advanced widespread publicity, Boo.com became perhaps the most eagerly awaited Internet IPO (initial public offering of stock) of its time. However, the company declared bankruptcy only six months after its Web site had been launched and before the company could ever undertake an IPO. Investors lost an estimated $185 million while shoppers faced a system too difficult for most to use. Many people are still wondering how it could have all gone so wrong so swiftly.

The idea for Boo.com came from two 28-year old Swedish friends, Ernst Malmsten and Kajsa Leander, who had already established and later sold Bokus.com, the world's third-largest online bookstore after Amazon.com and Barnes & Noble.com.

The two were joined by Patrik Hedelin, an investment banker at HSBC Holdings, a UK finance giant.

Boo planned to sell trendy fashion products over the Web, offering such brands as North Face, Adidas, Fila, Vans, Cosmic Girl, and Donna Karan. The Boo business model differed from other Internet startups in that its products would be sold at full retail price rather than at discount. Malmsten labelled his target group as "cash-rich, time-poor."

The Boo Web site enabled shoppers to view every product in full colour 3-D images. Visitors could zoom in to individual products, rotating them 360 degrees to view them from any angle. The site's advanced search engine allowed customers to search for items by colour, brand, price, style, and even sport. The site featured a universal sizing system based on size variations between brands and countries. Visitors were able to question

Miss Boo, an animated figure offering fashion advice based on locale or on a specific activity (such as trekking in Nepal). Boo.com also made available a telephone customer service advice line. In addition, Boo was to feature an independently run fashion magazine to report on global fashion trends. Future plans included expansion into Asia and a site targeted at young teenagers. Those who purchased products from Boo.com earned "loyalty points," which they could later use to obtain discounts on future purchases.

The company offered free delivery within one week and free returns for dissatisfied customers. The Web site was presented in seven languages (two of which were American and British English). Local currencies were accepted from the 18 original countries, and in those countries, national taxes were also calculated and collected. "Boo.com will revolutionize the way we shop…It's a completely new lifestyle proposition," Leander proclaimed.

The founders planned to advertise the site broadly both prior to launching and after. "We are building a very strong brand name for Boo.com," stated Malmsten. "We want to be the style editors for people with the best selection of products. We decided from day one that we would want to create a global brand name."

While many important financial giants rejected investment in Boo.com, J.P. Morgan & Co., an old-line investment bank, decided to back the project even though it had not backed any startups for many decades. According to *The New York Times*, Morgan liked the concept "because Boo wouldn't undercut traditional retailers with cut-rate pricing as many e-retailers do." The Morgan bankers were also impressed by the two founders because of their previous success launching Bokus.com. The bankers were also impressed by promised rewards of "55 percent gross margins and profitability within two years," according to the *Times*. Morgan found other early-stage investors, including Alessandro Benetton (son of the CEO of Benetton), Bain Capital (a Boston high-tech venture capital company), Bernard Arnault (who has made a fortune in luxury goods), Goldman Sachs, and the very wealthy Hariri family of Lebanon.

With startup funds in hand, Malmsten and Leander set a target date of May 1999 for launching the Web site. Boo planned to develop both its complex Internet platform and customer-fulfillment systems from scratch. Management originally planned to launch in the United States and five European countries simultaneously, but soon expanded the number of countries to 18. It also wanted a system that would handle 100 million Web visitors at once. When the launch date began to loom closer, management committed $25 million to an advertising budget, a huge sum for a startup. The company chose to advertise in expensive but trendy fashion magazines such as *Vanity Fair* as well as on cable television and the Internet. Malmsten and Leander even managed to appear on the cover of *Fortune* magazine before the Web site had been launched.

With so much technical development to be accomplished, the company moved the target date back to June 21. As June approached, management decided to open satellite offices in Munich, Paris, New York, and Amsterdam. Several hundred people were hired to take orders from these offices once the site went live. However, the launch date had to be postponed again because of incomplete development, and many of the staff sat idle for months. "With all those trophy offices, Boo looked more like a 1950s multinational than an Internet startup," claimed Marina Galanti, a Boo marketing director.

By September, the company had spent $70 million, and they undertook more fund-raising. With the pre-launch advertising campaign over months earlier, the Web site was finally launched in early November. The promised mass marketing blitz never materialized. With the original advertising campaign long over, observers commented that raising people's interest while delaying the opening resulted in many disappointed and alienated potential customers. Moreover, the site reviews were terrible. At launch time, 40 percent of the site's visitors could not even gain access. The site was full of errors, even causing visitor's computers to freeze. The site design, which had been advertised as revolutionary, was slow and very difficult to use. Only one in four attempts to make a purchase worked. Users of Macintosh computers could not even log on because Boo.com was incompatible with them. Users without high-speed Internet connections found that navigating the site was painfully slow because the flashy graphics and interactive features took so long to load. Angry customers jammed Boo.com's customer support lines. Malmsten indicated that the company actually wanted the negative press stories about usability problems in order to draw more attention to Boo.com. "We know the game and how to play it. If we didn't want to be in the press we wouldn't," he said. Sales in first three months amounted to only about $880,000 while expenses heavily topped $1 million per month. The Boo plan quickly began unravelling.

In December, J.P. Morgan's representative on Boo.com's board of directors resigned, leaving no one from Morgan to advise the company. In late December, with sales lagging badly and the company running out of cash, Malmsten was unable to raise enough additional investment, causing Boo to begin selling its clothing at a 40 percent discount. This changed Boo's public image and its target audience. However, Boo's advertising did not change to reflect this strategy shift. During December finance director and partner Patrik Hedelin left Boo's London headquarters to return to Stockholm permanently. His departure was not made public until late in January 2000. Rumours then spread that Hedelin had real differences with his two partners.

On January 25, Boo.com announced a layoff of 70 employees, starting its decline from a reported high of about 450 persons, a huge number for a startup. In late February, J.P. Morgan resigned as a Boo.com advisor. According to reports, it feared being sued by angry investors. In March, when sales reached $1.1 million, Boo was still spending far more than its income. In April, Boo's finance director Dean Hawkins resigned to take another Internet job. In that month, Internet stocks plunged on the stock market, and plans for a Boo IPO were shelved. On May 4, Boo.com confirmed that the company had been unsuccessfully looking for further financing. Finally on May 17, Malmsten hired a firm to liquidate the company, announcing his decision the next day. He also indicated that the company had many outstanding bills it could not pay.

One problem leading to Boo.com's bankruptcy was its lack of planning and control. "When you strip away the sexy dot-com aspect and the technology out of it, these are still businesses that need the fundamentals—budgeting, planning, and execution," observed Jim Rose, CEO of QXL.com PLC, an online auction house. "To roll out in 18 countries simultaneously, I don't think even the biggest global companies like IBM or General Motors would take that on." Noah Yasskin, an analyst with Jupiter Communications, said, "[Boo.com] had very little spending restraint to put it mildly." An example of its free spending mentality was its offices, which were rented in high-priced areas. For instance, its London offices were located on Carnaby Street, and in New York they were located in the West Village, both trendy, expensive neighbourhoods. Numerous reports surfaced of employees flying first class and staying in five-star hotels. Reports even surfaced that communications that could have been sent by regular mail were routinely sent by Federal Express.

Many in the financial community noted the lack of oversight by the board. Management controlled most of the board seats, with only four being allocated to investors. However, those four investor representatives rarely attended board meetings. Moreover, none had any significant retail or Internet experience. The board failed to offer management the supervision it clearly needed.

Serious technical problems contributed as well. Developing their own software proved slow and expensive. The plan required rich, complex graphics so visitors could view products from any angle. The technicians also had to develop a complex virtual inventory system because Boo maintained very little inventory of its own. Boo's order basket was particularly intricate because items were actually ordered from the manufacturer not from Boo, so that one customer might have a basket containing items coming from four or five different sources. The site also had to enable its customers to communicate in any one of seven languages and to convert 18 different currencies and calculate taxes from 18 different countries. Developing all this complex software in-house caused one prospective investor to observe, "It was like they were trying to build a Mercedes-Benz by hand."

Industry analysts observed that 99 percent of European and 98 percent of U.S. homes lack the high-capacity Internet connections required to easily access the graphics and animation on the Boo.com site. No Apple Macintosh computer could access the site. Navigating the site presented visitors with special problems. Web pages existed that did nothing, such as the one that visitors reported that displayed only the strange message that "Nothing happens on this page—except that you may want to bookmark it." Product descriptions were displayed in tiny one square inch windows, making descriptions not only difficult to read but also to scroll through. Boo developed their own, very unorthodox, scrolling method that people found unfamiliar and difficult to use. Moreover, interface navigation was too complex. The Boo hierarchical menus required precise accuracy because visitors making a wrong choice had no alternative but to return to the top to start over again, and the icons were tiny.

One annoying aspect of the site was the constant presence of Miss Boo. While she was developed to give style advice to browsers and buyers, she was constantly injected whether the visitor desired her or not. Many visitors reacted as they might have if they were shopping in a bricks and mortar store and had a live clerk hovering over them, commenting without stop.

On June 18, Fashionmall.com purchased most of the remnants of Boo.com, including its brand name, Web address, advertising materials, and online content. (Bright Station PLC purchased the company's software for taking orders in multiple languages to market to other online businesses that want to sell to consumers in other countries.) "What we really bought is a brand that has phenomenal awareness worldwide," explained Kate Buggeln, the president of Fashionmall.com's Boo division. The company plans to use the Boo brand name to add a high-end site similar to its long-existing clothing site. The new Boo.com was launched on October 30 with a shoestring $1 million budget. The site is much less ambitious than its earlier incarnation, acting primarily as a portal without any inventory. It features about 250 items for sale ferreted out by a network of fashion scouts. Rather than getting bogged down in taking orders and shipping goods, Boo will direct customers to the Web sites that sell the merchandise they wish to purchase. Buggeln is optimistic about the Boo.com's chances of success this time around. Boo has managed to attract a huge number of visitors, 558 000 in April 2000 alone compared with 208 000 for Fashionmall.com. Even when Boo.com was inactive, about 35 000 people visited the Web site each week.

Sources: Andrew Ross Sorkin, "Boo.com, Online Fashion Retailer, Goes Out of Business" *The New York Times*, May 19, 2000; Stephanie Gruner, "Trendy Online Retailer Is Reduced to a Cautionary Tale for Investors," *The Wall Street Journal*, May 19, 2000; Sarah Ellison, "Boo.com: Buried by Badly Managed Buzz," *The Wall Street Journal*, May 23, 2000; David Walker, "Talk About A Real Boo-boo," *Sydney Morning Herald*, May 30, 2000; Andrew Ross Sorkin, "Fashionmall.com Swoops in for the Boo.com Fire Sale," *The New York Times*, June 2, 2000; Bernhard Warner, "Boo.com Trims its Bottom Line," *TheStandard*, January 25, 2000; Polly Sprenger, "Boo Founder: Don't Cry for Me," *TheStandard*, February 11, 2000; Rikke Sternberg, "All About the Brand," *BizReport*, April 3, 2000; Polly Sprenger, "More Creaks and Groans at Boo.com," *TheStandard*, May 4, 2000; Christopher Cooper and Erik Portanger, "'Miss Boo' and Her Makeovers," *The Wall Street Journal*, June 27, 2000; Stephanie Gruner, "Resurrection of Boo May Prove Existence of Dot-Com Afterlife," *The Wall Street Journal Europe*, September 6, 2000; Suzanne Kapner, "Boo.com, Online Fashion Flop, Is Ready to Rise From Ashes," *The New York Times*, October 17, 2000; Suzie Amer, "If You Build It, Will They Come?" *Forbes ASAP*, May 25, 1999; Lauren Goldstein, "boo.com," *Fortune.com*, July 7, 1999; Polly Sprenger, "Where Is Boo.com," *TheStandard*, September 17, 1999.

CASE STUDY QUESTIONS

1. Analyze Boo.com's business model. How did it differ from more conventional retail Web site strategies? Why do you think the founders and investors of Boo were drawn to this unusual strategy?

2. What problems did Boo.com encounter trying to implement its business model? What management, organization, and technology factors contributed to these problems?

3. What could Boo.com have done differently that might have made the project successful?

5

SOCIAL, POLITICAL, AND ETHICAL ISSUES IN THE INFORMATION AGE

OBJECTIVES

After completing this chapter, you will be able to:

1. *Analyze the relationship among ethical, social, and political issues raised by information systems.*
2. *Identify the main moral dimensions of an information society and apply them to specific situations.*
3. *Apply an ethical analysis to difficult situations.*
4. *Examine specific ethical principles for conduct.*
5. *Design corporate policies for ethical conduct.*

M-Commerce: A New Threat to Privacy?

As the Web goes wireless, the old real estate adage "location, location, location" is taking on new importance. Location can matter in electronic commerce as people tap into the Internet while they are on the go. Web-enabled cell phones, PDA devices, or automobiles with location tracking systems have the potential to figure out exactly where people are and to put that information to use. For example, one could use location information to find the nearest restaurant or hotel, with the answer delivered on a tiny Web screen. Users can obtain this information on request or even have the information automatically delivered to them when they are in the vicinity of hotels and restaurants. Portable Internet, Inc. has just added Toronto and Vancouver to their list of cities in which they offer mobile interactive guides for users with handheld devices. Location-based services promise to be one of the hottest areas of m-commerce.

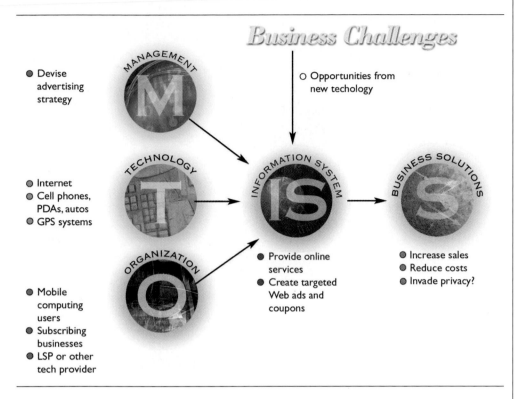

Business Challenges

MANAGEMENT
- Devise advertising strategy

TECHNOLOGY
- Internet
- Cell phones, PDAs, autos
- GPS systems

ORGANIZATION
- Mobile computing users
- Subscribing businesses
- LSP or other tech provider

INFORMATION SYSTEM
- Provide online services
- Create targeted Web ads and coupons

○ Opportunities from new techology

BUSINESS SOLUTIONS
- Increase sales
- Reduce costs
- Invade privacy?

How can a cell phone or PDA figure out your location? Users could tap in postal codes or nearby addresses. But there are better ways. Enhanced 911 systems that can automatically route emergency teams to a caller's location are being implemented in some Canadian townships and cities. Cell phones might be equipped with tiny global positioning systems (GPS) devices that triangulate positions by reading signals from U.S. military satellites sending timing and location information. Auto makers are starting to equip vehicles with GPS systems linked to wireless voice communications, Internet access, and onboard computers. Location-tracking technology is improving rapidly.

Businesses might even use these systems to send electronic coupons directly to a consumer's cell phone or car as the person nears a particular store or restaurant. Consumers might agree to these services in exchange for reduced equipment or service charges. But privacy groups have raised concerns about the potential threat to individual privacy posed by location-tracking technology. Many people may not like having their physical movements tracked so closely. Location information might help direct a tow truck to your broken down car, but it could also be used to find out where you are on your lunch hour. According to David Sobel, general counsel at the Electronic Privacy Information Center (EPIC) in Washington, much depends on "who is going to have control over whether location information is transmitted." Worries about privacy would diminish if there were mechanisms for users to determine exactly when and how their location information could be used.

Sources: Thomas E. Weber, "With Wireless Gadgets, Web Companies Plan to Map Your Moves," *The Wall Street Journal*, May 8, 2000; Patrick Thibodeau, "Satellites Will Change E-Commerce Landscape," *Computerworld*, February 21, 2000.

M-Commerce: A New Threat to Privacy?

MANAGEMENT CHALLENGES

5.1 **Understanding Ethical and Social Issues Related to Systems**
- A Model for Thinking About Ethical, Social, and Political Issues
- Five Moral Dimensions of the Information Age
- Key Technology Trends That Raise Ethical Issues

5.2 **Ethics in an Information Society**
- Basic Concepts: Responsibility, Accountability, and Liability
- Ethical Analysis
- Standard Ethical Principles
- Professional Codes of Conduct or Ethics
- Organizational Information Ethics Policies
- Some Real-World Ethical Dilemmas

MANAGEMENT DECISION PROBLEM:
What to Do about Employee Web Usage

5.3 **The Moral Dimensions of Information Systems**
- Information Rights: Privacy and Freedom in an Information Society
- Property Rights: Intellectual Property

Window on Technology:
Napster and Gnutella Rock the Entertainment Industry
- Accountability, Liability, and Control
- System Quality: Data Quality and System Errors
- Quality of Life: Equity, Access, and Boundaries

Window on Management:
Managing RSI
- Management Actions: A Corporate Code of Ethics

APPLICATION SOFTWARE EXERCISE:
Database Creation: Developing a Database to Track Ethical Violations

MANAGEMENT WRAP-UP

• *Summary* • *Key Terms* • *Review Questions* • *Group Project* • *Internet Connection* • *Case Study: Web Site Privacy: How Much Should We Worry?*

MANAGEMENT CHALLENGES

Technology can be a double-edged sword. It can be the source of many benefits. One great achievement of contemporary computer systems is the ease with which digital information can be analyzed, transmitted, and shared among many people. But at the same time, this powerful capability creates new opportunities for breaking the law or taking benefits away from others. Balancing the convenience and privacy implications of creating electronic dossiers on consumers is one of the compelling ethical issues raised by contemporary information systems. As you read this chapter, you should be aware of the following management challenges:

1. **Understanding the moral risks of new technology.** Rapid technological change means that the choices facing individuals also rapidly change, and the balance of risk and reward and the probabilities of apprehension for wrongful acts change as well. Protecting individual privacy has become a serious ethical issue precisely for this reason, in addition to other issues described in this chapter. In this environment, it will be important for management to conduct an ethical and social impact analysis of new technologies. One might take each of the moral dimensions described in this chapter and briefly speculate on how a new technology will affect each dimension. There may not always be right answers for how to act, but there should be management awareness about the moral risks of new technology.

2. **Establishing corporate ethics policies that include information systems issues**. As managers you will be responsible for developing, enforcing, and explaining corporate ethics policies. Historically, corporate management has paid much more attention to financial integrity and personnel policies than to the information systems area. But after reading this chapter, it should be clear that your organization should have an information systems ethics policy covering issues such as privacy, property, accountability, system quality, and quality of life. The challenge will be in educating non-IS managers to the need for these policies as well as educating your workforce.

Protecting personal privacy on the Internet represents one of the new ethical issues raised by the widespread use of information systems. Others include establishing information rights, protecting intellectual property rights; establishing accountability for the consequences of information systems; setting standards to safeguard systems quality that protect the safety of the individual and society; and preserving values and institutions considered essential to the quality of life in an information society. This chapter describes these issues and suggests guidelines for dealing with these questions.

5.1 UNDERSTANDING ETHICAL AND SOCIAL ISSUES RELATED TO SYSTEMS

ethics
Principles of right and wrong that can be used by individuals acting as free moral agents to make choices to guide their behaviour.

Ethics refers to the principles of right and wrong that individuals, acting as free moral agents, use to make choices to guide their behaviour. Information technology and information systems raise new ethical questions for both individuals and societies because they create opportunities for intense social change and thus threaten existing distributions of power, money, rights, and obligations. Like other technologies, such as steam engines, electricity, telephone, and radio, information technology can be used to achieve social progress, but it can also be used to commit crimes and to threaten cherished social values. The development of information technology will produce benefits for many and harm for others. When using information systems, it is essential to ask: what is the ethical and socially responsible course of action?

A MODEL FOR THINKING ABOUT ETHICAL, SOCIAL, AND POLITICAL ISSUES

Ethical, social, and political issues are closely linked. The ethical dilemma you may face as a manager of information systems typically is reflected in social and political debate. One way to think about these relationships is given in Figure 5-1. Imagine society as a more or less calm pond on a summer day, a delicate ecosystem in partial equilibrium with individuals and with social and political institutions. Individuals know how to act in this pond because social institutions (family, education, organizations) have developed well-established rules of behaviour, and these are backed by laws developed in the political sector that prescribe behaviour and promise sanctions for violations. Now toss a rock into the centre of the pond. But imagine instead of a rock that the disturbing force is a powerful earthquake of new information technology and systems hitting a society more or less at rest. What happens? Ripples, of course.

Suddenly individual actors are confronted with new situations that are often not covered by the old rules. Social institutions cannot respond overnight to these ripples—it may take years to develop etiquette, expectations, social responsibility, "politically correct" attitudes, or approved rules. Political institutions also require time before developing new laws and often require the demonstration of real harm before they enact legislation. In the meantime, you may have to act. You may be forced to operate in a legal "grey area."

We can use this model to illustrate the dynamics that connect ethical, social, and political issues. This model is also useful for identifying the main moral dimensions of the "information society," which cut across various levels of action—individual, social, and political.

FIVE MORAL DIMENSIONS OF THE INFORMATION AGE

A review of the literature on ethical, social, and political issues surrounding systems identifies five moral dimensions of the information age that we introduce here and explore in greater detail in Section 5.3. The five moral dimensions are as follows:

▌ Information rights and obligations: What **information rights** do individuals and organizations possess with respect to information about themselves? What can they protect? What obligations do individuals and organizations have concerning this information?

▌ Property rights: Who owns the software? Who owns the data? How will traditional intellectual property rights be protected in a digital society in which tracing and accounting for ownership is difficult and ignoring property rights is so easy?

▌ Accountability and control: Who can and will be held accountable and liable for any harm done to individual and collective information and property rights? to individuals and corporations?

information rights
The rights that individuals and organizations have with respect to information that pertains to themselves.

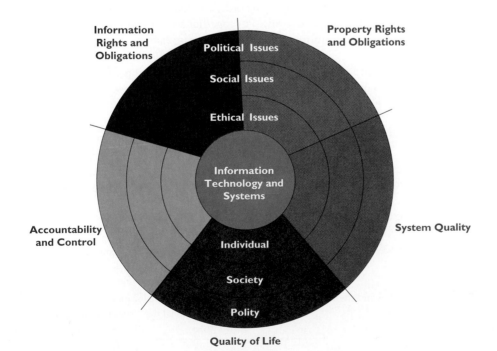

Information Rights and Obligations

Property Rights and Obligations

Political Issues

Social Issues

Ethical Issues

Information Technology and Systems

Accountability and Control

Individual

Society

Polity

System Quality

Quality of Life

FIGURE 5-1 The relationship between ethical, social, and political issues in an information society. The introduction of new information technology has a ripple effect, raising new ethical, social, and political issues that must be dealt with at the individual, social, and political levels. These issues have five moral dimensions: information rights and obligations, property rights and obligations, system quality, quality of life, and accountability and control.

❚ Systems quality: What standards of data and system quality should we demand to protect individual rights and the safety of society?

❚ Quality of life: What values should be preserved in an information- and knowledge-based society? What institutions should we protect from violation? What cultural values and practices are supported by the new information technology?

Before we analyze these dimensions, let us briefly review the major technology and systems trends that have increased our concern about these issues.

KEY TECHNOLOGY TRENDS THAT RAISE ETHICAL ISSUES

Ethical issues long preceded information technology—they are the abiding concerns of free societies everywhere. Nevertheless, information technology has heightened ethical concerns, put stress on existing social arrangements, and made existing laws obsolete or severely crippled. There are four key technological trends responsible for these ethical stresses. They are summarized in Table 5-1.

The doubling of computing power every 18 months has made it possible for most organizations to use information systems for their core production processes. As a result, our dependence on systems and our vulnerability to system errors and poor data quality have increased. Social rules and laws have not yet adjusted to this dependence. Standards for ensuring the accuracy and reliability of information systems (see Chapter 12) are not universally accepted or enforced.

Advances in data storage techniques and rapidly declining storage costs have been responsible for the creation of multiple databases on individuals—employees, customers, and potential customers—maintained by private and public organizations. These advances in data storage have made the routine violation of individual privacy both cheap and effective. For example, IBM has developed a wafer-sized disk that can hold the equivalent of more than 500 large novels (Markoff, 1998). Already massive data storage systems are cheap enough for regional and even local retailing firms to use in identifying customers.

Advances in datamining techniques for large databases are a third technological trend that heightens ethical concerns because they enable companies to find out much more detailed personal information about individuals. With contemporary information systems technology, companies can assemble and combine myriad pieces of information stored on an individual by computers much more easily than in the past. Think of all the ways computer information is generated—credit card purchases, telephone calls, magazine subscriptions, video rentals, mail-order purchases, banking records, and local, state, and federal government records (including court and police records). Put together and mined properly, this information can reveal not only credit information but also driving habits, tastes, associations, and political interests.

Companies with products to sell purchase relevant information from these sources to help them more finely target their marketing campaigns. Chapter 8 describes how companies

TABLE 5-1	TECHNOLOGY TRENDS THAT RAISE ETHICAL ISSUES
Trend	**Impact**
Computing power doubles every 18 months	More organizations depend on computer systems for critical operations
Rapidly declining data storage costs	Organizations can easily maintain detailed databases on individuals
Datamining advances	Companies can analyze vast quantities of data gathered on individuals to develop detailed profiles of individual behaviour
Networking advances and the Internet	Copying data from one location to another and accessing personal data from remote locations are much easier

Credit card purchases can make personal information available to market researchers, telephone marketers, and direct mail companies. Advances in information technology facilitate the invasion of privacy.

can use datamining on very large pools of data from multiple sources to rapidly identify buying patterns of customers and to suggest individual responses. The use of computers to combine data from multiple sources and to create electronic dossiers of detailed information on individuals is called **profiling**. For example, thousands of Web sites allow DoubleClick (www.doubleclick.net), an Internet advertising broker, to track the activities of their visitors in exchange for revenue from advertisements based on visitor information DoubleClick gathers. DoubleClick uses this information to create a profile of each online visitor, adding more detail to the profile as the visitor accesses an associated DoubleClick site. Over time, DoubleClick can create a detailed dossier of a person's spending and computing habits on the Web that can be sold to companies to help them target their Web ads more precisely.

profiling
The use of computers to combine data from multiple sources and to create electronic dossiers of detailed information on individuals.

Last, advances in networking, including the Internet, promise to significantly reduce the costs of moving and accessing large quantities of data and open the possibility for remotely mining large pools of data using small desktop machines, permitting an invasion of privacy on a scale and precision heretofore unimaginable.

The development of global digital-superhighway communication networks widely available to individuals and businesses poses many ethical and social concerns. Who will account for the flow of information over these networks? Can users trace information collected about them? What will these networks do to the traditional relationships between family, work, and leisure? How will traditional job designs be altered when millions of "employees" become subcontractors using mobile offices that they themselves pay for?

In the next section, we will consider some ethical principles and analytical techniques for dealing with these kinds of ethical and social concerns.

5.2 ETHICS IN AN INFORMATION SOCIETY

Ethics is a concern of humans who have freedom of choice. Ethics is about individual choice: When faced with alternative courses of action, what is the correct moral choice? What are the main features of "ethical choice"?

BASIC CONCEPTS: RESPONSIBILITY, ACCOUNTABILITY, AND LIABILITY

Ethical choices are decisions made by individuals who are responsible for the consequences of their actions. Responsibility is a key element of ethical action. **Responsibility** means that you accept the potential costs, duties, and obligations of the decisions you make. **Accountability** is a feature of systems and social institutions: It means that mechanisms are in place to determine who is responsible for an action. Systems and institutions in which it is impossible to find out who took what action are inherently incapable of ethical analysis or

responsibility
Accepting the potential costs, duties, and obligations for the decisions one makes.

accountability
The existence of mechanisms for assessing responsibility for decisions made and actions taken.

liability

The existence of laws that permit individuals to recover the damages done to them by other actors, systems, or organizations.

due process

A process in which laws are well-known and understood and in which there is an ability to appeal to higher authorities to ensure that laws are applied correctly.

ethical action. Liability extends the concept of responsibility further to the area of laws. **Liability** is a feature of political systems in which a body of law is in place that permits individuals to recover the damages done to them by other actors, systems, or organizations. **Due process** is a related feature of law-governed societies and is a process in which laws are known and understood, and in which there is an ability to appeal to higher authorities to ensure that the laws are applied correctly.

These basic concepts form the underpinning of an ethical analysis of information systems and those who manage them. First, as discussed in Chapter 3, information technologies are filtered through social institutions, organizations, and individuals. Systems do not have "impacts" by themselves. The impacts of information systems are products of institutional, organizational, and individual actions and behaviours. Second, responsibility for the consequences of technology falls clearly on the institutions, organizations, and individual managers who choose to use the technology. Using information technology in a "socially responsible" manner means that you may be held accountable for the consequences of your actions. Third, in an ethical political society, individuals and others can recover damages through a set of laws characterized by due process.

ETHICAL ANALYSIS

When confronted with a situation that seems to present ethical issues, how should you analyze and reason about the situation? Following is a five-step process that should help:

1. **Identify and describe the facts clearly.** Find out who did what to whom, where, when, and how. In many instances, you will be surprised at the errors in the initially reported facts, and often you will find that simply getting the facts straight helps to define the solution. It also helps to get the opposing parties involved in an ethical dilemma to agree on the facts.

2. **Define the conflict or dilemma and identify the higher-order values involved.** Ethical, social, and political issues always reference higher values. Typically, the parties to a dispute all claim to be pursuing higher values (e.g., freedom, privacy, protection of property, or the free enterprise system). Typically, an ethical issue involves a dilemma: two diametrically opposed courses of action that support worthwhile values. For example, the chapter-opening vignette and ending Case Study illustrate two competing values: the need for companies to use marketing to become more efficient and the need to protect individual privacy.

3. **Identify the stakeholders.** Every ethical, social, and political issue has stakeholders: players who have an interest in the outcome, who are invested in the situation, and usually who have vocal opinions. Find out the identity of these groups and what they want. This will be useful later when designing a solution.

4. **Identify the options that you can reasonably take.** You may find that none of the options satisfies all the interests involved, but that some options do a better job than others. Sometimes arriving at a "good" or ethical solution may not always be a "balancing" of consequences to stakeholders.

5. **Identify the potential consequences of your options.** Some options may be ethically correct, but disastrous from other points of view. Other options may work in this one instance, but not in other similar instances. Always ask yourself, "What if I choose this option consistently over time?"

Once your analysis is complete, what ethical principles or rules should you use to make a decision? What higher-order values should inform your judgment?

STANDARD ETHICAL PRINCIPLES

Although you are the only one who can decide which among many ethical principles you will follow and how you will prioritize them, it is helpful to consider some ethical principles with deep roots in many cultures that have survived throughout recorded history.

1. Do unto others as you would have them do unto you (the **Golden Rule**). Putting yourself into the place of others and thinking of yourself as the object of the decision can help you think about "fairness" in decision making.

2. If an action is not right for everyone to take, then it is not right for anyone (**Kant's categorical imperative**). Ask yourself, "If everyone did this, could the organization, or society, survive?"

3. If an action cannot be taken repeatedly, then it is not right to take at all. (**Descartes' rule of change**). This is the slippery-slope rule: An action may bring about a small change now that is acceptable, but if repeated would bring unacceptable changes in the long run. In the vernacular, it might be stated as "once started down a slippery slope, you may not be able to stop."

4. Take the action that achieves the higher or greater value (the **utilitarian principle**). This rule assumes you can prioritize values in a rank order and understand the consequences of various courses of action.

5. Take the action that produces the least harm, or the least potential cost (**risk aversion principle**). Some actions have extremely high failure costs but very low probability (e.g., building a nuclear generating facility in an urban area) or extremely high failure costs of moderate probability (speeding and automobile accidents). Avoid these high-failure-cost actions, paying greatest attention to high-failure-cost potentials of moderate to high probability.

6. Assume that virtually all tangible and intangible objects are owned by someone else unless there is a specific declaration otherwise. (This is the **ethical "no free lunch" rule**.) If something someone else has created is useful to you, it has value and you should assume the creator wants compensation for it.

Unfortunately, these ethical rules have too many logical and substantive exceptions to be absolute guides to action. Nevertheless, actions that do not easily pass these rules deserve very close attention and a great deal of caution because the appearance of unethical behaviour may do as much harm to you or your company as actual unethical behaviour.

PROFESSIONAL CODES OF CONDUCT OR ETHICS

When groups of people claim to be professionals, they take on special rights and obligations because of their special claims to knowledge, wisdom, and authority. Professional codes of conduct, also known as professional codes of ethics, are promulgated by associations of professionals such as the Canadian Information Processing Society (CIPS), the Canadian Bar Association (CBA), the Data Processing Management Association (DPMA), and the Association of Computing Machinery (ACM). These professional groups take responsibility for the partial regulation of their professions by determining entrance qualifications and competence. Codes of ethics are promises by professions to regulate themselves and their members in the general interest of society. For example, avoiding harm to others, honouring property rights (including intellectual property), and respecting privacy are among the General Moral Imperatives of the ACM's Code of Ethics and Professional Conduct (ACM, 1993).

Extensions to these moral imperatives state that ACM professionals should consider the health, privacy, and general welfare of the public in the performance of their work and that professionals should express their professional opinion to their employer regarding any adverse consequences to the public (Oz, 1994). There are many different ethical codes with competing ethical dictates, varying parties considered, and different priorities assigned to ethical obligations. Most codes of conduct for information systems professionals do not carry a penalty for code violations, other than the possible loss of certification or membership. Since many information systems professionals are not certified by a professional association and are not members of such an association, the codes serve at best as a warning of ethical concerns, rather than as a stringent requirement for action.

Golden Rule
A principle that states, "Do unto others as you would have them to do unto you."

Kant's categorical imperative
A principle that states that if an action is not right for everyone to take, it is not right for anyone.

Descartes' rule of change
A principle that states that if an action cannot be taken repeatedly, then it is not right to be taken at any time. Also known as the slippery-slope rule.

utilitarian principle
A principle that assumes one can put values in rank order and understand the consequences of various courses of action.

risk aversion principle
The principle that one should take the action that produces the least harm or incurs the least cost.

ethical "no free lunch" rule
A principle that assumes that all tangible and intangible objects are owned by someone else unless there is a specific declaration otherwise and that the creator wants compensation for this work.

ORGANIZATIONAL INFORMATION ETHICS POLICIES

It is not enough for a company to rely on a professional code of conduct or ethics. Many, if not most, information systems professionals do not belong to a professional association with a code of conduct. A well-thought-out, well-communicated organizational policy on information ethics is needed. The policy should also state how the policy will be carried out (e.g., electronic surveillance, monitoring of e-mail) and what the penalties are for violating the policy (e.g., firing, assessing a fine against wages).

Again, the policy must be communicated to employees. Many companies require their employees to sign a copy of the policy, stating that they have read and understood the policy and that they will abide by the policy.

SOME REAL-WORLD ETHICAL DILEMMAS

The recent ethical problems described in this section illustrate a wide range of issues. Some of these issues are obvious ethical dilemmas, in which one set of interests is pitted against another. Others represent a breach of ethics. In either instance, there are rarely any easy solutions.

Downsizing with Technology at the Telephone Company   Many of the large telephone companies in North America are using information technology to reduce the size of their workforce. For example, Bell Canada is using voice recognition software to reduce the need for human operators by allowing computers to recognize a customer's responses to a series of computerized questions. Bell Canada planned for the new technology to eliminate 1500 operator jobs nationwide.

Employee Monitoring on the Internet   Xerox Corporation fired 40 workers in 1999 for spending too much of their work time surfing the Web. That company and many others monitor what their employees are doing on the Internet to prevent them from wasting company resources for non-business activities (San Jose Mercury, 2000). Many firms also claim the right to monitor the electronic mail of their employees because they own the facilities, intend their use to be for business purposes only, and create the facility for a business purpose. In this case, a company policy on information ethics that included Internet usage would signal the rights of the individual and the rights of the company (see Figure 5-2). A Missisauga, Ontario engineer was fired from his job for sending pictures of Cindy Crawford in a bathing suit over e-mail (see Chapter 9).

In each instance, you can find competing values at work, with groups lined on either side of a debate. A company may argue, for example, that it has a right to use information systems to increase productivity and to reduce the size of its workforce to lower costs and stay in business. Employees displaced by information systems may argue that employers have

FIGURE 5-2 SurfControl's Super Scout Rules Administrator lets managers decide what their employees can access over the Web and insert comments on an employee's screen telling the employee why they cannot have access to a site.

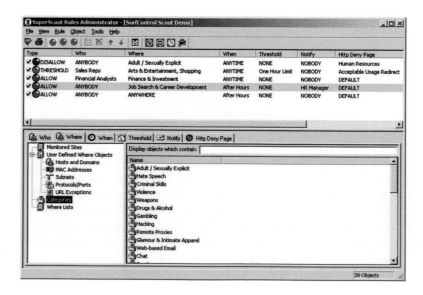

MANAGEMENT DECISION PROBLEM

WHAT TO DO ABOUT EMPLOYEE WEB USAGE

As the head of a small insurance company with six employees, you are concerned about how effectively your company is using its networking and human resources. Budgets are tight, and you are struggling to meet payrolls because employees are reporting many overtime hours. You do not believe that the employees have a sufficiently heavy workload to warrant working longer hours and are looking into the amount of time they spend on the Internet. Each employee uses a computer with Internet access on the job. You requested the following weekly report of employee Web usage from your company Web server.

Web Usage Report for the Week ending January 12, 2002:

User name	Minutes Online	URL Visited
Kelleher, Claire	45	www.doubleclick.net
Kelleher, Claire	57	www.yahoo.com
Kelleher, Claire	96	www.insuremarket.com
McMahon, Patricia	83	www.e-music.com
Milligan, Robert	112	www.shopping.com
Milligan, Robert	43	www.travelocity.com
Olivera, Ernesto	40	www.internetnews.com
Talbot, Helen	125	www.etrade.com
Talbot, Helen	27	www.wine.com
Talbot, Helen	35	www.yahoo.com
Talbot, Helen	73	www.ebay.com
Wright, Steven	23	www.geocities.com
Wright, Steven	15	www.autobytel.com

1. Calculate the total amount of time each employee spent on the Web for the week and the total amount of time that company computers were used for this purpose. Rank the employees in the order of the amount of time each spent online.

2. Do your findings and the contents of the report indicate any ethical problems employees are creating? Is the company creating an ethical problem by monitoring its employees' use of the Internet?

3. Use the guidelines for ethical analysis presented in this chapter to develop a solution to the problems you have identified.

---

some responsibility for their welfare. A close analysis of the facts can sometimes produce compromise solutions that give each side "half a loaf." Try to apply some of the described principles of ethical analysis to each of these cases. What is the right thing to do?

5.3 THE MORAL DIMENSIONS OF INFORMATION SYSTEMS

In this section, we take a closer look at the five moral dimensions of information systems first described in Figure 5-1. In each dimension, we identify the ethical, social, and political levels of analysis and use real-world examples to illustrate the values involved, the stakeholders, and the options chosen.

INFORMATION RIGHTS: PRIVACY AND FREEDOM IN AN INFORMATION SOCIETY

Privacy is the claim of individuals to be left alone, free from surveillance or interference from other individuals or organizations including government. Claims to privacy are also involved at the workplace: Millions of employees are subject to electronic and other forms of high-tech surveillance. For example, see the opening vignette of Chapter 1 for how Nygård video-tapes the shipping of its garments. Information technology and systems threaten individual claims to privacy by making the invasion of privacy cheap, profitable, and effective. The following describes first Canadian privacy laws and then U.S. privacy laws. In terms of international trade, organizations need to follow the privacy laws of the countries of their trading

privacy
The claim of individuals to be left alone, free from surveillance or interference from other individuals, organizations, or government.

partners. For this reason, we have chosen to highlight U.S. privacy laws as the United States is Canada's most significant trading partner. We also highlight European privacy protection. While similar, the differences are interesting.

The claim to privacy is protected in the Canadian, U.S., and German charters or constitutions in a variety of different ways, and in other countries through various statutes. In Canada, the claim to privacy is protected primarily by the right to be secure against unreasonable search or seizure found in the Charter of Rights and Freedoms. In addition, on April 13, 2000, Parliament passed Bill C-6, Canada's modern privacy law. Bill C-6 establishes the following principles to govern the collection, use, and disclosure of personal information: accountability, identifying the purposes for the collection of personal information, obtaining consent, limiting collection, limiting use, disclosure and retention, ensuring accuracy, providing adequate security, making information management policies readily available, providing individuals with access to information about themselves, and giving individuals a right to challenge an organization's compliance with these principles.

Bill C-6 further provides for the Privacy Commissioner to receive complaints concerning contraventions of the principles, conduct investigations, and attempt to resolve such complaints. Unresolved disputes relating to certain matters can be taken to the Federal Court for resolution. The law's provisions are being phased in from January 1, 2001, to January 1, 2004. This act complements the 1983 Privacy Act, which imposes rules on how federal government departments and agencies collect, use, and disclose personal information.

Every Canadian province and territory, except Prince Edward Island, has enacted legislation parallel to the federal *Privacy Act* and the *Access to Information Act*. These laws prevent the unnecessary distribution of one's personal information and guarantee access to unrestricted government information.

As in the federal jurisdiction, the laws apply only to information held by the public sector. "Public sector" organizations under the privacy laws include public or private companies that are regulated by the government, such as financial institutions, air transportation companies, and broadcast media. The only province with a privacy law governing the private sector is Quebec. Right now Quebec is the only province with privacy laws for the private sector that meet European Union standards. That's significant for international trade, which increasingly means information, not hard products. By the way, the United States doesn't meet those standards either. Other than in Quebec, there are no laws in Canada that regulate what private businesses can do with your personal information. This means that there is nothing to prevent a private company from distributing your personal information to other businesses.

Due process has become a key concept in defining privacy. Due process requires that a set of rules or laws exist that clearly define how information about individuals will be treated and what appeal mechanisms are available. Perhaps the best statement in Canada of due process in record keeping is given by the *Canadian Standards Association's Model Privacy Code*. Published in March 1996, the Code establishes 10 basic principles for all organizations that collect or use personal information. Retailers, direct marketers, financial institutions, telecommunications companies, product manufacturers, service providers, schools, universities, hospitals, personnel departments, and government agencies are potential users.

By choosing to adopt the voluntary Code, organizations demonstrate that they are following fair, nationally accepted principles. The Code is also an important resource for consumers, employees, patients, and other "data subjects," says Professor Jim Savary, former Vice-President of Policy and Issues at the Consumers' Association of Canada. "The Code is a vehicle for challenging an organization's behaviour. You can refer to these principles if you are uneasy about the information you are asked to supply or how it will be used."

The 10 practices in the Code are:

1. Accountability
2. Identifying purposes
3. Consent
4. Limiting collection
5. Limiting use, disclosure, and retention

6. Accuracy
7. Safeguards
8. Openness
9. Individual access
10. Challenging compliance

Most North American and European privacy law is based on a regime called Fair Information Practices (FIP) first set forth in a report written in 1973 by a U.S. government advisory committee (U.S. Department of Health, Education, and Welfare, 1973). **Fair Information Practices (FIP)** is a set of principles governing the collection and use of information about individuals. Fair Information Practices preceded but are similar to the *Model Privacy Code* in Canada. The five Fair Information Practices principles are shown in Table 5-2.

FIP principles are based on the notion of a "mutuality of interest" between the record holder and the individual. The individual has an interest in engaging in a transaction, and the record keeper—usually a business or government agency—requires information about the individual to support the transaction. Once gathered, the individual maintains an interest in the record, and the record may not be used to support other activities without the individual's consent.

Fair Information Practices form the basis of 13 U.S. statutes listed in Table 5.3 that set forth the conditions for handling information about individuals in such areas as credit reporting, education, financial records, newspaper records, cable communications, electronic communications, and even video rentals. The U.S. Privacy Act of 1974 is the most important of these laws, regulating the federal government's collection, use, and disclosure of information. Most federal privacy laws apply only to the federal government. Only credit, banking, cable, and video rental industries have been regulated by U.S. privacy law.

In the United States, privacy law is enforced by individuals who must sue agencies or companies in court to recover damages. European countries and Canada define privacy in a similar manner to that in the United States, but they have chosen to enforce their privacy laws by creating privacy commissions or data protection agencies to pursue complaints brought by citizens.

The European Directive on Data Protection

In Europe, privacy protection is much more stringent than in North America. On October 25, 1998, the European Directive on Data Protection came into effect, broadening privacy protection in the European Union (EU) nations. The Directive requires companies to inform people when they collect information about them and to disclose how it will be stored and used. Customers must provide their informed consent before any company can legally use data about them, and customers have the right to access that information, to correct it, and to request that no further data be collected. EU member nations must translate these principles into their own laws and cannot transfer personal data to countries such as Canada and the United States that don't have similar privacy protection regulations. This in effect constitutes the *opt-in* versus *opt-out* debate. In North America, consumers who are

Fair Information Practices (FIP)

A set of principles originally set forth in 1973 that governs the collection and use of information about individuals and forms the basis of most North American and European privacy laws.

TABLE 5-2	FAIR INFORMATION PRACTICES PRINCIPLES

1. There should be no personal record systems whose existence is secret.
2. Individuals have rights of access, inspection, review, and amendment to systems that contain information about them.
3. There must be no use of personal information for purposes other than those for which it was gathered, without prior consent.
4. Managers of systems are responsible and can be held accountable and liable for the damage done by systems for their reliability and security.
5. Governments have the right to intervene in the information relationships among private parties.

TABLE 5-3	FEDERAL PRIVACY LAWS IN THE UNITED STATES

1. General Federal Privacy Laws

Freedom of Information Act, 1968 as Amended (5 USC 552)

Privacy Act of 1974 as Amended (5 USC 552a)

Electronic Communications Privacy Act of 1986

Computer Matching and Privacy Protection Act of 1988

Computer Security Act of 1987

Federal Managers Financial Integrity Act of 1982

2. Privacy Laws Affecting Private Institutions

Fair Credit Reporting Act of 1970

Family Educational Rights and Privacy Act of 1978

Right to Financial Privacy Act of 1978

Privacy Protection Act of 1980

Cable Communications Policy Act of 1984

Electronic Communications Privacy Act of 1986

Video Privacy Protection Act of 1988

Communications Privacy and Consumer Empowerment Act of 1997

Data Privacy Act of 1997

Consumer Internet Privacy Protection Act of 1999

offered any degree of control over the data collected about them may be offered the option of "opting out," that is telling the company collecting the data that they do not want data to be collected about them or, alternatively, for that data to be used by anyone other than that company or for any purpose other than the purpose for which it was collected. Few North American companies offer customers the opportunity to "opt in." In the European Union, however, there is no such option. The only option available is to "opt in"; in other words, European counties may not collect extraneous personal data or use it for purposes other than those related to a transaction *unless* the customer says that they may do so.

Internet Challenges to Privacy

The Internet introduces technology that poses new challenges to the protection of individual privacy that existing Fair Information Practices principles are inadequate to address. Information sent over the Internet may pass through many different computer systems before it reaches its final destination. Each of these systems is capable of monitoring, capturing, and storing communications that pass through it.

It is possible to record many online activities, including which online newsgroups or files a person has accessed, which Web sites he or she has visited, and what items that person has inspected or purchased over the Web. This information can be collected by both a subscriber's own Internet service provider and the systems operators of remote Web sites that a subscriber visits. Tools to monitor visits to the World Wide Web have become popular because they help organizations determine who is visiting their Web sites and how to better target their offerings. (Some firms also monitor the Internet usage of their employees to see how they are using company network resources.) Web retailers now have access to software that lets them watch the online shopping behaviour of individuals and groups while they are visiting a Web site and making purchases (Dalton, 1999). The commercial demand for this personal information is enormous.

Web sites can learn the identity of their visitors if the visitors voluntarily register at the site to purchase a product or service or to obtain a free service such as information provided by an e-mail newsletter. Web sites can also capture information about visitors without their knowledge using "cookie" technology. **Cookies** are tiny files deposited on a computer's hard drive when a user visits certain Web sites. Cookies identify the visitor's Web browser software

cookie
A file deposited on a user's hard drive when the user visits certain Web sites, identifying the user's browser software and tracking the visit.

and track visits to the Web site. When the visitor returns to a site that has stored a cookie, the Web site software will search the visitor's computer, find the cookie, and "know" what that person has done in the past. It may also update the cookie, depending on the activity during visit. In this way, the site can customize its contents for each visitor's interests. For example, if a user purchases a book from Amazon.com and returns later from the same browser, the site will welcome the user by name and recommend other books of interest based on past purchases. DoubleClick, introduced earlier in this chapter, uses cookies to build its dossiers with details of online purchases and behaviour of Web site visitors. Figure 5-3 illustrates how cookies work.

A regular Web user can search his or her hard drive for files named "cookie.txt" and will likely find some. Sites may use the data from cookies for their own use, or they may also sell that data to other companies. Web sites using "cookie" technology cannot directly obtain visitors' names and addresses. However, if a person has registered at any other site, some of that information will be stored in a cookie. Examine the cookies on your own computer, and you will see how much personal data is there. Often, scattered within the cookies, you will find your real name, your user name, your bank, your stockbroker, and perhaps your account numbers. These cookies are not secured in any way, and Web site owners can surreptitiously search them for personal data stored there. Thus if one site stores your name, another can find it. The result is that many sites know a great deal more about you than you might suspect or desire.

Organizations can collect e-mail addresses to send out thousands and even hundreds of thousands of unsolicited e-mail and electronic messages. This practice is called **spamming**, and it is growing because it only costs a few cents to send thousands of messages advertising one's wares to Internet users. Marketing companies can use new technology for monitoring e-mail users to keep tabs on who opens their e-mail solicitations and at what time of the day to develop more personalized promotions. They can link this information to data collected through cookies to create even more detailed databases of individuals' activities on the Web (Harmon, 2000).

At present, Web site visitors can't easily find out how the information collected about them from their visits to Web sites is being used. Only a small percentage of Web sites openly post their privacy policies or offer consumers a choice about how their personal data are to be used (Rosen and Bacheldor, 2000). To encourage self-regulation in the Internet industry, industry groups such as the Online Privacy Alliance (OPA), consisting of over 100 global corporations and associations, have also issued guidelines for self-regulation. The U.S. Department of Commerce has issued guidelines for Fair Information Practices in online

spamming
The practice of sending unsolicited e-mail and other electronic communication.

FIGURE 5-3 How cookies identify Web visitors. Cookies are written by a Web site on a visitor's hard drive. When the visitor returns to that Web site, the Web server requests the ID number from the cookie and uses it to access the data stored by the server on that visitor. The Web site can then use these data to display personalized information.

Source: Alan Zeichick, "Personalization Explained," *Red Herring*, September 1999, p. 130. Reprinted by permission.

Don't I Know You?

How Web servers identify their visitors.

1. The server reads the PC's browser to determine the user's operating system, browser name and version number, IP address, and other information, sometimes including the user's e-mail address.

2. The server uses the browser information to transmit tiny bits of personalized data called cookies, which the user's browser receives and stores on the PC's hard drive.

3. When the user revisits the Web site, the server requests the contents of any cookie previously provided by that site.

4. The Web server reads the cookie, identifies the user, then calls up its data on the visitor.

business. Privacy-enhancing technologies for protecting user privacy during interactions with Web sites are being developed (Vijayan, 2000; Reiter and Rubin, 1999; Goldschlag, Reed, and Syverson, 1999; Gabber, Gibbons, Kristol, Matias, and Mayer, 1999). Additional legislation and government oversight may be required to make sure that privacy in the Internet age is properly safeguarded. The chapter-ending case study explores the issue of Web privacy in greater detail.

Ethical Issues

The ethical privacy issue in this information age is as follows: Under what conditions should I (you) invade the privacy of others? What legitimates intruding into others' lives through unobtrusive surveillance, through market research, or by whatever means? Do we have to inform people that we are eavesdropping? Do we have to inform people that we are using credit history information for employment screening purposes?

Social Issues

The social issue of privacy concerns the development of "expectations of privacy" or privacy norms as well as public attitudes. In what areas of life should we as a society encourage people to think they are in "private territory" as opposed to public view? For instance, should we as a society encourage people to develop expectations of privacy when using electronic mail, cellular telephones, bulletin boards, the postal system, the workplace, the street? Should expectations of privacy be extended to criminal conspirators?

Political Issues

The political issue of privacy concerns the development of statutes that govern the relations between record keepers and individuals. Should we permit the permit the Canadian Security Intelligence Service (CSIS), RCMP, or local police to eavesdrop at will? Should a law be passed to require direct-marketing firms to obtain the consent of individuals before using their names in mass marketing (a consensus database)? Should e-mail privacy—regardless of who owns the equipment—be protected by law? In general, large organizations of all kinds—public and private—are reluctant to disavow the advantages that come from the unfettered flow of information on individuals. Civil libertarians and other privacy groups have been the strongest voices supporting restraints on large organizations' information-gathering activities.

PROPERTY RIGHTS: INTELLECTUAL PROPERTY

Contemporary information systems have severely challenged existing law and social practices that protect private intellectual property. **Intellectual property** is considered to be intangible property created by individuals or corporations. Information technology has made it difficult to protect intellectual property because computerized information can be so easily copied or distributed on networks. Intellectual property is subject to a variety of protections under three different legal traditions: trade secret, copyright, and patent law (Graham, 1984).

Trade Secrets

Any intellectual work product—a formula, device, pattern, or compilation of data—used for a business purpose can be classified as a **trade secret**, provided it is not based on information in the public domain. Trade secret law has arisen out of the broad "duty of good faith" and the principle of equity that whoever "has received information in confidence shall not take unfair advantage of it."

The Supreme Court of Canada has stated that the test for whether there has been a breach of confidence consists of three elements.

1. The information conveyed must be confidential (that is, it must not be public knowledge).
2. The information must have been communicated in confidence.
3. The information must have been misused by the party to whom it was communicated.

---

intellectual property
Intangible property created by individuals or organizations that is subject to protections under trade secret, copyright, and patent law.

trade secret
Any intellectual work or product used for a business purpose that can be classified as belonging to that individual or business, provided it is not based on information in the public domain.

As trade secret law in Canada is a matter of provincial jurisdiction, the drafting and interpretation of agreements that contain trade secret provisions must be carried out by a lawyer in the province that governs the agreement in question. Similarly, the assessment of whether a breach of confidence has occurred must be carried out by a lawyer in the province that governs the obligation of confidence. In general, trade secret laws grant a monopoly on the ideas behind a work product, but it can be a very tenuous monopoly.

Software that contains novel or unique elements, procedures, or compilations can be included as a trade secret. Trade secret law protects the actual ideas in a work product, not only their manifestation. To make this claim, the creator or owner must take care to bind employees and customers with nondisclosure agreements and to prevent the secret from falling into the public domain.

The limitation of trade secret protection is that although virtually all software programs of any complexity contain unique elements of some sort, it is difficult to prevent the ideas in the work from falling into the public domain when the software is widely distributed.

Copyright

Copyright is a statutory grant that protects creators of intellectual property from having their work copied by others for any purpose for a period of at least 50 years. The Copyright Office registers copyrights and enforces copyright law in Canada. Parliament has extended copyright protection to books, periodicals, lectures, dramas, musical compositions, maps, drawings, artwork of any kind, and motion pictures. The intent behind copyright laws has been to encourage creativity and authorship by ensuring that creative people receive the financial and other benefits of their work. Most industrial nations have their own copyright laws, and there are several international conventions and bilateral agreements through which nations coordinate and enforce their laws.

Copyright law in Canada is one of the principal means of protecting computer software in Canada. Canadian copyright law is governed by the Copyright Act, which protects original literary, artistic, musical, and dramatic works. Computer software is protected in Canada as a literary work. Canadian copyright comes into existence automatically, and in the case of software, it comes into existence at the time the software is created and continues until the end of the calendar year in which the *author* of the software dies (regardless of whether the author has sold or assigned the copyright in the software or not) and continues for an additional period of 50 years following the end of that calendar year.

"Moral" rights are also protected under Canadian copyright law. Moral rights in Canada include the right of the author of a piece of software to be associated with the software by name or pseudonym, and the right to remain anonymous. They also include the author's right to the integrity of the software (that is, the author's right to stop the software from being distorted, mutilated or modified, to the prejudice of the author's honour or reputation, or from being used in association with a product, service, cause, or institution).

Moral rights remain with the *author* of a piece of software, even where the software, or the copyright in the software, has been sold or assigned; regardless of whether the author created the software in the employ of someone else, or created it under contract, or otherwise.

Copyright protection is clear-cut. It protects against copying of entire programs or their parts. Damages and relief are readily obtained for infringement. The drawback to copyright protection is that the underlying ideas behind a work are not protected, only their manifestation in a work. A competitor can use your software, understand how it works, and develop new software that follows the same concepts without infringing on a copyright.

"Look and feel" copyright infringement lawsuits are precisely about the distinction between an idea and its expression. Most of this type of copyright infringement has occurred in the United States. For instance, in the early 1990s, Apple Computer sued Microsoft Corporation and Hewlett-Packard Inc. for infringement of the *expression* of Apple's Macintosh interface. Among other claims, Apple claimed that the defendants copied the expression of overlapping windows. The defendants counterclaimed that the idea of overlapping windows can only be expressed in a single way and, therefore, was not protectable under the "merger" doctrine of copyright law. When ideas and their expression merge, the expression cannot be copyrighted. In general, courts appear to be following the reasoning of a 1989

copyright
A statutory grant that protects creators of intellectual property against copying by others for any purpose for a period of at least 50 years.

U.S. case—*Brown Bag Software* vs. *Symantec Corp.*—in which the court dissected the elements of software alleged to be infringing. The court found that neither similar concept, function, general functional features (e.g., drop-down menus), nor colours are protected by copyright law (*Brown Bag* vs. *Symantec Corp.*, 1992).

Patents

patent

A legal document that grants the owner an exclusive monopoly on the ideas behind an invention for between 17 and 20 years; designed to ensure that inventors of new machines or methods are rewarded for their labour while making widespread use of their inventions.

A **patent** grants the owner an exclusive monopoly on the ideas behind an invention for between 17 and 20 years. The intent behind patent law is to ensure that inventors of new machines, devices, or methods receive the full financial and other rewards of their labour and yet still make widespread use of the invention possible by providing detailed diagrams for those wishing to use the idea under license from the patent's owner. The granting of a patent is determined by the Patent Office and relies on court rulings.

The key concepts in patent law are originality, novelty, and invention. The Canadian Patent Office does not accept applications for software patents because software is considered to fall under Canadian copyright law. In the United States the U.S. Patent Office did not routinely issue patents on software until a 1981 Supreme Court decision that held that computer programs could be a part of a patentable process. Since that time, hundreds of U.S. patents for software have been granted, and thousands await consideration.

The strength of patent protection is that it grants a monopoly on the underlying concepts and ideas of software. The difficulty is passing stringent criteria of nonobviousness (e.g., the work must reflect some special understanding and contribution), originality, and novelty as well as years of waiting to receive protection.

Challenges to Intellectual Property Rights

Contemporary information technologies, especially software, pose a severe challenge to existing intellectual property regimes and, therefore, create significant ethical, social, and political issues. Digital media differ from books, periodicals, and other media in terms of ease of replication; ease of transmission; ease of alteration; difficulty classifying a software work as a program, book, or even music; compactness and electronic basis—making theft easy; and difficulties in establishing uniqueness.

The proliferation of electronic networks, including the Internet, has made it even more difficult to protect intellectual property. Before widespread use of networks, copies of software, books, magazine articles, or films had to be stored on physical media, such as paper, computer disks, or videotape, creating some hurdles to distribution. Using networks, information can be more widely reproduced and distributed (Johnson, 1997).

With the World Wide Web in particular, one can easily copy and distribute virtually anything to thousands and even millions of people around the world, even if they are using different types of computer systems. Information can be illicitly copied from one place and distributed through other systems and networks even though these parties do not willingly participate in the infringement. For example, the music industry is worried because individuals can illegally copy MP3 music files to Web sites where they can be downloaded by others who do not know that the MP3 files are not licensed for copying or distribution (see the Window on Technology). The Internet was designed to transmit information freely around the world, including copyrighted information. Intellectual property that can be easily copied is likely to be copied (Carazos, 1996; Chabrow, 1996).

The manner in which information is obtained and presented on the Web further challenges intellectual property protections (Okerson, 1996). Web pages can be constructed from bits of text, graphics, sound, or video that may come from many different sources. Each item may belong to a different entity, creating complicated issues of ownership and compensation (see Figure 5-4). Web sites can also use a capability called "framing" to let one site construct an on-screen border around content obtained by linking to another Web site. The first site's border and logo stay on screen, making the content of the new Web site appear to be "offered" by the previous Web site.

Mechanisms are being developed to sell and distribute books, articles, and other intellectual property on the Internet. Publishers continue to look for copyright violations because intellectual property can now be copied so easily. For example, Microsoft has published MS

NAPSTER AND GNUTELLA ROCK THE ENTERTAINMENT INDUSTRY

Would you pay $15.99 for a CD of your favourite recording artist when you could get it for free on the Web? That's what the music industry has been worrying about since the advent of Napster. Napster is a Web site that provides software and services that enable users to find and share MP3 music files. To use the company's service, users must download client software that allows them to search the hard drives of other Napster subscribers for MP3 files. The MP3 files can then be downloaded directly from the other subscriber's computer using peer-to-peer technology (see also Chapter 6).

Napster servers do not store any files. They act as matchmakers. After you type in the name of the song you want, Napster shows all the users who are connected and who have that song on their computer available for downloading. Napster software then sets up a connection between your computer and the computer with the MP3 file, so the download can proceed. The song can then be played through computer speakers, transferred to an audio CD with a CD-R drive, or left in the shared music folder on your hard drive so other Napster users can copy it from you. Napster attracted about 38 million users in its first 18 months of existence.

Napster software can be used in a perfectly legal fashion to trade uncopyrighted music files, but many Napster users are sharing digital MP3 music files that have been copied from commercial audio CDs. In December 1999, the Recording Industry of America, representing the five major music recording companies, sued Napster for violating copyright laws. This suit is one of a series of legal actions the recording industry has taken against online music companies that are violating copyrights. In April 2000, a Federal judge ruled that the music site MP3.com had violated copyright laws by compiling a vast online MP3 music database for visitors to download and that some of its contents were protected by copyright and were not authorized to be reproduced. On October 31, 2000, Napster announced it would join Bertelsman, one of the world's five major music companies, to create a fee-based Internet music service. MP3.com also has switched to an arrangement to pay the recording companies for use of their songs through its site.

But reforming Napster won't solve the problem. Other software and Web sites allow people to do the same thing using the same technology. Gnutella, for example, allows individuals to send and receive all kinds of files without going through a central computer. In addition to MP3 music files, digital files of any type, size, or origin, including files of films, books, TV shows, or software—anything that can be digitized—can be shared with other computers without going through a central server. Each Gnutella.net client can share files, search for files, and download files from any other user. Gnutella users have been actively trading movies as well as CDs over the Internet.

Gnutella was developed by Nullsoft, the maker of the Winamp MP3 player. Nullsoft's owner, America Online, shut down the Gnutella site immediately after it became active, but the Gnutella source code was openly distributed to developers outside the company and versions are available on the Internet. It is nearly impossible for ISPs, governments, or other groups to disable the network. According to Thomas Hale, CEO of Wired Planet, "The only way to stop [Gnutella] is to turn off the Internet."

Viewed in a positive light, Gnutella provides technology that can help break through censorship in other countries. Viewed more negatively, the same technology can be used to systematically violate copyright laws. The publishing and computer software industries are especially worried about potential losses from Gnutella and other similar programs such as Hotline, JungleMonkey, and Freenet because there is no central server, as in the case of Napster, that can be shut down to stop the flow of files.

To Think About: Should you use programs like Gnutella to obtain software, movies, or other digital files? Explain your answer.

Sources: Amy Harmon, "Napster Users Mourn End of Free Music," *The New York Times,* November 1, 2000; Amy Harmon with John Sullivan, "Music Industry Wins Ruling in U.S. Court," *The New York Times,* April 29, 2000; Hane C. Lee and Michael Laermonth, "Spawn of Napster," *The Industry Standard,* May 8, 2000; Peter H. Lewis, "Napster Rocks the Web," *The New York Times,* June 2000; Lee Gomes, "Software 'Free Spirits' Release Version of Program Mimicking Napster Product," *The Wall Street Journal,* March 15, 2000; Don Clark and Martin Peers, "Can the Record Industry Beat Free Web Music?" *The Wall Street Journal,* June 20, 2000.

Reader as freeware, allowing anyone to download for free software that will let the user read an electronic file of a book. Because the electronic file can be duplicated and distributed many times, publishers are worried that this application can cut into their sales in violation of copyright law, which provides for them to be paid for every new "copy" of a copyrighted work.

Ethical Issues

The central ethical issue posed to individuals about concerns copying software is: Should I (you) copy for my own use a piece of software protected by trade secret, copyright, and/or patent law? In the information age, it is so easy to obtain perfect, functional copies of software that the software companies themselves, to increase market penetration, have abandoned software protection schemes, and enforcement of the law is also rare. The software

FIGURE 5-4 Who owns the pieces? Anatomy of a Web page. Web pages are often constructed with elements from many different sources, clouding issues of ownership and intellectual property protection.

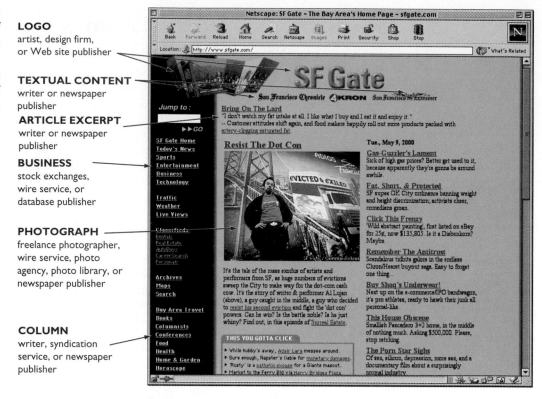

LOGO
artist, design firm, or Web site publisher

TEXTUAL CONTENT
writer or newspaper publisher

ARTICLE EXCERPT
writer or newspaper publisher

BUSINESS
stock exchanges, wire service, or database publisher

PHOTOGRAPH
freelance photographer, wire service, photo agency, photo library, or newspaper publisher

COLUMN
writer, syndication service, or newspaper publisher

companies haven't thrown in the towel yet, however, and are continuing to search for technological, licensing, and marketing solutions to the software protection dilemma. Keep in mind, though, if everyone copied software, very little new software would be produced because creators could not benefit from the results of their work.

Social Issues

There are several property-related social issues raised by new information technology. Most experts agree that the current intellectual property laws are breaking down in the information age. The vast majority of North Americans report in surveys that they routinely violate some minor laws—everything from speeding to taking paper clips from work to copying software. The ease with which software can be copied contributes to making us a society of lawbreakers. These routine thefts significantly threaten to reduce the speed with which new information technologies can and will be introduced and, thereby, threaten further advances in productivity and social well being. They also drive up the cost of the software since fewer copies are sold to pay for the research and development and marketing that have gone into the software.

Political Issues

The main property-related political issue concerns the creation of new property protection measures to protect investments made by creators of new software. Microsoft and 1400 other software and information content firms are represented by the Software and Information Industry Association (SIIA), which lobbies for new laws and enforcement of existing laws to protect intellectual property around the world. (SIIA was formed on January 1, 1999, from the merger of the Software Publishers Association (SPA) and the Information Industry Association (IIA).) The SIIA runs an anti-piracy hotline for individuals to report piracy activities and educational programs to help organizations combat software piracy. The SIIA has developed model Employee Usage Guidelines for software, described in Table 5-4.

Allied against the SIIA are a host of groups and millions of individuals who believe that anti-piracy laws cannot be enforced in the digital age, and that software should be free (freeware) or be paid for on a voluntary basis (shareware). According to these groups, greater social benefit results from the free distribution of software.

TABLE 5-4	**Employee Usage Guidelines for [Organization]**

Purpose

Software will be used only in accordance with its license agreement. Unless otherwise provided in the license, any duplication of copyrighted software, except for backup and archival purposes by software manager or designated department, is a violation of copyright law. In addition to violating copyright law, unauthorized duplication of software is contrary to [organization's] standards of conduct. The following points are to be followed to comply with software license agreements:

1. All users must use all software in accordance with its license agreements and the [organization's] software policy. All users acknowledge that they do not own this software or its related documentation, and unless expressly authorized by the software publisher, may not make additional copies except for archival purposes.

2. [Organization] will not tolerate the use of any unauthorized copies of software or fonts in our organization. Any person illegally reproducing software can be subject to civil and criminal penalties including fines and imprisonment. All users must not condone illegal copying of software under any circumstances and anyone who makes, uses, or otherwise acquires unauthorized software will be appropriately disciplined.

3. No user will give software or fonts to any outsiders including clients, customers, and others. Under no circumstances will software be used within [organization] that has been brought in from any unauthorized location under [organization's] policy, including, but not limited to, the Internet, the home, friends, and colleagues.

4. Any user who determines that there may be a misuse of software within the organization will notify the Certified Software Manager, department manager, or legal counsel.

5. All software used by the organization on organization-owned computers will be purchased through appropriate procedures.

I have read [organization's] software code of ethics. I am fully aware of our software compliance policies and agree to abide by them. I understand that violation of any above policies may result in my termination.

_____

EMPLOYEE SIGNATURE

_____

DATE

Published by the SPA Anti-Piracy. You are given permission to duplicate and modify this policy statement so long as attribution to the original document comes from SPA Anti-Piracy. (www.spa.org/piracy/policy/corp_soft.asp)

ACCOUNTABILITY, LIABILITY, AND CONTROL

Along with privacy and property laws, new information technologies are challenging existing liability law and social practices for holding individuals and institutions accountable. If a person is injured by a machine controlled, in part, by software, who should be held accountable and therefore held liable? Should a public bulletin board or an electronic service such as Prodigy or America Online permit the transmission of pornographic or offensive material (as broadcasters), or should they be held harmless against any liability for what users transmit (as is true of common carriers such as the telephone system)? What about the Internet? If you outsource your information processing, can you hold the external vendor liable for injuries done to your customers? Some real-world examples may shed light on these questions.

Some Recent Liability Problems

In November 1998, a railway backhoe operator accidentally cut an AT&T Canada fibre cable along the rail line between Toronto and Windsor, crashing computers, knocking out phone lines, and generally disrupting communications in southern Ontario. The main branch of the Bank of Nova Scotia was computerless.

On November 28, 2000, a double failure in Sprint Canada's network shut down trading on Vancouver's Canadian Venture Exchange for more than two hours. Three hundred thousand Rogers@Home cable customers were left without service recently when a rodent chewed through cables that were exposed during routine repairs.

In 1998, fires struck twice in communication "closets" in Toronto, disrupting long distance and Internet service to millions of Canadians—in particular, interestingly enough, in Western Canada. Who is liable for any economic harm caused to individuals or businesses that could not access their full account balances from the Bank of Nova Scotia or make stock trades when these long distance and Internet services were out?

In April 1990, a computer system at Shell Pipeline Corporation failed to detect a human operator error. As a result, 93 000 barrels of crude oil were shipped to the wrong trader. The error cost $2 million because the trader sold oil that should not have been delivered to him. A court ruled later that Shell Pipeline was liable for the loss of the oil because the error was due to a human operator who entered erroneous information into the system. Shell was held liable for not developing a system that would prevent the possibility of misdeliveries (King, 1992). Whom would you have held liable—Shell Pipeline? the trader for not being more careful about deliveries? the human operator who made the error?

These cases point out the difficulties faced by information systems executives who ultimately are responsible for the harm done by systems developed by their staffs. In general, insofar as computer software is part of a machine, and the machine injures someone physically or economically, the producer of the software and the operator can both be held liable for damages. Insofar as the software acts more like a book, storing, and displaying information, courts have been reluctant to hold authors, publishers, and booksellers liable for contents (the exception being instances of fraud or defamation), and hence courts have been wary of holding software authors liable for "book-like" software.

In general, it is very difficult (if not impossible) to hold software producers liable for their software products when those products are considered like books, regardless of the physical or economic harm that results. Historically print publishers have not been held liable because of fears that liability claims would interfere with the Charter of Rights and Freedoms, which guarantees freedom of expression.

What about "software as service"? ATMs are a service provided to bank customers. Should this service fail, customers will be inconvenienced and perhaps harmed economically if they cannot access their funds in a timely manner. Should liability protections be extended to software publishers and operators of defective financial, accounting, simulation, or marketing systems?

Software is very different from books. Software users may develop expectations of infallibility about software; software is less easily inspected than a book and more difficult to compare with other software products for quality; software claims actually to perform a task rather than describing a task like a book; and people come to depend on services essentially based on software. Given the centrality of software to everyday life, the chances are excellent that liability law will extend its reach to include software even when it merely provides an information service.

Between 1985 and 1987, six patients were crippled or died after receiving oncology treatments from a Therac-25 radiation machine produced by AECL (then a Canadian crown corporation, now privatized) and a French corporation, CGR. One of the patients who died was treated in Ontario. The massive radiation doses were caused by "glitches" in the software code: not one or two "bugs," but several coding errors caused the Therac-25 to deliver massive radiation doses whenever certain "keying" operations were performed. Who is responsible for these injuries and deaths? the programmer who wrote the code? AECL and CGR who sold the machine with its accompanying software and should have tested the code? the medical facility where the radiation treatments were made? the technicians who delivered the treatments? Who is liable?

Telephone systems have not been held liable for messages transmitted because they are regulated "common carriers." In return for their right to provide telephone service, they must provide access to all at reasonable rates and achieve acceptable reliability. But broadcasters and cable television systems are subject to a wide variety of federal and local constraints on content and facilities. Organizations can be held liable for offensive content on their Web sites, and online services such as Prodigy or America Online might be held liable for postings by their users.

Ethical Issues

The central liability-related ethical issue raised by new information technologies is whether individuals and organizations that create, produce, and sell systems (both hardware and software) are morally responsible for the consequences of their use (Johnson and Mulvey, 1995). If so, under what conditions? What liabilities (and responsibilities) should the user assume, and what should the provider assume?

Social Issues

The central liability-related social issue concerns expectations that develop around service-providing information systems. Should individuals (and organizations) be encouraged to develop their own backup devices to cover likely or easily anticipated system failures, or should organizations be held strictly liable for systems services they provide? If organizations are held strictly liable, what impact will this have on the development of new systems services? Can society permit networks and bulletin boards to post libellous, inaccurate, or misleading information that will harm many persons? Or should information service companies become self-regulating and self-censoring?

Political Issues

The leading liability-related political issue is the debate between information providers of all kinds (from software developers to network service providers) who want to be relieved of liability as much as possible (thereby maximizing their profits) and service users—individuals, organizations, communities—who want organizations to be held responsible for providing high-quality system services (thereby maximizing the quality of service). Service providers argue they will withdraw from the marketplace if they are held liable, while service users suggest that only by holding providers liable can a high level of service be guaranteed and injured parties compensated. Should legislation impose liability or restrict liability on service providers? This fundamental cleavage is at the heart of numerous political and judicial conflicts.

SYSTEM QUALITY: DATA QUALITY AND SYSTEM ERRORS

The debate over liability and accountability for unintentional consequences of system use raises a related but independent moral dimension: What is an acceptable, technologically feasible level of system quality (see Chapter 12)? At what point should systems managers say, "Stop testing, we've done all we can to perfect this software. Ship it!" Individuals and organizations may be held responsible for avoidable and foreseeable consequences that they have a duty to perceive and correct. The grey area is that some system errors are foreseeable and correctable only at very great expense, an expense so great that pursuing that level of perfection is not feasible economically—no one could afford the product. For example, although software companies try to debug their products before releasing them to the marketplace, they knowingly ship "buggy" products because the time and cost of fixing all minor errors would prevent these products from ever being released (Rigdon, 1995). Microsoft shipped Windows 2000 with 63 000 potential bugs. The "potential bugs" were spotted by Prefix, an internal Microsoft package for testing software. Some of these could be actual bugs, others could be code that Prefix detects as possibly needing optimization, and others are spots where Prefix found developer comments noting functionality that should be improved in the next release, Microsoft said.

What if the product were not offered on the marketplace? Would social welfare as a whole not advance and perhaps even decline? Carrying this further, just what is the responsibility of a producer of computer services—should they withdraw the product that can never be perfect, warn the user, or forget about the risk (let the buyer beware)?

Three principal sources of poor systems performance are software bugs and errors, hardware or facility failures due to natural or other causes, and poor input data quality. Chapter 12 shows why zero defects in software code of any complexity cannot be achieved and the seriousness of remaining bugs cannot be estimated. Hence, there is a technological barrier to perfect software, and users must be aware of the potential for catastrophic failure. The software industry has not yet arrived at testing standards for producing software of acceptable but not perfect performance (Collins et al., 1994).

Although software bugs and facility catastrophe are likely to be widely reported in the press, by far the most common source of business system failure is data quality. Few companies routinely measure the quality of their data, but studies of individual organizations report data error rates ranging from 0.5 to 30 percent (Redman, 1998).

Ethical Issues

The central quality-related ethical issue information systems raise is at what point should I (or you) release software or services for consumption by others? At what point can you conclude that your software or service achieves an economically and technologically adequate level of quality? What are you obliged to know about the quality of your software, its procedures for testing, and its operational characteristics?

Social Issues

The leading quality-related social issue once again deals with expectations: As a society, do we want to encourage people to believe that systems are infallible, that data errors are impossible? Do we instead want a society where people are openly skeptical and question the output of machines, where people are at least informed of the risk? By heightening awareness of system failure, do we inhibit the development of all systems, which in the end contribute to social well-being?

Political Issues

The leading quality-related political issue concerns the laws of responsibility and accountability. The Standards Council of Canada sets Canadian standards, including the international ISO 9000 and ISO 14000 standards. Many of these standards relate to computing and information systems, but penalties for failure to abide by the standards are unclear or nonexistent. Should industry associations be encouraged to develop industry-wide standards of quality? Or should Parliament wait for the marketplace to punish poor systems quality, recognizing that in some instances this will not work (e.g., if all retail grocers maintain poor quality systems, then customers have no alternatives)?

QUALITY OF LIFE: EQUITY, ACCESS, AND BOUNDARIES

The negative social costs of introducing information technologies and systems are beginning to mount along with the power of the technology. Many of these negative social consequences are not violations of individual rights, nor are they property crimes. Nevertheless, these negative consequences can be extremely harmful to individuals, societies, and institutions. Computers and information technologies can potentially destroy valuable elements of our culture and society even while they bring us benefits. If there is a balance of good and bad consequences of using information systems, whom do we hold responsible for the bad consequences? Next, we briefly examine some of the negative social consequences of systems, considering individual, social, and political responses.

Balancing Power Centre versus Periphery

An early fear of the computer age was that huge, centralized mainframe computers would centralize power at corporate headquarters and in the nation's capital, resulting in the type of Big Brother society suggested in George Orwell's novel *1984*. The shift toward highly decentralized computing, coupled with a philosophy of "empowerment" of thousands of workers, and the decentralization of decision making to lower organizational levels, have reduced fears of power centralization in institutions. Yet much of the "empowerment" described in popular business magazines is trivial. Lower-level employees may be empowered to make minor decisions, but the key policy decisions are likely to be as centralized as in the past.

Rapidity of Change: Reduced Response Time to Competition

Information systems have helped to create much more efficient national and international markets. The digital global marketplace has reduced the normal social buffers that gave businesses years to adjust to competition. "Time-based competition" has an ugly side: The business you work for may not have enough time to respond to global competitors and may be wiped out in a year, along with your job. We stand the risk of developing a "just-in-time society" with "just-in-time jobs" and "just-in-time" workplaces, families, and vacations.

Maintaining Boundaries: Family, Work, and Leisure

Parts of this book were produced on trains, planes, and in hotel rooms as well as on family "vacations" and what otherwise might have been "family" time. The danger to ubiquitous computing, telecommuting, nomad computing, and the "do anything anywhere anytime" computing environment is that it might actually come true. If so, the traditional boundaries that separate work from family and ordinary leisure will be weakened. Although authors have traditionally worked just about anywhere (typewriters have been portable for nearly a century), the advent of information systems, coupled with the growth of knowledge-work occupations, means that more and more people will be working when traditionally they would have been playing or communicating with family and friends. The "work umbrella" now extends far beyond the eight-hour day.

Weakening these institutions poses clear-cut risks. Family and friends historically have provided powerful support mechanisms for individuals, and they act as balance points in a society by preserving "private life," providing a place for one to collect one's thoughts, to think in ways contrary to one's employer, and to dream.

Dependence and Vulnerability

Today, our businesses, governments, schools, and private associations such as churches are incredibly dependent on information systems and are therefore highly vulnerable if these systems should fail. With information systems now as ubiquitous as the telephone system, it is startling to remember that there are no regulatory or standard-setting forces in place similar to telephone, electrical, radio, television, or other public-utility environments. The absence of standards and the criticality of some systems applications will probably call forth demands for national standards and perhaps regulatory oversight.

Computer Crime and Abuse

New technologies have created new opportunities for committing crime. Technologies including computers create new valuable items to steal, new ways to steal them, and new ways to harm others using them. **Computer crime** is the commission of illegal acts through the use of a computer or against a computer system. Computers or computer systems can be the object of the crime (destroying a company's computer centre or a company's computer files) as well as the instrument of a crime (stealing computer lists by illegally gaining access to

computer crime
The commission of illegal acts through the use of a computer or against a computer system.

While some people may enjoy the convenience of working at home, the "do anything anywhere anytime" computing environment can blur the traditional boundaries between work and family time.

computer abuse
The commission of acts involving a computer that may not be illegal but are considered unethical.

a computer system using a home computer). Simply accessing a computer system without authorization or intent to do harm, even by accident, is now a federal crime. **Computer abuse** is the commission of acts involving a computer that may not be illegal but are considered unethical.

The Canadian government has been very aggressive in implementing computer crime legislation. There are basically two sections in the Canadian Criminal Code, Sections 342.1 and 430, that define computer crime. Section 342.1 is itself divided into two parts. The first part deals with most of the items that would traditionally be considered computer crime. It defines unlawful entry into systems, interception of transmissions, as well as mandating a harsh 10-year prison sentence for violation of these laws. The second part defines data or computer programs, to give written documentation as to what kind of materials would qualify under the statute. Section 430 criminalizes the actual destruction, alteration, or interruption of data or data transmission. It does not set specific sentences, but one assumes they would be similar in nature to Section 342.1. Other related codes that more generally refer to the misuse of telecommunications include Section 184, the unlawful interception of telecommunications; Section 326, theft of telecommunications; and Section 327, possession of a device to intercept telecommunications.

The item, however, that truly distinguishes the Canadian government from others who try to enforce computer crime laws is the clear definition of a jurisdictional boundary for computer crime. All sections pertaining to such events fall under the mandate of the Royal Canadian Mountain Police (RCMP), specifically the Information Technology Security Branch (ITSB). In consultation with the Treasury Board Secretariat (TSB) and Communications Security Establishment (CSE), the ITSB is responsible for the information technology security of all of Canada. The ITSB's primary role is to educate the government on security matters by running seminars, printing documents, and providing consultation; however, they are also tasked with working with local law enforcement officials to crack down on computer crime.

The ITSB comprises three branches. The Security Evaluation and Inspection Team's (SEIT) primary function is to set up, secure, and be a consulting organization for any computers and networks set up by the government of Canada. The Computer Investigative Support Unit (CISU) is the legal branch of the RCMP. They provide legal counsel, acquire warrants, and direct the prosecution of computer criminals. Finally, the Counter Technical Intrusion Unit (CTIU) is responsible for performing periodic sweeps of governmental computer systems, assisting local police, and performing technical evaluations in cases of theft of communication.

No one knows the magnitude of the computer crime problem—how many systems are invaded, how many people engage in the practice, or what is the total economic damage. In just one measure of a Canada's success in their war on electronic crime, it is estimated that of the Cdn$3 billion to Cdn$4 billion lost in North America due to telecommunications theft, only $100 million, or about 3 percent, occurred in Canada even though Canada has 8 percent of the North American population.

Many companies are reluctant to report computer crimes because they may involve employees. The most economically damaging kinds of computer crime are introducing viruses, theft of services, disruption of computer systems, and theft of telecommunications services, such as denial-of-service (DOS) attacks. "**Hackers**" (also known as **crackers** if their intention is criminal and not just to prove that they can do it) is the pejorative term for persons who use computers in illegal ways. Hacker attacks are on the rise, posing new threats to organizations linked to the Internet (see Chapter 12).

hackers/crackers
Those who use computers in illegal ways.

Computer viruses (see Chapter 12) have grown exponentially during the past decade. Over 20 000 viruses have been documented, many causing huge losses due to lost data or crippled computers. Although many firms now use anti-virus software, the proliferation of computer networks will increase the probability of infections. The Window on Organizations in Chapter 12 details several examples of hacking and introducing computer viruses (see also Figure 5-5).

In general, it is employees—insiders—who have inflicted the most injurious computer crimes because they have the knowledge about and access to the company's systems, and they may have a job-related motive to commit such crimes.

TABLE 5-5	INTERNET CRIME AND ABUSE
Problem	**Description**
Hacking	Hackers exploit weaknesses in Web site security to obtain access to proprietary data such as customer information and passwords. They may use "Trojan horses" posing as legitimate software to obtain information from the host computer.
Jamming	Jammers use software routines to tie up the computer hosting a Web site so that legitimate visitors cannot access the site; also known as denial-of-service (DOS) attacks.
Malicious software	Cyber vandals use data flowing through the Internet to transmit computer viruses, which can disable computers that they "infect" (see Chapter 12).
Sniffing	Sniffing, a form of electronic eavesdropping, involves using software to intercept information passing from a user to the computer hosting a Web site. This information can include credit card numbers and other confidential data.
Spoofing	Spoofers fraudulently misrepresent themselves as other organizations, setting up false Web sites where they can collect confidential information from unsuspecting visitors to the site.

Most Canadian law related to computer crime comes under consumer law, contract law, and the Criminal Code of Canada. In the United States, Congress passed the Computer Fraud and Abuse Act in 1986. This act makes it illegal to access a computer system without authorization. Nonetheless, in Canada and elsewhere, new technologies make new laws necessary. Bill C-6, the Canadian privacy law, was only introduced in 1997 to remedy the onslaught of privacy concerns associated with the Internet and newer datamining applications.

The Internet's ease of use and accessibility have created new opportunities for computer crime and abuse. Table 5-5 describes some of the most common areas where the Internet has been used for illegal or malicious purposes.

Employment: Trickle-Down Technology and Re-engineering Job Loss

Re-engineering work processes (see Chapter 11) is typically hailed in the information systems community as a major benefit of new information technology. It is much less frequently noted that redesigning business processes could potentially cause millions of middle-level

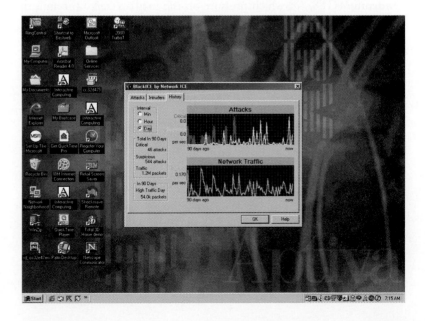

FIGURE 5-5 The Black ICE Defender Firewall protects home and small office systems from hacker attacks and provides reports documenting attempted attacks. Hackers illegally accessing systems can cause widespread disruption and harm.

managers and clerical workers to lose their jobs. One economist has raised the possibility that we will create a society run by a small "high tech elite of corporate professionals ... in a nation of the permanently unemployed" (Rifkin, 1993).

Other economists are much more sanguine about potential job losses. They believe relieving bright, educated workers from re-engineered jobs will result in these workers moving to better jobs in fast-growth industries. Left out of this equation are blue-collar workers, and older, less well-educated middle managers. It is not clear that these groups can be easily retrained for high-quality (high-paying) jobs. Careful planning and sensitivity to employee needs can help companies redesign work to minimize job losses.

Equity and Access: Increasing Racial and Social Class Cleavages

Does everyone have an equal opportunity to participate in the digital age? Will the social, economic, and cultural gaps that exist in North America and other societies be reduced by information systems technology? Or will the cleavages be increased, permitting the "better off" to become even better off relative to others?

These questions have not yet been fully answered because the impact of information technology on various groups in society has not been well studied. What we do know is that information, knowledge, computers, and access to these resources through educational institutions and public libraries are inequitably distributed along racial and social class lines as are many other information resources. Figure 5-6 illustrates the differences in computer ownership based on income. Left uncorrected, we could end up creating a society of information haves, those who are computer literate and skilled, versus a large group of information have-nots, those who are computer illiterate and unskilled.

Public interest groups want to narrow this "digital divide" by making digital information services—including the Internet—available to "virtually everyone" just as basic telephone service is now. The federal government and many provincial governments are mandating initiatives toward universal Internet access in schools, with high-speed telecommunications infrastructure available to homes throughout Canada within the next few years. This is only a partial solution to the problem, but it is a beginning.

Health Risks: RSI, CVS, and Technostress

The most important occupational disease today is **repetitive stress injury (RSI)**. RSI occurs when muscle groups are forced through repetitive actions, often with high-impact loads (such as tennis) or tens of thousands of repetitions under low-impact loads (such as working at a computer keyboard).

The single largest source of RSI is computer keyboards. Sixty percent of Canadians use computers at work. The most common kind of computer-related RSI is **carpal tunnel syndrome (CTS)**, in which pressure on the median nerve through the wrist's bony struc-

repetitive stress injury (RSI)
An occupational disease that occurs when muscle groups are forced through repetitive actions with high-impact loads or thousands of repetitions with low-impact loads.

carpal tunnel syndrome (CTS)
A type of RSI in which pressure on the median nerve through the wrist's bony carpal tunnel structure produces pain.

FIGURE 5-6 The widening digital divide. Households at the lowest income levels are over four times less likely to have a computer at home than those with incomes in the top 20 percent.

Source: Statistics Canada. *Household Facilities By Income and Other Characteristics*, 1997. Cat. No. 13-218-XPB. Ottawa: Minister of Industry, 1998.

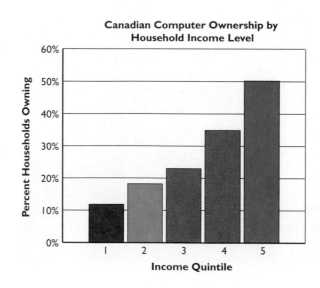

Canadian Computer Ownership by Household Income Level

Repetitive stress injury (RSI) is the leading occupational disease today. The single largest cause of RSI is computer keyboard work.

ture (called a "carpal tunnel") produces pain. The pressure is caused by constant repetition of keystrokes: In a single eight-hour shift, a word processor may perform 23 000 keystrokes. Symptoms of carpal tunnel syndrome include numbness, shooting pain, inability to grasp objects, and tingling. Millions of workers have been diagnosed with carpal tunnel syndrome.

RSI is avoidable. Designing workstations for a neutral wrist position (using a wrist rest to support the wrist), proper monitor stands, and footrests all contribute to proper posture and reduced RSI. **Ergonomics** is the use of research in designing systems, programs, or devices that are easy to use for their intended purposes and contexts. New, ergonomically correct keyboards are also an option, although their effectiveness has yet to be clearly established. These measures should be backed by frequent rest breaks, rotation of employees to different jobs, and moving toward voice or scanner data entry. RSI presents a serious challenge to management, as the Window on Management illustrates.

RSI is not the only occupational illness computers cause. Back and neck pain, leg stress, and foot pain also result from poor ergonomic designs of workstations. **Computer vision syndrome (CVS)** refers to any eye strain condition related to computer display screen use. Its symptoms, usually temporary, include headaches, blurred vision, and dry and irritated eyes.

The newest computer-related malady is **technostress**, which is stress induced by computer use. Its symptoms include aggravation, hostility toward humans, impatience, and fatigue. The problem is that humans working continuously with computers come to expect other humans and human institutions to behave like computers, providing instant response, attentiveness, and the absence of emotion. Workers who work primarily with computers are aggravated when put on hold during a phone call and become incensed or alarmed when their PCs take a few seconds longer to perform a task. Technostress is thought to be related to high levels of job turnover in the computer industry, high levels of early retirement from occupations that use computers to a large degree, and elevated levels of drug and alcohol abuse.

The incidence of technostress is not known but 80 percent of Canadian managers and executives surveyed late last year by Alberta's Athabasca University admitted to stress at work over pressure to adopt new technology (Wood, 2001). Health statistics in several industrialized countries show that computer-related jobs now top the list of stressful occupations.

To date, the role of radiation from computer display screens in occupational disease has not been proved. Video display terminals (VDTs) emit non-ionizing electric and magnetic fields at low frequencies. These rays enter the body and have unknown effects on enzymes, molecules, chromosomes, and cell membranes. Long-term studies are investigating low-level electromagnetic fields and birth defects, low birth weight, stress, and other diseases. All

ergonomics
The use of research in designing systems, programs, or devices that are easy to use for their intended purposes and contexts.

computer vision syndrome (CVS)
Any eye strain condition related to computer display screen use, with symptoms that include headaches, blurred vision, and dry, irritated eyes.

technostress
Stress induced by computer use, with symptoms including aggravation, hostility toward humans, impatience, and enervation.

MANAGING RSI

Ergonomic injuries—including repetitive stress injury (RSI) from computer use—are attracting more attention now than ever. These injuries have become more numerous, and their costs—in the form of lost productivity, higher medical bills, and workers' compensation claims—are rising. Workers for Web sites and Web graphics and development firms are even more at risk than those doing general office and computing tasks because they spend protracted hours at their terminals.

Each week in British Columbia, 735 workers suffer an ergonomic-related strain or exertion injury. In fact, musculoskeletal injuries (MSIs) account for a third of all WCB injury claims. The Workers' Compensation Board of British Columbia, among other provincial Boards, has occupational safety and health regulations that include ergonomic issues. To comply with the WCB's ergonomics requirements, an employer must consult with the occupational health and safety committee (or representative) to identify, assess, and control risks of MSI to workers; educate and train workers; and evaluate the effectiveness of the process.

Some experts claim preventive measures are relatively inexpensive compared with the bills for lost workdays, medical treatments, and increased insurance premiums, while others think they are too expensive and create a hardship for small- and medium-sized businesses. The Office Ergonomics Research Committee, a business-sponsored group counting Delta Air Lines, IBM, Compaq, and Aetna among its members, has been examining carpal tunnel syndrome and the effect of ergonomic intervention and stress management on workers. Bob Bettendorf, an ergonomic consultant who heads the Committee, says that many ergonomic solutions aren't costly and don't necessarily require special equipment. Rather they require employees to change the way they work. For example, one Committee study found that users strike computer keys with four to seven times the necessary force, contributing to hand and finger injuries.

SAS Institute Inc. established an ergonomic lab in 1996 to house ergonomic office equipment such as keyboards, computer mice, footrests, and adjustable chairs. The ergonomic lab conducted more than 545 employee ergonomic assessments in 1999. To help Jude Redman, an employee at SAS's Cary, North Carolina, headquarters, ease discomfort and pain from a musculoskeletal disorder, the office recommended refitting Redman's workplace with ergonomic equipment, which she could test herself in the lab. She switched to a split keyboard to ease her hand pain and found that adjusting the height of her computer monitor and incorporating wrist-support devices lessened her shoulder ache. To prevent future injuries, the ergonomic lab taught Redman how to sit correctly at her desk. SAS ergonomic coordinator Kathleen Kitts believes the ergonomic program can be justified from a cost-benefit standpoint. She estimates that one carpal tunnel injury costs the company at least U.S.$20 000 in medical bills and lost productivity while helping an employee facing ergonomic injuries costs U.S.$1500 at most.

The Canadian Auto Workers union has called on the Ontario and federal governments to require employers to protect their workers by using ergonomic principles in every aspect of workplace and job design. Cara Foods, the subject of the opening vignette in Chapter 2, has implemented ergonomic processes and equipment to minimize MSI among their catering employees. Cara's management asked the workers themselves what they should do and involved their own industrial engineers in the process.

Botwater, which owns and operates eight pulp and paper mills in Canada, the United States, and Korea, instituted an ergonomic plan about five years ago when its customer service personnel expressed concerns about increased worker injuries from their growing use of PCs. Worker-safety teams at the mills and headquarters attend a 40-hour training course at an ergonomics educational facility. So far no employees have reported an ergonomic injury.

To Think About: If you were a corporate vice president with responsibility for corporate safety, what policies would you recommend regarding RSI? Explain your recommendations.

Sources: Judith N. Mottl, "Computer-Related Injuries: It Helps Ease the Pain," *Information Week*, June 19, 2000; "New Regulation: Ergonomics Can Take the Pain Out of Work," *WorkSafe BC Newsletter*, May 18, 1999, www.worksafebc.com/pubs/newsletters/paw/paw4_4/newreg.asp, accessed July 31, 2001; "Custom Workstations a Better Fit for Flight Catering Staff," *WorkSafe BC Newsletter*, July/August 2000, www.worksafebc.com/pubs/newsletters/ws_mag/ws1_4/custom.asp, accessed July 31, 2001; "CAW Calls for Ergonomic Regulations Nationwide," CAW Press Release, www1.newswire.ca/releases/February2001/27/c7335.html, accessed July 31, 2001; and Steven Greenhouse, "Battle Lines Drawn over Ergonomic Rules," *The New York Times*, November 18, 2000.

manufacturers have reduced display screen emissions since the early 1980s, and European countries such as Sweden have adopted stiff radiation emission standards.

The computer has become a part of our lives—personally as well as socially, culturally, and politically. It is unlikely that the issues and our choices will become easier as information technology continues to transform our world. The growth of the Internet and the information economy suggests that all the ethical and social issues we have described will be heightened further as we move further into the first digital century.

MANAGEMENT ACTIONS: A CORPORATE CODE OF ETHICS

Some corporations have developed far-reaching corporate IS codes of ethics—Royal Bank, Federal Express, Nortel Networks, IBM, American Express, and Merck and Co. Most firms, however, have not developed these codes of ethics, leaving their employees in the dark about expected correct behaviour. There is some dispute concerning a general code of ethics versus a specific information systems code of ethics. As managers, you should strive to develop an IS-specific set of ethical standards for each of the five moral dimensions:

1. Information rights and obligations. A code should cover topics such as employee e-mail privacy, workplace monitoring, treatment of corporate information, and policies on customer information.

2. Property rights and obligations. A code should cover topics such as software licenses, ownership of firm data and facilities, ownership of software created by employees on company hardware, and software copyrights. Specific guidelines for contractual relationships with third parties should be covered as well.

3. Accountability and control. The code should specify a single individual responsible for all information systems and, under this individual, others who are responsible for individual rights, the protection of property rights, systems quality, and quality of life (e.g., job design, ergonomics, employee satisfaction). Responsibilities for control of systems, audits, and management should be clearly defined. The potential liabilities of systems officers and the corporation should be detailed in a separate document.

4. Systems quality. The code should describe the general levels of data quality and system error that can be tolerated with detailed specifications left to specific projects. The code should require that all systems attempt to estimate data quality and systems error probabilities.

5. Quality of life. The code should state that the purpose of systems is to improve the quality of life for customers and for employees by achieving high levels of product quality, customer service, employee satisfaction, and human dignity through proper ergonomics, job and workflow design, and human resources development.

APPLICATION SOFTWARE EXERCISE

DATABASE CREATION: DEVELOPING A DATABASE TO TRACK ETHICAL VIOLATIONS

Your employer, a national insurance company with headquarters in Vancouver, has discovered that its employees do not always behave ethically. There have been anecdotal reports that employees in a variety of departments and locations have violated what are understood to be appropriate information ethics. The head of your human resources department, together with the head of the information systems department, has just assigned you the project of creating a database to track information ethics violations across Canada.

You decide to use MS Access because you feel it is the most user friendly and can furnish you with all of the "bells and whistles" you need. First, decide what information you need to track. Keep in mind the who, what, where, when, and how principles of tracking. Second, create a database with appropriately formatted fields to track your information. Third, enter some test data—30 records should do. Finally, create a couple of reports to share with the heads of the HR and IS departments to get their feedback before you begin populating the database with actual violations of corporate information ethics.

The heads of HR and IS now ask you, based on the information you have collected, to devise an information ethics policy for the company. What would your policy look like? Use presentation software to prepare a formal presentation of your findings and your proposed policy, and present them to the class.

MANAGEMENT WRAP-UP

Managers should be ethical rule-makers for their organizations. They are charged with creating the policies and procedures to establish ethical conduct, including the ethical use of information systems. Managers are also responsible for identifying, analyzing, and resolving the ethical dilemmas that invariably crop up as they balance conflicting needs and interests.

Rapid changes fuelled by information technology are creating new situations where existing laws or rules of conduct may not be relevant. New "grey areas" are emerging in which ethical standards have not yet been codified into law. A new system of ethics for the Information Age is required to guide individual and organizational choices and actions.

Information technology continues to introduce changes that create new ethical issues for societies to debate and resolve. Increasing computing power, storage, and networking capabilities—including the Internet—can expand the reach of individual and organizational actions and magnify their impact. The ease and anonymity with which information can be communicated, copied, and manipulated in online environments challenges traditional rules of right and wrong behaviour.

For Discussion

1. Should producers of software-based services such as ATMs be held liable for economic injuries suffered when their systems fail?

2. Should companies be responsible for unemployment caused by their information systems? Why or why not?

SUMMARY

1. *Analyze the relationship among ethical, social, and political issues raised by information systems.* Ethical, social, and political issues are closely related in an information society. Ethical issues confront individuals who must choose a course of action, often in a situation in which two or more ethical principles are in conflict (a dilemma). Social issues spring from ethical issues. Societies must develop expectations in individuals about the correct course of action. Social issues then become debates about the kinds of situations and expectations that societies should develop so that individuals behave appropriately. Political issues spring from social conflict and have to do largely with laws that prescribe behaviour and seek to use the law to force individuals to behave appropriately.

2. *Identify the main moral dimensions of an information society and apply them to specific situations.* There are five main moral dimensions that tie together ethical, social, and political issues in an information society. These moral dimensions are information rights and obligations, property rights, accountability and control, system quality, and quality of life. It is important to analyze the values involved, the stakeholders, and the possible options. Each of these moral dimensions is complex, requiring awareness of the dimensions and the associated issues, laws, and consequences of violating them.

3. *Apply an ethical analysis to difficult situations.* An ethical analysis is a five-step methodology for analyzing a situation. The method involves identifying the facts, values, stakeholders, options, and consequences of actions. Once completed, you can begin to consider what ethical principle you should apply to a situation to arrive at a judgment. You need to be sure to bring to the surface any potential conflicts that may exist among the facts, values, stakeholders, options, and consequences.

4. *Examine specific ethical principles for conduct.* Six ethical principles are available to judge your own conduct (and that of others). These principles are derived independently from several cultural, religious, and intellectual traditions. They are not hard-and-fast rules and may not apply in all situations. The principles are the Golden Rule, Kant's categorical imperative, Descartes' rule of change, the utilitarian principle, the risk aversion principle, and the ethical "no free lunch" rule.

5. *Design corporate policies for ethical conduct.* For each of the five moral dimensions, corporations should develop an ethics policy statement to assist individuals in making the right choices. The policy areas are as follows. Individual information rights: Spell out corporate privacy and due process policies. Property rights: Clarify how the corporation will treat property rights of software owners. Accountability and control: Clarify who is responsible and accountable for information. System quality: Identify methodologies and quality standards to be achieved. Quality of life: Identify corporate policies on family, computer crime, decision-making, vulnerability, job loss, and health risks.

KEY TERMS

Accountability, 155

Carpal tunnel syndrome (CTS), 176

Computer abuse, 174

Computer crime, 173

Computer vision syndrome (CVS), 177

Cookie, 162

Copyright, 165

Descartes' rule of change, 157

Due process, 156

Ergonomics, 177

Ethical "no free lunch" rule, 157

Ethics, 152

Fair Information Practices (FIP), 161

Golden Rule, 157

Hacker/cracker, 174

Information rights, 153

Intellectual property, 164

Kant's categorical imperative, 157

Liability, 156

Patent, 166

Privacy, 159

Profiling, 155

Repetitive stress injury (RSI), 176

Responsibility, 155

Risk aversion principle, 157

Spamming, 163

Technostress, 177

Trade secret, 164

Utilitarian principle, 157

REVIEW QUESTIONS

1. In what ways are ethical, social, and political issues connected? Give some examples.

2. What are the key technological trends that heighten ethical concerns?

3. What are the differences between responsibility, accountability, and liability?

4. What are the five steps in an ethical analysis? Describe why each is important.

5. Name and describe six ethical principles.

6. What is a professional code of conduct?

7. What are meant by "privacy" and "fair information practices"?

8. How does the Internet challenge the protection of individual privacy?

9. What are the three different legal traditions that protect intellectual property rights? What challenges to intellectual property rights are posed by the Internet?

10. Why is it so difficult to hold software services liable for failure or injury?

11. What is the most common cause of systems quality problems?

12. Name and describe four "quality of life" impacts of computers and information systems.

13. What is technostress, and how would you identify it?

14. Describe three management actions that could reduce RSI injuries.

GROUP PROJECT

With three or four of your classmates, look up three or four corporate ethics codes on privacy that address both employee privacy and the privacy of customers and users of their corporate Web sites. Be sure to consider e-mail privacy and employer monitoring of work sites as well as corporate use of information about employees concerning their off-job behaviour (e.g., lifestyle, marital arrangements, and so forth). Present your ethics code to the class.

INTERNET CONNECTION

■ COMPANION WEBSITE

At www.pearsoned.ca/laudon, you'll find an online study guide with two quizzes to text your knowledge of information and computer ethics and laws. You'll also find updates to the chapter and online exercises and cases that enable you to apply your knowledge to realistic situations.

■ ADDITIONAL SITES OF INTEREST

There are many interesting Web sites to enhance your learning about information, ethics, and laws. You can search the Web yourself, or just try the following sites to add to what you have already learned.

Electronic Privacy Information Center

www.epic.org

A wealth of information on privacy issues.

Standards Council of Canada

www.scc.ca

Research any standard that has been adopted in Canada by this standards regulating body.

Business Ethics: Corporate Social Resonsibility Report

www.business-ethics.com

Magazine devoted to business ethics issues.

The Canadian Copyright Act

laws.justice.gc.ca/en/C-42/

Clearly spells out what can be copyrighted and what the penalties are for copyright infringement.

The Canadian Privacy Act

laws.justice.gc.ca/en/P-21/index.html

Updated to include Bill C-6, contains all of the nuances of Canadian privacy law.

Privacy Commissioner of Canada

www.privcom.gc.ca

Administrator of Federal privacy laws with links to provincial and territorial privacy commissioners.

CASE STUDY   *Web Site Privacy: How Much Should We Worry?*

The Internet has quickly become one of our most important sources of personal data. Obviously we openly volunteer personal information such as our names, addresses, and e-mail addresses when we register to gain access to a Web site or when we subscribe to an online newsletter. If you bank through the Net or invest through an online brokerage firm, you must give out a great deal more personal data. While you give this information freely, you rarely have any control over what the site will do with it. However, many sites are gathering much more personal information without our even being aware of it. Web sites can obtain basic personal data when you visit even though they do not yet know your identity. Stop by a Web site, and the owners can instantly obtain your Internet address, your browser type, your operating system, and the site you arrived from. That isolated data may seem perfectly harmless, but it is only the beginning.

In addition to "cookies," which we described earlier in this chapter, Web site owners and others have devised other surreptitious methods of gathering personal data when we are online. One-to-One from BroadVision Inc. linked with Andromedia's Aria eCommerce 3.0, are just two software packages that are now being used to observe and record individual online visitors' behaviour. Their purpose is to understand the behavioural patterns of individuals and groups in order to market more effectively to them. To understand how these tools electronically watch a Web site visitor, imagine being in a supermarket or clothing store where someone surreptitiously trailed you with a notebook recording your every move. Do you find this an acceptable method of data gathering?

Once these data are collected, they are often merged with other personal data about the individual. Many companies sell data to obtain income. For some companies the sale of personal data is their primary business. Acxiom Corp. has collected data on 176 million individuals, data that is for sale. "They follow you more closely than the government," says Anthony Picardi, a software analyst at International Data Corp.

Public institutions, such as hospitals, schools, and the police also collect massive amounts of data on their clients (patients, students, and citizens). Medical data in particular are becoming more and more centralized in huge databases. Many companies would love to purchase this data, and so it too might end up on the auction block. Many of these institutions are private and, without government regulation, are free to sell their data. Moreover, these organizations are occasionally privatized, merged, or closed, and so their data could end up in the hands of someone who would sell them. For example, the U.S. Federal Trade Commission (FTC) filed suit in July 2000 against Toysmart.com, the failed online retailer of children's toys, to block the company from selling its customer data as part of its assets. Toysmart.com's databases included information such as children's names, birth dates, and toy wish lists and the firm's privacy policy promised that personal information voluntarily submitted by Web site visitors would never be shared with a third party. The case was settled when the FTC said Toysmart could sell the information provided the buyer purchase the entire company and adhere to Toysmart's privacy policy. Two other expiring Internet companies, Boo.com and CraftShop.com were also discovered trying to sell private customer information such as home addresses, telephone and credit card numbers, and data on shopping habits.

Why this lucrative trade in personal data? Obviously, one reason is to increase sales. Many businesses use the information to locate good sales prospects or to target repeat customers with new offers of items to purchase. Web sites even use their own data to direct visitors to other sites in exchange for a fee. Insurance companies, lawyers, bail bondspersons, manufacturers of home security equipment, and even funeral parlours want personal data on recent crime victims in the hope of finding new clients.

Increasing sales is not the only reason for interest in these data, however. Organizations can use data on your Web travels to draw implications about you, implications that can be wrong and harmful. For example, employers could use these data to help them determine whom to hire. Job applicants may find that trouble they had in elementary school has followed them the rest of their lives. Or the employer may find that an applicant may have visited a number of sites relating to AIDS. The candidate may then be denied employment based on the conclusion that the candidate has AIDS even though the person may have visited them for many reasons, such as curiosity, research (for work, school), or to help a friend. Compounding this problem, data errors are likely to abound. Data can be inaccurate, false, and out-of-date and still be sold repeatedly or used in ways that harm the individual.

Because personal data can help as well as harm, data collection presents many people with a dilemma. "There's no question that this technology could be hugely invasive," explains Christine Varney who was the Internet expert for the Federal Trade Commission (FTC) until August 1997 and now heads the

Online Privacy Alliance. "But," she continues, "it could also be enormously empowering by allowing individuals to make their own choices and by saving us all time and money." Studies do show that most users want some protection from indiscriminate use of their personal data, but they are willing to supply it as long as they benefit from the proffered information and are fully informed as to how the data will be used.

Many individuals and organizations are addressing the Internet privacy issue. Self-regulation (that is, regulation by the industry rather than by the government) is a major approach involving some of the leading Internet companies. The Online Privacy Alliance is a trade association of about 100 companies including America Online Inc., Yahoo, Microsoft, Hewlett-Packard, IBM, and the Direct Marketing Association. The alliance recommends four guidelines that it urges all companies on the Internet to adopt:

1. Notifying visitors of their data collection practices;

2. Giving visitors the choice of opting out of the site collecting personal data;

3. Giving visitors access to their own personal data; and

4. Assuring visitors that their personal data are secure.

A major goal of the alliance is to persuade the government and American citizens that little government Internet privacy regulation is needed because the industry can adequately regulate itself. Varney believes "We can have a market-driven approach to privacy on the Internet." The OPA has one known Canadian member, ViewCall Canada, a Winnipeg-based company.

TRUSTe is also an industry organization promoting self-regulation. It issues a seal of approval that qualifying Web sites can display. To obtain permission to display the TRUSTe seal of approval, a Web site must agree to comply with TRUSTe's consumer privacy guidelines. If a Web site uses the personal information it has gathered in ways that the customer was not explicitly informed about, a violation would occur. Hundreds of companies now display the TRUSTe seal of approval. However, many question its value. When Microsoft's collection of private data was disclosed, TRUSTe refused to revoke its seal of approval. The reason TRUSTe gave was that the storing of the serial number was unrelated to Microsoft's Web site.

Some companies take Web site privacy very seriously. A few pay for outside audits to determine if they are protecting the privacy of their visitors and customers. Some companies, including Disney, IBM, and Microsoft, have announced they will not work with advertisers that do not have a baseline privacy policy for their Web sites. For example E-loan, a company based in Dublin, California, hired PricewaterhouseCoopers for a month-long, U.S.$200 000 privacy audit to be able to assure its customers that they are being protected. After the original audit, Chris Larsen, E-loan's CEO, decided to establish ongoing quarterly audits despite the expense. His reasons are complex, including both concerns about state and federal financial regulatory agencies and a desire to give customers confidence that their loan data will not be shared with other organizations. Some companies are taking action because they fear being sued and conclude that a good privacy policy will cost less than successful lawsuits.

The main reasons companies don't establish or enforce privacy policies are cost and revenue loss. It can be expensive to hire auditors or experts who can help the company establish and enforce a privacy policy. In addition, enforcing privacy policies can often require a complete redesign of the Web site and of its databases. The other side of the coin is that companies can sell private information and thereby generate a substantial income.

Privacy advocates have developed a Web browsers' bill of rights that can be used to measure the success of existing efforts to protect Web privacy. The bill of rights is based upon two principles: visitors must control their own data, and sites must disclose their privacy policies. The bill of rights states that site browsers must have the right to prevent uses of the information beyond the clear purposes of the site unless the visitor is explicitly notified and is given the opportunity to prohibit these expanded uses. Visitors must have the right to prevent the Web site from distributing the visitor's information outside the Web site's own organization unless the visitor has explicitly given permission. In addition visitors must also have the right to correct existing errors in their personal data, including the right to modify outdated information.

A survey released in April 2000 by Eponymous.com, a San Diego provider of privacy-related products and services, showed that 77 percent of the busiest Web sites still don't have a stated privacy policy. Of those that do, many do not offer policies providing much protection.

Addressing these concerns in November 1999, a group of leading Internet advertising and data-profiling companies, including DoubleClick and CMGI, agreed to develop voluntary privacy-protection guidelines that would notify consumers about their data collection practices and allow them to "opt out" of the profiling technology. These data-profiling companies also encourage other Web sites that work with them to clearly state they are using their services.

One "problem is that you now have the government taking its lead from industry on the privacy issue," declared Marc Rotenberg, the executive director of the Electronic Privacy Information Center, a Washington, D.C., civil liberties advocacy group. Rotenberg also believes that posted privacy policies actually protect site operators rather than visitors because the site operators are then free to do as they wish. "It becomes a privacy policy as a disclaimer," says Rotenberg. His organization is supporting technical changes to the Internet that would allow individuals to surf the Net anonymously.

Canadian law considers as part of contract law that companies must enforce any privacy policies that they publicly post. In the United States, in the spring of 2000, the U.S. FTC started expanding its activities for monitoring Internet commerce. It proposed rules for financial institutions to safeguard customer information and called on the U.S. Congress to protect the privacy of online consumers more rigorously.

Commercial vendors are also developing privacy tools that help users gain more control over their personal information. These tools include software to enable an individual to surf the Web using a fictitious identity and to send and receive e-mail that can never be traced back to them. Other tools block the use of "cookies," scramble IP addresses to prevent others from learning the user's fixed Internet address, and help users determine the kind of personal data that can be extracted by Web sites.

Sources: Cheryl Rosen and Beth Bacheldor, "The Politics of Privacy Protection," *Information Week*, July 17, 2000; DeWayne Lehman, "Privacy Policies Missing on 77% of Web Site," *Computerworld*, April 17, 2000; Jaikumar Vijayan, "Caught in the Middle," *Computerworld*, July 24, 2000; Keith Perine, "The Privacy Police," *The Industry Standard*, February 21, 2000; Michelle V. Rafter, "Trust or Bust?" *The Industry Standard*, March 13, 2000; Steve Lohr, "Internet Companies Set Policies to Help Protect Consumer Privacy," *The New York Times*, November 5, 1999; "Seizing the Initiative on Privacy"" *The New York Times*, October 11, 1999; Jon G. Auerbach, "To Get IBM Ad, Sites Must Post Privacy Policies," *The Wall Street Journal*, April 30, 1999; Edward C. Baig, Marcia Stepanek, and Neil Gross, "Privacy," *Business Week*, April 5, 1999; Gregory Dalton, "Online Data's FineLine," *Information Week*, March 29, and 1999; Alex Lash, "Privacy, Practically Speaking," *The Industry Standard*, August 2–9, 1999.

CASE STUDY QUESTIONS

1. Is Web site privacy a serious problem? Why or why not?

2. What are the gains for the Web-based businesses if they collect, use, sell, and otherwise disseminate non-explicit information on their visitors or use it in ways not explicitly approved by the visitor? the losses (costs)?

3. Apply an ethical analysis to the question of Web site visitors' privacy rights.

4. Should Web sites be allowed to collect visitor information that is not voluntarily provided?

5. How should Web site privacy be promoted? What role should the government play? What role should private business play? What role should technology play?

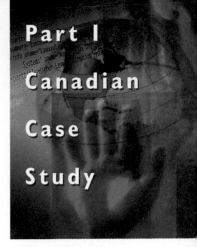

◼ SURVIVING HIGH TECH

Although much of the corporate world has switched to high-speed cable to connect to the World Wide Web, most hotels still offer only dial-up services. Hotel phones are designed for voice transmission. An average phone call from a room lasts around two to three minutes, but hotel Internet users, a growing breed, are typically online, tying up the phone system, for an hour or more. According to a survey last year by Radisson Hotels, an up-market chain with a sizable business clientele, 83.2 percent of its guests travel with portable computers.

More users mean an overload on the phone lines and a longer wait to download information. Hoteliers say that some business travellers, used to more sophisticated systems at the office, leave their computers on and connected even when they go out. That also ties up phone lines and creates difficulties for other users. Dialing into the Internet from a hotel-room telephone line can take several minutes depending on traffic.

"In 1999, we had an awful lot of problems with our phones," says Florencio de Dios, front-office manager of the Radisson President Hotel and Suites in Richmond, B.C., which caters mainly to business clients. "When people tried to call us or dial out, they constantly got a busy signal."

Meeting and exceeding customer expectations is an ongoing challenge and opportunity for large lodging management and franchise companies. Today most hoteliers have installed Internet access capabilities in all of their guestrooms. Service provision has grown in just three years from a guest "perk" that could give a hotelier a competitive advantage, to a commodity service, one that a broad range of suppliers—hardware, bandwidth, Web portal, and entertainment—are investing in. "Guests come to expect in-room Internet access, at the same speed they can get at their office," says Lewis Kievit, director of sales for the Park Hyatt Hotel in Chicago, Illinois.

So, in 1999, de Dios decided to look into getting a high-speed Internet link—which relatively few hotels offer. According to Philippe Labrosse, general manager of Montreal-based TravelNet Technologies Inc., a company specializing in Web-based applications, there are an estimated 300 000 hotel rooms across Canada, but fewer than 10 percent had been wired for high-speed Internet access by mid-2000.

GUEST-TEK: CANADIAN COMPANY TO THE HOTELS' RESCUE

By January 2000, all the rooms at the Richmond Radisson had been fitted with GlobalNet, a "plug and play" high-speed Internet access system that allows users to connect directly to the Internet from the comfort of their hotel rooms. GlobalNet uses a high-speed cable, accessed via an Ethernet card (a standard feature on most laptops), allowing guests to send and receive e-mail, surf the Internet, download company files, and access corporate networks via virtual private networks (VPNs).

GlobalNet, a product of Guest-Tek Ltd., is several hundred times faster than an average modem, but it has other advantages besides speed. Hotels, aware of the need to provide "added value" services in today's competitive marketplace, can charge $9.95 to $15 a day for GlobalNet and similar high-speed links—considerably less than Net-use phone charges that can run to several hundred dollars.

Guest-Tek isn't the only company supplying high-speed service to hotels—at least 20 other firms across North America are in the field, but it was the first in Canada when it was founded in 1996. Guest-Tek is a broadband networking supplier based in Calgary. Arnon Levy was 25 years old when he founded Guest-Tek.

Guest-Tek has signed up several major hotel chains, including Hyatt, Hilton, Fairmont, and Holiday Inn, and has installed its various systems in several dozen hotels in seven provinces across Canada. Their systems can also be found throughout the United States and in Australia. In addition to GlobalNet, Guest-Tek offers GlobalMeeting for meetings and convention centres. Guest-Tek offers hotels a wide range of applications to provide to their guests, including the administration of unlimited flexible billing options and connections, security, and statistics on guest access to the systems.

That's great for the hotels and guests. But how does a 28-year old Commerce grad from Alberta run a company that is growing at the rate of 296% annually (based on guest rooms serviced in 2000)? After founding the company and watching it take off, Levy knew he had to "build the company." He needed to triple his staff to keep up with sales that were growing at "warp speed."

LAUNCHWORKS STEPS UP TO THE PLATE

So, in August 1999, Guest-Tek received the first investment by a new venture capital company headquartered in Calgary—LaunchWorks. LaunchWorks focuses on growth-stage software technology businesses, using what they call "Launch Capital," a combination of guidance, executive talent, and financial capital to help technology companies achieve financial success.

LaunchWorks CEO Byron Osing sold the entrepreneurial company he started in 1995, TeleBackup, for over $200 million. He then started LaunchWorks, where he serves as CEO.

LaunchWorks is part of a trend toward investing "smart money." Their funds are backed by the operational and marketing expertise they bring to the table along with their investment capital. According to Levy, "LaunchWorks helped develop our strategic planning, and it lent us a chief financial officer."

"The LaunchWorks people are like mentors to me," says Levy. "They've been in my seat in the past, so they know what I'm going through and help me deal with my problems. That aspect of the deal is priceless."

LaunchWorks' venture capital process is different, too. Companies that approach LaunchWorks for capital go through a tightly scripted vetting process. It begins at the firm's Web site where needy entrepreneurs download and fill out an Opportunity Assessment form. LaunchWorks analyzes the results to find opportunities that meet its investment criteria. If the idea is solid, the prospective client fills out a business plan template and a personality profile so LaunchWorks can figure out who it is dealing with, what they're good at, and where they need to fill holes.

If the would-be client passes that stage, the two sides meet for a strategic planning session. "We review their mission, vision statement, tactics, and milestones and look at the resources they need," says LaunchWorks President Stephen Kenny, former president of Digitech Information Services. "It's a time-consuming process, but it let's us see them with their sleeves rolled up. It also helps them out because our senior guys throw ideas into the ring."

Historically, Western Canadian software and Internet start-ups making the transition from angel funding to venture capital have had to look outside the region if they wanted both management input and seed capital. But now there are a few firms in Alberta and British Columbia that take the combined approach, such as Ventures West Capital Ltd. in Vancouver and Sigma Technologies Corp. in Calgary.

"We want to make sure Canada participates in the shift to the new knowledge-based economy," says Kenny. "One of our mandates is to ensure that intellectual capital and the wealth that goes with it stays in Canada." The nationalist sentiment is nice, but it's clear they're capitalists first.

GUEST-TEK UNDER LAUNCHWORKS' MENTORSHIP

The LaunchWorks team met repeatedly with the Guest-Tek management team. LaunchWorks placed five of its team members in Guest-Tek's offices to mentor and consult. One of the recommendations was that Levy replace Kris Youell, the Director of Sales and Marketing. After much consideration, Levy decided to have Kris mentored to see if that would provide the needed expertise in her area until she gained the experience to handle the job.

Eventually, Paul Sullivan was brought on board as Vice President of Sales. Sullivan had more than 20 years' experience, including founding a high-tech start-up himself. Today he is the CEO at Guest-Tek, with Levy moving to the position of Executive Vice President, managing special projects and new product development. Two other members of Guest-Tek's board of directors are from LaunchWorks. Interestingly, a year after Sullivan's appointment to head sales, Youell was still with the company as Director of Sales until she took maternity leave.

Under the mentorship and consulting from LaunchWorks, Guest-Tek has partnered with Delphi Solutions, SaskTel, Norigen Communications, and Quorum Information Systems, all Canadian high-tech companies. Guest-Tek also signed a strategic alliance agreement with OnCommand Canada to market Guest-Tek's high-speed Internet access products to the Canadian hotels that carry OnCommand's entertainment, information, and business services.

In building their market, Guest-Tek has opened three offices in the United States in the last two years, in Atlanta, Chicago, and Minneapolis. LaunchWorks recently provided a third round of financing to cover potential growth in the market. According to PricewaterhouseCoopers, hotel rooms with high-speed Internet access should increase by 80 percent in 2001.

Sullivan plans to build Guest-Tek into the leading provider of high-speed Internet access in the industry. "We already have an industry-leading 97 percent success rate for connecting guests to the Internet." Guest-Tek's latest product is called MyAway, a customized Web portal covering a wide variety of topics aimed at business travellers—news headlines, stock updates, flight information, local information, and hotel services.

Sources: Helga Loverseed, "Hoteliers Finally Answer the Bell for Online Guests," *The Globe and Mail*, March 9, 2000; Paul W. Cockerham, "'Net Expectations: Interactive Options Fulfill Guest Needs in the Well Connected Hotel Room," *Hospitality Technology Magazine*, June 2001; Patricia Zyska, "Someone to Lean On," *Computing Canada*, September 15, 2000; Peter Verburg, "Payback Time," *Canadian Business*, November 12, 1999; Guest-Tek Web site, www.guest-tek.com, accessed August 13, 2001.

VIDEO RESOURCE
"Guest-Tek," *CBC Venture,* 736 (January 25, 2000).

CASE STUDY QUESTIONS

1. When Levy started Guest-Tek, what vision and mission did he have for the company? Do you think he was ready for the "hard things" he would have to do, such as discussing with Kris Youell the need for mentoring?

2. Why did Levy need additional financing? What do you think is the relationship between growth and the need for venture capital? Do you think Guest-Tek's growth rate necessitates occasional additional financing from outside the company?

3. Why did Levy pick LaunchWorks? Do you think the LaunchWorks' Capital model of providing expertise along with financing is a good model? Why has LaunchWorks continued to provide capital for Guest-Tek? Is this the way most organizations operate?

4. Why would Levy "demote" himself to executive vice president? What did Sullivan "bring to the table" that Levy does not have? Could Guest-Tek have continued to grow and prosper under Levy? How much influence did LaunchWorks have in this decision?

5. What do you think a hotel's management would be looking for from Guest-Tek? Why would a hotel contract with Guest-Tek for their services?

6. Are Guest-Tek's services electronic commerce? Or do they simply enable e-commerce? Why do you think that?

7. Why would Guest-Tek partner with other companies? Should they have done so? What other partners do you think Guest-Tek should acquire?

PART II

INFORMATION TECHNOLOGY

6 COMPUTER HARDWARE

OBJECTIVES

After completing this chapter, you will be able to:

1. *Identify the hardware components in a computer system.*
2. *Describe how information is represented and processed in a computer system.*
3. *Contrast the capabilities of personal computers, workstations, midrange computers, mainframes, and supercomputers.*
4. *Compare different arrangements of computer processing, including the use of client/server computing, network computers, and peer-to-peer computing.*
5. *Describe the principal media for storing data and programs in a computer system.*
6. *Compare the major input and output devices and the various ways they are connected to a computer system.*
7. *Compare various approaches to data input and processing.*
8. *Describe multimedia and information technology (IT) trends.*
9. *Analyze important issues in managing hardware.*

Navigation Canada Takes Flight with New Computers

Canada's air traffic control system monitors more than 38 million square kilometres of airspace. Before privatization in November 1996, this responsibility was handled with outdated Digital Equipment Corporation VAX cluster computers that required air traffic controllers to hunt for information on six different systems. The air navigation system was funded by an Air Transportation Tax levied by the government, which did not provide sufficient funds for computer upgrades.

Then a new private, nonprofit company called Navigation Canada (NavCan, www.navcanada.ca) took over. Because it could charge the airline industry for its services, NavCan was able to raise $800 million to upgrade the computers required to make the air traffic control system safer and more secure. The upgrade, called the Canadian Automated Air Traffic System (CAATS) started in the summer of 1998 and was completed in 2000. NavCan replaced the VAX clusters with HP 9000 server computers and HP C200 UNIX-based workstations. Each of NavCan's 23 operational sites has been outfitted with three servers—a primary server, a backup server, and a third server for training purposes. The built-in redundancy is deliberate. If one of the servers fails, another can take over. Air navigation systems can't afford to be down even for five minutes. Software has been added to ensure that flight data are transmitted and received without modification or corruption.

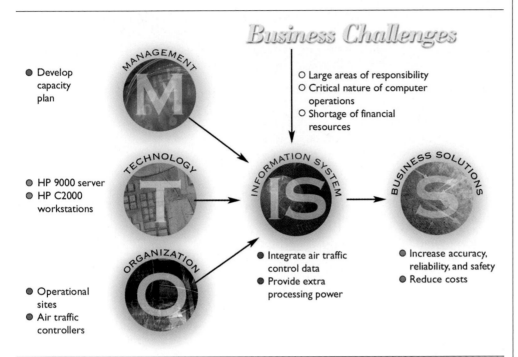

CAATS gives air traffic controllers radar data, flight path information, computer-based conflict prediction, weather updates, and navigational aid data on a single system. CAATS also automatically routes flight plans to the appropriate people, reducing the chance of human error or loss of critical information. With these new capabilities, NavCan can reduce flight delays and inefficiencies created by airplanes contending for the same runway. Air traffic controllers can support routes that are more direct and fuel-efficient. In addition to making our Canadian skies safer for flyers, Navigation Canada expects the efficiencies created by CAATS to cut annual operating costs by $135 million. As recently as August 2001, NavCan announced that they will spend almost $6 million on a new Air Operations Centre in Saskatoon and $3.4 million to update training simulators and software. This serves as a reminder that updating once is not enough; it is an ongoing process.

Sources: John Crichton, "Nav Canada Technology Update Notes for an Address," www.navcanada.ca/crichton-ATCA-June%208%2000%20media.doc.htm, June 8, 2000, accessed February 2001; "Nav Canada Announces Real Time Y2K Testing," Nav Canada, January 12, 1999; and Laura DiDio, "$600M Net Upgrade Takes Flight," *Computerworld*, February 16, 1998.

MANAGEMENT CHALLENGES

By shifting to more up-to-date computer hardware, Navigation Canada was able to provide more computing power for its air traffic control operations and to integrate all of the information used by air traffic controllers. To select the right computers, NavCan's managers needed to understand how much computer processing capacity its business processes required, how to evaluate the price and performance of various types of computers, and what was the financial and business rationale for hardware technology investments. They also had to plan for future processing requirements and understand how computers worked with storage, input, output, and communications technology. Selecting appropriate computer hardware raises the following management challenges:

1. **The centralization vs. decentralization debate.** A longstanding issue among information system managers and CEOs has been the question of how much to centralize or distribute computing resources. Should processing power and data be distributed to departments and divisions, or should they be concentrated at a single location using a large central computer? Client/server computing facilitates decentralization, but network computers and mainframes support a centralized model. Which is better for the organization? Every organization will have a different answer based on its own needs. Managers need to make sure that the computing model they select is compatible with organizational goals.

2. **Making wise technology purchasing decisions.** Computer hardware technology changes much more rapidly than other assets of the firm. Soon after having made an investment in hardware technology, managers find the completed system is obsolete and too expensive, given the power and lower cost of new technology. In this environment, it is very difficult to keep systems up to date. Considerable time must be spent anticipating and planning for technological change.

   Successful use of information systems to support an organization's business goals requires an understanding of computer processing power and the capabilities of hardware devices. By understanding the role of hardware technology in the organization's information technology infrastructure, managers can make sure that their firms have the processing capability they need to accomplish the work of the firm and to meet future business challenges.

In this chapter, we describe the typical hardware configuration of a computer system, explaining how a computer works, and how computer processing power and storage capacity are measured. We then compare the capabilities of various types of computers and input, output, and storage devices. We conclude by discussing the major issues in managing hardware.

6.1 COMPUTER HARDWARE AND INFORMATION TECHNOLOGY INFRASTRUCTURE

Computer hardware technology constitutes the underlying physical foundation for the firm's information technology infrastructure. The other components of IT infrastructure—software, data, and networks—require computer hardware for their storage or operation. Although managers and business professionals do not need to be computer technology experts, they should have a basic understanding of how computer hardware works and its role in the organization's IT infrastructure so that they can make technology decisions that benefit organizational performance and productivity.

THE COMPUTER SYSTEM

A contemporary computer system consists of a central processing unit, primary storage, secondary storage, input devices, output devices, and communications devices (see Figure 6-1).

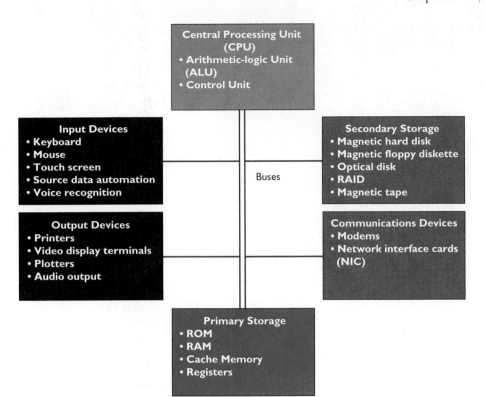

FIGURE 6-1 Hardware components of a computer system. A contemporary computer system can be categorized into six major components. The central processing unit manipulates data and controls the other parts of the computer system; primary storage temporarily stores data and program instructions during processing; secondary storage feeds data and instructions into the central processor and stores data for future use; input devices convert data and instructions for processing in the computer; output devices present data in a form that people can understand; and communications devices control the passing of information to and from communications networks.

The central processing unit manipulates raw data into a more useful form and controls the other parts of the computer system. Primary storage, consisting of RAM and cache memory, temporarily stores data and program instructions during processing whereas secondary storage devices (magnetic and optical disks, magnetic tape) store data and programs when they are not being used in processing. Registers are data holding places that are part of a computer microprocessor and that provide a place for passing data from one instruction to the next sequential instruction or to another program that the operating system has just given control to. Input devices, such as a keyboard or mouse, convert data and instructions into electronic form for input into the computer. Output devices, such as printers and monitors, convert electronic data produced by the computer system and display them in a form that people can understand. Communications devices such as modems and network interface cards provide connections between the computer and communications networks. Communications devices are discussed in Chapter 9. Buses are circuitry paths for transmitting data and signals among the parts of the computer system.

How Computers Represent Data

For information to flow through a computer system in a form suitable for processing, all symbols, pictures, or words must be reduced to a string of binary digits. A binary digit is called a **bit** and represents either a 0 or a 1. In the computer, the presence of an electronic or magnetic signal means one, and its absence signifies zero. Digital computers operate directly with binary digits, either singly or strung together to form bytes. A string of eight bits that the computer stores as a unit is called a **byte**. Each byte can be used to store a decimal number, a symbol, a character, or part of a picture (see Figure 6-2).

bit
A binary digit representing the smallest unit of data in a computer system. It can only have one of two states, representing 0 or 1.

byte
A string of eight bits used to store one number or character in a computer system.

FIGURE 6-2 Bits and bytes. Bits are represented by either a 0 or 1. A string of eight bits constitutes a byte, which represents a character. The computer's representation for the word "CANADA" is a series of six bytes, where each byte represents one character (or letter) in the word.

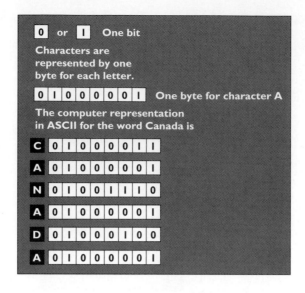

Figure 6-3 shows how decimal numbers are represented using binary digits. Each position in a decimal number has a certain value. Any number in the decimal system (base 10) can be reduced to a binary number. The binary number system (base 2) can express any number as a power of the number 2. The table at the bottom of the figure shows how the translation from binary to decimal works. By using a binary number system, a computer can express all numbers as groups of zeroes and ones. In addition to representing numbers, a computer must represent alphabetic characters and many other symbols used in natural language, such as $ and &. Manufacturers of computer hardware have developed standard binary codes for this purpose.

Two common codes are EBCDIC and ASCII. The **Extended Binary Coded Decimal Interchange Code** (**EBCDIC**—pronounced eb-si-dick) was developed by IBM in the 1950s, and it represents every number, alphabetic character, or special character with eight bits. **ASCII (American Standard Code for Information Interchange)** was developed by the American National Standards Institute (ANSI) to provide a standard code that could be used by many different manufacturers in order to make machinery compatible. ASCII was originally designed as a seven-bit code, but most computers use eight-bit versions. EBCDIC is used in IBM and other mainframe computers, whereas ASCII is used in data transmission, PCs, and some larger computers. Table 6-1 shows how some letters and numbers would be represented using EBCDIC and ASCII. Other coding systems such as Unicode are being developed to represent a wider array of foreign languages.

How can a computer represent a picture? The computer stores a picture by creating a grid overlay of the picture. Each single point in this grid or matrix is called a **pixel** (picture element) and consists of a number of bits. The computer then stores this information on

EBCDIC (Extended Binary Coded Decimal Interchange Code)
A binary code representing every number, alphabetic character, or special character with eight bits, used primarily in IBM and other mainframe computers.

ASCII (American Standard Code for Information Interchange)
A seven- or eight-bit binary code used in data transmission, PCs, and some large computers.

pixel
The smallest unit of data for defining an image in the computer. The computer reduces a picture to a grid of pixels. The term pixel comes from picture element.

FIGURE 6-3 The binary number system. Each decimal number has a certain value that can be expressed as a binary number. The binary number system can express any number as a power of the number 2.

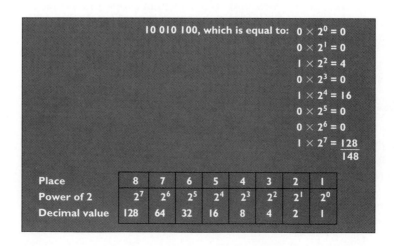

TABLE 6-1	EXAMPLES OF ASCII AND EBCDIC CODES	
Character or Number	ASCII-8 Binary	EBCDIC Binary
A	01000001	11000001
E	01000101	11000101
Z	01011010	11101001
0	00110000	11110000
1	00110001	11110001
5	00110101	11110101

each pixel. A high-resolution computer display monitor has a 1024 × 768 SVGA (super video graphics array) or XGA (extended graphics array) standard grid, creating more than 700 000 pixels. Whether processing pictures or text, modern computers operate by reducing data into bits and bytes.

THE CPU AND PRIMARY STORAGE

The **central processing unit (CPU)** is the part of the computer system where the manipulation of symbols, numbers, and letters occurs. The CPU controls the other parts of the computer system (see Figure 6-4). Located near the CPU is **primary storage** (sometimes called primary memory or main memory) where data and program instructions are stored temporarily during processing. A **bus** is the circuitry or data path on the computer's motherboard that interconnects the microprocessor with attachments to the motherboard in expansion slots (such as hard disk drives, CD-ROM drives, and graphics adapter cards). The **motherboard** is the physical platform in a computer that contains the computer's basic circuitry and components; it usually looks like a large electronic chip with slots and openings on it for memory hard drives and other devices to be plugged into.

Three kinds of buses link the CPU, primary storage, and other devices on the motherboard. The data bus moves data to and from primary storage. The address bus transmits signals for locating a given address in primary storage, indicating where data should be placed. The control bus transmits signals specifying whether to read or write data to or from a given primary storage address, input device, or output device. The characteristics of the CPU and primary storage are very important in determining a computer's speed and capabilities.

central processing unit (CPU)
The area of the computer system that manipulates symbols, numbers, and letters, and controls the other parts of the computer system.

primary storage
The part of the computer that temporarily stores program instructions and data being used by the CPU.

bus
The circuitry on the computer's motherboard that interconnects the microprocessor with attachments to the motherboard in expansion slots (such as hard disk drives, CD-ROM drives, and graphics adapters).

motherboard
The physical platform in a computer that contains the computer's basic circuitry and components.

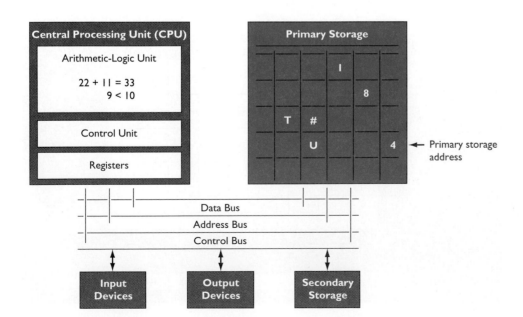

FIGURE 6-4 The CPU and primary storage. The CPU contains an arithmetic-logic unit, a control unit, and registers. Data and instructions are stored in unique addresses in primary storage that the CPU can access during processing. The data bus, address bus, and control bus transmit signals between the central processing unit, primary storage, and other devices in the computer system.

arithmetic-logic unit (ALU)
The component of the CPU that performs the computer's principal logic and arithmetic operations.

control unit
The component of the CPU that controls and coordinates the other parts of the computer system.

register
A temporary storage location in the ALU or control unit where small amounts of data and instructions reside just before use.

RAM (random access memory)
Primary storage of data or program instructions that can directly access any randomly chosen primary storage location in the same amount of time.

kilobyte
One thousand bytes (actually 1024 storage positions). Used as a measure of PC storage capacity.

megabyte
Approximately one million bytes. A unit of computer storage capacity.

gigabyte
Approximately one billion bytes. A unit of computer storage capacity.

terabyte
Approximately one trillion bytes. A unit of computer storage capacity.

semiconductor
An integrated circuit made by printing thousands and even millions of tiny transistors on a small silicon chip.

The Arithmetic-Logic Unit and Control Unit

Figure 6-4 also shows that the CPU consists of an arithmetic-logic unit, a control unit, and registers. The **arithmetic-logic unit (ALU)** performs the computer's principal logical and arithmetic operations. It adds, subtracts, multiplies, and divides, determining whether a number is positive, negative, or zero. In addition to performing arithmetic functions, an ALU must be able to determine when one quantity is greater than or less than another and when two quantities are equal. The ALU can perform logic operations on the binary codes for letters as well as numbers.

The **control unit** coordinates and controls the other parts of the computer system. It reads a stored program, one instruction at a time, and directs other components of the computer system to perform the program's required tasks. A **register** is a special temporary storage location in the ALU or control unit that acts like a high-speed staging area for program instructions or data being transferred from primary storage to the CPU for processing.

Primary Storage

Primary storage has three functions. First, it stores all or part of the program that is being executed. Second, primary storage also stores the operating system programs that manage the operation of the computer. (These programs are discussed in Chapter 7.) Finally, the primary storage area holds data that the program is using. Data and programs are placed in primary storage before processing, between processing steps, and after processing has ended, prior to being returned to secondary storage or released as output.

Figure 6-5 illustrates primary storage in an electronic digital computer. Primary storage is often called **RAM (random access memory)** because the CPU can directly access any randomly chosen primary storage location in the same amount of time.

Figure 6-5 shows that primary memory is divided into storage locations called bytes. Each location contains a set of eight binary switches or devices, each of which can store one bit of information. The set of eight bits found in each storage location is sufficient to store one letter, one digit, or one special symbol (such as $) using either EBCDIC or ASCII. Each byte has a unique address, similar to a mailbox, indicating where it is located in RAM. The computer can remember where the data in all of the bytes are located simply by keeping track of these addresses.

Computer storage capacity is measured in bytes. Table 6-2 lists computer storage capacity measurements. One thousand bytes (actually 1024 storage positions) is called a **kilobyte**. One million bytes is called a **megabyte**, one billion bytes is called a **gigabyte**, and one trillion bytes is called a **terabyte**.

Primary storage is composed of semiconductors. A **semiconductor** is an integrated circuit made by printing thousands and even millions of tiny transistors on a small silicon chip.

FIGURE 6-5 Primary storage in the computer. Primary storage can be visualized as a matrix. Each byte represents a mailbox with a unique address. In this example, mailbox [n,1] contains eight bits representing the number 0 (as coded in EBCDIC).

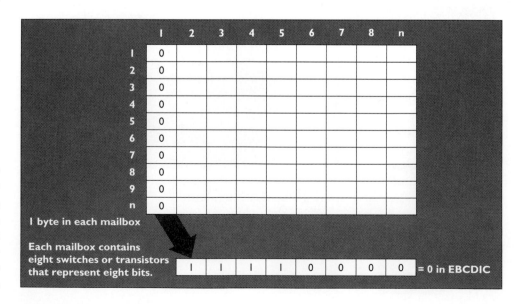

TABLE 6-2	SPEED AND SIZE IN THE DIGITAL WORLD	
Time	**Abbreviation**	**Seconds**
Millisecond	ms	1/1 000
Microsecond	mus	1/1 000 000
Nanosecond	ns	1/1 000 000 000
Picosecond	ps	1/1 000 000 000 000
Storage Capacity	**Abbreviation**	**Number of Bytes**
Byte	B	1*
Kilobyte	KB	1 000**
Megabyte	MB	1 000 000
Gigabyte	GB	1 000 000 000
Terabyte	TB	1 000 000 000 000

* String of eight bits
** Actually 1024 bytes

There are several different kinds of semiconductor memory used in primary storage. RAM is used for short-term storage of data or program instructions. RAM is volatile. Its contents will be lost when the computer's electric supply is disrupted by a power outage or when the computer is turned off. **ROM**, or **read-only memory**, can only be read from; it cannot be written to. ROM chips come from the manufacturer with programs already *burned in* or stored. There are also other kinds of ROM chips. *PROM* (programmable read-only memory) chips can be programmed once, avoiding the expense of having a specially manufactured chip manufactured for a specific purpose machine while *EPROM* (erasable programmable read-only memory) chips are used for device control and can be changed on a routine basis, such as in robots. ROM is used in general-purpose computers to store important or frequently used programs, such as computing routines for calculating the square roots of numbers.

MICROPROCESSORS AND PROCESSING POWER

Contemporary CPUs also use semiconductor chips called **microprocessors** that integrate all of the memory, logic, and control circuits for an entire CPU onto a single chip. The speed and performance of a computer's microprocessors help determine a computer's processing power. Some popular microprocessors are listed in Table 6-3. You may see microprocessor chips labelled as 8-bit, 16-bit, 32-bit, or 64-bit devices. These labels refer to the **word length** or the number of bits that the computer can process at one time. An 8-bit chip can process 8 bits, or 1 byte, of information in a single machine cycle. A 32-bit chip can process 32 bits or 4 bytes in a single cycle. The larger the word length, the greater the computer's speed.

ROM (read-only memory)
Semiconductor memory chips that contain program instructions. These chips can only be read from; they cannot be written to.

microprocessor
Very large-scale integrated circuit technology that integrates the computer's memory, logic, and control on a single chip.

word length
The number of bits that the computer can process at one time. The larger the word length, the greater the computer's speed.

TABLE 6-3	EXAMPLES OF MICROPROCESSORS			
Name	**Manufacturer**	**Word Length**	**Clock Speed (MHz)**	**Data Bus Width**
Pentium II	Intel	32	233–450	64
Celeron	Intel	32	500–700	64
Pentium III	Intel	32	500–1000	64
Pentium IV	Intel	64	1.5 GHz	64
Itanium	Intel	64	1.5 GHz	64
PowerPC	Motorola, IBM, Apple	32 or 64	100–400	64
Alpha	DEC/Compaq	64	600+	64
Athlon	AMD	64	800+	64

The Pentium IV chip has a clock speed over I gigahertz.

clock speed
The number of pulses per second generated by an oscillator that sets the tempo for the processor; usually measured in megahertz.

megahertz
A measure of cycle speed, or the pacing of events in a computer; one megahertz equals one million cycles per second.

machine cycle
A series of operations required to process a single machine instruction.

cycle time
The time, usually measured in fractions of a second, between the start of one random access memory access and the time when the next access can be started; consists of latency and transfer time.

latency
The time it takes to find the right place for the memory access and to prepare to access it.

microsecond
One-millionth of a second.

nanosecond
One-billionth of a second.

picosecond
One trillionth of a second.

data bus width
The number of bits that can be moved at one time between the CPU, primary storage, and the other devices of a computer.

reduced instruction set computing (RISC)
Technology used to enhance the speed of microprocessors by embedding only the most frequently used instructions on a chip.

MMX
A Pentium microprocessor modified to improve processing of multimedia applications. Stands for MultiMedia eXtension.

A second factor affecting chip speed is **clock speed**. Every event in a computer must be sequenced so that one step logically follows another. The control unit contains an oscillator that sets a beat to the chip. This beat is established by an internal clock and is measured in **megahertz** (abbreviated MHz, which stands for millions of cycles per second). The Intel 8088 chip, for instance, originally had a clock speed of 4.47 megahertz whereas the Intel Pentium III chip has a clock speed that ranges from 450 to 1500 megahertz and the Pentium IV chip clock speed is currently up to 2 gigahertz. The series of operations required to process a single machine instruction is called the **machine cycle**. **Cycle time** is the time, usually measured in fractions of a second, between the start of one random access memory (RAM) access and the time when the next access can be started. Cycle time consists of **latency** (the time it takes to find the right place for the memory access and to prepare to access it) and transfer time. Older computers and PCs have machine cycle times measured in **microseconds** (one-millionth of a second). More powerful machines have machine cycle times measured in **nanoseconds** (billionths of a second) or **picoseconds** (trillionths of a second). Another measure of machine cycle time is MIPS, or millions of instructions per second. Cycle time should not be confused with processor clock cycles or clock speed, which have to do with the number of cycles per second (in megahertz or MHz) to which a processor is paced.

A third factor affecting speed is the **data bus width**. The data bus acts as a highway between the CPU, primary storage, and other devices, determining how much data can be moved at one time. The 8088 chip used in the original IBM personal computer, for example, had a 16-bit word length but only an 8-bit data bus width. This meant that data were processed within the CPU chip itself in 16-bit chunks but could only be moved 8 bits at a time between the CPU, primary storage, and external devices. On the other hand, the Alpha chip has both a 64-bit word length and a 64-bit data bus width. To have a computer execute more instructions per second and work through programs or handle users expeditiously, it is necessary to increase the processor's word length, the data bus width, or the cycle speed—or all three.

Microprocessors can be made faster by using **reduced instruction set computing (RISC)** in their design. Conventional chips, based on complex instruction set computing, have several hundred or more instructions hard-wired into their circuitry, and they may take several clock cycles to execute a single instruction. If the little-used instructions are eliminated, the remaining instructions can execute much faster. RISC computers have only the most frequently used instructions embedded in them. A RISC CPU can execute most instructions in a single machine cycle and sometimes multiple instructions at the same time. RISC is most appropriate for scientific and workstation computing, where there are repetitive arithmetic and logical operations on data or applications calling for three-dimensional image rendering.

Microprocessors optimized for multimedia and graphics have been developed to improve processing visually intensive applications. Intel's **MMX (MultiMedia eXtension)** microprocessor is a Pentium chip that has been modified with additional instructions to

SEQUENTIAL PROCESSING

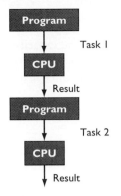

Task 1

Result

Task 2

Result

PARALLEL PROCESSING

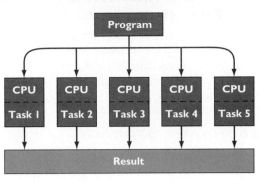

FIGURE 6-6 Sequential and parallel processing. During sequential processing, each task is assigned to one CPU that processes one instruction at a time. In parallel processing, multiple tasks are assigned to multiple processing units to expedite the result.

increase performance in many applications featuring graphics and sound. Multimedia applications such as games and video will be able to run more smoothly, display more colours, and perform more tasks simultaneously. For example, multiple channels of audio, high-quality video or animation, and Internet communication could all be running in the same application. Advanced Micro Devices' AMD-K6 microprocessor is compatible with the Pentium and also supports the MMX instruction set. Intel's Pentium III chip also has special capabilities for speech recognition, imaging, video, and Internet work.

Most of today's personal computers can be categorized as either IBM-compatible or Apple. There are a number of *clones* of the original IBM personal computer. Many of these clones use different chips or different operating systems than IBM's own computers.

MULTIPLE PROCESSORS AND PARALLEL PROCESSING

Many computers use multiple processors to perform their processing work. For example, PCs often use a *coprocessor* to speed processing by performing specific tasks such as mathematical calculations or graphics processing so that the CPU can be free to do other processing.

Processing can also be speeded by linking several processors to work simultaneously on the same task. Figure 6-6 compares parallel processing to serial processing used in conventional computers. In **parallel processing**, multiple CPUs break down a problem into smaller parts and work on it simultaneously. Getting a group of processors to attack the same problem at once requires both rethinking the problems and special software that can divide the problem among different processors in the most efficient way possible, reassembling these subtasks to reach the solution.

Massively parallel computers have huge networks of hundreds or even thousands of processor chips interwoven in complex and flexible ways to attack large computing problems. As opposed to parallel processing, where small numbers of powerful but expensive specialized chips are linked together, massively parallel machines chain hundreds or even thousands of inexpensive, commonly used chips to break problems into many small pieces and solve them. For instance, Wal-Mart uses a massively parallel machine to sift through an inventory and sales trend database with 24 trillion bytes of data.

parallel processing
A type of processing in which more than one instruction can be processed at a time by breaking down a problem into smaller parts and processing them simultaneously with multiple processors.

massively parallel computers
Computers that use hundreds or thousands of processing chips to attack large computing problems simultaneously.

The new supercomputer from Compaq. It combines up to 512 Alpha 21264a processors and 2048 GB of memory in a scalable supercomputer, offering unprecedented availability and performance, managed as a single 700 GigaFLOPS system.

6.2 STORAGE, INPUT, AND OUTPUT TECHNOLOGY

The capabilities of computer systems depend not only on the speed and capacity of the CPU but also on the speed, capacity, and design of storage, input, and output technology. Storage, input, and output devices are called *peripheral devices* because they are outside the main computer system unit.

SECONDARY STORAGE

Most of the information used by a computer application is stored on secondary storage devices located outside of the primary storage area. **Secondary storage** is used for relatively long-term storage of data outside the CPU. Secondary storage is nonvolatile and retains data even when the computer is turned off. The most important secondary storage technologies are magnetic disk, optical disk, and magnetic tape.

Magnetic Disk

The most widely used secondary-storage medium today is **magnetic disk**. There are two kinds of magnetic disks: floppy disks (used in PCs) and **hard disks** (used on large commercial disk drives and PCs). Large mainframe or minicomputer systems have multiple hard disk drives because they require immense disk storage capacity in the gigabyte and terabyte range. PCs also use **floppy disks**, which are removable and portable, with a storage capacity ranging from 360 kilobytes to 2.8 megabytes and a much slower access rate than hard disks. Removable disk drives such as those manufactured by Iomega and Syquest are becoming popular backup storage alternatives for PC systems. For example, Iomega's Zip drive's diskettes can hold up to 250 megabytes of data.

Magnetic disks on both large and small computers permit direct access to individual records so that data stored on the disk can be directly accessed regardless of the order in which the data were originally recorded. A disk drive is often referred to as a **direct access storage device (DASD)**. Disk technology is useful for systems requiring rapid and direct access to data.

Disk drive performance can be further enhanced by using a **RAID (Redundant Array of Inexpensive Disks)** device. RAID devices can package more than a hundred disk drives, a controller chip, and specialized software into a single large unit. The array appears to the computer as a single logical unit consisting of multiple disk drives. Traditional disk drives deliver data from the disk drive along a single path, but RAID delivers data over multiple paths simultaneously, improving disk access time and reliability. For most RAID systems, data on a failed disk can be restored automatically without the computer system having to be shut down.

Optical Disks

Optical disks, also called compact discs or laser optical disks, use laser technology to store data at densities many times greater than those of magnetic disks. They are available for both PCs and large computers. Optical disks can store massive quantities of data, including not only text but pictures, sound, and full-motion video, in a highly compact form. Optical disks are most appropriate for applications where enormous quantities of unchanging data must be stored compactly for easy retrieval, or for storing graphic images and sound.

The most common optical disk used with PCs is called **CD-ROM (compact disc read-only memory)**. A 4.75-inch compact disc for PCs can store up to 660 megabytes, nearly 300 times more than a high-density floppy disk. A CD-ROM is a read-only storage disk. No new data can be written to it; it can only be read. CD-ROMs have been most widely used for reference materials with large amounts of data, such as encyclopedias and directories, and for storing multimedia applications that combine text, sound, and images. For example, Canadian census demographic data and articles and financial databases from the *Financial Times* or the *Globe and Mail* are available on CD-ROM.

---

secondary storage
Relatively long-term, nonvolatile storage of data outside the CPU and primary storage.

magnetic disk
A secondary storage medium in which data are stored by means of magnetized areas on a hard or floppy disk.

hard disk
A set of stacked magnetic disks resembling thin metallic platters with iron oxide coating; used in large computer systems and in most PCs.

floppy disk
Removable magnetic disk storage primarily used with PCs.

direct access storage device (DASD)
A storage device that permits direct access to data or programs stored on the DASD regardless of the order in which were originally recorded.

RAID (Redundant Array of Inexpensive Disks)
Disk storage technology that boosts disk performance by packaging more than 100 smaller disk drives with a controller chip and specialized software into a single large unit to deliver data over multiple paths simultaneously.

optical disk
Disk storage that uses laser technology to store data at densities many times greater than those of magnetic disks.

CD-ROM (compact disc read-only memory)
Read-only optical disk storage used for imaging, reference, and database applications with massive amounts of unchanging data and for multimedia.

WORM (write once/read many) and **CD-R (compact disc-recordable)** optical disk systems allow users to record data only once on an optical disk. Once written, the data cannot be erased, but can be read indefinitely. CD-R technology allows individuals and organizations to create their own CD-ROMs at low cost using a special CD-R recording device. New **CD-RW (CD-ReWritable)** technology has been developed to allow users to create rewritable optical disks. Rewritable optical disk drives are not yet competitive with magnetic disk storage for most applications but are useful for applications requiring large volumes of storage where the information is only occasionally updated.

Digital video discs (DVDs) are optical disks the same size as CD-ROMs but of even higher capacity. They can hold a minimum of 4.7 gigabytes of data, enough to store a full-length, high-quality motion picture. DVDs are initially being used to store movies and multimedia applications using large amounts of video and graphics, but they may replace CD-ROMs because they can store large amounts of digitized text, graphics, audio, and video data.

Magnetic Tape

Magnetic tape is an older storage technology that still is employed for secondary storage of large volumes of information. More and more organizations are moving away from using the old reel-to-reel magnetic tapes and instead are using mass storage tape cartridges that hold far more data (up to 35 gigabytes) than the old magnetic tapes. These cartridges are part of automated systems that store hundreds of such cartridges and select and mount them automatically using sophisticated robotics technology. Contemporary magnetic tape systems are used for archiving data and for storing data that are needed rapidly but not instantly.

The principal advantages of magnetic tape are that it is very inexpensive, it is relatively stable, and it can store very large quantities of information. The principal disadvantages of magnetic tape are that it stores data sequentially and is relatively slow compared to the speed of other secondary storage media. In order to find an individual record stored on magnetic tape, such as an employment record, the tape must be read from the beginning up to the location of the desired record. Magnetic tape is frequently used to back up a system. If the system goes down, the tape can be loaded to replace the data and programs that were lost.

New Storage Alternatives: Storage Area Networks and Online Storage Service Providers

To meet the escalating demand for data-intensive multimedia, Web, and other services, the amount of data that companies need to store is increasing by 75 to 150 percent every year. Companies are turning to new kinds of storage infrastructures to deal with their mushrooming storage requirements and difficulties in managing large volumes of data.

Storage Area Networks   Storage area networks can provide a solution for companies with the need to share information across applications and computing platforms. A **storage area network (SAN)** is a high-speed network dedicated to storage that connects different kinds of storage devices, such as tape libraries and disk arrays. The network moves data among pools of servers and storage devices, creating an enterprise-wide infrastructure for data storage. Many companies store vital information on **servers** at many different locations, and SANs

Margin glossary

WORM (write once/read many)
An optical disk system that allows users to record data only once; data cannot be erased but can be read indefinitely.

CD-R (compact disc-recordable)
An optical disk system that allows individuals and organizations to record their own CD-ROMs.

CD-RW (compact disc-rewritable)
An optical disk system that allows users to create rewritable optical disks.

digital video disc (DVD)
A high-capacity optical storage medium that can store full-length videos and large amounts of data.

magnetic tape
An inexpensive, older secondary-storage medium in which large volumes of information are stored sequentially by means of magnetized and nonmagnetized spots on tape.

storage area network (SAN)
A high-speed network dedicated to storage that connects different kinds of storage devices, such as tape libraries and disk arrays.

server
A computer specifically optimized to provide software and other resources to other computers over a network.

Secondary storage devices such as floppy disks, optical disks, and hard disks are used to store large quantities of data outside the CPU and primary storage. They provide direct access to data for easy retrieval.

FIGURE 6-7 A storage area network (SAN). The SAN stores data on many different types of storage devices, providing data to the enterprise. Users can share data across the SAN.

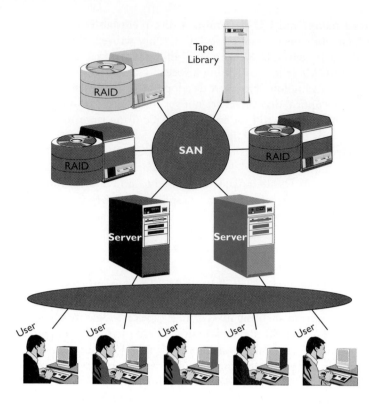

can make data available to all servers attached to them. The SAN creates a large, central pool of storage that can be shared by multiple servers so that users can rapidly share data across the SAN. Every user in a company can access data from any server in the organization. Figure 6-7 illustrates how a SAN works. The SAN storage devices are located on their own network and connected using high-speed transmission technology such as fibre optic channels. The SAN supports communication between any server and the storage unit as well as between different storage devices in the network.

A typical SAN consists of a server, storage devices, and networking devices and is used strictly for storage. In a SAN, the storage devices connect to the server independently, providing a dedicated path to the computer. Most SANs use high-speed transmission technology called *Fibre Channel* to facilitate the connection of multiple computers to dedicated storage systems. SANs can be expensive and difficult to manage, but they are very useful for companies that need rapid data access for widely distributed users and have the money to make long-term investments in their storage infrastructures.

Online Storage Service Providers Storage needs are growing so rapidly that many organizations no longer view computer storage as traditional hardware. Instead they view storage as a utility such as electricity or water. With utilities, we use what we need and pay for what we use. Following the utility view, some companies no longer provide their own data storage. Instead they store their data elsewhere, renting this capability from a storage service provider. A **storage service provider (SSP)** is a third-party provider that rents out storage space to subscribers over the Web. Storage service providers sell storage as a pay-per-use utility, allowing customers to store and access their data without having to purchase and maintain their own storage technology. (Similar outsourced service providers exist for software, as described in Chapter 7.) The Window on Management describes some of the benefits of using a storage service provider.

storage service provider (SSP)

A third-party provider that rents out storage space to subscribers over the Web, allowing customers to store and access their data without having to purchase and maintain their own storage technology.

INPUT AND OUTPUT DEVICES AND CONNECTIONS TO THE CENTRAL COMPUTER UNIT

Human beings interact with computer systems largely through input and output devices. Input devices gather data and convert them into electronic form for use by the computer while output devices display data after they have been processed.

STORAGE SERVICE PROVIDERS: DATA STORAGE BECOMES A UTILITY

The ever-increasing use of e-mail, data, graphics, video, sound, and electronic commerce documents has created a giant problem for many companies: How can they store so much data? According to Dataquest Gartner (www.gartner.com) of Lowell, Massachusetts, storage requirements will double every year for a number of years, with many companies unable to estimate their future data storage needs. Moreover, data storage and the management of stored data are growing more complex, leading to a shortage of technical experts in data storage. To meet these growing data storage problems, companies can turn to storage service providers (SSPs).

Most SSPs store your company's data on their equipment at their site. They operate like electric utilities: Your company uses the storage it needs and is billed monthly for that usage. SSPs obtain and manage the hardware, software, and staff for data storage. Companies can use an SSP service to replace or supplement their in-house storage infrastructure. To be successful, SSPs must offer very high availability and reliability and must also keep up with the latest technology. SSPs are responsible for monitoring the stored data and for managing their own capacity, response time, and reliability. SSPs also offer archiving and retrieval services and disaster recovery. The standard cost at present is about $75 000 per managed terabyte per month although some vendors offer it for as low as $45 000. These costs are starting to drop as more companies offer this service. Several Canadian technology companies have taken a lead in offering SSP services; Unylogix Technologies, Inc. of Quebec, Technique Microsystems of Toronto (www.techniquemicro.com), and StorageTek of Missisauga, Ont. are three such SSPs.

SSP customers can benefit in several ways. They will no longer have to purchase hardware and software to store their data and will not need to staff the storage function. They will also eliminate the cost of building and maintaining their own storage infrastructure. The thought of escalating storage costs makes fee-for-storage very appealing since the cost of this service is fairly predictable.

Internet startups have been the first users of SSPs. Many of them store massive amounts of data and yet are limited by their venture capital. By following the SSP route, they can use their limited funds for more fundamental activities such as designing their sites and products and developing quality management.

Transport Canada (www.tc.gc.ca) used a storage area network (SAN) provider rather than an SSP to establish a SAN. Transport Canada's client/server environment included over 150 servers on various operating platforms. Their managers sought to identify and implement a single solution to address their information management strategy. They contracted with Storage Technology Corporation (StorageTek of Mississauga) to implement a sophisticated storage management and backup/restore system consisting of a SUN E450 server, STK 9740 tape library with 9840 drives, and Veritas NetBackup software. In moving to this method of storage management, Transport Canada reduced the number of data servers and moved the servers to a uniform platform, reduced the effort involved in backing up all of their data servers, and improved security and data integrity while reducing their information management costs.

Large, established companies are more hesitant to try SSPs, often using them for less important data as a test. These companies have existing data centres in their infrastructure already, so their cost savings will be less. In addition, they fear a loss of control over their critical data. Finally, they fear for the security of data stored off-site. They also have the same fundamental fear for any outsourcing—that the SSP staff will not take ownership of the data and issues as do their internal staff.

To Think About: What management, technology, and organization issues would an established company face in outsourcing its data storage to an SSP? How does that differ for a newer company?

Sources: Stephanie Wilkinson, "Phone Bill, Electricity Bill, Storage Bill?" *Datamation*, October 24, 2000; Philip Gordon, "Convenient Online Storage," *Information Week*, July 3, 2000; Nick Wredon, "Outsourcing Options: A Hard Sell," *Information Week*, October 2, 2000; Lisa Kalis, "The Storage Space," *Red Herring Magazine*, March 1, 2000; Tom Stein, "The New Rage for Storage," *Red Herring Magazine*, March 1, 2000; Unylogix Technologies, Inc. Web site, www.unylogix.com, accessed February 2001; Technique Microsystems, Ltd. Web site, www.techniquemicro.com, accessed February 2001; Kevin Restivo, "StorageTek Opens Vista Certification Laboratory," *Computing Canada*, May, 28, 1999; Chris Molinski, "Automated Storage Management at Transport Canada—an Evolution," StorageTek's Web site, www.storagetek.com/teknews/user_groups/forum/bio_and_abstract/molinski.htm, accessed February 2001.

Input Devices

Keyboards remain the principal method of data entry for entering text and numerical data into a computer. However, pointing devices, such as the computer mouse and touch screens, are becoming popular for issuing commands and making selections in today's highly graphical computing environment.

Pointing Devices A **computer mouse** is a hand-held device with point-and-click capabilities that is usually connected to the computer by a cable (although wireless technology is becoming popular for both mice and keyboards). The computer user can move the mouse on

computer mouse
A hand-held input device whose movement on the desktop controls the position of the cursor on the computer display screen.

Touch screens allow users to enter small amounts of data by touching words, numbers, or specific points on the screen.

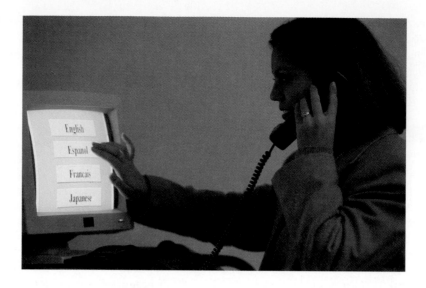

touch screen

Input device technology that permits users to enter or select commands and data by touching the surface of a sensitized video display monitor with a finger or a pointer.

source data automation

Input technology that captures data in computer-readable form at the time and place the data are created.

optical character recognition (OCR)

A form of source data automation in which optical scanning devices read specially designed data off of source documents and translate the data into digital form for the computer.

bar code

A form of OCR technology widely used in supermarkets and retail stores in which identification data are coded into a series of bars.

magnetic ink character recognition (MICR)

An input technology that translates characters written in magnetic ink into digital codes for processing.

pen-based input

Input devices such as tablets, notebooks, and notepads consisting of a flat-screen display tablet and a pen-like stylus that digitizes handwriting.

digital scanners

Input devices that translate images such as pictures or documents into digital form for processing.

voice input devices

Technology that converts the spoken word into digital form for processing.

a desktop to control the cursor's position on a computer display screen, pushing a button to select a command. The mouse also can be used to "draw" images on the screen. *Trackballs* and *touch pads* often are used in place of the mouse as pointing devices on laptop PCs.

Touch screens allow users to enter limited amounts of data by touching the surface of a sensitized video display monitor with a finger or a pointer. Touch screens often are found in information kiosks in retail stores, restaurants, and shopping malls.

Source Data Automation **Source data automation** captures data in computer-readable form at the time and place they are created. The principal source data automation technologies are optical character recognition, magnetic ink character recognition, pen-based input, digital scanners, voice input, and sensors.

Optical character recognition (OCR) devices translate specially designed marks, characters, and codes into digital form. The most widely used optical code is the **bar code**, which is used in point-of-sale systems in supermarkets and retail stores. Bar codes also are used in hospitals, libraries, military operations, and transportation facilities. The codes can include time, date, and location data in addition to identification data. The information makes them useful for analyzing the movement of items and determining what has happened to them during production or other processes. (The discussion of the United Parcel Service in Chapter 1 shows how valuable bar codes can be for this purpose.)

Magnetic ink character recognition (MICR) technology is used primarily in cheque processing for the banking industry. The bottom portion of a typical cheque contains characters identifying the bank, chequing account, and cheque number that are preprinted using a special magnetic ink. An MICR reader translates these characters into digital form for the computer.

Handwriting-recognition devices such as pen-based tablets, notebooks, and notepads are promising new input technologies, especially for people working in the sales or service areas or for those who have traditionally shunned computer keyboards. These **pen-based input** devices convert the motion made by an electronic stylus pressing on a touch-sensitive tablet screen into digital form. For instance, United Parcel Service replaced its drivers' familiar clipboard with a battery-powered Delivery Information Acquisition Device (DIAD) to capture signatures along with other information required for pickup and delivery (see the Chapter 1 Window on Technology). Personal digital assistants (PDAs) can also recognize handwriting.

Digital scanners translate images such as pictures or documents into digital form and are an essential component of image-processing systems. **Voice input devices** convert spoken words into digital form for processing by the computer. Voice recognition devices allow people to enter data into the computer without using their hands, making them useful for inspecting and sorting items in manufacturing and shipping and for dictation. Microphones and tape cassette players can serve as input devices for music and other sounds. A **sound card** is needed for voice input and voice recognition as well as to play certain types of audio files discussed in the later sections on output devices and multimedia.

Sensors are devices that collect data directly from the environment for input into a computer system. For instance, today's farmers can use sensors to monitor the moisture of the soil in their fields to help them with irrigation (Garber, 2000).

Output Devices

The major output devices are **monitors**, also called video display terminals (VDT), and printers. The monitor is the most popular form of computer output, and the cathode ray tube (CRT) is the most popular form of monitor. It works much like a television picture tube, with an electronic gun shooting a beam of electrons to illuminate the pixels on the screen. The more pixels per screen, the higher the resolution, or clarity of the image on the screen. Monitors are connected to the PC's **graphics adapter card**, which sends signals between the CPU and the monitor. Laptop computers use flat panel displays, which are less bulky than CRT monitors. Recently, flat panel monitors have become available for desktop PCs, too.

Printers produce a printed hard copy of information output. They include impact printers (such as a dot matrix printer) and nonimpact printers (laser, inkjet, and thermal transfer printers). Most printers print one character at a time, but some commercial printers print an entire line or page at a time. In general, impact printers are slower than nonimpact printers. Today the cost of laser technology has reduced the price of laser printers so that anyone can afford them. Colour laser printers, while much more expensive, are also available. For any printer or plotter, it should be noted that the cost of suppliers—toner, ink cartridges, pens—can be extremely expensive.

High-quality graphics documents can be created using **plotters** with multicoloured pens to draw (rather than print) computer output. Plotters are much slower than printers but are useful for outputting large-sized charts, maps, or drawings.

A **voice output device** converts digital output data back into intelligible speech. For instance, when you call for information on the telephone, you may hear a computerized voice respond with the telephone number you requested.

Audio output such as music and other sounds can be delivered by speakers connected to the computer through a sound card. Microfilm and microfiche have been used to store large quantities of output as microscopic filmed documents, but they are being replaced by optical disk technology.

Connections to the Central Computer Unit

All peripheral devices (located outside the central computer unit) must be connected in some way to the central computer unit. This is usually accomplished through a **port**. Various kinds of cables and connectors can be used, but the various types of ports found on the central computer unit are important because the ports dictate the types of connectors the peripherals must have to work with the computer. Ports also determine the speed of the connections between peripheral devices and the computer.

There are many different kinds of ports. Two are provided specifically for monitors and for keyboards. IBM developed a port called a *PS/2* that today is used primarily to connect a keyboard or a mouse; another type of port connects only a keyboard. Video monitor ports are located on graphics adapter cards, and microphone and headset ports are located on sound cards.

Other connections can be used by a variety of devices. Traditionally, the two main general-purpose types of port have been serial and parallel. Using a **serial port** or connection, a peripheral device can send only one bit at a time along the cable into the computer. This is much slower than a **parallel port,** which can send eight bits at a time. Because a great deal of data is required to print even one page, a parallel port typically connects printers. Computers can have several parallel and serial ports. The typical PC has one parallel and two serial ports.

Some recent technology can be used to speed up parallel and serial connections. **Firewire**, originally found only on newer Apple computers, is also available on a few IBM-compatible PCs and can transfer data much faster than the older forms of ports.

---

sound card
An extra device (for translating voice, music, and sound into digital signals and back again) that is plugged into the CPU's motherboard and usually contains jacks for earphones and microphones.

sensors
Devices that collect data directly from the environment for input into a computer system.

monitor
A display screen, also referred to as a video display terminal (VDT) or cathode ray tube (CRT). Provides a visual image of both user input and computer output.

graphics adapter card
A device that plugs into the CPU's motherboard to send signals between the CPU and the monitor through a port on the card.

printer
A computer output device that provides paper hard-copy output in the form of text or graphics.

plotter
An output device that uses multicoloured pens to draw high-quality graphic documents.

voice output device
A device that converts digital output data into spoken words.

port
A connection to the central computer unit.

serial port
A connection that only sends one bit at a time along the cable between the peripheral device and the central computer unit.

parallel port
A connection that sends eight bits at a time between a peripheral device and the central computer unit.

firewire
A port that provides a high speed connection between a peripheral device and the central computer unit.

universal serial bus (USB) port

A high-speed port capable of daisy-chaining USB devices through a USB hub to connect numerous peripheral devices to the central computer unit.

wireless port

A port that requires no cable connection between the peripheral device and the central computer unit; generally slower than other ports but the trend is toward faster wireless connections.

batch processing

A method of collecting and processing data in which transactions are accumulated and stored until a specified time when it is convenient or necessary to process them as a group.

online processing

A method of collecting and processing data in which transactions are entered directly into the computer system and processed immediately.

Universal serial bus (USB) ports are available on most PCs today; USB technology, like Firewire, is much faster, and it also permits up to 128 USB devices to be "daisy-chained" through only one USB port all at the same time. It accomplishes this by means of one or more USB hubs that connect to the USB port on the computer. USB technology also provides power to the USB peripheral devices, saving on the additional nuisance of requiring power cables to each connected device.

Finally, wireless ports are becoming popular for both home and office use. **Wireless ports** permit laptop and palmtop computers to be *synchronized* with desktop computers without using cables. They can also connect computers on a network as we will discuss in the chapter on telecommunications and networks. While most wireless ports use electromagnetic waves to carry the signal, infrared ports are common in personal digital assistants, laptops, and other computing devices.

BATCH AND ONLINE INPUT AND PROCESSING

The manner in which data are input into the computer affects how the data can be processed. Information systems collect and process information in one of two ways: through batch or through online processing. In **batch processing**, transactions such as orders or payroll time cards are accumulated and stored in a group or batch until the time when, because of some reporting cycle, it is efficient or necessary to process them. This was the only method of processing until the early 1960s, and it is still used today in older systems or some systems with massive volumes of transactions. In **online processing**, which is now very common, the user enters transactions into a device (such as a data entry keyboard or bar code reader) that is directly connected to the computer system. The transactions usually are processed immediately. Note that some systems permit online input of data but only process the data in batches.

The demands of the business determine the type of processing. If the user needs periodic or occasional reports or output, as in payroll or end-of-the-year reports, batch processing is most efficient. If the user needs immediate information and processing, as in an airline or hotel reservation system, then the system should use online processing.

Figure 6-8 compares batch and online processing. Although batch systems frequently use tape as a storage medium, online processing systems must use disk storage to permit

FIGURE 6-8 A comparison of batch and online processing. In batch processing, transactions are accumulated and stored in a group. Because batches are processed on a regular interval basis, such as daily, weekly, or monthly, information in the system will not always be up to date. A typical batch-processing job is payroll preparation. In online processing, transactions are input immediately and usually processed immediately. Information in the system is generally up to date. A typical online application is an airline reservation system.

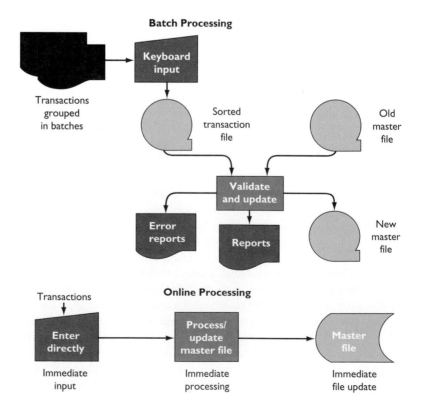

immediate access to specific items. In batch systems, transactions are accumulated in a **transaction file**, which contains all the transactions for a particular time period. Periodically this file is used to update a **master file**, which contains permanent information on entities. (An example is a payroll master file with employee earnings and deduction data. It is updated with weekly time-card transactions.) Adding the transaction data to the existing master file creates a new master file. In online processing, transactions are entered into the system immediately using a keyboard, pointing device, or source data automation, and the system usually responds immediately. The master file is updated continually. In online processing, there is a direct connection to the computer for input and output.

INTERACTIVE MULTIMEDIA

The processing, input, output, and storage technologies we have just described can be used to create interactive multimedia applications. **Multimedia** technologies facilitate the integration of two or more types of media, such as text, graphics, sound, voice, full-motion video, still video, or animation, into a computer-based application. Multimedia is the foundation of many new consumer products and services, such as electronic books and newspapers, electronic classroom-presentation technologies, full-motion video conferencing, imaging, graphics design tools, video, and voice mail. Many Web sites use multimedia.

PCs today come with built-in multimedia capabilities, including a high-resolution colour monitor, a CD-ROM drive or DVD drive to read video, audio, and graphic data, a sound card, and stereo speakers for amplifying audio output.

The most difficult element to incorporate into multimedia information systems has been full-motion video because so much data must be brought under the digital control of the computer. The massive amounts of data in each video image must be digitally encoded, stored, and manipulated electronically, using techniques that compress the digital data. Special adapter cards may be needed to digitize and compress sound and video.

The possibilities of this technology are endless, but multimedia seems especially well-suited for training and presentations. For training, multimedia is appealing because it is interactive and permits two-way communication. People can use multimedia training sessions any time of the day, at their own pace (Hardaway and Will, 1997). Instructors can easily integrate words, sounds, pictures, and both live and animated video to produce lessons that capture students' imaginations. For example, TD Canada Trust has developed a multimedia training program that teaches the basic skills that front-line branch bankers need to know, such as foreign exchanges and transfers (Newman-Provost, 1998).

Interactive Web pages replete with graphics, sound, animations, and full-motion video have made multimedia popular on the Internet. For example, visitors to CBC's Interactive Web site can access news stories from CBC, photos, on-air transcripts, video clips, and audio clips (see Figure 6-9). The video and audio clips are made available using **streaming technology**, which allows audio and video data to be processed as a steady and continuous stream as they are downloaded from the Web. (RealAudio and RealVideo are widely used streaming technology products on the Web.) Table 6-4 lists examples of other multimedia Web sites. If Internet transmission capacity and streaming technology continue to improve, Web sites could provide broadcast functions that compete with television along with new two-way interactivity.

Multimedia Web sites are also used to sell digital products, such as digitized

transaction file
In batch systems, a file in which all transactions are accumulated to await processing by updating the master file.

master file
A file that contains all permanent information and is updated during processing by transaction data.

multimedia
The integration of two or more types of media such as text, graphics, sound, voice, full-motion video, or animation into a computer-based application.

streaming technology
Technology for transferring audio or video data so that they can be processed as a steady and continuous stream.

Multimedia combines text, graphics, sound, and video into a computer-based experience that permits two-way communication. Many organizations use this technology for interactive training.

FIGURE 6-9 Web sites can incorporate multimedia elements such as graphics, sound, animation, and full-motion video.

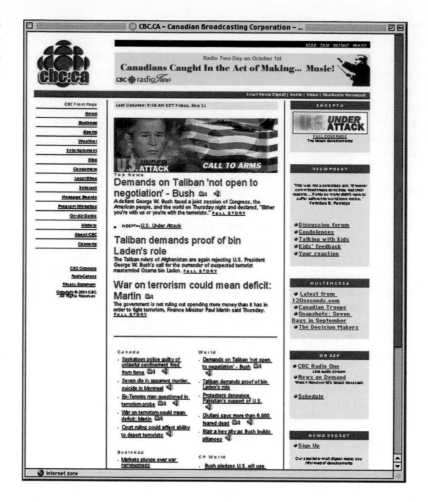

MP3 (MPEG3)

A compression standard that can compress audio files for transfer over the Internet with virtually no loss in quality.

music clips. A compression standard known as **MP3**, also called **MPEG3**, which stands for Motion Picture Experts Group, audio layer 3, can compress audio files down to one-tenth or one-twelfth of their original size with virtually no loss in quality. Visitors to Web sites such as www.MP3.com can download free MP3 music clips over the Internet and play them on their own computers.

TABLE 6-4   EXAMPLES OF MULTIMEDIA WEB SITES

Web Site	Description
Parliament (www.parl.gc.ca)	Created and maintained jointly by the Senate, House of Commons, and the Library of Parliament, provides information on Parliament and the bills before it.
Muchmusic.com (www.muchmusic.com)	Provides online chat, clips of artists' videos and interviews, a listening lounge where visitors can sample the latest musical releases, and online contests and shopping.
Canada World Web Travel (canada.worldweb.com)	Provides interactive tours of Canadian travel destinations through maps and photos.
ROBTV.com (www.robtv.com)	Provides live business information from Web casts of its television broadcast that include a real-time stock ticker of the Toronto Stock Exchange and video archives of past programs.
The Weather Network (www.weather.ca)	Provides audio summaries of national and local weather, along with satellite and radar maps.
Statistics Canada (www.statcan.ca)	Provides a wealth of information about Canadian business, governments, and organizations, including financial and census data.

Recently, Napster, an American company founded by college-student Shawn Fanning, turned the music industry on its ear by permitting Napster subscribers to share their MP3 music files with each other. Since many, if not most, of these music files are copyrighted, the music companies holding these copyrights (and even some of the bands, such as Metallica), sued Napster in the American courts, claiming infringement of copyright. The most recent ruling found that Napster must block copyrighted music from being shared through its site. Napster is planning to launch a new, copyright-friendly subscription version of its service. All file transfers on Napster have been down since July 2, and the company has not said when it plans to resume operations although the "New Napster" is almost ready for beta testing as of this writing.

The Napster concept is alive and well in Canada, too. In 1999, Canadians Grad Conn and Cory Doctorow founded OpenCola, a peer-to-peer application called OpenCola Folders™ that connects users—based on their affinity and community standing—to the content that is most relevant to them. Affinity means their personal or professional interests while community means that they have duly subscribed to a particular OpenCola "Folder." Another Canadian, 21-year-old Matt Goyer, said he plans to establish a Napster clone off the coast of Britain in an attempt to sidestep U.S. copyright laws. Goyer wrote on his Web site, Fairtunes.com, that he has conducted research into an offshore co-location "to set up an OpenNap server beyond the reach of the Recording Industry Association of America." He estimates the cost to be U.S.$15 000 in the first year and hopes to collect money from 1500 "irate Napster users." Reports are that Goyer is looking to set up his music-sharing service in Sealand, an ocean platform six miles off the eastern shore of England. Sealand, which was an island fortress created in World War II by Britain and founded as a sovereign principality in 1967, has become a popular location for online businesses. Goyer, who co-founded Fairtunes.com last year to enable Napster fans to compensate artists by voluntarily sending them money, follows others who have established file-swapping businesses outside of the United States.

A company called HavenCo launched its business operations in Sealand last year in an effort to provide an offshore facility for individuals or companies wishing to conduct their online businesses in a secure environment. According to HavenCo, Sealand has no laws governing data traffic, and its operation in Sealand offers "a haven" from legislation such as the U.S. Digital Millennium Copyright Act and Britain's Regulation of Investigatory Powers. "The whole purpose of Sealand was to set up a place where no other laws govern," attorney Kenneth Freudlich said.

6.3 CATEGORIES OF COMPUTERS AND COMPUTER SYSTEMS

All computers represent and process data the same way, but there are different computer classifications. Managers need to understand the capabilities of each of these types of computers and why some types are more appropriate for certain processing work than others. We can use size and processing speed to categorize contemporary computers as personal computers, workstations, midrange computers, mainframes, and supercomputers.

CATEGORIES OF COMPUTERS

A **personal computer (PC)**, which is often referred to as a microcomputer, is one that can be placed on a desktop or carried from room to room. Smaller **laptop** and *palmtop* PCs are often used as portable desktops on the road. PCs are used as personal machines as well as in business. A **workstation** also fits on a desktop but has more powerful mathematical and graphics-processing capability than a PC and can perform more complicated tasks than a PC in the same amount of time. Workstations are used for scientific, engineering, and design work that requires powerful graphics or computational capabilities.

A **midrange computer** is less powerful, less expensive, and smaller than a mainframe but capable of supporting the computing needs of smaller organizations or of managing networks of other computers. Midrange computers can be **minicomputers**, which are used in

personal computer (PC)
A small desktop or portable computer that can be placed on a desktop or carried from room to room; also known as a microcomputer.

laptop computers
(Also known as notebooks) Streamlined, lightweight, portable computers that users can take with them on the road or to clients' offices; a type of personal computer.

workstation
A desktop computer with powerful graphics and mathematical capabilities and the ability to perform several complicated tasks at once.

midrange computer
A mid-sized computer that is capable of supporting the computing needs of smaller organizations or of managing networks of other computers.

minicomputer
A mid-range computer, about the size of an office desk, often used in universities, factories, and research laboratories.

mainframe
The largest category of computer, used for major business processing.

supercomputer
A highly sophisticated and powerful computer that can perform very complex computations extremely rapidly.

systems for universities, factories, or research laboratories, or they can be servers, which are used for managing internal company networks or Web sites. Server computers are specifically optimized to support a computer network, enabling users to share files, software, peripheral devices, such as printers, or other network resources. Servers have large memory and disk-storage capacity, high-speed communications capabilities, and powerful CPUs.

A **mainframe** is much larger than a minicomputer and is a powerhouse of massive memory and extremely rapid processing. It is used for very large business, scientific, and military applications where a computer must handle massive amounts of data or many complicated processes. A **supercomputer** is a highly sophisticated and powerful machine that is used for specialized tasks requiring extremely rapid and complex calculations with hundreds of thousands of variable factors. Supercomputers use parallel processing and can perform billions and even trillions of calculations per second, many times faster than the largest mainframe. Supercomputers traditionally have been used in scientific and military work, but they are starting to be used in business as well. For example, PanCanadian Petroleum Limited of Calgary (www.pcp.ca) uses a Silicon Graphics supercomputer as the foundation of its Terradeck visualization centre for the advanced exploration of oil and natural gas. Using the visualization technology made possible by using a supercomputer, PanCanadian's geologists and drillers substantially improved their oil recovery rates (Boras, 2000).

The problem with this classification scheme is that the capacity of the machines changes so rapidly. Powerful PCs have sophisticated graphics and processing capabilities similar to workstations. PCs still cannot perform as many tasks at once as workstations, minicomputers, or mainframes (see the discussion of operating systems in Chapter 7), and they cannot be used by as many people simultaneously as these larger machines. But even these distinctions will become less pronounced in the future. The most powerful workstations have some of the capabilities of earlier mainframes and supercomputers.

Any of these computer categories can be designed to support a computer network, enabling users to share files, software, peripheral devices, such as printers, and other network resources. The actual function of any computer is unrelated to its classification based on its power, speed, capacity, size, and cost.

Mainframes can function as data warehouses (for storing data on millions of transactions or customers), Web servers (for large Web sites), gateways (permitting telecommunications by thousands of users), or front-end processors (to assist other mainframes). In fact, workstations and midrange computers can function as Web servers just as some mainframes do. Server computers store data and programs and connect networks; whether mainframe, midrange, or personal computer, servers are made specifically for network use, with large memory and disk-storage capacity, high-speed communications capabilities, and powerful CPUs. Server computers are specifically optimized to support a computer network, enabling users to share files, software, peripheral devices, such as printers, or other network resources.

Servers have become important components of firm's information technology (IT) infrastructure because they provide the hardware platform for electronic commerce. By adding special software, they can be customized to deliver Web pages, process purchase and sale transactions, or exchange data with systems inside the company. Organizations with heavy electronic commerce requirements and massive Web sites are running their Web and electronic commerce applications on multiple servers in **server farms** in computing centres run by commercial vendors such as IBM. Large electronic commerce sites such as Indigo.com, Dell.ca, and Baystreet.ca rely on server farms with sophisticated capabilities to balance computer loads and handle millions of purchases, inquiries, and other transactions.

server farm
A large group of servers maintained by a commercial vendor and made available to subscribers for electronic commerce and other activities requiring heavy use of servers.

distributed processing
The distribution of computer processing work among multiple computers linked by a communications network.

centralized processing
Processing that is accomplished by one large central computer.

COMPUTER NETWORKS AND CLIENT/SERVER COMPUTING

Today, stand-alone computers have been replaced by computers in networks for most processing tasks. The use of multiple computers linked by a communications network for processing is called **distributed processing**. In contrast with **centralized processing**, in which all processing is accomplished by one large central computer, distributed processing distributes the processing work among PCs, midrange computers, and mainframes linked together.

One widely used form of distributed processing is **client/server computing**. Client/server computing splits processing between "clients" and "servers." Both are on the network, but each machine is assigned functions it is best suited to perform. The **client** is the user point-of-entry for the required function and is normally a personal computer. The user generally interacts directly only with the client portion of the application, often to input data or retrieve data for further analysis.

The *server* provides the client with services. The server could be anything from a mainframe to another personal computer, but specialized server computers are often used in this role. Servers store and process shared data and also perform back-end functions not visible to users, such as managing network activities. Figure 6-10 illustrates the client/server computing concept. Computing on the Internet uses the client/server model (see Chapter 9).

The exact division of tasks between the client and the server depends on the requirements of each application, including its processing needs, the number of users, and the available resources. For example, client tasks for a large corporate payroll might include inputting data (such as enrolling new employees and recording hours worked), submitting data queries to the server, analyzing the retrieved data, and displaying results on the screen or on a printer. The server portion fetches the entered data and processes the payroll. It controls access so that only authorized users can view or update the data.

In some firms, client/server networks with PCs have actually replaced mainframes and midrange computers. The process of transferring applications from large computers to smaller ones is called **downsizing**. Downsizing has many advantages. Memory and processing power on a PC cost a fraction of their equivalent on a mainframe. The decision to downsize involves many factors in addition to the cost of computer hardware, including the need for new software, training, and perhaps new organizational procedures.

NETWORK COMPUTERS

In one form of client/server computing, client processing and storage capabilities are so minimal that the bulk of computer processing occurs on the server. The term *thin client* is sometimes used to refer to the client in this arrangement. Thin clients with minimal memory, storage, and processing power that do not store programs or data permanently are designed to work on networks and are called **network computers (NCs)**. Users download whatever software or data they need from a central computer over the Internet or an organization's internal network. The central computer also saves information for the user and makes it available for later retrieval, effectively eliminating the need for secondary storage devices such as hard disks, floppy disks, CD-ROMs, and their drives. A network computer may consist of little more than a stripped-down PC, a monitor, a keyboard, and a network connection.

If managed properly, both network computers and client/server computing can reduce the cost of information technology resources. Proponents of network computers believe NCs can reduce hardware costs because they are less expensive to purchase than regular PCs and because they can be administered and updated from a central network server. Software programs and applications would not have to be purchased, installed, and upgraded for each user because software would be delivered and maintained from one central point. Network

client/server computing
A model for computing that splits processing between "clients" and "servers" on a network, assigning functions to the machine most able to perform the function.

client
The user point-of-entry for the required function in client/server computing. Normally a personal computer.

downsizing
The process of transferring applications from large computers to smaller ones.

network computer (NC)
A simplified desktop computer that does not store software programs or data permanently. Users download whatever software or data they need from a central computer over the Internet or an organization's own internal network.

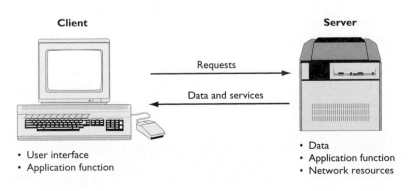

Client

Requests →

← Data and services

Server

• User interface
• Application function

• Data
• Application function
• Network resources

FIGURE 6-10 Client/server computing. In client/server computing, computer processing is split between client machines and server machines linked by a network. Users interface with the client machines.

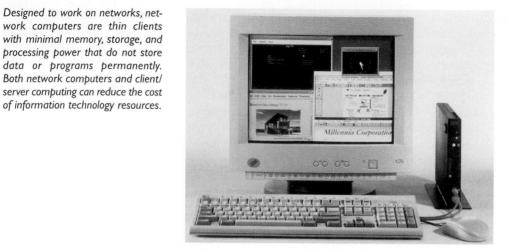

Designed to work on networks, network computers are thin clients with minimal memory, storage, and processing power that do not store data or programs permanently. Both network computers and client/ server computing can reduce the cost of information technology resources.

computers could thus increase management control over the organization's computing function. So much data and information are being delivered through the Web that computers do not necessarily need to store their own content. There will be additional uses for NCs as application software that can be rented over the Web becomes widely available (see Chapter 7).

Not everyone agrees that network computers will bring benefits. Some researchers believe that centralizing control over computing could stifle worker initiative and creativity. PCs have become so cheap and plentiful that many question whether the savings promised by network computers will actually be realized. If a network failure occurs, hundreds or thousands of employees would not be able to use their computers whereas people could keep on working if they had full-function PCs. Full-function PCs are more appropriate for situations where end users have varied application needs that require local processing. In fact, sales figures for network computers vary based on type of industry, size of company, and even the personal decision-making preferences of managers. Companies should closely examine how network computers fit into their information technology infrastructure.

PEER-TO-PEER COMPUTING

peer-to-peer computing
A form of distributed processing that links computers via the Internet or private networks so that they can share processing tasks.

Using another form of distributed processing called **peer-to-peer computing**, individual computers can share data, disk space, and even processing power for a variety of tasks when they are linked in a network, including the Internet. Peer-to-peer computing puts processing power back on users' desktops, linking these computers so that they can share files or processing tasks. While Napster and Gnutella, two music-file sharing peer-to-peer network services, apply only the file-sharing capabilities of peer-to-peer networks, peer-to-peer actually involves two distinct types of technology: the sharing of digital files and data between two separate computers (the Napster/Gnutella model), and the sharing of different CPU cycles.

The peer-to-peer computing model stands in contrast to the network computing model because processing power resides only on individual desktops, and these computers work together without a server or any central controlling authority. The lack of a central controlling authority is what has landed Napster in court. The central controlling authority for Napster, according to the music companies suing Napster, should be copyright.

It has been estimated that most companies—and individuals—use less than 25 percent of their processing and storage capacity. Peer-to-peer computing taps the unused disk space or processing power on PC or workstation networks for large computing tasks that can now only be performed by large expensive server computers or even supercomputers. The Window on Technology describes how other companies benefited from using this computing approach.

CREATING VIRTUAL MASSIVELY PARALLEL COMPUTERS VIA PEER-TO-PEER COMPUTING

Did you know that about 90 percent of the processing power of most computers goes unused? Most computers are used weekdays only and sit idle during coffee breaks, lunchtime, meetings, nights, and weekends. When they are processing, most tasks only use a small portion of available computer power. The revolutionary concept growing out of peer-to-peer computing is that by distributing small portions of giant processing tasks among many computers, their unused processing power can be employed to good advantage. In effect, peer-to-peer technology can be utilized to create virtual massively parallel computers. The idea of the *virtual* massively parallel computer is that the massively parallel computer is not *one* computer, but many that are linked together by telecommunications and can share processing over the telecommunications link.

Peer-to-peer technology is neither complex nor technologically new. All it does is establish direct links between two computers so they can "talk" to each other without going through a third party such as a server. What is new is that the connections between computers are now being established through the Internet as well as through private networks. Direct connections now can easily be established between any two computers selected from thousands and even millions that are online.

One well-known example of peer-to-peer distributed processing is the SETI@Home project, begun in the spring of 1999 to search for extraterrestrial intelligence. Every day the world's largest radio telescope, located in Arecibo, Puerto Rico, sweeps the sky recording digital noises travelling through space. Astronomers collect about 50 gigabytes of data per day. The data then must be searched for regular patterns that might indicate transmission by intelligent beings. However, searching through a year's worth of this data would take a large computer as much as 100 000 years, too large a task for ordinary means. The solution was to use the peer-to-peer model to create a virtual massively parallel computer.

The data gathered in Arecibo are forwarded to the University of California at Berkeley where they are broken into work units of perhaps 350 kilobytes each, producing about 150 000 units daily. Each unit is then downloaded to one of the 2 000 000 volunteers who allow their computers to process the data whenever its full power is not being used. Once the

unit is searched (about 20 hours on a Pentium 400 machine), the results are uploaded to the SETI computer for review. This analysis is only possible because of the massively parallel computing that occurs on the computers of all the volunteers. This piece is being written on a laptop computer that is simultaneously processing SETI data; the processing has no noticeable impact on other work.

This model is not applicable to all huge applications. It is useful only for large data-intensive projects. Computer chip manufacturer Intel began using this approach in 1990 to reduce the cost of chip designing. It linked 10 000 computers globally, thus eliminating the need to purchase several mainframes within two years. OpenCola, a Toronto-based company, wants to solve the problem of irrelevant search results on the Internet. It believes it can do so by linking those customers searching for results with expert groups that share similar interests. The company combines two of the most talked-about trends on the Internet: peer-to-peer networking and expert communities.

Energy companies gather immense amounts of geographic and seismic data that must be analyzed prior to digging for oil, gas, or coal. Oil giant Amerada Hess of New York (www.hess.com) is using this peer-to-peer model through its own network, connecting 200 desktop computers to analyze seismic data. The company cancelled the purchase of two IBM supercomputers as a result. According to CIO Richard Ross, Amerada Hess is "running seven times the throughput at a fraction of the cost." His company has also carried the concept one step further, joining the storage of these desktops to create a giant data repository.

To Think About: Would you want to sign up for the Seti@Home project? Why or why not? What are some of the drawbacks or problems of this approach? How does Napster work? What is the future of OpenCola or OpenCola-modelled organizations?

Sources: Jennifer Di Sabatino, "What's So New about Peer-to-Peer?" *Computerworld*, November 20, 2000; Paul McDougall, "The Power of Peer-To-Peer," *Information Week*, August 28, 2000; and Kathleen Melymuka, "IT on the 'Outer Limits,'" *Computerworld*, July 3, 2000; Jennifer Lewis, "OpenCOLA," *Red Herring Magazine*, http://www.redherring.com/story_redirect.asp?layout=story_generic&doc_id=RH1990013999&channel=70000007, November 1, 2000, accessed February 2001; "Blood, Sweat, and Tears," *Red Herring Magazine*, www.redherring.com/mag/issue86/mag-blood-86.html, December 4, 2000, accessed February 2001.

6.4 MANAGING HARDWARE ASSETS

As you can see from this chapter, selection and use of computer hardware technology can have a profound impact on business performance. Computer hardware technology thus represents an important organizational asset that must be properly managed. Managers need to balance the cost of acquiring hardware resources with the need to provide a responsive and reliable platform for delivering information systems applications. We now describe the most important issues in managing hardware technology assets: understanding the new technology requirements for electronic commerce and the digital firm; determining the total cost of ownership (TCO) of technology assets; and identifying technology trends impacting the organization's information technology infrastructure.

HARDWARE TECHNOLOGY REQUIREMENTS FOR ELECTRONIC COMMERCE AND THE DIGITAL FIRM

Electronic commerce and electronic business are placing heavy new demands on hardware technology because organizations are replacing so many manual and paper-based processes with electronic ones. Companies are processing and storing vast quantities of data for data-intensive applications such as video or graphics as well as for electronic commerce. Much larger processing and storage resources are required to process the surge in digital transactions flowing between different parts of the firm and between the firm and its customers and suppliers.

The Strategic Role of Storage Technology in the Digital Firm

While electronic commerce and electronic business may be reducing the role of paper, data of all types (such as orders, invoices, requisitions, and work orders) must be stored electronically and be available whenever needed. Customers and suppliers doing business electronically want to place their orders, check their accounts, and do their research at any hour of the day or night, and so they demand 24-hour availability. For business to occur 24 hours per day anywhere in our electronic world, all possibly relevant data must be stored for online access, and all this data must be backed up.

One example of this strategic role is online banking. Online banking enables bank customers to conduct their banking activities at automatic teller machines (ATMs) or through the Internet. A Canadian company, T-Base (www.tbase.com), has created a call-in service called Infotouch that provides documents quickly and easily to people unable to access information through conventional methods, such as ATMs. The Infotouch service can publish documents in multiple formats, including large print, audio, braille, and on computer diskette. Individual documents are published automatically from electronic masters and mailed directly to consumers within two days of the request. Canada's Royal Bank and other banking institutions use Infotouch (Williams, 2000). Electronic commerce and electronic business have put new strategic emphasis on technologies that can store vast quantities of transaction data and make them immediately available online.

Capacity Planning and Scalability

capacity planning
The process of predicting when a computer hardware system becomes saturated to ensure that adequate computing resources are available and that the firm has enough computing power for its current and future needs.

As firms' electronic commerce and electronic business activities expand, they must carefully review their servers and other infrastructure components to make sure they can handle increasing numbers of transactions and users while maintaining a high level of performance and availability. Managers and information systems specialists need to pay more attention to hardware capacity planning and scalability than they did in the past. **Capacity planning** is the process of predicting when a computer hardware system becomes saturated. It considers factors such as the maximum number of users that the system can accommodate, the impact of existing and future software applications, and performance measures such as minimum response time for processing business transactions. Today capacity planning must include networks to ensure that networks are always available.

Capacity planning ensures that adequate computing resources are available and that the firm has enough computing power for its current and future needs. During its brief existence, before the courts ruled that its provision of television programming on the Internet was illegal, the Toronto-based iCraveTV claimed that traffic from its servers used so much bandwidth that it caused backbone provider UUNet's system to crash (Verburg, 2000).

Although capacity planning is performed by information system specialists, input from business managers is essential. Capacity planners try to establish an optimum level of service for current and future applications. Outages and delayed response times translate into lost customers and lost revenue. Business managers need to determine acceptable levels of computer response time and availability for the firm's mission-critical systems to maintain the level of business performance they expect. New applications, mergers and acquisitions, and

MANAGEMENT DECISION PROBLEM

HARDWARE CAPACITY PLANNING FOR ELECTRONIC COMMERCE

Your company implemented its own electronic commerce site using its own hardware and software, and business is growing rapidly. The company Web site has not experienced any outages and customers are always able to have requests for information or purchase transactions processed very rapidly. Your Information Systems Department has instituted a formal operations review program that continuously monitors key indicators of system usage that affect processing capacity and response time. The following report illustrates two of those indicators, daily CPU usage and daily I/O usage for the system. I/O usage measures the number of times a disk has been read.

Your server supports primarily Canadian customers who access the Web site during the day and early evening. I/O usage should be kept below 70% if the CPU is very busy so that the CPU does not waste machine cycles looking for data. I/O usage is high between 1 and 6 a.m. because the firm backs up its data stored on disk when the CPU is not busy.

1. Anticipated increases in your e-commerce business over the next year are expected to increase CPU usage and I/O usage by 20 percent between 1:00 p.m. and 9:00 p.m. and by 10 percent during the rest of the day. Does your company have enough processing capacity to handle this increased load?

2. What would happen if your organization did not pay attention to capacity issues?

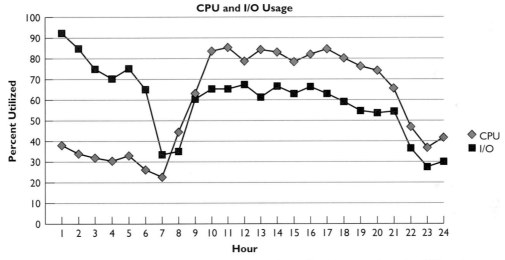

Daily CPU and I/O Usage (Hours Are for Canadian Eastern Standard Time.)

---

changes in business volume will all impact computer workload and must be taken into account when planning hardware capacity.

Electronic commerce and electronic business both call for scalable IT infrastructures that have the capacity to grow with the business. Servers need to provide the processing power to keep electronic commerce up and running as Web site visitors and customers grow in number. Delivering large Web pages with graphics over the Internet or private intranets can create performance bottlenecks. **Scalability** refers to the ability of a computer, product, or system to expand to serve a larger number of users without breaking down. There are several approaches to achieving scalability. One is to scale up, replacing, for example, a small server with a larger multiprocessor server or even a mainframe. The other approach is to scale out, which involves adding a large number of smaller servers. The choice of approach depends on the nature of the application or set of applications requiring upgraded hardware capacity.

scalability
The ability of a computer, product, or system to expand to serve a larger number of users without breaking down.

HARDWARE ACQUISITION AND THE TOTAL COST OF OWNERSHIP (TCO) OF TECHNOLOGY ASSETS

The purchase and maintenance of computer hardware equipment is but one of a series of cost components that managers must consider when selecting and managing hardware technology assets. The actual cost of owning technology resources includes both direct and

total cost of ownership (TCO)
Designates the total cost of owning technology resources, including initial purchase costs, the cost of hardware and software upgrades, maintenance, technical support, and training.

indirect costs, including the original cost of computer and software, hardware and software upgrades, maintenance, technical support, and training. The **total cost of ownership (TCO)** model can be used to analyze these direct and indirect costs to help firms determine the actual cost of specific technology implementations. Table 6-5 lists and describes the most important total cost of ownership (TCO) components.

When all these cost components are considered, the TCO for a PC might run up to three times the original purchase price of the equipment. "Hidden costs" for support staff and additional network management can make distributed client/server architectures more expensive than centralized mainframe architectures. When Jim Andrew became CIO of the new "megacity" of Toronto, he implemented a total cost of ownership (TCO) model for the 2001 budget process. "Right now we're mapping all our activities associated with TCO. This will enable us to put in a very cost-efficient model and give the departments the best bang for their buck," said Andrew.

The department is looking at a base cost per PC, which would include infrastructure charges. The base cost would include such things as help desk, communication line, network software, desktop software, and PC lease cost. "After that we will go to icon pricing," said Andrew. "If you want Oracle it will cost you this much; if you want SAP it will cost you that much. This puts the onus on the department to justify the business need for having these other products" (Carey, 2000).

A key to reducing total cost of ownership (TCO) is to create a comprehensive asset management plan. Many organizations cannot measure the total cost of ownership of their technology assets because these assets have never been inventoried. Organizations need to catalogue and manage their hardware and software assets. Software tools are now available to help identify and track these technology assets. Some of these tools even show managers what assets are breaking down and why and when these assets are due to be cycled out of service.

MONITORING TECHNOLOGY TRENDS

Computing technology continues to change at a blinding pace, requiring managers to constantly monitor technology trends and make decisions about upgrading the firm's information technology infrastructure. New hardware technologies can provide new ways of organizing work and sources of new products and services.

Superchips

In addition to improving their design, microprocessors have been made faster by shrinking the distance between transistors, giving the electrical current less distance to travel. The lines that form the transistors have also been made narrower, increasing the number of transistors that can be squeezed onto a single chip. Research by IBM will result in processors that can be folded or bent, paving the way for technologies such as foldable monitors that can fit in your pocket or purse. A phenomenon known as Moore's law (after Intel's founder who discovered the phenomenon) states that the processing power or speed of a microprocessor doubles every 18 months. While the physical limits of this law may soon be reached, researchers are

TABLE 6-5	COMPONENTS OF THE TOTAL COST OF OWNERSHIP (TCO) OF TECHNOLOGY ASSETS
Hardware acquisition:	Purchase price of computer hardware, including computers, monitors, storage, printers, etc.
Software acquisition:	Purchase or license of software for each user
Installation:	Costs to install computers and software
Training:	Costs to provide training to information system specialists and end users
Support:	Costs to provide ongoing technical support, help desks, etc.
Maintenance:	Costs to upgrade the hardware and software
Infrastructure:	Costs to acquire, maintain, and support related infrastructure such as networks and specialized equipment (storage back-up units etc.)

continuing to experiment with new materials and manufacturing methods to continue to increase processor speed.

Microminiaturization, Palm Computing, and Smart Cards: Information Appliances

During the past 40 years, each decade has seen computing costs drop by a factor of 10 and capacity increase by a factor of at least 100, allowing computers to become progressively smaller and more powerful. Today's microprocessors can put a mainframe-like processing power on a desktop, a briefcase, and even into a shirt pocket. Technology will soon be able to produce computers the size of a thumbnail. These advances in microprocessor technology have fuelled the growth of *microminiaturization*—the proliferation of computers that are so small, fast, and cheap that they have become ubiquitous. For instance, many of the intelligent features that have made automobiles, stereos, toys, watches, cameras, and other equipment easier to use are based on microprocessors. The future will see even more intelligence built into everyday devices as well as miniaturized computers.

More computing work will be performed by small hand-held computers and portable information appliances. Unlike a PC, which is a general-purpose device capable of performing many different kinds of tasks, an **information appliance** is customized to perform only a few specialized tasks very well with a minimum of effort. Such information appliances include mobile phones with e-mail and Internet access, fixed-screen telephones that can browse the Web and exchange e-mail, wireless hand-held devices for transmitting messages, and television set-top boxes to access the Web and provide e-mail and home shopping services.

A variety of hand-held computers have become commercially available in what is becoming the "war of the palmtops." Through miniaturization technologies, these small, lightweight computers can perform not only as **personal digital assistants (PDA)**, but also as programmable computers. Applications are being developed at a dizzying rate; now available on palmtops are word processing, spreadsheet, database, e-mail, games, and many other types of applications. One of PalmPilot's recent hand-held models, the M100, is the first relatively affordable palmtop computer. Not to be outdone, Hewlett-Packard, Handspring, Compaq, and others have developed their own hand-held models, many of them boasting colour and voice technologies.

A **smart card** is a plastic card the size of a credit card that contains a small amount of storage and a tiny microprocessor instead of a magnetic strip. The embedded chip can carry information, such as a person's health records, identification data, or telephone numbers, and the cards can serve as electronic "wallets" in place of cash. For example, several Canadian ski resorts are now using smart cards for entry to the resort and for use of their facilities. The vacationer purchases the smart card that contains not only their identification but grants access only to those facilities for which they have paid the appropriate admission fees. Visa Canada has confirmed that over the next four years, it will migrate 22 million magnetic-stripe Visa cards to chip cards (Marlin, 2000). Smart cards are very versatile, and their uses are growing.

These specialized computing devices are less expensive and difficult to use than PCs while providing enough capabilities for communication or accessing the Web to meet many people's computing needs. Some of these devices can run business applications as well as send e-mail or maintain names and addresses. PCs will play a smaller role in both personal and corporate computing as information appliances and hand-held computing devices become more widely utilized. Managers will need to manage these new computing resources and find the best way of incorporating them into the firm's information technology infrastructure. Data stored in mobile computing devices and appliances will need to be coordinated with data stored in the main corporate computers.

Social Interfaces

Computer technology is becoming so powerful and integrated into daily experiences that it can appear almost invisible to the user (Weiser, 1993). Social interfaces are being developed to model the interaction between people and computers using familiar human behaviour. People increasingly will interact with the computer in more intuitive and effortless ways—through writing, speech, touch, eye movement, and other gestures (Selker, 1996).

information appliance
A computing device customized to perform only a few specialized tasks very well with a minimum of effort.

personal digital assistant (PDA)
A small, lightweight computer that contains data needed by an individual user, such as their calendar, an address book, a to-do list, and a basic memorandum function.

smart card
A plastic card the size of a credit card that contains a small amount of storage and a tiny microprocessor, carrying information, electronic cash, and even software applications.

Voice-recognition technology is moving closer to natural speech. Commercial continuous-speech voice-recognition products have vocabularies large enough for general business use. These social interfaces will make it easier for organizations to incorporate computing devices into their work practices and business processes. People will use voice or other social interfaces to interact with corporate information systems.

APPLICATION EXERCISE

SPREADSHEET EXERCISE: IDENTIFYING HARDWARE REQUIREMENTS

Each semester, the management information systems department at your university encourages its new majors to attend an orientation seminar. During the seminar, students are provided with helpful information, such as how to establish an e-mail account, select a personal computer system, and join the local MIS-majors organization chapter. You have attended several of these orientations, and have found them valuable. Often current and former students are asked to participate in the orientations.

One afternoon, Dr. Janice Dubois, your favourite MIS-professor, stops by the lab to speak with you. She mentions that she is in charge of the upcoming orientation and would like you to speak at next month's seminar. In particular, she would like you to advise new students on the type of computer system they should consider purchasing. She would like you to discuss the minimum requirements that would be necessary as well as to identify possible upgrades for the system. During your presentation, you should discuss issues such as processor type and speed, RAM, hard drives, monitors, optical disk drives, and price.

In order to prepare your "Personal Computer Requirements" presentation, identify the minimum requirements that a computer system should have. Next, identify at least three computer systems that you would recommend to your fellow students. What features does each system have? What are the advantages and disadvantages of each system? For each system identified, what are the upgrade options? How much will the upgrades cost? Summarize your findings in a spreadsheet. Based on your findings, use presentation software to prepare a presentation that you could give to the orientation group. If time permits, share your findings with the class. How are your recommendations similar to your classmates'? How do your recommendations differ from your classmates'?

MANAGEMENT WRAP-UP

Selecting computer hardware technology for the organization is a key business decision, and it should not be left to technical specialists alone. General managers should understand the capabilities of various computer processing, input, output, and storage options as well as price/performance relationships. They should be involved in hardware-capacity planning and decisions to distribute computing, to downsize, or to use network computers.

Computer hardware technology can either enhance or impede organizational performance. Computer hardware selection should consider how well the technology meshes with the organization's culture and structure as well as its information-processing requirements.

Information technology today is not limited to computers but must be viewed as an array of networked digital devices. Organizations have many computer processing options to choose from, including mainframes, workstations, PCs, laptops, and network computers, and many different ways of configuring hardware components to create systems.

For Discussion
1. What management, organization, and technology issues should be considered when selecting computer hardware?
2. What factors would you consider in deciding whether to switch from centralized processing on a mainframe to client/server processing?

SUMMARY

1. *Identify the hardware components in a typical computer system.* The modern computer system has six major components: a central processing unit (CPU), primary storage, input devices, output devices, secondary storage, and communications devices.

2. *Describe how information is represented and processed in a computer system.* Computers store and process information in the form of binary digits called bits. A string of eight bits is called a byte. There are several coding schemes for arranging bits into characters. The most common are EBCDIC and ASCII. The CPU is the part of the computer where the manipulation of symbols, numbers, and letters occurs. The CPU has three components: an arithmetic-logic unit , a control unit, and registers. The arithmetic-logic unit performs arithmetic and logical operations on data while the control unit controls and coordinates the computer's other components. Registers store the data as it moves from one computer location to another.

   The CPU is closely tied to primary memory, or primary storage, which stores data and program instructions temporarily before and after processing. Several different kinds of semiconductor memory chips are used with primary storage: RAM (random access memory) is used for short-term storage of data and program instructions while ROM (read-only memory) permanently stores important program instructions.

   Computer processing power depends in part on the speed of their microprocessors, which integrate the computer's logic and control on a single chip. Microprocessor capabilities can be gauged by their word length, data bus width, and cycle speed. Most conventional computers process one instruction at a time, but computers with parallel processing can process multiple instructions simultaneously.

3. *Contrast the capabilities of personal computers, workstations, midrange computers, mainframes, and supercomputers.* Depending on their size and processing power, computers are categorized as personal computers, midrange computers, mainframes, or supercomputers. Personal computers may be desktop PCs, laptops, or hand-held computers. Workstations are the next most powerful category of computer and can handle more complex mathematical and graphical applications. Midrange computers are often used in midrange companies or large departments. Mainframes are the largest computers and function as data warehouses and communication gateways. Supercomputers are sophisticated, powerful computers that can perform massive and complex computations because they use parallel processing. Because of continuing advances in microprocessor technology, the distinctions between these types of computers are constantly changing.

4. *Compare different arrangements of computer processing, including the use of client/server computing, network computers, and peer-to-peer computing.* Computers can be networked together to distribute processing among different machines.

In the client/server model of computing, computer processing is split between "clients" and "servers" connected via a network. Each function of an application is assigned to the machine best suited to perform that function. The exact division of tasks between client and server depends on the application.

   Network computers are pared-down desktop machines with minimal or no local storage and processing capacity. They obtain most or all of their software and data from a central network server. While network computers help organizations maintain central control over computing, peer-to-peer computing puts processing power back on users' desktops, linking individual computers through the Internet or private networks to share data, disk space, and even processing power for a variety of tasks.

5. *Describe the principal media for storing data and programs in a computer system.* The principal forms of secondary storage are magnetic disk, optical disk, and magnetic tape. Disks permit direct access to specific records and are much faster than tape. Disk technology is used in online processing. Optical disks can store vast amounts of data compactly. Most CD-ROM disk systems can only be read from, but rewritable optical disk systems are becoming popular, too. Tape stores the records in sequence and can only be used in batch processing.

6. *Compare the major input and output devices and the various ways they are connected to a computer system.* The principal input devices are keyboards, computer mice, touch screens, magnetic ink and optical character recognition, pen-based instruments, digital scanners, sensors, and voice input.

   The principal output devices are monitors, printers, plotters, voice output devices, and microfilm and microfiche. Many input and output devices are located outside the central computer unit and are known as peripheral devices. They are connected to the central computer unit by ports, which vary in speed and bandwidth, from serial ports that process one bit at a time, to parallel ports that process eight bits at a time, to faster ports, such as Firewire and USB.

7. *Compare various approaches to data input and processing.* In batch processing, transactions are accumulated and stored in a group until it is efficient or necessary to process them. In online processing, the user enters transactions into a device that is directly connected to the computer system. The transactions are usually processed immediately.

8. *Describe multimedia and information technology trends.* Multimedia integrates two or more types of media, such as text, graphics, sound, voice, video, and/or animation into a computer-based application. The future will see chips that can package large amounts of computing power in very small spaces. Microminiaturization is embedding intelligence in more everyday devices, such as smart cards and hand-held or palmtop computers. Computers using superchips and massively parallel processing will be used more widely, and social interfaces will make using computers even easier.

9. *Analyze important issues in managing hardware.* Electronic commerce and electronic business have put new strategic emphasis on technologies that can store vast quantities of transaction data and make them immediately available online. Managers and information systems specialists need to pay special attention to hardware capacity planning, scalability, and total cost of ownership to ensure that the firm has enough computing power for its current and future needs. Managers also need to track technology trends that might require changes in the firm's information technology infrastructure, including the assignment of more corporate computing tasks to small hand-held computers and information appliances and the use of social interfaces.

Key Terms

Arithmetic-logic unit (ALU), 196

ASCII (American Standard Code for Information Interchange), 194

Bar code, 204

Batch processing, 206

Bit, 193

Bus, 195

Byte, 193

Capacity planning, 214

CD-R (compact disc-recordable), 201

CD-ROM (compact disc read-only memory), 200

CD-RW (compact disc rewritable), 201

Central processing unit (CPU), 195

Centralized processing, 210

Client, 211

Client/server computing, 211

Clock speed, 198

Computer mouse, 203

Control unit, 196

Cycle time, 198

Data bus width, 198

Digital scanners, 204

Digital video disk (DVD), 201

Direct access storage device (DASD), 200

Distributed processing, 210

Downsizing, 211

EBCDIC (Extended Binary Coded Decimal Interchange Code), 194

Firewire, 205

Floppy disk, 200

Gigabyte, 196

Graphics adapter card, 205

Hard disk, 200

Information appliance, 217

Kilobyte, 196

Laptop computer, 209

Latency, 198

Machine cycle, 198

Magnetic disk, 200

Magnetic ink character recognition (MICR), 204

Magnetic tape, 201

Mainframe, 210

Massively parallel computers, 199

Master file, 207

Megabyte, 196

Megahertz, 198

Microprocessor, 197

Microsecond, 198

Midrange computer, 209

Minicomputer, 209

MMX (MultiMedia eXtension), 198

Monitor, 205

Motherboard, 195

MP3 (MPEG3), 208

Multimedia, 207

Nanosecond, 198

Network computer (NC), 211

Online processing, 206

Optical character recognition (OCR), 204

Optical disk, 200

Parallel port, 205

Parallel processing, 199

Peer-to-peer computing, 212

Pen-based input, 204

Personal computer (PC), 209

Personal digital assistant (PDA), 217

Picosecond, 198

Pixel, 194

Plotter, 205

Port, 205

Primary storage, 195

Printer, 205

RAID (Redundant Array of Inexpensive Disks), 200

RAM (random access memory), 196

Reduced instruction set computing (RISC), 198

Register, 196

ROM (read-only memory), 197

Scalability, 215

Secondary storage, 200

Semiconductor, 196

Sensors, 205

Serial port, 205

Server, 201

Server farm, 210

Smart card, 217

Sound card, 205

Source data automation, 204

Storage area network (SAN), 201

Storage service provider (SSP), 202

Streaming technology, 207

Supercomputer, 210

Terabyte, 196

Total cost of ownership (TCO), 216

Touch screen, 204

Transaction file, 207

Universal serial bus (USB) port, 206

Voice input devices, 204

Voice output device, 205

Wireless port, 206

Word length, 197

Workstation, 209

WORM (write once/read many), 201

Review Questions

1. What are the components of a contemporary computer system?

2. Distinguish between a bit and a byte and describe how information is stored in primary memory.

3. What are ASCII and EBCDIC, and why are they used?

4. Name the major components of the CPU and the function of each.

5. What are the different types of semiconductor memory, and when are they used?

6. Name and describe the factors affecting a microprocessor's speed and performance.

7. Distinguish between serial, parallel, and massively parallel processing.

8. List the most important secondary storage media. What are the strengths and limitations of each?

9. List and describe the major input and output devices.

10. What is the difference between batch and online processing?

11. What is multimedia? What technologies are involved?

12. What are the differences among the various types of computers? What different types of computer are classified as PCs? Which of these computers can be used as a server?

13. What are downsizing and client/server processing?

14. What is a network computer? How does it differ from a conventional PC? Compare the network computer and peer-to-peer models of computing.

15. Why should managers pay attention to the total cost of ownership (TCO) of technology resources? How would using the TCO model affect computer hardware purchase decisions?

16. Why should managers be interested in computer storage, scalability, and hardware capacity planning?

17. Name two hardware trends, and explain their implications for business organizations.

GROUP PROJECT

Pair up with a classmate. Find a newspaper or magazine advertisement for a computer or office products company selling personal computers that lists the features and "extras" of a particular PC currently on sale. Do you know the meaning of all of the terms used in the ad? Do you know if the listed features all work well together? If you were buying a PC, would this one suit your needs? Is it a "good buy"? Can you find a Web site that would let you order your "customized" personal computer online? Present your findings to the class.

INTERNET CONNECTION

■ COMPANION WEBSITE

At www.pearsoned.ca/laudon, you'll find an online study guide with two quizzes to test your knowledge of computer hardware. You'll also find updates to the chapter and online exercises and cases that enable you to apply your knowledge to realistic situations.

■ ADDITIONAL SITES OF INTEREST

There are many interesting Web sites to enhance your learning about hardware. You can search the Web yourself, or just try the following sites to add to what you have already learned.

Tom's Hardware

www.tomshardware.com

The latest news on hardware testing and comparison of one brand of a particular piece of hardware against other brands

Whatis.com

www.whatis.com

An up-to-date combination dictionary and encyclopaedia of hardware, software, and applications

Intel Corporation

www.intel.com

The world's leading chip maker has an interesting Web site; you can find out about their latest research here

Dell Canada

www.dell.ca

See how to purchase a personal computer online from Dell Computer's Canadian Web site

SETI @ Home Project

setiathome.ssl.berkeley.edu/

Don't just read our material about the SETI@home project; sign up yourself, or check out what they may have already found in outer space

InformIT

www.informit.com

For the real "techie" in the class—an excellent Web site for staying up to date with the latest developments about hardware

CASE STUDY   *Wearable Computers: Will We Become Extensions of Our Computers?*

Bell Canada, IBM Canada Ltd. and Xybernaut Corporation teamed up to launch the first large-scale market trial of wearable computers. Bell Canada has outfitted an elite group of field service technicians with the Mobile Assistant IV (MA-IV), a fully wireless computing and communications device that is designed to connect the user to the Internet and provide a wireless voice connection. The device can be configured in different ways, including being worn as a vest or belt, and is equipped with a headset or a flat-panel touch display screen for projecting and viewing images.

IBM Canada's George Tatomyr, a strategic business development executive with the portable solutions group in Toronto, said the market trial is aimed at demonstrating the continuing migration of the PC from an enterprise environment to a mobile environment. "It's a means of justifying this wearable technology. We're expecting to conduct a post trial early next year," Tatomyr said. "People need to move around and with this wireless technology…they're still able to work with the same applications that they have on a PC."

Greater Toronto residents may catch a glimpse into the future of both technology and fashion as Bell Canada's technicians test the MA-IV in all weather and work conditions. The trial began in early October of 2000 with a total of 19 Bell technicians using the MA-IV. Currently, most Bell techies use IBM ThinkPad laptops to access data remotely.

"IBM has been looking at the wearable PC for years and we've been demonstrating that the technology is reliable," Tatomyr stated. "It's a miniaturized PC that you can wear. We hope to deploy MA-X as the project moves forward."

The wearable PC trial is the culmination of the collaborative work between Bell, IBM and Xybernaut to design, develop and manufacture the computer portion of Xybernaut's next generation of wearable systems.

"We're running the trial into December to get a bit of cold weather and to see how it performs," said Brad Chittey, a regional manager with the Mobile Communications Services for Bell Canada in Toronto. "Once we're able to validate the business value of the product we'll look at our other families and our counterparts in Eastern Ontario and Quebec."

For its part, Xybernaut provides the physical unit. The MA-IV runs all major operating systems such as Windows or Linux on Intel x86 architecture. It weighs less than a kilogram and boasts a 233MHz MMX Pentium processor, 160MB RAM, 8GB hard drive, a Lithium-ion battery, two PCMCIA card bus slots, and multiple I/O ports for connecting peripherals and power cables. The full-colour touch screen flat panel display can be wrist or belt-mounted and has a six- to eight-inch viewable diagonal display. The head-mounted gear features a microphone, earpiece speaker, and a display unit that projects an image onto a reflector that displays the image to the eye. It measures 1.1-inches diagonally and displays a VGA colour image at 640 by 480 resolution.

IBM has been toying with the idea of portable computers for a fair amount of time. In June of 2000, IBM unveiled a wearable PC and the IBM WatchPad—a watch that is capable of synchronizing data and images with a portable computer or PC via wireless connections. Unlike the wearable PC, the WatchPad is still in the prototype phase, and it is not close to reaching the market.

IBM has also developed a wireless hand-held device for airline check in. About the size of a deck of cards, the hand-held integrates three different technologies: an IBM badge computer, an AiroNet IEEE 802.11 wireless LAN card, and a RF reader.

"These applications are still in the test phase, it seems only the visionaries are looking at it right now, but cybersmart computing is definitely the way of the future," commented Kevin Restivo, an analyst with IDC Canada in Toronto. "The biggest asset to these devices is the practicality test as developers and researchers try to bring the product to the workplace.

Speaking of those developers and researchers, Canada's Steve Mann is working on a wearable computer that looks like a pair of eyeglasses. Considered by some to be the inventor of wearable computing, Mann, a professor at the University of Toronto, has decided to "regain control" of his space. Mann views the world through a pair of glasses that he invented, which mediate the reality that he sees.

"I wear dark glasses but can see the real world," Mann said during a Toronto event organized by Mississauga, Ontario-based Information Technology Association of Canada and Kanata, Ontario-based Communications and Information Technology Ontario. Mann's eyeglasses are opaque—no light can get through them. But they are powered by Eyetap technology (www.eyetap.org), which he said allows his eyes to act both as a camera and a display device.

The Eyetap glasses collect the light that would otherwise go into Mann's eyes, turn it into numbers, and resynthesize it into laser light, which the glasses project into his eyes. The glasses, along with a high-tech vest, connect Mann to the Internet. Now, instead of seeing an offending billboard, which he likens to e-mail spam, Mann can key out the billboard and project e-mail messages his wife and friends send him into that same space.

The glasses, which Mann wears almost everywhere he goes, don't look that different from a normal pair of sunglasses. Mann also has a pair of clear glasses with a single line across them that look like bifocals. But his glasses weren't always this pared down and sleek. He started off in the late '70s with a cumbersome headset and looked sort of like a Borg that had taken a wrong turn on its way to a *Star Trek* set. "I went through this phase of being a loner where nobody would talk to me because I was wearing that," he joked.

Mann wants to eliminate the distance between computers and human beings. "This whole concept is based on a philosophy that I refer to as humanistic intelligence (HI)," he said. The Eyetap technology allows human beings and computers to work in unison and give each other feedback. "The human being is a peripheral to the computer; and the computer is also a peripheral device to the human—the two use each other as peripherals. The human and computer are inextricably intertwined. The two are joined together, and so, in a sense, they are a single unit."

But Eyetap technology also goes one step further. Not only does it allow people to become closer to computers, according to Mann, it also allows people to become closer to each other. It opens the door to people experiencing the world with each other's eyes, to in effect be each other. "That's a lot more powerful than just seeing a picture of me. You know the Dick Tracy notion of the videophone that shows pictures of you. All these videophones are failing in the marketplace. When you think about it, it doesn't satisfy a need that there is. It doesn't really add any value, and most of my friends and relatives already know what I look like," he said.

"The whole notion here is that they can be me rather than just see me. It's a kind of existential communications content wherein they can get inside my head and see the world from my perspective." When Mann is driving home, for instance, his wife can see what he's seeing and will understand why he suddenly stops talking as he's making a left turn, Mann said. "It's as if she was in the car with me. So she becomes me."

Eyetap is fundamentally different from other computing and communications devices that people carry, such as cell phones, pagers, and PDAs, according to Mann. Those devices are not always on and need to be pulled out of a purse or a pocket to be used. Eyetap is always on and readily accessible.

It can, therefore, be used as a personal safety device, a camera, and a memory prosthetic. If Mann witnesses a crime, the Eyetap glasses can catalogue everything. If a business associate mentions someone, Mann can type in that person's name with his keyer, a specially-designed, hand-held input device operated with one hand, and bring up a file on that person. He can do this without interrupting his conversation to pull out a PDA.

"The interesting thing about this invention is it seems like a cumbersome apparatus, but when you add up all the things that it replaces, it's not really that bad. It's the one thing you need to carry with you to gather everything together all in one place; it functions as a pager, a cellphone, a personal sound system, a clock, camera, video recorder, and imaging device," he said.

Mann first began experimenting with WearComp—his word for wearable computing—in the '70s as a way to explore the visual arts. "I wanted to live in a photographic world and see the world through the eyes of a camera." He had some exhibits of his work and began doing commercial photography. People were interested not only in the images he created, but the process through which he created them. "The computer is the most extraordinary of man's technological clothing. It's an extension of our central nervous system."

Sources: Liam Lahey, "Bell Canada Techies Slip Into Something More Comfortable," *Computerworld Canada*, December 1, 2000; Poonam Khanna, "Mann Controls His Reality," *Computerworld Canada*, October 6, 2000.

CASE STUDY QUESTIONS

1. Where do you think the concept of wearable computers will go next? What applications can you see being developed for wearable computers?

2. What types of wearable computers would you be willing to wear? What applications would be on those wearable computers?

3. Do you agree with Steve Mann that "The human being is a peripheral to the computer; and the computer is also a peripheral device to the human—the two use each other as peripherals. The human and computer are inextricably intertwined. The two are joined together, and so, in a sense, they are a single unit?"

4. What management issues arise when managing a workforce that uses wearable computers? What human resource management issues arise, and what IT management issues arise?

CHAPTER

7

COMPUTER SOFTWARE

OBJECTIVES

After completing this chapter, you will be able to:

1. *Describe the major types of software.*
2. *Examine the functions of system software and compare leading PC operating systems.*
3. *Analyze the strengths and limitations of the major application programming languages and software tools.*
4. *Describe contemporary approaches to software development.*
5. *Identify important issues in the management of organizational software assets.*

Renting Software from an ASP: How Enerline Tamed the Beast and Saved Money, Too

Founded in Canada in 1995, Enerline Restorations, Inc. offers its patented Ener-Liner® corrosion protection solutions to major oil and gas producers, water utilities, and municipalities. Ener-Liner is a fast, cost-effective way to protect steel pipelines and oil field downhole tubular pipes from corrosion. In the oil and gas industry, downtime resulting from the failure of corroded pipes is very costly to customers and could be even more costly if Enerline fails to react to their needs.

With only one computer shared between 30 staff members, even basic tasks, such as generating inventory reports or checking customer delivery schedules, were slow and cumbersome. Enerline faced serious time-to-market challenges caused by the lack of a centralized information infrastructure easily accessible to all personnel. Demand soon began to overtake Enerline's ability to satisfy customers, affecting its reputation.

It became clear that the company either had to make a significant capital investment in information technology and hire a dedicated IT staff or look for outside help. The cost of the staff and equipment necessary to manage its IT needs internally would be cost-prohibitive, so the company took a different approach.

Enerline turned to FutureLink, an application service provider, or ASP. ASPs deploy, host, manage, and lease packaged application software to customers from centrally managed data centres. Customers access the applications through a browser. "People first looked at me like I had a hole in my head," says Cameron Chell, chairman and CEO of FutureLink. "They thought no customers were going to go for rented apps running in a remote facility...now [2000] you're seeing this market emerging as the hottest sector in IT outsourcing."

224

The company offers three levels of ASP services: so-called "application portal.com," where individual users can connect to a Web site for their applications; "application hosting," where FutureLink runs applications for a small company; and a total outsourcing offering, where FutureLink runs a customer's entire IT function, including providing the thin client hardware, help desk support, custom app development and business assessment services. FutureLink guarantees 99.8 percent uptime in its service level agreements.

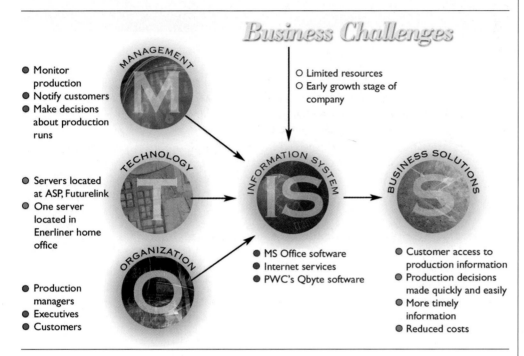

Business Challenges

MANAGEMENT
- Monitor production
- Notify customers
- Make decisions about production runs

TECHNOLOGY
- Servers located at ASP, Futurelink
- One server located in Enerliner home office

ORGANIZATION
- Production managers
- Executives
- Customers

- ○ Limited resources
- ○ Early growth stage of company

INFORMATION SYSTEM
- MS Office software
- Internet services
- PWC's Qbyte software

BUSINESS SOLUTIONS
- Customer access to production information
- Production decisions made quickly and easily
- More timely information
- Reduced costs

FutureLink has six offices in Canada and manages and supports a variety of mission-critical applications, which they lease to users on a monthly basis. Enerline was up and running within 30 days with access to Microsoft Office applications, Internet services, and PricewaterhouseCoopers' Qbyte accounting system. FutureLink provides the file, print, database, and application servers from their own central facilities. Enerline employees connect to FutureLink's facility and enjoy hassle-free computing with 24/7 availability, fast performance, and strong security.

By adopting the ASP model, Enerline has already saved more than $60 000–$80 000, including savings on capital equipment and software upgrades. "We have phenomenal access to technology for a company our size with our budget," said Ron Hozjan, CFO of Enerline. "We scaled up from one to six computers overnight without spending a dime on capital and have access to better technology than some companies five to ten times our size in Alberta."

Using FutureLink, Enerline is able to focus on its customers' needs and deliver strategic value-added services. For example, with Enerline's new Web site, customers will be able to find out where their orders are in the production cycle and even visualize the progress of their project with a few clicks of the mouse. Enerline can also take project queries directly from customers via the Web.

Enerline is also improving the efficiency and productivity of its employees. For instance, users can now gain quick access to current production schedules and inventory levels. As a result, production decisions are made more quickly and easily and are based on timely, accurate information.

(continued)

Renting Software from an ASP: How Enerline Tamed the Beast and Saved Money, Too

According to Hozjan, "Going the ASP route was an easy decision. The ASP computing model helped us to quickly improve our market position and prepared us to serve new, larger, and more geographically dispersed customers...by giving us a state-of-the-art IT infrastructure that we don't have to worry about. We can now focus exclusively on serving our customers."

Sources: Mark Mehler, "FutureLink: Linking the Future?," *Smart Partner*, May 3, 2000, available at http://www.zdnet.com/sp/stories/issue/0,4537,2228503,00.html, accessed April 1, 2001; "Enerline Restoration, Inc., A Case Study," http://www.futurelink.ca/case_studies/case_studies1/enerline.asp, accessed April 1, 2001.

MANAGEMENT CHALLENGES

Many businesses like Enerline have access to computer hardware. What prevented Ron Hozjan from efficiently managing Enerline's information was the inability to afford appropriate software and hardware. To find the information resources it needed, Enerline had to know the capabilities of various types of software, and it had to select a software provider that met its specific business requirements, was affordable, and was easy to use. The applications furnished by FutureLink transformed a jumble of tangled paperwork into manageable information and became an important technology asset. Selecting and developing the right software can improve organizational performance, but it raises the following management challenges:

1. **Increasing complexity and software errors.** Although software for desktop systems and Internet applications can sometimes be rapidly generated, a great deal of what software will be asked to do remains far-reaching and sophisticated, requiring programs that are large and complex. Large and complex systems tend to be error-prone, with software errors or "bugs" that may not be revealed for years until after exhaustive testing and actual use. Researchers do not know if the number of bugs grows exponentially or proportionately to the number of lines of code, nor can they tell for certain whether all segments of a complex piece of software will always work in total harmony. The process of designing and testing software that is reliable and "bug-free" is a serious quality control and management problem (see Chapter 11).

2. **The application backlog.** Advances in computer software have not kept pace with the breathtaking productivity gains in computer hardware. Developing software has become a major preoccupation for many organizations. A great deal of software must be intricately crafted. Moreover, the software itself is only one component of a complete information system that must be carefully designed and coordinated with other people, as well as with organizational and hardware components. The "software crisis" is actually part of a larger systems analysis, design, and implementation issue that will be discussed in detail later. Despite the gains from fourth-generation languages, personal desktop software tools, object-oriented programming, software development approaches, and software tools for the World Wide Web, many businesses continue to face a backlog of two to three years in developing the information systems they need, or they may not be able to develop them at all.

To play a useful role in the firm's information technology (IT) infrastructure, computer hardware requires instructions provided by computer software. This chapter shows how software turns computer hardware into useful information systems, describes major software types, and presents new approaches to software development and acquisition. It also introduces some key issues for managing software as an organizational asset in the information technology infrastructure.

7.1 WHAT IS SOFTWARE?

Software is the detailed instructions that control the operation of a computer system. Without software, computer hardware could not perform the tasks we associate with computers. The functions of software are to (1) manage the computer resources of the organization, (2) provide tools for human beings to take advantage of these resources, and (3) act as an intermediary between organizations and stored information. Selecting appropriate software for the organization is a key management decision.

software
Detailed instructions that control the operation of a computer system.

SOFTWARE PROGRAMS

A software **program** is a series of statements or instructions to the computer. The process of writing or coding programs is termed programming, and individuals who specialize in this task are called programmers. A program must be stored in the computer's primary storage along with the required data in order to execute or to have its instructions performed by the computer. Once a program has finished executing, the computer hardware can be used for another task when a new program is loaded into memory.

program
A series of statements or instructions to the computer.

MAJOR TYPES OF SOFTWARE

There are two major types of software: system software and application software. Each kind performs a different function, and both kinds need to work together to have a useful information system. **System software** is a set of generalized programs that manage the computer's resources, such as the central processor, communications links, and peripheral devices. System software makes the hardware usable. Programmers who write system software are called system programmers.

Application software describes the programs that are written for or by users to apply the computer to a specific task. Software for processing an order or generating a mailing list is application software. Programmers who write application software are called application programmers.

The types of software are interrelated and can be thought of as a set of nested boxes, each of which must interact closely with the other boxes surrounding it. Figure 7-1 illustrates this relationship. The system software surrounds and controls access to the hardware. Application software must work through the system software in order to operate. End users work primarily with application software. Each type of software must be specially designed for a specific machine to ensure its compatibility.

system software
Generalized programs that manage the computer's resources, such as the central processor, communications links, and peripheral devices.

application software
Programs written for a specific application to perform functions specified by end users.

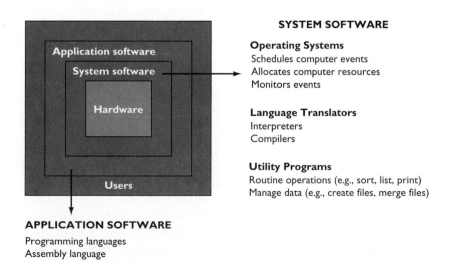

SYSTEM SOFTWARE

Operating Systems
Schedules computer events
Allocates computer resources
Monitors events

Language Translators
Interpreters
Compilers

Utility Programs
Routine operations (e.g., sort, list, print)
Manage data (e.g., create files, merge files)

APPLICATION SOFTWARE
Programming languages
Assembly language

FORTRAN   PASCAL
COBOL   C and C++
BASIC   Fourth-generation languages and PC software tools

FIGURE 7-1 The major types of software. The relationship between the system software, application software, and users can be illustrated by a series of nested boxes. System software—consisting of operating systems, language translators, and utility programs—controls access to the hardware. Application software, such as the programming languages and "fourth-generation" languages, must work through the system software to operate. The user interacts primarily with the application software.

7.2 System Software

System software coordinates the various parts of the computer system and mediates between application software and computer hardware. System software also provides the interface through which the user interacts with the hardware and software. The system software that manages and controls the computer's activities is called the **operating system**. Other system software consists of computer language translation programs that convert programming languages into machine language and utility programs that perform common processing tasks. Still other system software manages telecommunications and networking.

operating system
The system software that manages and controls the activities of the computer.

Functions of the Operating System

One way to look at the operating system is as the system's chief manager. Operating system software decides which computer resources will be used, which programs will be run, and the order in which activities will take place.

An operating system performs three functions. It allocates and assigns system resources; it schedules the use of computer resources and computer jobs, or program runs; and it monitors computer system activities.

Allocation and Assignment

The operating system allocates resources to the application jobs, or runs, in the execution queue. It provides locations in primary memory for data and programs and controls input and output devices such as printers, terminals, and telecommunication links.

Scheduling

Thousands of pieces of work can be going on in a computer simultaneously. The operating system decides when to schedule the jobs that have been submitted and when to coordinate the scheduling in various areas of the computer so that different parts of different jobs can be worked on at the same time. For instance, while one program is executing, the operating system may be scheduling the use of input and output devices for that program or for another program. Not all jobs are performed in the order they are submitted; the operating system should schedule these jobs according to organizational priorities. Online order processing may have priority over a job to generate mailing lists and labels.

Monitoring

The operating system monitors the activities of the computer system. It keeps track of each computer job and may also keep track of who is using the system, of what programs have been run, and of any unauthorized attempts to access the system. This is particularly important in the context of telecommunications and networking. Information system security is discussed in detail in Chapter 12.

Multiprogramming, Virtual Storage, Timesharing, and Multiprocessing

How is it possible for 1000 or more users sitting at remote terminals to use a computer information system simultaneously since most computers can execute only one instruction from one program at a time? How can computers run thousands of programs? The answer is that the computer has a series of specialized operating system capabilities.

Multiprogramming

multiprogramming
A method of executing two or more programs concurrently using the same computer. The CPU executes only one program but can service the input/output needs of others at the same time.

The most important operating system capability for sharing computer resources is **multiprogramming**. Multiprogramming permits multiple programs to share a computer system's resources at any one time through concurrent use of a CPU. By concurrent use, we mean that only one program is actually using the CPU at any given moment, but the input/output needs of other programs can be serviced at the same time. Two or more programs are active at the same time, but they do not use the same computer resources simultaneously. With multiprogramming, a group of programs takes turns using the processor.

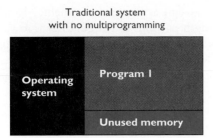
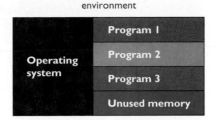

FIGURE 7-2 Single-program execution compared to multiprogramming. In multiprogramming, the computer can be used much more efficiently because a number of programs can be executing concurrently. Several complete programs are loaded into memory. This memory management aspect of the operating system greatly increases throughput by better management of high-speed memory and input/output devices.

Figure 7-2 shows how three programs in a multiprogramming environment can be stored in primary storage. The first program executes until an input/output event is read in the program. While waiting for the input/output event to complete, the CPU can move to the second program until an input/output statement occurs. At this point, the CPU can switch to the execution of the third program, and so forth, until eventually all three programs have been executed and all input/output operations have been completed. In this manner, many different programs can execute at the same time although different resources within the CPU are actually being used.

Multiprogramming on single-user operating systems such as those in older personal computers is called **multitasking**. **Multithreading** is the ability of an operating system to execute different parts of the same program, called *threads*, simultaneously. For example, a word processing program may be formatting one document while checking the spelling and grammar of another document.

Virtual Memory

Virtual memory handles programs more efficiently because the computer divides the programs into small fixed- or variable-length portions, storing only a small portion of the program in primary memory at one time. If only two or three large programs can be read into memory, a certain part of main memory generally remains underutilized because the programs add up to less than the total amount of primary storage space available and only a small number of programs can reside in primary storage at any given time.

multitasking
The multiprogramming capability of primarily single-user operating systems, such as those for older PCs.

multithreading
The capability of an operating system to execute different parts of the same program, called threads, at the same time.

virtual memory
Handling programs more efficiently by dividing the programs into small fixed- or variable-length portions with only a small portion stored in primary memory at one time.

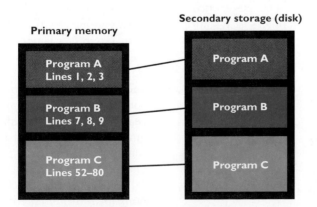

FIGURE 7-3 Virtual storage. Virtual storage is based on the fact that, in general, only a few statements in a program can actually be used at any given moment. In virtual storage, programs are broken down into small sections called pages. Individual program pages are read into memory only when needed. The rest of the program is stored on disk until it is required. In this way, very large programs can be executed by small machines, or a large number of programs can be executed concurrently by a single machine.

page
A fixed-length portion of a program used by virtual storage that is stored in primary memory.

segment
A variable-length portion of a program used by virtual storage that is stored in primary memory.

timesharing
The sharing of computer resources by many users simultaneously by having the CPU spend a fixed amount of time on each user's program before proceeding to the next.

multiprocessing
An operating system feature for executing two or more instructions simultaneously in a single computer system by using multiple central processing units.

source code
Program instructions written in a high-level language that must be translated into machine language to be executed by the computer.

compiler
Special system software that translates a high-level language into machine language for execution by the computer.

object code
Program instructions that have been translated into machine language so that they can be executed by the computer.

interpreter
A special translator of source code into machine code that translates source code statements into machine code and executes them, one at a time.

FIGURE 7-4 The language translation process. The source code in a high-level language program is translated by the compiler into object code so that the instructions can be "understood" by the machine. These are grouped into modules. Prior to execution, the object code modules are joined together by the linkage editor to create the load module. It is the load module that is actually executed by the computer.

Only a few statements of a program actually execute at any given moment. Virtual storage breaks a program into a number of fixed-length portions called **pages** or into variable-length portions called **segments**. Each of these portions is relatively small (a page is approximately two to four kilobytes). This permits a large number of programs to reside in primary memory, since only one page of each program is actually located there (see Figure 7-3), utilizing this resource more efficiently. All other program pages are stored in a secondary storage device until they are ready for execution.

Timesharing

Timesharing is an operating system capability that allows many users to share computer processing resources simultaneously. It differs from multiprogramming in that the CPU spends a fixed amount of time on one program before moving on to another. In a timesharing environment, thousands of users are each allocated a tiny slice of computer time (two milliseconds). In this time slot, each user is free to perform any required operations; at the end of this period, another user is given a two-millisecond time slice of the CPU. This arrangement permits many users to be connected to a CPU simultaneously, with each receiving only a tiny amount of CPU time. A CPU operating at the gigahertz (nanosecond) level can accomplish a great deal of work in two milliseconds.

Multiprocessing

Multiprocessing is an operating system capability that links together two or more CPUs to work in parallel in a single computer system. The operating system can assign multiple CPUs to execute different instructions from the same program or from different programs simultaneously, dividing the work between the CPUs. Whereas multiprogramming uses concurrent processing with one CPU, multiprocessing uses simultaneous processing with multiple CPUs.

LANGUAGE TRANSLATION AND UTILITY SOFTWARE

System software includes special language translator programs that translate high-level language programs written in programming languages such as COBOL, FORTRAN, or C into machine language that the computer can execute. This type of system software is called a compiler or interpreter. A program written in a high-level language (before translation into machine language) is called **source code**. A **compiler** translates all of the source code into machine code called **object code** at one time. Just before execution by the computer, the object code modules are joined with other needed object code modules (such as those to read files or to print) in a process called linkage editing. The resulting load module is what is actually executed by the computer. Figure 7-4 illustrates the language translation process.

Some programming languages such as BASIC do not use a compiler but instead use an **interpreter**, which translates each source code statement one at a time into machine code and executes it before translating the next statement. Interpreter languages are slow to execute because they are translated and executed one statement at a time. Interpreters are good for debugging while compilers are good for running programs that have already been debugged. An **assembler** is similar to a compiler, but it is used to translate only assembly language (see Section 7.3) into machine code.

System software includes utility programs for routine, repetitive tasks, such as copying files, clearing primary storage, computing a square root, or sorting. If you have worked on a computer and have performed such functions as setting up new files, deleting old files, or formatting diskettes, you have worked with utility programs.

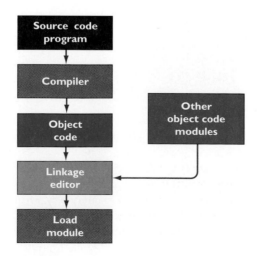
Source code program → Compiler → Object code → Linkage editor ← Other object code modules; Linkage editor → Load module

Utility programs are prewritten programs that are stored so that they can be shared by all users of a computer system and can be used rapidly in many different information system applications when requested.

GRAPHICAL USER INTERFACES

When users interact with a computer, even a PC, the interaction is controlled by an operating system. Users communicate with an operating system through the **user interface** of that operating system. Early PC operating systems were command-driven, but the **graphical user interface**, often called a GUI, makes extensive use of objects or icons, buttons, bars, boxes, and a mouse to perform the same tasks. It has become the dominant model for the user interface of PC operating systems and for many types of application software.

Older PC operating systems such as DOS, described in the following section, were command-driven, requiring the user to type in text-based commands using a keyboard. An operating system with a graphical user interface uses graphic symbols called icons to depict programs, files, and activities. For example, a file could be deleted by moving the icon representing the file to a trash icon. Many graphical user interfaces use a system of pull-down menus to help users select commands and "pop-up" dialogue boxes to help users select among command options. Windowing features allow users to create, stack, size, and move around boxes of information. A complex series of commands can be issued simply by linking icons.

PC OPERATING SYSTEMS

Like any other software, PC software is based on specific operating systems written for specific computer hardware. A software package written for one PC operating system usually cannot run on another. Table 7-1 compares the leading PC operating systems: Windows 98 and Windows ME, Windows 2000, Windows CE, OS/2, UNIX, Linux, the Macintosh operating system, the Palm operating system, and DOS.

Microsoft's **Windows 98** is a genuine 32-bit operating system that can address data in 32-bit chunks and run programs that take up more than 640 K of memory. It provides a streamlined graphical user interface that arranges icons to provide instant access to common tasks. Windows 98 features multitasking, multithreading, and powerful networking capabil-

assembler
A special translator that translates only assembly language source code into machine code.

utility program
System software consisting of programs for routine, repetitive tasks, which can be shared by many users.

user interface
The part of an operating system users interact with to issue commands to the computer.

graphical user interface (GUI)
The part of an operating system users interact with that uses graphic icons and the computer mouse to issue commands and make selections.

Windows 98
A version of the Windows operating system that is closely integrated with the Internet and that supports hardware technologies such as MMX, digital video disk, videoconferencing cameras, scanners, TV tuner-adapter cards, and joysticks.

TABLE 7-1	LEADING PC OPERATING SYSTEMS
Operating System	**Features**
Windows XP	Reliable, robust operating system with versions for both home and corporate users. Features support of Internet and multimedia and improved networking, security, and corporate management capabilities.
Windows ME, Windows 98, and Windows 95	Thirty-two-bit operating systems for personal computing with a streamlined graphical user interface. Has multitasking and powerful networking capabilities and can be integrated with the information resources of the Web.
Windows 2000	Thirty-two-bit operating system for PCs, workstations, and network servers. Supports multitasking, multiprocessing, intensive networking, and Internet services for corporate computing.
Windows CE	Pared-down version of the Windows operating system for handheld computers and wireless communication devices.
Palm OS	Operating system for Palm-compatible handheld computers and devices.
OS/2	Operating system of IBM PCs that can take advantage of the 32-bit microprocessor. Supports multitasking and networking.
UNIX	Used for powerful PCs, workstations, and midrange computers. Supports multitasking, multiuser processing, and networking. Is portable to different models of computer hardware.
Linux	Free, reliable alternative to UNIX and Windows 2000 that runs on many different types of computer hardware and provides source code that can be modified by software developers.
Mac OS	Operating system for the Macintosh computer. Supports networking and multitasking and has powerful multimedia capabilities. Supports connecting to and publishing on the Internet.
DOS	Operating system for older IBM and IBM-compatible PCs. Limits program use of memory to 640 kilobytes.

Windows 95

A 32-bit operating system with a streamlined graphical user interface and multitasking, multithreading, and networking capabilities.

ities, including the capability to integrate fax, e-mail, and scheduling programs. **Windows 95** was an earlier version of this operating system.

Windows 98 is faster and more integrated with the Internet than Windows 95, with support for additional hardware technologies such as MMX, DVD, videoconferencing cameras, scanners, TV tuner-adapter cards, and joysticks. It provides capabilities for optimizing hardware performance and file management on the hard disk and enhanced 3-D graphics. The most visible feature of Windows 98 is the integration of the operating system with Web browser software. Users can work with the traditional Windows interface or use the Web browser interface to display information. The user's hard disk can be viewed as an extension of the World Wide Web so that a document residing on the hard disk and on the Web can be accessed the same way. Small application programs, or applets, (see the discussion of Java in Section 7.4) on the Windows desktop can automatically retrieve information from specific Web sites whenever the user logs onto the Internet. These applets can automatically update the desktop with the latest news, stock quotes, or weather. Windows 98 also includes a group collaboration tool called NetMeeting and Front Page Express, a tool for creating and storing Web pages.

In 2000, Microsoft also released an enhanced Windows operating system for consumer users called **Windows Millennium Edition (Windows ME)**. It features tools to let users edit video recordings and put them up on the Web and tools to simplify home networking of two or more PCs. A media player bundled with Windows ME can record, store, and play CDs, digital music downloaded from the Internet, and videos. Windows ME users can also import, store, and share photos. Windows ME has improved capabilities for safeguarding critical files.

Windows Millennium Edition (Windows ME)

An enhanced Windows operating system for consumer users featuring tools for working with video, photos, music, and home networking.

Windows 2000

A powerful operating system developed by Microsoft for use with 32-bit PCs, workstations, and network servers. Supports networking, multitasking, multiprocessing, and Internet services.

Windows 2000 is another 32-bit operating system developed by Microsoft with features that make it appropriate for applications in large networked organizations (see Figure 7-5). Earlier versions of this operating system were known as Windows NT (for New Technology). Windows 2000 is used as an operating system for high-performance desktop and laptop computers and network servers. Windows 2000 shares the same graphical user interface as the other Windows operating systems, but it has more powerful networking, multitasking, and memory-management capabilities. Windows 2000 can support software written for Windows, and it can provide mainframe-like computing power for new applications with massive memory and file requirements. It can even support multiprocessing with multiple CPUs.

There are two basic versions of Windows 2000—a professional version for users of stand-alone or client desktop and laptop computers and several server versions designed to run on network servers and provide network management functions, including tools for creating and operating Web sites and other Internet services. An "Active Directory" allows server

FIGURE 7-5 Microsoft Windows 2000 is a powerful operating system with a graphical user interface for high-performance desktop and laptop computers and network servers.

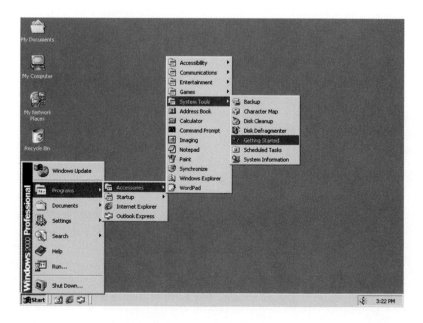

computers to manage user identities, security, and access to resources across computer networks.

In late 2001, Microsoft released **Windows XP** (from experience), which combines the reliability and robustness of Windows 2000 with the ease of use of Windows 98/ME. The Windows XP Home Edition is for home users, and the Windows XP Professional Edition targets mobile and business users. Windows XP increases the integration of the computer interface with the Web browser concept and offers additional multimedia support.

Windows CE (compact edition) has some of the capabilities of Windows, including its graphical user interface, but it is designed to run on small handheld computers, personal digital assistants, or wireless communication devices such as pagers and cellular phones. It is a portable and compact operating system requiring very little memory. Information appliances and consumer devices can use this operating system to share information with Windows-based PCs and to connect to the Internet.

The **Palm operating system** is used on many personal digital assistants, including the PalmPilot, Handspring's Visor, and IBM's Workpad, as well as Qualcomm's pdQ Smartphone.

OS/2 was introduced in the early 1990s to compete with Microsoft's Windows 3.x operating system. OS/2 is a robust 32-bit operating system for powerful IBM or IBM-compatible PCs with Intel microprocessors. OS/2 is used for complex, memory-intensive applications or those that require networking, multitasking, or large programs. OS/2 has its own graphical user interface and client and server versions; the latest version of OS/2 is OS/2 Warp.

UNIX is an interactive, multi-user, multitasking operating system developed by Bell Laboratories in 1969 to help scientific researchers share data. Many people can use UNIX simultaneously to perform the same kind of task, or one user can run many tasks on UNIX concurrently. UNIX was developed to connect various machines together and is highly supportive of communications and networking. UNIX is often used on workstations and servers and provides the reliability and scalability for running large systems on high-end servers. UNIX can run on many different kinds of computers and can be easily customized. Application programs that run under UNIX can be ported from one computer to run on a different computer with little modification. UNIX also can store and manage a large number of files.

UNIX is considered powerful and stable but very complex, with a legion of commands within a command-driven user interface (although graphical user interfaces have been developed for UNIX). UNIX cannot respond well to problems caused by the overuse of system resources (such as running too many jobs or a using a computer with too little disk space). UNIX also poses some security problems because multiple jobs and users can access the same file simultaneously. Vendors have developed different versions of UNIX that are incompatible, thereby limiting software portability.

Linux is a UNIX-like operating system that runs on Intel, Motorola, Digital Alpha, SPARC, and Mips processors. Linux can be downloaded from the Internet free of charge or purchased for a small fee from companies that provide additional tools for the software. Because it is free, reliable, compactly designed, and capable of running on many different hardware platforms, it has become popular during the past few years among sophisticated computer users and businesses as an alternative to UNIX and Windows NT. Major application software vendors are starting to provide versions that can run on Linux. The source code for Linux is available along with the operating system software, so that it can be modified by software developers to fit their particular needs.

Linux is an example of **open-source software**, which provides all computer users with free access to its source code so that they can modify the code to fix errors or to make improvements. Open-source software such as Linux is not owned by any company or individual. A global network of programmers and users manages and modifies the software, usually without being paid to do so. The Window on Organizations describes how organizations are starting to benefit from this new operating system.

Mac OS, the operating system for the Macintosh computer, features multitasking, powerful multimedia and networking capabilities, and a mouse-driven graphical user interface. New features of this operating system allow users to connect, explore, and publish on the Internet and World Wide Web; to use Java software (see Section 7.4); and to load Chinese,

Windows XP
Powerful new Windows operating system that provides reliability, robustness, and ease of use for both corporate and home PC users.

Windows CE
A portable and compact operating system designed to run on small handheld computers, personal digital assistants, or wireless communication devices.

Palm OS
A portable and compact operating system designed to run on small handheld computers, personal digital assistants, or wireless communication devices.

OS/2
A powerful operating system used with 32-bit IBM/PCs or workstations that supports multitasking, networking, and very memory-intensive applications.

UNIX
An operating system for all types of computers that is machine independent and supports multiuser processing, multitasking, and networking. Used in high-end workstations and servers.

Linux
A reliable and compactly designed operating system that is an offshoot of UNIX. It can run on many different hardware platforms and is available free or at very low cost. Used as an alternative to UNIX and Windows NT.

open-source software
Software that provides free access to its program code, allowing users to modify the program code to make improvements or fix errors.

Mac OS
An operating system for the Macintosh computer that supports multitasking, has access to the Internet, and has powerful graphics and multimedia capabilities.

Window on Organizations

WHY LINUX?

Why would a large company opt for a new shareware operating system that can be downloaded free from the Internet? Linux is attractive for both its price and its performance. Linux appears to be more stable than Windows NT and costs less to support. Linux's stability and ease of administration have made it a reliable, flexible, and robust substitute for Windows NT that is being used by a variety of companies from RE/MAX to Canadian National Railways. Even small firms are discovering that Linux may be a good choice for them as well because it runs well on older, less powerful machines and laptops.

So just how far have these companies gone with open-source software? RE/MAX Team Ideal Realty of Kingston, Ont., is using Linux for everything network-related, says system administrator Richard Potter.

"It's Web mail, FTP, virtual private networking for our downtown location, file serving for the whole company, print serving: everything," he says. As for Linux's performance in a business environment, it's "better than NT," according to Potter. "It's just an excellent way [of managing IT] for your business." Meanwhile, CN is using Linux to provide a full suite of functions, from network management and file serving to full Internet services, X-Windows, and software development.

Such thinking is one reason why a recent study by International Data Corp. (IDC) of Framingham, Massachusetts, showed Linux server shipments leaping in 1999. Twenty-five percent of the 5.4 million server operating systems shipped in 1999 were Linux, the study said. Server versions of Microsoft's Windows NT led the market with 38 percent. Novell NetWare had 19 percent of the market while all versions of UNIX slipped to a total of 15 percent. The study counted copies that were either sold or came with a computer, not freely distributed copies of Linux. By comparison, a year ago Linux trailed UNIX by three points. Clearly the upstart is charging. But where?

"As far as we are able to tell, it has not become a mainstream OS, one that's put on an IT department's (purchasing) short-list," said Dan Kusnetzky, an industry analyst at IDC. In the research, engineering, scientific, and academic communities, Linux growth is accelerating, but not in corporations. Or at least not yet. "Many IT organizations are open to it," said Kusnetzky, "but only a portion of them have purchased it."

However, Kusnetzky noted that Linux is creeping into business department by department in exactly the same way as the PC—and Microsoft—did a decade ago. Some managers start with it in the home. For example, Scot Adams, CIO of Toronto-based office and shopping mall developer Cadillac Fairview Corp. Ltd., bought a Linux-powered e-mail server from Cobalt Networks Inc. for his wife's home business. But there's no room yet for the OS at his office.

"It's missing a lot of the management tools I need to manage 65 offices across North America," he said. But if they appeared in the next six months, Linux would be a contender to replace Windows NT for print and file services in some offices. Otherwise, he said, he'll be upgrading Cadillac Fairview's NT servers to Windows 2000. Linux distributors are working to make the OS more popular with IT departments. Red Hat Inc. recently announced an enterprise edition line of its version of Linux tuned for enterprise applications, beginning with Oracle and SAP enterprise systems.

Even the Chinese government has embraced Linux. The government does not want to depend excessively on one vendor, Microsoft, and pay high prices for its operating system software when it can obtain Linux for free. The fact that Linux is publicly available and open to user modifications provides assurance that any security the government wants to build into its computer systems will not have undetected vulnerabilities. The government expects Linux will be running on half of China's Internet servers and one third of its desktop computers by the end of 2001.

Yet many organizations have not jumped on the Linux bandwagon. Not all business application software can run on Linux and the operating system is used primarily on servers providing Web, e-mail, or printing services, or to run custom applications that require only a simple interface.

To Think About: Should a company select Linux as its operating system for its major business applications? What management, organization, and technology factors would have to be addressed when making that decision?

Sources: Howard Solomon, "Linux Eats Up Bigger Piece of the Enterprise Pie," *Computing Canada,* March 3, 2000; "Fearing Control By Microsoft, China Backs the Linux System," *The New York Times,* July 8, 2000; James Careless, "'Stable as a Rock': Open Source Ready for Business," *Computing Canada,* February 4, 2000.

DOS

An operating system for 16-bit PCs based on the IBM personal computer standard.

Windows

A graphical user interface shell that runs in conjunction with the DOS PC operating system.

Japanese, Korean, Indian, Hebrew, and Arabic fonts for use in Web browser software (see Section 7.3). A new search capability called Sherlock provides a standard interface for efficiently searching for files on the Internet as well as on the user's own hard drive. These capabilities, initially found only in the Mac OS, are now also available in Microsoft Windows later editions.

DOS is a 16-bit operating system that is used rarely today and only with older PCs based on the IBM PC standard. DOS does not support multitasking and limits the size of a program in memory to 640 K. Fortunately, **Windows** and other operating systems have extended the reach of RAM to its current capacity.

7.3 APPLICATION SOFTWARE

Application software is primarily concerned with accomplishing the tasks of end users. Many different programming languages can be used to develop application software. Each has different strengths and drawbacks. Managers should understand how to evaluate and select software tools and programming languages that are appropriate for their organization's objectives.

PROGRAMMING LANGUAGES

The first generation of computer languages consisted of **machine language**, which requires the programmer to write all program instructions in the 0s and 1s of binary code and to specify storage locations for every instruction and item of data used. Programming in machine language was a very slow, labour-intensive process. As computer hardware improved and processing speed and memory size increased, programming languages changed from machine language to languages that have been easier for humans to understand and use. From the mid-1950s to the mid-1970s, higher-level programming languages emerged, allowing programs to be written with regular words using sentence-like statements.

Assembly Language

Assembly language is the next level of programming language up from machine language and is considered a "second generation" language. Like machine language, assembly language (Figure 7-6) is designed for a specific machine and specific microprocessors. Assembly language makes use of certain mnemonics (e.g., load, sum) to represent machine language instructions and storage locations. Although assembly language gives programmers great control and results in very efficient (fast) programs, it is costly in terms of programmer time; it is also difficult to read, debug, and learn. Assembly language is primarily used today in system software.

Third-Generation Languages: FORTRAN, COBOL, BASIC, Pascal, and C

Third-generation languages specify instructions as brief statements that are more like natural languages than assembly language. Although they are less efficient in using computer resources than earlier languages, they are easier to write and understand and have made it possible to create software for business and scientific problems. Important third-generation languages include FORTRAN, COBOL, C, and BASIC.

FORTRAN FORTRAN (FORmula TRANslator) (Figure 7-7) provides an easier way to write scientific and engineering applications. FORTRAN is especially useful in processing numeric data. Many kinds of business applications can be written in FORTRAN, and contemporary versions provide sophisticated structures for controlling program logic. FORTRAN is not very good at providing input/output efficiency or in printing and working with lists.

COBOL COBOL (COmmon Business Oriented Language) (Figure 7-8) came into use in the early 1960s. COBOL was designed for business applications, for processing large data

machine language
A programming language consisting of the 1s and 0s of binary code.

assembly language
A programming language developed in the 1950s that resembles machine language but substitutes mnemonics for numeric codes.

third-generation language
A nonprocedural programming language that specifies instructions as brief statements that are more like natural language than assembly language.

FORTRAN (FORmula TRANslator)
A programming language developed in 1956 for scientific and mathematical applications.

COBOL (COmmon Business Oriented Language)
A major programming language for business applications that can process large data files with alphanumeric characters.

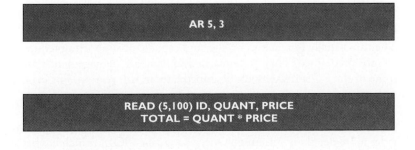

FIGURE 7-6 Assembly language. This sample assembly language command adds the contents of register 3 to register 5 and stores the result in register 5.

FIGURE 7-7 FORTRAN. This sample FORTRAN program code is part of a program to compute sales figures for a particular item.

```
MULTIPLY QUANT-SOLD BY UNIT-PRICE GIVING SALES-TOTAL.
```

files with alphanumeric characters (mixed alphabetic and numeric data), and for performing repetitive tasks such as payroll. COBOL is less efficient at complex mathematical calculations. Also, there are many versions of COBOL, and not all COBOL versions are compatible with each other.

BASIC and Pascal **BASIC** and **Pascal** are used primarily in education to teach programming. BASIC (Beginners All-purpose Symbolic Instruction Code) is easy to use, demonstrates computer capabilities well, and requires only a small interpreter. However, BASIC does few computer processing tasks well even though it does them all; different versions of BASIC exist. With sophisticated structures to control program logic and a simple, powerful set of commands, Pascal is used primarily in computer science courses to teach sound programming practices.

C and C++ **C** is a powerful and efficient language developed at AT&T's Bell Labs in the early 1970s. It combines machine portability with tight control and efficient use of computer resources, and it can work on a variety of different computers and operating systems. It is used primarily by professional programmers to create operating systems and application software, especially software for PCs.

C++ is a newer version of C that is object oriented (see Section 7.4). It has all the capabilities of C plus additional features for working with software objects. C++ is used for developing application software.

FOURTH-GENERATION LANGUAGES AND PC SOFTWARE TOOLS

Fourth-generation languages consist of a variety of software tools that enable end users to develop software applications with minimal or no technical assistance. They enhance professional programmers' productivity. Fourth-generation languages tend to be nonprocedural or less procedural than conventional programming languages. *Procedural languages* require specification of the sequence of steps, or procedures, that tell the computer what to do and how to do it. Nonprocedural languages need only specify what has to be accomplished rather than providing details about how to carry out the task. Thus, a nonprocedural language can accomplish the same task with fewer steps and lines of program code than a procedural language. Some of these *nonprocedural* languages are **natural languages** that enable users to communicate with the computer using conversational commands resembling human speech. Natural language development is one of the concerns of artificial intelligence (see Chapter 15). The developments in natural languages are considered by many to be yet a fifth generation of programming languages.

There are seven categories of fourth-generation languages: query languages, report generators, graphics languages, application generators, very high-level programming languages, application software packages, and PC tools. Figure 7-9 illustrates the spectrum of these tools and some commercially available products in each category.

Query Languages

Query languages are high-level languages for retrieving data stored in databases or files. They are usually interactive, online, and capable of supporting requests for information that are not predefined. They are often tied to database management systems (see Chapter 8) or some of the PC software tools described later in this section. For instance, the query

SELECT ALL WHERE age > 40 AND name = "Wilson"

requests all records where the name is "Wilson" and the age is more than 40. Chapter 8 provides more detail on Structured Query Language (SQL), which has become the de facto standard for query language.

BASIC (Beginners All-purpose Symbolic Instruction Code)

A general-purpose programming language used with PCs and for teaching programming.

Pascal

A programming language used on PCs and used to teach sound programming practices in computer science courses.

C

A powerful programming language with tight control and efficiency of execution; it is portable across different microprocessors and is used primarily with PCs.

C++

An object-oriented version of C used to develop software applications.

fourth-generation language

A nonprocedural programming language that can be employed directly by end users or less-skilled programmers to develop computer applications more rapidly than conventional programming languages.

natural language

Programming language that is very close to human language.

query language

A high-level computer language used to retrieve specific information from databases or files.

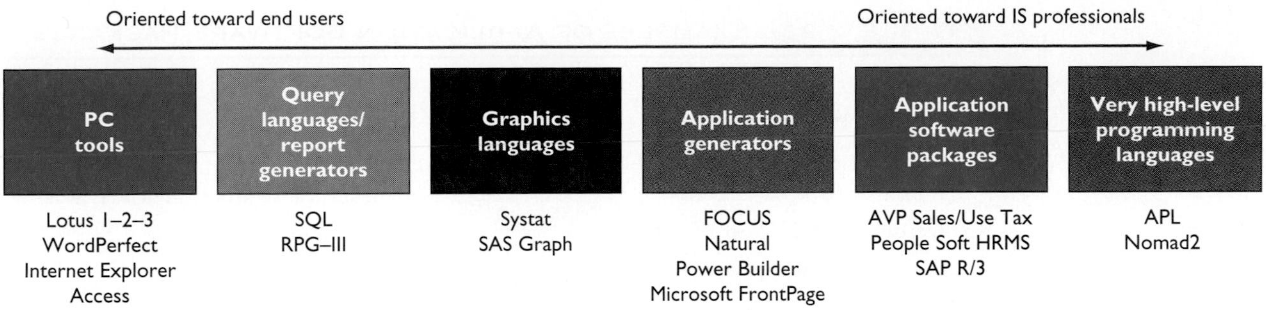

Oriented toward end users   Oriented toward IS professionals

PC tools	Query languages/ report generators	Graphics languages	Application generators	Application software packages	Very high-level programming languages
Lotus 1–2–3 WordPerfect Internet Explorer Access	SQL RPG–III	Systat SAS Graph	FOCUS Natural Power Builder Microsoft FrontPage	AVP Sales/Use Tax People Soft HRMS SAP R/3	APL Nomad2

FIGURE 7-9 Fourth-generation languages. The spectrum of major categories of fourth-generation languages. Commercially available products in each category are illustrated. Tools range from those that are simple and designed primarily for end users to complex tools designed for information systems professionals.

Report Generators

Report generators are software for creating customized reports. They extract data from files or databases and create reports in many formats. Report generators generally provide more control than query languages over the way data are formatted, organized, and displayed. The more powerful report generators can manipulate data with complex calculations and logic before they are output. Some report generators are extensions of database or query languages.

report generator
Software that creates customized reports in a wide range of formats that are not routinely produced by an information system.

Graphics Languages

Graphics languages retrieve data from files or databases and display them in graphic format. Users can ask for data and specify how they are to be charted. Some graphics software can perform arithmetic or logical operations on data as well. SAS and Systat are examples of powerful analytical graphics software.

graphics language
A computer language that displays data from files or databases in graphic format.

Application Generators

Application generators contain pre-programmed modules that can generate entire applications, greatly speeding development. A user can specify what needs to be done, and the application generator will create the appropriate code for input, validation, updating, processing, and reporting. Most full-function application generators consist of a comprehensive, integrated set of development tools: a query language, screen painter, graphics generator, report generator, decision support/modelling tools, security facilities, a high-level programming language, and tools for defining and organizing data. Application generators now include tools for developing full-function Web sites.

application generator
Software that can generate entire information system applications; the user has only to specify what needs to be done, and the application generator creates the appropriate program code.

Very High-Level Programming Languages

Very high-level programming languages are designed to generate program code with fewer instructions than conventional languages such as COBOL or FORTRAN. Programs and applications based on these languages can be developed in much shorter periods of time. End users can employ simple features of these languages. However, these languages are designed primarily as productivity tools for professional programmers. APL, developed by Canadian Ken Iverson, and Nomad2 are examples of these languages.

very high-level programming language
A programming language that uses fewer instructions than conventional languages. Used primarily by professional programmers as a productivity tool.

Application Software Packages

A **software package** is a prewritten, pre-coded, commercially available set of programs that eliminates the need for individuals or organizations to write their own software programs for certain functions. There are software packages for system software, but the vast majority of packaged software is application software.

Application software packages consist of prewritten application software that is marketed commercially. These packages are available for major business applications on mainframes, minicomputers, and PCs. Table 7-2 provides examples of applications for which

software package
A prewritten, pre-coded, commercially available set of programs that eliminates the need to write software programs for certain functions.

TABLE 7-2   Examples of Application Software Packages

Accounts receivable	Library systems
Bond and stock management	Life insurance
Computer-aided design (CAD)	Mailing labels
E-mail	Mathematical/statistical modelling
Electronic commerce storefront	Order processing
Enterprise resource planning (ERP)	Payroll
Graphics	Presentation
Groupware	Process control
Healthcare	Spreadsheet
Hotel management	Tax accounting
Internet telephone	Web browser
Job costing	Word processing

packages are commercially available. Although application packages for large complex systems must be installed by technical specialists, many application packages, especially those for PCs, are marketed directly to end users. Systems development based on application packages is discussed in Chapter 11.

PC Software Tools

Some of the most popular and productivity-promoting software tools are the general-purpose application packages that have been developed for PCs, especially those for word processing, spreadsheet, data management, presentation graphics, integrated software packages, e-mail, Web browsers, and groupware.

word processing software
Software that handles electronic storage, editing, formatting, and printing of documents.

Word Processing Software   **Word processing software** stores text data electronically as a computer file rather than on paper, allowing the user to make changes in the document electronically, eliminating the need to retype an entire page to incorporate corrections. The software has formatting options to make changes in line spacing, margins, character size, and column width. Microsoft Word and Corel WordPerfect are popular word processing packages. Figure 7-10 illustrates a Microsoft Word screen displaying text, spelling and grammar checking, and major menu options.

Most word processing software has advanced features that automate other writing tasks: spelling checkers, style checkers (to analyze grammar and punctuation), thesaurus programs,

FIGURE 7-10 Text and the spell-checking option in Microsoft Word. Word processing software provides many easy-to-use options to create and output a text document to meet a user's specifications.
Source: Courtesy of Microsoft.

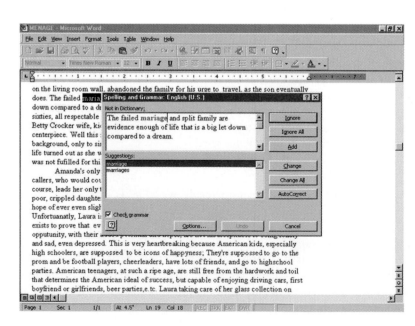

and mail merge programs, which link letters or other text documents with names and addresses in a mailing list. Label creation is another useful word processing function. The newest versions of this software can create, edit, and access Web pages.

While today's word processing programs can turn out very polished-looking documents, businesses that need to create highly professional-looking brochures, manuals, or books will likely use desktop publishing software for this purpose. **Desktop publishing software** provides more control over the placement of text, graphics, and photos in the layout of a page than does word processing software. Users of this software can design the layout, determine spacing between letters, words, and lines, reduce or enlarge graphics, or rearrange blocks of text and graphics, producing finished documents that look like those created by professional print shops. Adobe Pagemaker and MS Publisher are two popular desktop publishing packages.

Spreadsheets   Electronic spreadsheet software provides computerized versions of traditional financial modelling tools such as the accountant's columnar pad, pencil, and calculator. An electronic **spreadsheet** is organized into a grid of columns and rows. The power of the electronic spreadsheet is evident when one changes a value or values because all other related values on the spreadsheet will be automatically recomputed.

Spreadsheets are valuable for applications in which numerous calculations must be related to each other and for applications that require modelling and what-if analysis. A number of alternatives can easily be evaluated by changing one or two pieces of data without having to re-key in the rest of the worksheet. Many spreadsheet packages include graphics functions that can present data in the form of line graphs, bar graphs, or pie charts. The most popular spreadsheet packages are Microsoft Excel and Lotus 1-2-3. Current versions of this software can also read, edit, and write Web-based files. Figure 7-11 illustrates the output from a spreadsheet for a breakeven analysis and its accompanying graph.

Data Management Software   Although spreadsheet programs are powerful tools for manipulating quantitative data, **data management software** is more suitable for creating and manipulating lists and for combining information from different files. PC database

desktop publishing software Software that provides more control over the placement of text, graphics, and photos in the layout of a page than word processing software.

spreadsheet Software displaying data in a grid of columns and rows, with the capability of easily recalculating numerical data.

data management software Software used for creating and manipulating lists, creating files and databases to store data, and combining information for reports.

Total fixed cost	19 000.00				
Variable cost per unit	3.00				
Average sales price	17.00				
Contribution margin	14.00				
Breakeven point	1,357				
		Custom Neckties Pro Forma Income Statement			
Units sold	0.00	679	1 357	2 036	2 714
Revenue	0	11 536	23 071	34 607	46 143
Fixed cost	19 000	19 000	19 000	19 000	19 000
Variable cost	0	2 036	4 071	6 107	8 143
Total cost	19 000	21 036	23 071	25 107	27 143
Profit/Loss	(19 000)	(9 500)	0	9 500	19 000

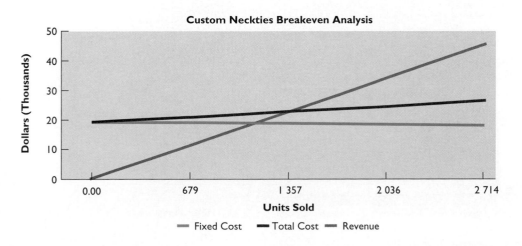

Custom Neckties Breakeven Analysis

— Fixed Cost   — Total Cost   — Revenue

FIGURE 7-11 Spreadsheet software. Spreadsheet software organizes data into columns and rows for analysis and manipulation. Contemporary spreadsheet software provides graphing abilities for clear visual representation of the data in the spreadsheets. This sample breakeven analysis is represented as numbers in a spreadsheet as well as a line graph for easy interpretation.

FIGURE 7-12 Data management software. This screen from Microsoft Access illustrates some of its powerful capabilities for managing and organizing information.

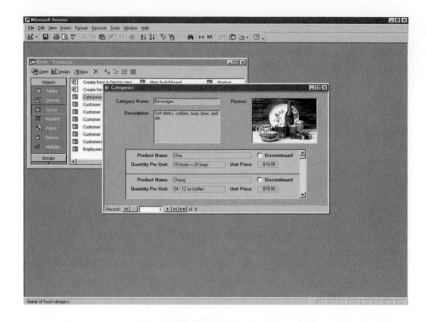

management packages have programming features and easy-to-learn menus that enable non-specialists to build small information systems.

Data management software typically has facilities for creating files and databases and for storing, modifying, and manipulating data for reports and queries. A detailed treatment of data management software and database management systems can be found in Chapter 8. Popular database management software for the personal computer includes Microsoft Access, which can also be used to publish data on the Web. Figure 7-12 shows a screen from Microsoft Access illustrating some of its capabilities.

presentation graphics
Software to create professional-quality graphics presentations that can incorporate charts, sound, animation, photos, and video clips.

Presentation Graphics   **Presentation graphics** software allows users to create professional-quality graphics presentations. This software can convert numeric data into charts and other types of graphics and can include multimedia displays of sound, animation, photos, and video clips, along with text. The leading presentation graphics packages include capabilities for computer-generated slide shows and translating content for the Web. Microsoft PowerPoint (see Figure 7-13), Lotus Freelance Graphics, Adobe Illustrator, and Aldus Persuasion are popular presentation graphics packages.

FIGURE 7-13 Users can create professional-looking electronic presentations incorporating text, diagrams, and other multimedia elements using presentation graphics software. This slide was created with Microsoft PowerPoint.

Integrated Software Packages and Software Suites **Integrated software packages** combine the functions of the most important PC software packages, such as word processing, spreadsheets, presentation graphics, and data management. This integration provides a more general-purpose software tool and eliminates redundant data entry and data maintenance. For example, the breakeven analysis spreadsheet illustrated in Figure 7-11 could be reformatted into a polished report with word processing software without separately keying the data into both programs. Integrated packages are a compromise. Although they can do many things well, they generally do not have the same power and depth as single-purpose packages. MS Works is a popular integrated software package.

Integrated software packages should be distinguished from **software suites**, which are collections of applications software sold as a unit. Microsoft Office is an example of a software suite and contains Word word processing software, Excel spreadsheet software, Access database software, PowerPoint presentation graphics software, and Outlook, a set of tools for e-mail, scheduling, and contact management. Office 2000 contains additional capabilities to support collaborative work on the Web, including online discussions about documents and the ability to automatically notify others about changes to documents. Documents created with Office tools can be viewed with a Web browser and published on a Web server. Software suites have some features of integrated packages, such as the ability to share data among different applications, but they consist of full-featured versions of each type of software.

E-mail Software **Electronic mail (e-mail)** is used for the computer-to-computer exchange of messages and is an important tool for communication and collaborative work. A person can use a networked computer to send notes or lengthier files of varied types to a recipient on the same network or a different network. Many organizations operate their own electronic-mail systems, but communications companies such as Rogers Communications and the provincial telephone companies offer these services, along with commercial online information services such as America Online, Microsoft's Passport/Hotmail, and public networks on the Internet.

Web browsers and PC software suites have included e-mail capabilities, and specialized e-mail software packages such as Eudora are also available for use on the Internet. In addition to providing electronic messaging, most e-mail software packages have capabilities for routing messages to multiple recipients, message forwarding, and attaching text or multimedia files to messages.

Web Browsers **Web browsers** are easy-to-use software tools for displaying Web pages and for accessing the Web and other Internet resources. Web browser software features a point-and-click graphical user interface to access and display information stored on computers at other Internet sites. Browsers can display or present graphics, audio, and video information as well as traditional text, and they allow the user to click on buttons, icons, graphics, or highlighted words to link to related Web sites. Web browsers have become the primary interface for accessing the Internet or for using networked systems based on Internet technology. You can see examples of Web browser software by looking at the illustrations of Web pages in each chapter of this text.

The two leading commercial Web browsers are Microsoft Internet Explorer and Netscape Navigator, which is also available as part of the Netscape Communicator software suite. They include capabilities for using e-mail, file transfer, online discussion groups, and bulletin boards, along with other Internet services. Newer versions of these browsers contain support for Web publishing and workgroup computing. (See the following discussion of groupware.) Other browsers, such as Opera, continue to offer most of the functionality of the Microsoft and Netscape browsers and may take up much less space on the user's PC.

Groupware **Groupware** provides functions and services to support the collaborative activities of work groups. Groupware includes software for information-sharing, electronic meetings, scheduling, and e-mail and is used over a network that connects the members of the group as they work on their own desktop computers, often in widely scattered locations. Table 7-3 describes groupware capabilities.

Groupware enhances collaboration by allowing the electronic exchange of ideas. All messages on a particular topic can be saved in a group, stamped with the date, time, and

---

integrated software package
A software package that provides two or more applications, such as word processing and spreadsheets, providing for easy transfer of data between them, but with limited functionality in each application.

software suite
A software package that combines fully functional applications, such as word processing and spreadsheets.

electronic mail (e-mail)
The computer-to-computer exchange of messages.

Web browser
Easy-to-use software for accessing the World Wide Web and the Internet.

groupware
Software that supports the collaborative activities of work groups.

TABLE 7-3	GROUPWARE CAPABILITIES

Electronic mail distribution

Electronic meetings and conferences

Group writing and commenting

Scheduling meetings and appointments

Shared files and databases

Shared time lines and plans

thread

A series of messages in online discussions on a specified topic that have been posted as replies to each other. Each message in a thread can be read to see how a discussion has evolved.

author. All of these messages can be followed in a thread to see how a discussion has evolved. (A **thread** is a series of messages in an online discussion that have been posted as replies to each other.) Any group member can review the ideas of others at any time and add to them, or individuals can post a document for others to comment on or edit. Members can post requests for help, allowing others to respond. Finally, if a group so chooses, members can store their work notes in a public space so that all others in the group can see what progress is being made, what problems occur, and what activities are planned (see Figure 7-14).

The leading commercial groupware product has been Lotus Notes from Lotus Development Corporation, owned today by IBM. The Internet is rich in capabilities to support collaborative work. Recent versions of Microsoft Internet Explorer and Netscape Communicator include groupware functions, such as e-mail, electronic scheduling and calendaring, audio and data conferencing, electronic meetings, and electronic discussion groups and databases (see Chapters 8 and 10). Microsoft's Office 2000 software suite includes groupware features using Web technology. Powerful Web-based groupware features can also be found in products such as Open Text's Livelink. As of this writing, a new groupware application, called Groove, is being offered. Developed by Ray Ozzie, who developed Lotus Notes, Groove will offer the user the ability to communicate and to share files with others approved by the user in a sort of "community."

SOFTWARE FOR ENTERPRISE INTEGRATION: ENTERPRISE SOFTWARE AND MIDDLEWARE

Chapters 2 and 3 have discussed the growing organizational need to integrate functions and business processes to improve organizational control, coordination, and responsiveness by allowing data and information to flow more freely between different parts of the organization. Poorly integrated applications can create costly inefficiencies or slow customer service

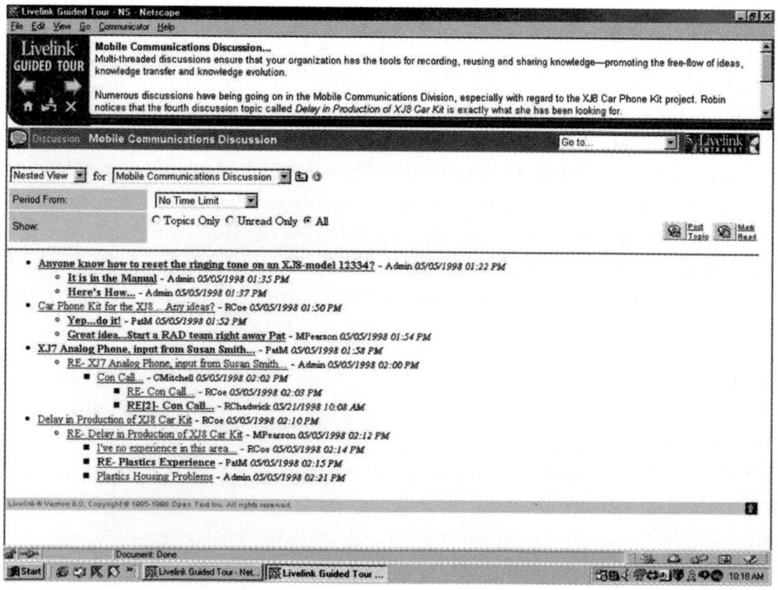

FIGURE 7-14 Groupware facilitates collaboration by enabling members of a group to share documents, schedule meetings, and discuss activities, events, and issues. Illustrated are capabilities for following a threaded discussion.

and become competitive liabilities. Alternative software solutions are available to promote enterprise integration.

Isolated systems that cannot communicate with each other can be replaced with an enterprise software package. Chapter 2 introduced enterprise systems. **Enterprise software,** also called enterprise resource planning or ERP software, consists of a set of interdependent modules for applications such as sales and distribution, financial accounting, investment management, materials management, production planning, plant maintenance, and human resources that allows data to be used by multiple functions and business processes for more precise organizational coordination and control. The modules can communicate with each other directly or by sharing a common repository of data. Contemporary enterprise systems use a client/server computing architecture. Major enterprise software vendors include SAP, Oracle, PeopleSoft, J.D. Edwards, and Baan. Smaller companies such as Great Plains, which was recently purchased by Microsoft, offer ERP applications as well. All now offer Web-based functionality, too. These vendors are now enhancing their products to provide more capabilities for supply chain management, customer relationship management, and exchange of data with other enterprises.

Individual companies can implement all of the enterprise software modules offered by a vendor or select only the modules of interest to them. They can also configure the software they select to match the way they do business. For example, they could configure the software to track revenue by product line, geographical unit, or distribution channel. However, the enterprise software may not be able to support some companies' unique business processes and can require firms to change the way they work. The chapter ending case study and Chapter 13 describe the challenges of implementing enterprise software in greater detail.

Most firms cannot jettison all of their existing systems and create enterprise-wide integration from scratch. Many existing legacy mainframe applications are essential to daily operations and very risky to change, but they can be made more useful if their information and business logic can be integrated with other applications (Noffsinger, Niedbalski, Blanks, and Emmart, 1998). One way to integrate various legacy applications is to use special software called **middleware** to create an interface or bridge between two different systems. Middleware is software that connects two otherwise separate applications, allowing them to communicate with each other and to pass data between them (see Figure 7-15). Middleware may be custom software written in-house or a software package. There are many different types of middleware. Middleware can link client and server machines in client/server computing and can link a Web server to data stored on another computer. This allows users to request data from the computer in which it is stored using forms displayed on a Web browser, and it enables the Web server to return dynamic Web pages based on the information a user has requested.

Instead of custom-writing software to connect one application to another, companies can now purchase **enterprise application integration software** to connect disparate applications or application clusters. Enterprise application integration is the process of tying together multiple applications to support the flow of information across multiple business units and systems. Enterprise application integration software can consist of middleware for passing data between two different systems or business process integration tools that link applications together through business process modelling. The software allows system builders to model their business processes graphically and define the rules that applications should follow to make these processes work. The software then generates the underlying program code to link existing applications to each other to support those processes. Because the enterprise application integration software is largely independent of the individual

enterprise software
A set of integrated modules for applications such as sales and distribution, financial accounting, investment management, materials management, production planning, plant maintenance, and human resources that allows data to be used by multiple functions and business processes.

middleware
Software that connects two disparate applications, allowing them to communicate with each other and to exchange data.

enterprise application integration software
Software that ties together multiple applications to support enterprise integration.

FIGURE 7-15 Middleware. Middleware is software that can be used to pass data and commands between two disparate applications so that they can work together.

applications it connects, the organization can change its business processes and grow without requiring changes to the applications. A few enterprise application integration tools allow multiple businesses to integrate their systems into an extended supply chain.

7.4 CONTEMPORARY TOOLS FOR SOFTWARE DEVELOPMENT

A growing backlog of software projects and the need for businesses to develop systems that are flexible or that can use the Internet have stimulated approaches to software development based on object-oriented and CASE programming tools and newer programming languages such as Java, hypertext markup language (HTML), extensible markup language (XML), and extensible business reporting language, as well as new environments such as Microsoft's .Net.

OBJECT-ORIENTED PROGRAMMING

Traditional software development methods have treated data and procedures as independent components. A separate programming procedure must be written for every separate action on a particular piece of data. The procedures act on data that the program passes to them.

What Makes Object-Oriented Programming Different?

object-oriented programming
An approach to software development that combines data and procedures into objects.

Object-oriented programming combines data and the specific procedures that operate on those data into one object. The object combines data and program code. Instead of passing data to procedures, programs send a message for an object to perform a procedure that is already embedded into it. (Procedures are termed methods in object-oriented languages.) The same message may be sent to many different objects, but each will implement that message differently.

For example, an object-oriented financial application might have Customer objects sending debit and credit messages to Account objects. The Account objects in turn might maintain Cash-on-Hand, Accounts-Payable, and Accounts-Receivable objects.

An object's data are hidden from other parts of the program and can only be manipulated from inside the object. The method for manipulating the object's data can be changed internally without affecting other parts of the program. Programmers can focus on what they want an object to do, and the object decides how to do it.

An object's data are encapsulated from other parts of the system, so each object is an independent software building block that can be used in many different systems without changing the program code. Thus, object-oriented programming is expected to reduce the time and cost of writing software by producing reusable program code or software chips that can be reused in other related systems. Future software development can draw on a library of reusable objects. Productivity gains from object-oriented technology could be magnified if objects are stored in reusable software libraries and explicitly designed for reuse (Fayad and Cline, 1996). However, such benefits will only be realized if organizations develop appropriate standards and procedures for reuse (Kim and Stohr, 1998). Objects that can be assembled into complete systems are becoming commercially available through networks. These network-based software services should lead to further software economies for firms.

Object-oriented programming has spawned a new programming technology known as **visual programming**. With visual programming, programmers do not write code. Rather, they use a mouse to select and arrange programming objects, copying an object from a library into a specific location in a program, or drawing a line to connect two or more objects. Visual Basic is a widely used visual programming tool for creating applications that run under Microsoft Windows. See Figure 7-16 for an example.

visual programming
The construction of software programs by selecting and arranging programming objects rather than by writing program code.

class
The feature of object-oriented programming wherein all objects belonging to a certain class have all of the features of that class.

inheritance
The feature of object-oriented programming in which a specific class of objects receives the features of a more general class.

Object-Oriented Programming Concepts

Object-oriented programming is based on the concepts of **class** and **inheritance**. Program code is not written separately for every object but for classes, or general categories, of similar objects. Objects belonging to a certain class have the features of that class. Classes of objects in turn can inherit all the structure and behaviours of a more general class and then add vari-

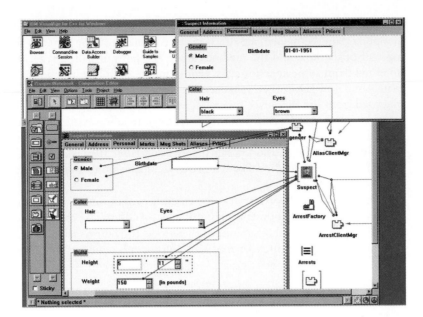

FIGURE 7-16 With visual programming tools such as IBM's Visual Age Generator, working software programs can be created by drawing, pointing, and clicking instead of writing program code.

ables and behaviours unique to each object. New classes of objects are created by choosing an existing class and specifying how the new class differs from the existing class, instead of starting from scratch each time.

Classes are organized hierarchically into superclasses and subclasses. For example, a car class might have a vehicle class for a superclass, so that it would inherit all the methods and data previously defined for vehicle. The design of the car class would only need to describe how cars differ from vehicles. A banking application could define a Savings-Account object that is very much like a Bank-Account object with a few minor differences. The Savings-Account object inherits all the Bank-Account object's state and methods and then adds a few extras.

We can see how class and inheritance work in Figure 7-17, which illustrates a tree of classes concerning employees and how they are paid. Employee is the common ancestor of

FIGURE 7-17 Class, subclasses, and overriding. This figure illustrates how a message's method can come from the class itself or from an ancestor class. Class variables and methods are shaded when they are inherited from above.

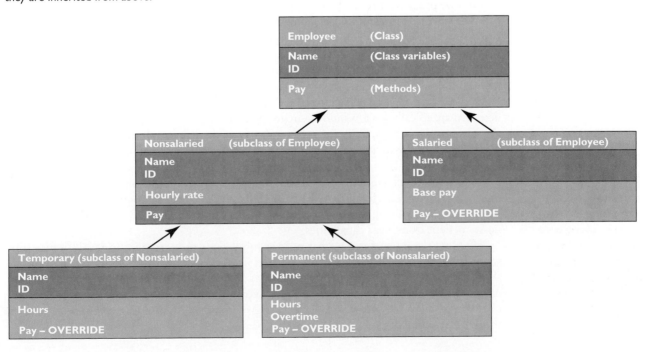

the other four classes. Nonsalaried and Salaried are subclasses of Employee, whereas Temporary and Permanent are subclasses of Nonsalaried. The variables for the class are in the top half of the box, and the methods are in the bottom half. Darker items in each box are inherited from some ancestor class. (For example, by following the tree upward, we can see that Name and ID in the Nonsalaried, Salaried, Temporary, and Permanent subclasses are inherited from the Employee superclass [ancestor class].) Lighter methods, or class variables, are unique to a specific class and they override or redefine existing methods. When a subclass overrides an inherited method, its object still responds to the same message, but it executes its definition of the method rather than its ancestor's. Pay is a method inherited from the superclass, but the method Pay-OVERRIDE is specific to the Temporary, Permanent, and Salaried classes.

Object-oriented software can be custom-programmed, or it can be developed with rapid-application development tools; this may cost 30 to 50 percent less than traditional program development methods. Some of these tools provide visual programming environments in which developers can create ready-to-use program code by "snapping" together pre-built objects. Other tools generate program code that can be compiled to run on a variety of computing platforms.

JAVA

Java
A programming language that can deliver only the software functionality needed for a particular task as a small applet downloaded from a network; can run on any computer and operating system.

Java is a platform-independent object-oriented programming language developed by Canadian James Gosling at Sun Microsystems. Java software is designed to run on any computer or computing device, regardless of the specific microprocessor or operating system it uses. A Macintosh PC, an IBM personal computer running Windows, a DEC computer running UNIX, and even a smart cellular phone or personal digital assistant can use the same Java application.

Java can be used to create miniature programs called "*applets*" designed to reside on centralized network servers. The network delivers only the applets required for a specific function. With Java applets residing on a network, a user downloads only the software functions and data needed to perform a particular task, such as analyzing the revenue from a sales territory. The user does not need to maintain large software programs or data files on a client desktop machine. When the user is finished with processing, the data can be saved through the network. Java can be used with network computers because it enables all processing software and data to be stored on a network server, downloaded via a network as needed, and then placed back on the network server.

Java is a very robust language that can handle text, data, graphics, sound, and video, all within one program if needed. Java applets often are used to provide interactive capabilities for Web pages. For example, Java applets can be used to create animated cartoons or real-time news tickers for a Web site or to permit a Web page to calculate a loan payment schedule online in response to financial data input by the user. (Microsoft's ActiveX sometimes is used as an alternative to Java for creating interactivity on a Web page. **ActiveX** is a set of controls that enables programs or other objects such as charts, tables, or animations to be embedded within a Web page. However, ActiveX lacks Java's machine independence and was designed specifically for a Windows environment.)

ActiveX
A set of controls for the Windows software environment that enables programs or other objects such as charts, tables, or animations to be embedded within a Web page; available only for the Windows platform.

virtual machine
Software that acts as an interface between Java binary code and the hardware platform that actually performs the program's instructions. Once a Java virtual machine has been provided for a platform, any Java program can run on that platform.

Companies are starting to develop more extensive Java applications running over the Internet or over their private networks because these applications can potentially run in Windows, UNIX, IBM mainframe, Macintosh, and other environments without having to be rewritten for each computing platform. Sun Microsystems terms this phenomenon "write once, run anywhere." Java can let PC users manipulate data on networked systems using Web browsers, reducing the need to write specialized software. Table 7-4 describes how businesses benefit from Java's capabilities.

Despite these benefits, Java has not yet fulfilled its early promise to revolutionize software development and use. Programs written in current versions of Java tend to run more slowly than "native" programs. Vendors such as Microsoft are supporting alternative versions of Java that include subtle differences in their **virtual machines** that affect Java's performance in different pieces of hardware and operating systems. Without a standard version of Java, true platform independence will not be achieved.

TABLE 7-4	HOW BUSINESSES ARE USING JAVA
Organization	**Java Application**
Jones Soda Juice Company (myjones.com)	Uses Java for the back end of the Web site and database that enables customers to order cases of sodas and juices with their own photograph on the label.
HomeTrust Company of Toronto	Uses Java to run its back office integration with an Oracle database to link its Web site so that all clients can access stock, investment, and rate information over their wireless devices.
Home Depot	Uses Java to write new applications such as one that automatically sends an application for employment to all of its 840 stores. Java also permits Home Depot to easily roll out software to more than 50 000 computing devices throughout the company.
Ford Motor Company of Canada	Uses Java applets on its Web site to help visitors select vehicles they might want to purchase.

HYPERTEXT MARKUP LANGUAGE (HTML) AND XML

HTML

Hypertext markup language (HTML) is a page description language for creating hypertext or hypermedia documents such as Web pages. (See the discussions of hypermedia in Chapter 8 and of Web pages in Chapter 10.) HTML uses instructions called tags (see Figure 7-18) to specify how text, graphics, video, and sound are placed in a document and to create dynamic links to other documents and objects stored in the same or remote computers. Using these links, a user need only point and click on a highlighted key word or graphic; another Web file is found and automatically loaded.

HTML programs can be custom-written, but they also can be created by using the HTML authoring capabilities of Web browsers or popular word processing, spreadsheet, data management, and presentation graphics software packages. HTML editors such as Claris Home Page, Adobe PageMill, Microsoft Front Page, and Macromedia Dreamweaver are more powerful HTML authoring tool programs for creating Web pages.

An extension to HTML called Dynamic HTML enables Web pages to react to user input without having to send additional requests to the Web server. Web pages using Dynamic HTML appear less static and more like interactive applications.

HTML (HyperText Markup Language)
A page description language for creating Web pages and other hypermedia documents.

XML

XML, which stands for eXtensible Markup Language, is a new specification originally designed to improve the usefulness of Web documents. It is actually a further development of HTML. While HTML only determines how text and images should be displayed on a Web document, XML describes what the data in these documents mean. XML makes the information in documents usable in computer programs. Any piece of information on a document or Web page can be given an XML tag to describe what the data mean. In XML, a number is not just a number; the XML tag specifies whether the number represents a price, a date, or a postal code.

For example, an HTML tag to highlight the price of a sweater in bold on a Web page would be $49. The number has no context. But an XML tag could designate that $49 is a price by labelling it with a tag such as <price>$49<price>. XML can also describe the meaning of non-numerical data, such as the sweater's colour or style. Figure 7-18 illustrates the differences between HTML and XML.

By tagging selected elements of the content of documents for their meanings, XML makes it possible for computers to automatically manipulate and interpret data and perform operations on the data without human intervention. The XML tags and standardized procedures for interpreting them can accompany the information wherever it goes. Web browsers and computer programs such as order processing or ERP software can follow programmed rules for applying and displaying the data.

XML (eXtensible Markup Language)
General-purpose language that describes the structure of a document and supports links to multiple documents, allowing data to be manipulated by the computer. XML tags describe what the data mean, not just how they are represented on a Web page and may be used in both Web and non-Web applications.

FIGURE 7-18 Comparing HTML with XML. HTML is used to display a Web page and tells where words should be placed and which words should be bold or italic. XML describes what the words means.

Source: "Putting It All in Context," from *Computerworld*, November 23, 1999. Copyright © 1999 COMPUTER-WORLD Inc. Reprinted with permission of *Computerworld Magazine*.

Plain English	HTML	XML
Sport utility vehicle	\<Title\> Automobile\</Title\>	\<AUTOMOBILE TYPE="Sport utility vehicle"\>
ABC Gremlin 300X SUV	\<Body\>	
	\<UL\>	
	\<LI\> Sport utility vehicle	
	\<LI\>ABC Gremlin 300X SUV	\<MANUFACTURER\>ABC\</MANUFACTURER\>
		\<LINE\>Gremlin\</LINE\>
		\<MODEL\>300X SUV\</MODEL\>
4 passenger	\<LI\>4 passenger	\<PASSENGER UNIT="PASS"\>4\</PASSENGER\>
200 K*hr maximum speed	\<LI\>200 K*hr maximum speed	\<SPEED UNIT="K*hr"\>200\</SPEED\>
$27 000	\<LI\>$27 000	\<PRICE CURRENCY="CDN"\>27 000\</PRICE\>
	\</UL\>\</Body\>	

XBRL (eXtensible Business Reporting Language)
A reporting language designed to make it easier to prepare financial statements and reports in a consistent format.

XHTML (Extensible Hypertext Markup Language)
A hybrid language between HTML and XML that provides more flexibility than HTML and the ability to create Web pages that can be read by many different computing platforms and display devices.

.Net
A business strategy from Microsoft that is aimed at the convergence of personal computing with the Web.

For example, documents or Web pages describing the price of the sweater could be easily accessed by buyers searching for a sweater that cost $49 or less. Data on Web pages describing new automobiles being offered for sale such as the brand, price, number of doors, colour, and engine power could be tagged so that someone could use the data to purchase a new car and have the data located automatically by a computer program to process the order. The Window on Technology describes how some businesses are benefiting from using XML.

XML is already becoming a serious technology for Web-based applications and could open the way for a whole new class of Internet software and services. The key to XML is the setting of standards (or vocabulary) that enable both sending and receiving parties to describe data the same way. The impact of XML will be felt more strongly over time as more and more industries develop their own widely accepted standards. Each standard is contained in an XML Document Type Definition (DTD), usually simply called a dictionary. For example, RosettaNet is an XML dictionary developed by 34 leading companies within the PC industry. It defines all the properties of a personal computer, such as modems, monitors, and cache memory. As a result, the PC industry is now able to speak the same language. The entire supply chain of the industry can now easily be linked. XML is supported by the latest versions of Web browsers.

The impact of XML extends far beyond the Web, facilitating companies' access to their own legacy data. Companies are now able to integrate legacy data quickly and cheaply into newer programs merely by assigning each piece of data an XML tag. XML has strategic impacts as well. Companies can now give their suppliers and customers access to their own data without high application development costs, thus better integrating their operations.

XBRL (eXtensible Business Reporting Language), an extension of XML, is a reporting language designed to make the preparation of financial statements and reports in a consistent format easier. Financial statements must frequently be duplicated separately—and altered—for different uses (a Web publication and printed document, for example), and the extraction of data can be very time-consuming. XBRL will automate these processes. In the future, XBRL is intended, among other things, to provide a standardized framework and integrated methodology for the preparation and publication of reports, as well as a consistent, automated process for the reliable extraction and exchange of financial statements.

XHTML (Extensible Hypertext Markup Language) is a hybrid between HTML and XML that has been recommended as a replacement for HTML by the World Wide Web Consortium (which works with business and government to create Web standards.) XHTML reformulates HTML with XML document-type definitions, giving it additional flexibility and the ability to create Web pages that can be read by many different computing platforms and display devices.

.Net

.Net (pronounced dot-Net) is a business strategy from Microsoft that is aimed at the convergence of personal computing with the Web. The goal is to provide individual and business

BUILDING BUSINESS WEBS WITH XML

In the fast-paced world of electronic commerce and electronic business, companies can benefit by being able to respond to customers quickly with their partners and suppliers. XML provides a new tool to accomplish this because it helps disparate applications identify and use a variety of information from otherwise incompatible sources.

Toronto-based Celestica is the world's third-largest electronics manufacturing services company. Celestica needed to provide coordination and integration of business processes and systems among its growing number of global facilities and to extend the benefits of internal process automation to key customers, reinforcing the customers' supply chain management initiatives. "We had 34 locations worldwide that needed to work together as if they were one," says Bernie Ulrich, Director of Global SCM E-Business for Celestica, "and we needed to provide a single point of contact with our customers. When a customer asks if we can build a product, they're not concerned with the internal processes we go through in order to respond. What they want, right away, is a yes or no answer, and a hard delivery date."

Celestica found the solution by combining IBM's MQSeries and MQSeries Integrator to facilitate internal process integration with IBM's Extricity B2B software platform to facilitate integration with their customers over the Internet. The MQSeries Integrator V2 is used to route messages between applications and transform internal application formats to XML. The Extricity software then transforms the XML data into different XML standard messages, allowing both internal and external parties to continue to use their standard message formats. Like many other companies, Celestica is using the RosettaNet standard, an XML-based messaging system with electronic data interchange commands.

Other Canadian organizations making extensive use of XML for their e-commerce applications include the Royal Bank of Canada, the Bank of Montreal, the Ontario Teachers' Pension Plan Board, and most of the other financial institutions headquartered in North America. In addition, Canadian companies, such as Xenos Group of Toronto and Open Text of Waterloo are paving the way for XML applications that can be bought or leased by companies for use in their Web applications.

Yet for all of its benefits, XML may not yet work for some companies. XML standards have not yet been developed for some industries. Use of XML can be affected by other features of a firm's information technology infrastructure. Siemens AG, the German computer and telecommunications company, decided against using XML for a global knowledge network to link its 6900 salespeople around the world even though it was the technology of choice. Network transmission capacity in many of the 160 countries where Siemens has offices is so low that application processing performance and reliability were negatively impacted by the extra time required to encode and decode XML messages. Siemens had to build the system with another software tool.

To Think About: How does XML support electronic commerce and electronic business? What management, organization, and technology issues need to be addressed when adopting XML for enterprise and inter-enterprise communication?

Sources: Stuart J. Johnston, "XML Drives Development," *The Industry Standard,* July 17, 2000; "Bills, Bills, Bills," *Canadian Business,* December 31, 1999; Dean Mackie, "Case Study: Automating Business Rules at a Public Sector Financial Institution," www.mum.edu/cs_dept/aarsanjani/oopsla2000, accessed April 3, 2001; Matthew Friedman, "RosettaNet solidifies supply chain links," *Computing Canada,* July 2, 1999; "Royal Bank of Canada Puts Customers at Heart of Its Workflow," www2.software.ibm.com/casestudies, accessed April 3, 2001; "Celestica Integrates Key Customers Using Extricity B2B and MQSeries," www2.software.ibm.com/casestudies, accessed April 3, 2001.

users with a seamlessly interoperable and Web-enabled interface for applications and computing devices and to make computing activities increasingly Web browser-oriented. According to Microsoft chairman Bill Gates, .Net is an open standard platform for building, deploying, operating, and integrating XML Web services. Many of the details for .Net are not yet fully worked out; however, the .Net platform will include servers, building block services such as Web-based data storage, and device software.

7.5 MANAGING SOFTWARE ASSETS

Software costs are one of the largest information technology expenditures in most firms— amounting to more than double the expenditures for hardware—and thus software represents another major technology asset. At many points in their careers, managers will be required to make important decisions concerning the selection, purchase, and utilization of their organization's software. Here are some important software management issues.

RENT OR BUILD DECISIONS: USING APPLICATION SERVICE PROVIDERS

Technology expenditures will increasingly focus on ways to use software to cut down on "people" costs as opposed to hardware costs by increasing the ease with which users can interact with hardware and software. More organizations are using software packages, fourth-generation languages, and object-oriented tools because they lower "people" costs by reducing the need for custom-crafted software written by skilled computer programmers. Leasing software and software services from other companies can lower some of these "people" costs even more.

Application Service Providers (ASPs)

application service provider (ASP)

A company providing software (and sometimes hardware) that can be rented by other companies over the Web or over a private network.

Chapter 6 described hardware capabilities for providing data and software programs to desktop computers and over networks. It is clear that software will be increasingly delivered and used over networks. Online application service providers (ASPs) are springing up to provide these software services over the Web and over private networks. An **application service provider (ASP)** is a business that delivers and manages applications and computer services from remote computer centres to multiple users via the Internet or a private network. Instead of buying and installing software programs, subscribing companies can rent the same functions from these services. Users pay for the use of this software either on a subscription or a per transaction basis. For example, companies can pay $5 per month per user (plus a one-time startup fee of $7500) to rent travel and entertainment (T&E) expense reporting software from ExpensAble.com instead of buying and installing T&E programs on their own computers. The ASP creates a single solution that can be rented, replacing all or part of a customer's information technology (IT) infrastructure. The ASP's solution combines packaged software applications and all of the related hardware, system software, network, and other infrastructure services that the customer would have to purchase, integrate, and manage on its own. The ASP customer interacts with a single entity instead of an array of technologies and service vendors.

The "timesharing" services of the 1970s that ran applications such as payroll on their computers for other companies were an earlier version of this application hosting. But today's ASPs run a wider array of applications than these earlier services and deliver many of these software services over the Web. With these Web-based services, servers belonging to the ASP perform the bulk of the processing; the only essential program needed by users is their Web browser. Table 7-5 lists examples of ASPs. Large and medium-sized businesses are using these services for enterprise systems, sales force automation, and financial management while smaller businesses are using them for functions such as invoicing, tax calculations, electronic calendars, and accounting. FutureLink, described in the chapter-opening vignette, is an ASP providing a variety of software to its clients.

Companies are turning to this "software utility" model as an alternative to developing their own software. Some companies will find it much easier to "rent" software from another firm and avoid the expense and difficulty of installing, operating, and maintaining complex systems, such as enterprise resource planning (ERP). The ASP contracts guarantee a level of service and support to make sure that the software is available and working at all times. For example, Telecomputing ASA charges $500 per seat per month for a three-to-five year contract that includes a guarantee of a 99.7 percent service level. Today's Internet-driven business environment is changing so rapidly that getting a system up and running in three months instead of six could make the difference between success and failure. Application service providers also enable small- and medium-sized companies to use applications that they otherwise could not afford.

Companies considering the ASP software utility model need to assess application service provider costs and benefits carefully, weighing all management, organizational, and technology issues. In some cases, the cost of renting software can add up to more than purchasing and maintaining the application in-house. Yet there may be benefits to paying more for software through an ASP if this decision allows the company to focus on core business issues instead of technology challenges.

TABLE 7-5	EXAMPLES OF APPLICATION SERVICE PROVIDERS	
Application Service Provider	**Service**	**Customer Access**
FutureLink	Provides all server and internetworking hardware, restore and backup services, network-based anti-virus software, a full range of help desk solutions, 24/7 network monitoring to ensure security and smooth performance of servers, personal and public file storage, various options of integrated e-mail, and a wide variety of industry applications.	Web, Private networks
IBM Canada	Provides a variety of applications from their strategic partners, such as Great Plains (financial and business management), SalesLogix (sales force automation/customer relationship management), Ultimate Software (human resource management/payroll), or J.D. Edwards (enterprise resource planning).	Web, Private networks
AT&T Canada (MarketPlace)	Eprocurement service connects buyers and suppliers through a centrally managed, secure, application.	Web
Telecomputing ASA (Norway)	Offers a complete suite of desktop applications such as Microsoft Office, e-mail, and Web access. Also provides enterprise system, e-commerce, and custom applications.	Private networks
Salesforce.com	Provides software on the Web to help sales representatives track leads, manage contacts, create reports, and measure their performance against other sales reps in the company.	Web

SOFTWARE MAINTENANCE

After software has been created for the organization, it usually has to be modified over time to incorporate new information requirements. Because of the way software is currently designed, this maintenance process is very costly, time-consuming, and challenging to manage. In most information systems departments, more than 50 percent of staff time is spent maintaining the software for existing systems. Chapter 12 provides more detail on this topic.

At the end of the last millennium, an unusually large maintenance problem called the Year 2000 Problem emerged. The **Year 2000 Problem**, sometimes referred to as the Millennium Bug or the Y2K Bug, was the inability of software programs to handle any dates other than those of the twentieth century—years that begin with "19." Many older computer programs (and even some recent PC programs) stored dates as six digits, two digits each for the day, month, and year (MM-DD-YY or DD-MM-YY) to save computer storage

Year 2000 (Y2K) Problem
An inability of software programs to handle dates other than those of the twentieth century that begin with "19" because the software represents years by only two digits. Presented a massive maintenance problem for most organizations.

<h1 style="text-align:center">MANAGEMENT DECISION PROBLEM</h1>

EVALUATING AN APPLICATION SERVICE PROVIDER
Your company has grown from 40 to 200 employees in the past two years. All of your human resources record keeping, such as processing hired and terminated employees, documenting promotions, and enrolling employees in medical and dental insurance plans used to be performed manually, but your two-person Human Resources Department is swamped with paperwork. You are looking at two options to automate these functions. One is to purchase a client/server human resources package to run on the company's midrange computer. The other is to use an application service provider that delivers human resources software over the Web. The company's Human Resources Department has PCs with Web browser software and Internet access. Your information systems staff consists of two IS professionals.

The Human Resources software package that best fits your needs costs $13 500 to purchase. One information systems specialist with an annual salary of $50 000 would have to spend four hours per forty-hour workweek supporting the program and applying upgrades as they became available. Upgrades cost $1500 each, and the vendor provides one upgrade every year after the first year the package is purchased.

The application services provider you have identified charges $2500 to set up the system initially and $7.50 per month for each employee in the firm. You do not need to purchase any additional hardware to run the system, and the vendor is responsible for supporting the system, including upgrades.

1. What are the costs of each option in the first year?

2. Which option is less expensive over a three-year period?

3. Which option would you select? Why? What factors would you use in making a decision? What are the risks of each approach?

4. What management and organizational challenges will you have in implementing your choice?

space. With dates represented this way, computers could interpret the year following 1999 as 1900 rather than 2000, creating errors in any software that was time-sensitive. To solve the problem before 2000 arrived, organizations combed through their programs to locate all coding in which dates were used. It is estimated that organizations spent from $600 billion to $900 billion worldwide to fix this problem.

SELECTING SOFTWARE FOR THE ORGANIZATION

Although managers need not become programmers, they should be able to use clear criteria in selecting application and system software for the organization. The most important criteria are discussed below.

Appropriateness

Some languages are general-purpose languages that can be used on a variety of problems while others are special-purpose languages suitable only for limited tasks. COBOL is excellent for business data processing but not suited for rigorous mathematical calculations. Language selection involves identifying the organizational use for the software and the users. Application software should also be easy to maintain and change and should be flexible enough so that it can grow with the organization. These organizational considerations have direct, long-term cost implications.

Efficiency

Although less important than in the past, the efficiency with which a language compiles and executes remains a consideration when purchasing software. Some programming languages are more efficient in the use of machine time than others and there are instances where these considerations outweigh personnel costs. Languages with slow compilers or interpreters like BASIC or Java or fourth-generation languages may prove too slow and expensive in terms of machine time for systems that must handle many thousands of transactions per second.

Compatibility

Application software must be able to run on the firm's hardware and operating system platform. Likewise, the firm's operating system software must be compatible with other software required by the firm's mainstream business applications. Mission-critical applications typically have large volumes of transactions to process and require stable, fast operating systems that can handle large complex software programs and massive files.

Support

In order to be effective, a programming language must be easy for the firm's programming staff to learn, and the staff should have sufficient knowledge so that they can provide ongoing support for all of the systems based on that software. It is also important to purchase packaged software that has widespread use in other organizations and is supported by many consulting firms and services. Another kind of support is the availability of software editing, debugging, and development tools.

APPLICATION EXERCISE

WEB PAGE DEVELOPMENT TOOL EXERCISE: DEVELOPING A WEB PAGE

Tony and Ann Jilnek, good friends of yours, own and operate a local jewellery store. On several occasions, Tony has mentioned that he would like to build a Web page for their store, but he does not know where to begin. You recall that Netscape Navigator and Microsoft Internet Explorer have online page wizards to help people like Tony get started with Web page development. The Page Wizard is a great tool for beginners since it enables them to build simple Web pages very quickly.

You decide to help Tony and begin by accessing either Netscape's Composer or Internet Explorer's Front Page Editor. Use the information provided below to build the Jilneks' Jewellery Store Web page.

a. The page title is "Jilneks' Jewellery."

b. The introduction should read: "Jilneks' Jewellery is located in Saskatoon, Saskatchewan. Jilneks' is family owned, and has been in operation since the 1950s."

c. Two hot links are: The Canadian Jewellers Association (http://cja.polygon.net/aboutcja.html) and the Canadian Jewellers Association's Code of Ethics (http://www.intergemlabs.com/cjacoe.htm).

d. The concluding paragraph should read: "Jilneks' Jewellery is open 6 days a week, Monday through Saturday from 7 a.m. to 7 p.m."

e. Use your current e-mail address as the e-mail link for Jilneks' Jewellery.

f. Choose a preset colour combination, or select your own colour combination.

g. From the styles provided, choose an appropriate bullet style and an appropriate horizontal rule style.

h. Build your Web page. Your instructor will provide you with instructions on how to save and print your Web page.

i. After examining the initial Web page, you realize that graphics would enhance the Web page. Using a browser of your choice, locate and download a picture of a diamond ring. Also, try to locate a picture of an antique watch or grandfather clock. Save these images to a disk, preferably to the same location where the Jilneks' Web page is currently stored.

j. Using the help feature of the Web page editor of your choice, research how to insert and delete images on a Web page.

k. Modify the Jilneks' Jewellery Web page to include the graphics that you downloaded. Insert the images where you think appropriate. Save and print this final version of the Jilneks' Jewellery Web page.

MANAGEMENT WRAP-UP

Managers should know how to select and manage the organization's software in the firm's information technology (IT) infrastructure. They should understand the advantages and disadvantages of building and owning these assets or of renting them from outside services. Managers should also be aware of the strengths and weaknesses of software tools, the tasks for which they are best suited, and whether these tools fit into the firm's long-term strategy and information technology (IT) infrastructure. Tradeoffs between efficiency, ease of use, and flexibility should be carefully analyzed. These organizational considerations have long-term cost implications.

Software can either enhance or impede organizational performance, depending on the software tools and services selected and how they are used. Organizational needs should drive software selection. Software tools selected should be easy for the firm's IS staff to learn and maintain and should be flexible enough so that they can grow with the organization. Software for non-IS specialists should have easy-to-use interfaces and be compatible with the firm's other software tools. Software services provided by outside vendors should fit into organizational computing plans.

A range of system and application software technologies is available to organizations. Key technology decisions include the appropriateness of the software tool for the problem to be addressed, compatibility with the firm's hardware and other components of information technology (IT) infrastructure, the efficiency of the software for performing specific tasks, vendor support of software packages and software services, and capabilities for debugging, documentation, and reuse.

SUMMARY

1. *Describe the major types of software.* The major types of software are system software and application software. Each serves a different purpose. System software manages the computer resources and mediates between application software and computer hardware. Application software is used by application programmers and some end users to develop specific applications. Application software works through system software, which controls access to computer hardware.

2. *Examine the functions of system software and compare leading PC operating systems.* System software coordinates the various parts of the computer system and mediates between application software and computer hardware. The system software that manages and controls the activities of the computer is called the operating system. Other system software includes computer-language translation programs that convert programming languages into machine language and utility programs that perform common processing tasks.

The operating system acts as the chief manager of the information system, allocating, assigning, and scheduling system resources and monitoring the use of the computer. Multiprogramming, multitasking, virtual storage, timesharing, and multiprocessing enable system resources to be used more efficiently so that the computer can attack many problems at the same time.

Multiprogramming (multitasking in PC environments) allows multiple programs to use the computer's resources concurrently. Virtual storage splits up programs into small portions so that main memory can be used more efficiently. Timesharing enables many users to share computer resources simultaneously by allocating each user a tiny slice of computing time. Multiprocessing is the use of two or more CPUs linked together working in tandem to perform a task. In order to be executed by the computer, a software program must be translated into machine language via special language-translation software—a compiler, an assembler, or an interpreter.

PC operating systems have developed sophisticated capabilities such as multitasking and support for multiple users on networks. Leading PC operating systems include Windows 98 and Windows ME, Windows CE, Windows 2000, OS/2, UNIX, Linux, Mac OS, and DOS. PC operating systems with graphical user interfaces have gained popularity over command-driven operating systems.

3. *Analyze the strengths and limitations of the major application programming languages and software tools.* The general trend in software is toward user-friendly, high-level languages that both increase professional programmer productivity and make it possible for amateurs to use information systems. There have been four generations of software development: (1) machine language; (2) symbolic languages such as assembly language; (3) high-level languages such as FORTRAN and COBOL; and (4) fourth-generation languages, which are less procedural and closer to natural language than earlier generations of software.

Conventional programming languages include assembly language, FORTRAN, COBOL, C, BASIC, and Pascal. These programming languages make more efficient use of computer resources than fourth-generation languages, and each is designed to solve specific types of problems.

Fourth-generation languages include query languages, report generators, graphics languages, application generators, very high-level programming languages, application software packages, and PC software tools. They are less procedural than conventional programming languages and enable end users to perform many software tasks that previously required technical specialists. Popular PC software tools include word processing, spreadsheet, data management, presentation graphics, and e-mail software along with Web browsers and groupware. Enterprise software, middleware, and enterprise application integration software are all software tools for promoting enterprise-wide application integration.

4. *Describe contemporary approaches to software development.* Object-oriented programming combines data and procedures into one object, which can act as an independent software building block. Each object can be used in many different systems without changing its program code.

Java is an object-oriented programming language designed to operate on the Internet. It can deliver the software functionality needed for a particular task as a small applet that is downloaded from a network or the Web. Java can run on any computer and operating system. HTML is a page description language for creating Web pages. XML is a language for creating structured documents in which data are tagged for definitions. The tagged data in XML documents can be manipulated and used by other computer systems. XHTML is a hybrid of HTML and XML.

5. *Identify important issues in the management of organizational software assets.* Software represents a major organizational asset that should be carefully managed. Managers need to balance the costs and benefits of developing software in-house versus renting the software from an application service provider. Software maintenance can account for over 50 percent of information system costs. Criteria such as efficiency, compatibility with the organization's technology platform, support, and whether the software language or tool is appropriate for the problems and tasks of the organization should govern software selection.

KEY TERMS

.Net, 248

ActiveX, 246

Application generator, 237

Application service provider (ASP), 250

Application software, 227

Assembler, 230

Assembly language, 235

BASIC (Beginners All-purpose Symbolic Instruction Code), 236

C, 236

C++, 236

Class, 244

COBOL (COmmon Business Oriented Language), 235

Compiler, 230

Data management software, 239

Desktop publishing software, 239

DOS, 234

Electronic mail (e-mail), 241

Enterprise application integration software, 243

Enterprise software, 243

FORTRAN (FORmula TRANslator), 235

Fourth-generation language, 236

Graphical user interface (GUI), 231

Graphics language, 237

Groupware, 241

HTML (HyperText Markup Language), 247

Inheritance, 244

Integrated software package, 241

Interpreter, 230

Java, 246

Linux, 233

Mac OS, 233

Machine language, 235

Middleware, 243

Multiprocessing, 230

Multiprogramming, 228

Multitasking, 229

Multithreading, 229

Natural language, 236

Object code, 230

Object-oriented programming, 244

Open-source software, 233

Operating system, 228

OS/2, 233

Pascal, 236

Page, 230

Palm OS, 233

Presentation graphics, 240

Program, 227

Query language, 236

Report generator, 237

Segment, 230

Software, 227

Software package, 237

Software suite, 241

Source code, 230

Spreadsheet, 239

System software, 227

Third-generation language, 235

Thread, 242

Timesharing, 230

UNIX, 233

User interface, 231

Utility program, 231

Very high level programming language, 237

Virtual machine, 246

Virtual memory, 229

Visual programming, 244

Web browser, 241

Windows, 234

Windows CE, 233

Windows 95, 232

Windows 98, 231

Windows Millennium Edition (ME), 232

Windows 2000, 232

Windows XP, 233

Word processing software, 238

XBRL (eXtensible Business Reporting Language), 248

XML (eXtensible Markup Language), 247

XHTML (eXtensible HyperText Markup Language), 248

Year 2000 Problem (Y2K), 251

REVIEW QUESTIONS

1. What are the major types of software? How do they differ in terms of users and uses?

2. What is the operating system of a computer? What does it do?

3. Describe multiprogramming, virtual storage, timesharing, and multiprocessing. Why are they important for the operation of an information system?

4. What is the difference between an assembler, a compiler, and an interpreter?

5. Define and describe graphical user interfaces.

6. Compare the major PC operating systems.

7. Name three high-level programming languages. Describe their strengths and weaknesses.

8. Define fourth-generation languages and list the seven categories of fourth-generation tools.

9. What is the difference between fourth-generation languages and conventional programming languages?

10. What is the difference between an application generator and an application software package? between a report generator and a query language?

11. Name and describe the most important PC software tools.

12. What is object-oriented programming? How does it differ from conventional software development?

13. What is Java? Why are firms building applications using this language?

14. What are HTML, XML, and XHTML? Compare their capabilities. Why are they important?

15. Name and describe three issues in managing software assets.

16. Why are organizations using application service providers? What benefits do they provide?

17. What criteria should be used when selecting software for the organization?

Group Project

How do you know what good Web page design is? In groups of four students, use Internet search engines to explore this issue. Each group should find three or four references on the Web that list criteria for good Web design. From these references, each group should establish their own set of five or more criteria for good Web design. Then each group should access four Web sites of their own choice and evaluate the sites based on the criteria they have established. Each group should report to the class on their best and worst designed sites.

Internet Connection

■ Companion Website

At www.pearsoned.ca/laudon, you'll find an online study guide with two quizzes to test your knowledge of the capabilities of various types of computer software. You'll also find updates to the chapter and online exercises and cases that enable you to apply your knowledge to realistic situations.

■ Additional Sites of Interest

There are many interesting Web sites to enhance your learning about software. You can search the Web yourself, or just try the following sites to add to what you have already learned.

Microsoft Canada

www.microsoft.ca

The Canadian arm of the largest software publisher in the world

IBM Canada

www.ibm.ca

The Canadian arm of the largest mainframe software publisher in the world

Red Hat Corporation

www.redhat.com

Offers software and support for the Linux open source operating system

Corel Corporation

www.corel.com

A Canadian software company offering graphics and desktop software

Netscape Corporation

www.netscape.com

Corporation offering Web browser software, Internet portal, and Web site development services

Textuality

www.textuality.com

Personal site of Tim Bray, one of the co-authors of XML and a member of the Board of the World Wide Web Consortium; provides an interesting explanation of XML

Electronic Commerce Knowledge Base

http://www.magal.com/courses/eckb/tools/HTML/html.html

Everything you ever wanted to know about HTML

Case Study   *SMED International: Meeting the Deadline*

It all started with Kai Smed. He brought his family and his European traditions of excellence in woodworking to Canada in 1952. He worked as a cabinet-maker at KP Manufacturing before buying the company in 1965. His sons carried on his vision and craftsmanship by making modular office systems, blending flexible design and client-defined details with the ability to respond to technological advancements.

SMED Manufacturing was founded in 1982. Mogens Smed took the company public in 1996, creating SMED International. The senior management of SMED International comes from construction and woodworking, turning the emphasis of SMED to interior construction, now known as Constructive Solutions™. In 2000, SMED was bought by Haworth Inc., making it part of the second largest office interiors company in the world.

Today Calgary-based SMED International custom builds modular office furniture and wall systems. It posts sales of $200 million-plus a year and employs 2300 people in showrooms and sales offices in 50 major cities around the world. For the last few years, SMED has been very technology-oriented. On the production floor, state-of-the-art equipment and refined work processes make their four-week lead time one of the shortest in the industry. SMED is ISO 9001 registered.

Eighteen months ago, SMED decided to replace an "unsophisticated," homegrown legacy system with ERP modules from the Netherlands-based Baan Company. SMED hoped to improve customer service by tracking the status of orders better and to increase profits by more closely tracking costs, thereby optimizing prices.

Since 1978, Baan had forged its position as a leading developer of innovative, integrated enterprise solutions. Over 15 000 business sites use Baan software for manufacturing, distribution, sales, marketing, and business intelligence. Baan has three offices in Canada alone. Baan's customers include Falconbridge of Toronto, General Mills, Barclays International Funds Group, and British Steel. Although Baan was purchased in 2000 by Invensys, it is maintained as a separate software division.

"Having clear objectives going into an ERP implementation is critical," says SMED president and project champion Andrew Moor. "ERP is often sold as a panacea. It rarely is. You've got to know what problems you're trying to solve and tailor the implementation to that—and not try to fix 20 disparate problems at once. We did a good job of focusing."

SMED began implementing major distribution, manufacturing, and finance modules in March 1998. It turned the system on in one part of the firm (representing about 30 percent of revenues) in January of 2000—on time. It will roll Baan out to the rest of the company over the rest of this year.

It's too early to gauge the success of Phase One," says ERP project manager Doug Hunt. "You wouldn't expect to see benefits for at least six months because of the learning curve involved and the need to tweak the system," he says. "But my intuition is that it's doing what we wanted it to do. It's forcing discipline and repeatability in our business processes."

The implementation went "fairly smoothly." One factor was the company's determination to minimize customization. All modifications had to be cleared by a high-level steering committee chaired by Moor. "It's very important that you put those controls in place," he says. "There are a lot of things that people would like to have. A lot of places you just have to compromise."

Hunt and Moor both attribute the success of the implementation in part to the company's project partner, Arthur Andersen & Co (now called Accenture). On the other hand, the project was subject to cost overruns, partly, Hunt suggests, because SMED relied too heavily on Arthur Andersen consultants to get the project completed on time.

Moor believes this was a worthwhile trade-off. Finishing on time, even if it means spending a little more on consulting help, is paradoxically the best way to control overall project costs, he says. "Every week a project runs overtime will cost you," he says. "The most critical thing is to finish on time. And to do that, you have to have a strong management structure in place." Arthur Andersen helped provide that. It also takes discipline and determination, Moor adds. "It's too easy to see that you've fallen behind and not be concerned. But you've got to be concerned. You've always got to bring the project back to the original time line."

Still, Hunt says the company has learned from the first phase and will reduce its reliance on consultants in future. Consultants are ultimately more expensive than well-trained in-house staff, he says, because they have to learn the business before they can be optimally effective—and then they leave. The over-reliance on consultants in the first phase stemmed in part from a failure to provide adequate technical and project management training for the core project team of users. The result was they couldn't carry the ball in some critical areas.

Hunt will also be more careful in the future about selecting core team members. Operational managers tended to nominate people who were available rather than those with requisite skills. One missing ingredient in the mix was decision-making skills—and authority. This slowed the process of getting sign-off from operational units. For the next phases of the project, Hunt will also integrate the programming staff working on modifications more tightly into the core project group to get the benefit of their technical expertise.

SMED has been plagued by some user resistance. Integration of front-end and back-end processes means sales people can no longer count on engineers in manufacturing to fill in the blanks in specifications for custom orders, for example. And if an order isn't entered completely, the system kicks it out. This is frustrating for users. More important, problems with customer orders would hurt relations with SMED's customers, such as the Walt Disney Company, Bank of America, and Coca-Cola.

Part of the problem, Hunt says, is that too many end users skipped training on the system, believing they could learn easily enough on the fly once the system was installed. It's too late now to go back and lay on additional training. User acceptance problems have been minimized, though, by Moor's contribution as project champion. "It's a critical role," Hunt says. "He has been energetically selling the project in the rest of the organization. When people see his commitment, it's that much easier to get theirs."

Sources: Tony Martell, "Scaling the ERP Mountain," *CIO Canada*, October 26, 2000; "Our Roots," SMED Web site, www.smed.ca, accessed April 5, 2001; "Success Stories—Baan at Work for Industry," Baan Web site, www.baan.com/customers/successes/index.html, accessed April 5, 2001.

CASE STUDY QUESTIONS:

1. Why was it important for SMED to implement an ERP system?

2. Describe the problems SMED faced in implementing their ERP? Why do you think they chose Baan for the job?

3. What management, organizational, and technical issues did Moor and Hunt have to consider when installing the Baan ERP?

4. What problems could implementing the Baan software have caused SMED with their customers?

8

MANAGING DATA RESOURCES

OBJECTIVES

After completing this chapter, you will be able to:

1. *Describe basic file organization concepts and the problems of the traditional file environment.*
2. *Describe how a database management system organizes information.*
3. *Compare the principal types of databases.*
4. *Identify important database design principles.*
5. *Identify the managerial and organizational requirements of a database environment.*
6. *Discuss new database trends.*

A New SPIN on Land Surveys

Bill Elliott was the natural guy to turn to when the Alberta government sought to streamline the process of searching the province's 230 000 survey plans. The surveys office had previously used only hard copies, serving the public from outlets in Edmonton and Calgary. When government cost-cutters looked for savings, the IT possibilities propelled the Surveys office immediately to the forefront of cost-cutting priorities.

Elliott brought the necessary IT and government experience; he was technical services administrator for Registries and had previously worked in Geographic Information Systems and Local Government Services where he was divisional business coordinator for information technology.

As project leader of the new Spatial Information System (SPIN), created in 1997, Elliott knew he faced a number of challenges, the biggest being the need to outsource the development work to obtain best-of-breed solutions. "We knew this would take a fair amount of time, but we wanted to set a scalable platform for future changes in Registries," Elliott says. Elliott contracted with WayTo Integration to create the information required for the system from three existing production databases. This required cleaning the data in two of the databases as there were errors that would have rendered the new application useless. WayTo has since added functionalities and data elements to the SPIN application (www.spin.gov.ab.ca/spin1).

Another critical step was to get the parties involved on board—especially the surveyors. Initially skeptical, the surveyor community could potentially benefit the most but would also have to make the most changes. The biggest change was that surveyors would have to submit all survey plans digitally, either online or by diskette. Surveys staff would then register and index them and post the plans to the SPIN application server. "Their big question was 'why'—what benefits were in it for them and their clients?" Elliott says. "It meant working closely with a number of stakeholders and explaining the goals of the project."

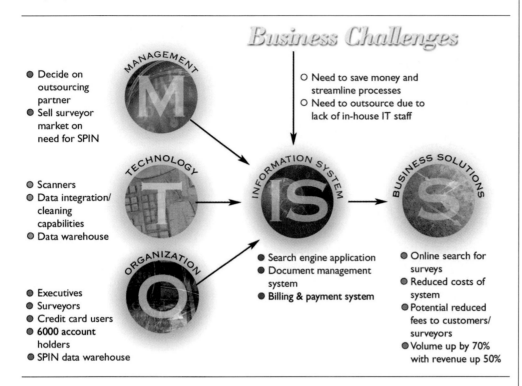

Business Challenges

MANAGEMENT
- Decide on outsourcing partner
- Sell surveyor market on need for SPIN

TECHNOLOGY
- Scanners
- Data integration/ cleaning capabilities
- Data warehouse

ORGANIZATION
- Executives
- Surveyors
- Credit card users
- 6000 account holders
- SPIN data warehouse

- Need to save money and streamline processes
- Need to outsource due to lack of in-house IT staff

INFORMATION SYSTEM
- Search engine application
- Document management system
- Billing & payment system

BUSINESS SOLUTIONS
- Online search for surveys
- Reduced costs of system
- Potential reduced fees to customers/ surveyors
- Volume up by 70% with revenue up 50%

Implementation of SPIN was slow, given the large volume of data involved. After a limited introduction in June of 1999 and some positive feedback, it was time to expand the reach of the project. SPIN was introduced to the general survey community in September 1999 and to the rest of the affected stakeholders in January of 2000. "We are aggressively promoting it now," Elliott says. "We wanted to fine-tune the system and not disappoint people. It probably took twice as long because we had to nursemaid so many technology and internal political components. But this prevented major disruptions down the road."

As anticipated, the biggest winner was the survey community. Once they had a taste of almost real-time delivery, most couldn't get enough. On the client side, there is no longer the need to send runners to search, order, and pick up plans at the land titles counters. Clients also now have a choice of how they want their surveys delivered (online, courier, fax, or mail), what format they want them in (CD, hardcopy, diskette), and how they wish to make payments online (account or credit card).

The Registries department and the Alberta government have benefited as well with plan delivery volumes up by 70 percent and revenues up by approximately 50 percent. Registries has also enjoyed decreased costs in archiving and distribution. If the savings trend continues, Registries may be able to drop the price of access to plans delivered by SPIN. "Benefits are about equal, it allows a time and dollar savings on both ends," explains Elliott. "It has certainly made our financial people happy." Transactions are now conducted online, which relieves staff of the need to manually enter them into the accounting system.

Sources: "A New SPIN on Land Surveys," *InformationStrategy*, Winter 2000; "Alberta Registries/E-Commerce Site," WayTo Integration, www.wayto.com, accessed April 10, 2001.

A New SPIN on Land Surveys

MANAGEMENT CHALLENGES

Alberta's SPIN system illustrates how much the effective use of information depends on how data are stored, organized, and accessed. Proper delivery of information not only depends on the capabilities of computer hardware and software but also on the organization's ability to manage data as an important resource. Inefficiencies in Survey's ability to search, retrieve, and deliver plans, together with the associated high labour costs, impaired organizational performance. It has been very difficult for organizations to manage their data effectively. Two challenges stand out.

1. **Organizational obstacles to a database environment.** Implementing a database requires widespread organizational change in the role of information (and information managers), the allocation of power at senior levels, the ownership and sharing of information, and patterns of organizational agreement. A database management system (DBMS) can challenge the existing power arrangements in an organization and therefore often generates political resistance. In a traditional file environment, each department constructed files and programs to fulfill its specific needs. Today, with a database, files and programs must be created that take into account the full organization's interest in data. Although the organization has purchased hardware and software for a database environment, it may not reap the benefits it should because it is unwilling or unable to make the requisite organizational changes.

2. **Cost/benefit considerations.** The costs of moving to a database environment are tangible, up front, and large in the short term (three years). Most firms buy a commercial DBMS package and related hardware. The software alone can cost $750 000 for a full-function package with all options. New hardware for data storage, processing, and backup may cost an additional $1.5 million to $3 million. Designing an enterprise-wide database that integrates all the organization's data can be a lengthy and costly process. It soon becomes apparent to senior management that a database system is a huge investment.

   Unfortunately, the benefits of the DBMS are often intangible, back-loaded, and long term (up to five years). Millions of dollars have been spent over the years designing and maintaining existing systems. People in organizations have developed an understanding of the existing system after long periods of training and socialization. For these reasons, and despite the clear advantages of a DBMS, the short-term costs of developing a DBMS often appear to be as great as the benefits. Managers, especially those unfamiliar with systems, tend to severely discount the obvious long-term benefits of the DBMS.

This chapter examines the managerial and organizational requirements as well as the technologies for managing data as a resource. Databases are the foundation for all of an organization's information systems. Organizations need to manage their data assets very carefully to make sure that they can be easily accessed and used by managers and employees across the organization. First we describe the traditional file management technologies and the problems they have created for organizations. Then we describe the technology of database management systems, which can overcome many of the drawbacks of traditional file management and provide the firm-wide integration of information required for digital firm applications. We include a discussion of the managerial and organizational requirements for successfully implementing a database environment. Finally, we discuss trends in database technology and applications.

8.1 ORGANIZING DATA IN A TRADITIONAL FILE ENVIRONMENT

An effective information system provides users with timely, accurate, and relevant information in a form suitable for their purposes. This information is stored in computer files. When the files are properly arranged and maintained, users can easily access and retrieve the information they need.

You can appreciate the importance of file management if you have ever presented a project using 3 × 5 index cards. No matter how efficient your storage device (a metal box or a rubber band), if you organize the cards randomly, your presentation would have little or no organization. Given enough time, you could put the cards in order, but your system would be more efficient if you set up your organizational scheme early on. If your scheme is flexible enough and well documented, you can extend it to account for any changes in your viewpoint as you prepare your presentation.

The same need for file organization applies to firms. Well-managed, carefully arranged files make it easy to obtain data for business analysis and decisions, whereas poorly managed files lead to chaos in information processing, high costs, poor performance, and little, if any, flexibility. Despite the use of excellent hardware and software, many organizations have inefficient information systems because of poor file management. In this section, we describe the traditional methods that organizations have used to arrange data in computer files. We also discuss the problems with these methods.

FILE ORGANIZATION TERMS AND CONCEPTS

A computer system organizes data in a hierarchy that starts with bits and bytes and progresses to fields, records, files, and databases (see Figure 8-1). A bit represents the smallest unit of data a computer can handle. A group of bits, called a byte, represents a single character, which can be a letter, a number, or another symbol. A grouping of characters into a word, a group of words, or a complete number representing an attribute or characteristic (such as a person's name or age), is called a **field**. A group of related fields, such as the student's name, the course taken, the date, and the grade, compose a **record**; a group of records of the same type is called a **file**. For instance, the student records in Figure 8-1 could constitute a course file. A group of related files makes up a **database**. The student course file illustrated in Figure 8-1 could be grouped with files on students' personal histories and financial backgrounds to create a student database.

A record describes an entity. An **entity** is a person, place, thing, or event on which we maintain information. An order is a typical entity in a sales order file, which maintains information on a firm's sales orders. Each characteristic or quality describing a particular entity is called an **attribute**. For example, order number, order date, order amount, item number, and item quantity would each be an attribute of the entity order. The specific values that these attributes have can be found in the fields of the record describing the entity order (see Figure 8-2).

field
A grouping of characters into a word, a group of words, or a complete number, representing an attribute or characteristic such as a person's name or age.

record
A group of related fields.

file
A group of records of the same type.

database
A group of related files.

entity
A person, place, thing, or event about which information must be kept.

attribute
A piece of information describing a particular entity.

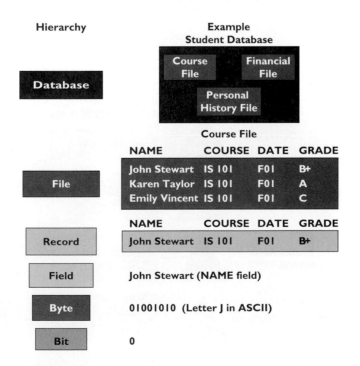

FIGURE 8-1 The data hierarchy. A computer system organizes data in a hierarchy that starts with the bit, which represents either a 0 or a 1. Bits can be grouped to form a byte to represent one character, number, or symbol. Bytes can be grouped to form a field, and related fields can be grouped to form a record. Related records can be collected to form a file, and related files can be organized into a database.

FIGURE 8-2 Entities and attributes. This record describes the entity called ORDER and its attributes. The specific values for order number, order date, item number, quantity, and amount for this particular order are the fields for this record. Order number is the key field because each order is assigned a unique identification number. The specific values shown in the figure are attributes of a specific record or entity.

key field
A field in a record that uniquely identifies that record so that it can be retrieved, updated, or sorted.

traditional file environment
A way of collecting and maintaining data in an organization that leads to each functional area or division creating and maintaining its own data files and programs.

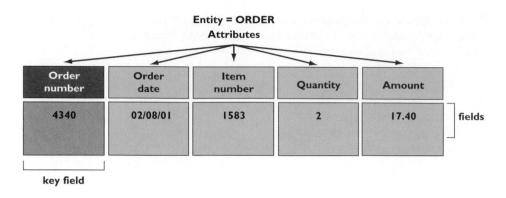

Every record in a file should contain at least one field that uniquely identifies that record so that the record can be retrieved, updated, or sorted. This identifier field is called a **key field**. An example of a key field is the order number for the order record illustrated in Figure 8-2 or an employee number or social insurance number for a personnel record (containing employee data such as the employee's name, age, address, job title, and so forth).

PROBLEMS WITH THE TRADITIONAL FILE ENVIRONMENT

Most organizations began information processing on a small scale, automating one application at a time. Systems tended to grow independently, not according to any particular overall plan in a **traditional file environment**. Each functional area tended to develop systems in isolation from other functional areas. Accounting, finance, manufacturing, human resources, and marketing each developed their own systems and data files. Figure 8-3 illustrates the traditional approach to information processing.

Each application required its own files and computer programs to operate. For example, the human resources functional area might have created a personnel master file, a payroll file, a medical insurance file, a pension file, a mailing list file, and so forth until tens, perhaps hundreds, of files and programs existed. In the company as a whole, this process often leads to multiple master files created, maintained, and operated by separate divisions or departments.

As this process goes on, the organization is saddled with hundreds of programs and applications with no one knowing what the files do, what data they use, or who uses the data. The organization collects the same information in far too many separate files. The resulting

FIGURE 8-3 Traditional file processing. The use of a traditional approach to file processing encourages each functional area in a corporation to develop specialized applications. Each application requires a unique data file that is likely to be a subset of the master file. These subsets of the master file lead to data redundancy, processing inflexibility, and wasted storage resources.

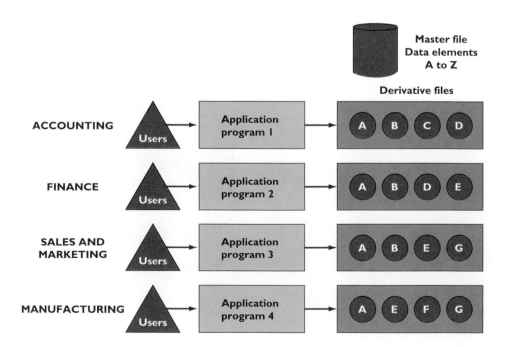

problems are poor data integrity, data redundancy, program-data dependence, inflexibility, poor data security, and inability to share data among applications.

Data Integrity

Data integrity means that data are accurate and up to date. As the same data are stored in multiple files, changes to the data may become inconsistent across all places in which it is stored. For example, if a customer moves, his/her address may reside in many separate files, such as accounts receivable, marketing, and mailing list files. The data would need to be changed in all three files to maintain data integrity.

> **data integrity**
> A characteristic of data wherein the data are accurate and up to date.

Not only is it difficult to remember to update all three files, but the possibility of making a data entry error while changing any one of the three files is three times greater than if the changes were only required to one file. If one of the files is not changed, it becomes very difficult to know which of the addresses is correct. Hence, the data loses integrity.

Data Redundancy and Confusion

Data redundancy is the presence of duplicate data in multiple data files. Data redundancy occurs when different divisions, functional areas, or groups in an organization independently collect the same piece of information. For instance, within the commercial loans division of a bank, the marketing and credit information functions might collect the same customer information. Because it is collected and maintained in different places, the same data item may have different meanings in different parts of the organization. Simple data items such as the fiscal year, employee identification, and credit limit can take on different meanings as programmers and analysts work in isolation on different applications. This causes confusion over which occurrence is the best (more reliable) for a particular purpose—or for a new purpose.

> **data redundancy**
> The presence of duplicate data in multiple data files.

Program-Data Dependence

Program-data dependence is the tight relationship between data stored in files and the specific programs required to update and maintain those files. Every computer program has to describe the location and nature of the data with which it works. In a traditional file environment, any change in a data field requires a change in all programs that access that data. Changes, for instance, in tax rates or postal code length require changes in programs. Some programs that use those files, but not the specific data field that changed, may need to be changed so that they maintain consistent descriptions of the data. These programming changes may cost millions of dollars to implement in programs that require the revised data.

> **program-data dependence**
> The tight relationship between data stored in files and the software programs that update and maintain those files. Any change in data organization or format requires a change in all the programs associated with those files.

Lack of Flexibility

A traditional file system can deliver routine scheduled reports after extensive programming efforts, but it cannot easily deliver ad hoc reports or respond to unanticipated information requirements in a timely fashion. The information required by ad hoc requests is somewhere in the system but is too complicated and expensive to retrieve. Several programmers would have to work for an extended time to put the required data items together in a new file.

Poor Security

Because there is little control or management of data, access to and dissemination of information may be out of control. Management may have no way of knowing who is accessing or making changes to the organization's data.

Lack of Data Sharing and Availability

The lack of control over access to data in this confused environment does not make it easy for people to obtain information. Because pieces of information in different files and different parts of the organization cannot be related or linked to one another, it is virtually impossible for information to be shared or accessed reliably in a timely manner. Information cannot flow freely across different functional areas or different parts of the organization.

8.2 THE DATABASE APPROACH TO DATA MANAGEMENT

database (rigorous definition)
A collection of data organized to service many applications at the same time by storing and managing data so that they appear to be in one location; managed by a database management system (DBMS).

Database technology can cut through many of the problems a traditional file organization creates. A more rigorous definition of a **database** is a collection of data organized to serve many applications efficiently by centralizing the data and minimizing redundant data through management by a database management system (DBMS). Rather than storing data in separate files for each application, data are stored so that they appear to users to be physically stored in only one location. A single database services multiple applications. For example, instead of a corporation storing employee data in separate information systems and separate files for personnel, payroll, and benefits, the corporation could create a single common human resources database. Figure 8-4 illustrates the database concept.

DATABASE MANAGEMENT SYSTEMS

database management system (DBMS)
Special software to create and maintain a database and enable individual business applications to extract the data they need without having to create separate files or data definitions in their computer programs.

logical view
A representation of data as they appear to an application programmer or end user.

physical view
A representation of data as they are actually organized on physical storage media.

A **database management system (DBMS)** is simply the software that permits an organization to centralize data, manage them efficiently, and provide controlled access to the stored data by application programs. The DBMS acts as an interface between application programs and the physical data files. When the application program calls for a data item, such as gross pay, the DBMS finds this item in the database and presents it to the application program. Using traditional data files, the programmer would have to specify the size and format of each data element used in the program and then tell the computer where they were located. A DBMS eliminates most of the data definition statements found in traditional programs.

The DBMS relieves the programmer or end user from the task of understanding where and how the data are actually stored by separating the logical and physical views of the data. The **logical view** presents data as they would be perceived by end users or business specialists whereas the **physical view** shows how data are actually organized and structured on physical storage media. While there is only one physical view of the data, there can be many different logical views. The database management software makes the physical database available for different logical views presented for various application programs. For example, an employee retirement benefits program might use a logical view of the human resources database illustrated in Figure 8-4 that requires only the employee's name, address, social insurance number, pension plan, and retirement benefits data.

FIGURE 8-4 The contemporary database environment. A single human resources database serves multiple applications and allows a corporation to easily draw together all the information for various applications. The database management system acts as the interface between the application programs and the data.

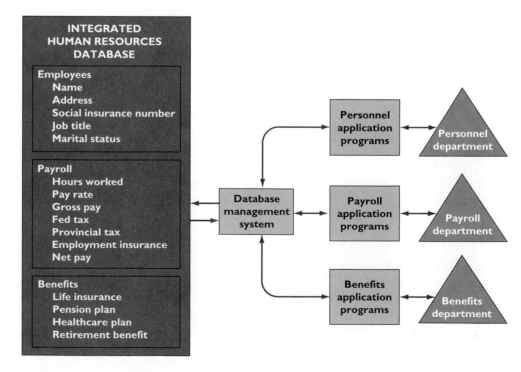

A database management system has three components:

1. A data definition language
2. A data manipulation language
3. A data dictionary

The **data definition language** is the formal language programmers use to specify the content and structure of the database. The data definition language defines each data element as it appears in the database before that data element is translated into the forms required by application programs.

Most DBMSs have a specialized language called a **data manipulation language** that is used in conjunction with a conventional third- or fourth-generation programming language to manipulate the data in the database. This language contains commands that permit end users and programming specialists to extract data from the database to satisfy information requests and develop applications. The most prominent data manipulation language today is **Structured Query Language** or SQL. Complex programming tasks cannot be performed efficiently with typical data manipulation languages. However, most mainframe DBMS are compatible with COBOL, FORTRAN, and other third-generation programming languages, permitting greater processing efficiency and flexibility.

The third element of a DBMS is a **data dictionary**. This is an automated or manual file that stores definitions of data elements and data characteristics such as usage, physical representation, ownership (the individual or group responsible for maintaining the data), authorization, and security. Many data dictionaries can produce lists and reports of data use, groupings, program locations, and so on. Figure 8-5 illustrates a sample data dictionary report that shows the size, format, meaning, and uses of a data element in a human resources database. A **data element** represents a field. In addition to listing the standard name (AMT-PAY-BASE), the dictionary lists the names that reference this element in specific systems and identifies the individuals, business functions, programs, and reports that use this data element.

data definition language
The component of a database management system that defines each data element as it appears in the database.

data manipulation language
A language associated with a database management system that end users and programmers use to manipulate data in the database.

Structured Query Language (SQL)
The standard data manipulation language for relational database management systems.

data dictionary
An automated or manual tool for storing and organizing information about the data maintained in a database.

data element
A field.

```
NAME:  AMT-PAY-BASE
FOCUS NAME:  BASEPAY
PC NAME:     SALARY

DESCRIPTION:  EMPLOYEE'S ANNUAL SALARY

SIZE: 9 BYTES
TYPE: N      (NUMERIC)
DATE CHANGED: 01/01/95
OWNERSHIP: COMPENSATION
UPDATE SECURITY:  SITE PERSONNEL
ACCESS SECURITY:  MANAGER, COMPENSATION PLANNING AND RESEARCH
                  MANAGER, JOB EVALUATION SYSTEMS
                  MANAGER, HUMAN RESOURCES PLANNING
                  MANAGER, SITE EQUAL OPPORTUNITY AFFAIRS
                  MANAGER, SITE BENEFITS
                  MANAGER, CLAIMS PAYING SYSTEMS
                  MANAGER, QUALIFIED PLANS
                  MANAGER, SITE EMPLOYMENT/EEO
BUSINESS FUNCTIONS USED BY:  COMPENSATION
                             HR PLANNING
                             EMPLOYMENT
                             INSURANCE
                             PENSION
                             401K

PROGRAMS USING:  PI01000
                 PI02000
                 PI03000
                 PI04000
                 PI05000

REPORTS USING:  REPORT 124 (SALARY INCREASE TRACKING REPORT)
                REPORT 448 (GROUP INSURANCE AUDIT REPORT)
                REPORT 452 (SALARY REVIEW LISTING)
                PENSION REFERENCE LISTING
```

FIGURE 8-5 Sample data dictionary report. The sample data dictionary report for a human resources database provides helpful information such as the size of the data element, which programs and reports use it, and which group in the organization is the owner responsible for maintaining it. The report also shows some of the other names that the organization uses for this piece of data.

By creating an inventory of data contained in the database, the data dictionary serves as an important data management tool. For instance, business users could consult the dictionary to find out exactly what pieces of data are maintained for the sales or marketing function or even to determine all the information maintained by the entire enterprise. The dictionary could supply business users with the name, format, and specifications required to access data for reports. Technical staff could use the dictionary to determine what data elements and files must be changed if a program is changed.

Most data dictionaries are entirely passive; they simply report. More advanced data dictionaries are active; changes in the dictionary can be automatically utilized by related programs. For instance, to change postal codes from six characters to nine characters, one could simply enter the change in the dictionary without having to modify and recompile all application programs using postal codes.

In an ideal database environment, the data in the database are defined only once and used for all applications whose data reside in the database, thereby eliminating data redundancy and inconsistency. Application programs, which are written using a combination of the DBMS data manipulation language and a conventional programming language, request data elements from the database. Data elements called for by the application programs are found and delivered by the DBMS. The programmer does not have to specify in detail how or where the data are to be found.

A DBMS can reduce program-data dependence along with program development and maintenance costs. Access and availability of information can be increased because users and programmers can perform ad hoc queries of data in the database. The DBMS allows the organization to centrally manage data, its use, and security.

TYPES OF DATABASES

Contemporary DBMSs use different database models to keep track of entities, attributes, and relationships. Each model has distinct processing and business advantages. In this section, we discuss hierarchical, network, and relational database models. A fourth type of database, object-oriented databases, is discussed in the section on database trends.

Hierarchical and Network DBMS

hierarchical data model
One type of logical database model that organizes data in a treelike structure. A record is subdivided into segments that are connected to each other in one-to-many parent–child relationships.

One can still find older systems that are based on either the hierarchical or network data model. The **hierarchical data model** presents data to users in a treelike structure. Within each record, data elements are organized into pieces of records called segments. To the user, each record looks like an organization chart with one top-level segment called the root. An upper segment is connected logically to a lower segment in a parent–child relationship. A parent segment can have more than one child, but a child can have only one parent.

Figure 8-6 shows a hierarchical structure that might be used for a human resources database. The root segment is Employee, which contains basic employee information such as name, address, and identification number. Immediately below it are three child segments: Compensation (containing salary and promotion data), Job Assignments (containing data about job positions and departments), and Benefits (containing data about beneficiaries and benefit options). The Compensation segment has two children below it: Performance Ratings (containing data about employees' job performance evaluations) and Salary History (containing historical data about employees' past salaries). Below the Benefits segment are child segments for Pension, Life Insurance, and Health, containing data about these benefit plans.

network data model
A logical database model that is useful for depicting many-to-many relationships.

While hierarchical structures depict one-to-many relationships, not all organizational uses can be conveniently represented by one-to-many relationships. **Network data models** depict data logically as many-to-many relationships. In other words, parents can have multiple children, and a child can have more than one parent. A typical many-to-many relationship for a network DBMS is the student–course relationship (see Figure 8-7). There are many courses in a university and many students. A student takes many courses and a course has many students.

Hierarchical and network DBMS are considered outdated and are not often used for building new database applications. They are much less flexible than relational DBMS and

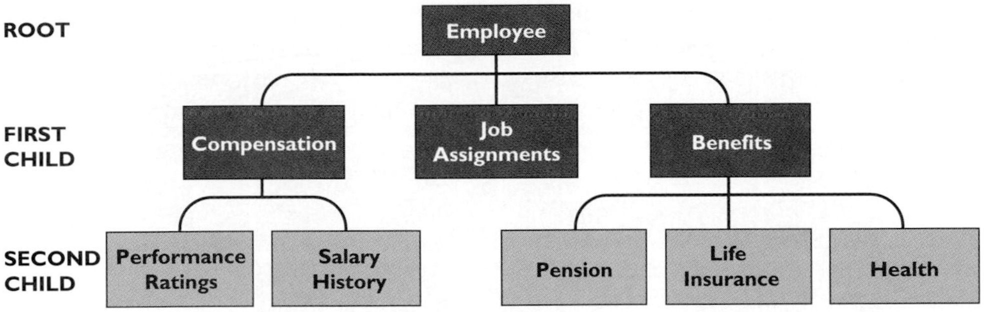

ROOT

FIRST CHILD

SECOND CHILD

FIGURE 8-6 A hierarchical database for a human resources system. The hierarchical database model looks like an organizational chart or a family tree. It has a single root segment (Employee) connected to lower-level segments (Compensation, Job Assignments, and Benefits). Each subordinate segment, in turn, may connect to other subordinate segments. Here, Compensation connects to Performance Ratings and Salary History. Benefits connects to Pension, Life Insurance, and Health Care. Each subordinate segment is the child of the segment directly above it.

do not easily support ad hoc, English language–like inquiries for information. All paths for accessing data must be specified in advance and cannot be changed without a major programming effort. For instance, if you queried the human resources database illustrated in Figure 8-6 to find out the names of the employees with the job title of administrative assistant, you would discover that there is no way that the system can find the answer in a reasonable amount of time. This path through the data was not specified in advance.

Hierarchical DBMS can still be found in large **legacy systems** that require intensive, high-volume transaction processing. A legacy system is a system that has been in existence for a long time and continues to be used to avoid the high cost of replacing or redesigning it. Banks, insurance companies, and other high-volume users continue to use reliable hierarchical databases such as IBM's IMSII (Information Management System), which was developed in 1979. Many organizations have converted to DB2, IBM's relational DBMS for new applications, while retaining IMS for traditional transaction processing. For example, Dallas-based Texas Instruments depends on IMS for its heavy processing requirements, including inventory, accounting, and manufacturing. As relational products acquire more muscle, firms will shift away completely from hierarchical DBMS, but this will happen over a long period of time.

Relational DBMS

The most popular type of DBMS today for PCs as well as for larger computers and mainframes is the relational DBMS. The **relational data model** represents all data in the database as simple two-dimensional tables called *relations*. The tables appear similar to flat files, but the information in several files can be extracted and combined. Sometimes, the tables are referred to as files.

Figure 8-8 shows a supplier table, a part table, and an order table. In each table, the rows are unique records, and the columns are fields. Another term for a row or record in a relation is a **tuple**. Often a user needs information from a number of relations to produce a report. This is the strength of the relational model: It can relate data in any one file or table to data in another file or table *as long as both tables share a common data element*.

legacy system
A system that has been in existence for a long time and continues to be used to avoid the high cost of replacing or redesigning it.

relational data model
A type of logical database model that treats data as if they were stored in two-dimensional tables. It can relate data stored in one table to data in another as long as the two tables share a common data element.

tuple
A row or record in a relational database.

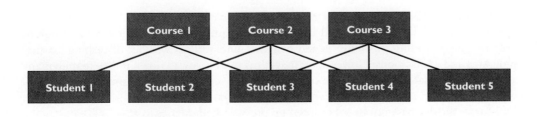

FIGURE 8-7 The network data model. This illustration of a network data model showing the relationship the students in a university have to the courses they take represents an example of logical many-to-many relationships.

FIGURE 8-8 The relational data model. Each table is a relation and each row or record is a tuple. Each column corresponds to a field. These relations can be combined and extracted to access data and produce reports, provided that all tables being combined share a common data element. In this example, the ORDER file shares the data element "Part_Number" with the PARTS file. The PARTS and SUPPLIER files share the data element "Supplier_Number."

Table (Relation)

Columns (Fields, Attributes)

ORDER

Order_ Number	Order_ Date	Delivery_ Date	Part_ Number	Part_ Amount	Order_ Total
1634	02/02/01	02/22/01	152	2	144.50
1635	02/12/01	02/28/01	137	3	79.70
1636	02/13/01	03/01/01	145	1	24.30

Rows (Records, Tuples)

PARTS

Part_ Number	Part_ Description	Unit_ Price	Supplier_ Number
137	Door latch	22.50	4058
145	Door handle	26.25	2038
150	Door seal	6.00	4058
152	Compressor	70.00	1125

SUPPLIER

Supplier_ Number	Supplier_ Name	Supplier_Address
4058	CBM Inc.	44 Winslow,
2038	Ace Inc.	Rte. 101,
1125	Bryant Corp.	51 Elm

select

A database operation that creates a subset of all records in the file that meet stated criteria.

join

A database operation that combines relational tables to provide more information than is found in only one table.

project

A database operation that creates a subset of columns in a table, permitting the creation of new tables (views) that contain only required information.

To demonstrate, suppose we wanted to find (in the relational database in Figure 8-8) the names and addresses of suppliers who could provide us with part number 137 or part number 152. We would need information from two tables: the supplier table and the parts table. Note that these two files have a shared data element: Supplier_Number.

In a relational database, three basic operations are used to develop useful sets of data: select, project, and join. The **select** operation creates a subset consisting of all records in the file that meet stated criteria. Select creates, in other words, a subset of rows that meet certain criteria. In our example, we want to select records (rows) from the part table where the part number equals 137 or 152. The **join** operation combines relational tables to provide the user with more information than is available in individual tables. To join multiple tables, we must use both primary keys (the key field in the original table) and foreign keys. A *foreign* key is a set of one or more columns in any table that may hold the value(s) found in the primary key column(s) of some other table. So we must have a primary key to match the foreign key. The only purpose of the primary key in the primary key/foreign key pair is to provide an unambiguous join—to maintain *referential integrity* with respect to the "foreign" table that holds the referenced primary key. This ensures that the value to which the foreign key refers will always be valid (or null, if allowed). In our example, we want to join the now shortened part table (only parts numbered 137 or 152 will be presented) and the supplier table into a single new result table.

The **project** operation creates a subset consisting of columns in a table, permitting the user to create new tables (also called views) that contain only the information required. In our example, we want to extract from the new result table only the following columns: Part_Number, Supplier_Number, Supplier_Name, and Supplier_Address. Figure 8-9 illustrates the select, join, and project operations just described. These operations are mathematically proven to be reliable, providing the data in each table conforms to a set of standards. Data that does conform is called normalized, and the mathematics involved is called relational mathematics. For more on normalization, see the section in this chapter on designing databases.

Relational DBMSs, in contrast to hierarchical or network DBMSs, have much more flexibility in providing data for ad hoc queries, combining information from different sources, and providing capability to add new data and records without disturbing existing programs and applications. However, these systems can be slowed down if they require many accesses to the data stored on disk to carry out the select, join, and project commands. Selecting one part number from among millions, one record at a time, can take a long time. Of course, the database can be set to speed up pre-specified queries.

ORDER

Order_Number	Order_Date	Delivery_Date	Part_Number	Part_Amount	Order_Total
1634	02/02/01	02/22/01	152	2	144.50
1635	02/12/01	02/28/01	137	3	79.70
1636	02/13/01	03/01/01	145	1	24.30

PART

Part_Number	Part_Description	Unit_Price	Supplier_Number
137	Door latch	22.50	4058
145	Door handle	26.25	2038
150	Door seal	6.00	4058
152	Compressor	70.00	1125

Select Part_Number = 137 or 152

SUPPLIER

Supplier_Number	Supplier_Name	Supplier_Address
4058	CBM Inc.	300 St. Mary, Winnipeg MB R2C 0A1
2038	Ace Inc.	800 Haven Dr., Vancouver BC V7H 2K1
1125	Bryant Corp.	302 Wilsey Rd., Fredericton NB E3B 5J1

Join by Supplier_Number

Part_Number	Supplier_Number	Supplier_Name	Supplier_Address
137	4058	CBM Inc.	300 St. Mary, Winnipeg MB R2C 0A1
152	1125	Bryant Corp.	302 Wilsey Rd., Fredericton NB E3B 5J1

Project selected columns

FIGURE 8-9 The three basic operations of a relational DBMS. The select, project, and join operations allow data from two different tables to be combined and only selected attributes to be displayed.

Leading mainframe relational database management systems include IBM's DB2 and Oracle from the Oracle Corporation. DB2, Oracle, and Microsoft SQL Server are used as DBMS for midrange computers. Microsoft Access is a PC relational database management system, and Oracle Lite is a DBMS for small handheld computing devices.

QUERYING DATABASES: ELEMENTS OF SQL

Structured query language (SQL) is the principal data manipulation language for relational DBMS. It is a major tool for querying, reading, and updating a relational database. There are versions of SQL that can run on almost any operating system or computer, so that computers are able to exchange data by passing SQL commands to each other. End users and information systems specialists can use SQL as an interactive query language to access data from databases, and SQL commands can also be embedded in application programs written in COBOL, C, and other programming languages.

We now describe the most important basic SQL commands. Convention calls for certain SQL reserved words with special meanings, such as SELECT and FROM, to be capitalized and for SQL statements to be written in multiple lines. Most SQL statements to retrieve data contain the following three clauses:

SELECT	Lists the columns from tables that the user would like to see in a result table.
FROM	Identifies the tables or views from which the columns will be selected.
WHERE	Includes conditions for selecting specific rows (records) within a single table and conditions for joining multiple tables.

The general form for a SELECT statement, retrieving specified columns for all of the rows in the table, is:

SELECT Column_Name, Column_Name, ...
FROM Table_Name;

The columns to be obtained are listed after the keyword SELECT, and the table to be used is listed after the keyword FROM. Note that column and table names do not have spaces and must be typed as one word and that the statement ends with a semicolon.

FIGURE 8-10 The results of using the SELECT statement to select only the columns Part_Number, Part_Description, and Unit_Price from all rows in the PART table.

Part_Number	Part_Description	Unit_Price
137	Door latch	22.50
145	Door handle	26.25
150	Door seal	6.00
152	Compressor	70.00

Review Figure 8-8. Suppose you wanted to see the Part_Number, Part_Description, and Unit_Price for each part in the PART table. Your query would read:

SELECT Part_Number, Part_Description, Unit_Price
FROM PARTS;

Figure 8-10 illustrates the results of your projection.

Suppose, for example, you wanted to see the same data, but only for parts in the part table with unit prices more than $25.00. Your query would include a where clause:

SELECT Part_Number, Part_Description, Unit_Price
FROM PARTS
WHERE Unit_Price > 25.00;

Your query would return the results illustrated in Figure 8-11.

Supposed you wanted to obtain information on the names, identification numbers, and addresses of suppliers for each part in the database. We can do this by joining the PARTS table with the SUPPLIER table and then extracting the required information. The query would look like this:

SELECT PARTS.Part_Number, SUPPLIER.Supplier_Number, SUPPLIER.Supplier_Name,
    SUPPLIER.Supplier_Address
FROM PARTS, SUPPLIER
WHERE PARTS.Supplier_Number = SUPPLIER.Supplier_Number;

The results would look like Figure 8-12.

If you only wanted to see the name, address, and supplier numbers for the suppliers of part numbers 137 or 152, the query would read:

SELECT PARTS.Part_Number, SUPPLIER.Supplier_Number, SUPPLIER.Supplier_Name,
    SUPPLIER.Supplier_Address
FROM PARTS, SUPPLIER
WHERE PARTS.Supplier_Number = SUPPLIER.Supplier_Number AND Part_Number = 137
    OR Part_Number = 152;

The results would look like the result of the join operation depicted in Figure 8-9. Note that several conditions can be expressed in the WHERE clause.

FIGURE 8-11 The results of using a conditional selection to select only parts that meet the condition of having unit prices more than $25.00.

Part_Number	Part_Description	Unit_Price
145	Door handle	26.25
152	Compressor	70.00

FIGURE 8-12 A projection from joining the PARTS and SUPPLIER tables.

Part_Number	Supplier_Number	Supplier_Name	Supplier_Address
137	4058	CBM Inc.	300 St. Mary
145	2038	Ace Inc.	800 Haven Dr.
150	4058	CBM Inc.	300 St. Mary
152	1125	Bryant Corp.	302 Wilsey Rd.

8.3 CREATING A DATABASE ENVIRONMENT

To create a database environment one must understand the entities and attributes of each entity and the relationships among the data and entities, the type of data that will be maintained in the database, how the data will be used, and how the organization will need to change to manage data from a company-wide perspective. We now describe important database design principles and the management and organizational requirements of a database environment.

DESIGNING DATABASES

To create a database, one must go through two design exercises: a conceptual design and a physical design. The conceptual or logical design of a database is an abstract model of the database from a business perspective whereas the physical design shows how the database is actually arranged on direct access storage devices. Logical design requires a detailed description of the business processes and information needs of the actual end users of the database. Ideally, database design will be part of an overall organizational data planning effort (see Chapter 11).

The conceptual database design describes how the data elements in the database are to be grouped. The design process identifies relationships among data elements (attributes and entities) and the most efficient way of grouping data elements together to meet information requirements. The process also identifies redundant data elements and the groupings of data elements required for specific application programs. Groups of data are organized, refined, and streamlined until an overall logical view of the relationships among all the data elements in the database emerges.

Database designers document the conceptual data model with an **entity-relationship diagram**, illustrated in Figure 8-13. The boxes represent entities and the diamonds represent relationships. The 1 or M on either side of the diamond represents the relationship among entities as either one-to-one, one-to-many, or many-to-many. Figure 8-13 shows that the entity ORDER can have more than one PART, but a PART can only have one SUPPLIER. Many parts can be provided by the same supplier. The attributes for each entity are listed next to the entity and the key field is underlined. Parts can belong to many orders.

To use a relational database model effectively, complex groupings of data must be streamlined to eliminate redundant data elements and awkward many-to-many relationships. The process of creating small, stable data structures from complex groups of data is called **normalization**. Figures 8-14 and 8-15 illustrate this process. In the particular business modelled here, an order can have more than one part, but each part is provided by only one supplier. If we built a relation called ORDER with all the fields included here, we would have to repeat the name, description, and price of each part on the order and the name and address of each part vendor. This relation contains what are called repeating groups because there can be many parts and suppliers for each order, and it actually describes multiple entities—parts and suppliers as well as orders. A more efficient way to arrange the data is to break down ORDER into smaller relations, each of which describes a single entity. If we go step by step and normalize the relation ORDER, we emerge with the relations illustrated in Figure 8-15.

If database requirements have been carefully considered, with a clear understanding of business information needs and usage, the database model will most likely be in some normalized form. Many real-world databases are not fully normalized

entity-relationship diagram
A methodology for documenting databases illustrating the relationship between various entities in the database as one to one, one to many, or many to many.

normalization
The process of creating small stable data structures from complex groups of data when designing a relational database.

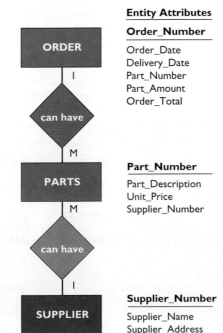

Entity Attributes

Order_Number

Order_Date
Delivery_Date
Part_Number
Part_Amount
Order_Total

Part_Number

Part_Description
Unit_Price
Supplier_Number

Supplier_Number

Supplier_Name
Supplier_Address

FIGURE 8-13 An entity-relationship diagram. This diagram shows the relationships between the entities ORDER, PARTS, and SUPPLIER that were used to develop the relational database illustrated in Figure 8-8.

ORDER

Order_ Number	Part_ Amount	Part_ Number	Part_ Description	Unit_ Price	Supplier_ Number	Supplier_ Name	Supplier_ Address	Order_ Date	Delivery_ Date	Order_ Total

FIGURE 8-14 An unnormalized relation for ORDER. In an unnormalized relation, there are repeating groups. For example, there can be many parts and suppliers for each order. There is only a one-to-one correspondence between ORDER_NUMBER and ORDER_DATE, ORDER_TOTAL, and DELIVERY_DATE.

because this may not be the most sensible way to meet business information requirements. Note that the relational database illustrated in Figure 8-8 is not fully normalized because there could be more than one part for each order. The designers chose to not use the four relations described in Figure 8-15 because most of the orders handled by this particular business are only for one part. The designers might have felt that for this particular business it was inefficient to maintain four different tables. For more on normalization and database design, see our Web site's section on this important topic.

Once the logical design has been specified, the physical design can be specified. Decisions about the database platform (mainframe, client/server, DBMS application) can be made. Physical design also involves implementing the logical design. For example, the logical process of normalization has resulted in a number of tables that can then be created using the chosen DBMS. Each logical entity becomes a table, foreign keys are introduced on the *many* side of a one-to-many relationship, and so on. At the end of the physical design process, implementation in the form of table creation and data entry begins.

DISTRIBUTING DATABASES

Database design also considers how the data are to be distributed. Information systems can be designed with a centralized database that is used by a single central processor or by multiple processors in a client/server network. Alternatively, the database can be distributed. A **distributed database** is one that is stored in more than one physical location. Parts of the database are stored physically in one location, and other parts are stored and maintained in other locations. There are two main ways of distributing a database (see Figure 8-16). The central database (see Figure 8-16a) can be partitioned so that each remote processor has the necessary data to serve its local area. Changes in local files can be reconciled with the central database on a batch basis, often at night. Another strategy is to replicate the central database (Figure 8-16b) at all remote locations. For example, Lufthansa Airlines replaced its centralized mainframe database with a replicated database to make information more immediately available to flight dispatchers. Any change made to Lufthansa's Frankfort DBMS is automatically replicated in New York and Hong Kong. This strategy also requires updating of the central database during off hours.

Distributed systems reduce the vulnerability of a single, massive central site. They increase service and responsiveness to local users and often can run on smaller, less expensive

distributed database
A database that is stored in more than one physical location. Parts or copies of the database are physically stored in one location, and other parts or copies are stored and maintained in other locations.

FIGURE 8-15 A normalized relation for ORDER. After normalization, the original relation ORDER has been broken down into four smaller relations. The relation ORDER is left with only three attributes, and the relation ORDERED-PARTS has a combined, or *concatenated*, key consisting of ORDER_NUMBER and PART_NUMBER.

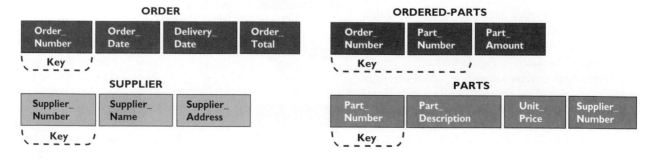

ORDER

Order_ Number	Order_ Date	Delivery_ Date	Order_ Total
Key			

ORDERED-PARTS

Order_ Number	Part_ Number	Part_ Amount
Key		

SUPPLIER

Supplier_ Number	Supplier_ Name	Supplier_ Address
Key		

PARTS

Part_ Number	Part_ Description	Unit_ Price	Supplier_ Number
Key			

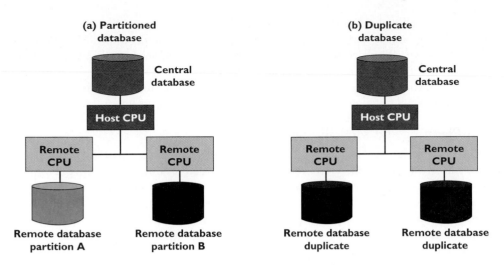

(a) Partitioned database

Central database

Host CPU

Remote CPU Remote CPU

Remote database partition A Remote database partition B

(b) Duplicate database

Central database

Host CPU

Remote CPU Remote CPU

Remote database duplicate Remote database duplicate

FIGURE 8-16 Distributed databases. There are alternative ways of distributing a database. The central database can be partitioned (a) so that each remote processor has the necessary data to serve its own local needs. The central database also can be duplicated (b) at all remote locations.

computers. Distributed systems, however, are dependent on high-quality telecommunications lines, which are themselves vulnerable. Moreover, local databases can sometimes depart from central data standards and definitions, and they pose security problems by widely distributing access to sensitive data. Database designers need to weigh these factors in their decisions.

MANAGEMENT REQUIREMENTS FOR DATABASE SYSTEMS

Much more is required for the development of database systems than simply selecting a logical database model. The database is an organizational discipline, a method, rather than a tool or technology. It requires organizational and conceptual change. Without management support and understanding, database efforts fail. The critical elements in a database environment are (1) data administration, (2) data planning and modelling methodology, (3) database technology and management, and (4) users. This environment is depicted in Figure 8-17.

Data Administration

Database systems require that the organization recognize the strategic role of information and begin actively to manage and plan for information as a corporate resource. This means that the organization must develop a data administration function with the power to define information requirements for the entire company and with direct access to senior management. The chief information officer (CIO) or vice president of information becomes the primary advocate in the organization for database systems.

Data administration is responsible for the specific policies and procedures through which data can be managed as an organizational resource. These responsibilities include developing information policy, planning for data, overseeing logical database design and data dictionary development, and monitoring how information system specialists and end-user groups use data.

The fundamental principle of data administration is that all data are the property of the organization as a whole. Data cannot belong exclusively to any one business area or organizational unit. All data are to be made available to any group that requires them to fulfil its mission. An organization needs to formulate an

data administration
A special organizational function for managing the organization's data resources, concerned with information policy, data planning, maintenance of data dictionaries, and data quality standards.

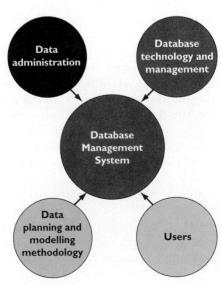

Data administration

Database technology and management

Database Management System

Data planning and modelling methodology

Users

FIGURE 8-17 Key organizational elements in the database environment. For a database management system to flourish in any organization, data administration functions and data planning and modelling methodologies must be coordinated with database technology and management. Resources must be devoted to train end users to use databases properly.

information policy
Formal rules governing the maintenance, distribution, and use of information in an organization.

information policy that specifies its rules for sharing, disseminating, acquiring, standardizing, classifying, and inventorying information throughout the organization. Information policy lays out specific procedures and accountabilities, specifying which organizational units share information, where information can be distributed, and who has responsibility for updating and maintaining the information. Although data administration is a very important organizational function, it has proved very challenging to implement.

Data Planning and Modelling Methodology

The organizational interests served by the DBMS are much broader than those in the traditional file environment; therefore, the organization requires enterprise-wide planning for data. Enterprise analysis, which addresses the information requirements of the entire organization (as opposed to the requirements of individual applications), is needed to develop databases. The purpose of enterprise analysis is to identify the key entities, attributes, and relationships that constitute the organization's data. These techniques are described in greater detail in Chapter 11.

Database Technology, Management, and Users

Databases require new software and new staff especially trained in DBMS techniques, as well as new data management structures. In most corporations, a database design and management group within the corporate information system division is responsible for defining and organizing the structure and content of the database and maintaining the database. In close cooperation with users, the design group establishes the physical database, the logical relations among data elements, and the access rules and procedures. The functions it performs are called **database administration**.

database administration
Refers to the more technical and operational aspects of managing data, including physical database design and maintenance.

A database serves a wider community of users than traditional systems. Relational systems with fourth-generation query languages permit employees who are not computer specialists to access large databases. In addition, users include trained computer specialists. To optimize access for non-specialists, more resources must be devoted to training end users.

8.4   DATABASE TRENDS

Organizations are installing powerful data analysis tools and data warehouses to make better use of the information stored in their databases and are taking advantage of database technology linked to the World Wide Web. We now explore these developments.

OBJECT-ORIENTED DATABASES

Conventional database management systems were designed for homogeneous textual or numeric data that could be easily structured into predefined data fields and records organized in rows or tables. But many applications today and in the future will require databases that can store and retrieve not only structured numbers and characters but also drawings, images, photographs, voice, and full-motion video. Conventional DBMS are not well suited to handling graphics-based or multimedia applications. For instance, design data in a computer-aided design (CAD) database consist of complex relationships among many types of data. Manipulating these kinds of data in a relational system requires extensive programming to translate these complex data structures into tables and rows. An object-oriented database management system, on the other hand, stores the data and procedures as objects that can be automatically retrieved and shared.

object-oriented DBMS
An approach to data management that stores both data and the procedures acting on the data as objects that can be automatically retrieved and shared; the objects can contain multimedia.

Object-oriented database management systems (OODBMS) are becoming popular because they can be used to manage the various multimedia components and Java applets used in Web applications, which typically integrate pieces of information from a variety of sources. OODBMS also are useful for storing data types such as recursive data. (An example would be parts within parts as found in manufacturing applications.) Finance and trading applications often use OODBMS because they require data models that must be easy to change to respond to new economic conditions. Jasmine *ii*, an OODBMS by Computer Associates, has been in use at 2000 beta sites, such as Surf N Shop (corp.surfnshop.com).

The Montreal-based company offers a portal-creation solution for organizations that already have an established relationship with buyers and sellers, such as magazines, banks, or shopping centres, said CEO Fernand Lecoq.

Target customers are "anyone who has a base of clients with trust built in." Surf N Shop offers a templates-based solution for very quick creation of a site and hosting, supplied in exchange for a percentage of the portal revenues. Because of Jasmine *ii*'s object-oriented nature, Lecoq said development time is reduced by half. He said the platform allows for the leveraging of legacy systems, with back-end integration, including ACCPAC. Cyril Déglise, a developer for Surf N Shop, said using an object-oriented database means "you're just accessing information in one way. To have done it with a relational database would have been a pain."

Although object-oriented databases can store more complex types of information than relational DBMS, they are relatively slow for processing large numbers of transactions compared with relational DBMS. Hybrid object-relational DBMS systems are now available to provide capabilities of both object-oriented and relational DBMS. A hybrid approach can be accomplished in three different ways: by using tools that offer object-oriented access to relational DBMS, by using object-oriented extensions to existing relational DBMS, or by using a hybrid **object-relational database management system**.

MULTIDIMENSIONAL DATA ANALYSIS

Sometimes managers need to analyze data in ways that traditional database models cannot represent. For example, a company selling four different products—nuts, bolts, washers, and screws—in the Atlantic, West, and Central regions, might want to know actual sales by product for each region and might also want to compare them with projected sales. This analysis requires a multidimensional view of data.

To provide this type of information, organizations can use either a specialized multidimensional database or a tool that creates multidimensional views of data in relational databases. Multidimensional analysis enables users to view the same data in different ways using multiple dimensions. Each aspect of information—product, pricing, cost, region, or time period—represents a different dimension. A product manager could use a multidimensional data analysis tool to learn how many washers were sold in the East in June, how that compares with the previous month and the previous June, and how it compares with the sales forecast. Another term for multidimensional data analysis is **online analytical processing (OLAP)**.

Figure 8-18 shows a multidimensional model that could be created to represent products, regions, actual sales, and projected sales. A matrix of actual sales can be stacked on top of a matrix of projected sales to form a cube with six faces. If you rotate the cube 90 degrees one way, the face showing will be product versus actual and projected sales. If you rotate the cube 90 degrees again, you can see region versus actual and projected sales. If you rotate 180 degrees from the original view, you can see projected sales and product versus region. Cubes can be nested within cubes to build complex views of data.

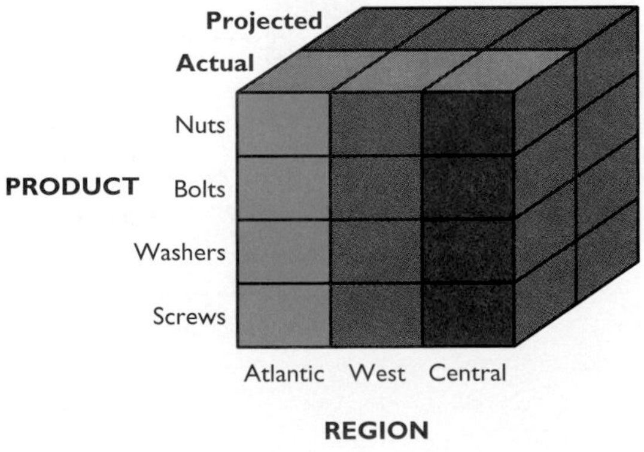

object-relational DBMS
A database management system that combines the capabilities of a relational DBMS for storing traditional information and the capabilities of an object-oriented DBMS for storing graphics and multimedia.

online analytical processing (OLAP)
Data analysis with the capability to manipulate and analyze large volumes of data from multiple perspectives.

FIGURE 8-18 Multidimensional data model. The view that is showing is product versus region. If you rotate the cube 90 degrees, the face that will be showing is product versus actual and projected sales. If you rotate the cube 90 degrees again, you can see region versus actual and projected sales. Other views are possible. The ability to rotate the data cube is the main technique for multidimensional reporting. It is sometimes called "slice and dice."

DATA WAREHOUSES AND DATAMINING

Decision makers need concise, reliable information about current operations, trends, and changes. What has previously been immediately available at most firms is current data only (historical data were available through special IS reports that took a long time to produce). Data are often fragmented in separate operational systems such as sales or payroll so that managers make decisions from incomplete knowledge. Users and information system specialists may have to spend inordinate amounts of time locating and gathering data (Watson and Haley, 1998). Data warehousing addresses this problem by integrating key operational data from around the company in a form that is consistent, reliable, and easily available for reporting.

What Is a Data Warehouse?

data warehouse

A database, with reporting and query tools, that stores current and historical data extracted from various operational systems and consolidated for management reporting and analysis.

A **data warehouse** is a database that stores current and historical data of potential interest to managers throughout the company. The data originate in many core operational systems and external sources, including Web site transactions, and are copied into the data warehouse database as often as needed—hourly, daily, weekly, monthly. The data are standardized and consolidated so that they can be used consistently and reliably across the enterprise for management analysis and decision making. The data are available for anyone to access as needed but cannot be altered. Figure 8-19 illustrates the data warehouse concept.

Companies can build enterprise-wide data warehouses where a central data warehouse serves the entire organization, or they can create smaller, decentralized warehouses called data marts. A **data mart** is a subset of a data warehouse in which a summarized or highly focused portion of the organization's data is placed in a separate database for a specific population of users. For example, a company might develop marketing and sales data marts to deal with customer information. A data mart typically focuses on a single subject area or line of business, so it usually can be constructed more rapidly and at lower cost than an enterprise-wide data warehouse. On the other hand, complexity, costs, and management problems will occur if an organization creates too many data marts.

data mart

A small data warehouse containing only a portion of the organization's data for a specified function or population of users.

Datamining

A data warehouse system provides a range of ad hoc and standardized query tools, analytical tools, and graphical reporting facilities, including tools for OLAP and datamining (see Figure 8-20). **Datamining** software tools find hidden patterns and relationships in large pools of data and infer rules from them that can be used to predict future behaviour and guide decision making. For example, mining data about purchases at a supermarket might reveal that when potato chips are purchased, soda is also purchased 65 percent of the time. When there is a promotion, soda is purchased 85 percent of the time. Datamining helps

datamining

Analysis of large pools of data to find patterns and rules that can be used to guide decision making and predict future behaviour.

FIGURE 8-19 Components of a data warehouse. A data warehouse extracts current and historical data from operational systems inside the organization. These data are combined with data from external sources and reorganized into a central database designed for management reporting and analysis. The information directory provides users with information about the data available in the warehouse.

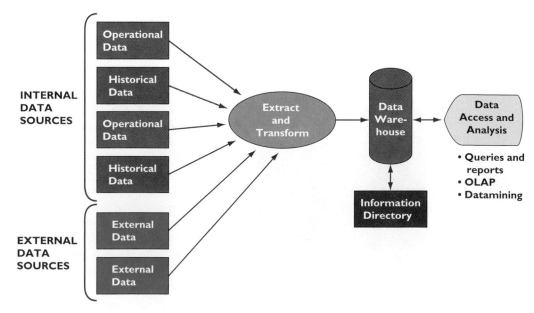

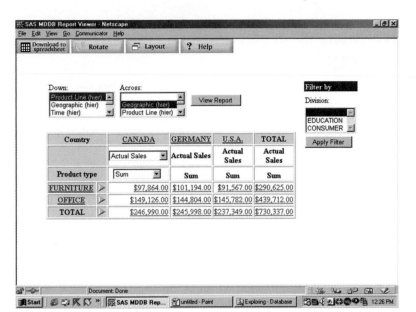

FIGURE 8-20 The SAS MDDP Report Viewer offers a Web interface for viewing and manipulating multdimensional databases produced with SAS software using business dimensions such as time, geography, or products. Online analytical processing (OLAP) gives users quick, unlimited views of multiple relationships in large quanities of summarized data.

companies engage in one-to-one marketing where personalized or individualized messages can be created based on individual preferences. Table 8-1 describes how some organizations are benefiting from datamining. These systems can perform high-level analyses of patterns or trends, but they can also drill into more detail where needed.

Benefits of Data Warehouses

Data warehouses not only offer improved information, they make it easy for decision makers to obtain it. They even include the ability to model and remodel the data. It has been estimated that 70 percent of the world's business information resides on mainframe databases, many of which are for older legacy systems. Many of these legacy systems are critical production

TABLE 8-1 HOW BUSINESSES USE DATAMINING

Organization	Datamining Application
Canadian Imperial Bank of Commerce (CIBC)	Customer profitability system helps the bank identify its most profitable customers so that it can offer them special sales and services.
Xerox Canada	Financial tracking system helps Xerox track revenues, P/L, receivables, and other financial data on its customers on a national account basis, from the time they become customers for as long as they remain in the Xerox fold. The system can pull together all customer financial data from several sources and develop reports from that data.
Molecular Mining Corp	Bioinformatics system, defined as the use of computer science to analyze biochemical data, uses data mining to find, for example, the right gene at which to target a drug. The system sifts through the reactions of 50 000 genes to dozens of different drug compounds to isolate the few drug and gene combinations that show a promising response.
American Express	Analyzes data from hundreds of billions of credit card purchases to create "one-to-one" marketing campaigns. Along with their credit card bills, customers receive personalized messages promoting goods and services in which they have shown interest.
Verizon Wireless	Analyzes Verizon's customer database to identify new customers so that customer-service representatives can find out if they need special help or services. Also uses datamining to identify mobile phone customers who might benefit from switching calling plans and mails them special promotions. Verizon uses these initiatives to increase customer satisfaction and thus reduce customer churn.

MANAGING CUSTOMER DATA FOR ABN AMRO BANK

Banking is a complex business, particularly when you are as big as the 14th largest bank in the world, with more than $600 billion in assets and offices in a number of countries. ABN AMRO Bank, NV, which is headquartered in Amsterdam, Netherlands, is also the largest foreign bank in North America with 17 000 employees and assets of $170 billion (www.abnamro.com). In this age of very large, complex corporations, all operating in an environment of globalization, the bank found it very difficult to manage its corporate customer relations or even to understand who its customers were and what services they were using.

The organization of many of these large corporations is the root of the problem. Many have multiple divisions and subsidiaries, each of which operates in multiple locations and maintains its own separate banking relationships. Moreover, each unit makes its own choices as to which of the bank's many services and products it will use. Each of these overall companies is an important customer of ABN AMRO, but how can the bank manage these complex customers? ABN AMRO's Chicago-based, North American management took what seemed to be the obvious step. It installed a customer data warehouse.

The bank contracted with consulting firm Ernst and Young to manage its project. The project's goal was to bring together the customer data from ABN AMRO's many branches for enterprise-wide reporting and analysis. To make the new system easily usable, the project focused on the user interface, selecting a product from Cognos of Burlington, Massachusetts, because it was both flexible and intuitive. The project was nicknamed CRISP (Corporate Relationship Information System Platform), and it proved to be a success.

Using a data warehouse, managers found they could bring the data together to better understand the firm's total relationship with each customer. Managers are now able to see what products the customer and all its units are using. They can iden-

tify which bank branches the customer is working with and which bank customers are subsidiaries or divisions of other customers. Management is even able to see reports on all customer contacts with individual companies regardless of the bank location or customer organizational unit.

Bank management is now able to take a more relationship-oriented approach to its customers. That means management is able to monitor general customer patterns and trends, regardless of how widespread the customer's organization is. Managers can easily compare the customer's current activities with its past activities and thereby spot any emerging trends, whether positive or negative. Also important has been the ability of managers to judge the risk exposure of the overall customer as well as the profitability of that customer's business with the bank. CRISP has also enabled management to monitor its own performance—its profitability, its revenue by product line, and the concentration of its commitments by geography, industry, and company.

ABN AMRO employees report that the project has enabled them to make faster decisions and to react quickly when needed. CRISP has improved employee productivity and thereby freed up staff to spend more time developing new customers and strengthening existing customer relations. It has even reduced report generation costs.

To Think About: Describe the business and environmental changes and forces that caused ABN AMRO in North America to turn to a data warehouse. What management, organization, and technology issues do you think the bank faced in making the project a success? Would these be the same issues faced by companies other than banks? Companies located anywhere in the world?

Sources: Sean Reid, "Warehousing Customer Data," *Strategic Vision*, Summer 2000; Robert Conlin, "Dutch Banking Giant Stays Neighborly with CRM," *CRM Daily*, April 20, 2001, available http://www.crmdaily.com/perl/story/9130.html, accessed September 27, 2001.

applications that support the company's core business processes. As long as these systems can efficiently process the necessary volume of transactions to keep the company running, firms are reluctant to replace them to avoid disrupting critical business functions and high system replacement costs. Many of these legacy systems use hierarchical DBMS or even older non-database files where information is difficult for users to access. Data warehouses enable decision makers to access data as often as needed without affecting the performance of the underlying operational systems. Many organizations are making access to their data warehouses even easier by using Web technology.

Organizations have used the information gleaned from data warehouses using OLAP and datamining to help them refocus their businesses. For example, PostBanken Norway built a data warehouse that included both internal data and data from external sources such as the public register of households. The company used these data to relate mortgage holders to variables such as age, sex, number of financial products used, and income. The results of the analysis showed that the prime candidates for mortgages were individuals aged 41–45, but the bank had been targeting its marketing campaigns toward people under the age of 30. By using the information from the data warehouse, PostBanken improved the quality of sales

MANAGEMENT DECISION PROBLEM

CREATING COMPANY-WIDE DATA STANDARDS

Your industrial supply company wants to create a data warehouse where management can obtain a single corporate-wide view of critical sales information to identify best-selling products in specific geographic areas, key customers, and sales trends. Your sales and product information are stored in two different systems: a divisional sales system running on a UNIX server and a corporate sales system running on an IBM mainframe. You would like to create a single standard format that consolidates these data from both systems. The following format has been proposed.

Product ID	Product Description	Cost per Unit	Units Sold	Sales Region	Division	Customer-ID

The following are sample files from the two systems that would supply the data for the data warehouse:

Mechanical Parts Division Sales System

Prod. No	Product Description	Cost per Unit	Units Sold	Sales Region	Customer-ID
60231	4" Steel bearing	5.28	900 245	West	Anderson
85773	SS assembly unit	12.45	992 111	East	Kelly Industries

Corporate Sales System

Product_ID	Product Description	Unit Cost	Units Sold	Sales Territory	Division
60231	Bearing, 4"	5.28	900 245	West	Parts
85773	SS assembly unit	12.02	992 111	East	Parts

1. What business problems are created by not having these data in a single standard format?

2. How easy would it be to create a database with a single standard format that could store the data from both systems? Identify the problems that would have to be addressed.

3. Should the problems be solved by database specialists or general business managers? Explain.

4. Who should have the authority to finalize a single company-wide format for this information in the data warehouse?

---

leads and the conversion of leads to actual sales. In six months, sales increased by 360 percent (Woods and O'Rourke, 2000). The Window on Organizations shows how ABN AMRO Bank, NV benefited from a data warehouse.

DATABASES AND THE WEB

Database technology plays an important role in making organizations' information resources available via the World Wide Web. We now explore the role of hypermedia databases on the Web and the growing use of Web sites to access information stored in conventional databases inside the firm.

The Web and Hypermedia Databases

Web sites store information as interconnected pages containing text, sound, video, and graphics using a **hypermedia database**. The hypermedia database approach to information management stores chunks of information in the form of nodes connected by links the user specifies (see Figure 8-21). The nodes can contain text, graphics, sound, full-motion video, or executable computer programs. Searching for information does not have to follow a predetermined organization scheme. Instead, one can branch instantly to related information in any kind of relationship the database developer establishes. The relationship between records is less structured than in a traditional DBMS.

The hypermedia database approach enables users to access topics on a Web site in whatever order they wish. For instance, from the home page from the Strategis Industry Canada Web site, located at strategis.ic.gc.ca and illustrated in Figure 8-22, the user can link to other Web pages by clicking on the topics in the left- or right-hand columns, or by clicking on a letter of the alphabet of the topic of interest. In addition to welcoming visitors to Strategis, these Web pages provide more information on recent business news, Industry Canada, Canadian companies and trade, and special topics of interest. The links from the current page to the other related Web pages are highlighted in blue. We provide more detail on these and other features of Web sites in Chapter 10.

hypermedia database
An approach to data management that organizes data as a network of nodes linked in any pattern the user specifies; the nodes can contain text, graphics, sound, full-motion video, or executable programs.

FIGURE 8-21 A hyper-media database. In a hypermedia database, the user can choose his or her own path to move from node to node. Each node can contain text, graphics, sound, full-motion video, or executable programs.

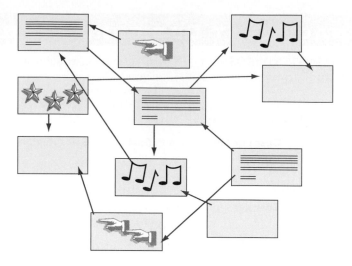

Linking Internal Databases to the Web

A series of middleware and other software products has been developed to help users gain access to organizations' legacy data through the Web. For example, a customer with a Web browser might want to search an online retailer's database for pricing information. Figure 8-23 illustrates how that customer might access the retailer's internal database over the Web. The user would access the retailer's Web site over the Internet using Web browser software on his or her client PC. The user's Web browser software would request data from the organization's database, using HTML commands to communicate with the Web server. Because many back-end databases cannot interpret commands written in HTML, the Web server would pass these requests for data to special middleware that would translate HTML commands into SQL so that they could be processed by the DBMS working with the database. The DBMS receives the SQL requests and provides the required data. The middleware would transfer information from the organization's internal database back to the Web server for delivery in the form of a Web page to the user. This approach, creating specific Web pages

FIGURE 8-22 From Industry Canada's Strategis Web site, you can link to other Web pages by clicking on the topics in the left- and right-hand columns or other links highlighted in blue.

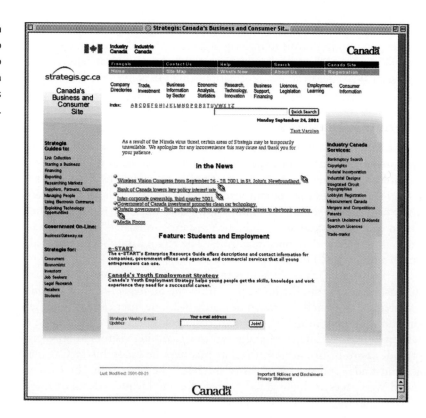

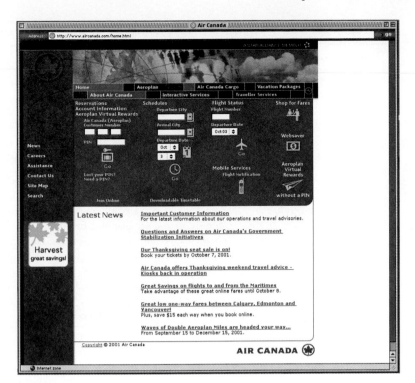

FIGURE 8-23 The Air Canada Web site allows the general public to access its schedule database. More and more organizations are using the Web to provide an interface to internal databases.

dynamically on request, is rapidly becoming a preferred approach to handling customer inquiries and ad hoc requests.

Figure 8-24 shows that the software working between the Web server and the DBMS could be an application server, a custom program, or a series of software scripts. An **application server** is software that handles all application operations between browser-based computers and a company's back-end business applications or databases. *Common Gateway Interface (CGI)* is a specification for transferring information between a Web server and a program designed to accept and return data. The program could be written in any programming language, including C, Perl, Java, or Visual Basic.

There are a number of advantages to using the Web to access an organization's internal databases. Web browser software is extremely easy to use, requiring much less training than even user-friendly database query tools. The Web interface requires no changes to the internal database. Companies leverage their investments in older systems because it costs much less to add a Web interface in front of a legacy system than to redesign and rebuild the system to improve user access.

Accessing corporate databases through the Web is creating new efficiencies and opportunities, in some cases even changing the way business is being done. Some companies have created new businesses based on access to large databases via the Web. Others are using Web technology to provide employees with integrated firm-wide views of information (see the Window on Technology). The major enterprise system vendors have enhanced their software so that users can access enterprise data through a Web interface. Table 8-2 describes some of these applications of Web-enabled databases.

application server
Software that handles all application operations between browser-based computers and a company's back-end business applications or databases.

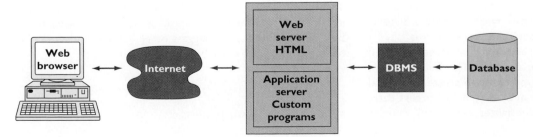

FIGURE 8-24 Linking internal databases to the Web. Users can access an organization's internal database through the Web using their desktop PCs and Web browser software.

TABLE 8-2	EXAMPLES OF WEB-ENABLED DATABASES
Organization	**Use of Web-Enabled Database**
MicroWarehouse (www.microwarehouse.ca)	Web site is linked to a relational database housing information about computer hardware, software, and peripherals. Visitors can immediately find online information about each electronic device and place orders over the Web.
Zellers (www.hbc.com/zellers/)	Web site links to a database of products that can be purchased online through Zellers' partner, HBC.com. The information users can access includes close up views and information on the products.
MapQuest (www.mapquest.com)	Web site links to a map database of information and maps about every country in the World, including city maps and world atlases. Visitors can use trip-planning functions, print maps, and even obtain maps of airports in larger cities. For businesses, MapQuest provides a full range of mapping and routing services, allowing clients to map-enable their Web, company intranet, and call-centre applications for improved marketing and customer service functionality. In addition, MapQuest provides maps and driving directions on a variety of wireless products.

WINDOW ON TECHNOLOGY

LINKING LEGACY DATABASES THROUGH THE INTERNET

Royal & SunAlliance Financial (www.royalsunalliance.com) wanted to sell its customers both life insurance and investment services. However, the Oakville, Ontario company faced a major obstacle. Its customer data were stored in two completely separate databases running on two independent mainframes. Given this situation, Royal and SunAlliance CEO Clive Smith said, "We can't tell who of our investment-product clients also has a life-insurance policy and vice versa." In addition the firm faced the data integrity problem that accompanies customer data being stored on multiple databases. If a change had to be made to the personal information in a customer's life insurance policy, it would have to be made in the other database as well.

Companies facing this problem have only two possible solutions. They could convert all existing data into a single new database, a long and expensive process, or they could connect the existing databases so they could be accessed as if they had been converted. Royal & SunAlliance turned to Unifi software, a product of DWL Inc. of Toronto, Canada. Unifi automates the process of linking existing databases and then making the data available through the Internet, leaving the existing databases intact. David Stahl, Royal & SunAlliance's CIO, estimated that building links to the data would have taken 18 months. By using Unifi, the entire process only took six to seven months.

Insurance is not the only business that faces the need addressed by DWL's software products. The Body Shop of Littlehampton, England, employed DWL to create the logical appearance of a single system out of its many product databases. The Body Shop, which specializes in natural cosmetics

and toiletries, has over 1700 stores in 48 countries. Prior to implementing DWL software in February 2000, the Body Shop would mail out monthly catalogues to its many stores worldwide. This expensive process meant that the data was always outdated. Now the data are all online, with accurate and up-to-date information on product availability, internal catalogues, and new offerings flowing seamlessly from headquarters to stores. The Body Shop expects to save hundreds of thousands of dollars by having this information readily available for more accurate orders and swifter delivery.

Both Royal & SunAlliance and The Body Shop are also benefiting from using Unifi's Internet access to their databases. Instead of accessing their databases with expensive proprietary systems, they can use PCs, Web browsers, and secure protected Internet connections for the task. Before switching to Unifi, Royal & SunAlliance employees communicated through old, hardwired technology across leased telephone lines and terminal screens with special codes that required a lot of training. Unifi's Internet interface is easy to use and requires no training. Scalability is an additional benefit. "With the old technology, we could roll out only a limited number of lines to the offices," adds Smith. "With this technology, the number of users is limitless."

To Think About: Suggest other ways the Unifi approach to legacy databases would save companies money or enhance their business operations. Also, suggest other businesses that would benefit from the use of such software.

Sources: Andy Patrizio, "Legacy Data: One Solution for Two Big Problems," *Information Week,* June 6, 2000; Diane Rezendes Khirallah, "Where Having Fun Really Pays," *Information Week,* January 15, 2001.

APPLICATION SOFTWARE EXERCISE

DATABASE EXERCISE: BUILDING A RELATIONAL DATABASE AT SYLVESTER'S BIKE SHOP

Bicycles have always fascinated Sylvester Jones. Sylvester has won several local, state, and regional bike races, once even competing in the Tour de France. His interest in bicycling and racing led him to open Sylvester's Bike Shop, located in San Francisco, California. While the store has only been open for a month, Sylvester's bicycle sales have been brisk. Sylvester sells road, mountain, hybrid, leisure, and children's bicycles. Currently, Sylvester purchases his bikes from three suppliers but plans to add new suppliers in the near future.

Sylvester expects his business to continue to grow and realizes a database will prove useful both now and in the future. Initially, he would like the database to house information about his suppliers and products. The database will contain two tables, a supplier table and a product table. Sylvester also recognizes the benefit of establishing a relationship between the two tables. He would like to perform several queries and produce several managerial reports based on the data contained in the two tables. In the future, he would like to keep information about his customers and will eventually build tables, queries, and reports to achieve this objective.

Using the information below, build a simple database for Sylvester. You may wish to use your DBMS' help feature to review the topics of relationships, queries, reporting, and table structures. Be sure to list at least three suppliers, ten types of bicycles, and two different reorder levels. Once you have built the database, perform the following activities.

A. Prepare a report that identifies the five most expensive bicycles. The report should list the bicycles in descending order from most expensive to least expensive. What is the quantity on hand for each? What is the profit margin for each?

B. Prepare a report that lists each supplier, its products, quantity on hand, and associated reorder levels. The report should be sorted alphabetically by supplier. Within each supplier category, the products should be sorted alphabetically.

C. Prepare a report listing only the bicycles that are low in stock.

MANAGEMENT WRAP-UP

Selecting an appropriate data model and data management technology for the organization is a key management decision. Managers will need to evaluate the costs and benefits of implementing a database environment and the capabilities of various DBMS or file management technologies. Management should ascertain that organizational databases are designed to meet management information objectives and the organization's business needs.

The organization's enterprise data model should reflect its key business processes and decision-making requirements. Data planning may be needed to ensure that the organization's data model delivers information efficiently for its business processes and enhances organizational performance. Designing a database is an organizational endeavour.

Multiple database and file management options are available for organizing and storing information. Key technology decisions should consider the efficiency of accessing information, flexibility in organizing information, the type of information to be stored and arranged, compatibility with the organization's data model, and compatibility with the organization's hardware and operating systems.

For Discussion
1. It has been said that you do not need database management software to create a database environment. Discuss.
2. To what extent should end users be involved in the selection of a database management system and database design?

SUMMARY

1. *Describe basic file organization concepts and the problems of the traditional file environment.* A computer system organizes data in a hierarchy that starts with bits and bytes and progresses to fields, records, files, and databases. A record describes an entity, which is a person, place, thing, or event on which we maintain information. Each characteristic or quality describing a particular entity is called an attribute. A file is a group of related records.

By allowing different functional areas and groups in the organization to maintain their own files independently, the traditional file environment creates problems such as lack of data integrity, data redundancy and inconsistency, program-data dependence, inflexibility, poor security, and lack of data sharing and accessibility.

2. *Describe how a database management system organizes and manages information.* A database management system (DBMS) is the software that permits centralization of data and data management. A DBMS includes a data definition language, a data manipulation language, and a data dictionary. The most important feature of the DBMS is its ability to separate the logical and physical views of data. The user works with a logical view of data. The DBMS software translates user queries into queries that can be applied to the physical view of the data. The DBMS retrieves information so that the user does not have to be concerned with its physical location or platform. This feature separates programs from data and from the management of data.

3. *Compare the principal types of databases.* The principal types of databases today are relational DBMSs and object-oriented DBMSs. Relational systems are very flexible for supporting ad hoc requests for information and for combining information from different sources. They support many-to-many relationships among entities and are efficient for storing alphanumeric data that can be organized into structured fields and records. Object-oriented DBMS can store graphics and other types of data in addition to conventional text data to support multimedia applications. Older types of databases include hierarchical, which supports a one parent–many children structure, and the network model, which supports a many parent–many children structure. Both hierarchical and network models are less flexible and user friendly than relational or object-oriented databases.

4. *Identify important database design principles.* Designing a database requires both a logical design and a physical design. The process of creating small, stable data structures from complex groups of data when designing a relational database is termed normalization. Database design considers whether a complete database or portions of the database can be distributed to more than one location to increase responsiveness and reduce vulnerability and costs. There are two major types of distributed databases: replicated databases and partitioned databases.

5. *Identify the managerial and organizational requirements of a database environment.* Developing a database environment requires much more than selecting technology. It requires a change in the corporation's attitude toward information. The organization must develop a data administration function and a data planning methodology. There is often political resistance in organizations to many key database concepts, especially to sharing information that has been controlled exclusively by one organizational group. If changes to the organization do not take place, the benefits offered by a DBMS will not be maximized.

6. *Discuss new database trends.* New tools and technologies provide users with more powerful tools to analyze the information in databases and to take advantage of information resources on the World Wide Web. Multidimensional data analysis, also known as online analytical processing (OLAP), can represent relationships among data as a multidimensional structure, which can be visualized as cubes of data and cubes within cubes of data, allowing for more sophisticated data analysis.

Data can be more conveniently analyzed across the enterprise by using a data warehouse, in which current and historical data are extracted from many different operational systems and consolidated for management decision making. Datamining analyzes large pools of data, including the contents of data warehouses, to find patterns and rules that can be used to predict future behaviour and guide decision making. Hypermedia databases allow data to be stored in nodes linked together in any pattern the user establishes and are used for storing information at Web sites. Conventional databases can be linked to the Web to facilitate user access to the data.

KEY TERMS

Application server, 281

Attribute, 261

Data administration, 273

Data definition language, 265

Data dictionary, 265

Data element, 265

Data integrity, 263

Data manipulation language, 265

Data mart, 276

Data redundancy, 263

Data warehouse, 276

Database, 261

Database (rigorous definition), 264

Database administration, 274

Database management system (DBMS), 264

Datamining, 276

Distributed database, 272

Entity, 261

Entity relationship diagram, 271

Field, 261

File, 261

Hierarchical data model, 266

Hypermedia database, 279

Information policy, 274

Join, 268

Key field, 262

REVIEW QUESTIONS

1. Why is file management important for overall system performance?

2. List and describe each of the components in the data hierarchy from the smallest to the largest.

3. Define and explain the significance of entities, attributes, and key fields.

4. List and describe some of the problems of the traditional file environment.

5. Define a database and a database management system.

6. Name and briefly describe the three components of a DBMS.

7. What is the difference between a logical and a physical view of data?

8. List some benefits of a DBMS.

9. Describe the principal types of databases and the advantages and disadvantages of each.

10. Name and describe the three most important SQL commands.

11. What is normalization? How is it related to the features of a well-designed relational database?

12. What is a distributed database, and what are the two main ways of distributing data?

13. What are the four key organizational elements of a database environment? Describe each briefly.

14. Describe the capabilities of online analytical processing (OLAP) and datamining.

15. What is a data warehouse? How can it benefit organizations?

16. What is a hypermedia database? How does it differ from a traditional database? How is it used for the Web?

17. How can users access information from a company's internal databases via the Web?

GROUP PROJECT

Review Figure 8-4, which provides an overview of a human resources database. Some additional information that might be maintained in such a database are an employee's date of hire, date of termination, date of birth, educational level, gender code, Employment Insurance, year-to-date gross and net pay, amount of life insurance coverage, supplementary healthcare plan payroll-deduction amount, life insurance plan payroll-deduction amount, and pension plan payroll-deduction amount.

Form a group with three or four of your classmates. Prepare two sample reports using the data in the database that might be of interest to either the employer or the employee. What pieces of information should be included on each report? In addition, prepare a data dictionary entry for one of the data elements in the database similar to the entry illustrated in Figure 8-5.

Your group's analysis should determine what business functions use this data element, which function has the primary responsibility for maintaining the data element, and which positions in the organization can access that data element. If possible, use electronic presentation software to present your findings to the class.

 INTERNET CONNECTION

■ COMPANION WEBSITE

At www.pearsoned.ca/laudon, you'll find an online study guide with two quizzes to test your knowledge of how database management systems are created and used in modern organizations. You'll also find updates to the chapter and online exercises and cases that enable you to apply your knowledge to realistic situations.

■ ADDITIONAL SITES OF INTEREST

There are many interesting Web sites to enhance your learning about database software. You can search the Web yourself, or just try the following sites to add to what you have already learned.

Oracle Corporation

   www.oracle.com/ca-en/

   The Canadian arm of one of the world's major database/ERP companies

Microsoft Corporation

   www.microsoft.com/office

   Publisher of MS Access, the most popular desktop database software

IBM Corporation

www-4.ibm.com/software/data/db2/

Publisher of DB2, the most popular mainframe database software

---

CASE STUDY   *Ford and Firestone's Tire Recall: The Costliest Information Gap in History*

On August 9, 2000, Bridgestone/Firestone Inc. announced it would recall more than 6.5 million tires, most of which had been mounted as original equipment on Ford Motor Co. Explorers and other Ford light trucks. Bridgestone/Firestone had become the subject of an intense federal investigation of 46 deaths and over 300 incidents where Firestone tires allegedly shredded on the highway. The Firestone tires affected were 15-inch Radial ATX and Radial ATX II tires produced in North America, and certain Wilderness AT tires manufactured at the firm's Decatur, Illinois plant. This tire recall was the second largest in history, behind only Firestone's 1978 recall of 14.5 million radial tires. The 1978 tire recall financially crippled the company for years afterward, and the August 2000 recall threatened to do the same. Consumers, the federal government, and the press wanted to know: Why didn't Ford and Firestone recognize this problem sooner? Let us look at the series of events surrounding the tire recall. These events reveal the role of information management in this tragedy.

1988—Financially weakened from its 1978 tire recall, Firestone agreed to be acquired by Bridgestone Tires, a Japanese firm. To increase its sales, Firestone became a supplier of tires for Ford Motor's new sport-utility vehicle (SUV), the Explorer.

March 11, 1999—In response to Ford's concern about tire separations on the Explorer, Bridgestone/Firestone (Firestone) sent a confidential memo to Ford claiming that less than 0.1 percent of all Wilderness tires (which are used on the Explorer) have been returned under warranty for any kind of problem. The note did not list tire separations on their own but did say this "rate of return is extremely low and substantiates [Firestone's] belief that this tire performs exceptionally well in the U.S. market."

August 1999—Ford Motor announced a recall in 16 foreign countries of all tires that had shown a tendency to fail primarily because of a problem of tread separation. The failures were primarily on the Ford Explorer, and the largest number of tires recalled was in Saudi Arabia. Firestone produced most of these tires. (A year earlier, Ford had noted problems with tread separation on Firestone tires mounted on Explorers in Venezuela and had sent samples of the failed tires to Bridgestone for analysis.) Ford did not report the recall to U.S. safety regulators because reporting was not required.

2000

Early February 2000—Firestone announced its "great pride in the quality and durability of our products." This announcement was in response to an investigation by KHOU-TV in Houston, Texas into three fatal incidents involving Firestone Radial ATX tires on Ford Explorers.

May 2—Three days after another fatal accident involving Firestone/Ford Explorer tread separations, the U.S. National Highway Transportation Safety Administration (NHTSA) opened a full investigation into possible defects with the Firestone ATX, ATX II, and Wilderness tires. The agency listed 90 complaints nationwide including 34 crashes and 24 injuries or deaths. NHTSA also learned of the foreign recalls.

August 4—Sears Roebuck and Co. announced it would cease selling Firestone's ATX, ATX II, and Wilderness tires. At this point, the NHTSA had 193 complaints about these tires, including 21 deaths. Firestone reiterated its belief that the tires were safe. Ford stated it was still investigating and could not respond yet.

August 9—At a news conference, Firestone announced that it would recall about 6.5 million tires that were on light trucks and SUVs because they had been implicated in more than 40 fatalities. Ford officials attended and stated Ford was cooperating. The tires were mostly on Ford Explorers. The company said it would replace all listed tires on any vehicle regardless of their condition or age. Firestone did not plan to recall tires made in Joliet, Quebec, or Wilson, NC.

Firestone said it continued to stand by the tires. Gary Crigger, executive vice president of Bridgestone/Firestone Inc., explained the recall by saying "At Bridgestone/Firestone, nothing is more important to us than the safety of our customers. We felt we must take this extraordinary step as a precaution to ensure consumer safety and consumer confidence in our brands." One Japanese analyst estimated the recall would cost Firestone as much as U.S.$500 million.

Firestone emphasized the importance of maintaining proper inflation pressure. Firestone recommended a pressure of 30 pounds-per-square-inch (psi) whereas Ford recommended a range of 26 to 30 psi. Ford claimed its tests showed the tire performed well at 26 psi and the lower pressure makes for a smoother ride. However, Firestone claimed under-inflation could put too much pressure on the tire, contributing to a higher temperature and causing the belts to separate.

Ford stated it had "worked closely with Firestone to thoroughly investigate" the tread separation problem, and that "After extensive review of the data, we are satisfied that Firestone has isolated the affected population of tires that should be recalled." Ford pointed out that while the NHTSA had not closed its investigation, the two companies did not want to wait to act. The NHTSA had received 270 complaints, including 46 deaths and 80 injuries.

August 10—Press reports asked why Ford did not act within the United States when it took action to replace tires on over 4000 Explorers sold overseas.

August 11—*Canadian Driver Magazine* reported that neither Nissan nor Subaru vehicles in Canada would be affected by the recall of the Firestone tires.

August 13—*The Washington Post* reported that the Decatur, Illinois, Firestone plant, source of many of the recalled tires, "was rife with quality-control problems in the mid-1990s." It said, "workers [were] using questionable tactics to speed production, and managers were giving short shrift to inspections." One tactic described was workers "puncturing bubbles on tires to cover up flaws on products that should have been scrapped."

August 15—The NHTSA announced it now linked 62 deaths to the recalled Firestone tires. It had also received over 750 complaints on these tires.

August 17—Bridgestone/Firestone submitted a recall notification to Transport Canada concerning problems with the three types of tires. Transport Canada posted the recall to its Web site and "encouraged" motorists who had experienced a tread separation and had the failed tire available for examination to call a 1-800 number to speak to a defect investigator. Over 250 000 Canadian tires were involved.

August 30—Ford announced that more than one million tires had already been replaced.

September 4—The United States Congress opened hearings on the Firestone and Ford tire separation problem. Congressional investigators released a memo from Firestone to Ford dated March 12, 1999, in which Firestone expressed "major reservations" about a Ford plan to replace Firestone tires overseas. According to Representative W.J. Tauzin of Louisiana, "The [1999] memo basically says 'you guys [Ford officials] made the decision to use these tires in the hot desert without consulting us [Firestone officials], so you assume responsibility for replacing them. And besides, we would prefer the [U.S. Department of Transportation] not know about this [foreign recall] program.'" A Ford representative at the hearing argued it had no need to report the replacement program because it was addressing a customer satisfaction problem and not a safety issue. The spokesperson added, "We are under no statutory obligations [to report overseas recalls] on tire actions."

Ford CEO Jacques Nasser testified before a joint congressional hearing that, "This is clearly a tire issue and not a vehicle issue." He pointed out that: "There are almost 3 million Goodyear tires on Ford Explorers that have not had a tread separation problem. So we know that this is a Firestone tire issue." However, he emphasized that Ford feels "a responsibility to do our best to prevent…this from ever happening again." He offered to work with the tire industry to develop and implement an "early warning system" to detect signs of tire defects earlier. He said: "This new system will require that tire manufacturers provide comprehensive real-world data on a timely basis." He also said that, in the future, his company would advise U.S. authorities of safety actions taken in overseas markets and vice versa.

Nasser said his company did not know of the problem until a few days prior to the announcement of the recall because "tires are the only component of a vehicle that are separately warranted." Ford had not obtained warranty data on tires the same way it does for any other part of a vehicle. It was Firestone that had collected the tire warranty data. Nasser said his company had "virtually pried the claims data from Firestone's hands and analyzed it." Ford thus lacked a database that could be used to deter-

mine whether reports of incidents with one type of tire could indicate a special problem relative to tires on other Ford vehicles. Ford only obtained the tire warranty data from Firestone on July 28. A Ford team with representatives of the legal, purchasing, and communication departments, safety experts, and Ford's truck group worked intensively with experts from Firestone to try to find a pattern in the tire incident reports. They finally determined that the problem tires originated in a Decatur, Illinois, plant during a specific period of production, and that the bulk of tire-separation incidents had occurred in Arizona, California, Texas, and Florida, all hot states. This correlated with the circumstances surrounding tire separations overseas.

Referring to the 1999 tire recalls in Saudi Arabia and other countries, Nasser said that when Ford dealers reported complaints, "We immediately asked Firestone to investigate." They did so, he said, and Firestone concluded "that the tread separations were caused by improper maintenance and road hazards unique to that environment." Because Ford was still troubled, Nasser said his company asked Firestone to conduct "all sorts of tests on the tires." When Firestone found no evidence of defects, Ford decided to replace the tires anyway to "satisfy our Saudi customers." He also asked Firestone to review data on U.S. customers. Firestone assured Ford that "There was no problem in this country," and, Nasser added, "our data, as well as government safety data, didn't show anything either." Nonetheless, he asked Firestone for an evaluation of tires in Texas, Nevada, and Arizona, where most of the failures were occurring. Again, Firestone found no problems. Nasser said Ford only became concerned when it "saw Firestone's confidential claims data." He added, "If I have one regret, it is that we did not ask Firestone the right questions sooner."

September 8—*The New York Times* released its own analysis of the Department of Transportation's Fatality Analysis Reporting System (FARS). FARS is one of the few tools available to government to independently track defects that cause fatal accidents. The *Times* found that "fatal crashes involving Ford Explorers were almost three times as likely to be tire related as fatal crashes involving other sport utility vehicles." The newspaper's analysis also said "The federal data shows no tire-related fatalities involving Explorers from 1991 to 1993 and a steadily increasing number thereafter, which may reflect that tread separation becomes more common as tires age."

Their analysis brought to light difficulties in finding patterns in the data that would have alerted various organizations to a problem earlier. Ford and Firestone said they had not detected such a pattern in the data, and the NHTSA said they had looked at a variety of databases without finding the tire flaw pattern.

The Department of Transportation databases independently track defects that contribute to fatal accidents, with data on about 40 000 fatalities each year. They only have information on type of vehicle, not the type of tire, involved in a fatality. Tire involvement in fatal accidents is common because tires, in the normal course of their life, will contribute to accidents as they age, so that accidents where tires may be a factor are usually not noteworthy. In comparison, Sue Bailey, the head of NHTSA, pointed out that accidents with seat belt failures stand out because seat belts should never fail. Safety experts note that very little data is collected on accidents resulting only in non-fatal injuries even though that there are six-to-eight times more such accidents than fatal accidents. Experts also note that no data is collected on the even more common accidents with only property damage. If more data were collected, the *Times* concluded, "Trends could be obvious sooner." Until Firestone announced its tire recall in August 2000, NHTSA had received only 5 complaints per year concerning Firestone's ATX, ATX II, and Wilderness AT tires out of 50 000 complaints of all kinds about vehicles.

While Firestone executives had just testified that Firestone's warranty claim data did not show a problem with the tires, Firestone documents made public by congressional investigators showed that in February, Firestone officials were already concerned with rising warranty costs for the now recalled tires. Firestone "had not perceived the rising claims as a problem," commented Firestone executive vice president for sales John Lampe, "because the number of Firestone tires in use had been increasing as the company gained market share." According to Crigger, the company relied on warranty data, factory quality tests, and field research on performance, none of which pointed to tread separation problems.

September 12—Yoichiro Kaizaki, president of Bridgestone (parent of Firestone), acknowledged inadequate attention to quality control. "The responsibility for the problem lies with Tokyo," he said. "We let the U.S. unit use its own culture. There was an element of mistake in that."

September 19—*USA Today* reported that, in more than 80 tire lawsuits against Firestone since 1991, internal Firestone documents and sworn testimony have been kept secret as part of the Firestone settlements. Observers noted that had these documents been made public at the time, many of the recent deaths might have been avoided.

September 20—NHTSA announced that the death toll linked to faulty Firestone tires was 103.

September 22—The Firestone tires that were at the centre of the recalled tires passed all United States government-required tests, causing NHTSA head Sue Bailey to say "Our testing is clearly outdated." During September, both Bridgestone and Firestone announced they would install supply chain information systems to prevent anything similar happening in the future.

2001

February 23, 2001—Firestone recalled certain model Firehawk GTA-02 tires in size P205/55R16 made at Wilson, NC. While most of these tires were fitted on certain model 2000 and 2001 Nissan Altima SE vehicles, the rest have been sold in replacement tire markets, including Canada. About 1315 Nissan Altima SE vehicles in Canada are also affected by the recall. Yoichiro Kaizaki, Bridgestone president, had already announced that he would step down in April 2001 to take responsibility for the recall.

May 11—The Toronto law firm of Rochon Genova filed a class action lawsuit against Ford Motor Company and Bridgestone/Firestone, alleging the companies knew tires on Ford vehicles were faulty. The suit was launched by Michelle Rambharos of Brampton, ON, who was injured when one of the

Firestone tires on her 1995 Ford Explorer ruptured, causing the vehicle to flip over. The lawsuit also sought to expand the recall of Firestone tires and to help Canadian consumers who might be hurt if the resale value of their Ford Explorers had decreased due to the reported problems with the vehicles.

May 22—Bridgestone/Firestone ended its tire supply relationship with the Ford Motor Company, saying that they no longer had a relationship "built upon trust" and reiterating the view that their tires are safe and that the Ford Explorer has "significant safety issues."

May 31—Bridgestone/Firestone asked the U.S. government to investigate the safety of the Ford Explorer. The tire company says that the problem is not "a tire problem, but a vehicle problem."

June 20—Winnipeg-based Faneuil Group received a 2001 Laureate Award from the ComputerWorld Honours Program that honours individuals and organizations using IT to improve society. Faneuil Group was singled out for the automated response system it developed in 2000 to handle customer e-mail on behalf of Bridgestone/Firestone during the recall program. In the three months following the recall, Faneuil received more than 1.4 million inquiries from Bridgestone/Firestone customers, including 80 000 e-mails. The e-mail filtering program used by Faneuil allowed for more than 80 percent of the e-mail inquiries to be fully answered automatically.

July 24—Bridgestone/Firestone settled about 40 percent of the person-injury lawsuits filed over the Wilderness AT and ATX tires. At least 203 deaths and more than 700 injuries were linked to Firestone tire failures in the U.S. alone.

Sources: Matthew L. Wald and Josh Barbanel, "Link Between Tires and Crashes Went Undetected in Federal Data," *The New York Times*, September 8, 2000; Robert L. Stimson, Karen Lundegaard, Norhiko Shirouzu, and Jenny Heller, "How the Tire Problem Turned Into a Crisis For Firestone and Ford," *The Wall Street Journal*, August 10, 2000; Mark Hall, "Information Gap," *Computerworld*, September 18, 2000; Keith Bradsher, "Documents Portray Tire Debacle as a Story of Lost Opportunities," *The New York Times*, September 10, 2000; Ed Foldessy and Stephen Power, "How Ford, Firestone Let the Warnings Slide By as Debacle Developed," *The Wall Street Journal*, September 6, 2000; Ford Motor Company, "Bridgestone/Firestone Announces Voluntary Tire Recall," Ford Motor Company, August 9, 2000; Edwina Gibbs, "Bridgestone Sees $350 million Special Loss, Stock Dives," Yahoo.com, August 10, 2000; John O'Dell and Edmund Sanders, "Firestone Begins Replacement of 6.4 Million Tires," *Los Angeles Times*, August 10, 2000; James V. Grimaldi, "Testimony Indicates Abuses at Firestone," *Washington Post*, August 13, 2000; Dina ElBoghdady, "Broader Tire Recall is Urged," *Detroit News*, August 14, 2000; "Ford Report Recommended Lower Tire Pressure," *The Associated Press*, August 20, 2000; Caroline E. Mayer, James V. Grimaldi, Stephen Power, and Robert L. Simison, "Memo Shows Bridgestone and Ford Considered Recall Over a Year Ago," *The Wall Street Journal*, September 6, 2000; Timothy Aeppel, Clare Ansbery, Milo Geyelin, and Robert L. Simison, "Ford and Firestone's Separate Goals, Gaps in Communication Gave Rise to Tire Fiasco," *The Wall Street Journal*, September 6, 2000; Matthew L. Wald, "Rancor Grows Between Ford and Firestone," *The New York Times*, September 13, 2000; Keith Bradsher, "Questions Raised About Ford Explorer's Margin of Safety,"

The New York Times, September 16, 2000; "Sealed Court Records Kept Tire Problems Hidden," *USA Today*, September 19, 2000; Tim Dobbyn, "Firestone Recall Exposes Flaws in Government Tests," *New York Daily News*, September 22, 2000; Bridgestone/Firestone, Inc., "Statement of February 4, 2000," Tire-defects.com; "Nissan Canada, Subaru Vehicles Not Affected by Firestone Recall," *Canadian Driver*, August 11, 2000; "The Firestone Tire Recall," Transport Canada, www.tc.gc.ca/en/mediaroom/backgrounders/firestone.htm, accessed May 16, 2001; "Firestone Issues Tire Recall After Finding Surface Cracks," *National Post Online*, February 23, 2001, www.nationalpost.com, accessed May 16, 2001; "Massive Tire Recall Sends Bridgestone Profits Skidding," *National Post Online*, February 23, 2001, www.nationalpost.com, accessed May 16, 2001; "Ford and Firestone Face Faulty Tire Suit in Canada," *National Post Online*, May 11, 2001, www.nationalpost.com, accessed May 16, 2001; Murray McNeill, "Faneuil Hailed for Effort in Tire Recall," *Winnipeg Free Press*, June 20, 2001, p. B3.

CASE STUDY QUESTIONS:

1. To what extent was this crisis an information management problem? What role did databases and data management play?

2. Why do you think it took so long for the issue to come to the attention of the general public?

3. List the different databases the parties had at their disposal as the problem grew, and list the data elements in those databases that were key to finding the tread separation problem earlier.

Ignoring for the moment all other data problems, what critical data elements were these organizations not storing? For each one, indicate why you think it was critical and why it was not being stored.

4. Make a list of useful queries that these organizations might have asked of the databases but did not. Discuss why you think they did not ask these questions.

5. Evaluate the types of data collected and the questions asked in analyzing the data by each of the key organizations (Firestone, Ford, the U.S. government, the Canadian government, and the legal community).

6. How did the relationship between Firestone, Ford, the U.S. and Canadian governments, and the legal community affect the development of the problem? the decisions on action that needed to be taken?

7. What data-related changes and improvements did the various parties and reporters suggest? Name other changes you believe should be made.

8. While legal responsibility rests with the courts, who do you think is ethically responsible for the deaths, injuries, and damage caused by the defective tires? Who is ethically responsible for the recall of the tires? Do you feel the decisions that were made at Firestone and Ford were unethical? Which decisions? Why? Who made those decisions? What influenced these decision makers to make unethical decisions?

9 TELECOMMUNI- CATIONS AND NETWORKS

OBJECTIVES

After completing this chapter, you will be able to:

1. *Describe the basic components of a telecommunications system.*

2. *Determine the capacity of telecommunications channels and evaluate transmission media.*

3. *Compare the various types of telecommunications networks and network services.*

4. *Compare alternative network services.*

5. *Identify principal telecommunications applications for supporting electronic commerce and electronic business.*

Toronto's Electronic Child Health Network Connects Remote Healthcare Workers

The patients of the Hospital for Sick Children (www.sickkids.on.ca) in Toronto are especially difficult to treat. Many have severe problems such as heart disease, cancer, or conditions requiring complex surgery, but they come from across Canada to Toronto and often move around a lot during the course of their treatment. In trying to provide care for these children, the Hospital for Sick Children found that the linkages among the hospitals it worked with were very poor. When these hospitals had to refer patients to the Hospital for Sick Children or when the Hospital sent patients back to them, systems for moving information with the patient were very primitive or non-existent. Patient records had to be mailed, faxed, or sent by courier.

To promote better patient care, the Hospital for Sick Children created an electronic Child Health Network (www.echn.com) linking it to three community hospitals, a homecare service, and a dozen physicians. The system is a secure network based on IBM's Health Data Network, a suite of software and hardware products that extracts information from the health records of each of the participating organizations using a Netscape Web browser. The system extracts information from the patient record systems of all of these organizations into a single chart that can be accessed by any of the participants using a Web browser. Five IBM RS/6000 servers link five eCHN sites, including a community hospital 60 miles away, with the admissions, registration, and critical information systems of the Hospital for Sick Children.

eCHN has three components: *Your Child's Health*, a public Web site that provides maternal, new-born, and child health information to parents and children; *Professional Online Forum (PROFOR)*, a professional development Web site for Ontario healthcare providers; and *Health Information Network (HiNet)*, a secure electronic database to allow the sharing of children's health records by healthcare providers across Ontario. Your Child's Health contains nine interactive kids' games/stories and logged over 665 000 page visits over a 12 month period.

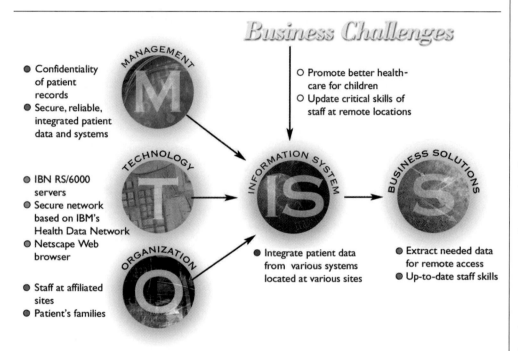

Business Challenges

MANAGEMENT
- Confidentiality of patient records
- Secure, reliable, integrated patient data and systems

TECHNOLOGY
- IBN RS/6000 servers
- Secure network based on IBM's Health Data Network
- Netscape Web browser

ORGANIZATION
- Staff at affiliated sites
- Patient's families

- ○ Promote better healthcare for children
- ○ Update critical skills of staff at remote locations

INFORMATION SYSTEM
- Integrate patient data from various systems located at various sites

BUSINESS SOLUTIONS
- Extract needed data for remote access
- Up-to-date staff skills

A doctor at an eCHN-affiliated hospital can view, from her computer screen, an X-ray taken at another affiliated hospital. The computer display even resembles an actual medical file, complete with tabs for such things as lab reports and radiology images. In a recent 12 month period, HiNet had 1.5 million transactions conducted for over 75 000 patients who had 370 000 encounters (hospital visits, tests, etc.) that were recorded on HiNet. PROFOR provides a private Web site where remote healthcare workers can update their clinical skills. Some remote hospitals have only two pediatricians. Using eCHN, they can view seminars and teaching rounds of the Toronto Hospital for Sick Children over streaming video at their convenience. The PROFOR component contains 213 streaming video presentations and has more than 1628 registered users.

Eventually, eCHN hopes to expand its network to include the patient records of adults as well as children. This would enable all eCHN-affilated hospitals to share information on adults, with the adults able to decide what information the physician can see. For example, if a patient is seeing a doctor about a broken leg, he can decide he doesn't want the doctor to see information pertaining to a bout with the flu 10 years earlier.

Sources: Walter A. Kleinschrod, "Keeping Workers Connected," *Beyond Computing*, June 2000; "Hospital for Sick Children and IBM Receive Award for the Child Health Network," IBM Press Release, November 23, 1999; Marjo Johns, "Prescription for Knowledge: Hospital Network to Boost Sharing," *National Post*, August 1, 2000; "The eCHN Annual Report for 2000/2001," available www.echn.ca, accessed September 28, 2001.

MANAGEMENT CHALLENGES

The members of the electronic Child Health Network, like many organizations all over the world, have found ways to benefit from communications technology to coordinate their internal activities and to communicate more efficiently with other organizations. It would be virtually impossible to conduct business today without using communications technology; applications of networks and communications technology for electronic business and electronic commerce are multiplying. However, incorporating communications technology into today's applications and information technology infrastructure raises several management challenges:

1. **Managing LANs.** Although local area networks appear to be flexible and inexpensive ways of delivering computing power to new areas of the organization, they must be carefully administered and monitored. LANs are especially vulnerable to network disruption, loss of essential data, access by unauthorized users, and infection from computer viruses (see Chapter 12). Dealing with these problems requires special technical expertise that is not normally available in end-user departments.

2. **Managing bandwidth.** Networks are the foundation of electronic commerce and the digital economy. Without network infrastructures that offer fast, reliable access, companies would lose many online customers and jeopardize relationships with suppliers and business partners as well. While telecommunication transmission costs are rapidly dropping, total network transmission capacity (bandwidth) requirements are growing at a rate of more than 40 percent each year. If more people use networks or if the firm implements data-intensive applications that require high-capacity transmission, a firm's network costs can easily spiral upward. Balancing the need to ensure network reliability and availability against mushrooming network costs is a central management concern.

Most of the information systems we use today require networks and communications technology. Large and small companies from all over the world are using networked systems and the Internet to locate suppliers and buyers, to negotiate contracts with them, and to service their needs. Applications of networks are multiplying in research, organizational coordination, and control. Networked systems are fundamental to electronic commerce and electronic business.

Today's computing tasks are so closely tied to networks that some believe "the network is the computer." This chapter describes the components of telecommunications systems, showing how they can be arranged to create various types of networks and network-based applications that can increase an organization's efficiency and competitiveness.

9.1   THE TELECOMMUNICATIONS REVOLUTION

telecommunications
The communication of information by electronic means, usually over some distance.

Telecommunications is the communication of information by electronic means, usually over some distance. Previously, telecommunications meant voice transmission over telephone lines. Today a great deal of telecommunications transmission is digital data transmission, using computers to transmit data from one location to another. We are currently in the middle of a telecommunications revolution that is spreading communications technology and telecommunications services throughout the world.

THE MARRIAGE OF COMPUTERS AND COMMUNICATIONS

Telecommunications used to be a monopoly of either the province or a regulated public or private firm. Telecommunications in Canada and the rest of the world traditionally has been administered primarily by a regulated post, telephone, and telegraph authority. In 1993, the Telecommunications Act established federal control of all of the provincial telephone companies, with the exception of Saskatchewan. This opened the door for competition from outside each province and for additional services to be offered by the telephone companies.

Today Canadian telephone and cable television companies offer Internet services and serve as Internet portals.

Thousands of companies have sprung up to provide telecommunications products and services, including local and long-distance telephone services, cellular phone and wireless communication services, data networks, cable and satellite television, communications satellites, and Internet services. Managers will always be faced with decisions on how to incorporate these services and technologies into their information systems and business processes.

THE INFORMATION SUPERHIGHWAY

Deregulation and the marriage of computers and communications also has made it possible for telephone companies to expand from traditional voice communications into new information services, such as those providing transmission of news reports, stock reports, television programs, and movies. These efforts are laying the foundation for the **information superhighway**, a vast web of high-speed digital telecommunications networks delivering information, education, and entertainment services to offices and homes. The networks composing the highway are national or worldwide in scope and accessible by the general public rather than restricted to use by members of a specific organization or set of organizations such as corporations. Some analysts believe the information superhighway will have as profound an impact on economic and social life in the twenty-first century as railroads and interstate highways did in the past.

> **information superhighway**
> High-speed digital telecommunications networks that are national or worldwide in scope and accessible by the general public rather than restricted to specific organizations.

The information superhighway concept is broad and rich, providing new ways for organizations and individuals to obtain and distribute information that virtually eliminate the barriers of time and place. Uses of this new superhighway for electronic commerce and electronic business are quickly emerging. The most well known and easily the largest implementation of the information superhighway is the Internet.

CA*net 3 (www.canet3.net) is Canada's research and education Internet backbone, connecting individual universities, federal and provincial government labs, and research institutes through provincially based Regional Advanced Networks, or RANs. CA*net 3 was the world's first national optical research and education network. CA*net 3 was designed and built from the ground up for TCP/IP data traffic. The federal government has pledged to connect all Canadians to the Internet by 2004. While most of the urban areas in Canada have high-speed and other Internet access at reasonable prices, the sparsely populated areas of the North and Northwest that have Internet access pay more for lower-speed access due to their remoteness.

To remedy this situation, the National Broadband Task Force was established in January 2001 by the Minister of Industry. The principal mandate of the Task Force was to map out a strategy for achieving the Government of Canada's goal of ensuring that broadband services are available to businesses and residents in every Canadian community by 2004. In addition, the Task Force was asked to advise the government on issues related to the development and deployment of broadband networks and services in Canada. The first priority of the broadband deployment strategy should be to link all First Nation, Inuit, rural, and remote communities to national broadband networks using appropriate technology. Further, access to broadband connectivity in these communities should be available at a price reasonably comparable to that for more densely populated areas. The Task Force Web site lists their recommendations, which are to be implemented by 2004 (broadband.gc.ca/Broadband-document/english/table_content.htm).

9.2 COMPONENTS AND FUNCTIONS OF A TELECOMMUNICATIONS SYSTEM

A **telecommunications system** is a collection of compatible hardware and software arranged to communicate information from one location to another. Figure 9-1 illustrates the components of a typical telecommunications system. Telecommunications systems can transmit text, graphic images, voice, or video information. This section describes the major components

> **telecommunications system**
> A collection of compatible hardware and software arranged to communicate information from one location to another.

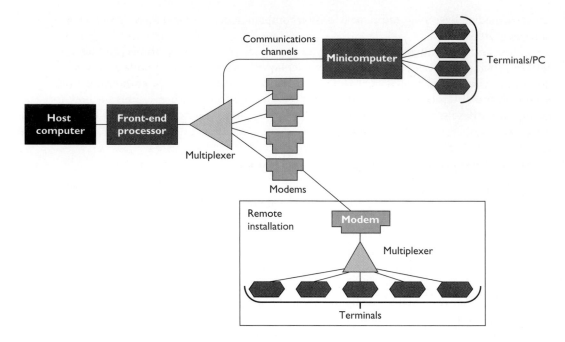

FIGURE 9-1 Components of a telecommunications system. This figure illustrates some of the hardware components that would be found in a typical telecommunications system. They include computers, terminals, communications channels, and communication processors such as modems, multiplexers, and front-end processors. Special communications software controls input and output activities and manages other functions of the telecommunications system.

of telecommunications systems. Subsequent sections describe how the components can be arranged into various types of networks.

TELECOMMUNICATIONS SYSTEM COMPONENTS

The following are essential components of a telecommunications system:

1. Computers to process information.
2. Terminals/PCs and/or any input/output devices that send or receive data.
3. Communications channels, the links by which data or voice are transmitted between sending and receiving devices in a network. Communications channels use various communications media, such as telephone lines, fibre optic cables, coaxial cables, and wireless transmission.
4. Communication processors, such as modems, multiplexers, controllers, and front-end processors, which provide support functions for data transmission and reception.
5. Communications software, which controls input and output activities and manages other functions of the communications network.

Functions of Telecommunications Systems

To send and receive information from one place to another, a telecommunications system must perform a number of separate functions. The system transmits information, establishes the interface between the sender and the receiver, routes messages along the most efficient paths, performs elementary processing of the information to ensure that the right message gets to the right receiver, performs editorial tasks on the data (such as checking for transmission errors and rearranging the format), and converts messages from one speed (say, the speed of a computer) into the speed of a communication line or from one format to another. Finally, the telecommunications system controls the flow of information. Computers handle most of these tasks.

A telecommunications network typically contains diverse hardware and software components that need to work together to transmit information. Different components in a network can communicate by adhering to a common set of rules that enable them to talk to each other. This set of rules and procedures governing transmission between two points in a network is called a **protocol**. Each device in a network must be able to interpret the other device's protocol. The principal functions of protocols in a telecommunications network are to identify each device in the communication path, to secure the attention of the other device, to verify correct receipt of the transmitted message, to verify that a message requires retransmission because it cannot be correctly interpreted, and to perform recovery when errors occur. Protocols are necessary since, without them, information could not be transmitted between dissimilar hardware. While some protocols are established by standards organizations, such as the International Standards Organization (ISO) or the Institute of Electrical and Electronics Engineers (IEEE), others become *de facto* standards, such as the Hayes command set for controlling modems. Where standards have not been set or have not been generally adopted by a critical mass of users, manufacturers make their hardware and software according to their own standards. In this case, users must be careful when purchasing hardware and software to ensure that the standards or protocols in the item they wish to purchase are compatible with the other hardware and software they already use.

protocol
A set of rules and procedures that govern transmission between the components in a network.

TYPES OF SIGNALS: ANALOG AND DIGITAL

Information travels through a telecommunications system in the form of electromagnetic signals. Signals are represented in two ways: analog and digital signals. An **analog signal** is represented by a continuous waveform that passes through a communications medium. Analog signals are used to handle voice communications and to reflect variations in pitch.

A **digital signal** is a discrete, rather than a continuous, waveform. It transmits data coded into two discrete states: 1-bits and 0-bits, which are represented as on–off electrical pulses. Most computers communicate with digital signals as do many local telephone companies and some larger networks. However, if a traditional telephone network is set up to process analog signals, a digital signal cannot be processed without some alterations. All digital signals must be translated into analog signals before they can be transmitted in an analog system. The device that performs this translation is called a **modem**. (Modem is an abbreviation for MOdulation/DEModulation.) A modem translates a computer's digital signals into analog form for transmission over ordinary telephone lines, or it translates analog signals back into digital form for reception by a computer (see Figure 9-2).

analog signal
A continuous waveform that passes through a communications medium; used primarily for voice communications.

digital signal
A discrete waveform that transmits data coded into two discrete states as 1-bits and 0-bits, which are represented as on–off electrical pulses; used primarily for data communications.

COMMUNICATION CHANNELS

Communication channels are the means by which data are transmitted from one device in a network to another. A **channel** can use different kinds of telecommunications transmission media: twisted wire, coaxial cable, fibre optics, terrestrial microwave, satellite, and other wireless transmission. Each has advantages and limitations. High-speed transmission media are more expensive in general, but they can handle higher volumes, which reduces the cost per bit. For instance, the cost per bit of data can be lower via satellite link than via leased telephone line if a firm uses the satellite link 100 percent of the time. There is also a wide range of speeds possible for any given medium depending on the software and hardware configuration.

modem
A device for translating digital signals into analog signals and vice versa.

channels
The links by which data or voice are transmitted between sending and receiving devices in a network.

FIGURE 9-2 Functions of the modem. A modem is a device that translates digital signals from a computer into analog form so that they can be transmitted over analog telephone lines. The modem also is used to translate analog signals back into digital form for the receiving computer.

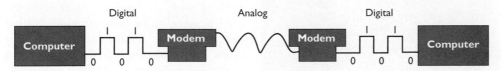

Twisted Wire

twisted wire
A transmission medium consisting of pairs of twisted copper wires; used to transmit analog phone conversations but can also be used for data transmission.

Twisted wire consists of strands of copper wire twisted in pairs. It is the oldest transmission medium. Most of the telephone systems in a building rely on twisted wires installed for analog communication, but they can be used for digital communication as well. Although it is low in cost and already is in place, twisted wire is relatively slow for transmitting data, and high-speed transmission causes interference called *crosstalk*. However, new software and hardware have raised the twisted-wire transmission capacity to make it useful for local- and wide-area computer networks as well as telephone systems.

Coaxial Cable

coaxial cable
A transmission medium consisting of thickly insulated copper wire; can transmit large volumes of data quickly.

Coaxial cable, like that used for cable television, consists of thickly insulated copper wire, which can transmit a larger volume of data than twisted wire. It often is used in place of twisted wire for important links in a telecommunications network because it is faster and more interference-free and can reach speeds of up to 200 megabits per second. However, coaxial cable is thick and hard to wire in many buildings, and it cannot support analog phone conversations. It must be moved when computers and other devices are moved.

Fibre Optics and Optical Networks

fibre optic cable
A fast, light, and durable transmission medium consisting of thin strands of clear glass fibre bound into cables. Data are transmitted as light pulses.

Fibre optic cable consists of thousands of strands of clear glass fibre, each less than the thickness of a human hair, which are bound into cables. Data are transformed into pulses of light, which are sent through the fibre optic cable by a laser device at a rate from 500 kilobits to several billion bits per second. Fibre optic cable is considerably faster, lighter, and more durable than wire media and is well suited to systems requiring transfers of large volumes of data. However, fibre optic cable is more difficult to work with, more expensive, and harder to install and repair.

Until recently, fibre optic cable has been used primarily as the high-speed network backbone while twisted wire and coaxial cable are used to connect the backbone to individual businesses and households. A **backbone** is the part of a network that handles the major traffic. It acts as the primary path for traffic flowing to or from other networks. Now competitive local exchange carriers are working on bringing fibre cables all the way into the basement of buildings so they can provide a variety of new services to business and eventually residential customers. These *optical networks* can transmit all types of traffic—voice, data, and video—over fibre cables and provide the massive bandwidth needed for new types of services and software. Using optical networks, on-demand video, software downloads, and high-quality digital audio can be accessed using set-top boxes and other information appliances without any delays or degradation in quality.

backbone
Part of a network handling the major traffic and providing the primary path for traffic flowing to or from other networks.

Fibre optic cable can transmit data that have been transformed into pulses of light at speeds of up to 6 terabits per second. Fibre optic technology is used in high-capacity optical networks.

For example, Bredbandsbolaget AB, a Swedish local telecommunications carrier, is running fibre to apartment blocks and wiring buildings to give each household a dedicated 10 megabits per second connection, upgradable to 100 megabits per second if needed. Users pay 200 Swedish kroner ($29 per month) for the connection and Internet access and an additional charge for hundreds of TV channels, programmable TV, video on demand, telephone services, games, and software rentals. Delays are so infrequent on the Bredbandsbolaget network that customers can't tell whether they are working with software programs delivered over the network or those running on their own hardware. Thus Bredbandsbolaget (www.bredband.com) can offer games and software rental without the user downloading programs. Customers don't need high-powered PCs to use these services (Heywood, 2000).

Currently, fibre optic networks are slowed down by the need to convert electrical data to optics to send it over a fibre line and then re-convert it. The long-term goal is to create pure optical networks in which light packets shuttle digital data at tremendous speed without ever converting them to electrical signals. Many new optical technologies are in development for this purpose. Next-generation optical networks will also boost capacity by using **dense wave division multiplexing (DWDM)**. DWDM boosts transmission capacity by using many different colours (or wavelengths) of light to carry separate streams of traffic (data) over the same fibre strand at the same time. DWDM combines up to 160 wavelengths per strand and can transmit up to 6.4 terabits per second over a single fibre. This technology will enable communications service providers such as AT&T Canada to add bandwidth to an existing fibre optic network without having to lay more fibre optic cable. Before DWDM, optical networks could only transmit a single wavelength per strand.

dense wave division multiplexing (DWDM)
Technology for boosting transmission capacity of optical fibre by using many different wavelengths to carry separate streams of data over the same fibre strand at the same time.

Wireless Transmission

Wireless transmission that sends signals through air or space without any physical tether has become an increasingly popular alternative to wired transmission channels such as twisted wire, coaxial cable, and fibre optics. Today common technologies for wireless data transmission include microwave transmission, communication satellites, pagers, cellular telephones, personal communication services (PCS), smart phones, personal digital assistants (PDAs), and mobile data networks.

The wireless transmission medium is the electromagnetic spectrum, illustrated in Figure 9-3. Some types of wireless transmission, such as microwave or infrared, by nature occupy specific spectrum frequency ranges (measured in megahertz). Other types of wireless transmissions are actually functional uses, such as cellular telephones and paging devices, that have been assigned a specific range of frequencies by national regulatory agencies and international agreements. Each frequency range has its own strengths and limitations, and these have helped to determine the specific function or data communications niche assigned to it.

Microwave systems, both terrestrial and celestial, transmit high-frequency radio signals through the atmosphere and are widely used for high-volume, long-distance, point-to-point, line-of-sight communication. Microwave signals follow a straight line and do not bend with the curvature of the earth; therefore, long-distance terrestrial transmission systems require

microwave
A high-volume, long-distance, point-to-point, line-of-sight transmission in which high-frequency radio signals are transmitted through the atmosphere from one terrestrial transmission station to another.

FIGURE 9-3 Frequency ranges for communications media and devices. Each telecommunications transmission medium or device occupies a different frequency range, measured in megahertz, on the electromagnetic spectrum.

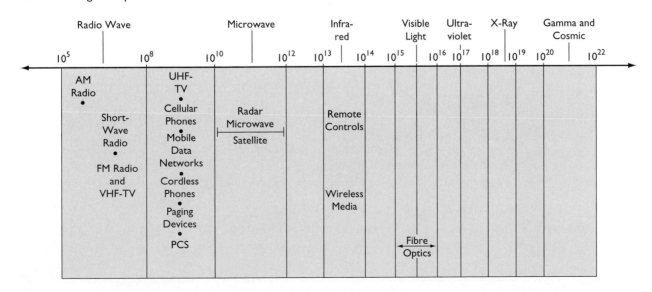

satellite
The transmission of data using orbiting satellites to serve as relay stations for transmitting microwave signals over very long distances.

that transmission stations be positioned 40 to 50 kilometres apart, adding to the expense of microwave.

This problem can be solved by bouncing microwave signals off **satellites**, enabling them to serve as relay stations for microwave signals transmitted from terrestrial stations. Communication satellites are cost effective for transmitting large quantities of data over very long distances. Satellites are typically used for communications in large, geographically dispersed organizations that would be difficult to tie together through cabling media or terrestrial microwave. For instance, Enbridge Pipelines Inc., the world's longest crude oil pipeline system, needs temperature and pressure data as well as contact and control information to operate its pipeline safely and efficiently. The main control centre is in Edmonton, with three additional control centres in Norman Wells, Northwest Territories; Sarnia, Ontario; and Superior, Wisconsin. Data from 110 different field locations is transmitted over leased line, radio, microwave, and satellite connections to one of these control centres. Figure 9-4 illustrates how this system works.

Conventional communication satellites move in stationary or *geosynchronous* orbits approximately 22 000 miles above the earth. A newer satellite medium, the low-earth orbit satellite (LEO), is beginning to be deployed. These satellites travel much closer to the earth and are able to pick up signals from weaker transmitters. They also consume less power and cost less to launch than conventional satellites. With these wireless networks, businesspeople will be able to "travel" virtually anywhere in the world from their desktop and have access to full communication capabilities including videoconferencing and multimedia-rich Internet access. As of this writing, this medium has not attracted as many users as was expected, and the companies owning these channels are experiencing financial difficulties.

Other wireless transmission technologies are being used in situations requiring remote access to corporate systems and mobile computing power. **Paging systems** have been used for several decades, originally just beeping when the user received a message and requiring the user to telephone an office to learn about the message. Today paging devices can send and receive short alphanumeric messages that the user reads on the pager's screen. Paging is useful for communicating with mobile workers such as repair crews; one-way paging also can provide an inexpensive way of communicating with workers in offices. For example, Toronto-based GetronicsWang, a computer hardware repair company, uses pagers to notify its technicians of dispatch information; the technicians can then respond using one of five predetermined messages or can use their Fido phones to contact headquarters.

paging system
A wireless transmission technology in which the pager beeps when the user receives a message; used to transmit short alphanumeric messages.

FIGURE 9-4 Enbridge Pipelines' satellite transmission system. Satellites help Enbridge transfer temperature and pressure data between field locations and control centres in Canada and the United States.

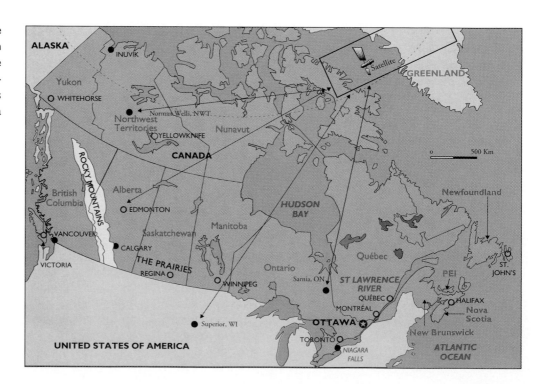

The Palm VII PDA, Nokia 7100 series mobile phone, and BlackBerry pager are examples of handheld devices for wireless communication. Some of these devices can provide wireless access to the Internet.

Cellular telephones work by using radio waves to communicate with radio antennas (towers) placed within adjacent geographic areas called cells. A telephone message is transmitted to the local cell by the cellular telephone and then is handed off from antenna to antenna—cell to cell—until it reaches the cell of its destination or the local telephone exchange office where it is transmitted to the receiving telephone. As a cellular signal travels from one cell into another, a computer that monitors signals from the cells switches the conversation to a radio channel assigned to the next cell. The radio antenna cells normally cover eight-mile hexagonal cells although their radius is smaller in densely populated localities. Older cellular systems are analog and newer cellular systems are digital.

Personal communication services (PCS) are a popular digital cellular service. PCS are entirely digital. They can transmit both voice and data and operate in a higher frequency range (1900 MHz) than analog cellular telephones. PCS cells are much smaller and more closely spaced than analog cells and can accommodate higher traffic demands.

In addition to handling voice messages, newer models of digital cellular phones can handle voice mail, e-mail, and faxes, save addresses, access a private corporate network, access information from the Internet, and provide wireless voice transmission. These **smart phones** are being equipped with Web browser software that lets digital cellular phones or other wireless devices access Web pages formatted to send text or other information that is suitable for tiny screens. Some smart phone models offer larger screens and keypads to make Internet access easier.

Personal digital assistants (PDA) are small, pen-based, handheld computers capable of entirely digital communications transmission. Many have built-in wireless telecommunications capabilities as well as work-organization software. A well-known example is the Palm Pilot. It can display and compose e-mail messages; some models can provide Internet access. The handheld Palm Pilot includes applications such as an electronic scheduler, address book, to-do list, memorandum generator, and expense tracker and can accept data entered with a special stylus through an on-screen writing pad. The Window on Organizations illustrates how Canada Post is using handheld computers in combination with wireless LANs in an electronic commerce application for delivery confirmation.

Wireless networks explicitly designed for two-way transmission of data files are called **mobile data networks**. These radio-based networks transmit data to and from handheld computers. For example, Manitoba Public Insurance (MPI) uses pen-based PCs with wireless links to process auto accident claims. As claimants drive into a bay at a claims centre, an adjuster enters the vehicle's license plate number onto the handheld PC. The data is transmitted via a wireless local area network to a server at the claims centre, which communicates with MPI's central mainframe. The system downloads information on the driver and the car

cellular telephone
A device that transmits voice or data, using radio waves to communicate with radio antennas placed within adjacent geographic areas called cells.

personal communication services (PCS)
A wireless digital cellular technology that uses lower power, higher frequency radio waves than does analog cellular technology and so can be used with smaller size telephones.

smart phone
A wireless phone with voice, text, and Internet capabilities.

personal digital assistants (PDA)
Small, pen-based, handheld computers with built-in wireless telecommunications capable of entirely digital communications transmission.

mobile data networks
Wireless networks that enable two-way transmission of data files cheaply and efficiently.

MOBILE DEVICES ARE IN THE MAIL

Alberta's dry winter air was a factor to consider when Canada Post was purchasing new technology. When the organization's IT department decided to move from coloured sticky labels to the more high-tech world of handheld computers and wireless LANs, it needed something that could withstand a variety of Canadian climates and geographies.

"Our requirements for our equipment have to be really well thought out from that perspective," said John Farnand, corporate manager for engineering and process design with Canada Post in Ottawa. "We almost had to put an underwater rating on this for Vancouver," he joked.

Canada Post purchased roughly 5000 PDT 7500 mobile computing devices from Symbol Technologies and installed 200 wireless LANs in its delivery depots and plants. So far, the technology has been deployed in 40 sites.

Eventually, it will span 450 Canada Post locations and an additional 1500 retail sites across the country. The technology will be installed throughout the summer into early fall of 2000, with the first phase of the implementation expected to be completed by November of that year.

"We don't have any illusions that there won't always be an increasing demand for more flexible operations, more immediate solutions, additional information, and so on," Farnand said. Rather, he says, the technology is being used as a platform to move forward with future IT projects.

The handhelds were designed for rugged conditions, such as extreme temperatures (from $-13°F$ to $122°F$) and static discharge. They can even be dropped on the floor and splashed with water. "That's not really recommended standard operating procedure," he said, "but we have to recognize that (mail carriers) are in and out of trucks."

Previously, Canada Post used a system of coloured sticky labels for delivery confirmation. Farnand said the organization is making some "pretty serious investments" in technology to increase flexibility and simplicity with customers and compete with other courier companies.

"What we're looking at is an ever-increasing level of reliability in terms of speed of capture of information, the reliability of that information, the capture of signatures, and the speed at which we get that into the network," he said. The handhelds feature signature capture on the computer screen that will automatically match the parcel or package to an individual customer and provide proof of pick-up and delivery.

Canada Post has teamed up with Silanis to offer its electronic post office, called PosteCS, which provides the ability to sign documents electronically. It allows for multiple signatures and sectional form signing to capture customer and supplier signatures on forms, applications, and contracts en route for approval processing.

Richard Chown, director of business development for Kanata, Ontario-based Symbol, said that by capturing signatures electronically, Canada Post will be able to see—at a glance—volumes and activities of customer interactions. Symbol is also supplying an additional 5000 handhelds to Purolator Courier Ltd., which is owned by Canada Post. "The nice thing is the use of a common technology platform," said Chown.

To Think About: What are the legal implications of using electronic signatures for delivery confirmation? What impact will the use of this technology have on Canada Post's delivery staff? What impact will it have on Canada Post's customers? Do you think Canada Post's customers will readily accept the idea of electronic signatures?

Sources: Vaun Himmelsbach, "Mobile Devices are in the Mail," *Computing Canada*, June, 23, 2000; Grant Buckler, "E-Signature Technology Means You Don't Need to Get It on Paper," *The Globe and Mail*, September 26, 2000.

and transmits it to the adjuster's handheld PC. Another type of mobile data network is based on a series of radio towers constructed specifically to transmit text and data. Wireless networks and transmission devices can be more expensive, slower, and more error prone than transmission over wired networks, although the major digital cellular networks are upgrading the speed of their services to 100 000 to 170 000 bits per second. (Satellite systems such as Teledesic are also spending billions to provide data transmission speeds as high as 50 million bits per second for multimedia-heavy, wireless Internet use.) Bandwidth and energy supply in wireless devices require careful management from both hardware and software standpoints (Imielinski and Badrinath, 1994). Security and privacy are more difficult to maintain because wireless transmission can be easily intercepted (see Chapter 12).

There are cultural and other differences in wireless use among different areas of the world. For example, the European wired infrastructure is not as high-tech as their wireless infrastructure, so their percentage of cellular phone usage is higher than that found in North America. The Japanese also use wireless telephones more often than North Americans; in this case, they use their cellular phones for text messaging to avoid face-to-face contact, a reflection of the differences between Japanese and North American cultures.

Data cannot be transmitted seamlessly between different wireless networks if they use incompatible standards. For example, digital cellular service in Canada is provided by different operators using one of several competing digital cellular technologies (CDMA, GSM 1900, and TDMA IS-136) that do not interoperate with each other. Many digital cellular handsets that use one of these technologies cannot operate in countries outside North America, which operate at different frequencies with still another set of standards. We provide a detailed discussion of these standards and other standards for networking in Chapter 10.

Transmission Speed

The total amount of information that can be transmitted through any telecommunications channel is measured in bits per second (bps). Sometimes this is referred to as the baud rate. A **baud** is a binary event representing a signal change from positive to negative or vice versa. The baud rate is not always the same as the bit rate. At today's higher speeds, a single signal change can transmit more than one bit at a time, so the bit rate generally surpasses the baud rate.

One signal change, or cycle, is required to transmit one or several bits per second; therefore, the transmission capacity of each type of telecommunications medium is a function of its **frequency**. The number of cycles per second that can be sent through that medium is measured in hertz. The range of frequencies that can be accommodated on a particular telecommunications channel is called its bandwidth. The **bandwidth** is the difference between the highest and lowest frequencies that can be accommodated on a single channel. The greater the range of frequencies, the greater the bandwidth and the greater the channel's transmission capacity. Table 9-1 compares the transmission speed and relative costs of the major types of transmissions media.

COMMUNICATION PROCESSORS AND SOFTWARE

Communication processors, such as front-end processors, concentrators, controllers, multiplexers, and modems support data transmission and reception in a telecommunications network. In a large computer system, the **front-end processor** is a special purpose computer dedicated to communications management and is attached to the main, or host, computer. The front-end processor performs communications processing such as error control, formatting, editing, controlling, routing, and speed and signal conversion.

A **concentrator** is a programmable telecommunication computer that collects and temporarily stores messages from terminals until enough messages are ready to be sent economically. The concentrator sends signals in bursts to the host computer.

A **controller** is a specialized computer that supervises communication traffic between the CPU and peripheral devices such as terminals and printers. The controller manages messages from these devices and communicates them to the CPU. It also routes output from the CPU to the appropriate peripheral device.

A **multiplexer** (also known as a MUX) is a device that enables a single communication channel to carry data transmissions from multiple sources simultaneously. The multiplexer divides the communication channel so that it can be shared by multiple transmission devices. The multiplexer may divide a high-speed channel into multiple channels of slower speed or

baud
A change in signal from positive to negative or vice versa that is used as a measure of transmission speed.

frequency
The number of complete cycles per second in alternating current direction; the standard measure unit of frequency is the hertz, abbreviated Hz.

bandwidth
The capacity of a communication channel as measured by the difference between the highest and lowest frequencies that can be transmitted by that channel.

front-end processor
A special purpose computer dedicated to managing communications for the host computer in a network.

concentrator
A telecommunications computer that collects and temporarily stores messages from terminals for batch transmission to the host computer.

controller
A specialized computer that supervises communications traffic between the CPU and the peripheral devices in a telecommunications system.

multiplexer
A device that enables a single communication channel to carry data transmissions from multiple sources simultaneously.

TABLE 9-1 TYPICAL SPEEDS AND COSTS OF TELECOMMUNICATIONS TRANSMISSION MEDIA

Medium	Speed	Cost
Twisted wire	300 bps–10 Mbps	Low
Microwave	256 Kbps–100 Mbps	
Satellite	256 Kbps–100 Mbps	
Coaxial cable	56 Kbps–200 Mbps	
Fibre optic cable	500 Kbps–up to 6+ Tbps	High

bps = bits per second; Kbps = kilobits per second; Mbps = megabits per second; Tbps = terabits per second

may assign each transmission source a very small slice of time for exclusive use of the high-speed channel.

Special telecommunications software residing in the host computer, front-end processor, and other processors in the network is required to control and support network activities. This software is responsible for functions such as network control, access control, transmission control, error detection/correction, and security. More detail on security software can be found in Chapter 12.

9.3 COMMUNICATION NETWORKS

A number of different ways exist to organize telecommunications components to form a network and hence, there are multiple ways to classify networks. Networks can be classified by their shape, or **topology**. Networks also can be classified by their geographic scope and the type of services provided. This section will describe different ways of categorizing networks and the management and technical requirements of creating networks linking entire enterprises.

topology
The shape or configuration of a network.

NETWORK TOPOLOGIES

One way of describing networks is by their shape or topology. As illustrated in Figures 9-5 to 9-7, the three most common topologies are the star, bus, and ring.

The Star Network

star network
A network topology in which all computers and other devices are connected to a central host computer. All communications between network devices must pass through the host computer.

The **star network** (see Figure 9-5) consists of a central host computer connected to a number of smaller computers or terminals. This topology is useful for applications where some processing must be centralized, and some can be performed locally. One problem with the star network is its vulnerability. All communication between points in the network must pass through the central computer. Because the central computer is the traffic controller for the other computers and terminals in the network, communication will come to a standstill if the host computer stops functioning.

The Bus Network

bus network
A network topology linking a number of computers by a single circuit with all messages broadcast to the entire network.

The **bus network** (see Figure 9-6) links a number of computers by a single circuit made of twisted wire, coaxial cable, or fibre optic cable. All of the signals are broadcast in both directions to the entire network, with special software to identify which components receive each message (there is no central host computer to control the network). If one of the computers in the network fails, none of the other components in the network are affected. However, the channel in a bus network can handle only one message at a time, so performance can degrade

FIGURE 9-5 A star network topology. In a star network configuration, a central host computer acts as a traffic controller for all other components of the network. All communication between the smaller computers, terminals, and printers must first pass through the central computer.

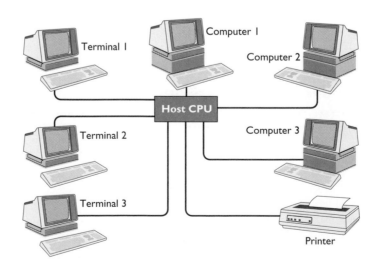

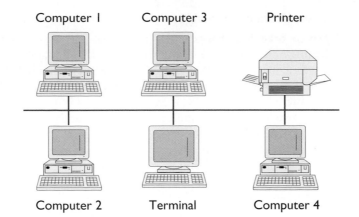

Computer 1   Computer 3   Printer

Computer 2   Terminal   Computer 4

FIGURE 9-6 A bus network topology. This topology allows for all messages to be broadcast to the entire network through a single circuit. There is no central host, and messages can travel in both directions along the cable.

if there is a high volume of network traffic. When two computers transmit messages simultaneously, a "collision" occurs, and the messages must be re-sent.

The Ring Network

Like the bus network, the **ring network** (see Figure 9-7) does not rely on a central host computer and will not automatically break down if one of the component computers malfunctions. Each computer in the network can communicate directly with any other computer, and each processes its own applications independently. However, in ring topology, the connecting wire, cable, or optical fibre forms a closed loop. Data are passed along the ring from one computer to another and always flow in one direction. Both ring and bus topologies are used in local area networks (LANs), which are discussed in the next section.

ring network
A network topology in which all computers are linked by a closed loop in a manner that passes data in one direction from one computer to another.

PRIVATE BRANCH EXCHANGES, LOCAL AREA NETWORKS, AND WIDE AREA NETWORKS

Networks may be classified by geographic scope into local area networks (LANs) and wide area networks (WANs). Wide area networks encompass a relatively wide geographic area, from several kilometres to thousands of kilometres, while local networks link local resources such as computers and terminals in the same department or building of a firm. Local networks consist of private branch exchanges and local area networks.

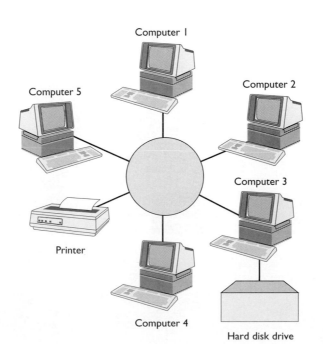

Computer 1

Computer 5

Computer 2

Computer 3

Printer

Computer 4

Hard disk drive

FIGURE 9-7 A ring network topology. In a ring network configuration, messages are transmitted from computer to computer, flowing in a single direction through a closed loop. Each computer operates independently so that if one fails, communication through the network is not interrupted.

Private Branch Exchanges

A **private branch exchange (PBX)** is a special-purpose computer designed for handling and switching office telephone calls at a company site. Today's PBXs can carry voice and data to create local networks. PBXs can store, transfer, hold, and redial telephone calls, and they also can be used to switch digital information among computers and office devices. Using a PBX, you can write a letter on a PC in your office, send it to the printer, and then dial up the local copying machine and have multiple copies of your letter created.

The advantage of digital PBXs over other local networking options is that they do not require special wiring. A PC connected to a network by telephone can be plugged or unplugged anywhere in a building, using the existing telephone lines. Commercial vendors support PBXs, so the organization does not need special expertise to manage them.

The geographic scope of PBXs is limited, usually to several hundred feet, although the PBX can be connected to other PBX networks or to packet-switched networks (see the discussion of value-added networks in this section) to encompass a larger geographic area. The primary disadvantages of PBXs are that they are limited to telephone lines, and they cannot easily handle very large volumes of data.

Local Area Networks

A **local area network (LAN)** encompasses a limited distance, usually within one building or several buildings in close proximity. Most LANs connect devices located within a 2000-foot radius, and they have been widely used to link PCs. LANs require their own communications channels.

LANs generally have higher transmission capacities than PBXs. They are recommended for applications transmitting high volumes of data and other functions requiring high transmission speeds, including video transmissions and graphics. LANs often are used to connect PCs in an office to shared printers and other resources or to link computers and computer-controlled machines in factories.

LANs are more expensive to install than PBXs and are less flexible, requiring new wiring each time a LAN is moved. One way to solve this problem is to create a wireless LAN, such as described in the Window on Technology. LANs are usually controlled, maintained, and operated by end users. This means that the user must know a great deal about telecommunications applications and networking.

Figure 9-8 illustrates one model of a LAN. The server acts as a librarian, storing programs and data files for network users. The server determines who gets access to what and in what sequence. Servers may be powerful PCs with large hard-disk capacity, workstations, minicomputers, or mainframes, although specialized computers are available for this purpose.

FIGURE 9-8 A local area network (LAN). A typical local area network connects computers and peripheral devices that are located close to each other, often in the same building. Note: This depiction of a LAN uses a star topology. Other topologies are also possible.

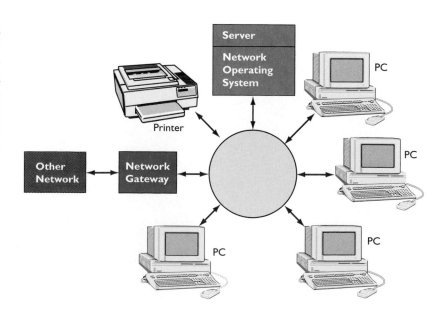

The network gateway connects the LAN to public networks, such as the telephone network, or to other corporate networks so that the LAN can exchange information with networks external to it. A **gateway** is generally a communications processor that can connect dissimilar networks by translating from one set of protocols to another. A **router** is used to route packets of data through several connected LANs or to a wide area network; routers can actually determine the path the packets will take and can be used to connect dissimilar networks. A **bridge** connects different segments of the same or similar networks.

LAN technology consists of cabling (twisted wire, coaxial, or fibre optic cable) or wireless technology that links individual computer devices, **network interface cards (NIC)** (which are special adapters that connect the computer to the cable or wireless hub), and software to control LAN activities. The NIC specifies the data transmission rate, the size of message units, the addressing information attached to each message, and network topology. Many networks use an Ethernet standard that uses a bus topology, for example.

LAN capabilities also are defined by the **network operating system (NOS)**. The network operating system can reside on every computer in the network, or it can reside on a single designated server for all the applications on the network. The NOS routes and manages communications on the network and coordinates network resources. Novell NetWare, Microsoft Windows NT Server (Windows 2000 Server and Windows 2000 Enterprise Server), and IBM's OS/2 Warp Server are popular network operating systems.

LANs may take the form of client/server networks, in which the server provides data and application programs to "client" computers on the network (see the Chapter 6 discussion of client/server computing), or they may use a peer-to-peer architecture. A **peer-to-peer** network treats all processors equally and is used primarily in small networks. Each computer on the network has direct access to every other computer and shared peripheral devices.

Wide Area Networks

Wide area networks (WANs) span broad geographical distances, ranging from several kilometres to entire continents. WANs may consist of a combination of switched and dedicated lines, microwave, and satellite communications. **Switched lines** are telephone lines that a computer can access to transmit data to another computer, the call being routed or switched through paths to the designated destination. **Dedicated lines** are continuously available for transmission, and the lessee typically pays a flat rate for total access to the line. The lines can be leased or purchased from common carriers or private communications media vendors. Most existing WANs are switched. Enbridge Pipelines' network for transmitting temperature and pressure data illustrated in Figure 9-4 is a WAN.

Individual business firms may maintain their own wide area networks. The firm is responsible for telecommunications content and management. However, private wide area networks are expensive to maintain, or firms may not have the resources to manage their own wide area networks. In such instances, companies may choose to use commercial network services to communicate over vast distances. Two other types of WAN are **metropolitan area networks (MAN)** that are the backbone for a community and **global area networks (GAN)** that link organizations operating in several countries together. MANs typically are managed by either commercial organizations, such as Sudbury Hydro in the Window on Technology, or by a municipality; global area networks are either the exclusive property of one company or may be a service offered to individuals, such as AT&T WorldNet.

NETWORK SERVICES AND BROADBAND TECHNOLOGIES

In addition to topology and geographic scope, networks can be classified by the types of service they provide.

Value-Added Networks

Value-added networks are an alternative to firms designing and managing their own networks. Value-added networks (VANs) are private, multipath, data-only, third-party-managed networks that can provide economies in the cost of service and in network management

gateway
A communications processor that connects dissimilar networks by providing the translation from one set of protocols to another.

router
A device that forwards packets of data from one LAN or wide area network to another.

bridge
A device that connects different segments of the same or similar networks.

network interface card (NIC)
A special adapter that connects the computer to the cable or wireless hub; NICs include various standards and routines for packet assembly and other functions

network operating system (NOS)
Special software that routes and manages communications on the network and coordinates network resources.

peer-to-peer
A network architecture that gives equal power to all computers on the network; used primarily in small networks.

wide area network (WAN)
A telecommunications network that spans a large geographical distance. May consist of a variety of cable, satellite, and microwave technologies.

switched lines
Telephone lines that a computer can access to transmit data to another computer, the call being routed or switched through paths to the designated destination.

dedicated lines
Telephone lines that are continuously available for transmission by a lessee. Typically conditioned to transmit data at high speeds for high-volume applications.

metropolitan area network
The backbone network for a community; typically managed by either commercial organizations or by a municipality.

global area network
A network linking several countries; either the exclusive property of one company or a service offered to individuals.

value-added network (VAN)
A private, multipath, data-only, third-party-managed network that multiple organizations use on a subscription basis.

MAN Turns Sudbury into a Wired Community

"How do you level the economic playing field when you're located in a remote area?" asks John Jeza, manager, communications services, at Sudbury Hydro in Sudbury, Ontario. "Distance is definitely a factor of doing business, but through technology, distance is no longer an issue. The issue becomes how to leverage technology for the betterment of the community while building on the strengths of the community."

Through the establishment of a metropolitan-area network (MAN) based on Cisco technology, the northern Ontario city of Sudbury is positioning itself to be one of the province's leading-edge wired communities, opening a wealth of new business and employment opportunities for its 95 000 residents.

The MAN allows Sudbury to provide high-speed Internet access and increased bandwidth capability to local government, utilities, school boards, libraries, private businesses, and citizens. Using the MAN, residents can register online for city programs, students can conduct live Webcasts, and businesses can access data network services at 100-Mbps connections. The Sudbury MAN began as an initiative of Sudbury Hydro in preparation for the electricity market's deregulation plans.

"Historically, municipal utilities have been used as a tool for economic development," explains Jeza. "But with deregulation, electricity becomes a ubiquitous service, available everywhere. Real-time information is absolutely critical. Although we owned the infrastructure—specifically, the hydro poles—we needed a high-speed, fibre optic network in order to remain competitive, one that would easily connect our 26 substations and support our customers."

"We had several important requirements," recalls Jeza. "We wanted a dynamic fibre optic network that could interface with the rest of the world. We needed something that was upgradable, scalable, and backwards compatible, allowing us to grow as our needs dictated. Cisco, together with AT&T Canada, joined forces to create a state-of-the-art network."

Sudbury Hydro now provides high-speed, managed-bandwidth data network services to 80 percent of local businesses. Wholesale Internet is offered to local Internet service providers (ISPs) and to major institutions that require dedicated Internet bandwidth. The MAN has also helped establish Sudbury Hydro as a CA*net II point-of-presence site to hook up research organizations such as the Sudbury Neutrino Observatory to CANARIE, the not-for-profit, government-supported organization that has succeeded in enhancing Canadian research Internet speeds.

"Before the MAN was created, most of our locations were not connected to city hall," explains Bruno Mangiardi, director of information services at the City of Sudbury. "Those that were connected did so via slow dial-up modems or via ISDN 128-Kbps connections through the Bell network. The four local municipalities that we service were connected through 56-Kbps connections. So when Sudbury Hydro built the fibre infrastructure, we jumped on the bandwagon. We now have all of our locations connected using high-speed fibre connections."

Residents will soon be able to log on remotely at various sites to register for city programs. The fibre backbone will enable the city to install 10 kiosks in local malls, libraries, colleges, and at the university, making it even easier for residents to do business with city hall, such as paying taxes and fines or ordering library books online.

As a by-product of the MAN, several call centres have been established in Sudbury, yielding hundreds of new job opportunities. "When you're here in the North, people often ask if you can do the job," says Jeza. "The fact that we have a metropolitan area network makes a very clear statement that Sudbury does indeed have the wherewithal to handle technology."

To Think About: How did communications technology help Sudbury Hydro pursue its business strategy? How did the MAN enhance the quality of life in Sudbury? If you were a local Sudbury business, would you link up to the MAN for a fee? What fee would you be willing to pay?

Sources: Barry Burke, "Metropolitan-Area Network Turns Sudbury into Leading-Edge Wired Community," Cisco Customer Profiles, www.cisco.com/warp/public/3/ca/profiles/sudbury.html, accessed September 28, 2001; Yankee Group Report, "The Spring of Hope: A Communications-Empowered Future?" *Canadian Market Strategies (3, 22)*, November, 1999, available www.yankeegroupcanada.com, accessed May 22, 2001.

---

because they are used by multiple organizations. The value-added network is set up by a firm that is in charge of managing the network. That firm sells subscriptions to other firms wishing to use the network. Subscribers pay only for the amount of data they transmit plus a subscription fee. The network may use a combination of twisted-pair lines, satellite links, and other communications channels leased by the value-added carrier.

The term *value added* refers to the extra value added to communications by the telecommunications and computing services these networks provide to clients. Customers do not have to invest in network equipment and software or perform their own error checking, editing, routing, and protocol conversion. Subscribers may achieve savings in line charges and transmission costs because the costs of using the network are shared among many users. The resulting costs should be lower than if the clients had leased their own lines or satellite services.

The leading international value-added networks provide casual or intermittent users international services on a dial-up basis and can provide a private network using dedicated circuits for customers requiring a full-time network. (Maintaining a private network may be most cost-effective for organizations with a high communications volume.) International VANs have representatives with language skills and knowledge of various countries' telecommunications administrations. The VANs already have leased lines from foreign telecommunications authorities or can arrange access to local networks and equipment abroad. It should be noted that the Internet has made VANs obsolete for many companies that feel they no longer need the value-added services when the Internet provides a more cost-effective networking capability.

Other Network Services

High-speed transmission technologies are sometimes referred to as **broadband**. The term broadband designates transmission media that can carry multiple channels simultaneously over a single communications medium.

Traditional analog telephone service is based on circuit switching where a direct connection must be maintained between two nodes in a network for the duration of the transmission session. **Packet switching** is a basic switching technique that can be used to achieve economies of scale and higher speeds in long distance transmission. VANs and the Internet use packet switching. Packet switching breaks up a lengthy block of text into small, fixed bundles of data called packets. (The X.25 packet switching standard uses packets of 128 bytes each.) In addition to the data in the packet, the packets include information to direct the packet to the right address and to check for transmission errors. Data are gathered from many users, divided into small packets, and transmitted via various communications channels. Each packet travels independently through the network. Packets of data originating at one source can be routed through different paths in the network before being reassembled into the original message when they reach their destination. Figure 9-9 illustrates how packet switching works.

Frame relay is a shared network service that is faster and less expensive than packet switching and can achieve transmission speeds up to 1.544 megabits per second. Frame relay packages data into frames that are similar to packets, but it does not perform error correction. It works well on reliable lines that do not require frequent re-transmission because of error.

Most corporations today use separate networks for voice, private-line services, and data, each of which is supported by a different technology. This means that users must have access to all of these separate networks and training on how to use each network and the associated technologies for voice and data, requiring additional training and significantly higher costs.

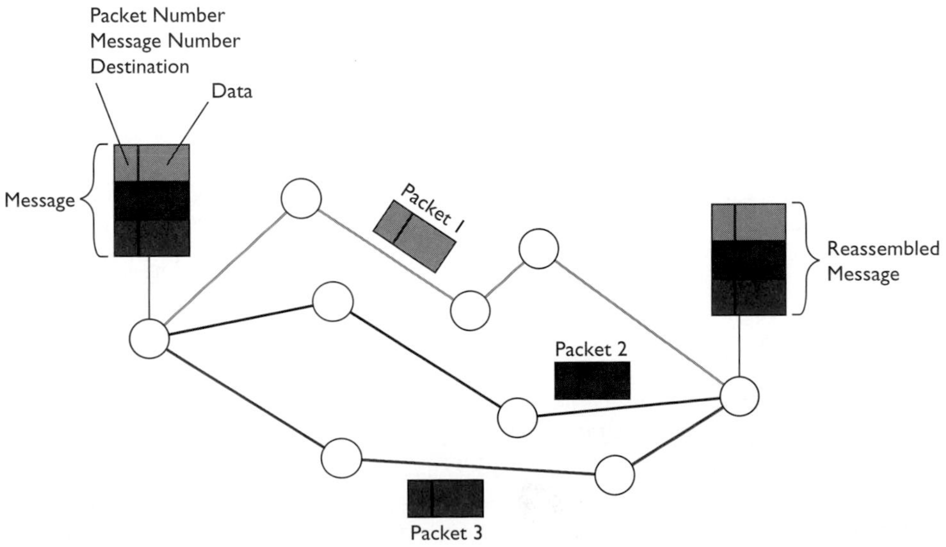

broadband
High-speed transmission technologies that can carry multiple channels simultaneously over a single medium.

packet switching
Technology that breaks blocks of text into small, fixed bundles of data and routes them in the most economical way through any available communications channel.

frame relay
A shared network service technology that packages data into bundles for transmission but does not use error-correction routines. Cheaper and faster than packet switching.

FIGURE 9-9 Packet-switched networks and packet communications. Data are grouped into small packets, which are transmitted independently via various communications channels and reassembled at their final destination.

asynchronous transfer mode (ATM)

A networking technology that parcels information into eight-byte cells, allowing data to be transmitted between computers from different vendors at any speed.

Integrated Services Digital Network (ISDN)

An international standard for transmitting voice, video, image, and data to support a wide range of service over public telephone lines.

digital subscriber line (DSL)

A group of technologies providing high-capacity transmission over existing copper telephone lines.

cable modem

A modem designed to operate over cable TV lines to provide high-speed access to the Web or corporate intranets.

A service called **asynchronous transfer mode (ATM)** may overcome some of these problems because it can seamlessly and dynamically switch voice, data, images, and video between users. ATM also promises to tie LANs and WANs together more easily. (LANs generally are based on lower-speed protocols while WANs operate at higher speeds.) ATM technology parcels information into uniform cells, each with 53 groups of 8 bytes, eliminating the need for protocol conversion. It can pass data between computers from different vendors and permits data to be transmitted at any speed the network handles. ATM can transmit up to 2.5 Gbps.

Integrated Services Digital Network (ISDN) is an international standard for dial-up network access that integrates voice, data, image, and video services in a single link. There are two levels of ISDN service: Basic Rate ISDN and Primary Rate ISDN. Each uses a group of B (bearer) channels to carry voice or data along with a D (delta) channel for signalling and control information. Basic Rate ISDN (BRI) can transmit data at a rate of 128 kilobits per second on an existing local telephone line. Organizations and individuals requiring high-bandwidth transmission or the ability to provide simultaneous voice and data transmission over one physical line might choose this service. Primary Rate ISDN (PRI) offers transmission capacities in the megabit range and is designed for large users of telecommunications services.

Other high-capacity services include digital subscriber line (DSL) technologies, cable modems, and T1 lines. Like ISDN, **digital subscriber line (DSL)** technologies also operate over existing copper telephone lines to carry voice, data, and video, but they have higher transmission capacities than ISDN. There are several categories of DSL. Asymmetric digital subscriber line (ADSL) supports a transmission rate of 1.5 to 9 megabits per second when receiving data and up to 640 kilobits per second when sending data. Symmetric digital subscriber line (SDSL) supports the same transmission rate for sending and receiving data of up to 3 Mbps. Canadian companies such as Telus and Sympatico offer high-speed ADSL support nationally while most of the local telephone companies also offer ADSL service as well as lower-speed service.

Cable modems are modems designed to operate over cable TV lines. They can provide high-speed access to the Web or corporate intranets of up to 4 megabits per second. However, cable modems use a shared line so that transmission will slow down if there are a large number of local users sharing the cable line. A cable modem at present has stronger

TABLE 9-2   **NETWORK SERVICES**

Service	Description	Bandwidth
X.25	Packet-switching standard that parcels data into packets of 128 bytes	Up to 1.544 Mbps
Frame relay	Packages data into frames for high-speed transmission over reliable lines but does not use error-correction routines	Up to 1.544 Mbps
ATM (asynchronous transfer mode)	Parcels data into uniform cells to allow high-capacity transmission of voice, data, images, and video between different types of computers	25 Mbps–2.5 Gbps
ISDN	Digital dial-up network access standard that can integrate voice, data, and video services	Basic Rate ISDN (BRI): 128 Kbps; Primary Rate ISDN (PRTI): 1.5 Mbps
DSL (digital subscriber line)	Series of technologies for high-capacity transmission over copper wires	ADSL—up to 9 Mbps for receiving and up to 640 Kbps for sending data; SDSL—up to 3 Mbps for both sending and receiving
T1	Dedicated telephone connection with 24 voice-quality, 64-Kbps channels for high-capacity transmission	1.544 Mbps
Cable modem	Modem for high-speed transmission of data over cable TV lines that are shared by many users	Up to 4 Mbps

capabilities for receiving data than for sending data. Canada's cable television companies have branched out to offer high-speed Internet access as well. As of September 2000, there were more than 1.1 million high-speed customers in Canada, representing 20 percent of Canadian Internet households. Canada's cable companies serve more than two-thirds of the high-speed market, with more than 800 000 customers. The telephone companies and other ISPs serve the rest. And, while high-speed connections are running at about 3 percent of all households in the United States, the penetration rate here is almost 10 percent. Shaw Communications' @Home service has 20 percent of the Canadian cable Internet service provider market while Rogers Communications has 14 percent.

A voice quality line carries 64 Kbps of data, enough for the analog version of a voice message. A **T1 line** is a dedicated telephone connection composed of 24 voice-quality channels that together can support a data transmission rate of 1.544 megabits per second. Each of these 64-kilobit-per-second channels can be configured to carry voice or data traffic. These services often are used for high-capacity Internet connections. Table 9-2 summarizes these network services.

Finally, wireless technology is being adopted for network connections. Wireless hubs receive wireless transmission from multiple wireless devices and then transfer these transmissions via wired or wireless connections to another server. Many small office home office (SOHO) networks use wireless networks.

T1 line

A dedicated telephone connection comprising 24 voice-quality channels of 64 Kbps each that can support a data transmission rate of 1.544 megabits per second. Each channel can be configured to carry voice or data traffic.

NETWORK CONVERGENCE

Most companies maintain separate networks for voice, data, and video, but products are now available to create **converged networks** that can deliver voice, data, and video in a single network infrastructure. These multiservice networks can potentially reduce networking costs by eliminating the need to provide support services and personnel for each different type of network. Multiservice networks can be attractive solutions for companies running multimedia applications such as video collaboration, voice data call centres, distance learning (see the

converged network

A network with technology to enable voice and data to run over a single network.

MANAGEMENT DECISION PROBLEM

CHOOSING AN INTERNET CONNECTION SERVICE

You run a graphic design company with 15 employees that does page layout and illustrations for magazine and book publishers throughout Canada. You want to take advantage of network services to send files of your illustrations and layout work for your clients to review. The average size of each graphics file you transmit is 4 megabytes and an average of 25 of these files are sent to clients each day. Schedules are tight, and productivity can be impacted if all of your network resources are tied up transmitting files. You are also on a very tight budget. The following network services are available in your area. At its current size, your business could use 1 dedicated telephone line with software that enables up to 20 employees to share Internet use.

Option	Transmission Capacity	Cost
Dial-up service with 56 Kbps analog modems for each employee	56 Kbps	$30 per month for Internet service + basic $25 per month phone charge
ISDN line	128 Kbps	$107 per month + $160 installation fee
Cable modem	1–2 Mbps	$100 per month + $200 installation fee
Symmetric DSL	512 Kbps sending and receiving	$200 for DSL modem + $100 per month
T1 line	1.5 Mbps	$2000 per month + installation fee

Use a spreadsheet to help you determine the answers to the following questions.

1. What is the average amount of time your business would spend daily transmitting files for each of these options?

2. Which of these options is most appropriate for your company? Why?

3. If your business expanded, and you had 60 employees and 100 files to transmit daily, which option would you choose?

following section), and unified messaging, or for firms with high costs for voice services. (Unified messaging systems combine voice mail, e-mail, and faxes so they can all be obtained from one system.)

9.4 ELECTRONIC COMMERCE AND ELECTRONIC BUSINESS TECHNOLOGIES

Allegiance Corporation's predecessor, Baxter Travenol, described in Chapter 3, realized the strategic significance of telecommunications. The company placed its own computer terminals in hospital supply rooms. Customers could dial up a local VAN and send their orders directly to the company. Many other companies also achieve strategic benefits by developing electronic commerce and electronic business applications based on the technologies available in the new information technology (IT) infrastructure.

Electronic mail (e-mail), groupware, voice mail, facsimile (fax), digital information services, teleconferencing, dataconferencing, videoconferencing, and electronic data interchange are key applications for electronic commerce and electronic business. They provide network-based capabilities for communication, coordination, and increasing the speed of purchase and sale transactions.

ELECTRONIC MAIL AND GROUPWARE

We already have described the capabilities of electronic mail, or e-mail, in Chapter 4. E-mail eliminates telephone tag and costly long-distance telephone charges while expediting communication between different parts of an organization (see Figure 9-10). Nestlé SA, the Swiss-based multinational food corporation, installed an electronic-mail system to connect its 60 000 employees in 80 countries. In one application, Nestlé's European units use e-mail to share information about production schedules and inventory levels to ship excess products from one country to another.

Many organizations operate their own internal e-mail systems, but communications companies such as Sprint, Bell Canada, and Rogers AT&T offer these services as do commercial online information services such as America Online Canada (www.aol.ca) and public networks on the Internet (see Chapter 10).

The chapter-ending Case Study looks at the privacy of e-mail messages from a different perspective, examining whether monitoring employees using e-mail, the Internet, and other network facilities is ethical.

FIGURE 9-10 Netscape Communicator includes e-mail functions such as attaching files, displaying messages, and providing logs of all incoming and outgoing messages. E-mail has become an important tool for organizational communication.

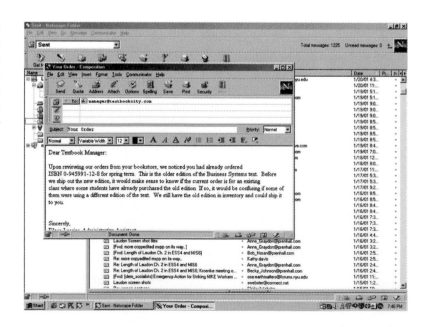

While e-mail has become a valuable tool for communication, groupware provides additional capabilities for supporting enterprise-wide communication and collaborative work. Individuals, teams, and work groups at different locations in the organization can use groupware to participate in discussion forums and work on shared documents and projects. More details on the use of groupware for collaborative work can be found in Chapters 7 and 15.

VOICE MAIL AND FAX

A **voice mail system** digitizes the sender's spoken message, transmits it over a network, and stores the message on disk for later retrieval. When the recipient is ready to listen, the messages are reconverted to audio form. Various store-and-forward capabilities notify recipients that messages are waiting. Recipients have the option of saving these messages for future use, deleting them, or routing them to other parties. Voice mail can also be used to send the same message to multiple parties at one time.

Facsimile (fax) machines can transmit documents containing both text and graphics over ordinary telephone lines. A sending fax machine scans and digitizes the document image. The digitized document is transmitted over a network and reproduced in hard copy form by a receiving fax machine. The process results in a duplicate, or facsimile, of the original.

TELECONFERENCING, DATACONFERENCING, AND VIDEOCONFERENCING

People can meet electronically even though they are hundreds or thousands of kilometres apart by using teleconferencing, dataconferencing, or videoconferencing. **Teleconferencing** allows a group of people to confer simultaneously via a communications channel or via electronic-mail group communication software. Teleconferencing that includes the ability of two or more people at distant locations to work on the same document or data simultaneously is called dataconferencing. With **dataconferencing**, users at distant locations are able to edit and modify data (including text, such as word processing documents; numeric data, such as spreadsheets; and graphic files). Teleconferencing in which participants see each other over video screens is termed video teleconferencing, or **videoconferencing**.

These forms of electronic conferencing are growing in popularity because they save travel time and cost. Legal firms might use videoconferencing to take depositions and to convene meetings between lawyers in different branch offices. A Winnipeg court permitted witnesses from Canada, the United States, and Europe to testify from the comfort of their hometowns by video link in the case of two men charged with Internet fraud. The two had duped at least 25 customers from five countries into buying computer and other equipment that was never shipped. Recent changes in the Canadian criminal code allow prosecutors to use video testimony rather than bringing the witness to the courtroom. Videoconferencing can also help companies promote remote collaboration from different locations or fill in per-

voice mail system
A system for digitizing a spoken message and transmitting it over a network.

facsimile (fax)
A machine that digitizes and transmits documents with both text and graphics over telephone lines.

teleconferencing
The ability to confer with a group of people simultaneously using the telephone or electronic-mail group communication software.

dataconferencing
Teleconferencing in which two or more users are able to edit and modify data files simultaneously.

videoconferencing
Teleconferencing in which participants see each other over video screens.

With PC desktop videoconferencing systems, users can see each other and simultaneously work on the same document. Organizations are using videoconferencing to improve coordination and save travel time and costs.

sonnel expertise gaps. Electronic conferencing is useful for supporting telecommuting, enabling home workers to meet with or collaborate with their counterparts working in the office or elsewhere.

Videoconferencing usually has required special videoconference rooms and videocameras, microphones, television monitors, and a computer equipped with a *codec* device that converts video images and analog sound waves into digital signals and compresses them for transfer over communications channels. Another codec on the receiving end reconverts the digital signals back into analog for display on the receiving monitor. PC-based, desktop videoconferencing systems in which users can see each other and simultaneously work on the same document are reducing videoconferencing costs so that more organizations can benefit from this technology.

Desktop videoconferencing systems typically provide a local window, in which you can see yourself, and a remote window to display the individual with whom you are communicating. Most desktop systems provide audio capabilities for two-way, real-time conversations and a whiteboard. The whiteboard is a shared drawing program that lets multiple users collaborate on projects by modifying images and text online. Software products such as Microsoft NetMeeting (a feature of Windows' latest operating systems), Netscape Communicator's Conference, and CU-SeeMe (available in both shareware and commercial versions) provide low-cost tools for desktop videoconferencing over the Internet.

DIGITAL INFORMATION SERVICES AND DISTANCE LEARNING

Powerful and far-reaching digital electronic services enable networked PC and workstation users to obtain information from outside the firm instantly without leaving their desks. Stock prices, periodicals, competitor data, industrial supply catalogues, legal research, news articles, reference works, and weather forecasts are information that can be accessed online (see Figure 9-11). Many of these services provide capabilities for electronic mail, electronic bulletin boards, online discussion groups, shopping, and travel reservations as well as Internet access. Table 9-3 describes the leading commercial digital information services. The following chapter describes how organizations can access even more information resources by using the Internet.

distance learning
Education or training delivered over a distance to individuals in one or more locations.

Organizations can also use communications technology to run distance learning programs where they can train or educate employees in remote locations without requiring them to be physically present in a classroom. **Distance learning** is education or training delivered over a distance to individuals in one or more locations. Although distance learning can be accomplished with print-based materials, the distance learning experience is increasingly based on information technology, including videoconferencing, satellite or cable television, or interactive multimedia, including the Web. Some distance learning programs use *synchronous communication,* where teacher and student are present at the same time during the instruction, even if they are in different places. Other programs use *asynchronous communication*, where teacher and student don't have person-to-person interaction at the same time or place. For example, students might access a Web site to obtain their course materials and communicate with their instructors via e-mail (see Figure 9-12).

TABLE 9-3	COMMERCIAL DIGITAL INFORMATION SERVICES
Provider	**Type of Service**
canada.com	General information/news
Canoe	General information/news
Globe Interactive	News/business information
Quick Law	Legal research
America Online Canada	General interest/business/information
Microsoft Network Canada	General interest/business/information

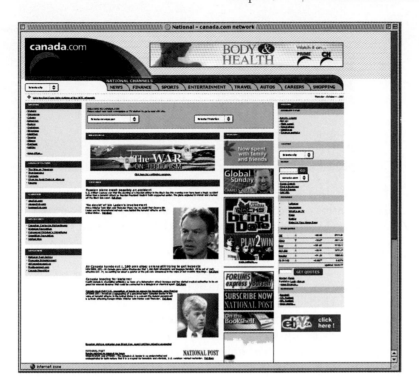

FIGURE 9-11 Users can access stock prices, news, health and other information, and purchase almost any item at the canada.com Web site.

ELECTRONIC DATA INTERCHANGE

Electronic data interchange (EDI) is a key technology for electronic commerce because it allows the computer-to-computer exchange between two organizations of standard transaction documents such as invoices, bills of lading, or purchase orders. EDI lowers transaction costs because transactions can be automatically transmitted from one information system to another through a telecommunications network, eliminating the printing and handling of paper at one end and the inputting of data at the other. EDI also may provide strategic benefits by helping a firm lock in customers, making it easier for customers or distributors to order from them rather than from competitors. EDI also reduces error since data are only entered once. Chapter 2 also shows how EDI can curb inventory costs by minimizing the amount of time components are in inventory.

electronic data interchange (EDI)
The direct computer-to-computer exchange between two organizations of standard business transaction documents.

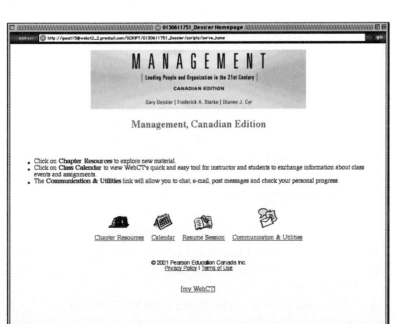

FIGURE 9-12 Students can use the Pearson Education Web site for this book to download materials about each chapter, including quizzes, updates to chapter material, and online exercises.

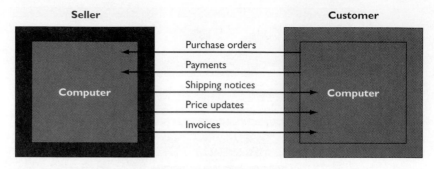

FIGURE 9-13 Electronic data interchange (EDI). Companies can use EDI to automate electronic commerce transactions. Purchase orders and payments can be transmitted directly from the customer's computer to the seller's computer. The seller can transmit shipping notices, price changes, and invoices electronically back to the customer.

EDI differs from electronic mail in that it transmits an actual structured transaction (with distinct fields such as the transaction date, transaction amount, sender's name, and recipient's name) as opposed to an unstructured text message such as a letter. Figure 9-13 illustrates how EDI works.

Organizations can most fully benefit from EDI when they integrate the data supplied by EDI with applications such as accounts payable, inventory control, shipping, and production planning (Premkumar, Ramamurthy, and Nilakanta, 1994), and when they have carefully planned for the organizational changes surrounding new business processes. Management support and training in the new technology are essential (Raymond and Bergeron, 1996). Companies must also standardize the form of the transactions they use with other firms and comply with legal requirements for verifying that the transactions are authentic. EDI standards are available but have not yet been universally adopted. Many organizations prefer to use private networks for EDI transactions but are increasingly turning to the Internet for this purpose (see Chapters 4 and 10).

APPLICATION SOFTWARE EXERCISE

WEB BROWSER EXERCISE: SURFING FOR INFORMATION ON THE WEB

The World Wide Web is a vast repository of information, and information on almost any topic is now available on the Web. The following questions are designed to help you learn more about information technology and test your information retrieval skills.

At the time of this writing, answers to each of the following questions were available on the World Wide Web. Some of the answers you will find quickly; others may take longer to locate. Once you have found the answers, summarize your answers in a report, and submit the report to your professor. You should also include in your report the URLs for the Web sites where you located the information.

1. Who invented HTML, the Web's first language? What year was that?
2. Locate an article that discusses analog and digital signals. How does the article differentiate analog signals from digital signals?
3. When was the Personal Information Protection and Privacy Act (formerly Bill C-6) passed in Parliament? What are its major provisions?
4. When and where is the next IEEE International Conference on Networks scheduled?
5. What is the purpose of the Canadian Radio-television and Telecommunications Commission?
6. What is the purpose of the World Wide Web Consortium?
7. When was the International Standards Organization founded? What is its purpose? How does it formulate its standards?

8. Visit an online store, and determine how much it would cost to set up a PC desktop videoconferencing system.

9. How much does it cost to subscribe to America Online Canada and Microsoft Network Canada? Compare and contrast the features provides by each service. Then compare and contrast the features and costs of using your local telephone company and cable company for high-speed Internet service.

10. What is the Internet Society's mission?

MANAGEMENT WRAP-UP

Managers need to be involved in telecommunications decisions continuously because so many important business processes are based on telecommunications and networks. Management should identify the business opportunities linked to telecommunications technology and establish the business criteria for selecting the firm's telecommunications platform.

Telecommunications technology enables organizations to reduce transaction and coordination costs by promoting electronic commerce and electronic business. The organization's telecommunications infrastructure should support its business processes and business strategy.

Communications technology is intertwined with all the other information technologies and deeply embedded in contemporary information systems. Networks are becoming more pervasive and powerful, capable of transmitting voice, data, and video over long distances. Many alternative network designs, transmission technologies, and network services are available to organizations.

For Discussion

1. Network design is a key business decision as well as a technology decision. Why?

2. What factors should be considered in making network design decisions?

3. If you were an international company with global operations, what criteria would you use to determine whether to use a value-added network (VAN) service or a private wide area network (WAN)?

SUMMARY

1. *Describe the basic components of a telecommunications system.* A telecommunications system is a set of compatible devices that are used to develop a network for communication from one location to another by electronic means. The essential components of a telecommunications system are computers, terminals, other input/output devices, communication channels, communications processors (such as modems, multiplexers, controllers, and front-end processors), and telecommunications software. Different components of a telecommunications network can communicate with each other with a common set of rules, termed protocols. Data are transmitted throughout a telecommunications network using either analog signals or digital signals. A modem is a device that translates analog signals to digital signals and vice versa.

2. *Determine the capacity of telecommunications channels and evaluate transmission media.* The capacity of a telecommuni-

cations channel is determined by the range of frequencies it can accommodate. The higher the range of frequencies, called bandwidth, the higher the capacity (measured in bits per second). The principal transmission media are twisted copper telephone wire, coaxial copper cable, fibre optic cable, and wireless transmission using microwave, satellite, low-frequency radio waves, or infrared waves. They differ in physical size, capacity or bandwidth, speed, and cost.

3. *Compare the various types of telecommunications networks and network services.* Networks can be classified by their shape or configuration. The three common network topologies are the star, bus, and ring networks. In a star network, all communications must pass through a central computer. The bus network links a number of devices to a single channel and broadcasts all of the signals to the entire network, with special software to identify which components receive each message. In a ring network, each computer in the network can communicate directly with any other computer but the channel is a closed loop. Data are passed along the ring from one computer to another. Networks can also be classified by their geographic scope. Local area networks (LANs) and private branch exchanges (PBXs) are used to link offices and buildings in close proximity. Wide area networks (WANs) span a broad geographical distance, ranging from several miles to continents and are private networks that are independently managed.

4. *Compare alternative network services.* Another way to classify networks is in terms of the type of services they provide. Value-added networks (VANs) also encompass a wide geographic area but are managed by a third party, which sells the services of the network to other companies. VANs and the Internet use packet switching, which achieves economies of scale and higher speeds in long-distance transmission by breaking messages into small packets that are sent independently along different paths in a network and then reassembled at their destination. Frame relay is a shared network service that is faster and less expensive than packet switching because it does not perform error correction routines.

Asynchronous transfer mode (ATM) can seamlessly and dynamically switch voice, data, images, and video between users faster than frame relay. ATM also promises to tie LANs and wide area networks together more easily. (LANs generally are based on lower speed protocols while WANs operate at higher speeds.) ATM technology parcels information into uniform cells, each with 53 groups of 8 bytes, eliminating the need for protocol conversion. It can pass data between computers from different vendors and permits data to be transmitted at any speed the network can handle. ATM can transmit up to 2.5 Gbps.

Integrated Services Digital Network (ISDN) is an international standard for dial-up network access that integrates voice, data, image, and video services in a single link. There are two levels of ISDN service: Basic Rate ISDN (BRI) and Primary Rate ISDN (PRI). Each uses a group of B (bearer) channels to carry voice or data along with a D (delta) channel for signalling and control information. Basic Rate ISDN can transmit data at a rate of 128 kilobits per second on an existing local telephone line. Organizations and individuals requiring high-bandwidth transmission or the ability to provide simultaneous voice or data transmission over one physical line might choose this service. Primary Rate ISDN offers transmission capacities in the megabit range and is designed for large users of telecommunications services.

Other high-capacity services include digital subscriber line (DSL) technologies, cable modems, and T1 lines. Like ISDN, digital subscriber line (DSL) technologies also operate over existing copper telephone lines to carry voice, data, and video, but they have higher transmission capacities than ISDN. There are several categories of DSL. Asymmetric digital subscriber line (ADSL) supports a transmission rate of 1.5 to 9 Mbps when receiving data and up to 640 Kbps when sending data. Symmetric digital subscriber line (SDSL) supports the same transmission rate for sending and receiving data of up to 3 Mbps. Cable modems are modems designed to operate over cable TV lines. They can provide high-speed access to the Web or corporate intranets of up to 10 Mbps. A T1 line is a dedicated telephone connection composed of 24 voice-quality channels that can support a data transmission rate of 1.544 megabits per second. Each of these 64-kilobit-per-second channels can be configured to carry voice or data traffic. These services are often used for high-capacity Internet connections.

5. *Identify the principal telecommunications applications for supporting electronic commerce and electronic business.* The principal telecommunications applications for electronic commerce and electronic business are electronic mail, voice mail, fax, digital information services, distance learning, teleconferencing, dataconferencing, videoconferencing, electronic data interchange (EDI), and groupware. Electronic data interchange is the computer-to-computer exchange between two organizations of standard transaction documents such as invoices, bills of lading, and purchase orders.

KEY TERMS

Analog signal, 295

Asynchronous transfer mode (ATM), 308

Backbone, 296

Bandwidth, 301

Baud, 301

Bridge, 305

Broadband, 307

Bus network, 302

Cable modem, 308

Cellular telephone, 299

Channels, 295

Coaxial cable, 296

Concentrator, 301

Controller, 301

Converged network, 309

Dataconferencing, 311

Dedicated lines, 305

Dense wave division multiplexing (DWDM), 297

Digital signal, 295

Digital subscriber line (DSL), 308

Distance learning, 312

Electronic data interchange (EDI), 313

Facsimile (fax), 311

Fibre optic cable, 296

Frame relay, 307

Frequency, 301

Front-end processor, 301

Gateway, 305

Global area network (GAN), 305

Information superhighway, 293

Integrated Services Digital Network (ISDN), 308

Local area network (LAN), 304

Metropolitan area network (MAN), 305

Microwave, 297

Mobile data networks, 299

Modem, 295

Multiplexer, 301

Network interface card (NIC), 305

Network operating system (NOS), 305

Packet switching, 307

Paging system, 298

Peer-to-peer, 305

Personal communication services (PCS), 299

Personal digital assistants (PDA), 299

REVIEW QUESTIONS

1. What is the significance of telecommunications deregulation for managers and organizations?

2. What is a telecommunications system? What are the principal functions of all telecommunications systems?

3. Name and briefly describe each of the components of a telecommunications system.

4. Distinguish between an analog and a digital signal.

5. Name the different types of telecommunications transmission media and compare them in terms of speed, capacity, and cost.

6. What is the relationship between bandwidth and a channel's transmission capacity?

7. Name and briefly describe the different kinds of communications processors.

8. Name and briefly describe the three principal network topologies.

9. Distinguish between a PBX and a LAN.

10. Contrast and compare LANs, WANs, and VANs.

11. List and describe the various network services.

12. Name and describe the telecommunications applications that can support electronic commerce and electronic business.

GROUP PROJECT

In groups of four students, describe in detail the ways that telecommunications technology can provide a firm with competitive advantage. Use the companies described in Chapter 3 or other chapters you have read so far to illustrate the points you make, or select examples of other companies using telecommunications from business or computer magazines. If possible, use electronic presentation software to present your findings to the class.

 **INTERNET CONNECTION**

■ **COMPANION WEBSITE**

At www.pearsoned.ca/laudon, you'll find an online study guide with two quizzes to test your knowledge of how telecommunications and networks work and how they are used in modern organizations. You'll also find updates to the chapter and online exercises and cases that enable you to apply your knowledge to realistic situations.

■ **ADDITIONAL SITES OF INTEREST**

There are many interesting Web sites to enhance your learning about telecommunications and networks. You can search the Web yourself, or just try the following sites to add to what you have already learned.

World Wide Web Consortium

www.w3.org

One of the World Wide Web coordinating bodies. Find out what the Web may be like in the future.

Canadian Laws

laws.justice.gc.ca

Parliament's site to search for laws that have been passed or bills that have been submitted to Parliament.

AT&T World Net

www.att.net

AT&T's global area network (GAN), which subscribers can use to update their Internet connection software, search for help when having a global connection problem, and use to connect to the Internet from all over the world.

CASE STUDY *Monitoring Employees on Networks: Unethical or Good Business?*

In the past few years, the Internet has grown almost at the speed of light, and it has rapidly become deeply embedded in our business and personal lives. However, corporate managements have been slow to realize that their employees are using corporate facilities to surf the Net and to use e-mail for personal reasons. This personal use can be disruptive and costly. Companies are now beginning to face the problem, which in turn has raised serious ethical issues. Is it ethical for employees to use the Net at work for personal purposes as they often were accustomed to doing with the telephone? Are employers obligated to bear the costs of the personal use of their facilities by their employees? Is it ethical for employers to monitor the personal activities of employees as long as those employees are meeting their work goals? Let us look at the many ways employees use the Net at work and the potential costs to employers. Then we will examine the ways corporations are addressing this problem.

When employers first became aware of employees using the Internet for personal purposes, their major concern was that employees would visit pornography sites that might offend other employees, perhaps even leading to lawsuits. Later, concern grew over the number of visits to sport sites and retail outlets on company time. However, it has turned out that the problem is far larger than a little bit of time on a few sites. A number of studies have concluded that at least 25 percent of employee online time is spent on non-work-related surfing. Moreover, investment monitoring and trading has now become the most popular non-work-related Web activity performed by employees on the job. These visits appear to be mushrooming.

New technology, particularly Web technology, makes it easy for people not only to trade, but also to research and monitor their own investments as investment professionals have always done. While many people are driven by hopes for the future, others now view active investment activity as a way to generate immediate supplementary income. The excitement climbs along with the market. With the recent volatility of global markets, the excitement has turned to apprehension with a continuing urge to surf and trade.

E-mail usage has also exploded as people turn to it for speedy, convenient, and inexpensive business and personal communications. Hundreds of millions of people are now connected to each other by e-mail, and the growth shows no sign of slowing. Not surprisingly, the use of e-mail for personal reasons at the workplace has also grown. Management fears that racist, sexually explicit, or other potentially offensive material could create problems in the workplace and could even result in adverse publicity and harassment lawsuits brought by workers. Companies also fear the loss of trade secrets through e-mail. Personal use of e-mail can even clog the company's network so that work cannot be carried out. At Lockheed Martin Corporation, an employee sent an e-mail message concerning an upcoming religious holiday to all of the company's 150 000 employees, locking up the entire network for six hours.

A study by the American Management Association concluded that 27 percent of large U.S. companies are now monitoring employee e-mail in some way compared to only 15 percent in 1997. If employees are using company Internet facilities for personal reasons, how much can it cost? The most obvious cost is the loss of time and employee productivity when employees are focusing on personal rather than company business. If you want to calculate the cost to a company, multiply the estimated average amount employees are paid for an hour's work by the number of hours lost for the average employee, and then multiply the results by the number of employees involved. The number can be very large indeed. In fact, a company with 1000 Internet users who surf the Web for personal reasons for one hour per day can lose more than $35 million in productivity costs each year.

An often ignored but potentially critical cost is the effect personal Internet activities can have on the availability of the company's network bandwidth. If personal traffic is too high, it will interfere with the company's ability to carry on its business. The company may then have to expand its bandwidth, an expensive and time-consuming activity. Only two alternatives exist. The first is to do nothing, causing the Internet connection to slow down and productivity to fall with it. The other alternative is to reduce the bandwidth drain by reducing or eliminating use of the Internet for personal business. Wolverton & Associates Inc., a civil engineering firm based in Norcross, Georgia, installed Telemate.Net monitoring software and found that broadcast.com was the third most visited site and consumed four percent of the company's bandwidth. Employees were using it to download music for themselves. E*Trade, which soaked up another three percent of Wolverton's bandwidth, is just one of many online securities trading sites that employees were visiting. Douglas Dahlberg, Wolverton's IT manager, points out that bandwidth is critical to the company's operations because Wolverton engineers regularly send very large, data-laden CAD files to their clients through e-mail.

Too much time on personal business, Internet or not, can mean lost revenue or overcharges to clients. Some employees may be charging time they spend trading stocks or pursuing other personal business to clients, thus overcharging the clients. A study by Angus Reid in May of 2000 showed that Canadians with work Internet access are racking up 800 million hours of annual personal surfing time at work. Seventy-eight percent of Canadians with Internet access at work have used the Internet for personal reasons, and personal usage accounts for 26 percent of Web surfing time at work. Among reasons cited by Angus Reid for workers to use the Net for personal reason during working hours are the convenience of using the Net from their normal perch in front of the office computer and the frustration with Internet access speeds from home. Research company Vault.com found that 72 percent of users use the Internet for news, followed by 45 percent making personal travel arrangements and 40 percent shopping online. Thirty-seven percent of Vault's respondents use the Internet on company time to find a new job while 13 percent use the Web to download music, and 11 percent use it to play games. Four percent of respondents checked their favourite pornographic sites on company time. Other responses included stock-checking (34 percent), planning social events (28 percent), instant messaging (26 percent), and visiting special personal interest sites (37 percent).

When employees access the Web using employer facilities, anything they do on the Web, including anything illegal, carries their company's name. Therefore, an employer can be traced and held liable. However, even if a company is not found to be liable, responding to lawsuits can cost a company tens of thousands of dollars at a minimum. In addition, lawsuits often result in adverse publicity for a company regardless of outcome. Even if lawsuits do not result, companies are often embarrassed by the publicity that can surround the online actions by a company's employees. Problems can arise not only from illegalities but also through very legal activities such as employee participation in chat rooms society finds unacceptable. For example, employee participation in white power or anti-Semitic chat rooms can produce a public relations nightmare.

How can management address these problems? Consultants recommend that companies begin with a written corporate policy. However, studies show that relatively few companies have written Internet usage policies that specifically address such problems as online investing during working hours. The Angus Reid study cited above shows that only 33 percent of respondents said that their company has an Internet usage policy even though two-thirds of Canadians feel their employer has the right to monitor employee activity.

What should these policies contain? They must include explicit ground rules, rules written in clear, easily understood English. They should state, by position or level, who has the right to access what, and under what circumstances they may access it. Naturally, the rules must be tailored to the specific organization because different companies may need to access different Web materials as part of their businesses. For example, while some companies may exclude anyone from visiting sites that have explicit sexual material, law firm or hospital employees may need access while investment firms will need to allow many of their employees access to other investment sites.

Some companies want to ban all personal activities—zero tolerance. Many companies reject this zero tolerance approach because they believe they must allow employees the ability to conduct some personal business during working hours. But if a company has a strict e-mail usage policy, management does not have to prove harassment to justify firing an errant e-mail user. A case in point is a 40-year-old technician at a Mississauga, Ont., engineering firm. He was fired after 13 years of service because he e-mailed pictures of Cindy Crawford in a bathing suit.

The technician says he sent only three such e-mails: "A manager calls me into his office and pulls out [copies of] the e-mail I sent. He asked me if I had sent this. I said: 'Yeah—but so what? There's no harm in it. It's just a joke.'" He was terminated on the spot. "The manager said I had been given warnings," he says. "That's true—but only indirectly. They had put out a written memo a long time before, saying e-mail was for 'work purposes only.' But I didn't take that seriously because everyone was doing it."

This applies to public organizations as well. The Ontario government joined the provincial governments of Manitoba and British Columbia in taking steps to identify employees who may be using e-mail or Internet privileges inappropriately. However, all of these governments only "sniff" e-mail after the user has been suspected of inappropriate use of these privileges. The Canadian government has an Internet use policy in place that spells out what kinds of sites are inappropriate to visit. Employees caught violating the standards can have their Internet access completely blocked, be suspended, or even be fired for serious infractions.

Clear policy rules and guidelines can be very difficult to write. An individual act, such as a visit to a stockbroker to execute an order, may be acceptable whereas repeated visits in order to monitor that stock might not be. Many find it impossible to draw a clear line between what is acceptable and what constitutes too much. These blurry guidelines may be difficult for employees and employers to apply fairly, and yet it is even more of a problem to achieve more precision. Some companies are even less specific, but at least they have made it clear that anything the employee does for personal reasons cannot be considered private. Moreover, they usually indicate that employees may be disciplined for misuse of the company's facilities, an effective warning that employees will be monitored and held to a standard.

When the *National Post* was under fire from letter writers for publishing a series of news articles and commentary pieces critical of the Tamil Tigers' and their alleged affiliates, some Post reporters were bombarded with angry e-mail messages. One recipient, exasperated because he had not written any of the controversial articles, fought back.

"Is it your company's policy to allow employees to send junk e-mail chain letters of a political nature to journalists?" he wrote to one critic, who had written him from a Nortel e-mail address. "Does your letter reflect the views of your employers? Finally, did Nortel's media relations officers know about your freelance PR? They do now." On his CC list, the journalist placed the e-mail addresses of several highly placed Nortel officers plucked from the company's Web site.

Nortel officials had words with their subordinate. A few days later, this reply from the original sender popped up in the journalist's inbox: "I am extremely sorry for having sent that e-mail to you. It was totally my own personal view and in no way represents that of Nortel Networks. I sincerely apologize." For their part, Nortel officials refused to comment on the exchange—or on any other aspect of their e-mail policy.

How valuable are policies and warnings? They do warn employees and so hopefully reduce misuse. At the same time, they protect the company from any lawsuits by employees if the company does take action. Some companies follow a potentially more effective strategy, combining policies and warnings with filtering or monitoring software (discussed below).

Education should also play a key role. Some companies require all employees to read the policy and then give them an opportunity to clarify any questions they may have. For example, the federal Department of Justice distributed a 19-page "do's and don'ts list" to its employees. Many companies require their employees to sign the policy.

Education also plays a role in identifying a new phenomenon, Internet addiction. Individuals can surf for hours; they feel they need to surf the Internet much as an alcoholic feels the need for a drink. In addition to wasting time, Internet addicts may be addicted to pornography or gambling or sex. The Internet is simply the channel through which they get their "hit." When employees are educated about Internet addiction and its warning signs, they may realize how their behaviour can sabotage their own success and career growth as well as the company's profitability. It is also important to realize that Internet misuse and Internet addiction are not problems that can be solved by technology or policy alone. These are new societal challenges that must be addressed through education in addition to the policy and technology options.

One approach that some companies use is to block all employee access to specific sites. Other solutions short of total blockage also exist. Content Technologies Inc., of Kirkland Washington, produces software that prevents employees from opening executable files. This software allows people to visit a site but also effectively prevents them from placing any orders. Not all agree that this approach is effective. U.S. law firm Epstein, Becker, and Green's Kroening believes: "They're probably just turning around and picking up the phone" to execute the trade, and that still costs employee time. Dahlberg solved his music-downloading problem by removing RealAudio music playing capability from all of Wolverton's systems.

Yet another approach used by many companies is to apply limits and conditions to the Web sites employees can visit. Software, such as SurfWatch, can be used by employers to allow visits to certain sites, such as investment sites, only during specific hours, such as during the lunch hour and before and after normal working hours.

Many companies are turning to software packages to monitor the Internet activities of their employees. Content Technologies produces a software package titled MailSweeper that automatically examines outgoing e-mail messages for language that the company wants to ban or at least to examine. Many employers feel, however, that once people are fully aware that they are being monitored, inappropriate usage will decline, and concurrently employee productivity will increase. In other words, it is the idea of monitoring and not the monitoring itself that may reduce inappropriate use.

Some companies may use monitoring software but prefer the personal approach for dealing with individual offenders. When David Kroening, assistant director of technology and operations at New York law firm Epstein, Becker, and Green, discovers a potential offender, he notifies the manager of the individual and asks that person to handle it. "It's more of a personal issue [than a technical one] now," he explains. Roy Crooks, director of information technology at Bard Manufacturing, uses monitoring software to find out who is creating a problem. Rather than turn the solution over to the offenders' managers, he attempts to solve the problems himself by talking with the offenders personally.

A number of corporations are trying to limit online personal activity to an acceptable amount of time rather than trying to shut if off completely. This policy is a natural extension of the one many employers have followed well before the Internet when they allowed employees to take care of personal business during working hours—within limits. In the minds of many, an absolute ban could create a situation in which employees would simply try to subvert the policy, thus creating an even worse problem. Some companies develop a rule-of-thumb measure for how much time is reasonable. Employees spending more than that amount of time on personal or recreational browsing will likely end up on a list of potential Internet abusers and could have their Internet access taken away. Still other companies permit employees to use company facilities for personal browsing during lunch hours and before and after work.

Some companies occasionally turn to the ultimate punishment, firing employees judged to be offenders. Some managers consider that firing sends a strong, quick message to the remaining employees. Remember the case of the engineering technician above? His colleagues probably got the message, too.

No solution is problem-free. Instituting any policy can create a great deal of controversy and may even result in lawsuits, particularly if employees have not been clearly warned about the new policy. Often employers hear charges of unethical or improper spying from their staffs. Even warnings do not always work. Wolverton's Dahlberg warned the company's small staff of only 36 employees that they would be monitored before the company installed the monitoring software. But warnings "just mustn't sink in," said Dahlberg. "I can see every little Web page you read—and still there were problems."

Sources: Jesse Berst, "How to Spy on Your Employees," *MSNBC Technology*, August 21, 2000; "U.S. Web Use Mostly at Work," *Reuters*, April 6, 2000; Michael J. McCarthy, "Web Surfers Beware: The Company Tech May Be a Secret Agent," *The Wall Street Journal*, January 10, 2000; Michael J. McCarthy, "How One Firm Tracks Ethics Electronically," *The Wall Street Journal*, October 21, 1999, "Now the Boss Knows Where You're Clicking," *The Wall Street Journal*, October 21, 1999, and "Virtual Morality: A New Workplace Quandary," *The Wall Street Journal*, October 21, 1999; Stacy Collett, "Net Managers Battle Online Trading Boom," *Computerworld*, July 5, 1999; Robert D. Hershey Jr., "Some Abandon the Water Cooler for Stock Trading on the Internet," *The New York Times*, May 20, 1999; Nick Wingfield, "More Companies Monitor Employees' E-Mail," *The Wall Street Journal*, December 2, 1999; Jonathan Kay, "FW: You're Fired," *National Post*, January 2001; Agnus Reid "Canadians with Work Internet Access will Rack Up 800 Million Hours of Annual Personal Surfing Time at Work," EProductivity Summit 2001, www.eproductivity.org/misuse/00/070400.cfm, accessed May 24, 2001; Ashlee Vance, "Study says Employees Abuse the Internet," IDG News Service, October 26, 2000, www.itworld.ca, accessed May 24, 2001; Mike McIntyre, "Pair Guilty in High-Tech Case Watched by World's Legal Eyes," *Winnipeg Free Press*, May 19, 2001; Tony Martell, "Something in the Air," *CIO Canada*, October 25, 2000; Liam Lahey, "Ontario Implements Internet Monitoring for Civil Servants," *ITWorld Canada*,

August 25, 2000, www.itworld.ca, accessed May 24, 2001; Dan Verton, "Survey Says: Employers Okay with E-Surfing," *Computerworld Online*, December 19, 2000, www.itworld.ca, accessed May 24, 2001.

CASE STUDY QUESTIONS:

1. Is it ethical for employers to simply check e-mail without having any specific reason to suspect that the employee has a problem that needs to be addressed? Explain your answer.

2. If employees complain about an undue invasion of privacy, how can management determine whether the employer's complaints are legitimate?

3. Write a rationale that would ban all employee personal use of the Internet, including e-mail and the Web.

4. Evaluate as an effective tool a zero tolerance position (firing of employees any time an Internet access rule is broken). If you do not believe zero tolerance is an appropriate policy, under what circumstances would you support firing an employee for using the Internet or e-mail while on the job?

5. Write what you consider to be an effective e-mail and Web use policy for a company. Explain your reasoning for the policy's details.

10 THE INTERNET AND THE NEW INFORMATION TECHNOLOGY INFRASTRUCTURE

OBJECTIVES

After completing this chapter, you will be able to:

1. *Describe the features of the new information technology (IT) infrastructure.*
2. *Describe important connectivity standards.*
3. *Describe how the Internet works and identify its major capabilities.*
4. *Evaluate the benefits the Internet offers organizations.*
5. *Describe the principal technologies for supporting electronic commerce.*
6. *Analyze the management problems raised by the new information technology (IT) infrastructure and suggest solutions.*

Small-Business Marine Retailer Explores the Depths of E-Commerce

Halifax's Binnacle Yachting Equipment and Accessories Ltd. is a pioneer of sorts. Despite the enormous market potential of global and online commerce, Binnacle discovered there was very little competition for yachting suppliers in e-commerce.

Binnacle asked Private Business Networks (www.pbnet.com) to design an affordable, easy-to-use electronic store. Private Business Networks created a complete Microsoft-based solution to take the company directly to the electronic marketplace. Binnacle.com, the yachting company, is no longer a supplier to just the East coast; it now provides for customers around the globe—and around the clock—in a reliable and secure environment.

Binnacle's management team made a decision to diversify their current operations to combat what had become a largely seasonal market base confined largely to the East coast. What they needed was an affordable solution that would increase their visibility beyond the Atlantic seaboard and expand their market in the lucrative yachting supply industry.

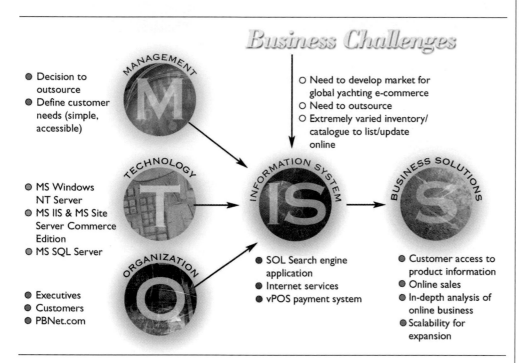

Business Challenges

MANAGEMENT
- Decision to outsource
- Define customer needs (simple, accessible)

TECHNOLOGY
- MS Windows NT Server
- MS IIS & MS Site Server Commerce Edition
- MS SQL Server

ORGANIZATION
- Executives
- Customers
- PBNet.com

- ○ Need to develop market for global yachting e-commerce
- ○ Need to outsource
- ○ Extremely varied inventory/catalogue to list/update online

INFORMATION SYSTEM
- SOL Search engine application
- Internet services
- vPOS payment system

BUSINESS SOLUTIONS
- Customer access to product information
- Online sales
- In-depth analysis of online business
- Scalability for expansion

Binnacle first needed to answer a very important question. How exactly do you bring a store that supplies yachting goods to the global market? Most Canadian yachting companies, Binnacle included, published annual print catalogues, but online competition was scarce. Management visualized an online presence, Binnacle.com, that would support their mission to make every customer a customer for life. The site needed to be inviting to a target group not accustomed to purchasing yachting products online, men between the ages of 40 to 65, the industry's biggest customers.

Binnacle approached Private Business Networks to assist them in designing and implementing an online store that would be accessible and easy-to-use while meeting some very specific criteria. Unlike online book sellers or CD vendors, Binnacle.com needed to offer an extremely varied assortment of goods—of different sizes and weights with non-uniform pricing—to customers around the world.

PBANET.com recommended a three-tiered Microsoft solution to resolve their dilemna. The solution provides Binnacle with everything they required in a site while maintaining a customer service orientation. Eric Dempsey, a member of Binnacle's management team, recalls that, "We weren't looking for off-the-shelf answers; we wanted a system that would allow us to tailor our site to the consumer while being responsive to their needs. We knew there was a way to sell service online, and this solution has provided us with those capabilities."

Today, there are more than 5000 yachting and marine supplies available through Binnacle.com's electronic storefront. The scalability of their e-commerce solution has allowed Binnacle.com to continue to grow while leaving room for

MANAGEMENT WRAP-UP
• *Summary* • *Key Terms* • *Review Questions* • *Group Project* • *Internet Connection* • *Case Study: B2B and B2C E-Commerce: State-of-the-Art Internet for Hudson's Bay Company*

future innovation. The Company projected that in 2001, sales at Binnacle.com would outpace that of their bricks and mortar operation, and things look like they are right on track.

Sources: "Small-Business Marine Retailer Uncovers Hidden Treasure by Exploring Depths of E-Commerce," Microsoft Canada Press Release, www.microsoft.com/Canada/press/releases/1999/12/1999_12_10b.asp, accessed September 30, 2001; "Binnacle Security," Binnacle.com's Web Site, www.binnacle.com, accessed May 28, 2001.

MANAGEMENT CHALLENGES

Like Binnacle Yachting Equipment, many companies are extending their information technology infrastructures to include access to the Internet and electronic storefronts. Electronic commerce, electronic business, and the emerging digital firm require a new information technology infrastructure that can integrate information from a variety of sources and applications. However, using Internet technology and the new IT infrastructure to digitally enable the firm raises the following management challenges:

1. **Taking a broader perspective of infrastructure development.** Electronic commerce and electronic business require an information technology infrastructure that can coordinate commerce-related transactions and operational activities across business processes and perhaps link a firm to others in its industry. The new IT infrastructure for the digitally enabled firm connects the whole enterprise and links with other infrastructures, including those of other organizations and the public Internet. Management can no longer think in terms of isolated networks and applications, or technologies confined to organizational boundaries.

2. **Selecting technologies for the new information technology (IT) infrastructure (connectivity)**. Internet technology, XML, and Java can only provide limited connectivity and application integration. Many firms have major applications that require disparate hardware, software, and network components to be coordinated through other means. Networks based on one standard may not be able to be linked to those based on another without additional equipment, expense, and management overhead. Integrating business applications requires software tools that can support the firm's business processes and data structures. These tools may not always provide the level of application integration desired. Networks that meet today's requirements may lack connectivity for future domestic or global expansion. Managers may have trouble choosing the right set of technologies for the firm's IT infrastructure.

10.1 THE NEW INFORMATION TECHNOLOGY INFRASTRUCTURE FOR THE DIGITAL FIRM

Today's firms can use the information technologies we have described in previous chapters to create an information technology (IT) infrastructure capable of coordinating the activities of entire firms and even entire industries. By enabling companies to radically reduce their agency and transaction costs, the new digital IT infrastructure provides a broad platform for electronic commerce, electronic business, and the emerging digital firm. The new IT infrastructure is based on powerful networks and Internet technology.

ENTERPRISE NETWORKING AND INTERNETWORKING

Figure 10-1 illustrates the new IT infrastructure. The new IT infrastructure uses a mixture of computer hardware supplied by different vendors.

▌ Large, complex databases that need central storage are found on mainframes or specialized servers while smaller databases and parts of large databases are loaded on PCs and workstations.

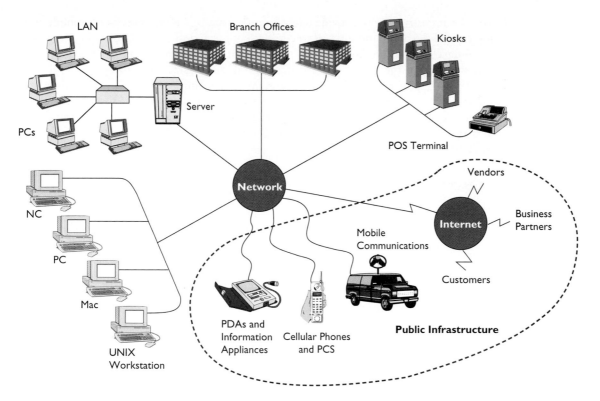

FIGURE 10-1 The new information technology (IT) infrastructure. The new IT infrastructure links desktop workstations, network computers, LANs, and server computers in an enterprise network so that information can flow freely between different parts of the organization. The enterprise network may also be linked to kiosks, point-of-sale (POS) terminals, PDAs and information appliances, digital cellular telephones and PCS, and mobile computing devices as well as the Internet using public infrastructures. Customers, suppliers, and business partners may also be linked to the organization through the new IT infrastructure.

▌ Client/server computing is often used to distribute more processing power to the desktop.

▌ The desktop itself has been extended to a larger workspace that includes mobile personal information devices, programmable cell phones, PDAs, pagers, and other information appliances.

▌ The new IT infrastructure also incorporates public infrastructures, such as the telephone system, the Internet, and public network services and electronic devices. Internet technology plays a pivotal role in the new infrastructure as the main communication channel between customers, employees, vendors, and distributors.

In the past, firms generally built their own software and developed their own computing facilities. As today's firms move toward the new infrastructure, their information systems departments are changing their roles to managers of software packages and software and networking services provided by outside vendors.

Through enterprise networking and internetworking, information flows smoothly between all of the devices within the organization and between the organization and its external environment. In **enterprise networking**, the organization's hardware, software, network, and data resources are arranged to put more computing power on the desktop and to create a company-wide network linking many smaller networks. The infrastructure is a network. In fact, for all but the smallest organizations, the infrastructure is composed of multiple networks. A high-capacity backbone network connects many local area networks and devices.

The backbone may be connected to the networks of other organizations outside the firm, to the Internet, to the networks of public telecommunication service providers, or to other public networks. The linking of separate networks, each of which retains its own identity, into an interconnected network is called **internetworking**. Some organizations are using

enterprise networking
An arrangement of the organization's hardware, software, network, and data resources to put more computing power on the desktop and create a company-wide network linking many smaller networks.

internetworking
The linking of separate networks, each of which retains its own identity, into an interconnected network.

the new IT infrastructure to provide telecommuters and other employees with mobile computing capabilities and remote access to corporate information systems.

Vienna University in Austria (www.univie.ac.at) illustrates enterprise networking and internetworking in the new IT infrastructure. The university's network consists of 3500 computers, including an IBM Enterprise System/9000 mainframe, UNIX workstations, and thousands of PCs. The university's backbone network uses Cisco routers to connect various university departments to the university's computer centre, where traffic is routed to other universities in Vienna, to the Austrian Academic Network (ACOnet), Austria's national research network, and to the Internet.

STANDARDS AND CONNECTIVITY FOR DIGITAL INTEGRATION

The new IT infrastructure is most likely to increase productivity and competitive advantage when digitized information can move seamlessly through the organization's web of electronic networks, connecting different kinds of machines, people, sensors, databases, functional divisions, departments, and work groups. The ability of computers and computer-based devices to communicate with one another and "share" information in a meaningful way without human intervention is called **connectivity**. Internet technology, XML, and Java provide some of this connectivity, but these technologies cannot be used as a foundation for all of the organization's information systems. Most organizations still use proprietary networks. They need to develop their own connectivity solutions to make different kinds of hardware, software, and communications systems work together.

Achieving connectivity requires standards for networking, operating systems, and user interfaces. Open systems promote connectivity because they enable disparate equipment and services to work together. **Open systems** are built on public, nonproprietary operating systems, user interfaces, application standards, and networking protocols. In open systems, software can operate on different hardware platforms and in that sense can be *portable*. Java, described in Chapter 6, can create an open system environment. The UNIX operating system supports open systems because it can operate on many different kinds of computer hardware. However, there are different versions of UNIX, and no one version has been accepted as an open systems standard. Linux also supports open systems.

Models of Connectivity for Networks

There are different models for achieving connectivity in telecommunications networks. The **Transmission Control Protocol/Internet Protocol (TCP/IP)** model was developed by the U.S. Department of Defense in 1972 for use in ARPANET, the precursor of the Internet, and is used in the Internet. Its purpose was to help scientists link disparate computers. Figure 10-2 shows that TCP/IP has a five-layer reference model. The five layers are described below.

1. *Application*: Provides end-user functionality by translating the messages into the user/host software for screen presentation.

2. *Transmission Control Protocol (TCP)*: Performs transport, breaking application data from the end user down into TCP packets called datagrams. Each packet consists of a header with the address of the sending host computer, information for putting the data back together, and information for making sure the packets do not become corrupted.

---

connectivity

A measure of how well computers and computer-based devices communicate and share information with one another without human intervention.

open systems

Software systems that can operate on different hardware platforms because they are built on public nonproprietary operating systems, user interfaces, application standards, and networking protocols.

Transmission Control Protocol/Internet Protocol (TCP/IP)

A U.S. Department of Defense reference model for linking different types of computers and networks; used in the Internet; consists of five layers.

FIGURE 10-2 The Transmission Control Protocol/Internet Protocol (TCP/IP) reference model. This figure illustrates the five layers of the TCP/IP reference model for communications.

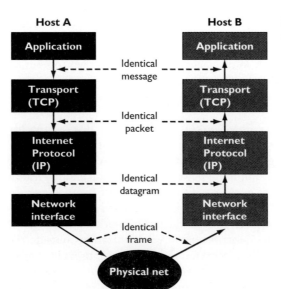

3. *Internet Protocol (IP)*: The Internet Protocol receives datagrams from TCP and breaks the packets down further. An IP packet contains a header with address information and carries TCP information and data. IP routes the individual datagrams from the sender to the recipient. IP packets are not very *reliable*, but the TCP level can keep resending them until the correct IP packets get through.

4. *Network interface*: Handles addressing issues, usually in the operating system, as well as the interface between the initiating computer and the network.

5. *Physical net*: Defines basic electrical transmission characteristic for sending the actual signal along communications networks.

Two computers using TCP/IP would be able to communicate even if they were based on different hardware and software platforms. Data sent from one computer to the other would pass downward through all five layers, starting with the sending computer's application layer and passing through the physical net. After the data reached the recipient host computer, they would travel up the layers. The TCP level would re-assemble the data into a format the receiving host computer could use. If the receiving computer found a damaged packet, it would ask the sending computer to retransmit it. The process would be reversed when the receiving computer responded.

The **Open Systems Interconnection (OSI)** model is an alternative model developed by the International Standards Organization for linking different types of computers and networks. It was designed to support global networks with large volumes of transaction processing. Like TCP/IP, OSI enables a computer connected to a network to communicate with any other computer on the same network or a different network, regardless of the manufacturer, by establishing communication rules that permit the exchange of information between dissimilar systems. OSI divides the telecommunications process into seven layers. Other established standards exist, including IBM's SNA (Systems Network Architecture). No matter how many layers there are or how they are labelled, the bottom line is the same: to establish connectivity.

Equipment makers are starting to develop some standards, including standards for small, high-speed wireless networks to serve offices, campuses, or homes that could provide high-speed data connections of up to two million bits per second. **Bluetooth** is a new standard that allows high-speed, radio-based communication among wireless phones, pagers, computers, and other handheld devices within a 10-metre area so that these devices can interoperate without direct user intervention. For example, a person could highlight a telephone number on a Palm Pilot PDA and automatically activate a call on a digital telephone. A mobile device could transmit a file wirelessly to a printer to produce a hard copy document. People could also synchronize all of their mobile devices wirelessly with desktop computers in their offices and homes. Wireless digital cellular handset manufacturers are working on standards for wireless Internet access (see section 10.3). Interestingly, Bluetooth is named for Harald Blatand (nicknamed Bluetooth), a Viking and Danish king who united Denmark and Norway. One of his skills was to make people talk to each other. Other connectivity-promoting standards have been developed for graphical user interfaces, electronic mail, packet switching, and electronic data interchange (EDI). Any manager wishing to achieve some measure of connectivity in his or her organization should try to use these standards when designing networks, purchasing hardware and software, or developing information systems applications.

Open Systems Interconnection (OSI)
An international reference model for linking different types of computers and networks; consists of seven layers.

Bluetooth
A networking standard for high-speed, radio-based communication within a small area between wireless handheld devices and computers.

10.2 THE INTERNET: INFORMATION TECHNOLOGY INFRASTRUCTURE FOR THE DIGITAL FIRM

The Internet is perhaps the most well-known and largest implementation of internetworking, linking hundreds of thousands of individual networks all over the world. The Internet has a range of capabilities that organizations are using to exchange information internally or to communicate externally with other organizations and individuals. Internet technology has become the primary infrastructure for electronic commerce, electronic business, and the emerging digital firm.

What Is the Internet?

The Internet began as a U.S. Department of Defense network called ARPANET that linked scientists and university professors around the world. Individuals cannot connect directly to the Internet although anyone with a computer, a modem, and the willingness to pay a small monthly usage fee can access it through an Internet service provider. An **Internet service provider (ISP)** is a commercial organization with a permanent connection to the Internet that sells temporary connections to subscribers. Individuals can also access the Internet through popular online services such as MSN Canada and America Online Canada and through networks established by such giants as Bell Canada and AT&T Canada.

One of the most interesting aspects of the Internet is that no one owns it and it has no formal management organization. The U.S. Defense Department forced the lack of centralization to make the Internet less vulnerable to wartime or terrorist attacks. To link to the Internet, an existing network need only pay a small registration fee and agree to certain standards based on the TCP/IP reference model. Costs are low because the Internet owns nothing and so has no costs to offset. Each organization, of course, pays for its own networks and its own connection bills, but those costs usually exist independent of the Internet. Regional Internet companies have been established to which member networks forward all transmissions. These Internet companies route and forward all traffic, and the cost is still only that of a local telephone call. The result is that the costs of e-mail and other Internet connections tend to be far lower than equivalent voice, postal, or overnight delivery, making the Net a very inexpensive communications medium. It is also a very fast method of communication, with messages arriving anywhere in the world often within seconds. We will now briefly describe the most important Internet technologies and capabilities.

Internet Technology and Capabilities

The Internet is based on client/server technology. Individuals using the Net control what they do through client applications such as Web browser software. All the data, including e-mail messages and Web pages, are stored on servers. A client uses the Internet to request information from a particular Web server on a distant computer, and the server sends the requested information back to the client via the Internet.

Client platforms today include not only PCs and other computers but also a wide array of handheld devices and information appliances, some of which can even provide wireless Internet access. Table 10-1 lists examples of some of these devices, most of which were described in Chapters 6 and 9. Some experts believe that the role of the PC or desktop computer as an Internet client is diminishing as people turn to other easy-to-use, specialized information appliances to connect to the Internet.

Servers dedicated to the Internet or even to specific Internet services such as e-mail or the Web are the heart of the information on the Net. Each Internet service is implemented by one or more software programs. All of the services may run on a single server computer, as illustrated in Figure 10-3, or different services may be allocated to different machines. There may be only one disk storing the data for these services, or there may be multiple disks for each type, depending on the amount of information being stored.

Web server software receives requests for Web pages from a client and accesses the Web pages from the disk where they are stored. Web servers can also access other information from an organization's internal information system applications and their associated databases and return that information to the client in the form of Web pages if so desired. Specialized middleware, including application servers, is used to manage the interactions between the Web server and the organization's internal information systems for processing orders, tracking inventory, maintaining product catalogues, and other electronic commerce functions. For example, if a customer filled out an online form on a Web page to order a product such as a light fixture, the middleware would translate the request on the Web page into commands that could be used by the company's internal order processing system and customer database.

Internet Service Provider (ISP)

A commercial organization with a permanent connection to the Internet that sells temporary connections to subscribers.

TABLE 10-1 EXAMPLES OF INTERNET CLIENT PLATFORMS

Device	Description	Example
PC	General purpose computing platform that can perform many different tasks, but often unreliable or complex to use	Dell, Compaq, IBM PCs
Net PC (also known as a thin client)	Network computer with minimal local storage and processing capability; designed to use software and services delivered over networks and the Internet	Sun Ray
Pager	Small device that provides limited e-mail and Web browsing	Blackberry (www.blackberry.net)
Smart Phone	Digital cellular phone that has a small screen and keyboard for browsing the Web and exchanging e-mail	Nokia
Game Machine	Game machine with a modem, keyboard, and capabilities to function as a Web access terminal	Sega Dreamcast
PDA	Wireless handheld personal digital assistant with e-mail and Internet service	Palm VII
E-mail machine	Tablet with keyboard that provides textual e-mail capabilities; requires linking to an e-mail service	MailStation (www.cidco.com)
Set top box	Provides Web surfing and e-mail capabilities using a television set and a wireless keyboard	WebTV

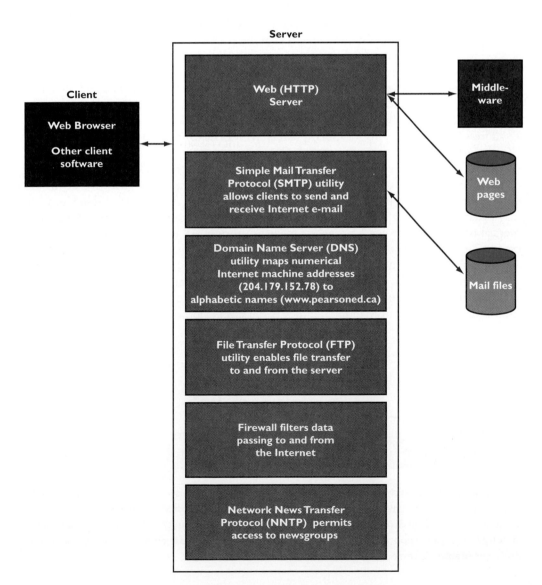

FIGURE 10-3 Client/server computing on the Internet. Client computers running Web browsers and other software can access an array of services on servers via the Internet. These services may all run on a single server or on multiple specialized servers.

TABLE 10-2	MAJOR INTERNET SERVICES
Capability	**Functions Supported**
E-mail	Person-to-person messaging; document sharing
Usenet newsgroups	Discussion groups on electronic bulletin boards
List servers	Discussion groups using e-mail mailing list servers
Chat rooms	Interactive conversations
Telnet	Working on one computer while actually logged into a different computer
FTP	Transfer of files from computer to computer
World Wide Web	Retrieval, formatting, and display of information (including text, audio, graphics, and video) using hypertext links

Internet Capabilities

The most important Internet services for business include e-mail, Usenet newsgroups, list servers, chat rooms, Telnet, FTP, and the World Wide Web. They can be used to retrieve and offer information. Table10-2 lists these capabilities and describes the functions they support.

Electronic Mail (E-Mail)   The Net has become the most important e-mail system in the world because it connects so many people worldwide, creating a productivity gain that observers have compared to Gutenberg's development of movable type in the fifteenth century. Figure 10-4 illustrates the components of an Internet e-mail address. The portion of the address to the left of the @ symbol in Net e-mail addresses is the name or identifier of the specific individual or organization. To the right of the @ symbol is the domain name. The **domain name** is the name that identifies a unique node on the Internet. The domain name corresponds to a unique four-part numeric **Internet Protocol (IP) address** for each computer connected to the Internet. (For example, the domain name, www.pearsoned.ca, has the IP address 204.179.152.78). A **Domain Name Server (DNS)** maps domain names to their IP addresses.

The domain name contains sub-domains separated by a period. The domain that is farthest to the right is the top-level domain, and each domain to the left helps further define the domain by network, department, and even specific computer. The top-level domain name may be either a country indicator or an organization type indicator, such as com for a commercial organization or gov for a government institution. All e-mail addresses end with a country indicator except those in the United States, which ordinarily does not use one. Table 10-3 lists the most prominent top-level domains.

In Figure 10-4, *ca*, the top level domain, is a country indicator, indicating that the address is in Canada. *edu* indicates that the address is an educational institution; *umanitoba* (in this case, University of Manitoba) indicates the specific location of the host computer.

domain name
The unique name of a collection of computers connected to the Internet.

Internet Protocol (IP) address
A four-part numeric address indicating a unique computer location on the Internet.

Domain Name Server (DNS)
A hierarchical system of servers maintaining databases enabling the conversion of domain names to their IP addresses.

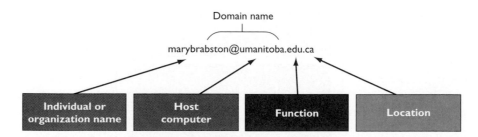

FIGURE 10-4 Analysis of an Internet address. In plain English, the e-mail address of professor and text co-author Mary Brabston would be translated as 'Mary Brabston @ University of Manitoba, educational institution, Canada'. The domain name to the right of the @ symbol contains a country indicator, an organization type indicator, and the location of the host computer. Note: This is not Professor Brabston's correct e-mail address.

TABLE 10-3	TOP-LEVEL DOMAINS
Domain	**Description**
com	Commercial organization/business
edu	Educational institution
gov	Governmental entity
mil	Military organization
net	ISP or other network services provider
org	Not-for-profit organization
ca, uk, us, it	Country indicators

The Internet Corporation for Assigned Numbers and Names (ICANN, the international body that regulates domain registration) approved several new top domain names as of November 2000: biz, info, name, pro, aero, coop, and museum. Some of these names are not yet available but should be soon.

Usenet Newsgroups (Forums or Bulletin Boards)   **Usenet** newsgroups (typically referred to simply as newsgroups) are worldwide discussion groups in which people share information and ideas on a defined topic such as radiology or rock bands. Discussion takes place in large electronic bulletin boards where anyone can post messages for others to read. Many thousands of groups exist discussing almost any conceivable topics. Each newsgroup is financed and administered independently.

List Server   A second type of public forum, a **list server**, allows discussions to be conducted through predefined groups but uses e-mail mailing list servers instead of bulletin boards for communications. If a user finds a listserv topic of interest, the user subscribes to the list server. From then on, through e-mail, the user will receive all messages sent by others concerning that topic. The user can, in turn, send a message to the list server, and it will automatically be broadcast to the other subscribers.

Chat Rooms   **Chat rooms** allow two or more people who are simultaneously connected to the Internet to hold live, interactive conversations. Chat groups are divided into channels, and each is assigned its own topic of conversation. The first generation of chat tools was for written conversations in which participants type their remarks using their keyboard and read responses on their computer screen. Systems featuring voice chat capabilities, such as those offered by Yahoo! Chat are now becoming popular.

A new enhancement to chat rooms called **instant messaging** even allows participants to create their own private chat channels. The instant messaging system alerts a person whenever someone on his or her private list is online so that the person can initiate a chat session with that particular individual. There are several competing instant messaging systems including MSN Messenger and America Online's Instant Messenger. Some of these systems can provide voice-based instant messages so that a user can click on a "talk" button and have an online conversation with another person.

Chatting can be an effective business tool if people who can benefit from interactive conversations set an appointed time to "meet" and "talk" on a particular topic (see Figure 10-5). Many online retailers are enhancing their Web sites with chat services to attract visitors, to encourage repeat purchases, and to improve customer service.

Telnet   **Telnet** allows someone to be on one computer system while doing work on another. Telnet is the protocol that establishes an error-free, rapid link between the two computers, allowing the user, for example, to log on to their business computer from a remote computer when on the road or working from home. Users can also log in and use third-party computers that have been made accessible to the public, such as accessing the catalogue of the National Library of Canada (Telnet:amicus.nlc-bnc.ca). Telnet will use the computer address supplied by the user to locate the remote computer and connect to it.

Usenet (newsgroups)
Forums in which people share information and ideas on a defined topic through large electronic bulletin boards where anyone can post messages on the topic for others to see and respond to.

list server
Online discussion groups using e-mail broadcast from mailing list servers.

chat rooms
Live, interactive conversations over a public network.

instant messaging
A chat service that allows participants to create their own private chat channels so that a person can be alerted whenever someone on his or her private list is online to initiate a chat session with that particular individual.

Telnet
A network tool that allows someone to log on to one computer system while doing work on another.

FIGURE 10-5 The Lands' End Web site provides online chat capabilities to answer visitors' questions and to help them find items they are looking for. Chat services can help Web sites attract customers.

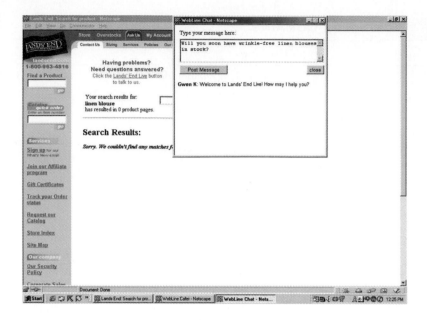

Information Retrieval on the Internet

Information retrieval is a second basic Internet function. Many hundreds of library catalogues are online through the Internet, including those of such giants as the National Library of Canada (www.nlc-bnc.ca/index-e.html), McGill University, and Ryerson Polytechnic University. In addition, users can search many thousands of databases that have been opened to the public by corporations, governments, and non-profit organizations. Individuals can gather information on almost any conceivable topic stored in these databases and libraries. Many people use the Internet to locate and download some of the free, quality computer software and files that have been made available by developers and others on computers all over the world.

The Internet is a voluntary, decentralized effort with no central listing of participants or sites, much less a listing of the data located at those sites, so a major problem is finding what you need from among the storehouses of data found in databases and libraries. We discuss additional information-retrieval methods in the next section on FTP and in our section on the World Wide Web.

file transfer protocol (FTP)
A tool for transferring files to and from a remote computer.

FTP **File transfer protocol (FTP)** is used to access a remote computer and transfer files to and from it. FTP is a quick and easy method if the user knows the remote computer site where the file is stored and if the user has been authorized to use FTP on that computer. After logging on to the remote computer, the user can move around directories that have been made accessible to him or her. Once located, FTP makes transfer of the file to the local computer very easy.

NEXT GENERATION INTERNET: BROADBAND AND INTERNET2

Sound, graphics, and full-motion video are now important features of Web-based computing. However, these all require immense quantities of data, greatly slowing down transmission and the downloading of Web pages. During peak periods of usage, Internet traffic slows to a crawl, and ISPs cannot keep up with the demand. In its current form, the Internet is not reliable or robust enough for many business-critical applications.

Internet2
A research network with new protocols and transmission speeds that provides an infrastructure for supporting high-bandwidth Internet applications.

Higher bandwidth alternatives are under development. Scientists at nearly 200 universities and scores of affiliated companies are working on a new version of the Internet, known as Internet2. **Internet2** is a research network with new protocols and transmission speeds that are much higher than the current Internet. The Internet2 infrastructure is based on a series of interconnected *gigapops*, which are regional high-speed points-of-presence that serve as aggregation points for traffic from participating institutions. (Several gigapops in operation at universities offer 622 megabit per second access to customer end points.) In the United States, these gigapops are in turn connected to the U.S. National Science Foundation's high-performance Backbone Network infrastructure, which will soon operate at 2 gigabits per second. The Canadian Internet2 equivalent is CA*net 3, which is administered by CANARIE, a not-for-profit corporation located in Ottawa and supported by its members, project partners, and the Federal Government. CA*net 3 was first introduced in Chapter 9.

TABLE 10-4	INTERNET2 INFRASTRUCTURE
Infrastructure	Speed
Desktop	10-100 Mbps
Campus (domain) backbone	500 Mbps
GigaPoP connection	155 Mbps
Backbones	2+ Gbps

In addition to testing a more advanced version of the Internet Protocol and finding new ways to route broadcast messages, Internet2 is focusing on developing protocols for permitting different levels of service quality. Today's Internet transmissions are "best effort"—packets of data arrive when they arrive without any regard to the priority of their contents. Different types of packets could be assigned different levels of priority as they travel over the network. For example, packets for applications such as videoconferencing, which need to arrive simultaneously without any break in service, could be assigned a high priority for immediate delivery. E-mail messages, which do not have to be delivered instantaneously, could be delivered when capacity was available.

The new Internet will have the reliability and security features of private leased-line networks with much more bandwidth, enabling companies to distribute video, audio, three-dimensional animations, and data signals in broadcast fashion with minimal disruptions. Web sites will be able to offer applications such as distance learning, digital libraries, 180-degree life-size video teleconferencing, and three-dimensional simulations, that are much more interactive and data-intensive than today's Internet applications, without any degradation in performance.

One important application made possible by Internet2 is the video portal, which delivers high-quality, lifelike video content rather than just text and graphics. Video portals could help automakers build a simulated auto remotely, manipulating parts and tools from afar. A shopper could virtually "try on" an outfit by immersing their 3-D image into the retailer's video site. Other companies could conduct electronic meetings where workers can meet and collaborate by video. High-quality video could be part of every application, along with interactivity and high quality sound.

As Internet2 components and high-speed network technologies come into the commercial mainstream, companies will have to rethink how they work, how they build and sell products, and how they manage their network assets. Internet2 connection speeds are in the hundreds of megabits per second range (see Table 10-4), with at least 100 Mbps connections to servers and at least 10 Mbps to the desktop. Broadband access technologies such as DSL and cable modem will be essential.

10.3 THE WORLD WIDE WEB

The World Wide Web (the Web) is at the heart of the explosion in the business use of the Net. The Web uses universally accepted standards for storing, retrieving, formatting, and displaying information using a client/server architecture. The Web combines text, hypermedia, graphics, and sound. It can handle all types of digital communication while making it easy to link resources that are half-a-world apart. The Web uses graphical user interfaces for easy viewing. It is based on a simple, standard hypertext language called Hypertext Markup Language (HTML), which formats documents and incorporates dynamic links to other documents and pictures stored in the same or remote computers (see Chapter 7). Using these links, the user need only point at a highlighted key word or graphic, click on it, and immediately be transported to another document, probably on another computer somewhere else in the world. Users are free to jump from place to place following their own logic and interest.

Web browser software is programmed according to HTML standards (see Chapter 7). The standard is universally accepted, so anyone using a browser can access any of the millions of Web sites. Browsers use hypertext's point-and-click ability to navigate or surf—move from site to site on the Web—to another desired site. The browsers also include back and forward buttons to enable the user to retrace his or her steps, navigating backwards or forwards, from site to site.

Those who offer information through the Web must establish a **home page**—a text and graphical screen display that usually welcomes the user and typically explains the organization that has established the page. For most organizations, the home page will lead the user to other pages, with all the pages of a company being known collectively as a Web site. For a corporation to establish a presence on the Web, therefore, it must set up a Web site of one or more pages. Most Web pages offer a way to contact the organization or individual. The person in charge of an organization's Web site is called a **Web master**.

To access a Web site, the user must specify a **uniform resource locator (URL)**, which points to the address of a specific resource on the Web. For instance, the URL for Pearson Education Canada, the publisher of this text, is

> http://www.pearsoned.ca

Hypertext transport protocol (http) is the communications standard used to transfer pages on the Web. HTTP defines how messages are formatted and transmitted and what actions Web servers and browsers should take in response to various commands. The domain name identifies the Web server storing the Web pages; in the example above, *www.pearsoned.ca* is the domain name.

Searching for Information on the Web

Locating information on the Web is a critical function, with the more than one billion Web pages in existence expected to double in eight months. No comprehensive catalogue of Web sites exists. The principal methods of locating information on the Web are Web site directories, search engines, and broadcast or "push" technology.

Several companies have created directories of Web sites and their addresses, providing search tools for finding information. Yahoo! Canada is an example. People or organizations submit or register sites of interest, which are then classified. To search the directory, the user enters one or more keywords and then sees displayed a list of categories and sites with those key words in the title.

Interestingly, there are two groups of Web content. The "surface" Web is what everybody knows as the "Web," a group that consists of static, publicly available Web pages, which is actually a relatively small portion of the entire Web. Another group is called the "deep" Web, and it consists of specialized Web-accessible databases and dynamic Web sites, which are not widely known by "average" surfers, even though the information available on the "deep" Web is 400 to 550 times larger than the information on the "surface."

The Web has also been represented as a bowtie. Researchers from AltaVista, IBM, and Compaq Computer have determined the Web's shape. What the team discovered was that the Web takes the shape of a bowtie, not a blob. These researchers discovered four distinct Web regions: origination, termination, disconnected sites, and the core. Where you go from each region depends on content characteristics. For example, it's easy to get from origination Web sites to the well-connected core, but it's not so easy to get back where you came from. The origination Web sites have hyperlinks to the core, but the core doesn't have hyperlinks to the origination sites. Termination sites are easy to reach, but you can't "click through" to any other Web pages. Here, the Back button comes in handy. Disconnected sites are rather isolated, sometimes because they were made that way and sometimes not. In the middle of it all—the bowtie's knot—resides the core, where it's easy to navigate via links.

Other search tools do not require Web sites to be pre-classified and will search Web pages on their own automatically. These tools, called **search engines**, can find Web sites that may be relatively unknown. They contain software that looks for Web pages containing one or more of the search terms; then they display matches ranked by a method that usually involves the location and frequency of the search terms, or the number of links from other pages to that site. Search engines do not display information about every site on the Web, but they create indexes of the Web pages they visit. The search engine software then locates Web

---

home page
A World Wide Web text and graphical screen display that welcomes the user and usually explains the organization or individual who has established the page.

Web master
The person in charge of an organization's Web site.

uniform resource locator (URL)
The address of a specific resource on the Internet.

hypertext transport protocol
The communications standard used to transfer pages on the Web. Defines how messages are formatted and transmitted.

search engine
A tool for locating specific sites or information on the Internet.

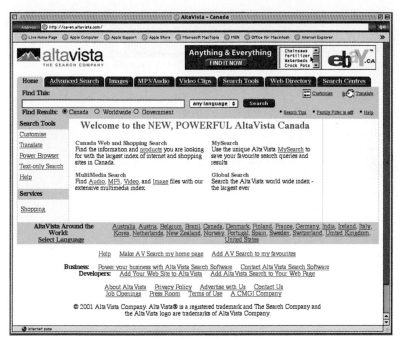

FIGURE 10-6 AltaVista provides a directory of Web sites classified into categories and is a major Internet portal. Users can search for sites of interest by entering keywords in many different foreign languages or by exploring the categories.

pages of interest by searching through these indexes. Alta Vista Canada, Cantrek.com, and Canada.com are examples of search engines (see Figure 10-6). Some are more comprehensive or current than others, depending on how their components are tuned and some also classify Web sites by subject categories.

Specialized search tools are also available to help users locate specific types of information easily. For example, Google is tuned to find the home pages of companies and organizations. Some Web sites that started as search engines like Yahoo! Canada and Canada.com have become so popular and easy to use that they also serve as portals for the Internet (see Chapter 4).

There are two ways of identifying Web pages to be tracked by search engines. One is to have Web page owners register their URLs with search engine sites. To promote their Web sites, many companies do more than simply registering with the search engines. Some search engines, such as GoTo, use "pay-for-position" fees; if a company wants its Web site to be one of the first results listed in a search on GoTo, it pays GoTo a fee—the higher the fee, the higher the placement on the search results list.

Commercial sites also pay fees so that the search engines will check their Web sites for updates more frequently than others. Other search engines, such as LookSmart, charge pay-for-inclusion fees; if a company wants to ensure that it is in LookSmart's database, it pays LookSmart a fee. As of this writing, Google does not accept fees from the sites they index; however, Google does position advertisements related to the keywords being searched on its results pages.

The other way to identify Web pages is to use software agents known as *spiders*, *bots,* and *Web crawlers* to traverse the Web and identify the Web pages for indexing. Chapter 15 details the capabilities of software agents with built-in intelligence, which can also help users search the Internet for shopping information. **Bots**, named for robots, are software that automate repetitive tasks, such as filtering e-mail, for users. For example, shopping bots can help people interested in making a purchase filter and retrieve information about products of interest, evaluate competing products according to criteria they have established, and negotiate with vendors for price and delivery terms (Maes, Guttman, and Moukas, 1999). Excite Canada now offers a **shopping bot** to comparison shop for their subscribers. To use these agents, the consumer enters the desired product into an online shopping form. Using this information, the shopping agent searches the Web for product pricing and availability. It returns a list of sites that sell the item along with pricing information and a purchase link. (See Figure 10-7). Table 10-5 compares various types of electronic commerce shopping bots.

bot
Software that automates a function based on the user's preferences (from "robot").

shopping bot
Software that has varying levels of built-in intelligence to help electronic commerce shoppers locate and evaluate products or services they might wish to purchase.

FIGURE 10-7 MySimon is a shopping bot that can search virtual retailers for price and availability of products specified by the user. Displayed here are the results for a search of prices and sources for a PDA.

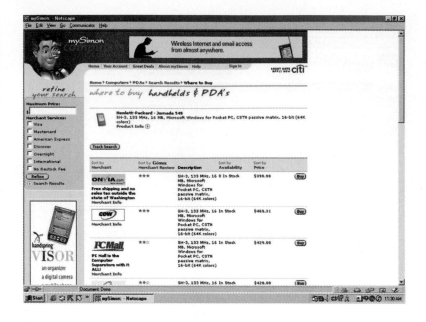

Broadcast and "Push" Technology

Instead of spending hours surfing the Web, users can have the information they are interested in delivered automatically to their desktops through **"push" technology**. A computer broadcasts information of interest directly to the user, rather than having the user "pull" content from Web sites.

Special client software allows the user to specify the categories of desired information, such as news, sports, financial data, and so forth, and how often the information should be updated. After finding the kind of information requested, push server programs serve it to the push client. Microsoft's Internet Explorer and Netscape Communicator include push tools that automatically download Web pages, inform the user of updated content, and create *channels* of user-specified sites. Using push technology to transmit information to a select group of individuals is one example of **multicasting**. (List servers sending e-mail to members of specific mailing lists is another.)

Online marketplaces and exchanges can use push services to alert buyers to price change and special deals. Companies are using push technology to set up their own internal push channels to broadcast important information on their own private networks. For example,

"push" technology
A method of obtaining relevant information on networks by having a computer broadcast information directly to the user based on pre-specified preferences.

multicasting
Transmission of data to a selected group of recipients.

TABLE 10-5	Examples of Electronic Commerce Shopping Bots
Agent	**Description**
Yahoo! Canada	Shopping bot that can compare prices at Yahoo! registered merchants
The Focus	Canadian search engine for shoppers to find the right item
MySimon	Real-time shopping bot that searches more than 1000 affiliated and unaffiliated merchants in 90 categories. Collects a 3 to 10 percent finders fee on sales.
Junglee	Shopping bot used in Amazon.com's Shop the Web comparison shopping service
W3Shopping.com	Uses Inktomi's C2B shopping bot technology to list 380 affiliated and unaffiliated merchants in 14 categories
AuctionBot	Allows sellers to set up their own auctions where buyers and sellers can place bids according to the protocols and parameters that have been established for the auction. Using AuctionBot, sellers create auctions by selecting the type of auction and parameters (such as clearing time or number of sellers) they wish to use. AuctionBot then manages the buyer bidding according to the specified parameters.

TABLE 10-6	EXAMPLES OF CANADIAN PUSH SITES
Push Site	**Description**
Lanacom	Pushes headlines from user-designated Web sites, then scrolls them in a floating ticker-tape bar in the title bar of the active application on your desktop. Click on a headline to retrieve articles without images
Canada Newswire	Pushes "Webcast" sponsored events to subscribers
IBM Canada	Uses BackWeb technology to push customer-requested product updates only when customer bandwidth is available (eliminating bandwidth performance degradation)

Mannesmann o.tel.o GmbH (www.o-tel-o.de/), one of the largest telecommunications providers in Germany, has developed an application using BackWeb's push delivery service that broadcasts new press releases about competitors' products as soon as the information appears on the Internet. Table 10-6 lists a few Canadian push sites and Figure 10-8 shows one example.

INTRANETS AND EXTRANETS

Organizations can use Internet networking standards and Web technology to create private networks called intranets. We introduced intranets in Chapter 1, explaining that an intranet is an internal organizational network that can provide access to data across the enterprise. It uses the existing company network infrastructure along with Internet connectivity standards and software developed for the World Wide Web. Intranets can create networked applications that can run on many different kinds of computers throughout the organization, including mobile handheld computers and wireless remote access devices.

Intranet Technology

Although the Web is open to anyone, an intranet is private and is protected from public visits by **firewalls**—security systems with specialized software to prevent outsiders from invading private networks. A firewall consists of hardware and/or software placed between an organization's internal network and external networks, including the Internet. A firewall is programmed to intercept each message packet passing between the two networks, examine its characteristics, and reject unauthorized messages or access attempts. We provide more detail on firewalls in Chapter 12.

firewall
Hardware and/or software placed between an organization's internal network and external networks to prevent outsiders from invading internal networks.

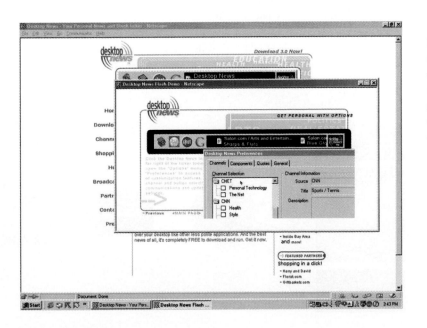

FIGURE 10-8 Delivering information through "push" technology. Desktop News delivers a continuous stream of news and information from Web sites selected by users directly to their desktops as a customizable ticker toolbar.

Intranets require no special hardware and can run over any existing network infrastructure. Intranet software technology is the same as that of the World Wide Web. Intranets use HTML or other Net languages to program Web pages and to establish dynamic, point-and-click hypertext links to other sites. The Web browser and Web server software used for intranets are the same as those on the Web. A simple intranet can be created by linking a client computer with a Web browser to a computer with Web server software via a TCP/IP network. A firewall keeps unwanted visitors out.

Extranets

Some firms are allowing people and organizations outside the firm to have limited access to their internal intranets. Private intranets that are extended to authorized users outside the company are called extranets, introduced in Chapter 4. For example, authorized buyers could link to a portion of a company's intranet from the Internet to obtain information about a product's cost and features. The company can use firewalls to ensure that access to its internal data is limited and remains secure; firewalls can also authenticate users, making sure that only authorized users can access the site.

Extranets are especially useful for linking organizations with customers or business partners. They often are used for providing product-availability, pricing, and shipment data, and for electronic data interchange (EDI), or for collaborating with other companies on joint development or training efforts. Figure 10-9 illustrates one way that an extranet might be set up.

THE WIRELESS WEB

Chapter 4 introduced mobile commerce (m-commerce), the use of the Internet for purchasing goods and services as well as sending and receiving messages using handheld wireless devices. With cell phones, PDAs, and other wireless computing devices becoming Internet-enabled, many believe m-commerce represents the next wave of Internet computing. Within the next few years, most Internet access could potentially take place via mobile wireless devices.

Web-enabled wireless devices will not replace the PC but will enable millions of people to access the Internet while on the go. M-commerce will become a significant subset of e-commerce. Businesses will increasingly incorporate wireless Internet access into their IT infrastructures so that employees can access information wherever they are and make decisions instantly without being wired to a desk or computer.

Web content will be reformatted for wireless devices, and new content and services will be developed specifically for those devices. **Wireless Web** applications enable users to access digital information from the Internet and be connected anywhere, any time, any place. Specialized portals steer users of Web-enabled wireless devices to the information they are most likely to need.

The Wireless Web is not a mobile version of the wired Internet; it is an entirely new medium. M-commerce technology and services could make the Internet ubiquitous, inte-

Wireless Web

Web-based applications enabling users to access digital information from the Internet using wireless mobile computing devices.

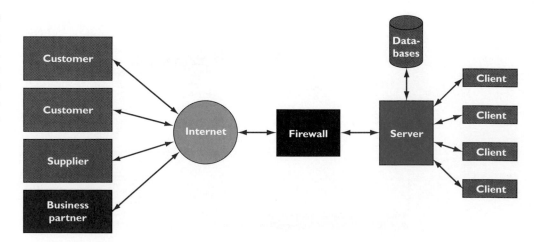

FIGURE 10-9 Model of an extranet. In this model of an extranet, selected customers, suppliers, and business partners can access a company's private intranet from the Internet. A firewall allows access only to authorized outsiders.

M-commerce services mean that business can be conducted wherever the participants are located.

grating individuals with Web information services wherever they go. The Web will evolve into a vast pool of data resources that can be accessed in many different ways as opposed to a collection of distinct pages.

M-commerce opportunities will abound as companies try to develop products and services to sell through the wireless Internet. Table 10-7 describes what are likely to be the most popular categories of m-commerce services and applications. Location-based applications are of special interest because they take advantage of the unique capabilities of mobile technology (see Figure 10-10). Whenever a user is connected to the Internet via a wireless device (cell phone, PDA, laptop), the transmission technology can be leveraged to determine that person's location and beam location-specific services or product information. For example, drivers could use this capability to obtain local weather data and local traffic information along with alternate route suggestions and descriptions of nearby restaurants.

While m-commerce is just starting up in North America, millions of users in Japan and Scandinavia already use cell phones to purchase goods, trade files, and get updated weather and sports reports. The Window on Organizations describes some of these m-commerce applications.

Wireless Web Standards

There is a plethora of standards governing every area of wireless communications. The two main standards for the Wireless Web are Wireless Application Protocol (WAP) and I-mode (see Figure 10-11).

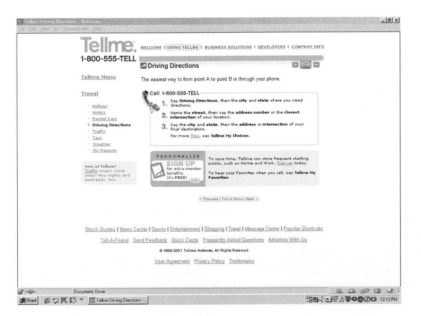

FIGURE 10-10 TellMe is a portal providing direct access to the Web using voice commands with wireless devices. It can provide driving directions and other location-based services.

TABLE 10-7	M-COMMERCE SERVICES AND APPLICATIONS
Type of M-Commerce Service	**Applications**
Information-based services	Instant messaging, e-mail, searching for a movie or restaurant using a cell phone or handheld PDA
Transaction-based services	Purchasing stocks, concert tickets, music, or games; searching for the best price of an item using a cell phone and buying it in a physical store or on the Web
Personalized services	Services that anticipate what you want based on your location or data profile, such as updated airline flight information or beaming coupons for nearby restaurants

Wireless Application Protocol (WAP)

A system of protocols and technologies that lets cell phones and other wireless devices with tiny displays, low bandwidth connections, and minimal memory access Web-based information and services.

WML (Wireless Markup Language)

A markup language for Wireless Web sites, based on XML and optimized for tiny displays.

Wireless Application Protocol (WAP) is a system of protocols and technologies that lets cell phones and other wireless devices with tiny displays, low bandwidth connections, and minimal memory access Web-based information and services. WAP uses **WML (Wireless Markup Language)**, which is based on XML (see Chapter 7) and optimized for tiny displays. Like XML, WML describes data rather than just the way data are displayed, and thus could potentially be used to manipulate and exchange data and create software applications. A person with a WAP-compliant phone uses a built-in microbrowser to make a

---

IT'S BECOMING A WIRELESS WORLD

In parts of Europe and Japan, m-commerce is flourishing. Consumers are using their cell phones as "electronic wallets" to shop, bank, and even pay their rent. Here are some examples.

Estonian Mobile Phone Co. (www.emt.ee) offers a service that enables subscribers to use their mobile phones to pay for parking spaces. After pulling into a parking space, they merely tap a few keys on the phone, and the screen displays a message confirming that the parking fee has been charged to their "virtual account." Parking attendants can check for payment by entering the driver's license plate number into their mobile devices to check the virtual account.

Spain's Telefonica SA (www.telefonica.es) is teaming up with Banco Bilbao Vizcaya Argentaria SA (www.bbva.es) to provide a wireless payment system that enables users to purchase inexpensive products such as soft drinks or newspapers by pressing a few keys on their mobile phones. The cost of the purchase is automatically deducted from the customer's bank account. Subscribers to Italy's Omnitel, a unit of Vodafone Air Touch PLC (www.vodafone.co.uk/cgi-bin/COUK/arrival.jsp), can use their cell phones to participate in wireless auctions for holiday packages, high-tech gear, and other products.

Japan already has dozens of mobile phone services that consumers are willing to pay for. NTT DoCoMo Inc., the wireless arm of Nippon Telegraph and Telephone Co., offers a wireless Internet service that has already attracted 10 million subscribers. Subscribers receive an Internet-enabled cell phone with which they can send and receive e-mail and access numerous Web sites formatted for tiny screens. For example, 28-year-old Takayo Yamamoto uses her cell phone to send e-mail to friends, check train schedules, obtain movie listings, and read Japan's largest daily newspaper. Other Japanese users can browse through restaurant guides, purchase tickets on Japan Airlines, trade stocks via DLJ Direct Inc., or view new cartoons.

The small keypads on mobile phones make it difficult for users to type in Web addresses. Subscribers to Japanese Web services can obtain menus of services tailored to their specific interests. Customers can sign onto a service with the click of a button without having to find and key in a complete Web address.

Some of these services are free; those that aren't, such as the newspaper, are bundled together and charged to a user's monthly telephone bill. The subscription fee for each Japanese wireless Internet service runs around $3 per month. This micro-billing system is simple for users and profitable for m-commerce service providers. According to Toby Rhodes, an analyst with Nikko Salomon Smith Barney in Tokyo, "It's a new business model." Many Web sites for PCs in North America put up their contents for free and feel consumers will balk if they start charging for their services. They're still struggling to become profitable. But Japan's mobile phone-based Internet services are charging for content, adding their fees to subscribers' cellular telephone bills. People who would normally resist paying for Web services apparently are willing to subscribe to wireless Web services because payment is so convenient.

To Think About: What types of businesses can benefit from supplying m-commerce services?

Sources: Gautam Naik, "M-Commerce: Mobile and Multiplying," *The Wall Street Journal*, August 18, 2000 and Miki Tanikawa, "Phone Surfing for a Few Yen," *The New York Times*, August 19, 2000.

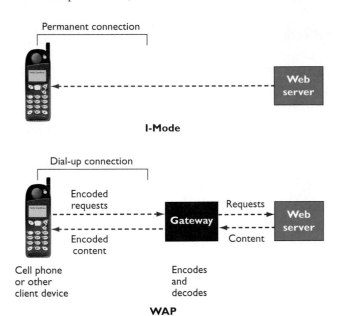

Permanent connection

Web server

I-Mode

Dial-up connection

Encoded requests

Gateway

Requests

Web server

Encoded content

Content

Cell phone or other client device

Encodes and decodes

WAP

FIGURE 10-11 WAP versus I-Mode. WAP and I-mode are two competing standards for accessing information from the Wireless Web.

request in WML. A **microbrowser** is an Internet browser with a small file size that can work with the low memory constraints of handheld wireless devices and the low bandwidth of wireless networks. The request is passed to a WAP gateway, which retrieves the information from an Internet server in either standard HTML format or in WML. The gateway translates HTML content back into WML so that it can be received by the WAP client. The complexity of the translation process can affect the speed of information delivery.

WML requires much less bandwidth and processing power than HTML, and it fits within tiny display screens. WAP supports most wireless network standards, including CDPD, CDMA, GSM, TDMA, PDC, and iDEN. It also supports operating systems for handheld computing devices such as PalmOS and Windows CE.

I-mode is a rival standard developed by Japan's NTT DoCoMo mobile phone network, which is widely used in Japan and is being introduced in Europe and North America. I-mode uses compact HTML to deliver content, making it easier for businesses to convert their HTML Web sites to mobile service. I-mode uses packet switching, allowing users to be constantly connected to the network and permitting content providers to broadcast relevant information to users (WAP users have to dial in to see if a site has changed.) I-mode can handle colour graphics not available on WAP handsets although WAP is being modified to handle colour graphics.

M-Commerce Challenges

There are still barriers to m-commerce services. Keyboards and screens on cell phones are tiny and awkward to use. The data transfer speeds on existing wireless networks are very slow, ranging from 9600 to 14 400 Kbps, compared to 56 Kbps for a dial-up connection to the Internet via a PC. Each second waiting for data to download costs the customer money, as much as $1 per minute. Most Internet-enabled phones have minimal memory, so Web content for wireless devices is in the form of text with very little graphics.

Rollout of m-commerce services has not been as rapid in North America as in Japan and Europe. Not enough North American Web sites have reconfigured their services to display only the few lines of text that can be accommodated by cell phone screens. Also, unlike Europe, North American wireless networks are based on several incompatible technologies. (Europe uses the GSM standard while wireless carriers in North America primarily use CDMA or TDMA standards.) For the wireless Web to take off, more Web sites need to be designed specifically for wireless devices, and wireless devices need to be made that are more Web-friendly.

Some of the limitations of m-commerce may be overcome by using voice recognition technology (see Figure 10-12). **Voice portals** accept voice commands for accessing information from the Web. Voice portals offer customers a combination of content and services, with

microbrowser
Web browser software with a small file size that can work with the low memory constraints and tiny screens of handheld wireless devices and the low bandwidth of wireless networks.

I-mode
A standard developed by Japan's NTT DoCoMo mobile phone network to enable cell phones to receive Web-based content and services.

voice portal
A portal that can accept voice commands for accessing information from the Web.

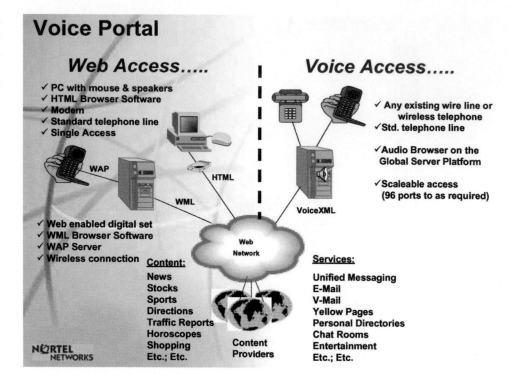

users accessing the content by speaking into a telephone. The user can orally request information such as stock quotes, weather reports, airline schedules, or news stories (see Table 10-8). Sophisticated voice recognition software processes the requests, which are then translated back into speech for the customer.

M-commerce will also benefit from faster wireless networks. Cellular network providers are speeding up their services, preparing new versions of the three main digital standards to double their speed. Third Generation (3G) mobile communication networks will offer transmission speeds of up to 2 Mbps. Faster wireless networks will make it possible to stream high quality video and audio to mobile devices along with new services. The Window on Technology describes other technology advances that will facilitate m-commerce and the opportunities they provide for entrepreneurs.

ORGANIZATIONAL BENEFITS OF INTERNET AND WEB TECHNOLOGY

The Internet, intranets, and extranets are becoming the principal platforms for electronic commerce and electronic business because this technology provides so many benefits. The

TABLE 10-8   EXAMPLES OF VOICE PORTALS

Voice portal	Services
GTG Technologies' GasToGo	GTG voice-recognition system provides the driver with the lowest reported gas prices on any street or within a radius from any intersection
Voice Genie	VoiceGenie's VoiceXML Gateway has a fully open, non-proprietary architecture, supporting a variety of speech recognition engines as well as open-standard VoiceXML applications
Mitercom	Airport Assistant offers real time access to information on commercial and charter airlines, businesses within an airport facility, customs and immigration, and public transportation
HeyAnita	Users can send and receive e-mail by speaking; recognizes voice commands in English, Korean, Mandarin Chinese, and Spanish

M-COMMERCE INSPIRES NEW NETREPRENEURS

Building the Internet's infrastructure has proven to be an extraordinary opportunity for entrepreneurship. New companies are popping up to develop the software and services needed to make the wireless Web a success. Entrepreneurs are identifying segments of wireless business in which they feel they can supply value. Argo Interactive Group (www.argogroup.com), a company with only 28 employees located in Chichester, United Kingdom, decided it would address the problem of too little bandwidth that all wireless companies face. While Argo cannot provide more bandwidth, it can help reduce the amount of bandwidth needed for any transmission by lessening the quantity of data needed to accomplish the specific task. Its software product, ActiGate, reduces or eliminates the HTML in wireless transmission that is so vital to the full Web displays on desktop and laptop computers. Because wireless devices vary widely, from the operating systems to screen size and shape, Argo also offers software that tailors messages to the specific device that will be receiving it. That way, someone using a wireless PDA with a vertical three-inch screen isn't restricted to the data that would fit the three-line display screen on a cell phone.

Iobox, a new company located in Helsinki, Finland, identified a way to make wireless devices more useful to business employees. Using Iobox software, individuals can enter personal data such as a calendar or address book onto the company's Web site and then access and utilize them via a cell phone when away from the office. The software also enables the user to go from an entry such as an anniversary reminder to a site at which the user can order flowers or a gift to be sent.

Webraska, located in Poissy, France, has identified geographic needs and makes available a service for WAP phones that provides real-time traffic data along with alternate route sugges-

tions. While users originally had to enter their locations manually, the company is switching to GPS (global positioning system) technology that automatically identifies the location. Once that transition has been made, Webraska will provide information about parking lots, gas stations, restaurants, hotels, and other services in the area. To achieve this, the company has joined with hotel networks, tourist guides, and auto clubs.

One Helsinki company, WapIT, decided to offer a wide range of information that European mobile phone users feel is important. The company maintains a wireless portal offering both its own Web services and those of over 100 other content providers with whom it has partnered. In this way, WapIT can truly satisfy most content demands that wireless device users want. For example, their offerings include address books, emergency telephone numbers, calendars, package tracking, and even sports data, horoscopes, and shoe size conversions.

In Korea, employees are forbidden to trade stocks on office PCs. Seoul-based Infobank offers a secure wireless trading platform for mobile phone users. Infobank currently charges South Korean securities firms a flat monthly fee for using its technology but will soon charge fees for every stock trade. South Korean investors are taking advantage of this technology to trade stocks while driving, shopping, and eating, making South Korea the country with the highest percentage of mobile stock trading in the world.

To Think About: How do the technologies described here facilitate m-commerce? How could businesses use these technologies? Would you use this technology? How much would you be willing to pay for it? On what basis should users be charged?

Sources: Fred Sandsmark, "Five Hot Wireless Startups," *Red Herring,* April 2000; Neel Chowdhury, "Infotank: Stock Trading on the Run," *Fortune,* October 9, 2000.

Internet's ease of use, low cost, and multimedia capabilities can be used to create interactive applications, services, and products. By using Internet technology, organizations can:

- Provide global connectivity
- Reduce communication and transaction costs
- Enhance coordination and collaboration
- Accelerate the distribution of knowledge
- Enhance customer relationship and supply chain management

Connectivity and Global Reach

The value of the Internet lies in its ability to easily and inexpensively connect so many people from so many places all over the world. Anyone who has an Internet connection can log on to a computer and reach any other computer on the Internet, regardless of location, computer type, or operating system.

The Internet's global connectivity and ease of use can provide companies with access to businesses or individuals who normally would be outside their reach. Companies can link directly to suppliers, business partners, or individual customers at the same low cost, even if they are halfway around the globe. The Internet provides a low-cost medium for forming global alliances and virtual organizations. The Web provides a standard interface and inexpensive global access, which can be used to create interorganizational systems among almost any organizations (Isakowitz, Bieber, and Vitali, 1998).

The Internet has made it easier and less expensive for companies to coordinate their staffs when opening new markets or working in isolated places because they do not have to build their own networks. Small companies that normally would find the cost of operating or selling abroad too expensive find the Internet especially valuable.

Reduced Communication Costs

Before the Net, organizations had to build their own wide area networks or subscribe to a value-added network service. Employing the Internet, although far from cost-free, is certainly more cost-effective for many organizations than building their own network or paying VAN subscription fees. Thus, the Internet can help organizations reduce operational costs or minimize operational expenses while extending their activities.

For example, Schlumberger Ltd. (www.slb.com), the New York and Paris oil-drilling equipment and electronics producer, operates in 85 countries. Using the Net, employees in remote locations use e-mail to stay in close contact with management at a very low cost. Schlumberger has found that since it converted to the Net from its own network, overall communications costs have dropped. For example, e-mail reduces voice communication and overnight-delivery service charges (employees attach complete documents to their e-mail messages).

Hardware and software have been developed for **Internet telephony**, allowing companies to use the Internet for telephone voice transmission. Internet telephony products are sometimes called IP telephony products. **Voice over IP** technology (VoIP) uses the Internet Protocol (IP) to deliver voice information in digital form using packet switching, avoiding the tolls charged by the circuit-switched telephone network. For example, Orbit Canada Inc. offers phone-to-phone unlimited long distance service using VoIP combined with unlimited Internet access for only $19.95 per month. New high-bandwidth networks will eliminate many of the early sound quality problems of this technology and enable the integration of voice with other Internet services. Users will be able to communicate by talking as well as by typing when they access a Web site.

Internet technology can also reduce communication costs by allowing companies to create virtual private networks as low-cost alternatives to private WANs. A **virtual private network (VPN)** is a secure connection between two points across the Internet and is available

---

Internet telephony
Technologies that use the Internet Protocol's packet-switched connections for voice service.

voice over IP (VoIP)
Facilities for managing the delivery of voice information using the Internet Protocol (IP).

virtual private network (VPN)
A secure connection between two points across the Internet to transmit corporate data. Provides a low-cost alternative to a private WAN.

FIGURE 10-13 Point-to-point tunnelling protocol in a virtual private network. Point-to-point tunnelling protocol encodes information for transmission across the Internet, which uses the Internet Protocol (IP). In a process called tunnelling, PPTP wraps various protocols inside the Internet Protocol (IP) so that non-IP data can travel through an IP network. By adding this "wrapper" around a network message to hide its content, organizations can create a private connection that travels through the Internet

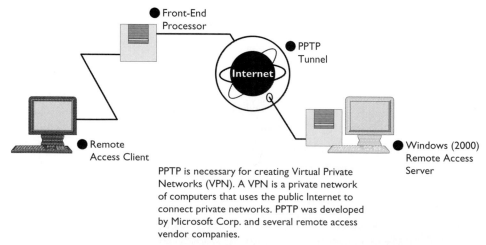

PPTP is necessary for creating Virtual Private Networks (VPN). A VPN is a private network of computers that uses the public Internet to connect private networks. PPTP was developed by Microsoft Corp. and several remote access vendor companies.

❶ The remote client makes a point-to-point connection to the front-end processor via a modem.

❷ The front-end processor connects to the remote access server, establishing a secure "tunnel" connection over the Internet. This connection then functions as the network backbone.

❸ The remote access server handles the account management and supports data encryption through IP, IPX, or NetBEUI protocols.

through Internet service providers (ISPs). A VPN provides many of the features of a private network at a much lower cost than using private leased telephone lines or frame-relay connections. Companies can save on long distance communication costs because workers can access remote locations for the cost of making a local call to an ISP. Figure 10-13 illustrates how a virtual private network works using point-to-point tunnelling protocol (PPTP), which is one of several competing protocols used to protect data transmitted over the public Internet. Companies are starting to use VPNs to reduce their WAN expenses. For example, Catholic HealthCare West used Contivity VPN switches from Nortel to slash their telephone bill in half, estimating that the VPN boxes would pay for themselves in three months time (Healthcare Solutions, 2001).

Reduce Transaction Costs

Businesses have found that conducting transactions electronically can be done at a fraction of the cost of paper-based processes. Using Internet technology reduces these transaction costs even further. Each time Federal Express clients use FedEx's Web site to track the status of their packages instead of inquiring by telephone, FedEx saves $8, amounting to a $2 million savings in operating costs each year. Figure 4-1 in Chapter 4 provides more examples of Internet transaction cost savings.

Reduced Agency Costs

As organizations expand and globalization continues, the need to coordinate activities in remote locations is becoming more critical. The Internet reduces agency costs—the cost of managing employees and coordinating their work—by providing low-cost networks and inexpensive communication and collaboration tools that can be used on a global scale. Schlumberger uses the Net for this purpose.

Interactivity, Flexibility, and Customization

Internet tools can create interactive applications that can be customized for multiple purposes and audiences. Web pages have capabilities for interacting with viewers that cannot be found in traditional print media. Visitors attracted by alluring displays of text, graphics, video, and sound also can click on "hot" buttons to make selections, take actions, or pursue additional information. Companies can use e-mail, chat rooms, and electronic discussion groups to create ongoing dialogues with their customers, using the information they have gathered to tailor communication precisely to fit the needs of each individual. They can create **dynamic pages** that reflect each customer's interests, based on information the customer has supplied to the Web site. The content of a dynamic page changes in response to user input at a Web site. Internet applications can be scaled up or down as the size of their audience changes because the technology works with the firm's existing network infrastructure.

dynamic page
A Web page with content that changes in response to information a visitor supplies to a Web site.

Accelerated Distribution of Knowledge

In today's information economy, rapid access to knowledge is critical to the success of many companies. The Internet helps with this problem. Organizations use e-mail and online databases to gain immediate access to information resources in key areas such as business, science, law, and government. The Internet can link a lone researcher sitting at a computer screen to mountains of data (including graphics) all over the world, which would be otherwise too expensive and too difficult to tap. For example, scientists can obtain photographs taken by NASA space probes within an hour of the pictures being taken. It has become easy and inexpensive for corporations to obtain the latest Canadian statistics, current weather data, and laws of legal entities and then to compare this data to those of other countries. Stock prices can be accessed within minutes of a change.

In addition to accessing public knowledge resources on the Internet and the Web, companies can create internal Web sites as repositories of their own organizational knowledge. Multimedia Web pages can organize this knowledge, giving employees easier access to information and expertise. Web browser software provides a universal interface for accessing information resources from internal corporate databases as well as external information sources. Use of intranets saves companies from adding additional hardware and software as well as saving in training costs. The hardware and software are the same the user would normally have, and most employees already know how to use Web browsers, which are provide access to intranets.

Enhance Customer Relationship Management and Supply Chain Management

Intranets can provide employees access to corporate data warehouses, permitting employees to analyze the latest customer data and to ascertain trends in the marketplace. This allows marketers to better target their markets and to develop new market niches. Additional programs to retain the most profitable customers can also be developed based on the customer relationship data obtained easily from the intranet. Purchasing departments, inventory managers, and production supervisors can all benefit from access to corporate intranets for supply chain management. Purchasers can examine previous purchases for quality and pricing information, inventory managers can easily check inventories and economic order quantities from a corporate intranet while production supervisors also need access to inventory information as well as human resource scheduling data.

10.4 SUPPORT TECHNOLOGY FOR ELECTRONIC COMMERCE AND ELECTRONIC BUSINESS

Businesses seriously pursuing electronic commerce and electronic business need special tools for maintaining their Web sites. These tools include Web server and electronic commerce server software, customer tracking and personalization tools, Web content management tools, and Web site performance monitoring tools.

WEB SERVERS AND ELECTRONIC COMMERCE SERVERS

Chapter 4 introduced Web servers as the software necessary to run Web sites, intranets, and extranets. The core capabilities of Web server software revolve around locating and managing stored Web pages. Web server software locates the Web pages requested by client computers by translating the uniform resource locator (URL) Web address into the physical file address for the requested Web page. The Web server then sends the requested pages to the client. Many Web servers also include tools for authenticating users, support for file transfer protocol (FTP), search engines and indexing programs, and capabilities for capturing Web site visitor information in log files. (Each request to the server for a file is recorded as an entry in the Web server log and is called a **hit**.) Apache HTTP Server, Microsoft's Internet Information Server (IIS), and Netscape's Enterprise Server (NES) are currently the most popular Web servers. The Apache and Netscape Web servers work with most operating systems while Internet Information Server is designed for Microsoft operating systems and software tools.

> **hit**
> An entry into a Web server's log file generated by each request to the server for a file.

Web server computers range in size from small desktop PCs to mainframes, depending upon the size of the Web sites. The Web server computer must be large enough to handle the Web server software and the projected traffic of the particular site.

Servers differ in their performance of various Web functions. For example, some servers load a static Web page more quickly while others deliver dynamic Web page content more quickly. Similarly, systems differ in their scalability, a major issue if a company is looking forward to quick growth. Thus the performance a company requires depends upon the size and type of site planned.

Specialized **electronic commerce server software** provides functions essential for e-commerce Web sites, often running on computers dedicated to this purpose (see Figure 10-14). Functions the software must perform for both business-to-consumer and business-to-business e-commerce include:

> **electronic commerce server software**
> Software that provides functions essential for running e-commerce Web sites, such as setting up electronic catalogues and storefronts and mechanisms for processing customer purchases.

▌ Setting up electronic storefronts and electronic catalogues to display product and pricing information.

▌ Designing electronic shopping carts so customers can collect the items they wish to purchase.

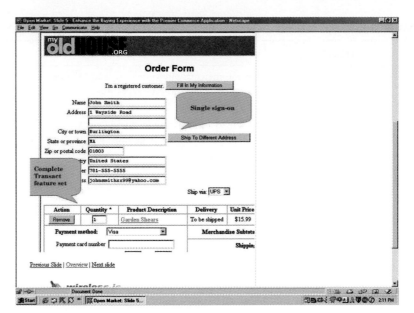

FIGURE 10-14 Open Market offers an integrated suite of applications for e-commerce management and content management. Business can use these tools to quickly develop full-function e-commerce sites.

▌ Making shipping arrangements.

▌ Linking to electronic payment processing systems.

▌ Displaying product availability and tracking shipments.

▌ Connecting to back-office systems where necessary.

▌ Reporting on both the business transacted through the site and the functioning of that site.

Systems designed for small business-to-consumer (B2C) e-commerce usually include wizards and templates to help set up the storefronts and catalogues. However, high-end business-to-business and business-to-consumer systems require the help of IT professionals for installation and support.

Business-to-business (B2B) e-commerce software must support tasks that are more complex than those for B2C commerce. B2B software must be able to access information on customers' contract agreements, order histories, payment records, geographic location(s), and even industries. While B2C prices are usually fixed, B2B prices are negotiable because they are affected by many contract factors, including volume, logistics preferences, and warranty coverage.

Bill presentment and payment is another area of difference between the two types of businesses. Retail sellers only need to accept payments via credit cards although some also accept debits using third-party payment processors. However, B2B buyers and sellers seldom use these forms of payment. Rather, purchases are presented, recorded, and verified using traditional business methods such as invoices, bills, purchase orders, and other accounting transactions. Payments are usually made by cheque, letter of credit, or even cost-centre codes. B2B e-commerce systems must support these processes.

E-commerce systems of both types are being marketed, but no single vendor can meet all of the requirements for buying and selling, linking transactions to order fulfillment, manufacturing and supply chains, inventory replenishment, and transportation. E-commerce sites usually must work with more than one system. Table 10-9 describes the leading e-commerce software vendors.

CUSTOMER TRACKING AND PERSONALIZATION TOOLS

Customer tracking and personalization tools have several main goals:

▌ Collecting and storing data on the behaviour of online customers and combining that data with data already stored in the company's back-office systems.

TABLE 10-9	EXAMPLES OF ELECTRONIC COMMERCE VENDORS	
Product	**Description**	**Vendor**
Commerce Server and BizTalk Server	Rapid development of e-commerce applications based on Microsoft architecture; strong enterprise application integration and B2B capabilities.	Microsoft
Open Market Transact	E-commerce engine, order processing, content management, and catalogue systems, with capabilities for integrating with back-end applications.	Open Market
WebSphere Commerce Suite	Tools for building sophisticated e-commerce applications, including pricing, e-billing, scalability, and connectivity to other applications. Requires professional developer assistance.	IBM
Customer Interaction System	Platform for building e-branding and e-marketing around commerce transactions.	Blue Martini Software
One-to-One Retail (B2C) and One-to-One Business Commerce (B2B)	E-commerce tools with strong personalization, content management, marketing, and reporting capabilities.	BroadVision
Spectra	E-commerce developer toolkit working with ColdFusion application server; can provide back-end integration with in-house applications.	Macromedia

▌ Analyzing the data in order to better understand the behaviour of online customers.

▌ Identifying developing customer trends.

Chapter 4 described some of the benefits of personalizing Web sites to deliver content specific to each user. Alternative approaches for providing Web site personalization include clickstream tracking, check-box personalization, collaborative filtering software, and rules-based systems.

clickstream tracking

Tracking data about customer activities at Web sites and storing them in a log.

Online personalization systems use **clickstream tracking** tools to collect customer data on customer activities at Web sites and store them in a log. The tools record the site that users last visited before coming to a Web site and where these users go when they leave the site. They also record the specific pages visited at the site, the time spent on each page, the types of pages visited, and what the visitors purchased. Web sites can also populate databases with explicit data gained when visitors fill out registration forms on the site or purchase products. This approach is called check-box personalization because users often checkmark their interests on an online checklist at the Web site.

collaborative filtering

Tracking user movements on a Web site, comparing the information gleaned about a user's behaviour against data about other customers with similar interests to predict what the user would like to see next.

Collaborative filtering software tracks users' movements on a Web site, comparing the information it gains about a user's behaviour against data about other customers with similar interests to predict what the user would like to see next. The software then makes recommendations to users based on their assumed interests.

Segmentation and rules-based systems use business rules to deliver certain types of information based on a user's profile, classifying users into smaller groups or segments based on these rules. The software uses demographic, geographic, or other information to divide or segment large populations into smaller groups. Data such as income level, geographic location, or purchasing history are aggregated to identify groups of people. Web sites using such personalization systems deliver content based on applying "if this, then that" rules processing.

Webhousing

Storing data collected from Web site visitors in a special data warehouse.

Data collected from Web site visitors can be stored in a special data warehouse called a Webhouse. The process is known as **Webhousing**. Web sites that are part of brick-and-mortar companies will have a great deal of customer information in relevant back-office systems such as enterprise resource planning (ERP) and supply chain systems. Some Webhouses make it possible to combine the clickstream data with back-office data and relevant external data to gain a fuller understanding of each customer. The goal of collecting all these data is to enable the company to unearth customer preferences and trends. Chapter 14 provides additional detail on Web customer data analysis.

WEB CONTENT MANAGEMENT TOOLS

Content management tools exist because most Web sites have long since ceased to be relatively simple documents with at most several dozen static pages that could be managed by a lone Webmaster. Today many companies have sites with thousands or tens of thousands of pages to manage, a task too great for a single person. Web content management software has emerged to assist the Webmaster and other responsible staff in the collection, assembly, and management of content on a Web site, intranet, or extranet.

The materials on Web sites are often very complex and include many forms of data such as documents, graphics, and sound. Often the content must be dynamic with parts of it capable of changing depending upon circumstances such as the identification of the visitor, the day of the month, the price of a product, or requests by the visitor. In addition, any complex site will require the use of multiple computer languages. Material to be displayed must be able to be prepared or modified offline and then updated instantly as often as needed. On larger sites, updating will occur continuously. Another complication is that the new displays or changes must often be published in multiple formats in order to be displayed on computers, personal digital assistants, and Web-enabled phones. Web content management tools must also be able to roll back the contents to an earlier version. And, of course, all of this must be done with neither technical nor content error so that the site will always remain up and operational.

Finally, Web content management software must include some form of access control (security) so that only those responsible for the specific content are able to update or change it. Given that these employees often will have little or no Web training, the tools must enable them to update the content directly without ever having to touch a Web page.

WEB PERFORMANCE MONITORING TOOLS

Most Web sites are plagued by problems such as slow performance, major outages (when a Web site is not accessible for some reason), content errors, broken links between Web pages, transaction failures, and slow-loading pages. These problems have grown exponentially as numerous Web sites have mushroomed into many thousands or tens-of-thousands of pages with graphics and advertising. To address these problems, companies can use their own **Web site performance monitoring** software tools or rely on Web site performance monitoring services (see Figure 10-15). Whether a company uses a monitoring service or employs these tools itself, the company's general goals usually are:

▌ To pinpoint problems occurring within both the transactions and the site infrastructure.

▌ To use this information to analyze and understand these problems.

▌ Ultimately, to correct the problems to maintain or improve the operation of the Web site.

A central concern at all Web sites is speed—how long does it take for a connection to be established, for a visitor to transfer from another site to the site, and to transfer from one page to another within the site. Web site operators will want to measure the response times of specific transactions such as inquiries, checking out, or authorizing credit through a credit card. Transactions such as these often include many steps. If the transaction is slow, users will want the software to pinpoint at which step or steps it is slow. A key function is to pinpoint the location of bottlenecks that slow down the reaction time of a Web site, such as the Web or application server, a specific database, or a network router. Some tools test the site's scalability by stressing the site by "creating" many test site visitors. Some tools also identify the causes for slow page loading speeds, such as loading too many banners, too many dense graphics files, or disk-space problems.

These tools can be used to identify particularly slow links and even missing links or graphics. Some software tracks the time of day or night to identify when the most serious problems occur. Some tools will compare a site with similar measurements at other Web sites that are top-rated for performance. These comparisons offer a scale against which companies can measure the quality of their own sites. In addition, these tools can be used to evaluate longer-range quality and problem trends.

Web content management software
Software that facilitates the collection, assembly, and management of content on a Web site, intranet, or extranet.

Web site performance monitoring tools
Software tools that monitor the time to download Web pages, perform Web transactions, identify broken links between Web pages, and pinpoint other Web site problems and bottlenecks.

FIGURE 10-15 Web-Trends offers sophisticated Web site analysis and reporting tools for businesses of all sizes. Illustrated here is a report showing the most frequently viewed pages of a Web site.

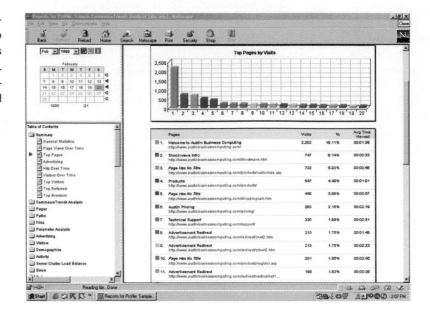

No single software tool exists that monitors all the functions we have described here. Companies that use these tools often purchase multiple packages or enlist external vendor specialists to conduct performance measurement for them. These service companies usually are able to generate synthetic traffic from various locations, often from as many as 50 cities around the country or around the world. Most of these companies offer consulting services when problems do appear so that the Web site owner is able to obtain help quickly in solving its problems.

WEB HOSTING SERVICES

Web hosting service
A company with large Web server computers that maintain the Web sites of fee-paying subscribers.

Companies that lack the financial or technical resources to operate their own Web sites or electronic commerce services can use Web hosting services. A **Web hosting service** maintains a large Web server or series of servers and provides fee-paying subscribers with space to maintain their Web sites. The subscribing companies may create their own Web pages or have the hosting service or a Web design firm create them.

Companies with small Web site needs often outsource their sites to an Internet service provider's computer. For $25 to $200 per month, they receive disk storage space to host their Web pages and the software to run their Web site, including e-mail services, and in some cases, software for basic electronic commerce transactions. These services cost much less than running one's own Web site and the ISPs have the technical staff on tap to design, develop, manage, and support the site.

Companies can also use specialized e-commerce application service providers to set up and operate their e-commerce sites. Companies such as Toronto-based Netfirms provide free e-commerce sites to small businesses with very simple e-commerce requirements that can use a predefined template for displaying and selling their wares. Yahoo! Store Canada and others offer e-commerce storefronts for a low monthly charge.

Many large companies use Web hosting services because they offer highly experienced technical staff and servers in multiple global locations, along with backup server capacity to ensure 100 percent Web site availability. Companies such as IBM Global Services, CanHost, and Softcom Canada provide fully managed Web hosting services. High-end managed hosting can range from $50 000 to $1 million per month.

Integrating all of the processes associated with electronic commerce requires additional software and tools, such as software providing interfaces between Web servers and the company's core-transaction databases and electronic payment systems. High-end hosting services provide the expertise for this integration although companies can also use their own technical staff or consulting teams for this purpose.

MANAGEMENT DECISION PROBLEM

REDUCING AGENCY COSTS

Your company has 3000 employees and is looking for ways to reduce some of its operating costs. You have prepared the following list of operating expenses.

Telephone Costs	$750 000 per year
Employee policy handbooks	$8.50 per handbook for printing and distribution
Employee benefits counselling	$80 per hour meeting

You are hoping you can reduce some of these costs by using Internet technology to build an intranet for the firm. The intranet would do the following:

- Provide e-mail communication among employees worldwide
- Provide employee handbooks that could be published and revised electronically and accessed from each employee's desktop computer
- Enable employees to select and revise their medical and life insurance plans online through their computers

You believe that employees could use e-mail to accomplish 40 percent of the communication that is taking place over the telephone. All employees are required to review their health benefits and re-enroll in their benefits plans once per year. New employee handbooks are distributed to each employee once a year. The intranet would cost $600 000 to develop and $100 000 annually to maintain. No new hardware or networking infrastructure would be required since employees already use networked desktop PCs.

1. How would the intranet make the management process more efficient?

2. How much would the intranet reduce agency costs? Is the intranet worthwhile to build?

3. Are there any other benefits that could be produced by the intranet? Are there any disadvantages to using the intranet?

10.5 MANAGEMENT ISSUES AND DECISIONS

The Internet presents new opportunities for the global conduct of business. In addition, an IT infrastructure for digitally enabling the enterprise requires coordinating many different types of computing and networking technologies, public and private infrastructures, and organizational processes. Careful, thoughtful management and planning are essential.

NEW TECHNICAL OPPORTUNITIES AND THE INTERNET

The technical advances described in Chapter 9 such as wireless Digital Subscriber Line (DSL) services should continue to fall in price and gain in power, facilitating the creation and operation of global networks. "Communicate and compute any time, anywhere" networks based on satellite systems, digital cellular phones, and personal communications services will make it even easier to coordinate work and information in many parts of the globe that cannot be reached by existing ground-based systems. Thus a salesperson in China could send an order-confirmation request to the home office in Calgary effortlessly and expect an instant reply.

Companies are using Internet technology to construct virtual private networks (VPNs) to reduce wide area networking costs and staffing requirements. Instead of using private, leased telephone lines or frame-relay connections, the company outsources the VPN to an Internet service provider. The VPN comprises WAN links, security products, and routers, providing a secure and encrypted connection between two points across the Internet to transmit corporate data. These VPNs from Internet service providers can provide many features of a private network to firms operating internationally.

However, VPNs may not provide the same level of quick and predictable response as private networks, especially during times of the day when Internet traffic is very congested. VPNs may not be able to support large numbers of remote users.

Throughout this text, we show how the Internet facilitates global coordination, communication, and electronic business. As Internet technology becomes more widespread outside North America, it will expand opportunities for electronic commerce and international trade. The global connectivity and low cost of Internet technology will further remove obstacles of geography and time zones for companies seeking to expand operations and sell their wares abroad (see Figure 10-16). Companies in Asia, Latin America, and Africa that do not have the financial or technical resources to handle EDI transactions can use Internet technology

to exchange information more rapidly with business partners in their supply chains. Small companies may especially benefit from using the Internet to speed delivery of products and manage their supply chains (Chabrow, 2000; Quelch and Klein, 1996).

THE CHALLENGE OF MANAGING THE NEW INFORMATION TECHNOLOGY INFRASTRUCTURE

Implementing enterprise networking and the new IT infrastructure has created problems as well as opportunities for organizations. Managers need to address these problems before they can create an IT infrastructure to digitally enable their firms.

Electronic commerce and e-business are forcing companies to reassess their IT infrastructures to remain competitive. Many organizations are saddled with a maze of old legacy applications, hardware, and networks that don't talk to each other. In order to support enterprise-wide business processes that can smoothly link to customers or suppliers via the Internet, they must rebuild their information architectures and IT infrastructures. Five problems stand out:

▌ Connectivity and application integration problems

▌ Loss of management control over information systems

▌ The need for organizational change

▌ The hidden costs of enterprise computing

▌ The difficulty of ensuring network reliability and security

Connectivity and Application Integration

We have already described the connectivity problems created by incompatible networks and standards, including connectivity problems for wireless networks. Digital organizations depend on enterprise-wide integration of their business processes and applications so that they can obtain their information from any point in the value chain. An order from a Web site should be able to trigger events automatically in the organization's accounting, inventory, and distribution applications to speed the product swiftly to the customer. Yet end-to-end process and application integration is extremely difficult to achieve and beyond the reach of many firms. For example, the U.S. National Association of Manufacturers reported that 90 percent of its members—including large firms with more than $1 billion in annual sales—could not even process orders electronically. They have to print out order information from their Web sites to input it into their transaction systems (Keen, 2000).

Loss of Management Control

Managing information systems technology and corporate data are proving much more difficult in a distributed environment because of the lack of a single, central point for IT management. Distributed client/server networks, new mobile wireless networks, and Internet computing have empowered end users to become independent sources of computing power capable of collecting, storing, and disseminating data and software. Data and software are no longer confined to the mainframe under the management of the traditional information systems department but reside on many different computing platforms throughout the organization.

An enterprise-wide IT infrastructure requires that a business knows where all of its data are located and can ensure that the same piece of information, such as a product number, is used consistently throughout the organization (see Chapter 8). These data may not always be in a standard format or may reside on incompatible computing platforms. However, many worry that excess centralization and management of information resources will stifle end user independence and creativity and reduce their ability to define their own information needs. The dilemma posed by enterprise networking and the new IT infrastructure is one of central management control versus end user creativity and productivity.

Organizational Change Requirements

Enterprise-wide computing is an opportunity to reengineer the organization into a more effective unit, but it will only create problems or chaos if the underlying organizational issues are not fully addressed (Duchessi and Chengalur-Smith, 1998). Behind antiquated legacy infrastructures are old ways of doing business, which must also be changed to work effectively in a new enterprise-wide IT infrastructure. For example, equipping the sales force with wireless devices for entering orders in the field will not produce efficiency or productivity benefits unless the firm redesigns or eliminates the steps in its order entry process that this technology makes redundant.

Infrastructure and architecture for a business environment that can respond to rapidly changing marketplace demands and industry changes require changes in corporate culture and organizational structure that are not easy to make. It took two years for TST Expedited Systems to reengineer their corporate processes and involved collaborating with a number of external stakeholders, including drivers and customers. It took several years of hard work and large financial investments for IBM to Web-enable its business processes and convince disparate business units to adopt a "One IBM" mindset where everyone uses common tools.

Hidden Costs of Enterprise Computing

Many companies have found that the savings they expected from distributed client/server computing did not materialize because of unexpected costs. Hardware-acquisition savings resulting from significantly lower costs of MIPS on PCs often are offset by high annual operating costs for additional labour and time required for network and system management. Considerable time must be spent on tasks such as network maintenance, data backup, technical problem solving, and hardware, software, and software-update installations. Gains in productivity and efficiency from equipping employees with wireless mobile computing devices must be balanced against increased costs associated with providing technical support and integrating these devices into the firm's IT infrastructure. As we discussed in Chapter 6, the total cost of ownership—including both hardware and software—must be calculated to accurately understand the hidden costs as well as the obvious costs of any IT endeavour, including enterprise computing.

Scalability, Reliability, and Security

Companies seeking to digitally enable their business require robust IT infrastructures with plentiful bandwidth and storage capacity for transmitting and maintaining all of the data generated by electronic commerce and electronic business transactions. Scalability has emerged as a critical infrastructure issue. Managers need to develop strategies for dealing with steadily increasing loads placed on company networks from increased traffic and bandwidth-hungry applications proliferating from broadband access to the Web. Network infrastructures need to handle not only current e-commerce demands but must also be able to scale rapidly to meet future demands while providing high levels of performance and availability for mission-critical applications.

downtime
Periods of time in which an information system is not operational.

Networks have dense layers of interacting technology, and the applications are also often intricately layered. Enterprise networking is highly sensitive to different versions of operating systems and network management software, with some applications requiring specific versions of each. It is difficult to make all of the components of large, heterogeneous networks work together as smoothly as management envisions. **Downtime**—periods of time in which the system is not operational—remains much more frequent in distributed systems than in established mainframe systems and should be considered carefully before moving essential applications from a mainframe.

Security is of paramount importance in firms with extensive networking and electronic transactions with individuals or other businesses outside organizational boundaries. Networks present end users, hackers, and thieves with many points of access and opportunities to steal or modify data in networks. Systems linked to the Internet are even more vulnerable because the Internet was designed to be open to everyone. Wireless computing devices linked to corporate applications create new areas of vulnerability. We discuss these issues in greater detail in Chapter 12.

SOME SOLUTIONS

Organizations can meet the challenges posed by the new IT infrastructure by planning for and managing business and organizational changes, increasing end user training, using data administration principles, and considering connectivity, application integration, bandwidth, and cost controls in their technology planning.

Managing the Change

To gain the full benefit of any new technology, organizations must carefully plan for and manage the change. Business processes may need to be reengineered to accompany infrastructure changes (see Chapter 11). For example, equipping the sales force with wireless handheld devices for entering orders in the field provides an opportunity for management to review the sales process to see if redundant order entry activities or a separate order entry staff can be eliminated. Management must address the organizational issues that arise from shifts in staffing, function, power, and organizational culture attendant to changing to a new IT infrastructure.

Education and Training

A well-developed training program can help end users overcome problems resulting from the lack of management support and poor understanding of networked computing (Westin et al., 1985; Bikson et al., 1985). Technical specialists will need training in Web site, wireless, client/server development, and network support methods.

Data Administration Principles

The role of data administration (see Chapter 8) becomes even more important when networks link many different applications, business areas, and computing devices. Organizations must systematically identify where their data are located, which group is responsible for maintaining each piece of data, and which individuals and groups are allowed to access and use that data. They need to develop specific policies and procedures to ensure that their data are accurate, available only to authorized users, and properly backed up.

Planning for Connectivity and Application Integration

Senior management must take a long-term view of the firm's IT infrastructure and information architecture, making sure they can support the level of process and information integration for current and future needs. Infrastructure planning should consider how much connectivity will be required to digitally enable core strategic business processes. To what extent should network services be standardized throughout the organization? Will the firm communicate with customers and suppliers using different technology platforms? How should wireless mobile computing networks be integrated with the rest of the firm?

While some connectivity problems can be solved by using intranets or the Internet, the firm will need to establish standards for other systems and applications that are enterprise-wide. Management can establish policies to keep networks and telecommunications services as homogeneous as possible, setting standards for data, voice, e-mail, and videoconferencing services along with hardware, software, and network operating systems

An enterprise-wide architecture for integrated business applications and processes cannot be created through piecemeal changes. It represents a long-term endeavour that should be supported by top management and coordinated with the firm's strategic plans.

APPLICATION SOFTWARE EXERCISE

SPREADSHEET, WEB BROWSER, AND PRESENTATION SOFTWARE EXERCISE: RESEARCHING WEB SITE DEVELOPMENT COMPANIES AT JEWEL OF THE WEB

Ralph and Janice Lorenzo have been designing and selling custom jewellery for the past 25 years. The jewellery business was once operated out of their home but has since expanded to a shop located in St. Johns, Newfoundland. They specialize in animal-designs in jewellery and have built collections around Freddy Frog, Betty Cat, and Tommy Teddy Bear. Items in each collection include an assortment of wrist and ankle bracelets, necklaces, rings, pins, and earrings.

Ralph and Janice have heard about electronic commerce and are interested in opening an online jewellery store, called Jewel of the Web. Since the Lorenzos have limited knowledge about starting an online business, they have decided to identify and research companies specializing in Web site development and hosting services. Initially, Jewel of the Web will have seven jewellery categories consisting of 25 products each. They will also accept credit cards and provide free shipping via all major carriers. The system should collect statistical data, such as the number of hits per day, the number of pages viewed, and peak traffic times.

Your task is to help Ralph and Janice perform their research. Locate three companies specializing in Web site development and hosting services. For each company you research online, what would the company charge to build and host the Jewel of the Web online store? What are the monthly operating costs associated with Jewel of the Web? Which company do you recommend? Why? Organize your findings in a spreadsheet(s). Also, prepare a written report and slide presentation about your findings. When preparing your analysis, you are free to make necessary assumptions; however, these assumptions must be clearly stated in your written report.

MANAGEMENT WRAP-UP

Planning the firm's IT infrastructure is a key management responsibility. Managers need to consider how the IT infrastructure supports the firm's business goals and whether the infrastructure should incorporate public infrastructures and links to other organizations. Planning should also consider the need to maintain some measure of management control as computing power becomes more widely distributed throughout the organization.

The new information technology infrastructure can enhance organizational performance by making information flow more smoothly between different parts of the organization and between the organization and its customers, suppliers, and other value partners. Organizations can use Internet technology and tools to reduce communication and coordination costs, to create interactive products and services, and to accelerate the distribution of knowledge.

Internet technology is a key component of the new IT infrastructure for the digital firm, creating the connectivity to link disparate systems within the organization and to connect the organization electronically to customers, suppliers, and other external entities. Key technology decisions should consider network reliability, security, bandwidth, and relationships to legacy systems, as well as the capabilities of Internet and other networking technologies.

For Discussion

1. It has been said that developing an information technology infrastructure for electronic commerce and electronic business is above all a business decision, as opposed to a technical decision. Discuss.

2. How can the Internet be used to facilitate global business processes? Is the Internet a valuable tool for all global business processes? Should it be used in every country to facilitate global business processes? Why or why not?

SUMMARY

1. *Describe the features of the new information technology (IT) infrastructure.* The new IT infrastructure uses a mixture of computer hardware supplied by different vendors, including mainframes, PCs, and servers, which are networked to each other. It also provides more processing power to the desktop through client/server computing and mobile personal information devices that provide remote access to the desktop from outside the organization. The new IT infrastructure also incorporates public infrastructures, such as the telephone system, the Internet, and public network services and electronic devices.

2. *Describe important connectivity standards.* Connectivity is a measure of how well computers and computer-based devices can communicate with one another and "share" information in a meaningful way without human intervention. It is essential in enterprise networking in the new IT infrastructure where different hardware, software, and network components must work together to transfer information seamlessly from one part of the organization to another. TCP/IP and OSI are important reference models for achieving connectivity in networks. Each of these models divides the communications process into layers. UNIX is an operating system that can be used to create open systems as can Linux. Connectivity can also be achieved by using Internet technology, XML, and Java.

3. *Describe how the Internet works and identify its major capabilities.* The Internet is a worldwide network of networks that uses the client/server model of computing and the TCP/IP network reference model. Using the Net, any computer (or computing appliance) can communicate with any other computer connected to the Net throughout the world. The Internet has no central management. The Internet is used for communications, including e-mail, public forums (newsgroups) on thousands of topics, and live, interactive conversations. It also is used for information retrieval from thousands of library, corporate, government, business, and non-profit databases. It has developed into an effective way for individuals and organizations to offer information and products through the Web using graphical user interfaces and easy-to-use links worldwide. Major Internet capabilities include e-mail, Usenet, list servers, chat rooms, Telnet, FTP, and the World Wide Web.

4. *Evaluate the benefits the Internet offers organizations.* Many organizations use the Net to reduce communications costs when they coordinate organizational activities and communicate with employees. Researchers and knowledge workers are finding the Internet a quick, low-cost way to gather and disperse knowledge. The global connectivity and low cost of the Internet helps organizations lower transaction and agency costs, allowing them to link directly to suppliers, customers, and business partners and to coordinate activities on a global scale with limited resources. The Web provides interactive multimedia capabilities that can be used to create new products and services and closer relationships with customers. Communication can be customized to a specific audience.

5. *Describe the principal technologies for supporting electronic commerce.* Businesses need a series of software tools for maintaining an electronic commerce Web site. Web server software locates and manages Web pages stored on Web server computers. Electronic commerce server software provides capabilities for setting up electronic storefronts and arranging for payments and shipping. Customer tracking and personalization tools collect, store, and analyze data on Web site visitors. Content management tools facilitate the collection, assembly, and management of Web site content. Web site performance monitoring tools monitor the speed of Web site transactions and identify Web site performance problems. Businesses can use an external vendor's Web hosting service as an alternative to maintaining their own Web sites.

6. *Analyze the management problems raised by the new information technology (IT) infrastructure and suggest solutions.* Problems posed by enterprise networking include connectivity and application integration challenges; loss of management control over systems; the need to carefully manage organizational change; controlling the hidden costs of enterprise computing, and the difficulty of ensuring network scalability, reliability, and security.

Solutions include planning for and managing the business and organizational changes associated with enterprise-wide computing, increasing end-user training, using data administration principles, and considering connectivity, application integration, bandwidth, and cost controls when planning the IT infrastructure.

KEY TERMS

Bluetooth, 327

Bot, 335

Chat rooms, 331

Clickstream tracking, 348

Collaborative filtering, 348

Connectivity, 326

Domain name, 330

Domain Name Server (DNS), 330

Downtime, 354

Dynamic page, 345

Electronic commerce server, 346

Enterprise networking, 325

File transfer protocol (FTP), 332

Firewall, 337

Hit, 346

Home page, 334

Hypertext transport protocol (http), 334

I-mode, 341

Instant messaging, 331

Internet Protocol (IP) address, 330

Internet Service Provider (ISP), 328

Internet telephony, 344

Internet2, 332

Internetworking, 325

List server, 331

Microbrowser, 341

Multicasting, 336

Open systems, 326

Open Systems Interconnect (OSI), 327

"Push" technology, 336

Search engine, 334

Shopping bot, 335

Telnet, 331

Transmission Control Protocol/Internet Protocol (TCP/IP), 326

Uniform resource locator (URL), 334

Usenet (newsgroups), 331

Virtual private network (VPN), 344

Voice over IP (VoIP), 344

Voice portal, 341

Web content management software, 349

Web hosting service, 350

Web site performance monitoring tools, 349

Webhousing, 348

Webmaster, 334

Wireless Application Protocol (WAP), 340

Wireless Markup Language (WML), 340

Wireless Web, 338

REVIEW QUESTIONS

1. What are the features of the new information technology (IT) infrastructure?

2. Why is connectivity so important for a digital firm? List and describe the major connectivity standards for networking and the Internet.

3. What is the Internet? List and describe alternative ways of accessing the Internet.

4. List and describe the Internet's principal capabilities.

5. What is Internet2? How does it differ from the first-generation Internet? What benefits will it provide?

6. Why is the World Wide Web so useful for individuals and businesses?

7. List and describe alternative ways of locating information on the Web.

8. What are intranets and extranets? How do they differ from the Internet and the Web?

9. What is the Wireless Web? How does it differ from the conventional Web?

10. List and describe the types of m-commerce services and applications supported by the Wireless Web.

11. Compare the WAP and I-mode Wireless Web standards.

12. Describe the organizational benefits of using Internet and Web technology.

13. List and describe the principal technologies for supporting electronic commerce.

14. Under what conditions should firms consider using a Web hosting service?

15. Describe five problems posed by the new information technology (IT) infrastructure.

16. Describe some solutions to the problems posed by the new IT infrastructure.

GROUP PROJECT

Form a group with three or four of your classmates. Prepare an evaluation of the wireless Internet capabilities of the Palm VII, the Handspring Visor, and the HP Jornada PocketPC handheld computing devices. Your analysis should consider the purchase cost of each device, any additional software required to make it Internet-enabled, the cost of wireless Internet services, and what Internet services are available for each device. You should also consider the other capabilities of each device, including the ability to integrate with existing corporate or PC applications. Which device would you select? What criteria would you use to guide your selection? If possible, use electronic presentation software to present your findings to the class.

INTERNET CONNECTION

■ COMPANION WEBSITE

At www.pearsoned.ca/laudon, you'll find an online study guide with two quizzes to test your knowledge of how the Internet and the new IT infrastructure can be used in modern organizations. You'll also find updates to the chapter and online exercises and cases that enable you to apply your knowledge to realistic situations.

■ ADDITIONAL SITES OF INTEREST

There are many interesting Web sites to enhance your learning about the capabilities of the Internet and the new IT infrastructure. You can search the Web yourself, or just try the following sites to add to what you have already learned.

Hudson's Bay Company

www.HBC.com

The HBC e-commerce marketplace from the customer perspective

Blue Martini Software

www.bluemartini.com

CRM software vendor that personalizes Web content to the customer's preferences, including converting platforms (such as from a desktop to a handheld device)

DoCoMo

www.nttdocomo.com

DoCoMo's I-mode site that details the growth of this technology, along with new products, specifications, and applications

WebSphere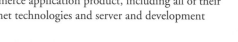

www.ibm.com/websphere

IBM's e-commerce application product, including all of their various Internet technologies and server and development applications

Network Solutions, Inc.

www.networksolutions.com

Provides all the details on how to register a domain name (obtain a URL); other Web sites and companies can also do this

---

CASE STUDY   *B2B and B2C E-Commerce: State-of-the-Art Internet for Hudson's Bay Company*

Established in 1670, Hudson's Bay Company (HBC) is a true Canadian landmark. It is also the nation's largest department store retailer. Led by its Bay and Zellers operating divisions, HBC accounts for approximately 39 percent of Canadian department store sales and almost eight percent of all Canadian retail sales. HBC has annual revenues of more than $7 billion, more than 500 retail locations, and more than 70 000 associates.

The year 2000 was a banner year for HBC's e-commerce initiatives. The company deployed both an extranet with suppliers for improved supply chain management, HBC.biz, and an online shopping site for improved customer service and sales, hbc.com. HBC also merged its Bay and Zellers customer databases to implement a major customer relationship management initiative.

Supply Chain Management: HBC.biz

Approximately 2000 people are employed in HBC's purchasing department. These individuals purchase billions of dollars of supplies from more than 3000 mid-sized and large suppliers in Canada and around the world. It is this dynamic supply chain that provides HBC's customers with a wide range of popular brands along with a growing collection of private label products.

The Challenge

For a retail organization as large as HBC, there is a continuing mandate to automate administrative processes and to increase efficiencies through the use of technology. For almost a decade, the organization's Bay, Zellers, HBC Outfitters, and Club Z retail divisions have used electronic data interchange (EDI) to connect and collaborate with many of their large suppliers.

HBC ran its EDI applications on value-added networks (VANs)—an infrastructure too expensive for most of its smaller suppliers to adopt. HBC's general manager of supply chain and logistics systems, Moses Levy, says the costs involved in running EDI through private networks were out of reach for a large portion of the small- to medium-sized HBC suppliers. Beyond the high initial purchase price of the VANs, suppliers had to factor in user licenses, EDI middleware, training, and maintenance costs. So HBC's smaller suppliers relied on fax machines and telephones to place and track orders and to check on stock availability. Levy recognized the need to automate supply chain processes for all of HBC's suppliers.

Technological Solution to a Business Problem

Levy found that the majority of e-commerce provider solutions were "too complex, too expensive, and took too long to implement." QLogitek, a systems integrator that had worked with HBC since 1978, was developing its own B2B e-commerce technology, L'eBIZ, to work over the Internet. QLogitek's B2B system would be based on a nominal transaction fee costing structure that would eliminate any technology investment beyond Web access on a PC.

Levy stated: "The Internet provides a very cost-efficient 24/7 communications mechanism through any Internet service provider for B2B e-commerce, and it's reliable. Instead of using such costly private networks, our suppliers can now communicate directly and easily over the Internet with our buyers through the L'eBIZ portal."

L'eBIZ utilizes features of Microsoft Windows® NT 4.0 Enterprise Edition, Microsoft SQL Server 7.0 Enterprise Edition, and Microsoft Site Server Commerce Edition, such as Microsoft Transaction Server, Windows Load Balancing, and Clustering for a scalable, flexible solution for HBC's suppliers.

The core component of L'eBIZ is its Universal Translator Engine (UTE) that translates and maps digital information exchanged and communicated between trading communities and individuals according to their unique proprietary and competitive business requirements. L'eBIZ is built on the open standards principles of the personal computer, Internet and browser technologies, emerging wireless technologies standards, and hand-held devices.

The L'eBIZ e-commerce product suite consists of L'eBIZ LITE , a browser-based forms application for supply chain management with full backend integration; L'eBIZ xEDI, a back office integration solution to transmit both EDI and non-EDI bulk information between trading partners; and L'eBIZ Admin, a module to administer security, membership profiles, and preferences. In addition to supporting small- and medium-sized suppliers, the L'eBIZ suite also provides full secure FTP support for large vendors for bulk EDI or non-EDI information exchange between the buyer and supplier back office applications.

Deployment

Because of their previous experience with QLogitek, Levy felt comfortable partnering with both QLogitek and Microsoft to provide the Web-based EDI solution. Within three months, HBC was testing L'eBIZ. At the end of June 2000, over 200 HBC suppliers were using L'eBIZ, with another 130 vendors signed up, and an additional 100 planning implementation of what is now called HBC.biz. Using tested Microsoft Windows operating system DNA architecture permitted Qlogitek to have L'eBIZ up and running in a very short time. Microsoft Consulting Services reviewed the L'eBIZ architecture and application design, performing operability testing and throughput simulation for quality assurance. The vendor package even came with 20 minutes of online training.

L'eBIZ Benefits for HBC

L'eBIZ gives HBC and its suppliers the means to transfer critical information to each other in real time over the Internet. The solution encompasses everything from purchasing to shipping to receiving, allowing purchase orders to be sent and fulfilled almost instantaneously.

Levy says that L'eBIZ is already proving to be a success. "We seized the opportunity to decrease the total cost of transacting business between our company and our suppliers. By taking advantage of the Internet, we have simplified our processes and made them more effective for all concerned," says Levy. "And because all of our suppliers can participate in the order and delivery cycle and progress can be monitored online, nothing gets overlooked. Our purchasing lifecycle has improved," Levy says. "We no longer have to wait for procurement documents in the mail and match them up to other paper forms. We don't have to

enter as much data because our suppliers are doing a lot of it at their end. And compared to our old system and processes, there are fewer hands touching the data, so the overall quality is higher." In fact, Levy notes that the solution is so easy to use that some employees within the purchasing department did not even realize that there was a new EDI solution in place.

The Future for HBC.biz

More small and mid-sized vendors are making their move to the new procurement solution. HBC is planning to utilize the portal to provide suppliers with full-fledged sales data (with breakdowns by transaction, date, store, etc.) to help them better predict inventory volumes and replace sold goods quicker. "In theory, we could give our suppliers a run-down of yesterday's sales, and they could fulfill the orders today," says Levy. In addition to continuing to making general enhancements to L'eBIZ, the QLogitek team is working to enable extended functionality and compatibility with wireless technology and hand-held computing devices.

The Online Shopping Initiative: HBC.com

In July 2000, George Heller, HBC's president and CEO, announced that Microsoft, Oracle, and IBM would partner with HBC to establish a world class "retail showcase for the North American market." "If you are not on an e-platform, you will never get there [to your goal]," Heller said. He explained his vision of HBC as a seamless retail organization whose online mandate is to bring HBC into the Web-enabled digital economy. "This goes beyond e-tailing, [it is an] enterprise-wide approach," he said.

The Challenge

HBC's CIO, David Poirier, said the transformation would make HBC a complete e-business and would affect everything from store operations to administration and supply chain management. Heller added that the solution would also integrate customer transactions so customers can be targeted as individuals. "This all started when HBC underwent a strategic assessment of the technology requirements to ensure our ability to compete and win in the emerging e-enabled world." HBC had already lost ground to Sears in the Canadian e-marketplace and was determined to regain that ground.

In response to attempts to determine how much the new e-venture would cost or how much money it would save, Heller would only say that HBC envisioned spending around $40 million to $45 million per year for the foreseeable future, with part of the cost for new technology and part for upgrading present systems. The analogy Heller used was that of a heart and lung transplant—huge and complex. He also said only that the company could save $20 million to $40 million annually in the e-procurement of non-merchandizing materials, but that there was no real way to know exactly how much will be saved or gained over all. "[It is] like asking how many angels dance on the head of a pin," he said. "How do you get your hands around a cloud?"

Technological Solution to a Business Problem

According to Poirier, the company is changing its systems from a mainframe to an e-platform; the time frame for completion is around two to two-and-a-half years. The HBC alliance with three frequently hostile competitors is an innovative model whose goal is to meet HBC's technology goals quickly and economically. The project will run until the end of 2002.

One might question the logic of going with three companies (to implement a solution) when one could have done it with a lot less friction. "Going with a single (company) might limit opportunities in the future," Poirier said. He said the advantages of getting several viewpoints and a great deal of expertise far outweighed any potential disadvantages. Even choosing the three to participate was no easy task. The Bay looked at IBM, Sun, and Hewlett-Packard platforms before deciding on the former mix. "[The] reality is that any of those technologies could have probably worked," he said.

Deployment

In those areas where there is going to be inevitable competition (databases come to mind), Poirier said an agreement was made at the outset that all partners would work through any problems. "No one will take their ball and bat and go home," he said. Poirier added that the overall solution would inevitably include other high technology companies and that present technology relationships will still be there in the future, with room for others to join.

In addition to building the Web site, HBC had to build a state-of-the-art pick-and-pack distribution facility and change its distribution processes. HBC.com was launched in the fall of 2000, along with HBC.net (intranet) and HBC.biz for B2B relationships.

HBC.com's Benefits

HBC.com incorporates The Bay's new loyalty program with Zellers Club Z loyalty program, adding not only value for customers but also customer relationship management data for HBC. Six months after implementing HBC.com, both The Bay and Zellers sent their customers information on the new loyalty program and their new loyalty cards. In addition, The Bay terminated use of the AIR MILES Reward program when they implemented their own loyalty program. HBC integrated their charge card systems so that Bay customers can use their Bay credit card when making purchases at Zellers and vice versa.

HBC.com looks like a real store, with products organized into various "rooms" and departments to help customers easily locate products. Customers can determine if the product can only be found at The Bay (or Zellers) or can also be found at the other division's stores. A "Tell a Friend" link on each product page permits customers to share the product page by e-mail with a friend. Ease of delivery and returns (non-electronic processes) made the implementation of HBC.com a success. In Canada, Canada Post or Loomis Couriers deliver orders to customers within 2 to 11 days, and returns can be made to any Bay or Zellers store, or by Canada Post.

HBC.com "members" (users who register at the site) can create their own personal "wish list" to share with their friends, who can simply log on to HBC.com and visit their friend's wish list; the friends can then order the gift and have it delivered, including gift-wrapping. Customers who don't trust the security of HBC.com can dial toll-free to place their orders.

Customer Relationship Management Initiative

Also in the summer of 2000, Heller announced that the customer databases of The Bay and Zellers stores would be merged in preparation for a massive new customer relationship management (CRM) push. According to Heller, the ultimate goal is to identify the best customers of their two chains and to tailor specific product and service offerings to maintain and build upon their loyalty.

Using these data, HBC will determine the best product mix to offer on HBC.com. Oracle, Microsoft, and IBM Canada are again partnering with HBC in the CRM initiative. "For many years, retail has been pushing product to the customer," said Heller, "It's slowly starting to change, so the customer is pulling product instead." As one part of the CRM initiative, The Bay has begun delivering billing statements to a sample group of credit card customers with customized marketing messages based on each customer's six-month purchase history.

Michael LeBlanc, HBC's director of customer retention, said that the primary means of gathering visitor data will come through "membership" in HBC.com. Visitors who register as members will receive benefits, such as express check-out, access to their order history, an e-mail newsletter, and the wish list function discussed above. "Understanding what's going on at our site—who's shopping and why—is the first goal," according to LeBlanc. "As we do that, we're going to be able to build a host of best-customer models—determining whether customers are cross-channel shoppers, pure dot-com shoppers, or cross-channel, cross-banner, cross-medium shoppers." Then, he says, HBC can begin to target individual customer segments with personalized marketing messages.

The implementation of HBC Rewards, HBC's new loyalty program that replaced AIR MILES, is expected to result in improved CRM because of the data that will be collected. According to Poirier, "We had all kinds of data in different places—we didn't have a single view of the customer. We thought a Zellers' customer was a Zellers' customer, and The Bay's customer was an entirely different customer. There's huge crossover, and yet we treated them like an entirely different population. Our organization is now switching from an organization that has traditionally been focused on selling more products to consumers to an organization that's now focused on managing relationships with customers." Poirier adds that it's tough moving an $8 billion company from a focus on selling in stores to a customer and market focus.

HBC's Bottom Line

Increased sales, customer tracking data, improved supply chain management including tremendously reduced inventory, improved loyalty, billing, and delivery processes—these are HBC's goals. As of this writing, these initiatives are too new to tell if they are paying off for HBC. But HBC has formed HBC Online to continue working with their strategic IT partners to build stronger, deeper relationships with customers, associates, and suppliers.

Sources: Craig Saunders, "Hudson's Bay Plans Massive CRM Push," *Strategy Magazine*, July 17, 2000; Bernadette Johnson, "HBC.com Aims to Give Customers Another Reason to Shop," *Strategy Magazine*,

January 1, 2001; Bernadette Johnson, "HBC Adds Newest Piece to CRM Strategy," *Strategy Magazine*, May 21, 2001; Tim Foran, "Tech Trio to Help Retailer," *Network World Canada*, August 11, 2000; Chris Conrath, "The Bay to Go All Out Embracing the World of 'E'," *ComputerWorld Canada*, July 28, 2000; Linda Stuart, "Virtual Voyageur (community)," *CXO.ca*, August 28, 2000; Cindy Steinman, "A Retail Tale," *Network World Canada*, May 5, 2000; "Hudson's Bay Company," *Microsoft Canada Case Study*, available www.microsoft.com/Canada/casestudies/inc/hb.htm, accessed June 1, 2001; "QLogitek and Microsoft Canada announce Major B2B E-Commerce Portal in Association with Hudson's Bay Company," Microsoft Canada press release May 2, 2000, available www.microsoft.com/Canada/casestudies/inc/hb.htm, accessed June 1, 2001.

CASE STUDY QUESTIONS:

1. Why did HBC feel that accomplishing these three initiatives in one year was so important to the future of HBC? Why did they wait so long to begin these initiatives?

2. What Internet technologies does HBC use in its three e-commerce initiatives? Are they compatible? Look these technologies up on the Web to find out more about them (e.g., Microsoft's DNA architecture, the various server software applications). Can you describe them in your own words?

3. What additional Internet technologies and capabilities could HBC use for these initiatives?

4. How was HBC able to accomplish these three initiatives in so short a time frame? What was the role of their partners in managing these projects?

5. What specific non-electronic processes did HBC have to change to meet the needs of their customers and the e-commerce initiatives?

6. Where do you think HBC should take their e-commerce platform now?

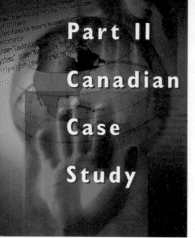

CBC

MUSIC IS NOT FREE!

Our modern technology has provided easy access to digital content, whether or not it is copyrighted and whether or not we have paid for it. Companies like Napster and Gnutella permit individuals to share *pirated* electronic files, which they have copied illegally. Typically, these are music files, most of them in the MP3 format. MP3 files can be played on any type of PC with the right media player or on handheld MP3 players as small as a deck of cards. To add insult to injury, these files can be transferred to a CD, permitting the user to play the music on an audio system in the comfort of his or her own home, from their own stereo.

The advent of MP3 technology is different from the previous technological advances in music media. When cassettes came out, the medium was still physical, and the sound quality of a dubbed cassette was not usually the equal of the original cassette. Today's MP3 files, though, are electronic, not physical. They can be sent through cyberspace, and a high volume of these files, the equivalent of many cassettes, can be stored in one small MP3 player. Since the sound is digital, the original quality of the recording is preserved; however, due to file size constraints, it's not quite like listening to the original CD *if* it had been purchased. Rather than spending time and energy going to a music store to rummage through its inventory, the MP3 shopper can look at a virtual catalogue of MP3 files maintained in any number of locations worldwide. MP3 files are cheap, too. For just the cost of a little Internet time, a user can download any number of MP3 files. For only the cost of a blank CD-R—a couple of dollars—a user can burn scores of songs onto a CD.

It is no wonder that the recording industry worldwide feels that it is being attacked and that each piece of music being downloaded without payment is a separate crime. Including the cost of the CD-R, the cost of downloading a CD's worth of music is about $3–$4. The user doesn't get a pretty CD cover, a protective plastic case, or liner notes. But then the music company doesn't get its royalties, and the recording artist and composer don't get royalties either. Without the royalties, says the music industry, why should music companies, artists, and composers keep recording music? It is the royalties that provide a living wage and encourage artists and composers to create their music and encourage the music companies to produce and distribute the music.

Critics of the recording industry say that the MP3 format and the ability to "burn," or create one's own CDs, has actually been good for business. They point out that to date, CD sales have not fallen substantially because of MP3 technology and the low cost of burning one's own CD, the price of other media and products, or anything else. For little-known music groups, this may be a great thing, according to those who promote the use of MP3 files and peer-to-peer networks like Napster. Groups that cannot afford a lot of publicity can promote their music in the MP3 chat rooms; these little-known artists hope that others will want to download their music, decide they like it, and then purchase a professionally produced CD at a nearby music store. Many of these groups even have Web sites at which visitors are welcome to download their music in MP3 format.

While this argument is probably true, those well-known artists who are popular and their recording companies stand to lose a great deal of money through copyright violation. It is considered cool to download and play a song before it hits the stores, particularly if the song comes from a prominent artist, such as Shania Twain or Celine Dion. While these artists arguably make a fortune, they earn it based on their contracts. Any reduction in their CD sales results in a decrease in their royalties. So a potential customer who doesn't buy their CD because he or she downloaded their favourite two or three songs from a Napster-like site, is stealing from the artist, just as though the CD had been stolen from a store. Then there's the problem of what might happen if music store revenues declined significantly. HMV and its competitors could be out of business in a couple of years if the current trend continues. Retail music stores reported that losses in 2000 were over $1 billion worldwide (counting losses to the recording industry, artists, and the stores); these losses will double in 2001, and potentially in every year after that as well.

Some companies, like Sony, have implemented security offices that actually track down chat rooms and other providers of files that violate Sony copyrights. They seek cease-and-desist orders, not against the individuals who are sharing the files, but against the site providers that provide the chat rooms and other services for sharing the files.

What can be done to save the recording industry, artists, and composers? At varying times and in varying places, a range of solutions have been proposed. Canada is no exception to this phenomenon nor to the range of proposed solutions. Parliament did pass one of those proposed solutions that we discuss below.

In the United States, a distinction is made between "consumer digital audio" media and data media. There is an extra charge for consumer audio-quality CD-R blanks and DAT tapes. The music industry gets the surcharge on the assumption that these media will be used to hold commercially recorded and copyrighted material.

Canada has gone a step farther, amending the Copyright Act with Bill C-32 in 1997, and placing a levy upon all media capable of storing audio. Even the "data" CD-R blanks, which don't work in consumer audio CD-R decks, are subject to the levy. In January 2001, the levy was raised from $0.052 to $0.21—a four-hundred-percent increase—for CD-R and CD-RW discs. The increase in the levy is was expected to raise $59 million for Canada's music industry over a two-year period. David Paterson, executive director of the CATA in Ottawa—Canada's entrepreneurial technology group—says: "Given the fact that if you buy the discs in bulk, you're paying about 60 cents each, this is one hell of a high [increase]". Paterson says that the levy was meant to deter music pirates, but the majority of CATA's membership is software companies, and they must pay the levy, too. Increased tariffs were also imposed on blank audio cassettes (from $0.233 to $0.29) and on CD-R Audio, CD-RW Audio, and MiniDiscs (from $0.608 to $0.77). The only allowable exemptions are granted to media designed to aid those with perceptual disabilities.

The tariff legislation established the Canadian Private Copying Collective (CPCC) in 1998 to receive revenues from the levy. Brian Cheter, CPCC spokesperson, said that two-thirds of the money will go to the writers, composers, and publishers, while one-third will go to the record companies. According to the amended Act, fifty percent of the money goes to the artists and fifty percent to the music companies. Another view, stated by Kevin Restivo, research director of IDC Canada, a consulting firm specializing in IT issues, is that "Technology is ahead of public institutions…CD-Rs will be outdated eventually, and with the rise of e-software, it'll become increasingly difficult for the government to impose a tax." As it stands, the Act doesn't impose a levy on Zip discs, flash memory cards, or any other medium that is also capable of holding MP3 files.

Even worse is that the 1997 amendments in Bill C-32 to the Copyright Act provided that copying of music works "for private use" will no longer be considered copyright infringement. In other words, for the price of the levy, or less than an extra dollar, a consumer now has the right to burn a CD, completely disregarding the artist or music company's copyright.

Other groups are more or less "held hostage" by the issues involved in the use of these new media. In Canada, Eiger Technology, Inc., headquartered in Stratford, Ont., is counting on MP3 technology to fill its coffers. Their Eiger Labs subsidiary was the first company to market an MP3 player (the EigerMan), which allows users to download free music from the Internet into a portable listening device. They are also one of the biggest manufacturers of 56K modems, which users needed to speed up download times. Think how of the business decisions Eiger Technology must face feel since finding out that many countries are considering a surcharge on the drives, including their MP3 player, that play the pirated music files. In June 2001, a German court ruled that the German Division of Hewlett-Packard must pay a flat fee to artists' guilds for every CD writer they sell, including all that were sold in the last three years.

Technological solutions are also being sought. In the 1980s, the makers of digital audio tape (DAT) were forced to use a 48 kilohertz sampling rate, slightly higher than the 44.1 kilohertz rate for music CDs. This was to prevent DATs from being used to copy commercially printed music CDs. More recently, the makers of stand-alone CD audio recorders were forced to design their products to use specially encoded media. These audio-specific CD-R discs look just like regular CD-Rs, but they have a special code so that stand-alone CD recorders can use them. Of course, the audio-specific discs cost more than the regular CD-Rs do, with the price difference going to compensate the recording industry for "lost revenue."

As the case in Germany illustrates, the companies that represent the artists legally challenge the companies that develop the technology, rather than the individuals actually responsible for copyright infringement. Content creators are unwilling or unable to prosecute individuals, so they go after the targets they can reach.

And what about those who wish to provide the content online? New York-based Contentville, launched in July 2000, promised to "transform the way consumers buy content online." Contentville is a digital reprint service with prominent backers such as the leading U.S. television networks. Contentville was founded by Steven Brill, the founder of the cable television channel, Courtroom Television. Contentville's copyright section warns: "The content on Contentville.com is the property of Contentville.com or its content suppliers and is protected by copyright laws." With all that cash and bragging, Contentville still sold articles, book excerpts, and dissertations without proper permission! Charles Mandel, a freelance writer, found 55 of his articles for sale at U.S.$2.95 per article. After a U.S.$7.25 million settlement was awarded in a class action suit brought by a group of freelance writers against another on-line content provider, UnCover.com, Contentville quickly settled with the National Writers Union, allowing writers to remove their articles from its site and setting payment to the authors for 30 percent of each U.S.$2.95 article sold if the article remained on the site. It is unclear as to who will audit the sales.

Technology analysts at Massachusetts-based Forrester Research predict that by 2005 cultural industries, including music companies and print publishers, will lose U.S.$4.6 billion to file sharing that violates copyright; the hit to the book industry alone will be U.S.$1.5 billion.

Montreal-based flipr.com plans to charge users a flat fee, probably less than $10 a month, for all the downloads belonging to any of 4000 independent labels worldwide that may participate. While it is more legal than Napster and less expensive than MP3.com, building a user base to draw traffic and advertising revenues can be difficult for such a start-up venture. Meanwhile, Napster is reinventing itself, and has been undergoing "beta testing" for months, as of this writing. They plan to implement a fee-based revenue model that will allow Napster to pay music companies for the music that is shared through their site. A Napster clone, called Wrapster, lets Napster users share not only music files, but also any digital files. You can even swap software through Wrapster without spending a cent.

To keep up with all the developments in the legal aspects of copyright on the Internet, you should subscribe to the Internet Law News, compiled by professor Michael Geist of the University of Ottawa. Published as daily e-mail, it provides links to Internet-related legal cases. Keeping up on the writs and torts and cease-and-desist orders could keep you from violating copyright. This may be too much trouble for most people, but it is a resource to consult when in doubt about Internet copyright laws. It's easy to blame Napster, Wrapster, flipr.com, and their like for being virtual thieves. But these sites are breaking ground in making the Web useful and popular. It would be nice if people of good conscience—those who own the content and those who want to exploit it—could find a compromise solution that makes money for everyone.

How many PC users have never violated copyright when placing any data, systems, software, or applications on their computers? In some cases, copyright is violated through ignorance. How does one know and support the copyright of those who initially provide content, whether recording artists or authors or software publishers? In the case of software, read the licence that comes with it. In the case of textual or music content, if in doubt, contact the publisher. Chances are you may think it's okay to download an e-book or MP3 file for free, but it's against the law and against computer ethics.

Sources: Joe Chidley, "There Goes the E-Neighbourhood," *Canadian Business*, April 17, 2000; Susan Taylor, "High Tech Sector Sounds Alarm over Canada CD Levy," *CD Media World*, December 17, 2000, available www.cdmediaworld.com/hardware/cdrom/news/9912/canada_cd_levy.shtml, accessed September 23, 2001; Jennifer Jannuska, "Federal Government to Levy Blank CD-Rewritable Media," Deeth Williams Wall LLP, available www.dww.com/articles/billc32article.

htm, accessed September 21, 2001; Dawn Calleja, "Music Hath Charms," *Canadian Business*, July 10, 2000; "Artists' Tax on CD Writers?" *Computer Peripherals*, June 22, 2001, available peripherals.about.com/library/weekly/aa062201a.htm, accessed September 23, 2001; Charles Mandel, "Somebody Call the Library Cops," *Canadian Business*, October 16, 2000; "Browser: I Say I Dunno," *Canadian Business*, November 13, 2000; "Is the Levy Too Heavy?" *NewMedia.Pro*, available www.newmediapromagazine.com/issues/2000/Feb/page22.htm, accessed August 8, 2001; Andy McFadden, "What's This about A Canadian CD-R Tax? CD-Recordable FAQ Sheet, available www.cdrfaq.org/faq07.html#S7-13, accessed August 28, 2001; Liam Lahey, "Copyright Board Quadruples Levies," *ComputerWorld Canada*, February 23, 2001.

VIDEO RESOURCE:

"Music For Free," *UNDERcurrents 111* (January 17, 1999).

CASE STUDY QUESTIONS

1. What are the benefits and negative impacts of sharing files? Does this apply to all kinds of files or just to MP3 files?

2. Should levies be legislated on recording media? Which media should carry a levy? How much should the levy be? What if the music being recorded is not Canadian? What if the music company whose file is being copied is not Canadian? Should the same tariff apply? How do you know if what will be recorded is Canadian or not?

3. Is there a better way to enforce or to pay for copyright? What is it?

4. Go online and review the Copyright Act. Next look at the CPCC's Web site. Can you see any potential conflicts in what the CPCC does and what the Copyright Act specifies? How does the CPCC distribute money to the actual artists? Is this fair?

INFORMATION RESOURCE MANAGEMENT

11 SYSTEMS DEVELOPMENT

Canadian Tire Struggles to Build Customer Relationships

Customer relationship management systems have become the new Holy Grail of high-end corporate computing. But like the famously difficult previous Holy Grail—enterprise resource planning systems—getting them up and running is harder than it looks. Just a few years ago, Canadian Tire Corp. Ltd. found itself drowning in its own systems.

In 1996, the chain of 430-plus automotive, hardware, and houseware stores decided to consolidate its 21 call centres and multiple back-end databases, according to Steve Folkerts, solutions consultant at Canadian Tire Acceptance Ltd., the company's financial services arm. "Our reps couldn't possibly take time to build a relationship with the customer because they had to take too much time building relationships with the systems," he said.

The proposed CRM project had six key business objectives to accomplish for the call centres:

▌ Greater customer loyalty to Canadian Tire as a result of world class customer service, measured by improved retention and increased customer satisfaction levels.

▌ Personalized customer attention and reduced call transfers.

▌ Improved operational efficiencies through centrally managed business process activation, staffing, and scheduling.

- ▌ Rapid introduction of new products or changes to existing business services.
- ▌ Reduced training requirements for customer service representatives.
- ▌ Integrating all customer touchpoints via a single system capable of including the Web, e-mail, and telephone.

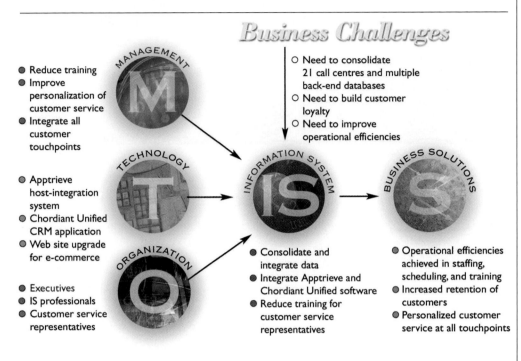

Business Challenges

MANAGEMENT
- ● Reduce training
- ● Improve personalization of customer service
- ● Integrate all customer touchpoints

TECHNOLOGY
- ● Apptrieve host-integration system
- ● Chordiant Unified CRM application
- ● Web site upgrade for e-commerce

ORGANIZATION
- ● Executives
- ● IS professionals
- ● Customer service representatives

- ○ Need to consolidate 21 call centres and multiple back-end databases
- ○ Need to build customer loyalty
- ○ Need to improve operational efficiencies

INFORMATION SYSTEM
- ● Consolidate and integrate data
- ● Integrate Apptrieve and Chordiant Unified software
- ● Reduce training for customer service representatives

BUSINESS SOLUTIONS
- ● Operational efficiencies achieved in staffing, scheduling, and training
- ● Increased retention of customers
- ● Personalized customer service at all touchpoints

Once company officials were able to justify the cost of the call centre integration, they realized they also need a strong CRM system. Once the CRM system was selected, however, officials decided it needed to be tied to the company's legacy databases. "We didn't own all of those back-end systems," Folkerts explained. "Nor was it cost effective to build that kind of industrial-strength integration." So in late 1998, the company purchased Seattle-based WRQ Inc.'s Apptrieve host-integration system, which includes a graphical mapping tool, a development kit, and a strong server. Apptrieve helped Canadian Tire link its legacy databases and tie them to its new CRM system. Canadian Tire had already selected Chordiant Unified CRM Solution to support its 800 customer service representatives across 10 customer service centres as the backbone of their effort to provide "world class" customer care.

Like Canadian Tire, many firms started catching on to CRM systems a few years ago but ran into so many kinks connecting to legacy systems that they're not done yet, according to Chris Selland, an analyst at the Yankee Group in Boston. Canadian Tire launched a pilot of its system in March 1999. But the system quickly stumbled when the company had to refocus its energies to solve unexpected Y2K date-change problems. Now, with Y2K projects over, the company has rolled out the first phase of its new unified systems. "All of a sudden, I had a strong back-end and easy user interface," said Folkerts. "It was like my dream come true." The next steps were adding Internet and e-mail channels to Canadian Tires' customer service system and boosting customer self-service functions on the Web.

Canadian Tire did just that. Today customers can purchase from the retailer's popular annual catalogue at home, either online from a special catalogue ordering

(continued)

Canadian Tire Struggles to Build Customer Relationships

MANAGEMENT CHALLENGES

11.1 Systems as Planned Organizational Change
- Linking Information Systems to the Business Plan
- Establishing Organizational Information Requirements
- Systems Development and Organizational Change

Window on Technology:
Cemex Becomes a Digital Firm

11.2 Business Process Reengineering and Total Quality Management
- Business Process Reengineering
- Steps in Effective Reengineering
- Process Improvement and Total Quality Management

11.3 The Importance of Change Management to Information Systems' Success and Failure
- Information Systems Problem Areas

Window on Organizations:
Web Sites Strive for Usability
- Change Management and the Concept of Implementation
- Causes of Implementation Success and Failure
- Change Management Challenges for Enterprise Systems, Business Process Reengineering, and Mergers and Acquisitions

Window on Management:
Managing the TransCanada Megamerger

11.4 Overview of Systems Development
- Systems Analysis
- Systems Design
- Completing the Systems Development Process

11.5 Alternative Systems Development Approaches
- Traditional Systems Development Life Cycle
- Prototyping
- Application Software Packages
- End User Development

MANAGEMENT DECISION PROBLEM:
Pricing a Software Package
- Outsourcing

Window on Management:
Subscription.com Invents Media and Publishing E-Marketplace

section on their Web site, www.canadiantire.ca, or over the phone via the existing customer service network. Shoppers can even earn Canadian Tire money online. Although Canadian Tire's Web site was plagued with technical problems during its first day of operation, including lack of access, error messages, and lengthy delays, Wayne Sales, Canadian Tire's President and CEO, says that "Canadian Tire is very well positioned to take a leadership position in serving Canadians online."

Sources: Melissa Solomon, "Like ERP, CRM Systems Can Be a Struggle to Launch," *ComputerWorld*, June 26, 2000; Bernadette Johnson, "Canadian Tire Ties Catalogue to Web, Phone," *Strategy Magazine*, April 23, 2001; Lori Enos, "Historic Canadian Retailer Joins the Web," *E-Commerce Times*, available www.ecommercetimes.com, November 21, 2000, accessed June 18, 2001.

MANAGEMENT CHALLENGES

Canadian Tire's CRM system illustrates the many factors at work in the development of a new information system. Developing the new system entailed analyzing the company's problems with existing information systems, assessing people's information needs, selecting appropriate technology, and redesigning business processes and jobs. Management had to monitor the systems development effort and evaluate its benefits and costs. The new information system represented a process of planned organizational change. However, developing information systems, especially those on a large scale, presents many challenges. Here are several challenges to consider:

1. **Major risks and uncertainties in systems development.** Information systems development has major risks and uncertainties that make it difficult for the systems to achieve their goals. One problem is the difficulty of establishing information requirements, both for individual end users and for the organization as a whole. The requirements may be very complex or subject to change. Another problem is that the time and cost factors to develop an information system are very difficult to analyze, especially in large projects. A third problem is the difficulty of managing the organizational change associated with a new system. Although building a new information system is a process of planned organizational change, this does not mean that change can always be planned or controlled. Individuals and groups in organizations have varying interests, and they may resist changes in procedures, job relationships, and technologies. Although this chapter describes some ways of dealing with these risks and uncertainties, the issues remain major management challenges.

2. **Controlling information systems development outside the information systems department.** There may not be a way to establish standards and controls for systems development that is not managed by the information systems department, such as end user development or outsourcing. Standards and controls that are too restrictive may not only generate user resistance but may also stifle end user innovation. If controls are too weak, the firm may encounter serious problems with data integrity and connectivity. It is not always easy to find the right balance.

This chapter describes how new information systems are conceived, developed, and implemented, with special attention to the issues of organizational design, business process reengineering, total quality management, and change management. It describes the core systems development activities and how to ensure that new systems are linked to the organization's business plan and information requirements. This chapter also examines alternative approaches for building systems.

11.1 SYSTEMS AS PLANNED ORGANIZATIONAL CHANGE

This text has emphasized that an information system is a sociotechnical entity, an arrangement of both technical and social elements. The introduction of a new information system involves much more than new hardware and software. It also includes changes in jobs, skills, management, and organization. In the sociotechnical philosophy, one cannot install new technology without considering the people who must work with it (Bostrom and Heinen, 1977). When we design a new information system, we are redesigning the organization.

Developing a new information system is one kind of planned organizational change. System developers must understand how a system will affect the organization as a whole, focusing particularly on organizational conflict and changes in the locus of control and decision making. Developers must also consider how the nature of work groups will change under the new system. Systems can be technical successes but organizational failures because of a failure in the social and political process of developing the system. Analysts and designers are responsible for ensuring that key members of the organization participate in the design process and are permitted to influence the system's ultimate shape. Managing this type of change is discussed later in this chapter.

LINKING INFORMATION SYSTEMS TO THE BUSINESS PLAN

Deciding which new systems to build should be an essential component of the organizational planning process. Organizations need to develop an information systems plan that supports their overall business plan and in which strategic systems are incorporated into top-level planning (Grover, Teng, and Fiedler, 1998). Once specific projects have been selected within the overall context of a strategic plan for the business and the information systems area, an **information systems plan** can be developed. The plan serves as a road map indicating the direction of systems development, the rationale, the current situation, the management strategy, the implementation plan, and the budget (see Table 11-1).

The plan contains a statement of corporate goals and specifies how information technology supports the attainment of those goals. The report shows how general goals will be achieved by specific information systems projects. It lays out specific target dates and milestones that can be used later to judge the plan's progress in terms of how many objectives were actually attained in the time frame specified in the plan. The plan indicates the key management decisions concerning hardware acquisition; telecommunications; centralization/decentralization of authority, data, and hardware; and required organizational change. Organizational changes are also usually described, including management and employee training requirements; recruiting efforts; changes in business processes; and changes in authority, structure, or management practice.

> **information systems plan**
> A road map indicating the direction of systems development: the rationale, the current situation, the management strategy, the implementation plan, and the budget.

ESTABLISHING ORGANIZATIONAL INFORMATION REQUIREMENTS

To develop an effective information systems plan, the organization must have a clear understanding of both its long- and short-term information requirements. Two principal methodologies for establishing the essential information requirements of the organization as a whole are enterprise analysis and critical success factors.

Enterprise Analysis (Business Systems Planning)

Enterprise analysis (also called *business systems planning* or *BSP*) argues that the firm's information requirements can only be understood by looking at the entire organization in terms of organizational units, functions, processes, and data elements. Enterprise analysis can help identify the key entities and attributes of the organization's data.

The central method used in the enterprise analysis approach is to take a large sample of managers and ask them how they use information, where they get the information, what

> **enterprise analysis**
> An analysis of organization-wide information requirements by looking at the entire organization in terms of organizational units, functions, processes, and data elements; helps identify the key entities and attributes in the organization's data.

TABLE 11-1	INFORMATION SYSTEMS PLAN

1. Purpose of the Plan

Overview of plan contents

Changes in firm's current situation

Firm's strategic plan

Current business organization

Key business processes

Management strategy

2. Strategic Business Plan

Current situation

Current business organization

Changing environments

Major goals of the business plan

3. Current Systems

Major systems supporting business functions
  and processes

Major current capabilities
  Hardware
  Software
  Database
  Telecommunications and the Internet

Difficulties meeting business requirements

Anticipated future demands

4. New Developments

New system projects
  Project descriptions
  Business rationale

New capabilities required
  Hardware
  Software
  Database
  Telecommunications and the Internet

5. Management Strategy

Acquisition plans

Milestones and timing

Organizational realignment

Internal reorganization

Management controls

Major training initiatives

Personnel strategy

6. Implementation Plan

Anticipated difficulties in implementation

Progress reports

7. Budget Requirements

Requirements

Potential savings and financial justification

Financing

Acquisition cycle

---

their environments are like, what their objectives are, how they make decisions, and what their data needs are. The results of this large survey of managers are aggregated into subunits, functions, processes, and data matrices. Data elements are organized into logical application groups—groups of data elements that support related sets of organizational processes.

Enterprise analysis produces an enormous amount of data that is expensive to collect and difficult to analyze. Most of the interviews are conducted with senior or middle managers, with little effort to collect information from clerical workers and supervisory managers. Moreover, the questions frequently focus not on management's critical objectives and where information is needed, but rather on what existing information is used. The result is a tendency to automate whatever exists. But in many instances, entirely new approaches to how business is conducted are needed, and these needs are not addressed.

Strategic Analysis or Critical Success Factors

critical success factors (CSFs)

A small number of easily identifiable operational goals shaped by the industry, the firm, the manager, and the broader environment that are believed to assure the success of an organization. Used to determine the information requirements of an organization.

The strategic analysis, or critical success factors, approach argues that an organization's information requirements are determined by a small number of **critical success factors (CSFs)** of managers. If these goals can be attained, the organization's success is assured (Rockart, 1979; Rockart and Treacy, 1982). CSFs are shaped by the industry, the firm, the managers, and the broader environment. An important premise of this approach is that there is a small number of objectives that managers can easily identify and information systems can focus on.

The principal method used in CSF analysis is interviewing—three or four personal interviews—with a number of top managers to identify their goals and the resulting CSFs.

TABLE 11-2 CRITICAL SUCCESS FACTORS AND ORGANIZATIONAL GOALS

Example	Goals	CSF
Profit concern	Earnings per share	Automotive industry
	Return on investment	Styling
	Market share	Quality dealer system
	New product	Cost control
		Energy standards
Nonprofit	Excellent health care	Regional integration with other hospitals
	Meeting government regulations	Improved monitoring of regulations
	Future health needs	Efficient use of resources

Source: Rockart (1979)

These personal CSFs are aggregated to develop a picture of the firm's CSFs. Systems are then developed to deliver information on these CSFs. (See Table 11-2 for an example of CSFs. For the method of developing CSFs in an organization, see Figure 11-1.)

The strength of the CSF method is that it produces a smaller data set to analyze than does enterprise analysis. Only top managers are interviewed, and the questions focus on a small number of CSFs rather than a broad inquiry into what information is used or needed. The CSF method takes into account the changing environment with which organizations and managers must deal. This method explicitly asks managers to look at the environment and to consider how their environmental analysis shapes their information needs. It is especially suitable for top management and for the development of decision support systems (DSS) and executive support systems (ESS). In contrast to enterprise analysis, the CSF method focuses organizational attention on how information should be handled.

The primary weakness of the CSF approach is that the aggregation process and the analysis of the data are art forms. There is no particularly rigorous way in which individual CSFs can be aggregated into a clear company pattern. Second, there is often confusion among interviewees (and interviewers) between *individual* and *organizational* CSFs. They are not necessarily the same. What can be critical to a manager may not be important for the

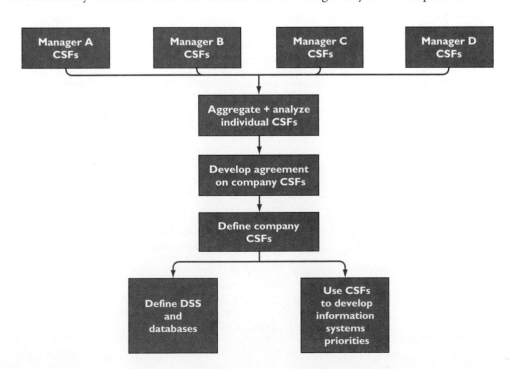

FIGURE 11-1 Using CSFs to develop systems. The CSF approach relies on interviews with key managers to identify their CSFs. Individual CSFs are aggregated to develop CSFs for the entire firm. Systems can then be built to deliver information on these CSFs.

organization. Moreover, this method is clearly biased toward top managers because they are the ones (generally the only ones) interviewed.

SYSTEMS DEVELOPMENT AND ORGANIZATIONAL CHANGE

New information systems can be powerful instruments for organizational change, enabling organizations to redesign their structure, scope, power relationships, workflows, products, and services. Table 11-3 describes some of the ways that information technology is being used to transform organizations and business processes.

The Spectrum of Organizational Change

Information technology can promote various degrees of organizational change, ranging from incremental to far-reaching. Figure 11-2 shows four kinds of structural organizational change that are enabled by information technology: (1) automation, (2) rationalization, (3) reengineering, and (4) paradigm shifts. Each carries different rewards and risks.

The most common form of IT-enabled organizational change is **automation**. The first applications of information technology involved assisting employees in performing their tasks more efficiently and effectively. Calculating paycheques and payroll registers, giving bank tellers instant access to customer deposit records, and developing a nationwide network of airline reservation terminals for airline reservation agents are all examples of early automation.

A deeper form of organizational change—one that follows quickly from early automation—is **rationalization of procedures**. Automation frequently reveals new bottlenecks in production and makes the existing arrangement of procedures and structures painfully cumbersome. Rationalization of procedures is the streamlining of standard operating procedures, eliminating obvious bottlenecks, so that automation can make operating procedures more efficient.

automation
Using the computer to speed up the performance of existing tasks.

rationalization of procedures
The streamlining of standard operating procedures, eliminating obvious bottlenecks, so that automation makes operating procedures more efficient.

TABLE 11-3 HOW INFORMATION TECHNOLOGY CAN TRANSFORM ORGANIZATIONS

Information Technology	Organizational Change
Global networks	*International division of labour*: The operations of a firm and its business processes are no longer determined by location; the global reach of firms is extended; costs of global coordination decline. Transaction costs decline.
Enterprise networks	*Collaborative work and teamwork*: The organization of work can now be coordinated across divisional boundaries; the costs of management (agency costs) decline. Multiple tasks can be worked on simultaneously from different locations.
Distributed computing	*Empowerment*: Individuals and work groups now have the information and knowledge to act. Business processes can be streamlined. Management costs decline. Hierarchy and centralization decline. The management hierarchical structure flattens.
Portable computing	*Virtual organizations*: Work is no longer tied to physical location. Knowledge and information can be delivered anywhere they are needed, anytime. Work becomes portable.
Multimedia and graphical interfaces	*Accessibility*: Everyone in the organization can access information and knowledge. Organizational costs decline as workflows move from paper to digital image, documents, and voice. Complex knowledge objects can be stored and represented as objects containing graphics, audio, video, or text.

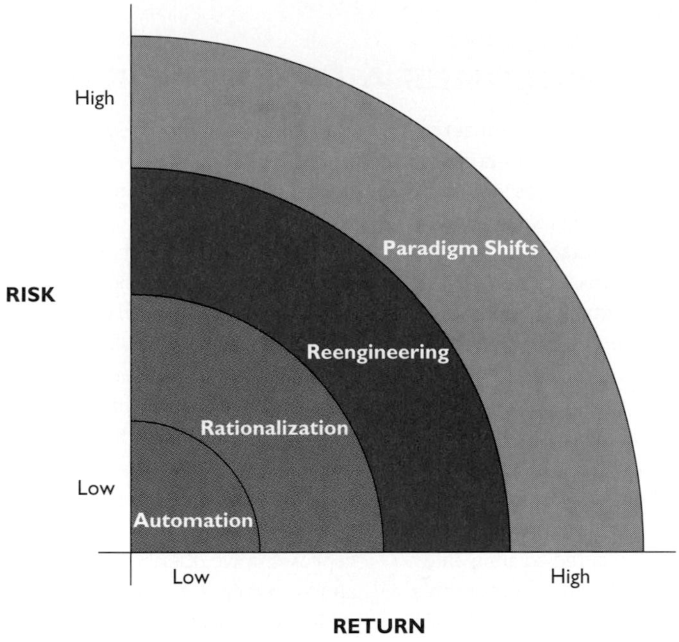

FIGURE 11-2 Organizational change carries risks and rewards. The most common forms of organizational change are automation and rationalization. These relatively slow-moving and slow-changing strategies present modest returns but little risk. Faster and more comprehensive change—like reengineering and paradigm shifts—carry potentially high rewards but offer a substantial chance of failure.

A more powerful type of organizational change is **business process reengineering**, in which business processes are analyzed, simplified, and redesigned. Using information technology, organizations can rethink and streamline their business processes to improve speed, service, and quality. Business reengineering reorganizes work flows, combining steps to cut waste and eliminating repetitive, paper-intensive tasks (often the new design eliminates jobs as well). It is much more ambitious than rationalization of procedures, requiring a new vision of how the process is to be organized.

A widely cited example of business reengineering is Ford Motor Company's *invoiceless processing*. Ford employed more than 500 people in its North American Accounts Payable organization. The accounts payable clerks spent most of their time resolving discrepancies between purchase orders, receiving documents, and invoices. Ford reengineered its accounts payable process, instituting a system wherein the purchasing department enters a purchase order into an online database that can be checked by the receiving department when the ordered items arrive. If the received goods match the purchase order, the system automatically generates a cheque for accounts payable to send to the vendor. There is no need for vendors to send invoices. After reengineering, Ford was able to reduce headcount in accounts payable by 75 percent and produce more accurate financial information (Hammer and Champy, 1993).

Rationalizing procedures and redesigning business processes are limited to specific parts of a business. New information systems can ultimately affect the design of the entire organization, by transforming how the organization carries out its business or even the nature of the business itself. For instance, Allegiance Healthcare's stockless inventory system (described in Chapter 2) transformed Allegiance into a working partner with hospitals and into a manager of its customers' supplies. This more radical form of business change is called a **paradigm shift**. A paradigm shift involves rethinking the nature of the business and the nature of the organization itself. The Window on Technology illustrates how Cemex used digital technology to make such organizational changes.

Paradigm shifts and reengineering often fail because extensive organizational change is so difficult to orchestrate. Why then do so many corporations entertain such radical change? Because the rewards are equally high (see Figure 11-2). In many instances, firms seeking paradigm shifts and pursuing reengineering strategies achieve stunning, order-of-magnitude increases in their returns on investment (or productivity). Some of these success stories, and some failure stories, are included throughout this book.

business process reengineering
The radical redesign of business processes, combining steps to cut waste and eliminating repetitive, paper-intensive tasks in order to improve cost, quality, and service, and to maximize the benefits of information technology.

paradigm shift
A radical reconceptualization of the nature of the business and the nature of the organization.

CEMEX BECOMES A DIGITAL FIRM

Cemex, based in Monterrey, Mexico, is a 90-year-old company that sells cement. It's an asset-intensive, low-efficiency business with unpredictable demand. Dispatchers took orders for 8000 grades of mixed concrete and forwarded them to six regional mixing plants, each with its own fleet of trucks. Customers routinely changed half of their orders, often hours before delivery and these orders might have to be rerouted due to weather change, traffic jams, or problems with building permits. Cemex's phone lines were often jammed as customers, truckers, and dispatchers tried to get orders straight. Many orders were lost.

Lorenzo Zambrano, a grandson of the founder of the company, took over the business in 1985 and decided to apply information technology to these problems. He and Cemex chief information officer Gelacio Iniguez developed a series of information systems that would enable Cemex to manage unforecastable demand better than its competitors.

Zambrano and Iniguez used ideas gleaned from visits to U.S. companies such as Federal Express, Exxon, and Houston's 911 emergency dispatch system to see how other organizations anticipated demand for their services. They built a system linking Cemex delivery trucks to a global positioning satellite system to help dispatchers monitor the location, direction, and speed of very vehicle. This information helps Cemex send the right truck to deliver a specific grade of cement or to redirect deliveries when directed by last-minute changes. The company has reduced average deliv-

ery time from three hours to 20 minutes, realizing huge savings in fuel, maintenance, and personnel costs. Cemex now uses 35 percent fewer trucks to deliver the same amount of cement. Customers are willing to pay premium prices to Cemex because they do not have to keep work crews idle waiting for cement deliveries to show up.

Cemex's production facilities used to operate independently, without precise knowledge of customer demand. A satellite communications system called CemexNet now electronically links all the firm's production facilities and coordinates them from a central clearinghouse.

Customers, distributors, and suppliers can use the Internet to place orders, check shipment delivery times, and review payment records without having to telephone a customer service representative. Zambrano and his managers now have access to almost every detail about Cemex operations within 24 hours while competitors are working with month-old data. Cemex's productivity and profitability have outpaced all of their major rivals in Mexico, and production output has grown six-fold since 1985. Cemex has become the world's third largest concrete manufacturer.

To Think About: How did digital technology transform the way Cemex ran its business? It has been said that Cemex has refocused efforts from managing assets to managing information. Explain. To what extent is Cemex a digital firm?

Sources: Adrian J. Slywotzky and David J. Morrison, "Concrete Solution," *The Industry Standard,* August 28, 2000; John A. Byrne, "Management by Web," *Business Week,* August 28, 2000.

11.2 BUSINESS PROCESS REENGINEERING AND TOTAL QUALITY MANAGEMENT

Many companies today focus on building new information systems where they can improve their business processes. Some of these system projects represent radical restructuring of business processes while others entail more incremental change.

BUSINESS PROCESS REENGINEERING

If organizations rethink and radically redesign their business processes before applying computing power, they can potentially obtain very large payoffs from their investments in information technology. The home mortgage industry is a leading example of how major corporations have implemented business process reengineering. The application process for a

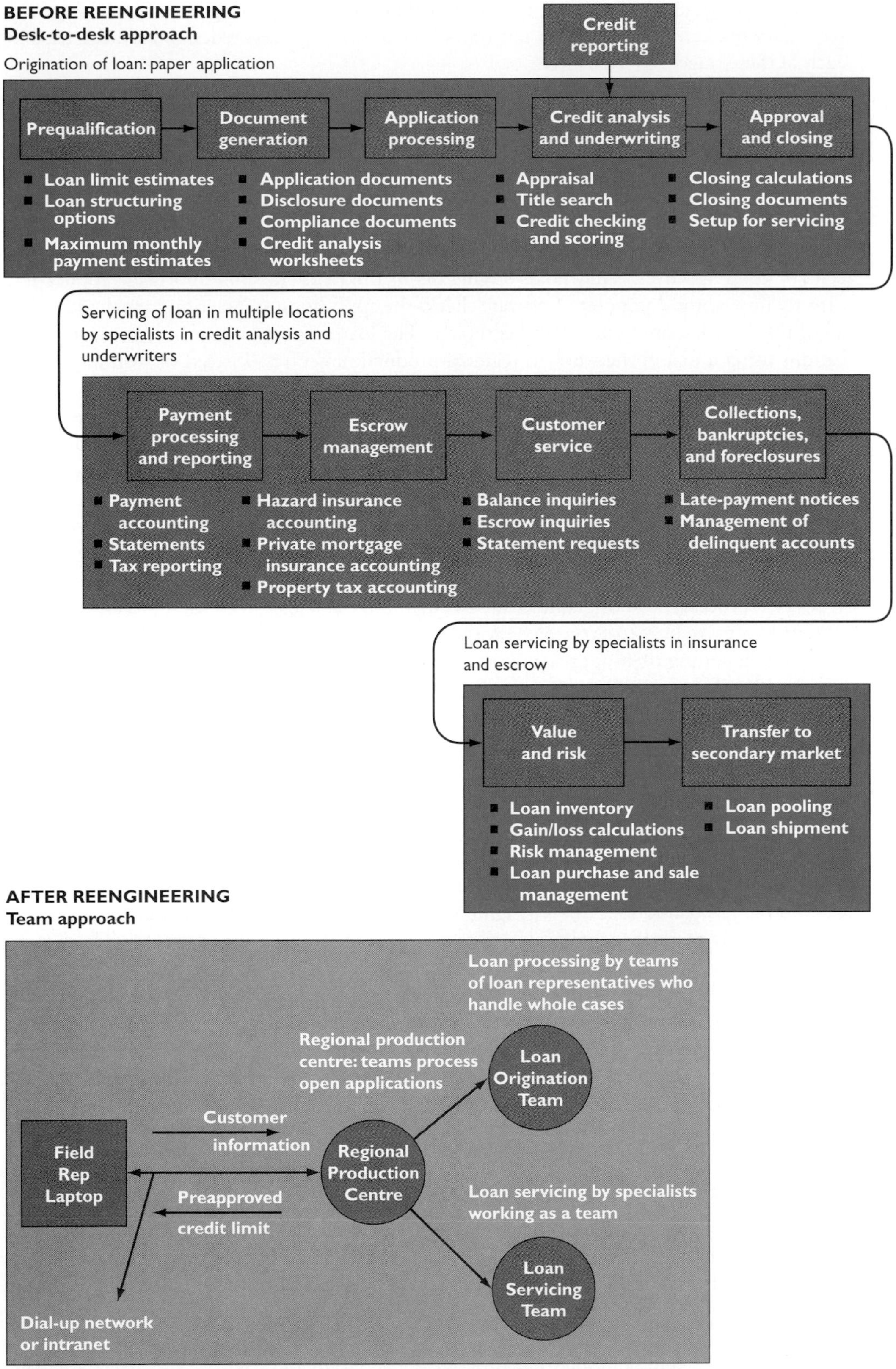

BEFORE REENGINEERING
Desk-to-desk approach

Origination of loan: paper application

AFTER REENGINEERING
Team approach

FIGURE 11-3 Redesigning mortgage processing. By redesigning their mortgage processing systems and the mortgage application process, mortgage banks are able to reduce the costs of processing the average mortgage from $3000 to $1000, and to reduce the time of approval from six weeks to one week or less. Some banks are even pre-approving mortgages and locking interest rates on the same day the customer applies.

home mortgage formerly took about six to eight weeks and cost about $3000. The goal of many mortgage banks has been to lower that cost to $1000 and the time to obtain a mortgage to less than one week. Leading Canadian mortgage banks have redesigned the mortgage application process. Today most applicants can have a mortgage pre-approved within a couple of days.

The mortgage application process is divided into three stages: origination, servicing, and secondary marketing. Figure 11-3 illustrates how business process redesign has been used in each of these stages.

In the past, a mortgage applicant filled out a paper loan application. The bank entered the application into its computer system. Specialists such as credit analysts and underwriters from perhaps eight different departments accessed and evaluated the application individually. If the loan application was approved, the closing was scheduled. After the closing, bank specialists dealing with insurance or funds in escrow serviced the loan. This "desk to desk" assembly-line approach might take up to 17 days.

Leading banks have replaced the sequential desk-to-desk approach with a speedier "work cell" or team approach. Now, loan originators in the field enter the mortgage application directly into laptop computers. Software checks the application transaction to make sure that all of the information is correct and complete. The loan originators transmit the loan applications using a dial-up network to regional production centres. Instead of working on the application individually, the credit analysts, loan underwriters, and other specialists convene electronically, working as a team to approve the mortgage. Some banks provide customers with a nearly instant credit lock-in of a guaranteed mortgage so they can find a house that meets their budget immediately. This type of pre-approval of a credit line is truly a radical reengineering of the traditional business process.

After closing, another team of specialists sets up the loan for servicing. The entire loan application process can take as little as two days. Loan information is easier to access than before, when the loan application could be in eight or nine different departments in a sequential process. Loan originators can also dial into the bank's network to obtain information on mortgage loan costs or to check the status of a loan for the customer.

By redesigning their approach to mortgage processing, mortgage banks have achieved remarkable efficiencies. They have not focused on redesigning a single business process but instead they have reexamined the entire set of logically connected processes required to obtain a mortgage. Instead of automating the previous method of mortgage processing, the banks have completely rethought the entire mortgage application process.

Workflow Management

workflow management
The process of streamlining business procedures so that documents can be moved easily and efficiently from one location to another.

To streamline paperwork in the mortgage application process, banks have turned to workflow and document management software. By using this software to store and process documents electronically, organizations can redesign their workflow so that documents can be worked on simultaneously or moved more easily and efficiently from one location to another. The process of streamlining business procedures so that documents can be moved easily and efficiently is called **workflow management**. Workflow and document management software automate processes such as routing documents to different locations, securing approvals, scheduling, and generating reports. Two or more people can work simultaneously on the same document, allowing a much quicker completion time. Work need not be delayed because a file is out or a document is in transit. And with a properly designed indexing system, users are able to retrieve files in many different ways, based on the content of the document.

STEPS IN EFFECTIVE REENGINEERING

To reengineer effectively, senior management needs to develop a broad strategic vision that calls for redesigned business processes. For example, Mitsubishi Heavy Industries management looked for breakthroughs to lower costs and accelerate product development that would enable the firm to regain world market leadership in shipbuilding. The company redesigned its entire production process to replace expensive labour-intensive tasks with robotic machines and computer-aided design tools. Companies should identify a few core business processes to be redesigned, focusing on those with the greatest potential payback (Davenport and Short, 1990).

Management must understand and measure the performance of existing processes as a baseline. If, for example, the objective of process redesign is to reduce time and cost in developing a new product or filling an order, the organization needs to measure the time and cost consumed by the unchanged process.

TABLE 11-4	NEW PROCESS DESIGN OPTIONS WITH INFORMATION TECHNOLOGY		
Assumption	**Technology**	**Options**	**Examples**
Field personnel need offices to receive, store, and transmit information.	Wireless communications	People can send and receive information from wherever they are.	Nikel Wood Barristers and Solicitors of Edmonton
Information can appear only in one place at one time.	Shared databases	People can collaborate on the same project from scattered locations; information can be used simultaneously wherever it is needed.	Canada Life
People are needed to ascertain where things are located.	Automatic identification and tracking technology	Things can tell people where they are.	Wilson Logistics, Inc.
Businesses need reserve inventory to prevent stockouts.	Networks, extranets, and EDI	Just-in-time delivery and stockless supply	Allegiance Health Care Wal-Mart

The conventional method of designing systems establishes the information requirements of a business function or process and then determines how they can be supported by information technology. However information technology can create new design options for various processes because it can be used to challenge longstanding assumptions about work arrangements that used to inhibit organizations. Table 11-4 provides examples of innovations that have overcome these assumptions using companies discussed in the text. Information technology should be allowed to influence process design from the start.

Following these steps does not automatically guarantee that reengineering will always be successful. The organization's information technology (IT) infrastructure should have capabilities to support business process changes that span boundaries between functions, business units, or firms (Broadbent, Weill, and St. Clair, 1999). The majority of reengineering projects do not achieve breakthrough gains in business performance. A reengineered business process or a new information system inevitably affects jobs, skill requirements, workflows, and reporting relationships (Teng, Jeong, and Grover, 1998). Fear of these changes breeds resistance, confusion, and even conscious efforts to undermine the change effort. We examine these organizational change issues later in this chapter.

PROCESS IMPROVEMENT AND TOTAL QUALITY MANAGEMENT

In addition to increasing organizational efficiency, companies are also changing their business processes to improve the quality in their products, services, and operations. Many are using the concept of **total quality management (TQM)** to make quality the responsibility of all people and functions within an organization. The TQM philosophy holds that the achievement of quality control is an end in itself. Everyone is expected to contribute to the overall improvement of quality—the engineer who avoids design errors, the production worker who spots defects, the sales representative who presents the product properly to potential customers, and even the secretary who avoids typing mistakes. Quality is understood to be quality as it is perceived by the customer, whether the customer is internal or external, and can only be evaluated in terms of the customers' perceptions of quality. TQM derives from quality management concepts developed by American quality experts W. Edwards Deming and Joseph Juran, but it was popularized by the Japanese. Studies have repeatedly shown that the earlier in the business cycle a problem is eliminated, the less it costs the company. Thus quality improvements can raise the level of product and service quality, and they can also lower costs.

total quality management (TQM)
A concept that makes quality control a responsibility to be shared by all people in an organization.

How Information Systems Contribute to Total Quality Management

TQM is considered to be more incremental than business process reengineering (BPR) because its efforts often focus on making a series of continual improvements rather than dramatic bursts of change. Sometimes, however, processes may have to be fully reengineered to achieve a specified level of quality. Information systems can help firms achieve their quality goals by helping them simplify products or processes, meet benchmarking standards, make improvements based on customer demands, reduce cycle time, and increase the quality and precision of design and production.

Simplifying the Product or the Production Process   The fewer steps in a process, the less time and opportunity for an error to occur. Ten years ago, 1-800-FLOWERS, a multimillion-dollar telephone- and Web-based floral service with a global reach, was a much smaller company that spent too much on advertising because it could not retain its customers. It had poor service, inconsistent quality, and a cumbersome manual order-taking process. Telephone representatives had to write the order, obtain credit card approval, determine which participating florist was closest to the delivery location, select a floral arrangement, and forward the order to the florist. Each step in the manual process increased the chance of human error, and the whole process took at least a half hour. Owners Jim and Chris McCann installed a new computer system that downloads orders taken at telecentres into a central computer and electronically transmits them to local florists. Orders are more accurate and arrive at the florist within one to two minutes (Gill, 1998).

benchmarking

Setting strict standards for products, services, or activities and measuring organizational performance against those standards.

Benchmarking   Many companies have been effective in achieving quality by setting strict standards for products, services, and other activities, and then measuring performance against those standards. This procedure is called **benchmarking.** Companies may use external industry standards, standards set by other companies, internally developed high standards, or some combination of the three. SAP, the leading enterprise software company, uses its own standards as benchmarks against which their customers and potential customers can measure their information systems. If the potential customers' benchmarks are much lower or slower than SAP's, they may feel that SAP can offer them a significant boost in productivity.

Use Customer Demands as a Guide to Improving Products and Services   Making customer service the number one priority will improve the quality of the product itself. In attempting to counteract their poor customer service image, Air Canada implemented self-service kiosks in many Canadian airports. Instead of there being 20 people in line to check in, passengers who check in at a kiosk can be on their way in about 60 seconds, having confirmed seating and frequent flyer points, and having received their boarding pass. Bags are left at the special express baggage drop-off counter (Shura, 2000).

Reduce Cycle Time   Reducing the amount of time from the beginning of a process to its end (*cycle time*) usually results in fewer steps. Shorter cycles mean that errors are often caught earlier in production (or logistics or design or whatever the function), often before the process is complete, eliminating many hidden costs. Iomega corporation in Roy, Utah, a manufacturer of disk drives, was spending $20 million a year to fix defective drives at the end of its 28-day production cycle. Reengineering the production process allowed the firm to reduce cycle time to a day and a half, eliminating this problem and winning the prestigious Shingo prize for excellence in American manufacturing.

Improve the Quality and Precision of the Design   *Computer-aided design* (*CAD*) software has made dramatic quality improvements possible in a wide range of businesses from aircraft manufacturing to production of razor blades. Alan R. Burns, head of the Airboss Company in Perth, Australia, used CAD to invent and design a new modular tire made up of a series of replaceable modules or segments so that if one segment were damaged, only that segment, not the whole tire, would need replacing. Burns established quality performance measurements for key tire characteristics such as load, temperature, speed, wear life, and traction. He entered these data into a CAD software package that he used to design the modules. Using the software, he was able to design and test iteratively until he was satisfied with the results. He did not need to develop an actual working model until the iterative design process was almost complete. Because of the speed and accuracy of the CAD

TABLE 11-5 DIFFERENCES IN BUSINESS PROCESS REENGINEERING AND TOTAL QUALITY MANAGEMENT

Difference	BPR	TQM
Type of change	Radical	Incremental
Time frame	All at once	Over time
Focus	Process	Customer/quality

software, the product he produced was of much higher quality than would have been possible through manual design and testing.

Increase the Precision of Production   For many products, achieving quality means making the production process more precise and decreasing the amount of variation from one part to another. Spunbonded roll goods producer Polybond Inc., part of the Dominion Nonwovens group of Dominion Textile headquartered in Montreal, used a statistical quality control tool to reduce their production variation. Traditionally, Polybond conducted end of roll samplings to test the basis weight profile. Checking the weight in the lab, however, is too late to improve the process. Polybond added an online basis-weight gauging and control system. Since the gauge became operational, Polybond has cut the variability of the basis weight profile across the web by half. The amount of scrap associated with the production process has been dramatically reduced as well ("Online Gauging Improves Spunbonded Fabric Quality," 2000).

Differences in BPR and TQM

There are differences in the approaches and philosophies of BPR and TQM. Table 11-5 illustrates these differences. While changes made during a BPR effort are large or radical and process-focused and occur all at once, TQM changes are small or incremental and customer-focused and occur over a much longer time frame. Today's BPR proponents insist that BPR is also customer- and quality-focused, but with a direct approach that is focused on process redesign. Many managers today believe that a coordinated change process is more effective. They recommend first conducting a BPR initiative. Once the BPR effort has been completed, they recommend implementing TQM to ensure that the reengineered processes maintain their level of quality and customer focus.

11.3 THE IMPORTANCE OF CHANGE MANAGEMENT TO INFORMATION SYSTEMS' SUCCESS AND FAILURE

Before we discuss the actual development of information systems, it is important to look at factors that influence the success or failure of IS development. Managing change is neither simple nor intuitive. The introduction or alteration of an information system has a powerful behavioural and organizational impact. It transforms how various individuals and groups perform and interact. Changes in the way that information is defined, accessed, and used to manage the organization's resources often lead to new distributions of authority and power. Internal organizational change breeds resistance and opposition and can lead to the demise of an otherwise good system.

A very large percentage of information systems fail to deliver benefits or to solve the problems for which they were intended because the process of organizational change surrounding systems development was not properly addressed. Successful system development requires careful change management.

INFORMATION SYSTEMS PROBLEM AREAS

The problems causing **information system failure** fall into multiple categories, as illustrated by Figure 11-4. The major problem areas are design, data, cost, and operations.

information system failure
An information system that either does not perform as expected, is not operational at a specified time, or cannot be used in the way it was intended.

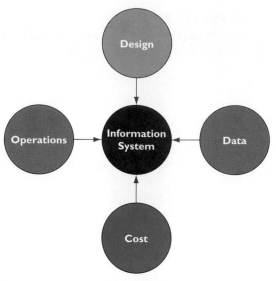

Design

The actual design of the system fails to capture essential business requirements or improve organizational performance. Information may not be provided quickly enough to be helpful; it may be in a format that is impossible to digest and use; or it may represent the wrong pieces of data. Failure to obtain needed user input for information requirements is often the leading cause of poor design.

The way in which nontechnical business users must interact with the system may be excessively complicated and discouraging. A system may be designed with a poor **user interface**. The user interface is the part of the system with which end users interact. For example, an input form or an online data entry screen may be so poorly arranged that no one wants to submit data. The procedures to request online information retrieval may be so unintelligible that users are too frustrated to make requests. Web sites may discourage visitors from exploring further if Web pages are cluttered and poorly arranged or users can't easily find the information they are seeking. A number of studies have found that close to 50 percent of Web shoppers give up purchasing items online because the site was too difficult to navigate and they could not locate products on the Web site (Lohse and Spiller, 1999). The Window on Organizations details how user interfaces can impact electronic commerce.

An information system will be judged a failure if its design is not compatible with the structure, culture, and goals of the organization as a whole. Historically, information systems design has focused on technical issues at the expense of organizational concerns. The result has often been information systems that are technically excellent but incompatible with their organization's structure, culture, and goals. Without a close organizational fit, these systems have created tensions, instability, and conflict.

Data

The data in the system may have a high level of inaccuracy or inconsistency. The information in certain fields may be erroneous or ambiguous, or they may not be broken out properly for business purposes. Information required for a specific business function may be inaccessible because the data are incomplete or are structured so as to be incompatible for use in other organizational systems where they may also be needed. Data from previous systems must be "cleaned" and carefully converted; it must be tested as well to ensure that it can be accessed easily and quickly and that the system maintains data integrity.

Cost

Some systems operate quite smoothly, but the cost to implement and run them on a production basis is way over budget. Other systems projects may be too costly to complete. In both cases, the excessive expenditures cannot be justified by the demonstrated business value of the information they provide. Some systems start development with a reasonable budget, but, over time, costs escalate as features are added or unforeseen problems or delays (such as assigning qualified personnel) occur. Costs to fix problems that occur can also add significantly to the development budget.

Operations

The system does not run well. Information is not provided in a timely and efficient manner because the computer operations that handle information processing break down. Jobs that abort too often lead to excessive reruns and delayed or missed schedules for delivery of

---

user interface

The part of the information system through which the end user interacts with the system; type of hardware and the series of on-screen commands and responses required for a user to work with the system.

WEB SITES STRIVE FOR USABILITY

At the end of January 2000, CarsDirect.com, an online auto store, saw the number of visitors of its Web site double. This surge in visitors was not the result of a heavy advertising expenditures campaign or more powerful information systems technology. CarsDirect.com had merely redesigned its Web site.

The new CarsDirect site is sleeker and easier on the eye, with new tools, such as the ability to connect to a live customer service representative with a single mouse click. CarsDirect.com also added software to help it understand the behaviour of potential customers. The software helps the company track what pages users are accessing and the points where they are leaving the site so that they can monitor how customers are reacting.

When it comes to Web sites, design matters. Usability and good looks count. Good design can make a Web site stand out among dozens of competitors. A well-designed Web site can boost traffic and sales and keep customers coming back. If visitors have a good experience on a Web site, they are much more likely to make a purchase. And if customers can't understand or easily find the information they need on a Web site, they'll get frustrated and turn to a competitor. The Web makes switching costs extraordinarily low, with competitors only a mouse-click away.

Studies of user behaviour on the Web have found that people have a low tolerance for difficult designs and slow sites. They don't want to wait to see a Web page. They won't want to spend time deciphering a home page. E-commerce firms must make sure that users can easily view a page from their Web sites, find an item, make a purchase, and navigate through page after page without losing track of where they

started. Sadly, the majority of Web sites today are difficult to use. Usability studies have found a success rate of less than 50 percent. That means that when a person is asked to perform a simple task on an average Web site, he or she will most likely fail.

Success in e-commerce can be measured by multiplying the number of people who visit a Web site times the conversion rate—the percentage of visitors who become customers. It's expensive and difficult for most companies to get people to visit their Web sites in the first place. To double the success of a site, firms must either double the number of visitors or double the conversion rate. Instead of doubling the advertising budget to increase site visitors, companies could spend much less to raise conversion rates by redesigning their Web site using a human-centred design process.

Fidelity Investments, the largest U.S. mutual fund manager, spends more on technology than any of its rivals, focusing on product usability. Its Fidelity Centre for Advanced Technology features two usability labs where Fidelity tests the human interface design of its Web site and other technologies for delivering its services. Fidelity even uses eye-tracking tests to track how people are viewing the pixels on its Web pages so it can fine-tune its Web site to eliminate every wasteful click. Fidelity.com is a complex site with many features and usability experts constantly work at making navigating its 30 000 pages as easy as possible.

To Think About: What organization and technology issues affect the usability of a Web site? Why is Web site usability so important in electronic commerce? In terms of design, what makes a Web site "user-friendly?"

Sources: Danny Hakim, "A High-Tech Vision Lifts Fidelity," *The New York Times*, September 17, 2000; Beth Batcheldor, "The Art of E-Biz," *Information Week*, February 14, 2000; and Jakob Nielsen and Donald A. Norman, "Usability on the Web Isn't a Luxury," *Information Week*, February 14, 2000.

FIGURE 11-5 CarsDirect.com redesigned its Web site to make it easier to use. A well-designed user interface contributes to system success.

information. An online system may be operationally inadequate because the response time is too long.

Some of these problems can be attributed to technical features of information systems, but most stem from organizational factors (Keil, Cule, Lyytinen, and Schmidt, 1998). Systems developers need to understand these organizational issues and learn how to manage the change associated with a new information system.

CHANGE MANAGEMENT AND THE CONCEPT OF IMPLEMENTATION

implementation
All organizational activities working toward the adoption, management, and routinization of an innovation.

change agent
In the context of implementation, the individual acting as the catalyst during the change process to ensure successful organizational adaptation to a new system or innovation.

To effectively manage the organizational change surrounding the introduction of a new information system, we need to examine the process of implementation. **Implementation** refers to all organizational activities working toward the adoption, management, and *routinization* of an innovation such as a new information system. In the implementation process, the systems analyst is a **change agent**. The analyst not only develops technical solutions but also redefines the configurations, interactions, job activities, and power relationships of various organizational groups. The analyst is the catalyst for the entire change process and is responsible for ensuring that the changes created by a new system are accepted by all parties involved. The change agent communicates with users, mediates between competing interest groups, and ensures that the organizational adjustment to these changes is complete.

Many people do not like change. They feel that the change will not be beneficial or is not needed. Or they do not think the new system will work as well as the old one. Still others are afraid of the unknown: how will the new system change their jobs and the tasks they perform? Will the new system replace their job or deskill it? Many feel inadequate for the proposed changes in their jobs; they may feel working with a particular system is too advanced for their educational or job level. Finally, many feel that they shouldn't be forced to change. Their resistance can take many forms, from refusing to use the system, to deliberately trying to crash the system, to quitting their jobs, to becoming less productive, to simply not learning the new system as well as they could if they had a positive attitude. What can be done to combat resistance to change? Let's look at two models of organizational change to see what they show.

One model of the implementation process is the Kolb-Frohman model of organizational change. This model divides the process of organizational change into a seven-stage relationship between an organizational consultant and his or her client. The consultant corresponds to the information system designer and the client to the user. The success of the change effort is determined by how well the consultant and client deal with the key issues at each stage (Kolb and Frohman, 1970). Other models of implementation describe the relationship as one between designers, clients, and decision makers, who are responsible for managing the implementation effort to bridge the gap between design and utilization (Swanson, 1988). Recent work on implementation stresses the need for flexibility and improvisation with organizational actors not limited to rigid prescribed roles (Markus and Benjamin, 1997; Orlikowski and Hofman, 1997).

The widely cited and more generic Lewin-Schein model of organizational change consists of three phases:

unfreezing
Preparing those affected by the change by communicating the reasons for the change, the importance of the change, management's support for the change, and soliciting their feedback and input into the change in hopes of their taking ownership of the change.

moving
The actual training of those affected by the change in their new responsibilities, tasks, schedules, etc., so that they feel capable of performing the changed routines.

refreezing
Routinization of the change so that it becomes second nature and is "frozen" as the new "normal" way of doing things.

▌ **Unfreezing**   Preparing those affected by the change by communicating the reasons for the change, the importance of the change, management's support for the change, and soliciting their feedback and input into the change in hopes of their taking ownership of the change

▌ **Moving**   The actual training of those affected by the change in their new responsibilities, tasks, schedules, etc., so that they feel capable of performing the changed routines

▌ **Refreezing**   Routinization of the change so that it becomes second nature and is "frozen" as the new "normal" way of doing things

Too many projects fail because not enough effort was expended in the unfreezing state to prepare those affected for the change (Schein, 1995). Training is especially important as it not only trains employees but elicits employee buy-in and communicates to employees the reasons for the change. Training can be in the form of reading manuals, attending classes, working through hands-on tutorials, or watching videos and seeing demonstrations. If change agents practice these steps or those in other widely accepted change models, change management should become more effective, if no less complex.

CAUSES OF IMPLEMENTATION SUCCESS AND FAILURE

Implementation outcomes can be largely determined by the following factors:

- The role of users in the implementation process
- The degree of management support for the implementation effort
- The level of complexity and risk of the implementation project
- The quality of management of the implementation process

These are largely behavioural and organizational issues and are illustrated in Figure 11-6.

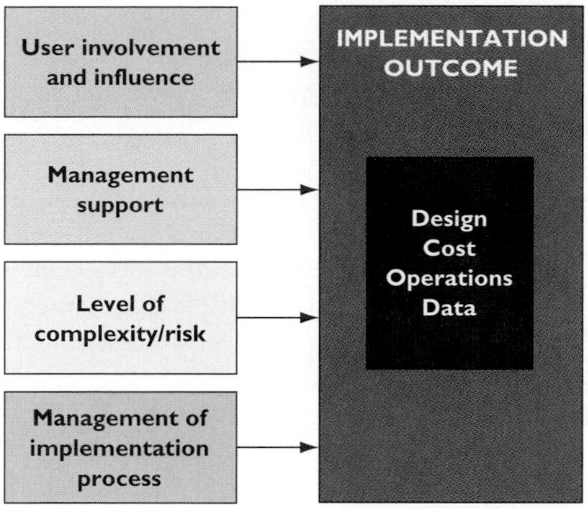

FIGURE 11-6 Factors in information system success or failure. The implementation outcome can be largely determined by the users' role; the degree of management support; the level of risk and complexity in the implementation project; and the quality of management of the implementation process. Evidence of success or failure can be found in the areas of design, cost, operations, or data of the information system.

User Involvement and Influence

User involvement in the design and operation of information systems has several positive results. First, if users are heavily involved in systems design, they have more opportunities to mould the system according to their priorities and business requirements and more opportunities to control the outcome. Second, they are more likely to react positively to the completed system because they have been active participants in the change process itself. This is known as *ownership*. It is often difficult to get users involved in a development project if they are pressed for time. Even when such involvement is limited, hands-on experience with the system helps users appreciate its benefits and provides useful suggestions for improvement (De and Ferrat, 1998).

Incorporating the user's knowledge and expertise leads to better solutions. However, users often take a very narrow and limited view of the problem to be solved and may overlook important opportunities for improving business processes or innovative ways to apply information technology. The skills and vision of professional system designers are still required in the same way that the services of an architect are required when building a new house (Markus and Keil, 1994). In addition, the designer can enable the user to see the "bigger picture"—why the new or upgraded system is needed in the first place.

The relationship between consultant and client has traditionally been a problem area for information systems implementation efforts. Users and information systems specialists tend to have different backgrounds, interests, and priorities. This is referred to as the **user–designer communications gap**. These differences lead to divergent organizational loyalties, approaches to problem solving, and vocabularies. Information systems specialists, for example, often have a highly technical or machine orientation to problem solving. They look for technical solutions in which hardware and software efficiency is optimized at the expense of ease of use or organizational effectiveness. Users prefer systems that are oriented to solving business problems or facilitating organizational tasks with user-friendly interfaces. Often the orientations of both groups are so at odds that they appear to speak in different tongues. These differences are illustrated in Table 11-6, which depicts the typical concerns of end

user–designer communications gap
The difference in backgrounds, interests, and priorities that impede communication and problem solving among end users and information systems specialists.

TABLE 11-6   THE USER–DESIGNER COMMUNICATIONS GAP

User Concerns	Designer Concerns
Will the system deliver the information I need for my work?	How much disk storage space will the master file consume?
How quickly can I access the data?	How many lines of program code will it take to perform this function?
How easily can I retrieve the data?	What keywords should I use to index the data?
How much clerical support will I need to enter data into the system?	What is the most efficient way of storing this piece of data?
How will the operation of the system fit into my daily business schedule?	What database management system model should we use?

users and technical specialists (information system designers) regarding the development of a new information system. This type of communication problem is a major reason that user requirements are not properly incorporated into information systems and that users feel driven out of the implementation process.

Systems development projects run a very high risk of failure when there is a pronounced gap between users and technicians and when these groups continue to pursue different goals. Under these conditions, users are often driven out of the implementation process. Because they cannot comprehend what the technicians are saying, users conclude that the entire project is best left in the hands of the information specialists alone. With so many implementation efforts guided by purely technical considerations, it is no wonder that many systems fail to serve organizational needs.

Management Support and Commitment

If an information systems project has the backing and commitment of management at various levels, it is more likely to be perceived positively by both users and the information systems staff. Both groups will believe that their participation in the development process will receive higher-level attention and priority. They will be recognized and rewarded for the time and effort they devote to implementation. Management backing also ensures that a systems project will receive sufficient funding and resources to be successful. Furthermore, all the changes in work habits and procedures and any organizational realignments associated with a new system depend on management backing to be enforced effectively. If a manager considers a new system to be a priority, the system will more likely be treated as such by his or her subordinates (Doll, 1985; Ein-Dor and Segev, 1978).

However, management support can sometimes backfire. Sometimes management becomes over-committed to a project, pouring excessive resources into a systems development effort that is failing or that should never have been undertaken in the first place (Newman and Sabherwal, 1996).

Level of Complexity and Risk

Systems differ dramatically in their size, scope, level of complexity, and organizational and technical components. Some systems development projects are more likely to fail or suffer delays because they carry a much higher level of risk than others. Researchers have identified three key dimensions that influence the level of project risk (McFarlan, 1981). These include project size, project structure, and the level of technical experience of the information systems staff and project team.

Project Size The larger the project—as indicated by the dollars spent, the size of the implementation staff, the time allocated to implementation, and the number of organizational units affected—the greater the risk. Therefore, an $8 million project lasting for two years and affecting five departments in 20 operating units and 120 users will be much riskier than a $30 000 project for two users that can be completed in two months. Another risk factor is the company's experience with projects of given sizes. If a company is accustomed to implementing large, costly systems, the risk of implementing the $8 million project is lower. The risk may even be lower than that of another concern attempting a $200 000 project when the firm's average project cost has been around $50 000. On the whole, however, very large-scale system projects show a failure rate that is 50 to 75 percent higher than for other projects because the larger projects are so complex and difficult to control. The behavioural characteristics of the system—who owns the system and how much it influences business processes—contribute to the complexity of large-scale system projects just as much as technical characteristics such as the number of lines of program code, length of project, and budget (The Concours Group, 2000; Laudon, 1989; United States General Services Administration, 1988).

Project Structure Some projects are more highly structured than others. Their requirements are clear and straightforward so the outputs and processes can be easily defined. Users know exactly what they want and what the system should do; there is almost no possibility for them to change their minds. These projects run a much lower risk than those with rela-

TABLE 11-7	DIMENSIONS OF PROJECT RISK		
Project Structure	**Project Technology Level**	**Project Size**	**Degree of Risk**
High	Low	Large	Low
High	Low	Small	Very low
High	High	Large	Medium
High	High	Small	Medium low
Low	Low	Large	Low
Low	Low	Small	Very low
Low	High	Large	Very high
Low	High	Small	High

tively undefined, fluid, and constantly changing requirements, with outputs that cannot be easily fixed because they are subject to users' changing ideas, or with users who cannot agree on what they want.

Experience with Technology   Project risk will rise if the project team and the information systems staff lack the required technical expertise. If the team is unfamiliar with the hardware, systems software, application software, or database management system proposed for the project, it is highly likely that the project will experience technical problems or take more time to complete because of the need to master new skills.

These dimensions of project risk are present in different combinations for every implementation effort. Table 11-7 shows that eight different combinations are possible, each with a different degree of risk. The higher the level of risk, the more likely it is that the implementation effort will fail. Chapter 13 discusses various ways to control risk factors.

Management of the Implementation Process

The development of a new system must be carefully managed and orchestrated. Often basic elements of success are forgotten. Training to ensure that end users are comfortable with the new system and fully understand its potential uses is often sacrificed or forgotten in systems development projects. If the budget is strained at the very beginning, there will likely be insufficient funds for training toward the end of a project (Bikson et al., 1985).

The conflicts and uncertainties inherent in any implementation effort will be magnified when an implementation project is poorly managed and organized. As illustrated in Figure 11-7, a systems development project without proper management will most likely suffer these consequences:

▌ Cost overruns that vastly exceed budgets

▌ Unexpected time slippage

▌ Technical shortfalls resulting in performance that is significantly below the estimated level

▌ Failure to obtain anticipated benefits

How badly are projects managed? On average, private sector projects are underestimated by one-half in terms of budget and time required to deliver the complete system promised in

FIGURE 11-7 Consequences of poor project management. Without proper management a systems development project will take longer to complete and most often will exceed the budgeted cost. The resulting information system will most likely be technically inferior and may not be able to demonstrate any benefits to the organization.

Poor project management →
Cost overruns
Time slippage
Technical shortfalls impairing performance
Failure to obtain anticipated benefits

the system plan. A large number of projects are delivered with missing functionality (promised for delivery in later versions). Why are projects managed so poorly and what can be done about it? Here we discuss some possibilities.

Ignorance and Optimism   The techniques for estimating the length of time required to analyze and design systems are poorly developed. Most applications are "first time" (i.e., there is no prior experience in the application area). The larger the scale of systems, the greater the role of ignorance and optimism. The net result of these factors is that estimates tend to be optimistic, "best case," and wrong. It is assumed that all will go well when in fact it rarely does.

man-month

The traditional unit of measurement used by systems designers to estimate the length of time to complete a project. Refers to the amount of work a person can be expected to complete in a month.

The Mythical Man-Month   The traditional unit of measurement used by systems designers to project costs is the **man-month**. Projects are estimated in terms of how many man-months will be required. However, adding more workers to projects does not necessarily reduce the time needed to complete a systems project (Brooks, 1974). Unlike planting trees—when tasks can be rigidly partitioned, communication between participants is not required, and little training is necessary—systems analysis and design involve *tasks that are sequentially linked, cannot be performed in isolation, and require extensive communications and training*. Adding labour to software projects can often slow down delivery as the communication, learning, and coordination costs escalate and reduce the output of participants. As a comparison, what would happen if five amateur spectators were added to one team in a championship professional basketball game? The team composed of five professional basketball players would probably do much better in the short run than the team with five professionals and five amateurs.

Falling Behind: Bad News Travels Slowly Upward   Among projects in all fields, slippage in projects, failure, and doubts are often not reported to senior management until it is too late. Those most closely involved in a project can see the problems but are afraid that management will either rate their performance poorly or may pull the plug on the whole project.

CHANGE MANAGEMENT CHALLENGES FOR ENTERPRISE SYSTEMS, BUSINESS PROCESS REENGINEERING, AND MERGERS AND ACQUISITIONS

Given the challenges of innovation and implementation, it is not surprising to find a very high failure rate among enterprise system and business process reengineering projects, which typically require extensive organizational change and which may require replacing old technologies and legacy systems that are deeply rooted in many interrelated business processes (Lloyd, Dewar, and Pooley, 1999). A number of studies have indicated that 70 percent of all BPR projects fail to deliver promised benefits. Likewise, 70 percent of all ERP projects fail to be fully implemented or to meet the goals of their users even after three years of work (Gillooly, 1998).

Many ERP and BPR projects have been undermined by poor implementation and change management practices that failed to address employees' concerns about change. Dealing with fear and anxiety throughout the organization; overcoming resistance by key managers; changing job functions, career paths, and recruitment practices; and poor training have posed greater threats to reengineering than the difficulties companies faced visualizing and designing breakthrough changes to business processes.

Enterprise systems create myriad interconnections among various business processes and data flows to ensure that information in one part of the business can be obtained by any other unit to help people eliminate redundant activities and to make better management decisions. Massive organizational changes are required to make this happen. Information that was previously maintained by different systems and different departments or functional areas must be integrated and made available to the company as a whole. Business processes must be tightly integrated, jobs must be redefined, and new procedures must be created throughout the company. Employees are often unprepared for these new procedures and roles (Davenport, 2000 and 1998).

System Implications of Mergers and Acquisitions

Mergers and acquisitions have been proliferating because they are a major growth engine for businesses. Potentially firms can cut costs significantly by merging with competitors, reduce risks by expanding into different industries (e.g., conglomeration), and create a larger pool of competitive knowledge and expertise by joining forces with other players. There are also economies of time: a firm can gain market share and expertise very quickly through acquisition rather than building over the long term.

MANAGING THE TRANSCANADA MEGAMERGER

TransCanada PipeLines Ltd. and Nova Corp. merged on July 1, 1998, accomplishing the largest merger in Canadian history to that date. The two had been the giants of Canadian natural gas and accompanying businesses. The merged company (also called TransCanada PipeLines Ltd. and located in Calgary, Alberta) had revenue of $17 billion and 4500 employees. The challenge for Russ Wells, TransCanada's new CIO, was to find a way to merge both companies' information technology infrastructures successfully.

The organizational differences between the two companies were immense. TransCanada's 250 IT employees were mostly allocated to various business units, with a separate information systems group for each business unit. A central IS group set their standards and architecture and provided common services such as telecommunications. On the other hand, Nova had outsourced almost all of IT work. Its only internal IS group was 18 employees who were responsible for governance and architecture.

Although both companies had some common desktop software such as Microsoft Office and Windows NT (the earlier version of Windows 2000), their IT infrastructures were very different. Nova ran Oracle software, Microsoft Internet Explorer, Windows NT, and Visual Basic and was in the midst of a multiyear implementation of SAP's enterprise software. TransCanada used Sun Microsystems' Forte and Java tools as well as software from Sybase, Novell, and Netscape Communications. TransCanada did not have a single enterprise system for the company, preferring best of breed applications for each business area.

Wells had to plan and begin to execute changes before senior management had developed a clear vision of the newly merged company. His plan called for spending the first year merging systems and platforms while postponing organizational restructuring until the second year. While Wells waited to make changes in the new company's IT organization, IT staff members started to worry about their jobs. Many became almost paranoid. Rumours flew about whether the

new company would outsource everything or whether the SAP enterprise system or best-of-breed applications would become new company standards.

Wells responded by setting up a decision board that included business leaders from the newly merged company. The group collectively devised decision criteria for TransCanada's new IT infrastructure, which would be based primarily on cost. A working committee then tried to objectively evaluate alternatives. Employees accepted their findings because they could see exactly how decisions were made.

Wells moved rapidly to create a reorganization plan that combined features of both merging companies' information systems groups and left most employees with jobs. Consultants that had previously been used by Nova were assigned a set of tasks but were placed under the direction of internal TransCanada staff. TransCanada would make its own strategic and architecture decisions. Hardware commodity services such as support for computers and telecommunications would be outsourced to IBM, which had performed that task for Nova. The new IT structure was in place in February 1999. The main lesson Wells and TransCanada learned was to keep staff well informed at all stages of a change.

TransCanada's management believes its new IT infrastructure is working very well. TransCanada has discarded Nova's SAP ERP application for its own best-of-breed applications. The company has been able to complete several mission-critical projects on time and on budget and the information technology budget for fiscal 2000 was 12.5 percent lower than pre-merger expenses in 1998.

To Think About: What management, organization, and technology issues were posed by the TransCanada merger? Evaluate the role of Wells and TransCanada's management in dealing with these issues. Do you think communicating with those affected by the changes in information systems is an effective part of change management? Why or why not?

Source: Kathleen Melymuka, "Rules of Engagement," *Computerworld*, July 24, 2000; Elizabeth U. Harding, "TransCanada Phases Out SAP, Goes for Best of Breed," *Software Magazine*, August 2000.

While some firms, such as Air Canada, which merged with Canadian Air Lines, or Toronto Dominion Bank, which merged with Canada Trust, are quite successful in carrying out mergers and acquisitions, research has found that more than 70 percent of all mergers and acquisitions result in a decline in shareholder value and often lead to divestiture at a later time (Braxton Associates, 1997; Economist 1997). A major reason that mergers and acquisitions fail is the difficulty of integrating the systems of different companies. Mergers and acquisitions are deeply affected by the organizational characteristics of the merging companies as well as by their information technology (IT) infrastructures. Combining the information systems of two different companies usually requires considerable organizational change and complex systems projects to manage. If the integration is not properly managed, firms can emerge with a tangled hodgepodge of inherited legacy systems built by aggregating the systems of one firm after another. Without successful systems integration, the benefits anticipated from the merger cannot be realized, or, worse, the merged entity cannot execute its business processes and loses customers.

When a company targeted for acquisition has been identified, information systems managers will need to identify the realistic costs of integration, the estimated benefits of economies in operation, scope, knowledge, and time, and any problematic systems that would require major investments to integrate. In addition, IT managers can critically estimate any likely costs and organizational changes required to upgrade the IT infrastructure or to make major systems improvements to support the merged companies. The Window on Management describes how TransCanada dealt with these issues.

▌▌.4 OVERVIEW OF SYSTEMS DEVELOPMENT

Whatever their scope and objectives, new information systems are an outgrowth of a process of organizational problem solving. A new information system is built as a solution to some type of problem or set of problems the organization perceives it is facing. The problem may be one where managers and employees realize that the organization is not performing as well as expected, or it may come from the realization that the organization should take advantage of new opportunities to perform more successfully.

systems development
The activities that go into producing an information systems solution to an organizational problem or opportunity.

The activities that go into producing an information system solution to an organizational problem or opportunity are called **systems development**. Systems development is a structured kind of problem solving with distinct activities. These activities consist of systems analysis, systems design, programming, testing, conversion, and production and maintenance. Other authors and IS professionals use different models of systems development, calling the activities by different names, but all of these models include the same steps and activities in almost the same order as the model we have used here. For example, a different model might be plan, analyze, design, implement, and maintain; activities involved in programming, testing, conversion, and production would all be subsumed under the implementation activity in this second model.

Figure 11-8 illustrates the systems development process. The systems development activities depicted here usually take place in sequential order, but some of the activities may need to be repeated or may take place simultaneously, depending on the approach to system building that is being employed. Each activity involves interaction with the organization. Members of the organization participate in these activities as the systems development process creates organizational changes.

SYSTEMS ANALYSIS

systems analysis
The analysis of a problem that the organization will try to solve with an information system.

Systems analysis is the analysis of the problem that the organization will try to solve with an information system. It consists of defining the problem, identifying its causes, specifying the solution, and identifying the information requirements that must be met by a system solution.

The systems analyst creates a road map of the existing organization and systems, identifying the primary owners and users of data in the organization. These stakeholders have a direct interest in the information affected by the new system. In addition to these organizational aspects, the analyst also briefly describes the existing hardware and software that serve the organization.

From this organizational analysis, the systems analyst details the problems of existing systems. By examining documents, work papers, and procedures; observing system operations; and interviewing key users of the systems, the analyst can identify the problem areas and objectives a solution would achieve. Often the solution requires building a new information system or improving an existing one.

The systems analysis would include a **feasibility study** to determine whether that solution was fea-

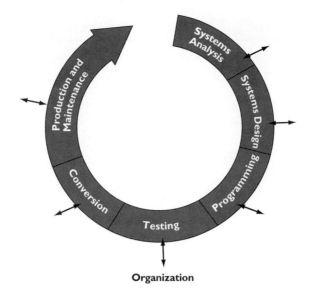

FIGURE 11-8 The systems development process. Each of the core systems development activities entails interaction with the organization.

sible or achievable from a financial, technical, legal, and organizational standpoint. The feasibility study would determine whether the proposed system was a good investment, whether the technology needed for the system was available and could be handled by the firm's information systems specialists, whether the new system abided by laws and regulations (such as privacy laws), and whether the organization could handle the changes introduced by the system.

Normally the systems analysis process will identify several alternative solutions that the organization can pursue. The analyst will then assess the feasibility of each. A written systems proposal report will describe the costs and benefits, advantages, and disadvantages of each alternative. It is up to management to determine which mix of costs, benefits, technical features, and organizational impacts represents the most desirable alternative.

feasibility study
A part of the systems analysis process; the way to determine whether the solution is achievable, given the organization's resources and constraints.

Establishing Information Requirements

Perhaps the most challenging task of the systems analyst is to define the specific information requirements that must be met by the system solution selected. At the most basic level, the **information requirements** of a new system involve identifying who needs what information, where, when, and how. Requirements analysis carefully defines the objectives of the new or modified system and develops a detailed description of the functions that the new system must perform. Faulty requirements analysis is a leading cause of systems failure and high systems development costs (see Section 11.3). A system designed around the wrong set of requirements will either have to be discarded because of poor performance or will need to undergo major modifications. Section 11.5 describes alternative approaches to eliciting requirements to help minimize this problem.

In many instances, building a new system creates an opportunity to redefine how the organization conducts its daily business. Some problems do not require an information system solution but instead need an adjustment in management, additional training, or refinement of existing organizational procedures. If the problem is information related, systems analysis may still be required to diagnose the problem and arrive at an appropriate solution.

information requirements
A detailed statement of the information needs that a new system must satisfy; identifies who needs what information, and when, where, and how the information is needed.

SYSTEMS DESIGN

Systems analysis describes what a system *should* do to meet information requirements while **systems design** shows *how* the system will fulfill this objective. The design of an information system is the overall plan or model for that system. Like the blueprint of a building or a house, it consists of all the specifications that give the system its form and structure.

The systems designer details the system specifications that will deliver the functions identified during systems analysis. These specifications should address all of the managerial, organizational, and technological components of the system solution. Table 11-8 lists the types of specifications that would be produced during systems design.

systems design
Details how a system will meet the information requirements determined during systems analysis.

TABLE 11-8   DESIGN SPECIFICATIONS

Output	Controls
Medium	Input controls (characters, limit, reasonableness)
Format	Processing controls (consistency, record counts)
Content	Output controls (totals, samples of output)
Timing	Procedural controls (passwords, special forms)
Input	Security
Origins	Access controls
Flow	Backups
Data entry	Hardware and software
User interface	Catastrophe plans
Simplicity	Audit trails
"Friendliness"	Documentation
Efficiency	Operations documentation
Logic	Systems documents
Feedback	User documentation
Errors	Conversion
Database design	Transfer files
Logical data relations	Clean/convert data
Volume and speed requirements	Initiate new procedures
File organization and design	Select testing method
Record specifications	Cut over to new system
Content/standardization/integration	Training
Processing	Select training techniques and trainers
Computations	Develop training modules
Program modules	Identify training facilities
Required reports	Identify those to be trained
Timing of processing and outputs	Schedule training
Manual procedures	Organizational changes
What activities	Task design/redesign
Who performs them	Job design/redesign
When	Process design/redesign
How	Office and organization structure design/redesign
Where	Reporting relationships

Like houses or buildings, information systems may have many possible designs. Each design represents a unique blend of technical and organizational components. What makes one design superior to others is the ease and efficiency with which it fulfills user requirements within a specific set of technical, organizational, financial, and time constraints.

The Role of End Users

User information requirements drive the entire systems development effort. Users must have sufficient control over the design process to ensure that the system reflects their business priorities and information needs, not the biases of the technical staff (Hunton and Beeler, 1997). Working on the design increases users' understanding and acceptance of the system, reducing problems caused by power transfers, intergroup conflict, and unfamiliarity with new system functions and procedures. As we described earlier, insufficient user involvement in the design effort is a major cause of system failure. However, some types of systems require more user participation in design than others and Section 11.5 shows how alternative systems development methods address user participation.

COMPLETING THE SYSTEMS DEVELOPMENT PROCESS

The remaining steps in the systems development process translate the solution specifications established during systems analysis and design into a fully operational information system.

Building successful information systems requires close cooperation among end users and information systems specialists throughout the systems development process.

These concluding steps consist of programming, testing, conversion, production, and maintenance.

Programming

During the **programming** stage, system specifications that were prepared during the design stage are translated into software program code. On the basis of detailed design documents for files, transaction and report layouts, and other design details, specifications for each program in the system are prepared. Organizations write the software programs themselves, purchase application software packages for this purpose, or hire consultants to develop their software.

Testing

Exhaustive and thorough **testing** must be conducted to ascertain whether the system produces the right results. Testing answers the question, "Will the system produce the desired results under known conditions?"

The amount of time needed to answer this question has been traditionally underrated in systems project planning (see Chapter 13). Testing is time consuming: Test data must be carefully prepared, results reviewed, and corrections made in the system. In some instances, parts of the system may have to be redesigned. The risks of taking this step too lightly are enormous.

Testing an information system can be broken down into three types of activities:

▌ **Unit testing**, or program testing, consists of testing each program separately in the system. It is widely believed that the purpose of unit testing is to guarantee that programs are error-free, but this goal is realistically impossible. Testing should be viewed instead as a means of locating errors in programs, focusing on finding all the ways to make a program fail. Once pinpointed, problems can be corrected.

▌ **System testing** tests the functioning of the information system as a whole. It tries to determine if discrete modules will function together as planned and whether discrepancies exist between the way the system actually works and the way it was conceived. Among the areas examined are performance time, capacity for file storage and handling peak loads, recovery and restart capabilities, and manual procedures.

▌ **Acceptance testing** provides the final certification that the system is ready to be used in a production setting. Systems tests are evaluated by users and reviewed by management. When all parties are satisfied that the new system meets their standards, the system is formally accepted for installation.

The systems development team works with users to devise a systematic test plan. The **test plan** includes all of the preparations for the series of tests we have just described.

Figure 11-9 shows an example of a test plan. The general condition being tested is a record change. The documentation consists of a series of test-plan screens maintained on a database (perhaps a microcomputer database) that is ideally suited to this kind of application.

programming
The process of translating the system specifications prepared during the design stage into program code.

testing
The exhaustive and thorough process that determines whether the system produces the desired results under known conditions.

unit testing
The process of testing each program separately in the system. Sometimes called program testing.

systems testing
Tests the functioning of the information system as a whole to determine if discrete modules will function together as planned.

acceptance testing
Provides the final certification that the system is ready to be used in a production setting.

test plan
Prepared by the development team in conjunction with users, it includes all of the preparations for the series of tests to be performed on the system.

FIGURE 11-9 A sample test plan to test a record change. When developing a test plan, it is imperative to include the various conditions to be tested, the requirements for each condition tested, and the expected results. Test plans require input from both end users and information systems specialists.

Procedure	Address and Maintenance "Record Change Series"		Test Series 2		
	Prepared By:	Date:	Version:		
Test Ref.	Condition Tested	Special Requirements	Expected Results	Output On	Next Screen
2	Change records				
2.1	Change existing record	Key field	Not allowed		
2.2	Change nonexistent record	Other fields	"Invalid key" message		
2.3	Change deleted record	Deleted record must be available	"Deleted" message		
2.4	Make second record	Change 2.1 above	OK if valid	Transaction file	V45
2.5	Insert record		OK if valid	Transaction file	V45
2.6	Abort during change	Abort 2.5	No change	Transaction file	V45

conversion
The process of changing from the old system to the new system.

parallel approach
A safe and conservative conversion method during which both the old system and its potential replacement are run together for a time until everyone is assured that the new one functions correctly.

direct cutover approach
A risky conversion method during which the new system completely replaces the old one on an appointed day.

pilot study approach
A fairly safe conversion method during which the new system is introduced to a limited area of the organization until it is proven to be fully functional; only then can the conversion to the new system across the entire organization take place.

phased approach
A fairly safe conversion method during which the new system is introduced in stages either by function or by organizational unit.

documentation
Descriptions of how an information system works from either a technical or end user standpoint.

production
The stage after the new system is installed and the conversion is complete; during this time the system is reviewed by users and technical specialists to determine how well it has met its original goals.

Conversion

Conversion is the process of changing from the old system to the new system. Four main conversion strategies can be employed: parallel, direct cutover, pilot study, and phased strategy.

In the **parallel approach,** both the old system and its potential replacement are run together for a time until everyone is assured that the new system functions correctly. This is the safest conversion approach because, in the event of errors or processing disruptions, the old system can still be used as a backup. However, this approach is very expensive, and additional staff or resources may be required to run the extra system.

The **direct cutover approach** replaces the old system entirely with the new system on an appointed day. At first glance, this strategy seems less costly than the parallel conversion strategy. However, it is a very risky approach that can potentially be more costly than parallel activities if serious problems with the new system are found, because there is no other system to fall back on. Disruptions and the cost of corrections may be enormous.

The **pilot study approach** introduces the new system to only a limited area of the organization, such as a single department or operating unit. When the pilot version is complete and working smoothly, it is installed throughout the rest of the organization, either simultaneously or in stages.

The **phased approach** introduces the new system in stages, either by functions or by organizational units. If, for example, the system is introduced by functions, a new payroll system might begin with hourly workers who are paid weekly, followed six months later by adding salaried employees (who are paid monthly) to the system. If the system is introduced by organizational units, corporate headquarters might be converted first, followed by outlying operating units four months later. The difference in the phased approach using organizational units and the pilot study approach is that the pilot study approach begins with a smaller, less significant unit while the phased approach could begin with a larger or critical unit.

Moving from an old system to a new one requires that end users be trained to use the new system. Detailed **documentation** showing how the system works from both a technical and end user standpoint is finalized during conversion time for use in training and everyday operations. Lack of proper training and documentation contributes to system failure, so this portion of the systems development process is very important.

Production and Maintenance

After the new system is installed and conversion is complete, the system is said to be in **production**. During this stage, the system will be reviewed by both users and technical specialists to determine how well it has met its original objectives and to decide whether any revisions or modifications are needed. Changes in hardware, software, documentation, or

TABLE 11-9 SYSTEMS DEVELOPMENT

Core Activity	Description
Systems analysis	Identify problem(s)
	Specify solution
	Establish information requirements
Systems design	Create logical design specifications
	Create physical design specifications
	Manage technical realization of system
Programming	Translate design specifications into program code
Testing	Unit test
	Systems test
	Acceptance test
Conversion	Plan conversion
	Prepare documentation
	Train users and technical staff
	Convert
Production and maintenance	Operate the system
	Evaluate the system
	Modify the system and relevant documentation

procedures to a production system to correct errors, meet new requirements, or improve processing efficiency are termed **maintenance**.

Studies of maintenance have examined the amount of time required for various maintenance tasks (Lientz and Swanson, 1980). Approximately 20 percent of the time is devoted to debugging or correcting emergency production problems; another 20 percent is concerned with changes in data, files, reports, hardware, or system software. But 60 percent of all maintenance work consists of making user enhancements, improving documentation, and recoding system components for greater processing efficiency. The amount of work in the third category of maintenance problems could be reduced significantly through better systems analysis and design practices. Table 11-9 summarizes the systems development activities.

maintenance
Changes in hardware, software, documentation, or procedures to a production system to correct errors, meet new requirements, or improve processing efficiency.

11.5 ALTERNATIVE SYSTEMS DEVELOPMENT APPROACHES

Systems differ in terms of their size and technological complexity, and in terms of the organizational problems they are meant to solve. Because there are different kinds of systems, a number of methods have been developed to build systems. This section describes these alternative methods: the traditional systems development life cycle (SDLC), prototyping, application software packages, end user development, and outsourcing.

TRADITIONAL SYSTEMS DEVELOPMENT LIFE CYCLE

The **systems development life cycle (SDLC)** is the oldest method for building information systems and is still used today for medium or large complex systems projects. It most closely resembles the system development activities discussed in the previous section. The systems development life cycle has six stages: (1) project definition, (2) systems study, (3) design, (4) programming, (5) installation, and (6) post-implementation. Again, there are other models of the SDLC, but all of these models contain the same steps in basically the same order. Figure 11-10 illustrates these stages. Each stage consists of basic activities that must be performed before the next stage can begin.

The SDLC methodology has a very formal division of labour between end users and information systems specialists. Technical specialists such as systems analysts and program-

systems development life cycle (SDLC)
A traditional methodology for developing an information system that partitions the systems development process into formal stages that must be completed sequentially with a very formal division of labour between end users and information systems specialists.

FIGURE 11-10 The systems development life cycle methodology. The SDLC methodology divides systems development into formal stages with specific milestones and products at each stage.

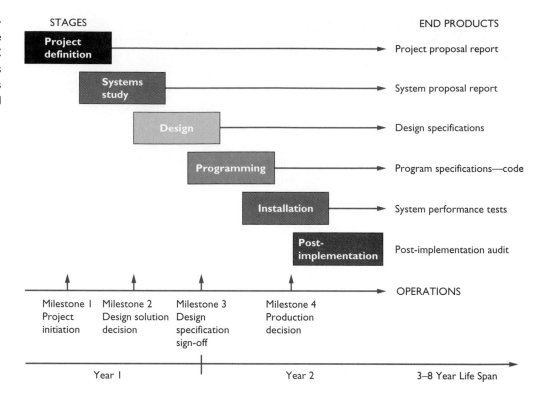

project definition
A stage in the systems development life cycle that determines whether the organization has a problem and whether the problem can be solved by launching a system project.

systems study
A stage in the systems development life cycle that analyzes the problems of existing systems, defines the objectives a solution will attain, and evaluates various solution alternatives.

design
A stage in the systems development life cycle that produces the logical and physical design specifications for the system solution.

programming
A stage in the systems development life cycle that translates the design specifications produced during the design stage into software program code.

installation
A stage in the systems development life cycle consisting of testing, training, and conversion; the final steps required to put a system into operation.

post-implementation
The final stage of the systems development life cycle in which the system is used and evaluated while in production and is modified to make improvements or meet new requirements.

mers are responsible for much of the systems analysis, design, and implementation work; end users are normally limited to providing information requirements and reviewing the technical staff's work.

Stages of the Systems Development Life Cycle

The **project definition** stage determines whether the organization has a problem and whether that problem can be solved by building a new information system or by modifying an existing one. The **systems study** stage analyzes the problems of existing systems (manual or automated) in detail, identifies objectives to be attained by a solution to these problems, and describes alternative solutions. Much of the information gathered during the systems study phase will be used to determine information system requirements. A systems study report and/or feasibility report are the potential deliverables at the end of this stage, perhaps in the form of a proposal to management for a system to be developed.

The **design** stage produces the logical and physical design specifications for the solution. The SDLC emphasizes formal specifications and paperwork, so many design documents are generated during this stage. Logical and physical designs, with accompanying charts and diagrams, are the deliverable from this stage. The **programming** stage translates the design specifications produced during the design stage into software program code. Systems analysts work with programmers to prepare specifications for each program in the system. The actual programs and program documentation are the deliverables of this stage.

The **installation** stage consists of the final steps to put the new or modified system into operation: testing, training, and conversion. Completed documentation and testing documents, including sign-off documents, are typical installation deliverables. The **post-implementation** stage consists of using and evaluating the system after it is installed and is in production. Users and technical specialists will go through a formal post-implementation audit that determines how well the new system has met its original objectives and whether any revisions or modifications are required. After the system has been fine-tuned, it will need to be maintained while it is in production to correct errors, meet requirements, or improve processing efficiency. Over time, the system may require so much maintenance to remain efficient and meet user objectives that it will come to the end of its useful life span. Once the SDLC comes to an end, a new system may be called for, and theSDLC may begin again.

Limitations of the SDLC Approach

The SDLC is still used for building large complex systems that require a rigorous and formal requirements analysis, predefined specifications, and tight controls over the systems development process. However, the SDLC approach is costly, time-consuming, and inflexible. Volumes of new documents must be generated and steps repeated if requirements and specifications need to be revised. Because of the time and cost to repeat the sequence of life cycle activities, the methodology encourages freezing of specifications early in the development process, discouraging change. The SDLC approach is also not suitable for many small desktop systems, which tend to be less structured and more individualized.

PROTOTYPING

Prototyping consists of building an experimental system rapidly and inexpensively for end users to evaluate. By interacting with the prototype, users can get a better idea of their information requirements. The prototype endorsed by the users can be used as a template to create the final system.

The **prototype** is a working version of an information system or part of the system, but it is meant to be only a preliminary model. Once operational, the prototype will be further refined until it conforms precisely to user requirements. Once the design has been finalized, the prototype can be converted to a polished production system. In addition to being a development methodology, prototyping can be used as a tool to investigate information requirements and to perform logical design.

The process of building a preliminary design, trying it out, refining it, and trying again has been called an **iterative** process of systems development because the steps required to build a system can be repeated over and over again. Prototyping is more explicitly iterative than the conventional SDLC, and it actively promotes system design changes. It has been said that prototyping replaces unplanned rework with planned iteration, with each version more accurately reflecting users' requirements.

Steps in Prototyping

Figure 11-11 shows a four-step model of the prototyping process, which consists of the following:

Step 1: *Identify basic user requirements.* The systems designer (usually an information systems specialist) works with users only long enough to capture their basic information needs.

Step 2: *Develop an initial prototype.* The system designer creates a working prototype quickly, using fourth-generation software, interactive multimedia, or computer-aided software engineering (CASE) tools described later in this chapter.

Step 3: *Use the prototype.* Users are encouraged to work with the system in order to determine how well the prototype meets their needs and to make suggestions for improving the prototype.

Step 4: *Revise and enhance the prototype.* The system

prototyping
The process of building an experimental system quickly and inexpensively for demonstration and evaluation so that users can better determine information requirements.

prototype
The preliminary working version of an information system for demonstration and evaluation purposes.

iterative
A process of repeating over and over again the steps to develop a system.

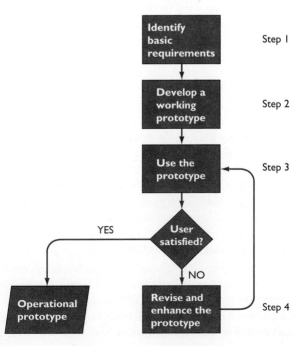

FIGURE 11-11 The prototyping process. The process of developing a prototype can be broken down into four steps. Because a prototype can be developed quickly and inexpensively, system builders can go through several iterations, repeating steps 3 and 4, to refine and enhance the prototype before arriving at the final operational one.

builder notes all changes requested by the users and refines the prototype accordingly. After the prototype has been revised, the cycle returns to step 3. Steps 3 and 4 are repeated until the users are satisfied.

When no more iterations are required, the approved prototype then becomes an operational prototype that furnishes the final specifications for the application. Sometimes the prototype itself is adopted as the production version of the system.

Advantages and Disadvantages of Prototyping

end user interface
The part of an information system through which the end user interacts with the system, such as online screens, commands, and reports.

Prototyping is most useful when there is some uncertainty about requirements or design solutions. Prototyping is especially useful in designing an information system's **end user interface** (the part of the system that end users interact with, such as online display and data-entry screens, reports, or Web pages). Since prototyping encourages intense end user involvement throughout systems development (Cerveny et al., 1986), it is more likely to produce systems that fulfill user requirements.

However, rapid prototyping can gloss over essential steps in systems development. If the completed prototype works reasonably well, management may not see the need for reprogramming, redesign, or full documentation and testing to build a polished production system. Some of these hastily constructed systems may not easily accommodate large quantities of data or a large number of users in a production environment. They may also not have necessary security controls built in. Finally, users may become dissatisfied when months pass between approving the prototype and delivery of the finished system.

APPLICATION SOFTWARE PACKAGES

application software package
A set of prewritten, precoded application software programs that are commercially available for sale or lease.

Information systems can be developed using software from **application software packages**, which we introduced in Chapter 7. There are many applications that are common to all business organizations—for example, payroll, accounts receivable, general ledger, or inventory control. For such universal functions with standard procedures, a generalized system will fulfill the requirements of many organizations. Even if the decision is to purchase a software package, the systems development life cycle is still followed. In the initial stage, feasibility and information requirements analyses are undertaken. During the design stage, the decision to purchase a software package is made, and potential packages are reviewed. A decision is made, and rather than a programming stage per se, the package is purchased or leased and customized to the organization. Implementation then proceeds, followed by maintenance.

If a software package can fulfill most of an organization's requirements, the company does not have to write its own software. The company can save time and money by using the prewritten, predesigned, pretested software programs from the package. Package vendors supply much of the ongoing maintenance and support for the system, providing enhancements to keep the system in line with ongoing technical and business developments.

customization
The modification of a software package to meet an organization's unique requirements without destroying the package software's integrity.

If an organization has unique requirements that the package does not address, many packages include capabilities for customization. **Customization** features allow a software package to be modified to meet an organization's unique requirements without destroying the integrity of the packaged software. If a great deal of customization is required, additional programming and customization work may become so expensive and time-consuming that they eliminate many of the advantages of software packages. Figure 11-12 shows how package costs in relation to total implementation costs rise with the degree of customization. The initial purchase price of the package can be deceptive because of these hidden implementation costs. Finally, an organization may pay for more "bells and whistles" than it needs when it purchases or leases a packaged application.

Selecting Software Packages

Request for Proposal (RFP)
A detailed list of questions submitted to vendors of software or other services to determine how well the vendor's product can meet the organization's specific requirements.

When a system is developed using an application software package, systems analysis will include a package evaluation effort. The most important evaluation criteria are the functions provided by the package, flexibility, user-friendliness, hardware and software requirements, database requirements, installation and maintenance effort, documentation, vendor quality, and cost. The package evaluation process often is based on a **Request for Proposal (RFP)**, which is a detailed list of questions submitted to packaged software vendors.

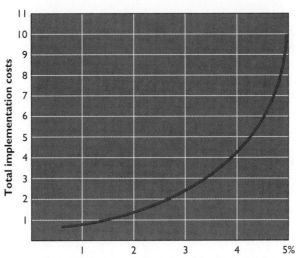

When a software package solution is selected, the organization no longer has total control over the system design process. Instead of tailoring the system design specifications directly to user requirements, the design effort will consist of trying to mould user requirements to conform to the features of the package. If the organization's requirements conflict with the way the package works and the package cannot be customized, the organization will have to adapt to the package and change its procedures.

END USER DEVELOPMENT

Some types of information systems can be developed by end users with little or no formal assistance from technical specialists. This is called **end user development**. Using fourth-generation languages, graphics languages, and PC software tools, end users can access data,

end user development
The development of information systems by end users with little or no formal assistance from technical specialists.

MANAGEMENT DECISION PROBLEM

PRICING A SOFTWARE PACKAGE

Your rapidly growing pharmaceutical company has 24 sales representatives, annual sales of $20 million, and an extensive inventory of products that it markets to hospitals and health care facilities. The sales department has used slick brochures, printed catalogues, and PowerPoint presentations to present information to customers about products, but you would like to be able to create custom catalogues and PowerPoint presentations for customer sales calls that are tailored to different selling situations. You have found a sales software package called PowerSales that provides these capabilities and that can link automatically into the firm's enterprise resource planning (ERP) system to reflect changes in pricing, availability, and new products. The software also provides sales managers with forecasts and detailed reports of each sales call. The package vendor has suggested the following pricing option:

Base software

One-time installation charge	$115 000
Annual license charge	$75 000

Custom content (one-time charges) for the entire sales force

Specific product promotions and product introduction	$130 000
Product line overview presentations	$65 000
Sales skills training	$57 500

Your company plans to use the same content for two years. After determining the initial software configuration, the package vendor supplies a consultant to guide the customization process, working with the client to provide text graphics, animation, audio, and video content for the system. The cost of the consultant is $2000 per day. You have been told that it would take about 50 days of consulting time to customize and complete implementation. Your firm would not need to purchase any new hardware to run the package, but you would need an information systems specialist at an annual salary of $75 000 to spend 20 hours per month supporting the package.

1. What are the total costs of using this package for the first year? For subsequent years?

2. The package vendor claims that after implementing the package, its customers have increased sales by an average of 10 percent over two years. How much increase in sales revenue should your company anticipate if you implement this package?

3. What additional information would be useful to guide your purchase decision?

create reports, and develop entire information systems on their own, with little or no help from professional systems analysts or programmers. Most of these end user developed systems can be created much more rapidly than with the traditional systems development life cycle. Figure 11-13 illustrates the concept of end user development.

Benefits and Limitations of End User Development

Many organizations have reported gains in application development productivity by using fourth-generation tools that in a few cases have reached 300 to 500 percent (Glass, 1999; Green, 1984–85; Harel, 1985). Allowing users to specify their own business needs improves requirements gathering and often leads to a higher level of user involvement and satisfaction with the system. However, fourth-generation tools still cannot replace conventional tools for some business applications because they cannot easily handle the processing of large numbers of transactions or applications with extensive procedural logic and updating requirements.

End user computing also poses organizational risks because it occurs outside of traditional mechanisms for information systems management and control. When systems are created rapidly, without a formal development methodology, testing and documentation may be inadequate. Control over data can be lost in systems outside the traditional information systems department (see Chapter 8). Finally, time and effort can be wasted either by users spending too much away from their normal duties developing systems or through duplication of end user developed systems. For example, a sales representative could spend a great deal of time developing their own sales contact system, neglecting their own sales duties, while at the same time, another sales representative had already created a suitable sales contact system.

Managing End User Development

To help organizations maximize the benefits of end user applications development, management should control the development of end user applications by requiring cost justification of end user information system projects and by establishing hardware, software, and quality standards for user-developed applications.

When end user computing first became popular, organizations used information centres to promote standards for hardware and software so that end users would not introduce disparate and incompatible technologies into the firm (Fuller and Swanson, 1992). **Information centres** are special facilities housing hardware, software, and technical specialists to supply end users with tools, training, and expert advice so they can create information system applications on their own or increase their productivity. The role of information cen-

information centre
A special facility within an organization that provides training and support for end user computing.

FIGURE 11-13 End user versus SDLC development. End users can access computerized information directly or develop information systems with little or no formal technical assistance. On the whole, end user developed systems can be completed more rapidly than those developed through the conventional SDLC.

Source: Application Development Without Programmers, by James Martin, 1982. Reprinted by permission of Prentice-Hall Inc., Upper Saddle River, NJ.

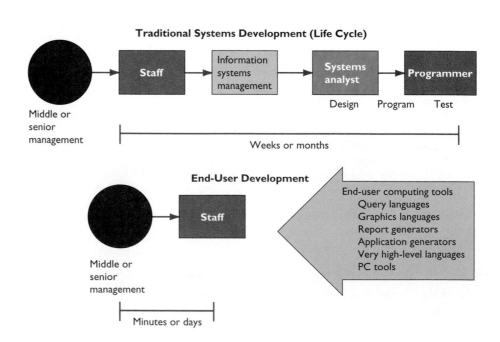

tres is diminishing as end users become more computer-literate, but organizations still need to closely monitor and manage end user development.

OUTSOURCING

If a firm does not want to use its internal resources to develop or operate information systems, it can hire an external organization that specializes in providing these services. The process of turning over an organization's computer centre operations, telecommunications networks, or applications development to external vendors is called **outsourcing**. The application service providers described in Chapter 7 are one form of outsourcing. Subscribing companies use the software and computer hardware provided by the ASP as the technical platform for their system. In another form of outsourcing, a company can hire an external vendor to design and create the software for its system, but that company would operate the system on its own computer. The Window on Management describes how one start-up company benefited from outsourcing its Web site.

Outsourcing has become popular because some organizations perceive it as more cost-effective than maintaining their own computer centre or information systems staff. The provider of outsourcing services benefits from economies of scale (the same knowledge, skills, and capacity can be shared with many different customers) and is likely to charge competitive prices for information systems services. Outsourcing allows a company with fluctuating needs for computer processing to pay for only what it uses rather than to build its own computer centre, which would be underutilized when there is no peak load. Some firms outsource because their internal information systems staff cannot keep pace with technological change or innovative business practices or because they want to free up scarce and costly talent for activities with higher payback.

Not all organizations benefit from outsourcing, and the disadvantages of outsourcing can create serious problems for organizations if they are not well understood and managed (Earl, 1996). When major applications are outsourced, some of the organization's most experienced and skilled IS staff may decide to leave, leaving the organization without the technical expertise it may still need. When a firm allocates the responsibility for developing and operating its information systems to another organization, it can lose control over its information systems function. If the organization lacks the expertise to negotiate a sound contract, the firm's dependence on the vendor could result in high costs or loss of control over technological direction (Lacity, Willcocks, and Feeny, 1996). Firms should be especially cautious when using an outsourcer to develop or to operate applications that give it some type of competitive advantage.

outsourcing
The practice of contracting computer centre operations, telecommunications networks, or applications development to external vendors.

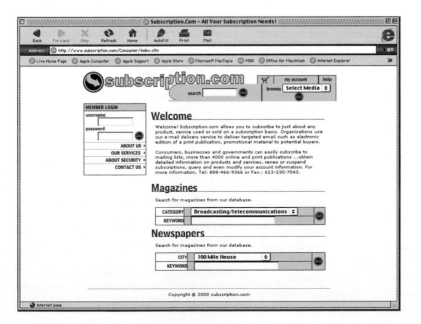

FIGURE 11-14 Customers can search for a variety of magazines and newspapers to which they wish to subscribe and then enter their subscription orders online at Subscription.com.

SUBSCRIPTION.COM INVENTS MEDIA AND PUBLISHING E-MARKETPLACE

If anything defines consumerism, it is freedom of choice. But with choice comes the responsibility of making informed decisions. And as consumers and marketers alike are inundated with information, that is becoming increasingly hard to do.

Take subscriptions, for example. Consumers spend long hours evaluating and subscribing to newspapers, magazines, entertainment and sports events, electronic information services, and other subscription-based products and services. At the same time, publishers and promoters of these services, as well as their fulfillment houses, require extensive budgets and technical resources just to manage the subscriptions and support their subscriber base.

It was inevitable that some enterprising company would see these challenges as a lucrative business opportunity. That company was Ottawa-based Business Interactive Corp. (BI). BI specializes in providing e-commerce transaction services that free companies to focus on boosting sales rather than on administering back-end activities such as order processing and fulfillment.

For the media and publishing industries, BI wanted to create a business-to-consumer (B2C) subscription management service called Subscription.com (see Figure 11-14). As an e-marketplace, Subscription.com would bring subscribers and subscription providers together, giving subscribers a more organized view of subscription offerings while providing publishers and service providers exposure to a broader range of more affluent, Web-savvy subscribers. Publishers and service providers would also gain access to a proven Web-based subscription application without the costs of developing and maintaining this type of application themselves. Overall, this would reduce the publisher's cost of subscription management by 20 percent.

But for BI, providing a turnkey service meant much more than developing a high-performance front-end application that subscribers could interact with over the Internet. It also required enabling the Web application to access the back-end databases of the companies offering subscriptions. BI used IBM's WebSphere Application Server, Advanced Edition, IBM Net.Commerce (now part of the IBM WebSphere Commerce Suite family of products), IBM Net.Data, and IBM DB2 Universal Database to accomplish all of this.

BI had already used Net.Commerce and Net.Data to build an e-business infrastructure for its other transaction services. By leveraging this infrastructure, BI was able to bring Subscription.com to market in just six weeks. Now, following the architectural roadmap provided by the IBM Application Framework for e-business, BI is engaging WebSphere Application Server to support enhancements to Subscription.com that will enable better back-end integration. "WebSphere Application Server supports XML and Java," says Guy Vales, BI's vice president of e-business and Web application development. "We believe these technologies will play an increasingly vital role in e-business."

More important, using WebSphere is expected to make a vital contribution to BI's bottom line. Revenues derived from the transaction processing service and from mining subscriber

demographics to marketing analysts are expected to reach between $1 million and $10 million in the first 18 months. "Following the Application Framework for e-business, we were able to deliver this e-business service early and capture a very ripe market," Vales notes. "As a result, we expect to achieve a full return on our investment in 24 months."

Subscription.com allows consumers to find and learn about numerous subscription-based services, subscribe to them online, and manage their subscription details—all from a single Web site. Consumers logging on to Subscription.com can search the subscription database by category and keyword. Subscription names and descriptions, along with links to the publisher's or service provider's Web sites, are stored in a DB2 Universal Database residing on a Netfinity 3500 server inside BI's firewall.

To safeguard their e-commerce transactions, consumers are asked to register with Subscription.com before subscribing, and that information is also stored in DB2. Net.Commerce provides the shopping cart and checkout functions and accesses the DB2 customer information database to process the subscription orders.

An e-mail publishing service, powered by Lotus Domino and running on another Netfinity server behind the firewall, allows publishers to add an e-mail edition to a print publication or to deliver information to large groups of people on a periodic basis using Internet e-mail. Businesses can also use Subscription.com to inform customers of price changes and obtain feedback from them.

The subscription information must be relayed back to the publisher's or provider's back-end systems, and the publishers and providers need to be able to easily post their content to Subscription.com. BI is using IBM's VisualAge for Java to develop the Java servlets that will enable these functions, taking advantage of the server's support for XML to perform application-to-application data transfer between BI and the back-end systems of the providers. WebSphere Application Server provides the runtime environment for these servlets.

For most customers, BI uses an application service provider (ASP) model to offer Subscription.com as a turnkey Internet subscription management service. But it also offers customized versions of Subscription.com for larger businesses that want to host the services at their own facilities. Creating libraries of objects in WebSphere Application Server allows BI to reuse existing business logic to customize the application quickly—typically in two to four weeks, according to Vales.

In addition, while Subscription.com primarily represents Canadian publishers at this time, BI is expanding its marketing to attract U.S. and European publishers—offering the subscription management system in French and English.

To Think About: What are the management benefits of outsourcing the development of a Web site? What are the disadvantages?

Sources: "Subscription.com Invents Media and Publishing E-Marketplace," IBM Case Study, available http://www-4.ibm.com/software/solutions/internet/g325-6698-00.pdf, accessed June 21, 2001; Subscription.com Web site, available www.subscription.com, accessed June 21, 2001; Business Interactive Corp. Web site, available www.businteractive.com, accessed June 21, 2001.

TABLE 11-10   COMPARISON OF SYSTEMS-DEVELOPMENT APPROACHES

Approach	Features	Advantages	Disadvantages
Systems development life cycle	Sequential step-by-step formal process Written specification and approvals Limited role of users	Necessary for large complex systems and projects	Slow and expensive Discourages changes Massive paperwork to manage
Prototyping	Requirements specified dynamically with experimental system Rapid, informal, and iterative process Users continually interact with the prototype	Rapid and relatively inexpensive Useful when requirements uncertain or when end-user interface is very important Promotes user participation	Inappropriate for large, complex systems Can gloss over steps in analysis, documentation, and testing
Applications software package	Commercial software eliminates need for internally developed software programs	Design, programming, installation, and maintenance work reduced Can save time and cost when developing common business applications Reduces need for internal information systems resources	May not meet organization's unique requirements May not perform many business functions well Extensive customization raises development costs
End user development	Systems created by end users using fourth-generation software tools Rapid and informal Minimal role of information systems specialists	Users control systems development Saves development time and cost Reduces application backlog	Can lead to proliferation of uncontrolled information systems and data Systems do not always meet quality assurance standards
Outsourcing	Systems build and sometimes operated by external vendor	Can reduce or control costs Can produce systems when internal resources are not available or technically deficient	Loss of control over the information systems function Dependence on the technical direction and prosperity of external vendors

Table 11-10 compares the advantages and disadvantages of each of the system-building alternatives.

OBJECT-ORIENTED SOFTWARE DEVELOPMENT, UNIFIED MODELLING LANGUAGE, RAPID APPLICATION DEVELOPMENT, AND JOINT APPLICATION DESIGN

Chapter 7 explained that object-oriented programming combines data and the specific procedures that operate on those data into one object. Object-oriented programming is part of a larger approach to systems development called object-oriented software development. **Object-oriented software development** differs from traditional systems development approaches by shifting the focus from separately modelling business processes and data to combining data and procedures into unified objects.

The system is viewed as a collection of classes and objects and includes the relationships among them. The objects are defined, programmed, tested, documented, and saved as building blocks to be used and re-used in future applications. Organizations are increasingly turning to object-oriented software development in the hope of building systems that are more flexible and easier to develop and maintain.

Objects are easily reusable, so object-oriented software development is expected to reduce the time and cost of writing software because organizations can reuse software objects that have already been created as building blocks for other applications. New systems can be created by using some existing objects as is, changing others, and adding a few new objects. Object-oriented development is very useful for creating Web applications. Of course, no organization will see savings from reusability until it builds up a library of objects to draw on and understands which objects have broad use (Pancake, 1995). In theory, design and pro-

object-oriented software development

An approach to software development that de-emphasizes procedures and shifts the focus from modelling business processes and data to combining data and procedures to create objects.

gramming can begin as soon as requirements are completed through the use of iterations of rapid prototyping. Object-oriented frameworks have been developed to provide reusable semi-complete applications that the organization can further customize into finished applications (Fayad and Schmidt, 1997). However, information systems specialists must learn a completely new way of modelling a system. Conversion to an object-oriented approach may require large-scale organizational investments, which management must balance against the anticipated payoffs.

Unified Modelling Language

Unified Modelling Language (UML) is a standard notation for the modelling of real-world objects as a first step in developing an object-oriented design methodology. Vendors of computer-aided software engineering products support UML, and it has been endorsed by almost every maker of software development products, including IBM and Microsoft (for its Visual Basic environment). Among the concepts of modelling that UML specifies how to describe are: class (of objects), object, association, responsibility, activity, interface, use case (similar to a scenario), package, sequence, collaboration, and state.

Rapid Application Development and Joint Application Development

Object-oriented software tools, reusable software, prototyping, and fourth-generation tools are helping systems developers create working systems much more rapidly than traditional systems development methods and software tools (see Figure 11-15). The term **rapid application development (RAD)** is used to describe this process of creating workable systems in a very short period of time. RAD can include the use of visual programming and other tools for building graphical user interfaces, iterative prototyping of key system elements, the automation of program code generation, and close teamwork among end users and information systems specialists. Simple systems often can be assembled from pre-built components. The process does not have to be sequential, and key parts of development can occur simultaneously.

Sometimes a technique called **JAD (joint application design)** is used to accelerate the generation of information requirements and to develop the initial systems design. JAD brings end users and information systems specialists together in an interactive session to discuss the systems design. Properly prepared and facilitated, JAD sessions can significantly speed the design phase while involving users at an intense level. Normally, JAD sessions take place away from the normal place of business to ensure that everyone involved can concentrate on the project and not be interrupted by their normal work.

---

unified modelling language (UML)

A standard notation for modelling real-world objects as a first step in developing an object-oriented design methodology.

rapid application development (RAD)

A process for developing systems in a very short time period by using prototyping, fourth-generation tools, and close teamwork among users and systems specialists.

joint application design (JAD)

A process to accelerate the generation of information requirements by having end users and information systems specialists work together in intensive interactive design sessions.

FIGURE 11-15 Gatsby Database Explorer generates a user-friendly interface to Microsoft Access and SQL Server databases that allows users to edit, view, and search database content over an intranet or extranet. This RAD development tool enables companies to create rapid solutions without special programming.

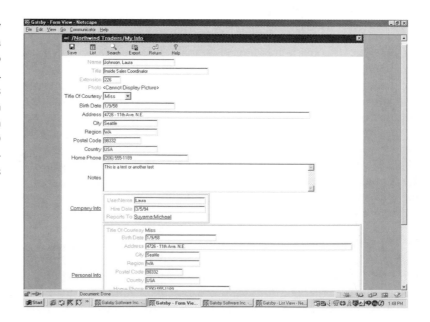

APPLICATION SOFTWARE EXERCISE

SYSTEMS DEVELOPMENT AT KTP CONSULTING: DEVELOPING A JOB DATABASE AND WEB SITE

KTP Consulting of Hamilton, Ontario operates in various locations around the world. KTP specializes in designing, developing, and implementing enterprise systems for medium- to large-sized companies. KTP offers its employees opportunities to travel, live, and work in various locations throughout North America, Europe, and Asia.

KTP's human resources department has a simple database that enables its staff to track job vacancies. When an employee is interested in relocating, he or she contacts the human resources department for a list of KTP job vacancies. KTP also posts its employment opportunities on the company Web site.

What type of data do you think is included in the KTP job vacancies database? What information should not be included in this database? Based on your answers to these questions, build a replica of how you think the KTP job vacancies database should look. Populate the database with at least 20 records. You should also build a simple Web page that incorporates job vacancy data from your newly created database. Submit a disk containing a copy of the KTP database and Web page to your professor.

MANAGEMENT WRAP-UP

Selection of a systems development approach can have a large impact on the time, cost, and end product of systems development. Managers should be aware of the strengths and weaknesses of each systems development approach and the types of problems for which each is best suited.

Organizational needs should drive the selection of a systems development approach. The impact of application software packages and outsourcing should be carefully evaluated before either is selected because these approaches give organizations less control over the systems development process.

Various software tools are available to support the systems development process. Key technology decisions should be based on the organization's familiarity with the technology and its compatibility with the organization's information requirements and information architecture.

For Discussion

1. Why is selecting a systems development approach an important business decision? Who should participate in the selection process?

2. Some have said that the best way to reduce system development costs is to use application software packages or fourth-generation tools. Do you agree? Why or why not?

SUMMARY

1. *Demonstrate how building new systems can produce organizational change.* Building a new information system is a form of planned organizational change that involves many different people in the organization. Because information systems are sociotechnical entities, a change in information systems involves changes in work, management, and the organization. Four kinds of technology-enabled change are (1) automation, (2) rationalization of procedures, (3) business reengineering,

and (4) paradigm shift, with far-reaching changes carrying the greatest risks and rewards. Many organizations are attempting business reengineering to redesign workflows and business processes in the hope of achieving dramatic productivity breakthroughs while others use TQM to achieve incremental improvements.

2. *Explain how the organization can develop information systems that fit its business plan.* Organizations should develop information systems plans that describe how information technology supports the attainment of their business goals. The plans indicate the direction of systems development, its rationale, implementation strategy, and budget. Enterprise analysis and critical success factors (CSFs) can be used to elicit organization-wide information requirements that must be addressed by the plans.

3. *Describe the problems and challenges involved in change management.* Every systems development project represents change, and every information systems professional is a change agent. Appropriate change management can forestall problems caused by users who resent the change, do not want to change the way they work, or cannot understand the need for the change. An appropriate amount of user involvement can help to reassure users and to help them to take ownership of the systems change as well as helping to resolve any user requirement problems that might arise. Adequate support from management, coupled with communication about the change, can also support change management and systems development issues.

4. *Discuss the reasons some information systems projects succeed and others fail.* In addition to change management issues, the complexity, size, and structure of the project can make information systems projects very difficult to implement. If these issues are not handled properly, perhaps by outsourcing, the project may fail. In addition, management of systems development, including proper planning techniques, can make or break a systems project. Finally, user requirements must be "frozen" in the analysis stage or the cost, time, and effort of the project may make the project unwieldy or poorly received.

5. *Identify the core activities in the systems development process.* The core activities in systems development are systems analysis, systems design, programming, testing, conversion, production, and maintenance. Systems analysis is the study and analysis of problems of existing systems and the identification of requirements for their solution. Systems design provides the specifications for an information system solution, showing how its technical and organizational components fit together.

6. *Evaluate alternatives for building systems: the traditional systems development life cycle, prototyping, application software packages, end user development, and outsourcing.* The traditional systems development life cycle—the oldest method for building systems—breaks the development of an information system into six formal stages: (1) project definition, (2) systems study, (3) design, (4) programming, (5) installation, and (6) post-implementation. The stages must proceed sequentially and have defined outputs; each requires formal approval before the next stage can commence. The systems development life cycle is useful for large projects that need formal specifications and tight management control over each stage of systems development. However, this approach is very rigid and costly and is not well suited for unstructured, decision-oriented applications where requirements cannot be immediately presented.

Prototyping is building an experimental system rapidly and inexpensively for end users to interact with and evaluate. The prototype is refined and enhanced until users are satisfied that it includes all of their requirements and can be used as a template to create the final system. Prototyping encourages end user involvement in systems development and iteration of design until specifications are captured accurately. The rapid creation of prototypes can result in systems that have not been completely tested or documented or that are technically inadequate for a production environment.

Developing an information system using an application software package eliminates the need for writing software programs when developing an information system. Using a software package cuts down on the amount of design, testing, installation, and maintenance work required to develop a system. Application software packages are helpful if a firm does not have the internal information systems staff or financial resources to custom-develop a system. To meet an organization's unique requirements, packages may require extensive modifications that can substantially raise development costs.

End user development is the development of information systems by end users, either alone or with minimal assistance from information systems specialists. End user-developed systems can be created rapidly and informally using fourth-generation software tools. The primary benefits of end user development are improved requirements determination, reduced application backlog, and increased end user participation in and control of the systems development process. However, end user development, in conjunction with distributed computing, has introduced new organizational risks by propagating information systems and data resources that do not necessarily meet quality assurance standards and that are not easily controlled by traditional means. End user development also wastes time and effort devoted to the end user's "real job" and may produce duplicated systems.

Outsourcing consists of using an external vendor to build (or operate) a firm's information systems. The work is done by the vendor rather than by the organization's internal information systems staff. Outsourcing can save application development costs or allow firms to develop applications without an internal information systems staff. However, firms risk losing control over their information systems and becoming too dependent on external vendors.

7. *Evaluate the use of object-oriented development, unified modelling language, rapid application development, and joint application design in building contemporary systems.* Object-oriented software development is expected to reduce the time and cost of writing software and of making maintenance changes because it models a system as a series of reusable objects that combine both data and procedures. Unified modelling language is also expected to result in faster, less expensive systems development by creating a standard development environment. Rapid application development (RAD) uses object-oriented software, visual

programming, prototyping, and fourth-generation tools for very rapid creation of systems. Joint application design (JAD) is RAD conducted in an intensive joint session between users and developers, usually away from the office.

KEY TERMS

Acceptance testing, 391

Application software package, 396

Automation, 372

Benchmarking, 378

Business process reengineering, 373

Change agent, 382

Conversion, 392

Critical success factors (CSFs), 370

Customization, 396

Design, 394

Direct cutover approach, 392

Documentation, 392

End user development, 397

End user interface, 396

Enterprise analysis, 369

Feasibility study, 389

Implementation, 382

Information centre, 398

Information requirements, 389

Information system failure, 379

Information systems plan, 369

Installation, 394

Iterative, 395

Joint application design (JAD), 402

Maintenance, 393

Man-month, 386

Moving, 382

Object-oriented software development, 401

Outsourcing, 399

Paradigm shift, 373

Parallel approach, 392

Phased approach, 392

Pilot study approach, 392

Post-implementation, 394

Programming, 391

Project definition, 394

Prototype, 395

Prototyping, 395

Production, 392

Programming, 394

Rapid application development (RAD), 402

Rationalization of procedures, 372

Refreezing, 382

Request for Proposal (RFP), 396

Systems analysis, 388

Systems design, 389

Systems development, 388

Systems development life cycle, 393

Systems study, 394

Systems testing, 391

Test plan, 391

Testing, 391

Total quality management (TQM), 377

Unfreezing, 382

Unified modelling language (UML), 402

Unit testing, 391

User–designer communication gap, 383

User interface, 380

Workflow management, 376

REVIEW QUESTIONS

1. Why can an information system be considered planned organizational change?

2. What are the major categories of an information systems plan?

3. How can enterprise analysis and critical success factors be used to establish organization-wide information system requirements?

4. Describe each of the four kinds of organizational change that can be promoted with information technology.

5. What is business process reengineering? What steps are required to make it effective?

6. Describe the Lewin–Schein model of organizational change and contrast it with the Kolb–Frohman model of organizational change

7. What major problems are there with change management? How can these issues be addressed?

8. What particular issues affect the success and failure of information systems development? How can these issues be addressed?

9. What is the difference between systems analysis and systems design? What activities are involved in each?

10. What are information requirements? Why are they difficult to determine correctly?

11. Why is the testing stage of systems development so important? Name and describe the three stages of testing for an information system.

12. What role do programming, conversion, production, and maintenance play in systems development?

13. What is the traditional systems development life cycle? Describe each of its steps and the advantages and disadvantages of using the SDLC.

14. What do we mean by information system prototyping? What are its benefits and limitations? List and describe the steps in the prototyping process.

15. What is an application software package? What are the advantages and disadvantages of developing information systems based on software packages?

16. What do we mean by end user development? What are its advantages and disadvantages? What are some policies and procedures for managing end user development?

17. What is outsourcing? Under what circumstances should it be used for developing information systems?

18. What is the difference between object-oriented software development and traditional software development? What are the advantages of using object-oriented software development in developing systems?

19. What is rapid application development? How can it help system developers? What is the difference between RAD and JAD?

Gʀᴏᴜᴘ Pʀᴏᴊᴇᴄᴛ

With three of four of your classmates, select an information system, such as an online store or reservations system, described in this text that uses the Web. Examples might be the systems used by Air Canada, Carsdirect.com, Cemex, or Subscription.com from this chapter alone. Review the company's Web site. Use what you learn from the Web site and the descriptions in this book to prepare a report describing some of the design specifications for the system you select. Present your findings to the class.

Iɴᴛᴇʀɴᴇᴛ Cᴏɴɴᴇᴄᴛɪᴏɴ

■ Cᴏᴍᴘᴀɴɪᴏɴ Wᴇʙsɪᴛᴇ

At www.pearsoned.ca/laudon, you'll find an online study guide with two quizzes to test your knowledge of how systems development is performed in modern organizations. You'll also find updates to the chapter and online exercises and cases that enable you to apply your knowledge to realistic situations.

■ Aᴅᴅɪᴛɪᴏɴᴀʟ Sɪᴛᴇs ᴏꜰ Iɴᴛᴇʀᴇsᴛ

There are many interesting Web sites to enhance your learning about systems development. You can search the Web yourself, or just try the following sites to add to what you have already learned.

Sybase

www.sybase.com

Sybase has products that can be used in RAD & JAD development.

EDS Systemhouse

www.eds.com/canada/ca_about.shtml

One of the largest outsourcing firms operating in Canada, EDS Systemhouse is the result of the merger of Canada's SHL Systemhouse and the United States' EDS.

Visual Café

www.visualcafe.com

Development software that can be used in a JAD environment.

Cᴀsᴇ Sᴛᴜᴅʏ   *Under Construction: A New System for Toromont Industries*

Toromont Industries Ltd. is headquartered in Toronto, Canada, and is one of the largest dealerships for Caterpillar heavy construction equipment in North America. Toromont also makes process systems and industrial and recreation equipment and operates a series of energy plants supplying Ontario's deregulated electricity market. Two thirds of Toromont's revenue, which amounted to $750 million in 1999, comes from its equipment group, which rents and sells heavy construction and mining equipment and parts. Toromont has over 2000 employees throughout North America.

Toromont's success has not been based on selling more tractor parts and engines but on selling the kind of service that leads customers to purchase 10-year contracts. The contracts call for Toromont to supply them with heavy equipment and to maintain that equipment. Customers do not need to purchase the equipment, which can amount to $225 000 per earth-moving machine, nor do they have to maintain their own warehouses or mechanics. Toromont supplies the machines and guarantees they will be maintained in top condition for the life of the contract.

Toromont faces stiff competition. Many heavy construction and mining equipment firms, including Komatsu, John Deere, and even Caterpillar itself, are putting more emphasis on customer service by selling parts online over the Internet. There are also Web sites such as EquipmentRental.com (www.equipmentrental.com), Point2 (http://point2.com), and Equipmenttrader.com, which provide clearinghouses for heavy construction equipment, parts, and services. The Internet appears to be turning heavy construction equipment into a commodity. "With so many others vying for your customers' attention, how to you convince them to buy from you instead of from a discount place on the Internet?" asks Rob Kugel, an analyst with FAC/Equities in Burlingame, California.

Toromont's management believes that the company can stay ahead of these competitors by offering the best possible customer service through a new online system for ordering and maintaining equipment and for tracking customer accounts. The system ideally would provide more interactive personalized service than could be obtained from any of its competitors. For example, the system could provide oil quality and other maintenance statistics online that could help customers determine pre-failure conditions faster, reducing the chances of costly downtime or worker injuries on construction jobs. Customers could get quick answers to questions such as how fast they can obtain the part they need, when their equipment needs to go into the repair shop for maintenance, and how much they owe on their accounts.

Toromont's senior management wants an interactive customer service capability as soon as possible and is willing to keep things simple to get this capability up and running. It doesn't want customers to see the same generic information. Each Toromont client should be able to see precisely the information that is specific to their company. Toromont currently provides customers with oil analyses and maintenance updates on their machines but delivers this information via fax.

The new system should not only provide this information online but should also be able to deliver e-mail and pager alerts to customers, technicians, and machine operators. Toromont would also like to offer personalized, real-time price quotes for parts and service based on the customer's size and contract. Customers should be able to use the system to access sales and service data, update their information, check outstanding invoices, and place orders. That would require the new system to access information housed in Toromont's basic operational systems running on an IBM AS/400 midrange computer. But management does not want to rewrite the software for these back-end systems or to have the new system interfere with the data in the AS/400 database.

Toromont's legacy back-end order entry and billing system is written in Cobol and uses a DB2 database running on an IBM AS/400 model 720 computer. The system supports order entry for parts and machine sales, service work-order processing, warranty, and inventory, and is integrated with a financial subsystem from Baan, a leading enterprise software vendor. The company has an IP network connecting 700 users to both local and wide-area networks and uses frame relay to connect 18 locations to corporate headquarters near Toronto. Customers order parts by telephoning Toromont's parts department. They must also use the telephone to check part prices, part availability, and the status of machines in for service.

Toromont management would like to make better use of the Internet and wonders how it could be incorporated in its system solution. It is willing to devote 25 percent of its information technology budget to the project and wants it completed in six months.

Sources: Claudia Graziano, "Under Construction," *Information Week*, February 7, 2000; and www.toromont.com.

CASE STUDY QUESTIONS:

1. Analyze Toromont and its business model using the competitive forces and value chain models (Chapter 3).

2. How well did Toromont's systems support its business model? What management, organization, and technology factors were responsible for its problems?

3. Propose a systems solution for Toromont. Your analysis should describe the objectives of the solution, the requirements to be met by the new system (or series of systems), and the feasibility of your proposal. Include an overview of the systems you would recommend, and explain how those systems would address the problems listed in your goals. Your analysis should consider organizational and change management issues to be addressed by the solution as well as technology issues.

4. If you were the systems analyst for this project, list five questions you would ask during interviews to elicit the information you need for your systems study report.

12

INFORMATION SYSTEM QUALITY, SECURITY, AND CONTROL

OBJECTIVES

After completing this chapter, you will be able to:

1. *Demonstrate why information systems are so vulnerable to destruction, error, abuse, and quality problems.*
2. *Compare general controls and application controls for information systems.*
3. *Describe the special measures required to ensure the reliability, availability, and security of electronic commerce and digital business processes.*
4. *Describe the most important software quality assurance techniques.*
5. *Demonstrate the importance of auditing information systems and safeguarding data quality.*

Systems Crash Causes: Quality and Control

The Toronto Stock Exchange's computers crashed twice on March 8, 2000, and are quite likely to continue crashing because there are no easy answers to the TSE's technology woes. The stock market opened an hour late after the computer that directs buy-and-sell orders broke down and traffic had to be rerouted. Traders found themselves staring at blank screens again for more than an hour that same afternoon as the TSE struggled to untangle trading traffic. It was the third time in three months that technical gremlins had halted trading.

These problems are rooted in a TSE computer system that was built in 1975, which is pretty much the Stone Age in technological terms. The dot-com stock mania and subsequent crash has inspired frenzied trading on the TSE and its peers around the world. Compared with two years ago, the exchange has seen a fourfold increase in the number of orders it receives each day. That unforeseen spike to record trading levels is overloading the system. Despite the enforced downtime, the TSE experienced a busy trading session, with 208 million shares changing hands.

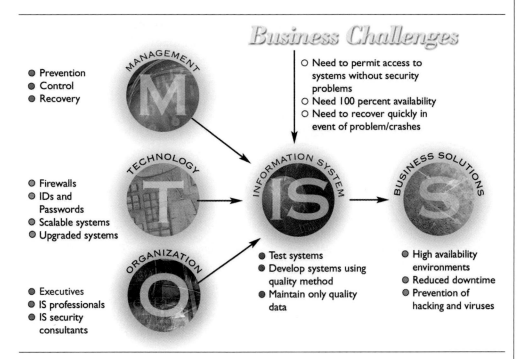

Business Challenges

MANAGEMENT
- Prevention
- Control
- Recovery

TECHNOLOGY
- Firewalls
- IDs and Passwords
- Scalable systems
- Upgraded systems

ORGANIZATION
- Executives
- IS professionals
- IS security consultants

INFORMATION SYSTEM

○ Need to permit access to systems without security problems
○ Need 100 percent availability
○ Need to recover quickly in event of problem/crashes

- Test systems
- Develop systems using quality method
- Maintain only quality data

BUSINESS SOLUTIONS
- High availability environments
- Reduced downtime
- Prevention of hacking and viruses

There's a certain irony to the new dot-com stocks overwhelming an old computer system. However, other exchanges are facing these skyrocketing volumes without breaking down. The TSE is guilty of focusing its attention on Year 2000–related computer problems over the past few years and not spending enough to update its whole system. The TSE has a $145 million (Canadian) war chest but spent just $16 million sprucing itself up in 1999. The exchange spent $38 million to exterminate Y2K bugs. But each time the computers fail, investors and Canadian companies find one more reason to bypass the TSE as the place they invest or raise money.

System crashes aren't only caused by too much activity. Problems with a routine upgrade of mainframe software at Automatic Data Processing Inc. (ADP) caused a system crash in November 2000 that temporarily left customers of at least five North American brokerages unable to get real-time updates of key information such as the cost of the online stock trades they were making.

Larry Tabb, an analyst at TowerGroup in Needham, Mass., called the incident "a fluke" and said he hadn't heard of many similar technical problems at ADP. "ADP has a pretty good track record," Tabb said. These glitches are typical during upgrades, he added, because complete testing and performance modelling is "virtually impossible" because of the massive amounts of information involved.

Other companies experience system outages for "non-hacking" reasons at the worst possible times, too. Internationally renowned toy retailer FAO Schwartz's Web e-tail site, FAO.com, went down one month before Christmas 2000 due to increased site traffic. Wouldn't you think they'd be ready for the Christmas rush? Amazon.com, the original Net bookstore, has been plagued by outages over the years, including—again—an outage three weeks before Christmas 2000. The latter outage was its third in two weeks due to internal "glitches" and a software conflict (running two incompatible programs simultaneously). The three outages probably cost Amazon U.S.$500 000 in sales.

(continued)

A fire in the switching station at Bell Canada's Simcoe Street central office in Toronto left long distance customers across Canada with greatly reduced long distance service and for much of Canada, no long distance service at all. It was the second such fire in less than 10 months.

Even software superstar Microsoft had its Web site disrupted in January 2001, when an employee made an error in configuring the company's domain name server architecture, taking down the company's home page as well as its MSN, Encarta, Carpoint, and Expedia sites. Finally—and dangerously—the Los Angeles, California, air traffic control mainframe crashed on October 19, 2000. All flights taking off and landing at Los Angeles International Airport were grounded for four hours while technicians tried to sort out the problem. They finally went back to the older version of the software.

Sources: Todd R. Weiss, "ADP Upgrade Glitch Causes Online Trading Problems," *ComputerWorld US*, November 13, 2000; Andrew Willis, "Computer Troubles Again Prove that Canada's Top Stock Exchange Isn't Ready for the 21st Century," *The Globe and Mail*, March 8, 2000; Stuart Glascock, "Microsoft Sites Fail, Again," *TechWeb News*, January 25, 2001, www.techweb.com, accessed June 27, 2001; Grant Buckler, "Grit Your Teeth and Upgrade," *Computing Canada*, January 5, 2001;

MANAGEMENT CHALLENGES

1. **Designing systems that are neither overcontrolled nor undercontrolled.** While security breaches and damage to information systems still come from organizational insiders, security breaches from outside the organization are increasing because firms pursuing electronic commerce have opened themselves to outsiders through the Internet. It is difficult for organizations to determine how open or closed they should be to protect themselves. If a system requires too many passwords, authorizations, or levels of security to access information, the system will go unused. Controls that are effective but that do not prevent authorized individuals from using a system are difficult to design.

2. **Applying quality assurance standards in large systems projects.** This chapter explains why the goal of zero defects in large, complex software applications is impossible to achieve. If the severity of remaining bugs cannot be ascertained, what constitutes acceptable—if not perfect—software performance? And even if meticulous design and exhaustive testing could eliminate all defects, time and budget constraints often prevent management from devoting as much time to thoroughly testing as should be done. Under these circumstances, it is difficult for managers to define and enforce standards for software quality.

Computer systems play such a critical role in business, government, and daily life that organizations must take special steps to protect their information systems and to ensure that they are accurate and reliable. This chapter describes how information systems can be controlled and made secure so that they serve the purposes for which they are intended.

▌12.1 SYSTEM VULNERABILITY AND ABUSE

Before computer automation, data were maintained and secured as paper records dispersed in separate business or organizational units. Information systems concentrate data in computer files that potentially can be accessed more easily by large numbers of people and by groups outside the organization. Consequently, automated data are more susceptible to destruction, fraud, error, and misuse.

ESTIMATED FINANCIAL LOSS DUE TO A SITE OUTAGE		
Type of Loss*	**Brokerage Site**	**Auction Site**
Direct revenues loss	$306 000	$512 478
Compensatory loss	0	$1 415 281
Inventory costs	0	0
Depreciation expenses	$6 215	$9 425
Lost future revenues	$7 215 480	$1 537 500
Workers downtime loss	$177 000	$69 150
Contract labour cost	$36 000	$78 270
Delay-to-market cost	$90 000	$539 800
Total financial impact	$7 830 695	$4 161 904

* Based on an eight-hour brokerage site outage during the trading day and on a 22-hour auction site outage.
Source: "Technology spotlight: The Financial Impact of Site Outages," *The Industry Standard*, October 4, 1999.
Reprinted by permission of *The Industry Standard*, www.thestandard.com.

FIGURE 12-1 Financial impact of Web site outages. Firms that need Web sites constantly available for electronic commerce stand to lose millions of dollars for every business day that the sites are not working.

When computer systems fail to perform as required, firms that depend heavily on computers may experience a devastating loss of business function. The longer computer systems are down, the more serious the consequences for the firm. Figure 12-1 describes the estimated financial losses due to Web site outages for brokerage and auction sites. Some firms relying on computers to process their critical business transactions might experience a total loss of business function if they lose computer capability for more than a few days.

WHY SYSTEMS ARE VULNERABLE

When large amounts of data are stored in electronic form, they are vulnerable to many more kinds of threats than when they exist in manual form. Table 12-1 lists the most common threats to computer-based information systems. They can stem from technical, organizational, and environmental factors compounded by poor management decisions.

Advances in telecommunications and computer software have magnified these vulnerabilities. Through telecommunications networks, information systems in different locations can be interconnected. The potential for unauthorized access, abuse, and fraud are not limited to a single location but can occur at any access point in the network and spread rapidly across the network and onto other networks.

Additionally, more complex and diverse hardware, software, organizational, and personnel arrangements are required for telecommunications networks, creating new areas and opportunities for penetration and manipulation. Wireless networks using radio-based technology are even more vulnerable to penetration because radio frequency bands are easy to scan. The Internet poses special problems because it was explicitly designed to be accessed easily by people on various computer systems. The vulnerabilities of telecommunications networks are illustrated in Figure 12-2.

TABLE 12-1	**THREATS TO COMPUTER-BASED INFORMATION SYSTEMS**	
Hardware failure	Fire	
Natural disasters	Electrical problems	
Software failure	User errors	
Personnel actions	Program changes	
Terminal access penetration	Telecommunications problems	
Theft of data, services, equipment		

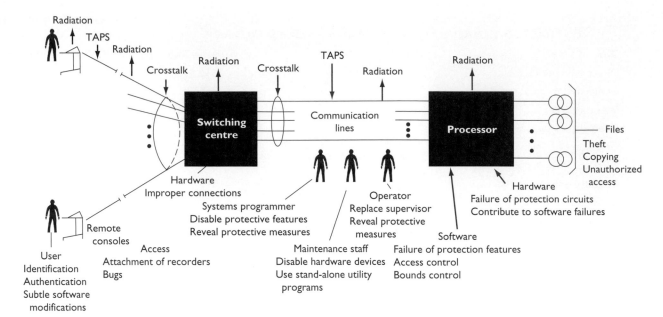

FIGURE 12-2 Telecommunications network vulnerabilities. Telecommunications networks are highly vulnerable to natural failure of hardware and software and to misuse by programmers, computer operators, maintenance staff, and end users. It is possible to tap communications lines and illegally intercept data. High-speed transmission over twisted wire communications channels causes interference called crosstalk. Radiation can disrupt a network at various points as well.

HACKERS AND COMPUTER VIRUSES

hacker
A person who gains unauthorized access to a computer network for profit, criminal mischief, or personal pleasure.

denial of service attack (DOS)
An attack on an organization's computer in which a hacker overloads a network server or Web server with a flood of requests for information or other data in order to crash the network.

computer virus
Rogue software programs that are difficult to detect and that spread rapidly through computer systems, destroying data or disrupting processing and memory systems.

The explosive growth of Internet use has been accompanied by rising reports of Internet security breaches. The main concern comes from unwanted intruders, or hackers, who use the latest technology and their skills to break into supposedly secure computers or to disable them. A **hacker** is a person who gains unauthorized access to a computer network for profit, criminal mischief, or personal pleasure. (A *cracker* is a hacker whose purpose is to commit a crime, not simply to prove that they can do it.) There are many ways that hacker break-ins can harm businesses. Some malicious intruders have planted logic bombs, *Trojan horses*, and other software that can hide in a system or network until executing at a specified time. (A Trojan horse is a software program that appears legitimate but contains a second hidden function that may cause damage.) In **denial of service attacks (DOS)**, hackers overload a network server or Web server with a flood of requests for information or other data in order to crash the network. The Window on Organizations describes one highly publicized denial of service attack and other problems hackers create for organizations that use the Internet. Canadian examples of hacking include a hacker gaining access to the server of Internet service provider Lino Solutions Internet, based in Val d'Or in northwestern Quebec; the hacker obtained a file listing the billing information of 1015 of Lino's customers, forcing Lino to notify all 25 000 customers to change their passwords. The file with the information on the 1015 clients had been left in an unsecure area of Lino's server and contained credit card numbers and expiry dates. In April 2001, "Mafiaboy," a 15-year-old from Montreal, pled guilty to 56 of 66 charges of hacking through other computers into the computers of 11 major international corporations, including CNN, Dell Computer, Buy.com, eTrade, Amazon.com, Yahoo!, eBay, Harvard University, and Yale University between February 6 and February 14, 2000. His denial-of-service attacks used freeware readily available off the Internet. The corporations had not implemented appropriate safeguards that were also readily available to guard from these DOS attacks.

Most recently, hackers have propagated **computer viruses**, rogue software programs that spread rapidly from system to system, clogging computer memory or destroying programs or data. Many thousands of viruses are known to exist, with 200 or more new viruses created each month. Table 12-2 describes the characteristics of the most common viruses.

INTERNET HACKERS: WHY WON'T THEY STOP?

In early January 2000, a mysterious intruder tried to extort $150 000 from CD Universe, an Internet music retailer, claiming to have copied over 300 000 credit card files that CD Universe had collected on its customers. The credit card numbers on these files could be used by other people to charge purchases online or by telephone. CD Universe refused to pay the blackmail, and the cyber-extortionist released some of the credit card files on the Internet, claiming that he had used other credit card numbers to obtain money for himself.

An e-mail trail traced the extortionist to Lavtia, Bulgaria, or Russia. The extortionist had been operating a Web site, called Maxus Credit Card Pipeline, where a visitor could obtain a valid credit card number, name, and address from the site's massive database. Before the Maxus site was shut down, a traffic counter indicated that several thousand visitors had downloaded more than 25 000 credit card numbers since December 25, 1999. The extortionist claimed he had found a way to subvert ICVerify, a credit card verification program sold by Cybercash Inc. CD Universe employs ICVerify, but the company was not ready to conclude that the blackmailer had obtained his credit card information by manipulating the software. The Maxus Web site extortionist claimed he hacked into a chain of shops in 1998 and obtained the ICVerify program with configuration files for transferring money.

During the second week of February 2000, a wave of hacker attacks temporarily disabled a series of major e-commerce sites, including Yahoo, Amazon.com, Buy.com, E*Trade, and ZDNet. These denial of service attacks were not designed to penetrate the Web sites but to disable them by inundating them with phony requests for data, overloading these sites' servers and preventing legitimate traffic from getting through. The Web sites were shut down for several hours, but no systems were compromised, no customer data were stolen, and financial losses from the outages were minor. After these incidents, many companies started looking for new ways to fortify their Web sites.

In early March 2000, a hacker broke into the Australian government's official Web site for its new Goods and Services tax and started downloading bank account details on up to 10 000 small businesses that had registered online. The hacker, known as K2 or Kelly, said on public radio that he had breached the security of the Web site by accident and wanted to publicize the risk to businesses. He started sending e-mail messages to the businesses with accounts at the Web site, detailing their bank account numbers, bank branches, tax numbers, and other private information. The Australian government immediately shut down the Web site, and the Australian Federal Police launched an investigation.

All of these incidents highlight a mounting problem with Internet hackers plaguing both government and business organizations. According to Trusecure Corporation, a security consulting firm, there were four times as many hacker attacks per day in North America in 2000 as there were a year earlier.

To Think About: How can break-ins from the Internet harm organizations? What management, organization, and technology issues should be considered when developing an Internet security plan? How can a small- to-medium-sized business keep up with emerging security problems and their potential solutions?

Sources: John Markoff, "Thief Reveals Credit Card Data When Web Extortion Plot Fails," *The New York Times,* January 10, 2000; Gerard Knapp, "Hacker Strolls into Australian Tax Site," *Australia.Internet.Com,* June 30, 2000; Elinor Abreu, "The Hack Attack," *The Industry Standard,* February 21, 2000; Kelly Jackson Higgins, "Human Element is Key to Stopping Hackers," *Information Week,* May 29, 2000.

TABLE 12-2   EXAMPLES OF COMPUTER VIRUSES

Virus Name	Description
Concept, Melissa, Love Bug	Macro viruses that exist inside executable programs called macros that provide functions within programs such as Microsoft Word. Can be spread when Word documents are attached to e-mail. Can copy from one document to another and delete files.
Form	Makes a clicking sound with each keystroke but only on the eighteenth day of the month. May corrupt data on the floppy disks it infects.
Explore.exe	"Worm" type virus that arrives attached to e-mail. When launched tries to e-mail itself to other PCs and destroy certain Microsoft Office and programmer files.
Monkey	Makes the hard disk look like it has failed because Windows will not run.
Chernobyl	Erases a computer's hard drive and ROM BIOS (Basic Input/Output System).
Junkie	A "multipartite" virus that can infect files as well as the boot sector of the hard drive (the section of a PC hard drive that the PC first reads when it boots up). May cause memory conflicts.

Many viruses today are spread through the Internet, from files of downloaded software or from files attached to e-mail transmissions. Viruses can also invade computer-based information systems from other computer networks as well as from "infected" disks from an outside source or infected machines. The potential for massive damage and loss from new computer viruses not yet developed remains. The Chernobyl, Melissa, and Love Bug viruses caused extensive PC damage worldwide after spreading around the world through infected e-mail. Now viruses are spreading to wireless computing devices. Mobile device viruses could pose a serious threat to enterprise computing because so many wireless devices are now linked to corporate information systems. A Philippine college student developed and launched the Love Bug virus in early 2000. Amazingly, he was tracked and caught within a week.

antivirus software
Software designed to detect and often eliminate computer viruses from an information system.

Organizations can use antivirus software and screening procedures to reduce the chances of infection. **Antivirus software** is special software designed to check computer systems and disks for the presence of various computer viruses (see Figure 12-3 for an example). Often the software can eliminate the virus from the infected area. However, antivirus software is only effective against viruses already known when the software is written—to protect their systems, management must continually update their antivirus software.

CONCERNS FOR SYSTEM DEVELOPERS AND USERS

The heightened vulnerability of automated data has created special concerns for the developers and users of information systems. These concerns include disaster, security, and administrative error.

Disaster

Computer hardware, programs, data files, and other equipment can be destroyed by fires, power failures, or other disasters. It may take many years and millions of dollars to reconstruct destroyed data files and computer programs, and some may not be able to be replaced. If an organization needs them to function on a day-to-day basis, it will no longer be able to operate. Companies such as VISA and the Bank of Nova Scotia employ elaborate emergency backup facilities. VISA has duplicate mainframes, duplicate network pathways, duplicate terminals, and duplicate power supplies. VISA even uses a duplicate data centre in McLean, Virginia, to handle half of its transactions and to serve as an emergency backup to its primary data centre in San Mateo, California. The Bank of Nova Scotia's Ontario operations use uninterruptible power supply technology provided by International Power Machines (IPM) because electrical power at its Mississauga location fluctuates frequently.

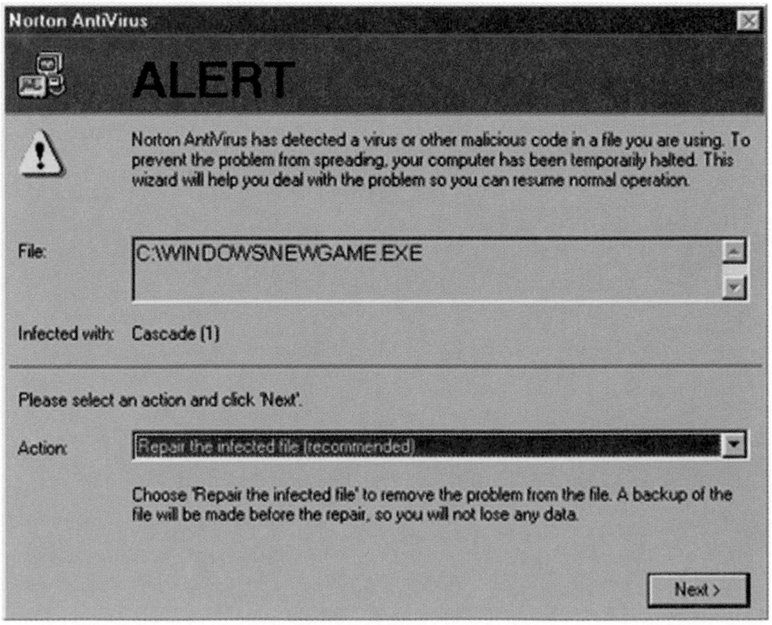

FIGURE 12-3 Many organizations use antivirus software to check computer systems and disks for the presence of various computer viruses.

Rather than build their own backup facilities, many firms contract with disaster recovery firms, such as JAWS Technologies, Inc. in Calgary, Alberta (www.jawzinc.com), and Comdisco Disaster Recovery Services headquartered in Rosemont, Illinois. These disaster recovery firms provide hot sites housing spare computers at locations around the country where subscribing firms can run their critical applications in an emergency. Disaster recovery services offer backup for client/server systems as well as traditional mainframe applications. As firms become increasingly digital and depend on systems that must be constantly available, disaster recovery planning has taken on new importance.

Security

Security refers to the policies, procedures, and technical measures used to prevent unauthorized access or alteration, theft, and physical damage to information systems. Security can be promoted with an array of techniques and tools to safeguard computer hardware, software, communications networks, and data. We have already discussed disaster protection measures. Other tools and techniques for promoting security will be discussed in subsequent sections.

Errors

Computers also can serve as instruments of error, severely disrupting or destroying an organization's record keeping and operations. For instance, on February 25, 1991, during Operation Desert Storm, a Patriot missile defence system operating at Dharan, Saudi Arabia, failed to track and intercept an incoming Scud missile because of a software error in the system's weapons control computer. The Scud hit an army barracks, killing 28 Americans. Errors in automated systems can occur at many points in the processing cycle: through data entry, program error, computer operations, and hardware. Figure 12-4 illustrates all of the points in a typical processing cycle where errors can occur.

SYSTEM QUALITY PROBLEMS: SOFTWARE AND DATA

In addition to disasters, viruses, and security breaches, defective software and data pose a constant threat to information systems, causing untold losses in productivity. An undiscovered error in a company's credit software or erroneous financial data can result in millions of dollars of losses. A hidden software problem in AT&T's long distance system brought down that system, bringing the New York-based financial exchanges to a halt and interfering with billions of dollars of business around the country for a number of hours. Modern passenger and commercial vehicles are increasingly dependent on computer programs for critical functions. A hidden software defect in a braking system could result in the loss of lives.

Bugs and Defects

A major problem with software is the presence of hidden **bugs** or program code defects. Studies have shown that it is virtually impossible to eliminate

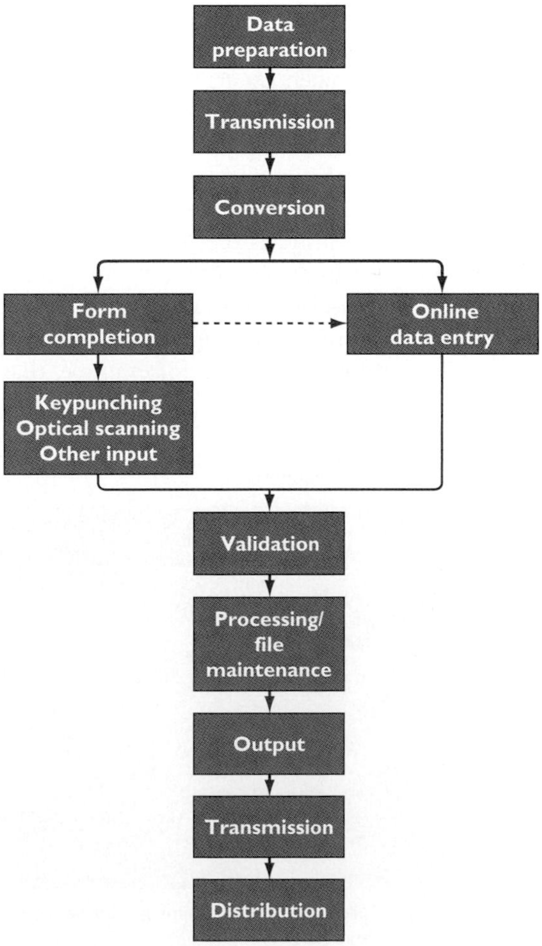

security
Policies, procedures, and technical measures used to prevent unauthorized access, alteration, theft, or physical damage to information systems.

bugs
Program code defects or errors.

FIGURE 12-4 Points in the processing cycle where errors can occur. Each of the points illustrated in this figure represents a control point where special automated and/or manual procedures should be established to reduce the risk of errors during processing.

all bugs from large programs. The main source of bugs is the complexity of decision-making code. Even a relatively small program of several hundred lines will contain tens of decisions leading to hundreds or even thousands of different paths. Important programs within most corporations are usually much larger, containing tens of thousands or even millions of lines of code, each with many times the choices and paths of the smaller programs. This level of complexity is difficult to document and design—designers document some reactions wrongly or fail to consider some possibilities. Studies show that about 60 percent of errors discovered during testing are a result of specifications in the design documentation that were missing, ambiguous, in error, or in conflict.

Zero defects, a goal of the total quality management movement, cannot be achieved in larger programs. Complete testing simply is not possible. Fully testing programs that contain thousands of choices and millions of paths would require thousands of years. Eliminating software bugs is an exercise in diminishing returns because it would take proportionately longer testing to detect and eliminate obscure residual bugs (Littlewood and Strigini, 1993). Even with rigorous testing, we could not know for sure that a piece of software was dependable until the product proved itself after much operational use. The message? We cannot eliminate all bugs, and we cannot know with certainty the seriousness of the bugs that do remain.

The Maintenance Nightmare

Another reason that systems are unreliable is that computer software traditionally has been a nightmare to maintain. Maintenance, the process of modifying a system in production use, is the most expensive phase of the systems development process. In most organizations, nearly half of information systems staff time is spent in the maintenance of existing systems.

Why are maintenance costs so high? One major reason is organizational change. The firm may experience large internal changes in structure or leadership, or change may come from its surrounding environment. These organizational changes affect information requirements. Another reason is software complexity, measured by the number and size of interrelated software programs and subprograms and the complexity of the flow of program logic between them (Banker, Datar, Kemerer, and Zweig, 1993). A third common cause of long-term maintenance problems is faulty systems analysis and design, especially information requirements analysis. Some studies of large transaction processing systems (TPS) by TRW, Inc., have found that a majority of system errors—64 percent—result from early analysis errors (Mazzucchelli, 1985).

Figure 12-5 illustrates the cost of correcting errors based on the experience of consultants and reports in the popular trade literature. If errors are detected early, during analysis and design, the cost to the systems development effort is small. But if they are not discovered until after programming, testing, or conversion has been completed, the costs can soar astronomically. A minor logic error, for example, that could take an hour to correct during the

FIGURE 12-5 The cost of errors over the systems development life cycle. The most common, most severe, and most expensive system errors are those that are not caught in the early design stages. They often involve faulty requirements analysis.

Source: Alberts, 1976.

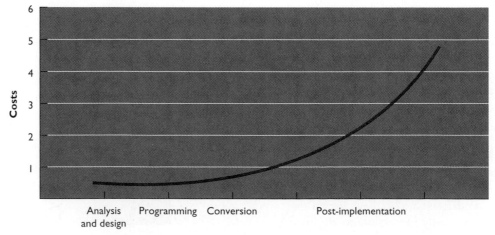

Estimate of the relative cost of repairing errors based on consultant reports and the popular trade literature

TABLE 12-3	EXAMPLES OF DATA QUALITY PROBLEMS
Organization	**Data Quality Problem**
Royal Bank of Canada	Employees often entered garbage character strings for the postal code if they didn't have the proper information at hand; target mailings were difficult because many customers' postal codes were entered as H0H 0H0, a garbage string that passed the system's edit checks.
Sears	Could not effectively pursue cross-selling among its customers because each of its businesses, including retail, home services, credit, and Web site, each had their own information systems with conflicting customer data. Sears needed to develop a massive data warehouse that consolidated and cleansed the data from all of these systems to create a single customer list
Paint Bull	Found that nearly half the names in its purchased mailing lists of prospective customers were inaccurate or out of date. Lost $10 for every promotional package of videos and catalogues that was returned as undeliverable.
Supermarkets	Several studies have established that 5 to 12 percent of bar-code sales at retail supermarkets are erroneous and that the average ratio of overcharges to undercharges runs 4 to 1.

analysis and design stage could take 10, 40, and 90 times as long to correct during programming, conversion, and post-implementation, respectively.

Data Quality Problems

The most common source of information system failure is poor data quality. Data that are inaccurate, untimely, or inconsistent with other sources of information can create serious operational and financial problems for businesses. When bad data go unnoticed, they can lead to bad decisions, product recalls, and even financial losses (Redman, 1998). Companies cannot pursue aggressive marketing and customer relationship management strategies unless they have high-quality data about their customers. Table 12-3 describes examples of data quality problems.

Poor data quality may stem from errors during data input or faulty information system and database design (Wand and Wang, 1996; Strong, Lee, and Wang, 1997). In the following sections, we examine how organizations can deal with data and software quality problems as well as other threats to information systems.

12.2 CREATING A CONTROL ENVIRONMENT

To minimize errors, disasters, interruptions of service, computer crime, and breaches of security, special policies and procedures must be incorporated into the design and implementation of information systems. The combination of manual and automated measures that safeguard information systems and ensure that they perform according to management standards constitute controls. **Controls** consist of all the methods, policies, and organizational procedures that ensure the safety of the organization's assets, the accuracy and reliability of its accounting records, and operational adherence to management standards.

In the past, the control of information systems was treated as an afterthought, addressed only toward the end of implementation, just before the system was installed. Today, however, organizations are so critically dependent on information systems that vulnerability and control issues must be identified as early as possible. The control of an information system must be an integral part of its design. Users and developers of systems must pay close attention to controls throughout the system's life span.

controls

All of the methods, policies, and procedures that ensure protection of the organization's assets, accuracy and reliability of its records, and operational adherence to management standards.

GENERAL CONTROLS AND APPLICATION CONTROLS

Computer systems are controlled by a combination of general controls and application controls. **General controls** are those that control the design, security, and use of computer programs and the security of data files in general throughout the organization's information technology infrastructure. On the whole, general controls apply to all computer-based applications and consist of a combination of hardware, software, and manual procedures that create an overall control environment.

general controls

Overall controls that establish a framework for controlling the design, security, and use of computer programs throughout an organization.

application controls
Specific controls unique to each computer-based application.

Application controls are specific controls unique to each computer-based application, such as payroll, accounts receivable, and order processing. They consist of controls applied in a particular system and from programmed procedures involved in using that system.

General Controls

General controls are overall controls governing the organization's information technology infrastructure. They apply to all application areas. General controls include the following:

- Controls over the system implementation process
- Software controls
- Hardware controls
- Computer operations controls
- Data security controls
- Administrative disciplines, standards, and procedures

implementation controls
The audit of the systems development process at various points to make sure that the process itself is properly controlled and managed.

Implementation Controls   **Implementation controls** audit the systems development process at various points to ensure that the process itself is properly controlled and managed. The systems development audit should look for the presence of formal review points at various stages of development that enable users and management to approve or reject the implementation. The systems development audit also should examine the level of user involvement at each stage of implementation and check for the use of a formal cost/benefit methodology in establishing system feasibility. The audit should look for the use of controls and quality assurance techniques for program development, conversion, and testing and for complete and thorough system, user, and operations documentation.

software controls
Controls to ensure the security and reliability of software.

Software Controls   Controls are essential for the various categories of software used in computer systems. **Software controls** monitor the use of systems software and prevent unauthorized access of software programs, systems software, and computer programs. Systems software is an important control area because it performs overall control functions for the programs that directly process data and data files.

hardware controls
Controls to ensure the physical security and correct performance of computer hardware.

Hardware Controls   **Hardware controls** ensure that computer hardware is physically secure and check for equipment malfunction. Computer hardware should be physically secured so that it can be accessed only by authorized individuals. Computer equipment should be specially protected against fires, natural disasters, and extremes of temperature and humidity. Organizations that are critically dependent on their computers must also make provisions for backup or continued operation to maintain constant service. Many kinds of computer hardware contain mechanisms that check for equipment malfunction.

computer operations controls
Procedures to ensure that programmed procedures are consistently and correctly applied to data storage and processing.

Computer Operations Controls   **Computer operations controls** involve the work of the information systems department and help ensure that programmed procedures are consistently and correctly applied to the storage and processing of data. They include controls over the set-up of computer processing jobs, operations software, computer operations, and backup and recovery procedures for processing that ends abnormally. Specific instructions for backup and recovery can be developed so that in the event of a hardware or software failure, the recovery process for production programs, systems software, and data files does not create erroneous changes in the system.

data security controls
Controls to ensure that data files on either disk or tape are not subject to unauthorized access, change, or destruction.

Data Security Controls   **Data security controls** ensure that valuable business data files on either disk or tape are not subject to unauthorized access, change, or destruction. These controls are required for data files when they are in use and when they are being held for storage.

When data can be input online through a terminal, entry of unauthorized input must be prevented. For example, a credit note could be altered to match a sales invoice on file. In such situations, security can be developed on several levels:

- Terminals can be physically restricted so that they are available only to authorized individuals.
- Systems software can include the use of passwords assigned only to authorized individuals. No one can log on to the system without a valid password.

❚ Additional sets of passwords and security restrictions can be developed for specific systems and applications. For example, data security software can limit access to specific files, such as files for the accounts receivable system. It can restrict the type of access so that only individuals authorized to update these specific files will have the ability to do so. All others will only be able to read the files or will be denied access altogether.

Figure 12-6 illustrates the security allowed for two sets of users of an online personnel database with sensitive information such as employees' salaries, benefits, and medical histories. One set of users consists of all employees who perform clerical functions such as inputting employee data into the system. All individuals with this type of profile can update the system but can neither read nor update sensitive fields such as salary, medical history, or earnings data. Another profile applies to a divisional manager, who cannot update the system but who can read all employee data fields for his or her division, including medical history and salary. These profiles would be established and maintained by a data security system. The data security system illustrated in Figure 12-6 provides very fine-grained security restrictions, such as allowing authorized personnel users to inquire about all employee information except that contained in confidential fields such as salary or medical history.

Administrative Controls   **Administrative controls** are formalized standards, rules, procedures, and control disciplines to ensure that the organization's general and application controls are properly executed and enforced. The most important administrative controls are (1) segregation of functions, (2) written policies and procedures, and (3) supervision.

Segregation of functions means that job functions should be designed to minimize the risk of errors or fraudulent manipulation of the organization's assets. The individuals responsible for operating systems should not be the same ones who can initiate transactions that change the assets held in these systems. A typical arrangement is to have the organization's information systems department responsible for data and program files and end users responsible for initiating transactions such as payments or cheques.

Written policies and procedures establish formal standards for controlling information system operations. Procedures must be formalized in writing and authorized by the appropriate level of management. Accountability and responsibility must be clearly specified.

Supervision of personnel involved in control procedures ensures that the controls for an information system are performing as intended. Without adequate supervision, the best-designed set of controls may be bypassed, short-circuited, or neglected.

administrative controls
Formalized standards, rules, procedures, and control disciplines to ensure that the organization's controls are properly executed and enforced.

segregation of functions
The principle of internal control that divides responsibilities and assigns tasks among people so that job functions do not overlap, minimizing the risk of errors and fraudulent manipulation of the organization's assets.

SECURITY PROFILE 1	
User: Personnel Dept. Clerk	
Location: Division 1	
Employee Identification Codes with This Profile:	00753, 27834, 37665, 44116
Data Field Restrictions	Type of Access
All employee data for Division 1 only	Read and Update
• Medical history data	None
• Salary	None
• Pensionable earnings	None

SECURITY PROFILE 2	
User: Divisional Personnel Manager	
Location: Division 1	
Employee Identification Codes with This Profile:	27321
Data Field Restrictions	Type of Access
All employee data for Division 1 only	Read Only

FIGURE 12-6 Security profiles for a personnel system. These two examples represent two security profiles or data security patterns that might be found in a personnel system. Depending on the security profile, a user would have certain restrictions on access to various systems, locations, or data in an organization.

Application Controls

Application controls are specific controls within each separate computer application, such as payroll or order processing. They include automated and manual procedures that ensure that only authorized data are processed by that application, and that the processing is both complete and accurate. The controls for each application should encompass the whole sequence of processing.

Not all of the application controls discussed here are used in every information system. Some systems require more of these controls than others, depending on the importance of the data and the nature of the application.

Application controls can be classified as (1) input controls, (2) processing controls, and (3) output controls.

input controls

The procedures to check data for accuracy and completeness when they enter the system.

Input Controls **Input controls** check data for accuracy and completeness when they enter the system. There are specific input controls for input authorization, data conversion, data editing, and error handling.

Input must be properly authorized, recorded, and monitored as source documents flow to the computer. For example, formal procedures can be set up to authorize only selected members of the sales department to prepare sales transactions for an order entry system.

Input must be properly converted into computer transactions, with no errors as it is transcribed from one form to another. Transcription errors can be eliminated or reduced by keying input transactions directly into computer terminals or by using some form of source data automation.

control totals

A type of input control that requires counting transactions or quantity fields prior to processing for comparison and reconciliation after processing.

Control totals can be established beforehand for input transactions. These totals can range from a simple document count to totals for quantity fields such as total sales amount (for a batch of transactions).

edit checks

Routines performed to verify input data and correct errors prior to processing.

Edit checks include various programmed routines that can be performed to edit input data for errors before they are processed. Transactions that do not meet edit criteria will be rejected. For example, data might be checked to make sure they are in the right format (for example, social insurance numbers should not contain any alphabetic characters) or that only valid codes used by the system were entered (e.g., gender codes of M or F are allowed; X or Y would not be allowed). The edit routines can produce lists of errors to be corrected later.

processing controls

The routines for establishing that data are complete and accurate during updating.

Processing Controls **Processing controls** establish that data are complete and accurate during updating. The major processing controls are run control totals, computer matching, and programmed edit checks.

run control totals

The procedures for controlling completeness of computer updating by generating control totals that reconcile totals before and after processing.

Run control totals reconcile the input control totals with the totals of items that have updated the file. Updating can be controlled by generating control totals during processing. The totals, such as total transactions processed or totals for critical quantities, can be compared manually or by computer. Discrepancies are noted for investigation.

computer matching

The processing control that matches input data to information held on master files.

Computer matching matches the input data with information held on master files with unmatched items noted for investigation. For example, a matching program might match employee timecards with a payroll master file and report missing or duplicate time cards.

Most programmed edit checking occurs at the time data are input. However, certain applications require some type of reasonableness or dependency check during updating. For example, consistency checks might be used by a utility company to compare a customer's electric bill with previous bills. If the bill were 500 percent higher this month compared to last month, the bill would not be processed until the meter was rechecked.

output controls

Measures that ensure that the results of computer processing are accurate, complete, and properly distributed.

Output Controls **Output controls** ensure that the results of computer processing are accurate, complete, and properly distributed. Typical output controls include the following:

▯ Balancing output totals with input and processing totals

▯ Reviews of the computer processing logs to determine that all of the correct computer jobs executed properly for processing

▯ Formal procedures and documentation specifying authorized recipients of output reports, cheques, or other critical documents

PROTECTING THE DIGITAL FIRM

As companies increasingly rely on digital networks for their revenue and operations, they need to take additional steps to ensure that their systems and applications are always available to support their digital business processes.

High-Availability Computing

In a digital firm environment, information technology infrastructures must provide a continuous level of service availability across distributed computing platforms. Many factors can disrupt the performance of a Web site, including network failure, heavy Internet traffic, and exhausted server resources. Computer failures, interruptions, and downtime can translate into disgruntled customers, millions of dollars in lost sales, and the inability to perform critical internal transactions. Firms such as those in the airline and financial service industries with critical applications requiring online transaction processing have traditionally used fault-tolerant computer systems for many years to ensure 100 percent availability. In **online transaction processing**, transactions entered online are immediately processed by the computer. Multitudinous changes to databases, reporting, or requests for information occur each instant. **Fault-tolerant computer systems** contain redundant hardware, software, and power supply components that can back up the system and keep it running to prevent system failure. Fault-tolerant computers contain extra memory chips, processors, and disk storage devices. They can use special software routines or self-checking logic built into their circuitry to detect hardware failures and automatically switch to a backup device. Parts from these computers can be removed and repaired without disruption to the computer system. E-Smart Direct Services, Inc. (www.esds.net) of Etobicoke, Ontario, a provider of electronic payment processing and authorization services for retailers and financial institutions, needs a technology platform with 100 percent system availability. The company uses fault-tolerant systems from Stratus for this purpose.

Fault tolerant should be distinguished from high-availability computing. Both fault-tolerant and high-availability computing are designed to maximize application and system availability. Both use backup hardware resources. However, **high-availability computing** helps firms recover quickly from a crash, while fault tolerance promises continuous availability and the elimination of recovery time altogether. High-availability computing environments are a minimum requirement for firms with heavy electronic commerce requirements or critical dependence on digital networks for their internal operations. High availability computing requires an assortment of tools and technologies to ensure maximum performance of computer systems and networks, including redundant servers, mirroring, load balancing, clustering, storage area networks (see Chapter 6), and a good disaster recovery plan. The firm's computing platform must be extremely robust with scalable processing power, storage, and bandwidth. High-availability computing also requires a security infrastructure that can support electronic commerce and electronic business as described below.

Load balancing distributes large numbers of access requests across multiple servers. The requests are directed to the most available server so that no single device is overwhelmed. If one server is swamped, requests are forwarded to another server with more capacity. **Mirroring** uses a backup server that duplicates all the processes and transactions of the primary server. If the primary server fails, the backup server can immediately take its place without any interruption in service. However, server mirroring is very expensive because each server must be mirrored by an identical server whose only purpose is to be available in the event of a failure. **Clustering** is a less expensive technique for ensuring continued availability. High-availability clustering links two computers together so that the second computer can act as a backup to the primary computer. If the primary computer fails, the second computer picks up its processing without any pause in the system. (Computers can also be clustered together as a single computing resource to speed up processing.)

Internet Security Challenges

Linking to the Internet or transmitting information via intranets and extranets requires special security measures. Large public networks, including the Internet, are more vulnerable because they are open to virtually anyone and because they are so huge that when abuses do

online transaction processing
A transaction processing mode in which transactions entered online are immediately processed by the computer.

fault-tolerant computer systems
Systems that contain redundant hardware, software, and power supply components that can back up a system and keep it running to prevent system failure.

high-availability computing
A computing environment that helps firms recover quickly from a systems crash.

load balancing
Distributing large numbers of requests for access among multiple servers so that no single device is overwhelmed.

mirroring
Duplicating all the processes and transactions of a server on a backup server to prevent any interruption in service if the primary server fails.

clustering
Linking two computers together so that the second computer can act as a backup to the primary computer or speed up processing.

occur, they can have an enormously widespread impact. When the Internet becomes part of the corporate network, the organization's information systems can be vulnerable to actions from outsiders. Computers that are constantly connected to the Internet via cable modem or DSL line are more open to penetration by outsiders because they use a fixed Internet address where they can be more easily identified. (With dial-up service, a temporary Internet address is assigned for each session.) A fixed Internet address creates a fixed target for hackers.

Both electronic commerce and electronic business require companies to be both more open and more closed at the same time. To benefit from electronic commerce, supply chain management, and other digital business processes, companies need to be open to outsiders such as customers, suppliers, and trading partners. Corporate systems must also be extended outside the organization so that they can be accessed by employees working with wireless and other mobile computing devices. Yet these systems must also be closed to hackers and other intruders. The new information technology infrastructure requires a new security culture and infrastructure that allows businesses to straddle this fine line.

Chapter 10 described the use of *firewalls* to prevent unauthorized users from accessing private networks. As growing numbers of businesses expose their networks to Internet traffic, firewalls are becoming a necessity.

A firewall is generally placed between internal LANs and WANs and external networks such as the Internet. The firewall controls access to the organization's internal networks by acting like a gatekeeper that examines each user's credentials before they can access the network. The firewall identifies names, Internet Protocol (IP) addresses, applications, and other characteristics of incoming traffic. It checks this information against the access rules that have been programmed into the system by the network administrator. The firewall prevents unauthorized communication into and out of the network, allowing the organization to enforce a security policy on traffic flowing between its network and the Internet (Oppliger, 1997).

There are essentially two major types of firewall technologies: proxies and stateful inspection. *Proxies* stop data originating outside the organization at the firewall, inspect them, and pass a proxy to the internal side of the firewall. If a user outside the company wants to communicate with a user inside the organization, the outside user first "talks" to the proxy application and the proxy application communicates with the firm's internal computer. Similarly, a user inside the organization goes through the proxy to "talk" to computers on the outside. Because the actual message doesn't pass through the firewall, proxies are considered more secure than stateful inspection. However, they have to do a lot of work and can consume system resources, degrading network performance. The Raptor Firewall product is primarily a proxy-based firewall.

In *stateful inspection*, the firewall scans each packet of incoming data, checking its source, destination addresses, or services. It sets up state tables to track information over multiple packets. User-defined access rules must identify every type of packet that the organization does not want to admit. Although stateful inspection consumes fewer network resources than proxies, it is theoretically not as secure because some data pass through the firewall. Cisco Systems' firewall product is an example of a stateful inspection firewall. Hybrid firewall products are being developed. For instance, AlphaShield by British Columbia's Saafnet International is primarily a stateful inspection product.

To create a good firewall, someone must write and maintain the internal rules identifying the people, applications, or addresses that are allowed or rejected in very fine detail. Firewalls can deter but not completely prevent network penetration by outsiders and should be viewed as only one element in an overall security plan. In order to deal effectively with Internet security, broader corporate policies and procedures, user responsibilities, and security awareness training may be required (Segev, Porra, and Roldan, 1998). Figure 12-7 illustrates a user-friendly graphical interface for defining security rules.

In addition to firewalls, commercial security vendors now provide intrusion detection tools and services to protect against suspicious network traffic. **Intrusion detection systems** feature full-time monitoring tools placed at the most vulnerable points or "hot spots" of corporate networks to continually detect and deter intruders. Scanning software looks for known problems such as bad passwords, checks to see whether important files have been removed or modified, and sends warnings of vandalism or system administration errors. Monitoring software examines events as they are happening to look for security attacks in

intrusion detection systems
Tools to monitor the most vulnerable points in a network to detect and deter unauthorized intruders.

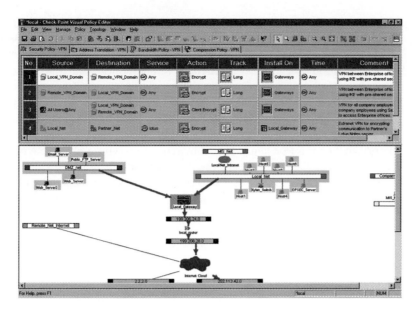

FIGURE 12-7 Check Point's Firewall-I software provides a user-friendly graphical interface for defining security rules. Firewall-I includes tools to monitor and control what goes into and out of an organization's network.

progress. The intrusion detection tool can also be customized to shut down a particularly sensitive part of a network if it receives unauthorized traffic.

Security and Electronic Commerce

Security of electronic communications is a major control issue for companies engaged in electronic commerce. It is essential that commerce-related data of buyers and sellers be kept private when they are transmitted electronically. The data being transmitted also must be protected against being purposefully altered by someone other than the sender, so that, for example, stock market execution orders or product orders accurately represent the wishes of the buyer and seller.

A large amount of online commerce continues to be handled through private electronic data interchange (EDI) networks, usually run over value-added networks (VANs). VANs are relatively secure and reliable. However, because they have to be privately maintained and run on high-speed private lines, VANs are expensive, easily costing a company $150 000 per month. They also are inflexible, being connected only to a limited number of sites and companies. As a result, the Internet is emerging as the network technology of choice. EDI transactions on the Internet run from one-half to one-tenth the cost of VAN-based transactions.

Many organizations rely on encryption to protect sensitive information transmitted over the Internet and other networks. **Encryption** is the coding and scrambling of messages to prevent unauthorized access to or understanding of the data being transmitted. A message can be encrypted by applying a secret numerical code called an encryption key so that it is transmitted as a scrambled set of characters. (The key consists of a large group of letters, numbers, and symbols.) In order to be read, the message must be decrypted (unscrambled) with a matching key.

A number of encryption standards exist. **SSL (Secure Sockets Layer)** and **S-HTTP (Secure Hypertext Transport Protocol)** are protocols for secure information transfer over the Internet. They allow client and server computers to manage encryption and decryption activities as they communicate with each other during a secure Web session. S-HTTP is an extension to the Hypertext Transfer Protocol that allows the secure exchange of files on the World Wide Web. Each S-HTTP file is encrypted and/or contains a digital certificate. S-HTTP does not use any single encryption system, but it does support the RSA public-and-private key encryption system.

S-HTTP allows the client to send a certificate to authenticate the user whereas SSL can only authenticate the server. S-HTTP is more likely to be used in situations where the server represents a bank and requires authentication from the user that is more secure than a userid and password. The "sockets" part of the secure sockets layer (SSL) refers to the method of passing data back and forth between a client and a server program in a network or between

encryption
The coding and scrambling of messages to prevent their being read or accessed without authorization.

Secure Sockets Layer (SSL)
A protocol for secure information transfer over the Internet that creates a secure connection between a client and a server.

Secure Hypertext Transport Protocol (S-HTTP)
A protocol for secure information transfer over the Internet that permits an individual message to be sent securely.

program layers in the same computer. SSL has recently been succeeded by Transport Layer Security (TLS), which is based on SSL. Both security protocols can be used by a browser user, but only one can be used with a given document.

There are several alternative methods of encryption, but "public key" encryption is the most popular. Public key encryption, illustrated in Figure 12-8, uses two different keys, one private and one public. The keys are mathematically related so that data encrypted with one key can only be decrypted using the other key. To send and receive messages, communicators first create separate pairs of private and public keys. The public key is kept in a directory and the private key must be kept secret. The sender encrypts a message with the recipient's public key. On receiving the message, the recipient uses his or her private key to decrypt it.

Encryption is especially useful to shield messages on the Internet and other public networks because they are less secure than private networks. Encryption helps protect transmission of payment data, such as credit card information, and addresses problems of authentication and message integrity.

Authentication refers to the ability of each party to know that the other party is who they claim to be. In the non-electronic world, we use our signatures. Bank-by-mail systems avoid the need for signatures on cheques they issue for their customers by using well-protected private networks where the source of the request for payment is recorded and can be proven. **Message integrity** is the ability to be certain that the message that is sent arrives without being copied or changed.

The Electronic Transactions Act, 2001, also known as Bill 13, came into force on April 10, 2001, and has given digital signatures the same legal status as those written on ink or paper. A **digital signature** is a digital code attached to an electronically transmitted message that is used to verify the origins and contents of a message. It provides a way to associate a message with the sender, performing a function similar to a written signature. For an electronic signature to be legally binding in court, someone must be able to verify that the signature actually belongs to the individual who sent the data and that the data were not altered after being "signed."

Digital certificates play a valuable role in authentication. **Digital certificates** are data files used to establish the identity of people and electronic assets for protection of online transactions (see Figure 12-9). A digital certificate system uses a trusted third party known as a *certificate authority (CA)* to validate a user's identity. The CA system can be run as a function inside an organization or by an outside company such as VeriSign Inc. of Mountain View, California. The CA verifies a digital certificate user's identity offline by telephone, postal mail, or in person. This information is put into a CA server that generates an encrypted digital certificate containing owner identification information and a copy of the owner's public key. The certificate authenticates that the public key belongs to the designated owner. The CA makes its own public key available publicly either in print or on the Internet. The recipient of an encrypted message uses the CA's public key to decode the digital certificate attached to the message, verifies it was issued by the CA, and then obtains the sender's public key and identification information contained in the certificate. Using this information, the recipient can send an encrypted reply. The digital certificate system would enable, for example, a credit card user and merchant to validate that their digital certificates were issued by an authorized and trusted third party before they exchange data.

authentication

The ability of each party in a transaction to ascertain the identity of the other party.

message integrity

The ability to ascertain that a transmitted message has not been copied or altered.

digital signature

A digital code that can be attached to an electronically transmitted message to uniquely identify its contents and the sender.

digital certificate

An attachment to an electronic message to verify the identity of the sender and to provide the receiver with the means to encode a reply.

FIGURE 12-8 Public key encryption. A public key encryption system can be viewed as a series of public and private keys that lock data when they are transmitted and unlock the data when they are received. The sender locates the recipient's public key in a directory and uses it to encrypt a message. The message is sent in encrypted form over the Internet or a private network. When the encrypted message arrives, the recipient uses his or her private key to decrypt the data and read the message.

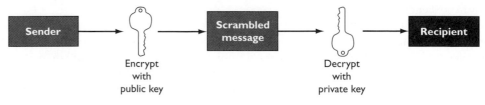

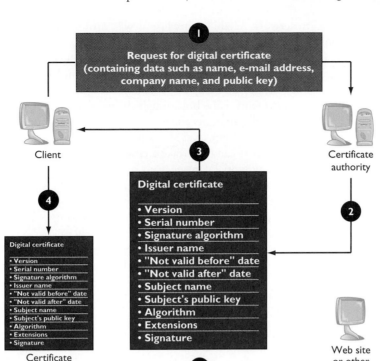

FIGURE 12-9 Digital certificates. Digital certificates establish the identity of people or electronic assets. They can be used to protect online transactions by providing secure, encrypted online communication.

Many credit card payment systems use the SSL protocol for encrypting credit card payment data. However, SSL does not verify that the purchaser is the owner of the card being used for payment. VISA, MasterCard, American Express, and other major credit card companies and banks have adopted a more secure protocol called the **Secure Electronic Transaction (SET)** protocol for encrypting credit card payment data over the Internet and other open networks. In SET, a user acquires a digital certificate and **digital wallet** from his or her bank, which acts as an intermediary in an e-commerce transaction. The wallet and certificate specify the identity of the user and the credit card being used. When the user shops at a Web site that uses the SET payment method, the merchant's servers send a signal over the Internet that invokes the user's SET wallet. The digital wallet encrypts the payment information and sends it to the merchant. The merchant verifies that the information is a SET packet and adds its digital certificate to the message. The merchant then encrypts this information and passes it on to a payment clearinghouse and to a certificate authority, which verifies the transaction as belonging to the sender. The clearinghouse approves or denies the transaction based on credit standing and passes that information over the Internet to the merchant and back to the user's wallet. The transaction is sent to the merchant's bank, which arranges for the fund transfer from user to merchant and the user's credit card account is charged for the transaction amount. The merchant ships the merchandise to the purchaser.

Secure Electronic Transaction (SET)
A standard for securing credit card transactions over the Internet and other networks that verifies that the owner of the card being used for payment is the purchaser.

digital wallet
Software that stores credit card, electronic cash, owner identification, and address information and provides these data automatically during electronic commerce purchase transactions.

DEVELOPING A CONTROL STRUCTURE:
COSTS AND BENEFITS

Information systems can make exhaustive use of all the control mechanisms previously discussed. But they may be so expensive to build and so complicated to use that the system is economically or operationally unfeasible. A cost/benefit analysis must be performed to determine which control mechanisms provide the most effective safeguards without sacrificing operational efficiency or cost.

One of the criteria that determine how much control is built into a system is the importance of its data. For example, major financial and accounting systems, such as a payroll system or one that tracks purchases and sales on the stock exchange, must have higher standards of control than a tickler system to track dental patients and remind them that their six-month check-up is due. For instance, Swissair invested in additional hardware and software

risk assessment
Determining the potential frequency of the occurrence of a problem and the potential damage if the problem were to occur. Used to determine the cost/benefit of a control.

to increase its network reliability because it was running critical reservation and ticketing applications.

The cost-effectiveness of controls will also be influenced by the efficiency, complexity, and expense of each control technique. For example, complete one-for-one checking may be time consuming and operationally impossible for a system that processes hundreds of thousands of utilities payments daily. But it might be possible to use this technique to verify only critical data such as dollar amounts and account numbers while ignoring names and addresses.

A third consideration is the level of risk if a specific activity or process is not properly controlled. System developers can undertake a **risk assessment**, determining the likely frequency of a problem and the potential damage if it were to occur. For example, if an event is likely to occur no more than once a year, with a maximum of $1000 loss to the organization, it would not be feasible to spend $20 000 on the design and maintenance of a control to protect against that event. However, if that same event could occur at least once a day, with a potential loss of more than $300 000 a year, $100 000 spent on a control might be entirely appropriate.

Table 12-4 illustrates sample results of a risk assessment for an online order processing system that processes 30 000 orders per day. The probability of a power failure occurring in a one-year period is 30 percent. Loss of order transactions while power is down could range from $5000 to $200 000 for each occurrence, depending on how long processing was halted. The probability of embezzlement occurring over a yearly period is about 5 percent, with potential losses ranging from $1000 to $50 000 for each occurrence. User errors have a 98 percent chance of occurring over a yearly period, with losses ranging from $200 to $40 000 for each occurrence. The average loss for each event can be weighted by multiplying it by the probability of its occurrence annually to determine the expected annual loss. Once the risks have been assessed, system developers can concentrate on the control points with the greatest vulnerability and potential loss. In this case, controls should focus on ways to minimize the risk of power failures and user errors. Increasing management awareness of the full range of actions they can take to reduce risks can substantially reduce system losses (Straub and Welke, 1998).

In some situations, organizations may not know the precise probability of threats occurring to their information systems, and they may not be able to quantify the impact of such events. In these instances, management may choose to describe risks and their likely impact in a qualitative manner (Rainer, Snyder, and Carr, 1991).

To decide which controls to use, information system developers must examine various control techniques in relation to each other and to their relative cost-effectiveness. A control weakness at one point may be offset by a strong control at another. It may not be cost-effective to build tight controls at every point in the processing cycle if the areas of greatest risk are secure or if compensating controls exist elsewhere. The combination of all of the controls developed for a particular application will determine its overall control structure.

TABLE 12-4	ONLINE ORDER PROCESSING RISK ASSESSMENT		
Exposure	**Probability of Occurrence (%)**	**Loss Range/ Average**	**Expected Annual Loss**
Power failure	30%	$5000–$200 000 ($102 500)	$30 750
Embezzlement	5	$1000–$50 000 ($25 500)	$1275
User error	98	$200–$40 000 ($20 100)	$19 698

This chart shows the results of a risk assessment of three selected areas of an online order processing system. The likelihood of each exposure occurring over a one-year period is expressed as a percentage. The next column shows the highest and lowest possible loss that could be expected each time the exposure occurred and an average loss calculated by adding the highest and lowest figures together and dividing by two. The expected annual loss for each exposure can be determined by multiplying the average loss by its probability of occurrence.

MANAGEMENT DECISION PROBLEM

ANALYZING SECURITY VULNERABILITIES

A survey of your firm's information technology infrastructure has produced the following security analysis statistics:

High-risk vulnerabilities include non-authorized users accessing applications, guessable passwords, user name matching the password, active user accounts with missing passwords, and the existence of unauthorized programs in application systems.

Medium-risk vulnerabilities include the ability of users to shut down the system without being logged on, passwords and screen saver settings that were not established for PCs, and outdated versions of software still being stored on hard drives.

Low-risk vulnerabilities include the inability of users to change their passwords, user passwords that have never been changed periodically, and passwords that were smaller than the minimum size specified by the company.

1. Calculate the total number of vulnerabilities for each platform. What is the potential impact on the organization of the security problems for each computing platform?

2. If you only have one information systems specialist in charge of security, which platforms should you address first in trying to eliminate these vulnerabilities? second? third? last? Why?

3. Identify the types of control problems illustrated by these vulnerabilities and explain the measures that should be taken to solve them.

4. What does your firm risk by ignoring the identified security vulnerabilities?

Security Vulnerabilities by Type of Computing Platform

Platform	Number of Computers	High Risk	Medium Risk	Low Risk	Total Vulnerabilities
Windows 2000 Server (corporate applications)	1	11	37	19	
Windows 2000 Workstation (high-level administrators)	3	56	242	87	
Linux (e-mail and printing services)	1	3	154	98	
Sun Solaris (UNIX) (E-commerce and Web servers)	2	12	299	78	
Windows 95/98 User desktops and laptops with office productivity tools that can also be linked to the corporate network running corporate applications and intranets	195	14	16	1237	

THE ROLE OF AUDITING IN THE CONTROL PROCESS

How does management know that information systems controls are effective? To answer this question, organizations must conduct comprehensive and systematic audits. An **MIS audit** identifies all of the controls that govern individual information systems and assesses their effectiveness. To accomplish this, the auditor must acquire a thorough understanding of operations, physical facilities, telecommunications, control systems, data security objectives, organizational structure, personnel, manual procedures, and individual applications.

The auditor usually interviews key individuals who use and operate a specific information system concerning their activities and procedures. Application controls, overall integrity controls, and control disciplines are examined. The auditor should trace the flow of sample transactions through the system and perform tests, using, if appropriate, automated audit software.

The audit lists and ranks all control weaknesses and estimates the probability of their occurrence. It then assesses the financial and organizational impact of each threat. Figure 12-10 is a sample auditor's listing of control weaknesses for a loan system. It includes a section for notifying management of these weaknesses and for management's response. Management is expected to devise a plan for countering significant weaknesses in controls.

MIS audit
Identifies all the controls that govern individual information systems and assesses their effectiveness.

An auditor interviews key individuals who use and operate a specific information system concerning their activities and procedures. The auditor often traces the flow of sample transactions through the system and performs tests using automated audit software.

Function: <u>Personal Loans</u>   Prepared by: <u>J. Ericson</u>   Received by: <u>T. Barrow</u>
Location: <u>   </u>   Preparation date: <u>June 16, 2001</u>   Review date: <u>June 28, 2001</u>

Nature of Weakness and Impact	Chance for Substantial Error		Effect on Audit Procedures	Notification to Management	
	Yes/ No	Justification	Required Amendment	Date of Report	Management Response
Loan repayment records are not reconciled to borrower's records during processing.	Yes	Without a detection control, errors in individual client balances may remain undetected.	Confirm a sample of loans.	5/10/01	Interest Rate Compare Report provides this control.
There are no regular audits of computer-generated data (interest charges).	Yes	Without a regular audit or reasonableness check, widespread miscalculations could result before errors are detected.		5/10/01	Periodic audits of loans will be instituted.
Programs can be put into production libraries to meet target deadlines without final approval from the Standards and Controls group.	No	All programs require management authorization. The Standards and Controls group controls access to all production systems and assigns these cases to a temporary production status.			

FIGURE 12-10 Sample auditor's list of control weaknesses. This chart is a sample page from a list of control weaknesses that an auditor might find in a loan system in a local commercial bank. This form helps auditors record and evaluate control weaknesses and shows the results of discussing those weaknesses with management, as well as any corrective actions taken by management.

12.3 ENSURING SYSTEM QUALITY

Organizations can improve system quality by using software quality assurance techniques and by improving the quality of their data.

SOFTWARE QUALITY ASSURANCE METHODOLOGIES AND TOOLS

Solutions to software quality problems include using an appropriate systems development methodology, proper resource allocation during systems development, the use of metrics, and attention to testing.

Structured Methodologies

development methodology
A collection of methods, one or more for every activity within every phase of a development project.

Various tools and development methodologies have been employed to help systems developers document, analyze, design, and implement information systems. A **development methodology** is a collection of methods, one or more for every activity within every phase of a systems development project. The primary function of a development methodology is to provide discipline to the entire development process. A good development methodology establishes organization-wide standards for requirements for gathering, design, programming, and testing. To produce quality software, organizations must select an appropriate methodology and then enforce its use. The methodology should call for systems requirement and specification documents that are complete, detailed, accurate, and in a format the user community can understand before they approve it. Specifications also must include agreed-on measures of system quality so that the system can be evaluated objectively while it is being developed and once it is completed.

structured
Refers to the fact that techniques are carefully drawn up, step by step, with each step building on a previous one.

Development methodologies reflect different philosophies of systems development. Chapter 11 has already described object-oriented software development. The traditional structured methodologies and computer-aided software engineering (CASE) are other important methodologies and tools for producing quality software. Structured methodologies have been used to document, analyze, and design information systems since the 1970s. **Structured** refers to the fact that the techniques follow a step-by-step pattern, with each step building on the previous one. Structured methodologies are top-down, progressing from the highest, most abstract level to the lowest level of detail—from the general to the specific. For example, the highest level of a top-down description of a human resources system would show the main human resources functions: personnel, benefits, compensation, and Equal Employment Opportunity (EEO). Each of these would be broken down into the next layer. Benefits, for instance, might include pension, employee savings, healthcare, and insurance. Each of these layers in turn would be broken down until the lowest level of detail could be depicted.

The traditional structured methodologies are process-oriented rather than data-oriented. Although data descriptions are part of the methods, the methodologies focus on how the data are transformed rather than on the data themselves. These methodologies are largely linear; each phase must be completed before the next one can begin. Structured methodologies include structured analysis, structured design, structured programming, and the use of flowcharts.

Structured Analysis

Structured analysis is widely used to define system inputs, processes, and outputs. It offers a logical, graphical model of information flow, partitioning a system into modules that show manageable levels of detail. It rigorously specifies the processes or transformations that occur within each module and the interfaces that exist between them. Its primary tool is the **data flow diagram (DFD)**, a graphic representation of a system's component processes and the interfaces (flow of data) between them.

Figure 12-11 shows a simple data flow diagram for a mail-in university course registration system. The rounded boxes represent processes, which portray the transformation of data. The square box represents an external entity, which is an originator or receiver of information located outside the boundaries of the system being modelled. The open rectangles represent data stores, which are either manual or automated inventories of data. The arrows represent data flows, which show the movement between processes, external entities, and data stores. They always contain packets of data with the name or content of each data flow listed beside the arrow.

The data flow diagram depicted shows that students submit registration forms with their name, identification number, and the numbers of the courses they wish to take. In process 1.0, the system verifies that each course selected is still open by referencing the university's course file. The file distinguishes courses that are open from those that have been cancelled or filled. Process 1.0 then determines which of the student's selections can be accepted or rejected. Process 2.0 enrols the student in the courses for which he or she has been accepted. It updates the university's course file with the student's name and identification number and recalculates the class size. If maximum enrolment has been reached, the course number is flagged as closed. Process 2.0 also updates the university's student master file with information about new students or changes in address. Process 3.0 then sends each student applicant

structured analysis
A method for defining system inputs, processes, and outputs, and for partitioning systems into subsystems or modules that show a logical, graphical model of information flow.

data flow diagram (DFD)
The primary tool for structured analysis that graphically illustrates a system's component processes and the flow of data between them.

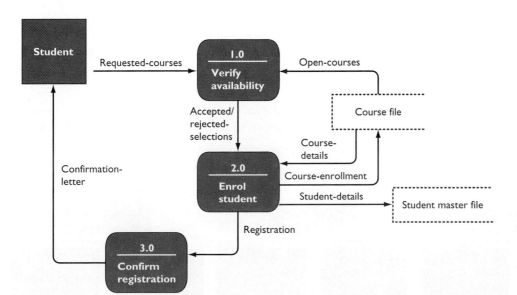

FIGURE 12-11 Data flow diagram for mail-in university registration system. The system has three processes: Verify availability (1.0), Enrol student (2.0), and Confirm registration (3.0). The name and content of each of the data flows appear adjacent to each arrow. There is one external entity in this system: the student. There are two data stores: the student master file and the course file.

a confirmation-of-registration letter listing the courses for which he or she is registered and noting the course selections that could not be fulfilled.

The diagrams can be used to depict higher-level processes as well as lower-level details. Through *levelled* data flow diagrams, a complex process can be broken down into successive levels of detail. An entire system can be divided into subsystems with a high-level data flow diagram. Each subsystem, in turn, can be divided into additional subsystems with second-level data flow diagrams, and the lower level subsystems can be broken down again until the lowest level of detail has been reached.

Another tool for structured analysis is a data dictionary, which contains information about individual pieces of data and data groupings within a system (see Chapter 8). The data dictionary defines the contents of data flows and data stores so that system developers understand exactly what pieces of data they contain. **Process specifications** describe the transformation occurring within the lowest level of the data flow diagrams. They express the logic for each process.

Structured Design

Structured design encompasses a set of design rules and techniques that promotes program clarity and simplicity, thereby reducing the time and effort required for coding, debugging, and maintenance. The main principle of structured design is that a system should be designed from the top down in hierarchical fashion and refined to greater levels of detail. The design should first consider the main function of a program or system, then break this function into subfunctions and decompose each subfunction until the lowest level of detail has been reached. The lowest level modules describe the actual processing that will occur. In this way, all high-level logic and the design model are developed before detailed program code is written. If structured analysis has been performed, the structured specification document can serve as input to the design process. Our earlier human resources top-down description provides a good overview example of structured design.

As the design is formulated, it is documented in a structure chart. The **structure chart** is a top-down chart, showing each level of design, its relationship to other levels, and its place in the overall design structure. Figure 12-12 shows a high-level structure chart for a payroll system. If a design has too many levels to fit onto one structure chart, it can be broken down further on more detailed structure charts. A structure chart may document one program, one system (a set of programs), or part of one program.

Structured Programming

Structured programming extends the principles governing structured design to the writing of programs to make software programs easier to understand and modify. It is based on the principle of modularization, which follows from top-down analysis and design. Each of the boxes in the structure chart represents a component **module** that is usually directly related to a bottom-level design module. It constitutes a logical unit that performs one or several functions. Ideally, modules should be independent of each other and should have only one entry to and exit from their parent modules. They should share data with as few other modules as possible. Each module should be kept to a manageable size. An individual should be

process specifications
Descriptions of the logic of the processes occurring within the lowest levels of a data flow diagram.

structured design
A software design discipline encompassing a set of design rules and techniques for designing systems from the top down in a hierarchical fashion.

structure chart
System documentation showing each level of design, the relationship among the levels, and the overall place in the design structure; can document one program, one system, or part of one program.

structured programming
A discipline for organizing and coding programs that simplifies the control paths so that the programs can be easily understood and modified; uses the basic control structures and modules that have only one entry point and one exit point.

module
A logical unit of a program that performs one or several functions.

FIGURE 12-12 High-level structure chart for a payroll system. This structure chart shows the highest or most abstract level of design for a payroll system, providing an overview of the entire system.

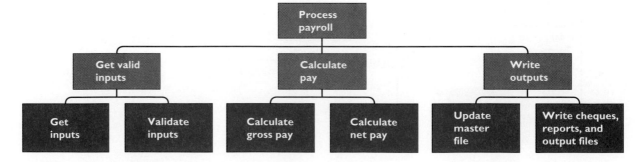

able to read and understand the program code for the module and easily keep track of its functions.

Proponents of structured programming have shown that any program can be written using three basic control constructs, or instruction patterns: (1) simple sequence, (2) selection, and (3) iteration. These control constructs are illustrated in Figure 12-13.

The **sequence construct** executes statements in the order in which they appear, with control passing unconditionally from one statement to the next. The program will execute statement A and then statement B.

The **selection construct** tests a condition and executes one of two alternative instructions based on the results of the test. Condition R is tested. If R is true, statement C is executed. If R is false, statement D is executed. Control then passes to the next statement. Selection construct instructions are also known as *if-then* statements.

The **iteration construct** repeats a segment of code as long as a conditional test remains true. Condition S is tested. If S is true, statement E is executed and control returns to the test of S. If S is false, E is skipped and control passes to the next statement. Iteration construct instruction sets are also known as *do loops* because the initial instruction is usually in the form of either "do while" the test is true or "do until" the test is false.

Flowcharts

Flowcharting is an older design tool that is still in use. **System flowcharts** detail the flow of data throughout an entire information system. Flowcharting is no longer recommended for program design because it does not provide top-down modular structure as effectively as other techniques. However, system flowcharts still may be used to document physical design specifications because they can show all inputs, major files, processing, and outputs for a system, and they can document manual procedures.

Using specialized symbols and flow lines, the system flowchart traces the flow of information and work in a system, the sequence of processing steps, and the physical media on which data are input, output, and stored. Figure 12-14 shows some of the basic symbols for system flowcharting used in a high-level system flowchart for a payroll system. The plain rectangle is a general symbol for a process. Flow lines show the sequence of steps and the direction of information flow. Arrows are employed to show direction if it is not apparent in the diagram.

Limitations of Traditional Methods

Although traditional methods are valuable, they can be inflexible and time-consuming. Completion of structured analysis is required before design can begin, and programming must await the completed deliverables from the design phase. A change in specifications requires that first the analysis documents and then the design documents must be modified before the programs can be changed to reflect the new requirement. Structured methodologies are function-oriented, focusing on the processes that transform the data. Chapter 11 described how object-oriented development addresses this problem. System developers can also use **computer-aided software engineering (CASE)** tools to make structured methods more flexible.

sequence construct
The sequential single steps or actions in the logic of a program that do not depend on the existence of any condition.

selection construct
The logic pattern in programming where a stated condition determines which of two alternative actions can be taken; also known as "if-then" statements.

iteration construct
The logic pattern in programming where certain actions are repeated while a specified condition occurs or until a certain condition is met; also known as "do while" or "do until" loops.

system flowchart
A graphic design tool that depicts the physical media and sequence of processing steps used in an entire information system.

computer-aided software engineering (CASE)
The automation of step by step methodologies for software and systems development to reduce the amount of repetitive work the developer needs to do.

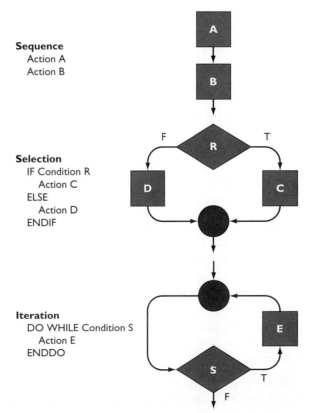

Sequence
Action A
Action B

Selection
IF Condition R
    Action C
ELSE
    Action D
ENDIF

Iteration
DO WHILE Condition S
    Action E
ENDDO

FIGURE 12-13 Basic program control constructs. The three basic control constructs used in structured programming are sequence, selection, and iteration.

FIGURE 12-14 System flowchart for a payroll system. This is a high-level system flowchart for a batch payroll system. Only the most important processes and files are illustrated. Data are input from two sources: timecards and payroll-related data (such as salary increases) passed from the human resources system. The data are first edited and validated against the existing payroll master file before the payroll master is updated. The update process produces an updated payroll master file, various payroll reports (such as the payroll register and hours register), cheques, a direct deposit tape, and a file of payment data that must be passed to the organization's general ledger system. The direct deposit tape is sent to the automated clearinghouse that serves the banks offering direct deposit services to employees.

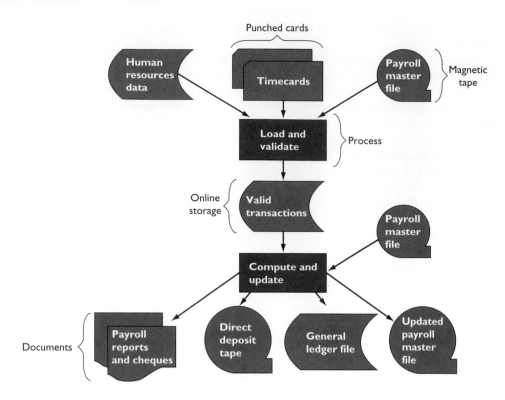

Unified Modelling Language (UML)

The Unified Modelling Language™ (UML) is the industry-standard language for specifying, visualizing, constructing, and documenting the artifacts of software systems. It simplifies the complex process of software design, making a "blueprint" for construction. UML represents a collection of best engineering practices that have proven successful in the modelling of large and complex systems. Developing a model for an industrial-strength software system prior to its construction or renovation is as essential as having a blueprint for large building. Good models are essential for communication among project teams and to ensure architectural soundness. As the complexity of systems increase, so does the importance of good modelling techniques. UML provides the a standardized application modelling language for business process modelling.

Computer-Aided Software Engineering (CASE)

Computer-aided software engineering (CASE)—sometimes called *computer-aided systems engineering*—is the automation of step-by-step methodologies for software and systems development to reduce the amount of repetitive work the developer needs to do. Its adoption can free the developer for more creative problem-solving tasks. CASE tools also facilitate the creation of clear documentation and the coordination of team development efforts. Team members can share their work easily by accessing each other's files to review or modify what has been done. Some studies have found that systems developed with CASE and the newer methodologies are more reliable, and they require repairs less often (Dekleva, 1992). Modest productivity benefits can also be achieved if the tools are used properly. Many CASE tools are PC-based, with powerful graphical capabilities.

CASE tools provide automated graphics facilities for producing charts and diagrams, screen and report generators, data dictionaries, extensive reporting facilities, analysis and checking tools, code generators, and documentation generators. Most CASE tools are based on one or more of the popular structured methodologies. Some support object-oriented development. In general, CASE tools try to increase productivity and quality by the following means:

▌ Enforce a standard development methodology and design discipline

▌ Improve communication between users and technical specialists

▌ Organize and correlate design components and provide rapid access to them via a design repository

▌ Automate tedious and error-prone portions of analysis and design

▌ Automate code generation, testing, and control rollout

Many CASE tools have been classified in terms of whether they support activities at the front end or the back end of the systems development process. Front-end CASE tools focus on capturing analysis and design information in the early stages of systems development while back-end CASE tools address coding, testing, and maintenance activities. Back-end tools help convert specifications automatically into program code. Front-end CASE tools are also referred to as *upper-CASE* while back-end CASE tools are *lower-CASE*. Those CASE tool packages that contain both are called *I-CASE* or *integrated CASE*.

CASE tools automatically tie data elements to the processes where they are used. If a data flow diagram is changed from one process to another, the elements in the data dictionary would be altered automatically to reflect the change in the diagram. CASE tools also contain features for validating design diagrams and specifications. CASE tools thus support iterative design by automating revisions and changes and providing prototyping facilities (see Figure 12-15).

A CASE information repository stores all the information defined by the analysts during the project. The repository includes data flow diagrams, structure charts, entity-relationship diagrams, data definitions, process specifications, screen and report formats, notes and comments, and test results. CASE tools now have features to support client/server applications, object-oriented programming, and business process redesign. Methodologies and tool sets are being created to leverage organizational knowledge of business process reengineering (Nissen, 1998).

To be used effectively, CASE tools require organizational discipline. Every member of a development project must adhere to a common set of naming conventions, standards, and development methodology. The best CASE tools enforce common methods and standards, which may discourage their use in situations where organizational discipline is lacking.

Resource Allocation During Systems Development

Views on resource allocation during systems development have changed significantly over the years. **Resource allocation** determines the way costs, time, and personnel are assigned to different phases of the project. Previously, developers focused on programming, with only about 1 percent of the time and costs of a project being devoted to systems analysis (determining specifications). More time should be spent on specifications and systems analysis, decreasing the proportion of programming time and reducing the need for as much maintenance time. Documenting requirements so that they can be understood from their origin through development, specification, and continuing use can also reduce errors as well as time and costs (Domges and Pohl, 1998). Current literature suggests that about one-quarter of a project's time and cost should be expended in specifications and analysis, with perhaps 50 percent of its resources being allocated to design and programming. Installation and post-implementation ideally should require only one-quarter of the project's resources. Investments in software quality initiatives early in a project are likely to provide the greatest payback (Slaughter, Harter, and Krishnan, 1998).

resource allocation
The determination of how costs, time, and personnel are assigned to different phases of a systems development project.

Software Metrics

Software metrics can play a vital role in increasing system quality. **Software metrics** are objective assessments of the system in the form of quantified measurements. Ongoing use of metrics allows the IS department and users jointly to measure the performance of the system and to identify problems as they occur. Examples of software metrics include the number of transactions that can be processed in a specified unit of time, online response time, the number of payroll cheques printed per hour, and the number of known bugs per hundred lines of code.

For metrics to be successful, they must be carefully designed, formal, and objective. They must measure significant aspects of the system. In addition, metrics are of no value unless they are used consistently and users agree to the measurements in advance.

software metrics
The objective assessments of the software used in a system in the form of quantified measurements.

FIGURE 12-15 CASE tools facilitate the creation of clear documentation and the coordination of team development efforts

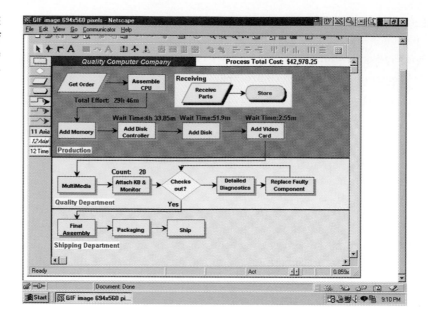

Testing

Chapter 11 described the stages of testing required to put an information system in operation—program testing, system testing, and acceptance testing. Early, regular, and thorough testing contributes significantly to system quality. In general, software testing is often misunderstood. Many view testing as a way to prove the correctness of work they have done. In fact, we know that all sizable software contains many errors, and we must test to uncover these errors.

Testing begins at the design phase. Because no coding yet exists, the test normally used is a **walkthrough**—a review of a specification or design document by a small group of people carefully selected based on the skills needed for the particular objectives being tested. Once coding begins, coding walkthroughs also can be used to review program code. However, code must be tested by computer runs. When errors are discovered, the source is found and eliminated through a process called **debugging**.

Electronic commerce and electronic business applications introduce new levels of complexity for testing to ensure high-quality performance and functionality. Behind each large Web site such as Indigo.com, eBay, or BayStreet.ca are hundreds of servers, thousands of miles of network cable, and hundreds of software programs, creating numerous points of vulnerability. These Web sites must be developed and tested to make sure that they can withstand both expected and unexpected spikes and peaks in their load. Web site traffic and technical components such as hardware, software, and networks must both be taken into consideration during application development and testing. The Window on Technology explores this issue.

Many companies delay testing until the end of the application development phase, when design decisions have been finalized and most of the software program code has been written. Leaving Web site performance and scalability tests until the end of the application development cycle is extremely risky because problems often stem from the fundamental workings of the system. To minimize the chance of discovering major structural problems late in the systems development process, companies should start their testing well before the system is complete. This makes it possible to address performance bottlenecks and other issues in each application level or system component before everything is integrated.

DATA QUALITY AUDITS AND DATA CLEANSING

Information system quality can also be improved by identifying and correcting faulty data and by making error detection a more explicit organizational goal (Klein, Goodhue, and Davis, 1997). The analysis of data quality often begins with a **data quality audit**, which is a

---

walkthrough

A review of a specification or design document by a small group of people carefully selected based on the skills needed for the particular objectives being tested.

debugging

The process of discovering and eliminating the errors and defects—the bugs—in program code.

data quality audit

A survey of files and samples of files for accuracy and completeness of data in an information system.

structured survey of the accuracy and level of completeness of the data in an information system. Data quality audits are accomplished by the following methods:

❚ Surveying end users for their perceptions of data quality

❚ Surveying entire data files

❚ Surveying samples from data files

Unless regular data quality audits are undertaken, organizations have no way of knowing to what extent their information systems contain inaccurate, incomplete, or ambiguous information.

Until recently, many organizations were not giving data quality the priority it deserves (Tayi and Ballou, 1998). Electronic commerce and electronic business are now forcing more companies to pay attention to data quality because a digitally enabled firm cannot run efficiently without accurate data about customers and business partners. **Data cleansing** has become a core requirement for data warehousing, customer relationship management, and Web-based commerce. Companies implementing data warehousing often find inconsistencies in customer or employee information as they try to integrate information from different business units. Companies are also finding mistakes in the data provided by customers or business partners through a Web site. Online exchanges (see Chapter 4) are especially prob-

data cleansing
Correcting errors and inconsistencies in data to increase accuracy so that the data can be used in a standard company-wide format.

WINDOW ON TECHNOLOGY

STRESS TESTING WEB SITES

Performance failures often accompany a Web site's success. Many Web site outages have been caused by large surges in the number of legitimate visitors as well as by hackers overwhelming the sites with requests for services. Serious e-commerce sites can expect spikes in traffic that run four to ten times their normal load. If a Web site cannot respond quickly and accurately to visitor requests, customers are quick to go elsewhere to make their purchases. The benefits of testing Web sites for scalability and rigor are obvious.

Some companies think that gathering five or six people in a room to click on a Web site is a suitable test of scalability and performance. But to test a Web site realistically, companies need to find a way to subject the Web site to the same number of concurrent users as would actually be visiting the site at one time and to devise test plans that reflect what these people would actually be doing. For example, a retail e-commerce site should create a test scenario where there are many visitors just browsing and some are making purchases. Developers should test for users with different types of client computers and the effect of slow telecommunication transmission speeds.

A realistic scalability test will reflect the driving factors behind each business, such as historic traffic numbers, profiles of typical Web site visitors, and metrics that are of most importance to the organization, such as page load time or number of transactions per second.

Managing spikes in Web site traffic requires a knowledge of Web site content, users, their interactions, and everything else that can affect Web site performance. Few managers understand their site's real performance level before testing.

Coast Software, located in Ottawa, Ontario, is a Web site performance management company that sells WebMaster software for Web testing and monitoring and offers hosting services for Web testing and monitoring. Coast and other performance management services can produce detailed data on every component of the Web site, any time, from any location. The resulting data can be used to create graphs to benchmark average performance from each location and to spot slow points. By creating a test population that mirrors the actual Web site visitor population, Web site owners can find out exactly how well their site works. Sometimes performance can be boosted through simple tuning of the Web site, but there are cases where the performance problems are deeply rooted and the Web site must undergo major design changes.

Testing wireless applications poses additional challenges. The millions of new wireless users are placing a massive new burden on the Internet infrastructure for wireless service providers and for organizations with wireless Web applications. Many wireless and conventional Web applications are linked to the same back-end systems so the total load on those systems will increase dramatically as wireless users are added. Automated load testing tools that simulate thousands of wireless Web and conventional Web browser sessions occurring simultaneously can help companies measure the impact on system performance.

To Think About: What management, organization, and technology issues should be addressed by Web site testing? At what point should an organization hire Coast Software or another Web testing firm? Why?

Sources: Phil Hollows, "Build High-Quality E-Business Applications," *e-Business Advisor*, November 2000; James Karney, "For Good Measure," *Internet World*, July 1, 2000; Coast Software Web Site, www.coast.ca, accessed June 27, 2001.

lematic because they use catalogue data from dozens to thousands of suppliers and these data are often in different formats, with different classification schemes for product numbers, product descriptions, and other attributes. Data cleansing tools can be used to correct errors in these data and to integrate them in a consistent company-wide format. For example, Ameritech was able to cut the volume of its mail by 4 percent and save $375 000 per year by cleansing millions of customer names and addresses (Faden, 2000). By using data cleansing, The Hong Kong Bank of Canada (www.hsbc.ca) was able to group customers by household while SaskTel was able to segment their customers into groups; without data cleansing so that data from different internal sources could be integrated, neither company could have carried through on these CRM initiatives.

APPLICATION SOFTWARE EXERCISE

SPREADSHEET EXERCISE: PERFORMING A SECURITY RISK ASSESSMENT

Mercer Paints is a paint manufacturing company located in Alberta. Although Mercer Paints is a small company, the quality of its products is widely recognized. The company has a network in place, linking many of its business operations.

While the company feels that its security is adequate, the recent addition of a Web site has been an open invitation to hackers. Just last week, someone hacked into the computer system and defaced the company's Web site. Because of this recent event, company management requested a risk assessment. The risk assessment identified several potential exposures; these exposures, associated probabilities, and average losses are summarized in the table provided on our Web site for Chapter 12. In addition to the potential exposures listed below, you should identify at least three other potential threats to Mercer Paints, assign probabilities to the threats, and estimate a loss range.

Using a spreadsheet product and the risk assessment data provided on the Laudon, Laudon, and Brabston Web site for Chapter 12, calculate the expected annual loss for each exposure. Which control points have the greatest vulnerability? What recommendations would you make to Mercer Paints? Prepare a written report that summarizes your findings and recommendations.

MANAGEMENT WRAP-UP

Management is responsible for developing and ensuring security, control, and quality standards for the organization. Key management decisions include establishing standards for systems accuracy and reliability, determining an appropriate level of control for organizational functions, and establishing a disaster recovery plan.

The characteristics of the organization play a large role in determining its approach to quality assurance and control issues. Some organizations are more quality and control conscious than others. Their cultures and business processes support high standards of quality and performance. Creating high levels of security and quality in information systems can be a process of lengthy organizational change.

A number of technologies and methodologies are available for promoting system quality and security. Technologies such as antivirus and data security software, firewalls, fault-tolerant and high-availability computing technology, and programmed procedures can be used to create a control environment while software metrics, systems development methodologies, and automated tools for systems development can be used to improve software quality. Organizational discipline is required to use these technologies effectively.

For Discussion

1. It has been said that controls and security should be one of the first areas to be addressed in the design of an information system. Do you agree? Why or why not?

2. How much software testing is "enough"? What management, organization, and technology issues should you consider in answering this question?

SUMMARY

1. *Demonstrate why information systems are so vulnerable to destruction, error, abuse, and system quality problems.* With data concentrated into electronic form and many procedures invisible through automation, computer-based information systems are vulnerable to destruction, misuse, error, fraud, and hardware or software failures. Online systems and those that use the Internet are especially vulnerable because data and files can be immediately and directly accessed through computer terminals or at many points in the network. Computer viruses can spread rampantly from system to system, clogging computer memory or destroying programs and data. Software presents problems because of the high costs of correcting errors and because software bugs may be impossible to eliminate. Data quality can also severely impact system quality and performance.

2. *Compare general controls and application controls for information systems.* Controls consist of all the methods, policies, and organizational procedures that ensure the safety of the organization's assets, the accuracy and reliability of its accounting records, and adherence to management standards. There are two main categories of controls: general controls and application controls.

General controls handle the overall design, security, and use of computers, programs, and files for the organization's information technology infrastructure. They include physical hardware controls, systems software controls, data file security controls, computer operations controls, controls over the systems implementation process, and administrative disciplines.

Application controls are those unique to specific computer-based applications. They focus on the completeness and accuracy of input, updating, and maintenance, and the validity of the information in the system. Application controls consist of input, processing, and output controls.

To determine which controls are required, designers and users of systems must identify all of the control points and control weaknesses and perform a risk assessment. They must also perform a cost/benefit analysis of controls and then design controls that can effectively safeguard systems without making them unusable.

3. *Describe the special measures required to ensure the reliability, availability, and security of electronic commerce and digital business processes.* Companies require special measures to support electronic commerce and digital business processes. They can use fault-tolerant computer systems or create high-availability computing environments to make sure that their information systems are always available and perform without interruptions. Firewalls and intrusion detection systems help safeguard private networks from unauthorized access when organizations use intranets or link to the Internet. Encryption is a widely used technology for securing electronic transmissions over the Internet. Digital certificates provide further protection of electronic transactions by authenticating a user's identity.

4. *Describe the most important software quality assurance techniques.* The quality and reliability of software can be improved by using a standard development methodology, software metrics, thorough testing procedures, and by reallocating resources to put more emphasis on the analysis and design stages of systems development.

Structured methodologies have been used to increase software quality since the 1970s. Structured analysis highlights the flow of data and the processes through which data are transformed. Its principal tool is the data flow diagram. Structured design and programming are software design disciplines that produce reliable, well-documented software with a simple, clear structure that is easy for others to understand and maintain. Structured charts show the top-down breakdown of a system by its modules. System flowcharts are useful for documenting the physical aspects of system design.

Computer-aided software engineering (CASE) automates methodologies for systems development. CASE promotes standards and improves coordination and consistency during systems development. CASE tools help system developers build a better model of a system and facilitate revision of design specifications to correct errors.

5. *Demonstrate the importance of auditing information systems and safeguarding data quality.* Comprehensive and systematic MIS auditing can help organizations to determine the effectiveness of the controls in their information systems. Regular data quality audits should be conducted to help organizations ensure a high level of completeness and accuracy of the data stored in their systems. Data cleansing should also be performed to create consistent and accurate data for company-wide use in electronic commerce and electronic business.

KEY TERMS

Administrative controls, 419

Antivirus software, 414

Application controls, 418

Authentication, 424

Bugs, 415

Clustering, 421

Computer-aided software engineering (CASE), 431

Computer matching, 420

Computer operations controls, 418

Computer virus, 412

Control totals, 420

Controls, 417

Data cleansing, 435

Data flow diagram, 429

Data quality audit, 434

Data security controls, 418

Debugging, 434

Denial of service attack, 412

Development methodology, 428

Digital certificate, 424

Digital signature, 424

Digital wallet, 425

Edit checks, 420

Encryption, 423

Fault-tolerant computer system, 421

General controls, 417

Hacker, 412

Hardware controls, 418

High-availability computing, 421

Implementation controls, 418

Input controls, 420

Intrusion detection systems, 422

Iteration construct, 431

Load balancing, 421

Message integrity, 424

Mirroring, 421

MIS audit, 427

Module, 430

Online transaction processing, 421

Output controls, 420

Process specifications, 430

Processing controls, 420

Resource allocation, 433

Risk assessment, 426

Run control totals, 420

Secure Electronic Transaction (SET), 425

Secure Hypertext Transport Protocol (S-HTTP), 423

Secure Sockets Layer (SSL), 423

Security, 415

Segregation of functions, 419

Selection construct, 431

Sequence construct, 431

Software controls, 418

Software metrics, 433

Structure chart, 430

Structured, 428

Structured analysis, 429

Structured design, 430

Structured programming, 430

System flowchart, 431

Walkthrough, 434

REVIEW QUESTIONS

1. Why are computer systems more vulnerable than manual systems to destruction, fraud, error, and misuse? Name some of the key areas where systems are most vulnerable.

2. Name some features of online information systems that make them difficult to control.

3. How can bad software and data quality affect system performance and reliability? Describe two software quality problems.

4. What are controls? Distinguish between general and application controls.

5. Name and describe the principal general controls for computer-based systems.

6. Name and describe the principal application controls.

7. How does MIS auditing enhance the control process?

8. What is the function of risk assessment?

9. Name and describe four software quality assurance techniques.

10. Why are data quality audits and data cleansing essential?

11. What is security? List and describe controls that promote security for computer hardware, computer networks, computer software, and computer-based data.

12. What special security measures must be taken by organizations linking to the Internet?

13. Describe the role of firewalls and encryption systems in promoting security.

14. Name and describe the major types of electronic payment systems for Internet electronic commerce.

GROUP PROJECT

Form a group with two or three other students. Select a system described in one of the chapter-ending cases. Write a description of the system, its functions, and its value to the organization.

Then write a description of both the general and application controls that should be used to protect the organization. Present your findings to the class.

 ## INTERNET CONNECTION

■ **COMPANION WEBSITE**

At www.pearsoned.ca/laudon, you'll find an online study guide with two quizzes to test your knowledge of how security and sys-

tems quality are maintained in modern organizations. You'll also find updates to the chapter and online exercises and cases that enable you to apply your knowledge to realistic situations.

■ **ADDITIONAL SITES OF INTEREST**

There are many interesting Web sites to enhance your learning about security and systems quality. You can search the Web yourself, or just try the following sites to add to what you have already learned.

Information Security Magazine

> **www.infosecuritymag.com**
>
> Up-to-date news and technical briefs on information security issues

AntiOnline E-Magazine

> **www.antionline.com**
>
> Web magazine for information security officers and others interested in preventing systems security problems

CIO's February 15, 2001, article on data quality

> **www.cio.com/archive/021501/data.html**
>
> Information about the Royal Bank's data quality initiative

Coast Software

> **www.coast.ca**
>
> Interesting Web site as well as a company with proven Web testing and monitoring products and services

CompInfo's CASE Tools Site

> **www.compinfo-center.com/CASE_tools.htm**
>
> Learn more about CASE tools at this Canadian computer information site

Microsoft's Visio Web site

> **www.microsoft.com/office/visio/**
>
> MS Visio 2000 is a leading flowcharting package

CASE STUDY *Hackers Raise the Stakes*

On Monday, February 7, 2000, at about 1:30 p.m., music retailer HMV Canada's bustling e-commerce site abruptly and without warning went haywire. Servers were running flat out but couldn't cope with a sudden inundation of ostensibly legitimate requests. Memory buffers and hard disks became full and caused systems to crash. Customers couldn't make purchases or even access the site. HMV's systems began to grind to a halt.

The company was under attack by cyber vandals. The symptoms were identical to the so-called denial of service attacks on high-profile e-commerce sites in the United States. Victims of those attacks included top sites such as eBay and Amazon.com. "We had a flood of requests from an unknown source—exponentially higher than normal traffic," explained Rodney McBrien, Toronto-based director of Information Systems for HMV North America. "It was a spike in the millions [of page hits] that basically overwhelmed our site." The company made the decision at this point to close the site.

HMV put log data on a tape and forwarded it to the RCMP. An hour later the site was back up, business as usual. The hackers had disappeared into the ether, leaving few traces. A random act of cyber violence? Possibly. But the larger implications of this and other recent hacker attacks on e-commerce companies go well beyond the immediate impacts on victims, raising disturbing questions for consumers and e-tailers.

The victims, ironically, were known for their e-security savvy and had taken almost every precaution they could. But the software that allowed the hackers to conduct the DOS attacks was readily available on the Internet; even worse, it was easy to install and use. Yet software that could have been installed to prevent these attacks was also readily available. Not only had HMV not installed the remedy for the denial-of-service type of attack, but neither had most e-tailers. Perhaps these attacks are the wake-up call they need.

One of the most disturbing aspects of these attacks is the way hackers used other systems on the Internet as robots or slaves to multiply the ferocity of the offensive and also to cover their tracks. "The power of the Internet," observed e-security expert Adel Melek, a partner in Deloitte & Touche's Toronto-based e-business consulting group, "was used against itself for the first time in these attacks. That is new."

Hackers broke into dozens or hundreds of vulnerable systems on the Net and planted zombie programs, all scheduled to begin flooding the target site with requests at a specific time. "Some [victims] experienced a gigabit of requests hitting their sites every second," notes security consultant Eckhardt Kriel, a partner with Ernst & Young LLP in Toronto. "You can't do that from a single computer." They may in some cases be able to trace the attack back to a particular computer. But any computer owner, including the real hackers, could claim their system had been invaded and a zombie planted.

One implication for the future of e-commerce security is the notion of being a "good Internet neighbour," securing your systems so they can't be used as robots. Melek speculates that as awareness of the risks rises, PC manufacturers may begin to build firewalls into their products.

The first, obvious impact on the victims was financial. The HMV site was down for about an hour, and customers couldn't use it for an undisclosed amount of time before that. Sales were lost. Many customers would find other places to buy or decide not to buy, McBrien said. He couldn't or wouldn't estimate the extent of the financial loss, although he admits it was not insignificant.

Nick Jones, new business manager for Web-based bookseller Chapters Online Inc. of Toronto, and McBrien both had conflicting feelings when they talked about the threat of these kinds of attacks and their impacts. On the one hand, they didn't want to diminish the seriousness of what happened or could happen in the future. On the other, they feared the general public—or, more accurately, the online public—might believe the attacks are even more serious than in fact they are. "It's not an attack where you lose customer information or have a security breach," McBrien is quick to point out. "It just means you can't perform commerce."

Jones blames the media for creating unnecessary alarm over what amounted to nuisance attacks. He says many newspapers erroneously reported that Amazon.com and others had been "hacked." "It sounded so brutal. And there were implications that customer information had been revealed, when in fact [the e-commerce sites attacked] had just been smothered." Jones hastened to add, "It was criminal what was done, but system integrity was not breached. Consumers need to know their information was secure."

But the question is, will online consumers understand or credit the distinction being made? And should they? After all, there certainly have been cases of hackers breaking into e-commerce systems and stealing customer credit card information. In one of the most recent, in January 2000, criminals hacked a system operated by eUniverse for its CD Universe site, stole customer credit card information, and then tried to blackmail the company. When eUniverse refused to play along and called the FBI, the hackers posted customer credit card information at a Web site. The site was shut down the same day, but for a short while, the data was freely available to anyone on the Net.

Whether or not consumers should be concerned about online credit card security, clearly many are. McBrien argues they aren't as paranoid about using credit cards on the Internet as they were a couple of years ago and so won't be influenced by these attacks. But recent studies suggest otherwise. According to *Winning The Online Consumer: Insights Into Online Consumer Behavior*, anxiety over credit card security is the main barrier to purchasing online, cited by 46 percent of participants. The study surveyed both those who had made online purchases and those who hadn't.

In another study, 19 percent of consumers already buying online expressed concern about credit card information being stolen. Whatever the level of fear, it exists. And the public spectacle of prominent e-commerce companies being humbled by sophisticated hackers certainly won't do anything to reduce it. For this reason, some companies are unwilling to disclose the fact that they have been hacked, fearing that this knowledge would undermine the public's confidence in either the company or e-commerce.

"Many consumers may not be technically aware of the differences between denial of service attacks and hacker intrusions," says Kriel. "Once they hear of a vulnerability, some may jump to the conclusion that it isn't safe yet to buy online." In fact, that conclusion may not always be wrong. While Melek says there is a clear distinction between companies that are vulnerable to "vandalization" and those negligent enough to allow data to be stolen, he also raises the possibility that denial of service "swarmings" could create vulnerabilities hackers could exploit to break in.

In an attack that is undetected or for whatever reason allowed to run its course—unlike the attack on HMV—a firewall could break down before the site itself shuts down entirely, giving hackers an entry point, Melek says. Or an application could begin to malfunction, "leaking" data even through a firewall.

Melek believes denial of service attacks are most often the last resort of hackers who have been repelled by a company's security systems and are looking for revenge or to humiliate their adver-

saries. It's what Deloitte & Touche's own ethical hackers—hackers hired to find the weak spots in a company's security systems—do, he admits. "It's generally the last phase of an engagement. If we've tried everything and we can't get in, then we try to bring the system down," Melek says.

But the real and first objective of most hackers, he believes, is to intrude, to breach a system's security and gain access to stored data and/or programs. The reason these e-commerce companies were hit with denial of service attacks may simply be that their security systems were too good and hackers couldn't get in. But what of other systems they tried—or will try?

Melek is afraid many of his clients—as many as 70 percent, he estimates—couldn't even say for sure if their systems had been hacked after the fact. eUniverse apparently had no idea data had been stolen from its site until the hackers contacted the company with ransom demands.

Companies with properly configured security systems would be able to say, and "with a great degree of accuracy," Melek says, whether or not hackers had intruded—and what they had done. In the aftermath of the denial of service attacks, e-commerce leaders such as Amazon.com and eBay were quick to state that no intrusion had occurred. Their disclaimers are probably credible, Melek says. "But I must tell you," he adds, "not many companies I come across have that ability."

Meanwhile, the popular image of the hacker as a morally neutral teenage computer nerd just looking for a challenge—a kind of merry prankster—clearly no longer fits. There is often much more at stake, as the CD Universe case shows. Cyber vandals is the wrong term: these are crooks.

In some cases, they may be after something other than financial gain, though—insights into how successful e-commerce companies work, for example, Melek suggests. Others say industrial espionage could be a motive. "Imagine being able to go into a system and get your competitor's customer list," says the CTO of one Toronto-area ISP, who requested anonymity for fear of being targeted by hackers. Kriel believes the only intent of the attacks on HMV and others was to bring the sites down, but he too sees dark motives at work. "We believe these attacks could be the work of hack-tivists," he says. "People for example who are trying to pressure computer users to pay more attention to security: that could be one likely scenario. They could be people with an agenda. They could be competitors, or investors wanting to change the course of evaluations. It could even be hostile foreign governments behind these attacks, although that is probably very unlikely."

Whatever the motives or strategies of hackers, the onus clearly is on e-commerce companies to protect themselves—and their customers. All invariably claim they are doing that. HMV has "an aggressive security policy," according to McBrien. He estimates the company has spent in excess of $100 000 on security-related infrastructure, including firewalls and intrusion detection software. McBrien has three people devoted to operations and security and is in the process of hiring a fourth.

Says Chapters' Jones, "The number one concern for consumers is privacy. Ipso facto, it's our number one concern. We've spent thousands of hours and millions of dollars on hardware and software, and the result is we have a world-class system for making purchases online."

There is no reason to disbelieve such claims, but customers may be excused for being skeptical. Chapters Online will not adopt any new security measures specifically in response to the recent attacks, but the firm is constantly upgrading security, Jones says. McBrien says his company did undergo an audit recently by a security consulting firm and will implement some new systems.

What should e-commerce companies be doing to secure their sites? Jones, who has a background in marketing, has an interesting take. He distinguishes between "perceived" and "actual" security. Perceived security includes things such as having or building a trusted brand-name, prominently posting security and privacy information at your site, publicizing relationships with trusted partners such as credit card companies, and having an e-commerce security audit firm—TRUSTe (www.etrust.com), for example, or WebTrust.com (www.webtrust.com)—certify your site so you can post their supposedly trusted symbols.

All good ideas no doubt, but they won't keep hackers out. Jones is a bit vague about "actual" security—deliberately so. Like many other e-commerce firms, Chapters won't talk in any detail about what it's doing to secure its site against cyber crooks. It fears hackers may be able to use any information it gives out.

Actual security in Jones' admittedly crude scheme of things involves three levels: facility, hardware, and software. Some companies, he notes, overlook the simplest level, security on the building where they keep their servers. He himself can't get into the computer room at the AT&T facility Chapters uses, he notes.

Hardware and software for security basically means firewalls, SSL (Secure Socket Layer) transaction encryption—and the possibility in the future of using SET (Secure Electronic Transaction), a more advanced transaction security system. But there is a good deal more to it than that. Good security, Kriel and Melek stress, starts at the top with an enterprise security policy. The policy identifies the assets to be protected, the procedures for protecting them, and the technologies used to support those procedures.

Melek says security policies should address four distinct phases: prevention, detection, reporting, and correction. Too many companies focus only on prevention, he notes. "They say, 'Oh, yeah, we've got a firewall,' but that's it. That's all they have." More and more companies have intrusion detection software, but still need to do a lot more work on reporting and correction, he says.

Reporting doesn't just mean reporting internally, though. It also means reporting to law enforcement and "up the chain," as Kriel puts it, to ISPs and Internet backbone operators. If IP addresses of slave systems can be identified quickly enough, it should be possible to block packets from those systems, or at least to call the owners to report the misuse.

Kriel says security systems vendors are working on automating this kind of reporting outside the organization. In the meantime, it's a question of picking up a phone and calling your ISP—and the RCMP—when you determine you're under attack.

All of this should be spelled out in any good e-security policy, Melek says. Too often, companies find themselves under attack and have no guidelines for how to respond. Decisions end up being made under pressure by relatively junior employees, he says. Policies and procedures, such as making sure employees are trained and all key programs and operating systems have the latest security upgrades, and subscribing to sources such as Carnegie Melon University's CERT (www.cert.org) or Ernst & Young's eDefense to keep up on recently discovered system vulnerabilities, are as important as having the latest security tools.

The fact is there is no technological silver bullet for hacker attacks now, Kriel says, and likely never will be. Hacker and e-security technology will continue to leapfrog each other at intervals. "I don't think we'll ever be at a simple state where we can say, 'Yeah, we've fixed the security problem,'" he says.

Nobody was driven out of business by the recent rash of denial of service attacks. Nobody, apparently, lost valued assets as a result. So what's all the fuss about? Jones and McBrien are right in a sense: these attacks were more a nuisance than a serious threat to the bottom line. But if from that you conclude there is nothing to worry about and nothing more you need do to secure your e-commerce operations, your survival is already in doubt.

Sources: Tony Martell, "Hackers Raise The Stakes," *CIO Canada*, October 17, 2000; Richard Power, *Tangled Web: Tales of Digital Crime from the Shadows of Cyberspace*, (Indianapolis: Que, 2000); John McHutchion, "Don't Know Hacker, Says Canadian ISP," *Canoe Money*, February 15, 2000, www.jamcaster.com/HackerAttack/feb15_cdnresponse.html, accessed June 28, 2001.

CASE STUDY QUESTIONS

1. What can companies do to "stay alert" to these security issues? How do IS professionals remain up to date in terms of their knowledge of security problems and solutions?

2. What should a security policy and plan contain to reduce or eliminate the security problems described in this case?

3. What steps should a company take to avoid denial-of-service attacks? to avoid being hacked? to avoid having data stolen?

INFORMATION AS A CRITICAL ASSET: INFORMATION RESOURCE MANAGEMENT

OBJECTIVES

After completing this chapter, you will be able to:

1. *Describe the various components of information resource management and the issues involved with each component.*

2. *Evaluate various models for understanding the business value of information systems.*

3. *Select appropriate strategies to manage the system implementation process.*

4. *Describe project management methods involved in information resource management.*

5. *Explain why international information resource management issues are more complex.*

Reshaping a Classic

Want some good advice in successfully bringing home a big system? You might do well to talk to Dan MacDonald, the Bank of Canada's Chief of Infrastructure Services. He helmed one of the more notable big-application successes in the nation's capital in recent times, and his approach is one that many CIOs can learn from.

MacDonald's team built the Bank's retail debt management system, a 10 000 function point system that significantly enhances the Bank's ability to act as fiscal agent and registrar for the Government of Canada. (A function point defines where an actual function has been performed.) The project was successfully completed this past June for under $10 million.

"Traditionally, the vendor builds a brick wall and has its own project office while the client has a separate project office. The two have separate meetings, and it often becomes adversarial," said project coach, Ron Wiens. "Dan's concept was one team, one project office, and both parties committed to the other's success."

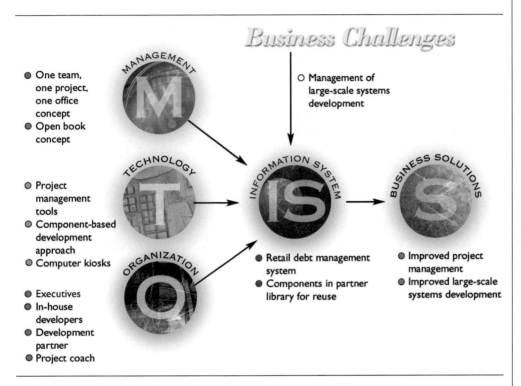

Business Challenges

- One team, one project, one office concept
- Open book concept

- Project management tools
- Component-based development approach
- Computer kiosks

- Executives
- In-house developers
- Development partner
- Project coach

MANAGEMENT
TECHNOLOGY
ORGANIZATION

○ Management of large-scale systems development

INFORMATION SYSTEM

- Retail debt management system
- Components in partner library for reuse

BUSINESS SOLUTIONS

- Improved project management
- Improved large-scale systems development

A first attempt at building the system with a large systems integrator ended in failure. The two organizations did not share similar values, and as a result, the project started going downhill and became very adversarial. After 18 months of trying, the project was canned, but it was a critical one so it couldn't stay canned.

Despite the initial setback, MacDonald stayed true to his values. Believing his approach was the right one, he went out and found a company that was not only qualified in terms of application knowledge, but that also shared his project management values. But it was a small company—Castek Software Factory Inc., of Toronto—and it took courage to select it. If the project went down in flames for the second time, MacDonald would be on the hot seat.

Part of the rationale behind choosing Castek was the concept of reusability. The company's component based development (CBD) approach enables the assembly of reusable building blocks of software services into a customized information system. MacDonald readily saw the value of building things and moving them to other parts of the organization, rather than constantly reinventing all the time.

A second key issue was productivity. "When we signed the contract, we established a productivity metric based on function points per person/month that was right at the leading edge of industry averages," said MacDonald. "Because you can reuse components, you can drive a higher level of productivity. If you get to a point where you're pulling 60 to 70 percent of reusable components out of a library, your productivity factor has risen exponentially."

A side benefit for the Bank is the potential to receive royalties on the modules it puts into Castek's component library. If other organizations are prepared to use those modules, that might contribute to lowering the Bank's overall cost of computing.

(continued)

A number of other important factors contributed to MacDonald's success. First and foremost, the approach with Castek was one team, completely open book—open budgets, open progress, nothing hidden. The project was so open, in fact, that a six by nine foot chart of the milestones was posted in the foyer of the bank where staff members would walk by it every day. That sent a message that management was highly committed to the project. When the team saw that everything was up front and on the table, they started taking ownership. All deliveries were celebrated, and programs for team recognition and peer-to-peer recognition were introduced.

Rather than try to drive the project forward by the force of his own will—a futile tactic on projects of this scope—MacDonald moved ownership to the front lines. For instance, he brought Ron Wiens on as project coach. "I've never seen this kind of role on an IT project before," said Wiens. "My job was just to keep a mirror in front of everybody in terms of attitudes, behaviour, values, and the leadership approach being used. It was up to them whether or not they did anything."

Sources: David Carey, "Reshaping a Classic," *CIO Canada*, October 26, 2000; "Managing Large-Scale Systems Development Risk Through the Deployment of Software Components: A Case Study," Castek Case Study, www.castek.com, accessed July 8, 2001.

MANAGEMENT CHALLENGES

One of the principal challenges posed by information systems is making sure they are managed to maximize genuine business benefits. Organizations need to find ways of measuring the business value of their information systems and to ensure that these systems actually deliver the benefits they promise. The Bank of Canada's experience is actually very common. Successful systems development requires skillful planning, project management, and change management, and managers should be aware of the following management challenges:

1. **Managing the information systems function as a critical resource.** Organizations today rely on their information systems to stay in business. The proper functioning of these systems—and their contribution to the bottom line—have become critically important to most organizations. Ensuring that appropriate personnel are properly trained, evaluated, and paid, ensuring that systems development projects are well managed, ensuring that proper planning at all levels has been conducted—these are the main issues involved in managing information and information systems as a critical resource for the organization.

2. **Determining benefits of a system when they are largely intangible.** As the sophistication of systems increases, they produce fewer tangible and more intangible benefits. By definition, there is no solid method for pricing intangible benefits. Organizations could lose important opportunities if they only use strict financial criteria for determining information systems benefits. However, organizations could also make very poor investment decisions if they overestimate intangible benefits.

3. **Dealing with the complexity of large-scale systems projects.** Large-scale systems affect large numbers of organizational units and staff members and have extensive information requirements and business process changes. These large-scale projects are difficult to plan for, coordinate, and oversee. Implementing these systems, which have multi-year development periods, is especially problem-ridden because the systems are so complex. In addition, there are few reliable techniques for estimating the time and cost to develop large-scale information systems. Guidelines presented in this chapter are helpful but cannot guarantee that a large information system project can be precisely planned with accurate cost figures. Adding the dimension of internationalization further complicates the project and its management.

In this chapter, we examine information resource management (IRM) and its various components. Next we review the types of information systems planning. We then examine various ways to measure the business value provided by information systems, describing both financial and nonfinancial models. Then we present strategies for reducing the risks in systems projects and improving project management. Finally, we review the added complications posed by international information systems in information resource management.

13.1 INFORMATION RESOURCE MANAGEMENT

Information resource management (IRM) is the process of managing information systems—including hardware, software, data and databases, telecommunications, people, and the facilities that house these IS components—as an asset or resource that is critical to the organization. As recently as 30 years ago, the information systems department was thought of as an "ivory tower" peopled by "pointy-headed geeks" who spoke "technobabble." Running the IS department as though it were any other business function was considered impossible by non-IS managers. What a difference 30 years makes!

Today IS departments are well managed, with personnel regulations and budgets, just like every other department. Like all departments, appropriate, well-thought-out management principles should be used to maximize the value of the IS department. That is the heart of IRM. In the following subsections, we review the basic components of IRM. While we assume that IS managers need to know these components, we also feel strongly that all managers should understand IRM in order to interact effectively and efficiently with the IS department. The IS department is a service provider to other departments and should be held accountable for the level of service provided. Managers who understand the components of IRM can accurately evaluate the level of service their department is provided by the IS department.

information resource management (IRM)
The process of managing information systems—including hardware, software, data and databases, telecommunications, people, and the facilities that house these IS components—as an asset or resource that is critical to the organization.

THE INFORMATION SYSTEMS DEPARTMENT

Almost every organization today has a computer. Whether there is only one computer and only one individual who uses it or whether there are thousands of computers located around the world, the duties and functions of the information systems department are vested in one or more individuals. Whether these duties are explicit, as they are in middle- to large-sized organizations, or implicit, as in a "mom-and-pop" shop, these duties must be handled. The IS department has the following duties and functions:

▌ Manage computer operations

▌ Manage systems development and systems development projects

▌ Manage IS personnel

▌ Budget for the department and others in the organization who use computers

▌ Plan for strategic-, tactical-, and operational-level systems and for the IS department

▌ Justify financial investment in information systems

IS departments are structured like other departments; they have managers at all levels and frequently division of duties and reporting responsibilities. A typical IS department will have divided its duties into several divisions, such as systems development, telecommunications, e-commerce/Web, database management, user relations, and operations. Each of these divisions might have subdivisions; for example, systems development might have two subdivisions, such as new development and maintenance. Each of the divisions would have a manager to whom those IS staff members assigned to that division would report. Division managers would report to the IS department manager. Figure 13-1 shows a typical IS department structure.

The IS department manager may or may not be the **chief information officer** (CIO). The CIO is the strategic-level manager for information systems. As a member of senior management, the CIO is responsible for strategic-level IS planning and for ensuring that all IS plans, systems, and operations support the organization's overall strategy. Some organizations

chief information officer
The strategic-level manager of information systems for an organization.

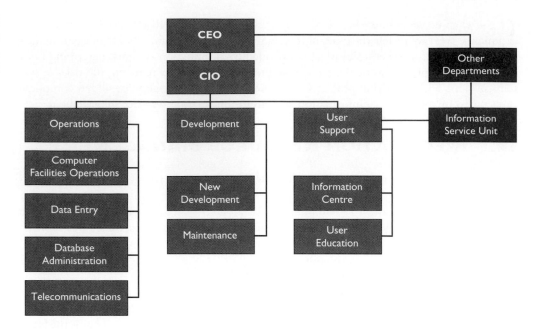

have begun calling the CIO a chief technology officer (CTO) or chief knowledge officer (CKO).

In addition to the CIO at the strategic level, the organization may also make use of an MIS Steering Committee. The **MIS Steering Committee** sets policy and priorities for the IS department, including approving budgets for major projects and hearing progress reports on those major projects. The MIS Steering Committee is usually composed of the CIO and other members of senior management. In the best case scenario, the organization's CEO is also a member of the MIS Steering Committee. It is the responsibility of the CIO to represent the IS department on the MIS Steering Committee and to communicate effectively with the committee's membership, "selling" them and other top managers on the IS department's plans and projects.

MIS Steering Committee
A strategic-level committee composed of the CIO and other top managers who set IS policy and prioritize and review major IS projects.

MANAGING PLANNING, STRATEGY, AND EXTERNAL RELATIONS

Again, like every other department, the IS department should conduct periodic planning at all levels. Strategic IS plans describe from a broad perspective the major strategic information systems that support or will support the organization's strategy. These are long-range plans that have a huge impact on the organization and on the IS department. Tactical IS plans have a shorter focus and concentrate on breaking down the strategic IS plan into more detailed plans that middle-level managers can focus on implementing. Finally, operational-level IS plans detail how the strategic IS plan will be implemented during the coming short term, usually one year. Specific goals and objectives permit measurement of how the IS department is performing in supporting the organization's strategy. Each of these sets of IS plans—strategic, tactical, and operational—should be *aligned* with the organization's strategy and with the organization's strategic-, tactical-, and operational-level plans (see Figure 13-2).

The CIO is responsible for ensuring that these plans are developed and aligned with the organization's plans. The CIO is also the major link to external parties, such as senior level managers at vendor organizations and strategic partners' CIOs. While many CIOs have been promoted from the ranks of the IS department, because of the communication-intensive nature of the position, many CIOs come from other areas of the organization, such as finance or human resources.

MANAGING SYSTEMS DEVELOPMENT

Systems development has many facets or perspectives. In Chapter 11, we looked at the systems development life cycle and at systems development as organizational change. In this

Figure 13-2A Model of Organizational Strategic Vision and Planning

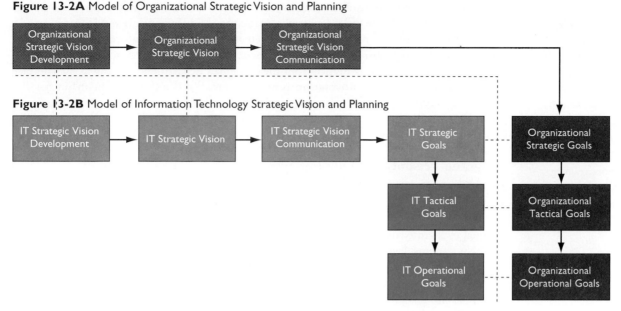

Figure 13-2B Model of Information Technology Strategic Vision and Planning

FIGURE 13-2 How information systems strategy and planning are aligned with organizational strategy and planning. Figure 13-2A represents the organization's strategy, planning steps, and levels while Figure 13-2B represents the IS department's strategy, planning steps, and levels. The dashed lines represent alignment between the organizational and IS strategies and plans at all steps and levels.

Source: Mary Brabston, Robert Zmud, and John Carlson, "Strategic Vision for Information Technology," in *Strategic Information Technology: Opportunities for Competitive Advantage*, edited by Raymond Papp, Idea Group Publishing, 2000. © Idea Group Publishing.

chapter, we look at systems development in terms of managing the implemented system and in terms of personnel assignments to develop systems.

In Chapter 12, we discussed information systems quality, security, and control in detail. These topics are also part of information resource management. Once a system has been implemented, it is the IS department's responsibility to ensure that policies, guidelines, and decisions about the implemented systems are followed. These responsibilities include ensuring that backups are made, that IS audits are conducted when and where appropriate, that appropriate security processes, such as passwords and locked doors, and appropriate controls are maintained and followed. Included in this are network, database, and Web management, which ensure that organizational and department policies are followed in each of these areas and that these parts of the organization's information systems are reliable, available, and accessible as needed.

In previous chapters, we briefly discussed the role of systems analysts and programmers. IS departments also employ **systems operators** who run the hardware, including loading tape and disk drives, starting and stopping computer "jobs," and ensuring that backups are carried out as dictated by policy. **Data-entry operators** enter data in computer-readable format and are managed by database managers. **Network managers** supervise networks while **Webmasters** handle the organization's Web-based presence. Every organization organizes its IS department and information system components differently. Every organization also calls people who hold these generic positions by different names. A network manager in one organization may be a LAN coordinator in another, but the employee's function is the same.

Many organizations centralize their information systems so that most of the information systems components (hardware, software, etc.) are located centrally and managed by a central IS department. In centralized IS departments, most decisions about information systems are made in the IS department. Other organizations choose to decentralize their information systems, permitting organizational departments or divisions to make their own decisions about what information systems to develop or purchase, frequently housing their own networks, hardware, and software. Many of these decentralized organizations also employ extra IS staff who report to the decentralized unit.

systems operators
IS personnel who actually operate the hardware.

data entry operators
IS personnel who enter data in computer-readable format.

network managers
IS personnel who supervise the operations of an organization's networks.

Webmasters
IS personnel who supervise an organization's Web-based presence.

information service unit
An IS group located within a non-IS department, such as marketing. The information service unit is employed by and reports to the IS department.

information centre
An IS group housed in the IS department that handles requests for support, training, assistance, and guidance from other departments.

Today, the trend is toward information service units and information centres. Figure 13-1 depicts this modern type of IS department structure. An **information service unit** is an IS group located within a non-IS department, such as marketing. The information service unit is employed by and reports to the IS department; the IS unit handles requests for systems development, training, or assistance from their assigned department, serving as an interface to the IS department. An **information centre** is housed in the IS department but handles requests for support, training, assistance, and guidance from other departments. If the marketing department needs to determine whether to upgrade the operating system their desktop computers use, they could call the information centre for advice.

Assigning Personnel to Develop Systems

How does an IS manager decide who will be assigned to a particular systems development project? Should an experienced person be assigned to new projects or to maintaining those projects on which he or she has already worked? Should less experienced personnel be assigned to maintenance projects so that they may gain experience?

New systems development is considered to be creative and more desirable than maintenance, which is viewed similarly to semi-annual checkups with your dentist. It has to be done, but you'd rather not have to do it. Every organization handles the assignment of programmers and analysts to individual projects differently. Frequently, rotation is used, so that personnel may be assigned to new development for a project and, when that project is completed, move on to a maintenance project. Just as frequently, less experienced IS staff are partnered with more experienced staff on projects, who act as mentors and help to guide them to higher levels of expertise.

Finally, the IS department is a service department, providing systems development and other services to other departments. Many businesses have implemented *service level agreements*, in which the IS department signs an agreement with a department for which they are developing a system. The service level agreement specifies milestones and deadlines, the budget, the level of service to be achieved, and other requested benchmarks. The IS department agrees to these terms and is held accountable by corporate management for meeting these benchmarks.

MANAGING PERSONNEL

We mentioned above that IS staff were formerly viewed as "pointy-headed geeks." Previous generations of hardware and software required a high level of technical knowledge and expertise. Today's systems permit lower levels of technical knowledge, enabling those with a middle level of technical expertise to succeed as programmers and analysts. This trend has opened IS career tracks to non-computer science majors.

While computer science focuses more on the technical side of information systems, the management information system (MIS) field focuses on the needs of business that can be met by computer-based information systems. Today's IS departments hire both computer science and MIS staff to fulfill their personnel requirements. In addition, yesterday's pointy-headed geeks receive education and training in business applications and how to communicate effectively without using technobabble. More and more, the language of the IS department is "business-ese" instead of technobabble.

Regardless of whether IS staff members were hired with a computer science or MIS background, like all other organizational employees they must be evaluated periodically. Determining metrics on which to base IS staff evaluation is a difficult task. Should a programmer be evaluated on number of lines of code generated? The code could be inefficient and time consuming to run. Should function points be used instead? **Function points** define where an actual function has been performed, but some functions are complex while others are not. Do you evaluate an analyst on how well the assigned user area is satisfied with their analyst? Or how well the analyst works with his or her programming teams? This is not an easy issue. Determining what criteria should be used in evaluating IS staff is a difficult task because each staff member's job presents a different mix of the technical and behavioural elements; the variation within the technical or behavioural elements and the mixing of the two, depending on the specific job, makes it difficult to develop and use evaluation criteria over a

function point
A measure that defines where an actual function has been performed in a program.

long period of time. A detailed discussion of this topic is beyond the scope of this text, but IS personnel must be evaluated and counselled on their performance on a periodic basis.

The last ten years have seen the salaries of IS staff increase rapidly. How does an organization recruit and retain IS staff when they cannot afford to give periodic raises that are as high as the local rate of increase for their classification? Some organizations have taken to giving bonuses based on work done, projects completed, or tenure in the organization. For example, NorthWest Company has on occasion given a "signing bonus" to new employees, accompanied by a retention bonus after one year on the job. Other organizations, such as the City of Winnipeg, have given their IS staff a year-end bonus, up to several thousand dollars, to those employees who have been there for several years. These loyalty bonuses serve to defuse the natural desire of IS staff to "follow the money." How does that fit the company's salary policy?

We hear in Canada about a "brain drain" to the South, in which skilled Canadians are being hired by U.S. companies at inflated salaries. Interestingly, there are experts on each side of the brain-drain issue—those who feel Canada is losing its best and brightest to the U.S. and those who feel disagree, arguing that the "brain drain" is only based on almost mythical anecdotal evidence. Regardless of which opinion is correct, the bottom line for IRM is that IS managers must attempt to keep their employees happy. In a time when IS jobs are going unfilled, this makes sense. The slowing economy (particularly following the terrorist attacks on September 11, 2001, in the United States) combines with the recent trend of dot-com failures to reduce the number of new IS jobs available. At least in this regard, perhaps the brain drain—if there ever was one, will subside.

With technology advancing so rapidly, how do IS staff keep their skills up to date? IS departments need to develop policies for staff to receive training and to upgrade their skills. Issues to be addressed by IS training policies are funding and time off to attend seminars, workshops, and courses; eligibility for funding and time off; the number of courses that can be taken in a given period; and the locus of the decision (who decides which courses employees will take) about continuing education.

In addition to keeping employees' skills up to date, providing training opportunities is an excellent way to motivate employees and to retain them. The flip side of the coin is, of course, that the employees will now have advanced skills with which to seek other jobs. Maintaining a challenging, positive environment with a few perks such as casual day (now more of a norm than an exception) or an on-site daycare service also helps to retain employees.

MANAGING BUDGETS

How can an IS manager know what the budget for the IS department should be for the coming year? A detailed analysis of projects that are ongoing and projects that may come forward during the next year is required, along with determining the need to upgrade technologies. The IS department must also examine the potential for extraordinary raises or bonuses for exceptional performance to retain key IS staff in light of the trend in IS salaries. These are not easy calculations. IS projects are notorious for running over budget (see the discussion on change management in Chapter 11).

How do you know when you should upgrade hardware or software? What do you do when your most productive and effective analyst comes to you with a job offer in hand for a ten percent raise and requests only a five percent raise to stay in your organization? How does that fit within the budget? Every IS organization handles their budgeting issues differently.

Many IS departments receive *revenue* from other departments in the form of *chargebacks*, or internal transfer of funds to reflect payment for services rendered. Chargebacks for a department can be calculated based on the department's computer usage, the number of nodes the department maintains on the LAN, IS department overhead charges based on the department's size in terms of number of employees or revenues generated, or myriad other ways. It is important that the method of chargeback is well communicated to department heads so that they understand the process and the charges.

Taken together, the topics discussed above compose the major components of IRM. Being able to justify financial investments in information systems is also part of strategic planning. The IS department must be able to explain and demonstrate that their budget and systems are worth the organization's financial commitment.

13.2 UNDERSTANDING THE BUSINESS VALUE OF INFORMATION SYSTEMS

Information systems can have several different values for business firms. A consistently strong information technology infrastructure can, over the longer term, play an important strategic role in the life of the firm. Looked at less grandly, information systems can permit firms simply to survive.

It is also important to realize that systems can have value, but the firm may not capture all or even some of the value. Although systems projects can result in benefits such as profitability and productivity, some or all of the benefits may go directly to the consumer in the form of lower prices or more reliable services and products (Hitt and Brynjolfsson, 1996). Competitors who fail to enrich consumers will not survive. From a management point of view, the challenge is to retain as much of the benefit of systems investments as is feasible in current market conditions.

The value of systems from the financial perspective comes down to one question: Does a particular IS investment produce sufficient returns to justify its costs? There are many problems with this approach, not the least of which is how to estimate benefits and costs.

TRADITIONAL CAPITAL BUDGETING MODELS

capital budgeting
The process of analyzing and selecting various proposals for capital expenditures.

Capital budgeting models are one of several techniques used to measure the value of investing in long-term capital investment projects. The process of analyzing and selecting various proposals for capital expenditures is called **capital budgeting**. Firms invest in capital projects to expand production to meet anticipated demand or to modernize production equipment to reduce costs. Firms also invest in capital projects for many non-economic reasons, such as to install pollution control equipment or to upgrade a human resources database to meet government regulations. Information systems are considered long-term capital investment projects.

All capital budgeting methods rely on measures of cash flows into and out of the firm. The investment cost is an immediate cash outflow caused by the purchase of the capital equipment. In subsequent years, the investment may cause additional cash outflows that will be balanced by cash inflows resulting from the investment. Cash inflows take the form of increased sales of more products (for reasons including new products, higher quality, or increasing market share) or reduction in costs of production and operation. The difference between cash outflows and cash inflows is used for calculating the financial worth of an investment. Once the cash flows have been established, several alternative methods are available for comparison among different projects and decision making about the investments.

Financial models assume that all relevant alternatives have been examined, that all costs and benefits are known, and that these costs and benefits can be expressed in a common metric, specifically money. When one has to choose among many complex and competing alternatives, these assumptions are rarely met in the real world although they may be approximated. Table 13-1 lists some of the more common costs and benefits of systems. **Tangible benefits** can be quantified and assigned a monetary value. **Intangible benefits**, such as more efficient customer service or enhanced decision making, cannot be immediately quantified but may lead to quantifiable gains in the long run.

tangible benefits
Benefits that can be quantified and assigned monetary value; they include lower operating costs and increased cash flows.

intangible benefits
Benefits that are not easily quantified; they include more efficient customer service and enhanced decision making.

Limitations of Financial Models

Many well-known problems emerge when financial analysis is applied to information systems (Dos Santos, 1991). Standard financial models do not express the risks and uncertainty of information systems estimates. Costs and benefits do not occur in the same time frame—costs tend to be upfront and tangible while benefits tend to be back-loaded and intangible. Inflation may affect costs and benefits differently. Technology—especially information technology—can change during the course of the project, causing estimates to vary

| TABLE 13-1 | COSTS AND BENEFITS OF INFORMATION SYSTEMS |

Costs	Intangible Benefits
Hardware	Improved asset utilization
Telecommunications	Improved resource control
Software	Improved organizational planning
Services	Increased organizational flexibility
Personnel	More timely information
	More information
Tangible Benefits (Cost Savings)	Increased organizational learning
Increased productivity	Legal requirements attained
Lower operating costs	Enhanced employee goodwill
Reduced work force	Increased job satisfaction
Lower computer expenses	Improved decision making
Lower outside vendor costs	Improved operations
Lower payroll and professional costs	Higher client satisfaction
Reduced rate of growth in expenses	Better corporate image
Reduced facility costs	

greatly. Intangible benefits are difficult to quantify. These factors play havoc with financial models.

The difficulties of measuring intangible benefits give financial models a bias toward certain types of applications: transaction and clerical systems that displace labour and save space always produce more measurable, tangible benefits than management information systems, decision-support systems, or computer-supported collaborative work systems (see Chapter 14).

There is some reason to believe that investment in information technology requires special consideration in financial modelling. Capital budgeting historically concerned itself with manufacturing equipment and other long-term investments such as electrical generating facilities and telephone networks. These investments had expected lives of more than one year and up to 25 years. However, information systems differ from manufacturing systems in that their expected life is much shorter. The very high rate of technological change in computer-based information systems means that most systems are essentially out of date in five to eight years. The high rate of technological obsolescence in budgeting for systems simply means that the payback period must be shorter and the rates of return higher than typical capital projects with much longer useful lives.

The "bottom line" with financial models is to use them cautiously and to put the results into a broader context of business analysis. Let us look at an example to see how these problems arise and can be handled. The following case study is based on a real-world scenario, but the names and locations have been changed.

CASE EXAMPLE: PRIMROSE, MENDELSON, AND HANSEN

Primrose, Mendelson, and Hansen is a 250-person law partnership in Toronto with branch offices in New York, London, and Paris. Founded in 1923, Primrose has excelled in corporate, tax, environmental, and health law. Its litigation department is also well known.

The Problem

The firm occupies three floors of a new building. Many partners still have five-year-old PCs on their desktops but rarely use them except to read e-mail. Virtually all business is conducted face-to-face in the office or when partners meet directly with clients on the clients' premises. Most of the law business involves marking up (editing), creating, filing, storing, and sending documents. In addition, the tax, pension, and real estate groups do a considerable amount of spreadsheet work.

With overall business off 15 percent since 1999, the chairman, Edward W. Hansen III, is hoping to use information systems to cope with the flood of paperwork, enhance service to clients, and reduce administrative costs.

First, the firm's income depends on billable hours, and every lawyer is supposed to keep a diary of his or her work for specific clients in 30-minute intervals. Generally, senior lawyers at this firm charge about $500 an hour for their time. Unfortunately, lawyers often forget what they have been working on, and must go back to reconstruct their time diaries. The firm hopes to implement some form of automated tracking of billable hours.

Second, a great deal of time is spent communicating with clients around the world, with other law firms both in Canada and overseas and with the Primrose branch offices. The fax machine has become the communication medium of choice, generating huge bills and developing lengthy queues. The firm wants to use some sort of secure e-mail, perhaps Lotus Notes or even the Internet. Law firms are wary of breaches in the security of confidential client information.

Third, Primrose has no client database! A law firm is a collection of fiefdoms—each lawyer has his or her own clients and keeps the information about them private. This makes it impossible for management to find out who is a client of the firm, who is working on a deal with whom, and so forth. The firm maintains a billing system, but the information is too difficult to search. What Primrose needs is an integrated client management system that would take care of billing, hourly charges, and make client information available to others in the firm. Even the overseas offices want to have information on who is taking care of a particular client in Canada.

Fourth, there is no system to track costs. The head of the firm and the department heads who compose the executive committee cannot identify what the costs are, where the money is being spent, who is spending it, and how the firm's resources are being allocated. A decent accounting system that could identify the cash flows and costs more clearly than the existing journal is needed.

The Solution

Information systems could obviously have some survival value and perhaps could grant a strategic advantage to Primrose if they were correctly developed and implemented. We will not go through a detailed systems analysis and design here. Instead, we will sketch the solution that in fact was adopted, showing the detailed costs by department and the estimated benefits.

If correctly developed and implemented, information systems can grant a strategic advantage to law firms.

The technical solution adopted was to create a local area network composed of 300 fully configured Pentium III multimedia desktop PCs, three Windows 2000 servers, and an Ethernet 10 Mbps local area network connected over a coaxial cable. Multimedia computers are required because lawyers access a fair amount of information stored on CD-ROM. The network connects all the lawyers and their secretaries into a single integrated system yet permits each lawyer to configure his or her desktop with specialized software and hardware. The older machines were given away to charity.

All desktop machines were configured with Windows 2000 and Office 2000 software while the servers used Windows 2000. Lotus Notes was chosen to handle client accounting, document management, group collaboration, and

	Estimated Costs and Benefits 2001-2006											
	A	B	C	D	E	F	G	H	I	J	K	L
1	Year :				0	1	2	3	4	5		
2					2001	2002	2003	2004	2005	2006		
3	**Costs Hardware**											
4		Servers		3@ 20000	60,000	10,000	10,000	10,000	10,000	10,000		
5		PCs		300@3000	900,000	10,000	10,000	10,000	10,000	10,000		
6		Network cards		300@100	30,000	0	0	0	0	0		
7		Scanners		6@100	600	500	500	500	500	500		
8												
9	Telecommunications											
10		Routers		10@500	5,000	1,000	1,000	1,000	1,000	1,000		
11		Cabling		150,000	150,000	0	0	0	0	0		
12		Telephone connect costs		50,000	50,000	50,000	50,000	50,000	50,000	50,000		
13												
14	Software											
15		Database		15,000	15,000	15,000	15,000	15,000	15,000	15,000		
16		Network		10,000	10,000	2,000	2,000	2,000	2,000	2,000		
17		Groupware		300@500	150,000	3,000	3,000	3,000	3,000	3,000		
18												
19	Services											
20		Lexis		50,000	50,000	50,000	50,000	50,000	50,000	50,000		
21		Training		300hrs@75/hr	22,500	10,000	10,000	10,000	10,000	10,000		
22		Director of Systems		100,000	100,000	100,000	100,000	100,000	100,000	100,000		
23		Systems Personnel		2@70000	140,000	140,000	140,000	140,000	140,000	140,000		
24		Trainer		1@50000	50,000	0	0	0	0	0		
25												
26	**Total Costs**				1,733,100	391,500	391,500	391,500	391,500	391,500	3,690,600	
27	Benefits											
28		1. Billing enhancements			300,000	500,000	600,000	600,000	600,000	500,000		
29		2. Reduced paralegals			50,000	100,000	150,000	150,000	150,000	150,000		
30		3. Reduced clerical			50,000	100,000	100,000	100,000	100,000	100,000		
31		4. Reduced messenger			15,000	30,000	30,000	30,000	30,000	30,000		
32		5. Reduced telecommunications			5,000	10,000	10,000	10,000	10,000	10,000		
33		6. Lawyer efficiencies			120,000	240,000	360,000	360,000	360,000	360,000		
34												
35	**Total Benefits**				540,000	980,000	1,250,000	1,250,000	1,250,000	1,150,000	6,420,000	

Sheet1 / Sheet2 / Sheet3

FIGURE 13-3 Costs and benefits of the Legal Information System. This spreadsheet analyzes the basic costs and benefits of implementing an information system for the law firm. The costs for hardware, telecommunications, software, services, and personnel are analyzed over a six-year period.

e-mail because it provided an easy-to-use interface and secure links to external networks (including the Internet). The Internet was rejected as an e-mail technology (without the additional security offered by Lotus Notes security features) because of its lack of security. The Primrose LAN is linked to external networks so that the firm can obtain information online from Lexis (a legal database) and several financial database services.

The new system required Primrose to hire a chief information officer and director of systems—a new position for most law firms. Four systems personnel were needed to operate the system and train lawyers. An outside trainer was also hired for a short period.

Figure 13-3 shows the estimated costs and benefits of the system. The system had an actual investment cost of $1 733 100 in the first year (Year 0) and total cost over six years of $3 690 600. The estimated benefits total $6 420 000 after six years.

Was the investment worthwhile? If so, in what sense? There are financial and nonfinancial answers to these questions. Six capital budgeting models are typically used by organizations to evaluate any type of capital project:

▌ Payback method

▌ Accounting rate of return on investment (ROI)

▌ Cost–benefit ratio

▌ Net present value

▌ Profitability index

▌ Internal rate of return (IRR)

Let us look at these financial models first. They are depicted in Figure 13-4.

Estimated Costs and Benefits 2001-2006

	A	B	C	D	E	F	G	H	I	J	K	L
1	Year :			0	1	2	3	4	5			
2	Net Cash Flow (not including orig. investment)			540,000	588,500	858,500	858,500	858,500	758,500			
3	Net Cash Flow (including orig. investment)			-1,193,100	588,500	858,500	858,500	858,500	758,500			
4												
5	(1) Payback Period = 2.5 years					Cumulative Cash Flow						
6	Initial investment = 1,733,100			Year 0	540,000	540,000						
7				Year 1	588,500	1,128,500						
8				Year 2	858,500	1,987,000						
9				Year 3	858,500	2,845,500						
10				Year 4	858,500	3,704,000						
11				Year 5	758,500	4,462,500						
12												
13	(2) Accounting rate of return											
14												
15	(Total benefits-Total Costs-Depreciation)/Useful life				Total Benefits	6,420,000						
16	--				Total Costs	3,690,600						
17	Total initial investment				Depreciation	1,733,100						
18				Tot. benefits-tot. costs-depreciation		996,300						
19					Life	6 years						
20												
21					Initial investment		1,733,100					
22	ROI =	(996,300/6)	9.58%									
23		1,733,100										
24												
25	(3) Cost-Benefit Ratio		Total Benefits	6,420,000	1.74							
26			Total Costs	3,690,600								
27												
28	(4) Net Present Value											
29			= NPV (0.05,D8:I8)-1,733,100			2,001,529						
30												
31	(5) Profitability Index											
32			PV/Investment	3,734,629/1,733,100		2.15						
33												
34	(6) Internal Rate of Return											
35												
36			= IRR(D9:I9)			55%						

Sheet1 **Sheet2** Sheet3

FIGURE 13-4 Financial models. To determine the financial basis for a project, a series of financial models helps determine the return on invested capital. These calculations include the payback period, the accounting rate of return (ROI), the cost–benefit ratio, the net present value, the profitability index, and the internal rate of return (IRR).

The Payback Method

payback method

A measure of the time required to pay back the initial investment on a project.

The **payback method** is quite simple: It is a measure of the time required to pay back the initial investment of a project. The payback period is computed as:

$$\frac{\text{Original investment}}{\text{Annual net cash inflow}} = \text{Number of years to pay back}$$

In the case of Primrose, it will take over three years to pay back the initial investment. (Since cash flows are uneven, annual cash inflows are summed until they equal the original investment to arrive at this number.) The payback method is a popular method because of its simplicity and power as an initial screening method. It is especially good for high-risk projects in which the useful life of a project is difficult to determine. If a project pays for itself in two years, then it matters less how long after two years the system lasts.

The weakness of this measure is its virtues: the method ignores the time value of money, the amount of cash flow after the payback period, the disposal value (usually zero with computer systems), and the profitability of the investment.

Accounting Rate of Return on Investment (ROI)

Firms make capital investments to earn a satisfactory rate of return. Determining a satisfactory rate of return depends on the cost of borrowing money, but other factors can enter into the equation, such as the historic rates of return expected by the firm. In the long run, the desired rate of return must equal or exceed the cost of capital in the marketplace. Otherwise, no one will lend the firm money.

The **accounting rate of return on investment (ROI)** calculates the rate of return from an investment by adjusting the cash inflows produced by the investment for depreciation. It gives an approximation of the accounting income earned by the project.

To find the ROI, first calculate the average net benefit. The formula for the average net benefit is as follows:

$$\frac{(\text{Total benefits} - \text{Total cost} - \text{Depreciation})}{\text{Useful life}} = \text{Net benefit}$$

This net benefit is divided by the total initial investment to arrive at the projected ROI (rate of return on investment). The formula is:

$$\frac{\text{Net benefit}}{\text{Total initial investment}} = \text{ROI}$$

In the case of Primrose, the average rate of return on the investment is 9.58 percent, which could be a good return on investment if the cost of capital (the prime rate) is around 7 to 8 percent, and returns on invested capital in corporate bonds are about 8 percent.

The weakness of ROI is that it can ignore the time value of money. Future savings are simply not worth as much in today's dollars as are current savings. However, ROI can be modified (and usually is) so that future benefits and costs are calculated in today's dollars. The present value function on most spreadsheets will perform this conversion.

Net Present Value

Evaluating a capital project requires that the cost of an investment (a cash outflow usually in year 0) be compared with the net cash inflows that occur many years later. But these two kinds of inflows are not directly comparable because of the time value of money. Money you have been promised to receive three, four, and five years from now is not worth as much as money received today. Money received in the future has to be discounted by some appropriate percentage rate—usually the prevailing interest rate or the cost of capital. **Present value** is the value in current dollars of a payment or stream of payments to be received in the future. It can be calculated by using the following formula:

$$\text{Payment} \times (1 + \text{interest})^{-n} = \text{Present value of expected cash flows}$$

Thus, to compare the investment (made in today's dollars) with future savings or earnings, you need to discount the earnings to their present value and then calculate the net present value of the investment. The **net present value** is the amount of money an investment is worth, taking into account its cost, earnings, and the time value of money. The formula for net present value is:

Present value of expected cash flows – Initial investment cost = Net present value

In the case of Primrose, the present value of the stream of benefits is $3 734 629 and the cost (in today's dollars) is $1 733 100, giving a net present value of $2 001 529. In other words, the net present value of the investment is $2 001 529 over a six-year period. For a $1.7 million investment today, the firm will receive more than $2 million. This is a very good rate of return on an investment.

Cost–Benefit Ratio

A simple method for calculating the returns from a capital expenditure is to calculate the **cost–benefit ratio**, which is the ratio of benefits to costs. The formula is:

$$\frac{\text{Total benefits}}{\text{Total costs}} = \text{Cost} - \text{benefit ratio}$$

In the case of Primrose, the cost–benefit ratio is 1.74, meaning that the benefits are 1.74 times greater than the costs. The cost–benefit ratio can be used to rank several projects for comparison. Some firms establish a minimum cost–benefit ratio that must be attained by capital projects. The cost–benefit ratio can of course be calculated using present values to account for the time value of money.

accounting rate of return on investment (ROI)
A calculation of the rate of return on an investment by adjusting cash inflows produced by the investment for depreciation. Approximates the accounting income earned by the investment.

present value
The value, in current dollars, of a payment or stream of payments to be received in the future.

net present value
The amount of money an investment is worth, taking into account its cost, earnings, and the time value of money.

cost–benefit ratio
A method for calculating the returns from a capital expenditure by dividing total benefits by total costs.

Profitability Index

profitability index
Used to compare the profitability of alternative investments; it is calculated by dividing the present value of the total cash inflow from an investment by the initial cost of the investment.

One limitation of net present value is that it provides no measure of profitability. Neither does it provide a way to rank different potential investments. One simple solution is provided by the profitability index. The **profitability index** is calculated by dividing the present value of the total cash inflow from an investment by the initial cost of the investment. The result can be used to compare the profitability of alternative investments.

$$\frac{\text{Present value of cash inflows}}{\text{Investment}} = \text{Profitability index}$$

In the case of Primrose, the profitability index is 2.15. The project returns more than its cost. Projects can be ranked on this index, permitting firms to focus on only the most profitable projects.

Internal Rate of Return (IRR)

internal rate of return (IRR)
The rate of return or profit that an investment is expected to earn.

Internal rate of return (IRR) is a variation of the net present value method. It takes into account the time value of money. **Internal rate of return (IRR)** is defined as the rate of return or profit that an investment is expected to earn. IRR is the discount (interest) rate that will equate the present value of the project's future cash flows to the initial cost of the project (defined here as a negative cash flow in year 0 of $1 193 100). In other words, the value of R (discount rate) is such that Present value − Initial cost = 0. In the case of Primrose, the IRR is 55 percent. This is a 55 percent rate of return.

Results of the Capital Budgeting Analysis

Using methods that take into account the time value of money, the Primrose project is cash flow positive over the time period and returns more benefits than it costs. Against this analysis, would other investments be better from an efficiency and effectiveness standpoint? Have all the benefits been calculated? It may be that this investment is necessary for the survival of the firm or necessary to provide a level of service demanded by its clients. What are other competitors doing? In other words, there may be other intangible and strategic business factors to take into account.

STRATEGIC CONSIDERATIONS

Other methods of selecting and evaluating information system investments involve non-financial and strategic considerations. When the firm has several alternative investments from which to select, it can employ portfolio analysis and scoring models. Several of these methods can be used in combination.

Portfolio Analysis

Rather than using capital budgeting, a second way of selecting among alternative projects is to consider the firm as having a portfolio of potential applications. Each application carries risks and benefits. The portfolio can be described as having a certain profile of risk and benefit to the firm (see Figure 13-5). Although there is no ideal profile for all firms, information-intensive industries (e.g., finance) should have a few high-risk, high-benefit projects to ensure that they stay current with technology. Firms in non-information-intensive industries should focus on high-benefit, low-risk projects.

Risks are not necessarily bad. They are tolerable so long as the benefits are commensurate. Chapter 11 described the factors that increase the risks of systems projects.

Once strategic analyses have determined the overall direction of systems

FIGURE 13-5 A systems projects portfolio. Companies should examine their portfolio of projects in terms of potential benefits and likely risks. Certain kinds of projects should be avoided altogether and others should be developed rapidly. There is no ideal mix. Companies in different industries have different profiles.

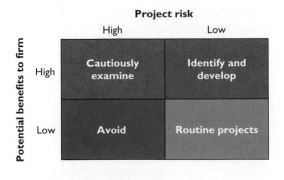

development, **portfolio analysis** can be used to select alternatives. Obviously, one can begin by focusing on systems of high benefit and low risk. These promise early returns and low risks. Second, high-benefit, high-risk systems should be examined; low-benefit, high-risk systems should be totally avoided; and low-benefit, low-risk systems should be re-examined for the possibility of rebuilding and replacing them with more desirable systems having higher benefits. An IS department managing several projects will want to have a mix of low risk/low return, high risk/high return, and low risk/high return projects in their portfolio.

portfolio analysis
An analysis of the portfolio of potential applications within a firm to determine the risks and benefits and to aid in selecting among alternatives for information systems.

Scoring Models

A quick and sometimes compelling method for arriving at a decision on alternative systems is a scoring model. **Scoring models** give alternative systems a single score based on the extent to which they meet selected objectives (Matlin, 1989; Buss, 1983).

In Table 13-2, the firm must decide among three alternative office systems: (1) an IBM AS/400 client/server system with proprietary software, (2) a UNIX-based client/server system using an Oracle database, and (3) a Windows 2000 client/server system using Windows and Lotus Notes. Column 1 lists the criteria that decision makers may apply to the systems. These criteria are usually the result of lengthy discussions among the decision-making group. Often the most important outcome of a scoring model is not the score but simply agreement on the criteria used to judge a system (Ginzberg, 1979; Nolan, 1982). Column 2 lists the weights that decision makers attach to the decision criteria. The scoring model helps to bring about agreement among participants concerning the ranking of the criteria. Columns 3 to 5 use a 1-to-5 scale (lowest to highest) to express the judgments of participants on the relative merits of each system. For example, concerning the percentage of user needs that each system meets, a score of 1 for a system argues that this system when compared with others being considered will be low in meeting user needs.

scoring model
A quick method for deciding among alternative systems based on a system of weighted ratings for selected objectives.

As with all objective techniques, there are many qualitative judgments involved in using the scoring model. This model requires experts who understand the issues and the technology. It is appropriate to cycle through the scoring model several times, changing the criteria and weights, to see how sensitive the outcome is to reasonable changes in criteria. Scoring models are used most commonly to confirm, to rationalize, and to support decisions, rather than as the final arbiters of system selection.

If Primrose had other alternative systems projects to select from, it could have used the portfolio and scoring models as well as financial models to establish the business value of its systems solution.

Primrose did not have a portfolio of applications that could be used to compare the proposed system. Senior lawyers felt the project was low in risk using well-understood technology. They felt the rewards were even higher than the financial models stated because the system might enable the firm to expand its business. For instance, the ability to communicate with other law firms, with clients, and with the international staff of lawyers in remote locations was not even considered in the financial analysis.

TABLE 13-2 SCORING MODEL USED TO CHOOSE AMONG ALTERNATIVE OFFICE SYSTEMS*

Criterion	Weight	AS/400		UNIX		Windows 2000	
Percentage of user needs met	0.40	2	0.8	3	1.2	4	1.6
Cost of the initial purchase	0.20	1	0.2	3	0.6	4	0.8
Financing	0.10	1	0.1	3	0.3	4	0.4
Ease of maintenance	0.10	2	0.2	3	0.3	4	0.4
Chances of success	0.20	3	0.6	4	0.8	4	0.8
Final score			1.9		3.2		4.0

Scale: 1 = low, 5 = high

* One of the major uses of scoring models is in identifying the criteria of selection and their relative weights. In this instance, an office system based on Windows 2000 appears preferable.

MANAGEMENT DECISION PROBLEM

EVALUATING ERP SYSTEMS WITH A SCORING MODEL
Your company, Audio Direct, sells parts used in audio systems for cars and trucks and is growing very fast. Your management team has decided that the firm can speed up product delivery to customers and lower inventory and customer support costs by installing an enterprise resource planning (ERP) system. Two enterprise software vendors have responded to your request for proposal (RFP) and have submitted reports showing which of your detailed list of requirements can be supported by their systems. Audio Direct attaches the most importance to capabilities for sales order processing, inventory management, and warehousing. The Information Systems staff prepared the following matrix comparing the vendors' capabilities for these functions. It shows the percentage of requirements for each function that each alter-native ERP system can provide. It also shows the weight, or relative importance the company attaches to each of these functions.

1. Calculate each ERP vendor's score by multiplying the percentage of requirements for each function by the weight for that function.

2. Calculate each ERP vendor's total score for each of the three major functions (order processing, inventory management, and warehousing). Then calculate the grand total for each vendor.

3. On the basis of vendor scores, which ERP vendor would you select?

4. Are there any other factors, including intangible benefits, that might affect your decision? What are they?

Function	Weight	ERP System A %	ERP System A Score	ERP System B %	ERP System B Score
1.0 Order Processing					
1.1 Online order entry	4	67		73	
1.2 Online pricing	4	81		87	
1.3 Inventory check	4	72		81	
1.4 Customer credit check	3	66		59	
1.5 Invoicing	4	73		82	
Total Order Processing					
2.0 Inventory Management					
2.1 Production forecasting	3	72		76	
2.2 Production planning	4	79		81	
2.3 Inventory control	4	68		80	
2.4 Reports	3	71		69	
Total Inventory Management					
3.0 Warehousing					
3.1 Receiving	2	71		75	
3.2 Picking/packing	3	77		82	
3.3 Shipping	4	92		89	
Total Warehousing					
Grand Total					

13.3 MANAGING IMPLEMENTATION

Not all aspects of the implementation process can be easily controlled or planned (Alter and Ginzberg, 1978). However, the chances for systems success can be increased by anticipating potential implementation problems and applying appropriate corrective strategies. Various project management, requirements gathering, and planning methodologies have been developed for specific categories of problems. Strategies have also been devised for ensuring that users play an appropriate role throughout the implementation period and for managing the organizational change process.

CONTROLLING RISK FACTORS

Implementers should adopt a contingency approach to project management, handling each project with the tools, project management methodologies, and organizational linkages geared to its level of risk (McFarlan, 1981).

Managing Technical Complexity

Projects with high levels of technology benefit from **internal integration tools**. The success of these projects depends on how well their technical complexity can be managed internally. Project leaders need both heavy technical and administrative experience. They must be able to anticipate problems and develop smooth working relationships among a predominantly technical team. The team should be under the leadership of a manager with a strong technical and project management background, and team members should be highly experienced. Team meetings should take place frequently, with routine distribution of meeting minutes concerning key design decisions. Essential technical skills or expertise not available internally should be secured from outside the organization.

internal integration tools
A project management technique that ensures that the implementation team operates as a cohesive unit.

Formal Planning and Control Tools

Large projects will benefit from appropriate use of **formal planning** and **formal control tools**. A detailed plan can be developed using project management techniques, such as PERT (Program Evaluation and Review Technique) or Gantt charts. PERT lists the specific activities that make up a project, their duration, and the activities that must be completed before a specific activity can start. A Gantt chart such as the one illustrated in Figure 13-6 visually represents the sequence and timing of different tasks in a development project as well as their resource requirements. Tasks can be defined and resources budgeted.

Project management techniques can help managers to identify bottlenecks and to determine the impact that problems will have on project completion times. They can also help systems developers to partition implementation into smaller, more manageable segments with defined, measurable business results (Fichman and Moses, 1999). Standard control techniques will successfully chart the progress of the project against budgets and target dates, so deviations from the plan can be spotted.

formal planning tools
A project management technique that structures and sequences tasks, budgeting time, money, and technical resources required to complete the tasks.

formal control tools
A project management technique that helps monitor the progress toward completion of a task and fulfillment of goals.

Increasing User Involvement and Overcoming User Resistance

Projects with relatively little structure must involve users fully at all stages. Users must be mobilized to support one of many possible design options and to remain committed to the single chosen design. **External integration tools** consist of ways to link the work of the implementation team to users at all organizational levels. For instance, users can become active members of the project team and take on leadership roles and take charge of installation and training.

Table 13-3 contains a breakdown of the factors that comprise risk and appropriate project management tools for dealing with each degree of risk.

external integration tools
A project management technique that links the work of the implementation team to that of users at all organizational levels.

This project team of professionals is using computing tools to enhance communication, analysis, and decision making.

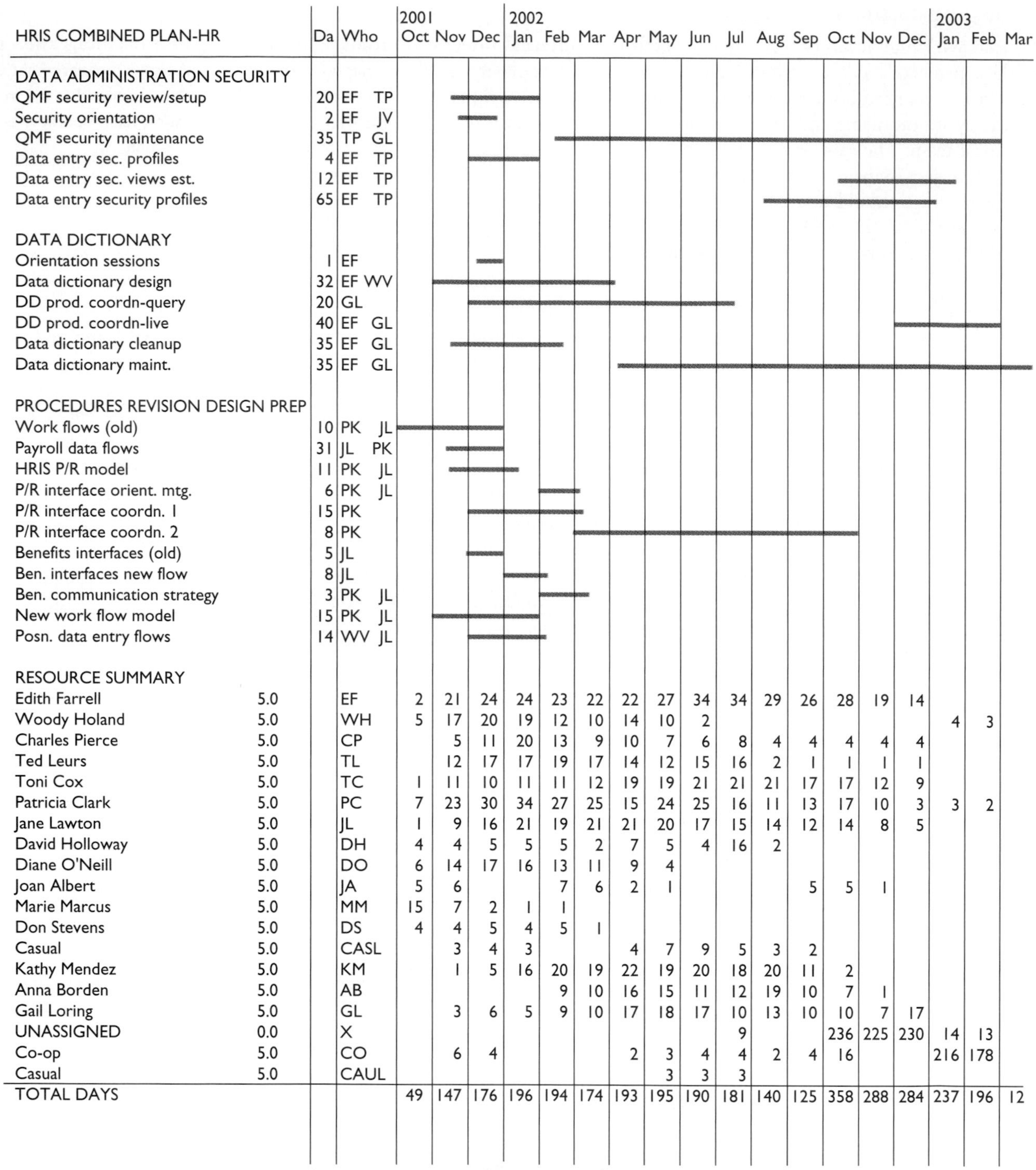

HRIS COMBINED PLAN-HR

Task	Da	Who
DATA ADMINISTRATION SECURITY		
QMF security review/setup	20	EF TP
Security orientation	2	EF JV
QMF security maintenance	35	TP GL
Data entry sec. profiles	4	EF TP
Data entry sec. views est.	12	EF TP
Data entry security profiles	65	EF TP
DATA DICTIONARY		
Orientation sessions	1	EF
Data dictionary design	32	EF WV
DD prod. coordn-query	20	GL
DD prod. coordn-live	40	EF GL
Data dictionary cleanup	35	EF GL
Data dictionary maint.	35	EF GL
PROCEDURES REVISION DESIGN PREP		
Work flows (old)	10	PK JL
Payroll data flows	31	JL PK
HRIS P/R model	11	PK JL
P/R interface orient. mtg.	6	PK JL
P/R interface coordn. 1	15	PK
P/R interface coordn. 2	8	PK
Benefits interfaces (old)	5	JL
Ben. interfaces new flow	8	JL
Ben. communication strategy	3	PK JL
New work flow model	15	PK JL
Posn. data entry flows	14	WV JL

RESOURCE SUMMARY

Name		Who	2001 Oct	Nov	Dec	2002 Jan	Feb	Mar	Apr	May	Jun	Jul	Aug	Sep	Oct	Nov	Dec	2003 Jan	Feb	Mar
Edith Farrell	5.0	EF	2	21	24	24	23	22	22	27	34	34	29	26	28	19	14			
Woody Holand	5.0	WH	5	17	20	19	12	10	14	10	2							4	3	
Charles Pierce	5.0	CP		5	11	20	13	9	10	7	6	8	4	4	4	4	4			
Ted Leurs	5.0	TL		12	17	17	19	17	14	12	15	16	2	1	1	1	1			
Toni Cox	5.0	TC	1	11	10	11	11	12	19	19	21	21	21	17	17	12	9			
Patricia Clark	5.0	PC	7	23	30	34	27	25	15	24	25	16	11	13	17	10	3	3	2	
Jane Lawton	5.0	JL	1	9	16	21	19	21	21	20	17	15	14	12	14	8	5			
David Holloway	5.0	DH	4	4	5	5	5	2	7	5	4	16	2							
Diane O'Neill	5.0	DO	6	14	17	16	13	11	9	4										
Joan Albert	5.0	JA	5	6			7	6	2	1				5	5	1				
Marie Marcus	5.0	MM	15	7	2	1	1													
Don Stevens	5.0	DS	4	4	5	4	5	1												
Casual	5.0	CASL		3	4	3			4	7	9	5	3	2						
Kathy Mendez	5.0	KM		1	5	16	20	19	22	19	20	18	20	11	2					
Anna Borden	5.0	AB				9	10	16	15	11	12	19	10	7	1					
Gail Loring	5.0	GL		3	6	5	9	10	17	18	17	10	13	10	10	7	17			
UNASSIGNED	0.0	X										9			236	225	230	14	13	
Co-op	5.0	CO		6	4				2	3	4	4	2	4	16			216	178	
Casual	5.0	CAUL							3	3	3									
TOTAL DAYS			49	147	176	196	194	174	193	195	190	181	140	125	358	288	284	237	196	12

FIGURE 13-6 Formal planning and control tools help to manage information systems projects successfully. The Gantt chart in this figure was produced by a commercially available project management software package. It shows the task, person-days, and initials of each responsible person, as well as the start and finish dates for each task. The resource summary provides a manager with the total person-days for each month and for each person working on the project to successfully manage the project. The project described here is a data administration project.

Unfortunately, systems development is not an entirely rational process. Users leading design activities have used their position to further their own private interests and to gain power rather than to promote organizational objectives (Franz and Robey, 1984). Users may not always be involved in systems projects in a productive way.

TABLE 13-3	STRATEGIES TO MANAGE PROJECTS BY CONTROLLING RISKS			
Project Structure	**Project Technology Level**	**Project Size**	**Degree of Risk**	**Project Management Tool**
High	Low	Large	Low	High use of formal planning
				High use of formal control
High	Low	Small	Very low	High use of formal control
				Medium use of formal planning
High	High	Large	Medium	Medium use of formal control
				Medium use of formal planning
High	High	Small	Medium-low	High internal integration
Low	Low	Large	Low	High external integration
				High use of formal planning
				High use of formal control
Low	Low	Small	Very low	High external integration
				High use of formal control
Low	High	Large	Very high	High external integration
				High internal integration
Low	High	Small	High	High external integration
				High internal integration

As we began discussing in Chapter 11, participation in implementation activities may not be enough to overcome the problem of user resistance. The implementation process demands organizational change. Change may be resisted because different users may be affected by the system in different ways. While some users may welcome a new system because it brings changes they perceive as beneficial to them, others may resist these changes because they believe the shifts are detrimental to their interests (Joshi, 1991).

If the use of a system is voluntary, users may choose to avoid it; if use is mandatory, resistance will take the form of increased error rates, disruptions, turnover, and even sabotage. Therefore, the implementation strategy must not only encourage user participation and involvement, it must also address the issue of counterimplementation (Keen, 1981). **Counterimplementation** is a deliberate strategy to thwart the implementation of an information system or an innovation in an organization.

Strategies to overcome user resistance include user participation (to elicit commitment as well as to improve design); user education and training; management commitment in the form of verbal support, edicts, and policies; and incentives for users who cooperate. The new system can be made more user friendly by improving the end-user interface. Users will be more cooperative if organizational problems are solved prior to introducing the new system.

counterimplementation
A deliberate strategy to thwart the implementation of an information system or an innovation in an organization.

DESIGNING FOR THE ORGANIZATION

Since the purpose of a new system is to improve the organization's performance, the systems development process must explicitly address the ways in which the organization will change when the new system is installed, including installation of intranets, extranets, and Internet applications. In addition to procedural changes, transformations in job functions, organizational structure, power relationships, and behaviour will all have to be carefully planned. When technology-induced changes produce unforeseen consequences, the organization can benefit by improvising to take advantage of new opportunities. Information systems specialists, managers, and users should remain open-minded about their roles in the change management process and not adhere to rigid narrow perceptions (Orlikowski and Hofman, 1997; Markus and Benjamin, 1997). Table 13-4 lists the organizational dimensions that would need to be addressed to plan and implement many systems.

Although systems analysis and design activities are supposed to include an organizational impact analysis, this area has traditionally been neglected. An **organizational impact analysis** explains how a proposed system will affect organizational structure, attitudes, deci-

organizational impact analysis
The study of the way a proposed system will affect organizational structure, attitudes, decision making, and operations.

TABLE 13-4 Implementation
Employee participation and involvement
Job design
Standards and performance monitoring
Ergonomics (including equipment, user interfaces, and the work environment)
Employee grievance resolution procedures
Health and safety
Government regulatory compliance

sion making, and operations. To integrate information systems successfully with the organization, thorough and fully documented organizational impact assessments must be given more attention in the development effort.

Allowing for the Human Factor

The quality of information systems should be evaluated in terms of user criteria rather than the criteria of the information systems staff. In addition to targets such as memory size, access rates, and calculation times, systems objectives should include standards for user performance. For example, an objective might be that data entry clerks learn the procedures and codes for four new online data entry screens in a half-day training session.

ergonomics
The interaction of people and machines in the work environment, including the design of jobs, health issues, and user interfaces of information systems.

User interfaces should be carefully designed with sensitivity to ergonomic issues. **Ergonomics** refers to the interaction of people and machines in the work environment. It considers the design of jobs, health issues, and the end-user interface of information systems. The impact of the system on the work environment and job dimensions must be carefully assessed. One noteworthy study of 620 U.S. Social Security Administration claims representatives showed that the representatives with online access to claims data experienced greater stress than those with serial access to the data via teletype. Even though the online interface was faster and more direct than teletype, it created much more frustration. Representatives with online access could interface with a larger number of clients per day, causing more stress due to the higher volume of client contacts. This changed the dimensions of the job for claims representatives. The restructuring of work—involving tasks, quality of working life, and performance—had a more profound impact than the nature of the technology itself (Turner, 1984).

Sociotechnical Design

Most contemporary systems development approaches tend to treat end users as essential to the systems-development process but to assign them a largely passive role with respect to other forces shaping the system such as the system designers and management. A different tradition, rooted in the European social democratic labour movement, assigns users a more active role, one that empowers them to co-determine the role of information systems in their workplace (Clement and Van den Besselaar, 1993).

sociotechnical design
A design to produce information systems that blend technical efficiency with sensitivity to organizational and human needs.

The tradition of participatory design emphasizes participation by the individuals most affected by the new system. It is closely associated with the concept of **sociotechnical design**. A sociotechnical design plan establishes human objectives for the system that lead to increased job satisfaction. Designers set forth separate sets of technical and social design solutions. The social design plans explore different work group structures, allocation of tasks, and the design of individual jobs. The proposed technical solutions are compared with the proposed social solutions. Social and technical solutions that can be combined are proposed as sociotechnical solutions. The alternative that best meets both social and technical objectives is selected for the final design. The resulting sociotechnical design is expected to produce an information system that blends technical efficiency with sensitivity to organizational and human needs, leading to higher job satisfaction (Mumford and Weir, 1979). Systems with compatible technical and organizational elements are expected to raise productivity without sacrificing human and social goals.

"FOURTH-GENERATION" PROJECT MANAGEMENT

Traditional techniques for managing projects deal with problems of size and complexity by breaking large projects into sub-projects; assigning teams, schedules, and milestones to each; and focusing primarily on project mechanics rather than business results. However, these techniques are inadequate for enterprise systems and other large-scale systems projects with extremely complex problems of organizational coordination and change management, complex and sometimes unfamiliar technology, and continually changing business requirements. A new "fourth-generation" of project management techniques is emerging to address these challenges.

In this model, project planning assumes an enterprise-wide focus, driven by the firm's strategic business vision and technology architecture. Project and sub-project managers focus on solving problems and meeting challenges as they arise rather than simply meeting formal project milestones. It may be useful for organizations to establish a separate program office to manage sub-projects, coordinate the entire project effort with other ongoing projects, and coordinate the project with ongoing changes in the firm's business strategy, information technology architecture and infrastructure, and business processes (The Concours Group, 2000).

13.4 MANAGING GLOBAL INFORMATION SYSTEMS

Table 13-5 lists the principal management problems posed by developing international systems. It is interesting to note that these problems are the chief difficulties managers experience in developing ordinary domestic systems as well! But these are enormously complicated in the international environment.

A TYPICAL SCENARIO: DISORGANIZATION ON A GLOBAL SCALE

A traditional multinational consumer-goods company based in Canada and operating in Europe would like to expand into Asian markets and knows that it must develop a transnational strategy and a supportive information systems structure. Like other Canadian multinationals, it has dispersed production and marketing to regional and national centres while maintaining a world headquarters and strategic management in Canada. Historically, it has allowed the subsidiary foreign divisions to develop their own systems. The only centrally coordinated systems are financial controls and reporting. The central systems group in Canada focuses only on domestic functions and production. The result is a hodgepodge of hardware, software, and telecommunications. The e-mail systems between Europe and Canada are incompatible. Each production facility uses a different manufacturing resources planning system (or a different version with local variations), and different marketing, sales, and human resource systems. The technology platforms are wildly different: Europe uses mostly UNIX-based file servers and IBM PC clones on desktops. Communications between different sites are poor, given the high cost and low quality of European inter-country communications. The Canadian group is moving from an IBM mainframe environment centralized

TABLE 13-5	MANAGEMENT CHALLENGES IN DEVELOPING GLOBAL SYSTEMS

Agreeing on common user requirements

Introducing changes in business processes

Coordinating applications development

Coordinating software releases

Encouraging local users to support global systems

Integration of standards

Differences in telecommunication standards and infrastructure levels

at headquarters to a highly distributed network architecture based on a national value-added network, with local sites developing their own local area networks. The central systems group at headquarters recently was decimated and dispersed to the Canadian local sites in the hope of serving local needs better and reducing costs.

The senior management leaders of this company now want to pursue a transnational strategy and develop an information systems infrastructure to support a highly coordinated global systems environment. What is your recommendation? Consider the problems you face by re-examining Table 13-5. The foreign divisions will resist efforts to agree on common user requirements; they have never thought about much beyond than their own units' needs. The systems groups in American local sites, which have been enlarged recently and told to focus on local needs, will not easily accept guidance from anyone recommending a transnational strategy. It will be difficult to convince local managers anywhere in the world that they should change their business procedures to align with other units in the world, especially if this might interfere with their local performance. After all, local managers are rewarded in this company for meeting local objectives of their division or plant. Finally, it will be difficult to coordinate development of projects around the world in the absence of a powerful telecommunications network and, therefore, difficult to encourage local users to take ownership in the systems developed.

STRATEGY: DIVIDE, CONQUER, APPEASE

Figure 13-7 lays out the main dimensions of a solution. First, consider that not all systems should be coordinated on a transnational basis; only some core systems are truly worth sharing from a cost and feasibility point of view. **Core systems** are systems that support functions that are absolutely critical to the organization. Other systems should be partially coordinated because they share key elements, but they do not have to be totally common across national boundaries. For these systems, a fair amount of local variation is possible and even desirable. A final group of systems are peripheral, truly provincial, and needed only to suit local requirements.

Define the Core Business Processes

How do you identify core systems? The first step is to define a short list of critical core business processes. Business processes were defined in Chapter 2. Briefly, business processes are sets of logically related tasks such as shipping out correct orders to customers or delivering innovative products to the market. Each business process typically involves many functional areas communicating and coordinating work, information, and knowledge.

core systems
Information systems that support functions that are absolutely critical to the organization.

FIGURE 13-7 Agency and other coordination costs increase as the firm moves from local option systems toward regional and global systems. However, transaction costs of participating in global markets probably decrease as firms develop global systems. A sensible strategy is to reduce agency costs by developing only a few core global systems that are vital for global operations, leaving other systems in the hands of regional and local units.

Source: From *Managing Information Technology in Multinational Corporations* by Edward M. Roche, © 1993. Adapted by permission of Prentice-Hall, Inc., Upper Saddle River, NJ.

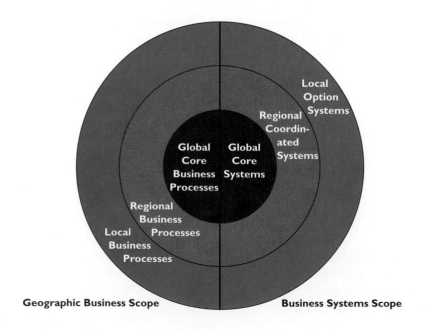

The way to identify these core business processes is to conduct a workflow analysis. How are customer orders taken, what happens to them once they are taken, who fills the orders, how are they shipped to the customers? What about suppliers? Do they have access to manufacturing resource planning systems so that supply replenishment is automatic? You should be able to identify and set priorities in a short list of 10 business processes that are absolutely critical for the firm.

Next, can you identify centres of excellence for these processes? Is the customer order fulfillment superior in the United States, manufacturing process control superior in Germany, and human resources superior in Asia? You should be able to identify some areas of the company, for some lines of business, where a division or unit stands out in the performance of one or several business functions.

When you understand the business processes of a firm, you can rank them. You then can decide which processes should be core applications, centrally coordinated, designed, and implemented around the globe, and which should be regional or local. At the same time, by identifying the critical business processes, you have gone a long way to defining a vision of the future that you should be working toward.

Identify the Core Systems to Coordinate Centrally

By identifying the critical core business processes, you begin to see opportunities for transnational systems. The second strategic step is to transform the core systems into truly transnational systems. The financial and political costs of defining and implementing transnational systems are extremely high. Therefore, keep the list to an absolute minimum, letting experience be the guide and erring on the side of minimalism. By defining a small group of systems as absolutely critical, you divide opposition to a transnational strategy. At the same time, you can appease those who oppose the central worldwide coordination implied by transnational systems by permitting peripheral systems development to progress unabated, with the exception of some technical platform requirements.

Choose an Approach: Incremental, Grand Design, Evolutionary

A third step is to choose an approach. Avoid piecemeal approaches. These surely will fail for lack of visibility, opposition from all who stand to lose from transnational development, and lack of power to convince senior management that the transnational systems are worth it. Likewise, avoid grand design approaches that try to do everything at once. These also tend to fail due to an inability to focus resources. Nothing gets done properly, and opposition to organizational change is needlessly strengthened because the effort requires huge resources. An alternative approach is to evolve transnational applications from existing applications with a precise and clear vision of the transnational capabilities the organization should have in five years.

Make the Benefits Clear

What is in it for the company? One of the worst situations is developing global systems for the sake of building global systems. From the beginning, it is crucial that senior management at headquarters and foreign division managers clearly understand the benefits that will come to the company as well as to individual units. Although each system offers unique benefits to a particular budget, the overall contribution of global systems are in four areas.

Global systems—truly integrated, distributed, and transnational systems—contribute to superior management and coordination. A simple price tag cannot be put on the value of this contribution, and the benefit will not show up in any capital budgeting model. Its value lies in the ability to switch suppliers on a moment's notice from one region to another in a crisis, the ability to move production in response to natural disasters, and the ability to use excess capacity in one region to meet raging demand in another.

A second major contribution is vast improvements in production, operations, and supply and distribution. Imagine a global value chain, with global suppliers and a global distribution network. For the first time, senior managers can locate value-adding activities in regions where they are most economically performed.

Third, global systems mean global customers and global marketing. Fixed costs around the world can be amortized over a much larger customer base. This will unleash new economies of scale at production facilities.

Last, global systems mean the ability to optimize the use of corporate funds over a much larger capital base. This means, for instance, that capital in a surplus region can be moved efficiently to expand production in capital-starved regions—that cash can be managed more effectively within the company and put to use more effectively.

These strategies will not by themselves create global systems. You will have to implement what you strategize, and this is an entirely different challenge.

IMPLEMENTATION TACTICS: CO-OPTATION

co-optation
Bringing the opposition into the process of designing and implementing the solution without giving up control over the direction and nature of the change.

The overall tactic for dealing with resistant local units in a transnational company is co-optation. **Co-optation** is defined as bringing the opposition into the process of designing and implementing the solution without giving up control over the direction and nature of the change. As much as possible, the use of raw power should be avoided. Minimally, however, local units must agree on a short list of transnational systems. Raw power may be required to force local units to agree on the list.

How should co-optation proceed? Several alternatives are possible. One alternative is to permit each country unit the opportunity to develop one transnational application first in its home territory, and then throughout the world. In this manner, each major country systems group is given a piece of the action in developing a transnational system, and local units feel a sense of ownership in the transnational effort. On the downside, this assumes the ability to develop high-quality systems is widely distributed, and that, for example, the German team can successfully implement systems in France and Italy. This will not always be the case. Also, the transnational effort will have low visibility.

A second tactic is to develop new transnational centres of excellence, or a single centre of excellence. There may be several centres around the globe that focus on specific business processes. These centres draw heavily from local national units, are based on multinational teams, and must report to worldwide management—their first line of responsibility is to the core applications. Centres of excellence perform the initial identification and specification of the business process, define the information requirements, perform the business and systems analysis, and accomplish all design and testing. Implementation and pilot testing, however, occur in World Pilot Regions where new applications are installed and tested first. Later, they are rolled out to other parts of the globe. This phased rollout strategy is the way most national applications are successfully developed.

THE MANAGEMENT SOLUTION

We now can reconsider how to handle the most vexing problems facing managers developing the transnational information system infrastructures that were described in Table 13-5.

▌ *Agreeing on common user requirements:* Establishing a short list of the core business processes and core support systems will begin a process of rational comparison across the many divisions of the company, develop a common language for discussing the business, and naturally lead to an understanding of common elements (as well as the unique qualities that must remain local).

▌ *Introducing changes in business processes:* Your success as a change agent will depend on your legitimacy, your actual raw power, and your ability to involve users in the change design process. **Legitimacy** is defined as the extent to which your authority is accepted on grounds of competence, vision, rank, or other qualities. The selection of a viable change strategy, which we have defined as evolutionary but with a vision, should assist you in convincing others that change is feasible and desirable. Involving people in change, assuring them that change is in the best interests of the company and their local units, is a key tactic.

legitimacy
The extent to which authority is accepted on the basis of competence, vision, rank, or other qualities.

▌ *Coordinating applications development:* Choice of change strategy is critical for this problem. At the global level, there is far too much complexity to attempt a grand design strategy of change. It is far easier to coordinate change by making small incremental steps toward a larger vision.

▌ *Coordinating software releases:* Firms can institute procedures to ensure that all operating units convert to new software updates at the same time so that all software is compatible.

▌ *Encouraging local users to support global systems:* Involve users in the creation of the design without giving up control over the development of the project to parochial interests. Recruit a wide range of local individuals to the transnational centres of excellence to send the message that all significant groups are involved in the design and will have an influence.

▌ *Integration of standards:* Individual country standards and laws and regulations governing these standards must be discovered and made a part of the implementation plan. Budgeting and timelines must include funding and adequate time to build interfaces between different standards or to include universal standards that are not already being used by the organization.

▌ *Differences in telecommunication standards and infrastructure levels:* Countries vary widely in the telecommunications standards they use or will accept and the level to which their telecommunications infrastructure supports global high-speed access. Implementation of an information system that requires high-speed access in a country or locale where

---

LUCENT'S ENTERPRISE SYSTEM SPEEDS ITS GLOBAL SUPPLY CHAIN

Competition in the manufacture and sales of cellular phones is so fierce that a new phone model can retain its original value for only two-to-three months. After that, newer models from competitors with newer functions and capabilities will make existing models somewhat obsolete. To compete successfully in such a market, speed is critical. Cellular phone manufacturers must be able to improve their products every several months and to shift to the manufacture of their new products within days or hours. This market presented a huge problem to the Lucent Microelectronics Group, which produces the chips that are the heart of many cellular phones. Lucent is a part of Lucent Technologies, the Murray Hill, New Jersey, giant telecommunications technology company divested from AT&T.

Lucent silicon wafers are produced in plants in Pennsylvania, Florida, and Spain. They are then assembled into integrated circuits in other plants in Pennsylvania, Thailand, and Singapore where they are also tested. From there, they are shipped to customers such as L.M. Ericsson, a telecommunications equipment maker in Stockholm, Sweden. Prior to 1999, Lucent factories were run by legacy systems that often did not even communicate with each other. Each factory had its own supply chain, production schedule, and manufacturing systems. "Gathering data across the enterprise was difficult, if not impossible," according to Lucent CIO William Stuckey.

The solution involved putting all Lucent factories on the same set of information systems and installing an Oracle enterprise system in June 1999 to help the company coordinate materials, processes, schedules, logistics, and accounting information. The new system gives Lucent a global view of its supply chain within three minutes of any transaction. For example,

once a purchase order from Ericsson for chips has been entered into the system, the system verifies customer data and checks to see whether the product is available. If it is, the system instructs the Lucent integrated circuit assembly plants to pick and pack the chips and hand them to DHL Worldwide Express for delivery. At the same time, the system sends Ericsson an EDI confirmation. DHL can deliver the order to an Ericsson plant in Sweden about 56 hours after it has been received.

The ERP system has reduced processes that used to take 10 to 15 days to less than eight hours. Lucent is able to manage all of its global factories as if they were a single factory. If, for instance, a natural catastrophe hits a plant, Lucent can shift critical production to another plant within eight hours. Customers can even use the Web to track the status of their own orders at any time.

While DHL's rapid delivery service is more expensive than the slower previous companies Lucent had relied upon, it is actually saving Lucent money. Previously, logistics costs, including personnel, warehousing, stocking and transportation, ran about 1.5% of revenue while today they have dropped to under 1%. Lucent has achieved this reduction through lowered warehousing and inventory expenses by substituting "information for inventory."

To Think About: What competitive forces drove Lucent to a new ERP system and to installing the same systems around the world? How did this technology help solve Lucent's supply chain problems?

Sources: David Baum, "The Future is Calling," *Profit*, August 2000; Eric Chabrow, "Supply Chains Go Global," *Information Week*, April 3, 2000; "Tighter Supply Chain Helps Lucent Speed Deliveries," *Information Week*, April 3, 2000.

this is not possible will meet with failure. In this case, a scaled down version of the system, or an entirely different system, may be needed to overcome these differences.

Even with the proper organizational structure and appropriate management choices, it is still possible to stumble over technological issues. Choices of technology, platforms, networks, hardware, and software are the final elements in building transnational information system infrastructures.

MAIN TECHNICAL ISSUES

Hardware, software, and telecommunications pose special technical challenges in an international setting. The major global hardware challenge is finding a way to standardize the firm's computer hardware platform when there is so much variation between countries. Managers need to think carefully about where to locate the firm's computer centres and how to select hardware suppliers. The major global software challenge is finding applications that are user friendly and that truly enhance the productivity of international work teams. The major global telecommunications challenge is making data flow seamlessly across networks shaped by disparate national standards. Many countries also do not have the fast and reliable postal and package delivery services that are essential for electronic commerce as well (DePalma, 2000). Many countries face high costs, government control, and government monitoring. Overcoming these challenges requires systems integration and connectivity on a global basis.

Hardware and Systems Integration

The development of transnational information system infrastructures based on the concept of core systems raises questions about how the new core systems will fit in with the existing suite of applications developed around the globe by different divisions, different people, and for different kinds of computing hardware. The goal is to develop global, distributed, and integrated systems. Briefly, these are the same problems faced by any large, domestic, systems development effort. However, the problems are more complex because of the international environment. For instance, in North America, IBM operating systems have played the predominant role in building core systems for large organizations while in Europe, UNIX was more commonly used for large systems. How can the two be integrated in a common transnational system?

The correct solution often will depend on the history of the company's systems and the extent of its commitment to proprietary systems. For instance, finance and insurance firms typically have relied almost exclusively on IBM proprietary equipment and architectures, and it would be extremely difficult and cost ineffective to abandon that equipment and software. Newer firms and manufacturing firms generally find it much easier to adopt open UNIX systems for international systems.

After a hardware platform is chosen, the question of standards must be addressed. Just because all sites use the same hardware does not guarantee common, integrated systems. Some central authority in the firm must establish data and other technical standards with which sites are to comply. For instance, technical accounting terms such as the beginning and end of the fiscal year must be standardized, as must the acceptable interfaces between systems, communication speeds and architectures, and network software.

Connectivity

The heart of the international systems problem is telecommunications—linking together the systems and people of a global firm into a single integrated network just like the phone system but capable of voice, data, and image transmissions. However, integrated global networks are extremely difficult to create (see Table 13-6). For example, many countries cannot fulfill basic business telecommunications needs such as obtaining reliable circuits, coordinating among different carriers and the regional telecommunications authority, obtaining bills in a common currency standard, and obtaining standard agreements for the level of telecommunications service provided.

Despite moves toward economic unity, Europe remains a hodgepodge of disparate national technical standards and service levels. The problem is especially critical for banks or

TABLE 13-6	PROBLEMS OF INTERNATIONAL NETWORKS

Costs and tariffs

Network management

Installation delays

Poor quality of international service

Regulatory constraints

Changing user requirements

Disparate standards

Network capacity

airlines that must move massive volumes of data around the world. Although most circuits leased by multinational corporations are fault-free more than 99.8 percent of the time, line quality and service vary widely from the north to the south of Europe. Network service is much more unreliable in southern Europe.

Existing European standards for networking and EDI (electronic data interchange) are very industry specific and country specific. Most European banks use the SWIFT (Society for Worldwide Interbank Financial Telecommunications) protocol for international funds transfer, while automobile companies and food producers often use industry-specific or country-specific versions of standard protocols for EDI. Complicating matters further, the United States' standard for EDI is ANSI (American National Standards Institute) X.12. The Open Systems Interconnect (OSI) reference model for linking networks is more popular in Europe than it is in the United States. Various industry groups have standardized on other networking architectures, such as Transmission Control Protocol/Internet Protocol (TCP/IP) or IBM's proprietary Systems Network Architecture (SNA). Even standards such as ISDN (Integrated Services Digital Network) vary from country to country.

Firms have several options for providing international connectivity: build their own international private network, rely on a network service based on the public switched networks throughout the world, or use the Internet and intranets.

One possibility is for the firm to put together its own private network based on leased lines from each country's PTT (post, telegraph, and telephone authorities). Each country, however, has different restrictions on data exchange, technical standards, and acceptable vendors of equipment. These problems are magnified in certain parts of the world. Despite such limitations, in Europe and the United States, reliance on PTTs still makes sense while these public networks expand services to compete with private providers.

The second major alternative to building one's own network is to use one of several expanding network services. With deregulation of telecommunications around the globe, private providers have sprung up to service business customers' data needs, along with voice and image communication.

Already common in North America, IVANs (International Value-Added Network Services) are expanding in Europe and Asia. These private firms offer value-added telecommunications capacity, usually rented from local PTTs or international satellite authorities, and then resold to corporate users. IVANs add value by providing protocol conversion, operating mail boxes and mail systems, and by offering integrated billing that permits a firm to track its data communications costs. Currently, these systems are limited to data transmissions, but in the future they will expand to voice and image.

The third alternative, which is becoming increasingly attractive, is to create global intranets to use the Internet for international communication. However, the Internet is not yet a worldwide tool because many countries lack the communications infrastructure for extensive Internet use.

Western Europe faces both high transmission costs and lack of common technology because it is not politically unified and because European telecommunications systems are still in the process of shedding their government monopolies. The lack of an infrastructure and the high cost of installing one are even more widespread in the rest of the world. The

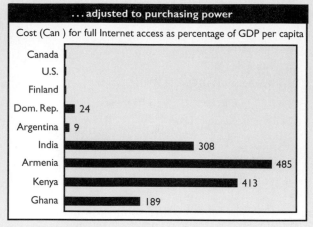

End user costs ...	
Absolute prices (Can) for full Internet access	
Canada	25
U.S.	30
Finland	27
Dom. Rep.	39
Argentina	75
India	123
Armenia	182
Kenya	150
Ghana	75

... adjusted to purchasing power	
Cost (Can) for full Internet access as percentage of GDP per capita	
Canada	
U.S.	
Finland	
Dom. Rep.	24
Argentina	9
India	308
Armenia	485
Kenya	413
Ghana	189

Sources: www.malinet.ml; www.ghana.com; www.Form-net.com; www.arminco.com/overview.htm; www.satlink.net/servicios/online.htm; www.aol.com; www.indiax.com/cal; www.att.net; and www.concentric.com

FIGURE 13-8 End-user costs for full Internet access. The cost of accessing the Internet is much higher in developing countries than in North America and Western Europe. These disparities are even greater when users' purchasing power is taken into account.

Source: Ben Petrazzini and Mugo Kibati, "The Internet in Developing Countries," *Communications of the ACM* 42, No. 6, June 1999. Reprinted by permission.

International Telecommunications Union estimates that only 500 million of the world's 1.5 billion households have basic telephone services (Wysocki, 2000). Low penetration of PCs and widespread illiteracy limit demand for Internet service in India (Burkhardt, Goodman, Mehta, and Press, 1999). Where an infrastructure exists in less-developed countries, it is often outdated, lacks digital circuits, and has very noisy lines. Figure 13-8 illustrates some of these global disparities in the pricing and cost of Internet service. The purchasing power of most people in developing counties makes access to Internet services very expensive (Petrazzini and Kibati, 1999).

Many countries monitor transmissions. The governments in China and Singapore monitor Internet traffic and block access to Web sites considered morally or politically offensive (Smith, 2000; Blanning, 1999). Corporations may be discouraged from using this medium. Companies planning international operations over the Internet will still have many hurdles.

FIGURE 13-9 WholeTree. com provides technology and services for developing multilingual Web sites. Web sites and software interfaces for global systems may have to be translated to accommodate users in other parts of the world.

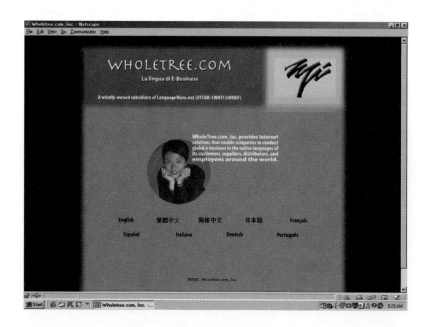

E-GLOBALIZATION PITFALLS

All Internet sites are accessible to anyone in the world unless the site owners establish security restrictions. However, doing business in distant lands contains many pitfalls. Even the smallest organization attempting to conduct business abroad must deal with many differences, from technology, law, and customs to foreign languages or differences in terminology. Let us look at some of the hazards.

Technology and the quality of technology differ all over the world. For example, while North America, Finland, and Sweden have developed adequate bandwidth for high-speed connections, the telecommunications infrastructures in Greece and Turkey are not as well developed. In some countries, a telecommunications infrastructure barely exists. One effect of a less developed infrastructure is that visitors from those countries will access a site at a very slow speeds and will even slow down visitors from other countries. Therefore, Web site owners may want to establish multiple regional sites to better serve those who are used to rapid responses on the Web.

Laws can present important obstacles as organizations attempt to expand. "We [Americans] take it for granted that when we log on a site, it recognizes us and displays preferences," says Victoria Bracewell-Short, a global E-commerce consultant with iXL Enterprises Inc. in Atlanta, Georgia. However, she points out, some other countries such as Germany have privacy laws that prevent the gathering of the kind of data necessary to be able to tailor the screen to the specific user. Just asking for personal data such as the visitor's name, mailing address, or e-mail address can be either illegal or outside the accepted customs of the specific country. Sites must be developed to accommodate different sets of laws in different countries.

Many question the use of language translation software to create foreign language sites because they can produce clumsy language or even the use of culturally unacceptable terms. However, screens developed in one country can even present translation problems in foreign countries that speak the same language. Let us look at Manheim Auctions Inc. as an example.

Manheim is an Atlanta, Georgia, based company that is the world's largest reseller of used cars. As the director of online operations for Manheim, Donald Foy ran into many unexpected problems when Manheim decided to go international. The company first targeted Australia and Great Britain because they both use English. However, a number of problems immediately emerged. For example, the company's logo displayed a globe showing North and South America. Australians were not willing to be so ignored, and so the logo had to be redesigned. Foy explained that his group had missed that issue altogether, and he added, "We have to be sensitive to their business and culture." To operate in both countries, the database had to be expanded to encompass national differences in terminology. For example what the people in North America call a car's hood, the British refer to as the bonnet. The database must also incorporate differences in measurements, with the Americans using miles while Canadians, British, and Australians use kilometres.

To Think About: What management, organization, and technology issues should be addressed when developing a global Web strategy? Who should take part in these decisions?

Sources: Dawne Shand, "All Information Is Local," *Computer-world*, April 10, 2000; Dermot McGrath, "Going Native," *Tornado-Insider.com*, May 2000.

The Window on Organizations explores Internet availability and other issues for companies attempting to develop an international Web strategy. Figure 13-9 looks at one company that is helping businesses produce multilingual sites.

Software

The development of core systems poses unique challenges for software: how will the old systems interface with the new? Entirely new interfaces must be developed and tested if old systems are kept in local areas (which is common). These interfaces can be costly and messy to develop. If new software must be developed, another challenge is to develop software that can be realistically used by multiple business units from different countries considering that these business units are accustomed to their unique business processes and definitions of data.

Aside from integrating new and old systems, there are problems in human interface design and functionality of systems. For instance, to be truly useful for enhancing the productivity of a global workforce, software interfaces must be easily understood and mastered quickly. Graphical user interfaces are ideal for this but presuppose a common language—usually English. When international systems involve knowledge workers only, English may be the assumed international standard. But as international systems penetrate deeper into management and clerical groups, a common language can not be assumed, and human interfaces must be developed to accommodate different languages and even conventions.

What are the most important software applications? Many international systems focus on basic transaction and MIS systems, including enterprise systems. Increasingly, firms such as Lucent Technologies, described in the Window on Technology, are turning to enterprise systems to standardize their business processes on a global basis and to create coordinated global supply chains. However, enterprise systems are not always compatible with differences in languages and business practices (Soh, Kien, and Tay-Yap, 2000). Company units in countries that are not technically sophisticated may also encounter problems trying to manage the technical complexities of enterprise software.

APPLICATION SOFTWARE EXERCISE

SPREADSHEET EXERCISE: CAPITAL BUDGETING AT SPARKLING CLEAN

Sparkling Clean, a janitorial supply manufacturer, is primarily known for its commercial laundry soap line, Forever Springtime. Currently, the inventory control system at Sparkling Clean is adequate. However, in recent strategic planning meetings, the company's management team has discussed the necessity of upgrading its information systems. As part of her duties, Katrina Cordova, a lead analyst at Sparkling Clean, was assigned the task of investigating design strategies for the new information system. Part of her duties requires her to prepare a financial analysis worksheet.

Because you are Katrina's assistant, she has asked you to prepare a financial worksheet that summarizes the costs, benefits, and financial analysis associated with the project. Although Katrina is still in the process of identifying the new system's costs and benefits, she feels you can begin working on the spreadsheet using the data on the Laudon, Laudon, and Brabston Web site for Chapter 13. The remaining costs and benefits will be added later. Prepare an initial financial analysis worksheet for Katrina. Please make sure your worksheet incorporates the capital budgeting models mentioned in the textbook. Use a discount rate of 12 percent, and assume a useful life of four years.

MANAGEMENT WRAP-UP

Managing information as a critical resource involves thinking of the information systems department as though it were any other department, such as the finance or accounting departments. Managers must link systems development to the organization's strategy and identify precisely which systems should be changed to achieve large-scale benefits for the organization as a whole. Managers must then be able to justify to senior management financial investment in these systems. Managers should fully understand the level of complexity and risk in new systems projects as well as their potential business value. Again, the complexity of developing and implementing international information systems greatly complicates these processes.

The CIO should be a member of top management and work closely with the MIS Steering Committee. Many organizational factors enter into the calculation of financial value of information systems. Managing global information systems vastly complicates the issues involved in information resource management.

Selecting the right technology for a systems solution that fits the problem's constraints and the organization's information technology infrastructure is a key business decision. Managers and systems builders should be fully aware of the risks and rewards of various technologies as they make their technology and project management selections.

For Discussion

1. This chapter views information as a critical resource or asset, just like lumber to a furniture company or paper to a publisher. What are the ramifications of this view?

2. When do you feel that professional project managers are needed for systems development projects? At what point should they enter the process?

SUMMARY

1. *Describe the various components of information resource management and the issues involved in each component.* The IS department may be structured in any of several ways: centralized as its own department, decentralized within other departments, or with personnel located both centrally and in various information service units and information centres. The CIO and MIS Steering Committee set IS policies and prioritize and review major projects. IS planning takes place at the strategic, tactical, and operational levels and should be aligned with organizational strategy at each level.

Systems development actually involves a number of IS personnel roles and includes the assignment of staff to various projects as well as ensuring that security issues are taken care of. IS personnel must be recruited, hired, and retained and must be permitted to keep their skill sets up. Like every other department in an organization, the IS department must set a budget, which is difficult at best given the trend toward rapidly changing technology and escalating IS personnel salaries.

2. *Evaluate various models for understanding the business value of information systems.* Capital budgeting models such as the payback method, accounting rate of return on investment (ROI), cost–benefit ratio, net present value, profitability index, and internal rate of return (IRR) are the primary financial models for determining the business value of information systems. Portfolio analysis and scoring models include nonfinancial considerations and can be used to evaluate alternative information systems projects.

3. *Select appropriate strategies to manage the system implementation process.* Management support and control of the implementation process are essential as are mechanisms for dealing with the level of risk in each new systems project. Some companies experience organizational resistance to change. Project risk factors can be brought under some control by a contin-

gency approach to project management. The level of risk in a systems development project is determined by three key dimensions: (1) project size, (2) project structure, and (3) experience with technology. The risk level of each project will determine the appropriate mix of external integration tools, internal integration tools, formal planning tools, and formal control tools to be applied.

Appropriate strategies can be applied to ensure the correct level of user participation in the systems development process and to minimize user resistance. Information system design and the entire implementation process should be managed as planned organizational change. Participatory design emphasizes the participation of the individuals most affected by a new system. Sociotechnical design aims for an optimal blend of social and technical design solutions.

4. *Describe project management methods involved in information resource management.* In managing projects, risk should first be assessed and then appropriate tools used, such as internal integration tools, formal planning and control tools such as PERT and Gantt charts, and external integration tools. All project management must take into account those who are affected by the project and its related change.

5. *Explain why international information resource management issues are more complex.* The level of complexity is greatly increased when information systems are international in scope. Management challenges include agreeing on common user requirements, introducing changes in business processes, coordinating applications development, coordinating software releases, encouraging local users to support global systems, integration of standards, and differences in telecommunications and infrastructure levels. A co-optation strategy may be needed to bring the various international parties into the process of managing global systems.

KEY TERMS

REVIEW QUESTIONS

1. Name and describe the components involved in information resource management.

2. Compare the role of the CIO with that of the MIS Steering Committee.

3. Name and describe the types or levels of IS planning.

4. Name and describe the various roles IS personnel have in the IS department.

5. What are the issues that complicate budgeting in the IS department?

6. Name and describe the principal capital budgeting methods used to evaluate information system projects.

7. What are the limitations of financial models for establishing the value of information systems?

8. Describe how portfolio analysis and scoring models can be used to establish the worth of systems.

9. What dimensions influence the level of risk in each systems development project?

10. What project management techniques can be used to control project risk?

11. What strategies can be used to overcome user resistance to systems development projects?

12. What organizational considerations should be addressed by information system design?

13. What are the management challenges involved in managing international information systems?

14. What strategies can be used to manage international information systems?

15. What problems are there in establishing international networks?

GROUP PROJECT

Form a group with two or three other students. Write a description of the implementation problems you might expect to encounter for the information system you designed for the Chapter 11 group project. Write an analysis of the steps you would take to solve or prevent these problems. Alternatively, you could describe the implementation problems that might be expected for one of the systems described in the Window boxes or chapter ending cases in this text. If possible, use electronic presentation software to present your findings to the class.

INTERNET CONNECTION

■ COMPANION WEBSITE

At www.pearsoned.ca/laudon, you'll find an online study guide with two quizzes to test your knowledge of how information resource management adds value in modern organizations. You'll also find updates to the chapter and online exercises and cases that enable you to apply your knowledge to realistic situations.

■ ADDITIONAL SITES OF INTEREST

There are many interesting Web sites to enhance your learning about information resource management. You can search the Web yourself, or just try the following sites to add to what you have already learned.

International Federation of Accountants
  www.ifac.org
  Full of information of interest to planning and project managers

Project Management Institute
  www.pmi.org
  Information for project management professionals

Canadian Risk Management Council
  www.infoinc.com/rims/canada/crmc.html
  Information about risk management in Canada

Information Resource Management Association of Canada
  www.irmac.ca
  Information related to IRM in Canada

CASE STUDY *Hershey's Enterprise System Creates Halloween Tricks*

When someone says "chocolate," many of us think of Hershey's—their chocolate bars, their Kisses, their many other candies. Hershey Foods Corp. of Hershey, Pennsylvania, was founded in 1894 and recorded U.S.$4.4 billion in sales in 1998, including its other brands such as Reese's Peanut Butter Cups, Milk Duds, and Good and Plenty. Altogether the company sells approximately 3300 candy products including variations in sizes and shapes. Candy is a very seasonal product, with Halloween and Christmas recording about 40 percent of annual candy sales, making the fourth quarter crucial to Hershey's profitability. Hershey's largest continuous challenge may be that it must rack up its multibillion dollars in sales of 50 cents or one dollar at a time, requiring huge numbers of its products to be sold. These quantities mean Hershey must have very reliable logistics systems.

Traditionally, the food and beverage industry has had a very low ratio of information technology (IT) spending to total revenue, ranging between 1.1 percent and 1.5 percent, according to Fred Parker, senior vice-president of IS at Schreiber Foods Inc. in Green Bay, Wisconsin. The last great technology advance in the industry was the bar-code scanner, which arrived about 1980. Parker believes the reason for the low IT spending ratio is the very low profit margin in the industry. However, the industry's stingy approach to IT began to change as the year 2000 approached. Many companies chose to solve their Year 2000 (Y2K) problems by replacing their legacy systems rather than spending a lot of money to retain and fix them.

According to Hershey vice-president of information systems, Rick Bentz, Hershey began to modernize its software and hardware in early 1996. The project, dubbed Enterprise 21, was scheduled to take four years (until early 2000). Enterprise 21 had several goals, including upgrading and standardizing the company's hardware, and moving from a mainframe-based network to a client-server environment. The company replaced 5000 desktop computers and also moved to TCP/IP networking based on newly installed network hardware. Bentz noted that benchmark studies by the Grocery Manufacturers of America show that Hershey's IT spending trailed that of most of its industrial peers. The study concluded that Hershey needed to be able to use and share its data much more efficiently. More and more retailers were demanding that suppliers such as Hershey fine-tune their deliveries so that the retailers could lower their inventory costs.

Hershey's information systems management set a goal to move to an ERP system using software from SAP AG of Walldorf, Germany. SAP was to be complemented with software from Manugistics Group Inc. of Rockville, Maryland. Manugistics would support production forecasting and scheduling as well as transportation management. In addition, the company decided to install software from Siebel Systems Inc. of San Mateo, California, that would aid Hershey in managing customer relations and in tracking the effectiveness of its marketing activities. Management believed that Enterprise 21 would help Hershey better execute its business strategy of emphasizing its core mass-market candy business.

A necessary piece of Enterprise 21 was the installation of bar-coding systems at all six U.S. production plants in 1999. Bar coding was necessary so the company could track all incoming and outgoing materials. In that way, it would be able to improve logistics management while controlling production costs. Enterprise 21 was later modified and called for Hershey to switch over to the new SAP system and its associated software in April of 1999, an annual period of low sales. This meant the company had 39 months to complete the project instead of the original 48 months. Although some SAP modules were actually put into production in January, the project ran behind the aggressive schedule, and the full system did not come online until mid-July. Included in the delayed conversion were SAP's critical order processing and billing systems, along with the Siebel and Manugistics systems. The timing caused a major problem because Halloween orders were already arriving by mid-July. The information systems staff chose to convert all these new systems using the direct cutover strategy in which the whole system goes live all at once. While this strategy is generally considered to be the most risky, were it to be successful, it could save the company time and money while enabling Hershey to fill its Halloween orders on schedule. By the time of the conversion, the whole project had cost Hershey U.S.$112 million.

Problems arose for Hershey when the cutover strategy did not work. Serious problems emerged immediately. As a result, many Hershey customers found their shelves empty as Halloween approached. Bruce Steinke, the candy buyer for Great North Foods, a regional distributor in Alpena, Michigan, had placed an order for 20 000 pounds of Hershey's candy and found his warehouse short just prior to Halloween. As a result 100 of Great North's 700 customers had no Hershey candy when Halloween arrived. The shortage meant not only a drop in Hershey's sales, but Great North (and other Hershey distributors) also lost credibility as their retail customers found it hard to believe that Hershey itself could be the problem.

The shortages also meant the loss of precious, highly contested shelf space. For example, Randall King, the candy buyer for the Winston-Salem, North Carolina-based Lowes Foods chain, faced the shortage problem. As a result, he told his 81 supermarkets to fill their empty Hershey candy shelves with other candies, and he even suggested that they turn to Mars brand candies. Retailers predicted that Hershey's lost shelf space would be hard to win back. Ron Coppel, a vice president of business development at Eby-Brown Co., a Naperville, Illinois, candy distributor, observed that "If you don't have my toothpaste, I'm walking out of the store. But," he added, "for a chocolate bar, I'll pick another one. [Customers are] not likely to walk out of a store because there was no Hershey's bar." So Hershey's long-range sales were also placed at risk by the logistics failures.

Hershey itself did not publicly acknowledge the problem until mid-September when it announced that something was wrong with its new computer systems. It did indicate that Hershey employees were having trouble entering new orders into the system. In addition, once in the system, the company stated that order details were not being properly transmitted to the warehouses where they could be filled. Hershey did announce that it expected the problem to be solved in time for Christmas shipments. However, industry analysts, such as William Leach of Donaldson, Lufkin & Jenrette, were quick to note that should the company fail to make that deadline, the problems would likely seriously cut into not only Christmas sales but also Valentine's Day and perhaps Easter shipments, two other crucial candy sales holidays.

As soon as the admission of problems was made, questions immediately arose as to the causes of those problems. Kevin McKay, the CEO of SAP in the United States, denied any problems with SAP's systems, saying, "If it was a system issue, I'd point directly to a system issue." He also made it clear that SAP was operating smoothly for Hershey's much smaller Canadian unit. Tom Crawford, the general manager of SAP America's consumer products business unit, verified that his consultants were at Hershey sites to help resolve the problems. But, he made clear, "There are really no software issues per se." Crawford explained that his consultants "are just making sure they [Hershey employees] are using the business processes (built into the software) correctly." Manugistics also said it was working with Hershey on "business process improvements." Brian Doyle, an IBM spokesperson, pointed to "the business process transformation underway at Hershey" as a possible cause which, he said, "is an enormously complex undertaking." He noted major changes in the way Hershey employees were doing their job, which implied the need for more and different training than Hershey's staff had originally received.

It was obvious that the problem was not in candy production. At the time of the cutover Hershey had an eight-day supply of products in its warehouses, a higher than usual supply in anticipation of possible minor problems with the new systems. However, within three weeks of turning on the new systems, shipments were more than two weeks late. Hershey began telling its customers to allow 12 days for delivery (the usual turnaround time was six days). Even that schedule proved to be too aggressive because Hershey could not deliver goods that quickly. Martha Kahler of Wal-Mart's Temple, Texas, store said, "It wasn't any particular [candy] item. It was across the board." Company spokespersons told financial analysts in late October that computer system problems had already reduced sales by $100 million in the third quarter.

When word of these problems became public, Hershey's stock price went into a sharp slide. By late October, its price had fallen to $47.50, down 35 percent from $74 one year earlier. During the same period, the Dow Jones Industrial Average had risen by 25 percent. Third quarter earnings dropped from $0.74 to $0.62. Hershey Chairman and CEO Kenneth L. Wolfe admitted that "third-quarter sales and earnings declined primarily as a result of problems encountered since the July start-up of new business processes in the areas of customer service, warehousing, and order fulfillment." He added, "These problems resulted in lost sales and significantly increased freight and warehousing costs." Hershey Senior Vice President Michael Pasquale pointed out that "Clearly, our customer relations have been strained." While Wolfe admitted the problems are taking longer to fix than expected, he did state his expectation that fourth-quarter sales

and earnings would bounce back. In late October, key individuals within Hershey held a two-day meeting to review the new system and produce a list of changes needed. Wolfe demanded that those involved "need to be tested before we put them in," possibly implying a lack of adequate testing prior to the original cutover.

In early February 2000, Hershey reported an 11 percent declines in sales and profits for its fourth quarter 1999. Wolfe again pointed to order processing, which this time around had caused many retailers not to place orders. He said that while system changes and increased personnel experience with the new software had reduced the problems, Hershey's has "not yet fully returned to historical customer service levels."

While Hershey has released very little information on the troubled implementation, observers continue to speculate on the key question: What went wrong? Some point to the pushing forward of the target date—trying to accomplish too much in the allotted time frame. Others have stated their belief that inadequate time and attention was allocated to testing prior to Hershey's new systems going live in July. Still other analysts point to the use of the direct cutover method. "These systems tie together in very intricate ways," stated AMR Research Inc. analyst Jim Shepherd, "and things that work fine in testing can turn out to be a disaster (when you go live)." He called the instant conversion approach "a huge bite to take, given that (processing orders) is the lifeblood of their [Hershey's] business." Finally, some analysts point their finger at training. A. Blanton Godfrey, CEO of the Juran Institute, a consulting firm based in Wilton, Connecticut, says that only 10 to 15 percent of ERP implementations go smoothly. He claims that the difference for them is better training. Some observers draw a distinction between training and education. "Training is the how part of the equation," explained John Conklin, vice president and CIO of World Kitchen, the Elmira, New York producer of Pyrex and Corningware. "Education is the bigger piece of the puzzle. If people don't go through this education, you won't win their hearts, and you won't have their minds." Thus some observers believe that lack of education on the "whys" of the system and how the many pieces of the full system fit together are possibly the reason order entry difficulties spilled over into warehouse problems.

Sources: Charles Waltner, "New Recipe for IT Implementation," *Information Week*, September 27, 2000; Craig Stedman, "IT Woes Contribute to Hershey, Profits Decline," *Computerworld*, February 2, 2000; "Failed ERP Gamble Haunts Hershey," *Computerworld*, November 1, 1999; Polly Schneider, "Another Trip to Hell," *CIO Magazine*, February 15, 2000; Malcolm Wheatley, "ERP Training Stinks," *CIO Magazine*, June 1, 2000; Emily Nelson and Evan Ramstad, "Hershey's Biggest Dud Has Turned Out to Be Its New Technology, *The Wall Street Journal*, October 29, 1999; Hershey Foods Corporate Investor Relations, "Hershey Foods Announces Third Quarter Results," www.corporate-ir.net/ireye/ir_site.zhtml?ticker=hsy&script=410&layout=-6&item_id=57564, October 25, 1999, accessed July 8, 2001; Stacy Collett, "Hershey Earnings Drop as New Warehouse, Order Systems Falter," *Computerworld*, October 27, 1999.

CASE STUDY QUESTIONS

1. Analyze Hershey's business model using the competitive forces and value chain models. Was an ERP system and related software a good solution to Hershey's problems? Explain your responses.

2. Classify and describe the problems with the Enterprise 21 project using the categories described in this chapter on the causes of system failure. What management, organization, and technology factors caused these problems?

3. What role did enterprise software play in the failure? Were Hershey's system problems the fault of the software vendors, Hershey, or both?

4. Who was responsible for the failure of Enterprise 21? Assess the role of Hershey's IT group and its managers.

5. Evaluate the risks of the project as seen at its outset, and then outline its key risk factors. Describe the steps you would have taken during the planning stage of the project to control those factors.

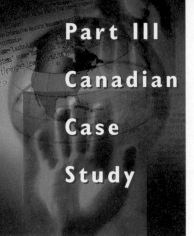

IN TECH WE TRUST: THE STORY OF SAP IN CANADA

The road to ERP success is littered with the corpses of many a company and many a CIO who have tried and failed at this complex and demanding undertaking. Why do ERP implementations go wrong? What steps can be taken to help put them on the right track? Let's examine NOVA Chemicals, a Calgary-based commodity chemical firm that has reached a level of ERP maturity, producing styrenics and olefins/polyolefins at 18 locations in Canada, the United States, France, the Netherlands, and the United Kingdom.

By the mid-1990s, NOVA had made a number of acquisitions and had gone through several reorganizations, resulting in myriad outdated legacy systems and a variety of systems running different parts of its business. The company was ripe for significant business process reengineering. Seeing some of its competitors already going the ERP route, NOVA decided to head in that direction as well.

In retrospect, some of NOVA's initial reasons for embarking on its ERP journey may not have been the right ones. As Senior VP & CIO John Wheeler observed, "NOVA is a commodity chemical company. We're not as big or as diverse as some of our competitors. But because of the commonality of our business, one of the things we can do is focus on best practices. So over time, it became apparent that ERP was not about technology. It wasn't even about information systems. It was really about building a company that could leverage best practices. It was about business process." But when NOVA first embarked on ERP, that realization was still years away.

NOVA'S INITIAL IMPLEMENTATION

NOVA first took the ERP plunge in 1995 when it decided to implement SAP's new distributed R3 Version 2.2. SAP is the third-largest software company in the world and specializes in client/server enterprise application software modules. That first plunge into ERP can be like taking a dip in a northern lake on a windy January day. NOVA attempted to do a pilot installation in a small U.S.-based styrenics business, but the project faltered and was abandoned, causing the company to step back and regroup.

During that first installation, NOVA did not have a CIO. But after that initial setback, it was decided that a CIO was necessary, and the company's Vice President and Controller, Larry MacDonald, was given that responsibility.

Reflecting on the company's early experiences with ERP, MacDonald pointed to the newness of the SAP/R3 product and its integrated nature as two early stumbling blocks. "The distributed R3 version was brand new, and people weren't used to the complexity of SAP implementations," he said. "Having something that was so broad and touched on the business from beginning to end—the total supply chain—was something that we did not understand well. We didn't understand the complexities that integration brought to an implementation."

As a result, NOVA underestimated the scope of the business process improvement and the need to get key people from across the business involved. It also underestimated what it would take to deliver the project and learn the software.

Complicating matters was the reluctance by many people on the business side to embrace SAP. NOVA was implementing all modules, so SAP was being installed virtually "wall to wall" throughout the business. First, the company had to learn how to do the implementation, and then it had to learn how to bring it into the culture of the organization. A lot of people resisted the early implementations, and naturally so, as they weren't receiving much value from them in those days.

"The change that this was bringing to how people did their work was tremendous," noted MacDonald. "We really had to work on the cultural piece, the education piece, and then the technical piece of it."

Consulting firm Deloitte and Touche was NOVA's main implementation partner, bringing a strong change-management capability, as well as strong project- and IT-management methodologies and good knowledge of SAP. According to Wheeler, NOVA's strong operations and change-management capability today can be attributed to practices introduced by its consulting partner.

THE TURNAROUND

Rallying line management was crucial to the success of the implementation. Recalled MacDonald, "Once providing resources to support the implementation became part of line management's job expectations and was clearly embedded in their performance requirements, we started to see a lot of progress. In the initial stages, it wasn't high on the priority list. It had to come from the president that this was important—we had to pay attention to it, and we had to dedicate resources to making this successful."

When Wheeler arrived, business support for ERP was still an issue. His goal was to make it stronger by moving ownership for the system towards the business. A significant measure of management's commitment to the success of NOVA's IT program was the appointment by current CEO Jeff Lipton of Wheeler to the company's Executive Leadership Team. Says Wheeler, "Being part of the senior team provides a clear understanding of the expectations of business leaders and an important forum to ensure that we work together to achieve the company's strategic goals."

"In the early days, the criticism is usually that ERP is an IT implementation. You need to move that ownership toward the business and make IT the enabler. To the extent you can do that earlier rather than later, you'll be more successful," he said. "The truly mature IT program is the one in which the business owns the process, the system, the costs, and the value. IT's role is to be in partnership with the business, using technology to enable business needs."

Wheeler believes that ERP projects require full-time commitment from business people. And those full time people should be quality people. "Sometimes the people you get turn out to be the people who are available, rather than the best people. And that's a mistake," he cautioned. "When you're changing your business process in a fundamental way, you cannot afford not to have your best people—and to have them relatively full time."

SAP: THE COMPANY

Founded in 1972 by four former IBM employees, SAP (Systems, Applications, and Products in Data Processing—pronounced S - A - P) is the dynamic German-based company whose products are client/server enterprise application software modules. Today more than 13 000 companies in over 100 countries run more than 30 000 installations of SAP's software. The company has subsidiaries in more than 50 countries; SAP Canada Inc. was established in 1989 and has offices in Toronto, Montreal, Ottawa, Calgary, and Vancouver. SAP CEO Hasso Plattner is the company's "visioneer," who sees all departments becoming one, not only across an organization, but across its environment as well. He calls this the "City of E."

The two main version of SAP are R/3 (Release 3) and mySAP, the latest Web-enabled version. Companies buy entire ERP packages for their particular industry, such as SAP Retail, SAP Mining, or SAP Banking, or they can buy individual modules, such as human resources or financial applications. Implementation of SAP can run into the tens of millions of dollars, including hardware, software, networking, personnel, and consulting components. SAP will not permit a company to adopt its software unless there are SAP-certified programmers and consultants on board for the project. SAP's latest "version" is called Accelerated SAP and is targeted at companies below $250 million in sales. Accelerated Solutions are pre-configured, scaled-down versions of R/3. Accelerated SAP claims to have a four-month implementation schedule and is offered at a fixed cost, rather than a per-user cost.

SAP's ERP software can translate foreign currencies and languages and handle taxes that vary worldwide. It is a birth-to-grave application that can cover the life of a product from financing the plant to produce it to payment from the customer after the product has arrived. But SAP does so in its own individual fashion.

SAP has implemented in its software "best practices" of companies it has studied, including its customers. Any organization—for profit, not-for-profit, governmental agency—that implements SAP must change its business processes to reflect those found in the way SAP's applications operate. Failure to do so is asking for implementation failure.

Just look at Sobeys, Canada's second-largest supermarket chain, which in early 2001 pulled the plug on its SAP implementation after writing off an after-tax loss of about $50 million. Bill McEwan, president and CEO of Nova Scota-based Sobeys Inc. said that the two-year-old project had "systemic problems of a much more serious nature" than the growing pains they had been led to expect. SAP implementation—after two years—resulted in "unprecedented" stock outs in December 2000 throughout eastern Canada, according to McEwan. He continued, "The SAP Retail software couldn't effectively deal with the extreme, high number of transactions in our retail operating environment." Business operations were affected for four to five weeks while problems were reconciled.

For employees of companies that have implemented SAP, one of the major changes is that they work mostly with data and software, rather than with people, according to Barry Hasler of Sony Canada. Another change is that they cannot get the exact reports and information they were used to getting; SAP reports are standard and do the job, but staff must change the information they need as well as what they do with it in the SAP environment.

But for those who are willing to exercise appropriate change management initiatives, including changing their own policies and procedures, reporting relationships, training, and communicating to instill ownership in their personnel, SAP does its job well. In other words, it's "The SAP Way, or No Way." Organizations that successfully implement SAP spend about one-third of their SAP budget on change management initiatives—training, communicating, consulting, and selling.

Sources: David Carey, "Surviving the ERP Journey," *CIO Canada*, May 1, 2001; Rebecca Maxwell, "Rayovac Gets a Charge from Accelerated SAP," *ComputerWorld Canada*, September 10, 2000; Curtis Cook and Michelle Schoffro, "SAP Not Just for Big Companies," *Canada Computes*, October 9, 1999; Lucas Mearlan, "Sobeys Says Goodbye to SAP," *ComputerWorld Online*, February 2, 2001; "mySAP.com to Power Canada's National Newspaper, *The Globe and Mail*," SAP Press Release, www.sap.com, accessed August 13, 2001; Chris Conrath, "SAP is Sold on the Internet," *Network World Canada*, July 28, 2000.

VIDEO RESOURCE

"In Tech We Trust," *CBC UNDERcurrents* 113 (October 31, 1999).

CASE STUDY QUESTIONS

1. What sort of businesses should invest in SAP's ERP applications? Should a company adopt all of the SAP modules? How does a company decide that it needs an ERP solution?

2. What specific change management actions might a company adopting SAP take to ensure implementation success?

3. Why does SAP consider it necessary for SAP-certified programmers and consultants to work with companies implementing SAP? Go online (www.sap.com) to find out how SAP implementation works. Does it make sense to pay for SAP consultants?

4. It has been said that SAP is itself a change management program or philosophy. Do you agree or disagree? Why? What might happen to implementation if a company chose to try to adapt SAP to its own processes rather than adapting its processes to SAP?

14 DECISION MAKING IN A DIGITAL AGE

OBJECTIVES

After completing this chapter, you will be able to:

1. *Differentiate a decision support system (DSS) and a group decision support system (GDSS).*
2. *Describe the components of decision support systems and group decision support systems.*
3. *Demonstrate how decision support systems and group decision support systems can enhance decision making.*
4. *Describe the capabilities of executive support systems (ESS).*
5. *Assess the benefits of executive support systems.*

Information Portals Sharpen Data Access at CIBC

Ever wondered why it's sometimes easier to locate a piece of information on the Internet than it is to find customer account data on your own desktop? So did staff at Canadian Imperial Bank of Commerce (CIBC). In response, CIBC turned the personalization and search power of the Internet inward by creating "information portals." These corporate Web pages let employees create a customized desktop with information relevant to their jobs. However, the search tools are directed to internal databases, not out to the Internet.

"There was a big challenge in accessing the information we needed to serve our clients well," said Joe Barretto, vice president of commercial and specialty business in CIBC's operations and technology division. CIBC's 800 financial managers had to collect necessary customer data from several reports on a non-Year-2000-compliant IBM system, so a solution was needed fast. CIBC used the E-Portal Suite from Viador, a California company. Instead of having to upgrade all of the desktops that used the old IBM system, no desktops were upgraded to use the E-Portal Suite since it is Web browser-based.

Through the new system, commercial sales and service managers across Canada can access audit reports, credit agreements, credit ratings, activity reports, margins, and ratings. From one screen on their desktops, they can also check for enterprise-wide irregularities in accounts, adding or deleting data as they see fit. Viador's software can be used with Excel spreadsheet software, and users can choose from different report styles as well. Compared with CIBC's previous report generation methods, they have reduced the necessity for and costs of initial report designs and subsequent revisions.

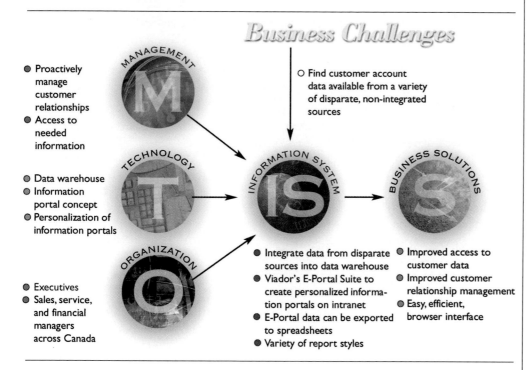

Business Challenges

MANAGEMENT
- Proactively manage customer relationships
- Access to needed information

TECHNOLOGY
- Data warehouse
- Information portal concept
- Personalization of information portals

ORGANIZATION
- Executives
- Sales, service, and financial managers across Canada

○ Find customer account data available from a variety of disparate, non-integrated sources

INFORMATION SYSTEM
- Integrate data from disparate sources into data warehouse
- Viador's E-Portal Suite to create personalized information portals on intranet
- E-Portal data can be exported to spreadsheets
- Variety of report styles

BUSINESS SOLUTIONS
- Improved access to customer data
- Improved customer relationship management
- Easy, efficient, browser interface

The data warehouse is supported "100% in-house," said Barretto, adding that the bank put a new infrastructure in place to support the portal, including more servers and IBM DB/2 Connect. Barretto thinks the information portal's effect will be far-reaching. "We were not really proactive in managing the customer before," he said. "Now we've made that much easier. If you have better information, you can serve your customers better."

Sources: Jeanne O'Brien, "'Information Portals' Sharpen Data Access at UBOC, CIBC," *Bank Systems and Technology*, January, 2000; Dave Kelly, "Using Business Portals to Achieve a Competitive Advantage," The Hurwitz Group, September 1999, www.viador.com/pdfs/HurwitzCaseStudy.pdf, accessed July 10, 2001.

MANAGEMENT CHALLENGES

CIBC's E-Portal Suite application is a management information system (MIS) supplying routine information to CIBC's managers at their request. In addition to MIS, even more sophisticated systems are needed by many organizations where decision making is a complex process. These more sophisticated systems have powerful analytic capabilities to support managers during decision making. Other systems in this category are group decision support systems (GDSS), which support decision making in groups, and executive support systems (ESS), which provide information for making strategic-level decisions. These systems can enhance organizational performance, but they raise the following management challenges:

1. **Building information systems that can actually fulfill executive information requirements.** Even with the use of critical success factors and other information requirements determination methods, it may still be difficult to establish information requirements for ESS and DSS serving senior management. Chapter 3 has already described why certain aspects of senior management decision making cannot be supported by information systems because the decisions are too unstructured and fluid. Even if a problem can be addressed by an information system, senior management may not fully understand their actual information needs. For instance, senior managers may not agree on the firm's critical success factors, or the critical success factors they describe may be inappropriate or outdated if the firm is confronting a crisis requiring a major strategic change.

2. **Create meaningful reporting and management decision-making processes.** Enterprise systems and data warehouses have made it much easier to supply DSS and ESS with data from many different systems than in the past. The remaining challenge is changing management thinking to use the data that are available to maximum advantage, to develop better reporting categories for measuring firm performance, and to inform new types of decisions. Many managers use the new capabilities in DSS and ESS to obtain the same information as before. Major changes in management thinking will be required to get managers to ask better questions of the data.

Most information systems described throughout this text help people make decisions in one way or another, but DSS, GDSS, and ESS are part of a special category of information systems that are explicitly designed to enhance managerial decision making. By taking advantage of more accurate firm-wide data provided by enterprise systems and the new information technology infrastructure, these systems can support very fine-grained decisions for guiding the firm, coordinating work [digital] activities across the enterprise, and responding rapidly to changing markets and customers. Many of these managerial decision-making applications are now Web-enabled. This chapter describes the characteristics of each of these types of information systems, showing how each enhances the managerial decision-making process and ultimately the performance of the organization.

DSS, GDSS, and ESS can support decision making in a number of ways. They can automate certain decision procedures (for example, determining the highest price that can be charged for a product to maintain market share or the right amount of materials to maintain in inventory to maximize efficient customer response and product profitability). They can provide information about different aspects of the decision situation and the decision process, such as what opportunities or problems triggered the decision process, what solution alternatives were generated or explored, and how the decision was reached. Finally, they can stimulate innovation in decision making by helping managers question existing decision procedures or explore different solution designs (Dutta, Wierenga, and Dalebout, 1997). The ability to explore the outcomes of alternative organizational scenarios, to use precise firm-wide information, and to provide tools to facilitate group decision processes can help managers make decisions that help the firm achieve its strategic objectives (Forgionne and Kohli, 2000).

14.1 Decision Support Systems

As noted in Chapter 2, a **decision support system (DSS)** assists management decision making by combining data, sophisticated analytical models and tools, and user-friendly software into a single powerful system that can support semistructured or unstructured decision making. A DSS provides users with a flexible set of tools and capabilities for analyzing important blocks of data.

TPS, MIS, AND DSS

We stated previously that there are many different ways to categorize information systems. In addition to the typology presented in Chapter 2, some experts have started to categorize information systems as falling into one of three categories: customer relationship management (CRM), supply chain management (SCM), and enterprise resource planning systems (ERP). It should be noted that any of the types of information systems presented in Chapter 2—TPS, OAS, KWS, DSS, MIS, and ESS—may also fall into one of the three categories of CRM, SCM, and ERP. A decision support system for inventory control would be both a DSS and an SCM system, as well as a management level system. For example, Wal-Mart's SCM application includes their sales transaction processing system because the sales data generates orders from Wal-Mart's supplier.

Throughout this text, we have discussed transaction processing systems (TPS) as they relate to a wide variety of information systems: e-commerce, routine operations, and administrative functions are all examples of *functional systems* that use TPS for their day-to-day operations. TPS are the foundation of almost all other information systems. They provide most of the internal data to MIS, DSS, ESS, and other types of information systems. A TPS may be as simple as the system that accepts your deposit at an automatic teller machine or as complex as one that lets you customize an online computer purchase, including approving your credit card purchase and tracking delivery of your order.

While they are critical to the functioning of organizations, understanding TPS is as simple as understanding ordinary business processes. TPS need to be accurate, to handle large volumes of transactions and data (depending on the size of the organization and its volume of activity), to be secure, and to be efficient in terms of processing transactions reliably and quickly.

Some of the earliest applications for supporting management decision making were **management information systems (MIS)**, which we introduced in Chapter 2. MIS primarily provide information on the firm's performance to help managers in monitoring and controlling the business. They typically produce fixed, regularly scheduled reports based on data extracted and summarized from the organization's underlying transaction processing systems. The format of these reports is often specified in advance. A typical MIS report might show a summary of monthly sales for each of the major sales territories of a company. Sometimes MIS reports are exception reports, highlighting only exceptional conditions, such as when the sales quota for a specific territory fall below an anticipated level or which employees have exceeded their spending limit in a dental care plan. Traditional MIS produced primarily hard copy reports. Today these reports might be available online through an intranet, and more MIS reports can be generated on demand. Table 14-1 provides some examples of MIS applications.

DSS provide new sets of capabilities for nonroutine decisions and user control. An MIS provides managers with reports based on routine flows of data and assists in the general control of the organization, whereas a DSS emphasizes change, flexibility, and rapid response. With a DSS there is less of an effort to link users to structured information flows and a correspondingly greater emphasis on models, assumptions, ad hoc queries, and display graphics.

Chapter 3 introduced the distinction between structured, semistructured, and unstructured decisions. Structured problems are repetitive and routine, with known algorithms to provide solutions. Unstructured problems are novel and nonroutine, with no algorithms to provide solutions. One can discuss, decide, and ruminate about unstructured problems, but they are not solved in the sense that one finds an answer to an equation. Semistructured problems fall between structured and unstructured problems. While MIS primarily address

decision support system (DSS)
A computer system at the management level of an organization that combines data, analytical tools, and models to support semistructured and unstructured decision making.

management information system (MIS)
A computer system that supports routine decision making by providing summarized and filtered information on the organization's performance to help managers monitor and control the business.

TABLE 14-1	EXAMPLES OF MIS APPLICATIONS
Organization	**MIS Application**
Ontario Hospital Association (www.oha.com)	Emergency Department Information System collects, reports, and monitors workloads in Ontario's emergency rooms.
Chubb Insurance Company of Canada (www.chubb.com/canada)	Web-enabled broker self-service site gives brokers 24/7 access to real-time information about Chubb Canada customers and their multi-faceted insurance policies. Reduced annual printing and mailing costs by at least $350 000 and reduced incoming calls to the call centre by 30 percent.
Ontario Provincial Police	Major Case Management System helps police to track down serial killers and rapists by finding certain items (such as names, addresses, licence plate numbers) that occur more than once in different major criminal investigations.
Taco Bell	TACO (Total Automation of Company Operations) system provides information on food cost, labour cost, and period-to-date costs for each restaurant.
MindfulEye	Subscription-based Internet monitoring and reporting service for the investment community enables users to track the actual "mood" of the market and stocks of interest to them.

structured problems, DSS support semistructured and unstructured problem analysis. Chapter 3 also introduced Simon's description of decision making, which consists of four stages: intelligence, design, choice, and implementation. Decision support systems are intended to help design and evaluate alternatives and monitor the adoption or implementation process.

TYPES OF DECISION SUPPORT SYSTEMS

The earliest DSS tended to draw on small subsets of corporate data and were heavily model driven. Recent advances in computer processing and database technology have expanded the definition of a DSS to include systems that can support decision making by analyzing vast quantities of data, including firm-wide data from enterprise systems and transaction data from the Web.

Today there are two basic types of decision support systems, model-driven and data-driven (Dhar and Stein, 1997). **Model-driven DSS** were primarily stand-alone systems isolated from major organizational information systems; they used some type of model to perform "what-if" and other kinds of analyses. These systems were often developed by end-user divisions or groups not under central IS control. Their analysis capabilities were based on a strong theory or model combined with a good user interface that made the model easy to use. Cara Airport Services described in the Chapter 2 opening vignette is an example of a model-driven DSS.

The second type of DSS is a **data-driven DSS**. These systems analyze large pools of data found in major organizational systems. They support decision making by allowing users to extract useful information that was previously buried in large quantities of data. Often data from transaction processing systems are collected in data warehouses for this purpose. Online analytical processing (OLAP) and datamining can then be used to analyze the data. Companies are starting to build data-driven DSS to mine customer data gathered from their Web sites as well as data from enterprise systems.

Traditional database queries answer such questions as, "How many units of product number 403 were shipped in November 1999?" OLAP, or multidimensional analysis, supports much more complex requests for information, such as, "Compare sales of product 403 relative to plan by quarter and sales region for the past two years." We described OLAP and multidimensional data analysis in Chapter 8. With OLAP and query-oriented data analysis, users need to have a good idea about the information for which they are looking.

Datamining is more discovery driven. **Datamining** provides insights into corporate data that cannot be obtained with OLAP by finding hidden patterns and relationships in large databases and inferring rules from them to predict future behaviour. The patterns and rules then can be used to guide decision making and forecast the effect of those decisions. The types of information that can be yielded from datamining include associations, sequences,

model-driven DSS
A primarily stand-alone system that uses some type of model to perform "what-if" and other kinds of analyses.

data-driven DSS
A primarily stand-alone system that allows users to extract and analyze useful information that was previously buried in large databases.

datamining
Technology for finding hidden patterns and relationships in large databases and inferring rules from them to predict future behaviour.

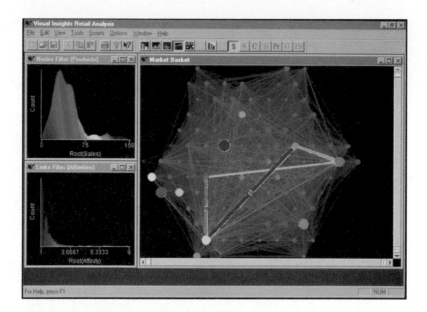

classifications, clusters, and forecasts. Figure 14-1 provides an example of software that helps businesses detect patterns in their data.

Associations are occurrences linked to a single event. For instance, a study of supermarket purchasing patterns might reveal that when tortilla chips are purchased, a cola drink is purchased 65 percent of the time, but when there is a promotion, cola is purchased 85 percent of the time. With this information, managers can make better decisions because they have learned the profitability of that type of promotion.

In *sequences*, events are linked over time. One might find, for example, that if a house is purchased, a new refrigerator will be purchased within two weeks 65 percent of the time, and an oven will be bought within one month of the home purchase 45 percent of the time.

Classification recognizes patterns that describe the group to which an item belongs by examining existing items that have been classified and by inferring a set of rules. For example, businesses such as credit card or telephone companies worry about the loss of steady customers. Classification can help discover the characteristics of customers who are likely to leave and can provide a model to help managers predict who those customers are so that they can devise special campaigns to retain those customers.

Clustering works in a manner similar to classification when no groups have yet been defined. A datamining tool will discover different groupings within data, such as finding affinity groups for bank cards or partitioning a database into groups of customers based on demographics and types of personal investments.

Although these applications involve predictions, forecasting uses predictions in a different way. It uses a series of existing values to forecast what other values will be. For example, forecasting might find patterns in data to help managers estimate the future value of continuous variables such as sales figures. Datamining uses statistical analysis tools as well as neural networks, fuzzy logic, genetic algorithms, or rule-based and other intelligent techniques (described in Chapter 15).

As noted in Chapter 3, it is a mistake to think that in large organizations only individuals make decisions. In fact, many, if not most, decisions are made collectively. Frequently, decisions must be coordinated with several groups before being finalized. In large organizations, decision making is inherently a group process, and a DSS can be designed to facilitate group decision making. Section 14.2 deals with this issue.

COMPONENTS OF DSS

Figure 14-2 illustrates the components of a DSS. They include a database used for query and analysis, a software system with models, datamining, other analytical tools, and a user interface.

FIGURE 14-2 Overview of a decision support system (DSS). The main components of the DSS are the DSS database, the DSS software system, and the user interface. The DSS database may be a small database residing on a PC or a massive data warehouse.

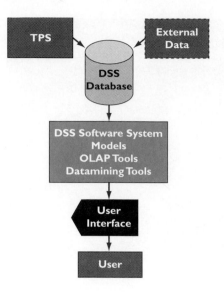

The **DSS database** is a collection of current or historical data from a number of applications or groups. It might be a small database residing on a PC that contains a subset of corporate data that has been downloaded and possibly combined with external data. Alternatively, the DSS database might be a massive data warehouse that is continuously updated by major organizational TPS (including enterprise systems and data generated by Web site transactions). The data in DSS databases are generally extracts or copies of production databases so that using the DSS does not interfere with critical operational systems.

The **DSS software system** contains the software tools that are used for data analysis. It may contain various OLAP tools, datamining tools, or a collection of mathematical and analytical models that can easily be made accessible to the DSS user.

DSS database

A collection of current or historical data from a number of applications or groups; can be a small PC database or a massive data warehouse.

DSS software system

A collection of software tools that are used for data analysis, such as OLAP tools, datamining tools, or a collection of mathematical and analytical models.

model

An abstract representation that illustrates the components or relationships of a phenomenon.

A **model** is an abstract representation that illustrates the components or relationships of a phenomenon. A model can be a physical model (such as a model airplane), a mathematical model (such as an equation), a graphical model (such as a spreadsheet or graph), or a verbal model (such as a description of a procedure for writing an order). Each decision support system is built for a specific set of purposes and will make different collections of models available depending on those purposes.

Perhaps the most common models are libraries of statistical models. These libraries usually contain the full range of traditional statistical functions including means, medians, deviations, and scatter plots. The software has the ability to project future outcomes by analyzing a series of data. Statistical modelling software can be used to help establish relationships, such as relating product sales to differences in age, income, or other factors between communities. Optimization models, often using linear programming, determine optimal resource allocation to maximize or minimize specified variables such as cost or time. A classic use of optimization models is to determine the proper mix of products within a given market to maximize profits.

Forecasting models often are used to forecast sales. The user of this type of model might supply a range of historical data to project future conditions and the sales that might result from those conditions. The decision maker could vary those future conditions (entering, for example, a rise in raw materials costs or the entry of a new, low-priced competitor in the market) to determine how these new conditions might affect sales. Companies often use this software to predict the actions of competitors. Various model libraries exist for specific functions, such as financial and risk analysis models.

sensitivity analysis

Models that ask "what-if" questions repeatedly to determine the impact of changes in one or more factors on outcomes.

Among the most widely used models are **sensitivity analysis** models that ask "what-if" questions repeatedly to determine the impact of changes in one or more factors on outcomes. "What-if" analysis—working forward from known or assumed conditions—allows the user to vary certain values and test results to better predict outcomes if changes occur in those val-

FIGURE 14-3 Sensitivity analysis. This table displays the results of a sensitivity analysis of the effect of changing the sales price of an umbrella and the cost per unit on the product's breakeven point. It answers the question "What happens to the breakeven point if the sales price and the cost to make each unit increase or decrease?"

Total fixed costs	19000					
Variable cost per unit	3					
Average sales price	17					
Contribution margin	14					
Breakeven point	1357					
		Variable Cost per Unit				
Sales	1357	2	3	4	5	6
Price	14	1583	1727	1900	2111	2375
	15	1462	1583	1727	1900	2111
	16	1357	1462	1583	1727	1900
	17	1267	1357	1462	1583	1727
	18	1188	1267	1357	1462	1583

ues. What happens if we raise the price by 5 percent or increase the advertising budget by $100 000? What happens if we keep the price and advertising budget the same? Desktop spreadsheet software, such as Microsoft Excel or Lotus 1-2-3, is often used for this purpose (see Figure 14-3). Backward sensitivity analysis software is used for goal seeking: If I want to sell one million product units next year, how much must I reduce the price of the product?

MANAGEMENT DECISION PROBLEM

MAKING A CAPITAL BUDGETING DECISION

Your firm, Quebec Tool and Die Corporation, is considering purchasing four new CAD workstations for a total of $250 000. It hopes to improve productivity by translating designs for new dies more efficiently into finished products with fewer defects. You believe that this investment would increase the firm's after-tax income by $60 000 per year over a five-year period by reducing production costs. At the end of five years, your firm plans to sell the workstations for a total of $50 000. The amount the firm would recover when it sells the used equipment is called the salvage value of the equipment.

You would like to evaluate this expenditure to see whether it is a good investment. To be considered worthwhile, a capital expenditure must produce at least the same rate of return on the money invested as if the amount of the investment were invested somewhere else, such as at a bank, at a certain rate of interest specified by the firm.

Review the discussion of capital budgeting methods for information system investments in Chapter 13. The following spreadsheet shows the results of using the net present value method for Quebec Tool and Die's investment in the new CAD equipment. The total cash flow is the sum of the additional income produced by the investment plus any salvage value of the equipment.

To arrive at the return from the investment in today's dollars, one must first calculate the present value of the total cash flow from this new equipment discounted at the prevailing interest rate for borrowing money. The initial purchase price of the equipment in today's

dollars is then subtracted from the present value of the total cash flow from the investment to arrive at the net present value of the investment. If the net present value for the investment is positive, it is a worthwhile investment. If it is negative, the investment should be rejected.

The following spreadsheet shows the results of your calculations assuming that interest rates are 8 percent and that the investment is producing $60 000 each year in additional income for the firm. Since investments are highly sensitive to changes in interest rates and economic conditions, you have added a sensitivity analysis to see whether the machine tool makes a good investment under a wide range of situations. The data table shows the impact on net present value if the interest rate and the annual income from using the new equipment are lower or higher than the original assumptions.

1. Should the company make this investment or should it be rejected? Explain your answer.

2. What other variables or circumstances besides interest rate and the additional income produced by the new equipment might also affect the returns on the investment?

3. What other actions can management take to ensure a positive return on the investment?

4. Could this decision be supported by a management information system? a DSS? How?

Assumptions

Interest rate	8.0%
Salvage value	50 000
Annual additional income	60 000

Quebec Tool and Die Company Capital Budgeting Analysis

	2001	2002	2003	2004	2005
Annual additional income	60 000	60 000	60 000	60 000	60 000
Salvage value					50 000
Annual cash flow	60 000	60 000	60 000	60 000	110 000
Total cash flow	350 000				
Present value	273 952				
Cost of investment	250 000				
Net present value	23 592				

		Interest rates			
	23 592	6.0%	7.0%	8.0%	9.0%	10.0%
	40 000	(44 143)	(50 343)	(56 262)	(61 917)	(67 322)
	45 000	(23 081)	(29 842)	(36 200)	(42 469)	(48 369)
	50 000	(2019)	(9341)	(16 335)	(23 021)	(29 415)
	55 000	19 043	11 160	3628	(3573)	(10 461)
	60 000	40 105	31 661	23 592	15 876	8493
Annual additional income	65 000	61 167	52 162	43 555	35 324	27 447
	70 000	82 228	72 663	63 519	54 772	46 401

The DSS user interface permits smooth interaction between users of the system and the DSS software tools. A graphical, easy-to-use, flexible user interface supports the dialogue between the user and the DSS. The DSS users might be managers or employees with no patience for learning a complex tool, so the interface must be relatively intuitive. Many DSS today are being built with Web-based interfaces to take advantage of the Web's ease of use, interactivity, and capabilities for personalization and customization. Building successful DSS requires a high level of user participation and, often, the use of prototyping to ensure these requirements are met.

DSS Applications and the Digital Firm

There are many ways in which DSS can be used to support decision making. Both data-driven and model-driven DSS have become very powerful and sophisticated, providing fine-grained information for decisions that enable the firm to coordinate both internal and external business processes much more precisely. Some of these DSS are helping companies improve supply chain management or plan scenarios for changing business conditions. Some can be used to fine-tune relationships with customers. Some take advantage of the company-wide data provided by enterprise systems. DSS today can also harness the interactive capabilities of the Web to provide decision support tools to both employees and customers.

To illustrate the range of capabilities of a DSS, we now describe some successful DSS applications. San Miguel's supply chain management system, IBM's supply chain management systems described in the Window on Technology, Cara Airport Services food production system described in the Chapter 2 opening vignette, and Pioneer Natural Resources' business simulation system, are examples of model-driven DSS. Royal Bank's customer segmentation system described in the Chapter 2 Window on Management and Della.com's customer analysis system are examples of data-driven DSS. We will also examine some applications of geographic information systems (GIS), a special category of DSS for visualizing data geographically.

DSS for Supply Chain Management

Supply chain decisions involve determining "who, what, when, and where " from purchasing and transporting materials and parts through manufacturing products and distributing and delivering those products to customers. DSS can help managers examine this complex chain comprehensively and search among a huge number of alternatives for the combinations that are most efficient and cost-effective. The prime management goal might be to reduce overall costs while increasing the speed and accuracy of filling customer orders. The Window on Technology illustrates how IBM uses DSS for supply chain management.

San Miguel Corporation uses DSS for supply chain management to help it distribute more than 300 products, such as beer, liquor, dairy products, and feed grains to every corner of the Philippine archipelago. A production load allocation system determines the quantity of products to produce for each bottling line and how production output should be assigned to warehouses. It balances ordering, carrying, and stock-out costs while considering frequency of deliveries and minimum order quantities, saving the company $270 000 in inventory costs in one year. The DSS can generate optimal production allocation plans based on either minimizing cost or maximizing profit. San Miguel's system also helps it reassign deliveries and warehouse facilities to counter imbalances in capacity and demand. Managers used information from the system to move more of San Miguel's delivery business to third-party logistics providers so that its own delivery trucks could be used more efficiently. The company found that it could reduce the number of routes serving sales districts in metropolitan Manila alone by 43 percent (Del Rosario, 1999).

DSS for Customer Relationship Management

DSS for customer relationship management use datamining to guide decisions about pricing, customer retention, market share, and new revenue streams. These systems typically consolidate customer information from a variety of systems into massive data warehouses and use various analytical tools to slice the data into tiny segments for one-to-one marketing (see Figure 14-4). The Window on Organizations illustrates how the Royal Bank of Canada

OPTIMIZING THE SUPPLY CHAIN AT IBM

In 1994, IBM began a global supply chain reengineering initiative to reduce inventory levels yet maintain enough inventory in the supply chain to respond quickly to customer demands. IBM Research developed an advanced supply chain optimization and simulation tool called the asset management tool (AMT) for this purpose.

AMT deals with a range of entities in the supply chain, including targets for inventory and customer service levels, product structure, channel assembly, supplier terms and conditions, and lead-time reduction. Users of AMT can evaluate supply chains in terms of financial tradeoffs associated with various configurations and operational policies.

The IBM Personal Systems Group (PSG) used AMT to reduce supply chain costs to cope with the large volumes, dropping prices, and slim profit margins in the personal computer market. PSG was able to reduce overall pipeline inventory by over 50 percent in 1997 and 1998. The system helped PSG reduce payments made to distributors and resellers to compensate for product price reductions by more than U.S.$750 million in 1998. PSG's cycle time from component procurement to product sale was reduced by four to six weeks, bringing reductions of 5 to 7 percent in overall product cost.

IBM's AS/400 midrange computer division used AMT to analyze and quantify the impact of product complexity. Information from the system helped IBM reduce the number of product features, substitute alternate parts, and delay customization. AMT also provided an analysis of the tradeoff between serviceability and inventory in IBM's QuickShip Program, helping the company reduce operational cost by up to 50 percent.

According to Jean-Pierre Briant, former IBM vice-president for Integrated Supply Chain, "AMT helps us understand our extended supply chain, from our suppliers' suppliers to our customers' customers." IBM has been able to use AMT to help its business partners improve management of their supply chains. For instance, supply chain analysis helped Piancor, one of IBM's major distributors, identify opportunities for optimizing the product flow between the two companies.

IBM's Microelectronics division improved its supply chain management by using a combination of software tools. This division needed to change its supply chain processes as it shifted from supplying semiconductors and packaged goods exclusively to IBM's PC and server divisions to supplying parts to outside organizations such as Advanced Micro Devices, Dell Computer, Cisco Systems, and Qualcomm. The division replaced an old, home-grown system with SAP's manufacturing resource planning software to capture and store orders and track current inventory. It installed Aspen Technology's Mimi toolkit to schedule the production of products and match demand with available resources. The Microelectronics Division also started transmitting purchase order, shipping date, logistics, and payment information to customers over the Internet.

To Think About: How did the systems described here help IBM promote its business strategy? How did they change the way IBM ran its business?

Sources: Brenda Dietrich, Nick Donofrio, Grace Lin, and Jane Snowdon, "Big Benefits for Big Blue," *OR/MS Today,* June 2000; Judy Democker, "Businesses Seek to Cut Weak Links from Supply Chains," *Information Week,* March 6, 2000.

---

benefited from using a DSS for this purpose. (While we previously described the Royal Bank's application for judging customer profitability, the DSS described below deals more directly with actual customer relationship management.)

Some of these DSS for customer relationship management use data gathered from the Web. Chapter 10 described how each action a visitor has taken when visiting a particular

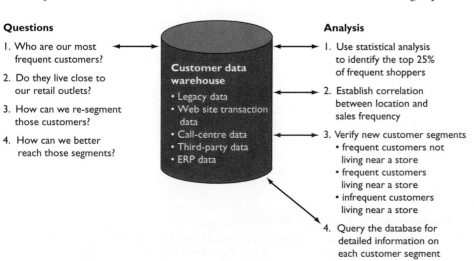

Questions

1. Who are our most frequent customers?

2. Do they live close to our retail outlets?

3. How can we re-segment those customers?

4. How can we better reach those segments?

Customer data warehouse
- Legacy data
- Web site transaction data
- Call-centre data
- Third-party data
- ERP data

Analysis

1. Use statistical analysis to identify the top 25% of frequent shoppers

2. Establish correlation between location and sales frequency

3. Verify new customer segments
   - frequent customers not living near a store
   - frequent customers living near a store
   - infrequent customers living near a store

4. Query the database for detailed information on each customer segment

FIGURE 14-4 DSS for customer analysis and segmentation. This DSS allows companies to segment their customer base with a high level of precision where it can be used to drive a marketing campaign. Based on the results of datamining, a firm can develop specific marketing campaigns for each customer segment. For example, it could target frequent customers living near a store with coupons for products of interest and with rewards for frequent shoppers.

ROYAL BANK BANKS ON A DATA-DRIVEN DSS

"Gone are the days where we had mass buckets of customers that would receive the same treatment or same offer on a monthly basis," says Shauneen Bruder, Royal Bank's senior vice president for North America. Instead of sending customers the same marketing information, Royal Bank has developed a DSS for customer segmentation that can tailor messages to very small groups of people and offer them products, services, and prices that are more likely to appeal to them. Royal Bank's customer segmentation is so effective that it can achieve a response rate as high as 30 percent to its marketing campaigns, compared to an average of 3 percent for the banking industry.

The technology behind this DSS system is based on consolidating data from various systems in the organization into a data warehouse. Royal Bank's main customer database is its marketing information file (MIF). The database even contains customer transactional data. MIF is fed data from every document a customer fills out as well as data from chequing accounts, credit cards, and Royal Bank's enterprise and billing systems. Bank analysts have a range of tools at their fingertips as they access MIF, including SAS data analysis software.

By querying the database, analysts can identify customers based on the products they might buy and the likelihood they will leave the bank, and combine these data with demographic data from external sources. Royal Bank can then identify one or a group of profitable customers who appear to be getting ready to leave the bank. To identify these customers, the bank will look at the customer's bank balance (recently being kept low), credit

card payments (also reduced in amount and perhaps paid later than in the past), and deposits (which have become sporadic). These signs could indicate a customer who is recently unemployed, but they could also highlight a profitable customer preparing to switch to another bank. Royal Bank, using its vast stored data, can quickly learn that it has profited from this customer's business. They do this by looking at the customer's past ongoing balances, use of Royal Bank's line of credit, and active car loan and/or mortgage. They also deduce from the customer's life and family data that the customer is probably at a stage in life when he or she will need more bank loans and other bank services.

Having identified these customer(s), the bank's marketing department might put together a tempting package of banking services at a low price, such as Internet banking, bill payment, unlimited ATM access, and a limited number of branch transactions, all for a fee of $9.95 per month. The bank knows that customers who use this type of service package stay with the bank for about three years longer than do those who don't have such a package. If the customer is not satisfied with the specific package, marketing can even tailor a package specifically for him or her. Royal Bank is linking its customer database and legacy systems to the Web so that it can offer customers service packages instantly online as they access their accounts over the Internet.

To Think About: How did Royal Bank's customer DSS change the way it conducted its business?

Sources: Meridith Wilson, "Slices of Life," *CIO Magazine*, August 15, 2000; Alan Radding, "Analyze Your Customers," *Datamation*, September 25, 2000.

Web site can be captured on that Web site's log. Companies can mine these data to answer questions such as what customers are purchasing and what promotions are generating the most traffic. The results can help companies tailor marketing programs more effectively, redesign Web sites to optimize traffic, and create personalized buying experiences for Web site visitors. Upon analyzing Web logs, Foofoo.com, which sells luxury bath products, fashions, and gourmet foods, learned that its Web site visitors were clicking to read editorial content about home electronics, but left without buying. The company chose to eliminate electronics equipment from its inventory and redesigned its Web site.

Other DSS combine Web site transaction data with data from enterprise systems. Weddingchannel.com, a wedding gift registry and wish-list aggregator, feeds sales order data from its enterprise system and Web logs into a customer data warehouse. It uses E.piphany's marketing analysis software to identify customer trends, such as where customers are coming from, how long they stay on the site, and what advertising vehicles draw their most profitable customers. Della.com, later bought by Weddingchannel.com, had started out as a wedding registry, but the system showed that its high-end customers were more seasonal than originally anticipated. Acting on this information Della.com turned the Web site into a general gift registry that was returned to its original purpose after the buyout by Weddingchannel.com (Stackpole, 2000).

DSS for Simulating Business Scenarios

We have already described the capabilities of model-driven DSS for performing "what-if" analyses on problems in specific areas of the firm. DSS with very powerful "what-if" and modelling capabilities have been developed for modelling entire business scenarios. Model-driven DSS use information from both internal and external sources to help managers tune strategy to a constantly changing array of conditions and variables.

Petro-Canada is one of Canada's largest oil and gas companies with operations spanning the upstream and downstream sectors of the industry. They are currently fine-tuning their category management processes to support approximately 500 of their convenience sites across Canada.

"While we are experts at marketing fuels, convenience retailing is still a new business for us," commented Georges Gasparovics, Petro-Canada's Director of Information Services. "Category management will help us enhance the product and service offering to our guests and maximize non-petroleum revenue opportunities."

According to Gasparovics, JDA Software Group's Open Database Merchandising System (ODBMS) integrated with Win/DSS is integral to their success. "Since establishing and managing pricing structures is a key element to category management, ODBMS helps us implement strategies to better maximize margins and competitively price our products. Win/DSS enables us to collect POS [point of sale] information and upload to ODBMS for analysis and decision making."

Geographic Information Systems

Geographic information systems (GIS) are a special category of DSS that can analyze and display data for planning and decision making using digitized maps. The software can assemble, store, manipulate, and display geographically referenced information, tying data to points, lines, and areas on a map. GIS can thus be used to support decisions that require knowledge about the geographic distribution of people or other resources in scientific research, resource management, and development planning. For example, GIS might be used to help state and local governments calculate emergency response times to natural disasters or to help banks identify the best locations for installing new branches or ATM terminals. GIS tools have become affordable even for small businesses, and some can be used on the Web. See Figure 14-5 for one example of a GIS in action.

GIS have modelling capabilities, allowing managers to change data and automatically revise business scenarios to find better solutions. Parks Canada's geographic information systems (www.parkscanada.pch.gc.ca) are implemented at various administrative levels including headquarters, regional offices, national parks, some heritage canals, and a limited number of historic sites. Geographic information systems are being used for planning, decision making, and ecosystem monitoring related to ecosystem management challenges. Current GIS applications include wildlife population census, ecological mapping, forest fire research and protection, insect and disease impact assessment, wildlife migration modelling, habitat management, coastal zone management, emergency measures preparedness, pollution monitoring, eco-tourism development, biodiversity analysis, land-use planning, temporal changes analysis, habitat fragmentation analysis, and environmental impact assessment—all from one type of information system.

The Manitoba Community Newspapers Association (www.mcna.com) hosts a GIS that tracks 3000 variables to assist media buyers in determining where to place their advertisements. Their data is based on Statistics Canada census data.

BC Rail worked with MultiModal's consulting team to perform a detailed review of the railroad's operating plan down to the customer level, and looked at ways to realign BC Rail's operations to reduce costs, improve customer service, and change the manner in which various terminals are utilized. The terminal work was targeted at both land use issues as well as physical plant considerations. Quaker Oats has used GIS to display and analyze sales and customer data by store locations. This information helps the company determine the best product mix for each retail store that carries Quaker Oats products and design advertising campaigns targeted specifically to each store's customers.

WEB-BASED CUSTOMER DECISION SUPPORT SYSTEMS

The growth of electronic commerce has encouraged many companies to develop DSS so that customers and employees can take advantage of Internet information resources and Web

geographic information system (GIS)
A system with software that can analyze and display data using digitized maps to enhance planning and decision making.

FIGURE 14-5 Geographic information system (GIS) software presents and analyzes data geographically, tying data to points, lines and areas on a map. This map can help decision makers with crime analysis by mapping each incident and relating crime hotspots to distribution of police staff.

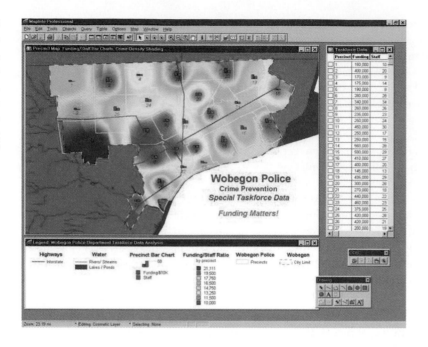

capabilities for interactivity and personalization. DSS based on the Web and the Internet can support decision making by providing online access to various databases and information pools along with software for data analysis. Some of these DSS are targeted toward management, but many have been developed to attract customers by providing information and tools to assist their decision making as they select products and services. Companies are finding that deciding which products and services to purchase has become increasingly information intensive. People are now using more information from multiple sources to make purchasing decisions (such as purchasing a car or computer) before they interact with the product or sales staff. **Customer decision support systems (CDSS)** support the decision making process of an existing or potential customer.

customer decision support system (CDSS)

A system to support the decision making process of an existing or potential customer.

People interested in purchasing a product or service can use Internet search engines, intelligent agents, online catalogues, Web directories, newsgroup discussions, e-mail, and other tools to help them locate the information they need to help with their decision. Information brokers, such as Statistics Canada and Travelocity.ca, described in Chapter 4, are also sources of summarized, structured information for specific products or industries and may provide models for evaluating the information. Companies also have developed specific customer Web sites where all the information, models, or other analytical tools for evaluating alternatives are concentrated in one location. Web-based DSS have become especially popu-

TABLE 14-2   EXAMPLES OF WEB-BASED DSS

DSS	Description
Bell Canada	Hundreds of business, operation, and sales managers can compose their own interactive queries from their Web browser rather than accessing static data reports prepared by financial analysts. They can navigate, analyze, and even update their sales forecasts without the need for proprietary client software.
General Electric Plastics	Web site provides a searchable repository of product-specification information that can be updated weekly. Visitors can use online continuous-simulation models that automatically generate graphs and diagrams in response to customer inputs. (For example, a simulation model might show how a particular plastic would behave at very high temperatures.) An e-mail capability allows visitors to forward technical questions to engineers, who then contact the customer.
Fidelity Investments	Web site features an online, interactive decision support application to help clients make decisions about investment savings plans and investment portfolio allocations. The application allows visitors to experiment with numerous "what-if" scenarios to design investment savings plans for retirement or a child's college education. If the user enters information about his or her finances, time horizon, and tolerance for risk, the system will suggest appropriate portfolios of mutual funds. The application performs the required number-crunching and displays the changing return on investment as the user alters these assumptions. See Figure 14-6 for another example.

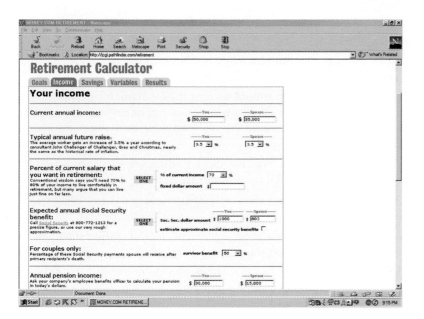

lar in the financial services area because so many people are trying to manage their own assets and retirement savings. Table 14-2 lists some examples.

14.2 Group Decision Support Systems

Early DSS focused largely on supporting individual decision making. However, because so much work is accomplished in groups within organizations, system developers and scholars began to focus on how computers can support group and organizational decision making. A new category of systems developed known as group decision support systems (GDSS).

What Is a GDSS?

A **group decision support system (GDSS)** is an interactive, computer-based information system that facilitates the solution of unstructured problems by a set of decision makers working together as a group (DeSanctis and Gallupe, 1987).

Groupware and Web-based tools for videoconferencing and electronic meetings described earlier in this text can support some group decision processes, but their focus is primarily on communication. This section focuses on the tools and technologies geared explicitly toward group decision making. GDSS were developed in response to a growing concern over the quality and effectiveness of meetings. The underlying problems in group decision making have been the explosion of decision maker meetings, the growing length of those meetings, and the increased number of attendees. Estimates on the amount of a manager's time spent in meetings range from 35 percent to 70 percent.

Meeting facilitators, organizational development professionals, and information systems scholars have been focusing on this issue and have identified a number of discrete meeting elements that need to be addressed (Grobowski et al., 1990; Kraemer and King, 1988; Nunamaker et al., 1991). Among these elements are the following:

1. *Improved preplanning*, to make meetings more effective and efficient.

2. *Increased participation*, so that all attendees will be able to contribute fully even if the number of attendees is large. Free riding (attending the meeting but not contributing) must also be addressed.

3. *Open, collaborative meeting atmosphere*, in which attendees from various organizational levels feel able to contribute freely. The lower level attendees must be able to participate without fear of being judged by their management; higher status participants must be able to participate without having their presence or ideas dominate the meeting and result in unwanted conformity.

group decision support system (GDSS)
An interactive, computer-based system that facilitates the solution of unstructured problems by a set of decision makers working together as a group.

4. *Criticism-free idea generation*, enabling attendees to contribute without undue fear of feeling personally criticized.

5. *Evaluation objectivity*, creating an atmosphere in which an idea will be evaluated on its merits rather than on the basis of the source of the idea.

6. *Idea organization and evaluation*, which require keeping the focus on the meeting objectives, finding efficient ways to organize the many ideas that can be generated in a brainstorming session, and evaluating those ideas not only on their merits but also within appropriate time constraints.

7. *Setting priorities and making decisions*, which require finding ways to encompass the thinking of all the attendees in making these judgments.

8. *Documentation of meetings*, so that attendees will have as complete and organized a record of the meeting as may be needed to continue the work of the project.

9. *Access to external information*, which will allow significant, factual disagreements to be settled in a timely fashion, thus enabling the meeting to continue and be productive.

10. *Preservation of "organizational memory,"* so that those who do not attend the meeting can also work on the project. Often a project will include teams at different locations who will need to understand the content of a meeting as if affects only their site.

One response to the problems of group decision making has been the adoption of new methods of organizing and running meetings. Techniques such as facilitated meetings, brainstorming, and criticism-free idea generation have become popular and are now accepted as standard. Another response has been the application of technology to the problems resulting in the emergence of group decision support systems.

CHARACTERISTICS OF GDSS

How can information technology help groups arrive at decisions? Scholars have identified at least three basic elements of a GDSS: hardware, software tools, and people. Hardware refers to the conference facility itself, including the room, the tables, and the chairs. The meeting facility must be physically laid out in a manner that supports group collaboration. It also must include some electronic hardware, such as electronic display boards, as well as audiovisual, computer, and networking equipment.

A wide range of *software tools*, including tools for organizing ideas, gathering information, ranking and setting priorities, voting, and other aspects of collaborative work are being used to support decision-making meetings. We describe these tools in the next section. The third component, people, includes not only the participants but also a trained facilitator and often staff to support the hardware and software. Together these elements have led to the creation of a range of different kinds of GDSS, from simple electronic boardrooms to elaborate

FIGURE 14-7 The Gjensidige Insurance (www.gjensidige.no) collaborative meeting room. There is one microphone for every two seats and a speaker system on the wall. This equipment is used for same-time meetings between Gjensidige's offices in Oslo and Trondheim.

Source: © 1996–1997. All rights reserved. Ventana Corporation.

collaboration laboratories. In a collaboration laboratory, individuals work on their own desktop PCs or workstations. Their input is integrated on a file server and is viewable on a common screen at the front of the room; in most systems the integrated input is also viewable on the individual participant's screen. See Figure 14-7 for an illustration of an actual GDSS collaborative meeting room.

GDSS Software Tools

Some features of groupware tools for collaborative work as described in Chapter 7 can be used to support group decision making. There also are specific GDSS software tools for supporting group meetings. These tools were originally developed for meetings in which all participants are in the same room, but they also can be used for networked meetings in which participants are in different locations. Specific GDSS software tools include the following:

- *Electronic questionnaires* aid the organizers in pre-meeting planning by identifying issues of concern and by helping to ensure that key planning information is not overlooked.

- *Electronic brainstorming tools* allow individuals simultaneously and anonymously to contribute ideas on the topics of the meeting.

- *Idea organizers* facilitate the organized integration and synthesis of ideas generated during brainstorming.

- *Questionnaire tools* support the facilitators and group leaders as they gather information before and during the process of setting priorities.

- *Tools for voting or setting priorities* make available a range of methods from simple voting, to ranking, to a range of weighted techniques for setting priorities or voting (see Figure 14-8).

- *Stakeholder identification and analysis tools* use structured approaches to evaluate the impact of an emerging proposal on the organization and to identify stakeholders and evaluate the potential impact of those stakeholders on the proposed project.

- *Policy formation tools* provide structured support for developing agreement on the wording of policy statements.

- *Group dictionaries* document group agreement on definitions of words and terms central to the project.

Additional tools are available, such as group outlining and writing tools, software that stores and reads project files, and software that allows the attendees to view internal operational data stored by the organization's production computer systems.

Overview of a GDSS Meeting

An **electronic meeting system (EMS)** is a type of collaborative GDSS that uses information technology to make group meetings more productive by facilitating communication as well as decision making. It supports any activity in which people come together, whether in the same place at the same time or in different places at different times (Dennis et al., 1988; Nunamaker et al., 1991). IBM has a number of EMSs installed at various sites. Each attendee has a workstation. The workstations are networked and are connected to the facilitator's console, which serves as both the facilitator's workstation and control panel and the meeting's file server. All data that the attendees forward from their workstations to the group are collected and saved on the file server. The facilitator is able to project computer images onto the projection screen at the front centre of the room. The facilitator also has an overhead projector available. Whiteboards are visible on either side of the projection screen. Larger electronic meeting rooms are arranged in a semicircle and are tiered in legislative style to accommodate a large number of attendees.

The facilitator controls the use of tools during the meeting, often selecting from a large tool box that is part of the organization's GDSS. Tool selection is part of the pre-meeting planning process. Which tools are selected depends on the subject matter, the goals of the meeting, and the facilitation methodology the facilitator will use.

electronic meeting system (EMS)
A collaborative GDSS that uses information technology to make group meetings more productive by facilitating communication as well as decision making. Supports meetings at the same place and time or at different places and times.

FIGURE 14-8 GDSS |software tools. The Ventana Corporation's Group Systems electronic meeting software helps people create, share, record, organize, and evaluate ideas in meetings, between offices, or around the world.

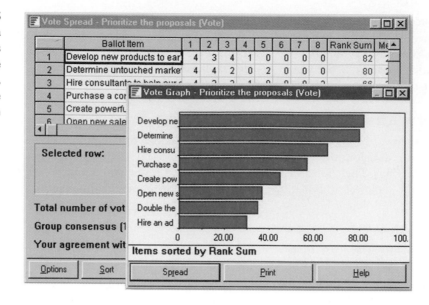

Attendees have full control over their own desktop computers. An attendee is able to view the agenda (and other planning documents), look at the integrated screen (or screens as the session progresses), use ordinary desktop PC tools (such as a word processor or a spreadsheet), tap into production data that have been made available, or work on the screen associated with the current meeting activity and associated tool (such as a brainstorming screen). However, no one can view anyone else's screens so participants' work is confidential until it is released to the file server for integration with the work of others. All input to the file server is anonymous—at each step, everyone's input to the file server (brainstorming ideas, idea evaluation and criticism, comments, voting, etc.) can be seen by all attendees on the integrated screens, but no information is available to identify the source of specific inputs. Attendees enter their data simultaneously rather than in round-robin fashion as is done in meetings that have little or no electronic systems support.

Figure 14-9 shows the sequence of activities at a typical EMS meeting. For each activity it also indicates the type of tools used and the output of those tools. During the meeting all

FIGURE 14-9 Group EMS tools. The sequence of activities and collaborative support tools used in an electronic meeting system (EMS) facilitates communication among attendees and generates a full record of the meeting.

Source: Nunamaker et al., "Electronic Meeting Systems to Support Group Work," *Communications of the ACM,* July 1991. Reprinted by permission.

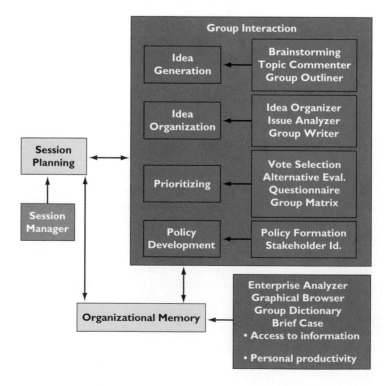

input to the integrated screens is saved on the file server. As a result, when the meeting is completed, a full record of the meeting (both raw material and resultant output) is available to the attendees and can be made available to anyone else with a need for access.

HOW GDSS CAN ENHANCE GROUP DECISION MAKING

GDSS are being used more widely, so we are able to understand some of their benefits and evaluate some of the tools. We look again at how a GDSS affects the 10 group meeting issues raised earlier.

1. *Improved preplanning.* Electronic questionnaires, supplemented by word processors, outlining software, and other desktop PC software, can structure planning, thereby improving it. The availability of the planning information at the actual meeting can also serve to enhance the quality of the meeting. Experts seem to feel that these tools add significance and emphasis to meeting pre-planning.

2. *Increased participation.* Studies show that in traditional decision-making meetings without GDSS support the optimal meeting size is three to five attendees. Beyond that size, the meeting process begins to break down. Using GDSS software, studies show that meeting size can increase while productivity also increases. One reason for this is that attendees contribute simultaneously rather than one at a time, which makes more efficient use of the meeting time. Interviews of GDSS meeting attendees indicate that the quality of participation is higher than in traditional meetings.

3. *Open, collaborative meeting atmosphere.* A GDSS contributes to a more collaborative atmosphere in several ways. First, anonymity of input is essentially guaranteed. Individuals need not be afraid of being judged by their boss for contributing a possibly offbeat idea. Second, anonymity reduces or eliminates the deadening effect that often occurs when high-status or dominant, outspoken individuals contribute. And third, the numbing pressures of social cues are reduced or eliminated.

4. *Criticism-free idea generation.* Anonymity ensures that attendees can contribute without fear of personally being criticized or of having their ideas rejected because of the identity of the contributor. Several studies show that interactive GDSS meetings generate more ideas and more satisfaction with those ideas than verbally interactive meetings (Nunamaker et al., 1991). GDSS can also help to reduce unproductive interpersonal conflict (Miranda and Bostrum, 1993–1994).

5. *Evaluation objectivity.* Anonymity prevents criticism of the source of ideas, thus supporting an atmosphere in which attendees focus on evaluating ideas. The same anonymity allows participants to detach from their own ideas so they are able to view them from a critical perspective. Evidence suggests that evaluation in an anonymous atmosphere increases the free flow of critical feedback and even stimulates the generation of new ideas during the evaluation process.

6. *Idea organization and evaluation.* GDSS software tools used for this purpose are structured and are based on methodology. They usually allow individuals to organize and then submit their results to the group (still anonymously). The group then iteratively modifies and develops the organized ideas until a document is completed. Attendees generally have viewed this approach as productive.

7. *Setting priorities and making decisions.* Anonymity helps lower level participants have their positions taken into consideration along with the higher-level attendees.

8. *Documentation of meetings.* Evidence at IBM indicates that post-meeting use of the data is crucial. Attendees use the data to continue their dialogues after the meetings, to discuss the meeting ideas with those who did not attend, and even to make presentations (Grobowski et al., 1990). Some tools enable the user to zoom in to more details on specific information.

9. *Access to external information.* Often a great deal of meeting time is devoted to factual disagreements. More experience with GDSS will indicate whether GDSS technology reduces this problem.

10. *Preservation of "organizational memory."* Specific tools have been developed to facilitate access to the data generated during a GDSS meeting, allowing nonattendees to locate needed information after the meeting. The documentation of a meeting by one group at one site has also been used successfully as input to another meeting on the same project at another site. GDSS could be further enhanced to integrate meeting memory with other organizational memory and supply this information to other parts of the organization (Schwabe, 1999).

Studies to date suggest that GDSS meetings can be more productive, make more efficient use of time, and produce the desired results in fewer meetings, although these results are not dramatically better than face-to-face meetings. GDSS seem most useful for tasks involving idea generation, complex problems, and large groups (Fjermestad and Hiltz, 1998–1999). One problem with understanding the value of GDSS is their complexity. A GDSS can be configured in an almost infinite variety of ways. In addition, the effectiveness of the tools will partially depend the facilitator's effectiveness, the quality of the pre-planning, the cooperation of the attendees, and the appropriateness of tools selected for different types of meetings. GDSS can enable groups to exchange more information, but cannot always help participants process the information effectively or reach better decisions (Dennis, 1996).

Researchers have noted that the design of an electronic meeting system and its technology is only one of a number of contingencies that affect the outcome of group meetings. Other factors, including the nature of the group, the task, the manner in which the problem is presented to the group, and the organizational context (including the organization's culture and environment) also affect the process of group meetings and meeting outcomes (Dennis et al., 1999; Fjermestad, 1998; Caouette and O'Connor, 1998; Dennis et al., 1988 and 1996; Nunamaker et al., 1991; Watson, Ho, and Raman, 1994). New types of group support systems with easy-to-use Web-based interfaces and multimedia capabilities may provide additional benefits.

14.3 EXECUTIVE SUPPORT IN THE ENTERPRISE

We have described how DSS and GDSS help managers make unstructured and semistructured decisions. **Executive support systems (ESS)** also help managers with unstructured problems, focusing on the information needs of senior management. Combining data from internal and external sources, ESS create a generalized computing and communications environment that can be focused and applied to a changing array of problems. ESS help senior executives monitor organizational performance, track activities of competitors, spot problems, identify opportunities, and forecast trends.

THE ROLE OF EXECUTIVE SUPPORT SYSTEMS IN THE ORGANIZATION

Before ESS, it was common for executives to receive numerous fixed-format reports, often hundreds of pages every month (or even every week). Today, an ESS can bring together data from all parts of the organization and allow managers to select, access, and tailor them as needed using easy-to-use desktop analytical tools and online data displays. Use of the systems has migrated down several organizational levels so that executives and their subordinates are able to look at the same data in the same way.

Today's systems try to avoid the problem of data overload so common in paper reports because the data can be filtered or viewed in graphic format (if the user so chooses). ESS systems have the ability to **drill down**, moving from a piece of summary data to lower and lower levels of detail. The ability to drill down is useful not only to senior executives but also to employees at lower levels of the organization who need to analyze data. OLAP tools for analyzing large databases provide this capability.

A major challenge of building executive support systems has been to integrate data from systems designed for very different purposes so that senior executives can review organizational performance from a firm-wide perspective. Often data critical to the senior executive had been unavailable. For example, sales data coming from an order-entry transaction pro-

executive support system (ESS)

An information system at the strategic level of an organization designed to address unstructured decision making through advanced graphics and communications.

drill down

The ability to move from summary data down to lower and lower levels of detail.

cessing system might not be linked to marketing information, a linkage the executive would find useful. In the traditional firm, which typically had hundreds or even thousands of incompatible systems, pulling such information together and making sense out of it was a major task. When the information was assembled, it was likely to be out of date, incomplete, and inaccurate. Making decisions under these conditions was like a dart game with the bull's eye swinging on a pendulum. Properly configured and implemented executive systems can provide managers with timely, comprehensive, and accurate firm-wide information. Executive support systems based on this data can be considered logical extensions of enterprise system functionality.

External data, including data from the Web, are now more easily available in many ESS as well. Executives need a wide range of external data from current stock market news to competitor information, industry trends, and even projected legislative action. Through their ESS, many managers have access to news services, financial market databases, economic information, and whatever other public data they may desire.

Contemporary ESS include tools for modelling and analysis. With only a minimum of experience, most managers find they can use these tools to create graphic comparisons of data by time, region, product, price range, and so on. (While DSS use such tools primarily for modelling and analysis in a fairly narrow range of decision situations, ESS use them primarily to provide status information about organizational performance.)

Developing ESS

ESS are executive systems and must be designed so that high-level managers and others can use them without much training. One area that merits special attention is the determination of executive information requirements. ESS need to have a facility for environmental scanning. A key information requirement of managers at the strategic level is the ability to detect signals of problems in the external environment that indicate strategic threats and opportunities (Walls et al., 1992). The ESS needs to be designed so that both external and internal sources of information can be used for environmental scanning purposes.

ESS potentially could give top executives the ability to examine other managers' work without their knowledge, so there may be some resistance to ESS at lower levels of the organization. Implementation of ESS should be carefully managed to neutralize such opposition (see Chapter 11).

Cost justification presents a different type of problem with an ESS. Because much of an executive's work is unstructured, how does one quantify benefits for a system that primarily supports such unstructured work? An ESS often is justified in advance by the intuitive feeling that it will pay for itself (Watson et al., 1991). If ESS benefits can ever be quantified, it would only be after the system is operational.

BENEFITS OF EXECUTIVE SUPPORT SYSTEMS

Much of the value of ESS is found in their flexibility. These systems put data and tools in the hands of executives without addressing specific problems or imposing solutions. Executives are free to shape the problems as they see fit, using the system as an extension of their own thinking processes. These are not decision-making systems; they are tools to aid executives in making decisions.

The most visible benefit of ESS is their ability to analyze, compare, and highlight trends. The easy use of graphics allows the user to look at more data in less time with greater clarity and insight than paper-based systems can provide. In the past, executives obtained the same information by taking up days and weeks of their staffs' valuable time. By using ESS, those staffs and the executives themselves are freed up for the more creative analysis and decision making in their jobs. ESS capabilities for drilling down and highlighting trends may also enhance the quality of the analysis and can speed up decision making (Leidner and Elam, 1993–1994).

Executives are using ESS to monitor performance more successfully in their own areas of responsibility. Some companies use these systems to monitor key performance indicators for the entire firm and to measure firm performance against changes in the external environment. The timeliness and availability of the data result in needed actions being identified and taken earlier. Problems can be handled before they become too damaging; opportunities also can be identified earlier. These systems can thus help organizations move toward a "sense and respond" strategy.

A well-designed ESS could dramatically improve management performance and increase upper management's span of control. Immediate access to this volume of data allows executives to better monitor activities of lower units reporting to them. That very monitoring ability could allow decision making to be decentralized and to take place at lower operating levels. Executives are often willing to push decision making further down into the organization as long as they can be assured that all is going well. Alternatively, executive support systems based on enterprise-wide data could potentially increase management centralization, enabling senior executives to monitor the performance of subordinates across the company and to direct them to take appropriate action when conditions change.

EXECUTIVE SUPPORT SYSTEMS AND THE DIGITAL FIRM

To illustrate the ways in which an ESS can enhance management decision making, we now describe important types of ESS applications for gathering business intelligence and monitoring corporate performance, including ESS based on enterprise systems.

ESS for Business Intelligence

Today, customer expectations, Internet technology, and new business models can alter the competitive landscape so rapidly that managers need special capabilities for competitive intelligence gathering. ESS can help managers identify changing market conditions, formulate responses, track implementation efforts, and learn from feedback.

BP Sony NV, the Dutch branch of the multinational electronics giant, wanted more insight from the marketplace to drive its competitive strategy. Until recently, its management reports were based primarily on financial and administrative data that took at least 24 hours to generate. Management wanted to be able to make meaningful decisions based on marketing and sales data as well so it could respond quickly to marketplace changes. Sony Netherlands constructed a data warehouse and executive information system (EIS) for this purpose.

The EIS is now available to 78 users in management, marketing, and sales. They can use the system to help them define strategies, search for opportunities, identify problems, and substantiate actions. Using a drill-down function, they can examine the underlying numbers behind the total result. For instance, while senior management can obtain sales results by business unit or product group, a marketing manager can use the system to look only at the group of products he or she was responsible for. The manager can produce a report to indicate exactly which products are strong or weak performers or to rank dealers by performance. The system is flexible, easy to use, and can provide much of this information to the user online (Information Builders, 2000).

Cookson Electronics of Foxborough, Massachusetts, a supplier of materials used in printed circuit boards and semiconductor packaging, has 14 divisions around the world. Each is responsible for a different point in the electronics life cycle, providing parts for computers, cell phones, and other consumer electronics. The semiconductor field has highly cyclical fluctuations in business, and Cookson divisions responsible for this part of the business can help the entire firm predict demand by anticipating industry cycles. Working with senior managers, Cookson's senior intelligence officer Yann Morvan developed a list of key intelligence topics (KITs) linked to strategic decisions. For example, a KIT might cover the firm's top five competitors, suppliers, customers, or technologies.

Corset Shop, Inc., a highly regarded intimate apparel retailer for over 35 years, implemented a suite of applications from Montreal's Gemmar Systems International. Corset Shop operates stores under the name Bare Necessities and also operates leased departments from coast to coast with more than 35 000 SKUs of lingerie, sleepwear, loungewear, leg wear, and accessories. Gemmar's Retail-1EIS gives Corset Shop executives the ability to drill down, look at category, department, or class statistics, rank their best and worst products, season and age their products and vendors, examine store performance, analyze inventories sell through, refunds, and a host of other types of analysis.

Monitoring Corporate Performance: Balanced Scorecard Systems

Companies have traditionally measured value using financial metrics such as return on investment (ROI), which we described in Chapter 13. Many firms are now implementing a **balanced scorecard** model that supplements traditional financial measures with measurements from additional perspectives, such as customers, internal business processes, and learning and growth. Managers can use balanced scorecard systems to see how well the firm is meeting its strategic goals. The goals and measures for the balanced scorecard vary from company to company. Companies are setting up information systems to populate the scorecard for management.

Amsterdam-based ING Bank, which is part of the ING Group global financial services firm, adopted a balanced scorecard approach when it reorganized. Management wanted to shift from a product to a client orientation and develop appropriate performance indicators to measure progress in this new direction. The bank developed a Web-based balanced scorecard application using SAS tools for data warehousing and statistical analysis to measure progress with 21 indicators. Data to fill out the scorecard from sources such as financial ledger applications and client retention and market penetration ratios feed a central data warehouse. The data come from systems running on Lotus Notes, Microsoft Excel spreadsheets, and Oracle and DB2 databases. The data warehouse and balanced scorecard software run on IBM RS/6000 servers. ING initially made the balanced scorecard system available only to midrange executives in sales but later extended it to 3000 users, including people at nearly every level of its relationship management group. Users regularly check progress with the scorecard. For example, by comparing how many visits they have made to different clients, sales people can make better decisions about how to allocate their time (McCune, 2000).

balanced scorecard
A model for analyzing firm performance that supplements traditional financial measures with measurements from additional business perspectives.

Enterprise-Wide Reporting and Analysis

Enterprise system vendors are now providing capabilities to extend the usefulness of data captured in operational systems to give management a picture of the overall performance of the firm. Some provide reporting of metrics for balanced scorecard analysis as well as more traditional financial and operating metrics. Table 14-3 describes strategic performance management tools for each of the major enterprise system vendors.

TABLE 14-3 STRATEGIC PERFORMANCE MANAGEMENT TOOLS FOR ENTERPRISE SYSTEMS

Enterprise System Vendor	Description
SAP	Web-enabled Strategic Enterprise Management module provides reports giving managers a comprehensive view of firm performance. Features corporate performance metrics, simulation, and planning tools. Managers can model and communicate key performance indicators for a Balanced Scorecard. Another measurement tool called the Management Cockpit can be used to structure and visualize performance indicators using ergonomic, easy-to-understand graphical displays.
PeopleSoft	Enterprise Performance Management (EPM) features four modules: Enterprise Warehouse to analyze business transactions, Business Intelligence to integrate external data such as surveys, Balanced Scorecard providing tools for measurement and communication of the scorecard, and Financial Workbench.
Oracle	Strategic Enterprise Management includes support for a Balanced Scorecard, activity-based management, and budgeting. A value-based management module under development will help companies develop and apply new accounting methods for quantifying intellectual capital.

FIGURE 14-10 The Management Cockpit is an ergonomic concept for structuring and visualizing firm performance indicators using easy-to-understand displays. This display is based on SAP's Strategic Enterprise Management module, which uses Web technology to provide management with a comprehensive view of firm performance.

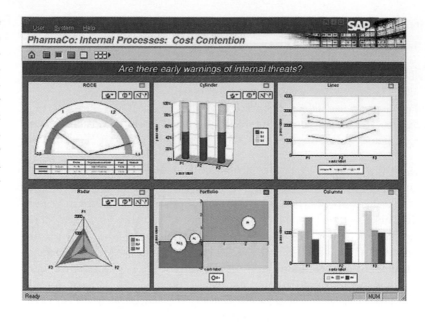

Companies can use these new enterprise reporting capabilities to create measures of firm performance that were not previously available. The head of strategic planning at Dow Chemical led a cross-functional steering team to develop a set of measures and reports based on data from the company's SAP enterprise system. (See Figure 14-10 for an example from another firm.) Process experts in different areas of the company defined reporting categories such as expense management, inventory management, and sales. Dow then developed a data mart for each type of data, amounting to over 20 data marts. The data marts are integrated so that the numbers for the "business results" mart balance to numbers in the expenses and sales marts. Dow also implemented a new set of performance measures based on shareholder value and activity-based costing. (Activity-based costing is a budgeting and analysis model that identifies all the resources, processes, and costs, including overhead and operating expenses, required to produce a specific product or service. It allows managers to see which products or services are profitable or losing money so they can determine the changes required to maximize firm profitability.) Instead of reporting in terms of product and income, the system can focus on contribution margins and customer accounts, with the ability to calculate the current and lifetime value of each account. The system is used by over 5000 people, ranging from Dow's CEO to plant floor workers (Davenport, 2000).

Management of Nissan Motor Company of Australia must oversee the activities of 550 people in 23 sites across the Australian continent. The company is primarily involved in Nissan's import and distribution activities for 35 000 automobiles each year. Like other automotive companies, Nissan Australia has extensive reporting requirements, including detailed controlling reports for financial accounts and monthly accounts. Managers need detailed reports down to the model level, with controlling reports for each department. When Nissan used an old legacy mainframe system, it would take up to two weeks to create and distribute reports to the company's board of directors.

In 1997, Nissan Australia installed SAP's R/3 enterprise software, serving as a pilot for the rest of the Nissan organization. The company also installed Information Builders' SNAPpack Power Reporter to create custom reports with a Web interface and powerful drill-down capabilities that did not require extensive programming to produce. These reports can be generated immediately and include profit-and-loss reports, gross margin analysis, balance sheets, and reports about wholesale and retail vehicles. Management requests for more profit analysis reports by model, state, and other variables can be easily satisfied (Information Builders, 2000).

APPLICATION SOFTWARE EXERCISE

SPREADSHEET EXERCISE: BREAKEVEN ANALYSIS AT JASMINE'S COOKWARE

Stanley's Cookware produces premiere cookware products and sells these products as sets to retailers. A typical Stanley Premiere Kitchen Set includes a Dutch oven, frying pan, stockpot, casserole, and saucepan. Each set is sold for $200 and costs the company approximately $125 to produce.

Production at the company's manufacturing plant will soon reach capacity, and management must decide whether to expand the existing facility or relocate to a new plant. Existing facility expansion has associated fixed costs of $2 500 000 and a capacity of 45 000 sets. If relocation occurs, fixed costs are estimated at $4 500 000, variable costs will drop to $110, and capacity will increase to 100 000 sets.

Prepare a spreadsheet to support the decision-making needs of Jasmine's Cookware's managers. The spreadsheet should summarize the fixed costs, variable costs, revenue, unit profit margin, and breakeven points for both options.

Your spreadsheet should provide reporting and scenario analysis features. How can these features provide support for this decision problem? If an optimistic forecast suggests that 75 000 sets will be sold, which site is the better choice? If a pessimistic forecast suggests that only 30 000 sets will be sold, which site is the better choice? Company management may increase the price of a Jasmine's Premiere Kitchen Set to $210. What impact, if any, does this information have on your analysis? Summarize your findings in a report, and submit the report and your spreadsheet to your professor.

MANAGEMENT WRAP-UP

Management is responsible for determining where management support systems can make their greatest contribution to organizational performance and for allocating the resources to build them. Management needs to work closely with systems developers to make sure that these systems effectively capture the right set of information requirements and decision processes for guiding the firm.

Management support systems can improve organizational performance by speeding up decision making or improving the quality of the management decisions. However, some of these decision processes may not be clearly understood. A management support system will be most effective when systems developers have a clear idea of its objectives, the nature of the decisions to be supported, and how the system will actually support decision making.

Systems to support management decision making can be developed with a range of technologies, including the use of large databases, modelling tools, graphics tools, datamining and analysis tools, and electronic meeting technology. Identifying the right technology for the decision or decision process to be supported is a key technology decision.

For Discussion

1. As a manager or user of information systems, what would you need to know to participate in the design and use of a DSS or an ESS? Why?
2. If businesses used DSS, GDSS, and ESS more widely, would they make better decisions? Explain.

Summary

1. *Differentiate a decision support system (DSS) and a group decision support system (GDSS).* A decision support system (DSS) is an interactive system under user control that combines data, sophisticated analytical models and tools, and user-friendly software into a single powerful system that can support semistructured or unstructured decision making. There are two kinds of DSS: model-driven DSS and data-driven DSS. DSS targeted toward customers as well as managers are becoming available on the Web. A group decision support system (GDSS) is an interactive computer-based system to facilitate the solution of unstructured problems by a set of decision makers working together as a group rather than individually.

2. *Describe the components of decision support systems and group decision support systems.* The components of a DSS are the DSS database, the DSS software system, and the user interface. The DSS database is a collection of current or historical data from a number of applications or workgroups that can be used for analysis. The data can come from both internal and external sources including enterprise systems and the Web. The DSS software system consists of OLAP and data-mining tools or mathematical and analytical models used to analyze the data in the database. The user interface allows users to interact with the DSS software tools directly.

   Group decision support systems (GDSS) have hardware, software, and people components. Hardware components consist of the conference room facilities, including seating arrangements and computer and other electronic hardware. Software components include tools for organizing ideas, gathering information, ranking and setting priorities, and documenting meeting sessions. People components include participants, a trained facilitator, and staff to support the hardware and software.

3. *Explain how decision support systems and group decision support systems can enhance decision making.* Both DSS and GDSS support steps in the process of arriving at decisions. A DSS provides results of model-based or data-driven analysis that help managers design and evaluate alternatives and monitor the progress of the solution that was adopted. DSS can support decisions for supply chain management and customer analysis as well model alternative business scenarios. A GDSS helps decision makers meeting together to arrive at a decision more efficiently and is especially useful for increasing the productivity of meetings larger than four or five people. However, the effectiveness of GDSS is contingent on the nature of the group, the task, and the context of the meeting.

4. *Describe the capabilities of executive support systems (ESS).* Executive support systems help managers with unstructured problems that occur at the strategic level of management. ESS provide data from both internal and external sources and provide a generalized computing and communications environment that can be focused and applied to a changing array of problems. ESS help senior executives monitor firm performance, spot problems, identify opportunities, and forecast trends. These systems can filter out extraneous details for high-level overviews, or they can enable senior managers and other users to drill down to provide detailed transaction data if required. ESS can also take advantage of firm-wide data provided by enterprise systems.

5. *Assess the benefits of executive support systems.* ESS help senior managers analyze, compare, and highlight trends so that they may more easily monitor organizational performance or identify strategic problems and opportunities. ESS can increase the span of control of senior management, allowing them to oversee more people with fewer resources or they can enable management to push decision making to lower levels.

Key Terms

Balanced scorecard, 503

Customer decision support system (CDSS), 494

Data-driven DSS, 486

Datamining, 486

Decision support system (DSS), 485

Drill down, 500

DSS database, 488

DSS software system, 488

Electronic meeting system (EMS), 497

Executive support system (ESS), 500

Geographic information system (GIS), 493

Group decision support system (GDSS), 495

Management information system (MIS), 485

Model, 488

Model-driven DSS, 486

Sensitivity analysis, 488

Review Questions

1. What is a decision support system (DSS)? How does it differ from a transaction processing system (TPS) and a management information system (MIS)?

2. How can a DSS support unstructured or semistructured decision making?

3. What is the difference between a data-driven DSS and a model-driven DSS? Give examples.

4. What are the three basic components of a DSS? Briefly describe each.

5. How can DSS help firms manage internal and external business processes?

6. What is a customer decision support system? How can the Internet be used for this purpose?

7. What is a group decision support system (GDSS)? How does it differ from a DSS?

8. What are the three underlying problems in group decision making that have led to the development of GDSS?

9. Describe the three elements of a GDSS.

10. Name five GDSS software tools.

11. What is an electronic meeting system (EMS)? Describe its capabilities.

12. For each of the three underlying problems in group decision making referred to in question 8, describe one or two ways GDSS can contribute to a solution.

13. Define and describe the capabilities of an executive support system.

14. How can the Internet and enterprise systems provide capabilities for executive support systems?

15. What are the benefits of ESS? How do these systems enhance managerial decision making?

GROUP PROJECT

With three or four of your classmates, identify several groups in your university that could benefit from a GDSS. Design a GDSS for one of those groups, describing its hardware, software, and people elements. Pre-plan a meeting for the group, including topics to be discussed and decisions that need to be made. Present your findings to the class.

INTERNET CONNECTION

■ COMPANION WEBSITE

At www.pearsoned.ca/laudon, you'll find an online study guide with two quizzes to test your knowledge of how decision and executive support systems are used in modern organizations. You'll also find updates to the chapter and online exercises and cases that enable you to apply your knowledge to realistic situations.

■ ADDITIONAL SITES OF INTEREST

There are many interesting Web sites to enhance your learning about DSS and ESS. You can search the Web yourself, or just try the following sites to add to what you have already learned.

Cognos

www.cognos.com

Ottawa-based world leader in datawarehouse OLAP, query, and reporting software

Gemmar Systems International

www.gsi.ca

International retail industry software provider located in Montreal

SAP

www.sap.com

Check out their Management Cockpit application for an enterprise-wide ESS application

CASE STUDY   *The Calgary Airport Authority: Knowledge Management Takes Flight*

With an increased number of people choosing air travel, Canada's airports have come to rely on a mixture of employee skill and timely information to see passengers to their travel destinations. Calgary International has grown to become Canada's fourth busiest airport, boasting more than 7.7 million visitors to its terminal last year alone. The airport has also won praise for its state-of-the-art facility, innovative service, and overall customer satisfaction ratings.

The Calgary Airport Authority has been responsible for the operation, maintenance, development, and management of Calgary International Airport since 1992 under a long-term lease from the Government of Canada. Calgary has the distinction of being one of the first cities in Canada to assume control over its local airport.

Access to timely and accurate information is the key to a successfully managed airport, and the Calgary Airport Authority is committed to providing its passengers with the highest quality information. Arrivals, departures, news, weather, and parking information are offered to customers in real-time via the organization's Web site located at www.calgaryairport.com.

When it came to managing its own internal information gathering and analysis techniques, the Calgary Airport Authority found itself in a bit of a quandary. The organization had inherited disparate information systems from the amalgamation of its business units in 1992, and it had become concerned with the quality of its flight information. To operate at peak efficiency, the airport relied on a constant feed of flight activity information from an array of business systems including air traffic control, flight information display, flight tracking records, and accounting. Because each system operated as an independent entity, comparative analysis and strategic planning had become both difficult and time-consuming. Differing views of critical airport information could lead to analysis discrepancies, and virtually all data was suspect.

"We had tried to link the systems together manually, but we still found it difficult to access information for analysis purposes, and more often than not, different departments within our organization were generating different results," says Paul Lawrence, Manager, Information Systems at the Calgary Airport Authority. The implementation of a powerful data warehouse system, known internally as Flight and Passenger Statistics (FLAPS), has made the Calgary Airport Authority a benchmark of efficiency within the Canadian airport community. This solution, based on the Microsoft SQL Server platform, has provided the company with a secure, cost-effective information repository for all of its business reporting and analysis needs.

The Calgary Airport Authority called on the expertise of EDS Systemhouse, Canada's leading professional IT services company for help with their knowledge management dilemma. EDS Systemhouse recommended a data warehouse, which would act as an information repository for the organization's flight activity information. This data store promised to provide a complete picture of the situation at the Calgary Airport Authority while providing the tools for a range of data reporting and analysis activities.

Another key player in the data warehouse implementation at the Calgary Airport Authority was Ottawa's Cognos. Its marquee product, NovaView™, is a front-end analysis application for Microsoft SQL Server 7.0 OLAP Services. NovaView™ lets users take advantage of Microsoft's new multidimensional data server to turn information into results.

Calgary Airport Authority and EDS Systemhouse worked together to create a data warehouse that would serve as the knowledge management hub for flight activity information. This solution allows for on-demand access to records and information for use in the decision-making process, and for projections used to develop future strategies.

Leveraging Microsoft's new OLAP Services capability and Cognos' expertise in multidimensional analysis, EDS Systemhouse created a scalable, secure, and cost efficient system for the Calgary Airport Authority to manage and access critical flight activity information. OLAP tools enable users to view the different dimensions of this multidimensional data, ensuring both accuracy and availability of flight and environmental information.

The new data warehouse system, FLAPS, gives the Calgary Airport Authority a bird's eye view of the day-to-day flight activities at the airport, based on the most up-to-date information from all sources. Airport staff are able to analyze data in a variety of ways, to plan strategic directions, and to analyze financial changes (including rate structures and accounting), which allows the Calgary Airport Authority to use its knowledge resources more efficiently. "Having this information and the tools to manipulate it gives us the power to quickly and effi-

ciently adjust our strategies and respond to changing demands," says Lawrence.

The biggest challenge faced by the implementation team concerned the creation of the Enterprise Flight Business model, which was designed to establish standards and integrate flight information from different flight systems. The model improved the common understanding of all information sources and provided an easy access repository for analysis and reporting. Taking advantage of the powerful capability of the Star Schema Database and MOLAP Cubes (with multiple dimensions and measures), the system can effectively manage complexity, query response time, security, and processing time.

Utilizing Cognos' NovaView™, the team quickly developed applications that provide standard templates of flight and passenger information. This information is critical to the Calgary Airport Authority as it summarizes key criteria such as airline/runway data with complete drill down, filtering, and calculation capability allowing access to source detail records.

The new data warehouse system has streamlined the workload and standardized information from many different flight information sources at the Calgary Airport Authority. This allows for the quick quantification of differences between disparate sources, which acts as an automatic double-check and validation of third-party information, ensuring that the organization is basing its analysis, reporting, and planning on complete and accurate information.

Business analysts and marketing personnel benefit from the ability to query the data warehouse using a variety of tools and techniques. These tools allow for the analysis and presentation of critical flight information in virtually limitless ways. Users in these key departments are now empowered to make informed and accurate decisions based on "big picture" information. This has helped resolve the challenges encountered under the organization's previous IT system.

With the support of the multidimensional, relational, and hybrid OLAP implementations, the Calgary Airport Authority was able to customize the data model that was best suited to its unique needs. Departments are able to custom configure analysis tools to help meet the needs specific to their jobs. In terms of time, Leslie Gavin, Business Development Analyst at the Calgary Airport Authority, has noticed a vast improvement under the new FLAPS system. "It has been an incredible time saver. Reports that used to take more than a half day to prepare can now be completed in less than 15 minutes," said Gavin.

Realizing the capabilities and the benefits of the new infrastructure, the Calgary Airport Authority is exploring new ways to include management of such activities as parking and operational services. The Calgary Airport Authority continues to experiment with the analyses made possible through these applications. These tools have provided the organization with the ability to examine information in ways never before thought possible. The Calgary Airport Authority can now easily and cost-effectively build their knowledge-management infrastructure by adding new applications to further enhance the level of internal and external information sharing. "Being able to look at information from every possible vantage point allows us to be more creative problem solvers—and that has helped make our business better," says Lawrence.

Sources: N.H. Argyle, "Air Route Changes Emphasize Service," *The Calgary Herald Discover Calgary*, Spring 2001; "The Calgary Airport Authority: Knowledge Management Takes Flight," Microsoft Canada Case Study, www.microsoft.com/canada/casestudies/Calgary_airport.asp?top=1, accessed July 12, 2001.

CASE STUDY QUESTIONS

1. What factors and issues prompted the Calgary Airport Authority to develop FLAPS and their other OLAP applications?

2. Why do you think the Authority decided to outsource their new decision support systems?

3. What management, organization, and technical issues did the Calgary Airport Authority have to address to develop and use the new system?

4. How did the success of the system impact the Authority's management, organization, and technology?

5. What other uses or benefits do you think the Calgary Airport Authority can obtain from this suite of OLAP applications?

15

KNOWLEDGE-BASED INFORMATION SYSTEMS

OBJECTIVES

After completing this chapter, you will be able to:

1. *Explain the importance of knowledge management in contemporary organizations.*

2. *Describe the applications that are most useful for distributing, creating, and sharing knowledge in the firm.*

3. *Evaluate the role of artificial intelligence in knowledge management.*

4. *Demonstrate how organizations can use expert systems and case-based reasoning to capture knowledge.*

5. *Demonstrate how organizations can use neural networks and other intelligent techniques to improve their knowledge base.*

Montreal Law Firm Adopts New Knowledge Management Solution

In April 1998, McMaster Meighen and Mackenzie Gervais combined to form McMaster Gervais. With roots dating back to 1823, the two Montreal-based legal practices joined to become one of the most enduring, prestigious, and progressive members of the Canadian legal community, offering a comprehensive range of legal services to their clients.

The integration of its information systems was critical to McMaster Gervais after the 1998 merger. The newly merged firm required an efficient way to rapidly combine two different hardware, software, and information infrastructures (operating in both English and French), into one single effective entity. This goal meant that, for example, data from legacy AS/400 systems needed to be extracted and moved to newer systems.

Document work constitutes about 70 percent of a law firm's activities. By implementing MGénie, their new knowledge management system, and channelling McMaster Gervais' document production through MGénie's knowledge centre, users can tap into a vast pool of knowledge-sharing tools and easily access needed organizational knowledge.

McMaster Gervais developed a clear set of criteria for its ideal knowledge management solution. Key elements in the knowledge management strategy included ready accessibility by lawyers and staff, Internet-based remote access to a wide range of information, and multilingual access and operation. The firm wanted a seamless integration of their various data sources and applications that was not only easy to use, but also easily managed and seamlessly integrated with the firm's day-to-day operations. In a business where privacy is paramount, McMaster Gervais knew that secure and reliable access was a vital component of the solution. The user-interface was also important; the firm demanded a system with characteristics that included customizable information delivery and a consistent look and feel.

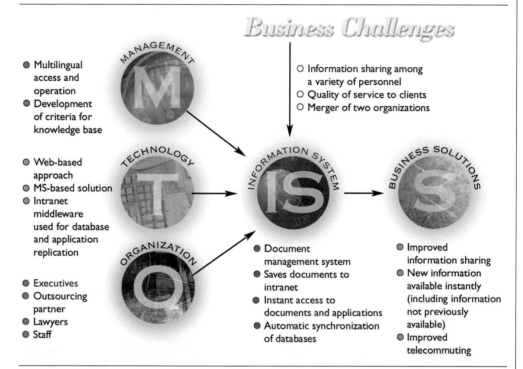

Business Challenges

MANAGEMENT
- Multilingual access and operation
- Development of criteria for knowledge base

TECHNOLOGY
- Web-based approach
- MS-based solution
- Intranet middleware used for database and application replication

ORGANIZATION
- Executives
- Outsourcing partner
- Lawyers
- Staff

- ○ Information sharing among a variety of personnel
- ○ Quality of service to clients
- ○ Merger of two organizations

INFORMATION SYSTEM
- Document management system
- Saves documents to intranet
- Instant access to documents and applications
- Automatic synchronization of databases

BUSINESS SOLUTIONS
- Improved information sharing
- New information available instantly (including information not previously available)
- Improved telecommuting

McMaster Gervais called upon Montreal-based consulting and systems integration firm, Zver & Associates. Zver & Associates services and supports more than 100 law firms and corporate law departments across North America. It assists clients with system selection, project management, and implementation, including development of law firm intranets and extranets. Zver's new division, PensEra Knowledge Technologies (www.pensera.com), specializes in online knowledge centre strategy and development for the legal profession.

McMaster Gervais was already working in a Microsoft-based environment, which was leveraged to construct a platform for MGénie. Document folders held in storage areas on Microsoft Exchange servers could be grouped according to criteria and then shared among McMaster Gervais' users. Microsoft SNA and SQL Servers provided access and database replication features so that McMaster Gervais could extract data from a legacy AS/400 system. Changes in data could be synchronized automatically between databases that were constantly accessed by employees throughout the firm. Existing applications for word processing, billing, and accounting were not replaced but were simply channelled to the intranet middleware. All information is securely protected behind McMaster Gervais' firewall to prevent unauthorized access.

(continued)

Development of the solution was undertaken with Microsoft tools, including Visual Interdev Web development system, Visual Basic for desktop, ActiveX controls, Visual C++ development system for server-side component development and Visual Basic for the development of specialized macros in Word that were used to accelerate standard business functions at McMaster Gervais.

In collaboration with McMaster Gervais, Zver developed a unique intranet-based law firm knowledge centre designed to meet the law firm's objectives. Although each component was designed to specifically address McMaster Gervais' needs, many of the knowledge centre components have become part of Zver's inventory of tools used as the basis for rapid development at other law firms and legal departments. The knowledge centre has individual sections dedicated to documents, the library, conference room schedules, client information, internal directories, etc. "All members of the firm visit MGénie because it is the central point for business information," Zver says. The knowledge centre is completely bilingual so all information and functions are available in English or French according to user selections.

MGénie's most innovative feature is a Web-based document management facility where users can create, classify, index, and retrieve any firm documents through a central intranet site. "Zver built a hybrid system that seamlessly layers the Web-based document facility over the regular word-processing functions," Felean said. Peter Zver said the solution's quality is demonstrated by its immediate impact on the users. "The scope of an intranet knowledge management solution is virtually unlimited, and the payback can be substantial," he said. "Not only is the knowledge centre worth its development cost, but it actually helps recoup prior investments by making information that was previously hidden in other application systems more accessible." McMaster Gervais' employees needed only brief training sessions because most were already familiar with Internet Explorer's search and browse features, which they use to access information off the corporate intranet.

Sources: "Prestigious Law Firm Adopts New Knowledge Management Solution," Microsoft Canada Case Study, www.microsoft.com/canada/casestudies/mcmaster.asp, accessed July 21, 2001; "Five Top Law Firms Merge to Form Borden Ladner Gervais LLP," *Canadian NewsWire*, www1.newswire.ca/releases/February2000/29/c8380.html, accessed July 21, 2001.

MANAGEMENT CHALLENGES

McMaster Gervais' MGénie is one example of how systems can be used to leverage organizational knowledge by making it more easily available. Collaborating and communicating with practitioners and experts and sharing ideas and information have become essential requirements in business, science, and government. In an information economy, capturing and distributing intelligence and knowledge and enhancing group collaboration have become vital to organizational innovation and survival. Special systems can be used for managing organizational knowledge, but they raise the following management challenges:

1. **Designing information systems that genuinely enhance the productivity of knowledge workers.** Information systems that truly enhance the productivity of knowledge workers may be difficult to build because the manner in which information technology can enhance higher level tasks such as those performed by managers and professionals (i.e., scientists or engineers) is not always clearly understood. Some aspects of organizational knowledge cannot be captured easily or codified, or the information that organizations finally manage to capture may become outdated as environments change (Malhotra, 1998). High-level knowledge workers may resist the introduction of any new technology, or they may resist knowledge work systems because these systems diminish personal control and creativity.

2. Creating robust expert systems. Expert systems must be changed every time there is a change in the organizational environment. Each time there is a change in the rules experts use, they must be reprogrammed. It is difficult to provide expert systems with the flexibility of human experts. Many thousands of businesses have undertaken experimental projects in expert systems, but only a small percentage have created expert systems that can actually be used on a production basis.

This chapter examines information system applications specifically designed to help organizations create, capture, distribute, and use knowledge and information. First, we examine information systems for supporting information and knowledge work. Then we look at the ways that organizations can use artificial intelligence for capturing and using knowledge and expertise.

15.1 KNOWLEDGE MANAGEMENT IN THE ORGANIZATION

Chapter 1 described the emergence of the information economy and the digital firm, in which the major source of wealth and prosperity is the production and distribution of information and knowledge. Firms increasingly rely on digital technology to enable business processes. For example, 55 percent of the U.S. labour force consists of knowledge and information workers, and 60 percent of the gross domestic product of the United States comes from the knowledge and information sectors, such as finance and publishing. While it is estimated that Canada slightly lags the United States in these statistics, the IT sector in Canada has been growing by 10 percent annually.

In an information economy, knowledge-based core competencies—the two or three things that an organization does best—are key organizational assets. Producing unique products or services or producing them at a lower cost than competitors is based on superior knowledge of the production process and superior design. Knowing how to do things effectively and efficiently in ways that other organizations cannot duplicate is a primary source of profit and a factor in production that cannot be purchased in external markets. Some management theorists believe that these knowledge assets are as important, if not more important, for competitive advantage and survival than physical and financial assets in ensuring the firm's competitiveness and survival.

As knowledge becomes a central productive and strategic asset, organizational success depends increasingly on the firm's ability to produce, gather, store, and disseminate knowledge. With knowledge, firms become more efficient and effective in their use of scarce resources. Without knowledge, firms become less efficient and effective in their use of resources and ultimately fail.

How do firms obtain knowledge? Like humans, organizations create and gather knowledge through a variety of organizational learning mechanisms. Through trial and error, careful measurement of planned activities, and feedback from customers and the environment in general, organizations create standard operating procedures and business processes that reflect their experience. This is called **organizational learning**. Arguably, organizations that can quickly sense and respond to their environments will survive longer than organizations that have poor learning mechanisms.

Knowledge management refers to the set of processes developed in an organization to create, gather, store, maintain, and disseminate the firm's knowledge. In short, knowledge management refers to how firms maximize their ability to learn from their environments. Information technology plays an important role in knowledge management as an enabler of business processes aimed at creating, storing, maintaining, and disseminating knowledge. Developing procedures and routines—business processes—to optimize the creation, flow, learning, protection, and sharing of knowledge in the firm is now a core management responsibility. Knowledge management increases the ability of the organization to learn from its environment and to incorporate knowledge into its business processes.

organizational learning
Creation of new standard operating procedures and business processes that reflect an organization's experience.

knowledge management
The set of processes developed in an organization to create, gather, store, maintain, and disseminate the firm's knowledge.

Companies cannot take advantage of their knowledge resources if they have inefficient processes for capturing and distributing knowledge or if they fail to appreciate the value of the knowledge they already possess. Some corporations have created explicit knowledge management programs for protecting and distributing knowledge resources that they have identified and for discovering new sources of knowledge. These programs are often headed by a **chief knowledge officer (CKO)**. The chief knowledge officer is a senior executive who is responsible for the firm's knowledge management program. The CKO helps design programs and systems to find new sources of knowledge or to make better use of existing knowledge in organizational and management processes (Earl and Scott, 1999).

SYSTEMS AND INFRASTRUCTURE FOR KNOWLEDGE MANAGEMENT

All the major types of information systems described in this text facilitate the flow of information and the management of a firm's knowledge. Earlier chapters have described systems that help firms understand and respond to their environments more effectively, notably enterprise systems, external and internal networks, databases, datamining, and communication-based applications. The concept of a "digital firm" refers to a firm with substantial use of information technology to enhance its ability to sense and respond to its environment.

While all the information systems we have described help an organization sense and respond to its environment, some technologies uniquely and directly address organizational learning and management tasks. Office systems, knowledge work systems (KWS), group collaboration systems, and artificial intelligence applications are especially useful for knowledge management because they focus on supporting information and knowledge work and on defining and capturing the organization's knowledge base. The knowledge base may include (1) structured internal knowledge (explicit knowledge) such as product manuals or research reports; (2) external knowledge of competitors, products, and markets, including competitive intelligence; and (3) informal internal knowledge, often called **tacit knowledge**, which resides in the minds of individual employees but has not been documented in structured form (Davenport, DeLong, and Beers, 1998).

Information systems can promote organizational learning by capturing, codifying, and distributing both explicit and tacit knowledge. Once information has been collected and organized in a system, it can be reused many times. Companies can use information systems to codify their best practices and make knowledge of these practices more widely available to employees. **Best practices** are the most successful solutions or problem-solving methods that have been developed by a specific organization or industry. In addition to improving existing work practices, knowledge can be preserved as organizational memory to train future employees or to help them with decision making. **Organizational memory** is the stored learning from an organization's history that can be used for decision making and other purposes. Information systems can also provide networks for linking people so that individuals with special areas of expertise can be easily identified and tacit knowledge can be shared.

Figure 15-1 illustrates the information systems and information technology (IT) infrastructure for supporting knowledge management. Office systems help disseminate and coordinate the flow of information in the organization. Knowledge work systems (KWS) support the activities of highly skilled knowledge workers and professionals as they create new knowledge and try to integrate it into the firm. Group collaboration and support systems support the creation and sharing of knowledge among people working in groups. Artificial intelligence systems capture new knowledge and provide organizations and managers with codified knowledge that can be reused by others in the organization. These systems require an information technology (IT) infrastructure that makes heavy use of powerful processors, networks, databases, and Internet tools.

KNOWLEDGE WORK AND PRODUCTIVITY

In information economies, organizational productivity depends on increasing the productivity of information and knowledge workers. Consequently, companies have made massive investments in technology to support information work. Information technology now

---

chief knowledge officer (CKO)
A senior executive in charge of the organization's knowledge management program.

tacit knowledge
Expertise and experience of organizational members that has not been formally documented.

best practices
The most successful solutions or problem-solving methods that have been developed by a specific organization or industry.

organizational memory
The stored learning from an organization's history that can be used for decision making and other purposes.

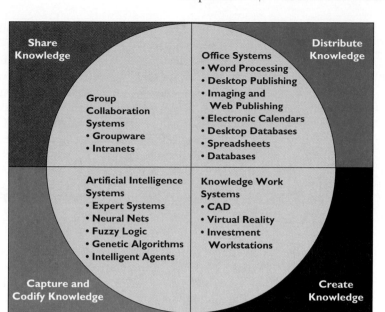

FIGURE 15-1 Knowledge management requires an information technology infrastructure that facilitates collection and sharing of knowledge as well as software for distributing information and making it more meaningful. The information systems illustrated here give support to information workers at many levels in the organization.

accounts for over 40 percent of total business expenditures on capital equipment in North American. Much of that information technology investment has poured into offices and the service sector.

Although information technology has increased productivity in manufacturing, especially the manufacture of information technology products, the extent to which computers have enhanced the productivity of information workers remains under debate. Some studies show that investment in information technology has not led to any appreciable growth in productivity among office workers. Corporate downsizings and cost-reduction measures have increased worker efficiency but have not yet led to sustained enhancements signifying genuine productivity gains (Roach, 2000, 1996, and 1988). Cell phones, home fax machines, laptop computers, and information appliances allow highly paid knowledge workers to get more work done by working longer hours and bringing their work home, but they are not necessarily getting more work done in a specified unit of time. Other studies suggest that information technology investments are starting to generate a productivity payback. Brynjolfsson and Hitt's studies of firms investing in information systems have found that firms that invest more in information technology have greater productivity improvements, and that their productivity continues to improve over time (Brynjolfsson and Hitt, 1999 and 1993). Productivity growth has been higher during the past decade than during the 1980s, when white-collar productivity only rose 0.28 percent each year. The debate centers on whether these gains are short term or represent fundamental changes in service-sector productivity that can be attributed to computers.

Productivity changes among information workers are difficult to measure because of the problems of identifying suitable units of output for information work (Panko, 1991). How does one measure the output of a law office? Should one measure productivity by examining the number of forms completed per employee (a measure of physical unit productivity) or by examining the amount of revenue produced per employee (a measure of financial unit productivity) in an information- and knowledge-intense industry? How does one track gains from investments resulting from changes in management, business processes, or increased employee training (Strassmann, 1999)? In addition, different types of organizations derive different levels of productivity benefit from information technology (Brynjolfsson and Hitt, 1998).

In addition to reducing costs, computers may increase the quality of products and services for consumers. These intangible benefits are difficult to measure and consequently are not addressed by conventional productivity measures. Moreover, because of competition, the value created by computers may primarily flow to customers rather than to the company making the investments (Brynjolfsson, 1996). Scholars are now looking at other ways to measure productivity from computers, including increases in corporate profits.

Introduction of information technology does not automatically guarantee productivity. Desktop computers, e-mail, and fax applications can actually generate more drafts, memos, spreadsheets, and messages—increasing bureaucratic red tape and paperwork. Firms are more likely to produce high returns on information technology investments if they rethink their procedures, processes, and business goals.

15.2 INFORMATION AND KNOWLEDGE WORK SYSTEMS

information work

Work that primarily consists of creating or processing information.

data workers

People such as secretaries or bookkeepers who process and disseminate the organization's information and paperwork.

knowledge workers

People such as engineers, scientists, or architects who design products or services or create knowledge for the organization.

Information work is work that consists primarily of creating or processing information. It is carried out by information workers who usually are divided into two subcategories: **data workers**, who primarily process and disseminate information; and **knowledge workers**, who primarily create knowledge and information.

Examples of data workers include secretaries, sales personnel, accountants, and draftspeople. Researchers, designers, architects, writers, and judges are examples of knowledge workers. Data workers usually can be distinguished from knowledge workers because knowledge workers usually have higher levels of education and memberships in professional organizations. In addition, knowledge workers exercise independent judgment as a routine aspect of their work. Data and knowledge workers have different information requirements and different systems to support them.

DISTRIBUTING KNOWLEDGE: OFFICE AND DOCUMENT MANAGEMENT SYSTEMS

Most data work and a great deal of knowledge work takes place in offices, including most of the work done by managers. The office plays a major role in coordinating the flow of information throughout the entire organization. The office has three basic functions:

▌ Managing and coordinating the work of data and knowledge workers

▌ Connecting the work of local information workers with all levels and functions of the organization

▌ Connecting the organization to the external world, including customers, suppliers, government regulators, and external auditors

Office workers span a very broad range: professionals, managers, sales, and clerical workers working alone or in groups. Their major activities include the following:

▌ Managing documents, including document creation, storage, retrieval, and dissemination

▌ Scheduling for individuals and groups

▌ Communicating, including initiating, receiving, and managing voice, digital, and document-based communications for individuals and groups

▌ Managing data, such as data about employees, customers, and vendors

office systems

Computer systems, such as word processing, voice mail, and imaging, that are designed to increase the productivity of information workers in the office.

These activities can be supported by office systems (see Table 15-1). **Office systems** are any application of information technology that intends to increase productivity of information workers in the office. Fifteen years ago, office automation meant only the creation, processing, and management of documents. Today professional knowledge and information work remains highly document-centred. However, digital image processing—words and documents—is also at the core of systems as are high-speed digital communications services. Because office work involves many people jointly engaged in projects, contemporary office automation systems have powerful group assistance tools like networked digital calendars. An ideal office environment would be based on a seamless network of digital machines linking professional, clerical, and managerial work groups and running a variety of types of software.

TABLE 15-1 TYPICAL OFFICE SYSTEMS

Office Activity	Technology
Managing documents	Word processing, desktop publishing, document imaging, Web publishing, workflow management systems
Scheduling	Electronic calendars, groupware, intranets
Communicating	E-mail, voice mail, digital answering systems, groupware, intranets
Managing data	Desktop databases, spreadsheets, user-friendly interfaces to mainframe databases

Although word processing and desktop publishing address the creation and presentation of documents, they only exacerbate the existing paper avalanche problem. Workflow problems arising from paper handling are enormous. It has been estimated that up to 85 percent of corporate information is stored on paper. Locating and updating information in that format is a great source of organizational inefficiency.

One way to reduce problems stemming from paper workflow is to employ document imaging systems. **Document imaging systems** are systems that convert documents and images into digital form so they can be stored and accessed on a computer. These systems store, retrieve, and manipulate a digitized image of a document, allowing the document itself to be discarded. The system must contain a scanner that converts the document image into a bit-mapped image, storing that image as a graphic. If the document is not in active use, it is usually stored on an optical disk system. Optical disks, kept online in a **jukebox** (a device for storing and retrieving many optical disks), require up to a minute to retrieve the document automatically.

An imaging system also requires indexes that will allow users to identify and retrieve a document when needed. Index data are entered so that a document can be retrieved in a variety of ways, depending upon the application. For example, the index may contain the document scan date, the customer name and number, the document type, and some type of subject information. Finally, the system must include retrieval equipment, primarily workstations capable of handling graphics and printers. Figure 15-2 illustrates the components of a typical imaging system.

Traditional document-management systems can be expensive, requiring proprietary client/server networks, special client software, and storage capabilities. Intranets provide a low-cost and universally available platform for basic document publishing, and many companies use them for this purpose. Employees can publish information using Web-authoring tools and post the information to an intranet Web server where it can be shared and accessed throughout the company with standard Web browsers. These Web files can be multimedia objects combining text, graphics, audio, and video along with hyperlinks. After a document has been posted to the server, it can be indexed for quicker access and linked to other documents (see Figure 15-3).

document imaging systems
Systems that convert documents and images into digital form so they can be stored and accessed on a computer.

jukebox
A device for storing and retrieving many optical disks.

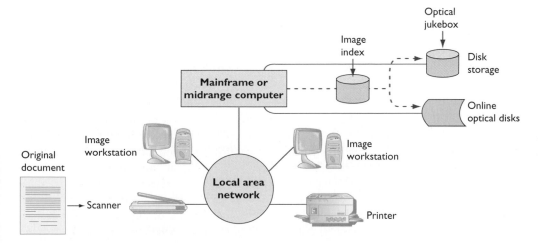

FIGURE 15-2 Components of an imaging system. A typical imaging system stores and processes digitized images of documents, using scanners, an optical disk system, an index server, workstations, and printers. A midrange or small mainframe computer may be required to control the activities of a large imaging system.

FIGURE 15-3 Web publishing and document management. An author can post information on an intranet Web server where it can be accessed through a variety of mechanisms.

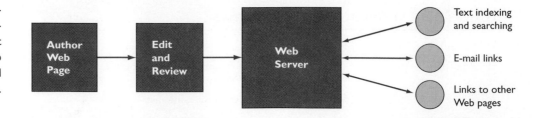

For more sophisticated document-management functions, such as controlling changes to documents, maintaining histories of activity and changes in the managed documents, and the ability to search documents using either content or index terms, commercial Web-based systems such as those from SNS/Assure, a BCE Emergis subsidiary, IntraNet Solutions, or Open Text are available. Vendors such as Toronto's Hummingbird or California-based FileNet and Documentum have enhanced their traditional document-management systems with Web capabilities.

To achieve the large productivity gains promised by imaging technology, organizations must redesign their workflow. In the past, the existence of only one copy of a document largely shaped workflow. Work had to be performed serially; two people could not work on the same document at the same time. Significant staff time was devoted to filing and retrieving documents. After a document has been stored electronically, workflow management can change the traditional methods of working with documents (see Chapter 11).

CREATING KNOWLEDGE: KNOWLEDGE WORK SYSTEMS

Knowledge work is that portion of information work that creates new knowledge and information. For example, knowledge workers create new products or find ways to improve existing ones. Knowledge work is segmented into many highly specialized fields, and each field has a different collection of **knowledge work systems (KWS)** that are specialized to support workers in that field. Knowledge workers perform three key roles that are critical to the organization and to the managers who work within the organization:

knowledge work systems (KWS)

Information systems that aid knowledge workers in the creation and integration of new knowledge in the organization.

environmental scanning

Keeping an organization up to date on knowledge as it develops in the external environment.

▌ Keeping the organization up to date in knowledge as it develops in the external environment; this is known as **environmental scanning**

▌ Serving as internal consultants regarding the areas of their knowledge, changes taking place, and potential opportunities

▌ Acting as change agents by evaluating, initiating, and promoting change projects

Knowledge workers and data workers have somewhat different information systems support needs. Most knowledge workers rely on office automation systems such as word processors, voice mail, and calendars, but they also require more specialized knowledge work systems. Knowledge work systems are specifically designed to promote the creation of knowledge and to ensure that new knowledge and technical expertise are properly integrated into the business.

Requirements of Knowledge Work Systems

Knowledge work systems have characteristics that reflect the special needs of knowledge workers. First, knowledge work systems must give knowledge workers the specialized tools they need, such as powerful graphics, analytical tools, and communications and document-management tools. These systems may require significant computing power to rapidly handle the sophisticated graphics or complex calculations necessary to knowledge workers such as scientific researchers, product designers, and financial analysts. Because knowledge workers are so focused on knowledge in the external environment, these systems also must give the worker quick and easy access to external databases.

A user-friendly interface is very important to a knowledge worker's system. User-friendly interfaces save time by allowing the user to perform needed tasks and access required information without having to spend a lot of time learning how to use the computer. Saving time is more important for knowledge workers than for most other employees because knowledge

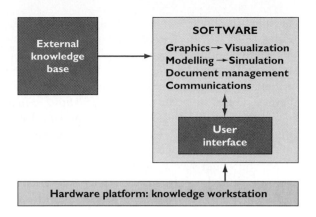

FIGURE 15-4 Requirements of knowledge work systems. Knowledge work systems require strong links to external knowledge bases in addition to specialized hardware and software.

workers are highly paid—wasting a knowledge worker's time is simply too expensive. Figure 15-4 summarizes the requirements of knowledge work systems.

Knowledge workstations often are designed and optimized for the specific tasks to be performed, so a design engineer will require a different workstation than a lawyer. Design engineers need graphics workstations with enough power to handle 3-D computer-aided design (CAD) systems. However, financial analysts are more interested in having access to myriad external databases and optical disk technology so they can access massive amounts of financial data very quickly.

Examples of Knowledge Work Systems

Major knowledge work applications include computer-aided design (CAD) systems, virtual reality systems for simulation and modelling, and financial workstations. **Computer-aided design (CAD)** automates the creation and revision of designs, using computers and sophisticated graphics software. With a traditional physical design methodology, each design modification requires a mould to be made and a prototype to be physically tested. That process must be repeated many times, which is a very expensive and time-consuming process. Using a CAD workstation, the designer only needs to make a physical prototype toward the end of the design process because the design can be easily tested and changed on the computer. The ability of CAD software to provide design specifications for the tooling and manufacturing processes saves a great deal of time and money while producing a manufacturing process with far fewer problems. For example, Stik AB of Stockholm, Sweden, is an engineering consultancy that specialized in custom mechanical product design. Stik's industrial designers use Canada's IronCAD software to maximize their design productivity. Using IronCAD, Stik's designers can "drag-and-drop." If they want to move a surface, they just drag its handle; if they want to add a new part to their design, they just drag it in from a catalogue. The designers

computer-aided design (CAD)
An information system that automates the creation and revision of designs using sophisticated graphics software.

A group of DaimlerChrysler engineers examines a new automobile design using a computer-aided design (CAD) tool. CAD systems improve the quality and precision of product design by performing much of the design and testing work on the computer.

can share their designs with non-engineers, who can then visualize what the product will actually look like. Additional detail on CAD systems can be found in Chapter 11.

virtual reality systems
Interactive graphics software and hardware that create computer-generated simulations that provide sensations that emulate real-world activities.

Virtual reality systems have visualization, rendering, and simulation capabilities that go far beyond those of conventional CAD systems. They use interactive graphics software to create computer-generated simulations that are so close to reality that users almost believe they are participating in a real-world situation. In many virtual reality systems, the user dons special clothing, headgear, or other equipment, depending on the application. The clothing contains sensors that record the user's movements and immediately transmit that information back to the computer. For instance, to walk through a virtual reality simulation of a house, you would need attire that monitors the movement of your feet, hands, and head. You also would need goggles that contain video screens and sometimes audio attachments and sensory gloves so that you can be immersed in the computer feedback.

Virtual reality is just starting to provide benefits in educational, scientific, and business work. For example, The Rehabilitation Sciences Virtual Reality (RSVR) Lab at the University of Ottawa (www.health.uottawa.ca/vrlab/home.htm) conducts applied research to develop new technology for individuals with disabilities. The RSVR Lab is currently researching and developing a virtual reality tool to help develop spatial abilities in children as well as programs for the promotion of disability awareness and children's pedestrian safety. In Japan, researchers have developed a "two force" display and applied it to a surgical simulator so that they can feel the resistance offered by virtual skin.

In New York City, Michael Kwartler, director of the Environmental Simulation Centre, built a three-dimensional model of a SoHo neighbourhood in lower Manhattan for a developer seeking to build a hotel in that location. Kwartler's group won community support for the project by allowing neighbourhood residents to work with the model and fly around to look at things from different angles. Surgeons at Boston's Brigham and Women's Hospital are using a virtual reality system in which a 3-D representation of the brain using CT and MRI scans is superimposed on live video. With this version of X-ray vision, surgeons can pinpoint the location of a tumour in the brain with 0.5-millimetre accuracy.

Virtual Reality Modelling Language (VRML)
A set of specifications for interactive, 3-D modelling on the World Wide Web.

Virtual reality applications are being developed for the Web using a standard called **Virtual Reality Modelling Language (VRML)**. VRML is a set of specifications for interactive, 3-D modelling on the World Wide Web that can organize multiple media types, including animation, images, and audio, to put users in a simulated real-world environment. VRML is platform-independent, operates over a desktop computer, and requires little bandwidth. Users can download a 3-D virtual world designed using VRML from a server over the Internet using their Web browser. (Recent versions of Netscape Navigator and Microsoft Internet Explorer are VRML compliant.)

DuPont, the Wilmington, Delaware, chemical company, created a VRML application called HyperPlant, which allows users to access 3-D data over the Internet with Web browsers. Engineers can go through 3-D models as if they were physically walking through a plant, viewing objects at eye level. This level of detail reduces the number of mistakes they make during construction of oilrigs, oil plants, and other structures.

The Sharper Image provides a 3D Enhanced Catalogue for Web site visitors with high-speed Internet connections and powerful processors that provides images of products in three dimensions. Visitors can rotate digitized images of many products so that they can examine them from any angle. The user can zoom in to see specific details and manipulate the object to see how the lid opens or how it folds for storage. Finally, most car manufacturers use virtual reality to depict their current models while most Canadian realtors are now offering virtual reality tours of their listings.

investment workstation
A powerful desktop computer for financial specialists, optimized to access and manipulate massive amounts of financial data.

The financial industry is using specialized **investment workstations** to leverage the knowledge and time of its brokers, traders, and portfolio managers. Firms such as TD Waterhouse and BMO Nesbitt Burns have installed investment workstations that integrate a wide range of data from both internal and external sources, including contact management data, real-time and historical market data, and research reports. Previously, financial professionals had to spend considerable time accessing data from separate systems and piecing together the information they needed. By providing one-stop information faster and with fewer errors, the workstations streamline the entire investment process from stock selection to updating client records.

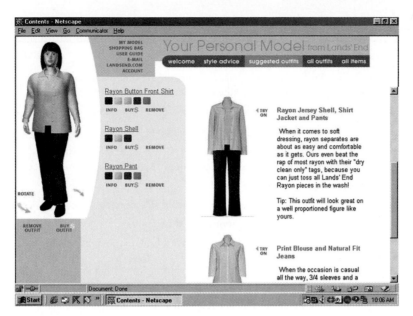

FIGURE 15-5 Women can create a VRML "personal model" that approximates their physical proportions to help them visualize how they will look in clothing sold at the Lands' End Web site. The digitized image can be rotated to show how the outfits will look from all angles and users can click to change the outfit's colour.

Table 15-2 summarizes the major types of knowledge work systems. Figure 15-5 shows Lands' End's Website and VRML personal model.

SHARING KNOWLEDGE: GROUP COLLABORATION SYSTEMS AND ENTERPRISE KNOWLEDGE ENVIRONMENTS

Although many knowledge and information work applications have been designed for individuals working alone, organizations have an increasing need to support people working in groups. Chapters 6, 8, and 10 introduced key technologies that can be used for group coordination and collaboration: e-mail, teleconferencing, dataconferencing, videoconferencing, groupware, and intranets. Groupware and intranets are especially valuable for this purpose.

Groupware

Until recently, **groupware** (which we introduced in Chapter 7) was the primary tool for creating collaborative work environments. Groupware is built around three key principles: communication, collaboration, and coordination. It allows groups to work together on documents, schedule meetings, route electronic forms, access shared folders and files, develop shared databases, and send e-mail. Table 15-3 lists the capabilities of major commercial groupware products that make them such powerful platforms for capturing information and experiences, coordinating common tasks, and distributing work through time and place. Information-intensive companies such as consulting firms, law firms, and financial management companies have found groupware an especially powerful tool for leveraging their knowledge assets.

groupware
Software that supports groups by providing functions and services that support the collaborative activities of work groups.

TABLE 15-2	EXAMPLES OF KNOWLEDGE WORK SYSTEMS
Knowledge Work System	**Function in Organization**
CAD/CAM (computer-aided design/ computer-aided manufacturing)	Provides engineers, designers, and factory managers with precise control over industrial design and manufacturing
Virtual reality systems	Provide designers, architects, engineers, and medical workers with precise, photo-realistic simulations of objects
Investment workstations	High-end PCs used in financial sector to analyze trading situations instantaneously and facilitate portfolio management

TABLE 15-3   **Knowledge Management Capabilities of Groupware**

Capability	Description
Publishing	Posting documents as well as simultaneous work on the same document by multiple users along with a mechanism to track changes to these documents
Replication	Maintaining and updating identical data on multiple PCs and servers
Discussion tracking	Organizing discussions by many users on different topics
Document management	Storing information from various types of software in a database
Workflow management	Moving and tracking documents created by groups
Security	Preventing unauthorized access to data
Portability	Availability of the software for mobile use (to access the corporate network from the road)
Application development	Developing custom software applications with the software
Scheduling	Ability to schedule resources (meeting participants, facilities, equipment) at a time when all needed resources are available

Intranets and Enterprise Knowledge Environments

Chapters 4 and 10 described how some organizations are using intranets and Internet technologies for group collaboration, including e-mail, discussion groups, and multimedia Web documents. Some of these intranets provide the foundation for enterprise knowledge environments in which information from a variety of sources and media, including text, sound, video, and even digital slides, can be shared, displayed, and accessed across an enterprise through a simple common interface. Examples of enterprise knowledge environments can be found in Table 15-4. These comprehensive intranets can transform decades-old processes, allowing people to disseminate information, share best practices, communicate, conduct research, and collaborate in ways that were never before possible.

enterprise information portal
An application that enables companies to provide users with a single gateway to internal and external sources of information.

Enterprise knowledge environments are so rich and vast that many organizations have built specialized corporate portals to help individuals navigate through various knowledge resources. These **enterprise information portals**, also known as *enterprise knowledge portals*, direct individuals to digital knowledge objects and information systems applications, helping them make sense of the volume of information that is available and also showing how organizational knowledge resources are interconnected. Figure 15-6 illustrates what an enterprise information portal might look like. It might include access to external sources of information such as news feeds and research as well as internal knowledge resources and capabilities for e-mail, chat, discussion groups, and videoconferencing. Software tools are available to build and personalize these portals. For example, Autonomy provides a tool that can analyze documents, Web pages, or e-mail to identify and rank the main ideas, categorize information by subject matter, insert hypertext links to related material, deliver information to users based

TABLE 15-4   **Examples of Enterprise Knowledge Environments**

Organization	Knowledge Management Capabilities
Royal Bank of Canada	EWISe, a knowledge management application, offers this large, diversified Canadian bank collaboration, document management, expertise management, workflow, and knowledge validation in a single integrated environment. Processes are streamlined, and the database is a trusted repository of the best in class financial knowledge. The work flows to the right experts leading to better efficiency.
College Pro Painters	Digital Dashboard consolidates individual, team, corporate, and external information with single-click access to analytical and collaborative tools, permitting the company to communicate more effectively with its franchisees—providing them with the integrated online sales, training, and administrative support they need.
Microsoft Canada	Canadaweb, Microsoft Canada's redesigned intranet, is the first place 400 employees go to source up-to-date company information—from expense reports and health benefits to corporate data and organizational charts. Project groups can revise or add comments to documents and post content to the intranet quickly and easily.

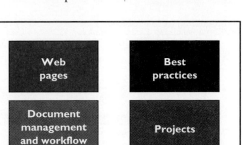

E-mail	Web pages	Best practices
Chat and conferencing	Document management and workflow	Projects
Groupware	Databases and data warehouse	Research and reference
Search tools and directories	Enterprise applications	News feeds

FIGURE 15-6 An enterprise information portal. The portal provides a single point of access to the firm's knowledge resources; it helps the firm coordinate information and people to make decisions and take action.

on the ideas in the text they read or write, and deliver information of interest to them. For example, Ericsson, the Swedish manufacturer of digital phones and data communications solutions, uses Autonomy to automatically aggregate, personalize, and deliver Internet news feeds, intranet pages, internal office documents, and company e-mail to its corporate intranet portal and users' mobile phones and handheld devices.

The collaborative and knowledge-sharing features of intranets, combined with their low cost, have made them attractive alternatives to proprietary groupware for collaborative work, especially among small- and medium-sized businesses. For simple tasks such as sharing documents or document publishing, an intranet generally is less expensive to build and maintain than applications based on commercial groupware products that require proprietary software and client/server networks.

For applications requiring extensive coordination and management, groupware software has important capabilities that intranets cannot yet provide. Groupware is more flexible when documents must be changed, updated, or edited on the fly. It can track revisions to a document as it moves through a collaborative editing process. Internal groupware-based networks are more secure than intranets. Web sites are more likely to crash or to have their servers overloaded when there are many requests for data. High-end groupware software such as Lotus Notes or Open Text's Livelink is thus more appropriate for applications requiring production and publication of documents by many authors, frequent updating and document tracking, and high security and replication. Lotus Notes and other groupware products have been enhanced so they can be integrated with the Internet or private intranets. Open Text is a Canadian company based in Waterloo, Ontario.

Intranet technology works best as a central repository with a small number of authors and relatively static information that does not require frequent updating, although intranet tools for group collaboration are improving. Netscape and Microsoft bundle their Web browsers with messaging and collaboration tools, including e-mail, newsgroup discussions, a group scheduling and calendaring tool, and point-to-point conferencing.

Commercial software tools called teamware make intranets more useful for working in teams. **Teamware** consists of intranet-based applications for building a work team, sharing ideas and documents, brainstorming, scheduling, tracking the status of tasks and projects, and archiving decisions made or rejected by project team members for future use. Teamware is similar to groupware but does not offer the powerful application development capabilities provided by sophisticated groupware products. However, it lets companies easily implement collaboration applications that can be accessed using a Web browser. eRoom Technology's eRoom (see Figure 15-7), Thoroughstar's QuickTeam, and Lotus Quickplace are examples of commercial teamware products.

The Window on Organizations shows how companies are using collaborative development tools in the design of new products.

teamware
Group collaboration software that is customized for teamwork.

FIGURE 15-7 eRoom is a secure, Web-based workplace and complete set of business collaboration tools that can be quickly tailored for specific business initiatives and easily installed. Companies can use the eRoom solution to enable distributed work teams to work closely and creatively to plan, collaborate, strategize, and make decisions across the extended enterprise.

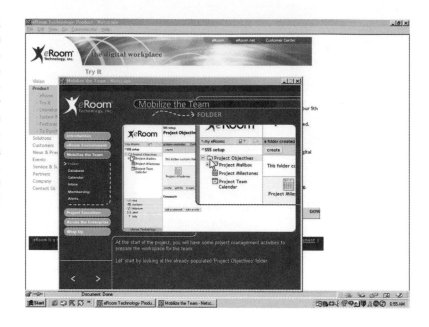

VIRTUAL COLLABORATION ON THE INTERNET

Imagine this scenario: A manufacturing manager in Edmonton looks at the model of a product under development on his computer screen at the same time a supplier in St. John's is reviewing the same model online. Meanwhile, engineers in Europe are making changes to the model by rotating the model and changing its shape. The supplier sees gaps in the design and informs the rest of the group what changes need to be made. All of these steps in the design process are occurring simultaneously. It sounds revolutionary, but the revolution is already here. More and more companies and their business partners are engaging in collaborative product development.

Firms can use Internet technology and new design and project management tools to share design data at all phases of the product life cycle with their design, sales, and manufacturing groups and also with their external suppliers and subcontractors. Immediate access to product data can help these groups plan resources and respond more quickly to customer expectations, saving both money and time.

The top 200 officers of Trans Canadian Pipe Lines, an $8 billion energy company, used Caucus collaboration software to support a comprehensive scenario planning process. Previously, business scenarios were developed by a small group working in isolation from the company as a whole. This time, critical issues were vetted by people with the experience and access to information necessary to develop effective strategies. While working on the future scenarios, the participants also discovered the value of bringing together cross-sections of the company to work on emerging problems. When a pipeline ruptured, the company used Caucus to support crisis management and co-ordinate communications.

Tight management of the product development process is essential at Seagate Technology, a leading manufacturer of data storage devices, which was acquired by Veritas Software Corporation and a group of private investors. Seagate releases 3000 new design documents each month. The company used to maintain these documents in paper form, storing them in filing cabinets where they might be difficult to locate. If an individual in another location needed to see the document, it had to be located in the file cabinet and then faxed. According to Doug Speidel, director of Seagate's engineering information systems, when companies store their documents on microfilm or paper, "your intellectual knowledge just collects dust." Seagate now uses IQXpert's product data management software and its own collaborative Web tools to store, secure, and organize design data from around the world. These systems ensure that Seagate's product data are accurate and consistent and allow Seagate to track and control changes to these data. Employees in design, purchasing, and field service access the system an average of 10 000 times per month. Seagate has also opened the product design and change process to its largest customers, such as PC manufacturers, that use Seagate disk and tape drives inside their products. Figure 15-8 illustrates how Seagate's business processes at these two companies changed as a result of this system.

To Think About: It has been said that collaborative development is "truly an electronic revolution." Do you agree? Why or why not? How did using collaborative development technologies change the way the companies described here conduct their business?

Sources: Alorie Gilbert, "Online Collaboration Tools Help Simplify Product Design," *Information Week,* April 24, 2000; Paul Kandarian, "All Together Now," *CIO Magazine,* September 1, 2000; and "Scenario Planning: Trans Canadian Pipe Lines," www.caucus.com/ourclients.html, accessed July 22, 2001.

BEFORE

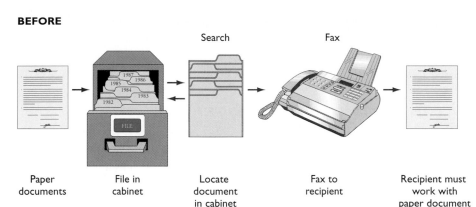

Search · Fax

| Paper documents | File in cabinet | Locate document in cabinet | Fax to recipient | Recipient must work with paper document |

FIGURE 15-8 Changes in Seagate's product development process. Seagate Technology replaced its multi-step paper-based process for product design and change with a much simpler process, using product data management softwre and collaborative Web tools.

AFTER

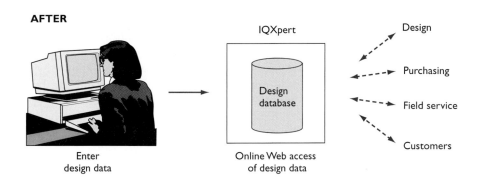

IQXpert

Design database

Design · Purchasing · Field service · Customers

Enter design data · Online Web access of design data

Group collaboration technologies alone cannot promote information sharing if team members do not feel it is in their interest to share, especially in organizations that encourage competition among employees. Collaboration technology can best enhance the work of a group if the applications are properly designed to fit the organization's needs and work practices and if management encourages a collaborative atmosphere (Alavi, 1999).

MANAGEMENT DECISION PROBLEM

MEASURING PRODUCTIVITY FROM A KNOWLEDGE INTRANET

You head a growing electronic commerce consulting company with over 150 employees in an expanding but fiercely competitive field. You need to recruit many junior consultants every year to replace employees who have left the firm and to fill new positions. In the past, your firm trained new employees by first sending them to a one-month training program. After completing the program, they could work full-time on projects. This process has proved to be very expensive and a drain on company resources. Junior consultants cannot work on any projects to generate client billings for the firm until they have finished the training program. In January 2001 your firm installed an intranet that provides the following:

❚ An online training class in company practices and methods
❚ A repository of "best practices" model proposals with search capabilities
❚ A directory of employees, the projects they have worked on, and their special expertise

You have started to compile a table showing training time and costs before and after installing the intranet. Training time goes down as the company gains experience using the intranet.

	2001	2002	2003
Time to train a new consultant	20 days	14 days	12 days
Daily training cost per consultant	$2000	$1400	$1000
Additional billings per consultant	0		

1. If your intranet trains new consultants more quickly and each trained consultant can start billing clients $1700 per day for work on projects, how much should this new intranet increase revenue from client billings generated by newly trained consultants in 2002 and 2003? Your firm hires and trains an average of 40 new consultants each year.

2. Using only these metrics, how much knowledge worker productivity has your intranet created since the intranet was installed?

3. What other capabilities would you add to the intranet to make your consultants even more productive? How could you measure productivity increases from these capabilities?

15.3 ARTIFICIAL INTELLIGENCE

Organizations are using artificial intelligence technology to capture individual and collective knowledge and to codify and extend their knowledge base. How can this be done?

WHAT IS ARTIFICIAL INTELLIGENCE?

artificial intelligence (AI)
The effort to develop computer-based systems that can behave like humans, with the ability to learn languages, accomplish physical tasks, use a perceptual apparatus, and emulate human expertise and decision making.

Artificial intelligence (AI) is the effort to develop computer-based systems (both hardware and software) that behave as humans do. AI systems can learn natural languages, accomplish coordinated physical tasks (robotics), use a perceptual apparatus that informs their physical behaviour and language (visual and oral perception systems), and emulate human expertise and decision making (expert systems). AI systems also exhibit logic, reasoning, intuition, and the just-plain-common-sense qualities that we associate with human beings. Finally, AI systems can find patterns in mountains of data beyond the reach of human analytic capabilities (neural networks). Figure 15-9 illustrates the elements of the artificial intelligence family. Another important element is intelligent machines, the physical hardware that performs these tasks.

Successful artificial intelligence systems are based on human expertise, knowledge, and selected reasoning patterns, but they do not exhibit the intelligence of human beings. Existing artificial intelligence systems do not come up with new and novel solutions to problems. Existing systems extend the powers of experts but in no way substitute for them or capture very much of their intelligence. Briefly, existing systems lack the common sense and generality of naturally intelligent human beings.

Human intelligence is vastly complex and much broader than computer intelligence. A key factor that distinguishes human beings from other animals is our ability to develop associations and to use metaphors and analogies such as *like* and *as*. Using metaphor and analogy, humans create new rules, apply old rules to new situations, and at times act intuitively and/or instinctively without rules. Much of what we call common sense or generality in humans resides in the ability to create metaphor and analogy.

Human intelligence also includes a unique ability to impose a conceptual apparatus on the surrounding world. Meta-concepts such as cause-and-effect and time, and concepts of a lower order such as breakfast, dinner, and lunch, are all imposed by human beings on the world around them. Thinking in terms of these concepts and acting on them are central characteristics of intelligent human behaviour.

WHY BUSINESS IS INTERESTED IN ARTIFICIAL INTELLIGENCE

Although artificial intelligence applications are much more limited than human intelligence, they are of great interest to business for the following reasons:

▌ To store information in an active form as organizational memory, creating an organizational knowledge base that many employees can examine and preserving expertise that might be lost when an acknowledged expert leave the firm.

▌ To create a mechanism that is not subject to human feelings such as fatigue and worry. This may be especially useful when jobs may be environmentally, physically, or mentally dangerous to humans. These systems also may be useful advisors in times of crisis.

▌ To eliminate routine and unsatisfying jobs held by people.

FIGURE 15-9 The artificial intelligence family. The field of AI currently includes many initiatives: natural language, robotics, perceptive systems, expert systems, intelligent machines, and neural networks.

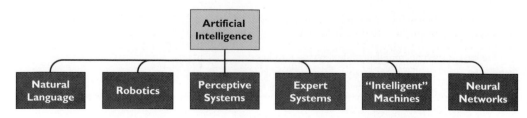

▌ To enhance the organization's knowledge base by suggesting solutions to specific problems that are too massive and complex to be analyzed by human beings in a short period of time.

CAPTURING KNOWLEDGE: EXPERT SYSTEMS

In limited areas of expertise, such as diagnosing a car's ignition system or classifying biological specimens, the rules of thumb used by real-world experts can be understood, codified, and placed in a machine. Information systems that solve problems by capturing knowledge for a very specific and limited domain of human expertise are called **expert systems**. Expert systems capture the knowledge of skilled employees in the form of a set of rules. The set of rules in the expert system adds to the memory, or stored learning of the firm. An expert system can assist decision making by asking relevant questions and explaining the reasons for adopting certain actions.

Expert systems lack the breadth of knowledge and the understanding of fundamental principles of a human expert. They are quite narrow, shallow, and brittle. They typically perform very limited tasks that can be performed by professionals in a few minutes or hours. Problems that cannot be solved by human experts in the same short period of time are far too difficult for an expert system. However, by capturing human expertise in limited areas, expert systems can provide benefits, helping organizations make high-quality decisions with fewer people.

> **expert system**
> A knowledge-intensive computer program that captures the expertise of humans in limited domains of knowledge.

How Expert Systems Work

Human knowledge must be modelled or represented in a way that a computer can process. The model of human knowledge used by expert systems is called the **knowledge base**. Two ways of representing human knowledge and expertise are rules and knowledge frames.

A standard structured programming construct (see Chapter 12) is the IF-THEN construct, in which a condition is evaluated. If the condition is true, an action is taken. For instance,

> **knowledge base**
> The model of human knowledge that is used by expert systems.

IF INCOME > $45 000 (condition)
THEN PRINT NAME AND ADDRESS (action)

A series of these rules can be a knowledge base. Any reader who has written computer programs knows that virtually all traditional computer programs contain IF-THEN statements. The difference between a traditional program and a **rule-based expert system** program is one of degree and magnitude. AI programs can easily have 200 to 10 000 rules, far more than traditional programs, which may have 50 to 100 IF-THEN statements. Moreover, in an AI program, the rules tend to be interconnected and nested to a far greater degree than in traditional programs, as shown in Figure 15-10. Hence the complexity of the rules in a rule-based expert system is considerable.

Could you represent the knowledge in the Encyclopaedia Britannica this way? Probably not, because the **rule base** would be too large, and not all the knowledge in the encyclopedia can be represented in the form of IF-THEN rules. In general, expert systems can be efficiently used only in those situations in which the domain of knowledge is highly restricted (such as in granting credit) and involves no more than a few thousand rules.

Knowledge frames can be used to represent knowledge by organizing information into chunks of interrelated characteristics. The relationships are based on shared characteristics rather than a hierarchy. This approach is grounded in the belief that humans use frames, or concepts, to make rapid sense out of perceptions. For instance, when a person is told, "Look for a tank, and shoot when you see one," experts believe that humans invoke a concept, or frame, of what a tank should look like. Anything that does not fit the concept of a tank is ignored. In a similar fashion, AI researchers can organize a vast array of information into frames. The computer is then instructed to search the database of frames and list connections to other frames of interest. The user can follow the pathways pointed to by the system.

Figure 15-11 shows a part of a knowledge base organized by frames. A "CAR" is defined by characteristics or slots in a frame as a vehicle, with four wheels, a gas or diesel motor, and an action such as rolling or moving. This frame could be related to almost any other object in the database that shares any of these characteristics, such as the tank frame.

> **rule-based expert system**
> An AI program that has a large number of interconnected and nested IF-THEN statements, or rules, that are the basis for the knowledge in the system.
>
> **rule base**
> The collection of knowledge in an AI system that is represented in the form of IF-THEN rules.
>
> **knowledge frames**
> A method of organizing expert system knowledge into chunks; the relationships are based on shared characteristics determined by the user.

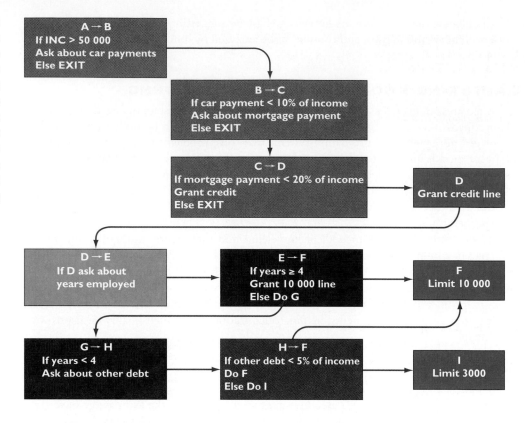

AI shell

The programming environment
of an expert system.

inference engine

The strategy used to search
through the rule base in an
expert system; can be forward
or backward chaining.

forward chaining

A strategy for searching the rule
base in an expert system that
begins with the information
entered by the user and
searches the rule base to arrive
at a conclusion.

The **AI shell** is the programming environment of an expert system. In the early years of expert systems, computer scientists used specialized artificial intelligence programming languages such as LISP or Prolog that could process lists of rules efficiently. Today a growing number of expert systems use AI shells that are user-friendly development environments. AI shells can quickly generate user-interface screens, capture the knowledge base, and manage the strategies for searching the rule base.

The strategy used to search through the rule base is called the **inference engine**. Two strategies are commonly used: forward chaining and backward chaining (see Figure 15-12).

In **forward chaining**, the inference engine begins with the information entered by the user and searches the rule base to arrive at a conclusion. The strategy is to fire, or carry out, the action of the rule when a condition is true. In Figure 15-12, beginning on the left, if the user enters a client with income greater than $100 000, the engine will fire all rules in

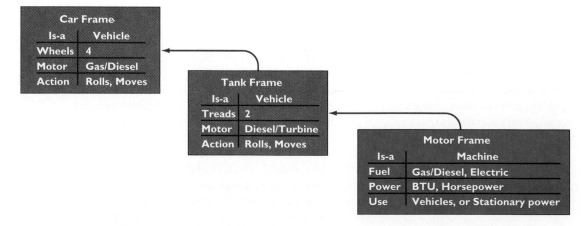

FIGURE 15-11 Knowledge and information can be organized into frames. Frames capture the relevant characteristics of the objects of interest. This approach is based on the belief that humans use "frames" or concepts to narrow the range of possibilities when scanning incoming information to make rapid sense out of perceptions.

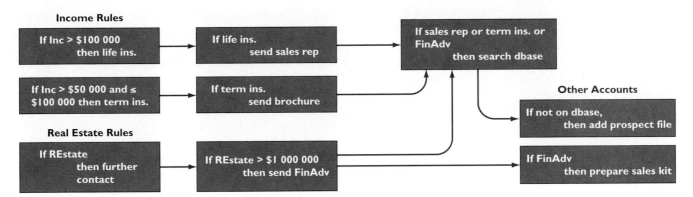

Income Rules

Real Estate Rules

Other Accounts

FIGURE 15-12 Inference engines in expert systems. An inference engine works by searching through the rules and "firing" those rules that are triggered by facts gathered and entered by the user. Basically, a collection of rules is similar to a series of nested "IF" statements in a traditional software program; however, the magnitude of the statements and degree of nesting are much greater in an expert system.

sequence from left to right. If the user then enters information indicating that the same client owns real estate, another pass of the rule base will occur and more rules will fire. Processing continues until no more rules can be fired.

In **backward chaining**, the strategy for searching the rule base starts with a hypothesis and proceeds by asking the user questions about selected facts until the hypothesis is either confirmed or disproved. In our example, in Figure 15-12, ask the question, "Should we add this person to the prospect database?" Begin on the right of the diagram and work toward the left. You can see that the person should be added to the database if a sales representative is sent, term insurance is granted, or a financial advisor visits the client.

Building an Expert System

Building an expert system is similar to building other information systems although building expert systems is an iterative process with each phase possibly requiring several iterations before a full system is developed. Typically the environment in which an expert system operates is continually changing so that the expert system must also continually change. Some expert systems, especially large ones, are so complex that in a few years the maintenance costs will equal the development costs.

An AI development team is composed of one or more experts who have a thorough command of the knowledge base and one or more knowledge engineers who can translate the knowledge (as described by the expert) into a set of rules or frames. A **knowledge engineer** is similar to a traditional systems analyst but has special expertise in eliciting information and expertise from other professionals.

The team members must select a problem appropriate for an expert system. The project team will balance potential savings from the proposed system against the cost. They will develop a prototype system to test assumptions about how to encode the knowledge of experts. Next, they will develop a full-scale system, focusing mainly on the addition of a very large number of rules. The complexity of the entire system grows with the number of rules, so the comprehensibility of the system may be threatened. Generally, the system will be pruned to achieve simplicity and power. The system is tested by a range of experts within the organization against the performance criteria established earlier. Once tested, the system will be integrated into the data flow and work patterns of the organization.

Examples of Successful Expert Systems

There is no accepted definition of a successful expert system. What is successful to an academic ("It works!") may not be successful to a corporation ("It costs a million dollars!"). The following are examples of expert systems that provide organizations with an array of benefits, including reduced errors, reduced cost, reduced training time, improved decisions, and improved quality and service.

backward chaining
A strategy for searching the rule base in an expert system that acts like a problem solver by beginning with a hypothesis and seeking out more information until the hypothesis is either proved or disproved.

knowledge engineer
A specialist who elicits information and expertise from other professionals and translates it into a set of rules or frames for an expert system.

The National Research Council of Canada has funded *Intelligent Research Group* projects, including one in collaboration with Air Canada, the Integrated Diagnostic System (IDS). IDS uses AI techniques, including knowledge bases and fuzzy logic (described below) to support companies in providing accurate diagnosis, advising optimal repair strategies, assessing equipment health, and predicting incipient failures.

Blue Cross Blue Shield of North Carolina used Aion, an AI shell, to build an automated medical underwriting system (AMUS). AMUS links to an IBM IMS hierarchical database and Blue Cross Blue Shield's in-house system for rate quoting, policy writing, and risk management. The system determines whether to underwrite applicants for health insurance after assessing their eligibility and medical risks. Underwriters can make changes to the rules as needed. This expert system enabled Blue Cross Blue Shield to reduce the time required by its small group health team to make an underwriting decision from one week to one day. The productivity gains from the system also enabled the company to eliminate or re-deploy 8 underwriters and 15 support personnel, replacing them with four underwriting processors. Since adopting AMUS, the accuracy of underwriting decisions has improved (Kay, 2000).

Countrywide Funding Corp. in Pasadena, California, is a loan-underwriting firm with about 400 underwriters in 150 offices around the country. The company developed a PC-based expert system in 1992 to make preliminary creditworthiness decisions on loan requests. The company had experienced rapid, continuing growth and wanted the system to help ensure consistent, high-quality loan decisions. CLUES (Countrywide's Loan Underwriting Expert System) has about 400 rules. Countrywide tested the system by sending every loan application handled by a human underwriter to CLUES as well. The system was refined until it agreed with the underwriter in 95 percent of the cases.

Countrywide will not rely on CLUES to reject loans because the expert system cannot be programmed to handle exceptional situations such as those involving a self-employed person or complex financial schemes. An underwriter will review all rejected loans and will make the final decision. CLUES has other benefits. Traditionally, an underwriter could handle six or seven applications a day. Using CLUES, the same underwriter can evaluate at least 16 per day. Countrywide now is using the rules in its expert system to answer e-mail inquiries from visitors to its Web site who want to know if they qualify for a loan (see Figure 15-13).

The United Nations developed an expert system to help calculate employees' salaries, taking into account numerous and complex rules for calculating entitlements such as benefits based on location of work and the employee's contract. The knowledge base for the system is online and is capable of applying entitlements automatically in payroll calculations. The system also reassesses when a change to an employee's status is approved and generates the appropriate salary for the next payroll.

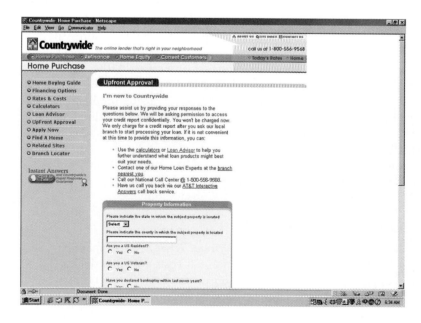

FIGURE 15-13 Countrywide Funding Corporation developed an expert system called CLUES to evaluate the creditworthiness of loan applicants. Countrywide is using the rules in this system to answer inquiries from visitors to its Web site who want to know if they can qualify for a loan.

Although expert systems lack the robust and general intelligence of human beings, they can provide benefits to organizations if their limitations are well understood. Only certain classes of problems can be solved using expert systems. Virtually all successful expert systems deal with problems of classification in which there are relatively few alternative outcomes and in which these possible outcomes are all known in advance. Many expert systems require large, lengthy, and expensive development efforts. Hiring or training more experts may be less expensive than building an expert system.

The knowledge base of expert systems is fragile and brittle; they cannot learn or change over time. In fast-moving fields such as medicine or the computer sciences, keeping the knowledge base up to date is a critical problem. For example, Digital Equipment Corporation, now part of Compaq, stopped using its XCON expert system for configuring VAX computers because its product line was constantly changing and it was too difficult to keep updating the system to capture these changes. Expert systems can only represent limited forms of knowledge. IF-THEN knowledge exists primarily in textbooks. There are no adequate representations for deep causal models or temporal trends. No expert system, for instance, can write a textbook on information systems or engage in other creative activities not explicitly foreseen by system designers. Many experts cannot express their knowledge using an IF-THEN format. Expert systems cannot yet replicate knowledge that is intuitive, based on analogy and on a sense of things.

Contrary to early promises, expert systems are most effective in automating lower level clerical functions. They can provide electronic checklists for lower level employees in service bureaucracies such as banking, insurance, sales, and welfare agencies. The applicability of expert systems to managerial problems is very limited. Managerial problems generally involve drawing facts and interpretations from divergent sources, evaluating the facts, and comparing one interpretation of the facts with another, and are not limited to simple classification. Expert systems based on the prior knowledge of a few known alternatives are unsuitable to most of the problems managers face on a daily basis

ORGANIZATIONAL INTELLIGENCE: CASE-BASED REASONING

Expert systems primarily capture the knowledge of individual experts, but organizations also have collective knowledge and expertise that they have built up over the years. This organizational knowledge can be captured and stored using case-based reasoning. In **case-based reasoning (CBR)**, descriptions of past experiences of human specialists, represented as cases, are stored in a database for later retrieval when the user encounters a new case with similar parameters. The system searches for stored cases with problem characteristics similar to the new one, finds the closest fit, and applies the solutions of the old case to the new case. Successful solutions are tagged to the new case, and both are stored together with the other cases in the knowledge base. Unsuccessful solutions also are appended to the case database along with explanations as to why the solutions did not work (see Figure 15-14).

Expert systems work by applying a set of IF-THEN-ELSE rules against a knowledge base, both of which are extracted from human experts. Case-based reasoning, in contrast, represents knowledge as a series of cases, and the case knowledge base is continually expanded and refined by users.

For example, Compaq Computer of Houston, Texas, operates in a highly competitive, customer service-oriented business environment and is daily flooded with customer phone calls crying for help. Keeping those customers satisfied requires Compaq to spend millions of dollars annually to maintain large, technically skilled, customer support staffs. When customers call with problems, they must describe the problems to the customer service staff and then wait on hold while their call is transferred to the appropriate technicians. The customers then describe the problem all over again while the technicians try to come up with answers— all in all, a most frustrating experience. To improve customer service and rein in costs, Compaq began giving away expensive case-based reasoning software to customers purchasing their Pagemarq printer.

The software knowledge base is a series of several hundred actual cases of Pagemarq printer problems—actual war stories about smudged copies, printer memory problems,

case-based reasoning (CBR)
Artificial intelligence technology that represents knowledge as a database of cases and solutions.

FIGURE 15-14 How case-based reasoning works. Case-based reasoning represents knowledge as a database of past cases and their solutions. The system uses a six-step process to generate solutions to new problems encountered by the user.

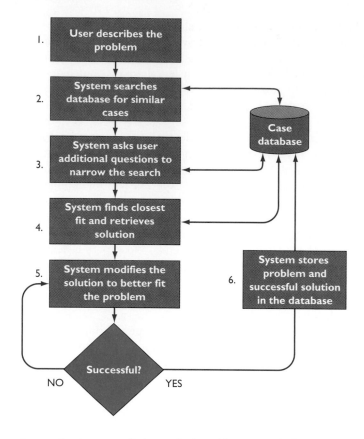

jammed printers—all the typical problems people face with laser printers. Trained CBR staff entered case descriptions in textual format into the CBR system. They entered key words necessary to categorize the problem, such as smudge, smear, lines, streaks, and paper jam. They also entered a series of questions that might be needed to allow the software to further narrow the problem. Finally, solutions also were attached to each case.

With the Compaq-supplied CBR system running on their computer, owners no longer need to call Compaq's service department. Instead they run the software and describe the problem to the software. The system swiftly searches actual cases, discarding unrelated ones, selecting related ones. If necessary to further narrow the search results, the software will ask the user for more information. In the end, one or more cases relevant to the specific problem are displayed, along with their solutions. Now, customers can solve most of their own problems quickly without a telephone call, and Compaq saves U.S.$10 million to U.S.$20 million annually in customer support costs.

New commercial software products, such as Inference's CasePoint WebServer, allow customers to access a case database through the Web. Using case-based reasoning, the server asks customers to answer a series of questions to narrow down the problem. CasePoint then extracts solutions from the database and passes them on to customers. Audio-product manufacturer Kenwood USA used this tool to put its manuals and technical-support solutions on the Web.

15.4 OTHER INTELLIGENT TECHNIQUES

Organizations are using other intelligent computing techniques to extend their knowledge base by providing solutions to problems that are too massive or too complex to be handled by people with limited resources. Neural networks, fuzzy logic, genetic algorithms, and intelligent agents are developing into promising business applications.

NEURAL NETWORKS

There has been an exciting resurgence of interest in bottom-up approaches to artificial intelligence in which machines are designed to imitate the physical thought process of the

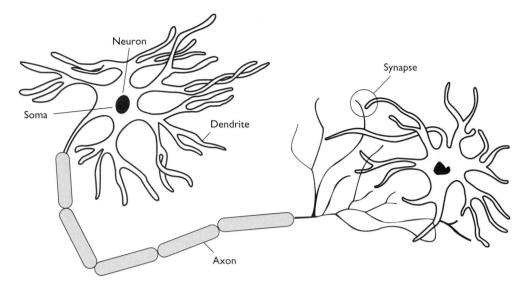

FIGURE 15-15 Biological neurons of a leech. Simple biological models, like the neurons of a leech, have influenced the development of artificial or computational neural networks in which the biological cells are replaced by transistors or entire processors.

Source: Defense Advance Research Projects Agency (DARPA), 1988. Unclassified.

biological brain. Figure 15-15 shows two neurons from a leech's brain. The soma, or nerve cell at the centre, acts like a switch, stimulating other neurons and being stimulated in turn. Emanating from the neuron is an axon, which is an electrically active link to the dendrites of other neurons. Axons and dendrites are the "wires" that electrically connect neurons to one another. The junction of the two is called a synapse. This simple biological model is the metaphor for the development of neural networks. A **neural network** consists of hardware or software that attempts to emulate the processing patterns of the biological brain.

The human brain has about 100 billion (10^{11}) neurons, each having about 1000 dendrites, which form 100 000 billion (10^{14}) synapses. The brain's neurons operate in parallel, and the human brain can accomplish about 10^{16}, or ten million billion, interconnections per second. This far exceeds the capacity of any known machine or any machine planned or ever likely to be built with current technology.

However, complex networks of neurons have been simulated on computers. Figure 15-16 shows an artificial neural network with two neurons. The resistors in the circuits are variable and can be used to teach the network. When the network makes a mistake (i.e., chooses the wrong pathway through the network and arrives at a false conclusion), resistance can be raised on some circuits, forcing other neurons to fire. If this learning process continues for thousands of cycles, the machine learns the correct response. The neurons are highly interconnected and operate in parallel.

A neural net has a large number of sensing and processing nodes that continuously interact with each other. Figure 15-17 represents a neural network comprising an input layer, an

neural network
Hardware or software that attempts to emulate the processing patterns of the biological brain.

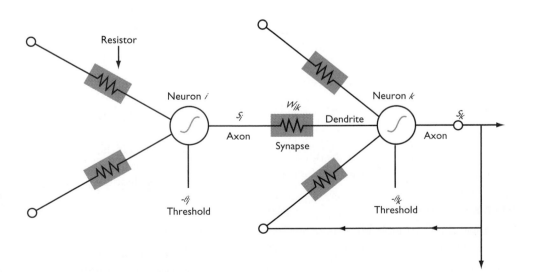

FIGURE 15-16 Artificial neural network with two neurons. In artificial neurons, the biological neurons become processing elements (switches), the axons and dendrites become wires, and the synapses become variable resistors that carry weighted inputs (currents) that represent data.

Source: DARPA, 1988. Unclassified.

FIGURE 15-17 A neural network uses rules it "learns" from patterns in data to construct a hidden layer of logic. The hidden layer then processes inputs, classifying them based on the experience of the model.

Source: Herb Edelstein, "Technology How-To: Mining Data Warehouses," *InformationWeek*, January 8, 1996. Copyright © 1996 CMP Media, Inc., 600 Community Drive, Manhasset, NY 11030. Reprinted with permission.

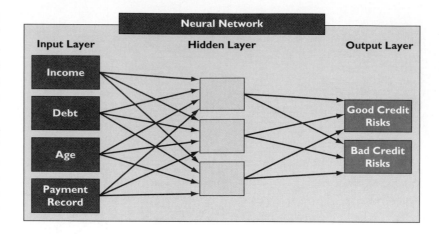

output layer, and a hidden processing layer. The network is fed a training set of data for which the inputs produce a known set of outputs or conclusions. This helps the computer learn the correct solution by example. As the computer is fed more data, each case is compared with the known outcome. If it differs, a correction is calculated and applied to the nodes in the hidden processing layer. These steps are repeated until a condition, such as corrections being less than a certain amount, is reached. The neural network in Figure 15-17 has "learned" how to identify a good credit risk.

The Difference Between Neural Networks and Expert Systems

What is different about neural networks? Expert systems seek to emulate or model a human expert's way of solving problems, but neural network builders claim that they do not model human intelligence, do not program solutions, and do not aim to solve specific problems per se. Instead, neural network designers seek to put intelligence into the hardware in the form of a generalized capability to learn. In contrast, the expert system is highly specific to a given problem and cannot be easily retrained.

Neural network applications are emerging in medicine, science, and business to address problems in pattern classification, prediction and financial analysis, and control and optimization. Papnet is a neural net-based system that distinguishes between normal and abnormal cells when examining Pap smears for cervical cancer. It has far greater accuracy than visual examinations by technicians. The computer is not able to make a final decision so a technician will review any selected abnormal cells. Using Papnet, a technician requires one-fifth the time to review a smear while attaining perhaps ten times the accuracy of the existing manual method.

Neural networks are being used by the financial industry to discern patterns in vast pools of data that might help investment firms predict the performance of equities, corporate bond ratings, or corporate bankruptcies. VISA International Inc. is using a neural network to help detect credit card fraud by monitoring all VISA transactions for sudden changes in the buying patterns of cardholders. The Window on Technology illustrates other neural net applications for pattern recognition.

Unlike expert systems, which typically provide explanations for their solutions, neural networks cannot always explain why they arrived at a particular solution. Moreover, they cannot always guarantee a completely certain solution, arrive at the same solution again with the same input data, or always guarantee the best solution (Trippi and Turban, 1989–1990). They are very sensitive and may not perform well if their training covers too little or too much data. In most current applications, neural networks are best used as aids to human decision makers instead of substitutes for them.

FUZZY LOGIC

Traditional computer programs require precision: on–off, yes–no, right–wrong. However, we human beings do not experience the world this way. We might all agree that 45 degrees Celsius

NEURAL NETS HELP SYSTEMS MANAGEMENT AND SCOTLAND YARD

When Computer Associates (CA) first developed its neural network software, it hoped to use this technology to enhance its software for managing IT infrastructure. A neural net examines historical data to recognize a pattern or relationship and apply this learned knowledge to detect changes and predict results. CA wanted to enlist neural network agents dubbed "neugents" to help its CA Unicenter TNG enterprise system management software administer large complex networked systems. By watching the behaviour of systems, the neugent trains itself better with every event so that it can eventually predict system problems before they occur. For instance, a neugent observing an e-mail server could discern a pattern of message queues that would soon cause the server to fail. Other neugents could detect situations such as service slowdowns, outages, or virus activity or forecast workloads and recommend system configurations.

AGF Brasil, a subsidiary of the AGF International insurance company, works with 15 000 registered brokers and agents in Brazil. Providing brokers and agents with up-to-the-minute information on the company's insurance products is vital to its success. AGF Brazil has built an 800-node network called AGF NET consisting of IBM AIX (UNIX) servers, Dell servers running Windows NT, and 50 local area networks for this purpose. The company uses CA Unicenter TNG to provide a single point of control for managing its entire information technology infrastructure, including severs, desktop computers, printers, routers, and hubs. CA neugents help with performance monitoring. They have alerted system administrators to a variety of processor, network, memory, and database bottlenecks as well

as the need to provide additional Web capacity. Neugents support AGF's mix of different types of servers equally well because they "learn" the machines' individual idiosyncracies. Using this neural network technology, AGF can keep important services running smoothly around the clock without high staffing levels.

Other applications can benefit from neugents as well. New Scotland Yard in London is experimenting with neugents to help with data analysis. Facing a rising crime rate and falling numbers of police officers, London's Metropolitan Police Service was looking for a way to make better use of its crime data. New Scotland Yard assigned neugents to look at data from five databases, including crime reports, forensic evidence, and mug shots, hoping the neugents would detect patterns, especially in burglaries to help the police identify serial burglars.

Neural network technology does not require defined fields in data to detect patterns. The software can look for string searches in text such as police reports. According to Patrick Dryden, an analyst at Illuminata Group in Nashua, New Hampshire, neural networks can throw brute force at large numbers to identify interesting trends. But business people have to look at those trends and decide what's important.

To Think About: How useful is neural network technology for the applications described here? Would you trust the management of a large complex client/server system to a neugent? Why or why not? What other applications can you think of that could use neural nets?

Sources: Sami Lais, "CA Bundles Neural Net, App Development Tools, *ComputerWorld*, August 7, 2000; www.ca.com/products/neugents, accessed July 21, 2001.

---

is hot and −40 degrees is cold; but is 10 degrees hot, warm, comfortable, or cool? The answer depends on many factors: the wind, the humidity, the individual experiencing the temperature, one's clothing, and one's expectations. Many of our activities are also inexact. Tractor-trailer drivers would find it nearly impossible to back their rig into a space precisely specified to have less than an inch of clearance on all sides.

Fuzzy logic, a relatively new, rule-based development in AI, tolerates imprecision and even uses it to solve problems we could not have solved before. **Fuzzy logic** consists of a variety of concepts and techniques for representing and inferring knowledge that is imprecise, uncertain, or unreliable. Fuzzy logic can create rules that use approximate or subjective values and incomplete or ambiguous data. By expressing logic with some carefully defined imprecision, fuzzy logic is closer to the way people actually think than traditional IF-THEN rules.

Ford Motor Co. developed a fuzzy logic application that backs a simulated tractor-trailer into a parking space. The application uses the following three rules:

IF the truck is *near* jackknifing, THEN *reduce* the steering angle.

IF the truck is *far away* from the dock, THEN steer *toward* the dock.

IF the truck is *near* the dock, THEN point the trailer *directly* at the dock.

fuzzy logic
A rule-based AI that tolerates imprecision by using nonspecific terms called membership functions to solve problems.

This logic makes sense to us as human beings, for it represents how we think as we back that truck into its berth.

How does the computer make sense of this programming? The answer is relatively simple. The terms (known as membership functions) are imprecisely defined so that, for example, in Figure 15-18, cool is between 50 and 70 degrees Fahrenheit although the temperature is most clearly cool between about 60 degrees and 67 degrees. Note that cool is overlapped by cold or norm. To control the room environment using this logic, the programmer would develop similarly imprecise definitions for humidity and other factors such as outdoor wind and temperature. The rules might include one that says: "If the temperature is cool or cold and the humidity is low while the outdoor wind is high and the outdoor temperature is low, raise the heat and humidity in the room." The computer would combine the membership function readings in a weighted manner and, using all the rules, raise and lower the temperature and humidity.

Fuzzy logic is widely used in Japan and is gaining popularity in North America. Its popularity has occurred partly because managers find they can use it to reduce costs and shorten development time. Fuzzy logic code requires fewer IF-THEN rules, making it simpler than traditional code. The rules required in the previous trucking example, plus its term definitions, might require hundreds of IF-THEN statements to implement in traditional logic. Compact code requires less computer capacity, allowing Sanyo Fisher USA to implement camcorder controls without adding expensive memory to their product.

Fuzzy logic also allows us to solve problems not previously solvable, thus improving product quality. In Japan, Sendai's subway system uses fuzzy logic controls to accelerate so smoothly that standing passengers need not hold on. Mitsubishi Heavy Industries in Tokyo (www.mhi.co.jp/indexe.html) has been able to reduce the power consumption of its air conditioners by 20 percent through implementing control programs in fuzzy logic. The auto-focus device in our cameras is only possible because of fuzzy logic. Kitchen stores sell an "intelligent" steamer made in Japan that uses fuzzy logic. A variable heat setting detects the amount of grain, cooks it at the preferred temperature, and keeps the rice warm up to 12 hours.

Management also has found fuzzy logic useful for decision making and organizational control. A Wall Street firm had a system developed that selects companies for potential acquisition, using the language stock traders understand. Recently, a system has been developed to detect possible fraud in medical claims submitted by health care providers anywhere in the United States. In Canada, fuzzy logic has been used largely by the natural sciences community, including scheduling timber harvesting, predicting weather, and promoting soil conservation.

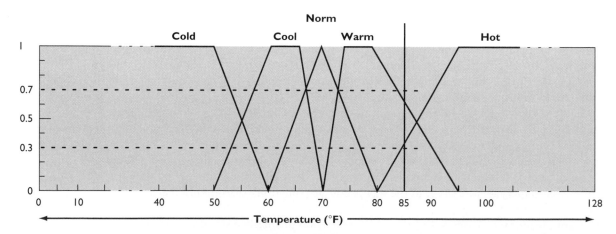

FIGURE 15-18 Implementing fuzzy logic rules in hardware. The membership functions for the input called temperature are in the logic of the thermostat to control the room temperature. Membership functions help translate linguistic expressions such as "warm" into numbers that the computer can manipulate.

Source: James M. Sibigtroth, "Implementing Fuzzy Expert Rules in Hardware," *AI Expert,* April 1992. © 1992 Miller Freeman, Inc. Reprinted with permission.

GENETIC ALGORITHMS

Genetic algorithms (also referred to as adaptive computation) refer to a variety of problem-solving techniques that are conceptually based on the method that living organisms use to adapt to their environment—the process of evolution. They are programmed to work the way populations solve problems—by changing and reorganizing their component parts using processes such as reproduction, mutation, and natural selection. Thus, genetic algorithms promote the evolution of solutions to particular problems, controlling the generation, variation, adaptation, and selection of possible solutions using genetically based processes. As solutions alter and combine, the worst ones are discarded, and the better ones survive to go on to produce even better solutions. Genetic algorithms breed programs that solve problems even when no person can fully understand their structure (Holland, 1992).

A genetic algorithm works by representing information as a string of 0s and 1s. A possible solution can be represented by a long string of these digits. The genetic algorithm provides methods of searching all possible combinations of digits to identify the right string representing the best possible structure for the problem

In one method, the programmer first randomly generates a population of strings consisting of combinations of binary digits (see Figure 15-19). Each string corresponds to one of the variables in the problem. One applies a test for fitness, ranking the strings in the population according to their level of desirability as possible solutions. After the initial population is evaluated for fitness, the algorithm then produces the next generation of strings, consisting of strings that survived the fitness test plus offspring strings produced from mating pairs of strings, and tests their fitness. The process continues until a solution is reached.

Solutions to certain types of problems in areas of optimization, product design, and monitoring industrial systems are especially appropriate for genetic algorithms. Many business problems require optimization because they deal with issues such as minimization of costs, maximization of profits, efficient scheduling, and use of resources. If these situations are very dynamic and complex, involving hundreds of variables or hundreds of formulas, genetic algorithms can expedite the solution because they can evaluate many different solution alternatives quickly to find the best one. For example, at Canada's Institute for Aerospace Research (www.nrc.ca/iar), researchers use genetic algorithms in the design of airfoils to facilitate optimization of multiple objectives (high efficiency, low performance penalty, etc.) where each design change required changes in a myriad of variables (Tse and Chan, 2001). Coors Brewing Company and the U.S. Navy used genetic algorithms to help them with scheduling problems (Burtka, 1993).

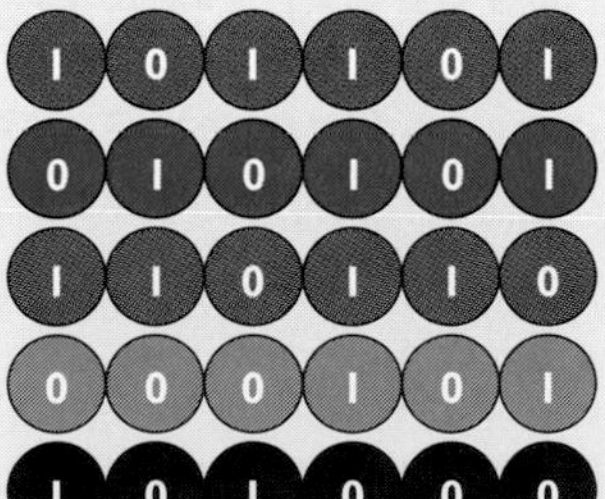

genetic algorithms
Problem-solving methods that promote the evolution of solutions to specified problems using the model of living organisms adapting to their environment.

		Colour	Speed	Intelligence	Fitness
1 0 1 1 0 1	1	White	Medium	Dumb	40
0 1 0 1 0 1	2	Black	Slow	Dumb	43
1 1 0 1 1 0	3	White	Slow	Very Dumb	22
0 0 0 1 0 1	4	Black	Fast	Dumb	71
1 0 1 0 0 0	5	White	Medium	Very Smart	53
A population of chromosomes			Decoding of chromosomes	Evaluation of chromosomes	

FIGURE 15-19 The components of a genetic algorithm. This example illustrates an initial population of "chromosomes," each representing a different solution. The genetic algorithm uses an iterative process to refine the initial solutions so that the better ones, those with the higher fitness, are more likely to emerge as the best solution.

Source: Vasant Dhar and Roger Stein, "Intelligent Decision Support Methods" p. 65 © 1997. Reprinted by permission of Prentice-Hall, Upper Saddle River, N.J.

Hybrid AI Systems

Genetic algorithms, fuzzy logic, neural networks, and expert systems can be integrated into a single application to take advantage of the best features of these technologies. These systems are called **hybrid AI systems**. Hybrid applications in business are growing. In Japan, Hitachi, Mitsubishi, Ricoh, Sanyo, and others are starting to incorporate hybrid AI in products such as home appliances, factory machinery, and office equipment. Matsushita has developed a "neurofuzzy" washing machine that combines fuzzy logic with neural networks. Nikko Securities has been working on a neurofuzzy system to forecast convertible-bond ratings.

INTELLIGENT AGENTS

Intelligent agents are software programs that work in the background to carry out specific, repetitive, and predictable tasks for an individual user, business process, or software application. The agent uses a built-in or learned knowledge base to accomplish tasks or make decisions on the user's behalf. Intelligent agents can be programmed to make decisions based on the user's personal preferences—for example, to delete junk e-mail, schedule appointments, or travel over interconnected networks to find the cheapest airfare to California. The agent can be likened to a personal digital assistant collaborating with the user in the same work environment. It can help the user by performing tasks on the user's behalf, training or teaching the user, hiding the complexity of difficult tasks, helping the user collaborate with other users, or monitoring events and procedures (Maes, 1994).

There are many intelligent agent applications today in operating systems, application software, e-mail systems, mobile computing software, and network tools. For example, the Wizards found in Microsoft Office software tools have built-in capabilities to show users how to accomplish various tasks, such as formatting documents or creating graphs, and to anticipate when users need assistance. Of special interest to business are intelligent agents for cruising networks, including the Internet, in search of information. Chapter 10 described how these *electronic commerce bots* can help consumers find products they want and assist them in comparing prices and other features. Because these mobile agents are personalized, semiautonomous, and continuously running, they can help automate several of the most time-consuming stages of the buying process and thus reduce transaction costs.

Agent-based electronic commerce will become even more widespread as agent and Web technology become more powerful and flexible. Increased use of XML, Java, and distributed objects (see Chapter 7) will allow software agents and other automated processes to access and interact with Web-based information more easily (Glushko, Tenenbaum, and Meltzer, 1999; Wong, Paciorek, and Moore, 1999).

APPLICATION SOFTWARE EXERCISE

EXPERT SYSTEM SOFTWARE EXERCISE: BUILDING EXPERT SYSTEM SUPPORT FOR RETIREMENT PLANNING

Katy Roberts is a benefits specialist for Clean Air Products, a regional heating and air conditioning parts manufacturer. Many of Clean Air's employees have been with the company since the early 1960s and receive cash bonuses upon retirement. These cash bonuses are based on the length of employment and the retiree's age. In order to receive a bonus, an employee must be at least 50 years of age and have worked for the company for 5 years. The following table summarizes the criteria for determining bonuses.

Length of Employment	Bonus
< 5 years	No bonus
6–10 years	20 percent of current annual salary
11–15 years	30 percent of current annual salary
16–20 years	40 percent of current annual salary
20–25 years	50 percent of current annual salary
26 or more years	100 percent of current annual salary

Many vendors sell and make demonstration copies of their expert systems available via the Web. Use a search engine to locate and download a demonstration copy of an expert system.

Using the information provided in the scenario, help Katy build a simple expert system. Feel free to make any assumptions that you feel are necessary; however, please document your assumptions in writing. Once you have built the expert system, prepare a written report that summarizes the development process. Was the product easy to use? Why or why not? What other features should the retirement planning expert system include? Why?

MANAGEMENT WRAP-UP

Leveraging and managing organizational knowledge have become core management responsibilities. Managers need to identify the knowledge assets of their organizations and make sure that appropriate systems and processes are in place to maximize their use.

Systems for knowledge and information work and artificial intelligence can enhance organizational processes in a number of ways. They can facilitate communication, collaboration, and coordination, bring more analytical power to bear in the development of solutions, or reduce the amount of human intervention in organizational processes.

An array of technologies is available to support knowledge management, including artificial intelligence technologies and tools for knowledge and information work and group collaboration. Managers should understand the costs, benefits, and capabilities of each technology and the knowledge management problem for which each is best suited.

For Discussion
1. Discuss some of the ways that knowledge management provides organizations with strategic advantage. How strategic are knowledge management systems?
2. How much can the use of artificial intelligence change the management process?

SUMMARY

1. *Explain the importance of knowledge management in contemporary organizations.* Knowledge management is the process of systematically and actively managing and leveraging the stores of knowledge in an organization. Knowledge is a central productive and strategic asset in an information economy. Information systems can play a valuable role in knowledge management, helping the organization optimize its flow of information and capture its knowledge base. Office systems, knowledge work systems, group collaboration systems, and artificial intelligence applications are especially useful for knowledge management because they focus on supporting information and knowledge work and on defining and codifying the organization's knowledge base.

2. *Describe the applications that are most useful for distributing, creating, and sharing knowledge in the firm.* Offices coordinate information work in the organization, link the work of diverse groups in the organization, and couple the organization to its external environment. Office systems support these functions by automating document management, communications, scheduling, and data management. Word processing, desktop publishing, Web publishing, and digital imaging systems support document management activities.

Electronic-mail systems and groupware support communications activities. Electronic calendar applications and groupware support scheduling activities. Desktop database management systems support data management activities.

Knowledge work systems support the creation of knowledge and its integration into the organization. KWS require easy access to an external knowledge base; powerful computer hardware that can support software with intensive graphics, analysis, document management, and communications capabilities; and a friendly user interface. Knowledge work systems often run on workstations that are customized for the work they must perform. Computer-aided design systems and virtual reality systems, which create interactive simulations that behave like the real world, require graphics and powerful modelling capabilities. Knowledge work systems for financial professionals provide access to external databases and the ability to analyze massive amounts of financial data very quickly.

Groupware is special software to support information-intensive activities in which people work collaboratively in groups. Intranets can perform many group collaboration and support functions and allow organizations to use Web publishing capabilities for document management.

3. *Evaluate the role of artificial intelligence in knowledge management.* Artificial intelligence is the development of computer-based systems that behave like humans. There are six members of the artificial intelligence family tree: natural language, robotics, perceptive systems, expert systems, intelligent machines, and neural networks. Artificial intelligence lacks the flexibility, breadth, and generality of human intelligence, but it can be used to capture and codify organizational knowledge.

4. *Explain how organizations can use expert systems and case-based reasoning to capture knowledge.* Expert systems are knowledge-intensive computer applications that solve problems that previously required human expertise. The systems capture a limited domain of human knowledge using rules or frames. The mechanism to search through the knowledge base, called the inference engine, can use either forward or backward chaining. Expert systems are most useful for problems of classification or diagnosis. Case-based reasoning represents organizational knowledge as a database of cases that can be continually expanded and refined. When the user encounters a new case, the system searches for similar cases, finds the closest fit, and applies the solution of the old case to the new case. The new case is stored with successful solutions in the case database.

5. *Explain how organizations can use neural networks and other intelligent techniques to improve their knowledge base.* Neural networks consist of hardware and software that attempt to mimic the thought processes of the human brain. Neural networks are notable for their ability to learn without programming and to recognize patterns that cannot be easily described by humans. They are being used in science, medicine, and business primarily to discriminate patterns in massive amounts of data.

Fuzzy logic is a software technology that expresses logic with some carefully defined imprecision so that it is closer to the way people actually think than traditional IF-THEN rules. Fuzzy logic has been used for controlling physical devices and is starting to be used for limited decision-making applications.

Genetic algorithms develop solutions to particular problems using genetically based processes such as fitness, crossover, and mutation. Genetic algorithms are beginning to be applied to problems involving optimization, product design, and monitoring industrial systems.

Intelligent agents are software programs with built-in or learned knowledge bases that carry out specific, repetitive, and predictable tasks for an individual user, business process, or software application. Intelligent agents can be programmed to search for information or to conduct transactions on networks, including the Internet.

Key Terms

AI shell, 528

Artificial intelligence, 526

Backward chaining, 529

Best practices, 514

Case-based reasoning (CBR), 531

Chief knowledge officer (CKO), 514

Computer-aided design (CAD), 519

Data workers, 516

Document imaging systems, 517

Enterprise information portal, 522

Environmental scanning, 518

Expert system, 527

Forward chaining, 528

Fuzzy logic, 535

Genetic algorithms, 537

Groupware, 521

Hybrid AI systems, 538

Inference engine, 528

Information work, 516

Intelligent agent, 538

Investment workstation, 520

Jukebox, 517

Knowledge base, 527

Knowledge engineer, 529

Knowledge frames, 527

Knowledge management, 513

Knowledge workers, 516

Knowledge work systems (KWS), 518

Neural network, 533

Office systems, 516

Organizational learning, 513

Organizational memory, 514

Rule base, 527

Rule-based expert system, 527

Tacit knowledge, 514

Teamware, 523

Virtual Reality Modelling Language (VRML), 520

Virtual reality systems, 520

Review Questions

1. What is knowledge management? List and briefly describe the information systems that support knowledge management and the kind of information technology infrastructure it requires.

2. How does knowledge management promote organizational learning?

3. What is the relationship between information work and productivity in contemporary organizations?

4. Describe the roles of the office in organizations. What are the major activities that take place in offices?

5. What are the principal types of information systems that support information worker activities in the office?

6. What are the generic requirements of knowledge work systems? Why?

7. Describe how the following systems support knowledge work: computer-aided design (CAD), virtual reality, and investment workstations.

8. How does groupware support information work? Describe its capabilities and Internet and intranet capabilities for collaborative work.

9. What is artificial intelligence? Why is it of interest to business?

10. What is the difference between artificial intelligence and natural or human intelligence?

11. Define an expert system, and describe how it can help organizations use their knowledge assets.

12. Define and describe the role of the following in expert systems: rule base, frames, inference engine.

13. What is case-based reasoning? How does it differ from an expert system?

14. Describe three problems of expert systems.

15. Describe a neural network. At what kinds of tasks would a neural network excel?

16. Define and describe fuzzy logic. For what kinds of applications is it suited?

17. What are genetic algorithms? How can they help organizations solve problems? For what kinds of problems are they suited?

18. What are intelligent agents? How can they be used to benefit businesses?

GROUP PROJECT

With a group of classmates, select two groupware products such as Lotus Notes and Open Text's LiveLink, and compare their features and capabilities. To prepare your analysis, use articles from computer magazines and Web sites for groupware vendors. If possible, use electronic presentation software to present your findings to the class.

# INTERNET CONNECTION

■ **COMPANION WEBSITE**

At www.pearsoned.ca/laudon, you'll find an online study guide with two quizzes to test your knowledge of how knowledge-based information systems are used in modern organizations. You'll also find updates to the chapter and online exercises and cases that enable you to apply your knowledge to realistic situations.

■ **ADDITIONAL SITES OF INTEREST**

There are many interesting Web sites to enhance your learning about knowledge-based information systems. You can search the Web yourself, or just try the following sites to add to what you have already learned.

Fuzzy Clips

ai.iit.nrc.ca/IR_public/fuzzy/fuzzyClips/fuzzyCLIPSIndex. html

Describes the evolution of fuzzy clips and links to freeware download of fuzzy clips (easy to use fuzzy logic modules developed by the National Research Council of Canada and the U.S. National Space and Aeronautics Administration)

Open Text's LiveLink

www.opentext.com/products/

Web-based enterprise knowledge management and collaboration software

CompInfo's AI index

www.compinfo-center.com/tpai-t.htm

Links to interesting AI Web sites

CASE STUDY   *Bubble, Bubble, Less Toil and Trouble*

Internationally recognized for more than 200 years, Molson Breweries offers beer drinkers more than 40 top-quality brands. It holds the highest market share in several provinces and is the leading exporter of Canadian beer to the United States. Molson Breweries has annual sales of almost $2.5 billion. Despite its traditions of fiscal stability and high market share, Molson Breweries faces the same challenges as any successful company in today's dynamic marketplace.

While Molson has a strong market presence, the battle to maintain its position is constant. "There is an increasing number of brands out there, all competing for consumer attention," says Trevor Smith, Molson's Vice President of Information Technology. "These include both beer and non-beer beverages, now heavily marketed by local direct rivals and microbreweries as well as U.S. imports."

In addition to waging market wars, Molson must frequently adjust to evolving customer needs. Smith says, "Consumer dynamics are always changing. Our challenge is to create incentive for current and potential beer drinkers to buy our products by continually enhancing the products' image." The company realized that to maintain its market dominance it had to invest in new information management tools and adopt a more fact-based approach to decision making. According to Smith, "You've got to move very quickly in our industry, and information is essential to making the right decisions. Consumer and brand insight are both key to competing effectively."

Having determined that a data warehouse was the right route, Molson settled on Oracle for its platform. Then, Molson chose Cognos Impromptu and PowerPlay for use in data querying, reporting, and analysis. Noel Zeldin, director of marketing and selling systems at the Molson Centre for Innovation, says: "They make it very easy to get data into users' hands. In addition, the Cognos–Oracle interface is extremely clean and reliable." Molson used Hexagon Computer systems, a Cognos partner, to build a central data warehouse running on HP-UX. They also created separate data marts that run on Compaq ProLiant file servers and a Windows NT workstation. "We've expanded beyond our Toronto headquarters to cover the rest of Ontario, the West, and Quebec," says Zeldin. "This supports an overall management shift through which regional offices have assumed more responsibility for sales and marketing initiatives, as well bottom-line profits."

Consisting of multidimensional cubed structures, with extracts generated on a Pentium, the data marts are distributed across an NT LAN/WAN environment. "The Web is the way of the future for us," says Smith. "As new applications are developed, we will be putting those on the Web first, using Impromptu Web Query and PowerPlay Server Web Edition." From an operating system standpoint, Molson standardized on Microsoft for its PCs and laptops. Microsoft's enterprise products integrate well with Cognos' tools.

Run on a daily, weekly, and monthly basis, Molson's data warehousing applications deal with sales, financial, and customer-tracking information. "For example, we have a consumer response system that allows customers to call in with comments, requests, or criticisms," says Zeldin. "The information is entered into a database and then distributed to our marketing, brewing, or packaging departments as appropriate."

Cognos' business intelligence tools allow Molson's end users to generate their own reports independently and to analyze data from different angles. "In addition to being able to access information readily, users also get the information in more depth," according to Zeldin. "Our development groups don't have to think of every possible way to represent data; we can just send out portions of it, give users basic access, and they can explore it to any level of detail."

In describing the impact of the company's data warehousing initiative, Smith said, "If you pulled the system away from the business, you would create much noise and concern. It is really woven into our operational fabric and is crucial to our ongoing success." According to Zeldin, the solution provides the easiest way to get critical information out to a broad audience within the company. The data warehousing initiative gives Molson the jump on its competitors by allowing its end users to draw faster and better conclusions, based on facts. "It delivers more accurate and timely information for sales and marketing staff to act upon in effectively deploying local programs," says Smith. "The knowl-

edge provided is facilitating our drive towards becoming more proactive, on a community basis, and we are definitely more targeted today."

When the Year 2000 approached, Molson knew that they had to keep the taps open and avoid the Y2K bug. To accommodate the need to share information and knowledge among members of their Y2K project team, Molson's Web Technology Manager Rob Van Tol chose Open Text's LiveLink. Open Text is a Canadian company headquartered in Waterloo, Ontario, with offices located around the world. LiveLink is Web-based enterprise information management software composed of a variety of applications. According to Van Tol, "We believe that knowledge management technology is one of the key strategies that will enable Molson to maintain its leadership position beyond the Y2K project. We, as a company, need to know what's happened in the past to know to best plan for the future…. As soon as we realized what LiveLink could do—beyond linking people together—the light bulbs went on immediately. There were so many applications for which we could use the powerful knowledge, project, work and collaboration management…. In addition, because it's Web-based, LiveLink fits right into the architecture we are building…. With LiveLink, we are improving customer service and internal communications. In addition, we are effectively meeting stringent government food safety regulations and managing work processes, resources, and intellectual property."

While the Oracle–Cognos solution helped in the creation of knowledge from transactional types of data, LiveLink is used to create a central repository for information that was scattered among individuals. Finding information had become more and more difficult, and the potential for duplication of effort to find individually-based information (documents, e-mails, etc.) more widespread.

The first application for which Molson used LiveLink was the Y2K project, which was distributed over five locations using 20 different computing systems and platforms. The IT department set the LiveLink server software to run on Molson's Micrsoft NT 4.0 servers, with team members accessing the software via Internet Explorer 4.0 attached to a Microsoft IIS 4.0 Web server on a corporate intranet. Y2K team leaders used LiveLink to assign tasks and monitor project status and to reduce the number of hard copy reports since everything was available online to anyone with permission to view it. Notes and information could be shared across various sub-teams resulting in better cross-project team information sharing, coordination, and collaboration. Van Tol says that the use of LiveLink "saved substantial operational and administrative overhead."

"Managing our knowledge base and making enterprise knowledge accessible to everyone who needs it can mean a tremendous competitive advantage moving forward," says Van Tol. "Success will depend on how fast and how effectively we can obtain information and transform it into real business results." Instead of searching through many loose-leaf folders for information, service representatives now simply enter the search criteria into the LiveLink knowledge base for immediate, accurate answers. LiveLink also enables them to save frequently used queries for faster access. In the future, as new information is updated, representatives will receive e-mail notification. Van Tol says, "We want everyone to be able to reference the knowledge of employees, past and present, along with all of the research that a consumer goods company acquires. So now if a key expert leaves the company or is reassigned or promoted, the knowledge remains with Molson. This benefit has even greater weight when you consider that people don't have to be called back to provide their knowledge and expertise on past projects." Dissemination of information to more than 500 people requires a simply mouse-click because changes are made on the server. Van Tol sees "many applications for which LiveLink is the ideal solution. These include collaboration over partner extranets, document management for ISO compliance as well as brewery-floor logs and documentation management."

Sources: "Bubble, Bubble, Less Toil and Trouble," *Communication News*, May 1999; "Y2K Compliance, Best Practices, and Knowledge Management," Open Text Case Study, www.opentext.com/customers/case_studies/livelink_case_study_molsons.pdf, accessed July 24, 2001.

CASE STUDY QUESTIONS

1. What market and competitive forces led Molson to move to computer-based knowledge management practices?

2. What is the real difference in the two knowledge management technologies that Molson employed?

3. What other uses could the Oracle–Cognos knowledge management enable? What about the LiveLink technology?

4. What other forms of knowledge-based systems could Molson Breweries use? Be specific about the technologies and the applications of the technologies.

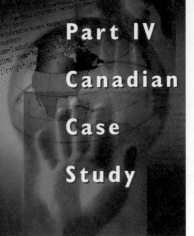

SMART CARDS: TOOLS FOR KNOWLEDGE AND DECISION SUPPORT

Canada has long been a pioneer in smart card technology experimentation. Over the last 10 years, smart cards have been used in several experiments to determine their technological feasibility and their appropriateness for use for a variety of purposes.

Many of these systems are health care applications. Almost all provinces and territories have implemented either pilot smart card projects or full-blown health care applications. The range of applications runs from linking patient care among providers, to automating communication of laboratory tests, to linking pharmacies, to intake and case management. The information provided by these smart card projects can help health care administrators and government officials make decisions about providing health care in their area.

What exactly are smart cards, and how can they help to manage knowledge and to make decisions? Identical in size and feel to credit cards, smart cards store information on an integrated microprocessor chip located within the body of the card. These chips hold a variety of information, from stored-value (monetary) used for retail and vending machines to secure information and applications for higher-end operations such as medical/healthcare records. New information and/or applications can be added depending on the chip's capabilities.

Smart cards allow thousands of times the information storable on magnetic stripe cards. In addition, smart cards are more reliable, perform multiple functions, and are more secure because of the high level of security mechanisms that can be built in, such as advanced encryption and biometrics.

Despite the touted advantages of smart cards, several barriers are preventing widespread adoption of the technology in North America, not the least of which are consumer concerns over privacy and business mindsets, according to industry experts. "The prevailing myth is, if all of your information is on a card, and you drop it in the street, anyone who picks it up will know everything about you," says Catherine Johnston, president of the Advanced Card Technology Association of Canada. "While this might be true of unencrypted data on a PC diskette, smart cards can be both secure and private."

Because of the high cost of back-end infrastructure necessary for smart cards, organizations must form partnerships in order to help launch projects, according to Duncan Brown, director of research in North America of London, England-based Ovum, Inc. Different organizations—such as universities and banks—can share the infrastructure costs.

In 1996, approximately 805 million smart cards were issued worldwide; in 2000, 1.8 billion cards were issued, an increase of 27 percent over the previous year, and an estimated 2.8 billion smart cards were issued in 2001. Smart cards are most prominent in Western Europe, but growth in North America is expanding rapidly.

Worldwide, smart card projects support a variety of applications. American Express launched the first chip-based credit card in Australia recently, with ANZ Bank following. In Italy, chambers of commerce, the national railway, and many other businesses plan to use smart cards to store digital certificates to secure B2B commerce. Mexico City's subway system plans to issue 300 000 smart cards to employees and disabled riders; these smart cards will be combination cards so that commuters can pay transit fares by waving the card near a radio-frequency device on a turnstile, using the same kind of card as those being used in Paris on their subway system.

In light of the September 11, 2001 terrorist attacks in the United States, the Newport Beach, California-based International Association of Professional Security Consultants has recommended that airline carriers should consider issuing smart cards to tighten security at airports. Airline carriers could convert their frequent flier cards, which are often paper-based cards with the customer's name and account number on it, into a chip card that would use stronger means of validating a person's identity. Identification methods could include a personal identification number or an application that would verify a person's identity with a physical characteristic, such as his fingerprint. Persons carrying smart cards would be processed separately from those not carrying cards. Bell ID proved the effects of tightened airport security by implementing a smart card system in combination with biometrics for frequent flyers at Amsterdam Schiphol Airport. The project was a successful pilot study.

Ken Scheflen at the U.S. Department of Defense says he would not be surprised if U.S. federal agencies accelerated any plans they may have to issue chip-based ID cards to employees. Scheflen is directing the Department of Defense's rollout of four million smart cards to military and civilian personnel to control access to their computer networks and physical facilities. "We probably know how to do it from a technical point of view," says Scheflen. "If asked, we will certainly share that expertise." Other U.S. agencies, among them the State and Treasury departments, already had plans to roll out smart cards. He added that some

U.S. officials are calling for a national citizen ID card, which could also be based on smart card technology.

Here in Canada, there are many smart card projects being implemented by private businesses, health care providers, and government entities. In the first trial of its kind, Scotiabank will begin offering a chip-based Visa-branded credit card early next year in Barrie, Ontario. The bank will solicit 12 000 customers who live in Barrie for the multiapplication smart card. The chip will store a Visa Cash electronic purse, merchant loyalty, and transit applications, all of which have been tested in an ongoing Visa Cash smart card trial in Barrie. In 1999, Scotiabank was also the first financial institution in Canada to routinely deploy smart-card-capable PIN (personal identification number) pads.

In the fall of 2001, an undisclosed Canadian card issuer piloted a chip-based credit card in Edmonton, Alberta, that can be used in local merchants' loyalty programs. The issuer says it will mail 15 000 solicitations to Edmonton residents to apply for the card and hopes to sign 400 local merchants to install chip-accepting point-of-sale terminals for the pilot. Cardholders will be able to go online to lifestylecanada.com to download electronic coupons and other types of loyalty programs onto the card. The issuer will also provide a smart card reader that connects to a PC.

Mondex Canada, an electronic cash card manufacturer located in Toronto, has had mixed success with several pilot projects in the last few years. Their original pilot was in Guelph, Ontario. While a technical success—the system worked—demand and usage for the Mondex card in Guelph never really accelerated.

In Brampton, Ontario, Canadian Imperial Bank of Commerce (CIBC) and Northern Telecom (now Nortel) partnered to offer Mondex cash to Nortel employees at their Brampton facility. Employees' Mondex cards could be used at telephones and banking machine terminals to download value, check accounts and card balances, and review previous transactions. Mondex e-cash was also used to purchase goods at all on-site merchants and vending machines. The city of Sherbrooke saw 25 000 Mondex cards using the new MULTOS operating system issued with over 600 merchants enlisted in their two-year pilot project. This project included 750 vending machines, a student card program at Bishop's University and Champlain College, the first test of Mondex e-cash loading technology via the Internet, and involved almost $3 million in e-cash value. Mondex findings from the Sherbrooke project mirror their previous findings: Canadian consumers and merchants like the e-cash concept but want more places to use e-cash, more convenience, more flexibility, and more features. In fact, the vast majority of these Mondex users want the functions of a debit card included on their Mondex card, another reason Mondex has moved to the MULTOS operating system. The Sherbrooke project wrapped up over the summer of 2001. Mondex Canada says that future pilots will be conducted, but only after the additional infrastructure to support the use of multiple applications has been developed and implemented.

What is missing from these projects are the business implications of issuing smart cards. Mondex, Schlumberger, and other smart card manufacturers should perhaps focus less on consumer demand and more on the potential applications that could add value to businesses. The data collected from smart card use has untold potential for adding to the enhancement of customer relationship management data and decision support as well as enhancing decision support for marketing, human resources, and manufacturing, just to name a few potential business-side applications.

Using data collected by smart card banking applications, financial institutions could determine how best to support their customers—from where to build new offices, to types of services to offer online or at banking machines, to staffing of offices and call centres. Knowing the extent of their customers' use of smart cards for banking and conceivably other applications could assist financial institutions in developing new products, re-engineering their processes, modifying their pricing structure or pricing scales, and partnering with other institutions to offer one-stop shopping and banking.

A business that offered smart card technology to support customer interactions—anything from e-cash transactions to biometric security identification—could use the data collected from smart card use to determine its staffing needs, including the number and type of employees needed at a particular location. For example, if airports implement smart cards with biometric identification, it is conceivable that they could shift the number of low-level-trained security employees significantly downward while slightly increasing the number of highly-trained security employees. Customs and immigration officials might find that they need fewer employees at major points of entry.

Manufacturers who partner with retailers that use smart card technology for retail purchases could use the data arising from the smart card transactions to determine needed inventory levels of both raw materials and finished goods and could adjust production schedules based on the wealth of data available from the consumers' use of smart cards. Understanding how and when consumers use smart cards can help businesses to better understand their customers' needs and how to develop marketing approaches to satisfy those needs.

This sounds like a commercial business' dream. From the smart card manufacturers' perspective, partnering with a business that would market the smart card to their customers—with incentives for use—sounds great. Yet the smart card manufacturers have focused instead on the end-consumers' use of smart cards. Even so, smart card manufacturers like Mondex are using the data gathered in their pilot projects to determine consumer needs and desires for future implementations of smart card technology.

From the consumers' perspective, though, smart card technology could finally bring "Big Brother" privacy issues to the table. Nowhere is this more evident than in the issues involved in the Ontario government's plans to implement smart card technology in a variety of applications. The Ontario card would give citizens access to a variety of provincial services, from healthcare and drivers' licences, to hunting and fishing licences, perhaps firearms registry, student loan applications, tax payments, and more. The exact dimensions and applications of this project are still being negotiated as of this writing, but many experts question the wisdom of the Ontario project and its implementation.

As of this writing, the specific applications and data collected and maintained for the smart card have not been determined. The Smart Card Project is supposed to represent a major step in the Ontario government's transformation to "e-government," using electronic tools to improve the way government delivers services and manages its operations. Stated principles of the project include: improved access to Ontario government services; enhanced privacy and security; reduction of fraud; and rigorous and accurate registration procedures that ensure one person, one card. According to the Ontario government, it will only introduce the technology when it is assured that personal information can be fully protected.

Government also claims that the smart card will not contain information on a person's medical history and that information on the card and access to that information will be completely controlled by the cardholder. According to David Tsubouchi, MPP, "no decisions have been taken as to whether the cards will employ biometric technology. We are exploring many options, and smart cards will only use this technology if it represents clear benefits for security, privacy, cost, and feasibility." Tsubouchi also stated that the Information and Privacy Commissioner of Ontario was involved in development of the smart card to ensure and "enhance" personal privacy. Ontario Minister of Municipal Affairs and Housing Chris Hodgson also insists that protection of privacy is a paramount concern.

Still, concerned citizens and officials, like Federal Privacy Commissioner George Radwanski, are worried about the potential for privacy invasion of the Ontario smart card. In March 2001, Radwanski said: "First a single card like that would tend to very quickly become a universal identity card, a kind of internal passport…. Second, a single card like that opens the door to far too many opportunities for data matching and cross-over uses of your personal information. Whether all the information is actually embedded in microchips on the card, or whether the single card simply provides access to information in various data banks, the outcome is the same; one card opens the door to all, or nearly all, the most sensitive information about you."

As much as $500 million will be needed to launch Ontario's basic smart card infrastructure, a bonanza for technology vendors advising the government on this project. The Ontario government conducted a $300 000 feasibility study on the use of biometrics in the smart card and have not released the findings of the report. Even if biometrics are not included in the initial project, biometric technology could be incorporated in later versions. Ontario has several smart card projects that are active in the health care field. The implications of combining these projects and placing these applications on the new smart card—a possibility given the slippery slope principle—are extremely worrisome for privacy. Once agreement is reached to combine the applications, the next step on the slippery-slope is to combine and use the data obtained from smart card use.

Yet, viewed from a "benevolent government" perspective, the information gathered—not on individual card users, but on card users as a whole—could enable the province to save money

and benefit Ontarians by transforming its business processes, by reengineering its consumer interactions, by developing new applications and transforming old ones, and by providing additional access to services and funding for these services. All of these changes would be the result of using data collected through smart card use and transforming that data into useful information through decision support and knowledge management systems.

Ontario's pilot project is scheduled to take place in 2002 with a larger-scale roll out to the general public in 2003. According to a government news release, the majority of Ontarians support the idea of introducing smart cards to the province. The issues are difficult. It remains to be seen what will happen when Canada's largest provincial government introduces this state-of-the-art technology.

Sources: "Toward Electronic Health Records," Office of Health and the Information Highway: Health Canada, www.hc-sc.gc.ca/ohih-bsi/ehr/ehr_dse/c_e.html, accessed October 2, 2001; "Last Month's Smart Card and Biometrics News," www.bellid.com/site/news/smartnews_old.htm, accessed October 4, 2001; "Research Statistics: WorldWide SmartCards Market Forecast," www.smartcardcentral.com/research, accessed October 4, 2001; "Scotiabank First to Deploy IVI Checkmate Smart-Card-Capable PIN Pad," www.ckmate.com/news/scotia_oct19_99.html, accessed August 10, 2001; "Greg Meckbach, "Smart Card Success Requires New Partnerships," *Computing Canada*, April 23, 1999; "U.S. Will Be Smart Card Hot Spot," *Bank Technology News*, April 3, 2001, http://special.northernlight.com/banking/hotspot.htm, accessed August 10, 2001; "Mondex in Action: Sherbrooke Implementation," www.mondex.ca/eng/mondexinaction/sherbrooke.cfm?pg-inaction, accessed October 4, 2001; "Mondex in Action: Canadian Projects," www.mondex.ca/eng/mondexinaction/canadianprojects.cfm?pg=inaction, accessed October 4, 2001; "Canadian Smart Card Test Goes to the Back of the Class," www.card-forum.com, accessed August 10, 2001; "Ottawa Lacks the Smarts on Smart Card,: Canada NewsWire, www.newswire.ca/releases/March2001/27/c7374.html, accessed August 10, 2001; "Research on the Ontario SmartCard Project," www.fis.utoronto.ca/research/iprp/sc, accessed August 10, 2001; Andrew Clement, "Ontario's Project on Smart Card is a Bad Idea," *The Toronto Star*, July 10, 2001; Nigel Hannaford, "Smart Card Would Not Be Wise," *Calgary Herald*, January 6, 2001; Theresa Boyle, "Smart Card Chills Privacy Experts," *The Toronto Star*, January 15, 2001.

VIDEO RESOURCE:
"A Medical Mystery," *UNDERcurrents* 145 (January 23, 2000).

CASE STUDY QUESTIONS:

1. What have been the outcomes of Canada's smart card pilot projects? Look on the Web for pilot projects conducted in other countries. Have these projects had the same results?

2. If your bank introduced smart cards in a project similar to those in Guelph and Sherbrooke, would you apply for the smart card? What if it was a different bank than your own?

3. What are the potential benefits of the Ontario smart card project? What government services do you think should be

accessed through smart cards? Which services should not be accessed through smart cards?

4. How can Ontario's government use the data they could collect from smart card users to improve access, delivery, quality, and the number of provincial government services available to their citizens?

5. What is the potential downside of Ontario's adoption of smart cards for access to provincial services? In addition to ethical issues, what other issues constitute the potential negative impacts of the Ontario smart card?

6. How do you think businesses could implement smart cards? Should they partner with other businesses? Give some examples of these partnerships. What would be the benefits in terms of decision support and knowledge management that businesses could obtain from smart card adoption by their customers? Do the same privacy and other concerns apply to the use of smart cards in business as in government? Explain your answer.

REFERENCES

Abdel-Hamid, Tarek K. Kishore Sengupta, and **Clint Swett.** "The Impact of Goals on Software Project Management: An Experimental Investigation." *MIS Quarterly* 23, no. 4. (December 1999).

"About Diversey Lever." *Diversey Lever.* http://www.unilever.ca/latestbr/diverseylever.html. (Accessed January 19, 2001).

"About the 'Health Information Network'. (HiNet)." *Electronic Child Health Network.* http://www.echn.ca/hsc/chnechnnsf/pages/hinetinfo. (Accessed June 12, 2000).

"About the Electronic Child Health Network." *Electronic Child Health Network.* http://www.echn.ca/hsc/chn-echn/pages/echninfo. (Accessed September 28, 2001).

Abreu, Elinor. "The Hack Attack." *The Industry Standard.* (February 21, 2000).

Ackerman, Mark S., and **Christine A. Halverson.** "Reexamining Organizational Memory." *Communications of the ACM* 43, no. 1. (January 2000).

Ackoff, R. L. "Management Misinformation System." *Management Science* 14, no. 4. (December 1967)., B140–B116.

"Advanced Technology." *Ottawa Economic Development Corporation.* http://www.ottawaregion.com/advancedtech/. (Accessed August 28, 2001).

"Advantex to Form Internet Alliance for Online Shopping Portal With Air Canada." *Advantex Marketing International Inc.* http://www.advantex.com/pr021000b.htm. (Accessed February 10, 2000).

Agarwal, P.K. "Building India's National Internet Backbone." *Communications of the ACM* 42, no. 6. (June 1999).

Agarwal, Ritu, Jayesh Prasad, Mohan Tanniru, and **John Lynch.** "Risks of Rapid Application Development." *Communications of the ACM* 43, no. 11es. (November 2000).

Agarwal, Ritu, Prabudda De, Atish P. Sinha, and **Mohan Tanniru.** "On the Usability of OO Representations." *Communications of the ACM* 43, no. 10. (October 2000).

Ahituv, Niv, and **Seev Neumann.** "A Flexible Approach to Information System Development." *MIS Quarterly.* (June 1984).

Aiken, Peter, Alice Muntz, and **Russ Richards.** "DOD Legacy Systems: Reverse Engineering Data Requirements." *Communications of the ACM* 37, no. 5. (May 1994).

"Air Canada and Canadian Airlines Frequent Flyer Programmes to be Integrated in April." *M2 Communications.* http://www.findarticles.com. (Accessed March 21, 2000).

"Air Canada and Canadian Airlines Frequent Flyers and History." *About: The Human Internet.* http://gocanada.about.com/about/canada/gocanada/library/weekly/aa090499.htm. (Accessed September 4, 1999).

"Air Canada Reports Third Quarter Results, Consolidated Results Include Canadian Airlines." *Yahoo! News.* http://cf.us.biz.yahoo.com/cnw/001026/a.air_cana.html. (Accessed October 26, 2000).

"Air Canada to Hire 2,000 Workers to Improve Customer Service." *The Canadian Press.* http://www.canoe.ca/AirMergers/aug3_aircanservice.html. (Accessed August 3, 2000).

Akin, David. "Empori.com Eggs Business Shoppers." *Financial Post.* (December 11, 2000).

Alavi, Maryam. "An Assessment of the Prototyping Approach to Information System Development." *Communications of the ACM* 27. (June 1984).

Alavi, Maryam, and **Dorothy Leidner.** "Knowledge Management Systems: Issues, Challenges, and Benefits." *Communications of the Association for Information Systems* 1. (February 1999).

Alavi, Maryam, and **Erich A. Joachimsthaler.** "Revisiting DSS Implementation Research: A Meta-Analysis of the Literature and Suggestions for Researchers." *MIS Quarterly* 16, no. 1. (March 1992).

Alavi, Maryam, R. Ryan Nelson, and **Ira R. Weiss.** "Strategies for End-User Computing: An Integrative Framework." *Journal of Management Information Systems* 4, no. 3. (Winter 1987–1988).

"Alberta Registries/E-Commerce Site." *wayto.com.* http://www.wayto.com/proj.asp?DocName=abregcom. (Accessed May 15, 1999).

Alberts, David S. "The Economics of Software Quality Assurance." Washington, DC: National Computer Conference, 1976 Proceedings.

Alison, Diana. "IT Takes on Handheld Management." *Information Week.* (May 29, 2000).

Allen, Bradley P. "CASE-Based Reasoning: Business Applications." *Communications of the ACM* 37, no. 3. (March 1994).

Allen, Brandt R., and **Andrew C. Boynton.** "Information Architecture: In Search of Efficient Flexibility." *MIS Quarterly* 15, no. 4. (December 1991).

Allison, Graham T. *Essence of Decision-Explaining the Cuban Missile Crisis.* Boston: Little Brown. (1971).

Alter, Steven, and **Michael Ginzberg.** "Managing Uncertainty in MIS Implementation." *Sloan Management Review* 20, no. 1. (Fall 1978).

Amer, Suzie. "If You Build It, Will They Come?." *Forbes.* (May 25, 1999).

Amor, Daniel. *The E-Business Revolution.* Upper Saddle River, NJ: Prentice-Hall. (2000).

"Anatel Communications." *Voiceage Corporation.* http://www.voiceage.com/news/newsduo.htm. (Accessed February 6, 2000).

Anderson, Evan A. "Choice Models for the Evaluation and Selection of Software Packages." *Journal of Management Information Systems* 6, no. 4. (Spring 1990).

Andrew, James P., Andy Blackburn, and **Harold L. Sirkin.** "The Business-to-Business Opportunity." Boston Consulting Group. (October 2000).

Angwin, Julia. "How an E-Posse Led to Arrests in Online Fraud." *The Wall Street Journal.* (May 4, 2000).

Ansley, Mike. "Virtual Manufacturing." *CMA Management.* (February 2000).

Anthes, Gary H. "Notes System Sends Federal Property Data Nationwide." *Computerworld.* (August 8, 1994).

———. "Supercomputers Make a Comeback." *Computerworld.* (July 3, 2000).

Anthony, R.N. *Planning and Control Systems: A Framework for Analysis.* Cambridge, MA: Harvard University Press. (1965).

Applegate, Lynda M., Clyde W. Holsapple, Ravi Kalakota, Franz J. Radermacher, and **Andrew B. Whinston.** "Electronic Commerce: Building Blocks of New Business Opportunity." *Journal of Organizational Computing and Electronic Commerce* 6, no. 1. (1996).

Applegate, Lynda, and **Janice Gogan.** "Electronic Commerce: Trends and Opportunities." Harvard Business School, 9-196-006. (October 6, 1995).

———. "Paving the Information Superhighway: Introduction to the Internet." *Harvard Business School* 9-195-202. (August 1995).

Argyle, N.H. "Air Route Changes Emphasize Service." *Calgary Herald.* http://www.calgaryherald.com/features/discover_spring2001/air.html. (Accessed July 12, 2001).

Argyris, Chris. *Interpersonal Competence and Organizational Effectiveness.* Homewood, IL: Dorsey Press. (1962).

Armstrong, Arthur, and **John Hagel, III.** "The Real Value of On-line Communities." *Harvard Business Review.* (May–June 1996).

Armstrong, Curtis P., and **V. Sambamurthy.** "Information Technology Assimilation in Firms: The Influence of Senior Leadership and IT Infrastructures." *Information Systems Research* 10, no. 4. (December 1999).

Asakawa, Kazuo, and **Hideyuki Takagi.** "Neural Networks in Japan." *Communications of the ACM* 37, no. 3. (March 1994).

Association of Computing Machinery. "ACM's Code of Ethics and Professional Conduct." *Communications of the ACM* 36, no. 12. (December 1993).

Atkinson, Anthony and **Marc Epstein.** "Measure for Measure." *CMA Management.* (September 2000).

Atkinson, Pat. "B2B Bears Fruit at GM Canada". (Accessed February 1, 2001).

Attewell, Paul. "Technology Diffusion and Organizational Learning: The Case of Business Computing." *Organization Science, no.* 3. (1992).

Attewell, Paul, and **James Rule.** "Computing and Organizations: What We Know and What We Don't Know." *Communications of the ACM* 27, no. 12. (December 1984).

Badler, Norman I., Martha S. Palmer, and **Rama Bindiganavale.** "Animation Control for Real-time Virtual Humans." *Communications of the ACM* 42, no. 8. (August 1999).

Baig, Edward C., Marcia Stepanek, and **Neill Gross.** "Privacy." *Business Week.* (April 5, 1999).

Baig, Edward, Neil Gross, and **Marcia Stepanek.** "Privacy." *Business Week.* (April 5, 1999).

Bakos, J. Yannis. "The Emerging Role of Electronic Marketplaces on the Internet." *Communications of the ACM* 41, no. 8. (August 1998).

Bakos, J. Yannis, and **Michael E. Treacy.** "Information Technology and Corporate Strategy: A Research Perspective." *MIS Quarterly.* (June 1986).

Balasubramanian, V., and **Alf Bashian.** "Document Management and Web Technologies: Alice Marries the Mad Hatter." *Communications of the ACM* 41, no. 7. (July 1998).

Bamn, David. "The Future Is Calling." *Profit. (*August 2000).

Banker, Rajiv. "Value Implications of Relative Investments in Information Technology." Department of Information Systems and Center for Digital Economy Research, University of Texas at Dallas, January 23, 2001.

Banker, Rajiv D., Srikant M. Datar, Chris F. Kemerer, and **Dani Zweig.** "Software Complexity and Maintenance Costs." *Communications of the ACM* 36, no. 11. (November 1993).

Banker, Rajiv D., Robert J. Kaufmann, and **Rachna Kumar.** "An Empirical Test of Object-Based Output Measurement Metrics in a Computer-Aided Software Engineering. (CASE). Environment." *Journal of Management Information Systems* 8, no. 3. (Winter 1991–1992).

Banker, Rajiv D., and **Chris F. Kemerer.** "Performance Evaluation Metrics in Information Systems Development: A Principal-Agent Model." *Information Systems Research* 3, no. 4. (December 1992).

"Banks Profit from Making Informed Decisions." *Angoss.* http://www.angoss.com/angoss.html. (Accessed January 19, 2001).

Bannan, Karen J. "Chatting Up a Sale." *The Wall Street Journal.* (October 23, 2000).

Barker, Virginia E., and **Dennis E. O'Connor.** "Expert Systems for Configuration at Digital: XCON and Beyond." *Communications of the ACM.* (March 1989).

Baron, John P., Michael J. Shaw, and **Andrew D. Bailey, Jr.** "Web-based E-catalog Systems in B2B Procurement." *Communications of the ACM* 43, no.5. (May 2000).

Barrett, Jim, Kevin Knight, Inderject Man, and **Elaine Rich.** "Knowledge and Natural Language Processing." *Communications of the ACM* 33, no. 8. (August 1990).

Barrett, Stephanie S. "Strategic Alternatives and Interorganizational System Implementations: An Overview." *Journal of Management Information Systems.* (Winter 1986–1987).

Barron, Kelly. "Logistics in Brown." *Forbes.* (January 10, 2000).

Bartholomew, Doug. "E-business Commentary to Exchange or Not to Exchange." *Industry Week.* http://www.industryweek.com. (Accessed May 8, 2001).

Barua, Anitesh, Sophie C. H. Lee, and **Andrew B. Whinston.** "The Calculus of Reengineering." *Information Systems Research* 7, no. 4. (December 1996).

Barua, Anitesh, Sury Ravindran, and **Andrew B. Whinston.** "Efficient Selection of Suppliers over the Internet." *Journal of Management Information Systems* 13, no. 4. (Spring 1997).

Baskerville, Richard L., and **Jan Stage.** "Controlling Prototype Development Through Risk Analysis." *MIS Quarterly* 20, no. 4. (December 1996).

Baum, David. "E-xchange This." *Profit Magazine.* (August 2000).

Baxter, James, "Computer Use Soars in the Job: Proliferation Highest Among Professionals." *Calgary Herald.* (May, 2001).

"BCTIA Monitor." *British Columbia Technology Industries Association.* http://www.bctia.org/Resources/BCTIA_Monitor. (Accessed July 5, 2001).

Beath, Cynthia Mathis, and **Wanda J. Orlikowski.** "The Contradictory Structure of Systems Development Methodologies: Deconstructing the IS-User Relationship in Information Engineering." *Information Systems Research* 5, no. 4. (December 1994).

Bedard, Dave. "SaskPool 'Will Survive.'" *Grainnews.* (March 23, 2001). Courtesy of Saskatchewan Wheat Pool.

Beer, Michael, Russell A. Eisenstat, and **Bert Spector.** "Why Change Programs Don't Produce Change." *Harvard Business Review.* (November–December 1990).

Beer, Randall D., Roger D. Quinn, Hillel J. Chiel, and **Roy E. Ritzman.** "Biologically Inspired Approaches to Robots." *Communications of the ACM* 40, no. 3. (March 1997).

Belkin, Nicholas J., and **W. Bruce Croft.** "Information Filtering and Information Retrieval: Two Sides of the Same Coin?" *Communications of the ACM* 35, no. 12. (November 1992).

Bellman, Steven, Eric J. Johnson, and **Gerald L. Lohse.** "To Opt-in or Opt-out? It Depends on the Question." *Communications of the ACM* 44, no. 2. (February 2001).

Benaroch, Michel, and **Robert J. Kauffman.** "Justifying Electronic Banking Network Expansion Using Real Options Analysis." *MIS Quarterly* 24, no. 2. (June 2000).

Benjamin, Robert, and **Rolf Wigand.** "Electronic Markets and Virtual Value Chains on the Information Superhighway." *Sloan Management Review.* (Winter 1995).

Bensaou, M. "Portfolios of Buyer-Supplier Relationships." *Sloan Management Review* 40, no. 4. (Summer 1999).

Berdichevsky, Daniel, and **Erik Neunschwander.** "Toward an Ethics of Persuasive Technology." *Communications of the ACM* 42, no. 5. (May 1999).

Berners-Lee, Tim, Robert Cailliau, Ari Luotonen, Henrik Frystyk Nielsen, and **Arthur Secret.** "The World-Wide Web." *Communications of the ACM* 37, no. 8. (August 1994).

Berry, Leonard L., and **A. Parasuraman.** "Listening to the Customer—the Concept of a Service-Quality Information System." *Sloan Management Review.* (Spring 1997).

Berst, Jesse. "How to Spy on Your Employees." *MSNBC Technology.* (August 21, 2000).

Bertino, Elisa, Elena Pagani, Gian Paolo Rossi, and **Pierangela Samarati.** "Protecting Information on the Web." *Communications of the ACM* 43, no.11. (Novemer 2000).

Bhandari, Inderpal. "Business Intelligence and the Search for Truth." *TGC.com.* http://www.tgc.com/dsstar/98/0825/980825.html. (Accessed July 11, 2001).

Bharadwaj, Anandhi. "A Resource-Based Perspective on Information Technology Capability and Firm Performance." *MIS Quarterly* 24, no. 1. (March 2000).

Bhattacharjee, Sudip, and **R. Ramesh.** "Enterprise Computing Environments and Cost Assessment." *Communications of the ACM* 43, no. 10. (October 2000).

Bikson, T.K., and **J.D. Eveland.** "Integrating New Tools into Information Work." The Rand Corporation. (1992). RAND/RP-106.

Bikson, Tora K., Cathleen Stasz, and **Donald A. Monkin.** "Computer-Mediated Work: Individual and Organizational Impact on One Corporate Headquarters." Rand Corporation. (1985).

"Binnacle Security." *Binnacle.com.* (Accessed May 28, 2001).

Bird, Jerry W., "Flying Gourmet: Cara's Airline Food Caters to Every Taste." *Air Highway Journal.* www.airhighwayjournal.com/ flying_gourmet_two.htm. (Accessed January 17, 2001).

Bjerklie, David. "Does E-Mail Mean Everyone's Mail?" *Information Week.* (January 3, 1994).

Blackburn, Joseph, Gary Scudder, and **Luk N. Van Wassenhove.** "Concurrent Software Development." *Communications of the ACM* 43, no. 11. (November 2000).

Blackwell, Gerry. "High Energy, Light Hand." *Infosystems Executive.* (July 17, 2001).

Blanning, Robert W. "Establishing a Corporate Presence on the Internet in Singapore." *Journal of Organizational Computing and Electronic Commerce* 9, no. 1. (1999).

Blanning, Robert W., David R. King, James R. Marsden, and **Ann C. Seror.** "Intelligent Models of Human Organizations: The State of the Art." *Journal of Organizational Computing* 2, no. 2. (1992).

Blau, Peter, and **W. Richard Scott.** *Formal Organizations.* San Francisco: Chandler Press. (1962).

"Blood, Sweat, and Peers." *Red Herring.* (December 4, 2000).

Boehm, Barry W. "Understanding and Controlling Software Costs." *IEEE Transactions on Software Engineering* 14, no. 10. (October 1988).

Borriello, Gaetano, and **Roy Want.** "Embedded Computation Meets the World Wide Web." *Communications of the ACM* 43, no. 5. (May 2000).

Bosak, Jon, and **Tim Bray.** "XML and the Second-Generation Web." *Scientific American.* (May 1999).

Boston Consulting Group. "Mobile Commerce: Winning the On-Air Consumer." (November 2000).

Bostrom, R. P., and **J. S. Heinen.** "MIS Problems and Failures: A Socio-Technical Perspective. Part I: The Causes." *MIS Quarterly* 1. (September 1977).

Bostrom, R. P., and **J. S. Heinen.** "MIS Problems and Failures: A Socio-Technical Perspective. Part II: The Application of Socio-Technical Theory." *MIS Quarterly* 1. (December 1977).

Bowen, Jonathan. "The Ethics of Safety-Critical Systems." *Communications of the ACM* 43, no. 3. (April 2000).

Brabston, Mary, Robert Zmud, and **John Carlson.** "Strategic Vision for Information Technology" in Raymond Papp, ed., "Strategic Information Technology: Opportunities for Competitive Advantage." *Idea Group Publishing.* (2000).

Brachman, Ronald J., Tom Khabaza, Willi Kloesgen, Gregory Piatetsky-Shapiro, and **Evangelos Simoudis.** "Mining Business Databases." *Communications of the ACM* 39, no. 11. (November 1996).

Braidotti, Victoria, and **Joan Harbin.** "Report on Enterprise Management." *AMR Research.* (May, 2001).

Brancheau, James C., Brian D. Janz, and **James C. Wetherbe.** "Key Issues in Information Systems Management: 1994–1995 SIM Delphi Results." *MIS Quarterly* 20, no. 2. (June 1996).

Brannigan, Mary. "Bill Payments Over the Internet Get a Big Boost." *The Wall Street Journal.* (January 28, 1999).

"Bridgestone/Firestone Announces Voluntary Tire Recall." *Ford Motor Company.* (August 9, 2000).

Brier, Tom, Jerry Luftman, and **Raymond Papp.** " Enablers and Inhibitors of Business—IT Alignment." *Communications of the Association for Information Systems* 1. (March 1999).

"British Trade Body Clears Air Canada/Canadian Airlines Merger at Heathrow." *The Canadian Press.* http://www.canoe.ca/ AirMergers/aug31_ukoksairmerger.html. (Accessed August 31, 2000).

Broadbent, Marianne, Peter Weill, and **Don St. Clair.** "The Implications of Information Technology Infrastructure for Business Process Redesign." *MIS Quarterly* 23, no. 2. (June 1999).

"Brocade Upgrades SAN System." *Management Consultants News*

Brod, Craig. *Techno Stress—The Human Cost of the Computer Revolution.* Reading MA: Addison-Wesley. (1982).

Brooks, Frederick P. "The Mythical Man-Month." *Datamation.* (December 1974).

Brown Bag Software vs. Symantec Corp. 960 F2D 1465. (Ninth Circuit, 1992).

Brutzman, Don. "The Virtual Reality Modeling Language and Java." *Communications of the ACM* 41, no. 6. (June 1998).

Brynjolfsson, Erik. "The Contribution of Information Technology to Consumer Welfare." *Information Systems Research* 7, no. 3. (September 1996).

———. "The Productivity Paradox of Information Technology." *Communications of the ACM* 36, no. 12. (December 1993).

Brynjolfsson, Erik, and **Lorin M. Hitt.** "Beyond the Productivity Paradox." *Communications of the ACM* 41, no. 8. (August 1998).

———. "Information Technology and Organizational Design: Evidence from Micro Data." MIT Sloan school of Management Working Paper (January 1998).

———. "New Evidence on the Returns to Information Systems." MIT Sloan School of Management. Working Paper (October 1993).

Brynjolfsson, E.T., T.W. Malone, V. Gurbaxani, and A. Kambil. "Does Information Technology Lead to Smaller Firms?" *Management Science* 40, no. 12. (1994).

Brynjolfsson, Erik, and S. Yang. "Intangible Assets: How the Interaction of Computers and Organizational Structure Affects Stock Markets." MIT Sloan School of Management. (2000).

"Bubble, Bubble, Less Toil and Trouble." *Communications News.* (May 1999).

Buckler, Grant. "Wheel of Fortune." *Infosystems Executive.* (July 2000).

"Building Value at Cara." *Business Wire.* http://biz.yahoo.com/ bw/001025/cara.html. (Accessed October 25, 2000).

Bullen, Christine, and John F. Rockart. "A Primer on Critical Success Factors." Cambridge, MA: Center for Information Systems Research, Sloan School of Management. (1981).

Burk, Dan L. "Copyrightable Functions and Patentable Speech." *Communications of the ACM* 44, no. 2. (February 2001).

Burke, Danny. "Metropolitan-Area Network Turns Sudbury Into Leading-Edge Wired Community." *Cisco Systems.* http://www. cisco.com/warp/public/3/ca/profiles/sudbury.htm. (Accessed November 12, 2000).

Burkhardt, Grey E., Seymour E. Goodman, Arun Mehta, and Larry Press. "The Internet in India: Better Times Ahead?" *Communications of the ACM* 41, no. 11. (November 1998).

Burtka, Michael. "Generic Algorithms." *The Stern Information Systems Review* 1, no. 1. (Spring 1993).

Busch, Elizabeth, Matti Hamalainen, Clyde W. Holsapple, Yongmoo Suh, and Andrew B. Whinston. "Issues and Obstacles in the Development of Team Support Systems." *Journal of Organizational Computing* 1, no. 2. (April–June 1991).

Buss, Martin D.J. "How to Rank Computer Projects." *Harvard Business Review.* (January 1983).

Byrd, Terry Anthony. "Measuring the Flexibility of Information Technology Infrastructure: Exploratory Analysis of a Construct." *Journal of Management Information Systems* 17, no. 1. (Summer 2000).

Byrna, John A. "Management by Web." *Business Week.* (August 2000).

Caldwell, Bruce. "A Cure for Hospital Woes." *Information Week.* (September 9, 1991).

Campbell, Steve. "Yaletown Technology Group: Taking CRM Lessons to Heart." *Yaletown Technology Group.* http://www. yaletech.com/news/articles/crm.htm. (Accessed July 5, 2001).

"Canadian Plus." *Air Canada.* http://www.aircanada.ca/cdnplus. (Accessed January 20, 2001).

"Canadian Projects." *Mondex Canada.* http://www.mondex.ca/eng/mondexinaction/canadianprojects.cf m?pg=inaction. (Accessed August 4, 2001).

"Canadian Smartcard Test Goes to the Back of the Class." *CardForum*, May 25, 2001. http://www.cardforum.com/html/news/052501_1.htm. (Accessed June 10, 2001).

"Canadian Standards Association: CSA Model Code for the Protection of Personal Information." *Media Awareness Network.* http://www.mediaawareness.ca/eng/issues/priv/laws/ csacode.htm. (Accessed July 31, 2001).

"Canadians with Work Internet Access Will Rack up 800 Million Hours of Annual Personal Surfing Time at Work." *E-Productivity Summit 2001.* http://www.eproductivity.org/ misues/00/070400.cfm. (Accessed May 24, 2001).

Caouette, Margarette J., and Bridget N. O'Connor. "The Impact of Group Support Systems on Corporate Teams' Stages of Development." *Journal of Organizational Computing and Electronic Commerce* 8, no. 1. (1998).

Carreno, Sonia. "Site Lines: HBC.com." *Strategy Magazine.* (January 29, 2001).

"Case Bank Text Mining Case Study in Banking." *Megaputer Intelligence.* http://www.megaputer.com/company/cases/ casebank.php3. (Accessed February 25, 2001).

"Case Study Voice Messaging." *Brooktrout Technology.* http://www.brooktrout.com/pages/news/case_studies/html/esna. html. (Accessed February 25, 2001).

"Case Study: HKBC Gets a Clean View of Customers Using Trillium on AS/400." *Trillium Software Systems.* (2000).

"Case Study: National Bank of Canada: Alphanet's Remote Network Management Provides Substantial Savings for National Bank of Canada." *Alphanet Solutions.* http://www. alphanetsolutions.com/NBoCtop.asp. (Accessed February 25, 2001).

"Case Study: Neoset Modular Furniture." *Vigilant.* http://www. vigilant.com/products/casestudies/multisites.neoset.htm. (Accessed February 25, 2001).

"Case Study: Windsor Regional Hospital Health Sciences Library." *EOS International.* http://www.eosintl.com/htdocs/cswindsor. html. (Accessed February 25, 2001).

"Case Study: Workers Compensation Board of British Columbia." *CMP Media.* http://www.lantimes.com/97/97may/705bCD8a. html. (Accessed May 2001).

Cash, J.I., and Benn R. Konsynski. "IS Redraws Competitive Boundaries." *Harvard Business Review.* (March–April 1985).

Caufield, Brian and Ian Mount, "The Missing Link: What You Need to Know About Supply Chain Technology." *Business 2.0.* (May 2001).

Cavazos, Edward A. "The Legal Risks of Setting up Shop in Cyberspace." *Journal of Organizational Computing* 6, no. 1. (1996).

"CAW Calls for Ergonomic Regulations Nationwide." *Canada Newswire.* http://www1.newswire.ca/releases/February2001. (Accessed July 13, 2001). © Canada Newswire Ltd.

Chabrow, Eric R. "Supply Chains Go Global." *Information Week.* (April 3, 2000).

———. "The Internet: Copyrights." *Information Week.* (March 25, 1996).

Chan, Yolande E., Sid L. Huff, Donald W. Barclay, and Duncan G. Copeland. "Business Strategic Orientation, Information Systems Strategic Orientation, and Strategic Alignment." *Information Systems Research* 8, no. 2. (June 1997).

Chang, Shih-Fu, John R. Amith, Mandis Beigi, and Ana Benitez. "Visual Information Retrieval from Large Distributed On-line Repositories." *Communications of the ACM* 40, no. 12. (December 1997).

Chatfield, Akemi Takeoka, and Philip Yetton. "Strategic Payoff from EDI as a Function of EDI Embeddedness." *Journal of Management Information Systems* 16, no. 4. (Spring 2000).

Chatterjee, Samir, and Suzanne Pawlowski. "All-Optical Networks." *Communications of the ACM* 42, no. 6. (June 1999).

Chatterjee, Samir. "Requirements for Success in Gigabit Networking." *Communications of the ACM* 40, no. 7. (July 1997).

Chaudhury, Abhijit, Debasish Mallick, and H. Raghav Rao. "Web Channels in E-Commerce." *Communications of the ACM* 44, no. 1. (January 2001).

Chen, David W. "Man Charged with Sabotage of Computers." *The New York Times.* (February 18, 1998).

Cheng, Hsing K., Ronald R. Sims, and **Hildy Teegen.** "To Purchase or to Pirate Software: An Empirical Study." *Journal of Management Information Systems* 13, no. 4. (Spring 1997).

Cheshire, Bruce "Case Study www.bombardier.com." http://msnhomepages.talkcity.com/RedmondAve/Bruce_Cheshire/bomb.htm. (Accessed May 15, 2001).

Cheyne, Tanya L., and **Frank E. Ritter.** "Targeting Audiences on the Internet." *Communications of the ACM* 44, no. 4. (April 2001).

Chidambaram, Laku. "Relational Development in Computer-Supported Groups." *MIS Quarterly* 20, no. 2. (June 1996).

Chin, Shu-Kai. "High-Confidence Design for Security." *Communications of the ACM* 42, no. 7. (July 1999).

Chismar, William G., and **Laku Chidambaram.** "Telecommunications and the Structuring of U.S. Multinational Corporations." *International Information Systems* 1, no. 4. (October 1992).

Cho, Sungzoon, Chigeun Han, Dae Hee Han, and **Hyung-Il Kim.** "Web-Based Keystroke Dynamics Identity Verification Using Neural Network." *Journal of Organizational Computing and Electronic Commerce* 10, no. 4. (2000).

Choi, Soon-Yong, Dale O. Stahl, and **Andrew B. Whinston.** *The Economics of Electronic Commerce.* Indianapolis, IN: Macmillan Technical Publishing. (1997).

Choy, Manhoi, Hong Va Leong, and **Man Hon Wong.** "Disaster Recovery Techniques for Database Systems." *Communications of the ACM* 43, no. 11. (November 2000).

Christensen, Clayton. "The Past and Future of Competitive Advantage." *Sloan Management Review* 42, no. 2. (Winter 2001).

Churchland, Paul M., and **Patricia Smith Churchland.** "Could a Machine Think?" *Scientific American.* (January 1990).

"CIT, BMO Launching Auto Financial Portal." *The Globe and Mail.* http://www.Globetechnology.com. (Accessed November 23, 2000).

Clark, Don. "Sun Microsystems Still Has a Legion of Believers." *The Wall Street Journal.* (March 23, 1998).

———. "The End of Software." *The Wall Street Journal Technology Report.* (November 15, 1999).

Clarke, Roger. "Internet Privacy Concerns Confirm the Case for Intervention." *Communications of the ACM* 42, no. 2. (February 1999).

Clement, Andrew, and **Peter Van den Besselaar.** "A Retrospective Look at PD Projects." *Communications of the ACM* 36, no. 4. (June 1993).

Clemons, Eric K. "Evaluation of Strategic Investments in Information Technology." *Communications of the ACM.* (January 1991).

Clemons, Eric K., and **Bruce W. Weber.** "Segmentation, Differentiation, and Flexible Pricing: Experience with Information Technology and Segment-Tailored Strategies." *Journal of Management Information Systems* 11, no. 2. (Fall 1994).

Clemons, Eric K., and **Michael Row.** "Limits to Interfirm Coordination through IT." *Journal of Management Information Systems* 10, no. 1. (Summer 1993).

———. "McKesson Drug Co.: Case Study of a Strategic Information System." *Journal of Management Information Systems.* (Summer 1988).

———. "Sustaining IT Advantage: The Role of Structural Differences." *MIS Quarterly* 15, no. 3. (September 1991).

Clemons, Eric K., Michael Row, and **Il-Horn Hann.** "Rosenbluth International: Strategic Transformation." *Journal of Management Information Systems* 16, no. 2. (Fall 1999).

Clifford, James, Albert Croker, and **Alex Tuzhilin.** "On Data Representation and Use in a Temporal Relational DBMS." *Information Systems Research* 7, no. 3. (September 1996).

Cline, Marshall, and **Mike Girou.** "Enduring Business Themes." *Communications of the ACM* 43, no. 5. (May 2000).

Coase, Ronald H. "The Nature of the Firm."(1937). in Putterman, Louis and Randall Kroszner. *The Economic Nature of the Firm: A Reader.* Cambridge University Press, 1995.

Cockerham, Paul W. "Net Expectations: Interactive Options Fulfill Guest Needs in the Well Connected Hotel Room." *Hospitality Technology Magazine.* (June 2001).

Cohen, Adam. "The Love Bug's Manila Birthplace Is Just One of Many Third World Virus Breeding Grounds." *Time Canada.* (May 22, 2000).

Cohen, Michael, James March, and **Johan Olsen.** "A Garbage Can Model of Organizational Choice." *Administrative Science Quarterly* 17. (1972).

Cole, Kevin, Olivier Fischer, and **Phyllis Saltzman.** "Just-in-Time Knowledge Delivery." *Communications of the ACM* 40, no. 7. (July 1997).

Cole-Gomolski, Barbara. "Customer Service with a :-)." *Computerworld.* (March 30, 1998).

Collins, W. Robert, Keith W. Miller, Bethany J. Spielman, and **Phillip Wherry.** "How Good Is Good Enough? An Ethical Analysis of Software Construction and Use." *Communications of the ACM* 37, no. 1. (January 1994).

"Company News and Events: Press Releases." *Portable Internet.* http://www.portableinternet.com/corporate_news.htm. (Accessed July 30, 2001). Provided with permission of Portable Internet, Inc.

"Company Profile" DWL Incorporated. http://www.dwl.com/website/company_profile/cp_main.html. (Accessed April 20, 2001).

"Compaq Intranet Case Study." *Intranet Design Magazine.* (January 17, 2001).

"Compinfo's AI Index." *Compinfocenter.com.* http://www.compinfocenter.com/tpait.htm. (Accessed January 28, 2001).

"Composite Case Study." *Enterprise Automation Technology.* http://www.eatl.com/case.htm. (Accessed March 11, 2000).

"Computer Software Law in Canada." *Law Office of Philip B. Kerr.* http://www.trytel.com/~pbkerr/computer.htm. (Accessed July 31, 2001).

Computer Systems Policy Project. "Perspectives on the National Information Infrastructure." (January 12, 1993).

Concours Group. "Delivering Large-Scale System Projects." (2000).

———. "ESII: Capitalizing on Enterprise Systems and Infrastructure." (1999).

———. "Managing and Exploiting Corporate Intranets." (1999).

Cooper, Brian L., Hugh J. Watson, Barbara H. Wixom, and **Dale L. Goodhue.** "Data Warehousing Supports Corporate Strategy at First American Corporation." *MIS Quarterly.* (December 2000).

Cooper, Randolph B. "Information Technology Development Creativity: A Case Study of Attempted Radical Change." *MIS Quarterly* 24, no. 2. (June 2000).

Copeland, Duncan G., and **James L. McKenney.** "Airline Reservations Systems: Lessons from History." *MIS Quarterly* 12, no. 3. (September 1988).

Corbato, Fernando J. "On Building Systems that Will Fail." *Communications of the ACM* 34, no. 9. (September 1991).

Corcoran, Cate T. "The Auction Economy." *Red Herring.* (August 1999).

"Corset Shop Signs with GSI." *Gemmar Systems International.* http://www.gemmar.com. (Accessed July 12, 2001).

Couger, J. Daniel. "Preparing IS Students to Deal with Ethical Issues." *MIS Quarterly* 13, no. 2. (June 1989).

Cox, Butler. *Globalization: The IT Challenge.* Sunnyvale, CA: Amdahl Executive Institute. (1991).

Cranor, Lorrie Faith, and **Brian A. LaMacchia.** "Spam!" *Communications of the ACM* 41, no. 8. (August 1998).

Crede, Andreas. "Electronic Commerce and the Banking Industry: The Requirement and Opportunities for New Payment Systems Using the Internet." *JCMC* 1, no. 3. (December 1995).

Crichton, John. "Nav Canada Announces Real Time Y2K Testing." *NavCanada.* (January 12, 1999). Courtesy of NAV CANADA.
———. "Nav Canada Technology Update." *NavCanada.* (June 8, 2000). Courtesy of NAV CANADA.

Cronin, Mary. *The Internet Strategy Handbook.* Boston, MA: Harvard Business School Press. (1996).

Cross, Rob, and **Lloyd Baird.** "Technology is Not Enough: Improving Performance by Building Organizational Memory." *Sloan Management Review* 41, no. 3. (Spring 2000).

Culnan, Mary J. "Transaction Processing Applications as Organizational Message Systems: Implications for the Intelligent Organization." Working paper no. 88-10, Twenty-second Hawaii International Conference on Systems Sciences. (January 1989).

Dalab, Suntanu. "What's Hot." *Canadian Business.* http://www.can-bus.com/magazine _items/2001/whatshot.shtml. (Accessed August 20, 2001).

Dalton, Gregory. "Going, Going, Gone!" *Information Week.* (October 4, 1999).
———. "Online Data's Fine Line." *Information Week.* (March 29, 1999).

Davenport, Thomas H. *Mission Critical: Realizing the Promise of Enterprise Systems.* Boston, MA: Harvard Business School Press. (2000).

Davenport, Tommas H. "Putting the Enterprise into Enterprise Systems." *Harvard Business Review.* (July–August 1998).

Davenport, Thomas H., and **James E. Short.** "The New Industrial Engineering: Information Technology and Business Process Redesign." *Sloan Management Review* 31, no. 4. (Summer 1990).

Davenport, Thomas H., and **Keri Pearlson**, **Jeanne G. Harris,** and **Ajay K. Kohli.** "How Do They Know Their Customers So Well?" *Sloan Management Review* 42, no. 2. (Winter 2001).

Davenport, Thomas H., and **Keri Pearlson.** "Two Cheers for the Virtual Office." *Sloan Management Review* 39, no. 4. (Summer 1998).

Davenport, Thomas H., and **Lawrence Prusak.** *Working Knowledge: How Organizations Manage What They Know.* Boston, MA: Harvard Business School Press. (1997).

Davenport, Thomas H., David W. DeLong, and **Michael C. Beers.** "Successful Knowledge Management Projects." *Sloan Management Review* 39, no. 2. (Winter 1998).

Davern, Michael J., and **Robert J. Kauffman.** "Discovering Potential and Realizing Value from Information Technology Investments. " *Journal of Management Information Systems* 16, no. 4. (Spring 2000).

Davidson, W.H. "Beyond Engineering: The Three Phases of Business Transformation." *IBM Systems Journal* 32, no. 1. (1993).

Davis, Fred R. "Perceived Usefulness, Ease of Use, and User Acceptance of Information Technology." *MIS Quarterly* 13, no. 3. (September 1989).

Davis, Gordon B. "Determining Management Information Needs: A Comparison of Methods." *MIS Quarterly* 1. (June 1977).

———. "Information Analysis for Information System Development." In *Systems Analysis and Design: A Foundation for the 1980's,* edited by W.W. Cotterman. J.D. Cougar, N.L. Enger, and F. Harold. New York: Wiley. (1981).

Davis, Gordon B. "Strategies for Information Requirements Determination." *IBM Systems Journal* 1. (1982).

Davis, Gordon B., and **Margrethe H. Olson.** *Management Information Systems: Conceptual Foundations, Structure, and Development,* 2nd ed. New York: McGraw-Hill. (1985).

Davis, Randall. "The Digital Dilemma." *Communications of the ACM* 44, no. 2. (February 2001).

Deans, Candace P., and **Michael J. Kane.** *International Dimensions of Information Systems and Technology.* Boston, MA: PWS-Kent. (1992).

Deans, Candace P., Kirk R. Karwan, Martin D. Goslar, David A. Ricks, and **Brian Toyne.** "Key International Issues in U.S.-Based Multinational Corporations." *Journal of Management Information Systems* 7, no. 4. (Spring 1991).

"Descartes Buys E-Transport to Expand Logistics Network." *Logistics Management and Distribution Report* 39, no. 4. (April 2000).

Defense Advance Research Projects Agency, 1998 DARPA. Unclassified.

Dejoie, Roy, George Fowler, and **David Paradice,** eds. *Ethical Issues in Information Systems.* Boston: Boyd & Fraser. (1991).

Dekleva, Sasa M. "The Influence of Information Systems Development Approach on Maintenance." *MIS Quarterly* 16, no. 3. (September 1992).

DeMarco, Tom. *Structured Analysis and System Specification.* New York: Yourdon Press. (1978).

Denning, Dorothy E., et al., "To Tap or Not to Tap." *Communications of the ACM* 36, no. 3. (March 1993).

Dennis, Alan R. "Information Exchange and Use in Group Decision Making: You Can Lead a Group to Information, But You Can't Make It Think." *MIS Quarterly* 20, no. 4. (December 1996).

Dennis, Alan R., Craig K. Tyran, Douglas R. Vogel, and **Jay Nunamaker, Jr.** "Group Support Systems for Strategic Planning." *Journal of Management Information Systems* 14, no. 1. (Summer 1997).

Dennis, Alan R., Jay E. Aronson, William G. Henriger, and **Edward D. Walker III.** "Structuring Time and Task in Electronic Brainstorming." *MIS Quarterly* 23, no. 1. (March 1999).

Dennis, Alan R., Jay F. Nunamaker, Jr., and **Douglas R. Vogel.** "A Comparison of Laboratory and Field Research in the Study of Electronic Meeting Systems." *Journal of Management Information Systems* 7, no. 3. (Winter 1990–1991).

Dennis, Alan R., Joey F. George, Len M. Jessup, Jay F. Nunamaker, and **Douglas R. Vogel.** "Information Technology to Support Electronic Meetings." *MIS Quarterly* 12, no. 4. (December 1988).

Dennis, Alan R., Sridar K. Pootheri, and **Vijaya L. Natarajan.** "Lessons from Early Adopters of Web Groupware." *Journal of Management Information Systems* 14, no. 4. (Spring 1998).

DePalma, Anthony. "Getting There is Challenge for Latin American E-tailing." *The New York Times.* (August 17, 2000).

DeSanctis, Geraldine, and **R. Brent Gallupe.** "A Foundation for the Study of Group Decision Support Systems." *Management Science* 33, no. 5. (May 1987).

Desmarais, Michel C., Richard Leclair, Jean-Yves Fiset, and **Hichem Talbi.** "Cost-Justifying Electronic Performance Support Systems." *Communications of the ACM* 40, no. 7. (July 1997).

Dhar, Vasant. "Plausibility and Scope of Expert Systems in Management." *Journal of Management Information Systems.* (Summer 1987).

Dhar, Vasant, and Roger Stein. *Intelligent Decision Support Methods: The Science of Knowledge Work.* Upper Saddle River, NJ: Prentice Hall. (1997).

Diamond, Edwin, and Stephen Bates. "Law and Order Comes to Cyberspace." *Technology Review.* (October 1995).

Dietrich, Brenda, Nick Donofrio, Grace Lin, and Jane Snowden. "Big Benefits for Big Blue." *ORMS Today.* (June, 2000).

Dijkstra, E. "Structured Programming." In *Classics in Software Engineering,* edited by Edward Nash Yourdon. New York: Yourdon Press. (1979).

"Discussion Forums." *Online Web Marketing.* http://forums.areaguide.net/default.asp?DT=98&10=583. (Accessed May 5, 1999).

"Distribution Savings on E-Goods is Dramatic," from "Spotlight: The Economic Impact of E-Commerce." *The Industry Standard.* (May 15, 1999).

Dobbyn, Tim. "Firestone Recall Exposes Flaws in Government Tests." *New York Daily News.* (September 22, 2000).

Doherty, Sean. "Thin-Client Devices." *Network Computing.* http://www.networkcomputing.com. (Accessed July 15, 2001).

Doll, William J. "Avenues for Top Management Involvement in Successful MIS Development." *MIS Quarterly.* (March 1985).

Domges, Rolf, and Klaus Pohl. "Adapting Traceability Environments to Project-Specific Needs." *Communications of the ACM* 41, no. 12. (December 1998).

"Don't Know Hacker, Says Canadian ISP." *Canoe Limited Partnership.* http://www.jamcaster.com/HackerAttack/feb_cdnresponse.html. (Accessed June 28, 2001). Courtesy of Canoe.ca.

Dos Santos, Brian. "Justifying Investments in New Information Technologies." *Journal of Management Information Systems* 7, no. 4. (Spring 1991).

"Dow Chemical Fires 50 workers after E-Mail Investigation." *San Jose Mercury News.* (July 27, 2000).

Downes, Larry, and Chunka Mui. *Unleashing the Killer App: Digital Strategies for Market Dominance.* Boston, MA: Harvard Business School Press. (1998).

Drucker, Peter. "The Coming of the New Organization." *Harvard Business Review.* (January–February 1988).

"Dubai Launches Internet City." *BBC Online News.* http://news.bbc.co.uk/low/english/world/middle_east/newsid_996000/996771.stm. (Accessed August 27, 2001).

Dubowski, Stefan. "Silicon Valley North's Tech-Title Aspirations Die in Provincial Parliament." *CanadaComputes.com.* (Accessed August 28, 2001).

Duchessi, Peter, and InduShobha Chengalur-Smith. "Client/Server Benefits, Problems, Best Practices." *Communications of the ACM* 41, no. 5. (May 1998).

Durst, Robert, Terrence Champion, Brian Witten, Eric Miller, and Luigi Spagnuolo. "Testing and Evaluating Computer Intrusion Detection Systems." *Communications of the ACM* 42, no. 7. (July 1999).

"Dutch Banking Giant Stays Neighbourly with CRM." *CRM Daily.com,* April 20, 2001. http://www.crmdaily.com/perl/printer/9130. (Accessed September 27, 2001).

Dutta, Amitava. "Telecommunications Infrastructure in Developing Nations." *International Information Systems* 1, no. 3. (July 1992).

Dutta, Soumitra, Berend Wierenga, and Arco Dalebout. "Designing Management Support Systems Using an Integrative

Perspective." *Communications of the ACM* 40, no. 6. (June 1997).

Dutta, Soumitra, Luk N. Van Wassenhove, and Selvan Kulandaiswamy. "Benchmarking European Software Management Practices." *Communications of the ACM* 41, no. 6. (June 1998).

Eardley, Alan, David Avison, and Philip Powell. "Developing Information Systems to Support Flexible Strategy." *Journal of Organizational Computing and Electronic Commerce* 7, no. 1. (1997).

Earl, Michael J., and Ian A. Scott. "What Is a Chief Knowledge Officer?" *Sloan Management Review* 40, no. 2. (Winter 1999).

Earl, Michael J., and Jeffrey L. Sampler. "Market Management to Transform the IT Organization." *Sloan Management Review* 39, no. 4. (Summer 1998).

"Eastman is Keen on E-Commerce." *Information Week.* (August 2, 2000).

"eCHN Newsletter." *Electronic Child Health Network.* July 16, 2001. http://www.echn.ca/hsc/chn-echn.nsf/index.html. (Accessed September 28, 2001).

Edelstein, Herb. "Technology How To: Mining Data Warehouses." *Information Week.* (January 8, 1996).

Ein Dor Philip, and Eli Segev. "Strategic Planning for Management Information Systems." *Management Science* 24, no. 15. (1978).

———. "Organizational Context and the Success of Management Information Systems." *Management Science* 24. (June 1978).

Ein-Dor, Philip, Seymour E. Goodman, and Peter Wolcott. "From Via Maris to Electronic Highway: The Internet in Canaan." *Communications of the ACM* 43, no. 7. (July 2000).

El Boghdady, Dina. "Broader Tire Recall Is Urged." *Detroit News.* (Accessed August 14, 2000).

El Najdawi, M. K., and Anthony C. Stylianou. "Expert Support Systems: Integrating AI Technologies." *Communications of the ACM* 36, no. 12. (December 1993).

El Sawy, Omar A. "Implementation by Cultural Infusion: An Approach for Managing the Introduction of Information Technologies." *MIS Quarterly.* (June 1985).

———. "Personal Information Systems for Strategic Scanning in Turbulent Environments." *MIS Quarterly* 9, no. 1. (March 1985).

El Sawy, Omar A., Arvind Malhotra, Sanjay Gosain, and Kerry M. Young, "IT-Intensive Value Innovation in the Electronic Economy: Insights from Marshall Industries, " *MIS Quarterly* 23, no. 3. (September 1999).

El Sawy, Omar, and Burt Nanus. "Toward the Design of Robust Information Systems." *Journal of Management Information Systems* 5, no. 4. (Spring 1989).

El Sherif, Hisham, and Omar A. El Sawy. "Issue-Based Decision Support Systems for the Egyptian Cabinet." *MIS Quarterly* 12, no. 4. (December 1988).

Elias, Paul. "Feds Can't Call Covisint Antitrustworthy Yet." *Red Herring.* (September 12, 2000).

Elofson, Greg, and William N. Robinson. "Creating a Custom Mass Production Channel on the Internet." *Communications of the ACM* 41, no. 3. (March 1998).

Emery, James C. "Cost/Benefit Analysis of Information Systems." Chicago: Society for Management Information Systems Workshop Report no. 1. (1971).

Engler, Natalie. "Small but Nimble." *Information Week.* (January 18, 1999).

Enns, Lori. "Historic Canadian Retailer Joins Web." *E-Commerce Times.* (November 21, 2000).

Enns, Lori. "Report: B2B Still Driving E-Commerce." *E-Commerce Times.* (December 11, 2000).

Etzioni, Amitai. *A Comparative Analysis of Complex Organizations.* New York: Free Press. (1975).

Etzioni, Oren. "The World-Wide Web: Quagmire or Gold Mine?" *Communications of the ACM* 39, no. 11. (November 1996).

Evans, Philip B. "The Blow-up of the Richness/Reach Trade-off." *Harvard School Press.* (July 2000).

Evans, Philip, and **Thomas S. Wurster.** "Getting Real about Virtual Commerce." *Harvard Business Review.* (November–December 1999).

———. "Strategy and the New Economics of Information." *Harvard Business Review.* (September–October 1997).

———. *Blown to Bits: How the New Economics of Information Transforms Strategy.* Boston, MA: Harvard Business School Press. (2000).

"Executive Royal Inn Hotels Offer GuestTek High Speed Internet Access for Free." *GuestTek.* http://www.guesttek.com/news/re-leases/230101.html. (Accessed August 12, 2001).

"FamiliPrix pour uin monde en sante." *FamiliPrix.* http://www.familiprix.com/accueil.asp. (Accessed July 28, 2001).

Farhoomand, Ali, Virpi Kristiina Tuunainen, and **Lester W. Yee.** "Barriers to Global Electronic Commerce: A Cross-Country Study of Hong Kong and Finland." *Journal of Organizational Computing and Electronic Commerce* 10, no. 1. (2000).

Favela, Jesus. "Capture and Dissemination of Specialized Knowledge in Network Organizations." *Journal of Organizational Computing and Electronic Commerce* 7, nos. 2 and 3. (1997).

Fayad, Mohamed, and **Marshall P. Cline.** "Aspects of Software Adaptability." *Communications of the ACM* 39, no. 10. (October 1996).

Fayol, Henri. *Administration industrielle et generale.* Paris: Dunods. (1950, first published in 1916).

Fedorowicz, Jane, and **Benn Konsynski.** "Organization Support Systems: Bridging Business and Decision Processes." *Journal of Management Information Systems* 8, no. 4. (Spring 1992).

Feeny, David. "Making Business Sense of the E-Opportunity." *Sloan Management Review* 42, no. 2. (Winter 2001).

Feeny, David E., and **Blake Ives.** "In Search of Sustainability: Reaping Long-Term Advantage from Investments in Information Technology." *Journal of Management Information Systems.* (Summer 1990).

Feeny, David E., and **Leslie P. Willcocks.** "Core IS Capabilities for Exploiting Information Technology." *Sloan Management Review* 39, no. 3. (Spring 1998).

Feigenbaum, Edward A. "The Art of Artificial Intelligence: Themes and Case Studies in Knowledge Engineering." *Proceedings of the IJCAI.* (1977).

Fichman, Robert G., and **Scott A. Moses.** "An Incremental Process for Software Implementation." *Sloan Management Review* 40, no. 2. (Winter 1999).

Fingar, Peter. "Component-Based Frameworks for E-Commerce." *Communications of the ACM* 43, no. 10. (October 2000).

Fiori, Rich. "The Information Warehouse." *Relational Database Journal.* (January–February 1995).

"Firestone Tire Recall." *National Highway Traffic Safety Administration.* http://www.nhsta.dot.gov/hot/Firestone/Index.html. (Accessed May 16, 2001). Courtesy of Transport Canada.

Fisher, Joe. "Toronto Supercomputers Chart DNA 'Book of Life.'" *The Canadian.* (Fall 2000/Winter 2001).

Fisher, Marshall L. "What Is the Right Supply Chain for Your Product?" *Harvard Business Review.* (March–April 1997).

Fisher, Marshall L., Ananth Raman, and **Anne Sheen McClelland.** "Rocket Science Retailing Is Almost Here: Are You Ready?" *Harvard Business Review.* (July–August 2000).

Fitzmaurice, George W., Rvain Balakrishnan, and **Gordon Kurtenbach.** "Sampling, Synthesis, and Input Devices." *Communications of the ACM* 42, no. 8. (August 1999).

"Five Top Law Firms Merge to Form Borden Ladner Gervais LLP." *Canada Newswire.* http://www1.newswire.ca/releases/February2000/29/c8380.html. (Accessed July 21, 2001). © Canada Newswire Ltd.

Fjermestad, Jerry. "An Integrated Framework for Group Support Systems." *Journal of Organizational Computing and Electronic Commerce* 8, no. 2. (1998).

Fjermestad, Jerry, and **Starr Roxanne Hiltz.** "An Assessment of Group Support Systems Experimental Research: Methodology, and Results." *Journal of Management Information Systems* 15, no. 3. (Winter, 1998–1999).

———. "Group Support Systems: A Descriptive Evaluation of Case and Field Studies." *Journal of Management Information Systems* 17, no. 3. (Winter 2000–2001).

Flynn, Jim, and **Bill Clarke.** "How Java Makes Network-Centric Computing Real." *Datamation.* (March 1, 1996).

Foran, Tim. "Tech Trio Help Retailer." *Network World Canada.* (June 1, 2001).

"Ford and Firestone Face Tire Suit in Canada." *The Canadian Press.* http://www.cp.org/english/hp.htm. (Accessed May 11, 2001).

Forgionne, Giuseppe. "Management Support System Effectiveness: Further Empirical Evidence." *Journal of the Association for Information Systems* 1. (May 2000).

Forrest, Stephanie, Steven A. Hofmeyr, and **Anil Somayaji.** "Computer Immunology." *Communications of the ACM* 40, no. 10. (October 1997).

"Forum Speaker: Chris Molinski." *StorageTek.* http://www.storagetek.com/teknews/usergroups/forum/bio_and_abstract/molinski.htm. (Accessed February 24, 2001).

Foster, Carly. "ESuccess Stories: Just White Shirts." *Canada One Magazine.* http://www.canadaone.com/ezine/sept99/ecommerce.html. (Accessed May 15, 2001).

Franz, Charles, and **Daniel Robey.** "An Investigation of User-Led System Design: Rational and Political Perspectives." *Communications of the ACM* 27. (December 1984).

Fraser, Martin D., and **Vijay K. Vaishnavi.** "A Formal Specifications Maturity Model." *Communications of the ACM* 40, no. 12. (December 1997).

Freedman, David H. "Cold Comfort." *Forbes.* (May 29, 2000).

Freeman, John, Glenn R. Carroll, and **Michael T. Hannan.** "The Liability of Newness: Age Dependence in Organizational Death Rates." *American Sociological Review* 48. (1983).

Friedman, Batya, Peter H. Kahn, Jr., and **Daniel C. Howek.** "Trust Online." *Communications of the ACM* 43, no. 12. (December 2000).

Fritz, Mary Beth Watson, Sridhar Narasimhan, and **Hyeun-Suk Rhee.** "Communication and Coordination in the Virtual Office." *Journal of Management Information Systems* 14, no. 4. (Spring 1998).

Froomkin, A. Michael. "The Collision of Trademarks, Domain Names, and Due Process in Cyberspace." *Communications of the ACM* 44, no. 2. (February 2001).

Fulk, Janet, and **Geraldine DeSanctis.** "Electronic Communication and Changing Organizational Forms." *Organization Science* 6, no. 4. (July–August 1995).

Fulton, Susan M. "Speak Softly, Carry a Big Chip." *The New York Times Circuits.* (March 30, 2000).

"Fuzzy Clips." *NRC.ca.* http://ai.iit.nrc.ca/IR_public/fuzzy/fuzztclips/fuzzyCLIPSIndex.html. (Accessed July 24, 2001).

Gallupe, R. Brent. "Images of Information Systems in the Early 21st Century." *Communications of the Association for Information Systems* 3, no. 3. (February 2000).

Gallupe, R. Brent, Geraldine DeSanctis, and **Gary W. Dickson.** "Computer-Based Support for Group Problem-Finding: An Experimental Investigation." *MIS Quarterly* 12, no. 2. (June 1988).

Gane, Chris, and **Trish Sarson.** *Structured Systems Analysis: Tools and Techniques.* Englewood Cliffs, NJ: Prentice Hall. (1979).

Garber, Angela R. "Ready, Set, Grow." *Small Business Computing.* (September 2000).

Gardner, Julia. "Strengthening the Focus on Users' Working Practices." *Communications of the ACM* 42, no. 5. (May 1999).

Gardner, Stephen R. "Building the Data Warehouse." *Communications of the ACM* 41, no. 9. (September 1998).

Garner, Rochelle. "Internet2. . . and Counting." *CIO Magazine.* (September 1, 1999).

Garvin, David A. "The Processes of Organization and Management." *Sloan Management Review* 39, no. 4. (Summer 1998).

Gates, Bill. "Why We're Building .NET Technology." *Microsoft.* http://www.microsoft.com/presspass/misc/06-18BillGNet.asp. (Accessed July 11, 2001).

Gattiker, Urs E., and **Helen Kelley.** "Morality and Computers: Attitudes and Differences in Judgments." *Information Systems Research* 10, no. 3. (September 1999).

"GE Logs a First on Automobile Network." *General Electric.* http://www.ketstrokes.net/proofs/linkage/nbanx020100.htm. (Accessed June 10, 2001).

Gefen, David, and **Detmar W. Straub.** "Gender Differences in the Perception and Use of E-Mail: An Extension to the Technology Acceptance Model." *MIS Quarterly* 21, no. 4. (December 1997).

Gelernter, David. "The Metamorphosis of Information Management." *Scientific American.* (August 1989).

"Geographic Information Systems." *Manitoba Community Newspaper Association.* http://www.mcna.com/media/gis.html. (Accessed July 11, 2001).

George, Joey. "Organizational Decision Support Systems." *Journal of Management Information Systems* 8, no. 3. (Winter 1991–1992).

"Getting Plugged into the Taxman: Filing Your Taxes Isn't Just for Old Men in Polyester Suits Anymore." *Financial Post.* http://www.nationalpost.com. (Accessed March 18, 2000).

Ghosh, Shikhar. "Making Business Sense of the Internet." *Harvard Business Review.* (March–April 1998).

Ghosh, Anup K., and **Jeffrey M. Voas.** "Inoculating Software for Survivability." *Communications of the ACM* 42, no. 7. (July 1999).

Ghosh, Anup K., and **Tara M. Swaminatha.** "Software Security and Privacy Risks in Mobile E-Commerce." *Communications of the ACM* 44, no. 2. (February 2001).

Giaglis, George. "Focus Issue on Legacy Information Systems and Business Process Change: On the Integrated Design and Evaluation of Business Processes and Information Systems." *Communications of the AIS* 2,. (July 1999).

Gibbs, Edwina. "Bridgestone Sees $350 Million Special Loss, Stock Dives." *Yahoo.com.* (August 10, 2000).

Gibson, Garth A., and **Rodney Van Meter.** "Network Attached Storage Architecture." *Communications of the ACM* 43, no. 11. (November 2000).

Gillmor, Dan. "Peer-to-Peer Computing: The Next IT Tsunami?" *San Jose Mercury News.* (February 25, 2001).

Gilmore, James H., and **B. Joseph Pine, II.** "The Four Faces of Mass Customization." *Harvard Business Review.* (January–February 1997).

Ginzberg, Michael J. "Early Diagnosis of MIS Implementation Failure: Promising Results and Unanswered Questions." *Management Science* 27. (April 1981).

Ginzberg, Michael J., W. R. Reitman, and **E. A. Stohr,** eds. *Decision Support Systems.* New York: North Holland Publishing Co. (1982).

Giuliao, Vincent E. "The Mechanization of Office Work." *Scientific American.* (September 1982).

Glasscock, Stuart. "Microsoft Sites Fail, Again." *TechWeb News.* http://content.techweb.com//wire/story/TWB20010125S0011. (Accessed June 25, 2001).

Glazer, Rashi. "Winning in Smart Markets." *Sloan Management Review* 40, no. 4. (Summer 1999).

"Global Internet Statistics." *Global Reach.* http://www.glreach.com/globstats. (Accessed Sept. 6, 2001).

Glushko, Robert J., Jay M. Tenenbaum, and **Bart Meltzer.** "An XML Framework for Agent-Based E-Commerce." *Communications of the ACM* 42, no. 3. (March 1999).

Goan, Terrance. "A Cop on the Beat: Collecting and Appraising Intrusion Evidence." *Communications of the ACM* 42, no. 7. (July 1999).

Gogan, Janis L., Jane Fedorowicz, and **Ashok Rao.** "Assessing Risks in Two Projects: A Strategic Opportunity and a Necessary Evil." *Communications of the Association for Information Systems* 1. (May 1999).

Goldberg, David E. "Genetic and Evolutionary Algorithms Come of Age." *Communications of the ACM* 37, no. 3. (March 1994).

Goldstein, R. C., and **J. B. McCririck.** "What Do Data Administrators Really Do?" *Datamation* 26. (August 1980).

Gomes, Lee. "Somebody Else's Problem." *The Wall Street Journal Technology Report.* (November 15, 1999).

Goodhue, Dale L., Judith A. Quillard, and **John F. Rockart.** "Managing the Data Resource: A Contingency Perspective." *MIS Quarterly.* (September 1988).

Goodhue, Dale L., Laurie J. Kirsch, Judith A. Quillard, and **Michael D. Wybo.** "Strategic Data Planning: Lessons from the Field." *MIS Quarterly* 16, no. 1. (March 1992).

Goodhue, Dale L., Michael D. Wybo, and **Laurie J. Kirsch.** "The Impact of Data Integration on the Costs and Benefits of Information Systems." *MIS Quarterly* 16, no. 3. (September 1992).

Goodman, S.E., L.I. Press, S.R. Ruth, and **A.M. Rutkowski.** "The Global Diffusion of the Internet: Patterns and Problems." *Communications of the ACM* 37, no. 8. (August 1994).

Gopal, Ram D., and **G. Lawrence Sanders.** "Global Software Piracy: You Can't Get Blood Out of a Turnip." *Communications of the ACM* 43, no. 9. (September 2000).

———. "Preventive and Deterrent Controls for Software Piracy." *Journal of Management Information Systems* 13, no. 4. (Spring 1997).

Gorry, G. Anthony, and **Michael S. Scott Morton.** "A Framework for Management Information Systems." *Sloan Management Review* 13, no. 1. (Fall 1971).

Goslar, Martin. "The New E-Security Frontier." *Information Week.* (July 10, 2000).

Gowan, J. Arthur, Chris Jesse, and **Richard G. Mathieu.** "Y2K Compliance and the Distributed Enterprise." *Communications of the ACM* 42, no. 2. (February 1999).

Graham, Robert L. "The Legal Protection of Computer Software." *Communications of the ACM.* (May 1984).

"Grand and Toy Ltd. Order Point." *Canadian Information Productivity Awards.* http://www.cipa.com/winners/ecom1_story.htm. (Accessed December 28, 2000).

Grant, Robert M. "Prospering in Dynamically-Competitive Environments: Organizational Capability as Knowledge Integration." *Organization Science* 7, no. 4. (July–August 1996).

Green, R.H. *The Ethical Manager.* New York: Macmillan. (1994).

Greengard, Samuel. "All for One." *Internet World.* (March 1, 2001).

———. "Assembling a Hybrid Data Warehouse." *Beyond Computing.* (March 1999).

Gregor, Shirley, and **Izak Benbasat.** "Explanations from Intelligent Systems: Theoretical Foundations and Implications for Practice." *MIS Quarterly* 23, no. 4. (December 1999).

Grimaldi, James V. "Testimony Indicates Abuses at Firestone." *Washington Post.* (August 13, 2000).

Grobowski, Ron, Chris McGoff, Doug Vogel, Ben Martz, and **Jay Nunamaker.** "Implementing Electronic Meeting Systems at IBM: Lessons Learned and Success Factors." *MIS Quarterly* 14, no. 4. (December 1990).

Grosky, William I. "Managing Multimedia Information in Database Systems." *Communications of the ACM* 40, no. 12. (December 1997).

Grover, Varun. "IS Investment Priorities in Contemporary Organizations." *Communications of the ACM* 41, no. 2. (February 1998).

Grover, Varun, and **James Teng.** "How Effective Is Data Resource Management?" *Journal of Information Systems Management.* (Summer 1991).

Grover, Varun, and **Martin D. Goslar.** "Initiation, Adoption, and Implementation of Telecommunications Technologies in U.S. Organizations." *Journal of Management Information Systems* 10, no. 1. (Summer 1993).

Grover, Varun, and **Pradipkumar Ramanlal.** "Six Myths of Information and Markets: Information Technology Networks, Electronic Commerce, and the Battle for Consumer Surplus." *MIS Quarterly* 23, no. 4. (December 1999).

Grover, Varun, Pradipkumar Ramanlal, and **James T.C. Teng.** "E-Commerce and the Information Market." *Communications of the ACM* 44, no. 4. (April 2001).

"GuestTek Aims to Dominate North American Mobile Internet Access Market with New VP of Sales." *GuestTek.* http://www.hotelpublication.com/news/010124g.html. (Accessed August 8, 2001).

"GuestTek Closes Third Round Financing; Broadband Internet Access Leader Poised for Dramatic Growth." *GuestTek.* http://www.eurhotec.com/news/4008012.2000325.htm. (Accessed August 8, 2001).

"GuestTek Opens Third U.S. Office in Minneapolis." *GuestTek.* http://nan.btbtravel.com/s/EditorialTechnology.asp?printVersion=now&ReportID=25835. (Accessed August 8, 2001).

Gulati, Ranjay, and **Jason Garino.** "Get the Right Mix of Bricks and Clicks." *Harvard Business Review.* (May–June 2000).

"Gulf Canada Improves Budgeting Process with Web Driven Reporting." *Information Builders.* http://www.ibi.com/applications/gulf.htm. (Accessed November 13, 2000).

Gupta, Amarnath, and **Ranesh Jain.** "Visual Information Retrieval." *Communications of the ACM* 40, no. 5. (May 1997).

Gurbaxani, V., and **S. Whang.** "The Impact of Information Systems on Organizations and Markets." *Communications of the ACM* 34, no. 1. (Jan. 1991).

Haavind, Robert. "Software's New Object Lesson." *Technology Review.* (February–March 1992).

Hafner, Katie. " For the Well Connected, All the World's an Office." *The New York Times Circuits.* (March 30, 2000).

Hagel, John III, and **Marc Singer.** "Unbundling the Corporation." *Harvard Business Review.* (March–April 1999).

———. *Net Worth.* Boston, MA: Harvard Business School Press. (1999).

Hammer, Michael. "Reengineering Work: Don't Automate, Obliterate." *Harvard Business Review.* (July–August 1990).

Hammer, Michael, and **James Champy.** *Reengineering the Corporation.* New York: HarperCollins Publishers. (1993).

Hammer, Michael, and **Steven A. Stanton.** *The Reengineering Revolution.* New York: HarperCollins. (1995).

Hannaford, Nigel. "[IPRP] Research on the Ontario Smartcard Project: Smart Card Would Not Be Wise." *Faculty of Information Studies: University of Ontario,* January 6, 2001. http://www.fis.utoronto.ca/research/iprp/sc/ch06012001.html. (Accessed August 10, 2001).

Hansen, James V., and **Ned C. Hill.** "Control and Audit of Electronic Data Interchange." *MIS Quarterly* 13, no. 4. (December 1989).

Hansen, Morton T., Nitin Nohria, and **Thomas Tierney.** "What's Your Strategy for Knowledge Management?" *Harvard Business Review.* (March–April 1999).

Hansen, Morton, and **Bolko von Oetinger.** "Introducing T-Shaped Managers: Knowledge Management's Next Generation." *Harvard Business Review.* (March 2001).

Hardaway, Don, and **Richard P. Will.** "Digital Multimedia Offers Key to Educational Reform." *Communications of the ACM* 40, no. 4. (April 1997).

Hardman, Vicky, Martina Angela Sasse, and **Isidor Kouvelas.** "Successful Multiparty Audio Communication over the Internet." *Communications of the ACM* 41, no. 5. (May 1998).

Harmon, Amy. "Software that Tracks E-Mail is Raising Privacy Concerns." *The New York Times.* (November 22, 2000).

Harrington, Susan J. "The Effect of Codes of Ethics and Personal Denial of Responsibility on Computer Abuse Judgments and Intentions." *MIS Quarterly* 20, no. 2. (September 1996).

Hart, Paul J., and **Carol Stoak Saunders.** "Emerging Electronic Partnerships: Antecedents and Dimensions of EDI Use from the Supplier's Perspective." *Journal of Management Information Systems* 14, no. 4. (Spring 1998).

Hayes-Roth, Frederick. "Knowledge-Based Expert Systems." *Spectrum IEEE.* (October 1987).

Hayes-Roth, Frederick, and **Neil Jacobstein.** "The State of Knowledge-Based Systems." *Communications of the ACM* 37, no. 3. (March 1994).

"HBC Corporate Overview." *Hudson's Bay Company.* http://www.hbc.com/hbc/eab/default.htm. (Accessed June 1, 2001).

"Healthcare Solutions." *Nortel Networks.* http://www.nortelnetworks.com/health. (2001).

Helms, Glenn L., and **Ira R. Weiss.** "The Cost of Internally Developed Applications: Analysis of Problems and Cost Control Methods." *Journal of Management Information Systems.* (Fall 1986).

Henderson, John C., and **David A. Schilling.** "Design and Implementation of Decision Support Systems in the Public Sector." *MIS Quarterly.* (June 1985).

Henderson, John C., and **John J. Sifonis.** "The Value of Strategic IS Planning: Understanding Consistency, Validity, and IS Markets." *MIS Quarterly* 12, no. 2. (June 1988).

"**Hershey Foods Announces Third Quarter Results.**" *Hershey Foods Corporate Investor Relations*. http://www.corporateir.net. (Accessed October 25, 1999).

Heywood, Peter. "Charge of the Light Brigade." *Red Herring*. (February 2000).

Hiatt, Bryan. "With Napster Weakened, RIAA Hopes to Settle Landmark Lawsuit." *MTV Online*. http://www.mtv.com/news/articles/1445466/20010727/index.jhtml. (Accessed August 24, 2001).

Hill, G. Christian. "First Voice, Now Data." *The Wall Street Journal*. (September 20, 1999).

Hilmer, Kelly M., and **Alan R. Dennis.** "Stimulating Thinking: Cultivating Better Decisions with Groupware through Categorization." *Journal of Management Information Systems* 17, no. 3. (Winter 2000–2001).

Hinds, Pamela, and **Sara Kiesler.** "Communication across Boundaries: Work, Structure, and Use of Communication Technologies in a Large Organization." *Organization Science* 6, no. 4. (July–August 1995).

Hinton, Gregory. "How Neural Networks Learn from Experience." *Scientific American*. (September 1992).

Hirscheim, Rudy, and **Mary Lacity.** "The Myths and Realities of Information Technology Insourcing." *Communications of the ACM* 43, no. 2. (February 2000).

Hitt, Lorin M. "Information Technology and Firm Boundaries: Evidence from Panel Data." *Information Systems Research* 10, | no. 2. (June 1999).

Hitt, Lorin M., and **Erik Brynjolfsson.** "Information Technology and Internal Firm Organization: An Exploratory Analysis." *Journal of Management Information Systems* 14, no. 2. (Fall 1997).

Ho, T.H., and **K.S. Raman.** "The Effect of GDSS on Small Group Meetings." *Journal of Management Information Systems* 8, no. 2. (Fall 1991).

Hoffman, Donna L., William D. Kalsbeek, and **Thomas P. Novak.** "Internet and Web Use in the U.S." *Communications of the ACM* 39, no. 12. (December 1996).

Hogan, Kevin, and **Matt Beer.** "The New Economy: Five Who Get It and Five Who Don't." *Business 2.0*. (June 2000).

Hogue, Jack T. "A Framework for the Examination of Management Involvement in Decision Support Systems." *Journal of Management Information Systems* 4, no. 1. (Summer 1987).

———. "Decision Support Systems and the Traditional Computer Information System Function: An Examination of Relationships During DSS Application Development." *Journal of Management Information Systems*. (Summer 1985).

Holland, Christopher, Geoff Lockett, and **Ian Blackman.** "Electronic Data Interchange Implementation: A Comparison of U.S. and European Cases." *International Information Systems* 1, no. 4. (October 1992).

Holland, John H. "Genetic Algorithms." *Scientific American*. (July 1992).

Hollows, Phil. "Build High Quality E-Business Applications." *E-Business Advisor*. (November 2000).

"**Home Trust Company: Outsourcing Leads to IT Partnership.**" *EZNet*. http://ww.eznet.com. (Accessed February 25, 2001).

Hopkins, Jon. "Component Primer." *Communications of the ACM* 43, no. 10. (October 2000).

Hopper, Max. "Rattling SABRE—New Ways to Compete on Information." *Harvard Business Review*. (May–June 1990).

"**Hospital Network to Boost Data-Sharing.**" *National Post Online*. August 2000. http://www.nationalpost.com/content/features/e-xchange/080700.html. (Accessed September 28, 2001).

"**Hospitality High Speed Internet Company Opens Third Office.**" *GuestTek*. http://www.hotelpublication.com/news/010501h.html. (Accessed August 8, 2001).

Houdeshel, George, and **Hugh J. Watson.** "The Management Information and Decision Support. (MIDS). System at Lockheed Georgia." *MIS Quarterly* 11, no. 1. (March 1987).

"**Household Income and Computer Ownership.**" *Ryerson University*. http://www.rcc.ryerson.ca/learnontario/idnm/mod5/mod52/mod5231.htm. (Accessed July 31, 2001).

Huber, George P. "Cognitive Style as a Basis for MIS and DSS Designs: Much Ado About Nothing?" *Management Science* 29. (May 1983).

———. "Organizational Information Systems: Determinants of Their Performance and Behavior." *Management Science* 28, no. 2. (1984).

———. "Organizational Learning: The Contributing Processes and Literature." *Organization Science,* 2. (1991), pp. 88–115.

———. "The Nature and Design of Post-Industrial Organizations." *Management Science* 30, no. 8. (August 1984).

"**Hudson's Bay Company Introduces hbc.com.**" *Hudson's Bay Company*. http://www.newswire.ca/releases/november2000/22/c6925.html. (Accessed November 22, 2000). © Canada Newswire Ltd.

Huff, Chuck, and **C. Dianne Martin.** "Computing Consequences: A Framework for Teaching Ethical Computing." *Communications of the ACM* 38, no. 12. (December 1995).

Huff, Sid, Malcolm C. Munro, and **Barbara H. Martin.** "Growth Stages of End User Computing." *Communications of the ACM*. (May 1988).

Huizing, Ard, Esther Koster, and **Wim Bouman.** "Balance in Business Process Reengineering: An Empirical Study of Fit and Performance." *Journal of Management Information Systems* 14, no. 1. (Summer 1997).

"**Human Resource Policies and Practices.**" *Royal Bank Corporation*. http://www.royalbank.com/careers/workressurv/hr_pandp.html. (Accessed August 1, 2001).

Hunton, James E., and **Jesse D. Beeler.** "Effects of User Participation in Systems Development: A Longitudinal Field Study." *MIS Quarterly* 21, no. 4. (December 1997).

Imielinski, Tomasz, and **B.R. Badrinath.** "Mobile Wireless Computing: Challenges in Data Management." *Communications of the ACM* 37, no. 10. (October 1994).

"**Information Portal Solutions.**" *Nortel Networks*. (2001). http://www.nortelnetworks.com/prd/consultant/collateral/emergc_present/voice_portal.pdf

Inman, W.H. "The Data Warehouse and Data Mining." *Communications of the ACM* 39, no. 11. (November 1996).

"**Integrated Information Technology: A Better Way to Work.**" *Allegiance Healthcare Corporation*. http://www.allegiancecorp.com/whoweare/infotech/infotech.htm. (Accessed January 19, 2001).

"**[IPRP] Research on the Ontario Smartcard Project: Project Information.**" *Faculty of Information Studies: University of Toronto*. http://www.fis.utoronto.ca/research/iprp/sc. (Accessed August 10, 2001).

Irani, Zahir, and **Peter E.D. Love.** "The Propagation of Technology Management Taxonomies for Evaluating Investments in Information Systems." *Journal of Management Information Systems* 17, no.3. (Winter 2000–2001).

Isakowitz, Tomas, Michael Bieber, and **Fabio Vitali.** "Web Information Systems." *Communications of the ACM* 41, no. 7. (July 1998).

Isenberg, Daniel J. "How Senior Managers Think." *Harvard Business Review.* (November–December 1984).

"'IT for All, All for IT' Should Be National Motto and Thrust of a National Campaign for Every Malaysian to Be Part of the Emerging Information Society." *DAP Malaysia.* http://www.malaysia.net/dap/sg321-01.htm. (Accessed August 28, 2001).

Ivari, Juhani, Rudy Hirschheim, and **Heinz K. Klein.** "A Dynamic Framework for Classifying Information Systems Development Methodologies and Approaches." *Journal of Management Information Systems* 17, no. 3. (Winter 2000-2001).

Ives, Blake, and **Sirkka Jarvenpaa.** "Applications of Global Information Technology: Key Issues for Management." *MIS Quarterly* 15, no. 1. (March 1991).

———. "Global Business Drivers: Aligning Information Technology to Global Business Strategy". *IBM Systems Journal* 32, no. 1. (1993).

———. "Global Information Technology: Some Lessons from Practice." *International Information Systems* 1, no. 3. (July 1992).

Jacobs, April. "The Network Computer: Where It's Going." *Computerworld.* (December 23, 1997/January 2, 1998).

Jahnke, Art. "It Takes a Village." *CIO WebBusiness.* (February 1, 1998).

Jainschigg, John. "Case Study: Office of the Future." *Computer Telephony.* (July 1, 1999).

Jajoda, Sushil, Catherine D. McCollum, and **Paul Ammann.** "Trusted Recovery." *Communications of the ACM* 42, no. 7. (July 1999).

Jarvenpaa, Sirkka L., Kathleen Knoll, and **Dorothy Leidner.** "Is Anybody Out There? Antecedents of Trust in Global Virtual Teams." *Journal of Management Information Systems* 14, no. 4. (Spring 1998).

Jarzabek, Stan, and **Riri Huang.** "The Case for User-Centered CASE Tools." *Communications of the ACM* 41, no. 8. (August 1998).

Jensen, M., and **W. Meckling.** "Theory of the Firm: Managerial Behavior, Agency Costs, and Ownership Structure." *Journal of Financial Economics* 3. (1976).

———. "Specific and General Knowledge and Organizational Science." In *Contract Economics,* edited by L. Wetin and J. Wijkander. Oxford: Basil Blackwell. (1992).

Jesser, Ryan, Rodney Smith, Mark Stupeck, and **William F. Wright.** "Information Technology Process Reengineering and Performance Measurement." *Communications of the Association for Information Systems* 1. (February 1999).

Jessup, Leonard M., Terry Connolly, and **Jolene Galegher.** "The Effects of Anonymity on GDSS Group Process with an Idea-Generating Task." *MIS Quarterly* 14, no. 3. (September 1990).

Joes, Kathryn. "EDS Set to Restore Cash-Machine Network." *The New York Times.* (March 26, 1993).

Johansen, Robert. "Groupware: Future Directions and Wild Cards." *Journal of Organizational Computing* 1, no. 2. (April–June 1991).

Johnson, Bernadette. "Canadian Tire Ties Catalogue to Web, Phone." *Strategy Magazine.* (April 23, 2001).

———. "HBC Adds Newest Piece to CRM Strategy." *Strategy Magazine.* (May 21, 2001).

———. "HBC.com Aims to Give Customers Another Reason to Shop." *Strategy Magazine.* (January 1, 2001).

Johnson, Deborah G. "Ethics Online." *Communications of the ACM* 40, no. 1. (January 1997).

Johnson, Deborah G., and **John M. Mulvey.** "Accountability and Computer Decision Systems." *Communications of the ACM* 38, no. 12. (December 1995).

Johnson, Gail. "Custom Workstations a Better Fit for Flight Catering Staff." *WorkSafe Magazine* 1, no. 4. (July/August 2000). http://www.worksafebc.com/pubs/newsletters/ws_mag/ws1_4/custom.asp. (Accessed July 7, 2001).

Johnson, Philip M. "Reengineering Inspection." *Communications of the ACM* 41, no. 2. (February 1998).

Johnson, Ralph E. "Frameworks 5. (Components 1 Patterns)." *Communications of the ACM* 40, no. 10. (October 1997).

Johnson, Richard A. "The Ups and Downs of Object-Oriented Systems Development." *Communications of the ACM* 43, no.10. (October 2000).

Johnson, Stuart J. "XML Drives Development." *The Industry Standard.* (July 17, 2000).

Johnston, David Cay. "A Kinder, Smarter Tax System for Kansas." *The New York Times.* (June 22, 1998).

Johnston, Russell, and **Michael J. Vitale.** "Creating Competitive Advantage with Interorganizational Information Systems." *MIS Quarterly* 12, no. 2. (June 1988).

Jones, Jack William, Carol Saunders, and **Raymond McLeod, Jr.,** "Media Usage and Velocity in Executive Information Acquisition: An Exploratory Study." *European Journal of Information Systems* 2. (1993).

Jones, Sara, Marc Wilikens, Philip Morris, and **Marcelo Masera.** "Trust Requirements in E-Business." *Communications of the ACM* 43, no. 12. (December 2000).

Joshi, James B.D., Walid G. Aref, Arif Ghafoor, and **Eugene H. Spafford.** "Security Models for Web-Based Applications." *Communications of the ACM* 44, no. 2. (February 2001).

Joshi, Kailash. "A Model of Users' Perspective on Change: The Case of Information Systems Technology Implementation." *MIS Quarterly* 15, no. 2. (June 1991).

Joy, Bill. "Design for the Digital Revolution." *Fortune.* (March 6, 2000).

Kachadourian, Gail. "Covisint is Up and Running." *Automotive News.* (October, 2000).

Kahn, Beverly K. "Some Realities of Data Administration." *Communications of the ACM* 26. (October 1983).

Kalakota, Ravi, and **Andrew B. Whinston.** *Electronic Commerce: A Manager's Guide.* Reading MA: Addison-Wesley. (1997).

Kalakota, Ravi, and **Marcia Robinson.** *e-Business2.0: Roadmap for Success.* Reading, MA: Addison-Wesley. (2001).

Kalakota, Ravi, Jan Stallaert, and **Andrew B. Whinston.** "Worldwide Real-Time Decision Support Systems for Electronic Commerce Applications." *Journal of Organizational Computing and Electronic Commerce* 6, no. 1. (1996).

Kalis, Lisa. "The Storage Space." *Red Herring.* (March 1, 2000).

Kambil, Ajit, and **James E. Short.** "Electronic Integration and Business Network Redesign: A Roles-Linkage Perspective." *Journal of Management Information Systems* 10, no. 4. (Spring 1994).

Kanade, Takeo, Michael L. Reed, and **Lee E. Weiss.** "New Technologies and Applications in Robotics." *Communications of the ACM* 37, no. 3. (March 1994).

Kanan, P.K., Ai-Mei Chang, and **Andrew B. Whinston.** "Marketing Information on the I-Way." *Communications of the ACM* 41, no. 3. (March 1998).

Kanter, Rosabeth Moss. "The New Managerial Work." *Harvard Business Review.* (November–December 1989).

———. "The Ten Deadly Mistakes of Wanna-Dots." *Harvard Business Review.* (January 2001).

Kaplan, David, Ramayya Krishnan, Rema Padman, and **James Peters.** "Assessing Data Quality in Accounting Information Systems." *Communications of the ACM* 41, no. 2. (February 1998).

Kaplan, Steven, and **Mohanbir Sawhney.** "E-Hubs: the New B2B Marketplaces." *Harvard Business Review.* (May–June 2000).

Kappelman, Leon A., Darla Fent, Kellie B. Keeling, and **Victor Prybutok.** "Calculating the Cost of Year 2000 Compliance." *Communications of the ACM* 41, no. 2. (February 1998).

Karahanna, Elena, and **Moez Limayem.** "E-Mail and V-Mail Usage: Generalizing Across Technologies." *Journal of Organizational Computing and Electronic Commerce* 10, no. 1. (2000).

Karat, John. "Evolving the Scope of User-Centered Design." *Communications of the ACM* 40, no. 7. (July 1997).

Karin, Jahangir, and **Benn R. Konsynski.** "Globalization and Information Management Strategies." *Journal of Management Information Systems* 7. (Spring 1991).

Karney, James. "For Good Measure." *Internet World.* (July 1, 2000).

Kautz, Henry, Bart Selman, and **Mehul Shah.** "ReferralWeb: Combining Social Networks and Collaborative Filtering." *Communications of the ACM* 40, no. 3. (March 1997).

Keen, Peter G.W. *Competing in Time: Using Telecommunications for Competitive Advantage.* Cambridge, MA: Ballinger Publishing Company. (1986).

———. "Information Systems and Organizational Change." *Communications of the ACM* 24, no. 1. (January 1981).

———. "Ready for the 'New' B2B?" *Computerworld.* (September 11, 2000).

———. *Shaping the Future: Business Design Through Information Technology.* Cambridge, MA: Harvard Business School Press. (1991).

———. *The Process Edge.* Boston, MA: Harvard Business School Press. (1997).

Keen, Peter G.W., and **M.S. Morton.** *Decision Support Systems: An Organizational Perspective.* Reading, MA: Addison-Wesley. (1978).

Keil, Mark, and **Daniel Robey.** "Blowing the Whistle on Troubled Software Projects." *Communications of the ACM* 44, no. 4. (April 2001).

Keil, Mark, and **Ramiro Montealegre.** "Cutting Your Losses: Extricating Your Organization When a Big Project Goes Awry." *Sloan Management Review* 41, no. 3. (Spring 2000).

Keil, Mark, Timo Saarinen, Bernard C.Y. Tan, Virpi Tuunainen, Arjen Waassenaar and **Kwok-Kee Wei.** "A Cross-Cultural Study on Escalation of Commitment Behavior in Software Projects." *MIS Quarterly* 24, no. 2. (June 2000).

Keil, Mark, Joan Mann, and **Arun Rai.** "Why Software Projects Escalate: An Empirical Analysis and Test of Four Theoretical Models." *MIS Quarterly* 24, no. 4. (December 2000).

Keil, Mark, Paul E. Cule, Kalle Lyytinen, and **Roy C. Schmidt.** "A Framework for Identifying Software Project Risks." *Communications of the ACM* 41, 11. (November 1998).

Keil, Mark, Richard Mixon, Timo Saarinen, and **Virpi Tuunairen.** "Understanding Runaway IT Projects." *Journal of Management Information Systems* 11, no. 3. (Winter 1994–95).

Kelly, Dave. "Using Business Portals to Achieve a Competitive Advantage." *The Hurwitz Group.* http://www.viador.com/pdfs/HurwitzCaseStudy.pdf. (Accessed July 10, 2001).

Kelly, Sue, Nicola Gibson, Christopher P. Holland, and **Ben Light.** "Focus Issue on Legacy Information Systems and Business Process Change: A Business Perspective of Legacy Information Systems." *Communications of the AIS* 2. (July 1999).

Kemerer, Chris F. "Progress, Obstacles, and Opportunities in Software Engineering Economics." *Communications of the ACM* 41, no. 8. (August 1998).

Kendall, Kenneth E., and **Julie E. Kendall.** "Information Delivery Systems: An Exploration of Web Push and Pull Technologies." *Communications of the Association for Information Systems* 1. (April 1999).

———. *Systems Analysis and Design,* 4th ed. Upper Saddle River, NJ: Prentice Hall. (1999).

Kenny, David, and **John F. Marshall.** "Contextual Marketing." *Harvard Business Review.* (November–December 2000).

Kettinger, William J., Varun Grover, Subashish Guhan, and **Albert H. Segors.** "Strategic Information Systems Revisited: A Study in Sustainability and Performance." *MIS Quarterly* 18, no. 1. (March 1994).

"Key Sector: High Technology." *Vancouver Economic Development Commission.* http://www.vancouvereconomic.com/investing/sectors/hitech.shtml. (Accessed August 27, 2001).

Kibati, Mugo, and **Donyaprueth Krairit.** "Building India's National Internet Backbone." *Communications of the ACM* 42, no. 6. (June 1999).

Kiesnoski, Kenneth, "CIBC Solves Branch Staffing Problem." *Bank Systems and Technology.* (July 2000).

Kim, B.G., and **P. Wang.** "ATM Network: Goals and Challenges." *Communications of the ACM* 38, no. 2. (February 1995).

Kim, Yongbeom, and **Edward A. Stohr.** "Software Reuse." *Journal of Management Information Systems* 14, no. 4. (Spring 1998).

King, John. "Centralized vs. Decentralized Computing: Organizational Considerations and Management Options." *Computing Surveys.* (October 1984).

———. "Successful Implementation of Large Scale Decision Support Systems: Computerized Models in U.S. Economic Policy Making." *Systems Objectives Solutions.* (November 1983).

King, John L., V. Gurbaxani, K.L. Kraemer, F.W. McFarlan, K.S. Raman, and **C.S. Yap.** "Institutional Factors in Information Technology Innovation." *Information Systems Research* 5, no. 2. (June 1994).

King, John L., and **Kenneth Kraemer.** "Information Resource Management Cannot Work." *Information and Management.* (1988).

King, Julia. "It's CYA Time." *Computerworld.* (March 30, 1992).

———. "Reengineering Slammed." *Computerworld.* (June 13, 1994).

King, W.R. "Creating a Strategic Capabilities Architecture." *Information Systems Management* 12, no. 1. (Winter 1995).

King, William R., and **Vikram Sethi.** "An Empirical Analysis of the Organization of Transnational Information Systems." *Journal of Management Information Systems* 15, no. 4. (Spring 1999).

Klein, Barbara D., Dale L. Goodhue, and **Gordon B. Davis.** "Can Humans Detect Errors in Data?" *MIS Quarterly* 21, no. 2. (June 1997).

Kleinschrod, Walter A. "Keeping Workers Connected." *Beyond Computing.* (June 2000).

Kling, Rob. "Social Analyses of Computing: Theoretical Perspectives in Recent Empirical Research." *Computing Survey* 12, no. 1. (March 1980).

———. "When Organizations Are Perpetrators: The Conditions of Computer Abuse and Computer Crime." In *Computerization & Controversy: Value Conflicts & Social Choices,* edited by Charles Dunlop and Rob Kling. New York: Academic Press. (1991).

Kling, Rob, and **William H. Dutton.** "The Computer Package: Dynamic Complexity." In *Computers and Politics,* edited by James Danziger, William H. Dutton, Rob Kling, and Kenneth Kraemer. New York: Columbia University Press. (1982).

Knapp, Gerald. "Hacker Strolls into Australian Tax Site" Australia.Internet.Com, *INT Media Group.* http://australia.

internet.com/r/article/jsp/sid/364921. (June 30, 2000). (Accessed August 10, 2001).

"Knowledge Portals And Knowledge Management Solutions." *Aptech Worldwide.* http://www.aptechworldwide.com/ aptech/knowledgemanange.htm. (Accessed July 22, 2001).

Knowles, Ann. "EDI Experiments with the Net." *Software Magazine.* (January 1997).

Kock, Ned, and **Robert J. McQueen.** "An Action Research Study of Effects of Asynchronous Groupware Support on Productivity and Outcome Quality in Process Redesign Groups." *Journal of Organizational Computing and Electronic Commerce* 8, no. 2. (1998).

Kohane, Jack. "Cara Airport Services Invests in Supply Chain Management System to Improve Production Efficiencies and Customer Service." *Food In Canada.* (April 1999).

———. "Food Service Operator Takes Off." *Food In Canada.* (April 1999).

Kolb, D.A., and **A.L. Frohman.** "An Organization Development Approach to Consulting." *Sloan Management Review* 12, no. 1. (Fall 1970).

Konsynski, Benn R., and **F. Warren McFarlan.** "Information Partnerships—Shared Data, Shared Scale." *Harvard Business Review.* (September–October 1990).

Korson, Tim, and **John D. McGregor.** "Understanding Object-Oriented: A Unifying Paradigm." *Communications of the ACM* 33, no. 9. (September 1990).

Kotter, John T. "What Effective General Managers Really Do." *Harvard Business Review.* (November–December 1982).

Kraemer, Kenneth L., and **John Leslie King.** "Computer-Based Systems for Cooperative Work and Group Decision Making." *ACM Computing Surveys* 20, no. 2. (June 1988).

Kraemer, Kenneth, John King, Debora Dunkle, and **Joe Lane.** *Managing Information Systems.* Los Angeles: Jossey-Bass. (1989).

Kraut, Robert, Charles Steinfield, Alice P Chan, Brian Butler, and **Anne Hoag.** "Coordination and Virtualization: The Role of Electronic Networks and Personal Relationships. *Organization Science* 10, no. 6. (November–December 1999).

Kreie, Jennifer, and **Timothy Paul Cronan.** "Making Ethical Decisions." *Communications of the ACM* 43, no. 12. (December 2000).

Kroenke, David. *Database Processing: Fundamentals, Design, and Implementation,* 7th ed. Upper Saddle River, NJ: Prentice Hall. (2000).

Kumar, Kuldeep, and **Jos Van Hillegersberg.** "ERP Experiences and Revolution." *Communications of the ACM* 43, no. 4. (April 2000).

Kuo, Geng-Sheng, and **Jing-Pei Lin.** "New Design Concepts for an Intelligent Internet." *Communications of the ACM* 41, no. 11. (November 1998).

Lahey, Liam. "Canada Facing Economic Peril: Report." *ITWorldCanada.com.* http://www.itworldcanada.com. (Accessed March 1, 2000).

———. "RCMP Hails CABS to Streamline Booking Processes and Capture Criminals." *Network World Canada.* (February 25, 2001).

Lange, Danny B. "An Object-Oriented Design Approach for Developing Hypermedia Information Systems." *Journal of Organizational Computing and Electronic Commerce* 6, no. 2. (1996).

Lash, Alex. "Privacy, Practically Speaking." *The Industry Standard.* (August 29, 1999).

Lassila, Kathy S., and **James C. Brancheau.** "Adoption and Utilization of Commercial Software Packages: Exploring

Utilization Equilibria, Transitions, Triggers, and Tracks." *Journal of Management Information Systems* 16, no. 2. (Fall 1999).

"Last Month's Smart Card & Biometrics News." *Bell ID.* http://www.bellid.com/site/news/smartnews.htm. (Accessed October 4, 2001).

"Latest Smart Card & Biometrics News." *Bell ID.* http://www.bellid.com/site/news/smartnews_old.htm. (Accessed October 4, 2001).

Laudon, Kenneth C. "A General Model for Understanding the Relationship Between Information Technology and Organizations." Working paper, Center for Research on Information Systems, New York University. (1989).

———. "CIOs Beware: Very Large Scale Systems." Center for Research on Information Systems, New York University Stern School of Business, working paper. (1989).

———. *Communications Technology and Democratic Participation.* New York: Praeger. (1977).

———. *Computers and Bureaucratic Reform.* New York: Wiley. (1974).

———. "Data Quality and Due Process in Large Interorganizational Record Systems." *Communications of the ACM* 29. (January 1986a).

———. *Dossier Society: Value Choices in the Design of National Information Systems.* New York: Columbia University Press. (1986).

———. "Environmental and Institutional Models of Systems Development." *Communications of the ACM* 28, no. 7. (July 1985).

———. "Ethical Concepts and Information Technology." *Communications of the ACM* 38, no. 12. (December 1995).

———. "From PCs to Managerial Workstations." In Matthias Jarke, *Managers, Micros, and Mainframes.* New York: John Wiley. (1986).

———. "The Promise and Potential of Enterprise Systems and Industrial Networks." Working paper, The Concours Group. Copyright Kenneth C. Laudon. (1999).

"Launchworks Provides 'Launch Capital' to High Speed, Internet Service Provider GuestTek." *GuestTek.* http://www1.newswire.ca/releases/September1999/20/c4655.html. (Accessed August 8, 2001).

"Law Office Of Philip B. Kerr." *Law Office of Philip B. Kerr.* http://www.trytel.com/~pbkerr/main.htm. (Accessed July 31, 2001).

Lawrence, Paul, and **Jay Lorsch.** *Organization and Environment.* Cambridge, MA: Harvard University Press. (1969).

"Leading with Vision: Arnon Levy, Executive VP." *GuestTek.* http://www.guesttek.com/company/team/arnon_levy.html. (Accessed August 12, 2001).

"Leading with Vision: Dan Freedman." *GuestTek.* http://www.guesttek.com/company/board/dan_freedman.html. (Accessed August 8, 2001).

"Leading with Vision: Paul Sullivan, CEO and Acting VP Sales." *GuestTek.* http://www.guesttek.com/company/team/paul_sullivan. html. (Accessed August 12, 2001).

Leavitt, Harold J. "Applying Organizational Change in Industry: Structural, Technological, and Humanistic Approaches." In *Handbook of Organizations,* edited by James G. March. Chicago: Rand McNally. (1965).

Leavitt, Harold J., and **Thomas L. Whisler.** "Management in the 1980s." *Harvard Business Review.* (November–December 1958).

Lederer, Albert, and **Jayesh Prasad.** "Nine Management Guidelines for Better Cost Estimating." *Communications of the ACM* 35, no. 2. (February 1992).

Lee, Hane C. and Laermonth, Michael. "Spawn of Napster." *The Industry Standard*. (May 8, 2000).

Lee, Hau, L., V. Padmanabhan, and Seugin Whang. "The Bullwhip Effect in Supply Chains." *Sloan Management Review*. (Spring 1997).

Lee, Ho Geun. "Do Electronic Marketplaces Lower the Price of Goods?" *Communications of the ACM* 41, no. 1. (January 1998).

Lee, Ho Geun, and Theodore H. Clark. "Market Process Reengineering through Electronic Market Systems: Opportunities and Challenges." *Journal of Management Information Systems* 13, no. 3. (Winter 1997).

Lee, Ho Geun, Theodore Clark, and Kar Yan Tam. "Research Report: Can EDI Benefit Adopters?" *Information Systems Research* 10, no. 2. (June 1999).

Lee, Jae Nam, and Young-Gul Kim. "Effect of Partnership Quality on IS Outsourcing Success." *Journal of Management Information Systems* 15, no. 4. (Spring 1999).

Lee, Soonchul. "The Impact of Office Information Systems on Power and Influence." *Journal of Management Information Systems* 8, no. 2. (Fall 1991).

Leidner, Dorothy E., and Joyce Elam. "Executive Information Systems: Their Impact on Executive Decision Making." *Journal of Management Information Systems*. (Winter 1993–1994).

———. "The Impact of Executive Information Systems on Organizational Design, Intelligence, and Decision Making." *Organization Science* 6, no. 6. (November–December 1995).

Leonard-Barton, Dorothy. *Wellsprings of Knowledge*. Boston, MA: Harvard Business School Press. (1995).

Leonard-Barton, Dorothy, and John J. Sviokla. "Putting Expert Systems to Work." *Harvard Business Review*. (March–April 1988).

Letmendia, Claire, "The Digital Divide, Part I: A Web For Everyone?" *canadacomputes.com*. http://www.canadacomputes. com/v3/print/1,1281,3077,00.html. (Accessed July 28, 2001).

Leveson, Nancy, and Clark S. Turner. "An Investigation of the Therac25 Accidents." *IEEE Computer*. (July 1993), p. 1841.

Levy, David. "Lean Production in an International Supply Chain." *Sloan Management Review*. (Winter 1997).

Lewe, Henrik, and Helmut Krcmar. "A Computer-Supported Cooperative Work Research Laboratory." *Journal of Management Information Systems* 8, no. 3. (Winter 1991–1992).

Lewis, Nicole. "Internet Telephony: The Business Connection." *Beyond Computing*. (July/August 1999).

Liebs, Scott, "In Your Face." *CFO Publishing*. (Acccssed January 19, 2001).

Lientz, Bennett P., and E. Burton Swanson. *Software Maintenance Management*. Reading, MA: Addison-Wesley. (1980).

Liker, Jeffrey K., David B. Roitman, and Ethel Roskies. "Changing Everything All at Once: Work Life and Technological Change." *Sloan Management Review*. (Summer 1987).

Lindblom, C.E. "The Science of Muddling Through." *Public Administration Review* 19. (1959).

Linthicum, David S. "EAI Application Integration Exposed." *Software Magazine*. (February/March 2000).

Lipin, Steven, and Nikhil Deogun. "Big Mergers of 90s Prove Disappointing to Shareholders." *The Wall Street Journal*. (October 30, 2000).

Littlewood, Bev, and Lorenzo Strigini. "The Risks of Software." *Scientific American* 267, no. 5. (November 1992).

———. "Validation of Ultra-high Dependability for Software-based Systems." *Communications of the ACM* 36, no. 11. (November 1993).

Liu, Ziming, and David G. Stork. "Is Paperless Really More?" *Communications of the ACM* 43, no. 11. (November 2000).

"Living the Commitments Gathering Competitive Information." *Nortel Networks*. http://www.nortelnetworks.com/corporate/ community/ethics/living4.html. (Accessed August 8, 2001).

Loch, Karen D., Houston H. Carr, and Merrill E. Warkentin. "Threats to Information Systems: Today's Reality, Yesterday's Understanding." *MIS Quarterly* 16, no. 2. (June 1992).

Lohr, Steve. "A Nation Ponders Its Growing Digital Divide." *The New York Times*. (October 21, 1996).

———. "The Network Computer as the PC's Evil Twin." *The New York Times*. (November 4, 1996).

Lohse, Gerald L., and Peter Spiller. "Electronic Shopping." *Communications of the ACM* 41, no. 7. (July 1998).

———. "Internet Retail Store Design: How the User Interface Influences Traffic and Sales." *Journal of Computer-Mediated Communication* 5, no. 2. (December 1999).

Lou, Hao, and Richard W. Scannell. "Acceptance of Groupware: The Relationships Among Use, Satisfaction, and Outcomes." *Journal of Organizational Computing and Electronic Commerce* 6, no. 2. (1996).

Lucas, Henry C., Jr. *Implementation: The Key to Successful Information Systems*. New York: Columbia University Press. (1981).

"Lycos Voice Portal Recognizes Speech." *Newsbytes*. http://www. canadacomputes.com/v3/print/1,1019,4603,00.html. (Accessed November 7, 2000).

Lyman, Jay. "Teenage Hacker Mafia Boy Pleads Guilty." *Newsfactor Network*. http://www.newsfactor.com. (Accessed June 27, 2001).

Machlup, Fritz. *The Production and Distribution of Knowledge in the United States*. Princeton, NJ: Princeton University Press. (1962).

Mackie, Dean. "Case Study: Automating Business Rules at a Public Sector Financial Institution". http://www.mum.edu/cs_dept/ aarsanjani/oopsla2000. (Accessed April 3, 2001).

Macklem, Katherine. "Air Rage: After Months of Chaos, Air Canada's Tough Guy Boss Insists the Worst Is Over." *Maclean's*. (June 11, 2000).

Maes, Patti. "Agents that Reduce Work and Information Overload." *Communications of the ACM* 38, no. 7. (July 1994).

Maes, Patti, Robert H. Guttman, and Alexandros G. Moukas. "Agents that Buy and Sell." *Communications of the ACM* 42, no. 3. (March 1999).

Maier, Jerry L., R. Kelly Rainer, Jr., and Charles A. Snyder. "Environmental Scanning for Information Technology: An Empirical Investigation." *Journal of Management Information Systems* 14, no. 2. (Fall 1997).

Main, Thomas J., and James E. Short. "Managing the Merger: Building Partnerships Through IT Planning at the New Baxter." *MIS Quarterly* 13, no. 4. (December 1989).

Malcolm, Andrew H. "How the Oil Spilled and Spread: Delay and Confusion Off Alaska." *The New York Times*. (April 16, 1989).

Malhotra, Yogesh. "Toward a Knowledge Ecology for Organizational White-Waters." Keynote Presentations for the Knowledge Ecology Fair '98. (1998).

Malone, Thomas W. "Is Empowerment Just a Fad? Control, Decision-Making, and IT." *Sloan Management Review*. (Winter 1997).

Malone, Thomas W., Kevin Crowston, Jintae Lee, and Brian Pentland. "Tools for Inventing Organizations: Toward a Handbook of Organizational Processes." *Management Science* 45, no. 3. (March 1999).

Malone, Thomas W., and J. F. Rockart. "Computers, Networks and the Corporation." *Scientific American* 265, no. 3. (September 1991).

Malone, Thomas W., JoAnne Yates, and **Robert I. Benjamin.** "Electronic Markets and Electronic Hierarchies." *Communications of the ACM.* (June 1987).
————. "The Logic of Electronic Markets." *Harvard Business Review.* (May–June 1989).

"Managing Large-Scale Systems Development Risk Through the Deployment of Software Components: A Case Study." *Castek Software Factory, Inc.* http://www.castek.com/success/ BOC_SIGSArticle.html. (Accessed July 8, 2001).

Mandelkern, David. "Graphical User Interfaces: The Next Generation." *Communications of the ACM* 36, no. 4. (April 1993).

Mannheim, Marvin L. "Global Information Technology: Issues and Strategic Opportunities." *International Information Systems* 1, no. 1. (January 1992).

"Maple Leaf Sports and Entertainment Ltd." *Great Plains Software.* http://www.greatplains.com/canada/document.asp?Link= profiles/m1se1_ca_en.htm. (Accessed May 9, 2001).

March, James G., and **G. Sevon.** "Gossip, Information, and Decision Making." In *Advances in Information Processing in Organizations,* edited by Lee S. Sproull and J. P. Crecine. vol. 1. Hillsdale, NJ: Erlbaum. (1984).

March, James G., and **Herbert A. Simon.** *Organizations.* New York: Wiley. (1958).

March, Salvatore T., and **Young-Gul Kim.** "Information Resource Management: A Metadata Perspective." *Journal of Management Information Systems* 5, no. 3. (Winter 1988–1989).

Mariano, Gwendolyn. "File-Swapping Services Seek Refuge Overseas." *CNET News.* http://news.cnet .com/news/0-1005-202-5025920.htm. (Accessed August 29, 2001).

Markoff, John. "Computer Scientists are Poised for Revolution on a Tiny Scale." *The New York Times.* (November 1, 1999).
————. "Growing Compatibility Issue: Computers and User Privacy." *The New York Times.* (March 3, 1999).
————. "Tiniest Circuits Hold Prospect of Explosive Computer Speeds." *The New York Times.* (July 16, 1999).

Markus, M. Lynne "Power, Politics, and MIS Implementation." *Communications of the ACM* 26, no. 6. (June 1983).

Markus, M. Lynne, and **Robert I. Benjamin.** "Change Agentry— The Next IS Frontier." *MIS Quarterly* 20, no. 4. (December 1996).
————. "The Magic Bullet Theory of IT-Enabled Transformation." *Sloan Management Review.* (Winter 1997).

Markus, M. Lynne, and **Mark Keil.** "If We Build It, They Will Come: Designing Information Systems That People Want to Use." *Sloan Management Review.* (Summer 1994).

Markus, M. Lynne, Conelis Tanis, and **Paul C. van Fenema.** "Multisite ERP Implementations." *Communications of the ACM* 43, no. 3. (April 2000).

Marlin, Steve, "Visa Moving Chipcards to Canada." *Bank Systems and Technology.* (May 2000).

Martin, J., and **C. McClure.** "Buying Software Off the Rack." *Harvard Business Review.* (November–December 1983).

Martin, James, and **Carma McClure.** *Structured Techniques: The Basis of CASE.* Englewood Cliffs, NJ: Prentice Hall. (1988).

Martin, James. *Application Development without Programmers.* Englewood Cliffs, NJ: Prentice Hall. (1982).

Martin, Jr. David M., Richard M. Smith, Michael Brittain, Ivan Fetch, and **Hailin Wu.** "The Privacy Practices of Web Browser Extensions." *Communications of the ACM* 44, no. 2. (February 2001).

Mason, R.E.A., and **T.T. Carey.** "Prototyping Interactive Information Systems." *Communications of the ACM* 26. (May 1983).

Mason, Richard O. "Applying Ethics to Information Technology Issues." *Communications of the ACM* 38, no. 12. (December 1995).
————. "Four Ethical Issues in the Information Age." *MIS Quarterly* 10, no. 1. (March 1986).

Massetti, Brenda, and **Robert W. Zmud.** "Measuring the Extent of EDI Usage in Complex Organizations. Strategies and Illustrative Examples." *MIS Quarterly* 20, no. 3. (September 1996).

Mata, Franciso J., William L. Fuerst, and **Jay B. Barney.** "Information Technology and Sustained Competitive Advantage: A Resource-Based Analysis." *MIS Quarterly* 19, no. 4. (December 1995).

Matlin, Gerald. "What Is the Value of Investment in Information Systems?" *MIS Quarterly* 13, no. 3. (September 1989).

Matos, Victor M., and **Paul J. Jalics.** "An Experimental Analysis of the Performance of Fourth-Generation Tools on PCs." *Communications of the ACM* 32, no. 11. (November 1989).

Mazzucchelli, Louis. "Structured Analysis Can Streamline Software Design." *Computerworld.* (December 9, 1985).

McCarthy, John. "Generality in Artificial Intelligence." *Communications of the ACM.* (December 1987).
————. "Phenomenal Data Mining." *Communications of the ACM* 43, no. 8. (August 2000).

McCormack, Alan. "Product-Development Practices that Work: How Internet Companies Build Software." *Sloan Management Review* 42, no. 2. (Winter 2001).

McCune, Jenny C. "Measuring Value." *Beyond Computing.* (July/August 2000).

McFadden, Fred R., Jeffrey A. Hoffer, and **Mary B. Prescott.** *Modern Database Management,* Fifth Edition. Upper Saddle River, NJ: Prentice-Hall. (1999).

McFarlan, F. Warren. "Information Technology Changes the Way You Compete." *Harvard Business Review.* (May–June 1984).
————. "Portfolio Approach to Information Systems." *Harvard Business Review.* (September–October 1981).

McFarlan, F. Warren, James L. McKenney, and **Philip Pyburn.** "Governing the New World." *Harvard Business Review.* (July–August 1983).
————. "The Information Archipelago—Plotting a Course." *Harvard Business Review.* (January–February 1983).

McGrath, Dermot. "Going Native." *Tornado Insider* 13. (May 2000).

McIntyre, Mike. "Pair Guilty in High-Tech Case." *Winnipeg Free Press.* (May 19, 2001).

McIntyre, Scott C., and **Lexis F. Higgins.** "Object-Oriented Analysis and Design: Methodology and Application." *Journal of Management Information Systems* 5, no. 1. (Summer 1988).

McKeen, James D., and **Tor Guimaraes.** "Successful Strategies for User Participation in Systems Development." *Journal of Management Information Systems* 14, no. 2. (Fall 1997).

McKenney, James L., and **Peter G.W. Keen.** "How Managers' Minds Work." *Harvard Business Review.* (May–June 1974).

McKenney, James L., and **F. Warren McFarlan.** "The Information Archipelago—Maps and Bridges." *Harvard Business Review.* (September–October 1982).

McWilliam, Gil. "Building Stronger Brands through Online Communities." *Sloan Management Review* 41, no. 3. (Spring 2000).

Mears, Rena, and **Jason Salzetti.** "The New Wireless Enterprise." *Information Week.* (September 18, 2000).

"Media Metrix Canada Releases June 2001 Internet Usage Stats." *Jupiter Media Metrix.* http://ca.mediametrix.com/press/releases/ 20010725.jsp. (Accessed July 28, 2001).

Mehler, Mark. "Futurelink: Linking the Future?" *ZDNet.* (May 3, 2000).

Meister, Frank, Jeetu Patel, and **Joe Fenner.** "E-Commerce Platforms Mature." *Information Week.* (October 23, 2000).

Memishi, Ruhan. "Covisint's Starts and Stops." *Internet World.* (January 1, 2001).

Memon, Nasir, and **Ping Wah Wong.** "Protecting Digital Media Content." *Communications of the ACM* 41, no. 7. (July 1, 1998).

Mendelson, Haim, and **Ravindra R. Pillai.** "Clock Speed and Informational Response: Evidence from the Information Technology Industry." *Information Systems Research* 9, no. 4. (December 1998).

Menon, Harikrishnan and **Vaidyanathan, Aruna.** "On Wings of Light." *The Economic Times.* (November 10, 2000).

Menzies, David. "Mondo Mondex." *Financial Post.* (June 1, 1998).

Messina, Paul, David Culler, Wayne Pfeiffer, William Martin, J. Tinsley Oden, and **Gary Smith.** "Architecture." *Communications of the ACM* 41, no. 11. (November 1998).

Metz, Cade. "A Quantum Leap, but at a Glacial Pace." *PC Magazine.* http://www.pcmag.com/print_article/0,3048,a%253D12710,00. asp. (Accessed August 31, 2001).

Meyer, Marc H., and **Robert Seliger,** "Product Platforms in Software Development." *Sloan Management Review* 40, no. 1. (Fall 1998).

Milberg, Sandra J., Sandra J. Burke, H. Jeff Smith, and **Ernest A. Kallman.** "Values, Personal Information Privacy, and Regulatory Approaches." *Communications of the ACM* 38, no. 12. (December 1995).

Mintzberg, Henry. "Managerial Work: Analysis from Observation." *Management Science* 18. (October 1971).

———. *The Nature of Managerial Work.* New York: Harper & Row. (1973).

———. *The Structuring of Organizations.* Englewood Cliffs, NJ: Prentice Hall. (1979).

"Minutes of the Eleventh Regular Meeting of Council Twenty-Fourth of May, 2001 at the Municipal Office, 420 L Thunder Bay, Ontario at the Hour of 5:30 pm." *The Corporation of the Township of Shuniah.* http://www.shuniah.org/councill/import/May%2024.htm. (Accessed July 30, 2001).

Miranda, Shaila M., and **Robert P. Bostrum.** "Meeting Facilitation: Process versus Content Interventions." *Journal of Management Information Systems* 15, no. 4. (Spring 1999).

———. "The Impact of Group Support Systems on Group Conflict and Conflict Management." *Journal of Management Information Systems* 10, no. 3. (Winter 1993–1994).

"Molson Breweries Case Study." *Opentext Corporation.* (2001). http://www.opentext.com/customers/case_studies/livelink_case_study_molsons.pdf. (Accessed August 3, 2001).

Moores, Trevor, and **Gurpreet Dhillon.** "Software Piracy: A View from Hong Kong." *Communications of the ACM* 43, no. 12. (December 2000).

"More Powerful Than a Speeding Network Manager." *Communications News.* (November 1998).

Morse, Alan, and **George Reynolds.** "Overcoming Current Growth Limits in UI Development." *Communications of the ACM* 36, no. 4. (April 1993).

Mougayar, Walid. *Opening Digital Markets,* 2nd ed. New York: McGraw-Hill. (1998).

Mueller, Milton. "Universal Service and the Telecommunications Act: Myth Made Law." *Communications of the ACM* 40, no. 3. (March 1997).

Muir, Jamie. "Cara Selects Synquest Supply Chain Management Software for 11 Site Contract." *Synquest Inc.* http://www.synquest.com/press_template.cfm?ID=308. (Accessed January 2001).

Muldowney, Lori. "Canada's E-business Backslide." *Wired Women.* (April 9, 2001).

Mullich, Joe. "Reinvent Your Intranet." *Datamation.* (June 1999).

"MultiModal Clients." *MultiModal Inc.* http://www.multimodalinc.com/clients.html. (Accessed July 11, 2001). Courtesy of MultiModal Applied Systems.

Mumford, Enid, and **Mary Weir.** *Computer Systems in Work Design: The ETHICS Method.* New York: John Wiley. (1979).

Munakata, Toshinori, and **Yashvant Jani.** "Fuzzy Systems: An Overview." *Communications of the ACM* 37, no. 3. (March 1994).

Mykytyn, Kathleen, Peter P. Mykytyn, Jr., and **Craig W. Slinkman.** "Expert Systems: A Question of Liability." *MIS Quarterly* 14, no. 1. (March 1990).

"MySAP.com brings e-Business Solutions to Celestica Inc." *SAP.* http://www.ext03.sap.com/canada/press/releases/2000/pr081700.asp. (Accessed May 31, 2001).

Nakamura, Kiyoh, Toshihiro Ide, and **Yukio Kiyokane.** "Roles of Multimedia Technology in Telework." *Journal of Organizational Computing and Electronic Commerce* 6, no. 4. (1996).

Nambisan, Satish, and **Yu-Ming Wang.** "Web Technology Adoption and Knowledge Barriers." *Journal of Organizational Computing and Electronic Commerce* 10, no. 2. (2000).

Nash, Jim. "State of the Market, Art, Union, and Technology." *AI Expert.* (January 1993).

National Telecommunications & Information Administration, U.S. Department of Commerce. "Falling Through the Net: Defining the Digital Divide." July 8, 1999

Needham, Roger M. "Denial of Service: An Example." *Communications of the ACM* 37, no. 11. (November 1994).

Nerson, Jean-Marc. "Applying Object-Oriented Analysis and Design." *Communications of the ACM* 35, no. 9. (September 1992).

"Netfirms Launches Free Business Web Hosting Service." *Netfirms Inc.* http://www.netfirms.com/companyPressJul19. (Accessed July 19, 1999).

Neumann, Peter G. "Inside RISKS: Computers, Ethics and Values." *Communications of the ACM* 34, no. 7. (July 1991).

———. "Inside RISKS: Fraud by Computer." *Communications of the ACM* 35, no. 8. (August 1992).

———. "Risks Considered Global(ly)." *Communications of the ACM* 35, no. 1. (January 1993).

Neumann, Seev. "Issues and Opportunities in International Information Systems." *International Information Systems* 1, no. 4. (October 1992).

"New $5.7 Million Air Operations Centre Will Keep Pace with Traffic Growth." *NAV Canada.* http://www.navcanada.ca/contentEN/news/newsreleases/2001/nr0827.asp. (Accessed August 26, 2001).

"New CEO Aims to Make GuestTek Dominant Player in High Speed Internet Access Market for Mobile Travelers." *GuestTek.* http://www.guesttek.com/news/newsreleases/190701.html. (Accessed August 12, 2001).

"New Regulation: Ergonomics Can Take the Pain Out of Work." *Worksafe BC.* http://www.worksafebc.com/pubs/newsletters/paw/paw4_4/newreg.asp. (Accessed July 31, 2001).

Newman-Provost, Josie. "Husky Merges Mobile Devices." *Canadian Banker.* (March/April 1998).

Ngwenyama, Ojelanki, and **Allen S. Lee.** "Communication Richness in Electronic Mail: Critical Social Theory and the Contextuality of Meaning." *MIS Quarterly* 21, no. 2. (June 1997).

Nidumolu, Sarma R., Seymour E. Goodman, Douglas R. Vogel, and **Ann K. Danowitz.** "Information Technology for Local Administration Support: The Governorates Project in Egypt." *MIS Quarterly* 20, no. 2. (June 1996).

Niederman, Fred, Catherine M. Beise, and **Peggy M. Beranek.** "Issues and Concerns about Computer-Supported Meetings: The Facilitator's Perspective." *MIS Quarterly* 20, no. 1. (March 1996).

Nilsen, Kelvin. "Adding Real-Time Capabilities to Java." *Communications of the ACM* 41, no. 6. (June 1998).

"Nissan Canada, Subaru Vehicles Not Affected by Firestone Recall." *Canadiandriver.com.* http://www.canadiandriver. com/news/0008114.htm. (Accessed August 11, 2000).

Nissen, Mark E. "Redesigning Reengineering through Measurement-Driven Inference." *MIS Quarterly* 22, no. 4. (December 1998).

Nissenbaum, Helen. "Computing and Accountability." *Communications of the ACM* 37, no. 1. (January 1994).

Noffsinger, W.B., Robert Niedbalski, Michael Blanks, and **Niall Emmart.** "Legacy Object Modeling Speeds Software Integration." *Communications of the ACM* 41, no. 12. (December 1998).

Nunamaker, J.F., Alan R. Dennis, Joseph S. Valacich, Douglas R. Vogel, and **Joey F. George.** "Electronic Meeting Systems to Support Group Work." *Communications of the ACM* 34, no. 7. (July 1991).

Nunamaker, Jay, Robert O. Briggs, Daniel D. Mittleman, Douglas R. Vogel, and **Pierre A. Balthazard.** "Lessons from a Dozen Years of Group Support Systems Research: A Discussion of Lab and Field Findings." *Journal of Management Information Systems* 13, no. 3. (Winter 1997).

O'Brien, Jeanne, "Information Portals Sharpen Data Access at UBOC, CIBC." *Bank Systems and Technology.* (January 2000).

O'Dell, John, and **Edmund Sanders.** "Firestone Begins Replacement of 6.4 Million Tires." *Los Angeles Times.* (August 10, 2000).

O'Keefe, Robert M., and **Tim McEachern.** "Web-based Customer Decision Support Systems." *Communications of the ACM* 41, no. 3. (March 1998).

O'Leary, Daniel E., Daniel Koukka, and **Robert Plant.** "Artificial Intelligence and Virtual Organizations." *Communications of the ACM* 40, no. 1. (January 1997).

O'Leary, Daniel, and **Peter Selfridge.** "Knowledge Management for Best Practices." *Communications of the ACM* 43, no. 11es. (November 2000).

O'Rourke, Maureen A. "Is Virtual Trespass an Apt Analogy?" *Communications of the ACM* 44, no. 2. (February 2001).

"OCRI Economic Development." *Ottawa Economic Development Corporation.* http://www.ottawaregion.com/oed/index.html. (Accessed August 28, 2001).

Okerson, Ann. "Who Owns Digital Works?" *Scientific American.* (July 1996).

"On Command Canada and GuestTek Announce Integrated TV Internet & High Speed Connectivity Solution for the Canadian Hotel Industry." *GuestTek.* http://www. hospitalitynet.org/news/4004739.htm. (Accessed August 8, 2001).

"Online Credit Hacker May Be Out for Profit: Investigator Thinks 'Maxus' Is a Two-Person Team." *apbnews.com.* http://www.apbnews.com. (Accessed January 14, 2000).

"Online Gauging Improves Spunbonded Fabric Quality." *NDC Infrared Engineering.* http://www.ndcinfrared.com/applications/ nonwovens_textiles_articles/spunbond/spunbond.html. (Accessed June 20, 2001).

"Open Database Merchandising System: Enhance Your Category Management Practices Using ODBMS." *JDA Software Group.*

http://www.jda.com/news.cfm?fstoryID=383. (Accessed July 11, 2001).

Oppliger, Rolf. "Internet Security, Firewalls, and Beyond." *Communications of the ACM* 40, no.7. (May 1997).

Orlikowski, Wanda J. "Learning from Notes: Organizational Issues in Groupware Implementation." Sloan Working Paper, no. 3428. Cambridge, MA: Sloan School of Management, Massachusetts Institute of Technology.

Orlikowski, Wanda J., and **Daniel Robey.** "Information Technology and the Structuring of Organizations." *Information Systems Research* 2, no. 2. (June 1991).

Orlikowski, Wanda J., and **J. Debra Hofman.** "An Improvisational Change Model for Change Management: The Case of Groupware Technologies." *Sloan Management Review.* (Winter 1997).

Orlikowski, Wanda J., and **Jack J. Baroudi.** "Studying Information Technology in Organizations: Research Approaches and Assumptions." *Information Systems Research* 2, no. 1. (March 1991).

Orr, Kenneth. "Data Quality and Systems Theory." *Communications of the ACM* 41, no. 2. (February 1998).

"Ottawa Lacks the Smarts On Smart Card." *Canada Newswire.* http://www.newswire.ca/releases/March 2001/27/c7374.html. (Accessed August 10, 2001).

"Our Winning Line-Up." *GuestTek.* http://www.guesttek.com/ products/globalsuite/overview.html. (Accessed August 12, 2001).

Oz, Effy. "Ethical Standards for Information Systems Professionals." *MIS Quarterly* 16, no. 4. (December 1992).

————. *Ethics for the Information Age.* Dubuque, Iowa: W. C. Brown. (1994).

Palaniswamy, Rajagopal, and **Tyler Frank.** "Enhancing Manufacturing Performance with ERP Systems." *Information Systems Management.* (Summer 2000).

Palleschi, Antionetta. "Trading Places." *CXO.CA.* (Accessed July 8, 2001).

Palmer, Jonathan W., and **David A. Griffith.** "An Emerging Model of Web Site Design for Marketing." *Communications of the ACM* 41, no. 3. (March 1998).

Palvia, Shailendra, Prashant Palvia, and **Ronald Zigli,** eds. *The Global Issues of Information Technology Management.* Harrisburg, PA: Idea Group Publishing. (1992).

Pancake, Cherri M. "The Promise and the Cost of Object Technology: A Five-Year Forecast." *Communications of the ACM* 38, no. 10. (October 1995).

"PanCanadian Unveils Canada's First Full-Sized, 3-D Visualization Centre for Oil and Gas Exploration." *Canada Newswire.* http://www.newswire.ca/releases/January2000/17/c0570.html. (Accessed January 17, 2000). © Canada Newswire Ltd.

Panko, Raymond R. "Is Office Productivity Stagnant?" *MIS Quarterly* 15, no. 2. (June 1991).

Papazoglou, Mike P. "Agent-Oriented Technology in Support of E-Business." *Communications of the ACM* 44, no. 4. (April 2001).

Parker, M.M. "Enterprise Information Analysis: Cost-Benefit Analysis and the Data-Managed System." *IBM Systems Journal* 21. (1982).

Parsons, Jeffrey, and **Yair Wand.** "Using Objects for Systems Analysis." *Communications of the ACM* 40, no. 12. (December 1997).

Passmore, David. "Scaling Large E-Commerce Infrastructures." *Packet Magazine.* (Third Quarter 1999).

Patton, Susannah. "The Truth About CRM." *CIO Magazine.* (May 1, 2001).

Paul, Lauren Gibbons. "What Price Ownership?" *Datamation.* (December/January 1998).

"Peer Review." *Red Herring.* (December 4, 2000).

Peirol, Paulette. "EBiz of the Week." *Globetechnology.com.* (December 28, 2000).

Peleg, Alex, Sam Wilkie, and **Uri Weiser.** "Intel MMX for Multimedia PCs." *Communications of the ACM* 40, no. 1. (January 1997).

Perine, Keith. "The Privacy Police." *The Industry Standard.* (February 21, 2000).

Petrazzini, Ben, and **Mugo Kibati.** "The Internet in Developing Countries." *Communications of the ACM* 42, no. 6. (June 1999).

"PetroCan Home Heating: A Workabout Case Study." *Sagedata Solutions.* http://www.sage.ca/appstr99/petrocan.html. (Accessed February 25, 2001).

Pindyck, Robert S., and **Daniel L. Rubinfeld.** *Microeconomics, Fifth Ed.* Upper Saddle River, NJ: Prentice Hall. (2001).

Pinsonneault, Alain, Henri Barki, R. Brent Gallupe, and **Norberto Hoppen.** "Electronic Brainstorming: The Illusion of Productivity." *Information Systems Research* 10, no. 2. (July 1999).

"Plans and Policies for Client/Server Technology." *I/S Analyzer* 30, no. 4. (April 1992).

Porat, Marc. "The Information Economy: Definition and Measurement." Washington, DC: U.S. Department of Commerce, Office of Telecommunications. (May 1977).

Porter, Michael. *Competitive Advantage.* New York: Free Press. (1985).

———. *Competitive Strategy.* New York: Free Press. (1980).

———. "How Information Can Help You Compete." *Harvard Business Review.* (August–September 1985).

———. "Strategy and the Internet." *Harvard Business Review.* (March 2001).

Post, Gerald V. "How Often Should a Firm Buy New PCs?" *Communications of the ACM* 42, no. 5. (May 1999).

Pottie, G.J., and **W.J Kaiser.** "Wireless Integrated Network Sensors." *Communications of the ACM* 43, no. 5. (May 2000).

Poulin, Jeffrey S. "Reuse: Been There, Done That." *Communications of the ACM* 42, no. 5. (May 1999).

Power, Richard. "Tangled Web: Tales of Digital Crime from the Shadows of Cyberspace." *Macmillan Press.* (2000).

Prahalad, C.K., and **M.S. Krishnan.** "The New Meaning of Quality in the Information Age." *Harvard Business Review.* (September–October 1999).

Prahalad, C.K., and **Venkatram Ramaswamy.** "Coopting Consumer Competence." *Harvard Business Review.* (January–February 2000).

Premkumar, G., K. Ramamurthy, and **Sree Nilakanta.** "Implementation of Electronic Data Interchange: An Innovation Diffusion Perspective." *Journal of Management Information Systems* 11, no. 2. (Fall 1994).

Press, Lawrence. "Lotus Notes. (Groupware) in Context." *Journal of Organizational Computing* 2, nos. 3 and 4. (1992).

"Press Release: Three Levels of Government Fund International Fashion Technology Centre." *Winnipeg Development Authority.* http://www.wda.mb.ca/new/news41.html. (Accessed June 4, 1999).

"Products And Services." *NBTEL.* http://www.nbtel.nb.ca/english/ callcentres/products_sub4_3.htm. (Accessed December 13, 2000).

"Profile Steve West." *CEO2GO.* http://www.biznet.maximizer.com/01415100135016/msg5.html http://www.biznet.maximizer.com/01415100135016/msg3.html. (Accessed January 19, 2001).

"Profiting Together." *GuestTek.* http://www.guesttek.com/partners/overview.html. (Accessed August 12, 2001).

Purao, Sandeep, Hemant Jain, and **Derek Nazareth.** "Effective Distribution of Object-Oriented Applications." *Communications of the ACM* 41, no. 8. (August 1998).

Quelch, John A., and **Lisa R. Klein.** "The Internet and International Marketing." *Sloan Management Review.* (Spring 1996).

Quinn, James Brian. "Strategic Outsourcing: Leveraging Knowledge Capabilities." *Sloan Management Review* 40, no. 4. (Summer 1999).

Rafter, Michelle V. "Can We Talk?" *The Industry Standard.* (February 15, 1999).

———. "Trust or Bust?" *The Industry Standard.* (March 13, 2000).

Rai, Arun, Ravi Patnayakuni, and **Nainika Patnayakuni.** "Technology Investment and Business Performance." *Communications of the ACM* 40, no. 7. (July 1997).

Rainer, Rex Kelley, Jr., Charles A. Snyder, and **Houston H. Carr.** "Risk Analysis for Information Technology." *Journal of Management Information Systems* 8, no. 1. (Summer 1991).

Randall, Dave, John Hughes, Jon O'Brien, Tom Rodden, Mark Rouncefield, Ian Sommerville, and **Peter Tolmie.** "Focus Issue on Legacy Information Systems and Business Process Change: Banking on the Old Technology: Understanding the Organisational Context of 'Legacy' Issues." *Communications of the AIS* 2. (July 1999).

Rangan, V. Kasturi, and **Marie Bell.** "Dell Online." Harvard Business School Case 9-598-116. (1998).

Ravichandran, T. and **Arun Rai.** "Total Quality Management in Information Systems Development." *Journal of Management Information Systems* 16, no. 3. (Winter 1999–2000).

Ray, Randy. "Web Expands Recruiting Role." *Globetechnology.com.* (November 10, 2000).

Raymond, Louis, and **Francois Bergeron.** "EDI Success in Small- and Medium-sized Enterprises: A Field Study." *Journal of Organizational Computing and Electronic Commerce* 6, no. 2. (1996).

Rayport, J.F., and **J.J. Sviokla.** "Managing in the Marketspace." *Harvard Business Review.* (November–December 1994).

Reagle, Joseph, and **Lorrie Faith Cranor.** "The Platform for Privacy Preferences." *Communications of the ACM* 42, no. 2. (February 1999).

Rebello, Joseph. "State Street Boston's Allure for Investors Starts to Fade." *The Wall Street Journal.* (January 4, 1995).

"Records, Computers, and the Rights of Citizens." *United States Department of Health, Education, and Welfare.* Cambridge: MIT Press. (1973).

Redburn, Tom. "How Much Am I Bid for this Imperfect Marketplace?" *The New York Times E-Commerce Section.* (December 13, 2000).

Redding, Alan. "Analyze Your Customers." *Datamation.* (September 2000).

Redman, Thomas C. "The Impact of Poor Data Quality on the Typical Enterprise." *Communications of the ACM* 41, no. 2. (February 1998).

Regan, Keith. "Amazon Endures Third Holiday Outage." *E-Commerce Times.* (December 6, 2000).

Regan, Keith. "eBay Slammed by 10-Hour Outage." *E-Commerce Times.* (January 4, 2001).

Reich, Blaize Horner, and **Izak Benbasat.** "Factors that Influence the Social Dimension of Alignment between Business and Information Technology Objectives." *MIS Quarterly* 24, no. 1. (March 2000).

Reichheld, Frederick E., and **Phil Schefter.** "E-Loyalty: Your Secret Weapon on the Web." *Harvard Business Review.* (July–August 2000).

"Research Statistics: Worldwide Smartcards Market Forecast." *SmartCard Central.* http://www.smartcardcentral.com/research. (Accessed August 8, 2001).

"Retail-1 EIS." *Gemmar Systems International.* http://www.gsi.ca/eis.html. (Accessed July 12, 2001).

Rifkin, Jeremy. "Watch Out for Trickle-Down Technology." *The New York Times.* (March 16, 1993).

Rigdon, Joan E. "Frequent Glitches in New Software Bug Users." *The Wall Street Journal.* (January 18, 1995).

Rivard, Suzanne, and **Sid L. Huff.** "Factors of Success for End-User Computing." *Communications of the ACM* 31, no. 5. (May 1988).

Roach, Stephen S. "Industrialization of the Information Economy." New York: Morgan Stanley and Co. (1984).

———. "Making Technology Work." New York: Morgan Stanley and Co. (1993).

———. "Services Under Siege—The Restructuring Imperative." *Harvard Business Review.* (September–October 1991).

———. "Technology and the Service Sector." *Technological Forecasting and Social Change* 34, no. 4. (December 1988).

———. "The Hollow Ring of the Productivity Revival." *Harvard Business Review.* (November–December 1996).

Roberts-Witt, Sarah L. "Proposed Auto Exchange Hits Bumps." *Knowledge Management.* (July 2000).

Robey, Daniel, and **Marie-Claude Boudreau.** "Accounting for the Contradictory Organizational Consequences of Information Technology: Theoretical Directions and Methodological Implications." *Information Systems Research* 10, no. 42. (June 1999).

Robey, Daniel, and **M. Lynne Markus.** "Rituals in Information System Design." *MIS Quarterly.* (March 1984).

Robey, Daniel, and **Sundeep Sahay.** "Transforming Work through Information Technology: A Comparative Case Study of Geographic Information Systems in County Government." *Information Systems Research* 7, no. 1. (March 1996).

Robinson, Teri. "NASDAQ Is Bullish on Technology." *Information Week.* (May 22, 2000).

Roche, Edward M. *Managing Information Technology in Multinational Corporations.* New York: Macmillan. (1992).

———. *Telecommunications and Business Strategy.* Chicago: The Dryden Press. (1991).

———. "Planning for Competitive Use of Information Technology in Multinational Corporations." AIB UK Region, Brighton Polytechnic, Brighton, UK, Conference Paper. (March 1992). Edward M. Roche, W. Paul Stillman School of Business, Seton Hall University.

Rockart, John F. "Chief Executives Define Their Own Data Needs." *Harvard Business Review.* (March–April 1979).

Rockart, John F., and **David W. DeLong.** *Executive Support Systems: The Emergence of Top Management Computer Use.* Homewood, IL: Dow-Jones Irwin. (1988).

Rockart, John F., and **Lauren S. Flannery.** "The Management of End-User Computing." *Communications of the ACM* 26, no. 10. (October 1983).

Rockart, John F., and **James E. Short.** "IT in the 1990s: Managing Organizational Interdependence." *Sloan Management Review* 30, no. 2. (Winter 1989).

Rockart, John F., and **Michael E. Treacy.** "The CEO Goes On-line." *Harvard Business Review.* (January–February 1982).

Rosario, Elise del. "Logistical Nightmare." *OR/MS Today.* (April 1999) http://www.lionhrtpub.com/orms/orms-4-99/rosario.html. (Accessed July 11, 2001).

Rotenberg, Marc. "Communications Privacy: Implications for Network Design." *Communications of the ACM* 36, no. 8. (August 1993).

———. "Inside RISKS: Protecting Privacy." *Communications of the ACM* 35, no. 4. (April 1992).

Ruhleder, Karen, and **John Leslie King.** "Computer Support for Work Across Space, Time, and Social Worlds." *Journal of Organizational Computing* 1, no. 4. (1991).

Rumelhart, David E., Bernard Widrow, and **Michael A. Lehr.** "The Basic Ideas in Neural Networks." *Communications of the ACM* 37, no. 3. (March 1994).

Rundensteiner, Elke A, Andreas Koeller, and **Xin Zhang.** "Maintaining Data Warehouses over Changing Information Sources." *Communications of the ACM* 43, no. 6. (June 2000).

Ryan, Sherry D., and **David A. Harrison.** "Considering Social Subsystem Costs and Benefits in Information Technology Investment Decisions: A View from the Field on Anticipated Payoffs." *Journal of Management Information Systems* 16, no. 4. (Spring 2000).

Sabherwahl, Rajiv. "The Role of Trust in IS Outsourcing Development Projects." *Communications of the ACM* 42, no. 2. (February 1999).

Salisbury, J. Kenneth, Jr. "Making Graphics Physically Tangible." *Communications of the ACM* 42, no. 8. (August 1999).

Sambamurthy, V. and **Robert W. Zmud.** "Research Commentary: The Organizing Logic for an Enterprise's IT Activities in the Digital Era-A Prognosis of Practice and a Call to Research." *Information Systems Research* 11, no. 2. (June 2000).

Samuelson, Pamela. "Computer Programs and Copyright's Fair Use Doctrine." *Communications of the ACM* 36, no. 9. (September 1993).

———. "Copyright's Fair Use Doctrine and Digital Data." *Communications of the ACM* 37, no. 1. (January 1994).

———. "Liability for Defective Electronic Information." *Communications of the ACM* 36, no. 1. (January 1993).

———. "Self Plagiarism or Fair Use?" *Communications of the ACM* 37, no. 8. (August 1994).

———. "The Ups and Downs of Look and Feel." *Communications of the ACM* 36, no. 4. (April 1993).

Sandsmark, Fred. "Five Hot Wireless Start-ups." *Red Herring.* (April 2000).

Sarkar, Mitra Barun, Brian Butler, and **Charles Steinfield.** "Intermediaries and Cybermediaries: A Continuing Role for Mediating Players in the Electronic Marketplace." *JCMC* 1, no. 3. (December 1995).

"Saskatchewan Wheat Pool Strengthens Its Alliance with Ag Growth Industries." *Saskatchewan Wheat Pool.* http://www.swp.com/releases/releases/010620.htm. (Accessed July 28, 2001). Courtesy of Saskatchewan Wheat Pool.

"Saskatchewan Wheat Pool." *Hoovers Online.* http://www.hoovers.com/co/capsule/3/0,2163,54123,00.html. (Accessed July 28, 2001). Coutresy of Hoover's, Inc. (www.hoovers.com)

Satzinger, John W., and **Lorne Olfman.** "User Interface Consistency Across Applications." *Journal of Management Infomation Systems* 14, no. 4. (Spring 1998).

Saunders, Craig. "Hudson's Bay Plans Massive CRM Push." *Strategy Magazine.* (July 17, 2000).

Sauter, Vicki L. "Intuitive Decision-Making." *Communications of the ACM* 42, no 6. (June 1999).

"Scenario Planning: Transcanada Pipelines." *Caucus Systems Inc.* http://www.caucus.com/ourclients.html. (Accessed July 27, 2001).

Scheck, Susan. "Celestica overhauls its supply chain." *Electronic Buyers' News.* (September 28, 1998).

Scheer, August-Wilhelm, and **Frank Habermann.** "Making ERP a Success." *Communications of the ACM* 43, no. 3. (April 2000).

Schein, Edgar H. *Organizational Culture and Leadership.* San Francisco: Jossey-Bass. (1985).

Schmidt, Douglas C., and **Mohamed E. Fayad.** "Lessons Learned Building Reusable OO Frameworks for Distributed Software." *Communications of the ACM* 40, no. 10. (October 1997).

Schneiderman, Ben. "Universal Usability." *Communications of the ACM* 43, no. 5. (May 2000).

Schoder, Detlef, and **Pai-ling Yin.** "Building Firm Trust Online." *Communications of the ACM* 43, no. 12. (December 2000).

Schultze, Ulrike, and **Betty Vandenbosch.** "Information Overload in a Groupware Environment: Now You See It, Now You Don't." *Journal of Organizational Computing and Electronic Commerce* 8, no. 2. (1998).

Schwabe, Gerhard. "Providing for Organizational Memory in Computer-Supported Meetings." *Journal of Organizational Computing and Electronic Commerce* 9, no. 2 and 3. (1999).

Schwenk, C.R. "Cognitive Simplification Processes in Strategic Decision Making." *Strategic Management Journal,* 5. (1984).

"Scotiabank First to Deploy IVI Checkmate Smartcard-Capable PIN Pad." *IVI Checkmate Corp.*, October 19, 1999. http://www.ckmate.com/news/scotia_oct19_99.html. (Accessed August 10, 2001).

Scott Morton, Michael, ed. *The Corporation in the 1990s.* New York: Oxford University Press. (1991).

Scott, Louise, Levente Horvath, and **Donald Day.** "Characterizing CASE Constraints." *Communications of the ACM* 43, no. 11. (November 2000).

"Sealed Court Records Kept Tire Problems Hidden." *USA Today.* (September 19, 2000).

Segars, Albert H., and **Varun Grover.** "Profiles of Strategic Information Systems Planning." *Information Systems Research* 10, no. 3. (September 1999).

Segev, Arie, Janna Porra, and **Malu Roldan.** "Internet Security and the Case of Bank of America." *Communications of the ACM* 41, no. 10. (October 1998).

Selker, Ted. "Coach: A Teaching Agent that Learns." *Communications of the ACM* 37, no. 7. (July 1994).

———. "New Paradigms for Using Computers." *Communications of the ACM* 39, no. 8. (August 1996).

Seybold, Patricia B. "Get Inside the Lives of Your Customers." *Harvard Business Review.* (May 2001).

Shand, Dawne. "Making It Up as You Go." *Knowledge Management.* (April 2000).

Shank, Michael E., Andrew C. Boynton, and **Robert W. Zmud.** "Critical Success Factor Analysis as a Methodology for MIS Planning." *MIS Quarterly.* (June 1985).

Shapiro, Carl, and **Hal R. Varian.** *Information Rules.* Boston, MA: Harvard Business School Press. (1999).

Sharda, Nalin. "Multimedia Networks: Fundamentals and Future Directions." *Communications of the Association for Information Systems.* (February 1999).

Sharda, Ramesh, and **David M. Steiger.** "Inductive Model Analysis Systems: Enhancing Model Analysis in Decision Support Systems." *Information Systems Research* 7, no. 3. (September 1996).

"Sharing in Our Success." *GuestTek.* http://www.guesttek.com/company/investors.html. (Accessed August 12, 2001).

Sharma, Srinarayan, and **Arun Rai.** "CASE Deployment in IS Organizations." *Communications of the ACM* 43, no. 1. (January 2000).

Sheetz, Steven D., Gretchen Irwin, David P. Tegarden, H. James Nelson, and **David E. Monarchi.** "Exploring the Difficulties of Learning Object-Oriented Techniques." *Journal of Management Information Systems* 14, no. 2. (Fall 1997).

"Shell Canada Empowers Its Employees LANSA for the Web." *Lansa.* http://www.lansa.com/casestudies/shell.htm. (Accessed May 14, 2001).

"Sherbrooke Implementation." *Mondex Canada.* http://www.mondex.ca/eng/mondexinaction/sherbrooke.cfm?pg=inaction. (Accessed August 4, 2001).

Sherman, Lee. "A Matter of Connections." *Knowledge Management.* (July 2000).

"Shoe Company Finds Right Technological Fit." *Chain Store Age.* (October 2000).

Shore, Edwin B. "Reshaping the IS Organization." *MIS Quarterly.* (December 1983).

Short, James E., and **N. Venkatraman.** "Beyond Business Process Redesign: Redefining Baxter's Business Network." *Sloan Management Review.* (Fall 1992).

Sia, Siew Kien, and **Boon Siong Neo.** "Reengineering Effectiveness and the Redesign of Organizational Control: A Case Study of the Inland Revenue Authority in Singapore." *Journal of Management Information Systems* 14, no. 1. (Summer 1997).

Sibigtroth, James M. "Implementing Fuzzy Expert Rules in Hardware." *AI Expert.* (April 1992).

Silberschatz, Avi, Michael Stonebraker, and **Jeff Ullman.** "Database Systems: Achievements and Opportunities." *Communications of the ACM* 34, no. 10. (October 1991).

Silver, Mark S. "Decision Support Systems: Directed and Nondirected Change." *Information Systems Research* 1, no. 1. (March 1990).

Simon, Herbert A. "Applying Information Technology to Organization Design." *Public Administration Review.* (May–June 1973).

———. *The New Science of Management Decision.* New York: Harper & Row. (1960).

Singh, Surendra N., and **Nikunj P. Dalal.** "Web Home Pages as Advertisements." *Communications of the ACM* 42, no. 8. (August 1999).

Sinha, Alok. "Client-Server Computing." *Communications of the ACM* 35, no. 7. (July 1992).

Sipior, Janice C., and **Burke T. Ward.** "The Dark Side of Employee E-mail." *Communications of the ACM* 42, no. 7. (July 1999).

———. "The Ethical and Legal Quandary of E-mail Privacy." *Communications of the ACM* 38, no. 12. (December 1995).

Sircar, Sumit, Joe L. Turnbow, and **Bijoy Bordoloi.** "A Framework for Assessing the Relationship between Information Technology Investments and Firm Performance." *Journal of Management Information Systems* 16, no. 4. (Spring 2000).

Slatalla, Michelle. "Shopper's Virtual Home Tour Satisfies that Peeping Urge." *The New York Times Circuits.* (August 31, 2000).

Slaughter, Sandra A., Donald E. Harter, and **Mayuram S. Krishnan.** "Evaluating the Cost of Software Quality." *Communications of the ACM* 41, no. 8. (August 1998).

Slofstra, Martin. "Analyze This." *Infosystems Executive.* (August 2000).

Slywotzky, Adrian J. and **David J. Morrison.** "Auction and Brokerage Sites Stand to Lose the Most "in" Technology Spotlight: The Financial Impact of Site Outages." *The Industry Standard.* (October 4, 1999).

———. "Concrete Solution." *The Industry Standard.* (August 28, 2000).

———. *How Digital Is Your Business?* New York: Crown Business. (2001).

"Smart Card Success Requires New Partnerships." *Computing Canada,* August 23, 1999. http://www.findarticles.com/cf_0/m0CGC/16_25/54481067/print.jhtml. (Accessed August 10, 2001).

Smith, Craig S. "Ambivalence in China on Expanding Net Access." *The New York Times*. (August 11, 2000).

Smith, H. Jeff. "Privacy Policies and Practices: Inside the Organizational Maze." *Communications of the ACM* 36, no. 12,. (December 1993).

Smith, H. Jeff, and John Hasnas. "Ethics and Information Systems: The Corporate Domain." *MIS Quarterly* 23, no. 1. (March 1999).

Smith, H. Jeff, Sandra J. Milberg, and Sandra J. Burke. "Information Privacy: Measuring Individuals' Concerns about Organizational Practices." *MIS Quarterly* 20, no. 2. (June 1996).

Smith, John B., and Stephen F. Weiss. "Hypertext." *Communications of the ACM* 31, no. 7. (July 1988).

Smith, Michael D., Joseph Bailey, and Erik Brynjolfsson. "Understanding Digital Markets: Review and Assessment" in Erik Brynjolfsson and Brian Kahin, eds. *Understanding the Digital Economy*. Cambridge, MA: MIT Press. (1999).

Soh, Christina, Sia Siew Kien, and Joanne Tay-Yap. "Cultural Fits and Misfits: Is ERP a Universal Solution?" *Communications of the ACM* 43, no. 3. (April 2000).

"Some Of Our Favourite Montreal Student-Related Web Sites." *Profscan.com*. http://www.profscan.com/concordia/links.html. (Accessed May 5, 2001).

Sprague, Ralph H., Jr., and Eric D. Carlson. *Building Effective Decision Support Systems*. Englewood Cliffs, NJ: Prentice Hall. (1982).

Sprenger, Polly. "Boo Founder: Don't Cry For Me." *The Industry Standard*. (February 11, 2000).

———. "More Creaks and Groans at Boo.com." *The Industry Standard*. (May 4, 2000).

———. "Where is Boo.com." *The Industry Standard*. (September 17, 1999).

Sprott, David. "Componentizing the Enterprise Application Packages." *Communications of the ACM* 43, no. 3. (April 2000).

Sproull, Lee, and Sara Kiesler. *Connections: New Ways of Working in the Networked Organization*. Cambridge, MA: MIT Press. (1992).

Stackpole, Beth. "Targeting One Buyer-Or a Million." *Datamation*. (March 2000).

"Standard Application Benchmarks—Published Results." *SAP*. http://www.sap.com/solutions/technology/pdf/50020428.pdf. (Accessed January 2001).

Staples, D. Sandy, John S. Hulland, and Christopher A. Higgins. "A Self-Efficacy Theory Explanation for the Management of Remote Workers in Virtual Organizations." *Organization Science* 10, no. 6. (November–December 1999).

Starbuck, William H. "Learning by Knowledge-Intensive Firms." *Journal of Management Studies* 29, no. 6. (November 1992).

———. "Organizations as Action Generators." *American Sociological Review* 48. (1983).

Starbuck, William H., and Frances J. Milliken. "Executives' Perceptual Filters: What They Notice and How They Make Sense." In *The Executive Effect: Concepts and Methods for Studying Top Managers,* edited by D. C. Hambrick. Greenwich, CT: JAI Press. (1988).

"Statement of February 4, 2000: Bridgestone/Firestone Inc." *Tiredefects.com*. http://www.tiredefects.com (Accessed June 5, 2001).

"Status: Pearson Airport and Frequent Flyer Miles." *Rider Travel Corporation*. http://www.riderbti.ca/news_and _advisories/pearson_airport_status.asp. (Accessed January 20, 2001).

Stein, Tom. "The New Rage for Storage." *Red Herring. (*March 1, 2000).

Steinbart, Paul John, and Ravinder Nath. "Problems and Issues in the Management of International Data Networks." *MIS Quarterly* 16, no. 1. (March 1992).

Steinfield, Charles. "The Impact of Electronic Commerce on Buyer-Seller Relationships." *JCMC* 1, no. 3. (December 1995).

Steinman, Cindy. "A Retail Tale." *Network World Canada*. (May 5, 2000).

Sternberg, Rikke, "All About the Brand." *Biz Report*. (Accessed April 3, 2000).

Sterne, Jim. "Customer Interface." *CIO WebBusiness*. (February 1, 1998).

Stillerman, Matthew, Carla Marceau, and Maureen Stillman. "Intrusion Detection for Distributed Applications." *Communications of the ACM* 42, no. 7. (July 1999).

Stirland, Sarah. "Armed with Insight." *Wall Street and Technology* 16, no. 8. (August 1998).

Storey, Veda C., and Robert C. Goldstein. "Knowledge-Based Approaches to Database Design." *MIS Quarterly* 17, no. 1. (March 1993).

Straub, Detmar W., Jr., "The Effect of Culture on IT Diffusion: E-Mail and FAX in Japan and the U.S." *Information Systems Research* 5, no. 1. (March 1994).

Straub, Detmar W., Jr., and Richard J. Welke. "Coping with Systems Risk: Security Planning Models for Management Decision Making." *MIS Quarterly* 22, no. 4. (December 1998).

Straub, Detmar W., Jr., and Rosann Webb Collins. "Key Information Liability Issues Facing Managers: Software Piracy, Proprietary Databases, and Individual Rights to Privacy." *MIS Quarterly* 14, no. 2. (June 1990).

Straub, Detmar W., Jr., and William D. Nance. "Discovering and Disciplining Computer Abuse in Organizations: A Field Study." *MIS Quarterly* 14, no. 1. (March 1990).

Straub, Detmar W., Jr., and James C. Wetherbe. "Information Technologies for the 1990s: An Organizational Impact Perspective." *Communications of the ACM* 32, no. 11. (November 1989).

Strong, Diane M., Yang W. Lee, and Richard Y. Wang. "Data Quality in Context." *Communications of the ACM* 40, no. 5. (May 1997).

Stylianou, Anthony C., Gregory R. Madey, and Robert D. Smith. "Selection Criteria for Expert System Shells: A Socio-Technical Framework." *Communications of the ACM* 35, no. 10. (October 1992).

"Success Stories: Baan at Work for Industry." *Baan*. http://www.baan.com/customers/successes/index.html. (Accessed April 5, 2001).

Sukhatme, Gaurav S., and Maja J. Mataric. "Embedding Robots into the Internet." *Communications of the ACM* 43, no. 5. (May 2000).

"Supercomputing." *University of Western Ontario*. http://www.apmaths.uwo.ca/agit/supercomputer.html. (Accessed February 24, 2001).

"Surveillance in the Workplace." *The Worklife Report* 12, no. 4. (2000).

Sviokla, John J. "An Examination of the Impact of Expert Systems on the Firm: The Case of XCON." *MIS Quarterly* 14, no. 5. (June 1990).

Sviokla, John J. "Expert Systems and Their Impact on the Firm: The Effects of PlanPower Use on the Information Processing Capacity of the Financial Collaborative." *Journal of Management Information Systems* 6, no. 3. (Winter 1989–1990).

Swanson, E. Burton. *Information System Implementation*. Homewood, IL: Richard D. Irwin. (1988).

Swanson, E. Burton and **Enrique Dans.** "System Life Expectancy and the Maintenance Effort: Exploring their Equilibration." *MIS Quarterly* 24, no. 2. (June 2000).

Swanson, Kent, Dave McComb, Jill Smith, and **Don McCubbrey.** "The Application Software Factory: Applying Total Quality Techniques to Systems Development." *MIS Quarterly* 15, no. 4. (December 1991).

Sweeney, Terry. "Voice Over IP Builds Momentum." *Information Week.* (November 20, 2000).

Taerum, Kathy. "Dust to Digits' Bringing the Seismic Archive to the Desktop." *Canadian Information Productivity Awards.* http://www.cipa.com/winners/dept1_home.htm. (Accessed November 16, 2000).

Taggart, Stewart. "The Other Side of the Divide." *The Industry Standard.* (September 11, 2000).

Tallon, Paul P, Kenneth L. Kraemer, and **Vijay Gurbaxani.** "Executives' Perceptions of the Business Value of Information Technology: A Process-Oriented Approach." *Journal of Management Information Systems* 16, no. 4. (Spring 2000).

Tan, Zixiang, William Foster, and **Seymour Goodman.** "China's State-Coordinated Internet Infrastructure." *Communications of the ACM* 42, no. 6. (June 1999).

Tan, Zixiang (Alex), Milton Mueller, and **Will Foster.** "China's New Internet Regulations: Two Steps Forward, One Step Backward." *Communications of the ACM* 40, no. 12. (December 1997).

Taudes, Alfred, Markus Feurstein, and **Andreas Mild.** "Options Analysis of Software Platform Decisions: A Case Study." *MIS Quarterly* 24, no. 2. (June 2000).

Tayi, Giri Kumar, and **Donald P. Ballou.** "Examining Data Quality." *Communications of the ACM* 41, no. 2. (February 1998).

"Teleuse Case Study." *AONIX.* http://www.aonix.com/content/ products/teleuse/bc.html. (Accessed February 25, 2001).

Teng, James T.C., Seung Ryul Jeong, and **Varun Grover.** "Profiling Successful Reengineering Projects." *Communications of the ACM* 41, no. 6. (June 1998).

Tennenhouse, David. "Proactive Computing." *Communications of the ACM* 43, no. 5. (May 2000).

Teo, Hock-Hai, Bernard C.Y. Tan, and **Kwok-Kee Wei.** "Organizational Transformation Using Electronic Data Interchange: The Case of TradeNet in Singapore." *Journal of Management Information Systems* 13, no. 4. (Spring 1997).

"The Company: AT&T." *Dot Hill.* http://www.dothill.com/ ravingfans/aH.htm. (Accessed February 25, 2001).

"The New Role for 'Executive Information Systems.'" *I/S Analyzer.* (January 1992).

"The Spring Of Hope: A Communications Empowered Future?" *The Yankee Group.* http://www.yankeegroupcanada.com. (Accessed May 22, 2001).

The Telecommunications Policy Roundtable. "Renewing the Commitment to a Public Interest Telecommunications Policy." *Communications of the ACM* 37, no. 1. (January 1994).

Thompson, Marjorie Sarbough, and **Martha S. Feldman.** "Electronic Mail and Organizational Communication." *Organization Science* 9, no. 6. (November–December 1998).

Thong, James Y.L., and **Chee-Sing Yap.** "Testing an Ethical Decision-Making Theory." *Journal of Management Information Systems* 15, no. 1. (Summer 1998).

Thong, James Y.L., Chee-Sing Yap and **Kin-Lee Seah.** "Business Process Reengineering in the Public Sector: The Case of the Housing Development Board in Singapore." *Journal of Management Information Systems* 17, no. 1. (Summer 2000).

Todd, Peter, and **Izak Benbasat.** "Evaluating the Impact of DSS, Cognitive Effort, and Incentives on Strategy Selection. *Information Systems Research* 10, no. 4. (December 1999).

Torkzadeh, Gholamreza, and **Weidong Xia.** "Managing Telecommunications Strategy by Steering Committee." *MIS Quarterly* 16, no. 2. (June 1992).

Tornatsky, Louis G., J.D. Eveland, M.G. Boylan, W.A. Hetzner, E.C. Johnson, D. Roitman, and **J. Schneider.** *The Process of Technological Innovation: Reviewing the Literature.* Washington, DC: National Science Foundation. (1983).

"Toward Electronic Health Records." *Health Canada,* January 2001. http://www.hc-sc.gc.ca/ohih-bsi/ehr/ehr_dse/c_e.html. (Accessed May 23, 3001).

Tractinsky, Noam, and **Sirkka L. Jarvenpaa.** "Information Systems Design Decisions in a Global Versus Domestic Context." *MIS Quarterly* 19, no. 4. (December 1995).

"Trading Places at Hudson's Bay Co." *QLogitek.* http://www. qlogitek.com/trading_places_at_hudson_bay.asp. (Accessed May 15, 2001).

Trippi, Robert, and **Efraim Turban.** "The Impact of Parallel and Neural Computing on Managerial Decision Making." *Journal of Management Information Systems* 6, no. 3. (Winter 1989–1990).

"Truck Tire Xchange.Com Launched to Merge E-Commerce with Truck Tire Buying, Selling Process." *Fleet Equipment* 26, no. 10. (October 2000).

Truex, Duane P., Richard Baskerville, and **Heinz Klein.** "Growing Systems in Emergent Organizations." *Communications of the ACM* 42, no. 8. (August 1999).

Truman, Gregory E. "Integration in Electronic Exchange Environments." *Journal of Management Information Systems* 17, no. 1. (Summer 2000).

Tse, Daniel and **Louis Chan.** "Multipoint Design of Airfoils by a Genetic Algorithm." *National Research Council Canada*

Tuomi, Ilkka. "Data Is More Than Knowledge." *Journal of Management Information Systems* 16, no. 3. (Winter 1999–2000).

Turban, Efraim and **Jay E. Aronson.** *Decision Support Systems and Intelligent Systems: Management Support Systems,* 5th ed. Upper Saddle River, NJ: Prentice Hall. (1998).

Turban, Efraim and **Paul R. Watkins.** "Integrating Expert Systems and Decision Support Systems." *MIS Quarterly.* (June 1986).

Turner, Jon A. "Computer Mediated Work: The Interplay Between Technology and Structured Jobs." *Communications of the ACM* 27, no. 12. (December 1984).

Turner, Jon A., and **Robert A. Karasek, Jr.** "Software Ergonomics: Effects of Computer Application Design Parameters on Operator Task Performance and Health." *Ergonomics* 27, no. 6. (1984).

Tushman, Michael L., and **Philip Anderson.** "Technological Discontinuities and Organizational Environments." *Administrative Science Quarterly* 31. (September 1986).

Tuttle, Brad, Adrian Harrell, and **Paul Harrison.** "Moral Hazard, Ethical Considerations, and the Decision to Implement an Information System." *Journal of Management Information Systems* 13, no. 4. (Spring 1997).

Tversky, A., and **D. Kahneman.** "The Framing of Decisions and the Psychology of Choice." *Science* 211. (January 1981).

Tyma, Paul. "Why Are We Using Java Again?" *Communications of the ACM* 41, no. 6. (June 1998).

Tyran, Craig K., Alan R. Dennis, Douglas R. Vogel, and **J.F. Nunamaker, Jr.** "The Application of Electronic Meeting Technology to Support Senior Management." *MIS Quarterly* 16, no. 3. (September 1992).

United States General Accounting Office. "Patriot Missile Defense: Software Problem Led to System Failure at Dharan, Saudi Arabia." GAO/IMTEC-92-26. (February 1992).

"U.S. Web Use Mostly at Work." *Reuters.* http://www.reuters.com. (Accessed April 6, 2000).

"U.S. Will Be Smart Card Hot Spot." *Northern Light*, April 3, 2001. http://special.northernlight.com/banking/hotspot.htm. (Accessed August 10, 2001).

Uslaner, Eric M. "Social Capital and the Net." *Communications of the ACM* 43, no. 12. (December 2000).

"USwap.Com." *Canadian Information Productivity Awards.* http://www.cipa.com/winners/small4_story.html. (Accessed May 5, 2001).

Valera, Francisco, Jorge E. López de Vergara, José I. Moreno, Víctor A. Villagrá, and **Julio Berrocal.** "Communication Management Experiences in E-commerce." *Communications of the ACM* 44, no. 4. (April 2001).

Van der Zee, J.T.M., and **Berend de Jong.** "Alignment Is Not Enough: Integrating Business and Information Technology Management." *Journal of Management Information Systems* 16, no. 2. (Fall 1999).

Vance, Ashlee. "Study Says Employees Abuse the Internet." *IDG News Service.* (October 26, 2000).

Vandenbosch, Betty, and **Michael J. Ginzberg.** "Lotus Notes and Collaboration: Plus ca change . . ." *Journal of Management Information Systems* 13, no. 3. (Winter 1997).

Varshney, Upkar. "Networking Support for Mobile Computing." *Communications of the Association for Information Systems* 1. (January 1999).

Varshney, Upkar, and **Ron Vetter.** "Emerging Mobile and Wireless Networks. *Communications of the ACM* 42, no. 6. (June 2000).

Vassiliou, Yannis. "On the Interactive Use of Databases: Query Languages." *Journal of Management Information Systems* 1. (Winter 1984–1985).

Vedder, Richard G., Michael T. Vanacek, C. Stephen Guynes, and **James J. Cappel.** "CEO and CIO Perspectives on Competitive Intelligence." *Communications of the ACM 42,* no. 8. (August 1999).

Venkatraman, N. "Beyond Outsourcing: Managing IT Resources as a Value Center." *Sloan Management Review.* (Spring 1997).

———. "Five Steps to a Dot-Com Strategy: How to Find Your Footing on the Web." *Sloan Management Review* 41, no. 3. (Spring 2000).

Vessey, Iris, and **Sue Conger.** "Learning to Specify Information Requirements: The Relationship between Application and Methodology." *Journal of Management Information Systems* 10, no. 2. (Fall 1993).

———. "Requirements Specification: Learning Object, Process, and Data Methodologies." *Communications of the ACM* 37, no. 5. (May 1994).

Vetter, Ronald J. "ATM Concepts, Architectures, and Protocols." *Communications of the ACM* 38, no. 2. (February 1995).

———. "The Wireless Web." *Communications of the ACM* 44, no. 3. (March 2001).

Viega, John, Tadayoshi Koho, and **Bruce Potter.** "Trust (and Mistrust) in Secure Applications." *Communications of the ACM* 44, no. 2. (February 2001).

Vijayan, Jaikumar. "Caught in the Middle." *Computerworld.* (July 24, 2000).

Vitalari, Nicholas P. "Knowledge as a Basis for Expertise in Systems Analysis: Empirical Study." *MIS Quarterly.* (September 1985).

Vittore, Vince. "A Voice For E-Commerce." *Telephony.* (August 31, 1998).

Vogel, Douglas R., Jay F. Nunamaker, William Benjamin Martz, Jr., Ronald Grobowski, and **Christopher McGoff.** "Electronic Meeting System Experience at IBM." *Journal of Management Information Systems* 6, no. 3. (Winter 1989–1990).

Volokh, Eugene. "Personalization and Privacy." *Communications of the ACM* 43, no. 8. (August 2000).

Volonino, Linda, and **Hugh J. Watson.** "The Strategic Business Objectives Method for EIS Development." *Journal of Management Information Systems* 7, no. 3. (Winter 1990–1991).

Walczak, Steven. "Gaining Competitive Advantage for Trading in Emerging Capital Markets with Neural Networks." *Journal of Management Information Systems* 16, no. 2. (Fall 1999).

Waldo, Jim. "The Jini Architecture for Network-centric Computing." *Communications of the ACM 42,* no. 7. (July 1999).

Walker, David. "Talk About A Real Booboo." *Sydney Morning Herald.* (May 30, 2000).

Walls, Joseph G., George R. Widmeyer, and **Omar A. El Sawy.** "Building an Information System Design Theory for Vigilant EIS." *Information Systems Research* 3, no. 1. (March 1992).

Walsham, Geoffrey, and **Sundeys Sahay.** "GIS and District Level Administration in India: Problems and Opportunities." *MIS Quarterly* 23, no. 1. (March 1999).

Wand, Yair, and **Richard Y. Wang.** "Anchoring Data Quality Dimensions in Ontological Foundations." *Communications of the ACM* 39, no. 11. (November 1996).

Wang, Huaiqing, Matthew K. O. Lee, and **Chen Wang.** "Consumer Privacy Concerns about Internet Marketing." *Communications of the ACM* 41, no. 3. (March 1998).

Wang, Richard. "A Product Perspective on Total Data Quality Management." *Communications of the ACM* 41, no. 2. (February 1998).

Wang, Richard Y., Yang W. Lee, Leo L. Pipino, and **Diane M. Strong.** "Manage Your Information as a Product." *Sloan Management Review* 39, no. 4. (Summer 1998).

"Warehousing Customer Data." *Strategic Vision.* (2000).

Warner, Bernhard. "Boo.com Trims its Bottom Line." *The Industry Standard.* (January 25, 2000).

Wastell, David G. "Learning Dysfunctions in Information Systems Development: Overcoming the Social Defenses with Transitional Objects." *MIS Quarterly* 23, no. 1. (December 1999).

Watad, Mahmoud M., and **Frank J. DiSanzo.** "Case Study: The Synergism of Telecommuting and Office Automation." *Sloan Management Review* 41, no. 2. (Winter 2000).

Watson, Hugh J., and **Barbara J. Haley.** "Managerial Considerations." *Communications of the ACM* 41, no. 9. (September 1998).

Watson, Hugh J., Astrid Lipp, Pamela Z. Jackson, Abdelhafid Dahmani, and **William B. Fredenberger.** "Organizational Support for Decision Support Systems." *Journal of Management Information Systems* 5, no. 4. (Spring 1989).

Watson, Hugh J., R. Kelly Rainer, Jr., and **Chang E. Koh.** "Executive Information Systems: A Framework for Development and a Survey of Current Practices." *MIS Quarterly* 15, no. 1. (March 1991).

Watson, Richard T., Geraldine DeSanctis, and **Marshall Scott Poole.** "Using a GDSS to Facilitate Group Consensus: Some Intended and Unintended Consequences." *MIS Quarterly* 12, no. 3. (September 1988).

Watson, Richard T., Gigi G. Kelly, Robert D. Galliers, and **James C. Brancheau.** "Key Issues in Information Systems Management: An International Perspective." *Journal of Management Information Systems* 13, no. 4. (Spring 1997).

Watson, Richard T., Teck-Hua Ho, and **K. S. Raman.** "Culture: A Fourth Dimension of Group Support Systems." *Communications of the ACM* 37, no. 10. (October 1994).

"Web Based Decision Support Systems: Part II." *Tgc.com.* http://www.tgc.com/dsstar/98/0825/200267.html. (Accessed July 11, 2001).

Weber, Max. *The Theory of Social and Economic Organization.* Translated by Talcott Parsons. New York: Free Press. (1947).

Weber, Ron. *EDP Auditing: Conceptual Foundations and Practice,* 2nd ed. New York: McGraw-Hill. (1988).

Weill, Peter, and **Marianne Broadbent.** *Leveraging the New Infrastructure.* Cambridge, MA: Harvard Business School Press. (1998).

———. "Management by Maxim: How Business and IT Managers Can Create IT Infrastructures." *Sloan Management Review.* (Spring 1997).

Weiser, Mark. "Some Computer Science Issues in Ubiquitous Computing." *Communications of the ACM* 36, no. 7. (July 1993).

Weitzel, John R., and **Larry Kerschberg.** "Developing Knowledge Based Systems: Reorganizing the System Development Life Cycle." *Communications of the ACM.* (April 1989).

"Welcome to JDA Software Group, Inc." *JDA Software Group.* http://www.jda.com. (Accessed July 11, 2001).

Werbach, Kevin. "Syndication: The Emerging Model for Business in the Internet Era." *Harvard Business Review.* (May–June 2000).

Westin, Alan F., Heather A. Schweder, Michael A. Baker, and **Sheila Lehman.** *The Changing Workplace.* New York: Knowledge Industries. (1995).

"What Banks Are Doing to Help Capitalize on the Web." *Globetechnology.com.* (October 23, 2000).

"What Is DIC?" *Dubai Internet City.* http://www.dubaiinternetcity.com/pages/aboutdic/aboutdic.asp?level=1&mcode=24. (Accessed August 28, 2001).

Wheatley, Malcolm. "Every Last Dime." *ITWorldCanada.com.* http://www.itworldcanada.com. (Accessed August 29, 2001).

"Where Having Fun Really Pays Off." *Information Week*, January 15, 2001.

Whiting, Rich. "Mind Your Business." *Information Week.* (March 6, 2000).

Whitman, Michael E., Anthony M. Townsend, and **Robert J. Aalberts.** "Considerations for Effective Telecommunications-Use Policy." *Communications of the ACM* 42, no. 6. (June 1999).

"Why Do Business with BDC?." *BDC.* http://connex.bdc.ca/eng/pourquoi_bdc.htm. (Accessed January 18, 2001).

"Why Invest in Canada." *Canadausinvestment.com.* http://www.canadausinvestment.com/caninfo.htm. (Accessed July 8, 2001).

Widrow, Bernard, David E. Rumelhart, and **Michael A. Lehr.** "Neural Networks: Applications in Industry, Business, and Science." *Communications of the ACM* 37, no. 3. (March 1994).

Wigand, Rolf T., and **Robert Benjamin.** "Electronic Commerce: Effects on Electronic Markets." *JCMC* 1, no. 3. (December 1995).

Wijnhoven, Fons. "Designing Organizational Memories: Concept and Method." *Journal of Organizational Computing and Electronic Commerce* 8, no. 1. (1998).

Wilder, Clinton. "Feds Allege Internet Scam." *Information Week.* (June 10, 1996).

———. "Tapping the Pipeline." *Information Week.* (March 15, 1999).

Wilkes, Maurice V. "The Long-Term Future of Operating Systems." *Communications of the ACM* 35, no. 11. (November 1992).

Wilkinson, Stephanie. "Melding Clicks and Bricks." *Datamation.* (August 2000).

———. "Phone Bill, Electricity Bill, Storage Bill?" *Datamation.* (October 2000).

Williams, John M, "Online Banking for the Disabled Just Isn't Enabling." *Business Week.* (November, 2000).

Williamson, Oliver E. *The Economic Institutions of Capitalism.* New York: Free Press,. (1985).

Willis, T. Hillman, and **Debbie B. Tesch.** "An Assessment of Systems Development Methodologies." *Journal of Information Technology Management* 2, no. 2. (1991).

Wise, Richard, and **David Morrison.** "Beyond the Exchange: The Future of B2B." *Harvard Business Review.* (November–December 2000).

Wiseman, Charles. *Strategic Information Systems.* Homewood, IL: Richard D. Irwin. (1988).

Wong, David, Noemi Paciorek, and **Dana Moore.** "Java-Based Mobile Agents." *Communications of the ACM* 42, no. 3. (March 1999).

Wong, Poh-Kam. "Leveraging the Global Information Revolution for Economic Development: Singapore's Evolving Information Industry Strategy." *Information Systems Research* 9, no. 4. (December 1998).

Wood, Chris. "Dealing With Tech Rage." *Maclean's.* (March 19, 2001).

Woods, Tony, and **Kate O'Rourke.** "Keeping Track of Customers." *E-Doc.* (May/June 2000).

Wrapp, H. Edward. "Good Managers Don't Make Policy Decisions." *Harvard Business Review.* (July–August 1984).

Wreden, Nick. "Business Intelligence: Turning on Success." *Beyond Computing.* (September 1997).

Wysocki, Bernard. "The Big Bang." *The Wall Street Journal.* (January 1, 2000).

Yates, Sarah. "Commitment to Technological Change Pay Dividends at Nygård." *Trade and Commerce.* (Spring 2001).

———. "Nygård International Has Led the IT Revolution in the Garment Industry." *Trade and Commerce.* (Spring 2001).

Yin, Robert K. "Life Histories of Innovations: How New Practices Become Routinized." *Public Administration Review.* (January–February 1981).

Young, Eric. "B2B's Broken Models." *The Industry Standard.* (November 6, 2000).

Yourdon, Edward, and **L.L. Constantine.** *Structured Design.* New York: Yourdon Press. (1978).

Zachman, J.A. "Business Systems Planning and Business Information Control Study: A Comparison." *IBM Systems Journal* 21. (1982).

Zadeh, Lotfi A. "Fuzzy Logic, Neural Networks, and Soft Computing." *Communications of the ACM* 37, no. 3. (March 1994).

———. "The Calculus of Fuzzy If/Then Rules." *AI Expert.* (March 1992).

Zeichick, Alan. "Personalization Explained." *Red Herring.* (September 1999).

Zeidenberg, Jerry. "Electronic Tools Enhance Quality of Long-Term Care." *Globetechnology.com.* (December 15, 2000).

Zhao, J. Leon, Akhil Kumar, and **Edward W. Stohr.** "Workflow-Centric Information Distribution through E-Mail." *Journal of Management Information Systems* 17, no. 3. (Winter 2000–2001).

Zviran, Moshe, and **William J. Haga.** "Password Security: An Empirical Study." *Journal of Management Information Systems* 15, no. 4. (Spring 1999).

INDEXES

ORGANIZATION INDEX

U.S. National Science Foundation, 333
U.S. Navy, 537
USA Today, 288
UUNet, 214

V
Vanity Fair, 148
Vault.com, 318
Ventures West Capital Ltd., 186
VeriSign Inc., 424
Veritas Software Corporation, 524
Viador, 482
Vienna University, 326
ViewCall Canada, 183
Virgin Mobile, 119
Visa Canada, 217
VISA International Inc., 414, 425, 534
Vizcaya Argentaria SA, 340
Vodafone Air Touch PLC, 340

W
Wal-Mart, 91–92, 98, 199, 476, 485
The Wall Street Journal, 119
Walt Disney Company, 183, 257
WapIT, 343
The Washington Post, 287
Watson Wyatt Worldwide, 133
Webraska, 343
WebTrust.com, 441
Weddingchannel.com, 492
WestJet, 123
WinePlanet.com.au, 137
Wired Planet, 167
Wolverton & Associates Inc., 318
Workers' Compensation Board of British
    Columbia, 178
World Kitchen, 476
Wrapster, 363, 364
WRQ Inc., 367

X
Xerox Canada, 91
Xerox Corporation, 158
Xybernaut Corporation, 221–222

Y
Yahoo!, 118, 129, 183, 331, 412, 413
Yahoo! Canada, 334, 335
Yahoo! Store Canada, 350
Yahoo.ca, 141
Yale University, 412
Yankee Group, 367
YkkNnet, 20

Z
ZDNet, 413
Zellers, 358–360
Zenos Group, 249
Zver & Associates, 511

SUBJECT INDEX

A
acceptance testing, 391
access, 176
Access to Information Act, 160
accountability, 153, 155, 169–171
accounting rate of return on investment
    (ROI), 455
ActiveX, 246
administrative controls, 419
agency costs, 345
agency theory, 77
AI shell, 528
analog signal, 295
antivirus software, 414
application controls, 418, 420
application generators, 237
application integration, 352, 354–355
application server, 281
application service providers (ASPs), 250
application software
    application generators, 237
    assembly language, 235
    BASIC, 236
    C, 236
    C++, 236
    COBOL, 235–236
    defined, 227
    enterprise application integration
        software, 243
    enterprise software, 242–244
    FORTRAN, 235
    fourth-generation languages, 236–242
    graphics languages, 237
    machine language, 235
    middleware, 243
    natural languages, 236
    packages, 237–238, 396–397
    Pascal, 236
    PC software tools, 238–242
    programming languages, 235–236
    query languages, 236
    report generators, 237
    third-generation languages, 235–236
    very high-level programming languages,
        237
arithmetic-logic unit (ALU), 196
ARPANET, 326, 328
artificial intelligence (AI)
    case-based reasoning, 531–532
    defined, 526
    expert systems, 527–531
    fuzzy logic, 534–536
    genetic algorithms, 537
    hybrid AI systems, 538
    intelligent agents, 538
    interest in, 526–527
    neural networks, 532–534
ASCII (American Standard Code for
    Information Interchange), 194
assembler, 230, 231
assembly language, 235
associations, 487

asynchronous communication, 312
asynchronous transfer mode (ATM), 308
ATMs (automated teller machines), 89–90,
    170
attribute, 261
audits, 427
authentication, 424
automation, 372

B
back-end CASE tools, 433
backbone, 296
balanced scorecard systems, 503
bandwidth, 301
banner ad, 116
bar code, 204
BASIC, 236
batch processing, 206–207
baud, 301
behavioural approach to information
    systems, 16
behavioural models of management, 80–82
behavioural theories, 78–79
benchmarking, 378
best practices, 514
Bill 13, 424
Bill C-6, 160, 175
Bill C-32, 363
bit, 193
bluetooth, 327
bots, 335, 538
brain drain, 449
branded exchanges, 125
bricks-and-mortar business, 118–119
bridge, 305
broadband, 307, 332–333
budget management, 449–450
bugs, 415–416
bureaucracy, 71
bureaucratic models of decision making, 85
bus, 195
bus network, 302–303
business driver, 98
business enterprise, transformation of, 7
business functions, 13
business intelligence, 502
business model, 114–119, 137
business process reengineering
    change management challenges, 386
    defined, 373
    effective, 376–378
    home mortgage industry, 374–376
    process improvement, 377–379
    vs. total quality management, 379
    workflow management, 376
business processes
    change requirements, 137–138
    core, 7
    defined, 7, 51
    enterprise systems, 58
    and information systems, 51–52
business relationships, 7
business systems planning (BSP), 369–370

PHOTO AND SCREEN SHOT CREDITS